Social Psychology

Social Psychology

ELEVENTH EDITION

Robert A. Baron
Rensselaer Polytechnic Institute

Donn Byrne
University at Albany, State University of New York

Nyla R. Branscombe
University of Kansas

PEARSON

Boston • New York • San Francisco
Mexico City • Montreal • Toronto • London • Madrid • Munich • Paris
Hong Kong • Singapore • Tokyo • Cape Town • Sydney

Series Editor: Susan Hartman
Editorial Assistant: Therese Felser
Marketing Manager: Pam Laskey
Editorial-Production Administrator:
   Annette Joseph
Editorial-Production Service: Colophon
Text Designer: Joyce C. Weston
Photo Editor: Katharine S. Cook

Electronic Composition:
   Omegatype Typography
Electronic Art: Precision Graphics
Composition/Prepress Buyer: Linda Cox
Manufacturing Buyer: Megan Cochran
Cover Administrator: Linda Knowles
Cover Designer: Susan Paradise

For related titles and support materials, visit our online catalog at
www.ablongman.com.

Between the time website information is gathered and then published, it is not
unusual for some sites to have closed. Also, the transcription of URLs can result
in typographical errors. The publisher would appreciate notification where
these errors occur so that they may be corrected in subsequent editions.

Library of Congress Cataloging-in-Publication Data

Baron, Robert A.
   Social psychology / Robert A. Baron, Donn Byrne, Nyla R. Branscombe.—11th ed.
      p.   cm.
   Includes bibliographical references and index.
   ISBN 0-205-44412-1 (alk. paper)
   1. Social psychology. I. Byrne, Donn Erwin. II. Branscombe, Nyla R. III. Title.

HM1033.B35 2006
302—dc22

2004065416

Printed in the United States of America

10 9 8 7 6 5 4 3 2 1   VHP   10 09 08 07 06 05

*Photo credits appear on page 653, which constitutes a continuation of the
copyright page.*

To Rebecca, whose love, help, and wise counsel mean more to me than I can ever say.

—R.A.B.

Throughout my early school years—from kindergarten at Matthews Elementary School in Austin, Texas, to East Bakersfield High School in California—a number of outstanding (and tolerant) teachers helped me survive, thrive, and then move on. Two high school teachers stand out because they exerted a major influence on my life. For all that they did, I especially want to thank Margaret Schilling, Social Science, and Joy Robinson, English.

—D.B.

To my siblings: Rose, Howard, Marlene, Leona, Gerald, and Elaine. No one could have better "litter mates."

—N.R.B.

BRIEF CONTENTS

CONTENTS

1. THE FIELD OF SOCIAL PSYCHOLOGY: How We Think about and Interact with Others   3

A. SOCIAL PSYCHOLOGY IN ACTION: Applications to Law and Health 502

SPECIAL FEATURES

Beyond the Headlines: As Social Psychologists See It

The Science of Social Psychology: Making Sense of Common Sense

Ideas to Take with You—and Use!

SPECIAL FEATURES

PREFACE

Why We Don't *"Leave Well Enough Alone"*

In the Preface to the third edition of this book (published in 1981), we wrote these words:

> *Books, like human beings, can (and do!) go stale. In fact, it is our impression that by the time they reach their third edition, many texts show signs of entering a complacent . . . "middle age." The topics covered, style of writing, illustrations, and many other features remain largely unaltered from edition to edition. The dangers of such stagnation are obvious. When a text ceases to change, it runs the very real risk of losing touch with the field it represents. This is especially true in the case of a vigorous and youthful field such as social psychology—one that often changes substantially over short periods of time. Any text that fails to reflect such shifts, we feel, will quickly outlive its usefulness. Even worse, it may present students with a misleading and dated image of social psychology.*

Although twenty-four years have passed since we expressed these views, we still believe them to be true. In fact, if anything, we accept them even more strongly than when we first stated them. And that belief has been a key guiding principle for this, the *eleventh edition*. In our view, the pace of change—and progress—in social psychology has accelerated, so it is even more crucial than ever that any text seeking to represent the field stay in touch with what is happening *today;* failure to do so will result in a book that will be perceived as badly out of date by social psychologists and one that—because it has lost its sense of excitement with the field—is more likely to generate yawns than enthusiasm from students.

With this principle in mind, we have adopted the following rule for revising our text: *Nothing—no discussion, no topic, no illustration—is sacred.* On the contrary, *everything* should be reviewed and revised to reflect the current knowledge of social psychology—and the true cutting edge of its recent progress. To implement this basic value, we have made many changes in the book. Below is a summary of the changes we view as being most important—and most constructive.

A New Coauthor

By far the most important change of all involves the addition of Nyla R. Branscombe as a coauthor. Professor Branscombe's expertise in such topics as prejudice, the self, gender, group processes, and many other key areas of research complements our own knowledge, and adds tremendous strengths to the book—and to our presentation of social psychology. Because she worked closely with the original authors and provided invaluable input on every chapter, her presence—and invaluable contributions—appear throughout the book. The result? This text is visibly stronger, more up to date, and better integrated than ever before. What a win for us—and our readers!—in every respect.

Changes in Content

Social psychology advances at a dizzying pace! To reflect this fact, every chapter has been thoroughly revised and updated to take into account new findings, lines of research, research methods, and approaches. These changes have taken several major forms. First, we have devoted special attention to the task of representing *emerging new themes* in the field. Among these are the following:

- The interface (and interplay) between social cognition and social behavior
- Social neuroscience
- The role of implicit (nonconscious) processes in both social thought and social behavior
- Growing attention to social diversity and the complex issues it involves

Second, we have totally revised several chapters to reflect major advances and reorientations. For instance, Chapter 5 (The Self) is almost entirely new in content, and now covers many new topics such as the effects of perceiving the self as a target of prejudice, introspection as a method of gaining self-insight, and identity as a rebel. In addition, coverage of several other topics is greatly expanded and updated (e.g., social comparison). Similarly, to better represent growing interest in the application of social psychology to practical problems and issues, we have added two new Modules—one (Module A) dealing with applications of social psychology to law and health and the other (Module B) dealing with applications of social psychology to work settings and to entrepreneurship.

Third, to take account of new lines of research and important new findings, we have included coverage of literally dozens of new topics. Listing all of these here would generate a truly gigantic list, so instead, we simply present a sample of these new topics below:

- An overview of several new trends in social psychology, including social neuroscience, increasing attention to implicit (nonconscious) processes (Chapter 1)
- A new section on the distinct neural bases of controlled and automatic processing (Chapter 2)
- New information on the role of automatic processes in counterfactual thinking (Chapter 2)
- New evidence on the role of linguistic style in the detection of deception (Chapter 3)
- New information on the origins of the correspondence biases (fundamental attribution error) (Chapter 3)
- A new section on implicit personality theories and their role in impression formation (Chapter 3)
- A new discussion of third-person effects of media exposure (Chapter 4)
- Discussion of attitudes toward many social issues (e.g., same-sex marriage, Muslims, age) (Chapter 4)
- Chapter 5: This chapter is almost entirely new in content.
- Discussion of research concerning the consequences of exposure to other people's prejudiced actions (Chapter 6)
- New research on prejudice reduction techniques (Chapter 6)
- New research on the role of laughter in attraction (Chapter 7)
- New coverage of mortality salience as a basis for affiliation (Chapter 7)
- New findings on the effects of loneliness on health and life span (Chapter 8)
- New coverage of the good and bad ways couples deal with disagreements (Chapter 8)
- A new section on automatic activation of norms (Chapter 9)
- An entirely new section on *symbolic social influence*—how we are influenced by our mental representations of other persons, even when they are not actually present (Chapter 9)

- New evidence on the nature of heroism (Chapter 10)

- New research on the implicit bystander effect (Chapter 10)

- New research on the effect of ethnicity on volunteerism and charitable donations (Chapter 10)

- A new section on the effects of violent pornography (Chapter 11)

- A new section on forgiveness as a means for reducing aggression (Chapter 11)

- A new discussion of the benefits and costs of group membership, including the reasons why groups sometimes splinter (Chapter 12)

- A new section on deindividuation, including recent work on the role of self-awareness and social identity in this process (Chapter 12)

A New Special Feature Designed to Highlight the Value of Social Psychology

We think that one of the most exciting aspects of social psychology is the fact that the findings it obtains are often *counterintuitive*—the opposite of what common sense would suggest. (Or, at least, social psychology's findings refine and correct the conclusions of common sense.) To capture this important element of the field (which, we think, clearly illustrates its intrinsic value), each chapter includes a special section labeled **The Science of Social Psychology: Making Sense of Common Sense.** These sections show how the findings of social psychology have reversed or refined ideas contained in common sense. Following are a few examples of some of the titles:

- Is Being in a Good Mood Always a Plus? The Potential Downside of Feeling "Up" (Chapter 2)

- Can We Be Scared into Changing Our Attitudes? (Chapter 4)

- Is Looking Inwardly the Best Route to Self-Insight? (Chapter 5)

- Complementarity: Do Opposites Attract? (Chapter 7)

- Written in the Stars or We Met on the Internet? (Chapter 8)

- Do Women and Men Differ in the Tendency to Conform? (Chapter 9)

- Catharsis: Does Getting It Out of Your System Really Help? (Chapter 11)

- Are Groups Really Less Likely Than Individuals to "Go over the Edge"? (Chapter 12)

Features Retained from the Previous Edition

Although we have made many changes, our basic approach to writing the book remains the same: We have tried very hard to produce a text that accurately reflects the nature and content of modern social psychology but at the same time is highly readable and useful for students. To attain this goal, we have retained several special features of previous editions:

- *Beyond the Headlines* sections. These special sections, which appear in every chapter, take an actual newspaper headline and examine it from the

perspective of social psychology. They illustrate how social psychologists think and how the principles of our field can be applied to virtually any aspect of human social behavior. Though the idea behind these sections remains much the same, the sections themselves are all *new* to this edition.

- *Ideas to Take with You—and Use! sections.* These appear at the end of each chapter and are designed to highlight important concepts you should remember—and use—long after this course is over. In our view, you will definitely find these principles helpful in many contexts in the years ahead.

- *Other Features Designed to Make the Book More Useful.* Each chapter begins with an outline that provides a "road map" that points out the major sections within the chapter. Within the text itself, key terms are printed in dark type like **this** and are followed by a definition. These key terms are also defined in a running glossary in the margins, as well as in a glossary at the end of the book.

To help students understand the materials presented, each major section is followed by a list of Key Points—a brief summary of major concepts and findings. These are repeated, together, in the Summary at the end of each chapter. Finally, all figures and tables are designed to be clear and simple, and most contain special labels and notes that call readers' attention to the points being illustrated.

Supplementary Materials

All good texts should be supported by a complete package of supplementary material, both for the students and for the instructor. This book provides ample aid for both.

For the Instructor:

The following are available for qualified instructors only. Please contact your Allyn & Bacon representative.

Instructor's Manual

Michele Van Volkom, Monmouth University

Prepared by Michele Van Volkom of Monmouth University, this rich collection of teaching material can be used by first-time or experienced teachers. Each chapter includes an At-A-Glance Grid, with detailed pedagogical information linking to other available supplements; a detailed chapter outline; teaching objectives covering major concepts within the chapter; a list of key terms; lecture material and student activities; numerous handouts; and an updated list of web links. In addition, this manual includes a preface, a sample syllabus, and a comprehensive list of video sources.

Test Bank and Computerized Test Bank

Robert B. Stennett, Gainesville College

Robert B. Stennett, Gainesville College, has created a thoroughly updated test bank with challenging questions that target key concepts. Each chapter includes over 100 questions, including multiple choice, true/false, short answer, and essay, each with an answer justification, page reference, a difficulty rating, and type designation.

This product is also available in TestGen 5.5 computerized version, for ease in creating tests for the classroom.

PowerPoint Presentation

Katherine Demitrakis, Albuquerque Technical Vocational Institute

This dynamic multimedia resource contains key points covered in the textbook, images from the textbook, questions to provoke classroom discussion, a link to the companion website for corresponding activities, and the electronic Instructor's Manual files.

Allyn and Bacon Transparencies for Social Psychology, © 2005

Approximately 100 revised, full-color acetates to enhance classroom lectures and discussions. Includes images from Allyn & Bacon's major Social Psychology texts.

Interactive Video for Social Psychology

A wonderful tool including 9 video clips. Clips cover such topics as self-esteem, plastic surgery, philanthropy, bullying, sororities, age discrimination, and more. Critical thinking questions accompany each clip. In addition, the video guide provides further critical thinking questions and Internet resources for more information.

MyPsychLab for Social Psychology

This interactive and instructive multimedia resource can be used to supplement a traditional lecture course or to administer a course entirely online. It is an all-inclusive tool, a text-specific e-book plus multimedia tutorials, audio, video, simulations, animations, and controlled assessments to completely engage students and reinforce learning. Fully customizable and easy to use, MyPsychLab meets the individual teaching and learning needs of every instructor and every student. Visit the site at **www.mypsychlab.com.**

■ For the Student:

Grade Aid Study Guide

Melinda Blackman, California State University, Fullerton

Written by Melinda Blackman, California State University, Fullerton, this guide aids students in synthesizing the material they are learning and helps them prepare for exams. Each chapter includes "Before You Read," with a brief chapter summary and chapter learning objectives; "As You Read," a collection of demonstrations, in-depth activities, and exercises; "After You Read," containing three short practice quizzes and one comprehensive practice test; "When You Have Finished," with web links for further information; and crossword puzzles using key terms from the text. An appendix includes answers to all practice tests and crossword puzzles.

Companion Website (www.ablongman.com/baronbyrne11e)

A unique resource for connecting the textbook to the Internet. Each chapter includes learning objectives; chapter summaries; updated and annotated web links for additional sources of information; flashcard glossary terms; online practice tests with multiple choice, true/false, and essay questions; and psychology activities. Visit this site at www.ablongman.com/baronbyrne11e.

Research Navigator Guide: Psychology, with access to Research Navigator™

Allyn & Bacon's new Research Navigator™ is the easiest way for students to start a research assignment or research paper. Complete with extensive help on the research process and three exclusive databases of credible and reliable source material including EBSCO's ContentSelect Academic Journal Database, New York Times Search by Subject Archive, and "Best of the Web" Link Library, Research Navigator™ helps students quickly and efficiently make the most of their research time. The booklet contains a practical and to-the-point discussion of search engines; detailed information on evaluating online sources and citation guidelines for web resources; web activities for Psychology; web links for Psychology; and a complete guide to Research Navigator.

Some Concluding Comments

In closing, we would like to ask, once again, for your help. As was true of past editions, we have spared no effort to make this new one the best ever. While it's possible to *imagine* perfection, we fully realize that it is impossible to attain. So, we sincerely request your ideas and suggestions for further improvements. If there is something you feel can be better, please let us know. Write, call, e-mail, or fax us at the addresses below. We'll be genuinely glad to receive your input and—even more important—we will definitely listen! Thanks in advance for your help.

Robert A. Baron
Pittsburgh Building
Rensselaer Polytechnic Institute
Troy, NY 12180-3590
Phone: (518) 276-2864
E-mail: baronr@rpi.edu
Fax: (518) 276-8661

Donn Byrne
Department of Psychology
University at Albany, SUNY
Albany, NY 12222
Phone: (518) 768-2643
E-mail: vyaduckdb@aol.com
Fax: (518) 442-4867

Nyla R. Branscombe
Department of Psychology
University of Kansas
1415 Jayhawk Blvd.
Lawrence, KS 66045
Phone: 785-864-9832
E-mail: nyla@ku.edu
Fax: 785-864-5696

ACKNOWLEDGMENTS

Words of Thanks

Each time we write this book, we gain a stronger appreciation of the following fact: We couldn't do it without the help of many talented, dedicated people. Although we can't possibly thank all of them here, we do wish to express our appreciation to those whose help has been most valuable.

First, our sincere thanks to the colleagues listed below who responded to our survey regarding how the eleventh edition could be improved. Their input was invaluable to us in planning this new edition.

Susan Doyle, Gainsville College

Karen A. Couture, Keene State College

M. Denise McClung, West Virginia University

John W. Porter, Thomas More College

Helen Harton, University of Northern Iowa

Timothy Franz, St. John Fisher College

J. Beth Mabry, Indiana University of Pennsylvania

Nancy J. Karlin, University of Northern Colorado

Daniel McElwreath, William Paterson University

Chris R. Logan, Southern Methodist University

Paul Windschitl, University of Iowa

Second, we wish to offer our personal thanks to Kelly May and Susan Hartman, our editors at Allyn & Bacon. It has been a pleasure to work with them and get to know them, and we wish to thank them for their help, enthusiasm, and efforts to make this new edition the best one yet.

Third, our sincere thanks to Max Effenson Chuck, our developmental editor. Her insightful comments helped to improve the book in many ways, and we are truly grateful to her for her excellent suggestions, her encouragement, and her obvious commitment to the project. Thanks, Max!

Fourth, our thanks to Kristina Smead for very careful and constructive copyediting. Her comments were insightful and thought provoking, thus providing valuable help in improving and clarifying our words.

Fifth, our thanks to all of those others who contributed to various aspects of the production process: to Katharine S. Cook for photo research, to Joyce C. Weston for design work, and to Susan Paradise for the cover design.

We also wish to offer our thanks to the many colleagues who provided reprints and preprints of their work. These individuals are too numerous to list here, but their input is gratefully acknowledged.

Special thanks are also extended to Rebecca A. Henry for her insightful comments on several of the chapters, to Amy Le Fevre for her work on the references, and to Lindsey Kelley Byrne and Rebecka Byrne Kelley for their help in many different ways.

Finally, our sincere thanks to Michele Van Volkom for her work on the Instructor's Manual; and to Melinda Blackman for her help in preparing the Study Guide. To all of these truly outstanding people, and to many others, too, our warmest personal regards and thanks.

ABOUT THE AUTHORS

Robert A. Baron is Professor of Psychology and Wellington Professor of Management at Rensselaer Polytechnic Institute. He received his Ph.D. from the University of Iowa in 1968. Professor Baron has held faculty appointments at Purdue University, the University of Minnesota, the University of Texas, the University of South Carolina, and Princeton University. In 1982 he was a Visiting Fellow at Oxford University. From 1979 to 1981 he served as a Program Director at the National Science Foundation (Washington, DC). He has been a Fellow of the American Psychological Association and is also a Fellow of the American Psychological Society. In 2001, he was appointed an Invited Senior Research Fellow by the French government, and held this post at the Université des Sciences Sociales at Toulouse, France.

Professor Baron has published more than one hundred articles in professional journals and thirty-five chapters in edited volumes. He is the author or coauthor of forty-two books, including *Behavior in Organizations* (8th ed.), *Psychology: From Science to Practice,* and *Entrepreneurship: A Process Perspective.* Professor Baron holds three U.S. patents based on his research, and served as president of his own company (Innovative Environmental Products, Inc.) from 1992 to 2000. Professor Baron's current research focuses mainly on the social and cognitive factors that influence entrepreneurs' success, and on various forms of workplace aggression.

Donn Byrne holds the rank of Distinguished Professor of Psychology at the University at Albany, State University of New York. He received his Ph.D. in 1958 from Stanford University and has held academic positions at the California State University at San Francisco, the University of Texas, and Purdue University, as well as visiting professorships at the University of Hawaii and Stanford University. He was elected president of the Midwestern Psychological Association and of the Society for the Scientific Study of Sexuality. He headed the personality program at Texas, the social-personality programs at Purdue and at Albany, and was chair of the psychology department at Albany. Professor Byrne is a Fellow of the American Psychological Association and a Charter Fellow of the American Psychological Society.

During his career, Professor Byrne has published over 150 articles in professional journals, and twenty-nine of them have been republished in books of readings. He has authored or coauthored thirty-six chapters in edited volumes, and fourteen books, including *Psychology: An Introduction to a Behavioral Science* (four editions plus translations in Spanish, Portuguese, and Chinese), *An Introduction to Personality* (three editions), *The Attraction Paradigm,* and *Exploring Human Sexuality.*

He has served on the editorial boards of fourteen professional journals, and has directed the doctoral work of fifty-two Ph.D. students. He was invited to deliver a G. Stanley Hall lecture at the 1981 meeting of the American Psychological Association in Los Angeles and a state of the science address at the 1981 meeting of the Society for the Scientific Study of Sexuality in New York City. He was invited to testify at Attorney

General Meese's Commission on Obscenity and Pornography in Houston in 1986 and to participate in Surgeon General Koop's Workshop on Pornography and Health in 1986 in Arlington, Virginia. He received the Excellence in Research Award from the University at Albany in 1987 and the Distinguished Scientific Achievement Award from the Society for the Scientific Study of Sexuality in 1989. In 2002, he participated in a Festschrift honoring his scientific contributions at the University of Connecticut organized by his graduate students (past and present) from Texas, Purdue, and Albany. He delivered the William Griffitt Memorial Lecture at Kansas State University in 2004. Professor Byrne's current research focuses on the determinants of interpersonal attraction, adult attachment styles, and sexually coercive behavior.

Nyla R. Branscombe is Professor of Psychology at University of Kansas. She received her B.A. from York University in Toronto in 1980, a M.A. from the University of Western Ontario in 1982, and her Ph.D. from Purdue University in 1986. Professor Branscombe held a postdoctoral appointment at the University of Illinois at Urbana–Champaign in 1987. In 1993 she was a Visiting Fellow at Free University of Amsterdam. She served as Associate Editor of *Personality and Social Psychology Bulletin* for three years, and presently serves as Associate Editor of *Group Processes and Intergroup Relations.*

Professor Branscombe has published more than eighty articles and chapters in professional journals and edited volumes. In 1999, she was a recipient of the Otto Klienberg prize for research on Intercultural and International Relations from the Society for the Psychological Study of Social Issues. In 2004, she coedited the volume, *Collective Guilt: International Perspectives.* Professor Branscombe's current research focuses primarily on two main issues: the psychology of privileged groups, in particular when and why they may feel guilt about their advantages, and the psychology of disadvantaged groups, especially how they cope with prejudice and discrimination.

Social Psychology

1 THE FIELD OF SOCIAL PSYCHOLOGY
How We Think about and Interact with Others

CHAPTER OUTLINE

When I (Robert Baron) was a junior in high school, I tried out for the track team—and made it. This didn't surprise me much because I had always been one of the fastest runners in my neighborhood. Being on the track team meant that I could wear a special patch on my jacket and that I had a chance to win medals—and glory!—when my team competed. But it also meant a lot of hard work. We had training several times a week after class, and our coach was really tough: While performing the exercises he gave us, I discovered muscles I didn't even know I had! But I stuck with it and did win a few races before I quit in my senior year to take a job after school.

But what, you are probably wondering, does this have to do with social psychology, the focus of this book? Actually, quite a lot. Although at first glance it might seem as though joining a high school track team has very little to do with the social side of life, it really *does*. Consider this question: Why did I try out for the team in the first place? The answer clearly involves *influence* from other people—friends who told me, "Baron, you are fast . . . you should go out for the team." Similarly, it involved key aspects of my *self-perceptions*. I knew from experience that my friends were right: I *was* a fast runner. This was part of my self-concept (formed by comparing myself with others—what social psychologists term *social comparison*), and I believed it was true, just as I was certain that I was far too short for my school's basketball team. Where does our self-concept come from? As you will discover in Chapter 5, it comes largely from information provided by other people; no one can really tell that he or she is smart, attractive, friendly, or anything else by looking into a mirror. Rather, we acquire such knowledge mainly from our contacts with other persons, who tell us—over and over—what we are really like. So my decision to join the

Chapter 1 / The Field of Social Psychology

team was clearly shaped by important social factors, such as influence and socially derived self-perceptions.

But there's more to the story than this. I also realized that winning a spot on the team would make me a member of a fairly elite *group;* athletes of every kind were minor heroes or heroines in my school. In addition, I liked the idea of competing against other runners and, if I were lucky, winning. *Group processes* such as these are another key focus of social psychology—and a basic fact of social life.

Finally, I believed that being on the team would make me more *attractive* to the girls in my school, and especially to one named Linda Fisher, on whom I had a major crush. As I worked out each day, I imagined her in the audience, watching me win a race and then, perhaps, showering me with approval. So, aspects of *social thought*—how we think about other people and the effects this has on our behavior—certainly played a role in my decision to join the team. As you will note throughout this book, social thought is a major theme of modern social psychology.

In short, my brief foray into the world of high school athletics illustrates a basic fact of life and a key theme of this book: *Virtually everything we do, feel, or think is related in some way to the social side of life.* In fact, our relations with other people are so central to our lives and happiness that it is hard to imagine existing without them, although as the cartoon in Figure 1.1 suggests, we can

"This model is called the 'Aunt Edna.' The support bar digs into one's back, assuring that unwanted guests stay only one night."

Figure 1.1 ■ **The Social Side of Life: Essential but Not Always Fun!**
Our relations with other people are such a central part of our lives that we cannot readily imagine existing without them. As this cartoon indicates, however, we don't enjoy our interactions with everyone we know or meet!
(*Source:* CLOSE TO HOME © 2003 John McPherson. Reprinted with permission of UNIVERSAL PRESS SYNDICATE. All rights reserved.)

certainly live without some of them. Survivors of shipwrecks or plane crashes who spend long periods of time alone often state that not having relationships with other people was the hardest part of their ordeal—more difficult to bear than lack of food or shelter. In short, the social side of life is, in many ways, the core of our existence. It is this basic fact that makes *social psychology*—the branch of psychology that studies all aspects of social behavior and social thought—so fascinating and so essential.

Having offered this passionate endorsement of social psychology, we would truly love to plunge right in and begin describing its fascinating findings for you. Before getting started, however, it's important to begin with some background information about the scope, nature, and methods of our field. Why is such information useful? Because research findings in cognitive psychology indicate that people have a much better chance of understanding, remembering, and using new information if they are first provided with a framework within which to organize it. In view of this fact, this introductory chapter is intended as a means of providing you with a framework for interpreting and understanding social psychology and everything about it that is contained in this book. Specifically, here's an outline of what we plan to do. (By the way, we provide this kind of outline at the start of each chapter.)

First, we present a more formal *definition* of social psychology: what it is and what it seeks to accomplish. Second, we describe some major, current trends in social psychology. These are reflected throughout this book, so knowing about them at the start helps you recognize them and understand why they are important. Third, we examine some of the methods used by social psychologists to answer questions about the social side of life. A working knowledge of these basic methods will help you to understand how social psychologists add to our knowledge of social thought and social behavior, and will also be useful to you outside the context of this course.

Social Psychology: A Working Definition

Providing a formal definition of almost any field is a complex task. In the case of social psychology, this difficulty is increased by two factors: the field's broad scope and its rapid rate of change. As you will note in each chapter of this book, social psychologists have a wide range of interests. Despite this fact, however, most social psychologists focus primarily on the following task: understanding how and why individuals behave, think, and feel as they do in social situations—ones involving the actual or imagined presence of other persons. Consistent with this basic fact, we define **social psychology** as *the scientific field that seeks to understand the nature and causes of individual behavior and thought in social situations.* We now clarify this definition by taking a closer look at several aspects of it.

social psychology
The scientific field that seeks to understand the nature and causes of individual behavior and thought in social situations.

Figure 1.2 ■ What Is Science, Really?
Many people seem to believe that only fields that use sophisticated equipment such as that shown here (*left photo*) can be viewed as scientific. In fact, though, the term *science* simply refers to adherence to a set of basic values (e.g., accuracy, objectivity) and use of a set of basic methods that can be applied to almost any aspect of the world around us, including the social side of life. In contrast, fields that are *not* scientific in nature (*right photo*) do not accept these values or use these methods.

Social Psychology Is Scientific in Nature

What is *science*? Many people seem to believe that this term refers only to fields such as chemistry, physics, and biology—ones that use the kind of equipment shown in the left photo in Figure 1.2. If you share this view, you may find our suggestion that social psychology is a scientific discipline somewhat puzzling. How can a field that studies the nature of love, the causes of aggression, and everything in between be scientific in the same sense as physics, biochemistry, or computer science? The answer is surprisingly simple.

In reality, the term *science* does not refer to a special group of highly advanced fields. Rather, it refers to two things: (1) a set of values and (2) several methods that can be used to study a wide range of topics. In deciding whether a given field is or is not scientific, therefore, the critical question is, "Does it adopt these values and methods?" To the extent that it does, it is scientific in nature; to the extent it does not, it falls outside the realm of science. We examine in detail the research procedures used by social psychologists in a later section, but here we focus on the core values that all fields must adopt to be considered scientific in nature. Four of the most important of these core values are:

1. *Accuracy:* A commitment to gathering and evaluating information about the world (including social behavior and thought) in as careful, precise, and error-free a manner as is possible.

2. *Objectivity:* A commitment to obtaining and evaluating such information in a manner that is as free of bias as is humanly possible.

3. *Skepticism:* A commitment to accepting findings as accurate only to the extent that they have been verified repeatedly.

4. *Open-mindedness:* A commitment to changing one's views—even views that are strongly held—if existing evidence suggests that these views are inaccurate.

Social psychology, as a field, is deeply committed to these values and applies them in its efforts to understand the nature of social behavior and social thought. For this reason, it makes sense to describe social psychology as scientific in orientation. In contrast, fields that are *not* scientific make assertions about the world and about people that are not subjected to the careful test and analysis required by the values listed above. In such fields (e.g., astrology and aromatherapy), intuition, faith, and unobservable forces are considered to be sufficient (see Figure 1.2) for reaching conclusions—the opposite of what is true in social psychology.

■ "But Why Adopt the Scientific Approach? Isn't Social Psychology Merely Common Sense?"

Having taught for many years (more than one hundred between us), we can almost hear you asking these questions. We understand why you might feel this way. All of us have spent our entire lives interacting with other people and thinking about them, so, in a sense, we are all amateur social psychologists. Why not rely on our own experience and intuition—or even on the wisdom of the ages—as a basis for understanding the social side of life? Our answer is straightforward: because such sources provide an inconsistent and unreliable guide.

For instance, consider the following statement, suggested by common sense: "Absence makes the heart grow fonder." Do you agree? When people are separated from those they love, is it true that they miss them and so experience increased longing for them? Many people would agree. They would answer, "Yes, that's right. Let me tell you about the time I was separated from . . . ." But now consider the following statement: "Out of sight, out of mind." How about this one? Is it true? When people are separated from those they love, do they quickly find another romantic interest? As you can see, these two views—both suggested by common sense—are contradictory. The same is true for many other informal observations about human behavior: They seem plausible but often suggest opposite conclusions. How about these: "Two heads are better than one" and "Too many cooks spoil the broth"? One suggests that when people work together, they perform better (e.g., make better decisions). The other suggests that when they work together, they may get in each other's way so that performance is actually reduced. By now, the main point should be clear: Common sense often suggests a confusing and inconsistent picture of human behavior, which is one important reason why social psychologists put their faith in the scientific method: It yields much more conclusive evidence. In fact, the scientific method is designed to help us determine not only *which* of the opposite sets of predictions listed previously is correct, but also *when* and *why* one or the other might apply. We think this principle is so important that we call attention to it throughout the book in special sections designed to show how careful research by social psychologists has helped to refine—and in some cases, to refute—the conclusions offered by common sense. These sections are titled, **The Science of Social Psychology: Making Sense of Common Sense.** We believe they will give you a true appreciation of why the scientific field of social psychology is so important and valuable.

But this is not the only reason for being suspicious of common sense. Another reason relates to the fact that, unlike Mr. Spock of *Star Trek* fame, we are not perfect information-processing machines. On the contrary, as we note repeatedly (e.g., in Chapters 2, 3, 4, and 6), our thinking is subject to several forms of error that can lead us seriously astray. Here's one example: Think back over major projects on which you have worked in the past (writing term papers, cooking a complicated dish, painting your room). Now, try to remember two things: (1) your initial estimates about how long it would take

Chapter 1 / The Field of Social Psychology

you to complete these jobs and (2) how long it actually took. Is there a gap between these two numbers? In all likelihood there is, because most of us fall victim to the *planning fallacy*—a strong tendency to believe that projects will take less time than they actually do or, alternatively, that we can accomplish more in a given period of time than is really true. Moreover, we are susceptible to this bias in our thoughts over and over again, despite repeated experiences that tell us that everything will take longer than we think it will.

Why are we subject to this kind of error? Research by social psychologists indicates that part of the answer involves a tendency to think about the future when we are estimating how long a job will take. This prevents us from remembering how long similar tasks took in the past, and that in turn leads us to underestimate the time we will need to accomplish the current task (e.g., Buehler, Griffin, & Ross, 1994). This is just one of the many ways in which we can—and often do—make errors in thinking about other people (and ourselves); we consider many others in Chapter 3. Because we are prone to such errors in our informal thinking about the social world, we cannot rely on it—or on common sense—to solve the mysteries of social behavior. Rather, we need scientific evidence; and that, in essence, is what social psychology is all about.

Social Psychology Focuses on the Behavior of Individuals

Societies differ greatly in terms of their views concerning courtship and marriage; yet, it is still individuals who fall in love. Similarly, societies vary greatly in terms of their overall levels of violence; yet, it is still individuals who perform aggressive actions or refrain from doing so. The same argument applies to virtually all other aspects of social behavior, from prejudice to helping: The actions are performed by, and the thoughts occur in, the minds of individuals. Due to this basic fact, the focus in social psychology is strongly on individuals. Social psychologists realize, of course, that we do not exist in isolation from social and cultural influences—far from it. As you will see throughout this book, much social behavior occurs in group settings, and these can exert powerful effects on us. But the field's major interest lies in understanding the factors that shape the actions and thoughts of individuals in social settings.

Social Psychology Seeks to Understand the Causes of Social Behavior and Social Thought

In a key sense, the heading of this section states the most central aspect of our definition: Social psychologists are interested primarily in understanding the many factors and conditions that shape the social behavior and social thought of individuals—their actions, feelings, beliefs, memories, and inferences concerning other persons. Obviously, a huge number of variables play a role in this regard. Most variables, though, fall under the following five headings.

The Actions and Characteristics of Other Persons
Imagine the following events:

> *You are attending a concert in a theater when a person seated nearby receives a call on his cell phone and begins a loud conversation about very private topics.*

> *You are eating a meal with two friends in a restaurant. The server is very attractive, and after taking your order, he or she smiles at you and touches you briefly on the arm in a very friendly way.*

> *You are in a hurry and notice that you are driving far above the speed limit. Suddenly, up ahead, you see the blinking lights of a state trooper who has pulled another driver over and is giving her a ticket.*

Figure 1.3 ■ Reacting to the Actions of Other Persons
As shown in these scenes, the behaviors of other persons often exert powerful effects on our own behaviors and social thoughts.

Will these actions by other persons have any effect on your behavior and thoughts? Absolutely. You will probably become annoyed with the person speaking on the cell phone and may even say something to him. The waitperson's behavior may well add to your enjoyment of the meal—and trigger some interesting thoughts about getting to know this person better. And the second you spot the state trooper's blinking light, you will almost certainly slow down—a lot! Instances such as these, which occur hundreds of times each day, indicate that other persons' behaviors often have a powerful impact on us (see Figure 1.3).

In addition, we are also often affected by others' appearance. Be honest: Have you ever felt uneasy in the presence of a person with a physical disability? Do you ever behave differently toward highly attractive persons than toward less attractive ones? Toward elderly persons than toward young ones? Toward persons belonging to racial and ethnic groups different from your own? Your answer to some of these questions is probably "yes," because we do often react to others' visible characteristics, such as their appearance (e.g., McCall, 1997; Twenge & Manis, 1998). In fact, findings reported by Hassin and Trope (2000) indicate that we cannot ignore others' appearance, even when we consciously try to do so. So, clearly, despite warnings to avoid "judging books by their covers," we are often strongly affected by other persons' outward appearance— even if we are unaware of such effects and might deny their existence.

■ Cognitive Processes

Suppose that you have arranged to meet a friend, and this person is late. In fact, after thirty minutes you begin to suspect that your friend will never arrive. Finally, she or he does appear and says, "Sorry . . . I forgot all about meeting you until a few minutes ago." How do you react? Probably with considerable annoyance. Imagine that instead, however, your friend says, "I'm so sorry to be late. There was a big accident, and the traffic was tied up for miles." Now how do you react? Probably with less annoyance—but not necessarily. If your friend is often late and has used this excuse before, you may be suspicious about whether this explanation is true. In contrast, if this is the first time your friend has been late, or if your friend has never used such an excuse in the past, you may accept it as true. In other words, your reactions in this situation depend strongly on your *memories* of your friend's past behavior and your *inferences* about whether her or his explanation is actually true. Situations such as these call attention to the fact that *cognitive processes* play a crucial role in social behavior and social thought. We are always trying to make sense out of the social world, and this effort leads us to engage in lots of social cognition—to think long and hard about other persons: what they are like, why they do what they do, how they might react to our behaviors, and so on (e.g., Shah, 2003). Social psychologists are well aware of the importance of such processes. In fact, social cognition is one of the most important areas of research in the field (e.g., Killeya & Johnson, 1998; Swann & Gill, 1997).

■ Environmental Variables: Impact of the Physical World

Are people more prone to wild impulsive behavior during the full moon than at other times (Rotton & Kelley, 1985)? Do we become more irritable and aggressive when the weather is hot and steamy than when it is cool and comfortable (Anderson, Bushman, & Groom, 1997; Rotton & Cohn, 2000)? Does exposure to a pleasant smell in the air make people more helpful to others (Baron, 1997)? Research findings indicate that the physical environment does influence our feelings, thoughts, and behaviors, so ecological variables fall within the realm of modern social psychology.

■ Cultural Context

Have you ever seen the old TV program *Leave It to Beaver*? What about *I Love Lucy*? If so, you know that these programs painted a picture of a very happy world, one in which parents were kind and understanding, children loved and respected them, and divorce was nonexistent (see Figure 1.4). These programs exaggerated; life in the 1950s and 1960s was not all sunshine and roses. It is true, though, that divorce rates were much lower than they are at present. Why? This is a complex question, but an important part of the answer involves changing *cultural beliefs* and *values*. In previous decades, divorce was viewed as a drastic action—something a person did only under extreme conditions (e.g., an abusive or repeatedly unfaithful spouse). Further, divorce was viewed in negative terms; cultural beliefs suggested that it was better to suffer in silence than to break up a home and family.

Although divorce is still viewed as a sad and unhappy event, cultural beliefs about it have changed greatly. Personal unhappiness is now considered adequate grounds for ending a marriage, and divorced persons are no longer viewed as unusual or somehow flawed. In fact, sad to relate, persons who remain married throughout life are now the exception rather than the rule.

These changes in beliefs concerning divorce are only one illustration of an important and basic fact: Social behavior does not occur in a cultural vacuum. On the

Figure 1.4 ■ Cultural Change as a Determinant of Social Behavior
Although the picture of family life portrayed by television shows in the 1950s was unrealistically positive, there *have* been major changes in cultural norms since that time. Such changes often exert powerful effects on social behavior.

evolutionary psychology
A new branch of psychology that seeks to investigate the potential role of genetic factors in various aspects of human behavior.

contrary, social behavior is often strongly affected by cultural norms (social rules concerning how people should behave in specific situations; see Chapter 9), membership in various groups, and changing societal values. Cultural norms say a lot about important life decisions, such as when people should marry and to whom, how many children they should have, whether it is all right to "fudge" one's income taxes, to be in debt, or to drive a large, gas-guzzling SUV, to mention just a few examples. So, clearly, social behavior and social thought can be, and often are, strongly affected by cultural factors. (The term *culture* refers to the system of shared meanings, perceptions, and beliefs held by persons belonging to some group [Smith & Bond, 1993].) As you'll soon discover, attention to the effects of cultural factors is an important trend in social psychology as the field attempts to take account of the growing cultural diversity in many different countries.

Biological Factors

Do biological processes and genetic factors influence social behavior? In the past, most social psychologists would have answered "no," at least to the genetic part of this question. Now, however, many have come to believe that our preferences, behaviors, emotions, and even attitudes are affected, to some extent, by our biological inheritance (Buss, 1999; Buss & Schmitt, 1993; Schmitt, 2004; Nisbett, 1990).

The view that biological factors play an important role in social behavior comes from the field of **evolutionary psychology** (e.g., Buss, 1999; Buss & Shackelford, 1997). This new branch of psychology suggests that our species, like all others on the planet, has been subjected to the process of biological evolution throughout its history, and that as a result of this process, we now possess a large number of *evolved psychological mechanisms* that help (or once helped) us deal with important problems relating to survival. How do these mechanisms become part of our biological inheritance? Through the process of evolution, which, in turn, involves three basic components: *variation, inheritance,* and *selection.* Variation refers to the fact that organisms belonging to a given species vary in many different ways; indeed, such variation is a basic part of life on our planet. Human beings, as you know, come in a wide variety of shapes and sizes, and they vary on what sometimes seems to be an almost countless number of dimensions.

Inheritance refers to the fact that some of these variations can be passed from one generation to the next through complex mechanisms that we are only now beginning to fully understand. Selection refers to the fact that some variations give the individuals who possess them an edge in terms of reproduction: They are more likely to survive, find mates, and pass these variations on to succeeding generations. The result is that, over time, more and more members of the species possess these variations. This change in the characteristics of a species over time—often immensely long periods of time—is the concrete outcome of evolution. (See Figure 1.5 for a summary of this process.)

Social psychologists who adopt the evolutionary perspective suggest that this process applies to at least some aspects of social behavior. For instance, consider the question of mate preference. Why do we find some people attractive? According to the evolutionary perspective, because the characteristics they show—symmetrical facial features; well-toned, shapely bodies

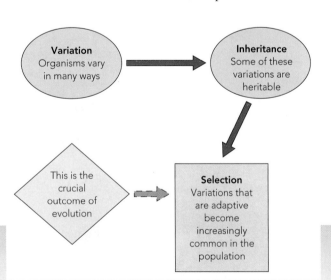

Figure 1.5 ▪ Evolution: An Overview
As shown here, evolution involves three major components: variation, inheritance, and selection.

(e.g., a relatively large waist-to-hip ratio in women; Schmitt & Buss, 2001; Tesser & Martin, 1996); clear skin; lustrous hair—are associated with reproductive capacity. In other words, these are outward signs of inner health and vigor. Thus, a preference for these characteristics in mates among our ancestors increased the chances that they would reproduce successfully; this, in turn, contributed to our preference for these aspects of appearance.

A related question involves what evolutionary psychologists term *short-term mating strategies*—how many sexual partners to whom they are not deeply committed people would prefer to have. Informal observation suggests that a gender difference may exist, with men preferring many different partners and women preferring a smaller number. An evolutionary perspective suggests that such differences, if they exist, are the result of evolutionary pressures. For instance, although men can father an almost infinite number of children and therefore pass their genes on to many offspring, women can have only a limited number, no matter how many sexual partners they have. So, having a lot of partners might be adaptive for men from an evolutionary perspective but be less adaptive for women, who might need the help of a long-term partner to raise their children to maturity. Do such differences exist? Many studies suggest that they do (e.g., Barash & Lipton, 2001; Buss & Schmitt, 1993).

For example, consider a recent study by Schmitt (2004) that involved more than sixteen thousand people living in virtually every major region of the world (North America, South America, Western Europe, Eastern Europe, Africa, the Middle East, Oceania, Southeast Asia, East Asia). Participants were asked a variety of questions relating to how many different sexual partners they would like to have over varying periods of time (from one month to their entire lifetimes), and how long they would want to know someone before having sexual relations with that person. Regardless of the measures used and across every region studied, men indicated a preference for more partners than did women (see Figure 1.6) and reported that they would require knowing someone for a shorter period of time before having sexual relations with them. Although there is no guarantee that these differences reflect the impact of genetic factors, they are consistent with predictions derived from an evolutionary perspective. Moreover, the fact that these differences in the

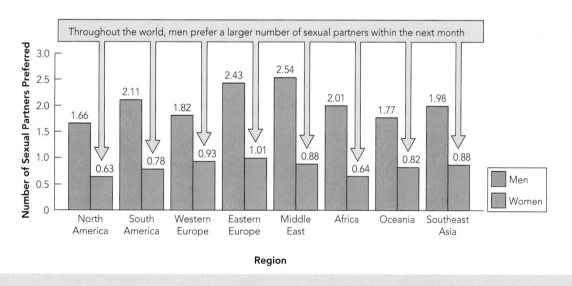

Figure 1.6 ■ Gender Differences in Short-Term Mating Strategies
As shown here, men preferred a larger number of sexual partners within the next month than did women. The fact that this finding occurs in many different cultures throughout the world indicates that genetic factors may play a role in its occurrence, as an *evolutionary* perspective suggests. (*Source: Based on data from Schmitt, 2003b.*)

desired number of partners occur in many different cultures points to the possibility that this particular difference between men and women may have some genetic component.

Many other topics have been studied from the evolutionary perspective (e.g., helping others, preferences for various ways of attracting persons who are already in a relationship—*mate poaching;* e.g., Schmitt, 2004; Schmitt & Shackelford, 2003), and we will consider such research in several later chapters (e.g., Chapters 10 and 11). Here, however, we emphasize an important fact: The evolutionary perspective does *not* suggest that we inherit specific patterns of social behavior. Rather, it contends that we inherit tendencies or predispositions that may or may not be translated into reality, depending on the environments in which we live. Similarly, this perspective does *not* suggest that we are "forced" or driven by our genes to act in specific ways. It merely suggests that because of our genetic inheritance, we have tendencies to behave in certain ways that, at least in the past, enhanced the chances that our ancestors would survive and pass their genes on to us. These tendencies, however, can be reduced or overridden by cognitive factors and the effects of experience (i.e., learning). Here's a clear example of this fact: Recent findings (Pettijohn & Jungeberg, 2004) indicate that men's preferences for certain facial and body characteristics in women may change with shifting economic conditions. Specifically, when economic conditions are bad, men's preferences tend to shift toward more mature-looking women (e.g., ones with smaller eyes, larger chins, and fuller figures), as compared to when economic conditions are good. These findings suggest that even if we do have biologically based tendencies to find others with certain traits attractive, these tendencies can readily be overridden by other factors. So, the evolutionary perspective does *not* accept the view that biology is destiny—far from it.

Social Psychology: Summing Up

In sum, social psychology focuses mainly on understanding the causes of social behavior and social thought—on identifying factors that shape our feelings, behaviors, and thoughts in social situations. It seeks to accomplish this goal through the use of scientific methods, and it takes careful note of the fact that a wide range of social, cognitive, environmental, cultural, and biological factors influence social behavior and thought.

The remainder of this text is devoted to describing some of the key findings of social psychology. This information is fascinating, so we're certain that you will find it of interest. We're equally sure, however, that you will also find some of it surprising, and that it will challenge many of your ideas about people and social relations. So, get ready for some new insights. We predict that after reading this book, you'll never think about the social side of life in quite the same way.

KEY POINTS

★ *Social psychology* is the scientific field that seeks to understand the nature and causes of individual behavior and thought in social situations.

★ *Social psychology* is scientific in nature because it adopts the values and methods used in other fields of science.

★ Social psychologists adopt the scientific method because common sense provides an unreliable guide to social behavior and because our thoughts are influenced by many potential sources of bias.

★ *Social psychology* focuses on the behavior of individuals and seeks to understand the causes of social behavior and thought, which can involve the behavior and appearance of others, social cognition, environmental factors, cultural values, and even biological and genetic factors.

Social Psychology: Its Cutting Edge

We feel strongly that any textbook should reflect the field it covers in an accurate and up-to-date manner. Consistent with this belief, we now describe several major trends in modern social psychology—themes and ideas that appear to be on the cutting edge of our field and that we represent throughout this book.

Cognition and Behavior: Two Sides of the Same Social Coin

At one time in the past, social psychologists could be divided into two distinct groups: those who were interested primarily in social behavior (how people act in social situations) and those who were interested primarily in social thought (how people attempt to make sense out of the social world and to understand themselves and others). This division has now largely disappeared. In modern social psychology, behavior and cognition are seen as intimately and continuously linked. In other words, there is virtually universal agreement in the field that we cannot hope to understand how and why people behave in certain ways in social situations without considering their thoughts, memories, intentions, attitudes, and beliefs. Similarly, virtually all social psychologists agree that we cannot hope to fully understand how people think about the social world without considering how such social cognition affects their behavior and their relations with others. Perhaps a concrete example of what we mean will be helpful.

Consider the following question: Who would you like better—someone who seems to be very similar to yourself in many ways or someone who is different? (This is the "birds of a feather" versus "opposites attract" example mentioned earlier.) Decades of research point to the conclusion that, in general, the more similar others are to us, the more we tend to like them. But is this always true? Perhaps not. We all have a mental picture of what we are like right now—our *actual self*—and a mental picture of the kind of person we would like to be—our *ideal self.* Suppose that someone is not merely similar to you as you view yourself but, in fact, is more similar to what you'd like to be in the future than you are; in other words, he or she is closer to your ideal self than you are. Would you like this person? Perhaps, but it is also possible that you would find the situation a little threatening; after all, he or she is currently where you want to be in the future.

In fact, recent research by Herbst, Gaertner, and Insko (2003) has confirmed this kind of effect. They asked participants to rate themselves on thirty different dimensions (e.g., talkative—reserved; generous—stingy) both in terms of how they were right now (their actual self) and in terms of how they would like to be in the future (their ideal self). During a second session, a week later, participants received information indicating that on the basis of their earlier ratings, a computer program had derived a key defining dimension for them. In addition, they also received information about a stranger they would supposedly meet later. This stranger appeared to vary in terms of similarity to a participant's ideal self. In three conditions, he or she was increasingly similar but lower than a participant's ideal self on the key dimension. In one condition, however, the stranger was actually higher than a participant on this dimension; in other words, the stranger's current actual self was higher than a participant's ideal self. After receiving this information, the participants in the study rated their liking for the stranger. The researchers predicted that, at first, increasing similarity to a participant's ideal self would lead to greater liking for the stranger until this person surpassed the participant's ideal self, but then liking would decrease; this is precisely what happened.

The findings of this research are interesting in themselves, but they also illustrate the main point we wish to make: There is a continuous, complex interplay between social thought (how people think about themselves and others) and social behavior (how people act in social situations); for example, do they like or dislike others they meet for the first time? This perspective is now a given in modern social psychology, and it is a major theme in this book.

Social Neuroscience: Where Social Psychology and Neuroscience Meet

Do you understand these words as you read them? If so, your ability to do so is the result of activity in your brain. Do you feel happy? Sad? Excited? Calm? Again, whatever you are feeling right now derives from activity in your brain and other biological events. Can you remember what your psychology professor looks like? What your first kiss felt like? Once more, your ability to do so is the result of activity in several areas of your brain. In recent years, such powerful tools as magnetic resonance imaging (MRI) and PET scans have allowed psychologists and other scientists to peer into the human brain as people engage in various activities (e.g., while solving problems, looking at emotion-provoking photos or films, etc.) (see Figure 1.7). The result of these studies is that we now know much more about the complex relationships between neural events and psychological ones (feelings, thoughts, and overt actions).

In recent years, social psychologists, too, have begun to search for the neural foundations of social thought and social behavior. In fact, the volume of research on this topic has increased greatly and was featured recently in a special section of one of social psychology's leading journals (e.g., Harmon-Jones & Devine, 2003). In conducting this research, social psychologists use the same basic tools as other scientists: They study events in the brain (through the use of MRI and other kinds of brain scans), other neural activity, and even changes in the immune system (e.g., Taylor et al., 2003) to determine how these events are related to important social processes. The findings of this research are truly fascinating. For instance, consider a recent study by Ito and Urland (2003) concerning *social categorization*—how we decide whether individuals belong to one social category or another (e.g., black or white, male or female, liberal or conservative, etc.). These researchers studied the neural basis of this process by recording special kinds of electrical activity in the brain known as *event-related potentials*. Such events can occur very soon after people see a stimulus (e.g., another person) and reflect immediate reactions to the stimulus, while others occur later and seem to reflect more complex cognitive events, such as the operation of memory processes.

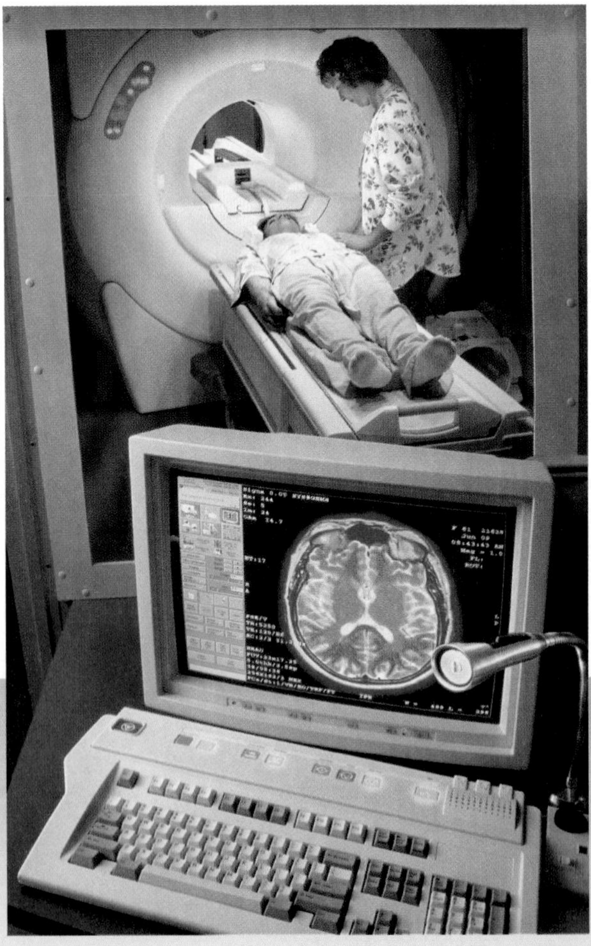

Figure 1.7 ■ Modern Techniques for Studying the Functioning Brain: One Foundation for Social Neuroscience
In recent years, techniques for studying activity in the functioning human brain have been devised (e.g., MRIs, PET scans). These techniques have allowed social psychologists to begin a scientific search for the neural roots of social processes.

In their study, Ito and Urland asked college students (almost all of whom were white) to indicate whether people shown in photographs were black or white and male or female. The photos were shown for one second each, and participants in the study indicated their judgment by pushing keys labeled "black," "white," "female," and "male." While they performed this task, recordings were made of several kinds of event-related brain potentials. Results indicated that, initially, attention was directed more to black than to white targets (i.e., photographs of black persons elicited larger potentials, indicating more attention). Later, but still relatively early in the process of social categorization, attention shifted to gender, with female targets inducing larger reactions than male targets. Only later did more complex factors relating to social context come into play, such as whether black persons were shown among other black persons or among white persons, and whether females were shown with other females or with males. Overall, the findings indicate that social categorization occurs very quickly—within one hundred milliseconds of seeing another person—and that people seem to pay attention to racial identity before they direct attention to gender. In other words, social categorization is not only fast; it also follows a distinct order in which we first pay attention to some kinds of information, then to others, and so on.

Research in the growing field of **social neuroscience** has investigated many additional topics—everything from how alcohol and other drugs affect our perceptions of other persons (Bartholow et al., 2003) to ways in which social thought can affect our health (e.g., people who view themselves in positive ways tend to be more resistant to stress than persons who do not engage in such self-enhancement) (Taylor et al., 2003). However, as noted recently by several experts (e.g., Cacioppo et al., 2003), social neuroscience cannot provide the answer to every question we have about social thought or behavior. For example, as Willingham and Dunn (2003) note, there are many aspects of social thought that cannot easily be related to activity in specific areas of the brain—aspects such as stereotypes, attitudes, attributions, and reciprocity. In principle, all of these components of social thought reflect activity in the brain, but this does not necessarily mean that it is best to try to study them in this way. In fact, the situation may be similar to that existing between chemistry and physics. All chemists agree that, ultimately, every chemical reaction can be explained in terms of physics. But the principles of chemistry are still so useful that chemists continue to use them in their research and do not rush out and become physicists. The same may well be true for social psychology: It does not have to seek to understand all of its major topics in terms of activities in the brain or nervous system; other approaches (described in later chapters) are still useful and can provide important new insights. Throughout this book, therefore, we describe research that uses a wide range of methods, from brain scans on one hand to direct observations of social behavior on the other. These methods reflect the current, eclectic nature of social psychology and are therefore the most appropriate content for this book.

The Role of Implicit (Nonconscious) Processes

Have you ever had the experience of meeting someone for the first time and taking an immediate liking or disliking to that person? Afterward, you may have wondered, "Why do I like (dislike) this person?" You probably didn't wonder for long, because we are all experts at finding good reasons to explain our own actions or feelings. This explanation in no way implies, however, that we really *do* understand why we behave or think in certain ways. In fact, a growing theme of recent research in social psychology is this: In many cases we really don't know why we think or behave as we do in social contexts. On the contrary, our thoughts and actions are shaped by factors and processes of which we are only dimly aware at best, and that often take place in an automatic manner without any conscious thought or intention on our part. This is one more reason why social psychologists are reluctant to trust common sense as a basis for reliable information

social neuroscience
An area of research in social psychology that seeks knowledge about the neural and biological bases of social processes.

about social behavior or social thought: We are unaware of many of the factors that influence how we think and how we behave and so cannot report on them accurately.

A very dramatic—and intriguing—illustration of this basic principle is provided by research conducted by Pelham, Mirenberg, and Jones (2002) in a paper entitled, "Why Susie Sells Seashells by the Seashore. . . ." In this research, the authors argued that as a result of *implicit egotism*—an unconscious tendency toward self-enhancement—our feelings about almost anything in the world around us are influenced by its relationship to our self-concept. The closer someone or something is to our self-concept, the more we will tend to like them or it. As a result, people will tend to live, at a higher rate than chance would predict, in places (cities or states) whose names resemble their own (e.g., people named Louis are more likely to live in St. Louis). Similarly, they will tend to live, at a greater than expected rate, in cities whose names begin with the numbers of their birthdays (e.g., Three Corners; Seven Springs) and will tend to choose careers whose names resemble their own (e.g., people named Dennis or Denise will be overrepresented among dentists, while people named Lawrence or Laura will be overrepresented among lawyers). In ten separate studies, Pelham, Mirenberg, and Jones found evidence for these predictions. While questions have been raised about the validity of these findings (Gallucci, 2003), additional evidence offers support for the original conclusion: Our preferences for the places in which we live and the careers we choose can be influenced by reactions and feelings we don't even realize we have (Pelham et al., 2003).

Research on the role of implicit (nonconscious) processes in our social behavior and thought has examined many other topics, such as the impact of our moods on what we tend to remember about other persons or complex issues (e.g., Ruder & Bless, 2003); how negative attitudes toward members of social groups other than our own, which we deny having, can still influence our reactions toward them (e.g., Fazio & Hilden, 2001); how we automatically evaluate persons belonging to various social groups once we have concluded that they belong to that group (Castelli, Zogmaister, & Smith, 2004); and how our tendency to assume that other people's behavior reflects their underlying traits rather than their reactions to the present situation can interfere with our ability to tell when they are lying (O'Sullivan, 2003). In short, the more deeply that social psychologists delve into this topic, the broader and more general the effects of nonconscious factors in our social behavior and thought seem to be. We examine such effects in several subsequent chapters because they are clearly on the cutting edge of progress in this field.

Taking Full Account of Social Diversity

There can be no doubt that the United States is undergoing a major social and cultural transformation. The census of 2000 indicates that 67 percent of the population identifies itself as white (of European heritage), while fully 33 percent identifies itself as belonging to some other group (13 percent African American, 4.5 percent American Indian, 13 percent Hispanic, 4.5 percent Asian/Pacific Islander, and 7 percent some other group). This represents a tremendous change from the 1960s, when approximately 90 percent of the population was of European descent. Indeed, in several states (e.g., California, New Mexico, Texas, Arizona), persons of European heritage are no longer a clear majority. In response to these tremendous shifts, psychologists have increasingly recognized the importance of taking cultural factors and differences into careful account in everything they do—teaching, research, counseling and therapy—and social psychologists are certainly no exception to this rule. They have been increasingly sensitive to the fact that individuals' cultural, ethnic, and racial heritages often play key roles in their self-identities, and that this, in turn, can exert important effects on their behaviors. This is in sharp contrast to the point of view that prevailed in the past, which suggested that cultural, ethnic, and gender differences are relatively unimportant. In contrast to that

Chapter 1 / The Field of Social Psychology

earlier perspective, social psychologists currently believe that such differences are *very* important and must be carefully taken into account in our effort to understand human behavior. As a result, psychology in general and social psychology, too, now adopt a **multicultural perspective**—one that carefully and clearly recognizes the potential importance of gender, age, ethnicity, sexual orientation, disability, socioeconomic status, religious orientation, and many other social and cultural dimensions.

This perspective led to important changes in the focus of social psychological research. For example, more recent studies conducted by social psychologists focus on ethnic and cultural differences in a wide range of social processes, including recognizing faces of persons belonging to one's own race versus those belonging to another race (e.g., Twenge & Crocker, 2002), cultural differences in binge drinking (Luczak, 2001), ethnic differences in optimism and pessimism (Chang & Asakawa, 2003), cultural and ethnic differences in reactions to sexual harassment (Cortina, 2004), and even cultural differences in attraction and love (e.g., Langlois et al., 2000). So, clearly, increased recognition of diversity is a hallmark of modern social psychology, and we discuss research highlighting the importance of such factors at many points in this book.

KEY POINTS

- ★ Social psychologists currently recognize that social thought and social behavior are two sides of the same coin and that there is a continuous, complex interplay between them.

- ★ Another major field of study involves growing interest in *social neuroscience*—efforts to relate activity in the brain and other biological events to key aspects of social thought and behavior.

- ★ Often our behavior and thoughts are shaped by factors of which we are unaware.

Growing attention to such implicit (nonconscious) processes is another major theme of modern *social psychology*.

- ★ *Social psychology* currently adopts a *multicultural perspective*, which recognizes the importance of cultural factors in social behavior and social thought and notes that research findings obtained in one culture do not necessarily generalize to other cultures.

Answering Questions about Social Behavior and Social Thought: Research Methods in Social Psychology

Now that we've described the current state of social psychology, we can turn to the third major task mentioned at the beginning of this chapter: explaining how social psychologists attempt to answer questions about social behavior and social thought—how, in short, they conduct their research. To provide you with basic information about this important issue, we examine three related topics. First, we will describe several *methods of research in social psychology*. Next, we consider the role of *theory* in such research. Finally, we touch on some of the complex *ethical issues* relating to social psychological research. Before beginning, though, we need to consider one other question about which you may already be wondering: Why should you bother to learn about the research methods used by social psychologists?

multicultural perspective
A focus on understanding the cultural and ethnic factors that influence social behavior.

Do you plan to become a psychologist? A social psychologist? If so, it is obvious why you need to know something about the basic methods of research used in psychological research. But even if you do not plan a career in social psychology, there are several reasons why it is very useful to know about these methods.

First, understanding how research is actually conducted will help you to understand many of the discussions in this text. Often, we will describe specific studies and what they tell us about the topics being considered. In this effort, we will assume that you have a working knowledge of the basic methods of research used by social psychologists. So, clearly, this information will be useful to you in this respect.

Second, and perhaps even more important, understanding the nature of research will help you to be a more informed consumer of knowledge. Almost every time you pick up a newspaper or magazine, you will find articles dealing with some aspect of the social side of life: Why do people fall in love? Why do they join cults? Are they affected by violent movies and video games? What are their attitudes toward the president, new fashion trends, or almost anything else? How should you interpret the findings reported? In part, by asking "How was this information obtained?" Some methods provide answers in which you can have more confidence than others, and understanding the nature of research—and its basic rules—will help you to decide what you should believe and what you should discount or reject. We give you practice in this regard in special **Beyond the Headlines** sections throughout the book that describe how social psychologists would react to newspaper articles dealing with social behavior. Understanding basic research methods, however, will be very helpful to you when you are on your own and must decide what information is useful and what should be ignored.

Finally, a working knowledge of research methods will help you avoid some tempting logical traps into which most people fall. For instance, many people do not seem clear about the difference between correlations and causation; they assume that if two variables seem to be related, one must cause the other. As you will soon discover, this assumption is wrong, and a working knowledge of research methods will help you avoid this and other common errors many people make. Overall, then, knowing about the methods used by social psychologists is useful in ways that go far beyond this book and course. So, read on and see for yourself what these benefits are.

Systematic Observation: Describing the World around Us

One basic technique for studying social behavior involves **systematic observation**—carefully observing behavior as it occurs. Such observation is not the kind of informal observation we all practice from childhood on; rather, in a scientific field such as social psychology, it is observation accompanied by careful, accurate measurement. For example, suppose that a social psychologist wanted to find out how frequently people touch each other in different settings. The researcher could study this topic by going to shopping malls, airports, college campuses, and many other locations and observing in those settings who touches whom, how they touch, and with what frequency. Such research (which has actually been conducted; see Chapter 3) uses what is known as *naturalistic observation*—observation of behavior in natural settings (Linden, 1992). Note that, in such observation, the researcher simply notices what is happening in various contexts; she or he makes no attempt to change the behavior of the persons being observed. In fact, such observation requires that the researcher take great pains to *avoid* influencing the persons observed in any way. Thus, the psychologist tries to remain as inconspicuous as possible, and might even try to hide behind barriers such as telephone poles, walls, or even bushes.

systematic observation
A method of research in which behavior is systematically observed and recorded.

Another technique that is often included under the heading of systematic observation is known as the **survey method.** Researchers ask large numbers of persons to respond to questions about their attitudes or behavior. Surveys are used for many purposes: to measure attitudes toward specific issues, to find out how voters feel about various political candidates, and even to assess student reactions to professors. Social psychologists sometimes use this method to measure attitudes concerning social issues—for instance, national health care or affirmative action programs. Scientists and practitioners in other fields use the survey method to measure everything from political views to elections and to assess consumer reactions to new products.

Surveys offer several advantages. Information can be gathered about thousands or even hundreds of thousands of persons with relative ease. In fact, surveys are now often conducted online through the Internet. For instance, one of us (Robert Baron) has recently been conducting one such study to find out how consumers who work with Microsoft and other large companies to help these companies develop better new products feel about the experience, and whether they would repeat it. (This is known as *co-innovation,* because consumers and the companies work together to develop something new; see Figure 1.8 on page 22.)

To be useful as a research tool, though, surveys must meet certain requirements. First, the persons who participate must be *representative* of the larger population about which conclusions are to be drawn—the issue of *sampling*. If this condition is not met, serious errors can result. For instance, every day, CNN news conducts a poll on some current issue; the next day, it presents the results. One recent topic, for instance, was "Should dividends paid to shareholders be exempt from income tax?" Results, shown the next day, indicated that a large majority was in favor of this policy. Can we have confidence in these results? Only to the extent that the people who responded to the survey are representative of the entire population. Suppose, for instance, that only people who expected to receive such dividends responded to the question (as seems likely). That leaves the issue of how other people—ones who don't expect to receive dividends—feel about this topic.

Yet another issue that must be carefully addressed with respect to surveys is this: The way in which the items are worded can exert strong effects on the outcomes obtained. For example, suppose a survey asked, "Do you think that persons convicted of multiple murders should be executed?" Many people might answer "yes"; after all, the convicted criminals have murdered several victims. But if, instead, the survey asked, "Are you in favor of the death penalty?" a smaller percentage might answer "yes." So, the way in which questions are posed can strongly affect the results.

In sum, the survey method can be a useful approach for studying some aspects of social behavior. The results obtained, however, are accurate only to the extent that issues relating to sampling and wording are carefully addressed.

Correlation: The Search for Relationships

At various times, you have probably noticed that some events appear to be related to each other: As one changes, the other changes, too. For example, perhaps you've noticed that people who drive new, expensive cars tend to be older than people who drive old, inexpensive ones, or that when interest rates rise, the stock market often falls. When two events are related in this way, they are said to be *correlated,* or that a correlation exists between them. The term *correlation* refers to a tendency for one event to change as the other changes. Social psychologists refer to such changeable aspects of the natural world as *variables,* because they can take different values.

From the scientific point of view, the existence of a correlation between two variables can be very useful. When a correlation exists, it is possible to predict one variable from information about one or more other variables. The ability to make such *predictions* is

survey method
A method of research in which large numbers of persons answer questions about their attitudes or behavior.

Online Product Communities & Customer Co-innovation: A Study

Online product communities enable customers to participate directly in several innovation activities including contributing product improvement ideas, answering other customers' product-related queries, and testing new products.

We are conducting a study to understand the issues related to such customer co-innovation. As a member of a online product community, your contribution to this study will be invaluable. We invite you to participate in this study by completing the survey below. The survey consists of 3 pages and will typically take only about 20 minutes to complete.

This is an **academic research project**. The study is **not** sponsored by (or, in any way related to) any company or external organization. All individual responses will be kept *strictly confidential*; only the aggregate data of all the survey respondents will be reported.

We greatly appreciate your willingness to participate in this study and to contribute to our research. Thank you for your time and help!

Satish Nambisan
Robert Baron
Lally School of Management
Rensselaer Polytechnic Institute
Troy, NY 12180
Note: If you have any queries related to this, please contact Satish Nambisan at nambis@rpi.edu or (518) 276-2230.

Instructions: Please answer the survey questions based on your experience or interactions in an online product community (e.g. Microsoft Windows XP newsgroup). The term 'product' in the survey questions refers to the product (or, products) that the online community is based on (e.g. Windows XP). The term 'product vendor' relates to the manufacturer of that product (e.g. Microsoft, HP). Once again, thank you!

1. Nature of your interactions in the online community

The following statements relate to the nature of your interactions in the online product community. For each item, please mark the box that best describes your interactions.

1.1. The amount of information about product design, features, and usage contained in my interactions in the online community is very large.	○ ○ ○ ○ ○ S. Disagree S. Agree
1.2. The amount of information about new product and product versions contained in my interactions in the online community is very large.	○ ○ ○ ○ ○ S. Disagree S. Agree
1.3. The amount of information about competing or other similar products contained in my interactions in the online community is very large.	○ ○ ○ ○ ○ S. Disagree S. Agree
1.4. The amount of information about the product vendor (e.g. Microsoft, HP) and their product plans contained in my interactions in the online community is very large.	○ ○ ○ ○ ○ S. Disagree S. Agree
1.5. The amount of information relevant to my profession/work that is contained in my interactions in the online community is very large.	○ ○ ○ ○ ○ S. Disagree S. Agree
1.6. The amount of information about other community members' personal/social issues contained in my interactions in the online community is very large.	○ ○ ○ ○ ○ S. Disagree S. Agree
1.7. The amount of information about hobbies, sports, politics, and other general interest topics contained in my interactions in the online community is very large.	○ ○ ○ ○ ○ S. Disagree S. Agree

Figure 1.8 ■ Surveys on the Internet: An Example
The page shown here is from a survey conducted on the Internet. The survey is concerned with reactions individuals have to *co-innovation*—helping large companies develop better products.

one important goal of all branches of science, including social psychology. Being able to make accurate predictions can be very helpful. For instance, imagine that a correlation is observed between certain attitudes on the part of individuals (one variable) and the likelihood that they will later engage in workplace violence against coworkers or their bosses (another variable). This correlation could be useful in identifying potentially dangerous persons so that companies can avoid hiring them. Similarly, suppose that a correlation is observed between certain patterns of behavior in married couples (e.g., the tendency to criticize each other harshly) and the likelihood that they will later divorce. Again, this information might be helpful in counseling the persons involved and perhaps, if this was what they desired, in saving their relationship. (See Chapter 7 for a discussion of why long-term relationships sometimes fail.)

How accurately can such predictions be made? The stronger the correlation between the variables in question, the more accurate the predictions. Correlations can range from zero to −1.00 or +1.00; the greater the departure from zero, the stronger the correlation. Positive numbers mean that as one variable increases, the other increases as well. Negative numbers indicate that as one variable increases, the other decreases. For instance, there is a negative correlation between age and the amount of hair on the heads of males: The older they are, the less hair they have.

These basic facts underlie an important method of research sometimes used by social psychologists: the **correlational method.** In this approach, social psychologists attempt to determine whether and to what extent different variables are related to each other. This method involves making careful observations of each variable and then performing appropriate statistical tests to determine whether and to what degree the variables are correlated.

Here is a concrete example: A social psychologist wants to find out if, as common sense seems to suggest, people who are in a good mood are more likely to be helpful to others than are persons who are in a bad mood. How could research on this **hypothesis**—an as-yet-unverified prediction—be conducted? One very basic approach would go something like this: The researcher might ask people to complete a questionnaire that measures their typical mood—how they usually feel during the course of the day. (Our moods fluctuate greatly over time in response to events in our lives, but there are also differences among people in how they feel most of the time, when nothing very good or bad is happening to them.) Participants in the research would also be asked to report how many times they are helpful to others each day—how many times they do favors for them, make a donation to charity, and so on. If positive correlations are obtained between these two factors—between mood and helpfulness—this would provide evidence for the hypothesis that being in a good mood is indeed related to helping.

Suppose that this was the finding actually obtained in the research (e.g., a correlation of +.51 between mood and helpfulness). What could we now conclude? That being in a good mood causes people to help others? Although it's tempting to jump to this conclusion, it may be a totally false one. Here's why: *The fact that two variables are correlated in no way guarantees that changes in one cause changes in the other.* On the contrary, the relationship between them may be due to chance or to random factors or to the fact that changes in *both* variables are related to a third variable (see Figure 1.9 on page 24). For instance, in this case, it is possible that being in a good mood doesn't really make people more helpful; rather, it may simply be that people who are often in a good mood are friendlier than people who are not often in a good mood, and it is *this* factor that results in their showing higher levels of helpfulness. Why? Because their friendliness encourages others to ask them for favors or other kinds of help. After all, would you be more likely to ask a smiling person for a favor or one who is frowning? Thus, the fact that people in a good mood engage in more helping than do persons who are not in a good mood may stem from this factor—not from any direct connection between mood and helpfulness.

There is still one further complication: It is also possible that helping others *puts us in a good mood*. In other words, it's not that being in a good mood causes increased

correlational method
A method of research in which a scientist systematically observes two or more variables to determine whether changes in one are accompanied by changes in the other.

hypothesis
An as-yet-unverified prediction.

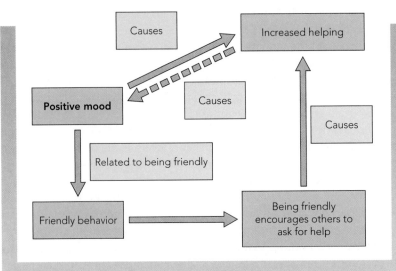

Figure 1.9 ■ Why Correlation Does Not Necessarily Mean Causation
Suppose that a correlation is found between mood and helping: The better people's moods, the more instances of helping others they report. Does this mean that being in a good mood causes increased helpfulness (*upper path*)? Not necessarily. As shown here, this finding may stem from the fact that people who are often in a good mood also tend to be friendlier than other persons. This, in turn, encourages others to ask them for help. So, they are more helpful not *because* they are in a good mood, but because of this other factor (their increased friendliness; *lower path*). In addition, and to add yet another complication, helping others may cause boosts in our mood rather than vice versa (*dotted arrow*).

helpfulness, but that helping produces boosts in our mood. Correlations simply tell us that two variables are related; they do *not* indicate the directions of these effects. For additional illustrations of the fact that even strong correlations between two variables do not necessarily mean that one causes the other, see the **Ideas to Take with You—and Use!** section at the end of this chapter.

Despite this major drawback, the correlational method of research is sometimes very useful to social psychologists. It can be used in natural settings, and it is often highly efficient: A large amount of information can be obtained in a relatively short period of time. However, the fact that it is generally not conclusive with respect to cause-and-effect relationships is a serious one, which leads social psychologists to prefer a different method. It is to this approach that we turn next.

KEY POINTS

★ In *systematic observation,* behavior is carefully observed and recorded. In naturalistic observation, such observations are made in settings in which the behavior naturally occurs.

★ In the *survey method,* large numbers of persons respond to questions about their attitudes or behavior.

★ In the *correlational method* of research, two or more variables are measured to determine whether they are related to one another in any way.

★ The existence of even strong correlations between variables does not indicate that they are causally related to each other.

As we have just seen, the correlational method of research is very useful from the point of view of one important goal of science: making accurate predictions. The correlational method is less useful, though, from the point of view of attaining another important goal: *explanation.* This is sometimes known as the "why" question, because scientists do not merely wish to describe the world and relationships among variables in it: They want to be able to *explain* these relationships, too. For instance, continuing with the mood and helpfulness example, if a link between being in a good mood and a tendency to help others does exist, social psychologists would want to know *why* this is so. Does being in a good mood automatically trigger kindness, without any conscious thought? Does it make us less able to resist requests from others—less able to say no to them? Or does it make us feel good about ourselves, and because being helpful to others is consistent with a positive self-image, an increased willingness to help stems from this source.

To attain the goal of explanation, social psychologists employ a method of research known as **experimentation,** or the **experimental method.** As the heading of this section suggests, experimentation involves the following strategy: One variable is changed systematically, and the effects of this change on one or more other variables are carefully measured. If systematic changes in one variable produce changes in another variable (and if the two additional conditions we describe below are also met), it is possible to conclude with reasonable certainty that there is a causal relationship between these variables: that changes in one do indeed *cause* changes in the other. Because the experimental method is so valuable in answering this kind of question, it is frequently the method of choice in social psychology. But please bear in mind that there is no single best method of research. Rather, social psychologists, like all other scientists, choose the method that is most appropriate for studying a particular topic.

Experimentation: Its Basic Nature

In its most basic form, the experimental method involves two key steps: (1) The presence or strength of some variable believed to affect an aspect of social behavior or thought is systematically changed, and (2) the effects of such changes (if any) are carefully measured. The factor systematically varied by the researcher is termed the **independent variable,** while the aspect of behavior studied is termed the **dependent variable.** In a simple experiment, then, different groups of participants are exposed to contrasting levels of the independent variable (such as low, moderate, and high). The researcher then carefully measures their behavior to determine whether it does in fact vary with these changes in the independent variable. If it does—and if two other conditions are also met—the researcher can tentatively conclude that the independent variable does indeed cause changes in the aspect of behavior being studied.

To illustrate the basic nature of experimentation in social psychology, let's return to the mood and helpfulness example. How could a social psychologist study this topic through experimentation? One possibility is as follows: The researcher would arrange for participants to come to a laboratory or other setting, where two things happen: (1) They are exposed to experiences designed to change their mood (to put them either in a good, a neutral, or a bad mood), and (2) they then have one or more opportunities to act in a helpful way. For instance, to vary their moods, the participants might be asked to perform some task and then receive either strong praise of their performance (which would induce a positive mood), neutral feedback (which would not change their mood much), or harshly negative feedback (which would induce a negative mood). Notice the word *either* in the preceding sentence—it is important because it means that participants would be put in either a good mood, a neutral mood, or a negative mood. Then, soon after the mood-changing procedures, they might be asked to

experimentation (experimental method)
A method of research in which one or more factors (the independent variables) are systematically changed to determine whether such variations affect one or more other factors (dependent variables).

independent variable
The variable that is systematically changed (i.e., varied) in an experiment.

dependent variable
The variable that is measured in an experiment.

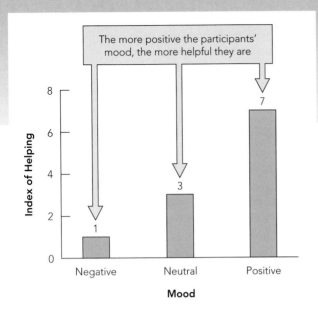

Figure 1.10 ▪ Experimentation: A Simple Example
In the study shown here, the participants were exposed to feedback designed to induce a positive, a neutral, or a negative mood. Then they were given an opportunity to act in a helpful way. Results indicated that the more positive their mood, the greater their helpfulness.

make a donation to a charitable organization or to volunteer their time for more research or to help the experimenter or someone else (e.g., another participant) in various ways.

If the results of this study look like those in Figure 1.10, the researcher could conclude, at least tentatively, that being in a good mood does produce increased helpfulness. Why? Because if the study were done correctly, the only difference between the experiences of participants assigned to the good mood, neutral mood, or negative mood conditions is that they receive contrasting feedback designed to alter their moods. As a result, any difference in their behaviors (i.e., in their helpfulness) must be due to this factor. It's important to note that in experimentation, such knowledge is obtained through direct intervention: A participant's mood—the independent variable—is systematically changed by the researcher. In the correlational method, in contrast, variables are *not* altered in this manner; rather, naturally occurring changes in them are simply observed and recorded.

▪ Experimentation: Two Requirements for Its Success

Earlier, we referred to two conditions that must be met before a researcher can conclude that changes in an independent variable have caused changes in a dependent variable. Let's consider these conditions now. The first involves what is termed **random assignment of participants to experimental conditions.** This means that all participants in an experiment must have an equal chance of being exposed to each level of the independent variable. The reason for this rule is simple: If participants are *not* randomly assigned to each condition, it may later be impossible to determine whether differences in their behavior stem from differences they brought with them to the study, from the impact of the independent variable, or both. For instance, imagine that in the study just described, one of the assistants decides to collect all the data for the positive mood condition on one day and all the data for the negative mood condition on the next day. It just so happens that on the first day, a very sad event occurred—perhaps there was an explosion on a space shuttle, and it seems likely that all the astronauts on board will die—while on the second day, a miracle occurred and the crew returned safely to earth. Results indicate that participants in the good mood condition are actually *less* helpful than those in the negative mood condition. Can you see why this might happen? All participants on the first day are in such a negative mood that the positive feedback fails to make them happy, while all those the next day are in such a happy mood that even the negative feedback seems unimportant and doesn't lower their moods. So, in fact, we can't tell *why* the results occurred, because the principle of random assignment of participants to experimental conditions has been violated.

The second condition essential for successful experimentation is as follows: Insofar as is possible, all factors other than the independent variable that might also affect participants' behavior must be held constant. To see why this is so, consider what would happen if, in the study on mood and helping, the research is conducted in rooms in which

random assignment of participants to experimental conditions

A basic requirement for conducting valid experiments. According to this principle, research participants must have an equal chance of being exposed to each level of the independent variable.

the temperature varies greatly. Sometimes the rooms are comfortable, and sometimes they are hot and stuffy. As a result, there are no effects of mood on helping. What causes this? It is possible that mood really has no impact on helpfulness. It is also possible, however, that changes in temperature play a role. Uncomfortable conditions put people in a bad mood, and because this factor is not being systematically varied by the researcher, it is impossible to determine what effects, if any, it has had on the results. In situations such as this, the independent variable is said to be *confounded* with another variable—one that is *not* under systematic investigation in the study. When such confounding occurs, the findings of an experiment may be largely meaningless (see Figure 1.11).

In sum, experimentation is, in several respects, the crown jewel among social psychology's methods. It certainly isn't perfect. For example, because experimentation is often conducted in laboratory settings, which are quite different from the locations in which social behavior actually occurs, the question of **external validity** often arises: To what extent can the findings of experiments be generalized to real-life social situations and perhaps to persons different from those who participated in the research? When experimentation is used with skill and care, however, it can yield results that help us answer complex questions about social behavior and social thought. Why, if this is so, don't social psychologists use it all the time? The answer is that, in some situations, experimentation cannot be used because of practical or ethical considerations: It is impossible to vary the independent variables systematically, or doing so would violate ethical principles. For example, imagine that that a researcher has good reason to believe that exposure to certain kinds of programs on television encourages teenagers to engage

external validity
The extent to which the findings of an experiment can be generalized to real-life social situations and perhaps to persons different from those who participated in the research.

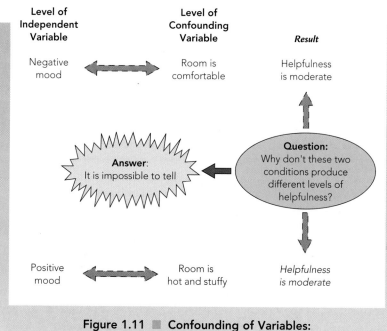

Figure 1.11 ■ **Confounding of Variables:
A Fatal Flaw in Experimentation**

In a hypothetical experiment designed to investigate the effects of mood on helping, mood—the *independent variable*—is confounded with another variable: temperature in the rooms where the study is conducted. Sometimes, the room is very hot when participants are placed in a good mood, and sometimes the room is comfortable when participants are placed in a negative mood. Results indicate no effects of mood on helping. Why? Is it impossible to tell because the *independent variable* (mood) is confounded with a variable not systematically varied or controlled by the researcher (temperature)?

in unprotected sex. Could the researcher ethically conduct an experiment on this topic, exposing some teenagers to lots of these programs and others to none and then comparing their rates of unprotected sex? In principle, such research is possible, but no ethical social psychologist would perform it because it might harm some of the participants.

It is partly because of these and related problems that social psychologists often turn to systematic observation and the correlational method in their research. So, to repeat: All research methods offer a mixed bag of advantages and disadvantages, and social psychologists simply choose the method that seems best for studying a particular topic or question.

KEY POINTS

★ *Experimentation* involves systematically altering one or more variables (*independent variables*) to determine whether changes in these variables affect some aspect of behavior (*dependent variables*).

★ Successful use of the *experimental method* requires *random assignment of participants to experimental conditions* and holding all other factors that might also influence behavior constant so as to avoid confounding of variables.

★ Although it is a very powerful research tool, the *experimental method* is not perfect—questions concerning its *external validity* often arise. Further, it cannot be used in some situations because of practical or ethical considerations.

Interpreting Research Results: The Use of Statistics, and Social Psychologists as Perennial Skeptics

Once a research project has been completed, social psychologists must turn their attention to another crucial task: interpreting the results. The key question is this: How much confidence can we place in the findings? Are correlations between variables, or observed differences between experimental conditions, real ones we can accept with confidence as accurate? To answer this question, social psychologists generally employ **inferential statistics**—a special form of mathematics that allows us to evaluate the likelihood that a given pattern of research results occurred by chance alone. To determine whether the findings of a study are indeed real—unlikely to be a chance event—psychologists perform appropriate statistical analyses on the data they collect. If these analyses suggest that the likelihood of obtaining the observed findings by chance is low (usually fewer than five times in one hundred), the results are described as *significant*. Only then are they interpreted as being of value in helping us understand some aspect of social behavior or social thought. All of the findings reported in this book have passed this basic test, so you can be confident that they refer to real (i.e., significant) results.

It's important to realize, however, that the likelihood that a given pattern of findings is a chance event is *never* zero. It can be very low—one chance in ten thousand, for instance—but it can never be zero. For this reason, a specific finding is always viewed as tentative in nature until it is replicated—reported again by different researchers in different laboratories. Only when findings have passed this additional test are they viewed with confidence by social psychologists. But here is where a serious problem arises: Only rarely do the results of social psychological research yield totally consistent findings. A more common pattern is that some studies offer support for a given hypothesis, but others fail to offer such support. Why do such discrepancies arise? In part,

inferential statistics
A special form of mathematics that allows us to evaluate the likelihood that a given pattern of research results occurred by chance alone.

because different researchers use different methods and measures of social behavior and thought. For instance, continuing with the mood and helpfulness example, some might use feedback on a task to vary participants' moods, while others might use exposure to happy or sad films to produce this effect. Both techniques are designed to vary mood, but it is possible that they also produce other, different effects. For instance, the content of the films, not just whether they are happy or sad, might affect participants' thoughts as well as their moods. The dependent measures employed in such research might vary, too. One researcher might measure helpfulness in terms of willingness to donate to charity, another might measure it in terms of willingness to volunteer for another experiment, and still another might measure it in terms of whether participants help the experimenter pick up papers she or he has spilled on the floor. Whatever the reason for contrasting research results, they pose a problem for social psychologists who must decide which results should be accepted as most valid.

■ Interpreting Diverse Results: The Role of Meta-Analysis

What do social psychologists do when confronted with this problem? One answer involves the use of a technique known as **meta-analysis** (e.g., Bond & Smith, 1996). This procedure allows the results of many different studies to be combined in order to estimate both the direction and the magnitude of the effects of independent variables. Meta-analytic procedures are mathematical in nature, so they eliminate potential sources of errors that might arise if researchers attempted to examine the findings of several studies in a more informal manner, such as through a simple count to see how many offer support for the hypothesis and how many do not. Overall, meta-analysis is an important tool for interpreting the results of social psychological research, and we refer to it often in later chapters.

The Role of Theory in Social Psychology

There is one more aspect of social psychological research we should consider before concluding. As we noted earlier, in their research, social psychologists seek to do more than simply describe the world: They want to be able to explain it, too. For instance, social psychologists don't want merely to state that racial prejudice is common in the United States: They want to be able to explain *why* some persons hold these negative views. In social psychology, as in all branches of science, explanation involves the construction of **theories**—frameworks for explaining various events or processes. The procedure involved in building a theory goes like this:

1. On the basis of existing evidence, a theory that reflects this evidence is proposed.

2. This theory, which consists of basic concepts and statements about how these concepts are related, helps to organize existing information and makes predictions about observable events. For instance, the theory might predict the conditions under which individuals acquire racial prejudice.

3. These predictions, known as *hypotheses*, are then tested by actual research.

4. If the results are consistent with the theory, confidence in its accuracy is increased. If they are not, the theory is modified and further tests are conducted.

5. Ultimately, the theory is either accepted as accurate or rejected as inaccurate. Even if the theory is accepted as accurate, however, it remains open to further refinement as improved methods of research are developed and additional evidence relevant to the theory's predictions is obtained.

This procedure may sound a bit abstract, so let's turn to a concrete example. Suppose that a social psychologist formulates the following theory: When people believe

meta-analysis
A statistical technique for combining data from independent studies in order to determine whether specific variables (or interactions among variables) have significant effects across these studies.

theories
Efforts by scientists in any field to answer the question "Why?" Theories involve attempts to understand why certain events or processes occur as they do.

that they hold a view that is in the minority, they will be slower to state it (something known as the *minority slowness* effect), and this stems not from the strength of their views but from reluctance to state minority opinions publicly, so that others will hear them and perhaps disapprove of them. This theory would lead to specific predictions; for instance, the minority slowness effect is reduced if people can state their opinions privately (e.g., Bassili, 2003). If research findings are consistent with this prediction and with others derived from the theory, confidence in the theory is increased. If findings are *not* consistent with the theory, it will be modified or perhaps rejected, as noted previously. (See Chapter 6 for a discussion of the causes of racial prejudice and of research designed to test this specific theory; Crandall et al., 2001.)

This process of formulating a theory, testing it, modifying the theory, testing it again, and so on, lies close to the core of the scientific method, so it is an important aspect of social psychological research (see Figure 1.12). Thus, many different theories relating to important aspects of social behavior and social thought are presented in this book.

Two final points need to be made: First, theories are never *proved* in any final, ultimate sense. Rather, they are always open to test and are accepted with more or less confidence depending on the weight of the available evidence. Second, research is *not* undertaken to prove or verify a theory; it is performed to gather evidence relevant to the theory. A researcher who sets out to "prove" her or his pet theory would be in serious violation of the principles of scientific skepticism, objectivity, and open-mindedness described on page 7.

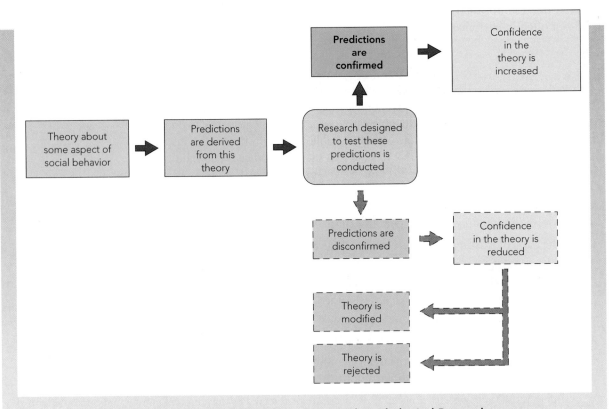

Figure 1.12 ■ The Role of Theory in Social Psychological Research
Theories both organize existing knowledge and make predictions about how various events or processes will occur. Once a theory is formulated, *hypotheses* derived logically from it are tested through careful research. If results agree with the predictions, confidence in the theory is increased. If results disagree with such predictions, the theory may be modified or, ultimately, rejected as false.

Chapter 1 / The Field of Social Psychology

KEY POINTS

★ To determine whether the results of a research project are real or due to chance, social psychologists use *inferential statistics*.

★ If the chances are small that research results occurred by chance (less than five times in one hundred), results are described as significant.

★ To assess the direction and magnitude of the effects of *independent variables* across different studies, social psychologists use a statistical technique known as *meta-analysis*.

★ *Theories* are frameworks for explaining various events or processes and play a key role in social psychological research.

The Quest for Knowledge and Rights of Individuals: Seeking an Appropriate Balance

In their use of experimentation, correlation, and systematic observation, social psychologists do not differ from researchers in other fields. One technique, however, does seem to be unique to research in social psychology: **deception.** This technique involves efforts by researchers to withhold or conceal information from participants about the purposes of a study. The reason for using this procedure is simple: Many social psychologists believe that if participants know the true purposes of a study, their behavior in it will be changed by that knowledge and the research thus will not yield valid information about social behavior or social thought.

Some kinds of research do seem to require the use of temporary deception. For example, consider the minority slowness effect described previously. If participants know that the purpose of a study is to investigate this effect, isn't it possible that they will lean over backward to avoid showing it? Similarly, consider a study of the effects of physical appearance on attraction between strangers. Again, if participants know that the researcher is interested in this topic, they might work hard to avoid being influenced by a stranger's appearance. In this and many other cases, social psychologists feel compelled to employ temporary deception in their research (Suls & Rosnow, 1988). However, the use of deception raises important ethical issues that cannot be ignored.

First, there is the chance, however slim, that deception may result in some kind of harm to the persons exposed to it. They may be upset by the procedures used or by their own reactions to them. For example, in several studies concerned with helping in emergencies, participants were exposed to seemingly real emergency situations: They overheard what seemed to be a medical emergency—another person having an apparent seizure (e.g., Darley & Latane, 1968). Many participants were strongly upset by these staged events, and others were disturbed by the fact that although they recognized the need to help, they failed to do so. Clearly, the fact that participants experienced emotional upset raises complex ethical issues about just how far researchers can go when studying even important topics such as this one.

We should hasten to emphasize that such research represents an extreme use of deception. Generally, deception takes much milder forms. For example, participants may receive a request for help from a stranger who is actually an accomplice of the researchers, or they may be informed that most other students in their university hold certain views when in fact they do not. Still, even in such cases, the potential for some kind of harmful effect to participants exists and is a potentially serious drawback to the use of deception.

deception
A technique whereby researchers withhold information about the purposes or procedures of a study from persons participating in it.

Figure 1.13 ■ Careful Debriefing: A Requirement in Studies Using Deception
After an experimental session is completed, participants should be provided with thorough *debriefing*—full information about the experiment's goals and the reasons why temporary deception was used. Thorough debriefing should be provided even if deception was *not* used.

Second, there is the possibility that participants will resent being fooled during a study and, as a result, will acquire negative attitudes toward social psychology and psychological research in general. For instance, they may become suspicious about information presented by researchers (Kelman, 1967). To the extent such reactions occur—and recent findings indicate that they do, at least to a degree (Epley & Huff, 1998)—they have disturbing implications for the future of social psychology, which places so much emphasis on scientific research.

Because of such possibilities, the use of deception poses something of a dilemma to social psychologists. On one hand, deception seems essential to their research. On the other, its use raises serious problems. How can this issue be resolved? Although opinion remains somewhat divided, most social psychologists agree on the following points. First, deception should *never* be used to persuade people to take part in a study; withholding information about what will happen in an experiment or providing misleading information in order to induce people to take part in it is not acceptable (Sigall, 1997). Second, most social psychologists agree that temporary deception may sometimes be acceptable, provided two basic safeguards are employed. One of these is **informed consent**—giving participants as much information as possible about the procedures to be followed before they make their decision to participate. In short, this is the opposite of withholding information in order to persuade people to participate. The second safeguard is careful **debriefing**—providing participants with a full description of the purposes of a study after they have participated in it (see Figure 1.13). Such information should also include an explanation of deception and why it was necessary to use it.

Fortunately, a growing body of evidence indicates that, together, informed consent and thorough debriefing can substantially reduce the potential dangers of deception (Smith & Richardson, 1985). For example, most participants report that they view temporary deception as acceptable, provided that potential benefits outweigh potential costs and if there is no other means of obtaining the information sought (Rogers, 1980; Sharpe, Adair, & Roese, 1992). However, as noted, there is some indication that participants do become somewhat more suspicious about what researchers tell them during an experiment; even worse, such increased suspiciousness seems to last over several months (Epley & Huff, 1998).

Overall, then, existing evidence seems to suggest that most research participants do not react negatively to temporary deception as long as its purpose and necessity are clear. However, these findings do not mean that the safety or appropriateness of deception should be taken for granted (Rubin, 1985). On the contrary, the guiding principles for all researchers planning to use this procedure should be as follows: (1) Use deception only when it is absolutely essential to do so—when no other means for conducting the research exists; (2) always proceed with caution; and (3) make certain that every possible precaution is taken to protect the rights, safety, and well-being of research participants.

informed consent
A procedure in which research participants are provided with as much information as possible about a research project before deciding whether to participate in it.

debriefing
Procedures at the conclusion of a research session in which participants are given full information about the nature of the research and the hypothesis or hypotheses under investigation.

Chapter 1 / The Field of Social Psychology

KEY POINTS

★ *Deception* involves efforts by social psychologists to withhold or conceal from participants information about the purposes of a study.

★ Most social psychologists believe that temporary deception is often necessary in order to obtain valid research results.

★ Social psychologists view *deception* as acceptable only when important safeguards are used: *informed consent* and thorough *debriefing*.

Using This Book: A Fugitive Preface

A textbook that is hard to read or understand is like a dull tool: It can't do what it is designed to do very well. Being well aware of this fact, we have tried our best to make this book easy to read, and have included a number of features designed to make it more enjoyable and useful for you. Following is an overview of the steps we've taken to make reading this book a pleasant and informative experience.

First, each chapter begins with an outline and ends with a summary. Within the text itself, key terms are printed in **dark type like this** and are followed by a definition. These terms are also defined in a running glossary in the margins, as well as in a glossary at the end of the book. To help you understand what you have read, each major section is followed by a list of **Key Points**—a brief summary of major points. All figures and tables are clear and simple, and most contain special labels and notes designed to help you understand them (see Figure 1.10 for an example). Finally, each chapter ends with the section **Summary and Review of Key Points;** reviewing this section can be an important aid to your studying.

Second, this book has an underlying theme that can be stated as follows: Social psychology is much more than just a collection of interesting findings to be enjoyed for the moment, recalled on tests, and then quickly forgotten. On the contrary, we believe that social psychology provides a new way of looking at the social world that everyone should use long after this course is over. To emphasize this theme, we include two special features that appear in each chapter. One of these is **Beyond the Headlines: As Social Psychologists See It.** These sections take an actual newspaper headline and examine it from the perspective of social psychology. These features also illustrate how social psychologists think and how the principles of our field can be applied to virtually any aspect of human social behavior. The second feature is **The Science of Social Psychology: Making Sense of Common Sense.** These sections are designed to highlight how the scientific approach taken by social psychology has helped to resolve—or at least clarify—the contradictions often contained in common sense. Does absence make the heart grow fonder, or is it a case of out of sight out of mind? Does blowing off steam (expressing anger and aggressive impulses) help reduce these feelings? When a judge says to a jury, "Disregard that information," can the jurors really do that? We'll examine these and many other instances in which social psychology has helped resolve questions that have persisted through the ages.

Another special feature that will help you recognize the usefulness and value of social psychology appears at the end of each chapter: **Ideas to Take with You—and Use!** These features (as an example, see the one on page 35) are designed to highlight important concepts you should remember—and use—long after this course is over. In our view, you may well them find useful in your life in the years ahead.

Finally, to help you understand how research in each area of social psychology is related to research in other areas, we've included special **Connections** tables at the end of each chapter. These tables provide a kind of global review, reminding you of related topics discussed elsewhere in the book. In addition, these tables emphasize that many aspects of social behavior and thought are closely linked: They do not occur in isolation of each other.

We think that together, these features will help you get the most out of this book and from your first encounter with social psychology. Good luck! And may your introduction to social psychology prove to be a rich, informative, and valuable experience—and also, we hope, fun!

SUMMARY AND REVIEW OF KEY POINTS

Social Psychology: A Working Definition

- *Social psychology* is the scientific field that seeks to understand the nature and causes of individual behavior and thought in social situations.

- *Social psychology* is scientific in nature because it adopts the values and methods used in other fields of science.

- Social psychologists adopt the scientific method because common sense provides an unreliable guide to social behavior, and because our thoughts are influenced by many potential sources of bias.

- *Social psychology* focuses on the behavior of individuals and seeks to understand the causes of social behavior and social thought, which can involve the behavior and appearance of others, social cognition, environmental factors, cultural values, and even biological and genetic factors.

Social Psychology: Its Cutting Edge

- Social psychologists currently recognize that social thought and social behavior are two sides of the same coin, and that there is a continuous, complex interplay between them.

- Another major field of study involves growing interest in *social neuroscience*—efforts to relate activity in the brain and other biological events to key aspects of social thought and behavior.

- Our behavior and thought are often shaped by factors of which we are unaware. Growing attention to such implicit (nonconscious) processes is another major theme of modern social psychology.

- *Social psychology* currently adopts a *multicultural perspective*. This perspective recognizes the importance of cultural factors in social behavior and social thought and notes that research findings obtained in one culture do not necessarily generalize to other cultures.

Answering Questions about Social Behavior and Social Thought: Research Methods in Social Psychology

- In *systematic observation*, behavior is carefully observed and recorded. In naturalistic observation, such observations are made in settings in which the behavior occurs naturally.

- In the *survey method*, large numbers of persons respond to questions about their attitudes or behavior.

■ In the *correlational method* of research, two or more variables are measured to determine whether they are related to one another in any way.

■ The existence of even strong correlations between variables does not indicate that they are causally related to each other.

■ *Experimentation* involves systematically altering one or more variables (*independent variables*) in order to determine whether changes in these variables affect some aspect of behavior (*dependent variables*).

■ Successful use of the *experimental method* requires *random assignment of participants to experimental conditions* and holding all other factors that might also influence behavior constant so as to avoid confounding of variables.

■ Although it is a very powerful research tool, the *experimental method* is not perfect. Questions concerning its *external validity* often arise. Further, it cannot be used in some situations because of practical or ethical considerations.

■ To determine whether the results of a research project are real or due to chance, social psychologists use *inferential statistics*.

■ If the chances are small that research results occurred by chance (less than five times in one hundred), results are described as significant.

■ To assess the direction and magnitude of the effects of *independent variables* across different studies, social psychologists use a statistical technique known as *meta-analysis*.

■ *Theories* are frameworks for explaining various events or processes. They play a key role in social psychological research.

The Quest for Knowledge and Rights of Individuals: Seeking an Appropriate Balance

■ *Deception* involves efforts by social psychologists to withhold or conceal from participants information about the purposes of a study.

■ Most social psychologists believe that temporary deception is often necessary in order to obtain valid research results.

■ Social psychologists view *deception* as acceptable only when important safeguards are used: *informed consent* and thorough *debriefing*.

Ideas to Take with You—and Use! **WHY CORRELATION DOES NOT EQUAL CAUSATION**

That two variables are correlated—even strongly correlated—does not necessarily mean that changes in one cause changes in the other. This is true because changes in both variables may actually be related to, or caused by, a third variable. Following are two examples:

Observation: As weight increases, income increases. (These two variables are positively correlated.)

Possible Interpretations:

1. Weight gain causes increased income.

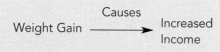

Weight Gain — Causes → Increased Income

2. As people grow older, they tend to gain weight *and* also earn higher incomes; both variables are actually related to *age*.

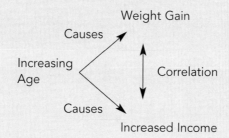

Increasing Age — Causes → Weight Gain

Correlation

Increasing Age — Causes → Increased Income

3. Increased income causes weight gain (because people with high incomes can buy a wider range of delicious foods).

Increased income → Weight Gain

Observation: The more violent television and movies people watch, the more likely they are to engage in dangerous acts of aggression. (These two variables are positively correlated.)

Possible Interpretations:

1. Exposure to media violence is one factor that increases aggression.

Exposure to Media Violence $\xrightarrow{\text{Causes}}$ Increased Aggression

2. People who prefer a high level of stimulation have little control over their impulses; thus, they choose to watch displays of violence and also act aggressively more often than other people. Both variables are related to a need for certain kinds of stimulation.

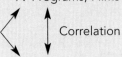

Need for Certain Kinds of Stimulation — Watching Violent TV Programs, Films / Behaving Aggressively — Correlation

3. High Levels of Aggressiveness → Preference for Watching Violent TV Programs and Films

Key Conclusion: Even if two variables are strongly correlated, this does not necessarily mean that changes in one cause changes in the other.

KEY TERMS

correlational method (p. 23)

debriefing (p. 32)

deception (p. 31)

dependent variable (p. 25)

evolutionary psychology (p. 12)

experimentation (experimental method) (p. 25)

external validity (p. 27)

hypothesis (p. 23)

independent variable (p. 25)

inferential statistics (p. 28)

informed consent (p. 32)

meta-analysis (p. 29)

multicultural perspective (p. 19)

random assignment of participants to experimental conditions (p. 26)

social neuroscience (p. 17)

social psychology (p. 6)

survey method (p. 21)

systematic observation (p. 20)

theories (p. 29)

For More Information

Buss, D. M. (1999). *Evolutionary psychology: The new science of the mind.* Boston: Allyn & Bacon.
• If you would like to learn more about the efforts of psychologists to understand the possible role of genetic and biological factors in our social behavior, this is an excellent place to begin. The chapters on mating strategies, kinship, and aggression and warfare are truly fascinating.

Abelson, R. P., Frey, K. P., & Gregg, A. P. (2004). *Experiments with people: Revelations from social psychology.* Mahwah, NJ: Erlbaum.
• This book examines a number of ground-breaking studies in social psychology—mainly experiments—that have added greatly to our understanding of human thought and social behavior. Among the topics covered are the effects of media biases, when actions influence attitudes, the hidden costs of rewards, the positive effects of mere exposure, and the nature of conformity. Truly a thought-provoking volume.

2 SOCIAL COGNITION
Thinking about the Social World

There's an old saying that goes something like this: "We choose our friends, but our relatives are inflicted upon us." This sentiment certainly applied to one relative I used to have, but who now—thank goodness—has left my family. He was probably the most opinionated person I have ever known. Even worse, many of his views seemed to be set in stone; nothing could change them. I remember one conversation with him about safety belts. "I never wear them," he said with a smug grin. "If I'm in an accident, I want to be able to get out of the car fast, and belts slow you down." I tried to point out that many more people are hurt when they are thrown out of their cars than are injured by remaining in them after an accident, and that many thousands of people are alive today because they were wearing safety belts during serious accidents, but it was of no use. His mind was made up, and he wouldn't even consider the possibility that safety belts could be helpful. Another time, he tried to persuade me that refusing to hire women as fire fighters was *not* discrimination against them— on the contrary, it was a very good thing because it protected them from unnecessary danger. When I tried to point out that if women are capable of performing this job, it is wrong to refuse to hire them, he answered by stating that no woman would *ever* be capable of being a fire fighter and walked away. Argument over!

I could continue with other examples, but by now you get the idea. I found this particular relative to be obnoxious not because he disagreed with me or because he liked to argue, but mainly because his ideas seemed to be totally fixed: Nothing— no facts, no evidence, nothing—could affect them. Truly, he was not someone I would have chosen to be around!

Figure 2.1 ■ Social Cognition: Far from Error-Free
As shown in this cartoon, once we have made a decision, we are often reluctant to change it, or even to consider information contrary to it. So, like the boss shown here, our thinking about the social world is often far from totally rational. (*Source: DILBERT reprinted by permission of United Features Syndicate, Inc.*)

Although I did not enjoy interacting with my former relative, he does have something to contribute to this discussion: His actions illustrate several important points about **social cognition**—the ways in which we interpret, analyze, remember, and use information about the social world; how, in other words, we think about other people, our relations with them, and the social environments in which we live.

First, and most obvious, my relative's behavior demonstrates that social thought is not always entirely rational. On the contrary, it is subject to a wide range of tendencies and "tilts" that can lead us into serious errors, including the tendency to stick to views and beliefs we have formed and hold even in the face of evidence indicating that they are wrong (see Figure 2.1). Why do we do this? Many factors play a role, but one of the most important illustrates another key fact about social cognition: Thinking about the social world often involves hard work, so we avoid it—or at least try to minimize it—as much as possible. Once our ideas and beliefs are formed, it takes a lot of effort to change them, so we don't, even if it makes little or no sense from a purely rational perspective.

Second, other aspects of my relative's behavior illustrate the fact that often, we process social information in a seemingly *automatic* manner. For instance, consider his view that no woman could ever be qualified to be a fire fighter. How could he hold such a narrow-minded, baseless opinion? In part because he had a very strong stereotype of women, one suggesting that they were too small and weak to be effective fire fighters. This stereotype then led him to conclude, in a seemingly automatic manner, that women should be excluded from this job because they could not perform it (e.g., Bargh et al., 1996; Greenwald et al., 1998). He didn't have to examine this view carefully or systematically; he just held it! If you are a woman, he believed, you cannot be a fire fighter—period.

Finally, I often noticed that if someone *did* challenge my relative's views, he would become emotional about them and that this, in turn, would tend to make him more unreasonable than ever. This observation illustrates the fact that there are important links between cognition and affect—how we think and how we feel. In other words, our thoughts often shape our feelings and our feelings, in turn, can strongly influence our thoughts. This interplay between cognition and affect is complex—far more complex than merely intensifying views we already hold (e.g., Forgas, 1995a)—and such interplay, too, is an important aspect of social thought.

In this chapter we examine several key aspects of social cognition. As noted in Chapter 1, a cognitive perspective is central to modern social psychology, and we consider it

social cognition
The manner in which we interpret, analyze, remember, and use information about the social world.

in every chapter in this book. Thus, it makes good sense to examine some of the basic principles of social thought here, before turning to other aspects of social psychology.

First, we examine a basic component of social thought—*schemas.* These are mental frameworks that allow us to organize large amounts of information in an efficient manner. Once formed, these frameworks exert strong effects on social thought—effects that are not always beneficial from the point of view of accuracy. Second, we consider *heuristics*—simple rules of thumb we often use to make decisions or draw inferences quickly, and with minimal effort. In other words, heuristics are another means of reducing cognitive effort, the mental work we must do to make sense out of the social world (e.g., Kunda, 1999). After discussing heuristics, we return to the important point that, often, social thought occurs in an automatic manner. In other words, it often unfolds in a quick and relatively effortless manner rather than in a careful, systematic, and more effortful one. Next, we examine several specific tendencies or "tilts" in social thought—tilts that can lead us to false conclusions about others or to additional errors in our efforts to understand the social world. Finally, we focus on the complex interplay between **affect**—our current feelings or moods—and various aspects of social cognition (e.g., Forgas, 1995a). Note that we also examine important aspects of social thought in Chapter 3, which considers several aspects of *person perception* (how we perceive others and try to understand them), and in Chapter 5, which examines key aspects of our social *self.*

Schemas: Mental Frameworks for Organizing— and Using—Social Information

What happens when you visit your doctor? Probably something like this: You enter and sign in. Then you sit and wait. If you are lucky, the wait is not very long and a nurse then takes you into an examining room. Once there, you wait some more. Eventually, the doctor enters and talks to you and perhaps examines you. Finally, you leave and perhaps pay some part of your bill on the way out. It doesn't matter who your doctor is or where you live. This sequence of events, or something very much like it, will take place. None of this surprises you; in fact, you expect these events to occur, including the waiting. Why? Because through past experience, you have built up a mental structure or framework for this kind of situation—for visiting a doctor. Similarly, you have other mental structures for going to restaurants, taking exams, shopping for groceries, going to the barber or hair dresser, and so on (see Figure 2.2).

You don't simply have such frameworks for specific situations; you also have them for people, occupations, social roles, specific social groups, and many other aspects of the social world. In each case, your experience enables you to build a mental framework that allows you to organize your knowledge and assumptions about each of these subjects or themes—about the situations, people, or social groups in question. Social psychologists describe such frameworks as **schemas** and define them as mental structures that help us to organize social information and that guide the processing of such information.

Once schemas are formed, they exert powerful effects on several aspects of social cognition. We examine these now because they are an important aspect of social cognition and our efforts to make sense out of the social world around us.

The Impact of Schemas on Social Cognition: Attention, Encoding, Retrieval

How do schemas influence social thought? Research findings suggest that they influence three basic processes: attention, encoding, and retrieval. *Attention* refers to what

affect
Our current feelings and moods.

schemas
Mental frameworks centering around a specific theme that help us to organize social information.

Chapter 2 / Social Cognition

Figure 2.2 ■ Schemas: Mental Frameworks for Organizing Information about the Social World
Through experience, we acquire *schemas*—mental frameworks for organizing, interpreting, and processing social information. For instance, you almost certainly have well-developed schemas for such events as taking an exam (*left photo*) and shopping for groceries (*right photo*). In other words, you know what to expect in these and many other situations and are prepared to behave in them in certain ways.

information we notice. *Encoding* refers to the processes through which information we notice stored in memory. Finally, *retrieval* refers to the processes through which we recover information from memory in order to use it in some manner—for example, in making judgments about other people.

Schemas have been found to influence all of these aspects of social cognition (Wyer & Srull, 1994). With respect to attention, schemas often act as a kind of filter: Information consistent with them is more likely to be noticed and to enter our consciousness. Information that does not fit with our schemas is often ignored (Fiske, 1993), unless it is so extreme that we can't help but notice it. And even then, it is often discounted as the exception that proves the rule.

Turning to encoding—what information is entered into memory—it is a basic fact that information that becomes the focus of our attention is much more likely to be stored in long-term memory. So again, in general, it is information that is consistent with our schemas that is encoded. However, information that is sharply inconsistent with our schemas—information that does *not* agree with our expectations in a given situation—may sometimes be encoded into a separate memory location and marked with a unique "tag." After all, such information is so unexpected that it literally seizes our attention and almost forces us to make a mental note of it (Stangor & McMillan, 1992). Here's an example: You have a well-developed schema for the role of "professor." You expect professors to come to class, to lecture, to answer questions, to give and grade exams, and so on. Suppose that one of your professors comes to class and instead of lecturing, reads poetry or does magic tricks. You will certainly remember these experiences because they are so inconsistent with your schema for professors—your mental framework for what professors do and say.

That leads us to the third process: retrieval from memory. What information is most readily remembered—information that is consistent with our schemas or information that is inconsistent with these mental frameworks? This is a complex question that has been investigated in many different studies (e.g., Stangor & McMillan, 1992).

Overall, this research suggests that people tend to report remembering and using information that is consistent with schemas to a greater extent than information that is inconsistent. However, this effect could stem from differences in actual memory or, alternatively, from simple response tendencies. In other words, information inconsistent with schemas might be present in memory as strongly, or even more strongly, than information consistent with schemas, but people simply tend to report (describe) information consistent with their schemas. In fact, this appears to be the case. When measures of memory are corrected for this response tendency, or when individuals are asked to actually *recall* information rather than simply use it or indicate whether they recognize it, a strong tendency to remember information that is incongruent with schemas appears. So, there is no simple answer to the question "Which do we remember better—information consistent or inconsistent with our schemas or expectations?" Rather, the answer depends on the measure of memory employed. In general, people *report* information consistent with their schemas; in fact, however, information inconsistent with schemas may be strongly present in memory, as well.

At this point, it's important to note that the effects of schemas on social cognition (e.g., what we notice and remember, and how we then use this information to make decisions or judgments) are strongly influenced by several other factors. For instance, such effects are stronger when schemas are themselves strong and well developed (e.g., Stangor & McMillan, 1992; Tice, Bratslavsky, & Baumeister, 2000), and they are stronger when *cognitive load*—how much mental effort we are expending at a given time—is high rather than low (e.g., Kunda, 1999). In other words, when we are trying to handle a lot of social information at one time, we rely on schemas because they allow us to process this information with less effort.

Before concluding this section, we must call attention to the fact that although schemas are based on our past experiences (they reflect knowledge we have extracted from our experiences in the social world) and are often helpful, they have a serious downside, too. By influencing what we notice, enter into memory, and later remember, schemas can produce distortions in our understanding of the social world. For example, as we'll discover in Chapter 6, schemas play an important role in prejudice, forming one basic component of stereotypes about specific social groups. And, unfortunately, once they are formed, schemas are often very resistant to change. They show a strong **perseverance effect**, remaining unchanged even in the face of contradictory information (e.g., Kunda & Oleson, 1995). For instance, when we encounter information inconsistent with our schemas, such as an engineer who is a wonderful cook and extremely charming (traits we don't expect in engineers, as a rule!), we do not alter our schema for "engineers." Rather, we may place such persons in a special category or *subtype* consisting of persons who do not confirm the schema or stereotype (e.g., Richards & Hewstone, 2001). Perhaps even worse, schemas can sometimes be *self-fulfilling:* They influence the social world in ways that *make* it consistent with the schema. Let's take a closer look at this process, known in social psychology as the self-fulfilling prophecy, or *the self-confirming nature* of schemas.

The Self-Confirming Nature of Schemas: When—and Why—Beliefs Shape Reality

During the depression of the 1930s, many banks faced the following situation: They were in excellent financial shape, but rumors circulated that indicated they were not. As a result, so many depositors lined up to withdraw their funds that, ultimately, the banks really did fail. They didn't have enough money on hand to meet all their customers' demands (Figure 2.3).

perseverance effect
The tendency for beliefs and schemas to remain unchanged, even in the face of contradictory information.

Figure 2.3 ■ **The Self-Confirming Nature of Beliefs**
During the 1930s, many people believed rumors that their banks would soon fail. As a result, many rushed to withdraw their money, and thus actually *caused* the collapse of the banks.

Interestingly, schemas, too, can produce such effects, which are sometimes described as a **self-fulfilling prophecies**—predictions that, in a sense, make themselves come true. Robert Rosenthal and Lenore Jacobson (1968) provided classic evidence for such effects during the turbulent 1960s. During that period, there was growing concern over the possibility that teachers' beliefs about minority students—their schemas for such youngsters—were causing them to treat these children differently (less favorably) than majority-group students and that, as a result, the minority group students were falling further and further behind.

To gather evidence on the possible occurrence of such effects, Rosenthal and Jacobson conducted an ingenious study that exerted a powerful effect on subsequent research in social psychology. They went to an elementary school in San Francisco and administered an IQ test to all students. They then told the teachers that some of the students had scored very high and were about to "bloom" academically. In fact, this was not true: They chose the names of these students randomly. But Rosenthal and Jacobson predicted that this information might change the teachers' expectations (and schemas) about these children, and hence their behavior toward them. The teachers were not given such information about other students, who constituted a control group.

To find out whether their predictions were self-fulfilling, Rosenthal and Jacobson returned eight months later and tested both groups of children again. Results were clear and dramatic: Those who had been described as "bloomers" to their teachers showed significantly larger gains on the IQ test than those in the control group. In short, teachers' beliefs about the students had operated in a self-fulfilling manner: The students that teachers believed would bloom academically actually did.

How did such an effect occur? In part, through the impact of the schemas on the teachers' behaviors. Further research (Rosenthal, 1994) indicated that the teachers gave the students they expected to bloom more attention, more challenging tasks, more and better feedback, and more opportunities to respond in class. In short, the teachers acted in ways that benefited the students they expected to bloom, and, as a result, these youngsters really did excel.

This early research inspired social psychologists to search for other self-confirming effects of schemas in many settings—education, therapy, and business, to name a few. They soon uncovered much evidence that schemas often shape behavior in ways that lead to their confirmation. For example, they found that teachers' lower expectations for success by minority students or girls undermined the confidence of these groups and actually contributed to poorer performance by them (e.g., Sadker & Sadker, 1994). Further, many studies indicated that the self-confirming effects of schemas do not result from deliberate attempts by people to confirm these mental frameworks

self-fulfilling prophecies
Predictions that, in a sense, make themselves come true.

(Chen & Bargh, 1997). On the contrary, these self-confirming effects occur even when individuals attempt to avoid letting their expectations shape their behavior toward others. So, schemas are definitely a two-edged sword: They help us make sense out of the social world and process information quickly and with minimal effort, but they can also lock us into perceiving the world in ways that may not, in fact, be accurate. We consider these effects again in our discussion of prejudice in Chapter 6.

KEY POINTS

★ Because we have limited cognitive capacity, we often attempt to reduce the effort we expend on *social cognition*—how we think about other persons. This can increase efficiency but reduce our accuracy with respect to this important task.

★ One basic component of social cognition is *schemas*—mental frameworks centering on a specific theme that help us to organize social information.

★ Once formed, schemas exert powerful effects on what we notice (attention), enter into memory (encoding), and later remem-

ber (retrieval). Individuals report remembering more information consistent with their schemas than information that is inconsistent with them. In fact, however, inconsistent information, too, is strongly represented in memory.

★ Schemas help us to process information, but they often persist even in the face of disconfirming information, thus distorting our understanding of the social world.

★ Schemas also can exert self-confirming effects, causing us to behave in ways that confirm the schemas.

Heuristics and Automatic Processing: How We Reduce Our Effort in Social Cognition

Several states have passed or are considering adopting laws that ban talking on hand-held cell phones while driving. Why? Because it has been found that when drivers are distracted, they are more likely to be involved in accidents, and talking on the phone can often be highly distracting (see Figure 2.4). This illustrates a basic principle concerning our cognitive abilities: They are definitely limited. At any given time, we are capable of handling a certain amount of information; additional input beyond this level places us into a state of **information overload:** The demands on our cognitive system are greater than its capacity. In addition, our processing capacity can be depleted by high levels of stress or other demands (e.g., Chajut & Algom, 2003). To deal with such situations, we adopt various strategies designed to "stretch" our cognitive resources—to let us do more, with less effort, than would otherwise be the case. To be successful, such strategies must meet two requirements: (1) They must provide a quick and simple way of dealing with large amounts of information, and (2) they must work; that is, they must be reasonably accurate much of the time. Many potential shortcuts for reducing mental effort exist, but among these, perhaps the most useful are **heuristics**—simple rules for making complex decisions or drawing inferences in a rapid and efficient manner.

Another means of dealing with the fact that the social world is complex yet our information processing capacity is limited is to put many activities, including some aspects of social thought and social behavior, on *automatic* (or *automatic processing,* as psychologists term it; e.g., Ohman et al., 2001). After discussing several heuristics, we consider such automatic processing and its implications for social thought.

information overload
Instances in which our ability to process information is exceeded.

heuristics
Simple rules for making complex decisions or drawing inferences in a rapid and seemingly effortless manner.

Figure 2.4 ■ Information Overload: A Potential Cause of Accidents
Our capacity to process incoming information is definitely limited and can easily be exceeded. This can happen when drivers talk on cell phones while driving in heavy traffic. If drivers exceed their capacity to process information and enter into a state of *information overload*, serious accidents may result. Because of these data, several states have passed or are considering passing laws that ban the use of handheld cell phones while driving.

Representativeness: Judging by Resemblance

Suppose that you have just met your next-door neighbor for the first time. While chatting with her, you notice that she is dressed conservatively, is neat in her personal habits, has a large library in her home, and seems to be gentle and a little shy. Later you realize that she never mentioned what she does for a living. Is she a business manager, a physician, a waitress, an attorney, a dancer, or a librarian? One quick way of making a guess is to compare her with other members of each of these occupations. How well does she resemble persons you have met in each of these fields or, perhaps, the typical member of these fields? If you proceed in this manner, you may quickly conclude that she is probably a librarian; her traits seem closer to those associated with this profession than they do to traits associated with being a physician, dancer, or executive. If you made a judgment about your neighbor's occupation in this manner, you would be using the **representativeness heuristic.** In other words, you would make your judgment on the basis of a relatively simple rule: *The more similar an individual is to typical members of a given group, the more likely she or he is to belong to that group.*

Are such judgments accurate? Often they are, because belonging to certain groups affects the behavior and style of persons in them, and because people with certain traits are attracted to particular groups in the first place. But sometimes, judgments based on representativeness are wrong, mainly for the following reason: Decisions or judgments made on the basis of this rule tend to ignore *base rates*—the frequency with which given events or patterns (e.g., occupations) occur in the total population (Tversky & Kahneman, 1973; Koehler, 1993). In fact, there are many more business managers than librarians—perhaps fifty times as many. Thus, even though your neighbor seems more

representativeness heuristic
A strategy for making judgments based on the extent to which current stimuli or events resemble other stimuli or categories.

similar to librarians than to managers in her personal traits, the chances are actually higher that she is a manager than a librarian. Yet, because of our strong tendency to use the representativeness heuristic, we tend to ignore such base rate information and instead base our judgments on similarity to typical members of a group or category. In this and related ways, the representativeness heuristic can lead to errors in our thinking about other persons.

Availability: "If I Can Think of It, It Must Be Important."

Which are more common: words that start with the letter *k* (e.g., *king*) or words with *k* as the third letter (e.g., *awkward*)? In English there are more than twice as many words with *k* in the third position as there are with *k* in the first position. Despite this fact, when asked this question, most people guess incorrectly (Tversky & Kahneman, 1982). Why? In part because of the operation of another heuristic—the **availability heuristic,** which suggests that the easier it is to bring information to mind, the greater is its impact on subsequent judgments or decisions. This heuristic, too, makes good sense. After all, that we can bring some information to mind quite easily suggests that it must be important and *should* influence our judgments and decisions. Relying on availability in making social judgments, however, can also lead to errors. For instance, it can lead us to overestimate the likelihood of events that are dramatic but rare, because they are easy to bring to mind. Consistent with this principle, many people fear travel in airplanes more than travel in automobiles, even though the chances of dying in an auto accident are hundreds of times higher. Here's another example: Physicians who examine the same patient often reach different diagnoses about the patient's illness. Why? One possibility is that the physicians have had different experiences in their medical practices, and so find different kinds of information easier to bring to mind. Their diagnoses then reflect these differences in ease of retrieval—or, in other terms, their reliance on the availability heuristic.

Interestingly, research suggests that there is more to the availability heuristic than merely the subjective ease with which relevant information comes to mind. In addition, the *amount* of information we can bring to mind seems to matter as well (e.g., Schwarz et al., 1991). The more information we can think of, the greater its impact on our judgments. Which of these two factors is more important? The answer appears to involve the kind of judgment we are making. If it is one involving emotions or feelings, we tend to rely on the "ease" rule, but if it is one involving facts or information, we tend to rely more on the "amount" rule (e.g., Rothman & Hardin, 1997; Ruder & Bless, 2003).

Priming: Some Effects of Increased Availability

The availability heuristic plays a role in many aspects of social thought, such as stereotyping (examined in detail in Chapter 6). In addition, the availablility heuristic relates to another especially important process: **priming**—increased availability of information resulting from exposure to specific stimuli or events.

Here's a clear example of such priming: During the first year of medical school, many students experience the "medical student syndrome." They begin to suspect that they or others have many serious illnesses. An ordinary headache may lead them to wonder whether they have a brain tumor, and a mild sore throat may lead to anxiety over the possibility of some rare but fatal type of infection. What accounts for such an effect? The explanation favored by social psychologists is that the students are exposed to descriptions of diseases day after day in their classes and assigned readings. As a result, such information increases in availability. This, in turn, leads them to imagine the worst when confronted with mild symptoms.

Priming effects occur in many other contexts. For example, the magnified fears many people experience after watching a horror film causes them to see every shadow as a potential monster and to jump at every sound (see Figure 2.5). Thus, priming

availability heuristic
A strategy for making judgments on the basis of how easily specific kinds of information can be brought to mind.

priming
Increased availability in memory or consciousness of specific types of information held in memory due to exposure to specific stimuli or events.

Figure 2.5 ■ Priming in Action
After watching a horror movie, many people find that they are more easily frightened by unexpected sights (e.g., moving shadows) and sounds. This is because thoughts of fear-inducing events and memories of times when they were fearful have been *primed* by the content of the film. Priming plays an important role in social cognition in many different contexts.

effects are an important aspect of social thought (e.g., Higgins & King, 1981; Higgins, Rohles, & Jones, 1977). In fact, research findings indicate that priming may occur even when individuals are unaware of the priming stimuli—an effect known as *automatic priming* (e.g., Bargh & Pietromonaco, 1982). In other words, the availability of certain kinds of information can be increased by priming stimuli, even though we are not aware of having been exposed to these stimuli. For instance, suppose that while waiting for a movie to start, you are thinking about some important matter. As a result, you do not even notice that a message urging you to "eat popcorn" has appeared on the screen. A few minutes later, you have a strong urge to buy some popcorn. Why? Perhaps because you are hungry and like popcorn; but it is also possible that your urge to buy popcorn stems, at least in part, from your being primed to do so by the message you did not consciously notice.

In sum, it appears that priming is a basic fact of social thought. External events and conditions—or even our own thoughts—can increase the availability of specific types of information. And increased availability, in turn, influences our judgments with respect to such information. "If I can think of it," we seem to reason, "then it must be important," and we often reach such conclusions even if they are not supported by social reality. (For another example of the availability heuristic in operation, please see the **Beyond the Headlines** section on page 50.)

Anchoring and Adjustment: Where You Begin Makes a Difference

Suppose you are in the market for a used car. You check the papers and find one that sounds promising. The ad says, "Best offer," so no price is listed. When you meet the owner, she names a figure that is much higher than you had in mind. What do you do?

Unsafe at Any Size?

Big and Bad: How the SUV Ran Over Automotive Safety

The New Yorker (January 12, 2004)—"In the summer of 1996, the Ford Motor Company began building the Expedition, its new full-sized SUV.... Ford executives thought the Expedition would be a highly profitable niche product. They were half right. The "highly profitable" part was true, but almost from the moment Ford's big new SUVs rolled off the assembly line, there

was nothing "niche" about the Expedition.... In the history of the automotive industry, few things have been quite as unexpected as the rise of the SUV. Detroit is a town of engineers, and engineers like to believe that there is some connection between the success of a vehicle and its technical merits ... so the SUV boom made no sense to them. Consumers said they liked four-wheel drive. But the overwhelming majority don't need it.... The truth, underneath all the rational-

izations, seems to be that SUV buyers thought of big, heavy vehicles as safe: they found comfort in being surrounded by so much rubber and steel.... But consider the set of safety statistics compiled by Tom Wenzel, a scientist at Lawrence Berkeley National Laboratory.... They show that the best performers are not the biggest and heaviest vehicles on the road. Among the safest cars are the midsize imports, like the Toyota Camry and the Honda Accord. Or consider the extraordinary perfor-

mance of the tiny Volkswagen Jetta. Drivers of the Jetta die at a rate of just forty-seven per million—half that of popular SUV models like the Ford Explorer or the GMC Jimmy. In a head-on crash, an Explorer or a Suburban would crush a Jetta or a Camry. But clearly, the drivers of Camrys and Jettas are finding ways to avoid head-on crashes with Explorers and Suburbans. The benefits of being nimble... are in many cases greater than the benefits of being big...."

I (Robert Baron) have several friends and relatives who drive huge SUVs, and when I ask them why, they usually reply, "I like being high up" and "I feel so safe in it." Some grudgingly admit that their SUVs handle like trucks (that's what, in essence, they are), but they still feel safe in them. In fact, though, there is no basis for this belief in safety. On the contrary, as shown in Table 2.1, the drivers of large SUVs are more likely to die, and to kill others, than the drivers of much smaller vehicles. So, size does *not* seem to offer the margin of safety many SUV owners assume exists.

How, then, can we explain these persistent beliefs that SUVs offer their drivers the advantage of safety? Advertising plays a role, because many ads for large SUVs do emphasize this angle, but it seems possible that this continued and largely unjustified belief in safety also stems from the powerful effects of the *availability*

heuristic. When people remember accidents they have seen in person or on television, the ones that come most easily to mind are the most dramatic—and those are often accidents in which a huge SUV has crushed a smaller vehicle. Because these events are so easy to remember, they strongly affect many drivers' perceptions of safety and lead them to conclude—falsely, it appears—that SUVs are unusually safe. Yes, they *are* safe in one respect: In a head-on collision, a large SUV will demolish a smaller vehicle. But the drivers of smaller cars with quick and responsive handling are able to *avoid* many accidents that SUVs cannot escape and, in fact, may be safer overall.

So where does all of this leave us? With the conclusion that, in this situation, as in many others, our thinking about the social world is subject to important forms of error and bias. Most people would probably be bet-

Do you counter with the price you want to pay, or do you offer something higher, in between what she has asked and your original price? Unless you are highly skilled in negotiation, you will probably offer more than you originally planned. Why? Because we often use a number or value as a starting point (an anchor) from which we then

ter off driving smaller, quicker-handling cars, but as long they continue to believe that SUVs offer greater safety, it seems safe to predict that these giant, gas-guzzling vehicles will remain popular, and will continue to generate huge profits for the companies that make them.

Table 2.1 ■ SUVs: An Illusion of Safety?

As shown here, death rates from accidents are much higher for many large SUVs than for smaller and quicker-handling cars. So, why do many drivers of SUVs believe that their vehicles afford them an extra margin of safety? It is possible that the *availability heuristic* and other errors in social cognition play a role in this error.

VEHICLE	TYPE	TOTAL DEATHS PER 1,000,000 VEHICLES (DRIVER DEATHS + OTHER DEATHS)
Toyota Avalon	Large car	60
Chrysler Town & Country	Minivan	67
Toyota Camry	Mid-size car	70
Volkswagen Jetta	Subcompact car	70
Ford Windstar	Minivan	72
Nissan Maxima	Mid-size car	79
Honda Accord	Mid-size car	82
Chevrolet Venture	Minivan	85
Buick Century	Mid-size car	93
Chevrolet Suburban	SUV	105
Jeep Grand Cherokee	SUV	106
Ford Explorer	SUV	112
GMC Jimmy	SUV	114
Toyota 4Runner	SUV	137
Chevrolet Tahoe	SUV	141
Ford Explorer	SUV	148

(*Source: Based on data in Gladwell, 2004.*)

make adjustments. Her asking price is the anchor in this situation, and you then make adjustments to it, offering something lower, but still above what you originally had in mind. Why? Because, the adjustments you make to the anchor are insufficient. Logically, they should be larger, but usually they are not (e.g., Epley & Gilovich, 2004). Our

Figure 2.6 ■ Anchoring and Adjustment: A Failure to Adjust Our Thinking
We often allow our personal experiences to serve as an anchor for our views, even if we know that these experiences are unusual or unreliable. For instance, if you visited Paris or any other major city during a major strike and found it to be dirtier and less pleasant than you had originally expected, you might fail to adjust your thinking about the city to reflect the impact of the strike. In other words, you might continue to view it negatively, even though you realize that you saw it at its worst.

tendency to make decisions in this way stems from another important heuristic, known as **anchoring and adjustment;** as just stated, this heuristic involves the tendency to use a number or value as a starting point, to which we then make adjustments.

Anchoring and adjustment can be seen in many situations, not only ones involving money or other figures. For instance, we often allow our personal experiences to serve as an anchor for our views, even if we know our experiences are unique or unusual in some way (e.g., Gilovich, Medvec, & Savitsky, 2000). Here's an example: Imagine that you visit Paris for the first time and find that the streets are filled with trash, the metro (public transportation) is not running, and the streets are totally choked with cars (see (Figure 2.6). Your conclusion: Paris does not live up to its reputation of beauty and romance, and you never want to return. Here's the surprising part: You may continue to feel this way, even if you later learn that you arrived during the worst strike in many years—a time when almost all public employees had walked off their jobs. Normally, the streets are clean and the metro runs just fine. But even though you have this information and know that your experience was an unusual one, you merely adjust your initial impression to make it a little more positive. You do not return to your initial expectations about Paris being a beautiful city.

Why do we let heuristics influence our thinking to such a great extent? Because they save us mental effort and that, it seems, is a guiding principle of social cognition— just as it is in almost every other aspect of life.

anchoring and adjustment heuristic
A heuristic that involves the tendency to use a number or value as a starting point, to which we then make adjustments.

Chapter 2 / Social Cognition

As noted earlier, a central dilemma we face with respect to social cognition is this: Our capacity to process information (including social information) is limited, yet daily life floods us with large amounts of information and requires us to deal with it both effectively and efficiently. Heuristics offer one means of solving this problem. In fact, however, heuristics represent just one aspect of a more general tendency: to engage in what social psychologists term **automatic processing,** or *automatic modes of thought.* This term refers to processing of social information that is nonconscious (recall the discussion in Chapter 1), unintentional, involuntary, and relatively effortless. Automatic processing tends to develop after we have extensive experience with a task or type of information and reach the stage at which we can perform the task or process the information without giving it conscious thought—and sometimes without even meaning to do so. Do you remember your efforts to learn to ride a bicycle? At first, you had to devote a lot of attention to this task; if you didn't, you would fall. But as you mastered it, riding required less and less attention until finally you could do it while thinking of entirely different topics, or even while engaging in other tasks, such as talking to a friend. In situations such as this one, the shift from *controlled processing* (which is effortful and conscious) to automatic processing is something we *want* to happen. It saves us a great deal of effort.

To an extent, this is true for social thought as well as well as for learning new skills. For instance, once we have a well-developed schema for a social group (e.g., for doctors or any other profession), we can think in shorthand ways about members of that group. We can, for instance, assume that all doctors will be busy, so it's necessary to get right to the point with them, that they are intelligent but not always very considerate, and so on. But, as is usually the case, these gains in efficiency or ease are offset by potential losses in accuracy. For instance, growing evidence indicates that one type of schema—*stereotypes*—can be activated in an automatic and nonconscious manner by the physical features associated with the stereotyped group (e.g., Pratto & Bargh, 1991). Thus, dark skin may automatically trigger a negative stereotype about African Americans, even if the person in question has no intention of thinking in terms of this stereotype. Similarly, attitudes (beliefs and evaluations of some aspect of the social world) may be triggered automatically by the mere presence of the focus of the attitude in question (e.g., Wegner & Bargh, 1998). Such automatic processing of social information can, of course, lead to serious errors.

Perhaps even more surprising, research findings indicate that schemas, once activated, may exert seemingly automatic effects on behavior. In other words, people often act in ways that are consistent with these schemas, even though they do not intend to do so, and are unaware that their behavior is influenced by the schemas.

Research conducted by Bargh, Chen, and Burrows (1996) provides a clear illustration of such effects. These researchers first activated either the schema for the trait of *rudeness* or the schema for the trait of *politeness* through priming. This was accomplished by having participants work on the task of unscrambling scrambled sentences. The sentences contained words related either to rudeness (e.g., *rude, impolitely, bluntly*) or to politeness (*cordially, patiently, courteous*). Exposure to words related to schemas was found, in past research, to prime or activate these mental frameworks. Persons in a third (control) group unscrambled sentences containing words unrelated to either trait (e.g., *exercising, flawlessly, occasionally, normally*). After completing these tasks, participants in the study were asked to report to the experimenter for more instructions. When they approached the experimenter, he or she was engaged in a conversation with another person (an accomplice). The experimenter continued this conversation, ignoring the participant. The major dependent measure was whether the participant interrupted the conversation. Bargh and colleagues (1996) predicted that persons for whom the trait *rudeness* had been primed would be more likely to interrupt than those for whom the trait *politeness* had been

automatic processing
After extensive experience with a task or type of information, the stage at which we can perform the task or process the information in a seemingly effortless, automatic, and nonconscious manner.

primed. This is precisely what happened. Perhaps even more revealing is the fact that these effects occurred despite the fact that participants' ratings of the experimenter in terms of politeness did not differ across the three experimental conditions. In other words, these differences in their behavior—how willing they were to interrupt the experimenter's conversations—seemed to occur in a nonconscious, automatic manner.

These results and those of many other studies (e.g., Fazio & Hilden, 2001; O'Sullivan, 2003) indicate that, often, social cognition is *not* the rational, reasonable, orderly process we would like it to be. On the contrary, schemas and other mental structures we have acquired through experience can strongly affect our behaviors, and our overt actions in ways that we do not fully recognize, and might, in some cases, wish to change. For instance, as we'll see in detail in Chapter 6, once stereotypes are activated, individuals may think about the social groups who are the targets of such stereotypes in negative ways and may treat members of these groups in a hostile or rejecting manner, *even if they do not intend to do so, and would be upset to realize that they are acting in these ways.* In these and many other situations, automatic processing is an important aspect of social thought, one well worth considering in our efforts to understand how we think about other persons and as we attempt to make sense out of the social world.

Controlled versus Automatic Processing in Evaluating the Social World: Evidence from Social Neuroscience

A very basic dimension of our reactions to the social world is *evaluation*—the extent to which we view events, people, or situations as good or bad. A large body of evidence suggests that we often make such evaluations in an automatic manner, without conscious thought of awareness. For instance, Fazio and his colleagues (1986) found that individuals were able to classify words as having a good or bad meaning more quickly if these words had been preceded by other words with similar meanings. Research participants responded more quickly to words with a good meaning, such as *beautiful,* if these words had been preceded by other words with a good meaning, such as *triumph,* than if they had been preceded by words with a bad meaning, such as *murder.* Additional studies (e.g., Bargh et al., 1992) indicated that such effects occurred even if participants did not have to decide whether the words had a good or bad meaning but were merely asked to pronounce them. Good words preceded by other good words were pronounced more quickly than were good words preceded by words with a bad meaning, and vice versa. These findings indicate that evaluations often occur in an automatic manner. In contrast, evaluations of words, people, or any other aspect of the world can also occur in a controlled or reflective manner, one in which we think about the judgments we are making carefully and consciously (e.g., Greenwald & Banaji, 1995). This is especially likely to occur when we are dealing with more complex information, or aspects of the social world toward which we have ambivalent reactions—ones that are both positive and negative.

These findings suggest that we may have two systems for evaluating various aspects of the social world: one that operates in an automatic manner and another that operates in a systematic and controlled manner. Do these systems involve different parts of the brain? If so, there would be strong evidence for their existence and for the distinction between them. In fact, studies conducted from the perspective of *social neuroscience* (see Chapter 1) indicate that these differences exist. Certain parts of the brain, especially the amygdala, may be involved in automatic evaluative reactions—simple good–bad judgments that occur in a rapid and nonconscious manner (Phelps et al., 2001). In contrast, portions of the prefrontal cortex (especially the medial prefrontal cortex and ventrolateral prefrontal cortex) may play a key role in more controlled evaluative reactions—the kinds about which we think carefully and consciously (e.g., Duncan & Owen, 2000).

Research performed by Cunningham and colleagues (2003) provides clear evidence for these conclusions. In this study, participants were shown the names of famous peo-

Chapter 2 / Social Cognition

ple (e.g., Adolf Hitler, Bill Cosby) and were asked to judge whether these persons were good or bad (an evaluative judgment) or whether the names referred to historical or present-day people (a nonevaluative judgment). As participants did this, activity in their brains was recorded by means of functional magnetic resonance imaging (fMRI). The authors reasoned that because the names were the same for both tasks, the *automatic* component of evaluation would be present in both. That is, the names would evoke evaluative reactions automatically, regardless of whether participants were asked to rate them as good or bad, or as referring to historical versus present-day people. Additional brain activation occurring during the good–bad task would then reflect more controlled evaluative processing—processing that took place *only when the conscious goal of participants was that of evaluating these names.*

Consistent with the findings mentioned previously, results indicated that such controlled processing occurred primarily in several areas of the prefrontal cortex—areas of the brain long known to be associated with our higher mental processes. In other words, activation in these areas increased when participants performed the evaluative task, relative to when they were judging the names in a nonevaluative manner (i.e., whether the names referred to historical or present-day people). In contrast, automatic processing seemed to occur primarily in the amygdala. Perhaps of even greater interest, when the names referred to people toward whom participants had ambivalent reactions—both positive and negative (e.g., Bill Clinton, Yasser Arafat)—rather than to ones toward whom they had nonambivalent reactions (e.g., Adolf Hitler, Mahatma Gandhi; see Figure 2.7), increased activity occurred in the prefrontal cortex during the

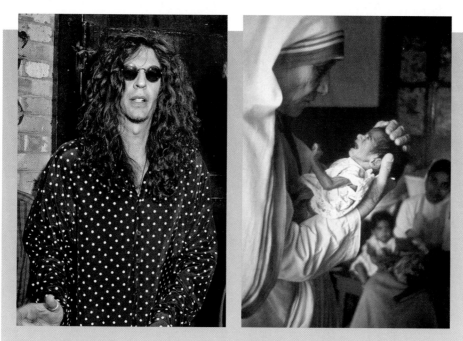

Figure 2.7 ■ Evaluation of Social Stimuli: Two Neural Systems
Findings of recent research conducted from the perspective of social neuroscience suggests that we have two distinct systems for evaluating social stimuli (other people, groups, ideas, etc.). One system, located primarily in the amygdala, evaluates such stimuli quickly and automatically. Another system, located mainly in the prefrontal cortex, evaluates such stimuli in a more controlled and systematic manner. Additional findings indicate that when we evaluate social stimuli toward which we have ambivalent (i.e., mixed) feelings (e.g., *photo on left*), the second (systematic thought) system shows greater activity than when we evaluate social stimuli toward which we have nonambivalent feelings (e.g., *photo on right*).
(*Source: Based on findings reported by Cunningham et al., 2003.*)

good–bad (evaluative) task. In other words, ambivalent names generated a greater amount of activity reflecting controlled processing than did the nonambivalent names, and this increased activity occurred mainly in the prefrontal cortex.

Overall, these results and those of many other studies support the view that we really do have distinct systems for evaluating social stimuli: one that responds quickly, automatically, and without conscious intention or effort, and another that comes into play when we engage in more controlled, systematic processing. The existence of these two distinct modes of processing social information makes a great deal of sense: After all, we don't have the time or motivation to evaluate everything around us in a careful, systematic manner. As we'll discover at several points in this book, however, our tendency to rely on automatic processing in evaluating aspects of the social world may play an important role in the powerful and often insidious impact of stereotypes on our judgments of others and our behavior toward them (see Chapter 6). Thus, as noted earlier, the efficiency provided by this automatic processing often comes at very high price.

KEY POINTS

★ Because our capacity to process information is limited, we often experience *information overload.* To avoid this, we make use of *heuristics*—rules for making decisions in a quick and relatively effortless manner.

★ One such heuristic is *representativeness,* which suggests that the more similar an individual is to typical members of a given group, the more likely she or he is to belong to that group.

★ Another heuristic is *availability,* which suggests that the easier it is to bring information to mind, the greater is its impact on subsequent decisions or judgments. In some cases, availability may also involve the amount of information we bring to mind.

★ A third heuristic is *anchoring and adjustment,* which leads us to use a number or a value as a starting point from which we then make

adjustments. These adjustments may not be sufficient to reflect actual social reality.

★ *Priming* refers to increased availability of information resulting from exposure to specific stimuli or events.

★ In a sense, heuristics are just one aspect of a more general tendency: to engage in *automatic processing,* or automatic thought, which refers to processing of social information that is nonconscious, unintentional, and relatively effortless. Such processing is a basic fact of social cognition and can affect both our thoughts and our overt actions in a wide range of contexts.

★ Growing evidence indicates that the distinction between automatic and controlled processing is a basic one. In fact, different regions of the brain appear to be involved in these two types of processing, especially with respect to evaluations of various aspects of the social world.

Potential Sources of Error in Social Cognition: Why Total Rationality Is Rarer Than You Think

Human beings are definitely not computers. Although we can *imagine* being able to reason in a perfectly logical way, we know from our own experiences that we often fall short of this goal. This is true with respect to many aspects of social thought. In our efforts to understand others and make sense out of the social world, we are subject to a wide range of tendencies that, together, can lead us into serious error. In this section, we consider several of these "tilts" in social cognition. Before doing so, however, we must emphasize the following point: Although these aspects of social thought sometimes result in errors, they are also quite adaptive. They often help us focus on the kinds of information that are most informative, and they reduce the effort required for understanding the social world. So, these tendencies in social thought are definitely something of a mixed bag, supplying us with tangible benefits as well as exacting important costs.

Negativity Bias: The Tendency to Pay Extra Attention to Negative Information

Imagine that in describing someone you haven't met, one of your friends mentions many positive things about this person: He or she is pleasant, intelligent, good-looking, friendly, and so on. Then, your friend mentions one negative piece of information: This person is also somewhat conceited. What are you likely to remember? Research findings indicate that, probably, the negative information will stand out in your memory (e.g., Kunda, 1999). Moreover, because of this, the negative information will have a stronger influence on your desire to meet this person than any one equivalent piece of positive information. Such findings suggest that we show a strong **negativity bias**—greater sensitivity to negative information than to positive information. This bias applies to both social information and information about other aspects of the world as well.

Why do we have this tendency? From an evolutionary perspective, having it makes a great deal of sense. Negative information reflects features of the external world that may threaten our safety or well-being. For this reason, it is especially important that we be sensitive to such stimuli and thus able to respond to them quickly. Several research findings offer support for this reasoning. For instance, consider our ability to recognize facial expressions in others. The results of many studies indicate that we are faster and more accurate in detecting negative facial expressions (e.g., ones showing anger or hostility) than positive facial expressions (e.g., ones showing friendliness).

Studies conducted by Ohman, Lundqvist, and Esteves (2001) provide a clear illustration of such effects. These researchers asked participants to search for neutral, friendly, or threatening faces among other faces with discrepant expressions (e.g., the friendly face was shown among neutral or threatening faces; the threatening face was shown among friendly or neutral faces; and so on). Results indicated that regardless of the background faces, participants were faster and more accurate in identifying threatening faces. In an additional study, participants were asked to search for several kinds of faces—threatening, friendly, scheming, or sad—among an array of neutral faces. Again, the threatening faces were identified faster and more accurately than any of the others see (Figure 2.8).

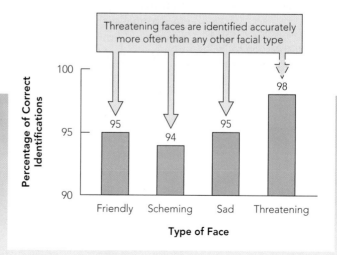

Figure 2.8 ■ **Evidence for the Negativity Bias: Which Face Do You Notice First?**
Threatening faces shown among a background of neutral faces were identified more quickly and more accurately than were friendly, scheming, or sad faces. These findings provide evidence for the existence of the *negativity bias*—enhanced sensitivity to negative stimuli or information. (*Source: Based on data from Ohman, Lundqvist, and Esteves, 2001.*)

In sum, we appear to have a strong tendency to show enhanced sensitivity to negative information. This tendency seems to be a basic aspect of social thought and may, in fact, be built into the structure and functioning of our brains (Ito et al., 1998; Cacioppo et al., 2003). In this respect, it is an important "tilt" in our social cognition, and one worth noting with care.

The Optimistic Bias: Our Tendency to See the World through Rose-Colored Glasses

Although the tendency to notice negative information is a strong one, don't despair. Despite the existence of the negativity bias, we also have a seemingly opposite tendency, known as the **optimistic bias.** This refers to a predisposition to expect things to turn out well overall. In fact, research findings indicate that most people believe that they are *more* likely than others to experience positive events and *less* likely to experience negative events (e.g., Shepperd, Ouellette, & Fernandez, 1996). Similarly, we often have greater confidence in our beliefs or judgments than is justified—an effect known as the **overconfidence barrier** (Vallone, Ross, & Lepper, 1985). Our strong leaning toward optimism is seen in many other contexts, too: Most people believe that they are more likely than others to get a good job, have a happy marriage, and live to a ripe old age, but less likely to experience negative outcomes such as being fired, becoming seriously ill, or being divorced (e.g., Schwarzer, 1994).

Yet another illustration is the **planning fallacy**—our tendency to believe that we can get more done in a given period of time than we actually can. Because of this aspect of the optimistic bias, governments frequently announce overly optimistic schedules for public works (e.g., new roads, new airports, new bridges; see Figure 2.9), and individuals adopt unrealistically optimistic schedules for their own work. If you have ever estimated that a project would take a certain amount of time but then found that it took much longer, you are already familiar with this effect, and with the planning fallacy.

Why do we fall prey to this particular kind of optimism? According to Buehler, Griffin, and Ross (1994), social psychologists who have studied this tendency in detail, several factors play a role. One is that when individuals make predictions about how long it will take them to complete a given task, they enter a *planning* or *narrative* mode of thought in which they focus primarily on the future and how they will perform the task. This, in turn, prevents them from looking backward in time and remembering how long similar tasks took them in the past. As a result, one important "reality check" that might help them avoid being overly optimistic is removed. In addition, when individuals *do* consider past experiences in which tasks took longer than expected, they tend to attribute such outcomes to factors outside their control. The result is that they tend to overlook important potential obstacles when predicting how long a task will take and fall prey to the planning fallacy. These predictions have been confirmed in several studies (e.g., Buehler et al., 1994), so they seem to provide important insights into the origins of the tendency to make optimistic predictions about task completion.

This is not the entire story, though. Research suggests that another factor, too, may play an important role in the planning fallacy: *motivation* to complete a task. When predicting what will happen, individuals often guess that what will happen is what they *want* to happen (e.g., Johnson & Sherman, 1990). In cases in which they are strongly motivated to complete a task, therefore, they make overly optimistic predictions about when they will attain this desired state of affairs. Research findings offer support for this reasoning, too (e.g., Buehler, Griffin, & MacDonald, 1997), so it appears that our estimates of when we will complete a task are indeed influenced by our hopes and desires: We want to finish early or on time, so we predict that we will. The result? Unfounded optimism strikes again!

optimistic bias
Our predisposition to expect things to turn out well overall.

overconfidence barrier
The tendency to have more confidence in the accuracy of our judgments than is reasonable.

planning fallacy
The tendency to make optimistic predictions concerning how long a given task will take for completion.

Chapter 2 / Social Cognition

Figure 2.9 ■ The Planning Fallacy in Action
Construction of a major tunnel in Boston took several years longer and cost billions of dollars more than originally projected. This is far from a rare occurrence. Public projects routinely take much longer to complete than initially planned. This may reflect effects of the planning fallacy—the tendency to believe that we can accomplish more than we actually can in a given period of time.

■ The Rocky Past versus the Golden Future: Optimism at Work!

Think back over your past. Did it have peaks (times when things were going great for you) and valleys (times when things were not good)? Now, in contrast, try to imagine your future. How do you think it will unfold? If you are like most people, you may notice a difference in these descriptions. Although most of us recognize that our pasts have been mixed in terms of highs and lows, we tend to forecast a very rosy or golden future—one in which we will be happy and in which few negative events will happen to us. In fact, recent research by Newby-Clark and Ross (2003) indicates that this tendency is so strong that it occurs even when people have just recalled negative episodes from their own pasts. What accounts for this difference? One possibility is that when we think about the past, we can recall failures, unpleasant events, and other disappointments. When we think about the future, however, we tend to concentrate on desirable goals, personal happiness, and doing things we have always wanted to do, such as traveling to exotic places. The result? Because our thinking is dominated by these positive thoughts, we make highly optimistic predictions about the future and tend to perceive it as indeed golden, at least in its promise or potential. In short, the optimistic bias seems to occur not only for specific tasks or situations, but in our projections of our entire future lives as well.

Interestingly, thinking about the future can also have another positive effect: It can increase *creativity*. Recent studies by Forster, Friedman, and Liberman (2004) indicate that when we think about the far-off future—for instance, our lives a year from now—we tend to think more abstractly, rather than concretely. This in turn can enhance creativity. So, thinking about the future can sometimes yield intriguing beneficial effects.

■ Bracing for Loss: An Exception to the Optimistic Rule

Though optimism seems to be the general rule for most people much of the time, there is one important exception to this pattern. When individuals expect to receive feedback or information that may be negative and that has important consequences for them, they seem to *brace for loss* (or for the worst) and show a reversal of the usual optimistic pattern. In fact, they tend to be *pessimistic*, showing an enhanced tendency to anticipate *negative* outcomes (e.g., Taylor & Shepperd, 1998).

Why does this occur? Research by Shepperd and his colleagues (Shepperd et al., 2000) suggests that it is due to the desire to be ready—braced—for the worst. In several related studies, Shepperd et al. (2000) asked students to estimate the likelihood that they would receive an additional bill (a negative outcome) or a refund (a positive outcome) from the registrar at their college. (Supposedly, the registrar had made a number of errors, resulting in fully 25 percent of the students receiving incorrect bills for tuition and fees.) Shepperd and his colleagues predicted that students who were financially needy—for whom the additional bill would be a major problem—would show a stronger *brace for loss* effect, because an extra bill would have more serious consequences for them, than would those who were not financially needy. Results confirmed this prediction. In several studies, financially needy students estimated the likelihood that they would receive an additional bill at between 40 percent and 67 percent—much higher than the 25 percent chance figure and significantly higher than for students who were not financially needy. Further, the financially needy students showed such pessimism only for themselves, not for a friend, and regardless of whether they were primed to think about past financial losses.

Together, these findings suggest that people indeed brace for the worst and turn pessimistic under conditions in which they anticipate possible news that will have strong negative effects on them. Research findings (e.g., Shepperd & McNulty, 2002) indicate that this tendency can have important effects on long-term personal relationships as well. For instance, it may help newly married couples who are not high in social skills to avoid the bitter disappointments that may occur if their expectations for marital happiness are unrealistically high (McNulty & Karney, 2004). But again, we should emphasize that this is the exception to a general rule of optimism. In most situations, we tend to be overly optimistic about our lives and social outcomes, but we can switch to pessimism when this helps us protect ourselves from the crushing blows of unexpected bad news.

Chapter 2 / Social Cognition

KEY POINTS

★ We show a strong *negativity bias*—a tendency to be highly sensitive to negative stimuli or information. This tendency appears to be basic and may be built into the functioning of our brains. Thus, it may be the result of evolutionary factors.

★ We also show a strong *optimistic bias*, expecting positive events and outcomes in many contexts. In addition, we tend to make overly optimistic predictions about how long it will take us to complete a given task, an effect known as the *planning fallacy*.

★ The optimistic bias also shows up in our tendency to assume that we are more likely than other persons to experience positive outcomes, but less likely than others to experience negative ones.

★ The optimistic bias is also evident when we compare our past and our future: Although we perceive the past as mixed in terms of highs and lows, we tend to perceive the future in highly optimistic terms.

★ The optimistic bias may be reversed and turn to pessimism, however, when we anticipate receiving bad news with important consequences for us; in such cases, we brace for loss and show an enhanced tendency to predict negative outcomes.

Counterfactual Thinking: The Effects of Considering What Might Have Been

Suppose that you take an important exam; when you receive your score, it is a C–, much lower than you had hoped. What thoughts enter your mind as you consider your grade? If you are like most people, you may quickly begin to imagine what might have been—receiving a higher grade—along with thoughts about how you could have obtained that better outcome. "If only I had studied more, or come to class more often," you may think to yourself. And then, perhaps, you may begin to formulate plans for actually doing better on the next test.

Such thoughts about what might have been—known in social psychology as **counterfactual thinking**—occur in a wide range of situations, not only ones in which we experience disappointments (see Figure 2.10). For instance, suppose you read an article in the newspaper about someone who left work at the normal time and was injured

counterfactual thinking
The tendency to imagine other outcomes in a situation than the ones that actually occurred ("what might have been").

Figure 2.10 ■ Counterfactual Thinking: An Example
General Halftrack is engaging in counterfactual thinking: He is imagining what might have been and is experiencing intense regret. This is a common aspect of social cognition—a kind of thinking in which most of us engage at least occasionally.
(*Source: Reprinted with special permission of King Features Syndicate.*)

in an automobile accident in which another driver ran a stop sign. You would feel sympathy for this person and would probably recommend compensation for him. Now imagine the same story with a slight difference: The same person was injured in the same kind of accident, but in this scenario, he had left work early to run an errand. Because the accident is the same, you should rationally feel the same amount of sympathy for him. In fact, though, you may not, because given that he left work earlier than usual, it is easy to imagine him *not* being in the accident. In other words, counterfactual thoughts about what might have happened (or not have happened) influence your sympathy—and perhaps your recommendations concerning compensation for him.

Why do such effects occur? Because counterfactual thoughts seem to occur automatically in many situations; we can't help imagining that things might have turned out differently. To overcome these automatic tendencies, therefore, we must try to correct for their influence, and this requires active processing in which we both suppress the counterfactual thoughts or discount them if they occur. If this reasoning is correct, then anything that reduces our information-processing capacity might strengthen the impact of counterfactual thoughts on our judgments and behavior (Bargh & Chartrand, 1999). In fact, growing evidence suggests that this is so. For instance, in a recent study, Goldinger and his colleagues (2003) first measured participants' working memory capacity—an index of information-processing capacity. Then they asked participants to read stories designed to induce counterfactual thoughts or not to induce such thoughts. For instance, one story involved a person who had a season basketball ticket. One night, he is sitting in his usual seat and a light fixture falls, injuring him severely. This is the control version that would *not* be expected to trigger counterfactual thoughts. In another version, he is also injured, but while sitting in a different seat that happened to be empty on that night. This version would be expected to induce counterfactual thoughts.

Another feature of the study by Goldinger et al. involved asking participants to perform an additional task (memorizing and recalling nonsense words such as *flozick* and *nucade*). They performed this memory-loading task at various times—before reading the stories or after reading them.

After reading the stories, participants indicated how much monetary compensation the victim of the accident should receive. Results indicated that asking them to perform a memory task that loaded their memories (reduced their information-processing capacity) greatly strengthened the impact of counterfactual thoughts, especially for persons who had low capacity to begin with (i.e., those with a low working memory capacity). Because they could readily imagine situations in which the victim was *not* injured (e.g., he sat in his regular seat), they recommended much smaller monetary compensation for him. These findings suggest that counterfactual thoughts do tend to occur automatically in many situations and that resisting their effects requires hard, cognitive work.

These are not the only effects of counterfactual thinking, however. As noted by Roese (1997), engaging in such thoughts can yield a wide range of effects, some of which are beneficial and some of which are costly to the persons involved. Depending on its focus, counterfactual thinking can yield either boosts to or reductions in our current moods. If individuals imagine *upward counterfactuals,* comparing their current outcomes with more favorable ones than they experienced, the result may be strong feelings of dissatisfaction or envy, especially if these persons do not feel capable of obtaining better outcomes in the future (Sanna, 1997). Olympic athletes who win a silver medal but imagine winning a gold one experience such reactions (e.g., Medvec, Madey, & Gilovich, 1995). Alternatively, if individuals compare their current outcomes with less favorable ones, or if they contemplate various ways in which disappointing results could have been avoided and positive ones attained, they may experience positive feelings of satisfaction or hopefulness. Such reactions have been found among

Olympic athletes who win bronze medals, and who therefore imagine what it would be like to have won no medal whatsoever (e.g., Gleicher et al., 1995). In sum, engaging in counterfactual thinking can strongly influence affective states (Medvec & Savitsky, 1997).

In addition, it appears that we often use counterfactual thinking to mitigate the bitterness of disappointments. After tragic events, such as the death of a loved one, people often find solace in thinking, "Nothing more could be done; the death was inevitable." In other words, they adjust their view concerning the inevitability of the death to make it seem more certain and therefore unavoidable. In contrast, if they have different counterfactual thoughts—"If only the illness had been diagnosed sooner" or "If only we had gotten him to the hospital quicker"—their suffering may be increased. So, by assuming that negative events or disappointments are inevitable, we tend to make these events more bearable (Tykocinski, 2001). We'll have more to say about such effects in a later section.

In sum, imagining what might have been in a given situation can yield many effects, ranging from despair and intense regret to hopefulness and increased determination to do better in the future. Our tendency to think not only about what is, but also about what *might* be, therefore, can have far-reaching effects on many aspects of our social thought and social behavior.

KEY POINTS

★ In many situations, when individuals imagine what might have been, they engage in *counterfactual thinking*. Such thoughts can affect our sympathy for persons who have experienced negative outcomes, and can cause us to experience strong regret over missed opportunities.

★ Counterfactual thoughts seem to occur automatically in many situations, and their effects can be reduced only through hard, cognitive work in which they are suppressed or discounted.

★ By assuming that disappointing or tragic events are unavoidable, individuals can make them more bearable. This is a very adaptive function of counterfactual thinking.

Thought Suppression: Why Efforts to Avoid Thinking Certain Thoughts Sometimes Backfire

In our discussion of counterfactual thinking, we noted that such thoughts occur automatically in many situations and that to prevent them from influencing our judgments, we must often try to suppress them. You have probably tried to do this in many other contexts, too. For example, if you have ever been on a diet, you probably tried to avoid thinking about delicious desserts or other forbidden foods. And if you have ever felt nervous about giving a speech in front of others, you probably tried to avoid thinking about all the ways in which you could fail at this task (see Figure 2.11 on page 64).

How do we accomplish such **thought suppression**, and what are the effects of this process? According to Daniel Wegner (1992b), a social psychologist who has studied thought suppression in detail, efforts to keep certain thoughts out of consciousness involve two components. First, there is an automatic *monitoring process* that searches for evidence that unwanted thoughts are about to intrude. When such thoughts are detected by the first process, a second one, which is more effortful and less automatic (i.e., more controlled), swings into operation. This *operating process* involves effortful,

thought suppression
Efforts to prevent certain thoughts from entering consciousness.

Figure 2.11 ■ Thought Suppression: Can We Really Avoid Thinking about Things We Don't Want to Think About? Yes, But It's Not Easy!
In many situations, we engage in *thought suppression:* We try not to think about unpleasant events or outcomes (e.g., ones that frighten us, such as looking foolish in front of an audience). Although we can sometimes succeed in driving such thoughts from our minds, this is far from an easy task.

conscious attempts to distract oneself by finding something else to think about. In a sense, the monitoring process is an early-warning system that tells the person that unwanted thoughts are present, and the second process is an active prevention system that keeps such thoughts out of consciousness through distraction.

Under normal circumstances, the two processes do a good job of suppressing unwanted thoughts. When information overload occurs or when individuals are fatigued, however, the monitoring process continues to identify unwanted thoughts, but the operating process no longer has the resources to keep them from entering consciousness. The result is that the individual actually experiences a pronounced *rebound* effect in which the unwanted thoughts occur at an even higher rate than was true before efforts to suppress them began. As we'll soon discover, the rebound effect can have serious consequences for the persons involved.

The operation of the two processes described by Wegner (1992a, 1994) has been confirmed in many different studies (e.g., Wegner & Zanakos, 1994), and with respect to thoughts ranging from strange or unusual images (e.g., a white elephant) to thoughts about former lovers (Wegner & Gold, 1995). This model of thought suppression therefore appears to be an accurate one.

Now for the second question posed earlier: What are the effects of engaging in thought suppression—and of failing to accomplish this task? Generally, people engage in thought suppression as a means of influencing their own feelings and behaviors. For example, if you want to avoid feeling angry, it's best not to think about incidents that cause you to feel resentment toward others. Similarly, if you want to avoid feeling depressed, it's useful to avoid thinking about events or experiences that make you feel sad. But sometimes, people engage in thought suppression because they are told to do so by someone else—for instance, a therapist who is trying to help them cope with personal problems. For example, a therapist may tell a woman with a drinking problem to avoid thinking about the pleasures of alcohol (e.g., how good drinking makes her feel). If she succeeds in suppressing such thoughts, she will overcome her drinking problem. But consider what happens if the individual fails in her efforts at thought suppression. She may think, "What a failure I am—I can't even control my thoughts!" As a result, this person's motivation to continue these efforts—or even to continue therapy—may decline, a very negative outcome (e.g., Kelly & Kahn, 1994).

Unfortunately, because some persons possess certain personal characteristics, they seem especially likely to experience such failures. Individuals who are high in *reactance*—those who react very negatively to perceived threats to their personal freedom—may be especially at risk for such effects. Such persons often reject advice or suggestions from others because they want to "do their own thing," so they may find instructions to suppress certain thoughts hard to follow.

That this reaction occurs is indicated by research carried out by Kelly and Nauta (1997). These social psychologists asked individuals who were previously found to be high or low in reactance to generate their own most frequently occurring intrusive thought and then either to suppress or to express that thought in writing. Later, participants were asked to rate the extent to which they felt out of control and distressed by their intrusive thoughts. Kelly and Nauta predicted that persons high in reactance would have more difficulty following instructions to suppress intrusive thoughts and would later report being more disturbed by these thoughts when they occurred. This is precisely what happened: Persons high in reactance did not differ from those low in reactance when told to express their intrusive thoughts. This was predicted, because reactance should *not* influence their behavior under these conditions. When told to suppress these thoughts, however, persons high in reactance reported a significantly higher incidence of the thoughts they were told to suppress. Apparently, they either acted in a manner opposite to the experimenters' instructions (what persons high in reactance often do) or tried to suppress their thoughts more completely, with the result that they experienced a greater rebound effect. Whatever the precise explanation, it seems clear that personal characteristics can indeed play a role in thought suppression, and that persons high in reactance may not be very good candidates for forms of therapy that include suppressing unwanted thoughts as part of their procedures.

Limits on Our Ability to Reason about the Social World: Magical Thinking and Ignoring Moderating Variables

Please answer the following questions truthfully:

> *If you are in class and don't want the professor to call on you, do you try to avoid thinking about being called on?*

> *Imagine that someone offered you a piece of chocolate shaped like a cockroach—would you eat it?*

On the basis of purely rational considerations, you know that your answers should be "no" and "yes," respectively, but are those the answers you actually gave? If you are like most people, perhaps not. In fact, research findings indicate that, as human beings, we are quite susceptible to what has been termed **magical thinking** (Rozin & Nemeroff, 1990). Such thinking makes assumptions that don't hold up to rational scrutiny but that are compelling nonetheless. One principle of such magical thinking assumes that one's thoughts can influence the physical world in a manner not governed by the laws of physics; for example, if you think about being called on by your professor, you will be! Another is the *law of similarity,* which suggests that things that resemble one another share basic

magical thinking
Thinking involving assumptions that don't hold up to rational scrutiny—for example, the belief that things that resemble one another share fundamental properties.

Figure 2.12 ■ Magical Thinking: An Example
Would you eat the candy shown here? Many people would not, even though they realize that the shape of the candy has nothing to do with its taste. This illustrates the *law of similarity*—one aspect of what social psychologists term *magical thinking*.

properties. So, people won't eat a chocolate shaped like a cockroach, even though they know, rationally, that its shape has nothing to do with its taste (see Figure 2.12).

Surprising as it may seem, our thinking about many situations, including social ones, is frequently influenced by such magical thinking. The next time you are tempted to make fun of someone's superstitious belief (e.g., fear of the number thirteen or of a black cat crossing one's path), think again. Although you may not accept these particular beliefs, this does not mean that your own thinking is totally free of the kind of "magical" assumptions considered here.

■ Failure to Take Account of Moderating Variables

Suppose that one day you read a story indicating that female professors at your university receive 25 percent less pay, on average, than male professors. This angers you because you feel very strongly that gender should have no effect on the salaries people receive. Then you read a little further and learn that male professors also have, on average, eight years more experience than female professors. This suggests that the difference in their pay may reflect a difference in number of years on the job rather than discrimination. You don't know whether this inference is accurate, but at least it's a possibility.

This kind of reasoning, in which we take account of the fact that an effect that seems to stem from one factor can, in fact, stem from another, is a type we are called on to perform in many social situations, so at first glance, you might expect that we can do it very well. Recent findings reported by Fiedler and his colleagues (2003), however, suggest that in reality we are *not* very adept at such thinking. In this research, Fiedler et al. presented participants with information about thirty-two women and thirty-two men who had applied for admission to two universities. Overall, nineteen men were accepted and thirteen were rejected. For women, the opposite was true: thirteen were accepted and nineteen were rejected. Additional information, however, suggested that this difference was due to the fact that most of the women applied to a university with much higher rejection rates (about 60 percent), while most men applied to a university with lower rejection rates (about 40 percent). The key question was, "Would participants be aware of the effects of this moderating variable?" Results from this study and several others indicated that they were not. They tended to assume that women were at a disadvantage simply because they were women, not because they chose to apply to a university with higher admissions standards than did the men. This tendency was evident even when steps were taken to help participants recognize the impact of this third variable (university selectivity) by, for instance, calling attention to the third variable or giving participants more time to examine the relevant information.

Overall, then, the following conclusion seems justified: Though our thinking about the social world *can* be rational, and we *can* reason effectively about it, our desire to save mental effort, the existence of many mental shortcuts, and our limited processing capacity all work against total rationality. To put it simply, we are capable of more accurate and reasoned social cognition than we often show.

Social Cognition: Some Words of Optimism

The *negativity bias, optimistic bias, counterfactual thinking, magical thinking, thought suppression*—having discovered these sources of error in social thought, you may be ready to lose hope: Can we ever get it right? The answer, in fact, is *absolutely*. No, we are definitely not perfect information-processing machines. We have limited cognitive capacities, and we can't increase these by buying pop-in memory chips. And, yes, we are somewhat lazy where social thought is concerned: We generally do the least amount of cognitive work possible in any situation. Despite these limitations, though, we frequently do an impressive job in thinking about others. Despite being flooded by truly enormous amounts of social information, we manage to sort, store, remember, and use a large portion of this input in an intelligent and highly efficient manner. Our thinking is subject to many potential sources of bias, and we do make errors. For the most part, however, we do a very good job of processing social information and making sense out of the social world around us. So, although we can imagine being even better at these tasks than we are, there's no reason to be discouraged. On the contrary, we can be proud of the fact that we accomplish so much with the limited tools at our disposal.

KEY POINTS

★ Individuals often engage in *thought suppression*—trying to prevent themselves from thinking about certain topics (e.g., delicious desserts, alcohol, cigarettes).

★ These efforts are often successful, but sometimes they result in a rebound effect, in which such thoughts actually increase in frequency. Persons who are high in reactance are more likely than those who are low in reactance to experience such effects.

★ There are important limits on our ability to think rationally about the social world. One involves *magical thinking*—thinking based on assumptions that don't hold up to rational scrutiny. For instance, we may believe that if two objects are in contact, properties can pass from one to the other.

★ Another limitation involves our inability to take account of moderating variables in many situations.

★ Although social cognition is subject to many sources of error, we generally do an excellent job of understanding the social world.

Affect and Cognition: How Feelings Shape Thought and Thought Shapes Feelings

In our earlier discussion of the optimistic bias, we used the phrase "seeing the world through rose-colored glasses" to reflect our tendency to expect positive outcomes in many situations. But there's an additional way in which these words apply to social cognition: They also illustrate the effect that being in a good mood has on our thoughts and perceptions (see Figure 2.13). Think of a time in your own life when you were in a very good mood. Didn't the world seem to be a happier place? And didn't you view everything and everyone with whom you came into contact more favorably than you would when in a less pleasant mood? Experiences such as this illustrate that there is often a complex interplay between *affect*—our current moods—and *cognition*—the ways in which we process, store, remember, and use social information (Forgas, 1995a; Isen & Baron, 1991). We use the term *interplay* because research on this topic indicates that, in fact, the relationship is very much a two-way street: Our feelings and moods strongly influence several aspects of cognition, and cognition, in turn, exerts strong effects on our feelings and moods (e.g., McDonald & Hirt, 1997; Seta, Hayes, & Seta, 1994). What are these effects like? Let's see what research findings tell us.

The Influence of Affect on Cognition

We have already mentioned the impact of moods on our perceptions of the world around us. Such effects apply to people as well as objects. Imagine, for instance, that you have just received some very good news: You did much better on an important exam than you expected. As a result, you are feeling great. Now, you run into one of your friends and she introduces you to someone you don't know. You chat with this person for a while and then leave for another class. Will your first impression of the stranger be influenced by the fact that you are feeling so good? The findings of many different studies suggest strongly that it will (Bower, 1991; Mayer & Hanson, 1995; Clore, Schwarz, & Conway, 1993). In other words, our current moods can strongly affect our

Figure 2.13 ■ The Influence of Affect on Cognition
Because Mr. Dithers is in a good mood, he is not upset by Dagwood's negative news; in fact, it seems unimportant to him. This is an illustration of the potentially powerfully effect of our current moods on our social thoughts. (*Source: Reprinted with special permission of King Features Syndicate.*)

reactions to new stimuli we encounter for the first time, whether these are people, foods, or even geographic locations we've never visited before, causing us to perceive them more favorably than we would if we were not in a good mood. Indeed, recent evidence indicates that we are even more likely to judge statements as true when we are in a positive mood than when we are in a more neutral mood (Garcia-Marques et al., 2004).

Such effects have important practical implications. For instance, consider the impact of moods on job interviews—a context in which interviewers meet many people for the first time. A growing body of evidence indicates that even experienced interviewers can't avoid being influenced by their current moods: They assign higher ratings to the persons they interview when they are in a good mood than when they are in a bad mood (e.g., Baron, 1993a; Robbins & DeNisi, 1994).

Another way in which affect influences cognition involves its impact on memory. Here, two different but related kinds of effect seem to occur. One is known as **mood-dependent memory,** which refers to the fact that what we remember while in a given mood may be determined, in part, by what we learned when previously in that mood. For instance, if you stored some information into long-term memory when in a good mood, you are more likely to remember this information when in a similar mood. In other words, your current mood serves as a kind of *retrieval cue* for memories stored while you were in a similar mood in the past. A second kind of effect is known as **mood congruence effects,** which refers to the fact that we tend to notice or remember information that is congruent with our current moods (Blaney, 1986). So, if we are in a good mood, we tend to notice and remember information congruent with this mood, and if we are in a bad mood, we tend to notice and remember information that matches *that* mood. A simple way to think about the difference between mood-dependent memory and mood congruence effects is this: In mood-dependent memory, the nature of the information doesn't matter—only your mood at the time you learned it and your mood when you try to recall it are relevant. In mood congruence effects, in contrast, the affective nature of the information— whether it is positive or negative—is crucial. When we are in a positive mood, we tend to remember positive information and when we are in a negative mood, we tend to remember negative information (see Figure 2.14 on page 70 for a summary of these points).

Research confirms the existence of mood-dependent memory (Eich, 1995) and also suggests that such effects may be quite important. For instance, mood-dependent memory helps explain why depressed persons have difficulty remembering times when they felt better (Schachter & Kihlstrom, 1989): Being in a very negative mood at present, they tend to remember information they entered into memory when in the same mood—and this information relates to feeling depressed. This is important because being able to remember what it felt like *not* to be depressed can play an important part in successful treatment of the depression. (We discuss other aspects of personal health in Module A.)

Our current moods also influence another important component of cognition— creativity. The results of several studies suggest that being in a happy mood can increase creativity, perhaps because being in a happy mood activates a wider range of ideas of associations than being in a negative mood, and because creativity consists, in part, of combining such associations into new patterns (e.g., Estrada, Isen, & Young, 1995).

Finally, additional findings indicate that information that evokes affective reactions may be processed differently than other kinds of information. Specifically, because emotional reactions are often diffuse in nature, information relating to them may encourage heuristic or automatic processing rather than systematic processing or thought. As a result, it may be almost impossible to ignore or disregard information relating to moods once it has been introduced into a situation (e.g., Edwards, Heindel, & Louis-Dreyfus, 1996; Wegner & Gold, 1995). This finding has important implications for the legal system. Often, attorneys introduce emotion-laden information into their statements to juries. For instance, they may mention previous crimes by the defendant or

mood-dependent memory
The effect that what we remember while in a given mood may be determined, in part, by what we learned when previously in that mood.

mood congruence effects
Effects that we are more likely to store or remember positive information when in a positive mood, and negative information when in a negative mood.

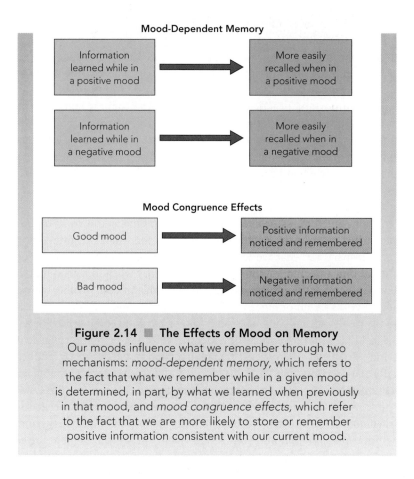

Figure 2.14 ▪ The Effects of Mood on Memory
Our moods influence what we remember through two mechanisms: *mood-dependent memory*, which refers to the fact that what we remember while in a given mood is determined, in part, by what we learned when previously in that mood, and *mood congruence effects*, which refer to the fact that we are more likely to store or remember positive information consistent with our current mood.

other damaging, negative information about the person. The opposing side quickly objects, and the judge may then instruct the jury to ignore this information. Can the jury actually do so? Because of its emotional content, ignoring the information may be virtually impossible. In fact, the findings of several studies (e.g., Edwards & Bryan, 1997) indicate that attempts to ignore or suppress such information may lead to a *rebound effect* in which jurors actually think about such information *more* than would otherwise be the case. (Recall our earlier discussion of thought suppression.) Clearly, then, that we process emotional information differently from other kinds of social information can have important and serious effects. (Common sense suggests that feeling happy is a very good thing. Is this actually true? For a discussion of this intriguing issue, please see the **Making Sense of Common Sense** section.)

The Influence of Cognition on Affect

Most research on the relationship between affect and cognition has focused on how feelings influence thought. However, there is also strong evidence for the reverse—the impact of cognition on affect. One aspect of this relationship is described in what is known as the *two-factor theory* of emotion (Schachter, 1964). This theory suggests that often we don't know our own feelings or attitudes directly. Rather, because these internal reactions are often ambiguous, we infer their nature from the external world—from the kinds of situations in which we experience these reactions. For example, if we experience increased arousal in the presence of an attractive person, we may conclude that

Is Being in a Good Mood Always a Plus?
The Potential Downside of Feeling "Up"

Everyone wants to feel happy, and there is no doubt that, for most of us, being in a good mood is more pleasant than being in a bad one. So, common sense strongly suggests that we should do everything we can to enhance our current moods. Consistent with this belief, research findings indicate that when people are in a good mood, they tend to be more creative and to be more helpful to others than when they are in a negative mood (e.g., Baron, 1997; Isen, 1984; Isen & Levin, 1972). But is being in a good mood always a plus? Does it always produce positive effects? In fact, growing evidence suggests that in this respect, as in many others, common sense may be throwing us a curve. Being in a good mood may have some real drawbacks that are well worth considering.

First, there is no doubt that being in a good mood increases our willingness to help others; this tendency has been demonstrated in many studies (e.g., Isen, 1984). The other side of the coin, however, is that when we are in a good mood, we are more susceptible to efforts by others to get us to do what they want. In other words, we are more susceptible to social influence from them. We discuss such influence in detail in Chapter 9, but here, we should note that others who want to change our behaviors or our attitudes don't always have our best interests at heart. Advertisers, salespersons, and sometimes politicians want to influence us because doing so is beneficial to them, not to us. So, in this respect, being in a good mood can be risky: It increases our tendency to say "yes" to requests or other forms of influence from others, and that can sometimes be downright dangerous!

An additional important downside to being in a good mood relates to the effects of such positive, happy feelings on social cognition. Growing evidence suggests that one effect of being in a good mood is that it tends to encourage heuristic thinking—a reliance on mental shortcuts that reduce effort. Why is this the case? Several possibilities exist. First, being in a happy mood may decrease our capacity to process information, thus increasing our reliance on heuristics (Mackie & Worth, 1989). Second, happy moods may reduce our motivation to process information carefully; that is, we are feeling too good to put out this kind of effort (e.g., Wegner & Petty, 1994). Third, being in a good mood may increase our reliance on general knowledge and heuristics without decreasing our capacity to process information or our motivation to do so—there may be a more direct link between feeling happy and thinking heuristically. Whatever the precise mechanisms involved, there seems to be little doubt that being in a good mood causes us to think heuristically (e.g., Martin & Clore, 2001). And this, in turn, can have important effects. For instance, it may increase our tendency to think about others in terms of stereotypes rather than in terms of their individual characteristics (e.g., Park & Banaji, 2000).

A closely related effect of being in a good mood involves dependence on an aspect of the availability heuristic—the *ease-of-use* heuristic. This mental shortcut suggests that the easier it is to use information in some way, the more influential or important it is determined to be (e.g., Bless, 2001). Research findings indicate that when people are in a good mood, they are more likely to rely on this heuristic than when they are in a neutral mood, and that when they are in a bad mood, they are more likely to pay careful attention to the content of such information, not only to how easily they can remember it.

Ruder and Bless (2003) recently provided evidence for these suggestions. These social psychologists first placed participants in their study in a good or a bad mood by asking them to remember happy or sad events, respectively, in their lives. For participants placed in a control condition, the researchers did not try to influence their current moods. Then participants in all three groups were asked to list either two or six arguments in favor of a change in the German educational system. In previous research, coming up with two arguments was found to be a task perceived by participants to be relatively easy; coming up with six arguments was perceived to be relatively hard. Thus, the researchers predicted that when later asked to express their attitudes toward this change in the educational system, those in a happy mood would be more in favor of it after remembering two rather than six arguments. Why? Because being in a good mood would cause them to pay attention to the *ease* with which they could bring these arguments to mind rather than the actual content of the arguments. Therefore, fewer arguments would have a greater impact on them than more arguments. In contrast, participants in a sad mood would be more in favor of the change after recalling six arguments than two arguments, because being in a sad mood, they would be more influenced by the *content* of the arguments, and six arguments would contain more information than two arguments. As you can see from Figure 2.15 on page 72, this is precisely what was found.

What does this mean in practical terms? That when we are in a good mood, we make judgments and decisions on the basis of heuristics—for instance, how easily we can bring information to mind—while when we are in a bad mood, we pay more attention to the content of this information. Because careful attention to content can often lead to better decisions, it is possible that being in a good mood may lead us to make serious errors. In other words, when we are feeling especially happy, we may "shoot from the hip" where processing social information is concerned—and that can be costly indeed.

In sum, systematic research by social psychologists indicates that although being in a good mood may be very pleasant, it is not always helpful from the point of view of making sense of the social world. In this respect, as in many others, the suggestions of common sense can be tested—and corrected—in the light of research findings.

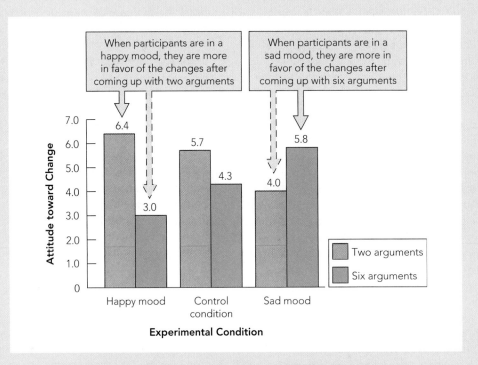

Figure 2.15 ■ Mood and Reliance on Heuristic Thinking
When participants were placed in a happy mood (by thinking about happy events in their lives), they were more in favor of a proposed change in the German educational system after coming up with two arguments in favor of this change than six arguments. This suggests that they were relying on the *ease-of-use* heuristic. In contrast, when they were placed in a sad mood, they were more in favor of the change after coming up with six arguments. This indicates that they were engaging in more careful, systematic thought. So, being in a good mood is not always beneficial from the point of view of social cognition. (*Source: Based on data from Ruder & Bless, 2003.*)

we are in love. In contrast, if we experience increased arousal after being cut off in traffic by another driver, we may conclude that what we feel is anger.

A second way in which cognition can influence emotions is by activating schemas containing a strong affective component. For example, if we label an individual as belonging to some group, the schema for this social category may suggest what traits he or she probably possesses. In addition, the schema may tell us how we *feel* about such persons. Thus, activation of a strong racial, ethnic, or religious schema or stereo-type may exert powerful effects on our current feelings. (We return to this topic in Chapter 6.)

A third way in which our thoughts can influence our affective states involves our efforts to regulate our emotions and feelings. This topic has important practical impli-cations, so we'll examine it carefully.

■ Cognition and the Regulation of Affective States

Learning to regulate our emotions is an important task; negative events and outcomes are an unavoidable part of life, so learning to cope with the negative feelings these events generate is crucial for effective personal adjustment—and for good social rela-tions with others. For example, individuals who lose their tempers often find it diffi-cult to get along with others and may, in fact, be avoided by them. Among the most important techniques we use for regulating our moods and emotions are those involv-ing cognitive mechanisms. In other words, we use our thoughts to regulate our feel-ings. There are many techniques for accomplishing this goal, but here we consider two that are especially interesting: a tactic that could be termed the "I never had a chance effect" and another involving yielding to temptation.

Do you remember our discussion of how people often attempt to soften the blow of negative or tragic events by assuming that these events were inevitable? In other words, they use counterfactual thinking—adjusting their thoughts about the proba-bility of negative events—to make the negative events seem unavoidable and there-fore less distressing. Direct evidence for such effects has been reported by Tykocinski (2001). He asked participants in the study to read a scenario in which they rushed to a store to obtain an item that was on sale. Participants in one condition learned that they had succeeded; they reached the store on time. Others read that they had failed; the store was closed when they arrived. Still others read a scenario indicating that they were still on the way to the store and did not know if it would be open when they arrived. The price reduction on the item they wanted to buy (a Swatch wristwatch) was either very large or small, so that participants' motivation for reaching the store on time also varied. After reading about one of these possible situations, participants in the success (arrived-on-time) and failure (arrived-too-late) conditions rated the likelihood, in retrospect, that they would have reached the store on time; those in the prior-to-outcomes condition rated the future chances that they would reach the store on time. Tykocinski (2001) predicted that those who had failed to reach the store on time would adjust the probability of getting there on time downward, especially in the large price reduction condition; they would do this to soften the blow of their disap-pointment. In contrast, those in the success and prior-to-outcomes conditions would not show this pattern. And that is what the results of the study showed. These find-ings indicate that we do sometimes use counterfactual thinking to reduce the bitter-ness of disappointments: By mentally reducing the odds of success—that is, by convincing ourselves that "we never had a chance"—we reduce our disappointment and so regulate our affective states.

Another cognitive mechanism we use to regulate our affective states—and espe-cially to reduce or eliminate negative feelings—involves giving in to temptation. When we feel "down" or distressed, we often engage in activities that we know are bad for us but make us feel better, at least temporarily (e.g., eating fattening snacks, wasting time watching television; see Figure 2.16 on page 74). These actions make us feel better, but we know full well that they have an important downside. Why, then, do we choose to do them? In the past, it was assumed that we engage in such actions because the

Figure 2.16 ■ **Regulating Our Own Affective States: Conscious Choice or Yielding to Temptation?**
When feeling down, many people engage in activities designed to boost their moods: They eat, watch television, consume alcohol, and so on. In the past, it was assumed that such actions were the result of yielding to temptation. Research findings now suggest, however, that engaging in such actions is the result of conscious cognitive strategies for regulating our emotions.

emotional distress we are experiencing reduces either our capacity or our motivation to control our impulse to do things that are enjoyable but potentially bad for us. However, Tice, Bratslavsky, and Baumeister (2000) argue that cognitive factors play a role in such behavior. They indicate that we often consciously choose to yield to temptation at times when we are experiencing negative affect. In other words, this is not an "automatic" behavior or a sign of weakness; rather, it is a strategic choice we make. We yield to temptation because, in the face of intense negative affect, we change our priorities. Reducing the negative becomes the primary goal, so we do whatever it takes to achieve this objective.

To test this prediction, Tice et al. (2000) conducted a study in which participants were first put in a good or a bad mood (by reading stories in which they either saved a child's life or ran a red light and so caused the death of a child). Then, they were told either that their moods could change over time or that, because of an aromatherapy candle the experimenter lit, their moods were "frozen" and could not change much. Participants were then told that they would work on an intelligence test and would receive feedback on their performance. Before doing the test, though, they would have a fifteen-minute practice session in which to prepare for it. The experimenter then left them in a room containing materials for practicing the test *and* distracters (other tasks on which they could work). For half of the participants, these distracters were attractive and tempting (e.g., a challenging puzzle, a video game, popular magazines). For the others, the distracters were less attractive (a preschool-level plastic puzzle, out-of-date technical journals). The main question was this: Would persons in a bad mood spend more of the practice time than persons in a good mood playing with the distracters (procrastinating)? More importantly, would this occur only in the condition in which participants believed they could change their own moods? After all, there would be no use in playing with the distracters if participants believed that their moods were frozen and could not be altered. Tice et al. (2000) predicted that this would be the case: Persons in a bad mood would procrastinate more, but only when they believed doing so would enhance their moods.

Results offered clear support for the prediction. These findings indicate that the tendency to yield to temptation and engage in forbidden pleasures is one technique we use to reduce negative feelings of distress. Further, it appears that such actions may represent a strategic and conscious choice, not a simple lapse in motivation or ability to restrain our own impulses. It is important to note, however, that although this technique may succeed, it may involve high costs: The actions we take to counter our negative feelings may be damaging to our health or well-being. Clearly, then, this is one tactic we should use with care.

KEY POINTS

★ Affect influences cognition in several ways. Our current moods can cause us to react positively or negatively to new stimuli (including other persons) and the extent to which we think systematically or heuristically, and can also influence memory through *mood-dependent memory* and *mood congruence effects.*

★ Affect can also influence creativity. Research indicates that emotion-provoking information can strongly influence judgments and decisions, even if we try to ignore it.

★ When we are in a positive mood, we tend to think heuristically to a greater extent than when we are a negative mood. Specifically,

we show increased reliance on stereotypes and other mental shortcuts.

★ Cognition influences affect through our interpretation of emotion-provoking events and through the activation of schemas containing a strong affective component.

★ We use several cognitive techniques to regulate our emotions or feelings; through counterfactual thinking, we can make negative outcomes seem inevitable and so less distressing; and when distressed, we can consciously choose to engage in activities that, while damaging in the long run, make us feel better in the short run.

Schemas: Mental Frameworks for Organizing—and Using—Social Information

■ Because we have limited cognitive capacity, we often attempt to reduce the effort we expend on *social cognition*—how we think about other persons. This can increase efficiency but reduce our accuracy with respect to this important task.

■ One basic component of social cognition is *schemas*—mental frameworks centering on a specific theme that help us to organize social information.

■ Once formed, schemas exert powerful effects on what we notice (attention), enter into memory (encoding), and later remember (retrieval). Individuals report remembering more information consistent with their

schemas than information inconsistent with them, but in fact, inconsistent information, too, is strongly represented in memory.

■ Schemas help us process information, but they often persist, even in the face of disconfirming information, thus distorting our understanding of the social world.

■ Schemas can also exert self-confirming effects, causing us to behave in ways that confirm them.

Heuristics and Automatic Processing: How We Reduce Our Effort in Social Cognition

■ Because our capacity to process information is limited, we often experience *information overload.* To avoid this, we make use of *heuristics*—rules for making decisions in a quick and relatively effortless manner.

■ One such heuristic is *representativeness,* which suggests that the more similar an individual is to typical members of a given group, the more likely she or he is to belong to that group.

■ Another heuristic is *availability,* which suggests that the easier it is to bring information to mind, the greater is its impact on subsequent decisions or judgments. In some cases, availability also may involve the amount of information we bring to mind.

■ *Priming* refers to increased availability of information resulting from exposure to specific stimuli or events.

■ A third heuristic is *anchoring and adjustment,* which leads us to use a number or value as a starting point from which we then make adjustments. These adjustments may not be sufficient to reflect actual social reality.

- In a sense, heuristics are just one aspect of a more general tendency: to engage in *automatic processing,* or automatic thought. This tendency refers to processing of social information that is nonconscious, unintentional, and relatively effortless. Such processing is a basic fact of social cognition and can affect both our thoughts and our overt actions in a wide range of contexts.

- Growing evidence indicates that the distinction between automatic and controlled processing is a basic one. In fact, different regions of the brain appear to be involved in these two types of processing, especially with respect to evaluations of various aspects of the social world.

Potential Sources of Error in Social Cognition: Why Total Rationality Is Rarer Than You Think

- We show a strong *negativity bias*—a tendency to be highly sensitive to negative stimuli or information. This tendency appears to be basic and may be built into the functioning of our brains. Thus, it may be the result of evolutionary factors.

- We also show a strong *optimistic bias*, expecting positive events and outcomes in many contexts. In addition, we tend to make overly optimistic predictions about how long it will take us to complete a given task, an effect known as the *planning fallacy.*

- The optimistic bias also shows up in our tendency to assume that we are more likely than other persons to experience positive outcomes, but less likely than others to experience negative ones.

- The optimistic bias is also evident when we compare our past and future: Although we perceive

the past as mixed in terms of highs and lows, we tend to perceive the future in highly optimistic terms.

- The optimistic bias may be reversed and turn to pessimism, however, when we anticipate receiving bad news with important consequences for us; in such cases, we brace for the worst, and show an enhanced tendency to predict negative outcomes.

- In many situations, when individuals imagine "what might have been," they engage in *counterfactual thinking.* Such thoughts can affect our sympathy for persons who have experienced negative outcomes and can cause us to experience strong regret over missed opportunities.

- Counterfactual thoughts seem to occur automatically in many situations, and their effects can be reduced only through hard, cognitive work in which they are suppressed or discounted.

- By assuming that disappointing or tragic events are unavoidable, individuals can make them more bearable; this is a very adaptive function of counterfactual thought.

- Individuals often engage in *thought suppression,* trying to prevent themselves from thinking about certain topics (e.g., delicious desserts, alcohol, cigarettes).

- These efforts are often successful, but sometimes they result in a rebound effect, in which such thoughts actually increase in frequency. Persons who are high in reactance are more likely than those who are low in reactance to experience such effects.

- There are important limits on our ability to think rationally about the social world. One involves *magical thinking*—thinking based on assumptions that don't hold up to rational scrutiny. For instance, we may believe that if two objects are in contact, prop-

erties can pass from one to the other.

- Another limitation involves our inability to take account of moderating variables in many situations.

- Although social cognition is subject to many sources of error, we generally do an excellent job of understanding the social world.

Affect and Cognition: How Feelings Shape Thought and Thought Shapes Feelings

- Affect influences cognition in several ways. Our current moods can cause us to react positively or negatively to new stimuli, including other persons, and the extent to which we think systematically or heuristically, and can influence memory through *mood-dependent memory* and *mood congruence effects.*

- Affect can also influence creativity. Research indicates that emotion-provoking information can strongly influence judgments and decisions, even if we try to ignore it.

- When we are in a positive mood, we tend to think heuristically to a greater extent than when we are a negative mood. Specifically, we show increased reliance on stereotypes and other mental shortcuts.

- Cognition influences affect through our interpretation of emotion-provoking events and through the activation of schemas containing a strong affective component.

- We employ several cognitive techniques to regulate our emotions or feelings; through counterfactual thinking we can make negative outcomes seem inevitable and so less distressing; and when distressed, we can consciously choose to engage in activities that, while damaging in the long run, make us feel better in the short run.

In this chapter, you read about . . .	In other chapters, you will find related discussions of . . .
schemas	the effects of schemas on other aspects of social behavior such as attitudes (Chapter 4) and prejudice (Chapter 6)
potential sources of error in social cognition	the role of these errors in first impressions (Chapter 2), persuasion (Chapter 4), long-term relationships (Chapter 8), and the legal system (Module A)
the interplay between affect and cognition	the role of such links in many forms of social behavior, including prejudice (Chapter 6), attraction (Chapter 7), helping (Chapter 10), aggression (Chapter 11), and behavior in work settings (Module B)

Thinking about Connections

1. Schemas help us understand and interpret many social situations. Do you think they play a role in long-term relationships (see Chapter 8)? For instance, do you think we possess relatively clear schemas, suggesting, for instance, that relationships should develop in various ways over time and even *when* such changes should occur?

2. Have you ever tried to suppress certain thoughts in order to make a beneficial change in your own behavior—for instance, to lose weight or change a bad habit? If so, were you successful? Do you think that after reading the information in this chapter, you might be able to do a better job in this respect? Could you, for instance, do a better job of keeping your temper in check (see Chapter 11) or avoiding negative feelings toward members of various minority groups (Chapter 6)?

3. Have you ever tried to reduce feelings of distress by concluding that the negative events that caused this distress were unavoidable? If so, did this strategy work? Did you feel better after reaching the conclusion that the disappointment or negative outcome you experienced was inevitable?

Social cognition—our efforts to interpret, analyze, remember, and use information about the social world—are subject to many sources of error. Here are some of the most important ones—errors of which you should be aware and try to guard against—in the years ahead.

The Self-Confirming Effects of Schemas

Once they are formed, *schemas*—mental frameworks for organizing and interpreting social information—tend to become self-confirm-ing: They lead us to notice only information that is consistent with them and cause us to act in ways that confirm their validity.

The Negativity Bias

We tend to be highly sensitive to negative information, devoting more attention to it and assigning it more importance than positive information.

The Optimistic Bias

We generally expect things to turn out well, even when such expecta-tions are somewhat unrealistic. However, if we anticipate feedback that may be negative and have important consequences for us, we may *brace for the worst* and show a reversal of our usual optimism.

Counterfactual Thinking: Imagining What Might Have Been

When we imagine outcomes different from those that actually occurred, we are engaging in *coun-*

terfactual thinking. Such thoughts can increase our satisfaction if we imagine worse outcomes than actually occurred but may lead to strong feelings of regret and envy if we imagine better outcomes than actually occurred.

Thought Suppression: Trying to Keep Certain Thoughts out of Consciousness

In many situations, we try to suppress thoughts that, we believe, will get us into trouble. For example, dieters try to suppress thoughts of delicious foods, and people trying to quit smoking try to avoid thinking about this activity. Unfortunately, trying to suppress such thoughts often leads us to have them *more* than would otherwise be the case.

The Role of Affective States

When we are in a good mood, we evaluate almost everything more positively than would otherwise be the case. The opposite is true when we are in a bad mood. Unfortunately, such effects can lead to serious errors in our efforts to make judgments about other persons.

KEY TERMS

affect (p. 42)

anchoring and adjustment heuristic (p. 52)

automatic processing (p. 53)

availability heuristic (p. 48)

counterfactual thinking (p. 61)

heuristics (p. 46)

information overload (p. 46)

magical thinking (p. 65)

mood congruence effects (p. 69)

mood-dependent memory (p. 69)

negativity bias (p. 57)

optimistic bias (p. 58)

overconfidence barrier (p. 58)

planning fallacy (p. 58)

perseverance effect (p. 44)

priming (p. 48)

representativeness heuristic (p. 47)

schemas (p. 42)

self-fulfilling prophecies (p. 45)

social cognition (p. 41)

thought suppression (p. 63)

FOR MORE INFORMATION

Bodenhausen, G. V., & Lambert A. J. (eds.). (2003). *Foundations of social cognition: A Festschrift in honor of Robert S. Wyer, Jr.* Mahwah, NJ: Erlbaum.

•This book honors one of the leading contributors to the study of social cognition—Robert S. Wyer, Jr. Chapters by leading researchers in the field cover

many aspect of social cognition—attention, perception, inference, memory—and also link them to other important concepts in social psychology—attitudes, impressions of persons and groups, and so on. An excellent, up-to-date source if you want to know more about social cognition.

Forgas, J. P. (2001). *Handbook of affect and social cognition.* Mahwah, NJ: Erlbaum.

• This book provides a very comprehensive overview of recent research and findings concerning the role of affect in social cognition. Chapters prepared by experts in the field are included, and these cover a wide range of topics (e.g., a neurobiological perspective, affect and processing of self-relevant information, the role of individual differences in affectivity).

Kunda, Z. (1999). *Social cognition: Making sense of people.* Cambridge, MA: MIT Press.

• This text describes our current knowledge about many aspects of social cognition. It is well-written and discusses in detail many of the topics covered in this chapter (e.g., schema, errors in social cognition). This is an excellent book to read if you want to know more about social thought and how we try to understand other people.

SOCIAL PERCEPTION
Perceiving and Understanding Others

Suppose that as a result of a serious accident, an individual suffers from profound amnesia. The patient can speak normally and recognizes friends and family members but has lost almost all memory for general knowledge—facts about the world, such as how far it is from New York to San Francisco, important dates in history, and the names of famous people, such as movie stars, athletes, and politicians. Now, imagine that we conduct the following experiment with this person. We show her photos of three evil tyrants—Adolf Hitler, Josef Stalin, and Saddam Hussein (see Figure 3.1). In all the photos, these despots are shown demonstrating positive emotions and acting in very friendly ways toward other people (e.g., kissing young children;

Figure 3.1 ■ Social Perception: Trickier Than You Might Guess
Because all we can observe is other persons' outward appearances and overt behaviors, perceiving them accurately is often difficult. Like the tyrants shown here, people may act in ways that do *not* reflect their underlying traits or motives, and this can lead us seriously astray.

Chapter 3 / Social Perception

pinning medals on the chests of heroes and heroines). Now, you ask the patient to describe the personalities and traits of these monstrous dictators. What would she be likely to say? Because she has no memory of who these people are, she might offer comments such as, "He has a nice warm smile," "I think he's probably kind and friendly," and "Look at how he is giving flowers to those children—he must be really nice."

How wrong could she get! These tyrants were responsible for the torture, imprisonment, and murder of many thousands (millions) of their own countrymen and women. How can our patient see them as good, kind, and friendly? The answer is obvious: Given the limited information she has—the appearance of these people in photos—she has reached reasonable conclusions. After all, in the photos they *do* appear to be friendly, happy, and kind. The moral? **Social perception**—perceiving others and understanding what makes them tick—is a tricky and complicated task, more complex and uncertain than you probably guess.

Although social perception is indeed a complex task, it is one we simply must perform: Other people play such an important role in our lives, we can't help but devote a lot of effort to trying to understand them. Sometimes these efforts succeed, but as we'll see in later sections, this is not always so, and we often make errors in our efforts to understand others. Why is perceiving other persons accurately so difficult? Because, in performing this task, we have to behave something like a detective. All we can observe is others' overt actions and outward appearances; we must then use this information as a basis for *inferring* how they are feeling right now, what kind of persons they are (what lasting traits they possess), why they have acted in various ways (their motives or goals), and how they will act in the future (their plans and intentions). Clearly, this is a complex task, and although we generally perform it quite well, we are also open to many forms of error. To repeat: Given the central role of other people in our lives, we have no choice but to try.

Social perception has long been recognized by social psychologists as a central aspect of social thought and an important foundation of social behavior. As a result, social perception has been the topic of careful study for several decades. To acquaint you with the key findings of this research, we focus on several major topics. First, we examine the process of *nonverbal communication*—communication between individuals involving an unspoken language of facial expressions, eye contact, body movements, and postures (e.g., Zebrowitz, 1997). Nonverbal cues often provide valuable information about others' current feelings, and this initial step can be useful in the process of understanding them.

Next, we examine *attribution,* the complex process through which we attempt to understand the reasons behind others' behavior—*why* they act as they do in a given situation. Third, we examine the nature of *impression formation*—how we form first

social perception
The process through which we seek to know and understand other persons.

impressions of others—and *impression management (or self-presentation)*—how we try to ensure that these impressions are favorable ones. In this discussion, we consider the role of our implicit beliefs about what traits or characteristics typically go together—what social psychologists describe as *implicit theories of personality*. These implicit beliefs can exert strong effects on our impressions of others, and on other aspects of social perception as well.

Nonverbal Communication: The Language of Expressions, Gazes, and Gestures

When are you more likely to do favors for others—when you are in a good mood or a bad one? And when are you more likely to lose your temper and lash out at other people—when you are feeling happy and content, or when you are feeling tense and irritable? The answers are obvious, and they suggest that often our social actions are affected by temporary factors or causes. Changing moods, shifting emotions, fatigue, illness, drugs—all can influence the ways in which we think and behave.

Because such temporary factors exert important effects on social behavior and thought, we are often interested in them: We try to find out how others are feeling *right now*. How do we go about this process? Sometimes, in a very straightforward way—we ask other persons directly. Unfortunately, this strategy often fails, because others may be unwilling to reveal their inner feelings to us. On the contrary, they may actively seek to conceal such information or even lie to us about their current emotions (e.g., DePaulo et al., 2003; Forrest & Feldman, 2000). For example, negotiators often hide their reactions from their opponents, and salespersons frequently show more liking and friendliness toward potential customers than they really feel.

In situations such as these, we often fall back on another, less direct method for gaining information about others' reactions: We pay careful attention to *nonverbal cues* provided by changes in their facial expressions, eye contact, posture, body movements, and other expressive actions. As noted by De Paulo et al. (2003), such behavior is relatively *irrepressible*—difficult to control—so that even when others try to conceal their inner feelings from us, these often "leak out" in many ways through nonverbal cues. The information conveyed by such cues, and our efforts to interpret this input, are often described by the term **nonverbal communication.** In this section, we first examine the basic channels through which nonverbal communication takes place. Then we turn to some interesting findings concerning how we use nonverbal cues to cut through *deception*—efforts by other persons to mislead us about their true feelings or beliefs (e.g., DePaulo, 1994). Before beginning, though, we must make one more point: Nonverbal cues emitted by other persons can affect our feelings, even if we are not consciously paying attention to these cues or trying to figure out how these persons feel. For instance, Neumann and Strack (2000) found that when individuals listen to another person read a speech, the tone of this person's voice (happy, neutral, or sad) can influence the listeners' moods even though the listeners are concentrating on the content of the speech and not on the reader's emotional state. Neumann and Strack refer to such effects as *emotional contagion*—a mechanism through which feelings are transferred in a seemingly automatic way from one person to another. Now, on to the basic channels of nonverbal communication.

Nonverbal Communication: The Basic Channels

Think for a moment: Do you act differently when you are feeling very happy than when you are feeling really sad? Most likely, you do. People tend to behave differently when experiencing different emotional states. But precisely how do differences in your inner

nonverbal communication
Communication between individuals that does not involve the content of spoken language. It relies instead on an unspoken language of facial expressions, eye contact, and body language.

Chapter 3 / Social Perception

states—your emotions, feelings, and moods—show up in your behavior? This question relates to the *basic channels* through which such communication takes place. Research findings indicate that five of these channels exist: facial expressions, eye contact, body movements, posture, and touching.

■ Unmasking the Face: Facial Expressions as Clues to Others' Emotions

More than two thousand years ago, the Roman orator Cicero stated, "The face is the image of the soul." By this statement he meant that human feelings and emotions are often reflected in the face and can be read there in specific expressions. Modern research suggests that Cicero—and many other observers of human behavior—were correct: It *is* possible to learn much about others' current moods and feelings from their facial expressions. In fact, it appears that six different basic emotions are represented clearly, and from a very early age, on the human face: anger, fear, happiness, sadness, surprise, and disgust (Izard, 1991; Rozin, Lowery, & Ebert, 1994). Additional findings suggest that another expression—contempt—may also be basic (e.g., Ekman & Heider, 1988). However, agreement on what specific facial expression represents contempt is less consistent than that for the other six emotions.

It's important to realize that these findings do not imply that human beings can show only a small number of facial expressions. On the contrary, emotions occur in many combinations (e.g., joy tinged with sorrow, surprise combined with fear), and each of these reactions can vary greatly in strength. Thus, while there may be only a small number of basic themes in facial expressions, the number of variations on these themes is immense (see Figure 3.2).

Now for another important question: Are facial expressions universal? In other words, if you traveled to a remote part of the world and visited a group of people who had never before met an outsider, would their facial expressions in various situations resemble your own? Would they smile in reaction to events that made them happy, frown when exposed to conditions that made them angry, and so on? Further, would you be able to recognize these distinct expressions as readily as the ones shown by persons belonging to your own culture? Early research on this question seemed to suggest that facial expressions *are* universal in both respects (e.g., Ekman & Friesen, 1975). However, some findings have called this conclusion into question (Russell, 1994). The results of more recent studies (e.g., Russell, 1994; Carroll & Russell, 1996) indicate that while facial expressions may indeed reveal much about others' emotions, our judgments in this respect are also affected by the context in which the facial expressions occur and various situational cues. For instance, if individuals view a photo of a face showing what would normally be judged as *fear* but also read a story suggesting that

Figure 3.2 ■ Facial Expressions: The Range Is Huge

Although only six basic emotions are represented in distinct facial expressions, these emotions can occur in many combinations and be shown to varying degrees. The result? The number of unique facial expressions any one person can show is truly immense.

this person is actually showing *anger,* many describe the face as showing anger, not fear (Carroll & Russell, 1996). Findings such as these suggest that facial expressions may not be as universal in terms of providing clear signals about underlying emotions as was previously assumed. However, additional evidence (e.g., Rosenberg & Ekman, 1995) provides support for the view that when situational cues and facial expressions are *not* inconsistent, others' facial expressions do provide an accurate guide to their underlying emotions. Overall then, it seems safest to conclude that while facial expressions are not totally universal around the world—cultural differences do exist with respect to their precise meaning—they generally need very little translation as compared with spoken languages.

Gazes and Stares: Eye Contact as a Nonverbal Cue

Have you ever had a conversation with someone wearing very dark or mirrored sunglasses? If so, you realize that this can be an uncomfortable situation. Because you can't see the other person's eyes, you are uncertain about how she or he is reacting. Taking note of the importance of cues provided by others' eyes, ancient poets often described the eyes as "the windows to the soul." In one important sense, they were correct: We do often learn much about others' feelings from their eyes. For example, we interpret a high level of gazing from another as a sign of liking or friendliness (Kleinke, 1986). In contrast, if others avoid eye contact with use, we may conclude that they are unfriendly, don't like us, or are simply shy (Zimbardo, 1977).

While a high level of eye contact with others is usually interpreted as a sign of liking or positive feelings, there is one exception to this general rule. If another person gazes at us continuously and maintains such contact regardless of what we do, she or he can be said to be **staring.** A stare is often interpreted as a sign of anger or hostility—as in *cold stare*—and most people find this particular nonverbal cue disturbing (Ellsworth & Carlsmith, 1973). In fact, we may quickly terminate social interaction with someone who stares at us and may even leave the scene (Greenbaum & Rosenfield, 1978). This is one reason why experts on "road rage"—highly aggressive driving by motorists, sometimes followed by actual assaults—recommend that drivers avoid eye contact with people who are disobeying traffic laws and rules of the road (e.g., Bushman, 1998). Apparently, such persons, who are already in a highly excitable state, interpret anything approaching a stare from another driver as an aggressive act and react accordingly.

Body Language: Gestures, Posture, and Movements

Try this simple demonstration for yourself: First, remember some incident that made you angry—the angrier the better. Think about it for a minute. Now, try to remember another incident, one that made you feel sad—again, the sadder the better. Compare your behavior in the two contexts. Did you change your posture or move your hands, arms, or legs as your thoughts shifted from the first event to the second? There is a good chance that you did, because our current moods or emotions are often reflected in the position, posture, and movement of our bodies. Together, such nonverbal behaviors are termed **body language,** and they, too, can provide useful information about others.

First, body language often reveals others' emotional states. Large numbers of movements, especially ones in which one part of the body does something to another part (touching, rubbing, scratching), suggest emotional arousal. The greater the frequency of such behavior, the higher the level of arousal or nervousness.

Larger patterns of movements, involving the whole body, can also be informative. Such statements as "She adopted a *threatening posture*" and "he greeted her with *open arms*" suggest that different body orientations or postures indicate contrasting emotional states. In fact, research by Aronoff, Woike, and Hyman (1992) confirms this possibility. These researchers first identified two groups of characters in classical ballet: ones who played a dangerous or threatening role (e.g., Macbeth, the Angel of Death, Lizzie

staring
A form of eye contact in which one person continues to gaze steadily at another regardless of what the recipient does.

body language
Cues provided by the position, posture, and movement of others' bodies or body parts.

Chapter 3 / Social Perception

Figure 3.3 ▪ Gestures: One Form of Nonverbal Communication
Do you recognize the gestures shown here? Can you tell what they mean? In the United States and other western cultures, each of these gestures has a clear meaning. However, they might well have no meaning, or entirely different meanings, in other cultures.

Borden) and ones who played warm, sympathetic roles (Juliet, Romeo). Then they examined examples of dancing by these characters in actual ballets to see if they adopted different kinds of postures. Aronoff and his colleagues predicted that the dangerous, threatening characters would show more diagonal or angular postures, while the warm, sympathetic characters would show more rounded postures, and their results strongly confirmed this hypothesis. These and related findings indicate that large-scale body movements or postures can sometimes provide important information about others' emotions, and even about their apparent traits.

More specific information about others' feelings is often provided by gestures. These fall into several categories, but perhaps the most important are *emblems*—body movements carrying specific meanings in a given culture. Do you recognize the gestures shown in Figure 3.3? In the United States and several other countries, these movements have clear and definite meanings. However, in other cultures, they might have no meaning, or even a different meaning. For this reason, it is wise to be careful about using gestures while traveling in cultures different from your own: You may offend the people around you without meaning to do so!

Interestingly, recent findings (e.g., Schubert, 2004) indicate that specific gestures can have different meanings for women and men. For instance, for men, gestures associated with bodily force, such as a clenched fist, seem to signal increased power (or efforts to obtain it); for women, such bodily actions seem to signal *loss* of power or reduced hope of gaining it. This, in turn, may reflect the fact that men are considerably stronger than women, and so often seek to gain power through force, while for women, force is more often defensive and has much less chance of success. Whatever the precise mechanisms involved, gender differences in the use and perception of various gestures do appear to exist.

▪ Touching: Is a Firm Handshake Really a Plus?

Suppose that during a brief conversation with another person, she or he touched you briefly. How would you react? What information would this behavior convey? The answer to both question is *it depends*. What it depends on is several factors relating to who does the touching (a friend, a stranger, a member of your own or the other gender), the nature of this physical contact (brief or prolonged, gentle or rough, what part of the body is touched), and the context in which the touching takes place (a business or social setting, a doctor's office). Given such factors, touch can suggest affection, sexual interest, dominance, caring, or even aggression. Despite such complexities, existing evidence indicates that when touching is considered appropriate, it often produces positive reactions in the person being touched (e.g., Alagna, Whitcher, & Fisher, 1979; Smith, Gier, & Willis, 1982). But remember: the touching must be viewed as appropriate to produce such reactions.

One acceptable way in which people in many different cultures touch strangers is through handshaking. Pop psychology and even books on etiquette (e.g., Vanderbilt, 1957) suggest that handshakes reveal much about other persons—for instance, their personalities—and that a firm handshake is a good way to make a favorable first impression on others. Are such observations true? Is this form of nonverbal communication actually revealing? Research findings (e.g., Chaplin et al., 2000) suggest that it is. The firmer, longer, and more vigorous others' handshakes are, the higher we tend to rate the handshakers in terms of extraversion and openness to experience. Further, the firmer and longer the handshakes are, the more favorable our first impressions of these persons tend to be.

In sum, we use this particular kind of touching as a basis for forming social perceptions of others. In this respect, popular books about the road to success are correct: A firm handshake *is* a valuable asset, at least in cultures in which handshakes are used for greetings and departures.

Recognizing Deception: The Role of Nonverbal Cues

Shakespeare once wrote: "Though I am not naturally honest, I am so sometimes by chance." As usual, he was a keen observer of human behavior, because research findings indicate that most people tell one or more lies *every day* (DePaulo & Kashy, 1998). Why do people lie? For many reasons: to avoid hurting others' feelings, to conceal their real feelings or reactions, to avoid punishment for misdeeds. In short, lying is an all-too-common part of social life (see Figure 3.4 for an example). This sad fact raises two important questions: (1) How good are we at recognizing deception by others? And (2) how can we do a better job at this task? The answer to the first question is somewhat discouraging. In general, we do only a little better than chance in determining whether others are lying or telling the truth (e.g., Malone & DePaulo, 2001; Ekman, 2001). There are many reasons why this is so, including the fact that we tend to perceive others as truthful and so don't search for clues to deception (Ekman, 2001); our desire to be polite, which makes us reluctant to discover or report deception by others; and our lack of attention to nonverbal cues that might reveal deception (e.g., Etcoff et al., 2000). Recently, another explanation—and a compelling one—has been added to this list: We tend to assume that if people are truthful in one situation or context, they will be truthful in others; this assumption can prevent us from realizing that they might lie on some occasions (e.g., O'Sullivan, 2003). We return to this possibility in more detail in our later discussion of *attribution*. We should add that trying to "read" others' nonverbal cues accurately does not always center on efforts to determine whether they are telling the truth. Recent findings (e.g., Pickett, Gardner, & Knowles, 2004) indicate that accuracy in decoding nonverbal cues is also related to the desire to be liked and accepted by other persons—the higher individuals are in such *need to belong*, the better they tend to be at reading nonverbal cues because they pay careful attention to others and *want* to understand them.

Given that nearly everyone engages in deception at least occasionally, the question of how we might do a better job of recognizing lies when they occur is an important one. The answer seems to involve careful attention to both nonverbal and verbal cues that can reveal the fact that others are trying to deceive us.

"In my ad, I lied about my age."

Figure 3.4 ■ Lying: An All-Too-Common Part of Everyday Life
As the young woman in this cartoon is discovering, lies occur in
many different contexts and are told for many different reasons.
(*Source: © The New Yorker Collection 2003 Lee Lorenz from
cartoonbank.com. All Rights Reserved.*)

With respect to nonverbal cues, the following information is very helpful (e.g.,
DePaulo et al., 2003):

1. *Microexpressions:* These are fleeting facial expressions that last only a few tenths of
   a second. Such reactions appear on the face quickly after an emotion-provoking
   event and are difficult to suppress. As a result, they can reveal others' true feelings
   or emotions. For instance, if you ask other persons whether they like something
   (e.g., an idea you have expressed, something you have just purchased), watch their
   faces closely as they respond. One expression (e.g., a frown) followed quickly by
   another (e.g., a smile) can be a useful sign that they are lying—they are stating one
   opinion or reaction when, in fact, they really have another.

2. *Interchannel discrepancies:* A second nonverbal cue revealing of deception is known
   as interchannel discrepancies. (The term *channel* refers to a type of nonverbal cue;
   for instance, facial expressions are one channel, and body movements are another.)
   Interchannel discrepancies are inconsistencies among nonverbal cues from different basic channels, and result from the fact that persons who are lying often find
   it difficult to control all of these channels at once. For instance, they may manage
   their facial expressions well but have difficulty looking you in the eye as they tell
   their lie.

microexpressions
Fleeting facial expressions
lasting only a few tenths
of a second.

3. *Eye contact:* Efforts at deception are often frequently revealed by certain aspects of eye contact. Persons who are lying often blink more often and show more dilated pupils than persons who are telling the truth. They may also show an unusually low level of eye contact or—surprisingly—an unusually high one, as they attempt to fake being honest by looking others right in their eyes.

4. *Exaggerated facial expressions:* Finally, persons who are lying sometimes show exaggerated facial expressions. They may smile more—or more broadly—than usual or may show greater sorrow than is typical in a given situation. A prime example: Someone says "no" to a request you've made and then shows exaggerated regret. This is a good sign that the reasons the person has supplied for saying "no" may not be true.

In addition to these nonverbal cues, other signs of deception are sometimes present in nonverbal aspects of what people actually say or in the words they choose. When people are lying, the pitches of their voices often rise, especially when they are highly motivated to lie. Similarly, they often take longer to begin—to respond to a question or to describe events. And they may show a greater tendency to start sentences, stop them, and begin again. In other words, certain aspects of people's **linguistic style** can reveal deception.

Perhaps even more interesting, people actually may tend to use different words when lying than when telling the truth (e.g., Vriz et al., 2000). Why would this be so? First, persons who are lying may want to avoid directing attention to themselves, so they may tend to use words such as *I* and *me* less often than persons who are telling the truth. Second, they may feel guilty, so they use more words that reflect negative emotions. Third, because they are making up the events they are describing, they may use more words relating to simple actions, such as *walk* and *go* and fewer words that make the story more specific, such as *except, but,* and *without.* Do such differences between lies and truthful statements exist? Recent research by Newman et al. (2003) confirms that they do. These researchers had large number of participants make true or false statements (spoken, typed, or handwritten) concerning their views about an important issue (abortion). They were asked to lie on some occasions and to tell the truth on others. The words they generated were then scored by a computer program that analyzes many aspects of linguistic style—many different kinds of words and how frequently they are used. Results were clear: Across several different studies, deceptive communications, as compared with accurate ones, used fewer first-person pronouns (*I, we*) and contained more negative emotion words, fewer exclusive words (e.g., *except, but*) and more motion verbs (*go, walk*). In other words, lies were less complex, less related to the self, and more negative in nature than truthful statements.

In sum, through careful attention to nonverbal cues and to various aspects of the words people use, we *can* often tell when others are lying—or merely trying to hide their feelings from us. Success in detecting deception is far from certain; some persons are very skillful liars. But if you pay careful attention to the cues described here, you will make their task of pulling the wool over your eyes much more difficult, and you may become as successful at this task as a group of people identified by Paul Ekman—a leading expert on facial expressions—who can reliably distinguish lies from the truth more than 80 percent of the time (Coniff, 2004). Is this a useful skill? Absolutely! Imagine the benefits if we could hire or train such persons to work at airports or other locations, identifying terrorists (see Figure 3.5 on page 91). Clearly then, understanding how we can learn to recognize deception has important implications not only for individuals, but also for society as a whole. (Do women and men differ in their ability to use and interpret nonverbal cues? For a discussion of this topic, please see the **Making Sense of Common Sense** section on page 92.)

linguistic style
Aspects of speech apart from the meaning of the words employed.

Chapter 3 / Social Perception

Figure 3.5 ■ **Recognizing Deception: A Useful Skill**
Being able to tell when others are engaging in deception is a useful skill. For instance, it could be very helpful in identifying or interrogating suspected terrorists.

KEY POINTS

★ *Social perception* involves the processes through which we seek to understand other persons. It plays a key role in social behavior and social thought.

★ To understand others' emotional states, we often rely on *nonverbal communication*—an unspoken language of facial expressions, eye contact, and body movements and postures.

★ Although facial expressions may not be as universal as once believed, they do often provide useful information about others' emotional states. Useful information on this issue is also provided by eye contact, body language, and touching.

★ Recent findings indicate that handshaking provides useful nonverbal cues about others' personality and can influence the first impressions of strangers.

★ If we pay careful attention to certain nonverbal cues, we can recognize efforts at deception by others, even if these persons are from cultures other than our own.

★ Women are better than men at both sending and interpreting nonverbal cues. This gives them an important advantage in many situations and may account for widespread belief in "women's intuition."

Does "Women's Intuition" Exist? And If So, Is It Based on the Ability to Use and Interpret Nonverbal Cues?

Have you ever heard the phrase "women's intuition"? It suggests that women have a special sixth sense that allows them to understand social situations and actions that remain mysterious to men. In the past, this phrase was often used by men to express their amazement at the ability of women to figure out what was happening in many situations and to predict the behavior of other persons accurately—much more accurately than the men could. In short, common sense seems to suggest that women are much better at social perception than are men—better at the task of understanding others and predicting their behavior. Is this true? The answer, as revealed by systematic research on gender differences in social perception seems to be that it depends on what aspect of social perception is being considered. Overall, there is no clear evidence that women are better than men at *all* aspects of social perception—aspects we consider in later sections of this chapter, such as forming accurate impressions of others or understanding their motives and intentions. But women do seem to have an important edge with respect to nonverbal cues. In fact, they are better at both sending and interpreting such cues (e.g., Mayo & Henley, 1981; Rosenthal & DePaulo, 1979).

First, women are better able than men to transmit clear signs of their feelings or reactions through facial expressions, body language, and other nonverbal cues. Second, they are better able to "decode" the nonverbal messages of others. Together, these superior skills at this aspect of social perception give them an important edge: Because they are better able than men to get their message across *and* better able to read nonverbal messages transmitted by others, women gain an important advantage in many social situations. They are better able to understand others, and this helps them predict how these people will act. It is little wonder, then, that men are often awed by the seemingly unfathomable ability of the women around them to figure out what's happening in various situations when the men themselves remain bewildered.

There seems to be only one important exception to this general rule: Women appear to lose their edge when others are lying. They tend, more than men, to accept deceptive messages as accurate ones and are less successful than men at distinguishing between communications that are false and ones that are true (Rosenthal & DePaulo, 1979), although, again, this is not always the case and may depend, in part, on the specific context in which the lies occur (see Figure 3.6; e.g., Ekman, O'Sullivan, & Frank, 1999).

What accounts for the generally superior skills of women in handling nonverbal cues? The answer, most social psychologists believe, lies in contrasting *gender roles*. In many societies, traditional stereotypes of mas-

Attribution: Understanding the Causes of Others' Behavior

attribution

The process through which we seek to identify the causes of others' behavior and so gain knowledge of their stable traits and dispositions.

Accurate knowledge of others' current moods or feelings can be useful in many ways. Yet, where social perception is concerned, this knowledge is often only the first step. In addition, we usually want to know more—to understand others' lasting traits and to know the causes behind their behavior. Social psychologists believe that our interest in such questions stems, in large measure, from our basic desire to understand cause-and-effect relationships in the social world (Pittman, 1993; Van Overwalle, 1998). In other words, we don't simply want to know *how* others have acted; we want to understand *why* they have done so, too, because we realize that this knowledge can help us to predict how they will act in the future. The process through which we seek such information is known as **attribution**. More formally, *attribution* refers to our efforts to understand the causes behind others' behavior and, on some occasions, the causes

culinity and femininity suggest that males are assertive, logical, and dominant, while females are expressive, supportive, and sensitive. Because gender roles and stereotypes are often self-confirming, one result is that women indeed pay more attention to the reactions of others and learn to be more sensitive to them. In addition, as we note in Chapter 5, contrasting gender roles often result in a situation in which women occupy positions of lower power and status within their societies. Because persons of relatively low status and power must be sensitive to the actions and reactions of persons higher in status and power than themselves, women tend to develop these skills to a greater extent than men (e.g., Eagly, 1987; Eagly & Karau, 2002).

Finally, because gender stereotypes suggest that women are *supposed* to be sensitive and polite, they are more reluctant to notice—or at least pay attention to—the fact that others are being deceptive. After all, that would not be gracious or polite (e.g., Buck, 1977).

So, viewed through the lens of social psychological theory and research, women's intuition loses its mystery. To the extent that it exists, it appears to derive primarily from women's superior skills in both sending and reading nonverbal cues. And these skills, in turn, are mainly a reflection of gender stereotypes and the roles women play in many societies (see Chapter 5). Once again, then, systematic research by social psychologists helps us to make sense out of common sense—to understand when and why it is correct, and when and why it leads us astray.

Figure 3.6 ■ Detecting Deception: An Exception to the Rule of Female Superiority in the Use of Nonverbal Cues
In general, women are superior to men in the use of nonverbal cues. However, they are less successful than men at detecting deception in some contexts (e.g., the one shown on the *left*). In other situations, however, women are just as successful at this task as men (*right photo*).

behind *our* behavior as well. Social psychologists have studied attribution for several decades, and their research has yielded many intriguing insights (e.g., Graham & Folkes, 1990; Heider, 1958; Read & Miller, 1998).

Theories of Attribution: Frameworks for Understanding How We Attempt to Make Sense of the Social World

Because attribution is complex, many theories have been proposed to explain its operation. Here, we focus on two classic views that have been especially influential.

■ From Acts to Dispositions: Using Others' Behavior as a Guide to Their Lasting Traits

The first of these classic theories—Jones and Davis's (1965) theory of **correspondent inference**—asks how we use information about others' behavior as a basis for inferring that they possess various traits. In other words, this theory is concerned with how we

correspondent inference (theory of)
A theory describing how we use others' behavior as a basis for inferring their stable dispositions.

decide, on the basis of others' overt actions, that they possess specific traits or dispositions likely to remain fairly stable over time.

At first glance, this might seem to be a simple task. Others' behavior provides us with a rich source on which to draw, so if we carefully observe the behavior of others, we should be able to learn a lot about them. Up to a point, this is true. The task is complicated, however, by the following fact: Often, individuals act in certain ways, not because doing so reflects their own preferences or traits, but rather because *external factors* leave them little choice. For example, suppose you observe a customer acting rudely toward a salesperson in a store. Does this mean that the customer is a nasty person who often treats others in a rude manner? Not necessarily. She may simply be responding to the fact that the salesperson ignored her and waited on two other customers even though she was first in line. So, her behavior now may be the exception, not the rule: Generally, she is very polite—unless pushed beyond all endurance! Situations such as this are common, and in them, using others' behavior as a guide to their lasting traits or motives can be very misleading.

How do we cope with such complications? According to Jones and Davis's theory (Jones & Davis, 1965; Jones & McGillis, 1976), we accomplish this task by focusing our attention on certain types of actions—those most likely to prove informative. First, we consider only behavior that seems to have been chosen freely, while largely ignoring ones that were somehow forced on the person in question. Second, we pay careful attention to actions that show what Jones and Davis term **noncommon effects**—effects that can be caused by one specific factor but not by others. (Don't confuse *noncommon* with *uncommon*, which simply means "infrequent.") Why are actions that produce noncommon effects informative? Because they allow us to zero in on the causes of others' behavior. For example, imagine that one of your friends has just become engaged. His future spouse is very attractive, has a great personality, is wildly in love with your friend, and is very rich. What can you learn about your friend from his decision to marry this woman? Not much. There are so many good reasons for his decision that you can't choose among them. In contrast, imagine that your friend's fiancée is very attractive but that she treats him with indifference and is known to be extremely boring; also, she is deeply in debt and is known to be someone who usually lives far beyond her means. Does the fact that your friend is marrying this woman tell you anything about him under these conditions? Definitely. You can probably conclude that he cares more about physical beauty than about personality or wealth. As you can see from this example, then, we can usually learn more about others from actions on their part that yield noncommon effects than from ones that do not.

Finally, Jones and Davis suggest that we also pay greater attention to actions by others that are low in *social desirability* than to actions that are high on this dimension. In other words, we learn more about others' traits from actions they perform that are somehow out of the ordinary than from actions that are very much like those of most other persons.

In sum, according to the theory proposed by Jones and Davis, we are most likely to conclude that others' behavior reflects their stable traits (i.e., we are likely to reach *correspondent* inferences about them) when that behavior (1) is freely chosen; (2) yields distinctive, noncommon effects; and (3) is low in social desirability.

■ **Kelley's Theory of Causal Attributions: How We Answer the Question "Why?"**
Consider the following events:

> *You arrange to meet someone for lunch, but he doesn't show up.*
>
> *You leave several messages for a friend, but she doesn't call back.*
>
> *You expect a promotion in your job but don't receive it.*

noncommon effects
Effects produced by a particular cause that could not be produced by any other apparent cause.

In all of these situations, you would probably wonder *why* these events occurred: *Why?* Didn't your lunch date show up? Did he forget? Did he do it on purpose? Why has your friend failed to return your messages? Is she angry at you? Is her answering machine or cell phone out of service? And you'd want to know why you didn't get the promotion. Is your boss disappointed in your performance? Were you the victim of some kind of discrimination? In many situations, this is the central attributional task we face. We want to know why other people have acted as they have or why events have turned out in a specific way. Such knowledge is crucial, because only if we understand the causes behind others' actions or events can we hope to make sense out of the social world. Obviously, the number of specific causes behind others' behavior is large. To make the task more manageable, therefore, we often begin with a preliminary question: Did others' behavior stem mainly from *internal* causes (their own traits, motives, intentions), mainly from *external* causes (some aspect of the social or physical world), or from a combination of the two? For example, you might wonder whether you didn't receive the promotion because you really haven't worked very hard (an internal cause), because your boss is unfair and biased against you (an external cause), or perhaps because of both factors. How do we attempt to answer this question? A theory proposed by Kelley (Kelley, 1972; Kelley & Michela, 1980) provides important insights into this process.

According to Kelley, in our attempts to answer the question *Why?* about others' behavior, we focus on three major types of information. First, we consider **consensus**—the extent to which other persons react to a given stimulus or event in the same manner as the person we are considering. The higher the proportion of people who react in the same way, the higher the consensus. Second, we consider **consistency**—the extent to which the person in question reacts to the stimulus or event in the same way on other occasions over time. And third, we examine **distinctiveness**—the extent to which this person reacts in the same manner to other, different stimuli or events.

According to Kelley's theory, we are most likely to attribute another's behavior to *internal* causes under conditions in which consensus and distinctiveness are low but consistency is high. In contrast, we are most likely to attribute another's behavior to *external* causes when consensus, consistency, and distinctiveness are all high. Finally, we usually attribute another's behavior to a combination of internal and external factors when consensus is low but consistency and distinctiveness are high. Perhaps a concrete example will help illustrate the very reasonable nature of these ideas.

Imagine that you see a server in a restaurant flirt with a customer. This behavior raises an interesting question: Why does the server act this way? Because of internal causes or external causes? Is she simply someone who likes to flirt (an internal cause)? Or is the customer extremely attractive (an external cause). According to Kelley's theory, your decision (as an observer of this scene) would depend on information relating to the three factors mentioned previously. First, assume that the following conditions prevail: (1) You observe other servers flirting with this customer (consensus is high); (2) you have seen this server flirt with the same customer on other occasions (consistency is high); and (3) you have *not* seen this server flirt with other customers (distinctiveness is high). Under these conditions—high consensus, consistency, and distinctiveness—you would probably attribute the clerk's behavior to external causes: This customer is very attractive, and that's why the server flirts with him.

Now, in contrast, assume that these conditions exist: (1) No other servers flirt with the customer (consensus is low); (2) you have seen this server flirt with the same customer on other occasions (consistency is high); and (3) you have seen this server flirt with many other customers, too (distinctiveness is low). In this case, Kelley's theory suggests that you would attribute the server's behavior to internal causes: The server is simply a person who likes to flirt (see Figure 3.7 on page 96).

consensus
The extent to which other persons react to some stimulus or even in the same manner as the person we are considering.

consistency
The extent to which an individual responds to a given stimulus or situation in the same way on different occasions (i.e., across time).

distinctiveness
The extent to which an individual responds in the same manner to different stimuli or events.

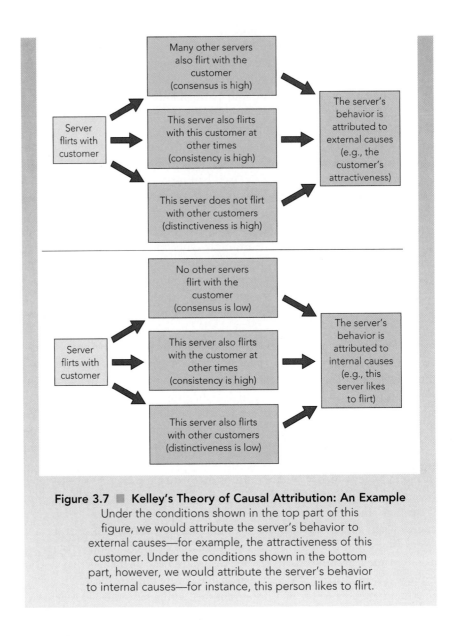

Figure 3.7 ■ Kelley's Theory of Causal Attribution: An Example
Under the conditions shown in the top part of this figure, we would attribute the server's behavior to external causes—for example, the attractiveness of this customer. Under the conditions shown in the bottom part, however, we would attribute the server's behavior to internal causes—for instance, this person likes to flirt.

The basic assumptions of Kelley's theory have been confirmed in a wide range of social situations, so it seems to provide important insights into the nature of causal attributions. However, research on the theory also suggests the need for certain modifications or extensions, as described below.

■ Other Dimensions of Causal Attribution

Although we are often very interested in knowing whether others' behavior stemmed mainly from internal or external causes, this is not the entire story. In addition, we are also concerned with two other questions: (1) Are the causal factors that influenced their behavior likely to be *stable* over time or to change, and (2) are these factors *controllable*—can the individual change or influence them if she or he wishes to do so (Weiner, 1993, 1995)? These dimensions are independent of the internal–external dimension we considered. For instance, some internal causes of behavior tend to be stable over time—personality traits and temperament (e.g., Miles & Carey, 1997). In contrast, other internal causes can, and often do, change greatly—for instance, motives, health, fatigue. Similarly, some internal causes are *controllable*—individuals can, if they wish, learn to hold their tempers in check; other internal causes, such as chronic illnesses or disabilities, are not controllable. The same is true for external causes of behavior: Some are stable over time (e.g., laws or social norms that indicate how we should behave in various situations), while others are not (e.g., bad luck). A large body of evidence indicates that in trying to understand the causes behind others' behavior, we do take note of all three of these dimensions—internal–external, stable–unstable, controllable–uncontrollable (Weiner, 1985, 1995). Moreover, our thinking in this respect strongly influences our conclusions concerning important matters, such as whether others are *personally responsible* for their own actions (e.g., Graham, Weiner, & Zucker, 1997).

■ Augmenting and Discounting: How We Handle Multiple Potential Causes

Suppose that one day, your boss stops by your desk and praises your work, telling you that you are doing a wonderful job and that she is glad to have you working with her. She does this in front of several other employees, who all congratulate you after she leaves. For the rest of the morning, you feel great. But then, after lunch, she calls you into her office and asks if you would be willing to take on an extra, difficult work assignment. Now you begin to wonder: Why did she praise your work? Because she really wanted to thank you for doing such a good job *or* because she knew all along that she was going to ask you to take on extra work? There are two possible causes behind her behavior, and because there are, you may well engage in what social psychologists term **discounting**—you view the first possible cause (her genuine desire to give you positive feedback) as less important or likely because another possible cause for this action exists, too (i.e., she wanted to set you up for her request to do extra work). Many studies indicate that discounting is a common occurrence and exerts a strong effect on our attributions in many situations (e.g., Gilbert & Malone, 1995; Morris & Larrick, 1995; Trope & Liberman, 1996). However, discounting is far from universal: Only some possible causes of a behavior can be used to discount other possible causes. For instance, suppose that you have a very thrifty friend—he literally pinches pennies. He is also a member of several proenvironmental groups. You visit his home during the winter and find that he has set his thermostats very low. In this kind of situation, you can't use one of your attributions about him (e.g., he is thrifty) to discount the other (he is strongly in favor of protecting the environment; McClure, 1998).

Now, imagine the same situation with one difference: Your boss has a strong policy against giving employees feedback in front of other persons. What will you conclude about her behavior now? Probably that the feedback was really motivated by a genuine desire to tell you that she is very pleased with your work. After all, she has done so despite the presence of another factor that would be expected to *prevent* her from doing this (her own policy against public feedback). This illustrates what social psychologists describe as **augmenting**—the tendency to assign added weight or importance to a factor that might facilitate a given behavior when this factor and another factor that might *inhibit* such behavior are both present, *yet the behavior still occurs* (see Figure 3.8 on page 98 for an overview of both attributional discounting and augmenting). In this case, you conclude that your boss actually is very pleased with your behavior because she praised it publicly despite the presence of a strong inhibitory factor (her policy against public feedback).

Evidence for the occurrence of attributional augmenting and discounting is found in many studies (e.g., Baron, Markman, & Hirsa, 2001), so it seems clear that these principles help explain how we deal with situations in which others' behavior could stem from several different causes.

discounting principle
The tendency to attach less importance to one potential cause of some behavior when other potential causes are also present.

augmenting principle
The tendency to attach greater importance to a potential cause of behavior if the behavior occurs despite the presence of other, inhibitory causes.

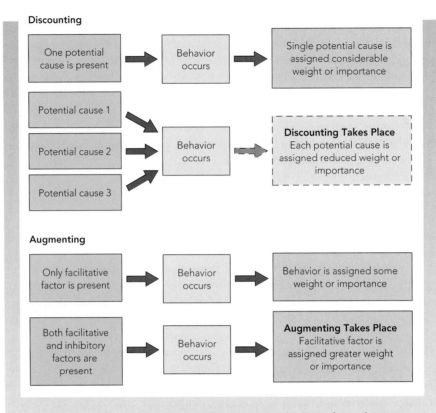

Discounting

One potential cause is present → Behavior occurs → Single potential cause is assigned considerable weight or importance

Potential cause 1
Potential cause 2 → Behavior occurs ⇢ **Discounting Takes Place** Each potential cause is assigned reduced weight or importance
Potential cause 3

Augmenting

Only facilitative factor is present → Behavior occurs → Behavior is assigned some weight or importance

Both facilitative and inhibitory factors are present → Behavior occurs → **Augmenting Takes Place** Facilitative factor is assigned greater weight or importance

Figure 3.8 ■ Augmenting and Discounting in Causal Attribution
According to the *discounting* principle (*upper diagram*), we attach less weight or importance to a given cause of some behavior when other potential causes of that behavior are also present. According to the *augmenting* principle (*lower diagram*), we attach greater weight to a potential cause of some behavior if that behavior occurs despite the presence of another factor that would tend to inhibit its occurrence.

KEY POINTS

★ To obtain information about others' lasting traits, motives, and intentions, we often engage in *attribution*—efforts to understand why they have acted as they have.

★ According to Jones and Davis's theory of *correspondent inference*, we attempt to infer others' traits from observing certain aspects of their behavior, especially behavior that is freely chosen, produces *noncommon effects*, and is low in social desirability.

★ Another theory, Kelley's theory of causal attribution, is interested in the question of whether others' behavior stems from internal or external causes. To answer this question,

we focus on information relating to *consensus, consistency*, and *distinctiveness*.

★ Two other important dimensions of causal attribution relate to whether specific causes of behavior are stable over time and are controllable or not controllable.

★ When two or more potential causes of another person's behavior exist, we tend to downplay the importance of each—an effect known as *discounting*. When a cause that facilitates a behavior and a cause that inhibits a behavior both exist, but the behavior still occurs, we assign added weight to the facilitative factors—an effect known as *augmenting*.

A basic theme we develop throughout this book is that although we generally do a good job in terms of thinking about the social world, we are far from perfect in this respect. In fact, our efforts to understand other persons—and ourselves—are subject to several types of errors that can lead us to false conclusions about why others have acted as they have and how they will behave in the future. Let's take a look at several of these errors now.

The Correspondence Bias: Overestimating the Role of Dispositional Causes

Imagine that you witness the following scene. A man arrives at a meeting one hour late. On entering, he drops his notes on the floor. While trying to pick them up, his glasses fall off and break. Later, he spills coffee all over his tie. How would you explain these events? The chances are good that you would reach a conclusion such as "This person is disorganized and clumsy." Is such an attribution accurate? Perhaps; but it is also possible that the man was late because of unavoidable delays at the airport, that he dropped his notes because they were printed on slick paper, and that he spilled his coffee because the cup was too hot to hold. The fact that you would be less likely to consider such potential *external* causes of his behavior illustrates what Jones (1979) labeled **correspondence bias**—the tendency to explain others' actions as stemming from (corresponding to) dispositions, even in the presence of clear situational causes (e.g., Gilbert & Malone, 1995). This bias seems to be so general in scope that many social psychologists refer to it as the *fundamental attribution error*. In short, we tend to perceive others as acting as they do because they are "that kind of person," rather than because of the many external factors that may influence their behavior. This tendency occurs in a wide range of contexts, but research findings (e.g., Van Overwalle, 1997) indicate that it is strongest in situations in which both consensus and distinctiveness are low, as predicted by Kelley's theory, and when we are trying to predict others' behavior in the far-off future rather than in the immediate future (Nussbaum, Trope, & Liberman, 2003). Why? Because when we think of the far-off future, we tend to do so in abstract terms, and this leads us to think about others in terms of global traits; as a result, we tend to overlook potential external causes of their behavior.

Social psychologists have conducted many studies to find out why this bias occurs (e.g., Robins, Spranca, & Mendelsohn, 1996), but the issue is still somewhat in doubt. One possibility is that when we observe another person's behavior, we tend to focus on his or her actions, the context in which the person behaves; hence potential situational causes of his or her behavior often fade into the background. As a result, dispositional causes (internal causes) are easier to notice (they are more *salient*) than situational ones. In other words, from our perspective, the person we are observing is high in *perceptual salience* and is the focus of our attention, while situational factors that might also have influenced this person's behavior are less salient and so seem less important to us. Another explanation is that we notice such situational causes but give them insufficient weight in our attributions. Still another explanation is when we focus on others' behavior, we tend to begin by assuming that their actions reflect their underlying characteristics. Then, we attempt to correct for any possible effects of the external world—the current situation—by taking these into account. (This involves a kind of mental shortcut known as *anchoring and adjustment,* covered in Chapter 2.) This correction, however, is often insufficient: We don't make enough allowance for the impact of external factors. We don't give enough weight to the possibility of delays at the airport or a slippery floor, for example, when reaching our conclusions (Gilbert & Malone, 1995).

Evidence for this two-step process—a quick, automatic reaction followed by a slower, more controlled correction—has been obtained in many studies (e.g., Gilbert, 2002; Chaiken & Trope, 1999), so it seems to offer a compelling explanation for the

correspondence bias (fundamental attribution error) The tendency to explain others' actions as stemming from dispositions, even in the presence of clear situational causes.

correspondence bias (i.e., fundamental attribution error). In fact, it appears that most people are aware of this process, or are at least aware of the fact that they start by assuming other people behave as they do because of internal causes (e.g., their personality, their true beliefs), but then correct this assumption, at least to a degree, by taking account of situational constraints. For instance, if they read an essay written by another person—an essay that supports some specific view—and then learn that this person was directed to write the essay in support of that view *regardless of his or her true beliefs*, they do start by assuming that the essay reflects the writer's views and then adjust this attribution in the light of the fact that this person was *told* to write the essay in this way (e.g., Jones & Harris, 1967; Ross, 1977).

Perhaps even more interesting, we tend to assume that *we* adjust our attributions to take account of situational constraints more than other persons do. In other words, we perceive that we are less likely to fall victim to the correspondence bias than are other persons. This tendency is clearly illustrated in recent studies by Van Boven et al. (2003). In one of these investigations, participants were asked to rate the extent to which a terrible crime (the massacre of twelve students and one teacher by students at a high school in Colorado) was due to the evil nature of the boys who performed this atrocity (internal causes) or external factors such as harassment by fellow students and problems in their families. Participants also were asked to estimate how other students in their school would rate these causes. As you can see from Figure 3.9, results indicated that participants felt that they would show the correspondence bias to a much lesser degree than other students at their school. In other words, they felt that they would attribute this crime more to situational (external) causes and less to dispositional (causes) than would other persons. So, not only do we tend to overestimate the impor-

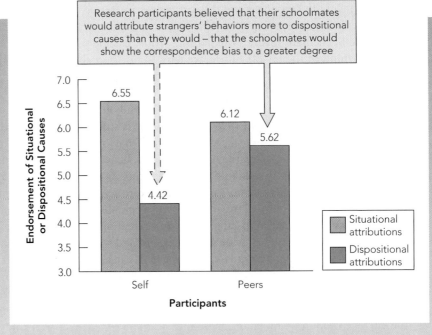

Figure 3.9 ■ "You Fall Victim to the Correspondence Bias; I Avoid (or at Least Minimize) It"

As shown here, research participants assumed that they would show the correspondence bias to a lesser extent than would other persons. Specifically, they believed that their schoolmates would attribute strangers' behavior to dispositional causes to a greater extent than they would. (*Source: Based on data from Van Boven et al., 2003.*)

Chapter 3 / Social Perception

tance of internal causes in shaping others' behavior, we tend to believe that we correct for this error to a greater extent than do other persons.

Cultural Factors in the Fundamental Attribution Error

Is this tendency to emphasize dispositional causes truly universal, or is it influenced, like many other aspects of social behavior and thought, by cultural factors? Research findings indicate that while this tendency is somewhat universal, culture indeed plays a role. Specifically, the fundamental attribution error appears to be more common or stronger in cultures that emphasize individual freedom—*individualistic* cultures such as those in Western Europe or the United States and Canada—than in *collectivistic* cultures that emphasize group membership, conformity, and interdependence (e.g., Triandis, 1990). This difference seems to reflect the fact that in individualistic cultures, there is a *norm of internality*—the view that people should accept responsibility for their own outcomes. In collectivistic cultures, in contrast, this norm is weaker or absent (Jellison & Green, 1981). We return to this topic in Chapter 5. For example, in one study, Morris and Pang (1994) analyzed newspaper articles about two mass murders—ones committed by a Chinese graduate student and ones committed by a white postal worker. The articles were published in English in the *New York Times* and in the *World Journal*, a Chinese-language newspaper published in the United States. Results were clear: The articles in English attributed both murderers' actions to dispositional factors to a greater extent than did the articles written in Chinese.

One of the studies carried out by Van Boven et al. (2003) provides further support for the role of cultural factors in the fundamental attribution error. In one of their experiments, these researchers asked students in the United States and Japan to imagine that they read an essay or heard a speech by a stranger who had been told to support a particular point of view on various controversial issues (e.g., abortion, the death penalty). Participants were asked to estimate how much they would correct their initial impression of the stranger's real attitudes after learning that he had been told to write the essay in a specific way, and how much other persons would correct *their* impressions. The researchers predicted that students in the United States would assume that they themselves would correct for the correspondence more than would other persons. However, Japanese students would not show this effect and, in fact, would demonstrate the correspondence bias to a much lesser degree. In other words, they would attribute the stranger's behavior primarily to external causes (the fact that he was told to write the essay to support a particular point of view). Results strongly confirmed these predictions, thus suggesting that cultural differences indeed matter where the correspondence bias is concerned.

Similar findings—more correspondence bias in western, individualistic countries than in Asian and more collectivistic ones—have been reported in several other studies (e.g., Choi and Nisbett, 1998). So there seems little doubt that cultural factors play a role even in this very basic aspect of attribution.

The Correspondence Bias in Attributions about Groups

Not only do we make attributions about the behavior of individual persons, we also sometimes make attributions about the behavior of groups. For instance, we try to understand why one group seems to dislike or even hate another—why, for example, did the Tutsis and Hutus (groups living in Rwanda) hate each other to the point that this hatred erupted into open genocide? And why did so many Germans hate Jews in pre–World War II Germany? Are our attributions about why various groups behave as they do also subject to the correspondence bias? Recent research conducted by Doosje and Branscombe (2003) suggests that it is. These researchers asked visitors to a museum related to events during the Holocaust (Anne Frank's home in Amsterdam) to rate the extent to which German atrocities against Jews during World War II were due to the

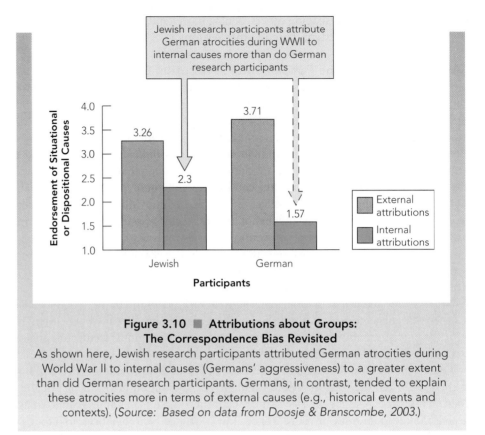

Figure 3.10 ■ Attributions about Groups: The Correspondence Bias Revisited
As shown here, Jewish research participants attributed German atrocities during World War II to internal causes (Germans' aggressiveness) to a greater extent than did German research participants. Germans, in contrast, tended to explain these atrocities more in terms of external causes (e.g., historical events and contexts). (*Source: Based on data from Doosje & Branscombe, 2003.*)

aggressive nature of Germans (an internal cause) or to the historical context in which these actions occurred (external factors). Participants in the study were either Jewish or German. The researchers predicted that Jewish people would show a greater tendency to attribute German atrocities to internal causes than would Germans themselves, and, in fact, this is what was found (see Figure 3.10). While neither group showed a strong tendency to explain these events in terms of internal causes, Jewish people—whose group had been harmed—showed this tendency to a greater extent than did Germans, thus demonstrating that attributions can be strongly affected by group membership, an effect we consider again in our discussion of prejudice (Chapter 6) and other group processes (Chapter 12). In any case, it seems clear that attributional processes—and errors—can operate with respect to social groups or even entire nations with respect to perceptions of individuals.

■ The Actor–Observer Effect: "You Fell; I Was Pushed."

The fundamental attribution error, powerful as it is, applies mainly to attributions we make about others—we don't tend to "overattribute" our own actions to external causes. This fact helps explain another and closely related type of attributional error known as the **actor–observer effect** (Jones & Nisbett, 1971), which involves our tendency to attribute our own behavior to situational (external) causes but that of others to dispositional (internal) ones. Thus, when we see another person trip and fall, we tend to attribute this event to his or her clumsiness. If *we* trip, however, we are more likely to attribute this event to situational causes, such as ice on the sidewalk.

Why does the actor–observer effect occur? In part because we are quite aware of the many external factors affecting our own actions but less aware of such factors when we turn our attention to the actions of other persons. Thus, we tend to perceive our

actor–observer effect
The tendency to attribute our own behavior mainly to situational causes but the behavior of others mainly to internal (dispositional) causes.

own behavior as arising largely from situational causes but that of others as deriving mainly from their traits or dispositions.

self-serving bias
The tendency to attribute positive outcomes to internal causes (e.g., one's own traits or characteristics) but negative outcomes or events to external causes (e.g., chance, task difficulty).

The Self-Serving Bias: "I'm Good; You Are Lucky."

Suppose that you write a term paper and when you get it back, you find the following comment on the first page: "An outstanding paper—one of the best I've see in years. A+." To what will you attribute this success? Probably you will explain it in terms of internal causes: your high level of talent, the effort you invested in writing the paper, and so on.

Now, in contrast, imagine that when you get the paper back, *these* comments are written on it, "Horrible paper—one of the worst I've seen in years. D–." How will you interpret *this* outcome? The chances are good that you will be tempted to focus mainly on external (situational factors): the difficulty of the task, your professor's unfairly harsh grading standards, the fact that you didn't have enough time to do a good job, and so on.

This tendency to attribute our own positive outcomes to internal causes but our negative ones to external factors is known as the **self-serving bias,** and it appears to be both general in scope and powerful in its effects (see Figure 3.11; Brown & Rogers, 1991; Miller & Ross, 1975).

Why does this tilt in our attributions occur? Several possibilities have been suggested, but most fall into two categories: cognitive and motivational explanations. The cognitive model suggests that the self-serving bias stems mainly from certain tendencies in the way we process social information (see Chapter 2; Ross, 1977). Specifically, it suggests that we attribute positive outcomes to internal causes but negative ones to external causes because we *expect* to succeed and have a tendency to attribute expected outcomes to internal causes more than to external ones. In contrast, the motivational explanation suggests that the self-serving bias stems from our need to protect and enhance our self-esteem or the related desire to look good to others (Greenberg, Pyszczynski, & Solomon, 1982). While both cognitive and motivational factors may well play a role in this kind of attributional error, research evidence seems to offer more support for the motivational view (e.g., Brown & Rogers, 1991).

Whatever the origins of the self-serving bias, it can be the cause of much interpersonal friction. It often leads persons who work with others on a joint task to perceive

Figure 3.11 ■ The Self-Serving Bias in Action
As shown in this cartoon, we have a strong tendency to attribute negative outcomes to external causes (e.g., other persons, society) while attributing positive outcomes to internal causes (e.g., our own characteristics). (*Source:* NON SEQUITUR © 1994 Wiley Miller. Dist. By UNIVERSAL PRESS SYNDICATE. Reprinted with permission. All rights reserved.)

that *they,* not their partners, have made the major contributions. I see this effect in my own classes every semester when students rate their own contribution and that of the other members of their team in a required term project. The result? Most students take lots of credit for themselves when the project has gone well but tend to blame (and downrate) their partners if it has not.

Interestingly, the results of several studies indicate that the strength of the self-serving bias varies across different cultures (e.g., Oettingen, 1995; Oettingen & Seligman, 1990). In particular, the self-serving bias is weaker in cultures, such as those in Asia, that place a greater emphasis on group outcomes and group harmony than it is in western cultures, in which individual accomplishments are emphasized and it is considered appropriate for winners to gloat (at least a little) over their victories (see Figure 3.12). For example, Lee and Seligman (1997) found that Americans of European descent showed a larger self-serving bias than either Chinese Americans or mainland Chinese. Once again, therefore, we see that cultural factors often play an important role, even in very basic aspects of social behavior and social thought.

Before concluding this discussion, we should note that despite all the errors described here, growing evidence suggests that social perception *can* be accurate—we do, in many cases, reach accurate conclusions about others' traits and motives from observing their behaviors. We examine some of the evidence pointing to this conclusion as part of our discussion of the process of impression formation. (Please see the **Ideas to Take with You—and Use!** section at the end of this chapter for some tips on how to avoid various attributional errors.)

**Figure 3.12 ▪ The Self-Serving Bias:
Stronger in Some Cultures Than in Others**
Research findings indicate that the self-serving bias is stronger in western cultures than in Asian ones. This is why western athletes or politicians seem to gloat after their victories, while Asian athletes or politicians are less likely to show such reactions.

Chapter 3 / Social Perception

KEY POINTS

★ *Attribution* is subject to many potential sources of error. One of the most important of these is the *correspondence bias*—the tendency to explain others' actions as stemming from dispositions, even in the presence of situational causes. This tendency seems to be stronger in western cultures than in Asian cultures and can occur for attributions for groups as well as for individuals.

★ Two other attributional errors are the *actor–observer effect*—the tendency to attribute our own behavior to external (situational causes) but that of others to internal causes—and the *self-serving bias*—the tendency to attribute positive outcomes to internal causes but negative ones to external causes.

★ The strength of the self-serving bias varies across cultures, being stronger in western societies, such as the United States, than in Asian cultures, such as China.

Applications of Attribution Theory: Insights and Interventions

Kurt Lewin, one of the founders of modern social psychology (see Chapter 1), often remarked, "There's nothing as practical as a good theory." By this he meant that once we obtain scientific understanding of some aspect of social behavior or social thought, we can potentially put this knowledge to practical use. Where attribution theory is concerned, this has definitely been the case. As basic knowledge about attribution has grown, so, too, has the range of practical problems to which such information has been applied (Miller & Rempel, 2004; Graham & Folkes, 1990). Here, we examine two important, and especially timely, applications of attribution theory.

■ Attribution and Depression

Depression is the most common psychological disorder. It has been estimated that almost half of all human beings experience such problems at some time during their lives (e.g., Blazer et al., 1994). Although many factors play a role in depression, one that has received increasing attention is what might be termed a *self-defeating* pattern of attributions. In contrast to most people, who show the self-serving bias described previously, depressed individuals tend to adopt an opposite pattern. They attribute *negative* outcomes to lasting, internal causes, such as their own traits or lack of ability, but attribute *positive* outcomes to temporary, external causes, such as good luck or special favors from others (see Figure 3.13 on page 106). As a result, such persons perceive that they have little or no control over what happens to them—they are mere chips in the winds of unpredictable fate. It is little wonder that they become depressed and tend to give up on life. And once they *are* depressed, the tendency to engage in this self-defeating pattern is strengthened, often initiating a vicious cycle.

Fortunately, several forms of therapy that focus on changing such attributions have been developed and appear to be successful (e.g., Bruder et al., 1997; Robinson, Berman, & Neimeyer, 1990). These new forms of therapy focus on getting depressed persons to change their attributions—to take personal credit for successful outcomes, to stop blaming themselves for negative outcomes (especially ones that can't be avoided), and to view at least some failures as the result of external factors beyond their control. These forms of therapy do not explore repressed urges, inner conflicts, or traumatic events during childhood, but they *do* seem to be successful. Because attribution theory provides the basis for these new forms of treatment, it has proved very useful in this respect.

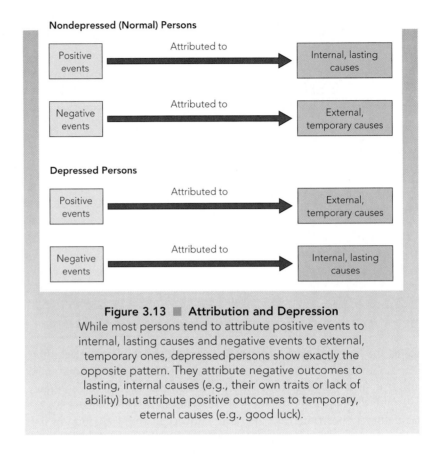

Nondepressed (Normal) Persons

Positive events — Attributed to → Internal, lasting causes

Negative events — Attributed to → External, temporary causes

Depressed Persons

Positive events — Attributed to → External, temporary causes

Negative events — Attributed to → Internal, lasting causes

Figure 3.13 ■ Attribution and Depression
While most persons tend to attribute positive events to internal, lasting causes and negative events to external, temporary ones, depressed persons show exactly the opposite pattern. They attribute negative outcomes to lasting, internal causes (e.g., their own traits or lack of ability) but attribute positive outcomes to temporary, eternal causes (e.g., good luck).

■ Attribution in Workplaces: Understanding Reactions to Sexual Harassment

There is little doubt that **sexual harassment**—unwanted contact or communication of a sexual nature—is an all-too-common occurrence in work settings (see Figure 3.14; e.g., O'Donohue, 1997). In fact, in recent surveys, almost one third of all working women report that they have had such experiences (Greenberg & Baron, 2002). One key issue relating to sexual harassment is that it is perceived differently by different social groups. For instance, men are less likely to define various actions as involving sexual harassment than are women (e.g., Runtz & O'Donnell, 2003). In part, such differences seem to involve not simply the actions themselves, but the perceived motives and intentions behind them. For instance, men may view a comment on a woman's appearance or dress as an inoffensive compliment, while women may view it as harassment. This difference suggests that attribution plays a key role in how people perceive and judge sexual harassment. To the extent this is so, theories of attribution developed by social psychologists can shed important light on this serious problem. Evidence that attribution theory can indeed be helpful in this respect has been provided by several studies (e.g., Wayne, Riordan, & Thomas, 2001). Among these, a study conducted recently by Smirles (2004) offers especially revealing findings.

In this study, male and female students read a brief description of an employer who threatened the career of an employee if this person did not consent to having a relationship with the employer. The gender of both the employer and the victim was systematically varied so that different groups of participants in the study were exposed to all possible combinations (a male harassing a male, a male harassing a female, a female harassing a female, a female harassing a male). After reading this information, they rated the extent to which the employer and the victim were responsible for what had happened. Results from this portion of the study indicated that male participants held the

sexual harassment
Unwanted contact or communication of a sexual nature.

Chapter 3 / Social Perception

victim more responsible and the employer less responsible than did female participants, regardless of the gender of the victim or the perpetrator. Why did this occur? One aspect of attribution theory—*defensive attribution*—offers an intriguing possibility.

Defensive attribution occurs when we notice that we are similar to someone who has experienced negative outcomes (e.g., a victim of sexual harassment). This causes us distress because we reason that because we are similar to the victim, we might experience these outcomes, too. To reduce these negative reactions, we attribute blame to external causes—the perpetrator—while minimizing blame for the victim. Because women are more often the victims of sexual harassment than are men, women would be expected to perceive greater similarity to the victim (regardless of this person's gender) and so blame the victim less for the negative events that occurred.

In a second part of the study, participants read a description of the victim's response to sexual harassment: acquiescence (giving in to the demands of the employer) and resistance (threatening to report the employer to his or her supervisor); a control group received no information on the victim's reaction. Attribution theory predicts that a victim who gives in to the demands of an employer will be held as more responsible for the harassment than one who resists, because it is clear that victims *can* resist; if they don't, this is attributed, at least in part, to internal factors such as weakness or a lack of resolve

Figure 3.14 ■ Sexual Harassment: Insights from Attribution Theory
Sexual harassment is a serious problem in many work settings. Attribution theory can help explain why men and women differ in their perceptions of this problem, and also suggests potential ways of reducing its occurrence.

on their part. These predictions, too, were confirmed: Victims who acquiesced were held as more responsible by both women and men for the harassment than ones who resisted.

Overall, these findings, and those of related research, suggest that attribution theory can offer important insights into the causes, and perhaps prevention, of sexual harassment. For instance, increasing males' awareness of their similarity to the victims of such treatment may cause them to blame persons who engage in sexual harassment more and victims less. Because most sexual harassment is performed by men, this could lead to reductions in such behavior in many workplaces. In this and many other ways, the knowledge regarding attributions gathered by social psychologists can be very valuable.

KEY POINTS

★ *Attribution* has been applied to many practical problems, often with great success. Depressed persons often show a pattern of attributions opposite to those of the self-serving bias: They attribute positive events to external causes and negative ones to internal causes. Therapy designed to change this pattern has proved highly effective.

★ Attribution theory also helps explain reactions to *sexual harassment* and can potentially be used to reduce such actions in workplaces.

Impression Formation and Impression Management: How We Integrate Social Information

Do you care about making a good first impression on others (see Figure 3.15)? Research findings indicate that you should, because such impressions seem to exert strong and lasting effects on other persons' perceptions of us; and as we've seen throughout this chapter, the way other persons perceive us can strongly influence their behavior toward us (e.g., Fiske, Lin, & Neuberg, 1999; Swann & Gill, 1997).

But what, exactly, *are* first impressions? How are they formed? And what steps can we take to make sure that we make good first impressions on others? These are the questions we consider now. First, we examine some classic research on these issues and then turn to more modern findings about the nature of first impressions.

A True Classic in Social Psychology: Asch's Research on Central and Peripheral Traits

As we have already seen, some aspects of social perception, such as attribution, require lots of hard mental work: It's not always easy to draw inferences about others' motives or traits from their behavior. In contrast, forming first impressions seems to be relatively effortless. As Solomon Asch (1946), one of the founders of experimental social psychology, put it, "We look at a person and immediately a certain impression of his character forms itself in us. A glance, a few spoken words are sufficient to tell us a story about a highly complex matter . . ." (1946, p. 258). How do we manage this feat? How, in short, do we form unified impressions of others in the quick and seemingly effortless way that we often do? This is the question Asch set out to study.

At the time Asch conducted his research, social psychologists were heavily influenced by the work of *Gestalt psychologists*—specialists in the field of perception. A basic prin-

Figure 3.15 ■ **First Impressions Really Do Matter**
A large body of research findings confirms what common sense suggests: First impressions really do matter. They tend to persist and can strongly influence our thinking about and interactions with other persons.

ciple of Gestalt psychology is this: "The whole is often greater than the sum of its parts," which means that what we perceive is often more than the sum of individual sensations. To illustrate this point for yourself, simply look at any painting (except a very modern one). What you see is *not* individual splotches of paint on the canvas; rather, you perceive an integrated whole—a portrait, a landscape, a bowl of fruit—whatever the artist intended. So as Gestalt psychologists suggest, each part of the world around us is interpreted, and understood, only in terms of its relationships to other parts or stimuli.

Asch applied these ideas to understanding impression formation, suggesting that we do *not* form impressions simply by adding together all of the traits we observe in other persons. Rather, we perceive these traits *in relation to one another,* so that the traits cease to exist individually and become, instead, part of an integrated, dynamic whole. How could these ideas be tested? Asch came up with an ingenious answer. He gave individuals lists of traits supposedly possessed by a stranger and then asked them to indicate their impressions of this person by putting check marks next to traits (on a much longer list) that they felt fit their overall impression of the stranger. For example, in one study, participants read one of the following two lists:

intelligent—skillful—industrious—warm—determined—practical—cautious

intelligent—skillful—industrious—cold—determined—practical—cautious

As you can see, the lists differ only with respect to two words: *warm* and *cold*. Thus, if people form impressions merely by adding together individual traits, the impressions formed by persons exposed to these two lists shouldn't differ very much. However, this was *not* the case. Persons who read the list containing *warm* were much more likely to view the stranger as generous, happy, good-natured, sociable, popular, and altruistic than were people who read the list containing *cold*. The words *warm* and *cold*, Asch concluded, described *central traits*—ones that strongly shaped overall impressions of the stranger and colored the other adjectives in the lists. Asch obtained additional support for this view by substituting the words *polite* and *blunt* for *warm* and *cold.* When he did this, the two lists yielded highly similar impressions of the stranger. So, *polite* and *blunt,* it appeared, were *not* central traits that colored the entire impressions of the stranger.

On the basis of many studies such as this one, Asch concluded that forming impressions of others involves more than simply combining individual traits. As he put it: "There is an attempt to form an impression of the *entire* person. . . . As soon as two or more traits are understood to belong to one person they cease to exist as isolated traits, and come into immediate . . . interaction. . . . The subject perceives not this *and* that quality, but the two entering into a particular relation . . ." (1946, p. 284). Although research on impression formation has become far more sophisticated since Asch's early work, many of his basic ideas about impression formation have withstood the test of time. Thus, his research exerted a lasting impact on the field and is still worthy of careful attention today.

Implicit Personality Theories: Schemas That Shape First Impressions

Suppose one of your friends described someone they had just met as *helpful* and *kind.* Would you now assume that this person is also sincere? Probably. And what if your friend described this stranger as *practical* and *intelligent?* Would you now assume that she or he is also ambitious? Again, the chances are good that you might. But why, in the absence of information on these specific traits, would you assume that this person possesses them? In part because we all possess what social psychologists describe as **implicit personality theories**—beliefs about what traits or characteristics tend to go together (e.g., Sedikides & Anderson, 1994). These theories, which can be viewed as a specific kind of *schema,* suggest that when individuals possess some traits, they are likely to possess others as well. These theories or expectations are strongly shaped by the cultures in which we live. For instance, in many societies (but not all) it is assumed that what is beautiful is good—that people who are attractive also possess other positive traits, such as good social skills and an interest in enjoying good times and the good things in life (e.g., Wheeler & Kim, 1997). Similarly, in some cultures (but again, not all) there is a schema for the jock—a young male who loves sports and prefers beer to wine, and who can, on occasion (e.g., during an important game), be very coarse. Again, once an individual is seen as having one of these traits, he or she is seen as possessing others, because typically we expect them to co-vary (to go together).

These tendencies to assume that certain traits or characteristics go together are common and can be observed in many contexts. For instance, you may well have implicit beliefs about the characteristics related to birth order. A large body of research findings indicates that we expect first-borns to be high achievers who are aggressive, ambitious, dominant, and independent, while we expect middle-borns to be caring, friendly, outgoing, and thoughtful. Only-children, in contrast, are expected to be independent, self-centered, selfish, and spoiled (e.g., Nyman, 1995).

The strength and generality of these implicit beliefs about the effects of birth order are illustrated clearly in research conducted recently by Herrera et al. (2003). These researchers asked participants to rate first-borns, only-children, middle-borns, last-borns, and themselves on various trait dimensions: agreeable–disagreeable, bold–timid, creative–uncreative, emotional–unemotional, extraverted–introverted, responsible–irresponsible, and several others. Results indicated clear differences in expectations about the traits supposedly shown by each group. First-borns were seen as being more intelligent, responsible, obedient, stable, and unemotional; only-children were seen as being the most disagreeable; middle-borns were expected to be envious and the least bold; while last-borns were seen as the most creative, emotional, disobedient, and irresponsible. So, clearly, implicit beliefs about links between birth order and important traits existed.

implicit personality theories
Beliefs about what traits or characteristics tend to go together.

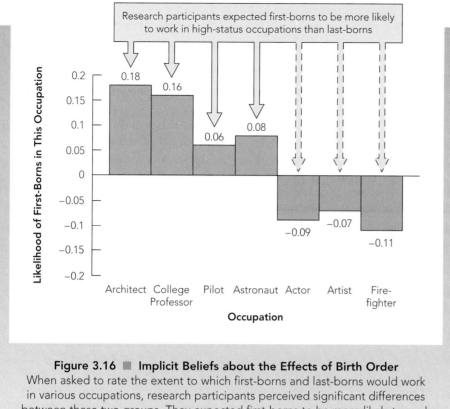

Figure 3.16 ■ Implicit Beliefs about the Effects of Birth Order
When asked to rate the extent to which first-borns and last-borns would work
in various occupations, research participants perceived significant differences
between these two groups. They expected first-borns to be more likely to work
in high-status occupations, such as accountant, pilot, architect, astronaut,
college professor, dentist, lawyer, physician, and high school teacher. In
contrast, they expected last-borns to be more likely to work as an actor,
artist, firefighter, journalist, musician, photographer, social worker, or
stunt man. (*Source: Based on data from Herrera et al., 2003.*)

Going further, the same researchers asked other participants to rate the extent to
which first-borns and last-borns would work in various occupations. As shown in Figure 3.16, birth order was significantly related to these expectations, too. Participants in
the study expected first-borns to be more likely to work in high-status occupations such
as accountant, pilot, architect, astronaut, college professor, dentist, lawyer, physician, and
high school teacher. In contrast, they expected last-borns to be more likely to work as an
actor, artist, firefighter, journalist, musician, photographer, social worker, or stunt man.

Perhaps most surprising of all, additional findings indicated that birth order was
actually related to important life outcomes: In a large sample of persons living in
Poland, the earlier individuals' position in their families' birth order, the higher their
occupational status and the more education they completed. This illustrates an important point we made in Chapter 2: Beliefs and expectations are often self-fulfilling, at
least to a degree. More generally, the findings reported by Herrera et al. (2003) and many
other researchers indicate that our beliefs about birth order can be viewed as one important kind of implicit personality theory: We *do* strongly believe that an individual's
place in her or his family's birth order is related to many different traits.

This implicit personality theory is not the only kind we hold, however. In addition,
we have beliefs about how many other traits and characteristics tend to vary together.
For instance, recall the correspondence bias discussed earlier in this chapter. In the classic research on this topic, participants were asked to read essays supporting one or the
other side in a controversial issue. Some were told that the persons who wrote the essays

chose to do this, while others were told that they were assigned to write the essay in support of one particular view. Even when they knew that the essay writers had been told what view to support, participants in many studies still assumed that the essay represented the writers' actual views—they attributed their behavior to their true beliefs, even though they knew this was not the case (e.g., Jones & Harris, 1967). So far, this finding seems to have little bearing on implicit personality theories. But consider this: What if the essays varied in quality or persuasiveness? It is possible that we have an implicit belief (implicit personality theory) that suggests that no one can write a very strong or persuasive essay in favor of a position unless that person really believes it, at least to some extent. In contrast, we may implicitly believe that almost anyone can write a weak or unpersuasive essay in favor of views they don't believe. This finding leads to the intriguing prediction that the tendency to attribute the essay to the writer's actual views will be very strong when the essay is persuasive and eloquent, because we implicitly believe that only people who really hold these views can be so passionate about them. In contrast, when the essay is not very persuasive, we will be less likely to attribute the essay to the writer's actual views; after all, anyone can write a weak essay in support of a position they don't really believe. Recent findings reported by Gawronski (2003) have confirmed these predictions, thus indicating that we have implicit beliefs about links between underlying beliefs and eloquence or persuasiveness—something that can be viewed as yet another kind of implicit personality theory. (These findings also provide additional evidence that there are indeed limits to the **fundamental attribution error**—our tendency to attribute other persons' behavior to internal causes.)

In sum, our impressions of others are often strongly shaped by our beliefs about what traits or characteristics go together. Indeed, these beliefs are frequently so strong that we sometimes bend our perceptions of other persons to be consistent with them. The result? We form impressions of others that reflect our implicit beliefs more than their actual traits.

Impression Formation: A Cognitive Perspective

Since Asch's classic research, social psychologists have made a great deal of progress toward understanding the nature of **impression formation**—the process through which we form impressions of others (e.g., Fiske, Lin, & Neuberg, 1999). A major reason for this progress has been adoption of a *cognitive perspective* on this topic. Briefly, social psychologists have found it very useful to examine impression formation in terms of basic cognitive processes. For instance, when we meet others for the first time, we don't pay equal attention to all kinds of information about them; rather, we focus on certain kinds—the kinds of input we view as being most useful (e.g., DeBruin & Van Lange, 2000). Further, to form lasting first impressions, we must enter various kinds of information into memory so that we can recall it at later times. And, of course, our first impressions of others will depend, to a degree, on our own characteristics. In fact, we can't help but see others through the lens of our own traits, motives, and desires (Vinokur & Schul, 2000).

Early work that adopted a cognitive perspective grappled with the following question: How do we manage to combine diverse information about other persons into unified impressions of them? Two possibilities seemed to exist: We could form unified impressions of others by *adding* discrete pieces of information about them, or, alternatively, we might form our impressions by *averaging* available information in some way (e.g., Anderson, 1965, 1968). Results were complex but generally pointed to the conclusion that averaging was the better explanation. The findings that led to this conclusion went something like this: If research participants were given information suggesting that a stranger possessed two highly favorable traits (e.g., truthful, reasonable), they formed a more favorable impression of this person than if they were given information suggesting that he or she possessed two highly favorable traits *and* two moderately favorable ones (e.g., truthful, reasonable, painstaking, persuasive). Researchers reasoned that

fundamental attribution error (correspondence bias)
The tendency to overestimate the impact of dispositional cues on others' behavior.

impression formation (self-presentation)
The process through which we form impressions of others.

if people combine the information they received simply by adding it together, they would like the second person more than first one because he was described as possessing a greater number of positive characteristics (two very favorable traits and two moderately favorable traits). If, in contrast, people combined the information through averaging, they would like the first one better, because the average of two highly favorable traits is higher than the average of two highly favorable *and* two moderately favorable traits. On the basis of these and related results, it was concluded that we form our impressions of others on the basis of a relatively simple kind of "cognitive algebra" (e.g., Anderson, 1973).

More recent research on impression formation has gone far beyond this initial approach. For instance, one question that was not addressed by early studies was this: What kind of information, exactly, do people focus on when meeting others for the first time? This question has many answers, depending, to some extent, on the precise context in which we encounter strangers. For instance, we might want different kinds of information about a physician we meet as a patient than we would want about someone we meet at a party or in a bar. The findings of many studies, however, indicate that across a wide range of contexts, we focus first on information concerning others' traits, values, and principles and only then turn to information about their competence—how well they can do various tasks (e.g., De Bruin & Van Lange, 2000). For instance, wouldn't you find information about whether another person is considerate and interested in people more revealing than information about this person's ability to master various tasks quickly? Many recent studies confirm this prediction: We do find certain kinds of information more informative than others, and it is this kind of information on which we tend to focus when meeting others for the first time. Of course, the context in which we meet others is important, too. In job interviews, for instance, we might well give competence more attention. Across many situations, though, we seem to assume that competence can be acquired, while traits, values, and principles are harder to change, and so offer more value information about other persons.

Other Aspects of Impression Formation: The Nature of First Impressions and Our Motives for Forming Them

Earlier, we noted that a cognitive perspective has proved very useful in the study of impression formation. In fact, this perspective has provided important insights into the basic nature of first impressions (e.g., Wyer et al., 1994; Ruscher & Hammer, 1994). For instance, most social psychologists now agree that impressions of others involve two major components: concrete examples of behaviors they have performed that are consistent with a given trait—*exemplars* of this trait—and mental summaries that are abstracted from repeated observations of others' behavior—*abstractions,* as they are usually termed (e.g., Klein, Loftus, & Plog, 1992; Smith & Zarate, 1992). Some models of impression formation stress the role of behavioral exemplars. These models suggest that when we make judgments about others, we recall examples of their behavior and base our judgments—and our impressions—on these. In contrast, other models stress the role of abstractions (sometimes referred to as *categorical judgments*). Such views suggest that when we make judgments about others, we simply bring our previously formed abstractions to mind and then use these as the basis for our impressions and our decisions. For instance, we recall that we have previously judged a person to be kind or unkind, friendly or hostile, optimistic or pessimistic, and then combine these traits into an impression of this individual.

Existing evidence suggests that both exemplars and mental abstractions play a role in impression formation (e.g., Budescheim & Bonnelle, 1998; Klein & Loftus, 1993; Klein et al., 1992). In fact, it appears that the nature of impressions may shift as we gain increasing experience with others. At first, our impression of someone we have just met consists largely of exemplars (concrete examples of behaviors he or she has performed). Later, as our experience with this person increases, our impression comes to consist mainly of mental abstractions derived from many observations of the person's behavior (Sherman & Klein, 1994).

The cognitive perspective has also shed new light on another important issue—the influence of our motives (what we are trying to accomplish in a given situation) on the kind of impressions we form, and even the processes through which we form them. As we saw in Chapter 2, people generally do the least cognitive work they can, and impression formation is no exception to this rule. Usually, then, we form impressions in the simplest and easiest way possible: by placing people into large social categories with which we are already familiar (e.g., "She is an engineer," "He is an Irish American," etc.). Then we base our impressions, at least in part, on what we know about these social groups. If we are motivated to be more accurate, though, we may focus on people we meet more as individuals possessing a unique collection of traits (e.g., Fiske, Lin, & Neuberg, 1999; Stevens & Fiske, 2000).

In sum, a cognitive perspective on impression formation has provided many valuable insights into the nature of this process. Such research suggests that although we seem to form impressions of others in a rapid and seemingly effortless manner, these impressions actually emerge out of the operation of cognitive processes relating to the storage, recall, and interpretation of social information. In short, there is a lot more going on beneath the surface than we might at first suspect.

Overall, modern research on impression formation employing a cognitive perspective has added much to our understanding of this important process. Because first impressions are often lasting and can strongly shape our future relations with others, this knowledge is valuable from both a theoretical perspective and a practical one. Perhaps the best way of illustrating the latter point is by considering impression formation from the point of view of the person about whom the impression is being formed rather than from that of the perceiver. This leads us to a discussion of the intriguing process of *impression management* (or *self-presentation*).

KEY POINTS

★ Most people are concerned with making good first impressions on others because they believe that these impressions will exert lasting effects.

★ Research on *impression formation*—the process through which we form impressions of others—suggests that this belief is true. Asch's classic research on impression formation indicated that impressions of others involve more than simple summaries of their traits.

★ Modern research conducted from a cognitive perspective has confirmed and extended this view, suggesting that in forming impressions of others we emphasize certain kinds of information (e.g., information about their traits and values rather than information about their competence).

★ Additional research indicates that impressions of others consist of examples of both behavior relating to specific traits (exemplars) and mental abstractions based on observations of many instances of behavior.

Impression Management: The Fine Art of Looking Good

The desire to make a favorable impression on others is a strong one, so most of us do our best to "look good" to others when we meet them for the first time (see Figure 3.17). Social psychologists use the term **impression management** (or *self-presentation*) to

HERMAN By Unger

© 1986 United Press Syndicate

"I always wear my lucky hat for job interviews."

describe these efforts to make a good impression on others, and the results of their research on this process suggest that it is well worth the effort: Persons who perform impression management successfully *do* often gain important advantages in many situations (e.g., Sharp & Getz, 1996; Wayne & Liden, 1995). What tactics do people use to create favorable impressions on others? Which work best? Let's see what research findings indicate about these intriguing questions.

■ Tactics of Impression Management and Their Relative Success

Although individuals use many different techniques for boosting their image, most of these fall into two major categories: *self-enhancement*—efforts to increase their appeal to others—and *other-enhancement*—efforts to make the target person feel good in various ways.

With respect to self-enhancement, specific strategies include efforts to boost one's physical appearance through style of dress, personal grooming, and the use of various props (e.g., eyeglasses, which have been found to encourage impressions of intelligence; Terry & Krantz, 1993). Additional tactics of self-enhancement involve efforts to appear highly skilled, or describing oneself in positive terms, explaining, for instance, how he or she (the person engaging in impression management) overcame daunting obstacles (Stevens & Kristof, 1995). Other findings (e.g., Rowatt, Cunningham, & Druen, 1998) indicate that many persons use this tactic to increase their appeal to potential dating partners; they describe themselves in very favorable terms (more favorable than they really deserve!) in order to impress persons they want to date. In short, they bend the truth to enhance their own appeal.

Turning to *other-enhancement*, individuals use many different tactics to induce positive moods and reactions in others. A large body of research findings suggests that such reactions, in turn, play an important role in generating liking for the person responsible for them (Byrne, 1992). The most commonly used tactic of other-enhancement is *flattery*—making statements that praise the target person, his or her traits, or accomplishments, or the organization with which the target person is associated (Kilduff & Day, 1994). Such tactics are often highly successful, provided they are not overdone. Additional tactics of other-enhancement involve expressing agreement with the target person's views, showing a high degree of interest in this person, doing small favors for them, asking for their advice and feedback in some manner (Morrison & Bies, 1991), or expressing liking for them nonverbally (e.g., through high levels of eye contact, nodding in agreement, and smiling; Wayne & Ferris, 1990).

That individuals often employ such tactics is obvious: You can probably recall many instances in which you either used, or were the target of, such strategies. A key question, however, is this: Do they work? Do these tactics of impression management succeed in generating positive feelings and reactions on the part of the persons toward whom they are directed? The answer provided by a growing body of literature is clear: *yes*, provided they are used with skill and care. For example, in one large-scale study involving more than 1,400 employees, Wayne et al. (1997) found that social skills (including impression management) were the single best predictor of job performance ratings and assessments

impression management
Efforts by individuals to produce favorable first impressions on others.

slime effect
A tendency to form nega-
tive impressions of others
who play up to their superiors but who treat subordinates with disdain.

of potential for promotion for employees in a wide range of jobs. These findings and those of many related studies (e.g., Wayne & Kacmar, 1991; Witt & Ferris, 2003; Paulhus, Bruce, & Trapnell, 1995) indicate that impression management tactics often succeed in enhancing the appeal of persons who use them effectively. However, we hasten to add that the use of these tactics involves potential pitfalls: If they are overused or used ineffectively, they can backfire and produce negative rather than positive reactions from others. For instance, in a thought-provoking study, Vonk (1998) found strong evidence for what she terms the **slime effect**—a tendency to form very negative impressions of others who "lick upward but kick downward"—persons in a work setting who play up to their superiors but treat subordinates with disdain and contempt. The moral of these findings is clear: Although tactics of impression management often succeed, this is not always the case, and sometimes they can boomerang, adversely affecting reactions to the persons who use them. (We return to this effect in Chapter 5.)

■ Impression Management: The Role of Cognitive Load

That we try to make a favorable impression on others in many situations is obvious; this effort makes a great deal of common sense. We have strong reasons for wanting to "look good" in job interviews, on first dates, and in many other contexts. Generally, we can do quite a good job in this respect because we have practiced impression management skills for many years. As a result, we can engage in positive self-presentation in a relatively automatic and effortless manner—we are simply following well-practiced scripts (see Schlenker & Pontari, 2000). Some situations in which we try to make a good first impression on others, however, are demanding ones: A lot is going on, so we don't have the luxury of concentrating solely or entirely on making a good first impression. For instance, consider the situation faced by politicians seeking the presidential nomination from their party. Often, they face a grueling schedule of meetings, speeches, and travel as they move from one location and one primary to another. As a result, they often become fatigued and experience cognitive overload—they are trying to handle more tasks and information than they can. (Another context in which such cognitive overload can occur is during *speed dating*—a topic discussed in the **Beyond the Headlines** section on the next page.) What effect does such extra *cognitive load* have on the ability to present oneself in a favorable light?

At first, you might guess that the effect would always be detrimental: When we are busy performing other tasks, we can't do as good a job at presenting ourselves, and, in general, this appears to be true (e.g., Tice et al., 1995). In fact, political candidates often *do* make serious blunders when fatigued or otherwise overloaded (see Figure 3.18). But consider this: Some persons are very uncomfortable

Figure 3.18 ■ Cognitive Overload and Impression Management
Research findings indicate that for some persons (e.g., ones who are shy or uncomfortable in social situations), cognitive overload can be a "plus," helping them to make good impressions on others. For most people most of the time, however, the opposite is true: When overloaded cognitively, people do a worse job at impression management than at other times. This is one reason why famous politicians make public blunders: They are so overloaded, they can't continue to maintain their "good image."

First Impressions on the Run: Speed Dating

"You CAN Hurry Love!"

Boston, MA—"Forget about candlelight dinners and flowers. That was so '90's and so time consuming. Courtly love poems and swooning: so 12th century.

For those ready to embrace a brave new world of courtship, it's all about speed . . . speed dating, that is. It's fast food for starving singles. It works like this: seven women and seven men gather in a café, pair up and chat for seven minutes. At the sound of a bell, it's all change for the next mini-date (see Figure 3.19). Each person fills out a card, indicating who he or she would like to go on a proper date with. The answers are compared, and people who match up are put in touch with each other. Does it work? Half of all participants come away with a potential match. Many believe that the success of this unconventional arrangement lies in something very "conventional"—simple chemistry between specific couples.

Wow! Who says there is nothing new under the sun? Speed dating, which first began in 1999, is now all the rage, and in every major city in many countries, single persons can sign up for as many of these sessions as they wish.

Clearly, speed dating is all about making a good first impression; with only seven minutes to impress potential dates, participants have to cram a lot into a short period of time. But research on first impressions indicates that this is not an impossible task; in fact, we seem to make initial judgments about others within a matter of one or two minutes even in important contexts, such as job interviews (e.g., Greenberg & Baron, 2003). Further, other findings concerned with very basic dimensions of personality ("The Big Five" dimensions; e.g., Barrick, Stewart, & Piotrowski, 2002) suggest that it is often possible to figure out where others stand with respect to these characteristics in just a few minutes. So, in the light of social psychological theory and research, speed dating may not be as bizarre as it may seem. Of course, speed dating does have important limitations: In a few minutes we can observe only a few things about another person—the aspects of their personality and behavior that are the most obvious. Many more subtle aspects are not readily apparent. But because attraction, a topic we consider in detail in Chapter 7, often involves intangibles such as "chemistry," and because we can't like or date people we never meet, speed dating may well succeed in its major goal: giving single persons a wider range of potential romantic partners than they might not otherwise have.

Figure 3.19 ■ Speed Dating: Can It Really Work?

In speed dating, persons seeking romantic partners have "dates" lasting seven minutes or less. This time frame allows them to meet many people, rather than just one, in a single evening. Can they really form accurate impressions of the people they meet so quickly? This is a question only time—and more information on the outcomes of speed dating—can answer.

in social situations because they feel anxious and tend to worry about how others will perceive them. For such persons, being busy with other tasks may distract them from such feelings and thoughts and so actually *enhance* their ability to present themselves favorably. In fact, research by Pontari and Schlenker (2000) indicates that this is true.

These researchers had persons who were extraverts (outgoing, friendly, sociable) and persons who were introverts (reserved, shy, withdrawn) take part in a mock job interview in which participants tried to present themselves either as they were (extraverted or introverted) or as the opposite kind of person. During the interview, participants were either busy performing another task (trying to remember an eight-digit number) or were not busy. Results indicated that for the extraverts, cognitive busyness interfered with their ability to present themselves as introverts (i.e., to appear shy, withdrawn, etc.). For introverts, however, the opposite was true: Trying to remember the eight-digit number actually improved their ability to appear to be extraverts. Pontari and Schlenker (2000) interpreted these findings as indicating that being busy with other tasks prevented introverts from feeling anxious and focusing on their fear of doing poorly. Thus, for such persons, cognitive distraction was actually a plus—it helped them to do a better job at self-presentation. But as interesting as this finding is, it does not negate the fact that, in most situations and for most people, cognitive overload can interfere with their efforts to "look good" in the eyes of others.

KEY POINTS

★ To make a good impression on others, individuals often engage in *impression management* (self-presentation).

★ Many techniques are used for this purpose, but most fall under two major headings: self-enhancement—efforts to boost one's appeal to others—and other-enhancement—efforts to induce positive moods or reactions in others.

★ *Impression management* is something we practice throughout life, so we can usually engage it in a fairly effortless manner. When other tasks require our cognitive resources, however, *impression management* can sometimes suffer—unless such tasks distract us from anxiety and fears over performing poorly.

★ Speed dating allows single persons to form first impressions of many potential romantic partners in a single evening. Although these impressions may not be accurate, they can lead to at least some lasting relationships.

S UMMARY AND REVIEW OF KEY POINTS

Nonverbal Communication: The Language of Expressions, Gazes, and Gestures

■ *Social perception* involves the processes through which we seek to understand other persons. It plays a key role in social behavior and social thought.

■ To understand others' emotional states, we often rely on *nonverbal communication*—an unspoken language of facial expressions, eye contact, and body movements and postures.

■ Though facial expressions may not be as universal as once believed, they often do provide useful information about others' emotional states. Useful information on this issue is also provided by eye-contact, *body language*, and touching.

■ Recent findings indicate that handshaking provides useful important nonverbal cues about others' personalities and can influence our first impressions of strangers.

■ If we pay careful attention to certain nonverbal cues, we can recognize efforts at deception by others, even if these persons are from cultures other than our own.

■ Women are better than men at both sending and interpreting nonverbal cues. This ability gives women an important advantage in many situations and may account for widespread belief in women's intuition.

Attribution: Understanding the Causes of Others' Behavior

■ To obtain information about others' lasting traits, motives, and intentions, we often engage in *attribution*—efforts to understand why they have acted as they have. According to Jones and Davis's theory of *correspondent inference*, we attempt to infer others' traits from observing certain aspects of their behavior, especially behavior that is freely chosen, produces *noncommon effects,* and is low in social desirability.

■ Kelley's theory of causal *attribution* asks the question of whether others' behavior stems from internal or external causes. To answer this question, we focus on information relating to *consensus, consistency*, and *distinctiveness*.

■ Two other important dimensions of causal attribution relate to whether specific causes of behavior are stable over time and controllable or not controllable.

■ When two or more potential causes of another person's behavior exist, we tend to downplay the importance of each—an effect known as *discounting*. When a cause that facilitates a behavior and a cause that inhibits it both exist, but the behavior still occurs, we assign added weight to the facilitative factors—an effect known as *augmenting*.

■ *Augmenting* occurs in many situations. For instance, it can boost perceptions of women who become entrepreneurs.

■ *Attribution* is subject to many potential sources of error. One of the most important of these is the *correspondence bias*—the tendency to explain others'

actions as stemming from dispositions, even in the presence of situational causes. This tendency seems to be stronger in western cultures than in Asian cultures, and can occur for attributions for groups as well as individuals.

■ Two other attributional errors are the *actor–observer effect*—the tendency to attribute our own behavior to external (situational) causes but that of others to internal causes—and the *self-serving bias*—the tendency to attribute positive outcomes to internal causes but negative ones to external causes.

■ The strength of the *self-serving bias* varies across differing cultures, being stronger in western societies, such as the United States, than in Asian cultures, such as China.

■ *Attribution* is applied to many practical problems, often with great success. Depressed persons often show a pattern of attributions opposite to that of the *self-serving bias:* They attribute positive events to external causes and negative ones to internal causes. Therapy designed to change this pattern has proved highly effective.

■ *Attribution* theory also helps explain reactions to *sexual harassment* and can potentially be used to reduce such actions in workplaces.

Impression Formation and Impression Management: How We Integrate Social Information

■ Most people are concerned with making good first impressions on others, because they believe that these impressions will exert lasting effects.

■ Research on *impression formation*—the process through which we form impressions of others—

suggests that this belief is true. Asch's classic research on *impression formation* indicated that impressions of others involve more than simple summaries of their traits.

■ Modern research conducted from a cognitive perspective has confirmed and extended this view, suggesting that in forming impressions of others, we emphasize certain kinds of information (e.g., information about their traits and values rather than information about their competence.)

■ Additional research indicates that impressions of others consist of examples of both behavior relating to specific traits (exemplars) and mental abstractions based on observations of many instances of behavior.

■ To make a good impression on others, individuals often engage in *impression management* (self-presentation).

■ Many techniques are used for *impression management,* but most fall under two major headings: self-enhancement—efforts to boost one's appeal to others—and other-enhancement—efforts to induce positive moods or reactions in others.

■ *Impression management* is something we practice throughout life, so we can usually engage it in a fairly effortless manner. When other tasks require our cognitive resources, however, *impression management* can sometimes suffer—unless such tasks distract us from anxiety and fears over performing poorly.

■ *Speed dating* allows single persons to form first impressions of many potential romantic partners in a single evening. Although these impressions may not be accurate, they can lead to at least some lasting relationships.

In this chapter, you read about . . .	In other chapters, you will find related discussions of . . .
basic channels of nonverbal communication	the role of nonverbal cues in interpersonal attraction (Chapter 7), persuasion (Chapter 4), prejudice (Chapter 6), and charismatic leadership (Chapter 12)
theories of attribution	the role of attribution in persuasion (Chapter 4), social identity and self-perception (Chapter 5), prejudice (Chapter 6), long-term relationships (Chapter 8), prosocial behavior (Chapter 10), and aggression (Chapter 11)
first impressions and impression management	the role of first impressions in interpersonal attraction (Chapter 7), the role of impression management in job interviews (Module B)

Thinking about Connections

1. As we'll point out in Chapters 4 (Attitudes) and 9 (Social Influence), influence is an important fact of social life: Each day, we attempt to change others' attitudes or behavior and they attempt to change ours. Having read about attribution in this chapter, do you think that influence attempts that conceal their true goals will be more successful than ones that do not? If so, why? If not, why?

2. In Chapter 11 (Aggression), we'll see that some persons experience much more than their fair share of aggressive encounters. Such persons, it appears, are lacking in basic social skills, such as the ability to accurately read nonverbal cues. On the basis of the discussion of nonverbal cues in this chapter, can you explain how this could contribute to their problems with respect to aggression?

3. Suppose you were preparing for an important job interview (see Module B). On the basis of information presented in this chapter, what steps could you take to improve your chances of actually getting the job?

4. Suppose you compared happy couples with ones that are unhappy and likely to break up. Do you think that the members of these couples would differ in their attributions concerning their partners' behavior? For instance, would the happy couples attribute their partners' behavior to more positive causes than the unhappy couples?

Ideas to Take with You—and Use! MINIMIZING THE IMPACT OF ATTRIBUTIONAL ERRORS

Attribution is subject to many errors, and these can prove costly both to you and to the people with whom you interact, so it's well worth the effort to avoid such pitfalls. Here are our suggestions for recognizing—and minimizing—several important attributional errors.

The Correspondence Bias: The Fundamental Attribution Error

We have a strong tendency to attribute others' behavior to internal (dispositional) causes, even when external (situational) factors that might have influenced their behavior are present. To reduce this error, always try to put yourself in the shoes of the persons whose behavior you are trying to explain. In other words, try to see the world through their eyes. If you do, you will probably realize that, from their perspective, there are many external factors that played a role in their behavior.

The Actor–Observer Effect: "I behave as I do because of situational causes; you behave as you do because you are that kind of person."

Consistent with the fundamental attribution error, we have a strong tendency to attribute our own behavior to external causes but that of others to internal causes. This tendency can lead us to false generalizations about others and the traits they possess. To minimize this error, try to imagine yourself in their place and ask yourself, "Why would I have acted in that way?" If you do, you'll quickly realize that external factors might have influenced your behavior. Similarly, ask yourself, "Did I behave that way because of traits or motives of which I'm not very aware?" This exercise may help you to appreciate the internal causes of your own behavior.

The Self-Serving Bias: "I'm good; you're lucky."

Perhaps the strongest attributional error we make is that of attributing positive outcomes to internal causes, such as our own abilities or efforts, but negative outcomes to external factors, such as luck or forces beyond our control. This error can have many harmful effects, but among the worst is a strong tendency to believe that the rewards

we receive (raises, promotions, share of the credit) are smaller than we deserve. I (Robert Baron) had first-hand experience with this effect when I was a department chair; virtually every faculty member seemed to feel they deserved a bigger raise than I recommended for them! Simply being aware of this attributional error can help you reduce it; such awareness may help you to realize that all your positive outcomes don't stem from internal causes, and that you may have played a role in producing negative ones. In addition, try to remember that other people are subject to the same bias; doing so can help remind you that they,

too, want to take as much credit for positive outcomes as possible but shift the blame for negative ones to external causes—such as you!

KEY TERMS

actor–observer effect (p. 102)

attribution (p. 92)

augmenting principle (p. 97)

body language (p. 86)

consensus (p. 95)

consistency (p. 95)

correspondence bias (p. 99)

corespondent inference (p. 93)

discounting principle (p. 97)

distinctiveness (p. 95)

fundamental attribution error (p. 112)

implicit personality theories (p. 110)

impression formation (p. 112)

impression management (p. 115)

linguistic style (p. 90)

microexpressions (p. 89)

noncommon effects (p. 94)

nonverbal communication (p. 84)

self-serving bias (p. 103)

sexual harassment (p. 106)

slime effect (p. 116)

social perception (p. 83)

staring (p. 86)

FOR MORE INFORMATION

Darley, J. M., & Cooper, J. (1998). *Attribution and social interaction: The legacy of Edward Jones.*
• In this book, experts on attribution theory review evidence concerning the role of attribution in social behavior. Many of the ideas considered were proposed by Edward E. Jones, a pioneer in the study of attribution. (We considered some of his work in this chapter.)

Hall, J. A., & Bernieri, F. J. (Eds.) (2001). *Interpersonal Sensitivity.* Mahwah, NJ: Erlbaum.

• This book examines the nature of interpersonal sensitivity, including key aspects of nonverbal communication. An excellent source for more information on nonverbal communication and related topics.

Spencer, S. J., Fein, S., Zanna, M. P., & Olson, J. M. (Eds.) (2003). *Motivated social perception.* Mahwah, NJ: Erlbaum.
• This book examines the effects of motivation on social perception—how the goals we seek to accomplish in our relations with others influence the ways in which

we perceive and understand them. Many chapters are closely related to aspects of social perception covered in this text.

Zebrowitz, L. A. (1997). *Reading faces.* Boulder, CO: Westview Press.
• In this book, a well-known researcher provides an overview of the influence of facial features and expressions on social perception. The discussions of the ways in which people look can actually be linked to their psychological traits are especially revealing.

4

ATTITUDES
Evaluating the Social World

In May 2004, the Massachusetts Supreme Court ruled that it is a violation of gay and lesbian people's constitutional rights to deny them the right to marry. With this ruling, Massachusetts became the first state to legally permit same-sex marriages. When the attitudes of the U.S. public concerning this issue are examined, we see a substantial generation gap in support for same-sex marriage (*Newsweek* Poll, 2004). Although, overall, American attitudes are currently against permitting same-sex marriage (only 28 percent favor it), a considerably larger percentage (41 percent) of those between the ages of eighteen and twenty-nine favor this legal change, compared with those in older age groups.

Legal changes that affect U.S. institutions often precede widespread public opinion change. Consider Americans' views on racial segregation. Before the *Brown vs. Topeka Board of Education* U.S. Supreme Court ruling in May 1954, which ordered that public schools be desegregated because "separate is inherently unequal," most White Americans were, in fact, in favor of racial segregation in schools (Pettigrew, 2004). Fifty years after this groundbreaking legal decision, the majority of Americans favor racial desegregation in the public schools. On both of these issues concerning matters of social justice, the opinions of younger people have tended to be more liberal than those of older people, but both those who favor and those who are against the changes in such policies hold strong opinions of which they are certain.

People do, however, hold many attitudes about which they feel some ambivalence—that is, they have both positive and negative responses, or have both approach and avoidance tendencies regarding the object or issue. For example, people may feel positively disposed toward particular foods (e.g., desserts) but simultaneously avoid them because of their high fat content. Likewise, people can positively evaluate a particular brand of automobile

Chapter 4 / Attitudes

but not purchase it because it is too expensive for their budget. The point is that for some attitudes we have no ambivalence toward the object or issue, but for others we have considerable ambivalence. As you'll see, the issue of strength and clarity of an attitude has important implications for our actions.

Social psychologists use the term **attitude** to refer to people's evaluation of virtually any aspect of the social world (e.g., Olson & Maio, 2003; Petty, Wheeler, & Tormala, 2003). People can have favorable or unfavorable reactions to issues, ideas, specific individuals, entire social groups, and objects. Yet attitudes in many domains are not always as uniformly positive or negative as they are for same-sex marriage and school desegregation; on the contrary, our evaluations are often mixed, consisting of both positive and negative reactions (e.g., Priester & Petty, 2001). By definition, ambivalent attitudes are easier to change than those that reflect a uniform position on an issue; as a result, behavioral responses tend to be unstable when attitudes are mixed (Armitage & Conner, 2000). Consider the dilemma of a friend of mine who went car shopping. She had limited funds and had "pre-decided" to purchase a modestly priced vehicle. However, at one car dealership, she saw a Lexus on the lot and decided to just take it out for a test drive. It was love on the first drive! In this case, can you guess which component of her attitude toward autos won out—her feelings about affordability or her desire for this luxurious car? As Figure 4.1 illustrates, like many people in the market for a new car, my friend convinced herself that she could manage the large monthly payments that this purchase would entail, and she ended up taking the Lexus home. Although I pointed out to my friend that there were many very nice, less expensive vehicles that she might consider, she was convinced that the Lexus was the car for her (and the financial sacrifices she would be making for several years by purchasing it were already seen as "not so bad"). The point is, when attitudes are ambivalent, they are more susceptible to change, compared with when they are uniformly positive or negative. In contrast, attitudes that lack ambivalence are indeed difficult to change—and, like the issue of school desegregation

attitude
Evaluation of various aspects of the social world.

Figure 4.1 ■ Attitudes That Lack Ambivalence Often Predict Behavior
Some of our attitudes are ambivalent: Our evaluations of various issues, people, groups, and objects can contain both positive and negative components. Many of us tend to confront our purchasing decisions with ambivalence (*left*). For example, when purchasing a car, we may like one model but also react negatively to its price tag. Strong attitudes (*right*) are often a better guide to predicting our future actions than attitudes that are ambivalent.

and same-sex marriage, may only be altered in response to behavioral changes across time or among those who are younger and lack a life-long commitment to a particular attitude position (Sears, 1985). Thus, strong attitudes tend to be better predictors of behavior in domains to which they are relevant than are ambivalent attitudes.

Social psychologists view the study of attitudes as central to their field for several reasons. First, attitudes influence our thoughts, even if they are not always reflected in our overt behavior. In fact, growing evidence suggests that attitudes, as evaluations of the world around us, represent a very basic aspect of social cognition. As we saw in Chapter 2, the tendency to evaluate stimuli as positive or negative—something we like or dislike—appears to be an initial step in our effort to make sense out of the world. In fact, such reactions occur almost immediately, before we attempt to integrate new stimuli with our previous experience (Ito et al., 1998). When stimuli are evaluated in terms of our attitudes, we experience different brain wave activity, compared with when we respond to the same stimuli in nonevaluative terms (Crites & Cacioppo, 1996). So, in a sense, attitudes truly reflect an essential building block of social thought (Eagly & Chaiken, 1998).

Second, social psychologists view attitudes as important, because attitudes *do* often affect our behavior. This is especially likely to be true when attitudes are strong, well established, and accessible (Ajzen, 2001; Fazio, 2000; Petty & Krosnick, 1995). What is your attitude toward the current U.S. president? If positive, you are likely to have voted for him in the recent 2004 election, but if negative, you are unlikely to have done so. Do you like "Reality TV"? If so, we can safely predict that you will probably choose to watch *Survivor* and other programs of that sort. Because attitudes influence behavior, knowing something about them helps us to predict people's behavior in a wide range of contexts. As we'll see in Chapter 6, people hold attitudes toward various social groups—for example, we may like or dislike particular groups; as a consequence, we may be positively or negatively predisposed to act in particular ways toward them. Clearly, then, attitudes can play a crucial role in our behavioral responses.

Attitudes have been a central concept in social psychology since its earliest days (e.g., Allport, 1924). In this chapter, we provide you with an overview of what social psychologists have discovered about attitudes. First, we consider the ways in which attitudes are *formed,* and why we construct them in the first place—in other words, what functions they serve. Next, we consider a question we have already raised: When do attitudes influence behavior? The answer: sometimes but not always. Recent research provides important insights concerning the complex issue of when attitudes and behavior are connected. Third, we turn to the related question of how attitudes are changed—the process of *persuasion.* Changing attitudes, though, can be a difficult business. In fact, changing them is far more difficult than advertisers, politicians, salespersons, and many other would-be persuaders assume. Still, as suggested in Figure 4. 2, such

CLOSE TO HOME

© 1997 John McPherson/Dist. by Universal Press Syndicate

BUT THEN AGAIN, IF BEING HERE BY 8:30 IS CRAMPING YOUR STYLE 10:30 OR 11:00 IS JUST FINE! AND, HEY! LIKE THE TV! NICE HOMEY TOUCH!

McPherson 9-26

Todd's relationship with management improved dramatically once he started bringing his new pet to work.

Figure 4.2 ■ Techniques for Changing Attitudes: The Range Is Immense
As suggested by this cartoon, people wishing to change our attitudes have many techniques for attaining this goal. (*Source:* CLOSE TO HOME © 1997 John McPherson. Reprinted with permission of UNIVERSAL PRESS SYNDICATE. All rights reseved.)

persons have many tricks up their sleeve, and make use of them in their effort to change our views. Fourth, we examine some of the reasons *why* attitudes are often so resistant to change. Finally, we consider the intriguing fact that on some occasions, our own actions shape our attitudes rather than vice versa. The process that underlies such effects is known as *cognitive dissonance,* and it has fascinating implications not only for attitude change, but for many aspects of social behavior as well.

Attitude Formation: How Attitudes Develop

How do you feel about the U.S. role in the war in Iraq, the legalization of marijuana, Quentin Tarantino's *Kill Bill* films, people who cover their bodies with tattoos, fraternities and sororities on campus, Donald Trump and his TV program *The Apprentice,* or people who talk on their cell phones while driving? Most people have attitudes about all of these issues, but where, precisely, did these views come from? Did you acquire them as a result of your own experiences, or from the people with whom you interact frequently? Are people's group memberships (e.g., racial, age, gender) important predictors of social attitudes? Why do we form attitudes in the first place—in other words, what functions do attitudes serve? With respect to the first question, almost all social psychologists believe that attitudes are *learned,* and much of our discussion focuses on the processes through which attitudes are acquired. Turning to the second question—*why* do we form attitudes (i.e., what functions do they serve?), we'll soon see that attitudes serve several different functions, and they are useful to us in many different respects.

Social Learning: Acquiring Attitudes from Others

One important means by which our attitudes develop is through the process of **social learning.** In other words, many of our views are acquired in situations in which we interact with others or simply observe their behavior. Such learning occurs through several processes, which are outlined below.

Classical Conditioning: Learning Based on Association

It is a basic principle of psychology that when one stimulus regularly precedes another, the one that occurs first can become a signal for the second. Over time, people learn that when the first stimulus occurs, the second will soon follow. For example, suppose you are allergic to cats. Whenever you go to visit one of your friends, who has two cats, you end up with watery eyes and other annoying consequences. As a result of classical conditioning, over time you associate the first stimulus (e.g., going to your friend's house) with the second stimulus (e.g., watery eyes), and you gradually acquire the same kind of reactions to the first stimulus as you show to the second stimulus, especially if the second is one that induces fairly strong and automatic reactions. Because visiting that friend reliably predicts these negative responses, the idea of going to your friend's house (and perhaps even that person) eventually will automatically elicit a negative response from you.

This process—known as **classical conditioning**—has important implications for attitude formation. To see how this process might influence attitudes toward an entire social category, consider the following sequence of events. A young child sees her

social learning
 The process through which we acquire new information, forms of behavior, or attitudes from other persons.

classical conditioning
 A basic form of learning in which one stimulus, initially neutral, acquires the capacity to evoke reactions through repeated pairing with another stimulus. In a sense, one stimulus becomes a signal for the presentation or occurrence of the other.

mother frown and show other signs of displeasure each time the mother encounters a member of a particular ethnic group. At first, the child is neutral toward members of this group and their visible characteristics (e.g., skin color, style of dress, accent). She has not yet learned to categorize this particular variation in people in terms of group membership. After these cues are paired repeatedly with the mother's negative emotional reactions on exposure to members of that group, classical conditioning occurs, and the child comes to react negatively to members of this particular ethnic group (see Figure 4.3). This reaction can occur without the child having conscious access to the role that her mother's subtle facial changes have had on what attitude she forms. The result is that the child acquires a negative attitude toward members of a particular group—an attitude that may form the core of prejudice, which we examine in detail in Chapter 6.

Not only can classical conditioning contribute to shaping our attitudes, it also can occur when we are not even aware of the stimuli that serve as the basis for this kind of conditioning. For instance, in one experiment (Krosnick et al., 1992), students saw photos of a stranger engaged in routine daily activities such as shopping in a grocery store or walking into her apartment. While these photos were shown, other photos known to induce either positive or negative feelings were exposed for very brief periods of time—so brief that participants were not aware of their presence. Participants who were nonconsciously exposed to photos that induced positive feelings (e.g., a newly-wed couple, people playing cards and laughing) liked the stranger better than did participants who had been exposed to photos that nonconsciously induced negative feelings (e.g., open-heart surgery, a werewolf). Even though participants were not aware that they had been exposed to the second group of photos, these stimuli significantly influenced the attitudes that were formed toward the stranger. Those exposed to the positive photos reported more favorable attitudes toward the stranger than those

Figure 4.3 ■ Classical Conditioning of Attitudes
Initially, a young child may have little or no emotional reaction to the visible characteristics of members of different social groups. If, however, the child sees her mother showing signs of negative reactions when in the presence of these persons, she may gradually acquire a negative reaction to them, too, as a result of the process of *classical conditioning*.

Chapter 4 / Attitudes

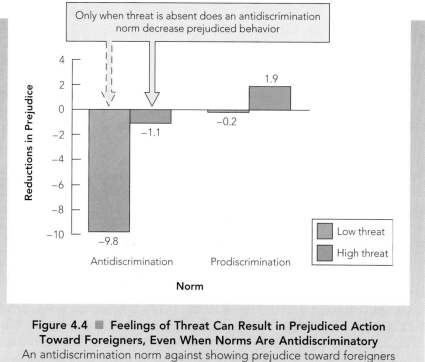

Figure 4.4 ■ Feelings of Threat Can Result in Prejudiced Action Toward Foreigners, Even When Norms Are Antidiscriminatory
An antidiscrimination norm against showing prejudice toward foreigners is only effective at reducing favoritism toward members of one's own group when people are feeling little threat. Regardless of feelings of threat, if a prodiscrimination norm is present, people discriminate by showing favoritism toward their own group members. (*Source: Based on data from Falomir-Pichastor et al., 2004.*)

exposed to the negative photos. These findings suggest that attitudes can be influenced by **subliminal conditioning**—classical conditioning that occurs in the absence of conscious awareness of the stimuli involved.

Indeed, once formed, attitudes relevant to discrimination against a particular category of people are most likely to affect people's behavior when they feel that they are experiencing a threat (Stephan & Stephan, 2000). For example, since the terrorist attacks on the United States on September 11, 2001, many Americans have increasingly felt threatened and, as a result, favor greater surveillance of foreigners, particularly those from Arab or Muslim countries. Recent research (Falomir-Pichastor et al., 2004) has revealed that even when the norms in a cultural setting are antidiscriminatory, it is only when feelings of threat from foreigners are low that prejudice is reduced (see Figure 4.4). As this research indicates, **social norms**—beliefs about how people should or are likely to behave—against discrimination are crucial for nonprejudiced behavior, but they are not sufficient. Rather, when perceived threat from foreigners is high, discrimination is still likely, even when the norm is antidiscriminatory.

Instrumental Conditioning: Rewards for the "Right" Views

Have you ever heard a seven-year-old state, with great conviction, that she or he is a Republican or a Democrat? Children of this age have little understanding of what these categories mean or the ways in which they differ from each other. Yet they sometimes confidently make such claims. Why? They have been praised or rewarded in various ways by their parents for stating such views. As a result, children learn which views are

subliminal conditioning
Classical conditioning of attitudes by exposure to stimuli that are below individuals' threshold of conscious awareness.

social norms
Expectations about how people will or should behave in a particular context.

seen as "correct" among the people with whom they identify. Behaviors that are followed by positive outcomes are strengthened and tend to be repeated, whereas behaviors that are followed by negative outcomes are weakened or decrease in their likelihood of being expressed. Thus, another way in which attitudes are acquired from others is through the process of **instrumental conditioning.** By rewarding children with smiles, approval, or hugs for stating the "right" views—the ones they themselves favor—parents and other adults play an active role in shaping youngsters' attitudes. It is for this reason that until they reach their teen years—when peer influences become especially strong—most children express political, religious, and social views that are highly similar to those of their family members.

As adults, we may expect to be rewarded for expressing support for a particular attitude position with some audiences, but at the same time, we know that we would be rewarded for expressing a different view to other audiences. Indeed, elections are won and lost on this premise. Politicians who are constantly shifting their responses to accommodate those they believe represent the majority of their audience may hurt themselves by looking as though they are not taking a firm stand on anything. Fortunately, for most of us, our every word is not recorded. This means that we are less likely to be caught expressing different views to different audiences than are politicians! In your own life, think about some of the attitudes that your parents would appreciate you expressing versus the attitudes you are likely to be rewarded for expressing when you are with other college students. For example, you may assure your parents that you will eat healthy food and limit your consumption of alcohol. Yet, when you are actually at school, you might join your friends in praising late-night binges at which you both eat high-fat food and drink more alcohol than your parents would deem acceptable.

One way of assessing whether people's reported attitudes vary depending on the expected audience reaction is to alter the audience that is expected to receive the message. For example, people seeking membership in a fraternity or sorority (e.g., pledges) differ in the attitudes they report toward other fraternities and sororities, depending on whether they believe their attitudes will remain private or whether they think that the well-established members of their group who will be controlling their admittance will know the attitude position they advocated (Noel, Wann, & Branscombe, 1995). When those who are attempting to gain membership in an organization believe that other members will learn of their responses, they derogate other fraternities or sororities as a means of communicating that the particular organization to which they want to be admitted is seen as the most desirable. Yet when they believe their responses will be private, they do not derogate other fraternities or sororities. Politicians are, of course, expert at telling people what they want to hear. For example, when the U.S. presidential candidates visited heavily blue-collar states such as Ohio and Michigan during the recent 2004 election, they emphasized policies and attitude issues of concern to those workers, but when they visited states with a sizable elderly population, such as Arizona and Florida, they instead emphasized how their policies are consistent with the attitudes and concerns of those groups.

Observational Learning: Learning by Example

A third process through which attitudes are formed can operate even when parents have no desire to directly transmit specific views to their children. This process is **observational learning,** and it occurs when individuals acquire new forms of behavior or thought simply by observing the actions of others (e.g., Bandura, 1997). Where attitude formation is concerned, observational learning appears to play an important role. In many cases, children hear their parents say things that are not intended for their ears, or observe their parents engaging in actions their parents tell them not to perform. In

instrumental conditioning
A basic form of learning in which responses that lead to positive outcomes or that permit avoidance of negative outcomes are strengthened.

observational learning
A basic form of learning in which individuals acquire new forms of behavior as a result of observing others.

Figure 4.5 ■ **Observational Learning in Action**
Children learn many things from their parents, including attitudes
and behaviors that their parents may not wish for them to acquire,
such as a positive view of smoking.

fact, parents might even explicitly say, "Don't do what I do." For example, parents who smoke often warn their children against this habit, even as they light up (see Figure 4.5). What message do children actually learn from such instances? The evidence is clear: They generally learn to do as their parents *do,* not as they *say.*

In addition, both children and adults acquire attitudes from exposure to mass media—magazines, films, and so on. Just think about how much observational learning most of us are doing as we watch television! For instance, the characters in many American action films routinely exhibit high levels of violence that, in the past, would have evoked stress and be perceived as frightening by viewers. However, young people who have grown up watching horror films (e.g., *Halloween; Friday the 13th, Scream 1* and *2*) do not find such graphic violence as distressing as do older persons who have not been desensitized to the presentation of violence. Thus, younger people do not have an aversion toward filmed violence—as a function of viewing it—but older people who have not been exposed to such content to the same extent are averse to it. Interestingly, we tend to think that it is *other* people who will be harmed by viewing violent or pornographic material, while we believe that we are not affected by doing so (Gunther, 1995). This has been referred to as the **third-person effect** of media exposure—the impact on others' attitudes and behaviors is overestimated, and the impact on the self is underestimated. See Chapter 11 for more on violence in the media and its effect on aggression.

Role of Social Comparison

Why do people often adopt the attitudes that they hear others express or acquire the behaviors they observe in others? One answer involves the mechanism of **social comparison**—the tendency to compare ourselves with others in order to determine whether our view of social reality is correct (Festinger, 1954). That is, to the extent that our views agree with those of others, we tend to conclude that our ideas and attitudes are accurate; after all, if others hold the same views, these views must be right! But are we equally likely to adopt all others' attitudes, or does it depend on our relationship to those others?

third-person effect
Effect that occurs when the impact of media exposure on others' attitudes and behaviors is overestimated and the impact on the self is underestimated.

social comparison
The process through which we compare ourselves to others in order to determine whether our views of social reality are or are not correct.

Social Learning: Acquiring Attitudes from Others

People often change their attitudes to hold views closer to those of people they value and with whom they identify. For example, Terry and Hogg (1996) found that the adoption of positive attitudes toward wearing sunscreen and the intention to do so on every occasion when one goes outside depended on the extent to which people identified with the group advocating in favor of this action. In Australia, where the study was done, the ozone that blocks harmful rays from the sun has been depleted, making sunscreen protection a vitally important means of reducing the incidence of skin cancer. Thus, as a result of social comparison with the attitudes held by others with whom we identify, new attitudes can be formed. For instance, imagine that you heard persons you like and respect expressing negative views toward a group with whom you have had no contact. Would this influence your attitudes? While it might be tempting to say, "Absolutely not!" research findings indicate that hearing others state negative views about a group can lead you to adopt similar attitudes—without your ever meeting any members of that group (e.g., Maio, Esses, & Bell, 1994; Terry, Hogg, & Duck, 1999). In such cases, attitudes are shaped as a result of social information, coupled with our desire to be similar to people we like.

Indeed, people expect to be influenced by others' attitude positions differentially, depending on how much they identify with those others. When a message concerning safe sex and AIDS prevention was created for university students, those who identified with their university's student group believed that they would be personally influenced by the position advocated in the message, whereas those who were low in identification with their university's student group did not expect to be personally influenced by the message (Duck, Hogg, & Terry, 1999). As shown in Figure 4.6, nonstudents were expected to be equally influenced by the message regardless of how identified with the student group the rater was. Thus, when we identify with a group, we expect to take on the attitudes advocated by that group.

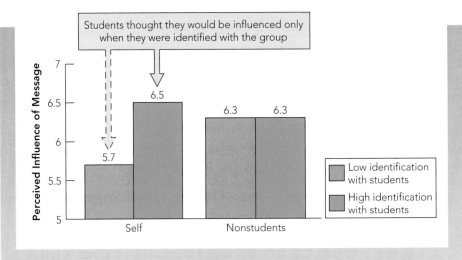

Figure 4.6 ■ Evidence for the Importance of Social Identity Influences on Attitudes

When judging how much the self would be influenced by a message aimed at members of one's group (e.g., students), the students thought they would be personally influenced when they highly identified with their student group but not when they were low in identification with their group. Identification with the group did not influence the message when it was nonstudents being estimated. (*Source: Based on data from Duck, Hogg, & Terry, 1999.*)

KEY POINTS

★ *Attitudes* are evaluations of any aspect of the social world. Often, attitudes are strong and unambivalent, which makes them resistant to change. Other attitudes are ambivalent, which means that they are based on conflicting beliefs—we evaluate the attitude object both positively and negatively—and such attitudes are less likely to predict behavior consistently.

★ Attitudes are often acquired from other persons through *social learning*. Such learning can involve *classical conditioning, instrumental conditioning,* or *observational learning*.

★ Attitudes are also formed on the basis of *social comparison*—the tendency to compare ourselves with others to determine whether our views of social reality are or are not correct. To be similar to others we like, we often adopt the attitudes that they hold.

★ Attitudes are influenced by exposure to mass media. We tend to believe, however, that only other people are affected by such exposure (e.g., to violence), but not ourselves—an effect known as the *third-person effect*.

★ When we identify with a group, we expect to be influenced by messages that are aimed at that group. We do not expect to be personally influenced when we do not identify with the group to which the attitude-relevant message is aimed.

Attitude Functions: Why We Form Attitudes in the First Place

Each of us holds many attitudes on a wide array of issues; in fact, it is safe to say that we are rarely completely neutral toward almost any aspect of the world around us. Indeed, **mere exposure** to an object—having seen before but not necessarily remembering having done so—can result in attitude formation. Even among patients with advanced Alzheimer's disease, who cannot remember having been exposed to an object, new attitudes are formed (Winograd et al., 1999). But why do we bother to form so many attitudes? In one sense, attitudes can be viewed as almost automatic reactions to the world around us. As noted earlier, research employing sophisticated techniques for observing activity in the human brain suggests that we seem to classify stimuli we encounter as either positive or negative almost immediately, and show different responses in the brain to the same object, depending on whether we are evaluating it (e.g., Crites & Cacioppo, 1996; Ito et al., 1998).

Having an already formed attitude toward a class of stimuli serves a number of useful functions. We now consider the knowledge, identity, self-esteem, ego-defensive, and impression motivation functions that attitudes can serve (Shavitt, 1990).

The Knowledge Function of Attitudes

Attitudes serve a **knowledge function** by aiding our interpretation of new information and influencing basic approach or avoidance responses. For example, Chen and Bargh (1999) found that positive attitudes toward an object were more quickly expressed when a lever had to be pulled toward the self, whereas negative attitudes were more readily expressed when a lever had to be pushed away from the self. This suggests that attitudes color our perceptions and responses. Indeed, research findings indicate that we view new information that offers support for our attitudes as more convincing and accurate

mere exposure
By having seen an object previously, but not necessarily remembering having done so, attitudes toward an object can become more positive.

knowledge function
Attitudes aid in the interpretation of new stimuli and enable rapid responding to attitude-relevant information.

than information that refutes our attitudes (Munro & Ditto, 1997). Likewise, we perceive information that is weak as relatively strong when it is consistent with our existing attitudes, compared with when it is inconsistent with our attitudes (Chaiken & Maheswaran, 1994). Conversely, there is considerable evidence that we view sources that provide evidence contrary to our views as highly suspect—biased and unreliable (Giner-Sorolla & Chaiken, 1994, 1997). In sum, attitudes enable us to rapidly make sense of our social world and prepare us for responding to attitude-relevant information in ways that maintain those attitudes.

The Identity Function of Attitudes

Attitudes permit us to express our central values and beliefs—that is, attitudes can serve an **identity or self-expression function.** For instance, if being politically liberal is crucial for a person's identity, that individual may find it important to express his or her proenvironmental attitudes by wearing Sierra Club T-shirts, because doing so allows the person to express a central belief. In fact, those people wearing their Sierra Club T-shirts might find that they are more well received by others wearing similar proenvironmental slogan T-shirts as opposed to those wearing pro–National Rifle Association T-shirts, which tend to represent the other side of the political spectrum. Likewise, the person wearing the pro–NRA T-shirt is unlikely to endear him- or herself to a person wearing a "Have you hugged a tree?" T-shirt. Indeed, we are more likely to adopt the attitude position of someone with whom we share an important identity (McGarty et al., 1994). Suppose you have to form an attitude concerning a product you've not encountered before. How might the identity relevance of the message influence your attitude? To address this question, Fleming and Petty (2000) first selected students who reported being high or low in identification with their gender group. Then, they introduced a new snack product ("Snickerdoodles") to men and women as either one that is "women's favorite snack food" or "men's favorite snack food." As Figure 4.7 illustrates,

identity or self-expression function

Attitudes can permit the expression of central values and beliefs and thereby communicate who we are.

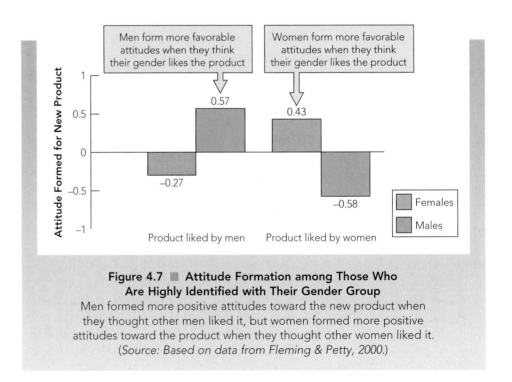

Figure 4.7 ■ Attitude Formation among Those Who Are Highly Identified with Their Gender Group
Men formed more positive attitudes toward the new product when they thought other men liked it, but women formed more positive attitudes toward the product when they thought other women liked it. (*Source: Based on data from Fleming & Petty, 2000.*)

Chapter 4 / Attitudes

among those who were highly identified with their gender group, a more favorable attitude toward this new product was formed when the message was framed in terms of their own group liking that food. In contrast, among both men and women who were low in gender group identification, no differences in attitudes toward the product were found as a function of who was said to favor the new food. By what means did the identity group information influence the formation of new attitudes among the highly identified participants? By examining the thoughts that the participants listed as they reviewed the information about the new food product, Fleming and Petty found that a greater proportion of positive thoughts were induced when the product was said to be favored by members of the participant's own gender group among those who were highly identified. Thus, the thoughts people have when they encounter a new object and form an attitude toward it can depend on people's own group membership and how important it is to them.

The Self-Esteem Function of Attitudes

A third function that attitudes often serve is a **self-esteem function.** Holding particular attitudes can help us to maintain or enhance our feelings of self-esteem or self-worth. This function is consistent with social comparison theory, which states that it can feel good to "know we are right," because our attitudes are validated by other people. For attitudes with a strong moral component, which could be derived from adherence to a set of religious or political beliefs, it can be self-validating to hold and act on those attitudes (Manstead, 2000). Indeed, a variety of emotions can be experienced as a result of expressing and acting on our attitudes. People can take pride in not cheating when they have an opportunity to do so, to the extent that their attitudes are based on moral principles. Likewise, consider the potential shame that many vegetarians might feel if they acted in a way that is inconsistent with their attitudes by eating meat. Considerable research has revealed that attitudes based on a moral conviction are good predictors of behavior. Does this mean that people never violate attitudes that they deem to be "right" based on a set of principles to which they intend to adhere? No, but violations of this sort can be more psychologically painful than attitude–behavior inconsistencies with which our moral selves are less strongly linked.

The Ego-Defensive Function of Attitudes

Attitudes also sometimes serve an **ego-defensive function** (Katz, 1960), helping people to protect themselves from unwanted information about themselves. For instance, many persons who are quite bigoted express the view that they are against prejudice and discrimination. By stating such attitudes, they protect themselves from recognizing that, in fact, they are actually highly prejudiced against members of various social groups. Indeed, because most of us want to be "cool" and accepted by others, we may claim to have more accepting or positive attitudes toward many issues (e.g., same-sex marriage, marijuana use, alcohol consumption) than we actually do—because we assume that our peers do and we want to defend our self-view as "like everyone else" (Miller & Prentice, 1996).

The Impression Motivation Function of Attitudes

Finally, attitudes also often serve an **impression motivation function.** As you may recall from our discussion of this topic in Chapter 3, we often wish to make a good impression on others, and expressing the "right" views is one way of doing so (Chaiken, Giner-Sorolla, & Chen, 1996). Research findings indicate that the extent to which attitudes serve this function can strongly affect how social information is processed. Such effects

self-esteem function
Function in which holding particular attitudes can help maintain or enhance feelings of self-worth.

ego-defensive function
Protection of ourselves from unwanted or unflattering views of ourselves by claiming particular attitudes.

impression motivation function
Attitudes can be used to lead others to have a positive view of ourselves. When motivated to do so, the attitudes we express can shift in order to create the desired impression on others.

are clearly demonstrated in a study by Nienhuis, Manstead, and Spears (2001). These researchers reasoned that when attitudes serve an impression motivation function, individuals tend to generate arguments that support their attitudes, and the stronger the motivation to impress others, the more arguments people will generate. To test this prediction, they asked Dutch college students to read a message arguing in favor of the legalization of hard drugs. Then, the participants were told that they would be asked to defend this position. To vary the level of participants' impression motivation, some were told that their performance in this role would not be evaluated (low motivation), others were told that their performance would be evaluated by one other person (the moderate motivation condition), and still others were informed that their performance would be evaluated by three other people (high motivation). After receiving this information and reading the message, participants reported their attitudes and also indicated to what extent they had generated new arguments in favor of drug legalization. As predicted, those in the high-motivation condition generated more new arguments and also reported that they would be more likely to use those arguments to convince the other person (see Figure 4.8). Thus, the attitudes we express can depend on the social context in which we find ourselves, and this situation can alter the amount of cognitive work we are willing to do (Schwarz & Bohner, 2001).

These findings indicate that the more attitudes served an impression motivation function, the more they led individuals to formulate arguments favoring the views they express. As we'll see in a later section, this, in turn, may make it more difficult to change such attitudes; after all, the persons who hold them can offer many arguments for holding those attitudes! In short, our attitudes can serve many different functions, and these can, in turn, strongly shape the impact of our attitudes on the processing of social information.

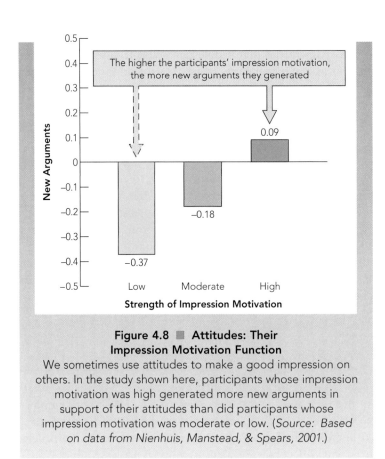

Figure 4.8 ■ Attitudes: Their Impression Motivation Function
We sometimes use attitudes to make a good impression on others. In the study shown here, participants whose impression motivation was high generated more new arguments in support of their attitudes than did participants whose impression motivation was moderate or low. (*Source: Based on data from Nienhuis, Manstead, & Spears, 2001.*)

KEY POINTS

★ Attitudes can be viewed as almost automatic reactions to the world around us. They can form rapidly as we are exposed to the attitude object and can influence basic approach or avoidance responses. Attitudes can serve several different functions.

★ Attitudes can serve a *knowledge function* and provide an interpretative framework for understanding the world.

★ Attitudes can provide a means for expressing who we are and who we are similar to, thereby serving an *identity or self-expression function*.

★ The *self-esteem function* of attitudes can be observed when we feel we are right and moral by expressing and behaving according to our attitudes.

★ Attitudes can serve an *ego-defensive function* by allowing us to defend our self-view as like others and not deviant.

★ When attitudes serve an *impression motivation function*, they guide the arguments constructed and, for this reason, may be relatively difficult to change. Attitudes can therefore allow us to manage how others perceive us.

Role of the Social Context in the Link between Attitudes and Behavior

More than seventy years ago, a classic study concerning ethnic prejudice (attitudes) and discrimination (behavior) was conducted by Richard LaPiere (1934). He wondered whether persons holding various prejudices—negative attitudes toward the members of specific social groups (see Chapter 6)—would, in fact, act on their attitudes. To find out, he spent two years traveling around the United States with a young Chinese couple. During these travels, they stopped at 184 restaurants and 66 hotels and motels. In the majority of the cases, they were treated courteously. In fact, they were refused service only once, and LaPiere reported that they received what he considered to be above-average service in most instances. After his travels were completed, LaPiere wrote to all of the businesses where he and the Chinese couple had stayed or dined and asked whether they would or would not offer service to Chinese visitors. The results were startling: Of the 128 businesses that responded, 92 percent of the restaurants and 91 percent of the hotels said "No to Chinese customers!" In short, these results seemed to indicate that there is often a sizable gap between attitudes and behavior—that is, what people say and what they actually do can be quite different.

Many people continue to expect that such social attitudes will directly predict behavior. For example, people think that those who hold bigoted attitudes will consistently behave in a prejudicial fashion, and that nonprejudiced people will not do so. However, there is a host of norms and laws that make many prejudicial actions illegal, and such actions are likely to be seen as immoral (e.g., cross burning, some forms of hate speech), so that even the most prejudicial people will not always act on their attitudes. In addition, there are social conditions under which people who do not think of themselves as prejudiced may find themselves advocating discriminatory treatment of people based on group membership. Consider some Americans' responses to Arabs or Muslims after September 11. Despite not seeing themselves as prejudiced, their exclusionary actions toward members of these groups are perceived as legitimate because of heightened safety concerns provoked by terrorism. Therefore, although it might seem reasonable to expect that attitudes toward a given ethnic group will directly predict discriminatory behavior, as you can see, the matter is considerably more complicated than that.

Many factors can alter the degree to which attitudes and behavior are related. You have probably experienced a gap between your own attitudes and behaviors on many occasions—this is because the social context can also affect our behavior. For instance, what would you say if one of your friends shows you a new possession of which he or she is proud and asks for your opinion? Would you state that you think the object is not attractive, if that is your view? Perhaps, but the chances are good that you would try to avoid hurting your friend's feelings by saying that you *like* his or her new possession, even though your actual attitude is negative. In such cases, there can be a sizable gap between our attitudes and our behavior, and we are often clearly aware of our conscious choice not to act on our "true" attitude. As this example illustrates, social contextual factors can limit the extent to which attitudes alone determine behavior. Your attitude might be a very good predictor of whether *you* would purchase that product, but the fact that your friend already has purchased the product influences what you say to your friend. For instance, if you like pepperoni pizza but dislike pizza with anchovies, which one are you most likely to order? Again, your attitude toward anchovies will affect *your* behavior. But, if you are with friends who love anchovies, will you express your hatred of these fish? Maybe not—it may be more important to avoid offending your friends than to swallow a couple of anchovies. Thus, depending on the degree to which the action is public and there are potential social consequences, attitudes will differentially predict behavior.

Because of the important role that the social context plays in determining the relationship between attitudes and behavior, recent research has focused on the factors that determine *when* attitudes influence behavior, as well as the issue of *why* such influence occurs.

When and Why Do Attitudes Influence Behavior?

Several factors determine the extent to which attitudes influence behavior. As already discussed, aspects of the situation can strongly influence the extent to which attitudes influence behavior. In addition, features of the attitudes themselves are also important. After considering these influences on the attitude–behavior relationship, we examine the question of *how* attitudes influence behavior—the underlying mechanisms involved in this process.

Situational Constraints That Affect Attitude Expression

Have you ever worried about what others would think of you if you expressed your "true" attitude toward an issue? If so, you understand the dilemma that Princeton University students experienced when studied by Miller, Monin, and Prentice (2000). The private attitudes of the students toward heavy alcohol consumption were relatively negative; however, they believed that other students' attitudes toward heavy alcohol consumption were more positive (an instance of **pluralistic ignorance,** in which we erroneously believe others have different attitudes than ourselves). When these students were placed in a discussion about this issue with other students, they expressed more comfort with campus drinking than they actually felt, and their beliefs about what others would think about them predicted their behavior in the group discussion better than their actual attitudes. Such constraints on revealing our private attitudes can occur even when we are talking with members of a group with whom we highly identify. For example, members of attitude groups that were either "pro-choice" or "pro-life" were stud-

pluralistic ignorance
When we collectively misunderstand what attitudes others hold, and believe erroneously that others have different attitudes than ourselves.

ied. In both groups, respondents were reluctant to publicly reveal the ambivalence they actually felt about their political position for fear that members of their own group would see them as disloyal. Thus, important forms of situational constraints of this sort can moderate the relationship between attitudes and behavior, and prevent attitudes from being expressed in overt behavior (Fazio & Roskos-Ewoldsen, 1994; Olson & Maio, 2003).

Strength of Attitudes

Consider the following situation: A large timber company signs a contract with the government that allows the company to cut trees in a national forest. Some of the trees scheduled to become backyard fences are ancient giants, hundreds of feet tall. A group of conservationists objects strongly to the cutting of these magnificent trees and quickly moves to block this action. They join hands and form a human ring around each of the largest trees, thus preventing the loggers from cutting them down. Indeed, such tactics can often work: Because so much negative publicity results, the contract is revoked and the trees are saved, at least temporarily.

Why might people take such drastic and potentially risky action (i.e., the blocking of logging activity)? The answer is clear: Such persons are passionately committed to saving old-growth trees. In other words, the activists hold very strong attitudes, which are important determinants of their behavior. Such events are far from rare. For example, residents of my (Nyla Branscombe) city have repeatedly and successfully prevented construction of a large mall that would drain business from the downtown area and ultimately leave it an empty shell, as has happened in many U.S. towns and cities. A dedicated few, and the possibility of very negative publicity against government or business policies, can result in political actions that are consistent with such activists' attitudes. Such incidents call attention to the fact that whether attitudes predict sustained behavior depends strongly on the strength of the attitudes. Let's consider why attitude strength has this effect.

The term *strength* captures the *extremity* or intensity of an attitude (how strong the emotional reaction provoked by the attitude object is), as well as the extent to which the attitude is based on *personal experience* with the attitude object. Both of these affect **attitude accessibility** (how easily the attitude comes to mind in various situations; Fazio, Ledbetter, & Towles-Schwen, 2000). As Figure 4.9 illustrates, research findings indicate that all of these components are interrelated, and each plays a role in attitude strength (Petty & Krosnick, 1995).

attitude accessibility
The ease with which specific attitudes can be remembered and brought into consciousness.

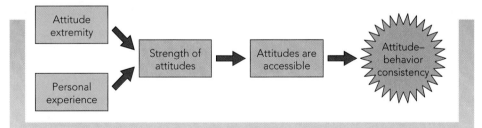

Figure 4.9 ■ How Attitude Strength Influences Attitude–Behavior Consistency
Attitudes that are formed on the basis of personal experience with the attitude object and extremity of the attitude combine to determine attitude strength. Strong attitudes are more likely to be accessible when a behavioral response is made, which results in greater attitude–behavior consistency than when attitudes are weak. (*Source: Based on suggestions by Petty & Krosnick, 1995.*)

Attitude Extremity

Let's consider first attitude *extremity*—the extent to which an individual feels strongly about an issue (Krosnick, 1988). One of the key determinants of this attitude is what social psychologists term *vested interest*—the extent to which the attitude is relevant to the concerns of the individual who holds it, which typically amounts to whether the object or issue might have important consequences for this person. The results of many studies indicate that the greater such vested interest, the stronger the impact of the attitude on behavior (Crano, 1995). For example, when students at a large university were telephoned and asked if they would participate in a campaign *against* increasing the legal age for drinking alcohol from eighteen to twenty-one, their responses depended on whether they would be affected by the policy change (Sivacek & Crano, 1982). Students who would be affected by this new law—those younger than twenty-one—had a stronger vested interest in this issue than those who would not be affected by the law because they were already twenty-one or would reach this age before the law took effect. Thus, it was predicted that those in the first group—whose vested interests were at stake—would be much more likely to join a rally against the proposed policy change than would those in the second group. This is exactly what happened: While more than 47 percent of those with high vested interest agreed to take part in the campaign, only 12 percent of those in the low vested interest group did so.

Not only do people with a vested interest behave in a way that supports their cause; they also are likely to elaborate on arguments that favor their position. By doing so, attitude-consistent thoughts come to mind when an issue is made salient. For example, Haugtvedt and Wegener (1994) found that when participants were asked to consider a nuclear power plant being built in their own state (high personal relevance), they developed more counterarguments against the plan than when the power plant might be built in a distant state (low personal relevance). Thus, attitudes based on vested interest are more likely to be thought about carefully, be resistant to change, and be an accessible guide for behavior.

Role of Personal Experience

Depending on how attitudes are formed initially, the link between attitudes and behavior can differ. Considerable evidence indicates that attitudes formed on the basis of direct experience with the object about which we hold a particular attitude can exert stronger effects on behavior than ones formed indirectly. This happens because attitudes formed on the basis of direct experience are easier to bring to mind when in the presence of the attitude object, which increases the likelihood that they will influence behavior (Tormala, Petty, & Brunol, 2002). Similarly, attitudes based on personal relevance are more likely to be elaborated in terms of supporting arguments, which makes them resistant to change (Wegener et al., 2004). Consider the difference between having a friend tell you that a particular car model, Brand X, is a lemon versus having experienced several failures with this brand yourself. When looking at new models of Brand X, would your friend's opinion even come to mind? Maybe not. Would your own experiences come to mind? Probably. Thus, when you have direct experience with an attitude object, it is likely to be quite personally relevant, and your attitude toward it is likely to predict your behavior toward it in the future.

In summary, existing evidence suggests that attitudes really *do* affect behavior (Petty & Krosnick, 1995). However, the strength of this link is strongly determined by a number of different factors. First of all, situational constraints may not permit us to overtly express our attitudes. Second, the strength of an attitude, which is a function of whether we have a vested interest in the issue or personal experience with it, can affect the accessibility of the attitude. Attitudes that are more accessible when we are selecting a behavioral response are more likely to determine behavior, compared with those that are not accessible.

KEY POINTS

★ Attitudes toward a group or object will not always directly predict behavior. Rather, there are situational constraints that affect our willingness to express our true attitudes. Not wanting to offend others and concerns about what others may think of us are important factors that can limit the extent to which attitudes and behavior are linked. We also often show *pluralistic ignorance* and erroneously believe others have attitudes that are different than those we hold, and this can limit the extent to which we express our attitudes in public.

★ Strong attitudes are more likely to be accessible at the time we take action, and for this reason, they are particularly likely to influence behavior. Strong attitudes are most likely when they are based on extreme beliefs and personal experience with the attitude object.

★ Extreme attitudes are ones to which we are committed and have elaborate arguments to support them. These attitudes often predict behavior.

★ People whose attitudes are formed via direct and personal experience with an attitude object are likely to have their attitudes come to mind and thereby affect their behavior.

How Do Attitudes Guide Behavior?

When it comes to the question of *how* attitudes guide behavior, it should come as no surprise that researchers have found that there are several basic mechanisms through which attitudes shape behavior. We first consider behaviors that are driven by attitudes based on reasoned thought, and then we examine the role of attitudes in more spontaneous behavioral responses.

Attitudes Based on Reasoned Thought

In some situations, we give careful, deliberate thought to our attitudes and their implications for our behavior. Insight into the nature of this process is provided by the **theory of reasoned action,** a theory developed further and later known as the **theory of planned behavior,** first proposed by Icek Ajzen and Martin Fishbein in 1980. The theory of reasoned action begins with the notion that the decision to engage in a particular behavior is the result of a rational process. Various behavioral options are considered, the consequences or outcomes of each are evaluated, and a decision is reached to act or not act. That decision is then reflected in *behavioral intentions*, which are often strong predictors of how we act in a given situation (Ajzen, 1987). According to the theory of planned behavior, intentions are determined by two factors: *attitudes toward a behavior*—people's positive or negative evaluations of performing the

theory of reasoned action
A theory suggesting that the decision to engage in a particular behavior is the result of a rational process in which behavioral options are considered, consequences or outcomes of each are evaluated, and a decision is reached to act or not to act. That decision is then reflected in behavioral intentions, which strongly influence overt behavior.

theory of planned behavior
An extension of the *theory of reasoned action,* suggesting that in addition to attitudes toward a given behavior and subjective norms about it, individuals also consider their ability to perform the behavior.

behavior (whether they think it will yield positive or negative consequences)—and *subjective norms*—people's perceptions of whether others will approve or disapprove of this behavior. A third factor, *perceived behavioral control*—people's appraisals of their ability to perform the behavior—was subsequently added (Ajzen, 1991). A specific example helps to illustrate the nature of these ideas.

Suppose a student is considering getting a body piercing—for instance, a nose ornament. Will she actually go to the shop and take this action? First, the answer depends on her intentions, which are strongly influenced by her attitude toward body piercing. Her decision, though, also is based on perceived norms and the extent to which she has control over the decision. If the student believes that a body piercing will be relatively painless and will make her look fashionable (she has positive attitudes toward the behavior), and also believes that the people whose opinions she values will approve of this action (subjective norms) and that she can readily do it (she knows an expert who does body piercing), her intention to carry out this action may be quite strong. On the other hand, if she believes that getting the piercing will be painful, it might not improve her appearance, her friends will disapprove of this behavior, and she will have trouble finding an expert to do it safely, then her intentions to get the nose ornament will be weak. Of course, even the best of intentions can be thwarted by situational factors (see the cartoon in Figure 4.10 for an amusing instance of this), but, in general, intentions are an important predictor of behavior.

These two theoretical perspectives (reasoned action and planned behavior) have been applied to predicting behavior in many settings, with considerable success. Research suggests that these theories are useful for predicting whether individuals will use Ecstasy, a dangerous drug used by a growing number of people between the ages of fifteen and twenty-five. For example, Orbell et al. (2001) approached young people in various locations and asked them to complete a questionnaire designed to measure (1) their attitudes toward Ecstasy (e.g., is this drug enjoyable–unenjoyable, pleasant–unpleasant, beneficial–harmful, and so forth), (2) their intention to use it in the next two months, (3) subjective norms (whether their friends would approve of their using it), and (4) two aspects of perceived control over using this drug—whether they could obtain it and whether they could resist taking it if they had it. Two months later, the same persons were contacted and asked whether they had actually used Ecstasy. The results indicated that having a positive attitude toward Ecstasy, seeing its use as nor-

Figure 4.10 ■ Thwarting Our Best Intentions
As this cartoon illustrates, even our best intentions can be undermined. We may intend to change our behavior, in this case, to avoid cookies, but circumstances can lead us to change our intentions. (*Source:* CATHY © 1985 Cathy Guisewite. Reprinted with permission of UNIVERSAL PRESS SYNDICATE. All rights reserved.)

matively accepted by one's peer group, and perceived control over using it were all significant predictors of the intention to use this drug. Indeed, attitudes, subjective norms, and intentions were all significant predictors of actual Ecstasy use. Thus, overall, the findings were consistent with the theories of reasoned action and planned behavior, with the factors identified by those perspectives being useful for predicting which persons will or will not use this particular drug.

Attitudes and Spontaneous Behavioral Reactions

Our ability to predict behavior in situations in which people have the time and opportunity to reflect carefully on various possible actions that they might undertake is quite good. However, in many situations, people have to act quickly and their reactions are more spontaneous. Suppose another driver cuts in front of you on the highway without signaling. In such cases, attitudes seem to influence behavior in a more direct and seemingly automatic manner, with intentions playing a less important role. According to one theoretical view—Fazio's **attitude-to-behavior process model** (Fazio, 1989; Fazio & Roskos-Ewoldsen, 1994)—the process works as follows. Some event activates an attitude; that attitude, once activated, influences how we perceive the attitude object. At the same time, our knowledge about what's appropriate in a given situation (our knowledge of various social norms) is also activated (see Chapter 9). Together, the attitude and the previously stored information about what's appropriate or expected shape our definition of the event. This perception, in turn, influences our behavior. Let's consider a concrete example.

Imagine that someone does cut into your traffic lane as you are driving (see Figure 4.11). This event triggers your attitude toward people who engage in such dangerous and discourteous behavior and, at the same time, your understanding of how people are expected to behave on expressways. As a result, you perceive this behavior as nonnormative, or unexpected, which influences your definition of and your response to the event. You might think, "Who does this person think she/he is? What nerve!" or perhaps your response is more situational: "Gee, this person must be in a big hurry; or maybe she/he is a foreigner who doesn't know that you should signal before pulling in the lane in front of someone." Indeed, when norms are violated by a foreigner in a situation, local people may respond differently, depending on their interpretation of the nonnormative behavior. For example, when I (Nyla Branscombe) was living in Amsterdam while on sabbatical, I went to a local bank to conduct some business. I

Figure 4.11 ■ Spontaneous Attitude-to-Behavior Process Effects
According to the *attitude-to-behavior process* model, events trigger our attitudes and, simultaneously, our understanding of how people are expected to behave or the appropriate norms for a given situation. In this case, being cut off in traffic by another driver triggers our attitudes toward such persons and our knowledge that this action is counternormative. This interpretation, in turn, determines how we behave. Thus, attitudes are an important factor in shaping our overt behavior. (*Source: Based on Fazio, 2000.*)

immediately went and stood behind the person talking to the teller and ignored everyone else milling around the lobby area. When the teller began to serve me, to my puzzlement, one Dutch person commented loudly on the "rudeness of Americans" (my nationality apparently was obvious from my accent), while another suggested that maybe I just didn't know the norms there: While waiting, there is a queue, but everyone waiting is supposed to *know* where they are in the line, making a literal queue unnecessary). Thus, people's definition of the event shapes their behavior—in one case, the assumption made was that I knew the norms and was ignoring them, and in the other, there was an acknowledgment that precisely because I was a foreigner I might not be familiar with this odd (to me) version of a line-up. Several studies provide support for this perspective on how attitudes can influence behavior by affecting the interpretation given to the situation.

In short, attitudes affect our behavior through at least two mechanisms, and these operate under somewhat contrasting conditions. When we have time to engage in careful, reasoned thought, we can weigh all the alternatives and decide how we will act. Under the hectic conditions of everyday life, however, we often don't have time for this kind of deliberate weighing of alternatives, and often people's responses appear to be much faster than such deliberate thought processes can account for. In such cases, our attitudes seem to spontaneously shape our perceptions of various events, and thereby our immediate behavioral reactions to them (Bargh, 1997; Dovidio et al., 1996).

KEY POINTS

★ Several factors affect the strength of the relationship between attitudes and behavior; some of these relate to the situation in which the attitudes are activated, and some to aspects of the attitudes themselves.

★ Attitudes seem to influence behavior through two different mechanisms. The *theories* of *reasoned action* and *planned behavior* predicts behavior when the decision to engage in an action is consciously and deliberately assessed. When we can give careful thought to our attitudes, intentions derived from our attitudes, norms, and perceived control over the behavior all predict behavior. In situations in which we do not engage in such deliberate thought, as described in the *attitude-to-behavior process model*, attitudes influence behavior by shaping our perceptions of the situation, which, in turn, dictate our behavior.

The Fine Art of Persuasion: How Attitudes Are Changed

How many times during the past day has someone tried to change your attitude on some issue or other? If you stop and think for a moment, you may be surprised at the answer, for it is clear that each day we are bombarded with such attempts, some of which are illustrated in Figure 4.12. Billboards, television commercials, newspaper and magazine ads, the recent presidential debates, appeals from charities, pop-up ads on our

Figure 4.12 ■ Persuasion: A Part of Daily Life
Each day, we are bombarded with dozens of messages designed to change
our attitudes and our behavior. Clearly, if these messages weren't effective
some of the time, advertisers would not pay the sums they do for these
opportunities to try to persuade us to do what they promote.

computers, our friends, even university professors—the list of potential "would-be per-suaders" seems almost endless. To what extent are such attempts at **persuasion**—efforts to change our attitudes through the use of various kinds of messages—successful? And what factors determine whether they succeed or fail? Social psychologists have studied these issues for decades, and as we'll soon see, their efforts have yielded important insights into the cognitive processes that play a role in persuasion (e.g., Eagly, Wood, & Chaiken, 1996; Petty et al., 2003). Before turning to the details of such research, how-ever, we illustrate the important progress made by social psychologists in understand-ing whether a particular persuasion technique—using fear appeals—is or is not effective in the **Making Sense of Common Sense** section on page 146.

Persuasion: Communicators and Audiences

Early research efforts aimed at understanding persuasion involved the study of the fol-lowing elements: Some *source* directs some type of *message* (the *communication*) to some person or group of persons (the *audience*). Following World War II, persuasion research conducted by Hovland, Janis, and Kelley (1953) focused on these key ele-ments, asking "*Who* says *what* to *whom* with what effect?" This approach yielded a number of important findings, with the following being the most consistently obtained.

• Communicators who are *credible*—who seem to know what they are talking about or who are expert with respect to the topics or issues they are presenting—are more persuasive than nonexperts. For instance, in a famous study on this topic, Hovland and Weiss (1951) asked participants to read communications dealing with various issues (e.g., atomic submarines, the future of movie theaters—remember, this was

persuasion
Efforts to change others'
attitudes through the use
of various kinds of
messages.

Fear Appeals: Do They Really Work?

Many people believe that the best method of getting people to change their attitudes (and behavior) is to frighten them about the consequences of *not* changing. When I (Nyla Branscombe) smoked cigarettes, people assumed that simply telling me all about the dangers of smoking would scare me enough to quit. People's assumption seemed to be that I'd be persuaded by their arguments, be frightened of the likely

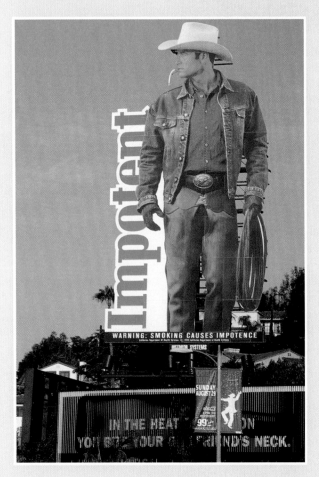

WARNING: SMOKING CAUSES IMPOTENCE

consequences of not changing, and then "just say no!" Governments appear to think this method will be effective as well. In Canada, for example, all tobacco products carry very large warnings of the sort, "Smoking KILLS," as shown in Figure 4.13. Indeed, Canada spends millions of dollars creating fear-based commercials showing diseased lungs and other grotesque long-term consequences of smoking. Social psychologists have conducted much research addressing the question of whether fear appeals effectively change attitudes, and they have come up with some surprising answers about how ineffective such fear appeals can be if used under the wrong circumstances.

Common sense would seem to suggest that if fear appeals present compelling arguments that frighten us with the reality of what will happen if we don't change, they should be effective at inducing change. The matter is more complicated than this, however. If the message is so fear arousing that people genuinely feel threatened, then they are likely to react defensively and argue against the threat, or else dismiss its applicability to the self (Liberman & Chaiken, 1992; Taylor & Shepperd, 1998). In this case, people are likely to say to themselves, "The evidence isn't that strong," "I'll quit before those consequences occur," or "It just won't happen to me," all of which can undermine the effectiveness of truly frightening messages. Indeed, smokers attending the funerals of their loved ones who died of lung cancer—and who are presumably feeling considerable fear—can be heard to utter just these sorts of defensive responses as they light up.

Might inducing more moderate levels of fear work better? There is some evidence that this is the case, but only when it is paired with specific information about how to reduce the fear and methods of behavioral change

Figure 4.13 ■ **Attempting to Frighten Us into Change**
Many grotesque and frightening images have been used in an attempt to scare people into changing their attitudes and behavior. Research indicates that this approach can be surprisingly ineffective because people have a variety of defenses they can use that then allow them to dismiss the message.

back in 1950!). The supposed source of these messages was varied so as to be high or low in credibility. For instance, for atomic submarines, a highly credible source was the famous scientist Robert J. Oppenheimer, while the low-credibility source was *Pravda*, the newspaper of the Communist party in the Soviet Union (notice, though, that the credible source was an ingroup member for Americans, but the low

that allow the negative consequences to be avoided (Petty & Krosnick, 1995). After all, if people do not know how to change, do not know where to get help to do so, do not know it will be a long process, or do not believe they can succeed in doing so (see Chapter 5 for research on the importance of feelings of self-efficacy), then fear will do little except induce avoidance and defensive responses.

Might health messages of various sorts be more effective if they were framed in a positive manner (e.g., how to attain good health) rather than in a negative manner (e.g., risks and the undesirable consequences that can follow from a particular behavior)? For example, any health message can be framed positively as "Do this and you will feel better" (e.g., "Having an annual mammogram may allow you to live a long life"). Negative framings for the same messages might be "If you don't do this behavior, you may become ill" (e.g., "Not getting a mammogram may shorten your life"). The point is that the same health information can be framed either positively—in terms of potential benefits of taking a particular action—or negatively—in terms of the consequences that can ensue if you don't

take that action. Broemer (2004) has provided evidence that when health messages are framed positively and when it is relatively easy to imagine ourselves having the rather serious symptoms described (so that fear is experienced), more change occurs than when health messages are framed negatively. In contrast, when it is easy to imagine experiencing only trivial symptoms (so that less fear is elicited), more attitude change was observed when the message was framed negatively than when it was framed positively. These findings are summarized in Figure 4.14.

Thus, fear appeals appear to be most effective when the symptoms of a potential illness are trivial, *not* when they are highly serious. Therefore, using them to induce change in order to prevent a serious illness, such as lung cancer, might be ineffective. In contrast, positively framed appeals seem to be most effective at inducing attitude change when the symptoms are serious. Thus, social psychological research shows how such commonsense notions of "Just scare people and they'll change" may be misleading. Indeed, positively framed messages can be even more effective when they concern serious health warnings.

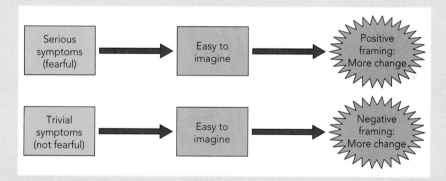

Figure 4.14 ■ Effectiveness of Positively versus Negatively Framed Health Messages
When serious symptoms that could occur because of one's own health-related behavior are easy to imagine, a positively framed message is most effective at inducing change. When, however, trivial symptoms are easy to imagine because of one's own health-related behavior, a negatively framed message is most effective at inducing change. (*Source: Based on data from Broemer, 2004.*)

credible source was an outgroup source). Participants expressed their attitudes toward these issues a week before the experiment and then immediately after receiving the communications. Those who were told that the source of the messages they read was a highly credible ingroup member showed significantly greater attitude change than those who thought the message was from the outgroup member, who lacked credibility for these participants. So, as the cartoon in Figure 4.15 suggests, source credibility is indeed an important factor in persuasion, and members of our own group are typically seen as more credible and produce greater influence than do those with whom we do not share a group membership (Turner, 1991).

• Communicators who are attractive in some way (e.g., physically) are more persuasive than communicators who are not attractive (Hovland & Weiss, 1951). This is one reason why advertisements often include attractive models. Frequently, advertisers are attempting to suggest to us that if we use their product, we, too, will be perceived as attractive, like the model shown in Figure 4.16.

• Messages that do not appear to be designed to change our attitudes are often more successful than those that seem to be designed to achieve this goal (Walster & Festinger, 1962). Indeed, a recent meta-analysis of research concerning forewarning that a message will be aimed at changing our attitudes has revealed that such forewarning does typically lessen the extent to which attitude change occurs (Benoit, 1998). So, simply knowing that a sales pitch is coming your way helps you to resist it.

• People are sometimes more susceptible to persuasion when they are distracted by an extraneous event than when they are paying full attention to what is being said (Allyn & Festinger, 1961). This is one reason why political candidates often arrange for spontaneous demonstrations or large crowds during their speeches. The distraction generated among audience members may enhance acceptance of the speaker's message. As you'll see later in this chapter, research in the elaboration–likelihood tradition has demonstrated how distraction can enhance persuasion by preventing systematic processing of the message content.

• When an audience holds attitudes contrary to those of a would-be persuader, it is often more effective for the communicator to adopt a *two-sided approach,* in which both sides of the argument are presented rather than a *one-sided approach* that discusses exclusively only one side. This is the case, especially when, within the message, arguments are included that refute the side of which the speaker is not in favor (Crowley & Hoyer, 1994). Well-educated listeners in particular are more likely to be persuaded by such two-sided messages (Faison, 1961). With a two-sided approach, we can feel that we've heard both sides of the argument but that the evidence more strongly supports the position being advocated by the communicator.

• People who speak rapidly are often more persuasive than persons who speak more slowly (Miller et al., 1976). Presumably, this works by influencing the perceived credibility of the communicator.

• People who exhibit greater confidence in what they are saying, regardless of its validity, are often more persuasive than those who appear to be less confident.

• Across the life span, people differ in the extent to which they are likely to be persuaded by a communicator. Specifically, young people (between

"A word to the wise, Benton, Don't squander your credibility."

Figure 4.15 ■ **Credibility: An Important Factor in Persuasion**
Research findings suggest that the character in this cartoon is correct: Credibility—the extent to which persons trying to change our attitudes are viewed as believable—is indeed an important factor in persuasion. (*Source: © The New Yorker Collection 1974 Lee Lorenz from cartoonbank.com. All Rights Reserved.*)

Chapter 4 / Attitudes

Figure 4.16 ■ **Role of Attractiveness of Communicator in Persuasion**
It is no accident that advertisers attempt to pair their product (everything from autos to beer) with an attractive woman (particularly when their target market is young men). The assumption is that the attractiveness of the model will be linked with the product.

the ages of eighteen and twenty-five) are especially likely to be influenced, whereas older people are more resistant to changing their attitudes (Sears, 1986).

Early research on persuasion provided important insights into the factors that influence persuasion. What such work *didn't* do, however, was offer a comprehensive account of *how* persuasion occurs. For instance, why, precisely, are highly credible or attractive communicators more effective in changing attitudes than are less credible or less attractive ones? Why does distraction increase attitude change? Why are fast speakers more effective in changing attitudes than are slower ones? In recent years, social psychologists have recognized that to answer such questions, it is necessary to carefully examine the cognitive factors and processes that underlie persuasion—in other words, what goes on in people's minds while they listen to a persuasive message and why they are influenced or not influenced by it. It is to this highly sophisticated work that we turn next.

The Cognitive Processes Underlying Persuasion

What happens when you are exposed to a persuasive message—for instance, when you watch a television commercial or listen to a political speech? Your first answer might be something like "I think about what's being said," and in a sense, that's correct. But as we saw in Chapter 3, social psychologists know that, in general, we often do the least amount of cognitive work that we can in a given situation. Indeed, people may *want* to avoid listening to such commercial messages—and thanks to VCRs, DVDs and TiVo, people can tape a program and skip the commercials entirely! But when you are subjected to a message, the central issue—the one that seems to provide the key to understanding the entire process of persuasion—is really "How do we process (absorb, interpret, evaluate) the information contained in such messages?" The answer that has emerged from hundreds of separate studies is that, basically, we process persuasive messages in two distinct ways.

■ Systematic versus Heuristic Processing

The first type of processing we can use is known as **systematic processing** or the **central route to persuasion,** and it involves careful consideration of message content and the ideas it contains. Such processing requires effort, and it absorbs much of our information-processing capacity. The second approach, known as **heuristic processing,** or the **peripheral route to persuasion,** involves the use of simple rules of thumb or mental shortcuts, such as the belief that "experts' statements can be trusted," or the idea that "if it makes me feel good, I'm in favor of it." This kind of processing requires less effort and allows us to react to persuasive messages in an automatic manner. It occurs in response to cues in the message or situation that evoke various mental shortcuts (e.g., beautiful models evoke the "What's beautiful is good and worth listening to" heuristic).

systematic processing
Processing of information in a persuasive message that involves careful consideration of message content and ideas.

central route (to persuasion)
Attitude change resulting from systematic processing of information presented in persuasive messages.

heuristic processing
Processing of information in a persuasive message that involves the use of simple rules of thumb or mental shortcuts.

peripheral route (to persuasion)
Attitude change that occurs in response to peripheral persuasion cues, often based on information concerning the expertise or status of would-be persuaders.

elaboration–likelihood model (of persuasion)
A theory suggesting that persuasion can occur in either of two distinct ways—systematic versus heuristic processing, which differ in the amount of cognitive effort or elaboration they require.

When do we engage in each of these two distinct modes of thought? Modern theories of persuasion such as the **elaboration–likelihood model** (ELM for short; e.g., Petty & Cacioppo, 1986; Petty, Wheeler, & Tormala, 2004) and the heuristic–systematic model (e.g., Chaiken, Liberman, & Eagly, 1989; Eagly & Chaiken, 1998) provide the following answer. We engage in the most effortful and systematic processing when our motivation and capacity to process information relating to the persuasive message is high. This type of processing occurs if we have a lot of knowledge about the topic, we have a lot of time to engage in careful thought, or the issue is sufficiently important to us and we believe it is essential to form an accurate view (Maheswaran & Chaiken, 1991; Petty & Cacioppo, 1990). In contrast, we engage in the type of processing that requires less effort (heuristic processing) when we lack the ability or capacity to process more carefully (we must make up our minds very quickly, or we have little knowledge about the issue) or when our motivation to perform such cognitive work is low (the issue is unimportant to us or has little potential effect on us). Advertisers, politicians, salespersons, and others wishing to change our attitudes prefer to push us into the heuristic mode of processing because, for reasons we describe below, it is often easier to change our attitudes when we think in this mode than when we engage in more careful and systematic processing. (See Figure 4.17 for an overview of the ELM model.)

The discovery of these two contrasting modes of processing provided an important key to understanding the process of persuasion, because the existence of these two modes of thought helps us to solve several intriguing puzzles. For instance, when persuasive messages are not interesting or relevant to individuals, the degree of persuasion they produce is *not* strongly influenced by the strength of the arguments these messages contain. When such messages are highly relevant to individuals, however, they are much more successful in inducing persuasion when the arguments they contain *are* strong and convincing. Can you see why this so? According to modern theories, such

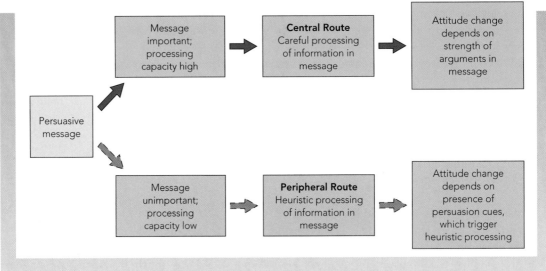

Figure 4.17 ■ The ELM Model: A Cognitive Theory of Persuasion
According to the *elaboration–likelihood* model (ELM), persuasion can occur in one of two ways. First, we can be persuaded by carefully and systematically processing the information contained in the persuasive messages (the central route), or second, through less systematic processing based on heuristics or mental shortcuts. Systematic processing occurs when the message is important to us and we have the cognitive resources available to think about it carefully. Heuristic processing is most likely when the message is not important to us or we do not have the cognitive resources (or time) to engage in careful thought. (*Source: Based on suggestions by Petty & Cacioppo, 1986.*)

as the ELM and the heuristic–systematic model, when relevance is low, individuals tend to process messages through the heuristic mode by means of cognitive shortcuts. Thus, argument strength has little impact on them. In contrast, when relevance is high, they process persuasive messages more systematically, and in this mode, argument strength *is* important (e.g., Petty & Cacioppo, 1990).

Similarly, the systematic versus heuristic distinction helps explain why people are more easily persuaded when they are somewhat distracted than when they are not. Under these conditions, the capacity to process the information in a persuasive message is limited, so people adopt the heuristic mode of thought. If the message contains the "right" cues that will induce heuristic processing (e.g., communicators who are attractive or seemingly expert), persuasion may occur because people respond to these cues and *not* to the arguments being presented. In summary, the modern cognitive approach does seem to provide a crucial key to understanding many aspects of persuasion.

KEY POINTS

★ Early research on *persuasion*—efforts to change attitudes through the use of messages—focused primarily on characteristics of the communicator (e.g., expertise, attractiveness), message (e.g., one-sided versus two-sided), and audience.

★ Modern theories of persuasion include the *elaboration–likelihood model (ELM)* and the *heuristic–systematic model*. Research based on these models has sought to understand the cognitive processes that play a role in persuasion. This work has illuminated how we process persuasive messages in two distinct ways: through *systematic processing* or the *central route to persuasion*, which involves careful attention to message content, or through *heuristic processing* or the *peripheral route to persuasion*, which involves the use of mental shortcuts (e.g., "Experts are usually right"). Argument strength therefore only affects persuasion when more systematic processing is engaged, whereas peripheral cues, such as features of the communicator, only affect persuasion when more heuristic processing occurs.

Resisting Persuasion Attempts

Based on the studies we are discussing, it should be clear that we tend to be highly resistant to persuasive messages. This raises an intriguing question: Why are we sometimes such a "tough sell" where efforts to change our attitudes are concerned? The answer involves several factors that, together, enhance our ability to resist even highly skilled efforts at persuasion.

Reactance: Protecting Our Personal Freedom

Have you ever experienced someone who increasingly mounts pressure on you to get you to change your attitude on some issue? As they do, you may experience a growing level of annoyance and resentment. The final outcome: Not only do you resist, you may actually lean over backward to adopt views that are *opposite* to those the would-be persuader wants you to adopt. Such behavior is an example of what social psychologists call **reactance**—a negative reaction to efforts by others to reduce our freedom by getting us to do what *they* want us to believe or do what they want. Research indicates that, in such situations, we often change our attitudes and behavior in the opposite direction of what we are being urged to believe or to do. This effect is known as *negative attitude change* (Brehm, 1966; Rhodewalt & Davison, 1983). Indeed, when we are feeling reactance, strong arguments in favor of attitude change can produce greater opposition to the advocated attitude position than when moderate or weak arguments are presented (Fuegen & Brehm, 2004).

The existence of reactance is one reason why hard-sell attempts at persuasion often fail. When individuals perceive such appeals as direct threats to their personal freedom (or their image of being independent persons), they are strongly motivated to resist. For example, some people grow up in homes in which it is expected that they will become a member of a particular occupational or religious group. Reactance can be experienced, though, from such pressure, which can then virtually assure that the individual's family or other would-be persuaders will fail in their mission.

Forewarning: Prior Knowledge of Persuasive Intent

When we watch television, we fully expect there to be commercials, and we know full well that these messages are designed to persuade us to purchase various products. Similarly, we know that when we listen to a political speech, the person delivering it is attempting to persuade us to vote for him or her. Does the fact that we know in advance about the persuasive intent behind such messages help us resist them? Research on the effects of such advance knowledge—known as **forewarning**—indicates that it does (e.g., Cialdini & Petty, 1979; Johnson, 1994). When we know that a speech, taped message, or written appeal is designed to alter our views, we are often less likely to be affected by it than when we do not possess such knowledge. Why is this the case? Because forewarning influences several cognitive processes that play an important role in persuasion.

First, forewarning provides us with more opportunity to formulate *counterarguments*—those that refute the message—and that can lessen the message's impact. In addition, forewarning provides us with more time in which to recall relevant facts and information that may prove useful in refuting a persuasive message. Those who want to persuade others and who want to counter the effects of forewarning should try distracting individuals between the time of the warning and receipt of the message; this tactic can prevent participants from counterarguing. In fact, those who have been forewarned, when distracted, are no more likely to resist the message than those who were not forewarned of the upcoming persuasive appeal. Wood and Quinn (2003) found that forewarning was generally effective at increasing resistance, and that simply *expecting* to receive a persuasive message (without actually receiving it) can influence attitudes in a resistant direction. The benefits of forewarning are more likely to occur with respect to attitudes we consider important (Krosnick, 1989), but they seem to occur to a smaller degree even for attitudes we view as fairly trivial. In many cases, then, it appears that to be forewarned is indeed to be forearmed where persuasion is concerned.

There are instances, though, in which forewarnings can encourage attitude shifts toward the position advocated, but this effect appears to be a temporary response to people's desire to defend their view of themselves as not gullible or easily influenced (Quinn & Wood, 2004). In this case, because people make the attitude shift before they receive the persuasive appeal, they can convince themselves that they were not in fact influenced at all! We can be assured that this effect is motivated because people are especially likely to show it when they know that the "future persuader" is an expert or

reactance
Negative reactions to threats to one's personal freedom. Reactance often increases resistance to persuasion and can even produce negative attitude change or that opposite to what was intended.

forewarning
Advance knowledge that one is about to become the target of an attempt at persuasion. Forewarning often increases resistance to the persuasion that follows.

Chapter 4 / Attitudes

will be highly persuasive. Furthermore, distraction after the forewarning was received—which presumably inhibits thought—had no effect on the extent to which attitudes were changed in the direction of the expected message. Thus, people appear to be using a simple heuristic (e.g., "This person will be an expert and I'll look stupid if I don't agree with what he/she says") and change their attitudes before even receiving the message.

Selective Avoidance of Persuasion Attempts

Still another way in which we resist attempts at persuasion is through **selective avoidance**—a tendency to direct our attention away from information that challenges our existing attitudes. As explained in Chapter 2, selective avoidance is one of the ways in which schemas guide the processing of social information, and attitudes often operate as schemas. Television viewing provides a clear illustration of the effects of selective avoidance. People do not simply sit in front of the television passively absorbing whatever the media decides to dish out. Instead, they channel surf, mute the commercials, tape their favorite programs, or simply cognitively tune out when confronted with information contrary to their views. The opposite effect occurs as well. When we encounter information that *supports* our views, we tend to give it our full attention. Such tendencies to ignore or avoid information that contradicts our attitudes while actively seeking information consistent with them constitute two sides of what social psychologists term *selective exposure*. Such selectivity in what we make the focus of our attention helps ensure that our attitudes remain largely intact for long periods of time.

Actively Defending Our Attitudes: Counterarguing against the Competition

Ignoring or screening out information incongruent with our current views is certainly one way of resisting persuasion. But growing evidence suggests that, in addition to this kind of passive defense of our attitudes, we also use a more active strategy as well: We actively counterargue against views that are contrary to our own (e.g., Eagly et al., 1999). Doing so makes the opposing views more memorable than they would be otherwise, but it reduces their impact on our attitudes. Eagly and her colleagues have reported clear evidence for such effects (2000).

These researchers exposed students previously identified as either for (pro-choice) or against (pro-life) abortion to persuasive messages delivered by a female communicator; the messages were either consistent with the participants' attitudes or were contrary to these views. After hearing the messages, participants reported their attitudes toward abortion, indicated how sure they were of their views (a measure of attitude strength), and listed all the arguments in the message they could recall (a measure of memory). In addition, they listed the thoughts they had while listening to the message; this provided information on the extent to which they counterargued internally against the message when it was contrary to their own views.

As expected, the results indicated that the counterattitudinal message and the proattitudinal message were equally memorable. However, participants reported thinking more systematically about the counterattitudinal message, and reported having more oppositional thoughts about it—a clear sign that they were indeed counterarguing against this message. In contrast, they reported more supportive thoughts in response to the proattitudinal message (see Figure 4.18 on page 154). Therefore, one reason we are so good at resisting persuasion is that we not only ignore information that is inconsistent with our current views, but also carefully process counterattitudinal input

selective avoidance
A tendency to direct attention away from information that challenges existing attitudes. Such avoidance increases resistance to persuasion.

Resisting Persuasion Attempts   153

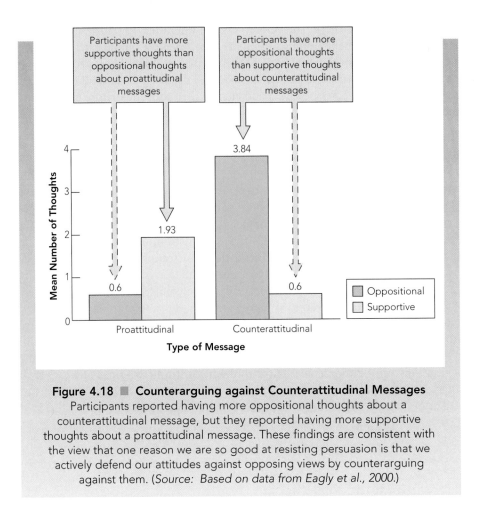

Figure 4.18 ■ Counterarguing against Counterattitudinal Messages
Participants reported having more oppositional thoughts about a counterattitudinal message, but they reported having more supportive thoughts about a proattitudinal message. These findings are consistent with the view that one reason we are so good at resisting persuasion is that we actively defend our attitudes against opposing views by counterarguing against them. (*Source: Based on data from Eagly et al., 2000.*)

and argue actively against it. In a sense, we provide our own strong defense against efforts to change our attitudes.

Inoculation against "Bad Ideas"

The idea that resistance to persuasion stems, at least in part, from generating arguments against the views presented in persuasive messages is far from new. In fact, more than forty years ago, William McGuire (1961) suggested that people could be inoculated against persuasion if they were first presented with views that opposed their own, along with arguments that refuted these counterattitudinal positions. He reasoned that when people were presented with counterarguments against the opposing view, they would be stimulated to generate additional counterarguments of their own, and this would make them more resistant to attitude change.

To test this prediction, he conducted several studies (e.g., McGuire & Papageorgis, 1961) in which individuals received attitude statements (e.g., truisms such as "Everyone should brush his or her teeth after every meal") along with one of two sets of arguments. One set of arguments supported this truism (the *supportive defense* condition), and the other set of arguments refuted the truism (the *refutational defense* condition). Two days later, participants received additional messages that attacked the original truisms with new arguments. Finally, participants were asked to report their attitudes toward these views. As predicted, the refutational defense was more effective in preventing persuasion. In other words, exposure to arguments opposed to our attitudes can serve to strengthen the views we already hold, making us more resistant to subsequent efforts to change them. In a sense, we can be inoculated against ideas that are contrary to our own! (Please see the **Ideas to Take with You—and Use!** section at the end of this chapter for advice on how to resist persuasion.)

KEY POINTS

★ Several factors contribute to our ability to resist persuasion. One such factor is *reactance*—negative reactions to efforts by others to reduce or limit our personal freedom, which can produce greater overall opposition to the message content.

★ Resistance to persuasion is often increased by *forewarning*—the knowledge that someone will be trying to change our attitudes—and by *selective avoidance*—the tendency to avoid exposure to information that contradicts our views.

★ In addition, when we are exposed to persuasive messages that are contrary to our existing views, we actively counterargue against the information they contain. This is a critical means by which our resistance to persuasion is increased.

★ If we receive arguments against our views along with arguments that refute these counterattitudinal positions, our resistance to subsequent persuasion attempts increases; this is known as inoculation against counterattitudinal views.

Cognitive Dissonance: What It Is and How We Reduce It

When we first introduced the questions of whether and to what extent attitudes and behavior are linked, we noted that, in many situations, there is a sizable gap between what we feel on the inside (positive or negative reactions to some object or issue) and what we show on the outside. For instance, I (Nyla Branscombe) have a neighbor who recently purchased a huge SUV. I have very strong, negative attitudes toward such giant vehicles because they get very low gas mileage, add to pollution, and block my view while driving. But when my neighbor asked how I liked her new vehicle, I hesitated and then said, "Nice, very nice," with as much enthusiasm as I could muster. She is a very good neighbor who looks after my house when I'm away, and I did not want to offend or upset her. But I certainly felt very uncomfortable when I uttered these words. Why? Because, in this situation, I was aware that my behavior was *not* consistent with my attitudes (e.g., that essentially I was lying), and this is an uncomfortable state for most of us. Social psychologists term the negative reaction I experienced **cognitive dissonance**—an unpleasant state that occurs when we notice that various attitudes we hold, or our attitudes and our behavior, are somehow inconsistent.

You have probably experienced cognitive dissonance sometimes in your everyday social life. Any time you say things you don't really believe (e.g., praise something you don't actually like just to be polite), make a difficult decision that requires you to reject an alternative you find attractive, or discover that something you've invested effort or money in is not as good as you expected, you may well experience dissonance. In all of these situations, there is a gap between your attitudes and your actions, and such gaps tend to make us quite uncomfortable. Most important from the present perspective,

cognitive dissonance
An internal state that results when individuals notice inconsistency among two or more attitudes or between their attitudes and their behavior.

cognitive dissonance can sometimes lead us to change our attitudes—to shift them so that they *are* consistent with our overt behavior. Put another way, because of cognitive dissonance and its effects, *we sometimes change our own attitudes,* even in the absence of any strong external pressure to do so. Let's take a closer look at cognitive dissonance and its intriguing implications for attitude change.

Dissonance theory begins with a very reasonable idea: People find inconsistency between their own actions and attitudes uncomfortable. In other words, when we notice that our attitudes and our behavior don't match, we are motivated to do something to reduce the dissonance. How do we accomplish this goal? In its early forms, dissonance research (Aronson, 1968; Festinger, 1957) focused on three basic mechanisms:

- First, we can change either our attitudes or our behavior so that these are more consistent with each other.

- Second, we can reduce cognitive dissonance by acquiring new information that supports our attitude or our behavior. Many persons who smoke, for instance, search for evidence suggesting that the harmful effects of this habit are minimal or occur only for very heavy smokers, or that the benefits (e.g., reduced tension, improved weight control) more than outweigh the costs (Lipkus et al., 2001).

- Third, we can decide that the inconsistency actually doesn't matter; in other words, we can engage in **trivialization**—concluding that the attitudes or behaviors in question are not important, so any inconsistency between them is of no importance (Simon, Greenberg, & Brehm, 1995).

All of these strategies can be viewed as *direct* methods of dissonance reduction: They focus on the attitude–behavior discrepancy that is causing the dissonance. Research by Steele and his colleagues (Steele & Lui, 1983; Steele, 1988) also indicates that dissonance can be reduced via *indirect* means—which means that the basic discrepancy between the attitude and behavior is left intact, but the unpleasant or negative feelings generated by dissonance can be reduced. According to this view, adoption of indirect tactics to reduce dissonance is most likely when the attitude–behavior discrepancy involves *important* attitudes or self-beliefs. Under these conditions, individuals experiencing dissonance may not focus so much on reducing the gap between their attitudes and behavior, but focus instead on other methods that will allow them to feel good about themselves despite the gap (Steele, Spencer, & Lynch, 1993). Specifically, *self-affirmation*—restoring positive self-evaluations that are threatened by the dissonance (e.g., Elliot & Devine, 1994; Tesser, Martin, & Cornell, 1996) can be accomplished by focusing on positive self-attributes—good things about oneself. For instance, when I (Nyla Branscombe) experienced dissonance as a result of saying nice things about my neighbor's giant new SUV, even though I am strongly against such vehicles, I reminded myself that I recently spoke out against SUVs at a party, and that I had a good reason for not revealing my true attitude: I wanted to make my neighbor feel good about something that was important to her, and this makes me a considerate person. Contemplating these positive aspects of myself can help to reduce the discomfort produced by my failure to act in a way that was consistent with my proenvironmental (and anti-SUV) attitudes.

In summary, dissonance can be reduced in many different ways—through indirect tactics, as well as direct strategies that are aimed at reducing the attitude–behavior discrepancy. As you'll soon see, the choice between various alternatives may be a function of what's available and the specific context in which dissonance occurs (Aronson, Cooper, & Blanton, 1995; Fried & Aronson, 1995). As the **Beyond the Headlines** section on the next page illustrates, dissonance may be experienced as we read the headlines or as we engage in discussions about public issues with members of our own family!

trivialization
A technique for reducing dissonance in which the importance of attitudes or behavior that are inconsistent with each other is cognitively reduced.

Chapter 4 / Attitudes

How TV Affects Attitudes toward Same-Sex Marriage: The *Will & Grace* Effect

Newsweek (May 24, 2004)— For Richard and Jeanine, opposing same-sex marriage was an easy call. "It's against nature, it's against society and it's against the Bible. The way we were raised, as Catholics, marriage was always between one man and one woman."

They took their children to church regularly and sent them to Catholic school. So it was a shock when their 18-year-old daughter, Diana, recently announced her support for gay marriage. Diana says her views solidified after she saw a just-married gay couple on TV.

"I just thought how sweet it was that they finally got what they wanted. Allowing them to be married is something that America is all about." Opinion polls reveal that, "Knowing someone who is openly gay or lesbian is the single biggest predictor of tolerance of same-sex

marriage." And if you don't personally know someone who's gay, you'll find plenty of gay characters and culture on TV. Seeing likable gay characters on shows like "Will & Grace" have similar effects to knowing gays in real life.

Cognitive dissonance should be very strong for those who are strongly opposed to same-sex marriage, if they find themselves liking the gay characters on TV programs such as *Will & Grace*. Massachusetts residents who oppose same-sex marriage are most likely experiencing dissonance now that their state has made it legally possible for their fellow gay and lesbian citizens to marry (as described in the opening vignette). After all, in each of these examples, two important cognitions are inconsistent with one another—positive attitudes toward gay characters as portrayed on TV and the fact that their state (or daughter!) supports same-sex marriage are inconsistent with these parents' own negative attitudes toward the issue.

Notice also how the definition of what is "normal for Americans" differs for those who support versus those who are against the issue. For supporters of same-sex marriage, it is a matter of civil rights, with everyone permitted to marry and pursue happiness as they please. For those who are against same-sex marriage, what is "normal" is framed in religious terms and what has always been, with the implication that it is therefore what ought to continue to be.

As we have already discussed, people have many ways of reducing such dissonance—for instance, they

can convince themselves that their attitudes toward TV characters is a completely different issue from legal changes with widespread ramifications, so as to minimize the inconsistency between these cognitions or trivialize the difference. Alternatively, they could work to undo the recent Massachusetts court decision, making their behavior consistent with their attitudes. Another possibility is that their attitudes may change over time as they become accustomed to attending their daughter's friends' same-sex marriage ceremonies. As a result, they will experience less dissonance. Or, to reduce the dissonance we can experience when someone important to us (sibling, child, parent, or partner) holds a very different attitude than we do, we may assume that something will come along to change the person's mind. That is, we might assume that the inconsistency between our attitude and that of an important other on a certain issue will decrease over time. However we choose to reduce dissonance, we all find strategies to help us deal with the extreme discomfort that comes with dissonance—the discrepancies between our attitudes and behaviors, or between two attitudes we hold, that can occur in our everyday social lives.

Is Dissonance Really Unpleasant?

When, without sufficient justification, we say or do things that are contrary to our true beliefs, we feel uncomfortable as a result of doing so. Until recently, however, there was little direct scientific evidence relating to this issue. That dissonance is arousing in a physiological sense was well documented (e.g., Elkin & Leippe, 1986; Losch & Cacioppo, 1990; Steele, Southwick, & Crichtlow, 1981), but there was little direct evidence that dissonance itself is unpleasant, although this is a central assumption of dissonance theory. To examine this issue, Eddie Harmon-Jones (2000) first had participants write counterattitudinal essays under conditions in which expressing views contrary to their real ones could not produce aversive consequences. That is, participants wrote essays in which they described a boring paragraph as actually interesting, and they were told to throw their essays away after writing them. Participants wrote their essays under one of two conditions: low choice (they were simply told to describe the boring paragraph as interesting) or high choice (they were told that they could describe the boring paragraph in any way they wished, but that the experimenter would really appreciate it if they wrote that the dull paragraph was interesting). Only in the high-choice condition, in which they felt responsible for what they wrote, would they be expected to experience dissonance.

After completing their essays, participants reported their attitude toward the paragraph they read, the discomfort they felt (e.g., how uneasy or bothered they were), and general negative affect (e.g., how tense, distressed, and irritable they felt) on a questionnaire. The results were as expected: Those in the high-choice condition rated the dull paragraph as more interesting than did those in the low-choice condition. More importantly, people in this condition also reported feeling more discomfort and more general negative affect than did those in the low-choice condition (see Figure 4.19). Because the essays they wrote could not have any aversive consequences, these findings suggest that the experience of dissonance indeed produces negative affect, as Festinger (1957) originally proposed.

Is Dissonance a Universal Human Experience?

According to cognitive dissonance theory, human beings dislike experiencing cognitive inconsistency. As discussed, people feel uncomfortable when they perceive their attitudes and behavior as inconsistent, and this often leads them to engage in active efforts to reduce the discomfort. As we have seen, a large body of evidence offers support for these ideas, so dissonance theory appears to be a source of important insights into several aspects of social thought. It's important to note, though, that the vast majority of studies on dissonance have been conducted in North America and Western Europe. This raises an important question: Does cognitive dissonance occur in other cultures, too? Although initial studies on this issue in Japan yielded mixed results (e.g., Takata & Hashimoto, 1973; Yoshida, 1977), more recent findings by Heine and Lehman (1997) point to the conclusion that dissonance is indeed a universal aspect of human thought. However, the factors that produce dissonance, and even its magnitude, can be influenced by cultural factors.

Consider the study conducted by Heine and Lehman (1997). These researchers reasoned that although dissonance might well occur all around the world, it may be less likely to influence attitudes in some cultures than in others. Specifically, they suggested that after making a choice between closely ranked alternatives, persons from cultures such as those in the United States and Canada would be more likely to experience post-decision dissonance than would persons from cultures in Asian countries. Why? Because

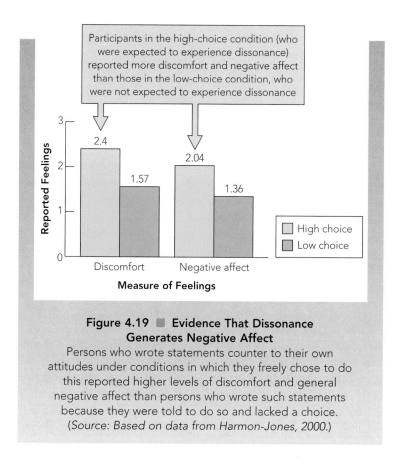

Figure 4.19 ■ **Evidence That Dissonance Generates Negative Affect**

Persons who wrote statements counter to their own attitudes under conditions in which they freely chose to do this reported higher levels of discomfort and general negative affect than persons who wrote such statements because they were told to do so and lacked a choice. (*Source: Based on data from Harmon-Jones, 2000.*)

in western cultures, the *self* is linked to individual actions, such as making correct decisions, so after making a choice between alternatives (different courses of action, different objects), individuals in western cultures can experience considerable dissonance. The possibility of having made an incorrect choice poses a threat to their self-esteem. After all, in such cultures, making correct choices as individuals is highly valued. In many Asian cultures, in contrast, the self is not as closely linked to individual actions or choices. Rather, the self is more strongly tied to roles and status—an individual's place in society and the obligations this involves. Thus, persons in such cultures should be less likely to perceive the possibility of making an incorrect decision as such a threat to their selves. If this were the case, they should also be less likely to experience dissonance.

To test this reasoning, Heine and Lehman (1997) had both Canadian students and Japanese students (who were temporarily living in Canada) choose the ten CDs from a group of forty that they would most like to own. The students also evaluated how much they would like each of these ten CDs. At this point, participants were told that they could only have *either* the CD they ranked first or the one they ranked sixth. After making their choices, participants rated these two CDs once again. Previous research suggests that to reduce dissonance, individuals who must make a decision between two options often downrate the item they did not choose, while raising their ratings of the item they did choose—an effect known as **spreading of alternatives** (Steele et al., 1993). The researchers predicted that such effects would be stronger for Canadians than for Japanese participants, and this is precisely what happened. The Canadian students showed the spreading of alternatives effect that results from dissonance reduction to a significant degree, while the Japanese students did not.

spreading of alternatives
When individuals make a decision between two options they tend to reduce the positivity of the item they did not choose and increase the positivity of the item they did choose.

These findings suggest that cultural factors indeed influence how dissonance affects people in different cultures. Although all human beings are made somewhat uneasy by inconsistencies among their attitudes or inconsistencies among their attitudes and their behavior, the intensity of such reactions, the precise conditions under which they occur, and the strategies used to reduce them may all be influenced by cultural factors.

Dissonance and Attitude Change: The Effects of Induced or Forced Compliance

As noted repeatedly, there are many occasions in everyday life when we say or do things that are inconsistent with our true attitudes. Social psychologists refer to situations such as this as involving **induced or forced compliance**—we are induced, somehow, to say or do something contrary to how we really feel. In such situations, dissonance is aroused, and when it is, we may change our attitudes so that they are more consistent with our actions. In a sense, we produce attitude change in ourselves when dissonance is experienced. We are especially likely to change our attitudes when other techniques for reducing dissonance are unavailable or require great effort.

■ Dissonance and the Less-Leads-to-More Effect

Will the reasons why you engaged in the behavior that is inconsistent with your attitudes matter? We can engage in attitude-discrepant behavior for many reasons, and some of these are more compelling than others. When will our attitudes change more: When there are "good" reasons for engaging in attitude-discrepant behavior or when there is no real justification for doing so? Cognitive dissonance theory offers an unexpected answer: Dissonance will be stronger when we have *few* reasons for engaging in attitude-discrepant behavior. When we have little justification, and therefore cannot explain away our actions to ourselves, dissonance will be most intense.

• As Figure 4.20 illustrates, cognitive dissonance theory predicts that it will be easier to change individuals' attitudes by offering them *just barely enough* to get them to engage in the attitude-discrepant behavior. This ensures that they will

induced or forced compliance

Situations in which individuals are somehow induced to say or do things inconsistent with their true attitudes.

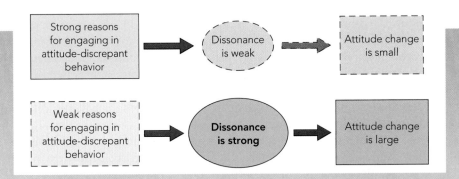

Figure 4.20 ■ Why Less (Smaller Inducements) Often Leads to More (Greater Attitude Change) after Attitude-Discrepant Behavior
When individuals have strong reasons for engaging in attitude-discrepant behavior, they experience relatively weak dissonance and weak pressure to change their attitudes. In contrast, when they have little apparent justification for engaging in the attitude-discrepant behavior, they will experience stronger dissonance and stronger pressure to change their attitudes. The result: Less justification leads to more dissonance following attitude-discrepant behavior.

feel there is little justification for their behavior; on the other hand, additional reasons or rewards would help to reduce dissonance and result in little subsequent attitude change. Social psychologists sometimes refer to this surprising prediction as the **less-leads-to-more effect**—having fewer reasons or rewards for an action often leads to greater attitude change. This effect has been confirmed in many studies (Riess & Schlenker, 1977; Leippe & Eisenstadt, 1994). Indeed, contrary to what many might think, the more money or other rewards that are offered to people for them to behave in a particular way can act as a justification for their actions, which then undermines the likelihood that attitude change will occur.

- First, the less-leads-to-more effect occurs only in situations in which people believe that they have a choice as to whether or not to perform the attitude-discrepant behavior. Strong forms of coercion undermine dissonance.

- Second, small rewards lead to greater attitude change only when people believe that they are personally responsible for both the chosen course of action and any negative effects it produces. For instance, when ordered by an authority to do a particular behavior, we may not feel either responsible for our actions or dissonance.

- And third, the less-leads-to-more effect does not occur when people view the payment they receive as a bribe rather than as a well-deserved payment for services rendered. To the extent that we believe we are being bribed, more may be required to induce the behavior.

Because such conditions often exist, the strategy of offering others just barely enough to induce them to say or do things contrary to their true attitudes can often be an effective technique for inducing attitude change.

When Dissonance Is a Tool for Beneficial Changes in Behavior

> *People who don't wear safety belts are much more likely to die in accidents than those who do. . . . People who smoke heavily are much more likely to suffer from lung cancer and heart disease than those who don't. . . . People who engage in unprotected sex are much more likely than those who engage in safe sex to contract dangerous diseases, including AIDS.*

Most of us know that these statements are true, so our attitudes are generally favorable toward using seat belts, quitting smoking, and engaging in safe sex (Carey, Morrison-Beedy, & Johnson, 1997). Yet, these attitudes are often *not* translated into overt actions: Some people continue to drive without seat belts, to smoke, and to have unprotected sex. To address these major social problems, what's needed is not so much a change in attitudes as a shift in overt behavior. Can dissonance be used to promote beneficial behavioral changes? A growing body of evidence suggests that it can (Batson, Kobrynowiez et al., 1997; Gibbons, Eggleston, & Benthin, 1997; Stone et al., 1994), especially when it is used to generate feelings of **hypocrisy**—the public advocating of some attitude and then making it salient to the person that they have acted in a way that is inconsistent with their own attitudes. Such feelings might be sufficiently intense that only actions that reduce dissonance directly, by inducing behavioral change, may be effective. These predictions concerning the possibility of dissonance-induced *behavior change* have been tested in several studies. For instance, in one interesting study, Jeff Stone and his colleagues (1997) asked participants to prepare a videotape advocating the use of condoms (safe sex) to avoid contracting AIDS. Next, participants were

less-leads-to-more effect
The fact that offering individuals small rewards for engaging in counterattitudinal behavior often produces more dissonance, and so more attitude change, than offering them larger rewards.

hypocrisy
The public advocating some attitudes or behaviors and then acting in a way that is inconsistent with these attitudes or behavior.

asked to think about reasons why they themselves hadn't used condoms in the past (*personal reasons*) or reasons why people in general sometimes fail to use condoms (*normative reasons* that didn't center on their own behavior). The researchers predicted that dissonance would be maximized in the personal reasons condition, in which participants had to come face to face with their own hypocrisy. Finally, all persons in the study were given a choice between a direct means of reducing dissonance—purchasing condoms at a reduced price—or an indirect means of reducing dissonance—making a donation to a program designed to aid homeless persons. The results indicated that when participants had been asked to focus on the reasons why they didn't engage in safe sex in the past, an overwhelming majority chose to purchase condoms, suggesting that their behavior in the future would be different—the direct route to dissonance reduction. In contrast, when asked to think about reasons why people in general didn't engage in safe sex, more participants actually chose the indirect route to dissonance reduction—a donation to the aid-the-homeless project—and didn't change their behavior (see Figure 4.21).

These findings suggest that using dissonance to make our own hypocrisy salient can be a powerful tool for changing behavior in desirable ways. For maximum effectiveness, however, such procedures must involve several elements: The persons in question must publicly advocate the desired behaviors (e.g., using condoms, wearing safety belts), must be induced to think about their own behavioral failures in the past, and must be given access to direct means for reducing their dissonance (i.e., a method for changing their behavior). When these conditions are met, dissonance can bring about beneficial changes in behavior.

Figure 4.21 ■ Using Hypocrisy to Change Behavior
When individuals are made to confront their own hypocrisy, most choose to reduce such dissonance through direct means (by changing their behavior). In contrast, when individuals are asked to think about reasons why people in general do not act according to their own beliefs, many choose to reduce dissonance and feel better about themselves via an indirect route and not change their behavior. (*Source: Based on data provided by Stone et al., 1997.*)

KEY POINTS

★ *Cognitive dissonance* is an unpleasant state that occurs when we notice discrepancies between our attitudes and our behavior. Recent findings indicate that dissonance produces negative affect and attitude change.

★ Dissonance often occurs in situations involving *induced or forced compliance,* in which we are led to say or do things that are inconsistent with our true attitudes.

★ Dissonance appears to be a universal aspect of social thought, but the conditions under which it occurs and tactics individuals choose to reduce it appear to be influenced by cultural factors. In western culture, the individual self is valued for correct decisions, but this is less so in Asian cultures. In one study, Canadians showed the *spreading of alternatives effect,* in which making a deci-

sion between two options resulted in downgrading the item not chosen and upgrading the item selected—but the Japanese did not show this effect.

★ Dissonance can lead to attitude change when we have reasons that are barely sufficient to get us to engage in attitude-discrepant behavior. Stronger reasons (or larger rewards) produce less attitude change: This is sometimes referred to as the *less-leads-to-more effect.*

★ Dissonance induced through *hypocrisy*—advocation by individuals of certain attitudes or behaviors, followed by a reminder that their own behavior has not always been consistent with these attitudes—can be a powerful tool for inducing beneficial changes in behavior.

SUMMARY AND REVIEW OF KEY POINTS

Attitude Formation: How Attitudes Develop

■ *Attitudes* are evaluations of any aspect of the social world. Often, attitudes are *ambivalent*—we evaluate the attitude object both positively and negatively.

Social Learning: Acquiring Attitudes from Others

■ Attitudes are often acquired from other persons through *social learning.* Such learning can involve *classical conditioning, instrumental conditioning,* or *observational learning.*

■ Attitudes can be formed via *subliminal conditioning,* which occurs in the absence of conscious awareness of the stimuli involved. By pairing a new attitude object with subliminally presented negative stimuli, more negative attitudes toward the new object can be formed.

■ Attitudes also are formed on the basis of *social comparison*—the tendency to compare ourselves with others to determine whether our views of social reality are or are not correct. To be similar to others we like, we accept the attitudes that they hold, to the

extent that we identify with that group.

Attitude Functions: Why We Form Attitudes in the First Place

■ Attitudes can provide an interpretative framework that allows us to easily make sense of new information (the knowledge function), they can be a means of expressing who we are (the identity function), they can make us feel superior to others (the self-esteem function) or feel that we are not deviant (the ego-defensive function), and they can allow us to manage how others perceive us (the impression motivation function).

Role of the Social Context in the Link between Attitudes and Behavior

- Depending on whether the action is public or private, attitudes can differentially predict behavior. When public, audiences can inhibit or encourage behavior that is inconsistent with our attitudes.

How Do Attitudes Guide Behavior?

- Several factors affect the strength of the relationship between attitudes and behavior; some of these relate to the situation in which the attitudes are activated, and some to aspects of the attitudes themselves.

- *Situational constraints* may prevent us from expressing our attitudes overtly. Several aspects of attitudes themselves also moderate the attitude–behavior link. These include whether we have personal experience with the attitude object and attitude extremity, both of which can make our attitudes more accessible and likely to guide our behavior.

- Attitudes seem to influence behavior through two different mechanisms. When we can give careful thought to our attitudes, intentions derived from our attitudes strongly predict behavior. In situations in which our behavior is more spontaneous and we don't engage in such deliberate thought, attitudes influence behavior by shaping our perceptions of the situation.

The Fine Art of Persuasion: How Attitudes Are Changed

- Early research on *persuasion*— efforts to change attitudes through the use of messages— focused primarily on characteristics of the communicator (e.g., expertise, attractiveness) and the message (e.g., strong versus weak arguments; one-sided versus two-sided argument presentation).

- More recent research has sought to understand the cognitive processes that play a role in persuasion. Such research suggests that we process persuasive messages in two distinct ways: through *systematic processing,* which involves careful attention to message content, or through *heuristic processing,* which involves the use of mental shortcuts (e.g., "Experts are usually right").

Resisting Persuasion Attempts

- Our attitudes tend to remain quite stable despite many efforts to change them. Several factors contribute to such *resistance to persuasion.*

- One such factor is *reactance*— negative reactions to efforts by others to reduce or limit our personal freedom. When people feel reactance, they often change their attitudes in the opposite direction from that advocated.

- Resistance to persuasion is often increased by *forewarning*—the knowledge that someone is trying to change our attitudes. This typically gives us a chance to counterargue against the expected persuasive appeal and thereby resist the message content when it is presented. We also maintain our current attitudes by *selective avoidance*— the tendency to overlook or disregard information that contradicts our views.

- If we receive arguments against our views along with arguments that refute these counterattitudinal positions, our resistance to subsequent persuasion increases; this is sometimes known as inoculation against counterattitudinal views.

Cognitive Dissonance: What It Is and How We Reduce It

- *Cognitive dissonance* is an unpleasant state that occurs when we notice discrepancies among our attitudes, or between our attitudes and our behavior. Recent findings indicate that dissonance produces negative affect.

- Dissonance often occurs in situations involving *induced* or *forced compliance*—situations in which we are induced by external factors to say or do things that are inconsistent with our true attitudes.

- In forced compliance, attitude change is maximal when we have reasons that are barely sufficient to get us to engage in attitude-discrepant behavior. Stronger reasons (or larger rewards) produce *less* attitude change—the *less-leads-to-more effect.*

- Dissonance induced by making us aware of our own *hypocrisy* can result in behavioral changes.

In this chapter, you read about . . .	In other chapters, you will find related discussions of . . .
the role of social learning in attitude formation	the role of social learning in several forms of social behavior—the self (Chapter 5), attraction (Chapter 8), helping (Chapter 10), and aggression (Chapter 11)
persuasion and resistance to persuasion	other techniques for changing attitudes and behavior and why they are effective or ineffective (Chapter 9); leadership (Chapter 12); the use of persuasive techniques in health-related messages (Module A)
cognitive dissonance	the role of cognitive dissonance in various attitudes and forms of social behavior, for example, job satisfaction (Module B)

Thinking about Connections

1. Suppose you wanted to launch a campaign to persuade adults of all ages to engage in safe sex (e.g., use condoms). What specific features would you include in this program in order to maximize its effectiveness and so improve the health of many people (see Module A)?

2. If we are so resistant to persuasion, why does advertising work? Think about heuristic processing when we are not cognitively engaged in the message presented. Provide an example of how heuristic processing can lead to persuasion and then explain why.

3. If attitudes are learned, it is reasonable to suggest that mass media (television, films, magazines) are important factors in attitude formation. What do you think the media is currently teaching children about key aspects of social behavior—love and sexual relations (Chapters 7 and 8), aggression (Chapter 11), honesty and integrity (Chapter 12)? Would you change any of this if you could? Why or why not?

Ideas to Take with You—and Use! — RESISTING PERSUASION: SOME USEFUL STEPS

Each day, we are exposed to many attempts to change our attitudes. Advertisers, politicians, and charities all seek to exert this kind of influence upon us. How can you resist such efforts, which are often highly skilled? Here are some suggestions based on the research findings of social psychology.

View Attempts at Persuasion as Assaults on Your Personal Freedom

No one likes being told what to do but, in a sense, this is precisely what advertisers and politicians are trying

to do when they attempt to change your attitudes. So, when you are on the receiving end of such appeals, remind yourself that you are in charge of your own life, and that there's no reason to listen to, or accept, what these would-be persuaders tell you.

Recognize Attempts at Persuasion When You See Them

As noted earlier, knowing that someone is trying to persuade you—being forewarned—is often useful from the point of view of resisting efforts at persuasion. So, whenever you encounter someone or some organization that seeks to influence your views, remind yourself that no matter how charming or friendly they are, persuasion is their goal. This will help you to resist.

Remind Yourself of Your Own Views and How These Differ from the Ones Being Urged upon You

While biased assimilation—the tendency to perceive views different from our own as unconvincing and unreliable—can prevent us from absorbing potentially useful information, it is also an effective means

for resisting persuasion. So when others offer views different from your own as part of a persuasive appeal, focus on how different these ideas are from your own. The rest will often take care of itself!

Actively Counterargue in Your Own Mind against the Views Being "Pushed" on You by Others

The more arguments you can generate against such views, the less likely these views are to influence you.

KEY TERMS

FOR MORE INFORMATION

Fleming, M. A., & Petty, R. E. (2000). Identity and persuasion: An elaboration likelihood approach. In D. J. Terry & M. A. Hogg (Eds.), *Attitudes, behavior, and social context* (pp. 171–199). Mahwah, NJ: Erlbaum.

• Up to date research concerning identity and persuasion is reviewed in this article. The development of new positive attitudes toward a product can depend on our perceptions concerning whether similar others hold this same attitude or not.

Broemer, P. (2004). Ease of imagination moderates reactions to differently framed health messages. *European Journal of Social Psychology, 34,* 103–119.

• This article reviews research on health message framing, including fear appeals, and shows under what circumstances such negatively framed messages are effective at inducing change as well as when more positively framed messages are most effective.

Fuegen, K., & Brehm, J. W. (2004). The intensity of affect and resistance to social influence. In E. S. Knowles & J. A. Linn (Eds.), *Resistance and persuasion* (pp. 39–63). Mahwah, NJ: Erlbaum.

• This chapter reviews research on emotion and its role in resisting persuasion. Empirical research showing that reactance can increase with reasons for not feeling as a communication advocates, which increases resistance to persuasion, is presented.

Quinn, J. M., & Wood, W. (2004). Forewarnings of influence appeals: Inducing resistance and acceptance. In E. S. Knowles & J. A. Linn (Eds.), *Resistance and persuasion* (pp. 193–213). Mahwah, NJ: Erlbaum.

• This is an excellent overview of research on forewarning and its consequences for resisting persuasion attempts. Although forewarning typically increases resistance, the conditions under which greater persuasion occurs are described.

5

THE SELF
Understanding
"Who Am I?"

When I (Nyla Branscombe) was a young girl, the American space program was big news. Family and friends would gather nightly to watch the unfolding of this riveting scientific endeavor. Like others at that time, I remember watching the lunar launches on television and Neil Armstrong's walks on the moon with great excitement. I was truly fascinated by the idea that humans could fly such distances, and that there were indeed other worlds besides the one I lived in that might be explored.

I remember distinctly the night that I announced to my father at dinner that when I grew up I wanted to be an astronaut. He smiled at me and said, "Girls *can't* be astronauts," but, perhaps to placate me, he added that I "*could* be an airline stewardess if I wanted." At the time, they seemed similar enough to me—with flying being the crucial element that had captured my imagination—so I was not too upset to learn that I could expect to be forever barred from my favorite career option because of a part of myself that I could not change. Indeed, this incident quite effectively conveyed very important information about the nature of the world here on earth and my place in it. I learned that there were positions that my gender might prevent me from occupying, and more generally, that my category membership was sufficiently important that it was likely to have a pervasive influence on the course of my life.

You might be tempted to think that this story reflects a very different time and that gender-based exclusion and discrimination is a thing of the past. And, to a certain extent, you'd be right. Legal barriers that prevented women from entering many occupations have been dismantled; there have even been female astronauts (see Figure 5.1). But, as you'll see, differential treatment based on gender is not history, although it may operate in a considerably more subtle fashion than my father's certainty that women simply were not *allowed* to be in some occupations.

People's stereotypes about what women are like have changed over time, and this has been due, in part, to the actual changes in the roles that women occupy (Diekman & Eagly, 2000). Although it may be amusing to take a look at how previous generations thought about women's work, as illustrated in "The Good Wife's Guide" in Figure 5.2

Chapter 5 / The Self

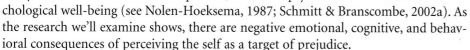

Figure 5.1 ■ Gender and Occupations: Some Women Have Become Astronauts
Gender is still an important predictor of membership in many occupations, but some vanguards have led the way!

on page 172, it would be erroneous to conclude that women no longer experience discrimination in the workplace. Nor are the consequences of being a target of discrimination as easy to accept as an eleven-year-old's perception that exclusion from one occupation is OK because any job that involves flying can be interchanged with any other. To realize that no matter what you do, your gender—which is a stable part of the self—may consistently result in undesirable consequences, can harm psychological well-being (see Nolen-Hoeksema, 1987; Schmitt & Branscombe, 2002a). As the research we'll examine shows, there are negative emotional, cognitive, and behavioral consequences of perceiving the self as a target of prejudice.

In this chapter, we examine what social psychologists have learned about the nature of the self. Some have suggested that the self is the heart of social psychology; consequently, the self has been the focus of much systematic research. Not only does how we think about ourselves influence our choices and behaviors, but it also serves as a reference point for how we perceive and interact with others. We begin by first considering whether we have just one "self" or many selves. The issue of whether one aspect of the self is more "true" or predictive of behavior than another, or if it depends on the nature of the situation in which people find themselves, is one with which we will grapple quite extensively. What does it mean to be *self-aware*, and does that influence how we evaluate ourselves and other people? Do we experience ourselves the same way all the time, or does our experience of ourselves depend on the context and the nature of the comparison it evokes? If we do categorize and think about ourselves in terms of different identities, what consequences does this have for our judgments about ourselves? Do our perceptions of ourselves depend on whether we have high or low self-esteem? Do people have methods of knowing themselves that allow them to feel positively, even when others perform better than they do in some domain? After considering these important questions, we will examine the effects of being a target of prejudice for a number of self-related processes, including the emotional, cognitive, and performance consequences that can ensue when people face rejection by others because of their group membership.

Thinking about the Self: Personal versus Social Identity

One of the most fundamental principles of the social identity perspective (Tajfel & Turner, 1986; Turner, 1985) is that individuals can perceive themselves differently depending on where they are at a particular moment in time on what is known as the **personal–social identity continuum.** The personal identity end of this continuum refers to when we think of ourselves primarily as *individuals*. The social identity end refers to when we think of ourselves as members of specific *social groups*. Because we do not experience all aspects of our self-concept simultaneously, which aspect of our identity is salient at any given moment will influence how we think about ourselves, and this, in

personal–social identity continuum

The two distinct ways that the self can be categorized. At the personal level, the self can be thought of as a unique individual, whereas at the social identity level, the self is thought of as a member of a group.

Figure 5.2 ▇ The 1945 Stereotype of a Good Woman
Looking back more than a half century, it is difficult to believe that these were the normative expectations for women. Clearly expectations of employment outside the home for married women was entirely absent, although most college-educated women in the United States today will be in the labor force for much of their adult lives. (*Source:* Housekeeping Monthly, *May 13, 1945.*)

The Good Wife's Guide
- Have dinner ready. Plan ahead, even the night before, to have a delicious meal ready, on time for his return. This is a way of letting him know that you have been thinking about him and are concerned about his needs. Most men are hungry when they come home and the prospect of a good meal (especially his favorite dish) is part of the warm welcome needed.
- Prepare yourself. Take 15 minutes to rest so you'll be refreshed when he arrives. Touch up your makeup, put a ribbon in your hair and be fresh-looking. He has just been with a lot of work-weary people.
- Clear away the clutter. Make one last trip through the main part of the house just before your husband arrives.
- Gather up schoolbooks, toys, paper, etc., and then run a dustcloth over the tables.
- Be happy to see him.
- Listen to him. You may have a dozen important things to tell him, but the moment of his arrival is not the time. Let him talk first—remember, his topics of conversation are more important than yours.
- Make him comfortable. Have him lean back in a comfortable chair or have him lie down in the bedroom. Have a cool or warm drink ready for him.
- Don't ask him questions about his actions or question his judgment or integrity. Remember, he is the master of the house and as such will always exercise his will with fairness and truthfulness. You have no right to question him.
- A good wife always knows her place.

turn, has consequences for our behavior. When we may think of ourselves as unique individuals, our personal identities are salient, and this is likely to result in self-descriptions that emphasize how we are different from other individuals. For example, you might describe yourself as fun when thinking of yourself at the personal identity level, to emphasize your self-perception as having more of this attribute than other individuals you are using as the comparative referent. Because personal identity self-description can be thought of as **intragroup** in nature—involving comparisons with other individuals who share our group membership—*which* group is the implicit referent used when describing the personal self can affect the content of self-descriptions (Oakes, Haslam, & Turner, 1994). For example, if you were asked to describe how you are different from other Americans, you might characterize yourself as particularly liberal, but if you were

intragroup comparisons
Judgments that result from comparisons between individuals who are members of the same group.

Chapter 5 / The Self

indicating how you are different from other college students you might say that you are rather conservative. If my family was the group I (Nyla Branscombe) was considering when describing myself, I might say that I'm a very patient person, even though I would not describe myself in this way if I were thinking of women, or scientists, or some other group that I belong to as the comparison. The point is that even for personal identity, the content we generate depends on some comparative reference, and this can result in different self-descriptors coming to mind, depending on the context.

At the other end of the personal–social identity continuum, we can perceive ourselves as members of a group, which means we emphasize the ways that we are similar to other group members. When we think of ourselves at the social identity level, we describe ourselves in terms of the attributes that members of our group share with each other and what differentiates "our group" from other groups. That is, descriptions of the self at the social identity level are **intergroup** in nature—they involve contrasts between groups. For example, you may think of yourself in terms of your social identity as a fraternity or sorority group member, and describe yourself as relatively athletic and self-motivated, attributes that you perceive to be shared with other members of your group, and as simultaneously differentiating your group from other fraternities or sororities that you see as being more studious and scholarly than your group perhaps. On other occasions, you might think of yourself in terms of a different social identity, that of your gender group. In that case, if you are female, you might emphasize the attributes that you share with other women (e.g., warm and caring) and that you perceive as differentiating women from men. What's important to note here is that when you think of yourself as an *individual,* the *content* of your self description is likely to differ from when you are thinking of yourself as a member of a *category* that you share with others. Of course, as these examples indicate, most of us are members of a variety of different groups (e.g., occupation, age group, sexual orientation, nationality, sports teams), but all of these will not be salient at the same time. When any particular social identity is salient, people are likely to act in ways that reflect that aspect of their self-concept. Thus, there may be a number of situational factors that will alter how we define ourselves, and the actions that stem from those differing self-definitions will also differ.

Can we say that one of these "selves" is the "true" self—either the personal self or any one of a person's potential social identities? Not really. All of these could be quite accurate portraits of the self, and accurately predict behavior, depending on the context and comparison dimension (Oakes & Reynolds, 1997). Note, too, how some ways of thinking about the self could even imply behaviors that are opposite of those that would result from other self-descriptions (e.g., fun versus scholarly).

Despite such potential variability in self-definition, most people manage to maintain a coherent image of the self, while recognizing that they may define themselves and behave differently in different situations (see Figure 5.3 for

Figure 5.3 ■ Seeing the Self as Competent Can Depend on the Context
This woman may define herself as competent in her role as executive but not so competent in her parental role (at least some days)!

an example of differing self-definitions, depending on the situation). For example, when you are at home with your parents, your self-image as a responsible adult might sometimes come into question. You might not pick up things after yourself, or you might even expect that someone else will do your laundry, and so forth. When, however, you are away at college, you perform these tasks competently and feel like a responsible adult. Despite such readily admitted pockets of irresponsibility, does that mean you will generally see yourself in this way? No, definitely not. You may maintain an image of yourself as responsible, either because the domains in which you are irresponsible are not particularly important to you, or they are not salient when you think of yourself as a college student (Patrick, Neighbors, & Knee, 2004). When people do face such mixed evidence for a valued self-perception as a function of context or audience, they can reduce the importance of competence in a given domain, or, alternatively, they can decide that only some reference groups are important for self-definition. Thus, some people may be affected by their families' perceptions of their competence, but not their professors, while others may show the reverse (Crocker & Wolfe, 2001).

Who I Am Depends on the Situation

College students' answers to the question, "Who am I?" typically consist of references to social identities (e.g., nationality, race, gender, university affiliation), interpersonal relationships (e.g., Karen's boyfriend, daughter of Howard and Rose), and a variety of personal traits such as honest or kind (Rentsch & Heffner, 1994). Indeed, people describe themselves differently, depending on whether the question being asked implies situational specificity or not. This effect was clearly illustrated in research by Mendoza-Denton and colleagues (2001). In their study, participants were given one of two different types of sentence completion tasks. When the prompt was open-ended, such as "I am a (an) . . . person," self-definition as an individual is implied. In this condition, participants' responses were primarily traitlike or global (e.g., "I am an ambitious person"). When, however, the prompt implied particular social settings, "I am a (an) . . . when . . .," the responses were more contingent on the situation considered by the participant (e.g., "I am an ambitious person when a professor provides me with a challenge").

Our tendency to see the self differentially, depending on what relationships with others we consider, and according to the context, increases with age (Byrne & Shavelson, 1996; Roccas & Brewer, 2002). We also differ across the life span in the extent to which we have multiple aspects of our self-concepts that are important to us. This has consequences for how we view the self when we experience stress. For instance, Linville (1987) found that people with more aspects of the self that are distinct (e.g., self as professional, mother, baseball fan) were less responsive to threats to any given identity (e.g., following a professional setback) than were people for whom those same identities were intertwined and not distinct. When important aspects of the self are distinct from one another—so that **self-complexity** is high—a failure in any one domain is less likely to affect how one feels about one's self overall. Indeed, those whose self-concepts are organized less complexly (have more overlap in different aspects of their self) exhibit more variability in how they feel about themselves than do those whose self-concepts are more complexly organized (aspects of the self are distinct or nonoverlapping). Stress is especially likely to be experienced by people when two important aspects of the self are perceived as in conflict with each other, creating **identity interference.** For example, Settles (2004) found that women in stereotypically masculine fields such as physics and astronomy who experienced interference between their identities as women and as scientists reported poorer well-being than did those who did not perceive their identities as in conflict.

Aspects of the self that are associated with a particular cultural tradition may be activated, depending on subtle context changes, and this can lead to different self-

self-complexity
How the self-concept is organized. For those whose self-concepts are organized complexly, important aspects of the self are distinct from one another. For those whose self-concept is low in complexity, there is greater overlap in different components of the self.

identity interference
When two important social identities are perceived as in conflict, such that acting on the basis of one identity interferes with performing well based on the other identity.

Chapter 5 / The Self

perceptions. For example, it is well known that North American culture emphasizes highly *individualistic norms* and an **independent self-concept,** whereas Asian cultures emphasize *collectivist norms* and an **interdependent self-concept** (Markus & Kitayama, 1991). Because of this cultural difference, the self-concepts of people who spend their lives in one cultural context might be expected to differ from those who spend their lives in a different cultural context. Such culture-based self-concept differences may be reflected in systematic differences in what is assumed to be "personal" tastes and preferences.

To test this idea, Kim and Markus (1999) showed Koreans and Americans abstract figures, each composed of nine different parts, and participants were asked to say which they preferred or liked better. Koreans selected more of the figures wherein the parts fit together, whereas Americans chose more of the figures for which some part of the figure was distinctive or different from the other parts. Such cultural differences in the choices people make may well reflect contrasting interdependent (e.g., fitting together with others) and independent (e.g., being distinctive or different than others) self-conceptions. However, it could also be that subtle aspects of the context simply cue one aspect of the self over another—the interdependent or independent component—because everyone is some of both. In support of the latter possibility, research with bicultural individuals (people who belong to or are fluent in two different cultures) finds that they behave differently, depending on which identity is made salient. For example, people who are experienced with both Asian and western cultural traditions, might express their "Asian-ness" in contexts that cue that aspect of the self, but express their "western-ness" in contexts that cue that aspect of the self. This notion that bicultural individuals possess both Asian and western identities, and can respond according to either, was tested with students in Hong Kong who were fluent in both Chinese and English (Trafimow et al., 1997). These students were asked to answer the question, "Who am I?" in either one language or the other. The Hong Kong students who responded to the question in English described themselves in terms of personal traits that differentiate them from others, which reflects an individualistic self-construal, while those who answered the question in Chinese described themselves in terms of group memberships that they share with others, reflecting a more interdependent self-construal. Thus, important group-based differences in the self-concept may emerge primarily when that group identity is activated, as it is when using a particular language (for those who have more than one).

Consider another example, this time involving gender, that demonstrates the importance of the social context for whether group differences in the self-concept are exhibited. A number of researchers have suggested that men and women differ in their self-concepts and, as a result, in how they respond to moral issues (Cross & Madson, 1997; Gilligan, 1988; Markus & Oyserman, 1989). Specifically, men may describe themselves as independent and autonomous and be inclined to approach moral problems according to a **justice ethic.** That is, because people believe that men tend to apply abstract universal rules when engaged in moral reasoning, they will use those same rules regardless of the context. In contrast, because women tend to describe themselves in more interdependent and connected terms, they might be expected to approach moral problems from a **care ethic.** That is, because people believe that women are concerned with the maintenance of relationships and the promotion of the welfare of others, their answers to moral dilemmas might generally reflect this orientation. Such a presumed gender difference in the self-concept and differential approach to moral issues could, however, depend on men and women defining themselves in terms of their gender for its expression. Indeed, when a different way of defining the self is salient, such gender differences could be entirely absent (Deaux & Major, 1987).

In a recent study, Ryan, David, & Reynolds (2004) illustrated the importance of how the self is categorized for the ways in which men and women describe themselves. Their study examined when gender differences in such self-descriptions are present and when they are not. In their research, when *both* men and women were first asked to focus on groups to which they belonged (i.e., they were asked to think about

independent self-concept
In individualistic cultures, the expectation is that people will develop a self-concept as separate from or independent of others. Men are expected to have an independent self-concept more so than women.

interdependent self-concept
In collectivist cultures, the expectation is that people will develop a self-concept in terms of one's connections or relationships with others. Women are expected to have an interdependent self-concept more so than men.

justice ethic
A justice and ethics orientation that emphasizes the application of universal rules regardless of one's own relationship with those individuals. Moral dilemmas are accordingly solved by using the same principle across cases.

care ethic
A justice and ethics orientation that emphasizes the maintenance of relationships. Moral dilemmas are accordingly solved by focusing on the welfare of others.

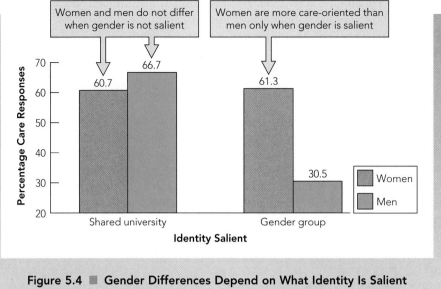

Figure 5.4 ■ Gender Differences Depend on What Identity Is Salient
When a shared identity with another in need is salient, both men
and women display care-oriented responses. However, when one's
gender group (and its differing norms) is salient, then men display fewer
care-oriented responses to the same need situation compared with women.
(*Source: Based on data from Ryan, David, & Reynolds, 2004*)

similarities between the self and others), they tended to describe themselves in terms of interdependent traits such as "dependable" and "understanding." In contrast, when *both* men and women had first focused on groups to which they did not belong (i.e., they were asked to think about differences between the self and others), they were more likely to describe themselves in terms of independent traits such as "unique" and "objective." Gender differences in self-definition *only* emerged when the participant's gender group membership was salient, but gender differences were not present in contexts such as these in which other identities were activated.

Such context shifts in self-definition have been shown to affect moral reasoning—a domain in which men and women have long been supposed to fundamentally differ. Ryan, David, and Reynolds (in press) showed that people's responses to a standard moral dilemma in which another person is in need depended on how they categorized themselves in relation to that other person. As shown in Figure 5.4, when the participant categorized the person in need as a university student and that person was therefore seen as a member of the same category as the participant, men and women were *equally* likely to display care-oriented responses toward the person in need in the dilemma. In contrast, when the participants categorized themselves in terms of their gender, then women displayed significantly more care-oriented responses than did men. In fact, men reduced their care-oriented responses to the person in need in the gender condition compared with the shared university-identity condition. Thus, both the self-concept and moral reasoning believed to stem from it appear to be flexible and context dependent. Gender differences in both the self-concept and moral reasoning depended on gender being a salient self category at the time the response was made. Nevertheless, gender is a powerful social category that is likely to be activated a great deal of the time (Fiske & Stevens, 1993). As a result, gender may be expected to influence perceptions of the self as well as responses to others with some frequency.

Chapter 5 / The Self

What determines *which* aspect of the self will be most influential at any given moment, if how we define ourselves can differ according to the context? First, one aspect of the self might be especially relevant to a particular context (e.g., thinking of ourselves as fun when at a party, but as hard working when we are in class or at work). Second, features of the context can make one aspect of the self highly distinctive, with that aspect of identity forming the basis of self-perception. For example, suppose an office is composed of only one woman among several men. The woman's gender distinguishes her from her colleagues. In such contexts, the lone woman is particularly likely to feel "like a woman" and she may be treated as representative of that group (Fuegen & Biernat, 2002; Yoder & Berendsen, 2001). Similarly, African American students at predominantly white universities and other contexts in which other minority group members are rare are likely to think of themselves in terms of their race (Pollak & Niemann, 1998; Postmes & Branscombe, 2002). Third, some people may be more ready to categorize themselves in terms of a particular personal trait (e.g., intelligence) or group identity and its associated attributes (e.g., gender) because of its importance to the self. The more a personal attribute or social identity is valued, the more self-verification on that dimension will be sought (Hogg & Turner, 1987; Swann, 1990). Fourth, other people, including how they refer to us linguistically, can cue us to think of ourselves in personal versus social identity terms. Bernd Simon (2004) has noted that aspects of the self-concept that are referred to as nouns (e.g., woman, psychologist) are particularly likely to activate social identities. Nouns suggest discrete categories, which trigger perceptions of members of those categories as sharing a fundamental nature or essence that is different than members of other categories (Lickel, Hamilton, & Sherman, 2001). In contrast, aspects of the self that are referred to with either adjectives or verbs (e.g., weak, taller, supportive) reference perceived differences between people within a category (Turner & Onorato, 1999) and are likely to elicit self-perceptions at the personal identity level.

Who I Am Depends on Others' Treatment

How others treat us, and how we believe they will treat us in the future, have important implications for how we think about ourselves. When it comes to self-perception, no person is truly an island. When we expect that others will reject us because of some aspect of ourselves, we can choose from a few different possible responses (Tajfel, 1978). To the extent that it is possible to change an aspect of the self and avoid being rejected by others, we could potentially choose to do that. In fact, we could choose to change *only* that particular feature when we anticipate being in the presence of others who will reject us because of it. In other words, for some aspects of the self, people can attempt to hide them from disapproving others. As the U.S. military policy of "Don't ask, don't tell" on homosexuality suggests, there are group memberships that we can choose to reveal or not. However, this option is practically impossible for some social identities. We can't easily hide or change our race, gender, or age. In some cases, even if we *could* alter the part of the self that brings rejection, we may rebel against those rejecting us and make that feature *even more* self-defining. That is, we may emphasize the feature we possess as a method of contrasting the self from those who reject us—in effect, by emphasizing that feature, we are publicly communicating that we value something different than those who might judge us harshly because of it.

This point was illustrated in research conducted by Jetten and colleagues (2001). These researchers studied young people who elect to get body piercings in visible parts of the body other than earlobes (e.g., navel, tongue, eyebrow), a practice that has recently gained in popularity. How we dress and alter our bodies can be conceptualized as important identity markers—ways of communicating to the world who we are. Although some identity markers may bring acceptance into peer groups, they may be perceived by other groups as weird or antinormative. Today, body piercings may be comparable to the wearing of blue jeans and men having long hair in the 1960s. These latter identity markers were the visible indicators of a "hippie" identity, a self-perception as a rebel against the establishment. Like their 1960s' counterparts, those young people at present who opt for visible body piercings appear to be engaged in a similar form of rebel identity construction. Even though they know that they are likely to be discriminated against because of their piercings, this expectation can lead them to greater self-definition in terms of a group that is actively rejecting the dominant culture's standards of beauty. Indeed, this research found that those with body piercings who were led to expect rejection from the mainstream because of their piercings identified more strongly with other people who have body piercings than did those who were led to expect acceptance from the mainstream. Such expected rejection and devaluation on the part of the culture as a whole can result in increasingly strong identification with a newly forming cultural group. As Figure 5.5 illustrates, people with body piercings seem to be creating an identity that communicates to all that "we are different from the mainstream." If, however, over time, the practice of getting body piercings ultimately becomes diffused throughout the culture, with almost everyone adopting the practice—as happened in the 1960s as everyone started wearing blue jeans—then those who are attempting to convey their collective difference from the mainstream may be compelled to become increasingly more extreme to achieve the same identity end.

This sort of identity dilemma—whether to increasingly emphasize and take pride in an identity or, in contrast, discard and distance ourselves from it—may be especially likely to be provoked when a person moves from one social context to another. Consider the dilemma experienced by Hispanic students as they leave their home environment to attend a primarily Anglo university. Social psychologists have examined the different strategies that such students can employ during their first year at college (Ethier & Deaux, 1994). Evidence has been obtained of people facing this identity dilemma using one of two strategies—movement away from the identity or increased movement toward it. Among those for whom a Hispanic identity was initially not important, when they moved to a non-Hispanic environment, they emphasized their Hispanic identity to a lesser degree. In contrast, for those who initially valued their Hispanic identity, in this new context in which they know they could be rejected based on that identity, they increased the emphasis they placed on their ethnic identity, as indicated by joining Hispanic student associations. Interestingly, it was those students who increasingly emphasized their Hispanic identity and who took pride in their differences from others in this new environment whose self-esteem was better during the transition to college. Those who chose to distance themselves from their Hispanic identity suffered reduced self-esteem when they faced rejection based on that identity.

Figure 5.5 ■ Claiming an Identity That Is "Nonmainstream"
Many forms of body adornment and body modification are visual indicators of social identity. This young woman may be conveying to the "mainstream" that she is not one of them, and that she "fits in" with other members of her peer group.

As we saw with the body piercing research, whether others devalue an identity one might hold is typically not correlated with how important that identity is to the self (Ashmore, Deaux, & McLaughlin-Volpe, 2004). That is, because people have the option of either distancing from or increasingly identifying with a group that might be devalued by some groups, the perceived standing of a group in the wider culture is not predictive of how important an identity will be for the individual. In other words, it is not solely those identities that might be widely regarded as negative that the individual must decide whether to give up the identity or strengthen it further as shifts in context are made. Consider someone who moves from a context in which royalty is a valued identity to a new poorer setting in which it might not be. That person would be faced with a similar choice about whether to retain value in and emphasize the former "blue blood" identity or distance from it.

Self-Awareness: Terror Management

Constantine Sedikides and John Skowronski (1997) argue that the first level of self to emerge in terms of our evolutionary history and during the individual's life span is **subjective self-awareness.** Such awareness allows organisms to differentiate themselves from the physical environment. Clearly, plants don't possess this quality, but most animals do share this characteristic. For example, my cat knows where his paw ends and my arm begins, as do quite young human children. A few animals (primates) also develop **objective self-awareness**—the organism's capacity to be the object of its own attention (Gallup, 1994). As shown in Figure 5.6, a chimp can inspect itself in a mirror and "know it knows" that it is seeing the self (Lewis, 1992, p. 124). Only humans, however, seem to have reached the third level of self-functioning—**symbolic self-awareness**—the ability to form an abstract representation of the self through language.

Figure 5.6 ■ Objective Self-Awareness: Recognizing the Self
Only among primates, such as the chimp shown here, does there seem to be *objective self-awareness*—the capacity to be aware of the self as an object. When a red spot is placed on the forehead of this chimp, it can only be detected in a mirror. The fact that seeing this image in the mirror leads the chimp to touch its own forehead is powerful evidence that there is some recognition that the reflected image is of the self.

subjective self-awareness
The first level of self to emerge. It is the recognition that the self is separate from other objects in one's physical environment.

objective self-awareness
The organism's capacity to be the object of its own attention—to know that it is seeing its own self in a mirror, for example.

symbolic self-awareness
The uniquely human capacity to form an abstract representation of the self through language. It also is connected with knowing that death of the physical self is inevitable.

Some social psychologists suggest that such self-awareness makes humans unique in the sense that they alone are aware of the inevitability of their own death. Such awareness of the fragility of our own existence creates the potential for **existential terror** (Greenberg, Solomon, & Pyszczynski, 1997). When our own mortality is salient, according to **terror management theory,** it has implications for how we will perceive the self in relation to others. To manage the terror that arises from the certainty that we will ultimately die, we attempt to assure ourselves that we are meeting the culture's standards of value. To the extent that we feel we are meeting the culture's criteria, we will have positive self-esteem. From this perspective, self-esteem acts as a buffer against the anxiety that stems from awareness of our own demise. Research indicates that those whose self-esteem has been temporarily increased or who are dispositionally high in self-esteem show less defensiveness when mortality is salient than those whose self-esteem has been decreased or who are dispositionally low in self-esteem (Greenberg et al., 1992).

As already illustrated in this chapter, group memberships can reflect important aspects of the self and can affect self-esteem. When a group membership has positive implications for self-esteem, people may increasingly define themselves in terms of that group membership when they are reminded of their own mortality. However, when that same group is portrayed as having negative implications for the self or might undermine self-esteem, then people may increasingly distance themselves from that social identity when their own mortality is salient. To illustrate the consequences of experiencing such existential terror for self-definition, Arndt and his colleagues (2002) made mortality salient for some women but not for others. They found that when women were reminded of their own mortality, they showed greater alignment between themselves and other women in reaction to the threat to self. These women reported perceiving themselves as most similar to other women after performing a verbal test (a dimension on which women perform well). In contrast, though, women showed less alignment and identification with women after performing a math test (a dimension on which women are easily threatened, as you'll see later in this chapter). These findings indicate that we tend to define ourselves in terms of particular social identities to the extent that they protect self-esteem, and this seems to be true when we are feeling threatened. This process is illustrated in Figure 5.7.

existential terror
Anxiety stemming from awareness that the self will inevitably die.

terror management theory
Because humans are aware of the inevitability of their own death, they confront existential terror. Terror management theory suggests ways that people attempt to deal with this threat to the self when their own mortality is salient.

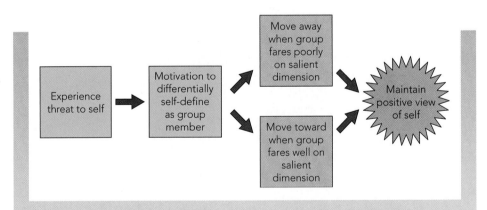

Figure 5.7 ■ Group Identification in Response to Threat
A variety of theoretical perspectives have suggested that when we experience a threat to the self, we are motivated to align ourselves with our group—to the extent that doing so will help us maintain a positive social identity. This process depends on whether the salient social identity is one that fares well on a particular dimension or not. (*Source: Based on data from Arndt et al., 2002.*)

Although we generally experience ourselves as relatively consistent over time, it is nonetheless true that people do change. Indeed, it is often gratifying to compare one's past self with the present self, for doing so will suggest that there has been improvement over time (Wilson & Ross, 2000). In fact, thinking about a future **possible self** that you may become can inspire you to forego current activities that are enjoyable but will not help, or might even hinder, bringing about this improved self (Markus & Nurius, 1986). Instead, you may invest in less immediately enjoyable activities in order to achieve the goal of becoming your desired possible self. Think about what is involved in attaining a variety of social identities. We give up years of "having fun" in order to attain the status of being a "college graduate," complete years of schooling and long internships to be able to call ourselves "doctors," and put grueling hours into law school and studying for state bar exams to become "lawyers." Lockwood and Kunda (1999) have found that *role models*—other people we wish to imitate or be like—can inspire us to invest in such long-term achievements, but, to do so, we must see the possible self that the role model represents as being potentially attainable. The image of a possible future self can influence our motivation to study harder, give up smoking, or invest in child-care and parenting classes, to the extent that we can imagine that a new and improved self will result from such changes.

People often consider new possible selves of this sort, as well as how to avoid negative and feared future possible selves, when they are making New Year's resolutions. Envisioning such self-changes can induce feelings of control and optimism, but failing to keep those resolutions is a common experience and repeated failures can lead to unhappiness (Polivy & Herman, 2000). When people feel they want to change but cannot succeed in doing so, they may be tempted to reduce this uncomfortable state of self-awareness by distracting themselves—either in mundane ways, such as getting lost in a novel, or in more damaging ways, such as consuming heavy amounts of alcohol (Baumeister, 1991). As we saw in Chapter 2, people appear to be generally *unrealistically optimistic* (Helweg-Larsen & Shepperd, 2001) in the extent to which they can achieve a host of positive outcomes (e.g., live to old age) and avoid negative outcomes (e.g., contracting a serious illness). The truth is, having confidence and efficacy in our ability to change is important for doing so, but overconfidence in our ability to do so can lead to false hope and, ultimately, disappointment. Although our ability to remake our physical selves may have limits, the photos in Figure 5.8 on page 182, like those seen on the new TV program *Extreme Make-Over,* suggest that rather dramatic changes are possible.

Successful performance in physical, academic, and job tasks is enhanced by feelings of **self-efficacy** (Courneya & McAuley, 1993; Huang, 1998; Sanna & Pusecker, 1994). It is necessary to believe that we *can* achieve a goal as a result of our own actions in order to even try (Bandura, 1997). Indeed, people high in self-efficacy in a domain tend to prefer to allocate their time and effort to tasks that *can* be solved, and they stop working on tasks that cannot be solved more quickly than those who are low in self-efficacy. A defining feature of people who are entrepreneurs (those who start new businesses) is their high levels of perceived self-efficacy (Markman, Balkin, & Baron, 2002).

When a task can be successfully accomplished only by working together with others, *collective self-efficacy* may be critical. As Figure 5.9 on page 182 illustrates, some successes critically depend on the team's performance as a whole—which is not equivalent to the self-efficacy that the individual members of the team may feel. Among basketball players, a shared belief in the collective efficacy of the team (measured at the beginning of the season) is associated with the team's overall success by the end of the season (Watson, Chemers, & Preiser, 2001). Likewise, collective self-efficacy can lead to political activism, such as persuading people to vote or joining a protest movement to bring about social change (Bandura, 2000; Simon & Klandermans, 2001).

possible selves
Images of how the self might be in the future—either "dreaded" possible selves to be avoided or "desired" potential selves that can be strived for.

self-efficacy
The belief that one can achieve a goal as a result of one's own actions. Collective self-efficacy is the belief that by working together with others, a goal can be achieved.

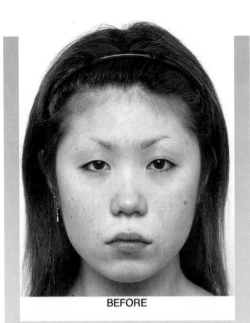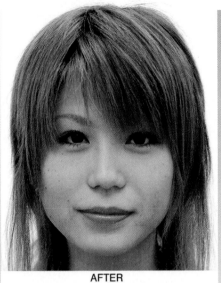

BEFORE   AFTER

Figure 5.8 ■ There May Be Limits to Our Ability to Change Ourselves, but Some Extreme Makeovers Suggest That Incredible Change Is Possible
These photos make the point that if we make extreme enough changes to ourselves, including cosmetic surgery, there might not seem to be much of the original "self" left.

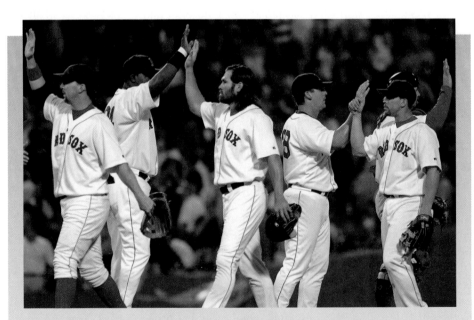

Figure 5.9 ■ Believing That Together We Can Accomplish Great Things
Why do some teams have so many victories? Part of the answer may involve the fact that they have high *collective self-efficacy*—high confidence in their ability to win.

Chapter 5 / The Self

Although we can bring about self-change as a result of our desire for self-improvement, many of these changes occur because of situational factors. Change can occur as we age, for example, because different demands are made on us as we occupy different roles throughout the life span. Consistent with this, much self-change occurs in response to relocating to a different community, where we begin to conform to new norms (Kling, Ryff, & Essex, 1997). Entering a new occupation also tends to bring about changes in our self-concept. Research indicates that becoming a police officer results in new self-perceptions (Stradling, Crowe, & Tuohy, 1993). Consider how you would see yourself differently when moving from working in a fast-food outlet to wearing a police officer's uniform, carrying a weapon, and having responsibilities that are more demanding than asking a customer, "Would you like fries with that?" Equally dramatic changes in the self-concept occur as one moves from civilian life to being in the armed forces and facing combat (Silverstein, 1994), as well as when college students graduate and leave the academic environment to become attorneys, engineers, or parents.

In addition, very negative effects on our self-concept can occur as a result of major life changes, such as losing a job (Sheeran & Abraham, 1994), contracting a serious illness (Taylor, Buunk, & Aspinwall, 1990), or losing someone close to you through death (Stroebe et al., 1995). Such identity changes can be conceptualized as either the addition of a new but not necessarily sought after identity (e.g., cancer survivor, rape victim, elderly) or deletion of a prior valued identity (e.g., employed person, no longer a son or daughter when one's parents are gone, lost youth).

KEY POINTS

★ Our self-conceptions can vary in terms of their emphasis on the *personal self* or the *social self,* with the resulting behavior being *intragroup* or *intergroup* in nature. We have multiple social identities, which could have rather different implications for behavior, depending on which social identity is activated.

★ The context in which we find ourselves can alter the aspect of the self that is salient. Gender differences will tend to be exhibited most when our gender group identity is salient, but may be absent entirely when another group identity is salient.

★ A frequent response to perceived rejection by others is to choose to emphasize the aspect of one's identity that differentiates the self from those rejecting us. To create a self-perception as a "rebel," one can "take on" a feature that differentiates members of one's peer group from the mainstream.

★ Images of future *possible selves* can inspire us to make difficult changes in the present in order to achieve this more desirable self.

★ Making our own mortality salient can threaten the self, and this can lead people to embrace aspects of the self that are positive and distance from aspects of the self that have the potential of harming self-esteem.

★ To succeed in changing something about ourselves, we need to have *self-efficacy,* or feelings that we can accomplish a goal. Some goals, however, can be accomplished only by joining with others—in these cases, it is important to feel *collective self-efficacy,* the feeling that together we can get the job done.

★ Self-change can occur as we find ourselves in a new social context. Such change can occur because we have moved, taken a new job, or become a parent. It can also result from negative events in our lives, such as illness, loss of a loved one, or loss of a job.

Self-Esteem: Attitudes toward the Self

So far we have considered some ways that people attempt to protect their self-esteem when they feel threatened, but we haven't yet discussed how self-esteem is routinely assessed. For the most part, **self-esteem** has been conceptualized by social psychologists as the individual's overall attitude toward the self. What kind of attitude do you have toward yourself—is it positive or negative? Is your attitude toward yourself stable, or does the situation affect how you feel, with self-esteem, as a result, varying across contexts?

The Measurement of Self-Esteem

The most common method of measuring self-esteem as a general traitlike evaluation is with the ten-item Rosenberg (1965) scale. As shown in Figure 5.10, this scale has rather straightforward items. People who agree strongly with such items are said to have high self-esteem, whereas those who disagree with the items have low self-esteem. Given that most people can guess what is being assessed with such items, it is not surprising that this measure correlates very highly with responses to the simple item, "I have high self-esteem" (Robins, Hendin, & Trzesniewski, 2001). On this measure, using a scale ranging from 1 (*not very true of me*) to 5 (*very true of me*), people are asked to provide their own explicit attitude toward themselves. There are also more specific measures of self-esteem that are used on occasion to assess self-esteem in particular domains such as academics, personal relationships, appearance, and athletics. In general, overall trait self-esteem, as measured with the Rosenberg scale, typically reflects the average of these more specific domains.

It is also the case that self-esteem can be responsive to specific situations. As Figure 5.11 illustrates, when we achieve important goals, self-esteem can improve, whereas failures can harm self-esteem. Such short-term increases in *state* self-esteem—how an individual feels about the self at a particular moment in time—can be induced easily in a laboratory setting. For example, simply giving people false feedback about their positive score on a personality test can raise self-esteem (Greenberg et al., 1992), and positive feedback about being accepted by other people has a similar effect (Leary, 1999). Self-esteem can be temporarily enhanced by wearing clothing that you like (Kwon, 1994) or by directing your thoughts toward desirable aspects of yourself (McGuire & McGuire, 1996).

self-esteem
The degree to which the self is perceived positively or negatively; one's overall attitude toward the self.

---

1. I feel that I am a person of worth, at least on an equal basis with others.
2. I feel that I have a number of good qualities.
3. All in all, I am inclined to feel that I am a failure.*
4. I am able to do things as well as most other people.
5. I feel I do not have much to be proud of.*
6. I take a positive attitude toward myself.
7. On the whole, I am satisfied with myself.
8. I wish I could have more respect for myself.*
9. I certainly feel useless at times.*
10. At times I think I am no good at all.*

Figure 5.10 ■ Measurement: The Rosenberg Self-Esteem Scale
Each of the items with an asterisk is reverse-scored, and then an average of all ten items is computed so that higher numbers indicate greater self-esteem. (*Source: Based on Rosenberg, 1965.*)

Figure 5.11 ■ **Self-Esteem: Attitudes toward the Self**
One's self-esteem, or attitude about oneself, can range from very positive to very negative. At least temporarily, the individuals shown here would seem to be expressing a very positive *(left)* and a very negative *(right)* attitude about themselves.

Likewise, self-esteem can be temporarily undermined in laboratory settings. When people are reminded of the ways they fall short of their ideals, self-esteem can decrease (Eisenstadt & Leippe, 1994). In fact, for women who place importance on their physical appearance, simply being required to put on a swimsuit can undermine their self-esteem (Fredrickson et al., 1998). Being ostracized, excluded, or ignored by other people, even in chat rooms on the Internet or while playing cybergames that lack long-term importance to the individual, can lower self-esteem (Williams, 2001).

Researchers have recently attempted to measure self-esteem with greater subtlety. They believed that attitudes toward the self might be better revealed using unconscious assessment procedures, compared with the previously discussed, explicitly conscious methods such as the Rosenberg scale. This is because such implicit measures of self-esteem might be less susceptible to bias due to people's self-presentation concerns (e.g., their desire to present themselves to others in the best possible light). Given the **self-reference effect** in information processing, in which people seem to prefer stimuli that are associated with the self (e.g., we like the letters in our own name better than other letters), researchers have investigated whether this preference for self-relevant information is sufficiently automatic that it occurs rapidly and without a conscious intention. To assess this possibility, Gray and colleagues (2004) measured brain responses (known as *event-related potentials*—ERPs) to self-relevant words versus non-self-relevant words. They found evidence that people automatically allocate their attention to self-relevant information. Because such basic and unconscious processes appear to be involved in the self-reference effect, it suggests that strategies designed to improve self-esteem might be effective when administered at the unconscious level.

In an attempt to assess whether implicit self-esteem can be improved without the participant's conscious awareness, Dijksterhuis (2004) used the logic of *classical*

self-reference effect
People's orientation toward stimuli that are associated with the self. People show a preference for objects owned by and reflective of the self.

conditioning procedures (see Chapter 4 for more on how social attitudes are classically conditioned). After repeatedly pairing representations of the self (*I* or *me*) with positively valenced trait terms (e.g., *nice, smart, warm*) that were presented subliminally (too quickly for participants to consciously recognize them), implicit self-esteem was found to be significantly higher compared with those in a control group who were not exposed to such pairings. In addition, such subliminal conditioning prevented participants from suffering a self-esteem reduction when they were later given negative false feedback about their intelligence. Thus, consistent with research on explicit self-esteem (such as studies using the Rosenberg scale) that shows people with high self-esteem are less vulnerable to threat following a failure experience, this subliminal training procedure appears to provide similar self-protection in the face of threat to the self.

Self-Serving Biases

People want to feel positively about themselves, and most manage to see themselves favorably much of the time. The fact that most of us show the **above-average effect**—which is thinking we are better than the average person on almost every dimension imaginable—is strong evidence of our desire to see the self relatively positively (Alicke et al., 2001; Klar, 2002; Taylor & Brown, 1988). Even when we are directly provided with negative social feedback that contradicts our rosy view of ourselves, we show evidence of forgetting such instances and emphasizing information that supports our favored positive self-perceptions (Sanitioso, Kunda, & Fong, 1990; Sanitioso & Wlodarski, 2004).

As described in Chapter 3, people reliably show self-serving biases when explaining their personal outcomes. Information that might imply we are responsible for negative outcomes is assessed critically, and our ability to refute such arguments appears to be rather remarkable (Greenwald, 2002; Pyszczynski & Greenberg, 1987). Consider the **Beyond the Headlines** section showing the extremes to which people can take this. As children we adopt the mantra, "It's not my fault," which we take with us into adulthood. We can use this when it comes to explanations for outcomes for which we might be blamed, regardless of whether we are innocent or guilty. Overusing this excuse, though, can have important consequences for how others evaluate us.

In contrast to our resistance to accepting responsibility for negative outcomes, we easily accept information that suggests we are responsible for our successes. This is especially the case for people with high self-esteem (Schlenker, Weigold, & Hallam, 1990). Not only do people show self-serving biases for their personal outcomes, but they also do so for their group's achievements. Fans of sports teams often believe that their presence and cheering was responsible for their team's success (Wann & Branscombe, 1993). People in groups that perform well tend to claim primary responsibility for those outcomes, while those who have been randomly assigned to groups that failed do not make this claim. There are, however, culture-based limits on people's willingness to "grab the credit." For example, in China, modesty is an important basis for self-esteem (Bond, 1996). Accordingly, Chinese students attribute their success in school to their teachers, whereas American students attribute it to their own skills and intelligence. Conversely, when it comes to failure, Chinese students are more likely to explain their failure as stemming from their own flaws, while Americans tend to explain their failures as being due to someone else's fault.

Is High Self-Esteem Always Positive?

Given the many techniques that people have in their arsenal for maintaining self-esteem, it is reasonable to ask whether high self-esteem is a crucial goal for which we should all strive. Indeed, some social scientists have suggested that the lack of high self-esteem (or presence of low self-esteem) is the root of many social ills, including drug abuse, poor

above-average effect
The tendency for people to rate themselves as above the average on most positive social attributes.

When Complaining Runs Headlong into Self-Serving Biases

Fugitive Blames Police for Not Capturing Him Fast Enough

Bangor, Maine—"A convicted sex offender, Harvey Taylor, who was wanted in Florida, fled into the Maine woods to escape from police. *The Bangor News* reports the 48-year-old spent at least three nights in the woods after running away from a Sheriff's detective. He claims he lost some toes to frostbite because he wasn't arrested quickly enough. Speaking from the hospital, he said: "If the detective had done his job, I wouldn't be in here now. I'm trying to find an attorney to bring a lawsuit against this detective. If he had done his job properly I wouldn't be in the condition that I'm in right now. I would have been in jail that very same day."

What do you think of people who fail to accept responsibility for their own negative outcomes? In general, we don't like people who blame other people and fail to take responsibility for their misfortunes—like the person in this story (Jellison & Green, 1981). In western cultures, internal explanations—attributions to something about the person—are highly valued and normative. Those who attribute their outcomes to internal rather than to external factors are perceived more favorably, and they are given greater access to social rewards (Beauvois & Dubois, 1988; Dubois & Beauvois, 1996).

Do our responses to people who appear to blame their negative outcomes on someone or something other than themselves depend on whether we believe the outcome was *actually* due to something about them (e.g., that it was their own fault)? Or, is it simply a matter of preferring people who accept responsibility for negative outcomes that happen to them?

Kaiser and Miller (2001) investigated this issue in the context of an African American student who attributed his negative grade on an essay to racial discrimination. Although these researchers varied the probability that the grader was racist—0 percent likelihood, 50 percent likelihood, or 100 percent likelihood—this had no effect on whites' evaluations of the student who complained that his grade was due to the grader's racism. Regardless of whether the white perceivers in this study agreed that the bad grade was likely to be due to discrimination or not, participants evaluated that person negatively compared with when he attributed the negative outcome to his own poor abilities. Thus, it would seem that even when we think that another person's negative outcome is *not* that person's own fault, when that individual does not accept responsibility for the outcome and instead attributes it to another person, it results in negative impressions. Such *social costs* include being labeled as a complainer or a troublemaker (Feagin & Sikes, 1994).

Does this mean we should never complain when we think we have been treated unjustly or harmed by another's negligence? Should we always publicly attribute responsibility for negative outcomes to something about ourselves? Complaining about another person who has treated us unfairly, or about unjust circumstances, can serve an *instrumental* function (Kowalski, 1996). That is, it can draw people's attention to undesirable conditions, and it may be an essential means of bringing about improved future outcomes. In fact, complaining is a critical aspect of the American legal system, because it is through formal complaints (i.e., lawsuits) that individuals and groups can seek redress when they have been wronged (Crosby et al., 2003). When people do not object to unfairness, their silence is likely to be interpreted as satisfaction, and this perpetuates unfair circumstances.

Complaining may lead to negative perceptions, in part, because doing so frequently involves an implication that another person is bad, which may be seen as rude, particularly if the situation or the evidence against the person is ambiguous (Kowalski, 1996). There is some evidence that it is high-status people who will be most willing to take the social risk of complaining about such negative outcomes. Goldman (2001) found that members of high-status groups were particularly inclined to formally file claims about discrimination. In a major survey of recently terminated employees, whites and men were *more* likely than were women or ethnic minorities to report that they had challenged the legitimacy of their termination to the Equal Employment Opportunity Commission (EEOC) or a Fair Employment Practice (FEP) office. Although these findings might seem surprising in light of who is actually most likely to suffer from discrimination, they do correspond with past research showing that men feel better, compared with women, after reporting their disadvantages (Branscombe, 1998).

school performance, depression, and various forms of violence, including terrorism. Some have argued that low self-esteem might be an important cause of aggression and general negativity toward others (Crocker et al., 1987; Nunn & Thomas, 1999). However, strong evidence has now accumulated in favor of the opposite conclusion—that high self-esteem is more strongly associated with bullying, narcissism, exhibitionism, self-aggrandizing, and interpersonal aggression (Baumeister, Smart, & Boden, 1996). For example, it is men with high self-esteem, not those with low self-esteem, who are most likely to commit violent acts when someone disputes their favorable view of themselves. Why might this be the case? To the extent that high self-esteem implies superiority to others, that view of the self may need to be defended with some frequency—whenever the individual's pride is threatened. It may even be that high self-esteem coupled with instability (making for greater volatility) results in the most hostility and defensive responding (Kernis et al., 1993). When those with unstable high self-esteem experience failure, their underlying self-doubt is reflected in physiological responses indicative of threat (Seery et al., 2004). Thus, while there are clear benefits for individuals to have a favorable view of themselves, there also appears to be a potential downside.

Do Women and Men Differ in Their Levels of Self-Esteem?

This question has fascinated researchers for some time, and is one that has generated considerable research. Who do you think, on average, has higher or lower self-esteem—women or men? Most people might guess that men have higher self-esteem than women. Why might social psychologists predict this, too? Because women occupy positions of lower status and are frequently targets of prejudice, their social structural position should have negative consequences for their self-esteem. Beginning with George Herbert Mead (1934), who first suggested that self-esteem is affected by how important others in our sociocultural environment see us, women have been expected to have lower self-esteem overall compared with men because self-esteem is responsive to the treatment we receive from others. To the extent that women have been traditionally viewed as less competent than men in the larger social world, their self-esteem should be, on average, lower than that of men. How important the dimensions are on which women are devalued in the larger society, and how aware women are of their devalued status, should influence the extent to which a gender-based self-esteem difference is observed.

Williams and Best (1990) conducted a fourteen-nation study of the self-concepts of women and men to provide support for these predictions. In nations such as India and Malaysia, where women are expected to remain in the home in their roles as wives and mothers, women have the most negative self-concepts. In contrast, in nations such as England and Finland, where women are most active in the labor force and are valued participants in life outside the home, women and men tend to perceive themselves equally favorably. This research suggests that when women are excluded from important life arenas, they feel more strongly devalued and, as a result, have worse self-concepts than men. Longitudinal research with employed women in the United States similarly finds that women in jobs in which gender discrimination is most frequent exhibit increasingly poorer emotional and physical health over time (Pavalko, Mossakowski, & Hamilton, 2003). Harm to women—as a function of employment in a discriminatory work environment—can be observed in comparison to health status before their employment began.

A meta-analysis comparing the global self-esteem of women and men in 226 samples collected in the United States and Canada from 1982 to 1992 has likewise found that men have reliably higher self-esteem than women (Major et al., 1999). Although the size of the effect that they obtained across all these studies was not large ($d = -.14$; range for this measure is -1.0 to 1.0), as Prentice and Miller (1992) point out, small differences between groups that are consistently observed can be quite impressive. Precisely because there are substantial differences within each gender group in level of self-esteem, being able to detect reliable group differences in self-esteem is rather remarkable. Consistent with the reasoning of the earlier cross-nation research, Major and her colleagues (1999) found that the self-esteem difference between men and women was less among those in the professional class and greatest among those in the middle and lower classes. Again, those women who have attained culturally desirable positions suffer less self-esteem loss than those who are more likely to experience the greatest devaluation. Interestingly, it was among white North Americans that the largest overall difference in level of self-esteem between men and women was observed ($d = -.20$), whereas no reliable difference in self-esteem by gender was obtained for minority Americans. For minority groups, members of *both* genders are likely to experience broad social devaluation based on their racial category, whereas only among whites are women likely to be discriminated against in important aspects of life. Consistent with this finding that the degree of gender discrimination matters, among preadolescents, there was no reliable gender difference in self-esteem, but beginning in puberty, when girls' options become increasingly limited (remember the opening vignette), a reliable self-esteem difference emerges that continues through adulthood, with women's self-esteem levels being lower than men's. So, is the commonsense notion correct after all—does overall self-esteem suffer for groups that are devalued in a given society? The research findings offer a straightforward answer for gender: Yes! How badly self-esteem suffers appears to depend on how much discrimination and devaluation the group that is the subject of such treatment experiences.

KEY POINTS

★ *Self-esteem* is the attitude we have toward ourselves. It can range from very positive to negative. Self-esteem is most frequently measured with Rosenberg's scale, which uses explicit items that capture people's perceptions that they do or do not have high self-esteem. Other more implicit measures assess the strength of the positive or negative association between the self and stimuli associated with it, including trait terms such as *warm* and *honest*.

★ Most people feel relatively positively about themselves. This is reflected in the *above-average effect*, in which people see themselves as above the average on most positive dimensions.

★ People maintain their positive view of themselves, in part, with self-serving biases in the explanations they provide for their outcomes. Americans especially accept credit for positive outcomes and refute their responsibility for negative outcomes, whereas Chinese people tend to show the reverse pattern.

★ People negatively evaluate others who fail to accept responsibility for their own negative outcomes. This is the case even when we know that person was *not* actually responsible for the negative outcome that happened! Although complaining about another's unjust treatment of us has "social costs," not doing so will maintain existing unfairness. Interestingly enough, it is high-status groups that are most likely to take the social risk and complain to formal authorities if they believe they were discriminated against.

★ Low self-esteem may not be predictive of the social ills many had thought. In fact, high self-esteem is predictive of violent reactions when one's superior view of the self is threatened.

★ There is a small but reliable gender-based difference in self-esteem. Women's self-esteem is worse than men's to the extent that they live in a nation with more exclusion of women from public life (lower labor force participation by women) and in the United States when they work in occupations in which discrimination is more likely.

Social Comparison: Knowing the Self

How do we know ourselves—whether we're good or bad in various domains, what our best and worst traits are, and how likable we are to others? Some social psychologists have suggested that *all* human judgment is relative to *some* comparison standard (Kahneman & Miller, 1986). There is indeed considerable evidence that how we think about and feel about ourselves depends on the standard of comparison we use. To take a simple example, if we compare our ability to complete a puzzle with a five-year-old's ability to solve it, we'll probably feel pretty good about our ability. This represents a **downward social comparison,** in which our own performances are compared with that of someone who is less capable than we are. On the other hand, if we compare our performances on the same task with that of a puzzle expert, we might not fare so well, nor feel so good about ourselves. This is the nature of **upward social comparisons,** which tend to be threatening to our self-image. As the amateur musician in the cartoon in Figure 5.12 suggests, protecting our self-image can depend on choosing the right standard of comparison.

You might be wondering why we compare ourselves with other people at all. Festinger's (1954) **social comparison theory** suggests that we compare ourselves with others because, for many domains and attributes, there is no objective yardstick with which to evaluate ourselves; other people are therefore highly informative. Indeed, feeling uncertain about themselves in a particular domain is among the most crucial conditions that lead people to engage in social comparison (Wood, 1989).

With whom do we compare ourselves, and how do we decide what standard of comparison to use? It depends on our motive for the comparison. Do we want an accurate assessment of ourselves, or do we want to simply feel good about ourselves? In general, the desire to see the self positively appears to be more powerful than either the desire to accurately assess the self or to verify strongly held beliefs about the self (Sedikides & Gregg, 2003). But, suppose, for the moment, that we really do want an accurate assessment. As Festinger (1954) originally suggested, we might gauge our abilities most accurately by comparing our own performance with that of someone who is similar to us. But, what determines similarity? Do we base it on age, gender, nationality, occupation, year in school, or something else entirely? In general, similarity tends to be based on broad social or demographic categories such as gender, race, or experience in a particular domain—which might include time spent playing the flute, grade in school, or number of cooking classes taken (Goethals & Darley, 1977; Wood, 1989).

Often, by using comparisons with others who share a social category with us, we can judge ourselves more positively than when we compare ourselves with others who

Figure 5.12 ■ Choosing the Right Standard of Comparison Can Protect Our Self-Esteem
As this cartoon suggests, if we could induce others to use a low standard when evaluating us, we can have higher self-esteem! *(Source: JEFF STAHLER reprinted by permission of Newspaper Enterprise Association, Inc.)*

Chapter 5 / The Self

are members of a different social category (especially one that is more advantaged than our own). This is partly because there are different performance expectations for members of different categories in particular domains (e.g., children versus adults, men versus women). To the extent that the context encourages a person to categorize the self as a member of a category with relatively low expectations in a particular domain, the individual will be able to conclude he or she measures up rather well. For example, a woman could console herself by thinking that her salary is "pretty good for a woman," while she would feel considerably worse if she made the same comparison with men, who on average are paid more (Reskin & Padavic, 1994; Vasquez, 2001). Thus, self-judgments are often less negative when the standards of our ingroup are used (see Biernat, Eidelman, & Fuegen, 2002). Indeed, some have suggested that such ingroup comparisons protect members of disadvantaged groups from negative and painful social comparisons with members of more advantaged groups (Crocker & Major, 1989; Major, 1994).

Many have suggested that the goal of perceiving the self positively is human beings' "master motive" (Baumeister, 1998). Social comparison is an important means by which this powerful motive is served (Wood & Wilson, 2003). How the generally positive self-perception that most of us have of ourselves is achieved depends on how we categorize the self in relation to the other to whom we are comparing. Such self-categorization influences how particular comparisons affect us by influencing the *meaning* of the comparison. Two influential perspectives on the self—the **self-evaluation maintenance model** and **social identity theory**—both build on Festinger's (1954) original social comparison theory to describe the consequences of social comparison in different contexts. Self-evaluation maintenance (Tesser, 1988) applies when we categorize the self at the personal level and we compare ourselves as an individual with another individual. Social identity theory (Tajfel & Turner, 1986) applies when we categorize the self at the group level (for example, as a Hispanic American), and the comparison other is categorized as sharing the same category as the self. When the context encourages comparison at the group level, the same other person will be responded to differently than when the context suggests a comparison between individuals. For example, another Hispanic American who performs poorly might be embarrassing to our Hispanic identity if we categorize the self as also belonging to that group. In contrast, that same poor-performing ingroup member could be flattering if we were to compare ourselves personally with that other individual.

Let's consider first what happens in an interpersonal comparison context. When someone with whom you compare yourself outperforms you in an area that is important to you, you will be motivated to distance yourself from the person with whom you are comparing yourself. Such a situation has the potential to be a relatively painful interpersonal comparison. After all, this other person has done better than you have on something that matters to you! Conversely, when you are comparing yourself with another person in an area that is important to you and that individual performs similarly to you or even worse, then you will be more likely to seek closeness to that other person because the comparison is positive. By performing worse than you, this person makes you look good by comparison. Such psychological movement toward and away from a comparison other who performs better or worse than you illustrates an important means by which positive self-evaluations are maintained.

A study by Pleban and Tesser (1981) illustrates this effect. They had participants compete in a game with another person (who was actually an accomplice of the experimenter). When the questions being asked in the game were on a dimension of importance to the self, participants reported disliking the accomplice who outperformed them more than the accomplice who performed worse than they did. Mussweiler, Gabriel, and Bodenhausen (2000) similarly paired participants with an individual who either performed better or worse than they did. They found that the upward comparison led participants to focus less on an aspect of the self that they shared with the comparison

self-evaluation maintenance model
The perspective that suggests that in order to maintain a positive view of the personal self, we distance ourselves from others who perform better than we do on valued dimensions, but move closer to others who perform worse. This view suggests that doing so will protect our self-esteem.

social identity theory
Our response when our group identity is salient. Suggests that we will move closer to positive others with whom we share an identity, but distance ourselves from other ingroup members who perform poorly or otherwise make our social identity negative.

other, while the downward comparison resulted in a greater focus on an aspect of the self that they shared with the comparison. Supporting the idea that such shifts in focus are self-protective, participants who scored high on a measure of self-esteem (and presumably have more skill at using self-protective strategies) were more likely to exhibit these shifting focus effects compared with those low in self-esteem.

When, if ever, should we want to align ourselves with another person who clearly outperforms us? Do we always dislike others who do better than us on identity-relevant dimensions? No, not at all—it depends on how we categorize ourselves in relation to the other. According to social identity theory, people are motivated to perceive their groups positively, and this should especially be the case for those who value a particular social identity. Therefore, another person who is categorized as a member of the same group as the self can help make our group positively distinct from other groups, and, as a result, those fellow group members who perform well can enhance our group's identity instead of threatening it.

To show that both of the self-protective processes described by the self-evaluation maintenance and social identity perspectives can occur, depending on whether personal or social identity is at stake, Schmitt, Silvia, and Branscombe (2000) manipulated the nature of the comparative context. When the performance dimension is relevant to the self—which was achieved by selecting people for the study who said that being creative was relevant to their own identity—then responses to a target who performs better than or equally poorly as the self will depend on the nature of the categorization context. As shown in Figure 5.13, when participants believed that their performance as an individual would be compared with the other target, they liked the poor-performing target better than the high-performing target, who represented a threat to their positive personal self-image. In contrast, when participants categorized themselves in terms of the gender group that they shared with the target and the expected comparison was intergroup in nature (between women and men), the high-performing other woman was evaluated more positively than the similar-to-self poor-performing other. Why? Because this person made the participants' group—women—look good. In another study, these investigators showed that such positive evaluation of the high-performing target in the

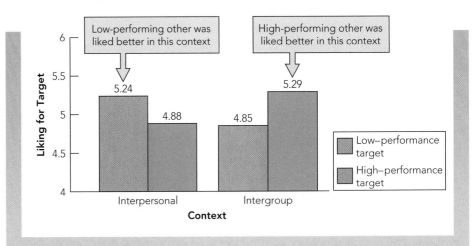

Figure 5.13 ■ How Do We Evaluate Another Who Performs Better or Worse Than We?
Research findings indicate that it depends on whether the context is interpersonal, whereby the personal self is at stake, or intergroup, with the social self at stake. As illustrated here, the low-performing target is liked best in an interpersonal context. The high-performing target is liked best in an intergroup context. (*Source: Based on data from Schmitt, Silvia, & Branscombe, 2000.*)

Chapter 5 / The Self

intergroup condition occurred most for those who highly valued their gender identity. Thus, different comparative contexts can induce us to categorize ourselves at varying degrees of inclusiveness, and this has important implications for the effects that upward and downward social comparisons have for self-evaluation.

Another important implication of group dynamics for how we evaluate ourselves and others is reflected in the **black sheep effect**—the rejection of negative ingroup members who threaten the positive image of our group. Members of our own group who perform poorly or otherwise make our group look bad can be intensely derogated (Marques & Paez, 1994). In fact, to the extent that their actions have implications for the positivity of our group's identity, members of our own group may be derogated more severely than members of another group who behave in the same way. People who value a particular group identity (e.g., highly identified fans of the University of Kansas basketball team) are especially likely to show the black sheep effect by derogating a disloyal Kansas fan (Branscombe et al., 1993). Such derogation of black sheep casts the unfavorable ingroup member as nonrepresentative of one's group, and this effectively protects the ingroup's overall identity (Castano et al., 2002).

Self-Presentation and Self-Regulation

As described in the previous section, we all have a strong desire for others to perceive us in a positive light. To ensure that others do see us positively, we often attempt to manage the impressions that they form of us. In Chapter 3 we noted how people attempt to ensure that others form impressions of them based on their most favorable self-aspects— that is, we engage in *self-promotion*. However, we also seem to know that an important way to induce others to like us is to convey positive regard for those others. People like to feel that others respect them, and we really like those who convey this to us (Tyler & Blader, 2000). To achieve this end, you can present yourself to others as someone who particularly values or respects them. People who are newcomers to a group, for example, may be especially motivated to present themselves to powerful others as a "good person." An important means of doing so is to communicate loyalty to the group and a willingness to conform to the group's norms (Noel, Wann, & Branscombe, 1995). In general, when we want to make a good impression, we use **ingratiation.** That is, we can make others like us by praising them. This is generally quite effective, unless we overdo it and others suspect our sincerity, which can bring the risk of our being seen as "slime" by those who witness our "sucking up" to the powerful (Vonk, 1999).

We also can try to present ourselves to others as superbly competent or otherwise having positive and desirable attributes. The tendency to use this strategy depends on our cultural background. When Kanagawa, Cross, and Markus (2001) asked Japanese and American students to describe themselves, the American students tended to describe themselves in terms of their strengths (e.g., "I am good at math"), while the Japanese students tended to describe themselves in more self-critical terms (e.g., "I am not good at music"). In both instances, people are conforming to norms about how to make a good impression and be liked by others, although the norms of how best to accomplish this can vary tremendously from culture to culture.

Some people are more adept at monitoring their behavior and conforming to what others expect or will see as desirable than are others (Snyder & Ickes, 1985). One individual difference variable—**self-monitoring**—captures people's willingness and ability to regulate their behavior. High self-monitoring means that people are concerned with how others will react, and it involves a focus on external cues such as expectations that others might have of them. Low self-monitoring involves a focus on internal cues such as their own beliefs or attitudes as a basis for behavior. Low self-monitors tend to be less responsive to situational norms (whatever those are in a given context), whereas high self-monitors tend to change as the situation changes (Koestner, Bernieri, & Zuckerman, 1992). Degree of self-monitoring is assessed with items

black sheep effect
When a member of the ingroup behaves in a way that threatens the value of the group identity and is intensely derogated as a means of protecting the group identity.

ingratiation
The attempt to make others like us by conveying that we like them.

self-monitoring
The monitoring by people of their behavior in response to others' expectancies. Low self-monitors are not very effective at doing this and instead prefer to act consistently according to their personal views. High self-monitors are quite effective at monitoring their behavior and adjust their actions according to others' expectations or the situation.

such as "I can only argue for ideas that I already believe," with low self-monitors tending to agree more than high self-monitors with this idea. Indeed, differences in self-monitoring are reflected in how people use language (Ickes, Reidhead, & Patterson, 1986). High self-monitors tend to use third-person pronouns (*they, them*) when they speak, which reflects their outward focus on others. Low self-monitors, on the other hand, tend to use first-person pronouns (*I, me*) more frequently, reflecting their differential focus on the self.

High self-monitors know how to obtain positive evaluations from other people; this can be a quite useful characteristic in many occupations. Politicians, actors, and salespeople are especially likely to be high in self-monitoring (Lippa & Donaldson, 1990). Overall, high self-monitors tend to have higher self-esteem than low self-monitors. This may stem from the higher levels of social approval that high self-monitors receive compared with low self-monitors (Leary et al., 1995). Indeed, the basis on which self-esteem rests and can be therefore undermined differs for these two types of

Is Looking Inwardly the Best Route to Self-Insight?

In a whole host of self-help books that sell millions of copies per year, we are told time and again to get to know ourselves by looking inwardly. Indeed, many people in our society believe that the more people introspect about themselves, the better they will understand themselves. In fact, as shown in Figure 5.14, pop psychology authors repeatedly tell us that the road to self-knowledge runs through such self-inspection. Is this really the best way to accurately understand ourselves? Not necessarily.

First of all, often we do not know or have conscious access to the reasons for our actions, although if pressed we can certainly generate what appear to be logical theories of why we acted as we did. For example, in early research on this issue, Richard Nisbett and Timothy Wilson (1977) presented participants with a choice situation: They were shown a variety of different pairs of socks from which they were to choose their favorite. After making their selection, participants were then asked *why* they chose the pair they did. Although people came up with various reasons for their selection, the researchers knew that their choices were actually based on an entirely different factor (the order of the items on the table—the

more to the right the pair was, the better it was liked, regardless of which pair that was). Although the participants in this study can and did introspect about why they liked one pair of socks over another, and they came up with seemingly logical reasons such as their color or the design, they apparently did not have conscious access to the factor that actually predicted their affective responses to the various pairs of socks (order it was examined).

Figure 5.14 ■ Self-Help Books Recommend Introspection
The titles of these various pop psychology books imply that the route to self-understanding may lie in introspection, but research reveals that this can be misleading. Depending on the nature of the factors that are actually driving our behavior, introspection may misdirect us.

Chapter 5 / The Self

individuals (Gonnerman et al., 2000). For low self-monitors, depression results when there is a discrepancy between the self and what the individual thinks he or she should be. For high self-monitors, depression results when there is a discrepancy between the self and what he or she thinks other people expect them to be. How do high self-monitors manage to be so successful in controlling the impressions others form of them? They seem to give others both what they expect and what they want!

So far, we have illustrated how we get to know ourselves by comparing how we perform on various tasks with others. In addition, by presenting ourselves in a particular way to other people, we come to see what we value about ourselves and what we hope others will perceive positively as well. Another important method that people have assumed is useful for learning about the self is to engage in **introspection**—to privately think about "who we are." Is looking inwardly the best route to understanding ourselves—to gaining self-insight? For a discussion of this intriguing issue, see the **Making Sense of Common Sense** section.

introspection
Attempts to understand the self by self-examination; turning inwardly to assess one's motives.

In fact, subsequent research has revealed that attempting to analyze our reasons for liking something or acting in a particular way can mislead us when we have to make a subsequent choice. That is, because we often genuinely don't know why we feel a particular way, generating reasons (that are likely to be inaccurate) could result in our changing our minds about how we feel based on the reasons that we generate. Wilson and Kraft (1993) illustrated this process in a series of studies concerning introspection on topics ranging from "Why I Feel as I Do about My Romantic Partner" to "Why I Like One Type of Jam over Another." They found that after analyzing the reasons for their feelings, people changed their attitudes, at least temporarily, to match their stated reasons. As you might imagine, this can lead to regrettable choices, because the original feelings that are based on other factors entirely are still there.

Another way in which introspection might be rather misleading to us is when we attempt to predict our future feelings. Try imagining how you would feel living in a new city, being fired from your current job, or living with another person for many years. When you are not in these specific circumstances, you might not be able to accurately predict how you will respond when you are in them. This applies to both positive and negative future circumstances. Gilbert and Wilson (2000) suggest that when we think about something terrible happening to us and try to predict how we would feel one year into the future, we focus exclusively on the awful event and neglect all the other factors that will contribute to our happiness level then. This means that people predict that they would feel much worse than they actually would when this future time arrives. Likewise, for positive events, if we focus on only its occurrence, we will mispredict our happiness as being considerably higher than the actual moderate feelings that are likely one year later. Again, this would occur because we would not focus on all the daily hassles and other factors that would moderate how we actually feel at some future point in time.

Does all this mean that introspection is inevitably misleading, and is in fact potentially harmful? It depends on *what* we analyze about ourselves. When the behavior in question is actually based on a conscious decision-making process—and is not based on unconscious affective factors—thinking about those reasons might well lead to accurate self-judgments. In addition, if we introspect about our behavior frequency in a particular domain, it is likely to be a very good cue to our preferences. If we find ourselves consistently watching a particular program on TV each week, we might be pretty accurate at inferring that we must like that show (Bem, 1972). When we find ourselves working on a particular task for long periods of time without any external rewards or constraints, we are likely to conclude that we are intrinsically motivated by the task and enjoy it. On the other hand, if we only perform a task when we are being monitored or rewarded for doing so (e.g., cleaning up our rooms), we can accurately conclude that our reasons for performing those actions may be *extrinsic* and not due to sheer liking of the task. So, although looking *inward* can be helpful, it may not be, as popular books suggest, helpful under all circumstances. Research has revealed that we may be "asking ourselves" more than we actually know! Although, when asked, people can generate reasons for why they do what they do, those reasons may be based on theories about the causes of behavior, rather than the affective factors that frequently predict actions.

KEY POINTS

★ *Downward social comparison* refers to instances in which we are compared with someone of lesser ability than ourselves. These instances can be flattering, as long as we are not worried that the worse-off other represents our own future! *Upward social comparison,* in contrast, refers to someone who outperforms us in areas central to the self. We often find these people threatening in interpersonal comparative contexts, but they are tolerated to the extent that we believe we, too, can achieve the other's more favorable position. We tend to like those who outperform us, particularly when we share a social category with them and the context implies an intergroup comparison. Then, the better-performing other is making our group identity more positive and is not experienced as threatening as the same target would be if the comparison were interpersonal.

★ *Social comparison theory* spawned two perspectives on the consequences of negative or upward social comparisons for the self—the *self-evaluation maintenance model* and *social identity theory.* When the self is categorized at the individual level, we distance from a better-performing other, but when the self is categorized at the social identity level, we distance from the poor-performing other.

★ Presenting ourselves as liking or admiring others is often an effective way of ingratiating ourselves with them and being liked in return. There are cultural differences in the way people present themselves, as a function of the valued norm of modesty in Asian cultures and self-promotion norms in American culture.

★ The *black sheep effect* proposes that we will derogate a member of our own group more than a member of another group when we think that person reflects badly on our group's image. By doing so, we protect the image of our own group identity.

★ Individuals differ in the extent to which they engage in *self-monitoring.* Low self-monitors are keen to be true to themselves and show cross-situational consistency, whereas high self-monitors want to be what others want and adapt themselves to different people and situations.

The Self as Target of Prejudice

Although the experience of not getting what you want, or getting what you don't want, is generally negative, how you explain these outcomes has important implications for how you feel about yourself. The explanation we give for such undesirable events, influences how we cope with them. As you saw in Chapter 3, attributions affect the *meaning* derived from events, and some attributions for a negative outcome are more psychologically harmful (i.e., can cause depression and undermine self-esteem) than others (Weiner, 1985). How people explain and respond to one class of negative outcomes—prejudice-based negative treatment stemming from one's group membership—has been the focus of considerable research. Although overt discrimination against women and minorities has generally declined in the United States since the end of World War II, it is sufficiently prevalent (although often subtle) that it may explain the more frequent undesirable outcomes that members of devalued groups experience. As the cartoon in Figure 5.15 suggests, the mere presence of devalued group members, which their exclusion was consistently the case in the past, is not the same thing as their being able to feel comfortable in an environment in which they can feel assured that discrimination will be absent.

"To begin with, I would like to express my sincere thanks and deep appreciation for the opportunity to meet with you. While there are still profound differences between us, I think the very fact of my presence here today is a major breakthrough."

Figure 5.15 ■ Progress toward Group Equality Can Be Measured in Degrees.
As this cartoon illustrates, women's (or the dragon's) presence in male-dominated professions (the knights' domain) represents a "good start," but it can hardly be said to represent "a warm and welcoming environment." (*Source: © The New Yorker Collection 1983 William Miller from cartoonbank.com. All Rights Reserved.*)

Emotional Consequences: How Well-Being Can Suffer

As discussed earlier in this chapter, social psychologists have long been interested in the self-esteem consequences of being a member of a devalued social group. George Herbert Mead (1934) initially suggested that our self-appraisals depend on how other people see us. Given that members of devalued groups are more likely to experience negative responses from others—because of their group membership—compared with mainstream group members, self-esteem processes between these two groups have been closely examined.

To account for how targets of prejudice maintain their self-esteem, Crocker and Major (1989) suggested that attributing negative outcomes to prejudice might be self-protective among those who are devalued and discriminated against. Specifically, they argued that an attribution for a negative outcome that points to another person's prejudice as the cause of one's poor outcome should be considered an *external* cause. For this reason, attributing a negative outcome to something outside the self should be self-protective. In fact, these theorists speculated that because an attribution to prejudice is a sufficiently self-protective explanation for poor outcomes that it "may not only be used in response to negative evaluations or outcomes that do, in fact, stem from prejudice against the stigmatized group, but also in response to negative outcomes that do not stem from prejudice" (Crocker & Major, 1989, p. 612). This implies that there could be a self-esteem protection motivation that encourages attributions to prejudice among devalued group members. Yet there is overwhelming correlational evidence that the more disadvantaged group members perceive discrimination against their group, the worse their well-being. Therefore, negative outcomes that are seen as stemming from stable factors such as one's group membership are not predicting positive self-esteem. Such relationships between perceived discrimination and negative well-being have been obtained among members of different social groups, including women (Schmitt et al., 2002), black Americans (Branscombe, Schmitt, & Harvey, 1999), homosexuals (Herek, Gillis, & Cogan, 1999), Jewish Canadians (Dion & Earn, 1975), and people who are overweight (Crocker, Cornwell, & Major, 1993). Let's consider the evidence that experimental research has generated concerning these dual propositions: (1) that attributions to prejudice are external attributions and can therefore discount internal causes for negative outcomes, and (2) that attributions to prejudice for a *specific* negative outcome protect the well-being of devalued group members.

Should our group memberships be considered truly external to the self? As this chapter has already revealed, our social identities as members of a group can be an important aspect of the self. Use of Kelley's "covariation principle" (see Chapter 3) suggests that when something about the self (group membership) covaries with an outcome (discrimination), the attribution made will have a substantial internal component. That is, people will conclude that it is both something about me (my group membership) and something about the other's prejudice that causes discriminatory outcomes. To illustrate the previously unidentified internal component of attributions to prejudice, Schmitt and Branscombe (2002b) compared this attribution with a situation in which a clear external attribution for the same exclusionary outcome was plausible. These researchers had participants think about a situation in which a professor refused their request to let them into a course that required the professor's permission in order for them to enroll. This exclusion could be due to different reasons that would have differing implications for how the person would feel. By varying information about the professor and who was or was not let in the desired class, prejudice or an exclusively external cause for the participant's rejection was made plausible. In the "prejudice plausible" condition, participants learned that the professor had a reputation for being hostile toward their gender and that only members of the other gender were admitted to the class. In the "everyone excluded" condition, participants learned that the professor had a reputation of being hostile toward all students and that no one was given the special permission that was needed to be admitted. To what did the students attribute their failure to be admitted to the class? In the prejudice condition, they perceived the cause of their rejection as both due to something about the professor *and* due to something about themselves. Only when everyone was excluded was the internal attributional component (e.g., something about me) essentially absent. The finding that the self is implicated when a prejudice attribution is made (e.g., one's group membership is a part of the self, so internality is high), compared with when an attribution that does not involve prejudice is made, was subsequently replicated (Major, Kaiser, & McCoy, 2003).

Given that we know that attributions to prejudice have a substantial internal component (i.e., the self at the group level), we can ask whether they are likely to be self-protective. That is, if attributions to prejudice are not external explanations, and instead reflect something that is internal and stable, attributions to prejudice may not protect self-esteem by discounting the self's role in causing the negative outcome. Indeed, Schmitt and Branscombe (2002b) found that, for women, making an attribution to the professor's prejudice against women harmed their well-being, compared with when everyone was excluded and the exclusion could not be attributed to prejudice. Using the same experimental materials involving the professor who refuses a student admittance to a course, Major, Kaiser, & McCoy (2003) found that there is an even worse attribution that can be made than either an attribution to prejudice or the professor's refusal to admit anyone. When the professor viewed the participant as *uniquely* stupid and, for this reason, the participant was the *only* person who was excluded from the class (i.e., all others who asked were admitted), this situation caused the participants' feelings about the self to be most negative.

The conclusions drawn about the emotional consequences of perceiving one's negative outcomes as stemming from prejudice against one's group clearly depend on the attribution to which it is compared. When negative outcomes are attributed to prejudice, this reflects an internal and relatively stable cause for disadvantaged group members. When compared with *another* important internal and stable feature of the self, such as one's lack of intelligence, an attribution to prejudice might be self-protective. To the extent that the other internal explanation is relevant to more situations or outcomes (is even more pervasive; Major, Kaiser, & McCoy, 2003), making that attribution could cause greater harm to well-being than attributing the outcome to prejudice. On the other hand, when compared with an actual external attribution, such as the professor's generally negative disposition (something that is not related to the participant's self at all), then attributions to prejudice are relatively harmful for well-being (Schmitt & Branscombe, 2002b). As Figure 5.16 illustrates, attributions for the same unfavorable outcome can be differentiated along a continuum in terms of the extent to which they have negative implications for psychological well-being. The worst possibility is when the outcome is attributed to an internal and stable factor that is likely to apply to many situations (e.g., being uniquely unintelligent for a college student). The next, slightly better attribution, for it is unlikely to be applicable across quite as many situations, is an attribution to prejudice. Making an attribution to prejudice that is seen as infrequent or isolated will be even better for psychological well-being. True external attributions, which could come in many different forms (e.g., professor is a jerk, having a bad day, bad luck), are most likely to be protective of the attributor's self and well-being.

An attribution to prejudice can reflect pervasive discriminatory circumstances, or it can be perceived as reflecting a rare or unusual instance. In effect, for any given experience, an attribution to prejudice could be seen as reflecting wider social circumstances or could be seen as an encounter with a lone bigot. Schmitt, Branscombe, and Postmes (2003) illustrated the importance of the perceived pervasiveness of prejudice for psychological well-being in women. Participants believed that they were taking part in a study concerning job interviewing skills and that one of the twenty male business people involved in the study would give them feedback. Each participant received the *identical* negative feedback from the interviewer. However, while waiting for their interviewing feedback, the experimenter ostensibly confided to the participant either that (1) "your interviewer is a real jerk and seems to give everyone a negative evaluation" (the nonsexist external attribution); (2) "your *particular* interviewer is really sexist and gives the women negative evaluations, but is positive toward the men" (the lone sexist); or (3) "*all*

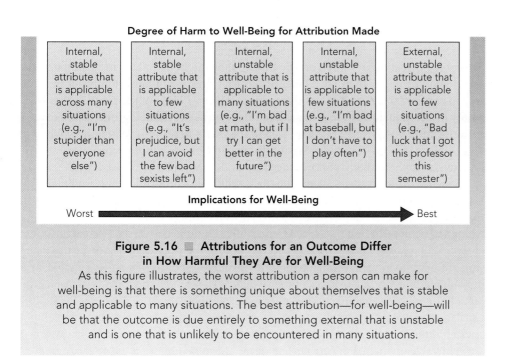

Degree of Harm to Well-Being for Attribution Made

Internal, stable attribute that is applicable across many situations (e.g., "I'm stupider than everyone else")	Internal, stable attribute that is applicable to few situations (e.g., "It's prejudice, but I can avoid the few bad sexists left")	Internal, unstable attribute that is applicable to many situations (e.g., "I'm bad at math, but if I try I can get better in the future")	Internal, unstable attribute that is applicable to few situations (e.g., "I'm bad at baseball, but I don't have to play often")	External, unstable attribute that is applicable to few situations (e.g., "Bad luck that I got this professor this semester")

Implications for Well-Being

Worst ⟶ Best

Figure 5.16 ▪ Attributions for an Outcome Differ in How Harmful They Are for Well-Being

As this figure illustrates, the worst attribution a person can make for well-being is that there is something unique about themselves that is stable and applicable to many situations. The best attribution—for well-being—will be that the outcome is due entirely to something external that is unstable and is one that is unlikely to be encountered in many situations.

of the interviewers, including yours, are really sexist" (pervasive sexism). Both feelings of self-esteem based on their gender and overall positive mood worsened when the prejudicial outcome was seen as also likely to occur in other situations (prejudice was seen as pervasive across the twenty interviewers), compared with either when prejudice could be seen as limited to the lone sexist or when a prejudice attribution was not made at all. When discrimination was seen as isolated, self-esteem and mood did not differ from when a "nonsexist jerk" delivered the negative feedback. Thus, all attributions to prejudice are not equal. What is fundamentally important for how an event is coped with and whether psychological well-being will be harmed by the experience or not is perceptions of how likely it is that such discriminatory treatment will be encountered in the future.

Cognitive Consequences: Performance Deficits

Perceived prejudice can not only affect psychological well-being, but also can interfere with our ability to learn and acquire new skills. Several studies have found that when people fear that others will discover their devalued group membership, as might be the case for concealable stigmas (i.e., think of gays and lesbians in the military), this fear can negatively affect people's ability to learn (Frable, Blackstone, & Scherbaum, 1990; Lord & Saenz, 1985). When we are in a position in which we feel we need to hide our identity and worry about how others might perceive us, it can be rather distracting. Studies measuring attention allocation reveal that when such distractions weigh on disadvantaged group members, their cognitive abilities are impaired and performance suffers.

What is considered a valued versus devalued social identity can be culture specific. Therefore, cognitive deficits stemming from concerns about a given social identity might only be present when it is an identity that is devalued by the larger culture, but not when the identity is esteemed in the larger culture. Levy and Langer (1994) provided evidence that this is the case for cognitive tasks involving memory. Specifically, the photos in Figure 5.17 reveal that, in the United States, the elderly are negatively stereotyped in terms of poor memory ability, while in China, the elderly are a revered social category. When these researchers compared young and older adults in the United States and China, they found that the older U.S. citizens did show deficits in memory, while in China this was not the case. Apparently, these differences stemmed from the fact that in the United States, being elderly is a negative aspect of identity, while in China, the opposite is true.

Behavioral Consequences: Stereotype Threat

Stereotype threat occurs when people believe they might be judged in light of a negative stereotype about their social identity or that they may inadvertently act in some way to confirm the stereotype of their group (Steele, 1997). When people value their ability in a certain domain (e.g., math), but it is one in which their group is stereotyped as performing poorly (e.g., women), stereotype threat may occur. When those who are vulnerable to stereotype threat are reminded in some overt or subtle way that the stereotype might apply to them, performance in that domain may be undermined.

Stereotype threat effects seem to be fairly difficult to control. For example, simply telling women before they take a math test that men do better on math than women do (Spencer, Steele, & Quinn, 1999) or having African Americans indicate their race before taking a difficult verbal test (Steele & Aronson, 1995) is sufficient to evoke stereotype threat and hurt their performance. Indeed, because women are negatively stereotyped as being worse at math than men, women tend to perform more poorly when they simply take a difficult math test in the presence of men, whereas they tend to perform better when the same test is taken in the presence of other women only (Inzlicht & Ben-Zeev, 2000). It is worth noting that these decrements in performance occur *only* with respect to stereotype-relevant dimensions—it is not all types of performances that are harmed. Thus, women are vulnerable on math, but African Americans are vulnerable on tests of verbal ability.

stereotype threat
People's belief that they might be judged in light of a negative stereotype about their group or that they may, because of their performance, in some way confirm a negative stereotype of their group.

Chapter 5 / The Self

Figure 5.17 ■ A Stigmatized Identity Depends on the Larger Cultural Context
Is "elderly" a positive or negative social identity? It depends on the cultural context. As you can see, in the United States, the elderly are often perceived as irrelevant and are negatively stereotyped. However, in Asia, the elderly are valued and viewed with veneration, not denigrated as incompetent. Where would you rather be a member of this social category?

Precisely because such stereotype threat effects have been quite difficult to eliminate, investigators have considered the response options that are available to devalued group members when they are in settings in which they experience stereotype threat. One option that has been suggested is disidentification with the domain (Steele, Spencer, & Aronson, 2002). That is, people could try to distance themselves from domains in which they are stereotypically vulnerable. Such an option, though, is likely to be rather problematic for people who strongly value performing well in a given domain to begin with. In this research, the women who are selected are strongly concerned about doing well in math; likewise, African Americans who are selected are keen to do well in occupations requiring strong verbal skills. Another option that might be used in a stereotype threat situation is to attempt to distance the self from the group identity as a whole. That is, women could decrease how much they identify with their gender group, or African Americans might do the same with their race. However, this option also comes with long-term risks—minority group identification is known to be important for psychological well-being (Postmes & Branscombe, 2002).

Current research has revealed a third option that is available to those subjected to stereotype threat conditions. People who are vulnerable to stereotype threat can maintain their overall level of identification with their group, and distance themselves only from the stereotypic dimensions that represent a threat to their performance in a particular valued domain. Consider the dilemma of women who have taken a lot of math classes and who perceive math to be an important aspect of their self-concept. They also value their identity as women. When they then find themselves exposed to information that suggests there are reliable sex differences in math ability, with men doing better than women, these women do indeed experience threat. How then do they manage to cope with such threat, *without* simultaneously distancing from either the domain or their group as a whole? One possibility is suggested by social psychologists, Pronin, Steele, and Ross (2004), who found that high math-identified women distanced themselves only

The Self as Target of Prejudice

from gender stereotypic dimensions that are deemed to be incompatible with math success (e.g., leaving work to raise children, being flirtatious) but did not do so for gender stereotypic dimensions deemed to be irrelevant to math success (e.g., being empathic, being fashion conscious). Disidentification from such aspects of their gender group occurred only in the stereotype threat condition but not when it was absent, suggesting it was a motivated process designed to alleviate the threat experienced.

Why do stereotype threat–based performance decrements occur? Some researchers suggest that anxiety is evoked in women, blacks, and Latinos when their group membership is portrayed as predictive of poor performance (Osborne, 2001). As a result of such anxiety, their actual performance on the relevant test is disrupted. If this is the case, when stress-based anxiety is prevented, as occurs among women who use humor as a coping strategy in stereotype threat situations, then performance decrements may be avoided (Ford et al., 2004).

Some studies have, however, failed to find increased self-reported anxiety among stigmatized group members in stereotype threat conditions (Aronson et al., 1999). This could be because members of stigmatized groups are reluctant to admit their feelings of anxiety in conditions in which they realize they will be compared with dominant group members, or it may be that they do not actually realize they are feeling anxious or aroused and so cannot accurately report those feelings.

Recent research that examines nonverbal measures of anxiety has revealed that anxiety can play a crucial role in stereotype threat effects. Although measures of self-reported anxiety have frequently failed to reveal the important role of anxiety, nonverbal measures of anxiety illustrate clearly the role that anxiety plays in stereotype threat effects. In a clever test of the hypothesis that anxiety does cause stereotype threat performance deficits, Bosson, Haymovitz, and Pinel (2004) first either reminded or did not remind gay and straight participants of their category membership before videotaping their interactions with young children in a nursery school. Participants were reminded of their sexual orientation by asking them to indicate their sexual orientation on a form just before they interacted with the children. After this subtle reminder that their group is stereotyped as one that is dangerous to children, the gay participants' child-care skills (as rated by judges blind to the hypotheses and procedure) suffered compared with when they were not so reminded of their category membership and its associated stereotype. This same group membership reminder had no effect on the straight participants because there is no such stereotype of danger to children. Consequently, straight participants were not at risk of potentially confirming a negative stereotype in the performance situation they faced.

Was increased anxiety in the gay men the cause of the reduction in their rated child-care skills? On standard self-report measures of anxiety and evaluation apprehension, the answer would seem to be "no"—Bosson, Haymovitz, and Pinel (2004) did not obtain differences in these self-reports as a function of either sexual orientation or stereotype threat condition. Importantly, however, independent judges of nonverbal anxiety—as indicated by various behaviors pointing to discomfort during the interaction with the children—were affected by sexual orientation and stereotype threat. Among the gay men who were reminded of their category membership, their anxiety was discernible in their nonverbal behavior, compared with the gay men who were not experiencing stereotype threat. Although the gay men experiencing stereotype threat did not rate themselves as more anxious than those not experiencing stereotype threat, they were visibly more fidgety, they averted their eyes, and otherwise exhibited signs of discomfort. This nonverbally exhibited anxiety disrupted their interactions with the children. However, among heterosexual men, reminders of their category membership tended to result in fewer nonverbal symptoms of anxiety, compared with when their category was not made salient.

Is it only for groups that are historically devalued in the culture as a whole that stereotype threat effects have been observed? No, definitely not. Such effects occur with men who are not a devalued group as a whole, but who are stereotyped as being less

Chapter 5 / The Self

emotional than women (Leyens, et al., 2000). When men were reminded of the stereotype concerning their emotional deficits, their performance on a task requiring them to identify emotions suffered. In an even more dramatic way, Stone and colleagues (1999) illustrated a similar point. They found that stereotype threat effects can occur among dominant group members as long as the implied comparison is based on dimensions on which their group is perceived less favorably. In their research, white men who were being compared with black men performed more poorly on an athletic performance task when they believed it reflected natural athletic ability. The reverse occurred when white men believed the exact same task reflected sports intelligence, which is a dimension on which white men expect to excel, as compared with black men. Likewise, although there is no stereotype that whites perform poorly on math, when they are threatened by a potentially negative comparison to Asians, who are stereotyped as performing better than whites in this domain, whites show math performance deficiencies (Aronson et al., 1999). Thus, the comparative context matters greatly for stereotype threat effects, and these effects are not limited to members of historically disadvantaged groups. Stereotype threat effects illustrate the importance of group membership for the experience of psychological threat, and how this can easily disrupt performance.

KEY POINTS

★ Emotional responses to a negative outcome depend on the attribution made for it. Although an attribution to prejudice is almost the most painful attribution that can be made—there is one that is worse. If you believe that bad outcomes happen because you are uniquely stupid (more so than all others) and this is a characteristic that predicts many negative outcomes, you will feel even worse than when an attribution to prejudice is made. When the identical outcome is attributed to prejudice, if that prejudice is seen as pervasive, then well-being will be harmed more than if it is seen as isolated or rare. When, however, an attribution for a negative outcome reflects an external cause, rather than prejudice against the person's group membership, well-being is protected.

★ The fear of being "found out" by others in terms of having a negatively valued group identity can disrupt performance. Such monitoring can consume cognitive resources and make it difficult to learn new skills. Such deficits occur only when the identity is devalued in the culture as a whole, and such deficits are absent when the same identity is valued.

★ *Stereotype threat* effects involve the undermining of performance in capable people in a domain they value. This occurs when a person is a member of a group that is negatively stereotyped in a particular domain. Stereotype threat effects have been observed in historically devalued group members (African Americans, women) and in dominant groups (whites, men) when they might negatively compare on an important dimension with members of another group. Stereotype threat effects can be difficult to control, and they can be induced very easily. Indeed, simply requiring people to indicate their group membership before taking a test in a domain in which they are vulnerable is enough to undermine performance.

★ When people experience stereotype threat, they can distance themselves from the task domain or they can distance themselves from the group as a whole. However, both of these options present long-term problems. One option that has received support is to disidentify with *only* the negative part of their group's stereotype.

★ Anxiety appears to be the mechanism by which stereotype threat effects occur. However, self-report measures of anxiety often fail to reveal its importance, but use of nonverbal measures has illustrated its important role.

Thinking about the Self: Personal versus Social Identity

How we think about ourselves varies depending on where we are on the *personal–social identity* continuum at any given moment in time. At the personal identity level, we can think of ourselves in terms of attributes that differentiate ourselves from other individuals, and therefore be based on *intragroup comparison*. Or, the self can be thought of as a member of a social group, with perceptions of the self being based on attributes shared with other group members; this perception of the self at the social identity level stems from *intergroup comparison* processes.

Self-definitions can vary across situations, with each being valid predictors of behavior in those settings. How the self is conceptualized can also depend on how others expect us to be and how we believe they will treat us.

Awareness of the self's mortality can encourage self-definitions in terms of group memberships that reflect positively on the self and discourage self-definitions that might reflect poorly on the self.

Other selves, besides who we are currently, can motivate us to attempt self-change. Dreaded possible selves can lead us to give up certain behaviors (e.g., smoking), while desired possible selves can lead us to work long hours to attain them.

Self-Esteem: Attitudes toward the Self

How we feel about ourselves can be assessed directly, as well as with more implicit or indirect methods. Most people show self-serving biases, such as the *above-average effect*, in which we see ourselves more positively (and less negatively) than we see most other people.

People tend not to like others who do not accept responsibility for their own negative outcomes. This is the case even when we do not believe that person was in fact responsible for the negative outcome that occurred. Thus, there can be important social costs for complaining about injustice on the part of another or existing circumstances.

High self-esteem comes with risks. It is correlated with an increased likelihood of interpersonal aggression, which appears to be in response to the greater need to defend one's superior self-view.

Women do, on average, have lower self-esteem than men. This is particularly the case in nations in which women do not participate in the labor force, and in the United States among middle and lower class women who work in environments in which gender-based devaluation is most frequent.

Social Comparison: Knowing the Self

Social comparison is a vital means by which we judge and know ourselves. *Upward social comparisons* at the personal level can be painful, and *downward social comparisons* at this level of identity can be comforting. When we self-categorize at the group level, though, the opposite is the case. Ingroup members who perform poorly threaten the positive view of our group identity, while ingroup members who perform well reflect positively on our group identity. Indeed, we are likely to derogate ingroup members who behave disloyally (the *black sheep effect*), and doing so protects the positive view of our group identity.

People often present themselves to others in an ingratiating manner, in order to be liked, although this tendency can depend on the cultural norms that guide our behavior. Individual differences in *self-monitoring* predict people's ability and willingness to adapt their behavior according to differing situational norms.

The Self as Target of Prejudice

Some researchers have suggested that, among devalued group members, attributions to prejudice are external attributions and therefore have the potential to protect self-esteem. Not only are such attributions to prejudice not perceived by the individual as external to the self (my group membership is about me), they generally are not protective—except when compared with the very worst possible attribution (an important dimension that is applicable to a wide range of situations and reflects both internal and stable aspects of the self). Indeed, perceiving the self as a target of discrimination can have negative consequences for well-being, particularly when the discrimination is seen as pervasive.

Suspecting that prejudice might be operating and affecting one's outcomes can be distracting, deplete cognitive resources, and create anxiety. As a result, *stereotype threat* effects can occur in historically devalued groups when members are simply reminded of their group membership and fear they might confirm negative expectancies about their group. Stereotype threat can undermine performance in dominant group members as well, when they fear a negative comparison with members of another group. This undermining of performance occurs only on dimensions relevant to the stereotype.

■ People cope with stereotype threat by distancing themselves from the performance domain (e.g., math) or from their group as a whole (e.g., women), but both of these options are emotionally costly. Distancing from only the stereotypic dimensions relevant to high performance in a domain appears to be preferable.

Connections INTEGRATING SOCIAL PSYCHOLOGY

In this chapter, you read about . . .	In other chapters, you will find related discussions of . . .
the role of norms in social functioning	the nature of norms and their role in social influence (Chapter 9) and aggression (Chapter 11)
the nature of attribution and social explanation	self-serving biases in attribution (Chapter 3)
individuals' concern with others' evaluations of their performance	the effects of others' evaluations on our liking for others (Chapter 7) and self-presentation (Chapter 3)
the importance of the situation or context for judgment	audience effects on attitudes (Chapter 4)
the role of stereotyping and discrimination	the nature of prejudice (Chapter 6), and various forms of social influence (Chapter 9)

Thinking about Connections

1. Do you see any connection between perceiving yourself as a member of a group (in social identity terms) and stereotype threat? (Hint: Have you ever suspected that other people might see your group negatively?)

2. Most of us are motivated to protect our self-esteem. Given that you want to protect your self-esteem, what would be the most favorable attribution you could make when you explain a bad outcome that has happened to you? What would be the worst? How might others respond to you if you voiced aloud either of those attributions (remember the social costs of not accepting responsibility for our own bad outcomes)? Is what is a self-protective attribution for the self different than the kind of attribution that leads to the most positive social evaluations?

3. We all want to know ourselves. How do we attempt to do this? Can you think of instances in which you compared unfavorably to another person and attempted to distance yourself from that person? Can you think of instances in which you compared favorably and liked being around the downward social comparison other? How did these different performances affect your relationship with that person? Do you think that after reading this chapter, you will question whether you can "get to know" yourself best by introspecting about the reasons for your own actions?

4. If images of "new possible selves" can motivate us to change ourselves, can you identify a "desired possible self" and a "feared possible self" that might suggest useful changes in yourself? If so, describe the changes you would make to avoid your feared possible self and then consider the changes you would make to achieve your desired possible self.

5. Have you ever experienced a change in your self-perception as you move from one situation or group of friends to another? If so, does one self-perception seem more accurate than another? Or are they equally true, depending on the situation?

■ Find a role model whose accomplishments seem attainable to you. If you think you can achieve his or her position or accomplishments ultimately, such an upward comparison can be inspiring.

■ Present yourself as liking and valuing others if you want them to like you. People like others who value them.

■ Avoid making attributions to prejudice for your own outcomes if you want to feel good about your future, because they are relatively internal and stable attributions, which are predictive of poor well-being. On the other hand, prejudicial treatment is likely to persist when complaints

of discrimination are avoided. If you do perceive an outcome as due to unjust discrimination, then seek social support from other members of your group. The female employees of Wal-Mart recently filed a class action lawsuit claiming pervasive sex discrimination. The result could be considerable change for women in the labor force.

■ Avoid making public attributions that blame others for negative outcomes, for there will be social costs.

■ *Stereotype threat* occurs when persons fear confirming a negative stereotype about their group. You can attempt to undermine its

likelihood of occurring by suggesting to vulnerable others that group differences are absent on a particular task. Here's how you can help prevent others from experiencing stereotype threat:

■ Avoid making their group membership salient. Otherwise, take care to construct situations in which gender and race are balanced so group membership doesn't seem relevant.

■ *Self-definition* can shift as the situation changes. Notice how you think about yourself when you are sitting in a classroom, in your dorm or apartment, when on a date, at your job versus when you are with your family.

■ Think about what others expect of you and consider how that affects how you feel about yourself.

■ Practice thinking about yourself positively. Think about all of your good attributes. Implicit self-esteem research suggests that you can increase your self-esteem this way.

KEY TERMS

above-average effect (p. 186)

black sheep effect (p. 193)

care ethic (p. 175)

downward social comparison (p. 190)

existential terror (p. 180)

identity interference (p. 174)

independent self-concept (p. 175)

ingratiation (p. 193)

interdependent self-concept (p. 175)

For More Information

Williams, K. D. (2001). *Ostracism: The power of silence.* New York: Guilford Press.

• This book reviews an intriguing program of research on ostracism and exclusion from groups. People find the experience painful, even when temporary or in an unimportant context, and engage in a variety of behaviors to attempt to regain inclusion by others.

Steele, C. M., Spencer, S. J., & Aronson, J. (2002). Contending with group image: The psychology of stereotype and social identity threat. *Advances in Experimental Social Psychology, 34,* 379–439.

• The article reviews research on stereotype threat and shows the circumstances in which performance is undermined. Various coping strategies that people who are vulnerable to stereotype threat can employ are identified.

Schmitt, M. T., & Branscombe, N. R. (2002a). The meaning and consequences of perceived discrimination in disadvantaged and privileged social groups. *European Review of Social Psychology, 12,* 167–199.

• This article comprehensively reviews research on perceived discrimination, and considers the different meanings that an attribution to prejudice can have among members of low and high status groups. An important coping strategy—group identification—that protects well-being in the face of devaluation threat is identified.

Dijksterhuis, A. (2004). I like myself but I don't know why: Enhancing implicit self-esteem by subliminal evaluative conditioning. *Journal of Personality and Social Psychology, 86,* 345–355.

• Dijksterhuis examines whether implicit self-esteem can be conditioned and thereby improved. By practicing pairing the self with positive attributes, implicit associations between them can be strengthened and can protect the self when threat is encountered.

PREJUDICE
Its Causes, Effects, and Cures

I (Nyla Branscombe) use international air travel frequently, commuting between the United States and Europe several times a year, in addition to trips to Canada and Australia. This means that for flights departing from the United States—since the terrorist attacks of September 11, 2001—I, like other Americans, have encountered dramatic increases in airport security procedures. Now, in U.S. airports, we routinely see military personnel carrying weapons and other indicators that we live in a nation "on alert." During various trips, I have wondered about the extent to which experiencing such security procedures—including removal of shoes and body searches with metal detectors—affects travelers and in what ways. Some might expect that such increased security will make us feel more "secure" and reduce feelings of threat because it serves as a reminder that our government is actively trying to prevent other would-be-attackers from succeeding at doing so. However, much social psychological research suggests that the experience of such security procedures, which have long been common in nations such as Israel, may actually have the opposite effect. That is, such reminders that our safety is in jeopardy can make death salient, heighten anxiety, and, as a result, have the potential to increase prejudice toward the group representing the threat (Pyszczynski et al., 2004). This psychological consequence is consistent with reports of Muslim Americans' experiences at airports since 9/11, and, more generally, with people who appear to be of Arab origin (Fries, 2001; Gerstenfeld, 2002). As you will see in this chapter, feelings of threat and vulnerability have played a critical role in theories of prejudice.

Recently, while traveling with a friend who is of Middle Eastern descent, I noticed that he received special scrutiny from U.S. security personnel, as well as some wary glances from other passengers. Do you think such additional scrutiny stems from prejudice? Do we perceive the actions of members of our own group—for example, its treatment of Arab and Muslim Americans or citizens of other nations—as prejudicial? Or, are we more likely to perceive such scrutiny as legitimate when we feel our own group is under threat? In this chapter, we will consider when prejudicial treatment is seen as legitimate, and when it is seen as illegitimate and something that we should work to combat.

At some time or other, virtually everyone comes face to face with prejudice—as either the target; as an observer of someone else's treatment of members of another group, as I did in the airport example; or as a perpetrator—when we recognize that we do feel and act less positively toward members of some groups compared with how we respond to members of our own group. Prejudice is not limited to the extreme forms shown in Figure 6.1 on page 212—that associated with atrocities such as ethnic cleansing in Europe and Africa, the institution of slavery, or the attacks on the World Trade Center and the Pentagon on September 11, 2001. As you will see in this chapter, the *roots* of such prejudice can be found in the cognitive and emotional processes that social psychologists have measured with reference to a number of different social groups.

Even if less extreme, prejudice can be consequential for its victims when it is based on category memberships, including age, occupation, gender, religion, language spoken and regional accent, sexual orientation, or body weight, to name just a few. Discriminatory treatment based on such category memberships can be blatant or it can be relatively subtle (Devine, Plant, & Blair, 2001; Swim & Campbell, 2001). Prejudice may be perceived by its perpetrators as acceptable and justified (Crandall, Eshleman, & O'Brien, 2002), or it can be seen as illegitimate and something that individuals should actively strive to prevent, both in themselves and in others (Devine & Monteith, 1993). In other words, all inequality and differential treatment is *not* perceived and responded to in the same way. Some forms of inequality are perceived as justified, and when norms concerning its legitimacy begin to change, threat can be aroused. Under these conditions, those high in prejudice may attempt to maintain the status quo, and even show a backlash against those seeking change. Those low in prejudice, in contrast, may strive to accelerate social change in those same changing social conditions, in the belief that doing so is how social justice is best achieved. Under such unstable and changing conditions, social conflict will be felt most intensely, with public opinion likely to be polarized concerning how relations among the groups should be (Hogg & Abrams, 1988).

In this chapter, we will examine the nature of *stereotyping* and consider how it is related to *discrimination,* particularly discrimination against women in the workplace. Although there is a high degree of interpersonal contact between men and women, which tends to be absent in other cases, such as racial and religious groups (Jackman, 1994), it is a group membership in which we all have a stake. We then turn to perspectives on the origins and nature of *prejudice* and consider why it is so persistent. Lastly, we explore various successful strategies that have been used to reduce prejudice.

Figure 6.1 ■ The Evil Results of Prejudice
At one time or other, all of us come face to face with prejudice, although
hopefully not in such extreme forms as the atrocities depicted here. Some
of the devastating effects of ethnic cleansing, slavery, and prejudice
against Americans on the part of al Qaeda are illustrated here.

The Nature and Origins of Stereotyping, Prejudice, and Discrimination

In everyday conversation, the terms *stereotyping*, *prejudice*, and *discrimination* are often
used interchangeably. However, social psychologists have drawn a distinction between
them by building on the more general attitude concept (see Chapter 4). That is, stereotypes are considered the cognitive component of attitudes toward a social group, and
they consist of beliefs about what a particular group is like. Prejudice is considered the
affective component, or the feelings we have about particular groups. Discrimination

concerns the behavioral component, or differential actions taken toward members of specific social groups.

Stereotyping: Beliefs about Social Groups

Like other attitudes, **stereotypes** about groups concern the beliefs and expectations that we have concerning what members of those groups are like. Stereotypes can include more than just traits; physical appearance, activity preferences, and likely behaviors are common components of stereotypic expectancies (Biernat & Thompson, 2002; Deaux & LaFrance, 1998; Twenge, 1999). The traits thought to distinguish between the groups can be either positive or negative attributes, they can be accurate or inaccurate, as well as being agreed with or rejected by members of the stereotyped group.

Gender stereotypes—beliefs concerning the characteristics of women and men—contain both positive and negative traits (see Table 6.1). Stereotypes of each gender are typically the converse of each other. For instance, on the positive side of the gender stereotype for women, they are viewed as being kind, nurturant, and considerate. On the negative side of the coin, they are viewed as being dependent, weak, and overly emotional. Thus, as Susan Fiske and her colleagues (Fiske et al., 2002) noted, our collective portrait of women is that they are high on warmth but low on competence. Indeed, perceptions of women are similar on these two dimensions to other groups who are seen as relatively low in status and *not* a threat to the high-status group (Conway & Vartanian, 2000; Eagly, 1987; Stewart et al., 2000). As you will see, when a group—such as Jews in Nazi Germany—is perceived as a threat to the high-status group (which is sometimes referred to as "envious prejudice"), those groups are frequently stereotyped as low in warmth but high in competence (see Glick, 2002).

Men are also assumed to have both positive and negative stereotypic traits—for example, they are viewed as decisive, assertive, and accomplished, but also as aggressive, insensitive, and arrogant. Such a portrait—being perceived as high on competence but low on communal attributes—reflects men's relatively high status. Interestingly,

stereotypes
Beliefs about social groups in terms of the traits or characteristics that they are deemed to share. Stereotypes are cognitive frameworks that influence the processing of social information.

gender stereotypes
Stereotypes concerning the traits possessed by females and males, and that distinguish the two genders from each other.

Table 6.1 ■ Common Traits Stereotypically Associated with Women and Men

As this list of stereotypic traits implies, women are seen as "nicer and warm," whereas men are seen as "competent and independent."

FEMALE TRAITS	MALE TRAITS
Warm	Competent
Emotional	Stable
Kind/polite	Tough/coarse
Sensitive	Self-confident
Follower	Leader
Weak	Strong
Friendly	Accomplished
Fashionable	Nonconforming
Gentle	Aggressive

(*Source: Based on Deaux & Kite, 1993; Eagly & Mladinic, 1994; Fiske et al., 2002.*)

The Nature and Origins of Stereotyping, Prejudice, and Discrimination

because of the strong emphasis on warmth in the stereotype for women, people tend to feel somewhat more positively about women on the whole compared with men—a finding described by Eagly and Mladinic (1994) as the "women are wonderful" effect.

Despite this greater perceived likeability, women face a key problem: The traits they supposedly possess tend to be viewed as less appropriate for high-status positions than the traits supposedly possessed by men. Women's traits tend to make them seem appropriate for "support roles," which is reflected in the actual occupational roles of women in the United States today. The vast majority of working women are in clerical, nursing, or service occupations, all of which bring less status and monetary compensation than comparably skilled male-dominated occupations (Jacobs & Steinberg, 1990; Peterson & Runyan, 1993). Although women comprise more than half the population in the United States, the power structure remains heavily male dominated: Men own and control most of the wealth, as well as the political power (Ridgeway, 2001). Again, because men and women are intimately intertwined in personal relationships, we often fail to recognize this structural fact concerning gender group membership.

■ Stereotypes and the "Glass Ceiling"

Between the 1970s and the 1990s, the proportion of managers who are women rose from 16 percent to more than 42 percent (U.S. Department of Labor, 1992). Yet, the proportion of high-level managers who are women changed very little—from 3 percent to 5 percent (Glass Ceiling Commission, 1995), reflecting what Schein (2001) has called the "think manager—think male" bias. Many authors have suggested that a **glass ceiling**—a final barrier that prevents women, as a group, from reaching top positions in the workplace—may explain these differential outcomes.

Several studies have confirmed that a glass ceiling does exist—in which women experience less favorable outcomes in their careers than men because of their gender (Heilman, 1995; Stroh, Langlands, & Simpson, 2004). For example, we know that although subordinates often *say* much the same things to female and male leaders, they actually exhibit more negative *nonverbal behaviors* toward women leaders (Butler & Geis, 1990). When women serve as leaders, they tend to receive lower evaluations from subordinates than do men, even when they act similarly (Butler & Geis, 1990; Eagly, Makijani, & Klonsky, 1992). Indeed, those women who have been rather successful in competitive, male-dominated work environments are most likely to report experiencing gender discrimination, compared with those in gender stereotypic occupations (Redersdorff, Martinot, & Branscombe, 2004), and they are especially likely to be evaluated negatively when their leadership style is task-focused or authoritarian (Eagly & Karau, 2002).

In other words, when women violate stereotypic expectancies concerning warmth and nurturance and instead act according to the prototype of a leader, particularly in masculine domains, they are likely to be rejected. For example, between 1978 and 1998, in 1,696 state executive office elections, Fox and Oxley (2003) found that women were less likely to put themselves forth as candidates, and were less successful when they did so, if they ran for stereotype-inconsistent offices (e.g., financial comptroller or attorney general) than if they ran for stereotype-consistent offices (e.g., education or human services). Violating stereotype-based expectancies appears to have been the problem for Ann Hopkins, who had acquired multi-million-dollar projects for Price Waterhouse but was declined partnership in that accounting firm, in part because she was deemed insufficiently feminine (Hopkins, 1996). In her case, the senior partners even suggested in her evaluations that she "wear more make-up" and act more "like a woman" should! Such explicit stereotyping may be one reason why the amicus brief on stereotyping research that was written by social psychologists influenced the U.S. Supreme Court, which ruled against Price Waterhouse and ordered that Ann Hopkins be given the partnership that she had earned (Fiske et al., 1991).

Recently, female professors at the prestigious Massachusetts Institute of Technology discovered that they were systematically awarded less research support and lower

glass ceiling
Barriers based on attitudinal or organizational bias that prevent qualified women from advancing to top-level positions.

Chapter 6 / Prejudice

salaries than their male colleagues (*MIT-report*, 1999). When the data that clearly illustrated the case were presented to the institution's officials, they did indeed make corrections, although they had failed to see the gender-based differences that were occurring before the data were combined across departments by gender. As Faye Crosby and her colleagues have demonstrated (Crosby et al., 1986), when individual cases are examined in isolation, people can easily generate explanations for differential treatment. It is only by combining the same case information across multiple instances that the clear pattern of differential treatment by gender is even noticed.

The overlap of stereotypes about men and stereotypes about leaders leads to the converse of the glass ceiling effect for men when they enter predominantly female occupations. In such cases, men tend to be given a ride to the top on a "glass escalator" (Williams, 1992) and rapidly become managers and executives in nursing and other traditionally female-dominated fields on entering them. Thus, the bias against people rising to the top when they enter stereotype-inconsistent work roles appears to be primarily a bias against women.

On the other hand, there is some basis for optimism for women presently entering the workforce. Lyness and Thompson (1997) compared the outcomes of men and women in a large company. The two groups were carefully matched in terms of education, work experience, and other factors. Very few differences were found in terms of their salaries, bonuses, or other benefits. However, the women reported supervising fewer subordinates and encountering more obstacles (e.g., trying to influence other people without any authority to back up such attempts). In a subsequent study, Lyness and Thompson (2000) looked more closely at the nature of the barriers that prevent women from attaining success. Again, the women and men in the study were closely matched in terms of their current job, number of years with the company, and performance ratings to assure that differences in these factors could not account for the results.

What emerged was evidence that although women and men may ultimately arrive at the same levels in a specific company, they differentially face obstacles along the way. Women reported experiencing greater difficulties with such factors as not fitting into the male-dominated culture, being excluded from informal networks, and greater difficulties in securing developmental assignments—ones that would help increase their skills and advance their careers. Again, relatively few gender differences in actual career success emerged. However, two factors—having a mentor and receiving assignments with a lot of responsibility, which women were more likely to lack than men—were strongly related to tangible measures of career success. Overall, then, while these women in management did experience more obstacles to success than men, they nevertheless appeared to surmount those obstacles and ultimately attained comparable levels of success with men. So, is there a glass ceiling? *Yes,* in the sense that women must overcome greater obstacles than men to arrive at similar levels of success. But the fact that a few do, ultimately, arrive at high levels of management (a few of the women in the sample had yearly salaries higher than $500,000) suggests that in recent years some cracks have begun to appear in the glass ceiling. Although a lot remains to be done, it does seem that some change has occurred in the world of work, and some women do overcome the obstacles that gender stereotyping places in their way.

▪ Consequences of Token Women in High Places

We can reasonably ask if the success of those individual women who have managed to break through the glass ceiling (see Figure 6.2 on page 216 for an example) makes discrimination seem less plausible as an explanation for other women's relative lack of success. To the extent that the success of such token high-status women is taken as evidence that gender no longer matters (Ely, 1994; Geis, 1993; Greenhaus & Parasuraman, 1993), people may infer that the relative absence of women in high places is due to their lacking the necessary qualities to succeed. For this reason, the success of token high-status women may obscure the structural nature of the disadvantages that women on the whole

Figure 6.2 ■ Do Visible and High-Status Women Lead Us to Believe That Discrimination Is a Thing of the Past?
Condoleeza Rice, U.S. Secretary of State. Her presence in this role might seem to suggest that "anyone can make it to the top" and that group membership is no longer important. Research suggests that gender and racial discrimination are alive and well, however, in American workplaces.

do face. As a result of the presence of a few successful tokens, those women who do not achieve similar success may come to believe that they have only themselves to blame (Schmitt, Ellemers, & Branscombe, 2003). A number of laboratory experiments have confirmed that tokenism can be a highly effective strategy for deterring collective protest by disadvantaged groups. For instance, allowing even a small percentage (e.g., 2 percent) of low-status group members to advance into a higher-status group deters collective resistance and leads disadvantaged group members to favor individual attempts to overcome barriers (Lalonde & Silverman, 1994; Wright, Taylor, & Moghaddam, 1990).

There are other negative consequences of tokenism, especially when the well-being of the person selected as a token is considered. Imagine that you are hired for a job you really want and at a higher starting salary than you expected. At first, you are happy about your good fortune. Now assume that one day you learn that you got the job mainly because you belong to a specific group—one that the company feels it must hire in order to avoid accusations of discrimination. How will you react? And how will other members of your company, who know that you were hired for this reason, perceive you? With respect to the first of these questions, research findings indicate that many persons find this kind of situation quite distressing. They are upset when they learn that they have been hired or promoted solely because of their ethnic background, gender, or some other reason that they see as being irrelevant to their abilities (Crosby, 2004). Further, they may object to it seeming to be sufficient on the part of the powers that be to have only one or a few members of their gender, ethnic, or religious group in the work setting.

Growing evidence indicates that persons who are hired as token representatives of their groups are perceived quite negatively by other members of the company (Yoder & Berendsen, 2001). In a sense then, such tokens are set up to be marginalized and disliked by their coworkers (Fuegen & Biernat, 2002). For example, job applicants who are identified as "affirmative action hirees" are perceived as less competent by people reviewing their files than are applicants who are *not* identified in this manner (Heilman, Block, & Lucas, 1992). Such a designation seems to imply to perceivers that the hiree is not qualified, which is not a happy situation for any prospective employee!

Hiring persons as token members of their group is just one form of **tokenism;** it can be manifested in other ways as well. Performing trivial positive actions for the targets of prejudice can serve as an excuse or justification for later discriminatory treatment (Wright, 2001). In this case, perpetrators can point to their prior positive actions as a credential that indicates their "nonprejudiced" treatment of members of the target group. In whatever form it occurs, research indicates that tokenism can have at least two negative effects. First, it lets prejudiced people off the hook; they can point to the token as public proof that they aren't really bigoted, and the presence of a token helps to maintain perceptions that the existing system is legitimate and fair, even among members of the disadvantaged group (see Ellemers, 2001). Second, it can be damaging to the self-esteem and confidence of the targets of prejudice, including those few persons who are selected as tokens.

tokenism
Tokenism can refer to hiring based on group membership. It also can concern instances in which individuals perform trivial positive actions for members of out-groups that are later used as an excuse for refusing more meaningful beneficial actions for members of these groups.

benevolent sexism
Views suggesting that women are superior to men in various ways (e.g., they are more pure, have better taste) and are truly necessary for men's happiness (e.g., no man is truly fulfilled unless he has a women he adores in his life).

Do Targets Agree with Stereotyped Portrayals of Their Group?

Are women around the world as likely to, if not more so than men, concur with what they perceive to be positive stereotypic images of their group? For example, in what Peter Glick and his colleagues (2000) describe as **benevolent sexism**—views suggesting that women are superior to men in various ways (e.g., they are more moral, have better taste) and that they play a necessary role in men's happiness (e.g., no man can be fulfilled without a woman in his life)—women often agree more strongly with the idea that their group has such positively distinct attributes than do men. Low-status groups are especially likely to show such **social creativity responses**—in which alternative dimensions are chosen as a means of differentiating their group from the higher-status group—when inequality between the groups is stable (Tajfel & Turner, 1986). As shown in Figure 6.3, in a massive study involving more than 15,000 participants in nineteen different countries, Glick et al. (2000) showed that such positive distinctiveness beliefs about women's finer qualities, which those researchers label *benevolent sexism,* are often agreed with more by women than men, whereas men uniformly show higher **hostile sexism** than do women.

As we discuss below in the section on prejudice, it is not surprising that men would consistently report greater hostile sexism than women, because it amounts to regarding women as a threat to the position of men (e.g., women are attempting to seize power from men that they should not have; they seek special favors that they don't deserve). You can pretty much substitute almost any disadvantaged group label in the items on the hostile sexism measure and have a reasonable assessment of prejudice

social creativity responses
When low-status groups attempt to achieve positive distinctiveness for their group on alternative dimensions that do not threaten the high-status group (e.g., *benevolent sexism*).

hostile sexism
The view that women are a threat to men's position (e.g., they seek special favors they do not deserve or are attempting to seize power that they should not have from men).

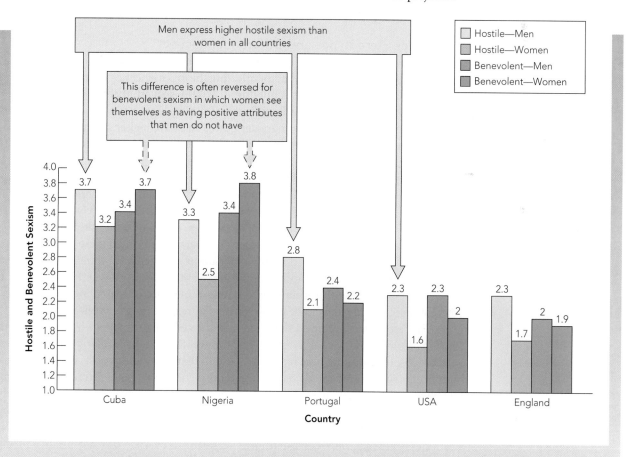

Figure 6.3 ■ Hostile and Benevolent Sexism around the Globe

Two forms of sexism have been identified—hostile (e.g., seeing women as a threat to men's position) and benevolent (e.g., seeing women as possessing uniquely positive attributes that are not shared by men). Men generally show *hostile sexism* more strongly than women, but this difference is often reversed with respect to *benevolent sexism.* (*Source: Based on data from Glick et al., 2000.*)

toward that specific group. Indeed, such items are very similar to how most measures of "modern prejudice" are worded, regardless of the group referenced in the measure. That is not the case for the benevolent sexism items, however, which refer to the positive attributes of the disadvantaged group. Indeed, many disadvantaged groups show this sort of favoritism toward their own group on dimensions that do not challenge the high-status group's position; that is, they *self-stereotype* by agreeing with what they perceive to be *positive* descriptions of their group (Ellemers et al., 1997; Jetten & Spears, 2003; Mummendey & Schreiber, 1984; Oakes, Haslam, & Turner, 1994).

In addition to the gender differences in hostile and benevolent sexism scores that Glick et al. (2000) report, the degree to which gender inequality is present in the participants' countries, based on data from the United Nations, was recorded. These researchers found that the greater the gender inequality in a nation (in terms of women not being found in high-status jobs, having few educational opportunities and a poor standard of living), the more both forms of sexism were present (men perceiving women as a threat and women perceiving their group as having distinct and positive attributes). However, only hostile sexism predicted negative stereotyping of women. Overall, then, **sexism**—or perceiving and treating the gender groups differently—may not simply refer to hostility toward women; it can also mean greater perceived gender stereotypic differences that might seem to favor women. Although the latter could appear to suggest a kinder, gentler face of stereotyping, as Glick et al. (2000) note, benevolent sexism may serve to keep women in a subordinate role by suggesting that their attributes make them uniquely suited for roles that are subordinate to men.

Gender Stereotypes and Differential Respect

Though gender stereotypes are an important part of persistent sexism and the glass ceiling effect, they are not the only factor affecting the experiences of women, especially in the workplace. Jackson, Esses, and Burris (2001) suggest that another variable—differential **respect**—is critical for women attaining high-status positions. Precisely because men occupy positions of greater power and have higher status in society, people may then infer that they are more *deserving* of respect than women, who are more likely to be found in relatively low status positions.

To determine whether differential respect actually does play a role in discrimination against women, Jackson, Esses, and Burris (2001) conducted a series of studies in which male and female participants evaluated applicants for relatively high status or low status jobs (e.g., regional director of a real estate company versus short-order cook). The applicants were either men or women, and participants rated these persons on the basis of information contained in job applications the men and women had, supposedly, completed. In addition to rating the applicants in terms of whether they should be hired, participants also completed a standard measure of masculine and feminine stereotyping. Finally, they indicated their level of respect for the applicants.

The researchers predicted that men would receive higher ratings in terms of both hiring recommendations and respect, and this was the case, particularly for the higher-status jobs. In addition, these researchers found that only ratings of respect for the job applicants significantly predicted hiring recommendations; gender stereotypes did *not* predict such ratings. In other words, the more respect participants in the study expressed for the applicants, the higher their ratings of these persons in terms of hiring recommendations. In contrast, the extent to which participants rated the applicants as showing traits consistent with gender stereotypes did *not* predict hiring recommendations. Because men, across the board, received higher ratings of respect, the results suggested that this factor indeed plays an important role in at least some forms of discrimination against women. In summary, it appears that although gender stereotypes certainly contribute to the persistence of discrimination against women, they are not the entire story. Differential respect for the two genders contributes substantially.

sexism
Prejudice based on gender; it typically refers to biases and negative responses toward women.

respect
The quality of being seen positively and as having worth. People seem to believe that men deserve greater respect than women.

Are Gender Stereotypes Accurate?

Do men and women really differ in the ways that gender stereotypes suggest? This question is complex, because such gender differences, even if observed, may be more a reflection of the *impact* of stereotypes and their self-confirming nature than of basic differences between females and males (Chen & Bargh, 1997; Claire & Fiske, 1998; Eagly, 1987). Existing evidence, however, points to the following conclusion: There are some differences between males and females with respect to various aspects of behavior, but in general, the magnitude of such differences is much smaller than prevailing gender stereotypes might suggest (Bettencourt & Miller, 1996; Plant et al., 2000; Swim, 1994). As illustrated in Figure 6.4, gender stereotypes can be exaggerations that reflect behaviors that are typical of the roles occupied by men and women. As these roles have shifted, so, too, have the behaviors most typical of both genders (Eagly & Wood, 1999). In the section **The Science of Social Psychology: Making Sense of Common Sense** on page 220, we consider how stereotyping might still be operating, despite people often showing no differences in the evaluations given to women and men.

Figure 6.4 ■ Gender Stereotypes: An Example

Gender stereotypes suggest that men share certain traits, while women share different traits. Obviously, such stereotypes about men's lack of domestic abilities are an exaggeration: Some men, at least, can indeed remember anniversaries and pick up their own clothes! (*Source:* © *Tribune Media Services*, Inc. All rights reserved. Reprinted with permission.)

Shifting Standards: Does No Difference in Evaluations Indicate No Difference in Meaning?

At present, overt discrimination on the basis of gender, race, and religious affiliation is illegal in many countries. Does this mean that stereotype-based discrimination has been eliminated? Not necessarily. Although overt and blatant discrimination may be substantially reduced, other more subtle forces continue to operate in ways that perpetuate discrimination in even well-meaning people (Crosby, 2004).

When people appear to evaluate members of two different groups similarly, does that really mean that stereotypes are not operating, and, if not, how can we know that is the case? Common sense suggests that when no differences in evaluations are obtained, it means that discrimination is absent. However, social psychologists have documented how there might be more going on than meets the eye, and that we would be wrong if we too quickly conclude that stereotypes are not continuing to affect behavior.

In a fascinating line of research by Monica Biernat and her colleagues on the **shifting standards** phenomena, we have learned that even when the same evaluation ratings are given to targets who are members of different groups, it does *not* mean that stereotypes are not influencing those ratings. Nor will those identical evaluation ratings translate into the same behavioral expectations. Consider, for example, whether it necessarily means the same thing

for you to give a woman baseball player a 7 on a scale ranging from 1 to 7, in which high scores mean "extremely good," as if you gave a male baseball player the identical 7 rating. Would you expect these two players to also have the same batting averages, and would you be similarly likely to pick them for your baseball team?

According to Biernat and Vescio (2002), those identical scores on **subjective scales**—which are open to interpretation and lack an externally grounded referent in reality, including scales labeled from good to bad or weak to strong—can take on different meanings depending on the group membership of the person being evaluated. These different meanings are revealed when judgments about the targets are also made on **objective scales**—those that are tied to measurement units that mean the same thing regardless of category membership. For example, dollars earned per year mean the same thing regardless of whether you are male or female, but rating oneself as "earning a lot" might take more dollars if you are male than if you are female. In this case, because women tend to compare themselves with other women, and because women are known to earn less than men, women may conclude that they are doing pretty well when they make less (Major, 1994). In other words, if stereotypes lead people to make **within-group comparisons**—compare themselves only with other members of the same group—subjective ratings can be the same for members of different groups, although those evaluations translate into something quite different in reality for members of those groups. That is, when subjective ratings are translated into dollars, feet and inches, pounds, or batting averages, we

Why Do People Form and Use Stereotypes?

schemas
Cognitive frameworks developed through experience that affect the processing of new social information.

shifting standards
When people use one group as the standard but shift to another group as the comparison standard when judging members of a different group.

Stereotypes often function as **schemas,** which, as we saw in Chapter 2, are cognitive frameworks for organizing, interpreting, and recalling information (Wyer & Srull, 1994). Also, as we noted in Chapter 2, human beings are "cognitive misers"—investing the least amount of cognitive effort possible in many situations. Thus, one important reason people hold stereotypes is that doing so can save considerable cognitive effort—the effort required to perceive the person complexly as an individual. We don't have to bother engaging in careful, systematic processing, because we "know" what members of this group are like; we can rely on quicker, heuristic-driven processing and use these preconceived beliefs when making behavioral choices. The results of several studies offer support for this view of stereotyping (Bodenhausen, 1993; Macrae, Milne, & Bodenhausen, 1994). This is not the only purpose served by stereotypes, however. As you'll see below, stereotypes can serve important motivational purposes; in addition to providing us with a sense that we understand the world, they can help us feel positive about our own group

can see that stereotypes did influence those "no differ-ence" ratings, because they produced very different (and stereotyped) expectancies on measurement units that do have a constant meaning.

So, what happened when Biernat and Vescio asked people to evaluate on subjective scales nine men and nine women from photographs that were prerated as "looking similarly athletic" in terms of their likely batting and field-ing abilities from "good" to "poor?" Did those ratings reflect closely the participants' responses on more "objec-tive" measures when they were also asked to choose thir-teen of the eighteen people to be on their team, and to decide the batting order for ten players (with the other three on the supposed team to be benched)? The argu-ment was that they would not, because with such "zero-sum" behavioral choices, which involve an allocation of

limited resources, like other objective scales, they require the respondent to use an absolute standard that has the same meaning regardless of category membership ("You're on the team or you are not"). How would you rate the targets shown in Figure 6.5? Were you aware that you might be thinking, "She could be pretty good...*for a girl?*" What happens when you evaluate both the male and female targets using a common standard (e.g., how good is each compared with professional baseball players, or how often will each hit home runs)?

On the subjective scales concerning good to poor batting and fielding ability ratings, participants actually dis-played a tendency to favor women over men. This would seem to imply that the stereotype concerning women's lesser skill in sports was not operating. However, when the objective scale or zero-sum judgments were considered (e.g., team selections, batting order, and benching deci-sions), a very different pattern emerged. On each of these measures, men were consistently given preference over women. This research therefore suggests that "same" does not necessarily mean "equal" or the absence of stereotyping. In fact, on measures in which the meaning of "good" can differ depending on group membership, such ratings can often mask stereotyping effects, while objective measures can reveal them.

Figure 6.5 ■ Shifting Standards: Do Similar Ratings of Girls and Boys Mean the Same Thing?
Gender stereotypes may induce us to equivalently rate members of different groups by leading us to use different standards of comparison. Male and female targets may be similarly rated on subjective rating scales, but when it comes time to pick one of these for the team, the male player will be more likely to be selected. (*Source: Based on Biernat & Vescio, 2002.*)

identity in comparison with other social groups. For now, though, let's consider what the cognitive miser perspective has illustrated in terms of how stereotypes are used.

Stereotypes: How They Operate

Consider the following groups: Korean Americans, homosexuals, Native Americans, artists, homeless people. Suppose you were asked to list the traits most characteristic of each. You would probably not find this a difficult task. Most people can easily construct a list for each group, and, moreover, they could probably do so even for groups with whom they have had limited personal contact. Stereotypes provide us with information about the typical or "modal" traits supposedly possessed by persons belonging to these groups (Judd, Ryan, & Parke, 1991), and, once activated, these traits come automatically to mind. It is this fact that explains the ease with which you can construct such lists, even though you may not have had much direct experience with any of these social groups.

Stereotypes act as theories, guiding what we attend to and exerting strong effects on how we process social information (Yzerbyt, Rocher, & Schradron, 1997). Information

subjective scales
Response scales that are open to interpretation and lack an externally grounded referent, including scales labeled from good to bad or weak to strong. They are said to be subjective because they can take on different meanings, depending on the group membership of the person being evaluated.

relevant to an activated stereotype is often processed more quickly and remembered better than information unrelated to it (Dovidio, Evans, & Tyler, 1986; Macrae et al., 1997). Similarly, stereotypes lead persons holding them to pay attention to specific types of information—usually, information consistent with the stereotypes. Furthermore, when information *inconsistent* with stereotypes does manage to enter consciousness, it may be actively refuted or changed in subtle ways that makes it seem *consistent* with the stereotype (Kunda & Oleson, 1995; Locke & Walker, 1999; O'Sullivan & Durso, 1984).

How do we make such stereotype-inconsistent information make sense when we encounter it? Suppose you learn that a well-known liberal politician has come out in favor of a large tax cut. This information is inconsistent with your stereotype of liberals, so you quickly draw another inference that will permit you to make sense of the unexpected information—for instance, you might conclude that this politician did so because most of the tax cut will go to people with low incomes. This is consistent with your stereotype of liberal politicians' concern with improving the plight of the poor. Such inferences can help you to retain your stereotype intact, despite the presence of disconfirming information. In view of such effects—which appear to be both strong and general in scope—two social psychologists, Dunning and Sherman (1997) have described stereotypes as *inferential prisons:* Once they are formed, they shape our perceptions so that new information about members of stereotyped groups is interpreted as confirming our stereotypes, even if this not the case.

Research findings also indicate that when we encounter someone who belongs to a group about whom we have a stereotype, and this person does not seem to fit the stereotype (e.g., a highly intelligent and cultivated person who is also a member of a low-status occupational group), we do not necessarily alter our stereotype about what is typical of members of that occupational group. Rather, we place such persons into a special category or **subtype** consisting of persons who do not confirm the schema or stereotype (Richards & Hewstone, 2001; Queller & Smith, 2002). It is only when the person who disconfirms the stereotype in one specific way, but is otherwise seen as a typical group member, that stereotype revision seems to occur (Locke & Johnston, 2001). This is especially the case when we repeatedly encounter members of the stereotyped group who consistently show this one deviation from our stereotype. When the disconfirming target is seen to be atypical of the group as a whole, or the target represents an extreme disconfirmation of the stereotype, then stereotypes are not revised.

Think about what effect encountering a taxi driver who dresses rather formally and fashionably, has Shakespeare's sonnets lying open on the front seat of the taxi, and speaks elegantly would have on your stereotype of taxi drivers. Would she lead you to stop expecting taxi drivers to be aggressive men who are not well educated and who dress casually? Not likely. Instead, you would simply think she's atypical, and her extreme atypicality on a variety of dimensions might even confirm the "validity" of your initial stereotype about what *most* taxi drivers are like. Now suppose I told you that I met this particular taxi driver in Germany? Ah, you say, no wonder—the stereotype doesn't apply in foreign countries—and your stereotype of *American* taxi drivers remains unchanged.

Forming Illusory Correlations

Suppose you were asked to evaluate the criminal tendencies of two groups: Would your ratings of them differ depending on the size of the group? Your first answer is probably, "Of course not—why should they?" Let's assume for the moment that the actual rate of criminal behavior is 10 percent in both a majority and a minority group. Surprisingly, research suggests that you might form more negative stereotypes and perceive the minority group less favorably than the majority group with exactly the same rates of negative behaviors (Johnson & Mullen, 1994; McConnell, Sherman, & Hamilton, 1994). Social psychologists refer to this tendency to overestimate the rate of negative behaviors in relatively small groups as the formation of **illusory correlations.** This term

objective scales
Scales with measurement units that are tied to external reality so that they mean the same thing regardless of category membership (e.g., dollars earned, feet and inches, chosen or rejected).

within-group comparisons
Comparisons made between a target and other members of that same category only.

subtype
A subset of a group that is not consistent with the stereotype of the group as a whole.

illusory correlation
The perception of a stronger association between two variables than actually exists.

makes a great deal of sense, because such effects involve perceiving links between variables that aren't really there—in this case, links between being a member of a minority group and the tendency to engage in criminal behavior.

As you can readily see, illusory correlations, to the extent they occur, can have important implications. In particular, the formation of illusory correlations can help explain why negative behaviors are often attributed to members of various minority groups. For example, some social psychologists have suggested that illusory correlation effects help explain why many whites in the United States overestimate crime rates among African American men (Hamilton & Sherman, 1989). For many complex reasons, young African American men are, in fact, arrested for various crimes at higher rates than young white men or those of Asian descent (United States Department of Justice, 1994). But white Americans tend to *overestimate* the size of this difference, and this can be interpreted as an instance of illusory correlation. Interestingly, Mark Schaller and Anne Maass (1989) have shown that illusory correlation effects do not occur among minority-group members, or when forming an illusory correlation would result in one's own group being negatively stereotyped.

But why, then, do such effects occur among majority-group members? One explanation is based on the distinctiveness of infrequent events or stimuli. According to this view, infrequent events are distinctive and readily noticed. For this reason, they may be encoded more extensively than other items when they are encountered, and so become more accessible in memory. When judgments about the groups involved are made later, the distinctive events come readily to mind, and this leads us to overinterpret their importance. Consider how this explanation applies to the tendency of white Americans to overestimate crime rates among African Americans. African Americans are a minority group (they compose about 12 percent of the total population); for this reason, they are high in distinctiveness. Many criminal behaviors, too, are highly distinctive (relatively rare). When news reports show African Americans being arrested for such crimes, this information becomes highly accessible in memory. It also is highly consistent with existing stereotypes about African American men, and this, too, is a condition known to increase the size of illusory correlation effects (McArthur & Friedman, 1980). Thus, because of the multiple forms of distinctiveness and consistency with existing stereotypes, white Americans may tend to believe such illusory correlation-based information (Hamilton & Sherman, 1989; Stroessner, Hamilton, & Mackie, 1992).

■ Out-Group Homogeneity: "They're All the Same"—or Are They?

Do stereotypes, in effect, lead us to conclude that members of another group are "all the same"? To what extent do we see members of groups we do not belong to as more similar to one another (e.g., as more homogeneous) than the members of our own group? The tendency to perceive persons belonging to groups other than one's own as all alike is known as the **out-group homogeneity** effect (Linville et al., 1989). The mirror image of this is **in-group differentiation**—the tendency to perceive members of our own group as being different from one another (as being more heterogeneous) than those of other groups.

Out-group homogeneity has been demonstrated for a variety of different groups. For example, individuals tend to perceive persons older than themselves as more similar to one another than persons in their own age group—an intriguing type of "generation gap" (Linville, Fischer, & Salovney, 1989). People also perceive students from another university as more homogeneous than students at their own university, especially when these persons appear to be biased against *them* (Rothgerber, 1997).

The converse—an **in-group homogeneity** effect—in which "we" are seen as all similar to each other often emerges among minority groups (Simon, 1992; Simon & Pettigrew, 1990), and this is particularly likely in social contexts in which the minority is preparing to respond to perceived injustices (Simon, 1998). Indeed, both effects

out-group homogeneity
The tendency to perceive members of an out-group as "all alike" or more similar to each other than members of the in-group.

in-group differentiation
The tendency to perceive members of our own group as showing much larger differences from one another (as being more heterogeneous) than members of other groups.

in-group homogeneity
In-group members are seen as more similar to each other than out-group members are. This tends to occur most among minority-group members.

(in-group and out-group homogeneity) have been observed in one study. By assessing stereotypical perceptions of the in-group and the out-group among both gay and straight men, Simon, Glassner-Bayerl, and Stratenwerth (1991) found that straight participants exhibited an out-group homogeneity effect, while the gay participants exhibited an in-group homogeneity effect.

What accounts for the tendency to perceive members of other groups as more homogeneous than members of our own group and the less frequent but equally important tendency to perceive members of the in-group as similarly united and homogeneous? One explanation that has been offered for the out-group homogeneity effect involves the fact that we have a great deal of experience with members of our own group, and so are exposed to a wider range of individual variation within that group. In contrast, we generally have much less experience with members of other groups, and hence less exposure to their individual variations (Linville, Fischer, & Salovney, 1989). Another explanation for these different kinds of homogeneity effects has emerged recently because the differential familiarity notion cannot explain why in-group homogeneity would occur. That is, depending on the perceiver's purposes in a given setting, they may be motivated to emphasize their similarities with each other (e.g., when those perceptions are useful for mobilizing against a majority group) or their differences from each other (e.g., when majority groups want to emphasize their own individuality, and the lack thereof in out-groups). Because either the in-group or the out-group can be perceived as relatively more homogeneous, it suggests that stereotyped perception may have strategic elements, with stereotypes being recruited in the service of social motives (Oakes, Haslam, & Turner, 1994; Simon, 2004).

Do Stereotypes Ever Change?

We have reviewed evidence that stereotypes can be automatically activated, that we interpret new information in ways that allow us to maintain our stereotypes, and we form illusory correlations concerning the negativity of minority groups. Does this mean that it is never possible to change stereotypes? We must first consider whether stereotypes might serve other purposes besides efficiency, conserving mental effort, and helping us maintain our preexisting beliefs. If so, the motivations that stereotypes serve could provide us with clues about when and why stereotypes might change.

Many theorists have suggested that stereotypic judgments will be stable as long as the nature of the intergroup relationship that exists between any two groups is stable (e.g., Eagly, 1987; Oakes et al., 1994; Sherif, 1966; Tajfel, 1981). That is, because we construct stereotypes that reflect how we see members of groups actually behaving, stereotype change should occur primarily when the relations between the groups change (so the behaviors we observe change accordingly). In addition, because we generally hold stereotypes that are favorable to our own group, in comparison with another group, unless social conditions shift in terms of the extent to which such in-group favoritism is seen as warranted and acceptable, unfavorable stereotypes of groups of which we are not members can be expected to persist (Spears, Jetten, & Doosje, 2001).

Lastly, because stereotypes serve as justifications for existing social arrangements, only when values and the categorizations used shift, or our stake in the present status relations is altered, should stereotypes change (Haslam, 2001). For example, as people change group memberships and move up within the status hierarchy, does their tendency to stereotype those with less power and status change? According to Susan Fiske and her colleagues, those with more power are especially inclined to attend to information that is consistent with negative stereotypes about members of subordinate groups (Fiske & Depret, 1996; Goodwin et al., 2000). In contrast, members of subordinate groups—because they need to be accurate and individuate members of the powerful group—tend to stereotype them less (Fiske, 2000). This, of course, does not mean that disadvantaged groups do not have stereotypes about powerful groups. Disadvantaged groups' stereotypes of powerful groups reflect their negative (frequently discriminatory) experiences with members of those groups. For example, African Americans are likely to stereotype whites as spiteful, greedy, and selfish (Johnson & Lecci, 2003; Monteith & Spicer, 2000). We will return to the issue of when stereotypes change in the final section of the chapter when we consider interventions that have been developed to alter prejudice and discrimination.

KEY POINTS

★ *Gender stereotypes*—beliefs about the different attributes that men and women possess—play an important role in the differential outcomes that men and women receive. Women are stereotyped as high on warmth dimensions but low on competence, while men are viewed as possessing the reverse combination of traits.

★ A *glass ceiling* exists such that women encounter more barriers than men in their careers and, as a result, find it difficult to move into top positions. Women are especially likely to be penalized when they violate stereotypic expectancies.

★ *Sexism* can occur in two contrasting forms: *hostile sexism*, which involves the belief that women are a threat to men's position and negative feelings about women, and *benevolent sexism*, which involves positive beliefs about the attributes of women that makes women suitable primarily for subordinate roles. The latter—differentiating women positively from men on alternative dimensions—is an instance of *social creativity*, which many disadvantaged groups show, particularly when inequality is stable.

★ *Tokenism*—the hiring or acceptance of only a few members of a particular group—has two effects: It maintains perceptions that the system is not discriminatory, and it harms the tokens' self-esteem as well as how they are perceived by others.

★ Although males and females do differ in some aspects of their behavior, gender stereotypes exaggerate these differences, and stereotypes may be used as justification for continued differential treatment.

★ Both women and men express greater *respect* for men, and this plays an important role in biases in employee selection.

★ Stereotypes can influence behavior even in the absence of different *subjective scale* evaluations of men and women. When *objective scale* measures are employed, in which *shifting standards* cannot be used and the meaning of the response is constant, women receive worse outcomes than men.

★ Stereotypes lead us to attend to information that is consistent with them, and to construe inconsistent information in ways that allow us to maintain our stereotypes. When a person's actions are strongly stereotype-discrepant, we *subtype* that person as a special case that proves the rule and do not change our stereotypes.

★ Majority-group members tend to form *illusory correlations* about the negative attributes of minority-group members by linking two distinctive attributes—group membership and infrequent actions.

★ Majority groups tend to perceive out-group members as "all alike" (*out-group homogeneity*) and their own group members as more diverse (*in-group differentiation*). Minority groups, in contrast, often show an *in-group homogeneity* effect, particularly in contexts in which cohesion is needed to confront injustice.

★ *Stereotypes* change as the relations between the groups are altered. Those in positions of power are especially likely to negatively stereotype those with lesser status, while those with little power are motivated to attend to and individuate the powerful.

Prejudice and Discrimination: Feelings and Actions toward Social Groups

Prejudice is the feelings component of attitudes toward social groups. Prejudice reflects the feelings experienced that are based solely on a person's membership in a particular group. In that sense, prejudice is *not* personal—it is an affective reaction toward the category as a whole. In other words, a person who is prejudiced toward some social group tends to evaluate its members in a specific manner (usually negatively) *because* they belong to that group. The individual's traits or behaviors play little role; the person is disliked (or liked) precisely because she or he has been categorized as a member of a specific group that is different than the perceiver's own (Turner et al., 1987). In contrast, *discrimination* refers to the less favorable treatment or the negative actions received by members of groups that are the targets of prejudice. When prejudice is expressed in overt action, it will be fundamentally dependent on the perceived norms and acceptability of doing so (Crandall et al., 2002; Jetten, Spears, & Manstead, 1997; Turner et al., 1987). Indeed, as you will see in the final section of this chapter, changes to the perceived norms or consensus is sufficient to alter prejudice expression.

When prejudice is defined as a special type of attitude, several important implications follow. Individuals who are more prejudiced toward a particular group tend to process information about that group differently from the way they process information about other groups. Considerable research has addressed how those who are high or low in prejudice toward a particular group respond in the presence (or implied presence) of members of the target group. For example, information relating to the targets of the prejudice is often given more attention, or is processed more carefully, than information not relating to it (Blascovich et al., 1997; Hugenberg & Bodenhausen, 2003). Similarly, information that is consistent with individuals' prejudiced views often receives closer attention and so is remembered more than information that is not consistent with these views (Fiske & Neuberg, 1990; Judd et al., 1991).

Indeed, those who are high in prejudice toward a particular social group are very concerned with being certain they know the group membership of a person (when that is ambiguous). This is because they believe the groups have underlying essences—typically some biologically based feature that can be seen as unchangeable—which are then used as justification for differential treatment of the groups (Yzerbyt et al., 1997). For example, the "one drop of blood rule" for racial classification has often been employed, and it reflects the considerable concern that many people feel about being certain of the racial identity of persons with whom they might interact. In many U.S. states, if one great-grandparent was African American, that is enough to categorize a person as a member of that racial group. As a result of such attention to categorizing people in terms of their group membership and processing information in ways that confirm one's feelings about that group, prejudice becomes a kind of closed cognitive loop that can increase in strength over time.

As an attitude, prejudice is reflected in the negative feelings or emotions experienced on the part of prejudiced persons when they are in the presence of, or merely think about, members of the groups they dislike (Brewer & Brown, 1998; Vanman et al., 1997). Some theorists have suggested that all prejudices are *not* the same, or at least are not based on the same type of negative affect. According to this view, we may not be able to speak of "prejudice" as a *generic* negative emotional response toward a social group. Instead, we may need to delineate between prejudices that are associated with specific intergroup emotions, including fear, anger, envy, guilt, or disgust (Glick, 2002; Mackie & Smith, 2002). Depending on *what* emotion is primarily underlying prejudice

prejudice
Negative attitudes toward the members of specific social groups.

toward a particular group, the discriminatory actions that follow may be rather different. For example, when people's prejudice primarily reflects anger, they may attempt to harm the out-group directly in retaliation of presumed wrongs against the in-group. In contrast, prejudice based on guilt might lead to avoidance of the out-group because of the distress their plight can evoke (Branscombe & Miron, 2004). Likewise, prejudice based on disgust might result in out-group avoidance to the extent that one might be contaminated by association (Neuberg & Cottrell, 2002). In contrast, fear and envy could evoke defensive reactions aimed primarily at protecting the in-group's status position (Glick, 2002). Based on this perspective, prejudice reduction efforts may need to tackle the specific intergroup emotion on which prejudice toward a particular group is based. For example, to the extent that intergroup anxiety and fear are reduced, when prejudice is based primarily on those emotions, then prejudice can be reduced (Miller, Smith, & Mackie, 2004). If, however, prejudice toward a specific group is based on another emotional response, then that emotion may need to be addressed for prejudice toward that group to be reduced. As shown in Figure 6.6, different types of hate groups that can be readily seen on the Internet imply that prejudice can reflect rather different emotions, with the prejudicial behaviors and ideologies advocated differing accordingly.

Recent research concerning the development of prejudice suggests that only some negative emotions lead directly to automatic prejudice responses (DeSteno et al., 2004). In two experiments, these researchers found that after experiencing anger, but not sadness or a neutral state, evidence of more negative attitudes toward an out-group was

Figure 6.6 ■ **Hate on the Web: Prejudice toward Different Groups May Stem from Different Kinds of Emotions**
Each year, thousands of hate crimes—crimes based largely on ethnic, racial, or antigay prejudice—are perpetrated in the United States. Indeed, numerous hate groups have websites that they use as a method of spreading their beliefs. The information presented at these hate websites suggests that prejudice toward different groups is based on rather different kinds of intergroup emotions.

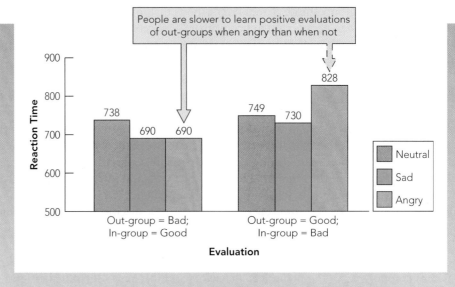

Figure 6.7 ■ One Way Prejudice Can Develop
When feeling angry for incidental reasons, people take longer to learn to associate positive evaluations about members of an out-group than to learn to associate positive evaluations with members of their in-group. Likewise, it takes longer to develop negative associations between the in-group when angry, although negative associations about the out-group develop rapidly. These differences in time to develop associations were present only when anger was induced and not when sadness or a neutral mood preceded the evaluation pairing task. (*Source: Based on data from DeSteno et al., 2004.*)

minimal groups
When people are categorized into different groups based on some "minimal" criteria, they tend to favor others who are categorized in the same group as themselves, compared with those categorized as members of a different group.

incidental feelings
Those feelings induced separately or before a target is encountered—so they are irrelevant to the group being judged, but can still affect judgments of the target.

implicit associations
Links between group membership and trait associations or evaluations of which the perceiver may be unaware. They can be activated automatically when the target is categorized as a group member.

obtained. First, participants were assigned to **minimal groups**—they were falsely told that they *belong* to a social category that is limited to the present context (e.g., they tend to overestimate or underestimate the frequency of various events), and they were asked to wear a wristband throughout the study to remind them of their group membership. After participants had been minimally so categorized, they were given an emotion-inducing writing task (e.g., to write in detail about when they felt very angry, very sad, or neutral in the past). Next, participants were asked to evaluate other members of their in-group (e.g., those wearing the same colored wristband) or the out-group (e.g., those wearing another color wristband). As shown in Figure 6.7, reaction times to associate positive or negative evaluation words with the in-group and out-group differed depending on the type of negative emotion experienced. When feeling angry, people more rapidly associated the out-group with negative evaluations and the in-group with positive evaluations, whereas it took considerably longer to learn to associate the out-group with positive evaluations and the in-group with negative evaluations. When feeling either sad or neutral, in contrast, no differences in time to associate the in-group and out-group with positive or negative evaluations were obtained. This suggests that even **incidental feelings** of anger—those caused by other factors entirely rather than the actions of the out-group per se—can generate automatic prejudice toward members of groups to which we do not belong.

As you can see, such **implicit associations**—links between group membership and evaluative responses—can be triggered in a seemingly automatic manner as a result of in-group and out-group categorization and exposure to members of the groups toward whom it is directed. Further, such implicit prejudice can influence overt behav-

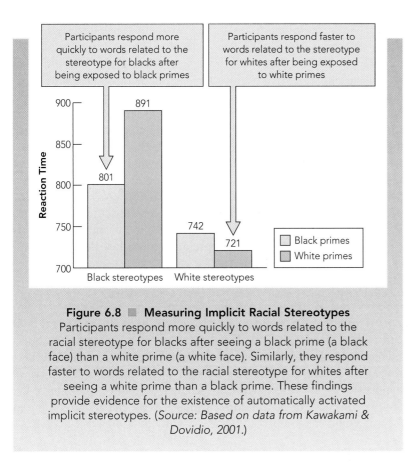

Figure 6.8 ■ Measuring Implicit Racial Stereotypes
Participants respond more quickly to words related to the racial stereotype for blacks after seeing a black prime (a black face) than a white prime (a white face). Similarly, they respond faster to words related to the racial stereotype for whites after seeing a white prime than a black prime. These findings provide evidence for the existence of automatically activated implicit stereotypes. (*Source: Based on data from Kawakami & Dovidio, 2001.*)

ior even when the persons involved are largely unaware of the existence of those views and might vigorously deny that they hold them (Fazio & Hilden, 2001; Greenwald, 2002). A method to assess such implicit prejudice was devised by Banaji and Hardin (1996). In this procedure, participants are first shown primes (stimuli associated with a particular group membership) at **subliminal levels** for such a short period of time that participants can't recognize or identify the stimuli. For instance, in one study (Kawakami & Dovidio, 2001), the primes were schematic faces of blacks or whites. After the primes were shown for a very short period (15 to 30 milliseconds), a specific kind of word category was cued by a letter or symbol—in this study, one letter stood for "houses" and the other for "persons." Finally, words related to racial stereotypes for blacks and whites or to the neutral category "houses" were presented and participants were asked to indicate whether these words could ever describe a member of the cued word category (i.e., a person or a house). For instance, one target word related to the racial stereotype for whites was "conventional," while one target word related to the racial stereotype for blacks was "musical." An example of a word related to houses was "drafty."

If implicit racial stereotypes are activated by the priming stimuli (faces of black and white persons), then response times to the target words should vary as a function of these primes. Specifically, participants should respond more quickly to words related to the racial stereotype for whites after seeing a white prime than a black prime, and faster to words related to the racial stereotype for blacks after seeing a black prime than a white prime. As you can see from Figure 6.8, this is precisely what was found. Similar results have been reported in many other studies that, together, indicate that implicit

subliminal levels
Stimuli shown to participants so rapidly that the stimuli cannot be recognized or identified by them.

stereotyping and prejudice toward blacks can be activated automatically (Kawakami, Dion, & Dovidio, 1998), as well as toward elderly people (Hense, Penner, & Nelson, 1995) and many other groups, including soccer hooligans, child abusers, skinheads, and even professors (Dijksterhuis & van Knippenberg, 1996; Kawakami et al., 2000).

The important thing about such implicit stereotyping and prejudice is this: Although we may not be aware of the fact that it is occurring, stereotyping and prejudice can still influence our judgments and decisions about other people, or even how we interact with them. In particular, growing evidence suggests that such implicit stereotypes may be better predictors of subtle or spontaneous expressions of bias than explicit measures obtained through attitude questionnaires or other kinds of self-report (Dovidio et al., 1997). Before turning to a discussion of the many ways in which prejudice is expressed in overt behavior, however, we must address two additional questions: What motivations might affect the extent to which prejudice is felt, and what psychological benefits might people get from expressing prejudice toward particular groups?

The Origins of Prejudice: Contrasting Perspectives

Several important perspectives have been developed to answer the questions, "Where does prejudice come from, and why does it persist?" The most general response to these questions has focused on **threat**—be it either material or symbolic. We consider first how perceptions of threat to self-esteem and group interests are critical for prejudice. Then we consider how competition for scarce resources can encourage prejudice expression. At the end of this section, we consider whether categorizing the self as a member of a group, and others as members of a different group, is a sufficient condition for prejudice to occur.

■ Threats to Self-Esteem

It is true that prejudice cannot be understood, unless threat and how it affects people's intergroup responses is taken into account. People want to see their own group positively (Tajfel & Turner, 1986), which in practice means more positive than some comparative reference group. When an event threatens people's perceptions of their group's value, they may retaliate by derogating the source of the threat. To threaten social identity, does the threatening event need to be consciously seen as illegitimate, or is it sufficient that it imply that your group is not as positive as you would like to see it?

To test this idea, American college students, who differed in the extent to which they placed value on their identity as Americans, were shown one of two six-minute videos based on the movie *Rocky IV* (Branscombe & Wann, 1994). In one clip, Rocky (an American boxer played by Sylvester Stallone) won the match against Ivan (a supposedly Russian contender). This version was not threatening, for it supports Americans' positive views of their group as winners. In the other clip, Rocky loses the fight to Ivan, the Russian. This version was threatening, particularly to those who highly value their identity as Americans, and it lowered feelings of self-esteem based on group membership. The question is this: Can exposure to such a minor threat to identity in the laboratory result in prejudice? The answer obtained was "yes"—those who were highly identified as Americans and who saw the threatening Rocky-as-loser film clip showed increased prejudice toward Russians and advocated they be kept out of the United States in the future. In fact, the more these participants derogated Russians, the more their self-esteem based on their group membership subsequently increased. This research suggests that holding prejudiced views of an out-group allows group members to bolster their own group's image.

In a similar vein, Fein and Spencer (1997) showed that when college students experienced a threat to their positive views about themselves personally, they also subsequently showed increased prejudice. In other words, prejudice can play an important role in protecting or enhancing the individual's self-concept. Putting down members of another

threat
Threat can take different forms, but it primarily concerns fear that one's group interests will be undermined or that one's self-esteem is in jeopardy.

group can allow people to affirm their own comparative value—to feel superior in various ways—and such prejudice may be expressed only when threat is experienced.

Consider the situation created by Sinclair and Kunda (1999). Their white participants received either praise or criticism from someone they believed was either a black or white doctor. When the criticism seemingly came from the black doctor, negative views about blacks were more strongly activated compared with when praise was received. When the doctor was thought to be white, negative views concerning blacks were not differentially activated. Thus, threat, in the form of perceived criticism from an out-group member can directly encourage prejudice expression, and this is particularly likely when the criticism is seen as group-based (see also Bourhis et al., 1978).

Having higher status and feeling superior can be a source of positive group identity, and threat to one's group's position is critical to feelings of prejudice toward a variety of social groups. Among men, to the extent that valued aspects of the self depend on seeing their gender group as superior, events that imply that social change might eliminate that superiority could feel threatening (Kilmartin, 1994). Indeed, research indicates that men's collective opposition to challenges by women and to affirmative action for women is most severe when men perceive their fortunes as declining relative to women's and they realize that the particular social policy will undermine their group's position (Faludi, 1992; Garcia et al., in press). Likewise, opposition to social policies designed to increase racial equality appears to be strongest among those whites who perceive their group's interests to be at stake (Bobo, 2000).

Such threat to group position can visibly affect men's actions toward women they perceive as competition. For example, Rudman and Fairchild (2004) hypothesized that men would be particularly likely to sabotage a woman who beat them at a computer game task when it was one at which men were said to be normatively good compared with one at which women were said to be good. Thus, when women seem to be "moving in" on men's traditional territory, women are more likely to be sabotaged in ways that affect their subsequent performance, which, in turn, serves to rationalize future prejudice toward the threatening group. Evidence for each step in this process, illustrated in Figure 6.9, was obtained. The threatened participants knew they were compromising the "deviant" target's ability to perform well in the future, and these "backlash" responses against the threatening target were associated with subsequent increased self-esteem in these male participants.

In an experimental test of the consequences of perceived threat for prejudice against immigrants, a new fictitious immigrant group was created and described to Canadians under one of two conditions (Esses et al., 1999). In the condition in which participants read that the new immigrant group, because of their strong skills, might be construed as a threat to existing Canadians in the job market, the fictitious immigrant group was

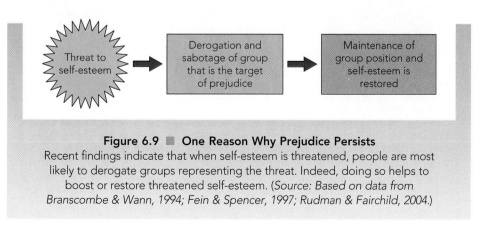

Figure 6.9 ■ One Reason Why Prejudice Persists
Recent findings indicate that when self-esteem is threatened, people are most likely to derogate groups representing the threat. Indeed, doing so helps to boost or restore threatened self-esteem. (*Source: Based on data from Branscombe & Wann, 1994; Fein & Spencer, 1997; Rudman & Fairchild, 2004.*)

responded to more negatively and more severe immigration policies were advocated than when the potential group position–threatening information was not provided. Similarly, when the immigrant group was seen as a threat to the culture of the in-group, white Americans expressed more negative attitudes toward Mexican immigrants (Zarate et al., 2004). Overall, then, these studies suggest that advantaged groups exhibit prejudice toward out-groups most strongly when the advantaged groups experience a threat to their group's image and interests.

■ Competition for Resources as a Source of Prejudice

It is sad but true that the things people want and value most—good jobs, nice homes, high status—are in short supply. Frequently, these are zero-sum outcomes—if one group has them, the other group can't. Consider the conflict between the Israelis and Palestinians. Both want the same little bit of land (i.e., Jerusalem). This sort of conflict over desirable material resources has been considered within **realistic conflict theory** (e.g., Bobo, 1983) to be a major cause of prejudice. According to this view, prejudice develops out of the struggle over land, jobs, adequate housing, and other desirable outcomes. The theory further suggests that as such competition escalates and both sides begin to experience losses, the members of the groups involved come to view each other in increasingly negative terms (White, 1977). They may label each other as "enemies," view their own group as morally superior, and draw the boundaries between themselves and their opponents more firmly, and, under extreme conditions, they may come to see the opposing group as not even human (Bar-Tal, 2003). From this perspective, what starts out as simple competition can gradually escalate into full-scale, emotion-laden prejudice (see Figure 6.10).

Evidence from several different studies confirms the role that competition can play in escalating intergroup prejudice. As competition persists, group members come to perceive each other in increasingly negative ways. A very dramatic demonstration of such effects is provided by a well-known field study conducted by Sherif and his col-

realistic conflict theory
The view that prejudice stems from direct competition between various social groups over scarce and valued resources.

Figure 6.10 ■ Intergroup Competition as a Source of Prejudice
When groups compete with each other for valued resources (e.g., land), they may come to view each other in increasingly negative terms. Ultimately, full-scale hatred or prejudice toward the group with which they are in competition may develop. As shown here, both Israelis and Palestinians are in competition for Jerusalem.

leagues (1961). This innovative study involved sending eleven-year-old boys to a special summer camp in a remote area of Oklahoma where, free from external influences, the nature of conflict and its role in prejudice could be carefully studied. When the boys arrived at the camp (named *The Robber's Cave* in honor of a nearby cave that was once, supposedly, used by robbers), they were divided into two separate groups and assigned to cabins located quite far apart. Indeed, for the first week, the campers in each group engaged in such enjoyable activities as hiking, swimming, and other sports amongst themselves, without knowing the other group even existed.

During this initial phase, the boys quickly developed strong attachments to their own groups. They chose names for their teams (*Rattlers* and *Eagles*), stenciled them onto their shirts, and made up flags with their groups' symbols on them. At this point, the second phase of the study began. The boys in both groups were brought together and began to engage in a series of competitions. They were told that the winning team would receive a trophy and its members would earn prizes (pocket knives and medals). Because these were prizes the boys strongly desired, the stage was set for intense competition. Would such conflict generate prejudice? The answer was quick in coming. As the boys competed, the tension between the groups rose. At first, it was limited to verbal taunts and name-calling, but soon it escalated into more direct acts—for example, the Eagles burned the Rattlers' flag. The next day, the Rattlers struck back by attacking the rival group's cabin, overturning beds, tearing out mosquito netting, and seizing personal property. At the same time, the two groups voiced increasingly negative views of each other. They labeled their opponents "bums" and "cowards," while heaping praise on their own group at every turn. In short, the groups showed all the key components of strong prejudice toward each other.

Fortunately, The Robber's Cave story has a happy ending. In the study's final phase, Sherif and his colleagues attempted to reduce the negative reactions the competition had instilled. Merely increasing the amount of contact between the groups failed to accomplish this goal; indeed, it seemed to fan the flames of anger. But when conditions were altered so that the groups found it necessary to work together to reach **superordinate goals**—ones they both desired but neither group could achieve alone—dramatic changes occurred. After the boys worked cooperatively together to restore their water supply (secretly sabotaged by the researchers), combined their funds to rent a movie, and jointly repaired a broken-down truck, tensions between the groups gradually decreased, and many cross-group friendships began to develop.

Because Sherif selected normal middle-class, well-adjusted boys to participate in the study, and then randomly assigned them to one team or the other, he could rule out pathology as an explanation for the prejudice that developed. The research provided a chilling picture of how competition over scarce resources could quickly escalate into full-scale conflict that fostered negative attitudes toward opponents. What he did *not* show is whether competition is *necessary* for prejudice to develop—whether that is the sole basis for the prejudice he observed. In other words, prejudice might have been present and would have been expressed—had the two groups come into contact—before any competition even took place. Recall how both groups spent the first week developing a cohesive group identity and establishing norms within each group. Perhaps simply being a member of a group and coming to identify with it is sufficient for prejudice to occur. This is the notion that was developed further by Henri Tajfel and John Turner in their social identity theory (1986), to which we will turn next.

■ Role of Social Categorization: The Us-versus-Them Effect

Although we categorize virtually every kind of object in the world, **social categorization** is special because we are members of one category or the other. This puts the self in the categorization process. Thus, people can divide the social world into distinct categories on almost any basis, and doing so can result in different perceptions of "us" (usually termed the **in-group**) versus "them" (the **out-group**). Such distinctions can be based on

superordinate goals
Goals that can be achieved only by cooperation between groups.

social categorization
The tendency to divide the social world into separate categories: our in-group ("us") and various out-groups ("them").

in-group
The social group to which an individual perceives herself or himself as belonging ("us").

out-group
Any group other than the one to which individuals perceive themselves as belonging.

an almost endless list of possibilities, depending on what categorical divisions are important in the world in which we find ourselves. For example, although the length of one's neck is not an important attribute or way of dividing people in the United States, it definitely is important among the Masai people in Kenya. As shown in Figure 6.11, people can go to great lengths—by wearing neckbands from early childhood onward—to increase their neck length. When we arrive in the world, such categorizations tell us what features of the world are important determinants of the treatment that people receive. In our world, the categorizations that tend to be important are based on race, religious group membership, gender, age, occupation, and income, to name just a few.

If the process of dividing the social world into "us" and "them" had no emotional consequences, it would have little bearing on prejudice: There would simply be many different ways that people could differ from each other. However, some differences take on considerable importance and have meaning for our own identities (Oakes et al., 1994). Sharply contrasting feelings and beliefs are associated with members of one's in-group versus members of various out-groups. Persons in the "us" category are viewed in more favorable terms, while those in the "them" category are perceived more negatively. Out-group members are assumed to possess more undesirable traits, whereas in-group members are seen as possessing positive traits (Lambert, 1995; Oakes et al., 1994). There is frequently considerable social agreement for holding differential views of in-groups and out-groups. Indeed, it may be normatively expected that some groups are disliked, while we may feel that prejudice toward other groups is less justified (Crandall et al., 2002). For example, Midwestern college students who were asked to rate the extent to which it was normatively appropriate or legitimate to express prejudice toward 105 different social groups did so easily. The top ten groups for which it is acceptable to display prejudice and the ten for which it is least legitimate to express prejudice are shown in Table 6.2.

Figure 6.11 ■ Social Categorization: In-Groups and Out-Groups
Although the length of one's neck is not an important categorization in the United States, in some parts of the world it indicates who is a member of one's tribe and who is not. In the United States, one's skin color, age, gender, and occupational markers serve similar purposes by allowing us to quickly categorize those who are members of our group and who are not.

Chapter 6 / Prejudice

Table 6.2 ◼ Whom Do We Believe It Is OK or
Not OK to Express Prejudice Toward?

The top ten list on the left indicates the groups that Midwestern college students
perceive it to be acceptable and legitimate to feel prejudice toward. The top ten
list on the right indicates what groups they perceive it to be unacceptable and
illegitimate to feel prejudice toward. How do you think these lists would differ for
people living in regions of the United States besides the Midwest, or how might
they differ for people who are members of different ethnic groups?

PREJUDICE LEGITIMIZED	PREJUDICE SEEN AS ILLEGITIMATE
Rapists	Blind people
Child abusers	Female homemakers
Child molesters	Deaf people
Wife beaters	Mentally retarded people
Terrorists	Family men
Racists	Farmers
Ku Klux Klan members	Male nurses
Drunk drivers	Librarians
Nazi party members	Bowling league members
Pregnant women who drink alcohol	Dog owners

(Source: Based on data provided by Crandall, Eshleman, & O'Brien, 2002.)

Such in-group versus out-group distinctions affect the ways in which we explain
the actions of persons belonging to each social category—the *attributions* that we make.
We tend to attribute desirable behaviors by members of our in-group to stable, internal causes (e.g., their admirable traits), but attribute desirable behaviors by members
of out-groups to transitory factors or to external causes (Hewstone, Bond, & Wan,
1983). This tendency to make more favorable and flattering attributions about members of one's own group than about members of other groups is sometimes described
as the **ultimate attribution error** (Pettigrew, 1979), because it carries the self-serving
bias described in Chapter 2 into the area of intergroup relations.

That strong tendencies to divide the social world into "us" and "them" color our
perceptions of groups has been demonstrated in many studies (Stephan, 1985; Tajfel,
1982). But how, precisely, does social categorization result in prejudice? An intriguing
answer is provided by Tajfel and his colleagues (Tajfel & Turner, 1986; Oakes et al., 1994)
in **social identity theory.** This theory suggests that individuals seek to feel positively
about the groups to which they belong, and part of their self-esteem depends on identifying with social groups. Because people who are identified with their group are most
likely to express favoritism toward their own group and a corresponding bias against
out-groups, valuing our own group has predictable consequences for prejudice (Spears,
Doosje, & Ellemers, 1999). Research findings indicate that balanced against these
tendencies is our desire to be fair-minded, and this may somewhat moderate our
propensity to boost our own group and put other groups down (Singh, Choo, & Poh,
1998). However, in general, the strong need to enhance our self-esteem wins out, and
we see other groups as inferior to our own, particularly on dimensions on which there
is existing social consensus (see Ellemers et al., 1997).

ultimate attribution error
The tendency to make
more favorable and flat-
tering attributions about
members of one's own
group than about mem-
bers of other groups. In
effect, it is the self-serving
attributional bias at the
group level.

social identity theory
A theory concerned with
the consequences of per-
ceiving the self as a member of a social group and
identifying with it.

When individuals feel secure in their own group or cultural identity, they can be generous and tolerant toward other groups or cultures. In other words, when they feel secure with respect to their own group identity (e.g., secure about its goodness or superiority), then more positive attitudes toward other groups or, conversely, reduced prejudice is most likely (Hornsey & Hogg, 2000). This reasoning leads to an intriguing prediction: Under conditions in which individuals feel that the distinctiveness (superiority) of their own group or culture is somehow threatened because their group is lumped together with another, they will react most negatively to the other group, and, moreover, these reactions will be intensified by perceived similarity between their own group and the other group. Why? Such similarity threatens the distinctiveness of their own group. In contrast, when individuals do not feel that the distinctiveness of their own group is being threatened or challenged, similarity to other groups has the opposite effect: The greater the similarity perceived between the in-group and another group, the more positive their reactions to the out-group will be.

To test these predictions, Hornsey and Hogg (2000) had students at a large university in Australia read short written passages indicating either that math–science students and humanities students are very different in their ideas and attitudes (the *low-similarity* condition) or that they are actually very similar (the *high-similarity* condition). Participants belonged to one of these groups or the other. After reading these passages, half of the participants were induced to think that they are all members of the same category—students (a procedure designed to threaten the distinctiveness of their own subgroup, be it either humanities or math–science students); this was the *threat to subgroup distinctiveness* condition. The remaining participants were induced to think both about being in the same student category *and* about their subgroup identity as either a math–science or humanities student; this was the *no threat to subgroup distinctiveness* condition. In this case, participants were made aware of their membership in one of the two subgroups and also of their membership in the entire university community.

After these procedures were completed, students rated the extent to which they thought they would enjoy working with humanities or math–science students, and how difficult working with such students would be. Participants rated both their own group and the other group in this manner. It was predicted that in the condition in which the distinctiveness of their own subgroup was not threatened, participants would express less bias toward the other group when it had been described as similar rather than dissimilar to their own. In contrast, in the threat to subgroup distinctiveness condition, the opposite should be true: Participants would actually express more bias against an out-group described as similar to their own, because this would pose an even bigger threat to their group's distinctiveness. As you can see from Figure 6.12, both of these predictions were confirmed.

These findings suggest that efforts to reduce prejudice between groups by breaking down the distinction between "us" and "them" can succeed, but only if doing so does not threaten each subgroup's unique identity or sense of superiority. In other words, our tendency to divide the social world into opposing categories seems to serve important esteem-boosting functions for us; if these are overlooked, efforts to reduce prejudice by urging distinct cultural or ethnic groups to view themselves as "one" or as not distinct could backfire. This makes the most sense for people who strongly value their subgroup identity and who are motivated to perceive their group as distinct from others.

Discrimination: Prejudice in Action

Attitudes, we noted in Chapter 4, are not always reflected in overt actions, and prejudice is definitely no exception to this rule. In many cases, persons holding negative attitudes toward the members of various groups cannot express these views directly. Laws, social pressure, fear of retaliation—all serve to deter people from putting their preju-

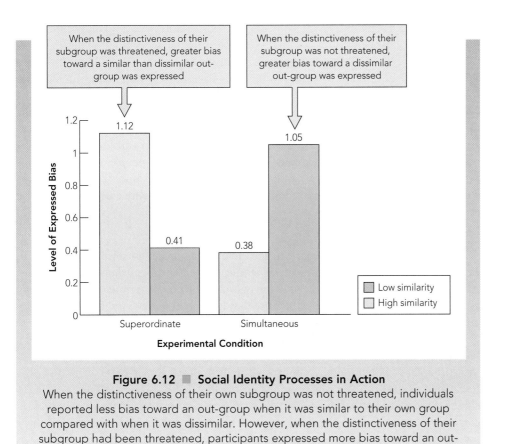

Figure 6.12 ■ Social Identity Processes in Action
When the distinctiveness of their own subgroup was not threatened, individuals reported less bias toward an out-group when it was similar to their own group compared with when it was dissimilar. However, when the distinctiveness of their subgroup had been threatened, participants expressed more bias toward an out-group that was described as similar to their own. (*Source: Hornsey & Hogg, 2000.*)

diced views into open practice. For these reasons, blatant forms of **discrimination**—negative actions toward the objects of racial, sexual orientation, gender, ethnic, or religious prejudice—have decreased somewhat in recent years in the United States and many other countries (e.g., Devine et al., 2001; Swim et al., 2001). Thus, actions such as restricting members of various groups to certain seats on buses or in movie theaters, or barring them from public restaurants, schools, or neighborhoods—all common in the past—have now largely vanished in many countries. This is not to suggest, however, that extreme expressions of prejudice have totally vanished. On the contrary, dramatic instances of hate crimes—crimes based on racial, ethnic, and other types of prejudice—continue to occur with disturbing frequency. For instance, Matthew Shepard, a college student, was murdered in Wyoming in 1998 because of his sexual preference (he was homosexual). Various antigay websites—like other hate groups—continue to present such incidents as desirable. But, in general, prejudice finds expression in much more subtle forms of behavior. What are these *subtle* or *disguised* forms of discrimination like? Research by social psychologists points to several important conclusions about how and when people will attempt to not respond in a prejudiced fashion, and what happens when they attempt to suppress these responses.

■ Modern Racism: More Subtle, but Just as Deadly

At one time, many people felt no qualms about expressing openly racist beliefs (Sears, 1988). Now, of course, very few Americans openly state such views. Does this mean that racism has disappeared or is on the wane? This circumstance is certainly plausible (Martin & Parker, 1995), but many social psychologists believe that, in fact, all that has happened is that "old-fashioned racism" (read "blatant feelings of superiority" for "old-fashioned") has been replaced by more subtle forms, which they term **modern racism**

discrimination
Differential (usually negative) behaviors directed toward members of different social groups.

modern racism
More subtle beliefs than blatant feelings of superiority. Modern racism consists primarily of thinking that minorities are seeking and receiving more benefits than they deserve and a denial that discrimination affects their outcomes.

(McConahay, 1986; Swim et al., 1995). What is such racism like? It involves concealing prejudice from others in public settings but expressing bigoted attitudes when it is safe to do so—for instance, in the company of friends and family members known to share these views. In addition, it involves attributing various bigoted views to sources other than prejudice. On measures of modern racism, individuals express agreement with the following notions: resentment of benefits that they perceive minorities to be disproportionately receiving, the perception that those same minorities are pushing too hard to get things they don't deserve, and a denial that discrimination continues to affect the outcomes of minority-group members. Precisely because many people may want to conceal their racist attitudes, social psychologists have developed unobtrusive means for studying such attitudes. Let's take a look at how these attitudes are assessed.

■ Measuring Implicit Racial Attitudes: From the Bogus Pipeline to the Bona Fide Pipeline

The most straightforward approach to measuring prejudice is to simply ask people to express their views toward various racial, ethnic, gender, or other groups—for example, African Americans, homosexuals, or women. But, many people are not willing to openly admit to holding prejudiced views, because they believe these views might be seen as illegitimate, so social psychologists have had to develop alternative ways of assessing people's actual views. One approach is known as the "bogus pipeline." In this procedure, research participants are told that they will be attached to a special apparatus and that by measuring tiny changes in their muscles (or in brain waves or other reactions), the researchers can assess their true opinions no matter what they say (see Figure 6.13). To convince respondents that this is actually so, the researcher asks for their views on several issues—ones on which their real views are known (e.g., because they expressed them several weeks earlier). The researcher then "reads" the machine and reports these views to participants, who are often quite impressed. Once they believe that the machine can, in a sense, "see inside them," there is no reason to conceal their true attitudes. Presumably, then, their responses to questions or to an attitude scale are truthful and provide an accurate picture of their attitudes, including various forms of prejudice.

Although the bogus pipeline can be useful for revealing attitudes people normally conceal, it involves deception and can succeed only to the extent that research participants believe the false statements about the functions of the apparatus used. Further, the bogus pipeline is useful only for measuring *explicit* attitudes: ones of which people are aware and could report if they wished to do so. In recent years, social psychologists have recognized that many attitudes people hold are *implicit*—they exist and can influence several forms of behavior, but the persons holding them may not be aware of their existence. In fact, in some cases, these people would vigorously deny that they hold such views, especially when the views relate to such issues as racial prejudice (Dovidio & Fazio, 1991; Greenwald & Banaji, 1995). In addition, such attitudes may be elicited automatically by exposure to members of the groups toward whom the prejudice is directed or stimuli associated with such persons. How then can such subtle forms of prejudice be measured? Several different methods have been developed (Kawakami & Dovidio, 2001), but most are based on **priming**—in which exposure to certain stimuli or events "primes" information held in memory, making it easier to bring to mind or more available to influence our current reactions.

One technique that makes use of priming to study implicit or automatically activated racial attitudes is known as the **bona fide pipeline** (in contrast to the bogus pipeline; Banaji & Hardin, 1996; Towles-Schwen & Fazio, 2001). With this procedure, participants see various adjectives and are asked to indicate whether they have a "good" or a "bad" meaning by pushing one of two buttons. Before seeing each adjective, however, they are briefly exposed to faces of persons belonging to various racial groups (blacks, whites, Asians, Hispanics). It is reasoned that implicit racial attitudes will be revealed by how quickly participants respond to the words. To the extent that a nega-

priming
Using a stimulus to make accessible related information in memory.

bona fide pipeline
A technique that uses *priming* to measure implicit racial attitudes.

Chapter 6 / Prejudice

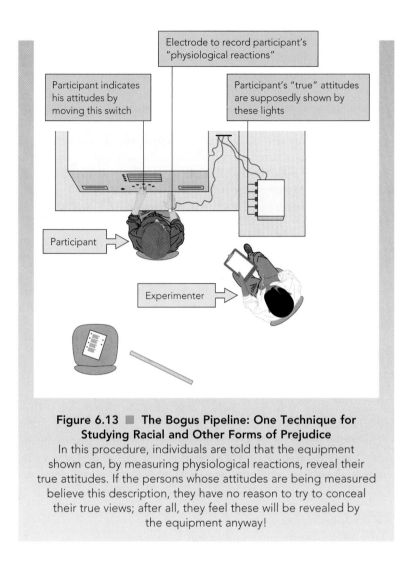

Figure 6.13 ■ **The Bogus Pipeline: One Technique for Studying Racial and Other Forms of Prejudice**
In this procedure, individuals are told that the equipment shown can, by measuring physiological reactions, reveal their true attitudes. If the persons whose attitudes are being measured believe this description, they have no reason to try to conceal their true views; after all, they feel these will be revealed by the equipment anyway!

tive attitude is triggered by the prime (e.g., a picture of a black person's face), participants will respond faster to words that have a negative meaning. In contrast, participants will respond more slowly to words with a positive meaning, because this meaning is inconsistent with the negative attitude elicited by the priming stimulus.

Research findings using this procedure indicate that people indeed have implicit racial attitudes that are automatically elicited by members of racial or ethnic groups, and that such automatically elicited attitudes, in turn, can influence important forms of behavior, such as decisions concerning others and the degree of friendliness that is expressed in interactions with others (Fazio & Hilden, 2001; Towles-Schwen & Fazio, 2001). The important point to note is this: Despite the fact that blatant forms of racism have decreased in public life in the United States and many other countries, this damaging type of automatic prejudice is still very much alive and, through more subtle kinds of reactions, continues to represent a very serious problem.

Consequences of Exposure to Others' Prejudice

How do we respond when we encounter prejudice in other people? Does it uniformly elicit disgust in us and lessen the likelihood that we, too, will act in a prejudicial fashion? Or, might it insidiously create the conditions under which prejudice is supported and perpetuated? A number of studies have suggested that exposure to derogatory ethnic labels can make "prejudice a highly communicable social disease" (Simon & Greenberg, 1996, p. 1195). This is the case, in part, because exposure to such comments can elicit conformity pressures (see Chapter 9), with people wanting to fit in with others and behave according to what they perceive to be existing social norms. For example, what is likely to happen when a person joins an institution that subtly supports prejudice toward particular out-groups? Serge Guimond (2000) investigated this issue among Canadian military personnel. He found that English Canadians became significantly more prejudiced toward specific out-groups (e.g., French Canadians, immigrants, and civilians) and internalized justifications for the economic gap between their own group and these out-groups as they progressed through the four-year officer training program. Further, he found that the more they identified with the military and the category they aspired to join within it (e.g., Canadian Forces Officers), the more they showed increases in prejudice.

Exposure to another person using derogatory ethnic labels can cue negative stereotypes, and this may be one means by which prejudice is perpetuated. For example, when white participants were presented with a trial transcript of a lawyer defending a client, when the attorney was black and he was referred to in terms of an ethnic slur, the attorney was perceived more stereotypically and as relatively incompetent compared with when no ethnic slur was used (Kirkland, Greenberg, & Pyszczynski, 1987).

Subsequent research has addressed whether the effect of exposure to such ethnic slurs depends on the person's initial level of prejudice (Simon & Greenberg, 1996). After preselecting participants who differed in their level of racism (pro-black, anti-black, or those with ambivalent attitudes), these researchers had participants work on what they thought was a group task. The participants were then given what they believed to be a black participant's task solution accompanied by a note from another white participant. The "note" either did not have any comment on it or it contained a derogatory ethnic label for the black accomplice. As shown in Figure 6.14, the white participants' reactions to the black accomplice depended both on their level of preju-

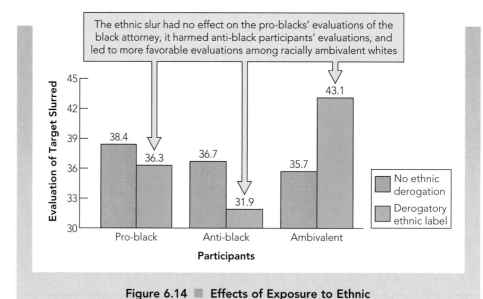

Figure 6.14 ■ **Effects of Exposure to Ethnic Slurs Depend on Level of Prejudice**
Exposure to others' prejudice can have no effect (among pro-black participants), can harm our impressions of the target so slurred (among anti-black participants), and can result in more positive impressions of the slurred target among those whites with ambivalent racial attitudes. (*Source: Simon & Greenberg, 1996.*)

Chapter 6 / Prejudice

dice and whether a racial slur were expressed or not. Those participants with pro-black attitudes were not affected by exposure to the derogatory ethnic label, but exposure to the derogatory ethnic label did negatively affect evaluation of the black target among those with anti-black attitudes. Interestingly, those with **ambivalent racial attitudes**—those who have both positive and negative feelings about the group—evaluated the black accomplice most positively after they had been exposed to the derogatory ethnic label. For these participants, the ethnic slur may have reminded them of what they wish not to be but fear that they are, and thereby elicited the most positive ratings of the black target. In the special section **Beyond the Headlines: As Social Psychologists See It** on page 242, we consider the issue of how people respond when they are exposed to information that implies their whole group may be prejudiced.

ambivalent racial attitudes Both positive and negative feelings about a minority group.

KEY POINTS

★ *Prejudice* is an attitude (usually negative) toward members of a social group based solely on their membership in that group. It can be triggered in a seemingly automatic manner and can be implicit as well as explicit.

★ Prejudice may reflect more specific underlying emotional responses to different out-groups, including fear, anger, guilt, and disgust.

★ Prejudice persists because disparaging groups can protect our self-esteem. *Threat* to our group's interests can motivate prejudice, and perceived competition between groups for resources can escalate conflict.

★ According to *social identity theory*, prejudice is derived from our tendency to divide the world into "us" and "them" and to view our own group more favorably than various out-groups. People may feel it is legitimate to display prejudice toward some social groups—that it is normative to do so—while for other groups it is seen as highly illegitimate to express prejudice.

★ Feeling secure in one's subgroup distinctiveness results in less prejudice toward similar out-groups. In contrast, feeling insecure about the distinctiveness of one's subgroup, leads to greater prejudice toward similar out-groups.

★ *Discrimination* involves differential actions toward members of various social groups. Although blatant discrimination has clearly

decreased, more subtle forms, such as *modern racism* and *ambivalent racism*, persist. Persons who are high in modern racism may want to hide their prejudice. Bogus pipeline procedures were developed to convince participants to express their "true" attitudes, on the assumption that the researcher will be able to discover those anyway. The *bona fide pipeline* is based on the assumption that people are unaware of their prejudices, but they can be revealed with implicit measures, in which *priming* a category to which the individual has negative attitudes produces faster responses to words with negative meanings.

★ Group norms and socialization in institutions that support prejudice toward out-groups helps to perpetuate prejudice. When people are exposed to derogatory ethnic labels, they can affect responses to the slurred target differently depending on their level of racism.

★ When we are exposed to instances in which members of our own group have behaved in a prejudicial fashion, we can distance ourselves and not feel *collective guilt* to the extent that we can conclude that the harmful acts were performed by a small few, the acts were not so severe, or that the acts were legitimate either because the people harmed did not warrant concern or because doing so served the in-group's higher goals.

B

Reactions to the Harmful Actions of Members of Our Own National Group

Torture at Abu Ghraib

Washington Post, June 11, 2004—U.S. intelligence personnel ordered military dog handlers at the Abu Ghraib prison in Iraq to use unmuzzled dogs to frighten and intimidate detainees during interrogations late last year. A military intelli-gence interrogator also told investigators that two dog handlers at Abu Ghraib were "having a contest" to see how many detainees they could make involuntarily urinate out of fear of the dogs. The statements by the dog handlers provide the clearest indication yet that military intelligence personnel were deeply involved in tactics deemed by a U.S. Army general to be "sadistic, blatant and wanton criminal abuses." Pentagon officials have said the criminal abuse at Abu Ghraib was confined to a small group of rogue military police soldiers who stripped detainees naked, beat them and pho-tographed them in humili-ating sexual poses. Human rights experts said the use of dogs and other abuses at Abu Ghraib violates long-standing tenets regulating the treatment of prisoners and civilians under the control of an occupying force, including the Army's field manual, which pro-hibits "acts of violence or in-timidation" by American soldiers.

As you probably are aware, when the CBS news *60 Minutes* program first showed the public the shocking photos of the abuses taking place at Abu Ghraib prison (see Figure 6.15), the U.S. Senate held hearings to determine how Americans could behave this way toward Iraqi civilians (60 percent of the inmates at Abu Ghraib were civilians deemed not to be a threat to society; see Hersh, 2004). How do people respond when they witness or learn about the harmful and prejudicial actions of members of their own group? What implications do you think this might have for how citizens of other countries are likely to think about the United States when they view such images?

First, let's consider the various responses and strategies that people have available to them when they are exposed to such depictions, which imply their group has perpetrated injustice. To avoid or reduce aversive feelings of **collective guilt**—an emotional response that can be experienced when people are confronted with the wrongdoings of members of their own group (Branscombe, 2004)—people have a variety of defensive strategies that they can employ. *Guilt* has been defined as regret for wrongdoing (Eisenberg, 2000) or the viola-tion of moral standards (Ferguson & Stegge, 1998). One possible means of limiting the guilt felt for wrongdoing is that taken by the Pentagon and the White House—to argue that it isn't the group as a whole (the nation, or even the U.S. army) that has behaved "immorally" but just a "few bad apples." To the extent that this is seen as believable and is accepted, little distress and guilt may be felt. Anger might be directed toward the spe-cific persons accused of the wrongdoing, but the group as a whole will not be tainted and the extent to which collective guilt is felt will be limited.

Even when the in-group's harmful actions cannot be denied, people can still appraise the gravity of the harm done as less severe. Consequently, people may minimize the number of Iraqi prisoners who were abused, or the

collective guilt
The emotion that can be experienced when people are confronted with the harmful actions done by their in-group against an out-group. Collective guilt is most likely to be experienced when the harmful actions are seen as illegitimate.

Why Prejudice Is Not Inevitable: Techniques for Countering Its Effects

Prejudice appears to be an all-too-common aspect of life in most, if not all, societies (Sidanius & Pratto, 1999). Does this mean that it is inevitable? Or can prejudice and the effects it produces be reduced? Social psychologists have generally approached this question from the perspective "Yes, prejudice *can* be reduced, and it is our job to find out how." Let's now take a look at several promising techniques for reducing prejudice.

length of time during which the abuse occurred. The perceived severity of the harm done can also be minimized by selectively using different standards for judging injustice. Groups favor use of judgment standards that allow their in-group's actions to be perceived as moral. For example, some Americans might be inclined to compare their group's abuses with those that occurred at the same prison during Saddam Hussein's regime, or the recent mass killings in Bosnia or Rwanda. Doing so should allow the in-group's harmdoing to be judged more favorably by comparison with these even more severe forms of abuse. Marques, Paez, and Sera (1997) describe this strategy's use among Portuguese participants who can perceive their nation's colonial past more positively by comparing it with other colonial nations' more severe treatment of indigenous peoples.

Another response might be to legitimize the harmdoing, which can be accomplished in several ways. If the actions are not perceived as illegitimate, there will be no basis for guilt (either personal on the part of the perpetrators, or collective on the part of group members who witness those actions). First, people can deny the collective or the possibility of collective responsibility (Branscombe, Slugoski, & Kappen, 2004), which can prevent feelings of guilt based on the in-group's actions. Second, people can blame the victims by suggesting that they deserved the outcomes they received. Indeed, derogation of victims helps perpetrators to be "less burdened by distress" when faced with their harmdoing (Bandura, 1990). Social psychological research has

revealed that people who are defined as "enemies" are more easily dehumanized and the harm done to them justified (Alexander, Brewer, & Herrmann, 1999; Staub, 1989). For this reason, people may choose to believe that the prisoners at Abu Ghraib were not primarily civilians but "terrorists." At its most extreme, victims may be excluded from the category "human" entirely so they can be seen as not deserving of humane treatment at all, which permits any harm done to them to be seen as completely justified (Bar-Tal, 2003).

Lastly, the abuses may be seen as in the service of the nation's higher goals—for example, to get important information that would prevent the loss of additional American lives. In this case, people can accept that their actions did result in harmful outcomes, but because they are seen as necessary to achieve larger moral purposes, little guilt may be felt. Of course, the international community, including the citizens of Iraq, who have now also viewed the same disturbing photographs of the abuses at Abu Ghraib, may not see those actions as justified to the same extent as some Americans. Indeed, they may assign greater guilt to the United States as a whole, and show increased negative stereotyping of the nation.

Figure 6.15 ■ Shocking Photos of Abuse at Abu Ghraib Prison in Iraq
How do Americans respond when they see members of their own group behaving in such an abusive and prejudicial fashion? People have a variety of strategies they can use when confronted with such damaging information about their own in-group.

On Learning Not to Hate

According to the **social learning view,** children acquire negative attitudes toward various social groups because they hear such views expressed by significant others and because they are directly rewarded (with love, praise, and approval) for adopting these views. However, direct experience with persons belonging to other groups also shapes attitudes. Evidence for the strong impact of childhood experiences on several aspects of racial prejudice has been reported (Towles-Schwen & Fazio, 2001). The more participants' parents were prejudiced and the less positive their interactions with minority-group persons, the greater restraint reported in interacting with African Americans. Because restraint reflects

social learning view (of prejudice)
The view that prejudice is acquired through direct and vicarious experiences in much the same manner as other attitudes.

feelings of social awkwardness and anticipation of potential conflict, these findings support the role of parents and other adults in training children in bigotry.

How can parents, who are themselves highly prejudiced, be encouraged to teach less biased views to their children? One possibility involves calling parents' attention to their own prejudice. Few persons are willing to describe themselves as bigoted; instead, they view their own negative attitudes toward various groups as justified. A key initial step, therefore, is questioning that justification. Once people come face to face with their own prejudices, some are willing to modify their words and behavior to encourage lower levels of prejudice among their children. It is also possible to remind parents of the high costs of holding racist attitudes. Research has revealed that the enjoyment that highly prejudiced people experience from everyday activities and life itself is lower than that experienced by people low in prejudice (Feagin & McKinney, 2003). Overall, it is clear that persons holding intense racial and ethnic prejudices suffer many harmful effects from their intolerant views. Because most parents want to do everything they can to further their children's well-being, calling these costs to their attention may be effective in discouraging them from transmitting prejudiced views to their children.

The Potential Benefits of Contact

At the present time, many American cities have a disintegrating and crime-ridden core that is inhabited primarily by minority groups, and that is surrounded by relatively affluent suburbs inhabited mainly by whites. Needless to say, contact between the people living in these different areas is minimal. Such segregation raises an intriguing question: Can prejudice be reduced by increasing the degree of contact between different groups? The idea that it can is known as the **contact hypothesis,** and there are several good reasons for predicting that such a strategy can be effective (Pettigrew, 1981; 1997). Increased contact between persons from different groups can lead to a growing recognition of similarities between them—which can change the categorizations that people employ. As we saw earlier, those who are categorized as "us" are responded to more positively than those categorized as "them." Increased contact, or even just knowledge that other members of our group have such contact with out-group members, can signal that the norms of the group are not so "anti-out-group" as individuals might initially have believed. The existence of cross-group friendships suggests that members of the out-group do not necessarily dislike members of our in-group, and this knowledge can reduce intergroup anxiety. Indeed, recent evidence suggests that increased contact can reduce prejudice by reducing the anxiety that is felt when the out-group is thought about.

Consider, for example, the situation of Catholics and Protestants in Northern Ireland. Members of these groups, too, live in highly segregated housing districts, and contact between the members of the two groups is often perceived negatively. Social psychologists there (Paolini et al., 2004), however, have found that direct contact between members of the two religious groups, as well as indirect contact (via knowledge of other in-group members' friendships with out-group members), can reduce prejudice via reductions in anxiety about future encounters with out-group members. Other research has likewise suggested that among groups throughout Europe, positive contact that is seen as important—when it reflects increased cooperation and interdependence between the groups—can change norms so that group equality is favored, and thereby prejudice is reduced (Van Dick et al., 2004). Moreover, the beneficial effects of such cross-group friendships can readily spread to other persons who have not experienced such contacts: Simply knowing about them can be enough. In other words, merely learning that some people in one's own group get along well with persons belonging to other groups can be a highly effective means of countering prejudice.

contact hypothesis
The view that increased contact between members of various social groups can be effective in reducing prejudice among them.

Think back to your high school days. Imagine that your school's basketball team is playing an important game against a rival school from a nearby town. In this case, you would certainly view your own school as "us" and the other school as "them." But now imagine that the other school's team wins, and goes on to play against a team from another state in a national tournament. *Now* how would you view that team? The chances are good that under these conditions, you would view the other school's team as "us"; after all, it now represents your state. And, of course, if a team from a state other than your own were playing against teams from other countries, you might now view it as "us" relative to those "foreigners."

Situations like this, in which we shift the boundary between "us" and "them," are common in everyday life, and they raise an interesting question: Can such shifts—or **recategorizations,** as they are termed by social psychologists—be used to reduce prejudice? The **common in-group identity model** suggests that they can (Dovidio, Gaertner, & Validzic, 1998; Gaertner et al., 1994). To the extent that individuals who belong to different social groups come to view themselves as members of a *single social entity,* their attitudes toward each other become more positive. These favorable attitudes then promote increased positive contacts between members of the previously separate groups, and this, in turn, reduces intergroup bias still further. In short, recategorizing what were formerly out-group members into a new, more inclusive in-group in which they are now included in the "us" category can reduce prejudice and hostility.

How can we induce people belonging to different groups to perceive each other as members of a single group? Gaertner and his colleagues (1990) suggest that one crucial factor is the experience of working together cooperatively. When individuals belonging to initially distinct groups work together toward shared goals, they come to perceive themselves as a single social entity. Then, feelings of bias or hostility toward the former out-group—toward "them"—seem to fade away, taking prejudice with them. Such effects have been demonstrated in several studies (Brewer et al., 1987; Gaertner et al., 1989, 1990), both in the laboratory and in the field. When *recategorization* can be induced, it has proved to be another useful technique for reducing prejudice toward those who were previously categorized as out-group members.

The power of shifting to a more inclusive category for reductions in negative feelings toward an out-group has been shown even among groups with a long history, including one group's brutality toward another. Consider how Jewish people may feel about Germans, given the Holocaust. Although that conflict has long been over, to the extent that the victim group continues to categorize Jews and Germans as separate and distinct groups, contemporary Germans are likely to be responded to with prejudice, even though most Germans could not possibly have been involved in the Nazi atrocities against the Jews, for they were not alive during that period. In a strong test of the recategorization hypothesis, Jewish Americans were induced either to think about Jews and Germans as separate groups or to categorize them as members of a single and maximally inclusive group—that of humans (Wohl & Branscombe, 2005). Following this manipulation, Jewish participants were asked to indicate the extent to which they believe contemporary Germans should feel collective guilt for their group's harmful past, and the extent to which they were willing to forgive Germans for the past. In the condition in which Germans and Jews were thought of as separate groups, participants expected Germans to feel more collective guilt, and they reported less forgiveness of Germans compared with when the two groups were included in one social category (that of humans). Therefore, including members of an out-group in the same category as the in-group has important consequences for prejudice reduction and willingness to have social contact, even with members of an "old enemy" group.

recategorization
Shifts in the boundaries between an individual's in-group ("us") and some out-group ("them"). As a result of such recategorization, persons formerly viewed as out-group members may now be viewed as belonging to the in-group, and consequently are viewed more positively.

common in-group identity model
A theory suggesting that to the extent individuals in different groups view themselves as members of a single social entity, intergroup bias will be reduced.

The Benefits of Guilt for Prejudice Reduction

When people have egalitarian self-images, they may be motivated to suppress prejudice (Monteith, Devine, & Zuwerink, 1993). Indeed, failing to do so, and being confronted with instances in which one has personally behaved in a prejudiced fashion can lead to "compunction" or feelings of guilt for having violated one's personal standards (Plant & Devine, 1998). But, what about when a person is a member of a group that has a history of being prejudiced toward another group. Might that person feel "guilt by association," even if that person has not personally behaved in a prejudiced fashion? Considerable research has now revealed that people can feel *collective guilt,* based on the actions of other members of their group, when they are confronted with the harm that their group's prejudice toward another group has produced (Branscombe, Doosje, & McGarty, 2002). Can such feelings of collective guilt be used as a means of reducing racism?

In a recent set of studies, Powell, Branscombe, and Schmitt (in press) found evidence that feeling collective guilt can reduce racism. In their research, white college students were first asked to think about the racial inequality that exists in the United States. The identical difference between two groups can be framed either in terms of the disadvantages experienced by one group *or* the advantages experienced by the other. In almost all of the social psychological literature on prejudiced attitudes, racial inequality has been framed essentially in terms of the hardships or disadvantages associated with minority-group membership. These researchers suggested that how the existing inequality is framed has important implications for whether the self, defined at the collective level, is seen as playing a role in maintaining that inequality. It was hypothesized that when the self, via one's membership in a group, is perceived as playing a role in racial inequality, then prejudice might be reduced to the extent that guilt is induced.

To test this idea, white participants in one condition were asked to write down all the advantages they receive because of their race. In the other condition, participants were asked to write down all the disadvantages that blacks receive because of their race. This manipulation simply varied how the existing racial inequality was framed. As expected, the white advantage framing resulted in significantly more collective guilt than did the black disadvantage framing. Furthermore, as shown in Figure 6.16, the more collective guilt was experienced in the white advantage condition, the lower the subsequent racism. This research suggests that reflecting on racial inequality can be an effective means of lowering racism to the extent that the problem cannot be isolated as one concerning the other group, but instead is seen as one involving the in-group as beneficiary.

Can We Learn to "Just Say No" to Stereotypes?

Throughout this chapter, we have noted that the tendency to think about others in terms of their group membership is a key factor in the occurrence and persistence of several forms of prejudice. To the extent that people want to be egalitarian, it may be possible to train them so that the automatic activation of stereotypes is reduced and they can therefore behave according to their egalitarian principles. As described earlier, individuals acquire stereotypes by learning to associate certain characteristics (e.g., negative traits such as "hostile" or "dangerous") with various racial or ethnic groups; once such automatic associations are formed, members of these groups can serve as primes for racial or ethnic stereotypes, which are then activated automatically. Can individuals actively break the "stereotype habit" by saying "no" to the stereotypic traits they associate with a specific group? Kawakami and her colleagues (2000) reasoned that such procedures might reduce individuals' reliance on stereotypes.

To test this possibility, the researchers conducted several related studies in which participants' stereotypic associations were first assessed. After this, participants were divided into two groups. In one group—those in the *stereotype-maintaining* condition—

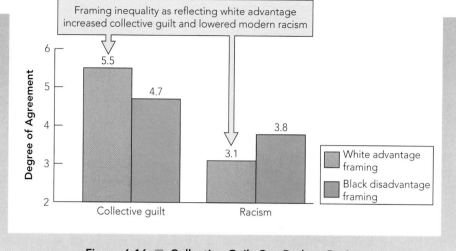

Figure 6.16 ■ Collective Guilt Can Reduce Racism
The same inequality between groups can be framed as either reflecting the advantages of one group or the disadvantages of the other. Having white Americans think about inequality as white advantage led to increased feelings of collective guilt, and this, in turn, resulted in lowered racism. A little collective guilt then may have social benefits. (*Source: Based on data from Powell, Branscombe, & Schmitt, in press.*)

participants were instructed to respond "yes" when they were presented with a photograph of a white person and a white stereotype word (e.g., *ambitious* and *uptight*) or a photograph of a black person and a black stereotype word (e.g., *athletic* and *poor*). They were told to respond "no" to stereotype-inconsistent word–picture pairings (e.g., a word consistent with the stereotype for whites, but a photo of a black individual). Those in a second group, the *stereotype-negation* condition, were told to respond "no" when presented with a photo of a white person and a word consistent with this stereotype, or a photo of a black person and a word consistent with the stereotype for blacks. On the other hand, they were told to respond "yes" to stereotype-inconsistent pairings of words and pictures. In others words, they practiced negating their own implicit racial stereotypes. Participants in both groups performed these procedures several hundred times.

The results were clear. Reliance on stereotypes can be reduced through the process of repeatedly saying "no" to them. As shown in Figure 6.17 on page 248, prior to negation training, participants categorized white faces more quickly than black faces after seeing white stereotype words, but black faces more quickly after seeing black stereotype words. After negation training designed to weaken these implicit stereotypes, however, these differences disappeared. Although we do not yet know how reduced stereotype activation influences actual interactions with group members, the possibility that people can readily learn to say "no" to racial and ethnic stereotypes is encouraging indeed.

Social Influence as a Means of Reducing Prejudice

As we saw earlier in this chapter, **social norms**—rules within a given group suggesting what actions or attitudes are appropriate—are important determinants of attitude expression (Pettigrew, 1969; Turner, 1991). Therefore, providing evidence that the members of one's group *like* persons belonging to another group that is the target of strong prejudice can sometimes serve to weaken such negative reactions (Pettigrew, 1997; Wright et al., 1997). In contrast, when stereotypic beliefs are said to be endorsed by the individual's in-group and that individual's membership in that group is salient,

social norms
Rules within a particular social group concerning what actions and attitudes are appropriate.

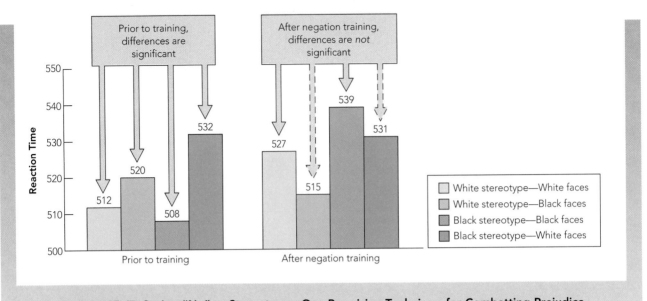

Figure 6.17 ■ **Saying "No" to Stereotypes: One Promising Technique for Combatting Prejudice**
Prior to negation training, during which participants responded "no" to racial stereotypes, participants categorized white faces more quickly than black faces after seeing words related to the stereotype for whites; black faces were categorized more quickly after seeing words related to the stereotype for blacks. After negation training, which was designed to weaken these implicit stereotypes, these differences disappeared. (*Source: Based on data from Kawakami et al., 2000.*)

then the in-group's beliefs are more predictive of prejudice than are the individual's personal beliefs about the out-group (Haslam & Wilson, 2000). This finding suggests that stereotypes that are believed to be widely shared within our own group play a critical role in the expression of prejudice.

Evidence that the same social influence process can be used to reduce prejudice was reported by Stangor, Sechrist, and Jost (2001). Students were first asked to estimate the percentage of African Americans possessing each of nineteen stereotypical traits. After completing these estimates, participants were given information suggesting that other students in their university disagreed with their ratings. In one condition (favorable feedback), they learned that other students held more favorable views of African Americans than they did (i.e., the other students estimated a higher incidence of positive traits and a lower incidence of negative traits than the participants did). In another condition (unfavorable feedback), they learned that other students held less favorable views of African Americans than they did (i.e., these persons estimated a higher incidence of negative traits and a lower incidence of positive traits). After receiving this information, participants again estimated the percentage of African Americans possessing positive and negative traits. These white participants' racial attitudes were indeed affected by social influence. Endorsement of negative stereotypes increased in the unfavorable feedback condition, while endorsement of such stereotypes decreased in the favorable feedback condition.

Together, these findings indicate that racial attitudes do not exist in a social vacuum; on the contrary, the attitudes that individuals hold are influenced not only by their early experience, but also by current information indicating how closely their views match those of other members of their group. The moral is clear: If bigoted persons can be induced to believe that their prejudiced views are out of line with those of most other persons—especially with the views of persons they admire or respect—they may well change those views toward a less prejudiced position. (For an overview of techniques useful in combating prejudice, see the **Ideas to Take with You—and Use!** section at the end of the chapter.)

KEY POINTS

★ Social psychologists believe that prejudice is *not* inevitable; it can be reduced by several techniques.

★ One of these techniques involves changing children's early experiences so that they are not taught bigotry by their parents and other adults. Pointing out the costs of prejudice, as well as undermining the justifications subscribed to for prejudice are two methods that can be used to encourage less prejudiced parenting.

★ Another technique, outlined in the *contact hypothesis,* involves bringing previously segregated groups into contact. This has proved sufficient to reduce prejudice, as has simply knowing that members of one's group have formed friendships with members of an out-group.

★ As suggested by the *common in-group identity model,* prejudice can also be reduced through *recategorization*—shifting the boundary between "us" and "them" to include former out-groups in the "us" category. This is the case even for long-

standing enemy groups when the maximal category—humans—is used.

★ Emotional techniques for reducing prejudice are also effective. People with egalitarian standards can feel guilty when they violate those beliefs and personally behave in a prejudicial fashion.

★ People can also feel *collective guilt* for their group's prejudiced history. By framing inequality as due to the in-group's advantages, collective guilt can be induced, and this, in turn, can reduce racism.

★ Reductions in prejudice can also be accomplished by training individuals to say "no" to associations between stereotypes and specific social groups.

★ Social influence plays an important role in both the maintenance and reduction of prejudice. Beliefs that are believed to be held by other members of one's own group predict prejudice, and providing individuals with evidence suggesting that members of one's group hold less prejudiced views than they do can reduce prejudice.

SUMMARY AND REVIEW OF KEY POINTS

The Nature and Origins of Stereotyping, Prejudice, and Discrimination

■ *Gender stereotypes* are beliefs about the different attributes that males and females possess. Women are stereotyped as high on warmth dimensions but low on competence, while men are viewed as possessing the reverse combination of traits. People express greater respect for men than for women, and this factor

plays an important role in discrimination against women in the workplace.

■ Although blatant forms of discrimination based on gender have decreased, women continue to be adversely affected by more subtle forms. The *glass-ceiling* effect occurs when women are prevented from attaining high-level positions. Women are most likely to be sabotaged when men are experi-

encing threat and women behave in a stereotype-inconsistent manner.

■ *Sexism* can occur in two contrasting forms: *hostile sexism,* which involves the belief that women are a threat to men's position and negative feelings about women, and *benevolent sexism,* which involves positive beliefs about the attributes of women that make women suitable primarily for subordinate roles. The latter—differentiating women positively from men on alternative dimensions—is an instance of *social creativity*, which many disadvantaged groups show, particularly when inequality is stable and severe.

■ *Tokenism*—the hiring or acceptance of only a few members of a particular group—has two effects: It maintains perceptions that the system is not discriminatory, and it harms the token persons' self-esteem and how they are perceived by others.

■ Stereotypes lead us to attend to information that is consistent with them, and to construe inconsistent information in ways that allow us to maintain our stereotypes. Majority-group members tend to form *illusory correlations* about the negative attributes of minority-group members by linking two distinctive attributes: group membership and infrequent actions.

■ Stereotypes can influence behavior even in the absence of different *subjective scale* evaluations of men and women. When *objective scale* measures are employed, in which *shifting standards* cannot be used and the meaning of the response is constant, women receive worse outcomes than men.

Prejudice and Discrimination: Feelings and Actions toward Social Groups

■ *Prejudice* is an attitude (usually negative) toward members of a social group. It can be triggered in a seemingly automatic manner and can be implicit as well as explicit in nature. Prejudice may reflect more specific underlying emotional responses to different

out-groups, including fear, anger, guilt, and disgust

■ According to *social identity theory*, prejudice is derived from our tendency to divide the world into "us" and "them" and to view our own group more favorably than various out-groups. Prejudice persists because disparaging outgroups can protect our self-esteem. *Threat* to our group's interests can motivate prejudice, and perceived competition between groups for resources can escalate conflict.

■ People may feel it is legitimate to display prejudice toward some social groups—that it is normative to do so—while for other groups, it is seen as highly illegitimate to express prejudice. Although blatant *discrimination* has clearly decreased, more subtle forms, such as *modern racism*, persist.

■ Prejudice sometimes stems from basic aspects of social cognition—the ways in which we process social information. Implicit stereotypes can be activated automatically, and even though we are not aware of it, they can affect our thinking about and behavior toward persons belonging to those groups. For example, highly prejudiced persons respond more quickly to stereotype-related words than do less prejudiced persons.

■ Group norms that support prejudice toward out-groups help to perpetuate prejudice. When people are exposed to derogatory ethnic labels, their responses to the slurred targets differ depending on their level of racism. When we are exposed to instances in which members of our own group have behaved in a prejudicial fashion, we can feel *collective guilt* to

the extent that we can conclude the harmful acts were illegitimate.

Why Prejudice Is Not Inevitable: Techniques for Countering Its Effects

■ Social psychologists believe that prejudice is *not* inevitable; it can be reduced by several techniques.

■ Pointing out the costs of prejudice, as well as undermining the justifications subscribed to for prejudice, are two methods that can be used to encourage less prejudice.

■ Another technique involves direct contact between persons from different groups. Under certain conditions, this contact can reduce prejudice. In fact, simply knowing that members of one's own group have formed friendships with members of an out-group may be sufficient to reduce prejudice.

■ Prejudice can be reduced through *recategorization*—shifting the boundary between "us" and "them" so as to include former out-groups in the "us" category. This is the case even for long-standing "enemy" groups when the more inclusive category is that of "human."

■ Cognitive techniques for reducing prejudice are also effective. Reductions in prejudice can be accomplished by training individuals to say "no" to associations between stereotypes and specific social groups.

■ Emotions can be used to motivate others to be nonprejudiced; by making people aware of egalitarian norms and standards, guilt can be experienced if either their own or their group's actions violate those norms and standards.

Feeling collective guilt can motivate reductions in racism when the in-group is focused on as a cause of existing racial inequality.

■ Beliefs that are deemed to be held by other members of one's own group predict prejudice, and providing individuals with evidence suggesting that one's in-group has fewer prejudiced views can reduce prejudice.

Connections INTEGRATING SOCIAL PSYCHOLOGY

In this chapter, you read about . . .	**In other chapters, you will find related discussions of . . .**
stereotypes as mental shortcuts—one means of saving cognitive effort	heuristics and other mental shortcuts (Chapters 2 and 4)
the role of competition in prejudice	the role of frustration in aggression and conflict (Chapter 11)
the tendency to divide the social world into "us" and "them" and its effects	other effects of group membership (Chapter 12)
evaluations of women in positions of authority or leadership	other aspects of leadership (Module B)
the effects of prejudice on its targets	coping when the self is a target of prejudice (Chapter 5)
the effects of perceived similarity on prejudice	the effects of perceived similarity on attraction (Chapter 7)

Thinking about Connections

1. Some observers suggest that as open forms of discrimination have decreased, more subtle forms have increased. In other words, they believe that the attitudes underlying discrimination remain unchanged (see Chapter 4) and that only overt behavior relating to these attitudes has changed. What do you think?

2. Some evidence indicates that prejudice persists because it produces benefits for the people who hold it (e.g., it protects their self-concept). But prejudice also produces harmful effects for the people who hold it (e.g., they experience ungrounded fear of harm from out-group members; see Chapter 11). Which do you think is dominant where prejudice is concerned—its benefits or its costs?

3. In your view, why do we show such a strong tendency to divide the social world into two categories—"us" and "them"? Do you think this tendency could stem, in part, from our biological heritage—for instance, the conditions under which our species evolved (see Chapter 1)? Or is it due to the motivation to perceive our own groups positively (see Chapter 3)?

4. Sexism appears to have two aspects: hostile and benevolent attitudes toward women. Do you think it is important to eliminate both kinds? Or do you feel that benevolent sexism, which puts women on a pedestal, has some beneficial effects?

5. To what extent do you see your own prejudices as legitimate (and therefore not really prejudice)? When you cannot see either your own or your group's prejudicial actions as legitimate, do you feel guilty? Under what circumstances does this occur?

6. Which of the strategies outlined for reducing prejudice have you tried? Are the social conditions in which you find yourself important for whether one strategy or another works best? Just as we saw with other attitudes (see Chapter 4), might the kind of processing engaged in (systematic versus heuristic) matter for the extent to which prejudice is altered?

Prejudice is an all-too-common part of social life, but most social psychologists believe that it *can* be reduced—it is not inevitable. Here are some techniques that seem to work.

Teaching Children Tolerance Instead of Bigotry

If children are taught, from an early age, to respect all groups—including ones very different from their own—prejudice can be nipped in the bud, so to speak.

Using Social Influence Processes to Reduce Prejudice

We can communicate to others that prejudice is neither normative nor acceptable. When people are told that others do not hold similarly prejudiced beliefs toward a particular social group (as they had assumed was the case), they change in response to such normative information.

Increased Intergroup Contact—Or Merely Knowledge that It Occurs

Recent findings indicate that if people merely know that friendly contacts between members of their own group and members of various outgroups occur, their prejudice toward these groups can be sharply reduced.

Recategorization

Once individuals include people they once excluded from their ingroup *within* it, prejudice toward them may disappear. This can be accomplished by reminding people that they are part of larger groups—for instance, that they are all Americans, members of the same work group, or even members of a single group: humans. As shown here, there will be greater team cohesion among the members of this group than if they were categorized and divided according to their gender.

The Benefits of Guilt

Differences between groups can be considered by focusing on the ingroup's role in creating them or the out-group's role in doing so. Research has shown that considering one's own group's role and responsibility for inequality can induce collective guilt, and this, in turn, can lower prejudice. Feeling guilt about one's group overbenefiting can have positive social consequences.

Undermining Stereotypes

Stereotypes suggest that all persons belonging to specific social groups are alike—they share the same characteristics. Such beliefs can be weakened by encouraging people to think about others as *individuals*, not simply as members of social groups. Further, if individuals learn to reject implicit links between certain traits and racial or ethnic groups (saying "no" to stereotypes), the impact of these cognitive frameworks can be reduced.

KEY TERMS

ambivalent racial attitudes (p. 241)

benevolent sexism (p. 216)

bona fide pipeline (p. 238)

collective guilt (p. 242)

common in-group identity model (p. 245)

contact hypothesis (p. 244)

discrimination (p. 237)

gender stereotypes (p. 213)

glass ceiling (p. 214)

hostile sexism (p. 217)

illusory correlation (p. 222)

implicit associations (p. 229)

incidental feelings (p. 228)

in-group (p. 233)

in-group differentiation (p. 223)

in-group homogeneity (p. 223)

minimal groups (p. 228)

modern racism (p. 237)

objective scales (p. 222)

out-group (p. 233)

out-group homogeneity (p. 223)

prejudice (p. 226)

priming (p. 238)

realistic conflict theory (p. 232)

recategorization (p. 245)

respect (p. 218)

schemas (p. 220)

sexism (p. 218)

shifting standards (p. 220)

social categorization (p. 233)

social creativity responses (p. 217)

social identity theory (p. 235)

social learning view (of prejudice) (p. 243)

social norms (p. 247)

stereotypes (p. 213)

subjective scales (p. 221)

subliminal levels (p. 229)

subtype (p. 222)

superordinate goals (p. 233)

threat (p. 230)

tokenism (p. 216)

ultimate attribution error (p. 235)

within-group comparisons (p. 222)

FOR MORE INFORMATION

Paolini, S., Hewstone, M., Cairns, E., & Voci, A. (2004). Effects of direct and indirect cross-group friendships on judgments of Catholics and Protestants in Northern Ireland: The mediating role of an anxiety-reduction mechanism. *Personality and Social Psychology Bulletin, 30*, 770–786.

• This article reviews work on the contact hypothesis and explains why contact between members of different social groups can lessen prejudice. The authors illustrate the important role that cross-group friendships can play in reducing the anxiety that can be experienced during contact with members of another group with whom there is a history of conflict with one's own group.

Branscombe, N. R. (2004). A social psychological process perspective on collective guilt. In N. R. Branscombe & B. Doosje (Eds.), *Collective guilt: International perspectives* (pp. 320–334). New York: Cambridge University Press.

• This chapter reviews research concerning when and why collective guilt may be experienced, and discusses the important social consequences that can flow from collective guilt. Important challenges for future research on collective guilt are identified.

Crosby, F. J. (2004). *Affirmative action is dead: Long live affirmative action.* New Haven, CT: Yale University Press.

• This is a well-written comprehensive review of theory and research

on affirmative action. Both the extent to which the policy is needed—given the pervasiveness of discrimination—and the likely shape that this social policy will take in the United States are considered.

Feagin, J. R., & McKinney, K. D. (2003). *The many costs of racism.* Lanham, MD: Rowman & Littlefield.

• The authors describe the many subtle and not-so-subtle costs of racism in America in this easy to read volume. Special attention is given to the issue of why whites remain unaware of the costs of racism that African Americans bear, as well as the unique costs accumulated by white Americans because of the persistence of racism.

7

INTERPERSONAL ATTRACTION
Meeting, Liking, Becoming Acquainted

Recently, I (Donn Byrne) traveled to a college class reunion—my first reunion of any kind. Though all of my high school and college years were spent in California, most of my adult life has been spent thousands of miles from there in Texas, Indiana, and New York. Over the years, I lost contact with a great many people who had at one time played a central role in my interpersonal world. I decided to let the reunion trip serve as an excuse to locate as many people as possible from my past. College friends were easier to find because some of us had remained in contact, and many would be at the reunion.

High school friends were more difficult to locate, however, but by contacting a couple of key individuals, I obtained the addresses of a number of people I had known several decades in the past. I wrote or e-mailed them and made plans to get together with those who were available. With others, we began renewed relationships via letters, the telephone, and the Internet. I was even able to reach one of my favorite high school teachers, a lady who had a major influence on my life. She was unaware of her effect on me, and I'm truly sorry that I waited several decades before telling her that. Only one of my high school friends failed to respond at all. Perhaps she suspected that I was really planning to offer her a real estate deal involving Florida swampland. Though painful to suggest, it is also quite possible that she simply never liked me as much as I liked her.

For those who did respond, the interactions were surprisingly enjoyable for me. They brought back a flood of memories involving people, places, and events that we shared. In some instances, one other person and I were the only two people in the world who could share that particular memory. In other instances, my very clear recollections turned out to be partially or totally incorrect (just as research on eyewitness testimony indicates; see Module A). Another aspect of these interactions was the opportunity to learn about the subsequent lives of those I once knew well—marriages, offspring, vocations, divorces, and much more. It was something like seeing the first part of a movie and then having the opportunity to see the rest of it after many years had passed.

My only regret about all of this is that I waited much too long to seek out these friends from the past. I belatedly realized how much I had missed. I suspect that many of us take relationships for granted—people come and go as we move on to different aspects or our respective lives. We probably should not let that happen.

On the basis of my experience, I now believe that if you liked someone at point 1 in your life, you probably will also like them at point 2, no matter how many years have passed (see Figure 7.1). Perhaps the moral of this story is that each relationship can be valuable. Do your best not to lose any of them.

Figure 7.1 ■ Attraction is Likely to Remain the Same Despite the Passage of Time
When people get together after many years have passed, the qualities that led them to have a friendly (or unfriendly) relationship early in their lives (for example, in high school) are likely to have the same effect later in their lives (for example, at a class reunion).

As a social psychologist, I discovered that these reunions with past friends involved another kind of experience as well. Now, I am able to look back and understand the factors that led me to be attracted to some specific individuals rather than to others. One of them I first met because we happened to be in the same fourth- or fifth-grade class; I was acutely aware of her attractiveness and intelligence, but we barely interacted. We finally became friends about five years later when we were no longer too shy to have an actual conversation and discovered that we were similar in many ways, including the things we found amusing. One person I met only because he was the college roommate of someone in my freshman French class with whom I sometimes studied. Another person became a high school friend primarily because we had similar (though immature) political views. Another became a friend because we both enjoyed tennis and played at about the same (not so great) level. And, this chapter is about just such factors that lead to *interpersonal attraction.*

Psychologists and others generally agree that human beings are motivated to form bonds with one another. We seem to have a built-in *affiliation need*—a need to associate with our fellow humans in a friendly, cooperative way. Of course, we don't form such bonds with everyone we meet. We make distinctions and choose to be with some people and to avoid others. It appears to be a very basic human characteristic to evaluate just about everything and everyone we encounter. That is, we form attitudes (see Chapter 4) about people, objects, and events. **Interpersonal attraction** refers to the attitude one holds about another person. These evaluations of people fall along a dimension that involves liking at one end and disliking at the other (see Figure 7.2). We like some people and dislike others, and some of those we meet like us and some do not.

Beginning with the earliest empirical studies of attraction by social psychologists and sociologists, a major goal was to identify in detail the specific factors responsible for

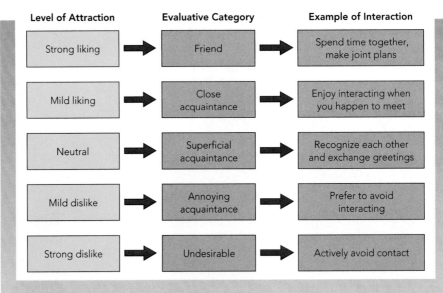

Figure 7.2 ■ Interpersonal Attraction: The Evaluation of Another Person
Interpersonal attraction refers to one's evaluation of or one's attitude about some other person. We express attraction along a dimension that ranges from strong liking to strong dislike. Depending on the level of attraction we feel, we categorize that person and behave toward him or her in quite different ways. Attraction research is designed to identify the factors that are responsible for such evaluations.

interpersonal attraction
A person's attitude about another person. Attraction is expressed along a dimension that ranges from strong liking to strong feelings of dislike.

one person's evaluation of another. As you read about each of these variables in the remainder of this chapter, it is easy to lose sight of the "forest" (attraction) because the discussion tends to focus on the individual "trees" (proximity, physical appearance, etc.).

It may be helpful to keep in mind one very simple but all-important concept. Many social psychologists are convinced that when we experience positive emotions, we make positive evaluations. And, when we experience negative emotions, we make negative evaluations. Another person is liked when he or she either causes us to feel good or is simply associated with good feelings. Another person is disliked when he or she either causes us to feel bad or is simply associated with bad feelings.

Simply put, one's interpersonal likes and dislikes are determined by one's *affective state*. Each of the specific influences on attraction that we discuss in this chapter influences affect (emotions), and that is the reason they are relevant to attraction. One such factor is physical *proximity*. Very often, two people first become acquainted as the result of accidental encounters in the neighborhood or apartment building in which they live, in classrooms or elsewhere in school, or at their place of work. It may seem either odd or obvious to you, but we are most likely to come in contact with people who live near us and use the same sidewalk or who are assigned a classroom seat next to ours, or who work in close proximity on the job. It may be less obvious that *repeated exposure* to another person is likely to result in a favorable evaluation of that person.

Emotions (and therefore evaluations) are also determined, in part, by how a person looks, or sounds, or smells—his or her *observable characteristics*. Often, unfairly and incorrectly, we react to the observable characteristics of those we encounter in a positive or a negative way.

What is likely to elicit more intense interpersonal attitudes? Beyond a basic need to affiliate and a basic tendency to evaluate and beyond the relatively mild affect elicited by a person's proximity or observable characteristics, we tend to form friendly relationships with those who make us feel most comfortable and to avoid relationships with those who make us feel most uncomfortable. A more intense level of attraction is determined in part by the discovery of areas of *similarity* or of *dissimilarity* with respect to attitudes, beliefs, values, interests, and much else besides. To the extent that similarities outweigh dissimilarities, attraction between two individuals is enhanced. When dissimilarities predominate, attraction is low.

Finally, the most positive emotions and the most comfortable feelings occur when two people indicate *mutual liking* by what they say or what they do. It is at this point that attraction advances toward the kind of close relationships described in Chapter 8.

Internal Determinants of Attraction: The Need to Affiliate and the Basic Role of Affect

Much of our life is spent interacting with other people, and this tendency to affiliate seems to have a neurobiological basis (Rowe, 1996). The need to affiliate with others and to be accepted by them is hypothesized to be as basic to our psychological well-being as hunger and thirst are to our physical well-being (Baumeister & Leary, 1995).

The Importance of Affiliation for Human Existence

From an evolutionary perspective, it would almost certainly have been an advantage to our distant ancestors to interact socially and to cooperate with one another in

Figure 7.3 ■ Affiliation as an Adaptive Response
For our ancient ancestors, any tendencies that facilitated social interaction and cooperation had positive effects. Because affiliation increased the odds of surviving and reproducing, this motive became a part of our genetic heritage.

obtaining food, protecting one another from danger, and reproducing, as suggested in Figure 7.3.

Human infants are apparently born with the motivation and the ability to seek contact with their interpersonal world (Baldwin, 2000), and even newborns are predisposed to look toward faces in preference to other stimuli (Mondloch et al., 1999). Adults also pay special attention to faces, and facial information is processed in a different way than stimuli of less biological significance (Ro, Russell, & Lavie, 2001). The importance of a facial stimulus is also suggested by the fact that we respond automatically to facial cues such as smiles and frowns (Hassin & Trope, 2000).

■ Individual Differences in the Need to Affiliate

People are not all the same, of course, and they differ in the strength of their **need for affiliation.** These differences, whether based on genetics or experience, constitute a relatively stable *trait* (or *disposition*). People tend to seek the amount of social contact that is optimal for them, preferring to be alone some of the time and in social situations some of the time (O'Connor & Rosenblood, 1996). Questionnaires that ask respondents to indicate how much they want to affiliate and about their affiliation-relevant activities measure the conscious, *explicit* need to affiliate. College students who score high on such a test tend to be sociable and to affiliate with many people (Craig, Koestner, & Zuroff, 1994). In contrast, projective measures that ask respondents to tell stories in response to ambiguous pictures measure the less conscious, *implicit* need to affiliate. Students scoring high on this type of test tend to interact primarily in limited, close, two-person situations.

How do we react when affiliation needs are not met? When, for example, other people ignore you, the experience is very unpleasant—whatever one's age (Faulkner & Williams, 1999) and whatever one's cultural background (Williams, Cheung, & Choi, 2000). When you are "left out" by others, it hurts, leaves you with the sense that you have lost control, and makes you feel both sad and angry because you simply don't belong (Buckley, Winkel, & Leary, 2004). Social exclusion leads to increased sensitivity to interpersonal information (Gardner, Pickett, & Brewer, 2000) and actually results in less effective cognitive functioning (Baumeister, Twenge, & Nuss, 2002).

need for affiliation
The basic motive to seek and maintain interpersonal relationships.

Situational Influences on the Need to Affiliate

In addition to individual differences in affiliation need, external events can elicit temporary *states* reflecting an increase in the need to affiliate. When people are reminded of their own mortality, for example, a common response is the desire to affiliate with others (Wisman & Koole, 2003). Newspaper and television stories frequently describe how the desire to affiliate is a common response to natural disasters. In the wake of such threats as a flood, earthquake, or blizzard, strangers come together and interact in a positive way to help and comfort one another (Benjamin, 1998; Byrne, 1991). These disaster-induced interactions are described as friendly and cheerful, with people doing their best to help one another.

The underlying reason for responding to stress with friendliness and affiliation was first identified by Schachter (1959). His early work revealed that participants in an experiment who were expecting to receive an electric shock preferred to spend time with others facing the same unpleasant prospect rather than being alone. Those in the control group, not expecting shock, preferred to be alone or didn't care whether they were with others or not. One conclusion from this line of research was that "misery doesn't just love any kind of company, it loves only miserable company" (Schachter, 1959, p. 24).

Why should real-life threats and anxiety-inducing laboratory experiences arouse the need to affiliate? Why should frightened, anxious people want to interact with other frightened, anxious people? One answer is that such affiliation provides the opportunity for *social comparison*. People want to be with others—even strangers—in order to communicate about what they are experiencing and to compare their affective reactions. Arousing situations lead us to seek "cognitive clarity" in order to know what is going on and "emotional clarity" in order to make sense of just what it is that we are feeling (Gump & Kulik, 1997; Kulik, Mahler, & Moore, 1996). And, contact with other humans is likely to include both conversations and hugs—both can be comforting.

Affect as a Basic Response System

Your emotional state (happy, sad, fearful, etc.) at any given moment influences what you perceive, your thought processes, your motivation, the decisions you make, *and* interpersonal attraction (Berry & Hansen, 1996; Forgas, 1995b). As you may remember from Chapter 2, psychologists often use the term **affect** when referring to emotions or feelings. The two most important characteristics of affect are *intensity*—the strength of the emotion—and *direction*—whether the emotion is positive or negative (see Figure 7.4 on page 262).

Why is affect a basic aspect of human behavior? Social psychologist John Cacioppo has provided an explanation based on evolutionary principles. He suggests, "The affect system is responsible for guiding our behavior toward whole classes of stimuli. The most fundamental discrimination animals must be able to make [in order to] survive is to discriminate hostile from hospitable events" (quoted by Volpe, 2002, p. 7). Our ancestors (both human and otherwise) were best able to live long enough to reproduce if they could avoid whatever was unpleasant and seek out whatever was pleasant. In effect, we are "built for pleasure" because the chances of survival and of reproduction are enhanced by just such tendencies. This generalization is useful whether the discrimination involves evaluations of unfamiliar food, a new environmental setting, or a stranger.

It was once assumed that all emotions fall along a single dimension (with positive feelings on one end and negative feelings on the other). We now know, however, that affect consists of at least two separate dimensions that activate somewhat different portions of the brain (Drake & Myers, 2000; George et al., 1995). The presence of two separate kinds of affect means that we can feel both positively and negatively at the same time; that is, we often respond to situations with ambivalence. This, too, has evolutionary significance

affect
A person's emotional state—positive and negative feelings and moods.

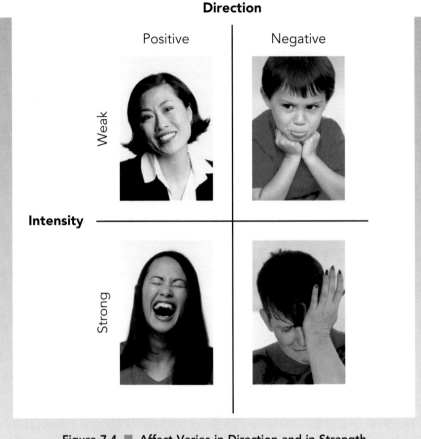

Figure 7.4 ■ Affect Varies in Direction and in Strength
The underlying dimensions of affect involve direction in that they can be positive or negative. They also vary in intensity from weak to strong.

because positive affect motivates us to seek out and explore novel aspects of the environment, while negative affect simultaneously warns us to be vigilant, watching out for possible danger so that we are also prepared to retreat (Cacioppo & Berntson, 1999). Depending on the specific circumstances and on individual predispositions, positive and negative affect can be equally important in determining our evaluations. In different situations, sometimes positive and sometimes negative emotions may predominate (Eiser et al., 2003; Gable, Reis, & Elliot, 2000).

Besides simply a positive and a negative dimension, there seem to be additional affective subdivisions (Egloff et al., 2003). For example, positive affect includes joy (feeling proud and enthusiastic), interest (feeling strong and determined), and activation (feeling alert and attentive). It may be that positive evaluations based on joy (for example) are different than positive evaluations based on interest.

Affect and Attraction

However complex positive and negative affect may turn out to be, a basic principle remains. The presence of positive affect leads to positive evaluations of other people (liking), while negative affect leads to negative evaluations (disliking) (Byrne, 1997; Dovidio et al., 1995).

The Direct Effect of Emotions on Attraction

Emotions have a *direct effect* on attraction when another person says or does something that makes you feel good or bad. You will not be surprised to be told that you tend to like someone who makes you feel good and dislike someone who makes you feel bad (Ben-Porath, 2002; Shapiro, Baumeister, & Kessler, 1991). Many experiments have confirmed just such an effect. For example, attraction toward another person is less if he or she provides punishments in rating one's performance on a task rather than rewards (McDonald, 1962), and less toward a stranger who invades one's personal space than one who remains at a comfortable distance (Fisher & Byrne, 1975). Many such findings allow us to predict with confidence that a stranger will like you better if you do or say something pleasant (e.g., "That's a beautiful dog you've got") as opposed to something unpleasant (e.g., "Where did you find such an ugly mutt?").

The Associated Effect of Emotions on Attraction

A phenomenon that is perhaps more surprising than the *direct effect* of emotions on attraction is the *associated effect* of emotions on attraction. This effect occurs when another person is simply present at the same time that one's emotional state is aroused by something or someone else. Though the individual toward whom you express like or dislike is not in any way responsible for what you are feeling, you nevertheless tend to evaluate him or her more positively when you are feeling good and more negatively when you are feeling bad. For example, if you come in contact with a stranger shortly after you receive a low grade on an exam, you tend to like that person less than someone you meet shortly after you receive your paycheck.

These associated (or indirect) influences of one's affective state have been demonstrated in many experiments involving emotional states based on a variety of quite diverse external causes. Examples include the subliminal presentation of pleasant versus unpleasant pictures—for example, kittens versus snakes (Krosnick et al., 1992); the presence of background music that college students perceived as pleasant versus unpleasant—for example, rock and roll versus classical (May & Hamilton, 1980); and the positive versus negative mood states that the research participants express when they first report for an experiment (Berry & Hansen, 1996).

The general explanation for such effects on attraction (as well as on other attitudes) rests on classical conditioning. When a neutral stimulus is paired with a positive stimulus, it is evaluated more positively than a neutral stimulus that is paired with a negative stimulus, even when the person is not aware that the pairing occurred (Olson & Fazio, 2001). Figure 7.5 on page 264 illustrates both direct and associated effects of emotion on attraction as examples of conditioning.

Additional Implications of the Affect–Attraction Relationship

There is reason to believe that the effect of positive emotions on interpersonal relationships has implications for many aspects of our lives.

Laughter and Liking

Because people like one another better when affect is positive, it is reasonable to suggest that laughter helps humans interact (Bachorowski & Owren, 2001). One of the ways in which people can feel most comfortable when dealing with one another is to laugh together. A person giving a speech often begins the presentation by saying something humorous, strangers stuck on a malfunctioning elevator are likely to joke about their situation, and salespeople sometimes make an amusing remark before they talk about the product or service they are selling. Why does humor arise in such situations?

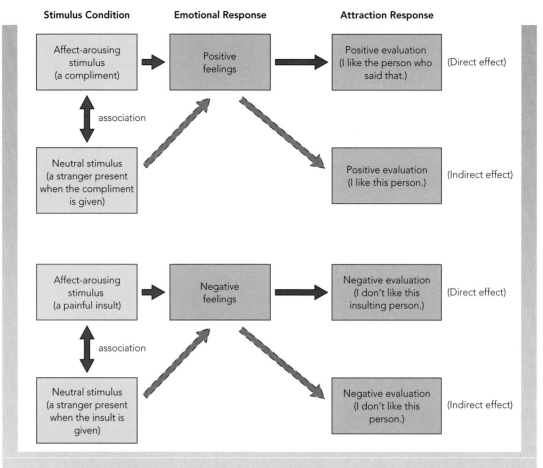

Figure 7.5 ■ Affect and Attraction: Direct Effects and Associated Effects
When any stimulus (including another person) arouses an individual's positive affect, the stimulus is liked. If the stimulus arouses negative affect, it is disliked. Such positive and negative arousal is defined as the direct effect of affect on attraction. Indirect effects occurs when any neutral stimulus (including another person) is present at the same time that affect is aroused by some other, unrelated source. The neutral stimulus becomes associated with the affect and is therefore either liked or disliked as a result. An indirect or associated effect is a form of classical conditioning. (*Source: Based on material in Byrne & Clore, 1970.*)

Humor is not only pleasant, it also provides a nonthreatening way for people to deal with one another. Neuroembryologist Robert Provine proposes that laughter helps strengthen social bonds and serves as a social "lubricant" that makes interpersonal behavior function more smoothly (Johnson, 2003; Selim, 2003). Just as many young mammals engage in playful behavior, young humans do the same thing and eventually turn to verbal play. Even in infancy, among the earliest interactions with parents is likely to be some form of play that evokes laughter, such as "peek-a-boo" and "this little piggy went to market." Such positive emotional experiences are believed to be the beginning of social interaction.

If humor is a social lubricant, it follows that strangers who share a humorous experience are more likely to interact in a pleasant way. According to Oscar Wilde, "Laughter is not at all a bad beginning for a friendship" (quoted by Fraley & Aron, 2004). Such an effect was demonstrated in an experimental setting in which pairs of college students met for the first time and engaged in a task that involved examining a "laugh

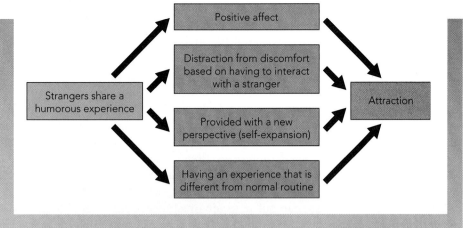

Figure 7.6 ■ Sharing a Laugh Leads to Attraction
In a variety of social situations, humor is commonly used to "break the ice" and facilitate a friendly interaction. Laboratory experiments verify the usefulness of shared humor as a way to enhance mutual attraction. Among the processes involved are the arousal of positive affect, the relief provided by a distraction from the discomfort caused by interacting with a stranger, the creation of a new perspective—or an expanded self—induced by the humor, and the pleasure of sharing a nonroutine experience with another person. (*Source: Based on the formulations described in Byrne et al., 1975, and in Fraley and Aron, 2004.*)

box"—a simple toy containing a recording of raucous laughter that was activated whenever the box was picked up. This was more or less an early version of the Tickle Me Elmo doll. Most of the students found the experience funny, most laughed, and most liked the stranger with whom they shared this experience (Byrne et al., 1975). Such an effect could have simply meant that, once again, positive affect leads to attraction.

Fraley and Aron (2004) proposed that, beyond positive affect, additional factors are involved when strangers share a humorous experience. Specifically, the shared experience was hypothesized to act as a distraction from the discomfort of interacting with a stranger and to create the perception that one has a new perspective on the situation (a feeling of self-expansion). Several different kinds of humorous experiences were utilized (e.g., playing charades, communicating a TV commercial in a made-up language). Compared with students in a nonhumorous control condition, the students who shared something humorous felt a sense of closeness to one another and also indicated that both distraction from discomfort and the perception of self-expansion took place. These combined effects are shown in Figure 7.6. As these experimenters suggested, "We hope the present study will encourage other relationship researchers to take humor seriously when considering the variables that play an important role in the development of close relationships" (Fraley & Aron, 2004, pp. 76–77).

■ Manipulating Affect to Influence Behavior

The fact that interpersonal evaluations are strongly influenced both directly and indirectly by emotional states can be and often is utilized in attempts to influence our behavior. Can we really be persuaded to purchase specific products, vote for specific political candidates, and support particular issues just because the right emotions have been aroused? The answer is "yes." And, such manipulation has become a familiar aspect of our lives. In addition to the relatively simple attempts of a salesperson to evoke a positive response with a free sample or a compliment, all branches of the media are utilized to arouse our emotions. The goal is to make us like whatever or whoever is being "sold" and, sometimes, to dislike whatever the alternative may be. In a movie theater, before the film begins, we are exposed to bright images and happy music with the general message, "Let's all go to the lobby" to purchase food and drink. Political candidates are paired with a wholesome family setting, complete with cuddly pets, as in Figure 7.7. And, the people in most advertisements smile because we believe that smiling people are better and more likable human beings (Glaser & Salovey, 1998; Harker & Keltner, 2001). Every attempt is made to associate a presidential hopeful who is being "sold" with positive words such as *moral, courageous, strong,* and *caring,* while associating the opponent with negative words such as *destructive, radical, incompetent,* and *corrupt* (Weisberg, 1990).

Because the attempts to manipulate us are often more subtle than ideal families and good versus bad adjectives, columnist Molly Ivins has suggested that whenever you see a company's advertisement depicting scenes of a beautiful countryside dotted with green forests and sparkling water, you should perhaps be a little suspicious as to whether that company is destroying trees and polluting nearby streams.

Are any of these manipulations effective? Research suggests that they are. For example, Pentony (1995) presented undergraduates with positive information about two candidates. For one of the candidates, however, *a single* unpleasant allegation was also included (a claim that he obtained tax breaks for his friends). That one bit of negative information resulted in a negative evaluation of the candidate and fewer votes. Even when a candidate presents evidence that the accusation is untrue, the candidate who is associated with purely positive information wins the contest.

Figure 7.7 ■ Positive Affect: Attraction to Candidate = Votes
In both political and commercial advertising, positive affect is used to "sell" the product, and sometimes negative affect is used to discourage interest in the competition. In politics, this often means that a candidate should be a tall, good looking (but not too "pretty") male who is married and has children and pets. Watch for such commercials whenever an election is being held and list the number of positive cues you observe. Beyond appearance and family, look for the presence of a flag, reference to military service, wholesome outdoor scenes, and so forth.

Other research indicates that the effect of mood on evaluations of political candidates is greatest when the audience is relatively uninformed (Ottati & Isbell, 1996). Also, context matters (Isbell & Wyer, 1999). In a political debate, for example, the viewer is consciously oriented toward evaluating and comparing the opponents; as a result, they tend to adjust their evaluations to take account of biased affective information. In contrast, seemingly casual remarks on a talk show can have a more powerful effect because the audience is not concentrating on making evaluations and comparisons.

Altogether, irrelevant affective factors are most likely to influence those who are relatively uninformed, unaware that their emotional state is being manipulated, and who are actively and consciously engaged in making decisions. You might find it helpful to keep these points in mind the next time you are exposed to any kind of affect-arousing message.

KEY POINTS

★ *Interpersonal attraction* refers to the evaluations we make of other people—the positive and negative attitudes we form about them.

★ Human beings are apparently born with a *need for affiliation*, the motivation to interact with other people in a cooperative way, often relying on shared laughter to smooth the way. The strength of this need differs among individuals and across situations.

★ Positive and negative affective states influence attraction both directly and indirectly.

Direct effects occur when another person is responsible for arousing the emotion; indirect effects occur when the source of the emotion is elsewhere and another person is simply associated with its presence.

★ The application of associated *affect* is a common element in both commercial and political advertising. This approach is most effective when directed at an audience that is relatively unaware and uninformed.

External Determinants of Attraction: Proximity and Observable Characteristics

Whether or not two specific people ever come into contact is very often determined by accidental, unplanned aspects of their physical environment. For example, two students assigned to adjoining classroom seats are more likely to interact than are two students given seats several rows apart. Once physical proximity brings about contact, their first impressions of one another are very often determined by preexisting beliefs and attitudes—stereotypes they hold about such observable factors as race, gender, physical attractiveness, accent, height, and so forth. We will describe just how proximity and observable characteristics influence attraction.

The Power of Proximity: Unplanned Contacts

More than six billion people now live on our planet, but you are likely to come into contact with only a very small percentage of them in your lifetime. Without some kind of contact, you obviously can't become acquainted with anyone or have a basis on which to decide which individuals you like or dislike.

Figure 7.8 ■ Proximity: Repeated Interactions in Everyday Life Facilitate Attraction
At school, at work, or where you live, proximity results in repeated contact with specific others simply on the basis of the physical arrangement of a classroom, workplace, or dwelling place. Repeated exposure most often leads to recognition, an increasingly positive evaluation, and a greater likelihood that two people will become acquainted.

Though it is not exactly surprising when you think about it, most of us are not really conscious of the way our interpersonal behavior is shaped by our physical surroundings. Many seemingly unimportant details of the setting in which we live, work, and go to school can have a powerful influence on our interpersonal lives. Basically, two people are likely to become acquaintances if external factors such as the location of their classroom seats, dormitory rooms, office desks, or whatever bring them into repeated contact. Such contacts occur on the basis of physical **proximity**. As suggested in Figure 7.8, people ordinarily become aware of one another and begin to interact in settings that bring them into close proximity. That may seem simple enough, but what is it about being brought into physical contact that influences social behavior?

■ Why Does Proximity Matter? Repeated Exposure Is the Key

Picture yourself in a large lecture class on the first day of school. Let's say that you don't see anyone you know and that the instructor has a chart that assigns students to seats alphabetically. At first, this roomful of strangers is a confusing blur of unfamiliar faces. Once you take your assigned seat, you probably notice the person sitting on your right and the one on your left, but you may or may not speak to one another. By the second or third day of class, however, you recognize the person or persons sitting beside you when you see them and may even say, "Hi." In the weeks that follow, you may have bits of conversation about the class or about something that is happening on campus. If you see a seat "neighbor" in some other setting, there is mutual recognition and you are increasingly likely to interact. If you think about it, it feels good to see a familiar face. Numerous early studies in the United States and in Europe revealed that students are most likely to become acquainted if they are seated beside one another (Byrne,

proximity
In attraction research, the physical closeness between two individuals with respect to where they live, where they sit in a classroom, where they work, and so on. The smaller the physical distance, the greater the probability that the two people will come into repeated contact, experiencing repeated exposure to one another, positive affect, and the development of mutual attraction.

1961a; Maisonneuve, Palmade, & Fourment, 1952; Segal, 1974). In addition to proximity in the classroom, investigations conducted throughout the twentieth century indicated that people who live or work in close proximity are likely to become acquainted, form friendships, and even marry one another (Bossard, 1932; Couple repays . . . , 1997; Festinger, Schachter, & Back, 1950). Despite the many examples of proximity resulting in attraction, you might wonder *why* proximity results in attraction.

The answer has been provided by numerous experiments showing that **repeated exposure** to a new stimulus results in an increasingly positive evaluation of that stimulus (Zajonc, 1968). This finding is sometimes called the **mere exposure effect** because the positive response to a stranger, a drawing, a word in an unknown language, or whatever that is observed multiple times occurs simply on the basis of exposure. Even infants tend to smile at a photograph of someone they have seen before but not at a photograph of someone they are seeing for the first time (Brooks-Gunn & Lewis, 1981).

A very clear demonstration of the effects of repeated exposure on attraction is provided by an experiment conducted in a classroom setting (Moreland & Beach, 1992). In a college course, one female assistant attended class fifteen times during the semester, a second assistant attended class ten times, a third attended five times, and a fourth did not attend the class at all. None of the assistants interacted with the other class members. At the end of the semester, the students were shown slides depicting the four assistants and asked to indicate how much they liked each one. As shown in Figure 7.9, the more times a particular assistant attended class, the more she was liked. In this and many other experiments, repeated exposure was found to have a positive effect on attraction.

Zajonc (2001) explains the effect of repeated exposure by suggesting that we ordinarily respond with at least mild discomfort when we encounter anyone or anything new and unfamiliar. It is reasonable to suppose that it was adaptive for our ancestors to be wary of approaching anything or anyone for the first time. Whatever is unknown and unfamiliar is always at least potentially dangerous. With repeated exposure, however, in the absence of harmful consequences, negative emotions decrease and positive emotions increase—familiarity with a stimulus reduces any feelings of uncertainty, suggesting that it is safe (Lee, 2001). A familiar face, for example, elicits positive affect, is evaluated positively, and activates facial muscles and brain activity in ways associated with positive emotions (Harmon-Jones & Allen, 2001). Not only does familiarity elicit positive affect, but positive affect elicits the perception of familiarity (Monin, 2003). For example, even when seen for the first time, a beautiful face is perceived as being more familiar than an unattractive one.

Many animals, too, appear to categorize specific individuals in their social encounters as friends or foes

repeated exposure
Zajonc's finding that frequent contact with any mildly negative, neutral, or positive stimulus results in an increasingly positive evaluation of that stimulus.

mere exposure effect
Another term for the *repeated exposure* effect, emphasizing the fact that exposure to a stimulus is all that is necessary to enhance the positive evaluation of that stimulus.

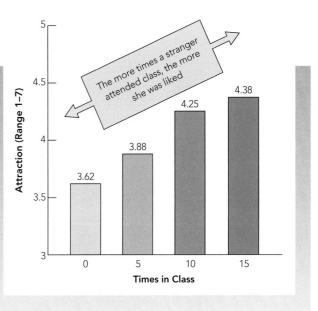

Figure 7.9 ■ Frequency of Exposure and Liking in the Classroom
To test the repeated exposure effect in a college classroom, Moreland and Beach (1992) employed four female research assistants to pretend to be fellow students. One of them did not attend class all semester, another attended class five times, a third attended ten times, and a fourth came to class fifteen times. None of them interacted with the actual students. At the end of the semester, the students were shown photos of the assistants and were asked to indicate how much they liked each one. It was found that the more times the students had been exposed to an assistant, the more they liked her. (*Source: Based on data from Moreland and Beach, 1992*).

(Schusterman, Reichmuth, & Kastak, 2000). It may be helpful to remember that the word *familiar* is related to the word *family.* In a way, repeated exposure allows us to include new individuals and new aspects of the environment in our expanded "family."

■ Extensions of the Repeated Exposure Effect

Repeated exposure to a stimulus results in a more positive evaluation of that stimulus, even when a person is not aware that the exposure has taken place. In fact, the effect is stronger under these conditions (Bornstein & D'Agostino, 1992). In addition, the positive affect generated by repeated exposure to subliminal stimuli *generalizes* to other, similar stimuli and even to new, completely different stimuli (Monahan, Murphy, & Zajonc, 2000).

Not all individuals are equally responsive to the repeated exposure effect. For example, people differ in their need for structure, and people high on this dimension are apt to organize their surroundings in simple rather than complex ways and to rely more heavily on stereotypes and categories when making judgments (Neuberg & Newsom, 1993). Hansen and Bartsch (2001) propose that familiarity would have the greatest effect on liking among those with a high need for structure. When unfamiliar Turkish words were first presented to English-speaking American students, they were rated more negatively by students high in need for structure than by those low in this need. After the research participants were shown these words multiple times, the words were rated more and more positively by most of the participants, but the effect was greatest among students high in the need for structure.

As powerful as the repeated exposure effect has been found to be, it fails to operate when a person's initial reaction to the stimulus is extremely negative. Repeated exposure in this instance not only fails to bring about a more positive evaluation, it can even lead to greater dislike (Swap, 1977). You may have experienced this yourself when a song or a commercial you disliked at first seems even worse when you hear it over and over again. For me, one of the worst experiences like that was the roommate assigned to me when I started my freshman year in college. John and I were clearly incompatible from the first moment we met, and sharing a room with someone you dislike for an entire academic year does not create a warm and friendly relationship. Sometimes, familiarity breeds contempt rather than attraction.

■ Applying Knowledge about the Effects of Proximity

Though most of us—most of the time—simply accept our surroundings and their effect on our interpersonal behavior, it is often possible to behave proactively. That is, you sometimes can change things. Even when classroom seats are *not* assigned, students tend to continue sitting wherever they first sat down, but they don't have to do so. Though it would have required time and effort for me to find a new dormitory room (and roommate), I could have done so.

In a classroom, if you have a choice and if you want to make new friends, select a seat between two likely prospects and not a seat on the end of the row or beside an empty desk. And, if you discover that your chosen seat neighbor or neighbors are not people you want to know, try a new location. If you are not eager to meet anyone new and would prefer privacy (Larson & Bell, 1988), select a place to sit that is as isolated as possible from other classmates. In fact, students who prefer privacy tend to select seats in the back of the room (Pedersen, 1994). In a similar way, you can choose relatively isolated or relatively interactive locations in a variety of settings, as in Figure 7.10.

In a more dramatic application that utilizes what is known about proximity, architects have designed offices and neighborhoods in a way that encourages interaction and communication (Giovannini, 2000; Gladwell, 2000). Because we know that interpersonal behavior is influenced by the details of our physical surroundings, it makes sense to take advantage of what we know and create or select the kind of environment that maximizes the outcomes we desire.

"Can I get you anyone?"

Figure 7.10 ■ If You Prefer Privacy, Avoid Proximity
Though we often surrender passively to the influence of physical proximity on our interpersonal interactions, it is possible to exert control over many situations. If, for example, you prefer to interact and make new acquaintances, place yourself in a position that encourages interactions with others. If you prefer privacy, select a relatively isolated position. The party hostess in this cartoon is trying to encourage interaction, whereas the man on the couch does not appear to have the same goal. (*Source: © The New Yorker Collection 2004 Michael Maslin from cartoonbank.com. All Rights Reserved.*)

Observable Characteristics: Instant Evaluations

Though positive affect from any source and the positive affect aroused by repeated exposure tend to result in attraction, it doesn't always work out that way. Sometimes people do not interact with the person sitting next to them all semester or the person living in the next apartment. And, sometimes you may be attracted to someone who is not in close proximity—"some enchanted evening" you might see a stranger "across a crowded room" and still be attracted. What might account for these contradictory behaviors? Instant likes and dislikes (first impressions) can also arouse strong affect, sometimes strong enough to overcome the proximity effect.

How could a person we don't know elicit a strong emotional reaction? Whenever we like—or dislike—someone at first sight, this reaction strongly suggests that something about that person has elicited positive or negative affect. Presumably, the affect is based on past experiences, stereotypes, and attributions that often are both inaccurate and irrelevant (Andreoletti, Zebrowitz, & Lachman, 2001). For example, if a stranger reminds you of someone you know and like, you probably will respond positively to that person (Andersen & Baum, 1994). Or if the stranger belongs to a category of people about whom you hold a generalized attitude (e.g., individuals with a Southern accent), you may tend to like the stranger if you like that kind of accent or express dislike if you react to such an accent negatively. As discussed in Chapter 6, stereotypes about people are poor predictors of their behavior. Despite that fact, most people react strongly on the basis of their own stereotypes. If you hold a positive stereotype, you are apt to be surprised when the person fails to match your expectations. If your stereotype is a negative one, this may prevent you from ever getting to know the actual person.

■ Physical Attractiveness: Judging Books by Their Covers

You know that your reaction to the cover of this textbook is not a good indicator of how much you will like or dislike its contents. (We hope, by the way, that you like both.) Each of us has learned since childhood "not to judge books by their covers" and that "beauty is only skin deep" and "pretty is as pretty does." Nevertheless, it is repeatedly found that people are most likely to respond positively to those who are most attractive and negatively to those who are least attractive (Collins & Zebrowitz, 1995). Thus, a pervasive factor that influences one's initial response to others is **physical attractiveness** (Maner et al., 2003), as illustrated in Figure 7.11.

Both in experiments and in the real world, physical appearance determines many types of interpersonal evaluations, including guilt or innocence in the courtroom (see Module A) and the grade that is assigned to an essay (Cash & Trimer, 1984). People even respond more positively to attractive infants than to unattractive ones (Karraker & Stern, 1990). And, as we will discuss in Chapter 8, appearance also plays a major role in mate selection. One of the reasons we focus on appearance is that we hold stereotypes based on how people look. Before you read any further, take a look at Figure 7.12, and follow the instructions you will find there.

Most people tend to believe that attractive men and women are more poised, interesting, sociable, independent, dominant, exciting, sexy, well adjusted, socially skilled, successful, and more masculine (men) or more feminine (women) than unattractive individuals (Dion & Dion, 1987; Hatfield & Sprecher, 1986a). Altogether, as social psychologists documented over three decades ago, most people assume that "what is beautiful is good" (Dion, Berscheid, & Hatfield, 1972). Despite the powerful effects of attractiveness, people are not very accurate in estimating how they are perceived by others (Gabriel, Critelli, & Ee, 1994). The appearance issue seems to be more acute for women than for men, but some members of both genders experience **appearance anxiety**—an undue concern with how one looks. Those with the greatest anxiety agree

Figure 7.11 ■ A Negative Reaction to Observable Characteristics Can Prevent You from Knowing the Actual Person
The movie *Shallow Hal* depicts Hal (Jack Black) as a man who responds only to the external appearance of women. When he is granted the power to see the "inner person," he perceives an overweight Gwyneth Paltrow as a beautiful, kind, interesting woman.

Figure 7.12 ■ How Would You Describe These People?
Make a list of the personality characteristics that you think might describe each of these individuals. For example, what do you think about each person's sociability, adjustment, intelligence, poise, independence, masculinity–femininity, popularity, vanity, potential for success, integrity, concern for others, sexual appeal, and other qualities? When you are finished, return to the text to find out whether your perceptions correspond to those of most people and to what has been found in psychological research.

with test items such as "I feel that most of my friends are more physically attractive than myself" and disagree with test items such as "I enjoy looking at myself in the mirror" (Dion, Dion, & Keelan, 1990). It probably comes as no surprise that when women watch TV commercials dealing with appearance, they begin focusing on how they look and express anger and dissatisfaction with themselves (Hargreaves & Tiggemann, 2002). A woman's comparison between herself and the women in the ads has the most negative effect if she perceives herself to be relatively unattractive (Patrick, Neighbors, & Knee, 2004).

Although cross-cultural research indicates that positive stereotypes about attractiveness are universal, the *specific content* of the stereotypes depends on the characteristics most valued by each culture (Dion, Pak, & Dion, 1990). In a collectivist culture such as Korea, attractiveness is assumed to be associated with integrity and concern for others, but these attributes do not appear among the stereotypes that are common among individualistic North Americans (Wheeler & Kim, 1997).

Despite widespread acceptance of attractiveness as an important cue to personality and character, most of the widely held appearance stereotypes are *incorrect* (Feingold, 1992; Kenealy et al., 1991). Note that extraordinarily evil individuals (such as Saddam Hussein's sons) can be good looking, and many people who do not look like movie stars—Bill Gates, for example—are often intelligent, interesting, kind, amusing, and so forth. Though the stereotypes about attractive people tend to be invalid, attractiveness actually *is* associated with popularity, good interpersonal skills, and high self-esteem (Diener, Wolsic, & Fujita, 1995; Johnstone, Frame, & Bouman, 1992). A probable reason for this association between how one looks and social skills, and so on, is that very attractive people have spent their lives being liked and treated well by other people who are responding to their appearance (Zebrowitz, Collins, & Dutta, 1998). And, those who are very attractive to others are aware that they are pretty or handsome (Marcus & Miller, 2003). In other words, appearance does not create social skills and high self-esteem, but such characteristics are developed *because of* the way other people have reacted to appearance.

People who are beautiful are usually seen as "good," but attractiveness is also associated with a few negative assumptions. For example, beautiful women are sometimes perceived as vain and materialistic (Cash & Duncan, 1984). Also, handsome male political candidates are more likely to be elected than unattractive ones, but an attractive female candidate is *not* helped by her appearance (Sigelman et al., 1986). Possibly, being "too feminine" is assumed to be inappropriate for someone in a legislative, judicial, or executive position, although being "too masculine" is OK.

What, Exactly, Constitutes "Attractiveness"?

Judgments of one's own attractiveness may not match the judgments of others very well, but there is surprisingly good agreement when two people are asked to rate a third person (Cunningham et al., 1995; Fink & Penton-Voak, 2002). The greatest agreement

Figure 7.13 ■ **Two Types of Attractive Women: Cute or Mature**
The study of physical attractiveness has identified two types of women who are rated most attractive. One category is considered cute—childlike features, large widely spaced eyes, and a small nose and chin (e.g., Meg Ryan). The other category of attractiveness is the mature look—prominent cheekbones, high eyebrows, large pupils, and a big smile (e.g., Julia Roberts).

occurs when men are judging the attractiveness of women (Marcus & Miller, 2003). Despite the consensus as to who is and is not attractive, it has proved difficult to identify the precise cues that determine these judgments.

In attempting to discover just what these cues might be, investigators have used two quite different procedures. One approach is to identify individuals who are perceived to be "attractive" and then to determine what they have in common. Cunningham (1986) asked male undergraduates to rate photographs of young women. The women who were judged to be most attractive fell into one of two groups, as shown in Figure 7.13. Some had "childlike features" consisting of large, widely spaced eyes and a small nose and chin. Women like Meg Ryan fit this category and are considered "cute" (Johnston & Oliver-Rodriguez, 1997; McKelvie, 1993a). The other category of attractive women had mature features, with prominent cheekbones, high eyebrows, large pupils, and a big smile—Julia Roberts is an example. These same two general facial types are found among fashion models, and they appear with equal frequency among white, African American, and Asian women (Ashmore, Solomon, & Longo, 1996).

A second approach to the determination of what is meant by attractiveness was taken by Langlois and Roggman (1990). They began with several facial photographs and then used computer digitizing to combine multiple faces into one face. The image in each photo is divided into microscopic squares, and each square is assigned a number that represents a specific shade. Then the numbers are averaged across two or more pictures, and this average is translated back into a corresponding shade. The overall result is assembled into a composite image of the combined faces.

You might reasonably guess that a face created by averaging would be rated as average in attractiveness. Instead, composite faces are rated as *more* attractive than most of the individual faces used to make the composite (Langlois, Roggman, & Musselman,

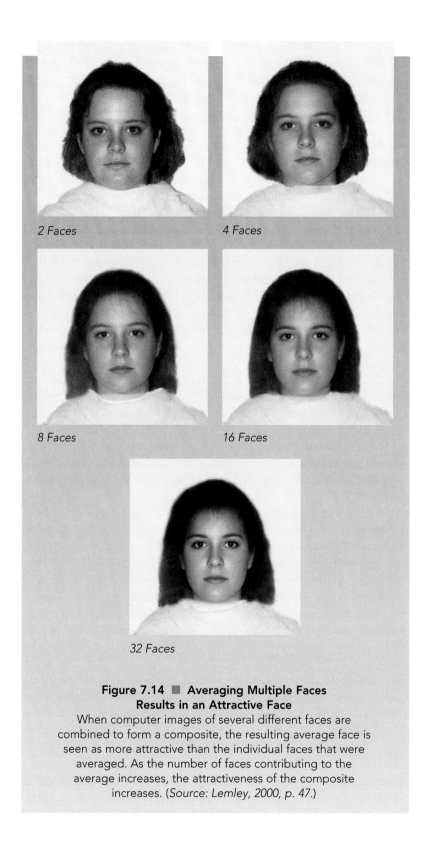

2 Faces

4 Faces

8 Faces

16 Faces

32 Faces

**Figure 7.14 ■ Averaging Multiple Faces
Results in an Attractive Face**
When computer images of several different faces are combined to form a composite, the resulting average face is seen as more attractive than the individual faces that were averaged. As the number of faces contributing to the average increases, the attractiveness of the composite increases. (*Source: Lemley, 2000, p. 47.*)

1994; Rhodes & Tremewan, 1996). In addition, the more faces that are averaged, the more beautiful the resulting face. As shown in Figure 7.14, when you combine as many as thirty-two faces, "you end up with a face that is pretty darned attractive" (Judith Langlois, as quoted in Lemley, 2000, p. 47).

It is possible to create an even more attractive face by taking initial attractiveness into account. For example, if you start with fifteen extremely attractive faces, their composite is more attractive than a composite of fifteen average faces (Perrett, May, & Yoshikawa, 1994). Another way to enhance the attractiveness of a composite face is to rate each face going into the mix and then to assign more weight to the most attractive faces than to the less attractive ones. When biopsychologist Victor Johnston did this with a series of twenty generations of composites rated by ten thousand visitors to his website, the final face was extremely attractive, and it was perceived to be more feminine than average (Lemley, 2000). With respect to both male and female faces, a composite that is relatively feminine is preferred (Angier, 1998a).

Why should composite faces be especially attractive? It is possible that each person's schema of women and of men is created in our cognitions in much the same way that the averaged face is created. That is, we form such schemas on the basis of our experiences with many different images, so a composite face is closer to that schema than is any specific face. If this analysis is accurate, a composite of other kinds of images should also constitute the most attractive alternative, but it does *not* work with composite dogs or composite birds (Halberstadt & Rhodes, 2000). It may be that our perception of human composites is different because it was historically more important to our species to recognize potential friends, enemies, and mates than to recognize specific, individual dogs and birds.

In addition to the details of facial features, perceptions of attractiveness are also influenced by the situation. When research participants have been shown pictures of very attractive people, they then rate a stranger as less attractive than do participants who have not been looking at attractive pictures (Kenrick et al., 1993). Why? The difference between the attractiveness of the people in the photographs and the stranger creates what is known as a *contrast effect*. In a similar way, men rate their own female partners less positively if they have just been looking at photos of very attractive women (Kenrick & Gutierres, 1980).

Other aspects of context also matter. As suggested by Mickey Gilley's song about searching for romance in bars, "the girls all get prettier at closing time." Actually, research in bars indicates that "girls" (and "boys," too) are perceived as more attractive by members of the opposite sex as the evening progresses (Nida & Koon, 1983; Pennebaker et al., 1979). Ratings of same-sex strangers by heterosexuals do not improve as closing time approaches, so alcohol consumption does not explain the effects (Gladue & Delaney, 1990). Rather, as people pair off and the number of available partners decreases, the resulting scarcity results in a more positive evaluation of those who remain unattached.

Other Aspects of Appearance and Behavior That Influence Attraction

When we meet someone for the first time, we usually react to a variety of factors. Any observable cue, no matter how superficial, may evoke a stereotype, and the resulting emotional reactions lead to instant likes and dislikes. One of the factors that have been studied is clothing (Cheverton & Byrne, 1998; Jarrell, 1998). Beyond such factors as neatness (Mack & Rainey, 1990), clothing colors seem to have an effect. People make an automatic association between brightness and affect; specifically, bright equals good, and dark equals bad (Meier, Robinson, & Clore, 2004). Attraction is also influenced by the presence of observable disabilities (Fichten & Amsel, 1986), behaviors that suggest mental illness (Schumacher, Corrigan, & Dejong, 2003), perceived age (McKelvie, 1993b), the presence of eyeglasses (Lundberg & Sheehan, 1994), and a man's facial hair (Shannon & Stark, 2003).

Before discussing the effect of additional factors on attraction, consider the important role played by observable characteristics on voters' attraction toward presidential candidates in the following **Beyond the Headlines** section.

Voting for the Candidate Who Looks Like a President

Short End of Stick Can Hurt in Politics

Cleveland, November 2, 2003—Dennis Kucinich is often called a long-shot candidate for president, but he might more accurately be called a short-shot candidate. And, it doesn't matter what you think of him or what he has to say on the issues. History shows that size matters in presidential politics, and Kucinich, who measures 5'7", is below the average of American men which is 5'9". The tallest candidate doesn't *always* win (e.g., 2004), although it happens more often than chance. Only a half-dozen of our 43 presidents were close to the average height of their times, and only one (James Madison at 5'4") could actually be called short. In fact, most U.S. presidents have been several inches above the norm; eighteen have been over six feet including six of the last nine. Beginning with George Washing-ton and Thomas Jefferson (both 6'2"), Americans have elected tall men, and they continue to do so. Only Abraham Lincoln (6'4") was taller than Lyndon Johnson (6'3") and Bill Clinton (6'2"). Height is an advantage in other occupations besides the presidency. Tall people are found to earn more than short people throughout their careers, and each inch adds about $789 a year to one's pay (Judge & Cable, 2004). These findings are some-what troubling, because no one, except the members of a professional basketball team, would argue that height is an essential quality for any occupation. In Hollywood, height is not a problem—such actors as Dustin Hoffman, Al Pacino, Tom Cruise, and Mike Myers are shorter than average. Martin Sheen, at 5'7", is able to play the role of president (on *The West Wing*), but the odds are against his actually being elected to that office.

Data involving the effects of height are also troubling to social psychologists, but not surprising. It is well established that attraction is based in part on stereotypes associated with observable characteristics such as height. A man's height is perceived as an indicator of qualities such as leadership and masculinity, so voters clearly like and want to elect as president a man who has these qualities.

As with all stereotypes, of course, height is a poor predictor of behavior, but people often vote with their feelings and not with their cognitive functions. Few people want to admit, even to themselves, that they plan to vote for X because he is taller than Y, but it seems that many people do, in fact, make choices in that way. Tall men elicit positive affect (as well as perceptions of specific character traits), and we evaluate them favorably. Still, it seems a bit odd that one could have predicted the outcome of the 2004 Democratic primaries before any debates were held and before any candidate had spoken out on the major issues. The tallest (Kerry) would have been predicted to win, and the shortest (Kucinich) would have been expected to get the least number of votes. No, the outcome was not a surprise.

It should be noted that *attractive* candidates are also likely to win political contests. In 2004, John Edwards was generally considered the best looking of the Democratic hopefuls and he is also tall (6 feet), but he came in second among those running for the nomination. His only problem with respect to appearance was that he looked too young (the baby-face effect) to be president (Crowley, 2003) though not too young to be vice president. Though he had his fiftieth birthday during primary season, Edwards' youthful appearance elicited beliefs about relatively immature characteristics—both positive (trustworthy, honest) and negative (submissive, naïve) rather than mature, masculine ones (Zebrowitz et al., 2003).

Among other observable characteristics, a person's physique also is associated with stereotypes that trigger emotional reactions and differential attraction. It was once thought that body type provided information about personality (Sheldon, Stevens, &

Figure 7.15 ■ Obesity as a Stigma
Along with facial attractiveness, weight is an observable characteristic that elicits consistent stereotypes. In many cultures, negative attitudes about obesity influence various aspects of interpersonal behavior. As with others who are the object of stereotyping, overweight individuals sometimes fight back with anger or humor. Shown here is a rally for the Million Pound March in southern California.

Tucker, 1940), but decades of research indicated that this assumption was an inaccurate one. Nevertheless, even today people respond to others as if physique provided useful information. Though these observations are untrue, people believe that a round and fat body indicates a sad and sloppy person, that a hard and muscular body indicates good health and lack of intelligence, and a thin and angular body indicates intelligence and fearfulness (Gardner & Tockerman, 1994; Ryckman et al., 1989).

In these and other investigations, a consistent finding is that the least liked physique is one characterized by excess fat (Harris, Harris, & Bochner, 1982; Lundberg & Sheehan, 1994), as in Figure 7.15. Obesity even functions as a stigma, and the stigma can rub off onto others—a man sitting with an overweight woman is evaluated more negatively than a man sitting with a woman of average weight (Hebl & Mannix, 2003). Once again, it is important to remember that stereotypes associated with weight do not lead to accurate predictions about how an individual can be expected to behave (Miller et al., 1995a).

Crandall (1994) equates prejudice against obesity with racial prejudice, and he developed a measure of antifat prejudice. Test items consist of such statements as "I really don't like fat people much" and "Fat people tend to be fat pretty much through their own fault." Though there is a prevailing prejudice in the United States against those who are overweight, in Mexico and other collectivist cultures there is much less concern about weight and a less negative reaction to those who are overweight (Crandall & Martinez, 1996; Crandall et al., 2001).

Observable differences in overt behavior also elicit stereotypes that influence attraction. A person with a youthful walking style elicits a more positive response than one who walks with an elderly style, regardless of gender or actual age (Montepare & Zebrowitz-McArthur, 1988). A person with a firm handshake is perceived as being extroverted and emotionally expressive (Chaplin et al., 2000). People respond positively

Chapter 7 / Interpersonal Attraction

to someone whose behavior is animated (Bernieri et al., 1996), who actively participates in class discussions (Bell, 1995), and who acts modestly rather than arrogantly (Hareli & Weiner, 2000).

In initial encounters, men who behave in a dominant, authoritative, competitive way are preferred to those who seem submissive, noncompetitive, and less masculine (Friedman, Riggio, & Casella, 1988). When subsequent interactions provide additional information about the individual, however, the preference shifts to men who are prosocial and sensitive (Jensen-Campbell, West, & Graziano, 1995; Morey & Gerber, 1995). It might be said that nice guys finish first when you get to know them.

Interpersonal judgments are also influenced by what a person eats (Stein & Nemeroff, 1995). Regardless of factors such as height and weight, a person who eats "good food" (e.g., oranges, salad, whole wheat bread, chicken) is perceived as more likeable and morally superior to one who eats "bad food" (e.g., steak, hamburgers, French fries, donuts, and double-fudge sundaes).

One final, and perhaps most surprising, influence on interpersonal perceptions is a person's first name. Familiar names activate a category of experience and information that provides us with a stereotype (Macrae, Mitchell, & Pendry, 2002). And, various male and female names elicit widely shared positive and negative stereotypes (Mehrabian & Piercy, 1993), as shown in Table 7.1. In addition, a distinctive first name attached to a highly publicized individual (real or fictional) becomes associated with some of the characteristics of that individual; the resulting stereotype then transfers to anyone else who happens to have that name. What would your first thought be if you met someone named Osama, Keanu, Hillary, Bart, Whoopi, or Gwyneth?

Table 7.1 ■ What's in a Name? The Answer Is Stereotypes

Initial impressions are sometimes based on a person's first name. Once again, stereotypes lead to inaccurate assumptions, and the assumptions influence interpersonal behavior.

MALE NAMES	FEMALE NAMES	ATTRIBUTIONS ABOUT THE INDIVIDUAL
Alexander	Elizabeth	*Successful*
Otis	Mildred	*Unsuccessful*
Joshua	Mary	*Moral*
Roscoe	Tracy	*Immoral*
Mark	Jessica	*Popular*
Norbert	Harriet	*Unpopular*
Henry	Ann	*Warm*
Ogden	Freida	*Cold*
Scott	Brittany	*Cheerful*
Willard	Agatha	*Not cheerful*
Taylor	Rosalyn	*Masculine*
Eugene	Isabella	*Feminine*

(*Source:* Based on information in Mehrabian & Piercy, 1993.)

KEY POINTS

★ The initial contact between two people is very often based on the *proximity* that is the result of such physical aspects of the environment as classroom seating assignments, the location of residences, and how workplaces are arranged.

★ Proximity, in turn, leads to *repeated exposure* of two individuals to one another. Repeated exposure usually results in positive affect, which results in attraction—a process known as the *mere exposure effect*.

★ Interpersonal attraction and judgments based on stereotypes are strongly affected by various observable characteristics of those we meet, including *physical attrac-*

tiveness. People like and make positive attributions about attractive men and women of all ages, despite the fact that assumptions based on appearance are usually inaccurate.

★ In addition to attractiveness, many other observable characteristics influence initial interpersonal evaluations, including physique, weight, behavioral style, food preferences, first names, and other superficial characteristics.

★ Height, especially for males, is a positive factor—the taller the better, with respect to career success and even to being elected to the presidency.

Interactive Determinants of Attraction: Similarity and Mutual Liking

We have learned that the formation of any kind of relationship between two people is facilitated by the need for affiliation, positive affect, physical proximity, and a positive reaction to the observable characteristics of one another. The next steps toward interpersonal closeness involve communication. Two crucial aspects of this communication are the extent to which the interacting individuals discover their degree of *similarity* and the extent to which they indicate *mutual liking* by what they say and what they do.

Similarity: Birds of a Feather Actually Do Flock Together

The role of similarity in fostering interpersonal attraction is now generally accepted. This phenomenon has been observed and discussed for well over two thousand years, beginning with Aristotle's (330 B.C./1932) essay on friendship. Support for this early observation was expressed over the centuries from sources as varied as Spinoza (1675/1951) and Samuel Johnson (Boswell, 1791/1963). Empirical support for the "similarity hypothesis" was not provided, however, until Sir Francis Galton (1870/1952) obtained correlational data on married couples, indicating that spouses resemble one another in many respects. In the first half of the twentieth century, additional correlational studies continued to find that friends and spouses were more similar than would occur by chance (e.g., Hunt, 1935). Such similarity could have meant either that liking led to similarity or vice versa, but Newcomb (1956) studied university transfer students and found that similar attitudes (assessed before the students had even met) predicted subsequent liking. In addition to this convincing finding, later experiments manipulated similarity and then assessed attraction, coming to the same conclusion (Byrne, 1961b; Schachter, 1951). As Aristotle and others had speculated, the data indicate clearly that two people who find that they are similar like each other *because* they are similar.

Before we go on to describe some of the research on similarity, you may be asking, "What about the 'fact' that opposites attract?" Do they? Most people, including especially those who write scripts for movies and television, clearly believe that the answer is "yes." In the realm of empirical evidence, however, similarity is found to be the rule. See **The Science of Social Psychology: Making Sense of Common Sense** section that follows.

Complementarity: Do Opposites Attract?

The idea that "opposites attract" is nearly as ancient as the idea that "birds of a feather flock together" and as new as the last movie you saw in which two very different people become friends, roommates, or romantic partners. In plays, movies, and television series, a familiar story line in one in which two very different people are attracted to one another, in part because they are so different. Think, for example, of Will and Grace, the couples in *Maid in Manhattan* and *Along Came Polly*, not to mention Marge and Homer Simpson or a movie such as *Lady and the Tramp*, plus many, many others. In contrast, real-life examples of such pairings are relatively rare (Angier, 2003; Buston & Emlen, 2003). Even when opposites do form a relationship (e.g., a married couple like Democratic strategist James Carville and Republican strategist Mary Matalin; see Figure 7.16), one can guess that despite their opposing political views, they have a great deal in common. For example, both are intensely interested in the political process, and party differences represent only a relatively limited set of disagreements.

In the early days of research on this topic, the proposed attraction of opposites was often phrased in terms of complementarity. That is, it was suggested that dominant individuals would be attracted to submissive ones, talkative people to quiet ones, sadists to masochists, and so on. The idea was that such complementary characteristics would be mutually reinforcing and hence a good basis for a relationship. Direct tests of these propositions, however, failed to support complementarity as a determinant of attraction, even with characteristics like dominance and submissiveness (Palmer & Byrne, 1970). With respect to attitudes, values, personality characteristics, bad habits, intellectual ability, income level, and even minor preferences, such as choosing the right-hand versus left-hand aisle in a movie theater, similarity results in attraction (Byrne, 1971). On the basis of multiple experiments over the past several decades, one can only conclude that there is no evidence that opposites attract.

There is, however, consistent evidence that complementarity *sometimes* does operate in a specific situation (e.g., when a male and a female are interacting). Specifically, when one person engages in dominant behavior, the other then responds in a submissive fashion (Markey, Funder, & Ozer, 2003; Sadler & Woody, 2003). And, this situation-specific kind of complementarity leads to greater attraction than when the second person copies the first person (Tiedens & Fragale, 2003). With other kinds of interaction (e.g., a person who is verbally withdrawn and unresponsive interacting with someone who is verbally expressive and critical), opposite styles not only fail to attract, they are especially incompatible and more likely to bring about rejection and avoidance than attraction (Swann, Rentfrow, & Gosling, 2003).

Figure 7.16 ■ With Rare Exceptions, Opposites Don't Attract
Though the belief that opposites attract is a familiar one in fiction, similarity is a much better predictor of attraction. Even when seemingly opposite people do attract one another (as with Democrat James Carville and his wife, Republican Mary Matalin), they still are found to have a great deal in common.

Interactive Determinants of Attraction

■ Similarity–Dissimilarity: A Consistent Predictor of Attraction

Much of the early work on the **similarity–dissimilarity effect** focused on **attitude sim-ilarity,** but this phrase was generally used as a short-hand term that included not only similarity of attitudes, but also beliefs, values, and interests. The initial laboratory exper-iments on this topic consisted of two steps: First, the attitudes of the participants were assessed, and second, these individuals were exposed to the attitudes, and so forth, of a stranger and asked to evaluate him or her (Byrne, 1961b). The results were straight-forward in that people consistently indicated that they liked similar strangers much bet-ter than they liked dissimilar ones. Not only do we like people who are similar to ourselves, we also judge them to be more intelligent, better informed, more moral, and better adjusted than people who are dissimilar. As you might suspect on the basis of our discussion of affect earlier in this chapter, similarity arouses positive feelings and dissimilarity arouses negative feelings.

Many such investigations with a variety of populations, procedures, and topics, revealed that people respond to similarity–dissimilarity in a surprisingly precise way. Attraction is determined by the **proportion of similarity.** That is, when the number of topics on which two people express similar views is divided by the total number of top-ics on which they have communicated, the resulting proportion can be inserted in a sim-ple formula that allows us to predict their attraction to one another (Byrne & Nelson, 1965). The higher the proportion of similarity, the greater the liking, as illustrated in Figure 7.17. No one knows exactly how attitudinal information is processed to produce that outcome, but it is *as if* people automatically engage in some kind of cognitive addi-tion and division, manipulating the units of positive and negative affect they experience.

The effect of attitude similarity on attraction is a strong one, and it holds true regardless of the number of topics on which people express their views and regardless of how important or trivial the topics may be. It holds equally true for males and females, regardless of age, educational, or cultural differences (Byrne, 1971).

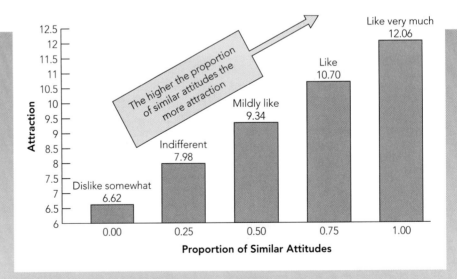

Figure 7.17 ■ As Proportion of Similar Attitudes Increases, Attraction Increases

The relationship between proportion of similar attitudes and attraction is a consistent and highly predictable one. The greater the proportion of similar attitudes, the greater the attraction. The relationship can be expressed in a simple linear formula, and it holds true for both genders and across different age groups, different cultures, and different educational levels.

The most serious challenge to the validity of such findings was offered by Rosenbaum (1986) when he proposed that using proportion as the independent variable made it impossible to separate the effect of similarity from the effect of dissimilarity. Based on some data he gathered, the **repulsion hypothesis** was put forth as an alternative to the *similarity–dissimilarity effect.* The basic idea is that information about similarity has no effect on attraction—people are simply repulsed by information about dissimilarity. Later research was able to show that the idea is wrong (Smeaton, Byrne, & Murnen, 1989), but there was a grain of truth in the repulsion hypothesis. Specifically, under most circumstances, information about dissimilarity has a *slightly stronger effect* on attraction than the same amount of information about similarity (Chen & Kenrick, 2002; Singh & Ho, 2000; Tan & Singh, 1995).

Beyond attitudes, values, and so forth, many kinds of similarity–dissimilarity have been investigated, and in each instance, people prefer those who are similar to themselves rather than dissimilar. Examples include similarity–dissimilarity with respect to physical attractiveness (Zajonc et al., 1987), smoking marijuana (Eisenman, 1985), religious practices (Kandel, 1978), self-concept (Klohnen & Luo, 2003), being a "morning person" versus an "evening person" (Watts, 1982), and finding the same jokes amusing (Cann, Calhoun, & Banks, 1995).

Is it possible that people seek similarity not only with respect to friends and spouses, but with their pets as well? People have often suggested, for example, that people resemble their dogs, but is that true? This proposition has recently been tested, and it seems to be accurate (see Figure 7.18 on page 284). Roy and Christenfeld (2004) took separate photographs of dogs and of pet owners. College students (who didn't know the people in the pictures) were shown an owner along with two dog pictures—one was that person's dog and the other was a picture of some other dog. The students were asked to guess which dog was the person's pet, and the matches were correct much more often than would have occurred by chance. Note that this finding holds only for purebred dogs and not mixed breeds, presumably because people are unconsciously seeking a pet similar to themselves, but a puppy's eventual appearance can consistently be predicted only for pure breeds.

There are a few partial exceptions to the similarity effect. One example is the degree to which two people are similar with respect to ideal self. Similarity to ideal self has a positive effect (as is true of other types of similarity), but discovering that someone is closer to your ideal than you are is also threatening (Herbst, Gaertner, & Insko, 2003). Leaving aside such minor exceptions, why do people usually respond to similarity and dissimilarity in a positive versus a negative way?

Explaining the Effect of Similarity–Dissimilarity on Attraction

To ask the general question another way, *why* does similarity elicit positive affect, while dissimilarity elicits negative affect?

The oldest explanation—**balance theory**—was proposed independently by Newcomb (1961) and by Heider (1958). This formulation states that people naturally organize their likes and dislikes in a symmetrical way (Hummert, Crockett, & Kemper, 1990). When two people like each other and discover that they are similar in some specific respect, this constitutes a state of *balance,* and balance is emotionally pleasant. When two people like each other and find out that they are dissimilar in some specific respect, the result is *imbalance.* Imbalance is emotionally unpleasant, causing the individuals to strive to restore balance by inducing one of them to change and thus create similarity or by misperceiving the dissimilarity or simply by deciding to dislike one another. Whenever two people dislike one another, their relationship involves *nonbalance.* This is not especially pleasant or unpleasant, because each individual is indifferent to the other person's similarities or dissimilarities.

These aspects of balance theory are correct, but they do not deal with the question of why similarity should matter in the first place. So, a second level of explanation is

repulsion hypothesis
Rosenbaum's provocative proposal that attraction is not increased by similar attitudes but is simply decreased by dissimilar attitudes. This hypothesis is incorrect as stated, but it is true that dissimilar attitudes tend to have negative effects that are stronger than the positive effects of similar attitudes.

balance theory
The formulations of Heider and of Newcomb that specify the relationships among (1) an individual's liking for another person, (2) his or her attitude about given topic, and (3) the other person's attitude about the same topic. Balance (liking plus agreement) results in a positive emotional state. Imbalance (liking plus disagreement) results in a negative state and a desire to restore balance. Nonbalance (disliking plus either agreement or disagreement) leads to indifference.

Figure 7.18 ■ Look-Alikes? Dogs and Their Owners
It is a common belief that pet owners tend to be similar in appearance to their pets, and research by Roy and Christenfeld (2004) has confirmed it. College students were able to match photographs of purebred dogs with photographs of their owners with greater than chance accuracy. The photos shown here were *not* those used in the study, but do you think you would have been able to match Paris Hilton with her Chihuahua, the lady with her Maltese, and the man with his bulldog?

needed. Why should you care if someone differs from you with respect to musical preferences, belief in God, or anything else? One answer is provided by aspects of Festinger's (1954) *social comparison theory.* Briefly stated, you compare your attitudes and beliefs with those of others because the only way you can evaluate your accuracy and normality is by finding that other people agree with you. This is not a perfect way to determine the truth, but it is often the best we can do. For example, if you are the *only one* who believes that invisible Martians have landed and are living in your attic, the odds are that you are incorrect and perhaps delusional. No one wants to be in that position, so we turn to others to obtain *consensual validation* (see Chapter 9). When you learn that someone else shares your attitudes and beliefs, it feels good, because such information at least suggests that you have sound judgment, are normal and in contact with reality, and so forth. Dissimilarity suggests the opposite, and that creates negative affect. We all are anxious to be "right, sensible, and sane," but we each have some degree of self-doubt. You may have observed two people arguing and getting very angry about issues for which there is no way to prove that either is correct—"It is when we are not sure that we are doubly sure" (Niebuhr, as quoted by Beinart, 1998, p. 25).

A third approach to an explanation of the similarity–dissimilarity effect rests on an evolutionary perspective as an **adaptive response** to potential danger. Gould (1996) suggests that our negative reaction to dissimilar others may have originated when humans were living in small groups of hunters and gatherers on the savannas of Africa. It seems that a great deal (perhaps most) of human animosity is based on reactions to dissimilarity. In the words of Howard Stern, "If you're not like me, I hate you" (Zoglin, 1993). It seems that the worst acts of barbarism are directed toward those who differ from the perpetrator in race, ethnicity, language, religious beliefs, sexual orientation, political affiliation, and so on: "Programmed into the human soul is a preference for the near and familiar" (McDonald, 2001).

Imagine what it was like when a band of our primitive ancestors accidentally encountered humans from a different band. Horney (1950) described three basic alternative reactions to the strangers: Our ancient relatives could have moved *toward* them with a friendly intent; *away from* them, out of fear, with a self-protective intent; or *against* them with an aggressive intent. Under specific circumstances, monkeys have been observed to engage in each of these three patterns when they spot an unfamiliar monkey (Carpenter, 2001a).

Different potential consequences are associated with the different response choices. If the strangers are good and kind, a friendly approach could benefit both groups. If, however, the strangers posed a threat (perhaps the most likely possibility), then greeting them with friendliness and trust would be the most dangerous and least adaptive response that could be made. Survival, and hence reproduction, would best be enhanced by either retreating or attacking, and the latter is probably the most effective way to survive. Humans are not the only species to aggress against strangers. Male chimpanzees, for example, band together to kill chimps from a different group. By destroying the outsiders, the killers are able to weaken the rival band, expand their own territory, and provide additional food for their mates and offspring (Wilson & Wrangham, 2003; Wade, 2003). Similar behavior is common even among mice (Stowers et al., 2002): "Male mice are genetically programmed to follow a simple rule when a strange mouse enters their territory. If it's a male, attack it; if female, seduce it" (Wade, 2002, p. F3).

This general account at least seems plausible. If it is accurate, we may simply be programmed to fear and hate those who are different from ourselves, especially if they are males. And, there is increasing evidence that we are automatically vigilant in reacting to cues that alert us to positive or negative consequences of interaction and therefore to approach or avoid those cues (Bargh, 1997; Wentura, Rothermund, & Bak, 2000). Though these various reactions may have once been crucial to survival and reproductive success for our species, today they form the basis for prejudice, hate crimes, terrorism, genocide, and a general dislike of anyone who is "different."

An example of the hatred of whoever and whatever differs from oneself and one's society is provided by an Islamic teacher, Hassan al-Banna. In the 1920s he wrote an essay that describes some of the cross-cultural animosity that is as relevant today (and frighteningly prophetic) as it was eight decades ago. Banna complained that the European colonialists had expropriated Islamic lands and corrupted the people who lived there. He clearly perceived these outsiders as dissimilar from the residents of the Middle East and hence evil:

> They imported their half-naked women into these regions, together with their liquors, their theaters, their dance halls, their amusements, their stories, their newspapers, their novels, their whims, their silly games, and their vices. . . . The day must come when the castles of this materialistic civilization will be laid low upon the heads of their inhabitants. (quoted in Remnick, 2004, p. 76)

adaptive response
Any physical characteristic or behavioral tendency that enhances the odds of reproductive success for an individual or for other individuals with similar genes.

Attraction: Progressing from Bits and Pieces to an Overall Picture

Throughout this chapter, we have stressed the idea that attraction is based on positive and negative affective responses that lead us to make positive and negative evaluations. This general formulation is known as the **affect-centered model of attraction**. The emphasis on affect does not mean, however, that cognitive processes are irrelevant. As shown in Figure 7.19, Person B's affective state (either directly aroused by Person A or simply associated with Person A) is conceptualized as playing a major role in determining how B evaluates A, as well as B's subsequent behavior toward A. It is also necessary, however, for B to engage in cognitively processing all available information about A. Such information includes stereotypes, beliefs, and factual knowledge and can therefore have an additional influence on affective arousal, enhancing or mitigating B's initial evaluation (Montoya & Horton, 2004).

As an example of the interplay of affect and cognition, let's return to the issue of responding aggressively to those who are dissimilar. Human cognitive and language skills enable us to dehumanize whomever we attack, and this helps justify our aggression. In an analogous way, the cartoon lions in Figure 7.20 "delionize" their rabbit prey—a rabbit is not at all like a lion; a rabbit doesn't even feel pain.

Compared with the behavior of predators such as lions, however, human aggression is notably vicious. Bandura (1999a) makes the point that it is all too easy to disengage moral control and thus justify cruel and inhumane acts. It is easy, for example, to attribute one's angry, fear-inspired, violent impulses to others: "It is justifiable to harm them, because they intend to harm me" (Schimel et al., 2000). And once the violent, harmful, evil behavior begins, it grows increasingly intense (Staub, 1999). Though the initial dislike of a stranger may be based on affective factors, the justification for that affect and the subsequent decision about the most appropriate way to respond are based on cognitive factors. (Keep in mind that dissimilarity is only one source of provocation to aggress. As we discuss in Chapter 11, there are multiple determinants of human aggression.)

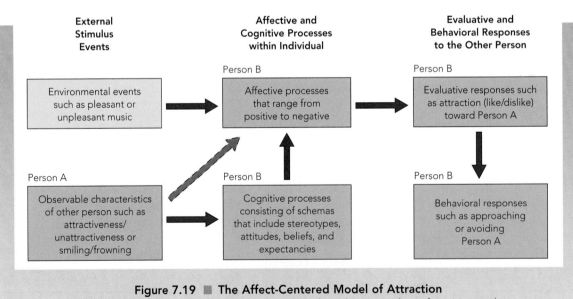

Figure 7.19 ■ The Affect-Centered Model of Attraction
Attraction toward a given person is based on the relative number of positive and negative affective responses that are aroused by that person, by other external events, or by internal factors, including cognitive processes. The net affective state forms the basis of an evaluative response such as like or dislike and also of a behavioral response such as approach or avoidance. (*Source: Based on material in Byrne, 1992.*)

"Naw, they're not like us—they don't feel pain."

Figure 7.20 ■ **Cognitions Can Justify Negative Reactions to Dissimilar Others**
Just as these cartoon lions can convince themselves that rabbits don't feel pain, real-life human beings can convince themselves that it is justifiable to dislike and sometimes attack those who are dissimilar. Not many of us are willing to admit that we hate people simply because they are different from ourselves. It is much more acceptable to hate people because they possess unpleasant characteristics, evil motives, or are so different from us that they don't even feel pain. (*Source:* © *The New Yorker Collection 2004 Charles Barsotti from cartoonbank.com. All Rights Reserved.*)

Mutual Evaluations: Reciprocal Liking or Disliking

Note that Person B in Figure 7.19 is not the only one experiencing arousal, processing information, and making evaluations. Person A is engaged in reciprocal reactions to Person B. The specific details of such a dyadic interaction can result in moving the two people toward a relationship based on mutual liking, as described in Chapter 8, or (if there is mutual disliking) away from a relationship. We will focus on mutual liking—the intermediate step between *initial attraction* and the establishment of an *interpersonal relationship*.

When each interacting individual communicates a positive evaluation of the other by what is said or done, this realization of mutual attraction is an added positive experience for each of them. Most of us are pleased to receive positive feedback and displeased to receive feedback that is negative (Gordon, 1996).

Not only do we enjoy being evaluated positively, we even welcome such an evaluation when it is inaccurate or an insincere attempt at flattery. To an outside observer, false flattery may be perceived accurately for what it is, but to the person being flattered, it is likely to appear honest and accurate (Gordon, 1996; Vonk, 1998, 2002). Using this type of ingratiation technique to deal with a boss or supervisor may disgust one's coworkers, but it pays off in raises and promotions (Orpen, 1996). In 1831, Tocqueville observed that Americans had a special talent for ingratiating themselves with anybody and everybody who could help them in any way (Lapham, 1996). Only if someone is as transparent and obvious as Eddie Haskell (on the *Leave It to Beaver* TV show) does flattery fail.

At times, the first sign of attraction is nonverbal. For example, if an acquaintance chooses to sit next to you in class or on a bus, you reasonably interpret this as a positive sign of his or her feelings about you. In this instance, liking leads to proximity rather than the reverse (Byrne, Baskett, & Hodges, 1971). Another example is when a woman maintains eye contact while talking to a man and leans toward him. The man tends to interpret these acts (sometimes incorrectly) to mean that she likes him. Her positive signals, in turn, may lead him to like her (Gold, Ryckman, & Mosley, 1984).

In a more general sense, our lives are made more pleasant by genuine, sincere communication of positive feelings about one another—and sometimes even by positive messages that are not entirely genuine and sincere. In contrast, negative interpersonal communications almost always elicit unpleasant reactions. Put simply, it never hurts to be nice, but it always hurts to be nasty.

KEY POINTS

★ One of the many factors determining attraction toward another person is similarity of attitudes, beliefs, values, and interests.

★ Despite the continuing popularity of the idea that opposites attract, especially in fiction, it rarely occurs in the real world.

★ Though dissimilarity tends to have a greater impact on attraction than similarity, we respond to both, and the larger the *proportion of similarity information*, the greater the attraction.

★ The *similarity–dissimilarity effect* has been explained by *balance theory*, social compar-

ison theory, and by an evolutionary perspective as an adaptive response to potential danger.

★ An overall summary of the major determinants of attraction is provided by the *affect-centered model of attraction,* which stipulates that attraction is determined by direct and associated sources of affect, often mediated by cognitive processes.

★ We especially like other people who indicate in word or deed that they like and positively evaluate us. We very much dislike those who dislike and negatively evaluate us.

ẞUMMARY AND REVIEW OF KEY POINTS

Internal Determinants of Attraction: The Need to Affiliate and the Basic Role of Affect

■ *Interpersonal attraction* refers to the evaluations we make of other people—the positive and negative attitudes we form about them.

■ Human beings are apparently born with a *need for affiliation*, the motivation to interact with other people in a cooperative way, often relying on shared laughter to smooth the way. The strength of this need differs among individuals and across situations.

■ Positive and negative affective states influence attraction both directly and indirectly. Direct effects occur when another person is responsible for arousing the emotion. Indirect effects occur when the source of the

emotion is elsewhere and another person is simply associated with its presence.

■ The application of associated affect is a common element in both commercial and political advertising. This approach is most effective when directed at an audience that is relatively unaware and uninformed.

External Determinants of Attraction: Proximity and Observable Characteristics

■ The initial contact between two people is very often based on the *proximity* that is the result of such physical aspects of the environment as classroom seating assignments, the location of residences, and how workplaces are arranged.

■ Proximity, in turn, leads to the *repeated exposure* of two individuals to one another. Repeated

exposure usually results in positive affect, which results in attraction—a process known as the *mere exposure effect.*

■ Interpersonal attraction and judgments based on stereotypes are strongly affected by various observable characteristics of those we meet, including *physical attractiveness*. People like and make positive attributions about attractive men and women of all ages, despite the fact that assumptions based on appearance are usually inaccurate.

■ In addition to attractiveness, many other observable characteristics influence initial interpersonal evaluations, including physique, weight, behavioral style, food preferences, first names, and other superficial characteristics.

■ Height, especially for males, is a positive factor—the taller the better, with respect to career success and even to being elected to the presidency.

Interactive Determinants of Attraction: Similarity and Mutual Evaluations

■ One of the many factors determining attraction toward another person is similarity of attitudes, beliefs, values, and interests.

■ Despite the continuing popularity of the idea that opposites attract, especially in fiction, it rarely occurs in the real world.

■ Though dissimilarity tends to have a greater impact on attraction than similarity, we respond to both, and the larger the *proportion of similarity*, the greater the attraction.

■ The *similarity–dissimilarity effect* has been explained by *balance theory*, social comparison theory, and by an evolutionary perspective as an adaptive response to potential danger.

■ An overall summary of the major determinants of attraction is provided by the *affect-centered*

model of attraction, which stipulates that attraction is determined by direct and associated sources of affect, often mediated by cognitive processes.

■ We especially like other people who indicate in word or deed that they like and positively evaluate us. We very much dislike those who dislike and negatively evaluate us.

Connections · INTEGRATING SOCIAL PSYCHOLOGY

In this chapter, you read about . . .	In other chapters, you will find related discussions of . . .
attitudes about people	attitudes (Chapter 4)
conditioning of affect/attraction	conditioning of attitudes (Chapter 4)
similarity and attraction	similarity and friendship, love, and marriage (Chapter 8)
effects of physical attractiveness	attractiveness and love (Chapter 8), effects of attractiveness in the courtroom (Module A)
appearance and stereotypes	prejudice and stereotypes (Chapter 6)

Thinking about Connections

1. Pick one person you know or have known very well. Can you remember exactly how you met?

When did you decide that you liked this individual? Why do you think you liked him or her? Are there any connections between your personal experience with this person and the discussion in the chapter about the factors influencing attraction?

2. Give some thought to the physical appearance of someone you don't know very well but see in class, in your neighborhood, or at work. On the basis of the person's attractiveness, physique, accent, clothing, or whatever else you have observed about him or

her, what can you conclude about the person? Have you ever talked to him or her? Why, or why not? Do you perceive any connections between prejudice and your evaluation of this individual?

3. Consider some issues about which you have strong attitudes and beliefs. Do you ever discuss these topics with your acquaintances or friends? How do you react when others agree with you? What hap-

pens when they disagree with you? Have disagreements ever caused you to stop interacting with someone you once liked? Think about why agreement and disagreement might matter to you.

4. What is your first reaction when you see a stranger in your school or neighborhood? Do you feel friendly, fearful, angry? Does it matter if this person is very different from you in appearance, clothing, or accent?

5. Do you ever compliment other people, tell them you like them, or comment favorably on something they have done? If so, how did they respond? Describe what you believe is going on in this kind of interaction. Consider also the opposite situation, in which you have criticized someone, indicated your dislike, or given a negative evaluation. What happens in that kind of interaction?

WHAT CAN YOU DO TO MAKE PEOPLE LIKE YOU?

Most of us would rather be liked than disliked, and attraction research provides a lot of information that can be helpful when we interact with other people.

Make Proximity Work for You

Whenever it is possible, don't passively accept the accidental demands of the environment. Instead, play an active role by taking advantage of proximity opportunities. In a lunchroom, for example, take your tray and sit near other people with whom you can talk instead of sitting by yourself in an isolated location.

Create Positive Affect

Do your best to create a positive mood, and don't bore others with your problems and worries. If you can, say something to make others laugh, and avoid criticizing others. Smile!

with respect to weight, hair, clothing, and so on. At the same time, try hard not to judge others on the basis of inaccurate stereotypes. Get to know people as they actually are and not on the basis of skin color, height, accent, or whatever.

Make the Most of Your Own Appearance and Look Beyond the Appearance of Others

Within reasonable limits, do what you can to look the best you can

Chapter 7 / Interpersonal Attraction

Emphasize Similarities and Minimize Differences

You don't need to lie about your attitudes and beliefs, but there is no reason to concentrate on disagreements and dissimilarities. When you don't agree, deal with the question in an open-minded and nondogmatic way that doesn't sound like an attack on the other person.

 # KEY TERMS

adaptive response (p. 285)

affect (p. 261)

affect-centered model of attraction (p. 286)

appearance anxiety (p. 272)

attitude similarity (p. 282)

balance theory (p. 283)

interpersonal attraction (p. 258)

mere exposure effect (p. 269)

need for affiliation (p. 260)

physical attractiveness (p. 272)

proportion of similarity (p. 282)

proximity (p. 268)

repeated exposure (p. 269)

repulsion hypothesis (p. 283)

similarity–dissimilarity effect (p. 282)

 # FOR MORE INFORMATION

Etcoff, N. (1999). *Survival of the prettiest: The science of beauty.* New York: Random House.

• In this book, the author takes the position that attractiveness has survival value and that sensitivity to beauty is a biological adaptation. Using scientific data and cultural analysis, Etcoff supports her evolutionary position in a highly readable and entertaining style.

Falk, G. (2001). *Stigma: How we treat outsiders.* Amherst, MA: Prometheus.

• Sociologist Gerhard Falk examines various segments of the population that have been stigmatized. He also discusses how some groups and some individuals are able to resist the cultural stigmas placed upon them.

Forgas, J. P., Williams, K. D., & von Hippel, W. (Eds.). (2003). *Social*

judgments: Implicit and explicit processes. New York: Cambridge University Press.

• This volume contains a series of essays that identify the role of evolutionary, neuropsychological, and developmental influences on social judgments. The authors stress the interaction between conscious and unconscious mechanisms in determining the decisions we make in our everyday lives.

8 CLOSE RELATIONSHIPS
Family, Friends, Lovers, and Spouses

The following story is based on actual experiences, but it consists of a combination of events described by a variety of couples—to avoid embarrassment for specific couples.

Greg and Linda met when they were in college, taking the same introductory course in anthropology and sitting in the same row. They talked a few times, and when she had to miss class once, Linda asked if she could borrow Greg's notes for that day. Soon after that, they began hanging out at various campus events. One spring night, during a keg party at Greg's fraternity house, they went to an empty room upstairs and, without actually saying much, simply had sex. The next week, they met for coffee and began talking seriously about their feelings for one another, about love, and about the future. From then on, they were a "couple"—two people in an exclusive relationship that includes physical intimacy and joyful, exciting conversations about the future and about their marriage. They didn't talk about money, careers, or parenthood—why should two people feeling genuine love for one another spoil everything by going into boring details?

Shortly after graduation, they had a beautiful wedding, went to a Jamaican resort for what they agreed was a perfect honeymoon (financed by his parents), and returned home to a small apartment near the university where Greg had been accepted for graduate school. The first several months were a continuation of their life before marriage, but more convenient, more exciting, and more "grown up." Married life was a new adventure. They were happy, and their future seemed bright and endless. Greg's father even let him pick out a new car as a special wedding present.

Over time, a few problems gradually began to arise. Linda had been an excellent student with plans to attend law school, but there was no law school at Greg's new university. Her plans would have to be postponed until some future time. Greg worked hard as a graduate student and spent a good deal of time in the library and in the physical anthro lab where he was a research assistant. Sometimes he had to work on the weekends, and some evenings he came home late, with beer on his breath. One night, Linda brought up her desire to have kids—at least two but maybe more. That brought on their first real argument, and Greg told her for the first time that he had no desire to be a father. They couldn't agree, but more or less compromised on a "substitute baby" by adopting a kitten for Linda to take care of. Greg's late nights became more frequent, and Linda worried that he might be seeing someone else. She feared that Greg would eventually dump her because she was "just a housewife," while he was surrounded by women working on advanced degrees. He believed that Linda was "too possessive" and was trying to take away his independence and freedom.

In addition to these issues, they began to quarrel about other things. She complained about his dirty clothes left on the floor for her to pick up. He complained about her cooking. She complained about his willingness to spend money on beer but not on things for their apartment. He complained about the smell of the litter box, and she complained about the smell of his cigarettes. She accused him of being oversexed, and he accused her of being undersexed. She said he was a spoiled brat, and he said she was a self-centered bitch.

They drifted steadily apart. Without telling Greg, she shopped around for a lawyer; one day he came home to find her gone. A note told him that she had filed for divorce. What happened, and why did a romantic, loving relationship turn into an unpleasant year of arguments, insults, and accusations?

"I don't care if she is a tape dispenser. I love her."

Figure 8.1 ■ Love Is Often Blind

In choosing a romantic partner or a spouse, we often see what we want to see and believe what we want to believe, just like this snail who has fallen in love with a tape dispenser. Eventually, the lover comes to his or her senses and perceives the loved one more accurately. By that time, it's often too late. (*Source: © The New Yorker Collection 1998 Sam Gross from cartoonbank.com. All Rights Reserved.*)

We hope to help answer some of these questions in this chapter. You might want to look back at the story of Linda and Greg from time to time whenever you find possible explanations for some of the things that went wrong. One familiar sort of problem is illustrated in Figure 8.1. Love (as well as lust) is often blind, in that we see what we want to see and believe what we want to believe. What do you think—is the relationship between the snail and the tape dispenser likely to work out?

The study of *interpersonal attraction* has been a major focus of social psychology since early in the twentieth century, but the investigation of *interpersonal relationships* was largely ignored until the second half of that century. In part, the difference can be explained by the fact that relationships are more complex and more difficult to study than the simple attraction of one person to another.

In recent years, however, social psychologists have made up for lost time by turning their attention to relationships in general (Berscheid & Reis, 1998), relationships within families (Boon & Brussoni, 1998), love and intimacy (Hatfield & Rapson, 1993), and marriage (Sternberg & Hojjat, 1997).

In this chapter, we describe what psychologists have learned about relationships. One's first experiences with *interdependent relationships* are with family members. During infancy and early childhood, *attachment patterns* develop, and these can affect one's interpersonal behavior throughout life. We then discuss the establishment of friendships and one of the consequences of not being able to form such relationships—*loneliness.* We also examine *romantic relationships* and what is meant by *love.* The final topic is *marriage,* and we describe the major factors involved in the success or the failure of such a union, as well as the often painful consequences of divorce.

Interdependent Relationships with Family and Friends versus Loneliness

All close relationships share one common characteristic: **interdependence.** This term refers to an interpersonal association in which two people consistently influence each

---

interdependence

The characteristic that is common to all close relationships. Interdependence refers to an interpersonal association in which two people influence each others' lives. They often focus their thoughts on one another and regularly engage in joint activities.

Chapter 8 / Close Relationships

Figure 8.2 ■ Humans and Our Closest Primate Relatives Evolved as Social Beings
There is a good deal of evidence that the human need for close relationships was adaptive for our ancestors, human and otherwise. DNA studies show that chimpanzees and bonobos are our closest primate relatives, and they are similar to us in much of their social behavior, including mother–infant bonding and the formation of cooperative friendships.

other's lives (Holmes, 2002). They often focus their thoughts and emotions on one another and regularly engage in joint activities. Interdependent relationships with family members, friends, and romantic partners include a sense of commitment to the relationship itself (Fehr, 1999). Interdependence occurs across age groups and across different kinds of interactions. The importance of forming such bonds with other people is emphasized by Ryff and Singer (2000, p. 30), who propose, "Quality ties to others are universally endorsed as central to optimal living."

The affection felt by mothers for their offspring ("mother love") appears to be based in part on specific hormones (Maestripieri, 2001). Do other interpersonal bonds (e.g., between friends and between lovers) also rest on biological factors? As discussed in Chapter 7 with respect to the *need for affiliation*, there is good reason to believe that our need for companionship is an adaptive mechanism that benefited our ancestors, increasing the odds that they would survive and reproduce. Animal studies provide evidence that social attachment depends on specific neurochemical systems (Curtis & Wang, 2003). DNA evidence indicates that chimpanzees and bonobos are our closest nonhuman relatives, and they are more closely related to us than they are to gorillas or orangutans (Smuts, 2000/2001). Field studies of these primates reveal that they interact socially much as we do. That is, they hug, kiss, and form long-term social bonds such as mother–offspring, friendship pairs, and mates (see Figure 8.2).

Scientists who have observed the forest apes in their natural environments report many similarities between their social behavior and our own. Smuts (2001) writes,

> *In chimps and bonobos, in particular, emotional expression is uninhibited, at least from the point of view of staid human observers. When two groups meet after a separation of days or even hours, it is as if they have not seen one another in ages. Animals rush into each other's arms, jump up and down, and shriek with delight. (p. 80)*

We now take a closer look at human relationships, beginning with those within the family.

Family: Where Relationships and Attachment Styles Begin

Parent–child interactions are of basic importance because this is usually one's first contact with another person. It is logical to suppose that our attitudes and expectancies about relationships begin to form in this context. We come into the world ready to interact with other humans, but the specific characteristics of those interactions differ from person to person and from family to family. It is those details that seem to have important implications for our later interactions with other people.

During the first year of life, human infants are extremely sensitive to facial expressions, bodily movements, and the sounds people make. The person taking care of the baby is typically the mother, and she, in turn, is equally sensitive to what the infant does

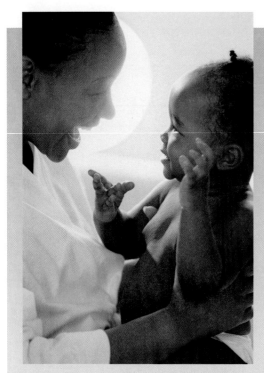

Figure 8.3 ■ Infants and Their Mothers Communicate
Beginning in early infancy, babies are sensitive to the sounds, facial expressions, and bodily movements of their mothers (or other caregivers). Mothers, in turn, are equally sensitive to their infants' sounds, expressions, and movements. The result is interactive communication between the two. Such exchanges constitute the earliest form of social interaction.

(Kochanska et al., 2004). As they interact, the two individuals communicate and reinforce the actions of one another (Murray & Trevarthen, 1986; Trevarthen, 1993). The adult shows interest in the infant's communication in various ways, such as engaging in baby talk and displaying exaggerated facial expressions. The infant, in turn, shows interest in the adult by attempting to make appropriate sounds and expressions. Such reciprocal interactions tend to be a positive educational experience for both participants (see Figure 8.3). There is even evidence that a mother's "baby talk" is "incredibly systematic and rhythmical"—much like that found in poetry and song lyrics (Miall & Dissanayake, 2004; Selim, 2004). In addition to interpersonal bonding, these interactions may also form the basis for the emotional response to music and other artistic expressions.

■ The Lasting Importance of Parent–Child Interactions

The study of early relationships has been conducted primarily by developmental psychologists. Because the nature of these relationships affects the nature of later interpersonal behavior, social psychologists have begun to look more closely at what happens in early childhood.

As a very brief overview, it appears that the quality of the interaction between a mother (or other caregiver) and her infant determines the infant's future interpersonal attitudes and actions as he or she progresses into childhood, adolescence, and beyond (Oberlander, 2003). People are found to be consistent with respect to their interaction patterns in quite different relationships—parent–child, friends, and romantic partners (Foltz et al., 1999).

Bowlby's (1969, 1973) studies of mothers and infants led him to the concept of **attachment style**—the degree of security an individual feels in interpersonal relationships. It is assumed that an infant acquires two basic attitudes during its earliest interactions with an adult. The first is an attitude about self that we label **self-esteem**. The

attachment style
The degree of security experienced in interpersonal relationships. Differential styles initially develop in the interactions between infant and caregiver when the infant acquires basic attitudes about self-worth and *interpersonal trust*.

self-esteem
The self-evaluation made by each individual. It represents one's attitude about oneself along a positive–negative dimension.

behavior and the emotional reactions of the caregiver provide information to the infant that he or she is a valued, important, loved individual or, at the other extreme, someone who is without value, unimportant, and unloved. The second basic attitude acquired by an infant is about other people, involving general expectancies and beliefs. This attitude is labeled **interpersonal trust.** It is based on whether the caregiver is perceived as trustworthy, dependable, and reliable or as untrustworthy, undependable, and unreliable. Research findings suggest that we develop these basic attitudes about self and about others long before we acquire language skills. As adults, it often seems that we were "just born with" a given level of self-esteem and a given level of trust, but it is likely that these dispositions were learned at such an early age that we simply cannot remember their origins.

Based on the two basic attitudes about self and others, people can be roughly classified as having a particular interaction style. There is some disagreement in the field as to the number of attachment styles, but there *is* general agreement about their overall effects (Bartholomew & Horowitz, 1991; Bowlby, 1982). If we conceptualize self-esteem as one dimension and interpersonal trust as another, it follows that a person could be high on both dimensions, low on both, or high on either one but low on the other. This yields four attachment styles. A **secure attachment style** is characterized by a person who is high in both self-esteem and trust. Secure individuals are best able to form lasting, committed, satisfying relationships throughout their lives (Shaver & Brennan, 1992). In many respects, a secure style is ideal not only with respect to relationships, but also as associated with a high need for achievement, low fear of failure, and the desire to learn about and explore one's world (Elliot & Reis, 2003; Green & Campbell, 2000). Being low in both self-esteem and interpersonal trust results in a **fearful–avoidant attachment style.** Fearful–avoidant individuals tend to avoid close relationships altogether or to establish unhappy partnerships (Mikulincer, 1998a; Tidwell, Reis, & Shaver, 1996). A negative self-image combined with high interpersonal trust produces a **preoccupied attachment style.** These individuals want closeness (sometimes excessively so), and they readily form relationships. They cling to others but are often depressed about relationships because they expect eventually to be rejected (Davila et al., 2004; Lopez et al., 1997; Whiffen et al., 2000). Those with a **dismissing attachment style** are high in self-esteem and low in interpersonal trust. This combination leads to the belief that one is very much deserving of good relationships, while expecting the worst of others. As a result, dismissing individuals fear genuine closeness (Onishi, Gjerde, & Block, 2001).

It is sometimes assumed that the attachment style one develops in infancy and childhood remains constant throughout life (Klohnen & Bera, 1998), and styles frequently *are* stable from infancy through childhood and beyond (Fraley, 2000). Nevertheless, there is considerable evidence that very good or very bad relationship experiences can lead to a change in style (Brennan & Bosson, 1998; Cozzarelli et al., 2003; Davila & Cobb, 2003). For example, a relationship breakup is likely to reduce (sometimes only temporarily) the extent of one's secure attachment, while a positive, lasting relationship is likely to increase the possibility of feeling securely attached (Ruvolo, Fabin, & Ruvolo, 2001).

■ Interactions with Other Family Members

In addition to the mother figure, other family members also interact with infants and young children. Research is beginning to reveal the importance of interaction with fathers as well as with grandparents and others (Lin & Harwood, 2003; Maio, Fincham, & Lycett, 2000). Because these people are likely to differ among themselves with respect to personality characteristics, the youngster can be influenced in a variety of positive and negative ways (Clark, Kochanska, & Ready, 2000). For example, the negative effects of having a withdrawn, unreliable mother can be offset partly by the presence of an

interpersonal trust
An attitudinal dimension underlying *attachment styles* that involves the belief that other people are generally trustworthy, dependable, and reliable as opposed to the belief that others are generally untrustworthy, undependable, and unreliable.

secure attachment style
A style characterized by high *self-esteem* and high *interpersonal trust*. This is the most successful and most desirable attachment style.

fearful–avoidant attachment style
A style characterized by low *self-esteem* and low *interpersonal trust*. This is the most insecure and least adaptive attachment style.

preoccupied attachment style
A style characterized by low *self-esteem* and high *interpersonal trust*. This is a conflicted and somewhat insecure style in which the individual strongly desires a close relationship but feels that he or she is unworthy of the partner and is thus vulnerable to being rejected.

dismissing attachment style
A style characterized by high *self-esteem* and low *interpersonal trust*. This is a conflicted and somewhat insecure style in which the individual feels that he or she "deserves" a close relationship but is frustrated because of mistrust of potential partners. The result is the tendency to reject the other person at some point in the relationship in order to avoid being the one who is rejected.

Figure 8.4 ■ **Interactions within the Family Provide the Framework for a Child's Future Social Behavior**
When a child has the opportunity to interact with other members of the family, he or she is not simply playing a game (as in this photograph) but is also learning how people interact. If the learning experience provides a model for following the rules, playing fair, solving disagreements in an agreeable way, being a good loser (or winner), and so forth, the child will benefit by interacting with other people in this way. In the absence of such experiences or with negative early experiences, the child will lack the necessary social skills to interact with others in an appropriate way.

outgoing, dependable grandfather. Every interaction is potentially important as the young person is developing attitudes about the meaning and value of such factors as trust, affection, self-worth, competition, and humor (O'Leary, 1995). Consider a simple example, as in Figure 8.4. When an older person plays games with a youngster (from Go Fish to Monopoly to chess), this constitutes a learning experience that involves not only the game itself, but also the way in which people interact in a social situation, follow a set of rules, and behave honestly or cheat, and how they deal with disagreements. All of this has an effect on the child's subsequent interactions with other adults and with peers (Lindsey, Mize, & Pettit, 1997).

Although adolescence is sometimes described as a time of emotional turmoil and rebellion, most adolescents express very positive feelings about their parents, despite being less close and less dependent on them than they were in childhood (Galambos, 1992). Adolescents ordinarily report that they like their parents, and these adolescents are described as being "good kids" who are ethical and trustworthy. In fact, most teenagers indicate that they love their parents, and, in turn, they feel loved (Jeffries, 1993). This kind of satisfying relationship between a teenager and his or her parents is associated with becoming an adult who experiences empathy (see Chapter 10), has high self-esteem (see Chapter 5), and expresses interpersonal trust.

Cultural differences also play a role in family interactions. Compared with the typical individualistic family, a more collectivist family is different in several ways. For example, in Mexican American families, the offspring are more likely than those in Anglo-American families to help their parents, less likely to want to interact with individuals outside of the home, and more likely to feel that they have an obligation to their parents (Freeberg & Stein, 1996).

■ Relationships between and among Siblings

Approximately 80 percent of us have grown up in a household with at least one sibling, and sibling interactions are also important with respect to what we learn about interpersonal behavior (Dunn, 1992). Among elementary school children, those who have no siblings are found to be less liked by their classmates and to be more aggressive (or to be more victimized by aggression) than those with siblings. Such differences presumably exist because having brothers or sisters provides useful interpersonal learning experiences (Kitzmann, Cohen, & Lockwood, 2002). Sibling relationships, unlike those between parent and child, often combine feelings of affection, hostility, and rivalry (Boer et al., 1997). A familiar theme is some version of "Mom always liked you best" or "They took a hundred pictures of you for every one they took of me." Parents, though, seldom admit that they feel any such favoritism; one exception to this is that mothers in their sixties and seventies often report being closer to at least one of their grown offspring than to the others (Suitor & Pillemer, 2000). This may not, however, indicate a lifelong favoritism but a reflection of how their grown offspring differentially treat their mothers.

Most of us have experienced (or observed in others) multiple examples of sibling rivalry, as in Figure 8.5, and many of us have known adults who complain about events involving competition between siblings that occurred in the distant past. In fact, though, most siblings get along fairly well. An affectionate relationship between siblings is most likely if each has a warm relationship with the parents, and if the mother and father are satisfied with their marriage (McGuire, McHale, & Updegraff, 1996).

The nature of sibling relationships is important in part because the positive or negative affect associated with siblings is likely to be aroused over and over again in interactions with peers, romantic partners, and spouses (Klagsbrun, 1992). For example, schoolyard bullies (see Chapter 11) tend to have had negative relationships with their siblings (Bowers, Smith, & Binney, 1994). Boys who exhibit behavior problems in school are likely to have had intense conflicts with a sibling plus a rejecting, punitive mother (Garcia & Shaw, 2000).

Figure 8.5 ■ Sibling Rivalry Can Last a Lifetime
Relationships between siblings are often based on a mixture of affection, hostility, and rivalry. Remnants of these childhood emotions and reactions sometimes continue well beyond childhood and influence behavior in other relationships as well. (*Source:* © Grimmy, Inc. Reprinted with special permission of King Features Syndicate.)

Siblings who feel close to one another are able to share attitudes and memories, protect one another from outsiders, enjoy being together, and provide support when problems arise (Floyd, 1996). Siblings tend to grow apart in adolescence and young adulthood, even if they were very close as children (Rosenthal, 1992). By the time they reach middle age, however, most are able to reestablish positive relationships. These same general patterns are true for twins, with identical twins experiencing the greatest closeness, followed by fraternal twins, and then ordinary brothers and sisters (Neyer, 2002). Sibling relationships sometimes involve one taking the parent role and the other functioning as the child, they may interact as casual acquaintances, they may become close buddies, or they may simply maintain contact only because they believe that is what family members are supposed to do (Stewart, Verbrugge, & Beilfuss, 1998). About 20 percent of adult siblings never establish any degree of closeness—about half of these are simply indifferent to their siblings, and half actively dislike them (Folwell et al., 1997).

Beyond the Family: Friendships

Beginning in early childhood, most of us establish casual friendships with peers who share common interests. Such relationships generally begin on the basis of proximity, as described in Chapter 7, or because the respective parents know one another. If two children have mutual interests and if they have positive rather than negative experiences together, they may maintain a friendship over a relatively long period of time. I (Donn Byrne) remember playing marbles, acting out stories based on movies we liked (*Tarzan, Robin Hood,* and *One Million Years B.C.* were favorites), and working cooperatively while trying to stay within the outlines provided by coloring books. Positive affect tends to be a simple matter of having fun together, and negative affect is most likely to be aroused by verbal or physical aggression (Hartup & Stevens, 1999). A simple truth is that, regardless of age, we prefer pleasant interactions to unpleasant ones.

▪ Close Friendships

Many childhood friendships simply fade away, and I doubt that I will ever look up anyone I knew in early childhood. We hardly knew one another then, and we are unlikely to enact movie scenes in my back yard. At times, however, a relationship begun in early childhood can mature into a **close friendship** (see Figure 8.6) that involves increasingly mature types of interaction. What, exactly, is involved in close friendships?

Such friendships have several distinctive characteristics. For example, many individuals tend to engage in self-enhancing behavior (such as bragging) when interacting with a wide range of other people, but they exhibit modesty when interacting with their close friends (Tice et al., 1995). Friends are less likely to lie to one another, unless the lie is designed to make the friend feel better (DePaulo & Kashy, 1998). And, friends begin to speak of "we" and "us" rather than "she and I" or "he and I" (Fitzsimmons & Kay, 2004). Once established, a close relationship results in the two individuals spending a great deal of time together, interacting in varied situations, self-disclosing, and providing mutual emotional support (Laurenceau, Barrett, & Pietromonaco, 1998; Matsushima & Shiomi, 2002). A close friend is valued for his or her generosity, sensitivity, and honesty—someone with whom you can relax and be yourself (Urbanski, 1992).

Culture also influences what is meant by *friendship*. Among Japanese college students, a best friend was described as someone in a give-and-take relationship, a person with whom it is easy to get along, who does not brag, and is considerate and not short-tempered (Maeda & Ritchie, 2003). American students describe friends in a very sim-

close friendship
A relationship in which two people spend a great deal of time together, interact in a variety of situations, and provide mutual emotional support.

Chapter 8 / Close Relationships

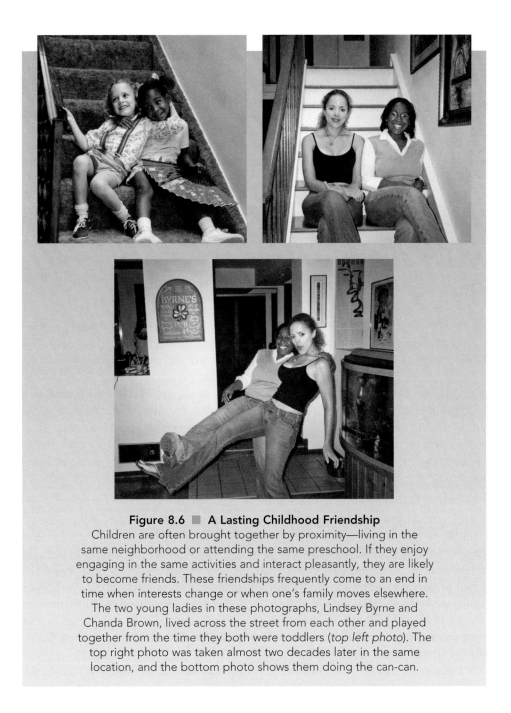

Figure 8.6 ■ A Lasting Childhood Friendship
Children are often brought together by proximity—living in the same neighborhood or attending the same preschool. If they enjoy engaging in the same activities and interact pleasantly, they are likely to become friends. These friendships frequently come to an end in time when interests change or when one's family moves elsewhere. The two young ladies in these photographs, Lindsey Byrne and Chanda Brown, lived across the street from each other and played together from the time they both were toddlers (*top left photo*). The top right photo was taken almost two decades later in the same location, and the bottom photo shows them doing the can-can.

ilar way except that, unlike those in Japan, they also value a friend who is spontaneous and active.

■ Gender and Friendships

Women indicate that they have more close friends than do men (Fredrickson, 1995). Women also place more importance on intimacy (characterized by self-disclosure and emotional support) than is true for men (Fehr, 2004).

There are many benefits to having close friends, but there can also be pain when you lose a friend or are forced by circumstances to separate. For example, when a friendship is interrupted by college graduation, the two individuals must adapt to the

Figure 8.7 ■ Graduation Often Separates Friends
We benefit by establishing close friendships, but it can be very upsetting when friends are separated by life changes such as moving to different locations, entering a new career, or graduating from college.

sometimes painful reality of no longer being together (see Figure 8.7). As a result, graduating seniors, especially women, report more intense emotional involvement when interacting with close friends than is true for students who are not facing graduation (Fredrickson, 1995). The importance of friendships extends far beyond the undergraduate years, and even plays a role in the social success of professionals in the world of business (Gibbons & Olk, 2003).

Do the conversations of two male friends differ from those of two female friends? Martin (1997) identified several gender-specific aspects of what friends talk about. Two men often talk about women and sex, being trapped in a relationship, sports, and alcohol. Two women tend to talk about relationships with men, clothes, and problems with roommates.

Can a man and a woman become friends without having a romantic or sexual relationship? Men and women differ in their expectations about opposite-sex friendships (Bleske-Rechek & Buss, 2001). Men tend to initiate such friendships when the woman is attractive, and they assume that a sexual relationship will eventually develop. If that does *not* happen, they usually end the relationship. Women, in contrast, initiate such a friendship because they want a man who can protect them. As with men who lose interest without sex, women are likely to end a relationship if the man does not fill a protective role.

Loneliness: Life without Close Relationships

Despite a biological need to establish relationships and despite the rewards of being in a relationship, many individuals find that they are unable to achieve that goal. The result is **loneliness**—an individual's emotional and cognitive reaction to having fewer and less satisfying relationships than he or she desires (Archibald, Bartholomew, & Marx, 1995). In contrast, people who simply are uninterested in having friends do not experience loneliness (Burger, 1995). It is possible for an individual to desire solitude for very positive reasons (Long et al., 2003).

Loneliness appears to be a common human experience, as shown by studies not only of Americans and Canadians (Rokach & Neto, 2000), but also of British Asians (Shams, 2001), Spaniards (Rokach et al., 2001), Portuguese (Neto & Barrios, 2001), Chinese Canadians (Goodwin, Cook, & Yung, 2001), and Turks and Argentines (Rokach & Bacanli, 2001).

■ The Consequences of Being Lonely

If a child has only *one* friend, that is enough to diminish feelings of loneliness (Asher & Paquette, 2003). In the absence of any close friends, people who feel lonely tend to spend their leisure time in solitary activity, to have very few dates, and to have only casual friends or acquaintances (R. A. Bell, 1991; Berg & McQuinn, 1989). Lonely individuals feel left out and believe they have very little in common with those they meet (B. Bell, 1993).

Loneliness is, of course, unpleasant, and the negative affect includes feelings of depression, anxiety, unhappiness, dissatisfaction, pessimism about the future, self-blame, and shyness (Anderson et al., 1994; Jackson, Soderlind, & Weiss, 2000). From

loneliness
The unpleasant emotional and cognitive state based on desiring close relationships but being unable to attain them.

the perspective of others, lonely individuals are perceived as maladjusted (Lau & Gruen, 1992; Rotenberg & Kmill, 1992).

Even worse, loneliness is associated with poor health and reduced life expectancy (Cacioppo, Hawkley, & Berntson, 2003; Hawkley et al., 2003). A possible reason for these negative effects was provided by Cacioppo and his colleagues (2002). They found that in both a controlled laboratory situation and their own homes, lonely individuals exhibit sleep problems. People need an appropriate amount of sleep to restore the daily wear and tear on the organism.

Why Are Some People Lonely?

The origins of dispositional loneliness include a combination of genetics, attachment style, and the opportunity for early social experiences with peers. In an intriguing study designed to examine the possible role of genetic factors in loneliness, McGuire and Clifford (2000) conducted a behavioral genetic investigation of loneliness among children aged nine to fourteen. The participants included pairs of biological siblings, pairs of unrelated siblings raised in adoptive homes, and pairs of identical and fraternal twins. The data consistently indicated that loneliness is based, in part, on inherited factors. For example, identical twins are more similar in loneliness than are fraternal twins, indicating that greater genetic similarity is associated with greater similarity with respect to loneliness. Nevertheless, loneliness was also found to be influenced by environmental factors, as indicated by the fact that unrelated siblings raised in adoptive homes are more similar in loneliness than are random pairs of children. As the investigators point out, the fact that there is a genetic component to loneliness does not fully explain exactly how it operates. For example, the relevant genes might affect feelings of depression or hostility; if so, differences in loneliness could be the result of rejection based on genetically determined differences in interpersonal behavior.

Another possible source of loneliness can be traced to attachment style (Duggan & Brennan, 1994). Both dismissing and fearful–avoidant individuals fear intimacy and so tend to avoid establishing relationships (Sherman & Thelen, 1996). Such individuals do not have sufficient trust in other people to risk seeking closeness. Shyness and loneliness are related, in part, because lonely individuals expect to be rejected, and shyness can provide protection from that possibility (Jackson et al., 2002). Loneliness is also associated with failure to self-disclose because of the fear that others will react negatively to one's disclosures (Matsushima & Shiomi, 2001). In general, insecure attachment is associated with social anxiety and loneliness (Vertue, 2003). A study of Dutch students by Buunk and Prins (1998) suggests that a preoccupied attachment style may also lead to loneliness when such individuals believe they are giving more than they are receiving. This perceived lack of reciprocity also leads to feelings of loneliness and being underappreciated.

A third possible factor that results in loneliness is the failure to develop appropriate social skills, and this can occur for a variety of reasons (Braza et al., 1993). In part, children learn interpersonal skills by interacting with peers. Because they have such opportunities, children who attend preschool (or in some other way have the chance to engage in play-related interactions with multiple peers) are better liked in elementary school than those who lack such experiences (Erwin & Letchford, 2003). Also, loneliness is more likely to occur among those who did not have a close relationship with a sibling, especially if the relationship is characterized by conflict (Ponzetti & James, 1997). Without the necessary social skills, a child may engage in self-defeating behaviors such as avoiding others, engaging in verbal aggression such as teasing, or aggressing physically. As a consequence of these behaviors, the child is rejected by potential playmates (Johnson, Poteat, & Ironsmith, 1991; Kowalski, 2000; Ray et al., 1997). Inappropriate interpersonal behavior leads to rejection and unpopularity and thus increased

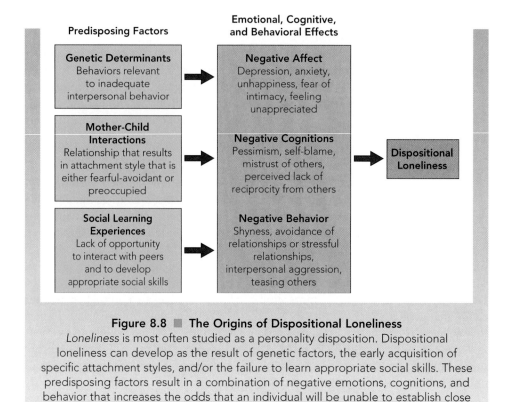

Figure 8.8 ■ The Origins of Dispositional Loneliness
Loneliness is most often studied as a personality disposition. Dispositional loneliness can develop as the result of genetic factors, the early acquisition of specific attachment styles, and/or the failure to learn appropriate social skills. These predisposing factors result in a combination of negative emotions, cognitions, and behavior that increases the odds that an individual will be unable to establish close relationships and will thus develop dispositional loneliness.

loneliness—the individual is caught in a seemingly endless self-destructive cycle (Carver, Kus, & Scheier, 1994). The determinants of loneliness are summarized in Figure 8.8.

Without some form of intervention to alter this behavior, interpersonal difficulties typically continue throughout childhood and adolescence and into adulthood. These interpersonal problems do not simply go away with the passage of time (Asendorpf, 1992; Hall-Elston & Mullins, 1999).

■ Reducing Loneliness

Those who function badly in social interactions are usually well aware that this is a problem (Duck, Pond, & Leatham, 1994). They realize that they are unhappy, dissatisfied, and unpopular (Furr & Funder, 1998; Meleshko & Alden, 1993). One unsatisfactory response to the situation is to stay away from other people as much as possible (Herbert, 1995). Lonely people may feel hopeless and even contemplate suicide (Page, 1991). Are there any satisfactory ways to deal with loneliness?

Once loneliness develops, it is not possible to change the individual's history by providing new genes or by altering early mother–child interactions. It is possible, however, to acquire new and more appropriate social skills. Such intervention concentrates on a number of fairly specific behaviors. The major intervention procedures are *cognitive therapy* (Salmela-Aro & Nurmi, 1996) and *social skills training* (Hope, Holt, & Heimberg, 1995), and these techniques can be used simultaneously. The goal of cognitive therapy is to disrupt the pattern of negativity and to encourage new cognitions, perceptions, and expectations about social interactions. In social skills training, the lonely person is provided with examples of socially appropriate behavior on videotape and then given the opportunity to practice the observed behavior in role play. Finally, there are instructions to try out the new skills in actual social situations. They can learn to interact with others in a friendly way, to avoid expressing anger and hostility, and to make casual conversation (Keltner et al., 1998; Reisman, 1984). Lonely individuals are instructed to express interest in the other person and to make fewer self-references (Kowalski, 1993), and they learn to self-disclose in an acceptable way (R. A. Bell, 1991; Rotenberg, 1997). Just as people can be taught mathematics, table manners, and how to drive a car, they can also be taught social skills and how to interact with other people.

Loneliness as a Response to External Factors

Most of the research on loneliness is, as just described, based on the assumption that it represents a personality disposition. In addition to dispositional loneliness, situational loneliness can result from external factors. For example, a move to a new location usually means that a person is surrounded by strangers and without friends. For example, loneliness can arise when a student leaves home and goes away to college. As he or she meets new people and makes new friends, however, the problem most often goes away. A study of North American college students studying in Israel revealed that they were lonely, but only for a few weeks, by which time new relationships had been established (Wiseman, 1997).

A more difficult situation arises in response to **social rejection**—when another individual has no interest in establishing a relationship with you. The rejection is not based on something you have done or said but on the prejudices, stereotypes, and attitudes held by the rejecting individual. The tactics of rejection involve three basic strategies to discourage a personal relationship (Hess, 2002): *avoidance* (failing to interact, ignoring the other person, cutting short the interaction), *disengagement* (not disclosing information about self, not paying attention, interacting in an impersonal way), and, the most direct of all, *cognitive dissociation* (derogating and degrading the other person). Each of these behaviors communicates a lack of interest in establishing a relationship.

Social exclusion occurs when the rejection comes not from merely one individual, but from an entire group. The devastating effects of being rejected by a group were shown in an experiment in which undergraduates interacted with several strangers. After the interaction, each participant was asked to name two group members with whom they would like to interact again (Twenge, Catanese, & Baumeister, 2003). The experimenters provided (false) information to some that they were named by everyone in the group as a choice for future interactions, while others were supposedly rejected by everyone in the group. Not only did social exclusion create a negative mood, the rejected students also functioned badly in various ways afterward. They felt tired, judged time to be passing more slowly, and were more likely to express the belief that "life is meaningless."

To be left out obviously hurts a great deal. Such reactions were also found when undergraduates were ignored or left out while playing a game (Cyberball) on the Internet. Sitting at a computer, each research participant believed that he or she was playing this ball-tossing game with two others. The participant was twice given the ball to toss, but the others hogged the ball for the remainder of the game. Being left out had a negative impact, even though the supposed other players were two unseen strangers. Surprisingly, this negative reaction to rejection also occurred among other participants who believed they were simply playing against the computer rather than actual people (Zadro, Williams, & Richardson, 2004). These authors suggest that humans apparently have a very primitive automatic negative response "to even the slightest hint of social exclusion" (p. 560).

If being excluded by strangers in a brief experimental session or by a computer program can have strong emotional effects, you can well imagine how it feels to be excluded in real life by people who know you. Whatever the reason for being rejected or excluded, this treatment hurts and elicits anger and sadness (Buckley, Winkel, & Leary, 2003; Nolan, Flynn, & Garber, 2003). Many teen-oriented movies depict social exclusion being directed at a person who enters a new school and is then treated badly. The rest of the movie is about the hero or heroine overcoming the rejection either by becoming popular or by getting revenge on the unfriendly rejecters (see Figure 8.9 on page 308).

social rejection
Rejection by one individual of another individual, not on the basis of what he or he has done, but on the basis of prejudice, stereotypes, and biases.

social exclusion
Social rejection of an individual by an entire group of people, not on the basis of what he or she has done, but on the basis of prejudice, stereotypes, and biases.

Figure 8.9 ■ Social Exclusion Is a Painful Experience with Many Negative Consequences, Including Loneliness

When an individual is rejected and excluded by his or her peers, the result is a strong emotional reaction that includes negative feelings, disrupted cognitive functioning, and the pain of loneliness. Such experiences are especially upsetting in adolescence, and teen-oriented movies often focus on this theme (for example, *Mean Girls*). In films, if not in real life, the excluded individual is likely to be transformed into someone whose newfound popularity is greater than that of those who originally took part in the exclusion. A darker alternative involves getting revenge by harming the rejecters in some dramatic way (for example, *The Rage: Carrie 2*).

KEY POINTS

★ Close relationships are characterized by *interdependence,* in which two people influence each other's lives, share their thoughts and emotions, and engage in joint activities.

★ Evolutionary theory proposes that emotional bonding with other human beings increased the odds of survival and reproductive success. As a result of this selective process, modern humans and other primates are hard-wired to seek emotional closeness.

★ The first relationships are within the family, and we acquire an *attachment style* (a combination of level of *self-esteem* and degree of *interpersonal trust*) based on interactions with a caregiver. Children also learn what to expect from other people and how to interact with them as a result of their interactions with parents, siblings, grandparents, and other family members.

★ Friendships outside of the family begin in childhood and are based initially on such factors as common interests and other sources of positive affect, resulting in attraction. With increasing maturity, it becomes possible to form *close friendships* that involve spending time together, interacting in many different situations, providing mutual social support, and engaging in self-disclosure.

★ *Loneliness* occurs when a person has fewer and less satisfying relationships than he or she desires. The result is depression and anxiety. Dispositional loneliness originates in a combination of genetics, an insecure attachment style based on mother–child interactions, and the lack of early social experiences with peers. A helpful intervention involves a combination of cognitive therapy and social skills training. Situational loneliness is brought about by external factors such as a move to a new location or social rejection and is based on factors unrelated to the behavior of the rejected individual.

Romantic Relationships and Falling in Love

We discussed attraction in Chapter 7 and friendship in this chapter. What factors might lead two individuals to an even closer relationship, one involving romance, love, and sometimes sex? In a developing relationship, one or any combination of these three aspects of closeness may occur, and they can do so in any sequence. Even in early adolescence, romantic relationships often develop, and they tend to focus on affiliation needs and sexual feelings (Furman, 2002). Most of the existing research on these topics deals with heterosexual couples, but we will note here whenever relevant data involving gays and lesbians are available. It appears that most of what we know about heterosexual couples applies equally well to homosexual couples (Kurdek, 2003). For example, regardless of sexual orientation, people expect that a romantic relationship will include sexual attraction, similarity of attitudes and values, spending time together, and, very often, the belief that two people share something special (Baccman, Folkesson, & Norlander, 1999).

Romance: Moving beyond Friendship

Among the most obvious differences between friendship and romance are sexual attraction and at least some level of physical intimacy, as suggested in Figure 8.10. Depending on what is acceptable in one's cultural subgroup, the sexual attraction may or may not lead to some form of sexual behavior and the physical intimacy may be limited to holding hands, hugging, and kissing, or it can include more explicitly sexual interactions. At least one of the partners is likely to believe that he or she is in love and to expect that the relationship may lead to marriage (Hendrick & Hendrick, 2002).

■ Similarities and Differences between Friendship and Romance

Most often, romantic attraction begins in the same way that all interpersonal attraction does: a combination of affiliation need, affect arousal, proximity, reactions to observable characteristics, similarity, and mutual liking. Among college students, an ideal romantic partner is one who is similar to oneself and who has a secure attachment style (Dittmann, 2003; Klohnen & Luo, 2003). A primary feature of romance is the interpretation of one's emotional arousal as an indicator of a strong attraction that includes at least the potential for love and sex. In addition, both men and women set higher standards for romantic partners than for friends with respect to physical attractiveness, social status, and characteristics such as warmth and intelligence (Sprecher & Regan, 2002). A spirit of playfulness also is important in romantic relationships (Aune & Wong, 2002).

Figure 8.10 ■ Romantic Relationships Include Physical Intimacy
Unlike friendships, romantic relationships usually include some degree of physical intimacy. Depending on cultural norms and individual differences, intimacy can range from holding hands to sexual interactions.

**Figure 8.11 ■ Workplace Romance: A
Step Beyond Interpersonal Attraction**
Romance in the workplace is facilitated by the same factors that
lead to interpersonal attraction elsewhere: positive affect, the
need for affiliation, proximity, physical attractiveness, similarity,
and so on. Romance in this particular setting can create special
problems, including charges of harassment, lower productivity,
and the perception of biased performance evaluations.

The workplace is a familiar setting in which romance often occurs. In most occupations, people who were once strangers work in close proximity, evaluate one another on the basis of appearance and other observables, talk and discover the degree to which they are similar, and—sometimes—experience sexual attraction (Seal, 1997). See Figure 8.11. The effects of these attraction-relevant factors have been described by Pierce, Byrne, and Aguinis (1996). Romance in the workplace also is associated with some situation-specific problems, such as charges of sexual harassment (Pierce et al., 2004) and romance-induced bias in evaluating performance (Goodwin et al., 2002).

Beyond the overtones of sexuality, other aspects of a romantic relationship differ from those of a friendly relationship. For example, Swann, De La Ronde, and Hixon (1994) report that among friends, dormitory roommates, and even married couples, most people prefer a partner who provides accurate feedback. We appreciate being with someone who knows us well enough to point out our good and bad characteristics. In contrast, at least at the beginning of a romantic relationship, the two individuals are not looking for accuracy and truth as much as they are looking for total approval and acceptance. In a romantic relationship, we want to like and to be liked unconditionally, and we need to be reassured by compliments, praise, and frequent demonstrations of affection.

It may be helpful to think about a romantic relationship in terms of three overlapping schemas (Fletcher et al., 1999), as in Figure 8.12. There is a self schema, as was described in Chapter 5, a second schema that is a person's perception of the partner, and a third schema that encompasses the relationship between self and partner.

The schema involving one's partner is often an unrealistic and inaccurate one. Each individual wants to believe that the other person represents the perfect partner, and each wants uncomplicated, totally positive feedback from that partner (Katz & Beach, 2000; Simpson, Ickes, & Blackstone, 1995). The closer the partner is to one's ideal, the better and more lasting the relationship is perceived to be (Campbell et al., 2001; Fletcher, Simpson, & Thomas, 2000). That person's virtues are emphasized, and possi-

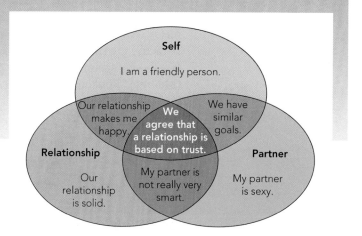

Figure 8.12 ■ Schemas for Self, Partner, and the Romantic Relationship
A romantic relationship involves three overlapping schemas: for self, for one's partner, and for the relationship. There is overlapping content between pairs of schemas and a central area of content involving all three schemas. (*Source: Based on concepts from Fletcher et al., 1999.*)

ble faults are dismissed as unimportant (Murray & Holmes, 1999). Remember the cartoon snail attracted to a tape dispenser in Figure 8.1? Many of us seem to behave like that snail from time to time.

Romance is built, in part, on fantasies and illusions, and these illusions may be crucial to both men and women in creating the relationship (Martz et al., 1998; Murray & Holmes, 1997). Women seem to fantasize on a general basis, while men must be strongly committed to a specific relationship before the fantasies kick in (Gagne & Lydon, 2003). Studies in various countries indicate that couples believe their own relationship is better than the relationships of other people (Buunk & van der Eijnden, 1997; Endo, Heine, & Lehman, 2000). In fact, to the extent that two people like one another and believe that their relationship is special, this affection and this belief may actually help maintain the relationship (Franiuk, Cohen, & Pomerantz, 2002; Knee, 1998).

Selecting a Potential Mate: Different Criteria for Men and Women

Dreams of romance may not include the desire to become a parent, but some evolutionary psychologists suggest that our genetic history is a crucial aspect of romantic attraction (Geary, Vigil, & Byrd-Craven, 2004). Our motives need not be conscious, but our search for a suitable romantic partner involves something different than the search for a suitable friend. What matters most in seeking a romantic partner? As we will discuss, men stress the physical attractiveness of a potential mate, and women stress a mate's status and resources (Fletcher et al., 2004). For both genders, personality and character matter. Both men and women say that finding a kind and intelligent mate is important (Li et al., 2002), as is avoiding a mate with a history of infidelity (Hanko, Master, & Sabini, 2004).

■ Men Seek Female Attractiveness: Youth and Beauty Equals Reproductive Fitness

From the perspective of evolutionary determinants, female beauty is believed to be sexually attractive to men because beauty is associated with youth, health, and fertility. The basic principle is that the reproductive success of our male ancestors was enhanced by selecting female mates on the basis of such cues. Though men in a dating relationship are not ordinarily interested in reproduction (sex, maybe, but not reproduction), they *are* predisposed to respond positively to beauty. Over hundreds of thousands of years, males who were attracted to youthful beauty were more likely to pass on their genes to the next generation than were males for whom youth and beauty were irrelevant (Buss, 1994, 1998).

Men are attracted not only to beauty, but also to some other specific characteristics that indicate youth and health. A woman's long hair is one example (Jacobi & Cash,

1994), presumably because healthy, shiny hair is a sign of youth and health (Etcoff, 1999; Hinsz, Matz, & Patience, 2001). Another positive cue is a face that exhibits **bilateral symmetry** (having identical left and right sides). A symmetrical face is perceived as more attractive than an unsymmetrical one (Hughes, Harrison, & Gallup, 2002). Beyond the face, bodily symmetry in general is associated with genetic fitness, health, and fertility (Manning, Koukourakis, & Brodie, 1997; Scutt et al., 1997).

■ Women Seek Men with Resources: Power Equals Ability to Raise and Protect Offspring

In Chapter 7, we pointed out that women respond positively to physical appearance, though not as strongly as do men. In seeking a romantic partner, women pay more attention to a man's resources, whether that consists of a warm cave and the strength to fight off predators in prehistoric times or of economic and interpersonal power in today's world. The reason that women are relatively unconcerned about male youth and attractiveness is explained by evolutionary theorists by the fact that, unlike women, men are usually able to reproduce from puberty well into old age. For a prehistoric female, reproductive success was enhanced by being young and healthy and by choosing a mate who had the ability to protect and care for her and for their offspring (Kenrick et al., 1994, 2001).

Many studies of contemporary men and women suggest that mate preferences are consistent with this evolutionary description. For example, a study in the Netherlands of men and women between twenty and sixty years of age reported that men preferred women who were more attractive than themselves, while women preferred men who were higher in income, education, self-confidence, intelligence, dominance, and social position than themselves (Buunk et al., 2002).

As compelling as the evolution-based explanation of gender differences may be, it is far from universally accepted. Miller, Putcha-Bhagavatula, and Pedersen (2002) discuss culture-based explanations of gender differences in mate selection. With respect to resources, for example, *both* men and women prefer a wealthy mate, and these findings make more sense in terms of cultural values than of genetic influences (Hanko, Master, & Sabini, 2004). This is not something new. Even George Washington and Thomas Jefferson found it useful to marry wealthy widows (Wood, 2004).

■ Finding a Mate

Whatever the basis of mating preferences, people face a very practical obstacle to romance. How does one find a suitable partner? Historically (and in some cultures even today), the answer was simply to enter a marriage arranged by the two sets of parents, often motivated by financial or political goals. In contrast, throughout much of the world, we now leave the process up to the two individuals directly involved. **The Science of Social Psychology: Making Sense of Common Sense** section on page 314 contrasts popular beliefs about the romantic ideal with the possibility that romantic relationships are initiated by observable, predictable factors.

Love: Who Can Explain It? Who Can Tell You Why? Just Maybe, Social Psychologists

Love is one of the most popular themes in our songs, movies, and everyday lives. Most people in our culture accept love as a normative human experience, and a 1993 poll found that almost three out of four Americans said they were currently "in love." In part, love is an emotional reaction that seems as basic as anger, sadness, happiness, and fear (Shaver, Morgan, & Wu, 1996). Maybe love is even good for you. Aron, Paris, and

bilateral symmetry
The alikeness of the left and the right sides of the body (or parts of the body).

love
A combination of emotions, cognitions, and behaviors that often play a crucial role in intimate relationships.

Chapter 8 / Close Relationships

Table 8.1 ■ What Is Love?

When people of different ages were asked about the meaning of love, their answers varied, but young children and college students both suggested many of the same themes: Love can begin positively and end negatively; love can be blind; love involves sharing, forgiveness, and a willingness to sacrifice; and love often includes sexuality.

ACCORDING TO CHILDREN AGED FOUR TO EIGHT
Love is that first feeling you feel before all the bad stuff gets in the way.
Love is when your puppy licks your face even after you left him alone all day.
Love is when mommy sees daddy smelly and sweaty and still says he looks like Robert Redford.
Love is when you go out to eat and give somebody most of your French fries without making them give you any of theirs.
Love is when a girl puts on perfume and a boy puts on shaving cologne and they go out and smell each other.

ACCORDING TO COLLEGE UNDERGRADUATES
Love is like an elevator; you can ride it to the top or end up in the basement, but eventually you'll choose which floor to get off.—T.W.
Love, especially unrequited love, is good, like Baklava; it's very sweet and tasty today, but usually gone tomorrow.—C.H.
Love is when you look at your partner when they first wake up and still think that they are beautiful!—C.M.
Love is offering the last bite.—J.B.
Love is when I want to be naked in front of you.—T.T.

(*Source: Hughes, 2000; Harrison, 2003.*)

Aron (1995) found that falling in love leads to an increase in self-efficacy and self-esteem (see Chapter 5). So, what do we mean by the word *love*?

Some clues to the meaning of love can be found in the spontaneous definitions people offer when asked what it means. Hughes (2000) reported the answers of children (ages four to eight) to the question, "What is love?" Harrison (2003) asked a group of college undergraduates the same question. A sample of the responses from both groups appears in Table 8.1. Individuals in each age group focus on both positive and negative emotions, unselfishness, and attraction.

You may be surprised to learn that social psychologists ignored the topic of love until late in the twentieth century, when Zick Rubin (1970) developed a measure of romantic love and Ellen Berscheid and Elaine Hatfield (1974) proposed a psychological theory of love. Since that time, however, love has become a major research interest. For one thing, now we know what love is *not*. That is, love is something more than a close friendship and something different than simply being sexually interested in another person (Diamond, 2004). The specific details may vary from culture to culture (Beall & Sternberg, 1995), but there is reason to believe that the basic phenomenon we call *love* is a universal one (Hatfield & Rapson, 1993). What do we know about the cognitive and emotional aspects of love?

Written in the Stars or We Met on the Internet?

There is widespread belief in *romantic destiny*—the conviction that two people are meant for each other, and they will somehow meet and automatically fall in love. It was written in the stars. You may find your true love across a crowded room. Among contemporary college students, a great many individuals endorse this general view of romance by expressing agreement with statements such as the following (Weaver & Ganong, 2004):

There will be only one real love for me.

The relationship I have with my "true love" will be nearly perfect.

I am likely to fall in love almost immediately if I meet the right person.

I believe that to be truly in love is to be in love forever.

The idea that love between two people is predestined was expressed in a slightly less positive way by a cynical ten-year-old, who suggested, "God decides who will get married, and you get to find out later who you're stuck with" (Hughes, 2002). In any event, if love is determined by romantic destiny, there's not much we can do to help it along, except possibly mingle with members of the opposite sex, waiting for the right person to appear.

In the not too distant past, the mingling process took the following form in many parts of the world. When a man and a woman met and there was some indication of mutual attraction, the man would ask the woman out on a date, which could involve seeing a movie, attending a dance, playing tennis, or some other social activity. If the date was enjoyable for both, they tended to arrange further dates. If not, they would move on to different potential romantic partners. One day, the right person would presumably appear, and that would be that.

That now quaint custom began to fade at least two decades ago, but without a new custom to take its place. Even among high school students, dating is becoming extinct. The senior prom has become an event attended not only by couples, but also by groups of same-sex friends and opposite-sex friends (Gootman, 2004), as shown in Figure 8.13.

College students across the United States report that dating is dead, but this leaves them with a curious problem. How do you find romance? In place of dating, undergraduates often simply "hang out" in groups, frequently while consuming alcohol. These casual interactions sometimes result in pairs moving on to a "hookup," frequently involving strangers. These interactions are common during vacations such as spring break in the United States and in Australia, where such breaks are called "schoolies" (Maticka-Tyndale, Herold, & Oppermann, 2003). The hookup itself involves acts of physical intimacy, ranging from kissing to intercourse, and the two participants are unlikely to get together again (Paul & Hayes, 2002). Romance can sometimes grow out of hanging out or hooking up, but students complain about the lack of options (Milanese, 2002). In addition, many men and women say they feel uncomfortable about such experiences, though they believe that other students do not (Lambert, Kahn, & Apple, 2003).

Figure 8.13 ■ Going to the High School Prom without a Date
Over the past several years, traditional dating has been declining in popularity in U.S. high schools and colleges. Instead, students go out in various combinations of same-sex and opposite-sex friends. Shown here are students without dates attending a high school prom. In the upper photo, a group of three boys and one girl rented transportation and traveled to the prom as a group. In the lower photo, girls dance without partners in their special prom gowns. (*Source: Photos by Mike Appleton/*The New York Times.)

Despite the frustration, young people also feel awkward about simply asking each other out (Bombardieri, 2004). As a result, a surprising number of students spend their four undergraduate years without ever having anything even resembling a date and without having a girlfriend or boyfriend. After college, the same patterns are common, except that people are likely to meet at their places of work or at public gathering places such as singles bars.

As discussed in Chapter 7 and in this chapter, social psychologists have learned a great deal about attraction, friendship formation, and love. Considering what is known about the need for affiliation, affect, proximity, similarity, and so on, might there be a better way to find a romantic partner than simply waiting for one's true love, either through traditional dating or hooking up with strangers? An alternative that has become increasingly popular utilizes some of the insights provided by psychological research combined with computer technology. People interested in meeting potential partners sign up on a website (bypassing the role of proximity) and are matched with respect to several dimensions (bypassing the need to explore attitudes and beliefs). For pairs who are mutually attracted on the basis of the information available and sometimes a photograph, identities are then revealed and meetings arranged (bypassing the possible rejection involved in asking for a date and the indecision about whether or not to say yes).

On many college campuses, enterprising individuals have created websites for the purpose of bringing interested students together. At Williams College, Williamstown, MA, for example, the site provides each user with the names of the top matches with respect to questionnaire items; a well-matched couple might be 70 to 90 percent similar, and the site provides this service for both straights and gays (Bombardieri, 2004). On a nationwide basis, online dating has become extremely popular among singles of all ages (see Figure 8.14), including singles over age fifty (Mahoney, 2003).

How useful is this process? As yet, the comparative success of computer matching procedures (or *speed dating*, described in Chapter 3) as a way to select a partner, fall in love, or find a suitable spouse has not been established. The use of technology to find romance is clearly not as idealistic as waiting for your soul mate to appear, but it would seem more efficient than "old-fashioned" dating. And, meeting a similar, interested individual online seems infinitely more sensible than getting drunk at a keg party and hooking up with a stranger.

Figure 8.14 ■ Using Your Computer to Find Romance
In recent years, changes in dating practices have led to the development of new ways for couples to meet. Though computer-based services do not conform to traditional ideas about romance and finding one's true love, people are increasingly turning to them to locate possible partners.

Romantic Relationships and Falling in Love

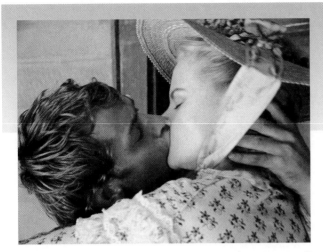

Figure 8.15 ■ Falling in Love
A familiar experience and a familiar movie theme is the emotional reaction to another person that is labeled *passionate love*. It can begin suddenly and includes an all-encompassing emotional surge and a preoccupation with the other person, as depicted here by Jude Law and Nicole Kidman in *Cold Mountain*.

■ Passionate Love

Aron and his colleagues (1989) pointed out that many people fall in love, but no one ever seems to "fall in friend-ship." Unlike attraction, or even romance, **passionate love** involves an intense and often unrealistic emotional reaction to another person. Passionate love usually begins as an instant, overwhelming, surging, all-consuming positive reaction to another person—a reaction that feels as if it's beyond your control, like an unpredictable accident. It often occurs suddenly, as Elaine Hatfield observed, "like slipping on a banana peel," and the experience is described as "falling head over heels in love." A person in love is preoccupied with the loved one and can think about little else (see Figure 8.15).

Meyers and Berscheid (1997) propose that sexual attraction is a necessary but not sufficient condition for being in love with another person. That is, you can be sexually attracted without being in love, but you aren't likely to be in love in the absence of sex-ual attraction (Regan, 2000). Surveys indicate that college students agree (Regan, 1998). For many people, love makes sex more acceptable; and sexual activity can be romanti-cized (Goldberg et al., 1999). That's why it is more acceptable for two people to "make love" than simply to copulate like animals in heat.

In addition to sex, passionate love includes strong emotional arousal, the desire to be physically close, and an intense need to be loved as much as you love the other per-son. Loving and being loved are positive experiences, but they are accompanied by a recurring fear that something may happen to end the relationship. Hatfield and Sprecher (1986b) developed the *Passionate Love Scale* to measure these positive and neg-ative elements, and it contains items such as "For me, _____ is the perfect romantic partner" and "I would feel deep despair if _____ left me."

Though it sounds like something that only happens in a movie, most people, when asked, report having had the experience of suddenly falling in love with a stranger—*love at first sight* (Averill & Boothroyd, 1977). Even in an experimental laboratory, some-thing like this can happen. When two opposite-sex strangers are asked to gaze into each other's eyes for two minutes or to self-disclose, the result is mutual affection (Aron et al., 1997; Kellerman, Lewis, & Laird, 1989), and this is especially true for those who strongly believe in love (Williams & Kleinke, 1993).

It is possible to fall in love, even though the feeling is not returned—**unrequited love.** Such one-way love is most common among those with a conflicted attachment style (Aron, Aron, & Allen, 1998). In one large survey investigation, about 60 percent of the respondents said that they had experienced this kind of love within the past two years (Bringle & Winnick, 1992). Many years ago, when I saw the movie *And God Created Woman*, I (Donn Byrne) "fell in love" with Brigitte Bardot, but I recovered soon after. As a matter of fact, men, especially in late adolescence and early adulthood, report more instances of unrequited love than do women (Hill, Blakemore, & Drumm, 1977). The person who loves in vain feels rejected, while the one who fails to respond feels guilty (Baumeister, Wotman, & Stillwell, 1993). I can live with the rejection, but I hope that Ms. Bardot feels just a little guilty.

passionate love
An intense and often unrealistic emotional response to another per-son. When this emotion is experienced, it is usually perceived as an indication of "true love," but to out-side observers it appears to be "infatuation."

unrequited love
Love felt by one person for another who does not feel love in return.

For any variety of passionate love to occur, Hatfield and Walster (1981) suggested that three factors are necessary. First, you have to learn about love, and most of us are exposed from childhood on to love-related images in fairy tales, songs about love, and romantic movies. These images motivate us to seek the experience of falling in love and provide a script that tells us how to act if it happens (Sternberg, 1996). Second, an appropriate love object must be present. *Appropriate* tends to mean a physically attractive person of the opposite sex who is not currently married, for example. Third, based on Schachter's (1964) two-factor theory of emotion, the individual must be in a state of physiological arousal (sexual excitement, fear, anxiety, or whatever) that is interpreted as the emotion of love (Dutton & Aron, 1974; Istvan, Griffitt, & Weidner, 1983).

What Is the Origin of Love?

The answer is that no one knows for sure. It is possible that love is only a pleasant fantasy that we share with others, much like Santa Claus and the Tooth Fairy. Perhaps psychoanalytic theory is correct to interpret it as an acceptable substitute for the lust we feel toward one of our parents. At the current time, the most accepted explanation is based on evolutionary factors (Buss & Schmitt, 1993).

When our early hominid ancestors first began to walk in an upright position, they hunted for meat and gathered edible vegetables that could be carried back to a place of shelter (Lemonick & Dorfman, 2001). Among many factors, reproductive success was more likely for these individuals if heterosexual pairs were erotically attracted to one another *and* if they were willing to invest time and effort in feeding and protecting any offspring they produced. These two important characteristics (lust and interpersonal commitment) are presumably based in biology. We experience sexual desire and the desire to bond with a mate and with our children because such motivations were adaptive (Rensberger, 1993). Our ancestors were more than simply sex partners. It was an advantage if they liked and trusted one another and if they could divide up tasks such as hunting and child care. Thus, bonding was important to the success of the species. As a consequence, today's humans may be genetically primed to seek sex, fall in love, and become caring parents. Most young adults say they expect to have a monogamous relationship with the person they love (Wiederman & Allgeier, 1996). In addition to genetic underpinnings, cultural influences can affect both lust and commitment by way of religious teachings, civil laws, and the way we depict love and marriage in our songs and stories (Allgeier & Wiederman, 1994).

The Components of Love

Though passionate love is a common experience, it is too intense and too overwhelming to be maintained as a permanent emotional state. There are other kinds of love, however, that *can* be long lasting. Hatfield describes **companionate love** as the "affection we feel for those with whom our lives are deeply entwined" (1988, p. 205). Unlike passionate love, companionate love is based on a very close friendship in which two people are sexually attracted, have a great deal in common, care about each other's well-being, and express mutual liking and respect (Caspi & Herbener, 1990). It's not quite as exciting as passionate love nor as interesting a theme for music and fiction, but it *is* a crucial aspect of a satisfying and lasting relationship.

In addition to these two aspects of love, four other styles have been identified. Game-playing love includes such behavior as having two lovers at once, possessive love concentrates on the fear of losing one's lover, logical love is based on decisions as to whether a partner is suitable, and selfless love is a rare phenomenon in which an individual would rather suffer than have a lover suffer (Hendrick & Hendrick, 1986). Among the many findings with respect to style differences, men are more likely to engage in game-playing love than are women, but the reverse is true for logical and possessive love (Hendrick et al., 1984). In general, people agree that companionate love

companionate love
Love that is based on friendship, mutual attraction, shared interests, respect, and concern for one another's welfare.

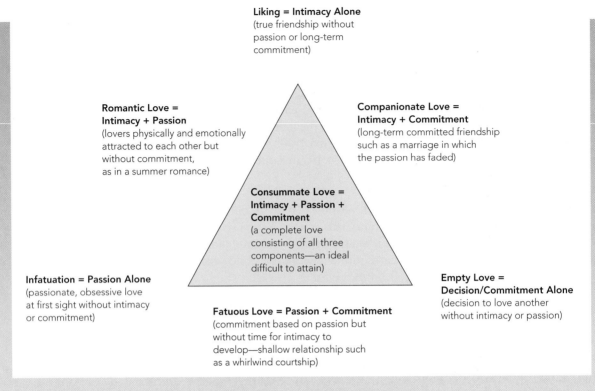

Figure 8.16 ■ Sternberg's Triangular Model of Love
Sternberg's model of love has three basic components: *intimacy, passion,* and *decision/commitment*. For a given couple, love can be based on any one of these three components, on a combination of any two of them, or on all three. As shown in the illustration, these various possibilities yield seven types of relationships, including the ideal (*consummate love*) that consists of all three basic components equally represented.

triangular model of love
Sternberg's conceptualization of love relationships consisting of three basic components: *intimacy, passion,* and *decision/commitment*.

intimacy
In Sternberg's *triangular model of love*, the closeness felt by two people—the extent to which they are bonded.

passion
In Sternberg's *triangular model of love*, the sexual motives and sexual excitement associated with a couple's relationship.

and selfless love are the most desirable, while game-playing is the least desirable (Hahn & Blass, 1997).

A different conception of the meaning of love is provided by Sternberg's (1986) **triangular model of love,** as depicted in Figure 8.16. This formulation suggests that each love relationship is made up of three basic components that are present in varying degrees in different couples (Aron & Westbay, 1996). One component is **intimacy**—the closeness two people feel and the strength of the bond that holds them together. Intimacy is essentially companionate love. Partners high in intimacy are concerned with each other's welfare and happiness, and they value, like, count on, and understand each other. The second component, **passion,** is based on romance, physical attraction, and sexuality—in other words, passionate love. Men are more likely to stress this component than are women (Fehr & Broughton, 2001). The third component, **decision/ commitment,** represents cognitive factors such as the decision that you love and want to be associated with the other person, along with a commitment to maintain the relationship on a permanent basis.

Actual lovers subjectively experience these three elements as overlapping and related components of love. Many relationships can be categorized primarily by a single component or by a combination of two of the components (as described in Figure 8.16). When all three angles of the triangle are equally strong, the result is **consummate love**—defined as the ideal form but difficult to attain.

Although attraction research (see Chapter 7) has long stressed the effects of physical attractiveness on liking, its effect on love has been somewhat overlooked until recently. In Spain, almost two thousand individuals ranging in age from eighteen to sixty-four were asked questions about physical attractiveness, falling in love, and each of the components of Sternberg's model (Sangrador & Yela, 2000). The findings suggest that appearance is important not only with respect to passion, but also with respect to intimacy and decision/commitment. Surprisingly, attractiveness is as important in the later stages of a relationship as it is at the beginning. In the words of these Spanish psychologists, "What is beautiful is loved." This focus on external appearance may not be wise, but these investigators suggest that we should at least acknowledge the reality of the influence of physical attractiveness on long-term relationships.

Romance, Love, and Sex

Despite a long history of religious, legal, and commonsense pressures to avoid premarital sex, there is an equally long history of couples whose behavior defied these pressures. Early in the twentieth century in many parts of the world, attitudes about sexuality became increasingly permissive, and sexual interaction became a common and widely accepted component of romantic relationships (Coontz, 1992; Jones, 1997; Michael et al., 1994). These changes in attitude and behavior were sufficiently dramatic that they were characterized as a "sexual revolution" (see Figure 8.17). Gender differences in sexuality have essentially disappeared (Weinberg, Lottes, & Shaver, 1995), but both men and women vary widely in their sexual knowledge, attitudes, and practices. (Byrne, 1997b; Fisher & Barak, 1991; Simpson & Gangestad, 1992).

The "flower children" of the 1960s and 1970s once were described by some as representing the future, with permissive sexuality providing the solution to problems as varied as achieving world peace and establishing lasting relationships. As the twentieth century drew to a close and the twenty-first century began, there were many signs that the sexual revolution was fading. The reasons included the growing realization that sexual "freedom" often meant sexual "conformity" to social pressure (Townsend, 1995).

decision/commitment
In Sternberg's *triangular model of love*, these are the cognitive processes involved in deciding that you love another person and are committed to maintaining the relationship.

consummate love
In Sternberg's *triangular model of love*, a complete and ideal love that combines *intimacy, passion,* and *decision/commitment.*

Figure 8.17 ■ In Turbulent Times—The Sexual Revolution
In the 1960s and 1970s, the United States was the scene of experiments with illegal drugs, a new kind of music, the demand for sexual freedom, and protests against the war in Vietnam. Change was the goal, and the status quo was unacceptable to many young people. Among the lasting effects of that era is a shift toward greater permissiveness and tolerance with respect to sexual attitudes and behavior.

Two other, unrelated issues contributed to a decrease in permissiveness: the explosive number of unwanted teenage pregnancies (Byrne & Fisher, 1983) and the rise of the dangerous, and frequently fatal, sexually transmitted human immunodeficiency virus (HIV) infection, which can develop into acquired immunodeficiency syndrome (AIDS). Though this disease first spread from apes to humans as early as the seventeenth century, it was in the 1980s that it was identified as an epidemic (Boyce, 2001).

A growing realization of the dangers posed by sexual pressure, unwanted pregnancies, and incurable diseases led gradually to changes in sexual practices. Teenage birth rates in the United States dropped to a record low (Schmid, 2001). The incidence of HIV infections has decreased in several parts of the world, though it continues to increase in many areas, including the United States, the Caribbean, and sub-Saharan Africa (Fang, 2001; Whitelaw, 2003). The changes that *do* occur reflect changes in sexual attitudes and practices. For example, in U.S. high schools, unlike a decade ago, the majority of students have *not* engaged in intercourse; an additional change is that most of today's sexually active students use condoms (Lewin, 2002).

The permissiveness that characterized the revolution did have some lasting effects, however. Though free love in the park has not become the norm, it is nevertheless true that most married couples in the early twenty-first century have engaged in some form of premarital sexual intimacy with each other and often with others as well. It also is true that premarital sex, including cohabitation, is not related to the probability of marriage taking place, and it has no effect on subsequent marital satisfaction or on marital success or failure (Cunningham & Antill, 1994; Stafford, Kline, & Rankin, 2004).

KEY POINTS

★ One defining characteristic of romantic relationships is some degree of physical intimacy, ranging from holding hands to sexual interactions.

★ As is true for attraction and friendship, romantic attraction is influenced by factors such as physical proximity, appearance, and similarity. In addition, romance includes sexual attraction, the desire for total acceptance by the other person, and an acceptance of positive fantasies about such relationships.

★ The reproductive success of our ancient ancestors was enhanced by male attraction to young, fertile females; female attraction to males with resources; and by bonding between mates and between parents and their offspring.

★ *Love* consists of multiple components. For example, *passionate love* is a sudden, over-whelming emotional response to another person. *Companionate love* resembles a close friendship that includes caring, mutual liking, and respect. Sternberg's *triangular model of love* includes these two components plus a third—*decision/commitment*—that is a cognitive decision to love and to be committed to a relationship.

★ Widespread changes in sexual attitudes and practices in the 1960s and 1970s have been described as a "sexual revolution" that, among other changes, resulted in premarital sex becoming the norm. Because of reactions against pressures to conform to the new sexual norms, the problem of unwanted pregnancies, and the fear of sexually transmitted diseases, there has been a partial backlash against the sexual revolution toward safer and more discriminating sexual behavior.

Marriage: Happily Ever After—and Otherwise

As you might expect, all of the factors that have been discussed with respect to attraction, friendship, romance, love, and sex are also relevant to the selection of a marital partner. Marriage, however, brings with it new challenges, such as economic issues, parenthood, and careers that sometimes conflict with the very difficult task of maintaining a long-term relationship.

Before we discuss how marriage is affected by such challenges, in the **Beyond the Headlines** section on page 322, we turn to a relatively recent phenomenon that has created a major conflict in the United States, as noted in Chapter 4. In May 2004, the first same-sex couples in the United States were legally married in the state of Massachusetts. Simultaneously, the Massachusetts state legislature has been working to draft an amendment to the state constitution that would make such marriages *illegal,* and President George W. Bush supported an amendment to the U.S. Constitution confining marriage to the union of a man and a woman. In Belgium and the Netherlands, as well as in three Canadian provinces, gay marriages have been legal for some time and are not the subject of controversy (Haslett, 2004; Kisner, 2004). We briefly note some of the opinions supporting legalization and supporting prohibition of same-sex marriages and then offer a prediction about the probable outcome of this dispute.

Marital Success and Satisfaction: Similarity, Personality, and Sexuality

Given the fact that most people do get married and that half or more of these marriages fail, it would be helpful if each of us knew as much as possible about the factors that differentiate marital success and failure. Though the importance of commitment to the relationship is often stressed, note that commitment based on fear of a breakup is not as effective as commitment based on the positive rewards of a continuing relationship (Frank & Brandstatter, 2002).

In a long-term relationship, many problems can arise over time, and we discuss this shortly. Other predictive factors are present even before the wedding, and they can be useful indications of the probability that a marriage will succeed or fail.

◼ Similarity and Assumed Similarity

Not surprisingly, over a century of research has consistently indicated that spouses are similar in their attitudes, beliefs, values, interests, ages, attractiveness, and other attributes (Galton, 1870/1952; Pearson & Lee, 1903; Terman & Buttenwieser, 1935a, 1935b). Further, a longitudinal study of couples from the time they were first engaged through twenty years of marriage indicates very little change in the degree of similarity over time (Caspi, Herbener, & Ozer, 1992). In other words, similar people marry, and the similarity neither increases nor decreases as the years pass. Greater than chance similarity is also found for pairs of friends and for dating couples, but husbands and wives are even more similar (Watson, Hubbard, & Wiese, 2000). As emphasized in Chapter 7, opposites don't attract. Also, because there is a positive relationship between the degree of similarity and the success of the relationship, a couple contemplating marriage might do well to pay greater attention to their similarities and dissimilarities and less attention to attractiveness and sexuality.

Gay Marriage, Civil Unions, and Family Values

Gay Couples Sue State over Marriage Law

Albany (April 8, 2004)— Thirteen gay couples filed suit against the New York State Health Department on Wednesday. They argue that regulations which define marriage as limited to unions between a man and a woman should be declared unconstitutional.

This group includes couples who have been together for many years, and couples with children. They indicate that they are simply seeking the same rights and safeguards granted to heterosexual couples. On a more personal level, one of the individuals involved in the suit said, "I have a dream of a wedding. I want to achieve what everyone else has in life: marrying the person I love."

New York's Attorney General, Elliot Spitzer, has indicated that he personally has no problem with such marriages, but has ruled that they are currently illegal because the state constitution has no provision that allows people of the same sex to marry (Bolton, 2004, p. A1).

Social psychologists don't pretend to be experts on either constitutional law or religious doctrine, so what can they offer that would be of use in this controversy? Think of the arguments for or against same-sex marriage as reflecting attitudes, and think of the beliefs underlying those attitudes. What are the issues? Is this a simple matter of equal rights under the law, part of a militant gay agenda to make homosexuality an accepted part of society, an attack on family values, or a way to weaken the religious meaning of marriage? Individuals on both sides express strong pro and con opinions in emotion-laden terms (see Figure 8.18). As examples, consider the following sample of statements:

> *"Just as it isn't fair to discriminate against someone for their skin color, heritage or religious beliefs, it isn't fair to discriminate against someone for their sexual orientation"* (Editorial Board of Baylor University student newspaper, quoted by Hertzberg, 2004, p. 62).

Figure 8.18 ■ Gay Marriage: A Threat or a Civil Right?

When the ban on gay marriage was declared unconstitutional by a Massachusetts court, officials in various parts of the United States began issuing marriage licenses to nonheterosexual couples. The result was an outpouring of gay and lesbian couples who wanted to marry and heated protests by those who viewed the change as a threat to the institution of marriage. Shown here is one of the resulting confrontations taking place at the San Francisco Court House. (*Source:* The New Republic, May 3, 2004, p. 18.)

"... ministers performing the [gay] 'weddings' knowingly and willfully violated the law in order to promote their way of thinking onto and into the lives of the general public. . . . The 'ministers' must be prosecuted . . . ." (Miller, 2004, p. A16).

"Marriage is more than a benefits package. It serves, among other purposes, to reconcile the differences between the sexes in a publicly recognized and sanctioned union" (Favata, 2004, p. A16).

By assessing such opinions in samples of the population, we can document how the attitudes are broken down. For example, when Americans are questioned about whether even gay *relationships* should be legal, those who say "yes" and those who say "no" are split fairly evenly, but when the question deals with gay *marriage*, 30 percent say they are in favor, while 64 percent are opposed (Chait, 2004). These percentages apply to the general population, but specific subgroups of the population yield quite different results. For example,

among white evangelical Christians, gay marriage is opposed by 85 percent, while only 10 percent are in favor (Evangelicals in America, 2004). Such differences suggest, among other things, that decisions about legalizing gay marriage might be quite different in various parts of the United States, depending on the concentration of particular subgroups.

One subgroup difference has even broader implications, however. While older voters (age sixty-five and up) overwhelmingly oppose gay marriage, younger voters (under age thirty) overwhelmingly favor gay marriage (see Figure 8.19). Unless the younger voters drastically change their minds when they grow older, the trend is clear: "At some point in the fairly near future...gay marriage will be routine—so will gay divorce, if the experience of straight marriage is any guide." (Hertzberg, 2004, p. 62).

If this prediction, based on attitudinal differences among different age groups, is accurate, the issue will be peacefully resolved over time. You may believe that is a good outcome or a bad one, but that is what the data strongly indicate.

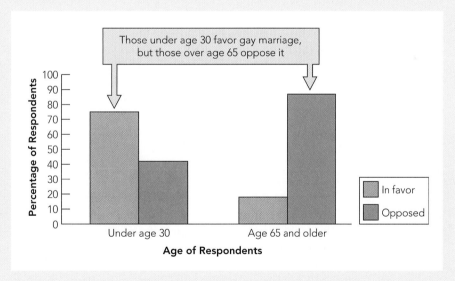

Figure 8.19 ■ Attitudes about Gay Marriage: An Age Gap
Approval versus disapproval of the legalization of gay marriage is strongly associated with age. Younger Americans are overwhelmingly in favor of such marriages, while older ones are overwhelmingly against such marriages. As time passes, it appears inevitable that the favorable attitudes will prevail. (*Source: Based on data in Hertzberg, 2004.*)

Not only do similar people marry, but happily married couples *believe* they are even more similar than they actually are—a phenomenon known as **assumed similarity** (Byrne & Blaylock, 1963; Schul & Vinokur, 2000). Both actual and assumed similarity increases marital satisfaction. Interestingly, dating couples have even higher assumed similarity than do married couples, perhaps reflecting the romantic illusions discussed earlier.

Dispositional Factors

Beyond similarity, marital success is affected by some specific personality dispositions. In other words, some individuals are better able to maintain a positive relationship than are others, and they are better bets as marriage partners than are others.

For example, **narcissism** refers to an individual who feels superior to most other people, someone who seeks admiration and lacks empathy (American Psychiatric Association, 1994). Narcissists report feeling less commitment to a relationship (Campbell & Foster, 2002). As one exception to the similarity rule, two narcissists are not likely to have a happy relationship (Campbell, 1999).

Other important personality dispositions that affect the success of a relationship are those associated with interpersonal behavior and attachment styles. Thus, individuals with preoccupied or fearful–avoidant styles have less satisfying relationships than those with secure or dismissing styles (Murray et al., 2001). In general, secure attachment is associated with marital satisfaction (Banse, 2004).

Other personality characteristics, such as anxiety, negativity, and neuroticism (assessed when couples were newlyweds) are associated with later relationship problems (Huston et al., 2001). It should be noted that these negative characteristics, which were present when the marriage began, were predictive of relationship problems over the subsequent thirteen years of marriage (Caughlin, Huston, & Houts, 2000).

It seems clear that, over time, the expression of negative affect results in disillusionment as love fades, overt affection declines, and ambivalence increases. When marital partners *do not express* negative emotions such as fear, anxiety, and anger, the relationship has a greater chance of success (Robins, Caspi, & Moffitt, 2000). The longer a couple has been together, the less likely the individuals are to keep their opinions to themselves (Stafford, Kline, & Rankin, 2004). Despite what you may have heard, it is usually *not* a good idea to "let it all hang out." When a partner is inconsiderate or hostile, the other individual usually responds by pointing out the lack of consideration or expressing hostility in return. The relationship suffers from the original negative behavior of one partner and the resultant negative behavior of the other partner. Holding back in such interactions requires more self-control than many of us are able to master (Finkel & Campbell, 2001).

Marital Sex

Surveys of married couples reveal that sexual interactions become less frequent as time passes, and that the most rapid decline occurs during the first four years of marriage (Udry, 1980); this decreased frequency of sexual interaction over time is equally true for cohabiting couples. Surprisingly, studies show that neither full-time nor part-time employment has a negative effect on a couple's sex life.

Regardless of sexual *frequency*, the degree of *similarity* of sexual attitudes and preferences predicts marital compatibility (Smith et al., 1993). Also, men are more likely than women to equate sexual satisfaction with the quality of the relationship (Sprecher, 2002).

Love and Marriage: Careers, Parenthood, and Family Composition

The ongoing realities of a marital relationship present a more complex challenge than simply falling in love, having a marriage ceremony, and living happily every after. Two

assumed similarity
The extent to which two people believe they are similar with respect to specific attitudes, beliefs, values, and so forth, as opposed to the extent to which they are actually similar.

narcissism
A personality disposition characterized by unreasonably high *self-esteem*, a feeling of superiority, a need for admiration, sensitivity to criticism, a lack of empathy, and exploitative behavior.

people must interact on a daily basis and find ways to deal with an almost endless list of potential problems, such as dividing up the household chores, dealing with the unexpected events that arise each day, meeting the demands of those outside of the relationship (e.g., parents, siblings, and friends), and juggling the requirements of a job (or jobs). In addition, economic concerns (Conger, Rueter, & Elder, 1999), the stresses of parenthood (Kurdek, 1999), and the complications of a nontraditional family composition can bring unexpected complications. Such factors are very likely to contribute to the fact that relationship quality begins to decline shortly after the bride and groom say, "I do."

Is It Better to Be Married or to Be Unmarried?

If marriage does not promise eternal bliss, should this lead people to avoid it? Although more Americans are remaining single than ever before, 90 percent of adults are (or were) married (Edwards, 2000; Households, 2001). Most adults want to get married and most *do* get married (Frazier et al., 1996; People, 2001).

Compared with single individuals, men who are married consistently report being happier and healthier, but for women, only a satisfactory marriage provides health benefits (DeNoon, 2003; Steinhauer, 1995). A Norwegian study found that married people report a greater sense of well-being and have a lower suicide rate than singles—at least until their late thirties. After that, the advantages of being married begin to disappear (Mastekaasa, 1995).

Love and Marriage

In song, these two concepts may "go together like a horse and carriage," but what happens in real life? Usually, passionate love decreases over time (Tucker & Aron, 1993), although women who continue to feel intense love toward their husbands are more satisfied with their relationships than those who do not. Male satisfaction with marriage, however, is unrelated to feelings of passionate love (Aron & Henkemeyer, 1995). Companionate love is, however, important for both men and women—sharing activities, exchanging ideas, laughing together, and cooperating on projects. One of the best examples and most detailed records of companionate love in a marriage can be found in the collected letters of John and Abigail Adams that were written during their long separations before and after the American Revolution (Shuffelton, 2004).

Work Inside and Outside of the Home

Although the patterns are gradually changing, men do most of the repairs and women do most of the cooking and cleaning, even if they both have active careers (Yu, 1996). Marital conflict and dissatisfaction often involve the perceived unfairness in the way such chores are divided (Grote & Clark, 2001). Similar problems arise in the households of gay couples, but, unlike gays and heterosexuals, lesbian partners report being able to share household labor in a fair and equitable way (Kurdek, 1993).

With respect to work outside of the home, there is always the potential for conflict between the demands of the job and the demands of the marriage. This conflict can easily lead to alienation and eventually to emotional exhaustion (Senecal, Vallerand, & Guay, 2001). For both men and women, this results in dissatisfaction with one's job and with one's life (Perrew & Hochwarter, 2001). When both spouses work outside of the home, the potential for conflict is even greater, and no one has devised a satisfactory way to solve all of the problems created by a two-career family (Gilbert, 1993). Spouses with secure attachment styles deal most effectively with these competing demands, while fearful–avoidant individuals have the most difficulty. Individuals with dismissing or preoccupied styles fall in between these two extremes (Vasquez, Durik, & Hyde, 2002).

Parenthood

Bell (2001) suggests that evolution has produced a neurobiological basis for the emotional bond between parents and their children that goes beyond logic or other cognitive

Figure 8.20 ■ Parenthood Can Be a Challenge
Although most couples want to have offspring, the transition to parenthood presents a unending series of potential problems and challenges.

considerations (see Figure 8.20). Despite these biological pressures favoring parenthood, along with social disapproval of childlessness (LaMastro, 2001), becoming a parent creates unexpected problems. As actress Kate Hudson (2004, p. 46) said a few months after the birth of her first child, "You know, nothing really prepares you for motherhood." Or, fatherhood either. Becoming a parent is likely to interfere with marital sexuality, beginning with sexuality during pregnancy (De Judicibus & McCabe, 2002; Regan et al., 2003), and having children brings many additional sources of potential conflict to the relationship (Alexander & Higgins, 1993; Hackel & Ruble, 1992). Parenthood is often associated with a decline in marital satisfaction, but the decline is less if the couple has a strong, companionate relationship (Shapiro & Gottman, 2000) and if the parents have secure attachment styles (Alexander et al., 2001; Berant, Mikulincer, & Florian, 2001).

Despite the difficulties, parents consistently report that they are very glad they have children (Feldman & Nash, 1984). With larger families, however, men and women differ somewhat in this sentiment. The more children they have, the more women express dissatisfaction with the marriage, while men express greater satisfaction (Grote, Frieze, & Stone, 1996). Perhaps the difference arises because women spend more time than men taking care of their expanding brood (Bjorklund & Shackelford, 1999).

■ Changes in Family Composition

Marriage rates are down in the United States and in several European countries, while cohabitation rates are up (Montgomery, 2004). Nevertheless, when most people think of marriage, parenthood, and families, they have an idealized image of a traditional household with a mother and father plus a couple of children. In spite of this 1950s' sitcom image, many families today take other forms.

By the early 1970s, only 45 percent of American families consisted of a married couple and their offspring, and that figure dropped to 23.5 percent over the next thirty years (Irvine, 1999; Schmitt, 2001). Comparing U.S. Census Bureau figures for 1990 and 2000, the greatest increase has been in the number of households consisting of a single mother; such families grew five times faster in the 1990s than did families containing a married couple (Schmitt, 2001).

In addition to single-parent households, there has been an increase in the number of remarriages in which the wife, the husband, or both have offspring from a previous marriage; the number of cohabiting couples who became parents; and the number of gay and lesbian couples with children (either adopted or the offspring of one of the partners) (McLaughlin, 2001a; Stacy & Biblarz, 2001). We don't yet know the possible ramifications of these relatively new family arrangements—either for the adults or for their children.

When Relationships Fail: Causes, Preventives, and Consequences

People usually enter marriage with high hopes, and they tend to be optimistic about their chances of marital success (McNulty & Karney, 2004). More than 50 percent of the marriages in the United States end in divorce, and the figure for those marrying today is expected to reach 64 percent. In an attempt to point out the discrepancy between positive expectancies and negative reality, Chast (2004) created a mock "marital adjustment test" that suggests a high frequency of marital discord. For example, the first question asks,

> *When did you realize that you couldn't stand your partner?*
>
> *A minute ago ___ About an hour ago ___*
>
> *Last night when I was watching "E. R." ___*
>
> *Sometime in the last month ___ Before that even ___*

Despite statistics to the contrary, unmarried respondents estimate for themselves only a 10 percent chance of a divorce when they marry (Fowers et al., 2001). In other words, people expect their own marriages to succeed, despite the fact that at least half of all marriages fail. Why is it that couples fail to succeed at marriage, no matter how optimistic they may be?

Costs and Benefits of Marital Interactions

Before we discuss specific problems, it may be useful to consider each interaction in a marriage in terms of costs and benefits. It is assumed that the greater the number of benefits relative to the number of costs, the higher the quality of the relationship.

Clark and Grote (1998) identified several types of costs and benefits, some of which are intentionally positive or negative and some of which are unintentional. From the viewpoint of attempting to maintain a good relationship, it is possible to engage in intentionally positive acts and to avoid intentionally negative acts, but both partners have to consider the consequences of what they say and do and to be motivated to exercise self-control. Even more difficult is being willing to engage in difficult or undesired behavior in order to meet the needs of one's partner. These acts constitute **communal behavior**—a "cost" for one individual that is a "benefit" for the partner. As you might expect, a communal orientation is associated with a partner's marital satisfaction (Mills et al., 2004). Altogether, relationship satisfaction depends on maximizing benefits and minimizing costs, as outlined in Figure 8.21 on page 328.

Problems between Spouses

What happens to transform a loving romantic relationship into an unhappy and dissatisfied one, often characterized by mutual hate? Why do costs begin to rise and benefits begin to drop?

One factor is the failure to understand the reality of a relationship. That is, no spouse (including oneself) is perfect. No matter how ideal the other person may have seemed through the mist of romance, it eventually becomes obvious that he or she has negative qualities as well as positive ones. For example, there is the disappointing discovery that the *actual* similarity between spouses is less than the *assumed* similarity (Silars et al., 1994).

communal behavior
Benevolent acts in a relationship that "cost" the one who performs those acts and "benefit" the partner and the relationship itself.

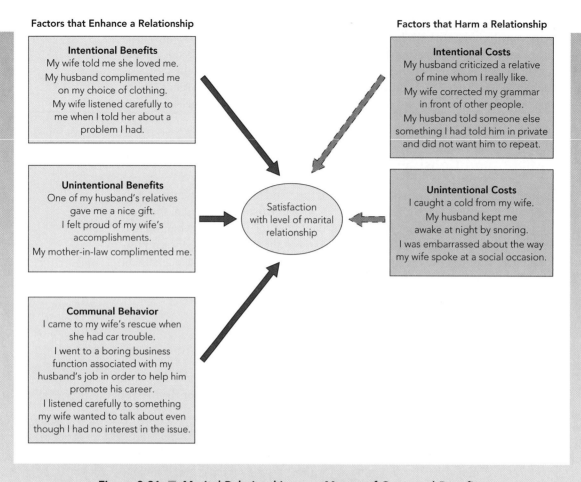

Factors that Enhance a Relationship

Intentional Benefits
My wife told me she loved me.
My husband complimented me on my choice of clothing.
My wife listened carefully to me when I told her about a problem I had.

Unintentional Benefits
One of my husband's relatives gave me a nice gift.
I felt proud of my wife's accomplishments.
My mother-in-law complimented me.

Communal Behavior
I came to my wife's rescue when she had car trouble.
I went to a boring business function associated with my husband's job in order to help him promote his career.
I listened carefully to something my wife wanted to talk about even though I had no interest in the issue.

Factors that Harm a Relationship

Intentional Costs
My husband criticized a relative of mine whom I really like.
My wife corrected my grammar in front of other people.
My husband told someone else something I had told him in private and did not want him to repeat.

Unintentional Costs
I caught a cold from my wife.
My husband kept me awake at night by snoring.
I was embarrassed about the way my wife spoke at a social occasion.

Satisfaction with level of marital relationship

Figure 8.21 ■ Marital Relationships as a Matter of Costs and Benefits
Relationship success and failure can be conceptualized as the result of the relative number of costs and benefits that are present. Shown here are some of the possible intentional and unintentional costs and benefits in a relationship. In addition, there is *communal behavior,* which represents a cost to the spouse engaging in the behavior but a benefit to the partner and to the relationship itself. Marital satisfaction depends on the relative number of costs and benefits that spouses experience in their marriage. (*Source: Based on information in Clark & Grote, 1998.*)

Also, over time, the negative personality characteristics (discussed earlier in this chapter) become less and less tolerable. Minor behavioral flaws that once seemed cute can come to be perceived as annoying and unlikable (Felmlee, 1995; Pines, 1997). If you are initially drawn to someone because that person is very different from yourself or perhaps even unique, chances are good that disenchantment will eventually set in (Felmlee, 1998).

A special problem in any intimate relationship is jealousy, the negative reaction to a partner's real or imagined attraction toward someone else. Some propose that men are most threatened by a partner's sexual attraction to a rival man, while women are most threatened by a partner's emotional attraction to a rival woman. The difference presumably results from biological differences, in that men fear having to raise some other man's offspring, while women fear losing a mate's resources if he transfers his affection to a different mate (Berscheid & Reis, 1998). Although the possibility of such sex differences is both interesting and plausible, recent research suggests that men and women are equally threatened by either type of infidelity (DeSteno et al., 2002; Harris, 2002, 2003; Levy & Kelly, 2002).

The ultimate step in sexual attraction toward someone other than one's spouse is infidelity. It has long been known that extramarital sex is associated with marital dissolution, but which occurs first? A longitudinal study by Previti and Amato (2004) indicates that the events can go either way. Individuals in an unhappy marriage often engage in extramarital sex, and extramarital sex often leads to a marriage breaking up.

Some marital problems are universal, and probably unavoidable, because being in any kind of close relationship involves some degree of compromise. To take a minor example, when you live alone, you can have whatever you wish for dinner. When two people are together, they must somehow decide what to eat, who prepares it, and when and how to serve the meal. Analogous decisions must be made about whether to watch TV and which programs to watch, whether to wash the dishes after dinner or let them wait for the next day, where to set the thermostat, whether to have sex right now or some other time—along with hundreds of other major and minor decisions about their daily lives, economic issues, child-rearing issues, and much else besides. Because both partners have needs and preferences, there is an inevitable conflict between the desire for independence and the need for closeness (Baxter, 1990). As a consequence, 98.8 percent of married couples report that they have disagreements, and most indicate that serious conflicts arise once a month or more often (McGonagle, Kessler, & Schilling, 1992). Because disagreements and conflicts are essentially inevitable, what becomes crucial is how those conflicts are handled.

Dealing with Marital Problems

When there are marital arguments or disagreements, it is not helpful to focus on winning versus losing or on being right versus being wrong. Marital disagreements are not some kind of sport in which it is important to score more points than your opponent. In videotaped interactions of husbands and wives discussing problems in their marriage, one positive and three negative patterns were identified (McNulty & Karney, 2004). A positive, constructive style involves focusing on the topic under discussion and attempting to resolve the conflict. Negative, destructive behaviors consisted of avoidance (changing the subject and talking about something else), direct negative interactions (faulting, rejecting, or criticizing the partner), and indirect negative interactions (making attributions, avoiding responsibility, or asking hostile questions). Avoidance is most often practiced by men, and it simply postpones any effort to solve problems (Bodenman et al., 1998), but the most maladaptive responses to conflict is for the disagreeing partners to lash out in a directly or indirectly negative way. This behavior only provokes additional negative responses from the partner, simply intensifying the conflict.

In addition, it seems to be true that "people do a lot of mean and nasty things to one another" (Kowalski et al., 2003, p. 471). A variety of aversive interpersonal behaviors such as lying, cheating, complaining, and teasing are familiar examples of unnecessarily unpleasant actions that occur in relationships. At the opposite extreme are positive interpersonal behaviors that communicate commitment to the relationship; examples include showing affection, providing support and companionship, showing respect, and maintaining a positive atmosphere (Weigel & Ballard-Reisch, 2002). Which set of behaviors would you guess are more likely to help maintain a relationship?

If partners pause and consider the long-term effects of what they say and do, this can often lead to a constructive response (Yovetich & Rusbult, 1994). It is important to be able to disagree and yet deal with problems in an agreeable way (Graziano, Jensen-Campbell, & Hair, 1996), to show empathy (Arriaga & Rusbult, 1998), and to avoid hostility and defensiveness (Newton et al., 1995; Thompson, Whiffen, & Blain, 1995).

A more comprehensive way of characterizing these various patterns of interacting with a partner can be summarized simply: Whatever is said or done that creates negative affect is bad for a relationship, and whatever is said or done that creates positive affect is good for a relationship (Levenson, Carstensen, & Gottman, 1994). Videotapes of interactions between satisfied and dissatisfied partners reveal much more negative verbal and nonverbal behavior in the latter pairs than in the former (Halford & Sanders,

Table 8.2 ■ Ten Tips for Spouses

A marriage and family therapist provides these suggestions as ways to maintain a positive marital relationship. You may notice that these tips from a clinical practitioner are quite consistent with the research findings discussed in this chapter.

1. You can be right or you can be happy—not both. Choose wisely.

2. Learn the gentle art of cooperation.

3. Talk about the important stuff.

4. Forgive as much or more than you would like to be forgiven.

5. Celebrate what you want to see more of. Appreciation can go a long way.

6. Listen to the heart more than you listen to the words. This can lead to conflict resolution and to taking care of each other.

7. Don't be like Darren in *Bewitched* who wanted Samantha to stop using her magic witch powers. Encourage your partner in her or his gifts.

8. Check out your communication. It's easy to talk, but it's more difficult to communicate.

9. Take responsibility for your contributions to the problems.

10. Don't assume that just because you are married, you know how to be married.

(Source: Based on information from Herring, May 20, 2001, Knight Ridder.)

1990). As the amount of negative affect increases and the amount of positive affect decreases, the relationship becomes less and less satisfactory (Kurdek, 1996, 1997).

Jeff Herring (2001), marriage and family therapist, provides ten tips to strengthen a marriage, and his suggestions (see Table 8.2) are consistent with what is known about avoiding and dealing with problems. A successful marriage is one that emphasizes friendship, commitment, trust, social support, similarity, and a consistent determination to create positive affect (Adams & Jones, 1997; Cobb, Davila, & Bradbury, 2001; Wieselquist et al., 1999).

■ The Consequences of a Failed Relationship

Friends may drift apart peacefully, but spouses are much more likely to feel intense distress and anger when a marriage fails (Fischman, 1986). In part, spouses find the end of their relationship more difficult than the end of a friendship because they have invested considerable time and effort in one another, engaged in many mutually rewarding activities, planned a future together, and expressed a lasting commitment to the relationship (Simpson, 1987). Suddenly, all of the experiences, the interactions, and the plans seem to have been a waste of time, and, of course, blame is attributed primarily to the other person.

When it is clear that a relationship has severe problems, each partner can respond either actively or passively to the situation (Rusbult & Zembrodt, 1983). An active response consists of either ending the relationship as quickly as possible (moving out, filing for divorce, etc.) or working to improve it (deliberately trying to behave in a more positive way, seeing a marriage counselor, etc.). A passive response involves simply waiting and hoping that things will get better or waiting for things to get worse. Men and women with secure attachment styles are more likely to work actively to save a relationship, while those with insecure attachment styles are more likely to end the relationship or simply wait for it to get worse (Rusbult, Morrow, & Johnson, 1990).

It is difficult, though possible, to reverse a deteriorating relationship. A couple is most able to reconcile if (1) the needs of each partner can be satisfied, (2) each is committed to continuing the relationship, and (3) alternative lovers are not readily available (Arriaga & Agnew, 2001; Rusbult, Martz, & Agnew, 1998). When children are part of the marriage, they become the innocent victims of relationship failure. Approximately one out of three American children has this experience (Bumpass, 1984). The negative consequences of divorce for these boys and girls include long-term effects on their health and well-being (Friedman et al., 1995; Vobejda, 1997), behavior problems at school (O'Brien & Bahadur, 1998), a higher risk of mortality throughout their lives, and a greater likelihood of getting a divorce themselves (Tucker et al., 1997). And the negative effects of divorce on children are worse if either of the parents moves to a new location (Braver, Ellman, & Fabricius, 2003). Despite the numerous problems found among children whose parents divorce, sociologist Constance Ahrons (2004) points out that this does not mean that *all* children of divorce are doomed to have serious problems throughout their lives. "The reality is that although a minority of children will indeed suffer negative consequences, the great majority do not" (quoted by Carroll, 2004, p. D1). Divorce is not solely to blame for unpleasant effects when they occur. Even if unhappily married parents stay together, their negative interactions are predictive of future marital problems for their offspring (Amato & Booth, 2001). Among the specific parental behaviors associated with a harmful effect on their children's future are expressing jealousy, being easily angered, making critical remarks, and refusing to talk to one another. Parental conflicts, whether or not they lead to divorce, are bad for their offspring (Doucet & Aseltine, 2003; Riggio, 2004). Anyone who considers marriage and plans to have children might do well to give more than a passing thought to the consequences of marital failure.

Despite the shattered hopes of living happily ever after and despite the emotional and often financial pain of a marital breakup, it must be noted that most divorced individuals, especially men, marry again. In fact, almost half of all marriages in the United States are remarriages for one or both partners (Koch, 1996). The desire for love and happiness in a relationship seems to have a greater influence on what people do than any negative experiences with a former spouse. As Samuel Johnson put it over a century ago, "Remarriage, sir, represents the triumph of hope over experience."

KEY POINTS

★ In the United States, about 50 percent of marriages end in divorce, but people do not believe that their own marriages will fail.

★ Most married couples have some degree of conflict and disagreement. When difficulties can be resolved constructively, the marriage is likely to endure. When the problems are made worse by destructive interactions, the marriage is likely to fail.

★ Constructive responses include attempts to understand the partner's point of view, not threatening his or her self-esteem; compromising; increasing the benefits and decreasing the costs of the marriage; being agreeable; and, above all, maximizing positive affect and minimizing negative affect.

★ If dissatisfaction becomes too great, individuals tend to respond either actively or passively in the hope of restoring the relationship or ending it.

★ Divorce is usually a painful process with overwhelmingly negative emotional and economic effects. The most vulnerable victims are the children of divorce. Despite what they have experienced, those who divorce are likely to marry again.

Interdependent Relationships with Family and Friends versus Loneliness

■ Close relationships are characterized by *interdependence*, in which two people influence each other's lives, share their thoughts and emotions, and engage in joint activities.

■ Evolutionary theory proposes that emotional bonding with other human beings increased the odds of survival and reproductive success. As a result of this selective process, modern humans and other primates are hard-wired to seek emotional closeness.

■ The first relationships are within the family, and we acquire an *attachment style* (a combination of level of *self-esteem* and degree of *interpersonal trust*) based on interactions with a caregiver. Children also learn what to expect from other people and how to interact with them as a result of their interactions with parents, siblings, grandparents, and other family members.

■ Friendships outside of the family begin in childhood and are initially based simply on such factors as common interests and other sources of positive affect, resulting in attraction. With increasing maturity, it becomes possible to form *close friendships* that involve spending time together, interacting in many different situations, providing mutual social support, and engaging in self-disclosure.

■ *Loneliness* occurs when a person has fewer and less satisfying relationships than he or she desires. The result is depression and anxiety. Dispositional loneliness originates in a combination of genetics, an insecure attachment style based on mother–child interactions, and the lack of early

social experiences with peers. A helpful intervention involves a combination of cognitive therapy and social skills training. Situational loneliness is brought about by external factors such as a move to a new location or social rejection and is based on factors unrelated to the behavior of the rejected individual.

Romantic Relationships and Falling in Love

■ One defining characteristic of romantic relationships is some degree of physical intimacy, ranging from holding hands to sexual interactions.

■ As is true for attraction and friendship, romantic attraction is influenced by factors such as physical proximity, appearance, and similarity. In addition, romance includes sexual attraction, the desire for total acceptance by the other person, and an acceptance of positive fantasies about such relationships.

■ The reproductive success of our ancient ancestors was enhanced by male attraction to young, fertile females; female attraction to males with resources; and bonding between mates and between parents and their offspring.

■ *Love* consists of multiple components. For example, *passionate love* is a sudden, overwhelming emotional response to another person. *Companionate love* resembles a close friendship that includes caring, mutual liking, and respect. Sternberg's *triangular model of love* includes these two components plus a third— *decision/commitment*—that is a cognitive decision to love and to be committed to a relationship.

■ Widespread changes in sexual attitudes and practices in the 1960s and 1970s have been

described as a "sexual revolution" that, among other changes, resulted in premarital sex becoming the norm. Because of reactions against feeling the pressure to conform to sexual pressures, the problem of unwanted pregnancies, and the fear of sexually transmitted diseases, there has been a partial backlash against the sexual revolution and toward safer and more discriminating sexual behavior.

Marriage: Happily Ever After—and Otherwise

■ In the United States, about 50 percent of marriages end in divorce, but people do not believe that their own marriages will fail.

■ Most married couples have some degree of conflict and disagreement. When difficulties can be resolved constructively, the marriage is likely to endure. When the problems are made worse by destructive interactions, the marriage is likely to fail.

■ Constructive responses include attempts to understand the partner's point of view, not threatening his or her self-esteem; compromising; increasing the benefits and decreasing the costs of the marriage; being agreeable; and, above all, maximizing positive affect and minimizing negative affect.

■ If dissatisfaction becomes too great, individuals tend to respond either actively or passively in the hope of restoring the relationship or ending it.

■ Divorce is usually a painful process with overwhelmingly negative emotional and economic effects. The most vulnerable victims are the children of divorce. Despite what they have experienced, those who divorce are likely to marry again.

In this chapter, you read about . . .	In other chapters, you will find related discussions of . . .
the association between self-esteem and attachment and the effects of love on self-esteem	self-esteem (Chapter 5)
similarity as a factor in friendships, romantic relationships, and marriage	similarity and attraction (Chapter 7)
love as emotional misattribution	misattribution and emotions (Chapter 3)
affect and relationships	affect and attraction (Chapter 7)
responses to conflicts between spouses	responses to conflict in organizations (Module B)

Thinking about Connections

1. Do you believe that your relationship with your parents has anything to do with the way you relate to other people? Did your mother and father make you feel good about yourself? Do you still feel the same way about yourself? In your childhood, were the adults in your life dependable? Did they keep their promises? Do you think of them as kind? How do you feel about most of the people you meet? Do you believe that the average person is more or less trustworthy?

2. Think of someone who is (or was) your closest friend. What was it about that person that first attracted you? Did proximity, similarity, positive affect, or appearance play a role in your getting to know one another? How do (or did) you spend your time together? Are there any parallels between your childhood friendships and your current friendships?

3. Think about yourself in a close romantic relationship—either in the past, in the present, or in the possible future. What is it about the other person that you find appealing? Do you think romance is something that develops gradually, or is it love at first sight? Is there any match between your own experience and such research topics as the role of misattributed emotions, evolution-related reproductive strategies, or expectancies based on stories about love you first heard in childhood? Write down the lyrics of a love song that you believe express a realistic perspective.

4. When you find yourself disagreeing with a romantic partner, a friend, or anyone else, what do you do and say? Is the interaction constructive, or do you just get mad and exchange insults? Have you ever ended a relationship with someone with whom you once felt very close? Why did it happen? Who initiated the breakup, and how was it done? Could either of you have handled the situation more constructively?

Ideas to Take with You—and Use! ARE YOU IN LOVE?

At some point in a relationship, individuals often ask themselves questions about their own feelings with respect to love, sex, and marriage. You might find it useful to consider what social psychologists have discovered about these topics.

Love or Just Arousal?

When you are near someone who appeals to you, it is easy to confuse a variety of arousal states with feelings of "love." Social psychologist Elaine Hatfield once suggested that people often fall in lust and interpret their feelings as love. More generally, research on emotional misattribution indicates that the physiological arousal associated with general excitement, fear, happiness, and even anger can be mislabeled in that way. If you are with someone nice and find yourself surging with emotion, don't automatically assume that you are madly in love. Take a deep breath and consider other possible explanations for your feelings.

Be Informed about Your Partner

You don't have to administer a questionnaire to every potential date, lover, or spouse, but try to learn as much as you can. Pay attention to personal details when you interact. If any particular topic is especially important to you (e.g., religion, politics, abortion rights, sex, vegetarianism, having children), it is essential to discover incompatibilities early in a relationship, no

matter how awkward it may be to ask about such matters.

Know What You (and the Other Person) Mean by "Love"

Look back in the chapter to remind yourself of the different kinds of love that have been identified and determine just what each of you has in mind when you say, "I love you." If the two of you have different definitions or if you differ with respect to your beliefs about true love, and so on, you both need to evaluate this information and to think about what incompatibility might mean to your relationship.

Think about You and Your Partner in Terms of Companionate Love

Set aside your feelings of passionate love for a moment and try to picture yourself with the other person engaging in friendly interactions having nothing to do with love or sex. Do you have enough interests in common that you would enjoy spending time together playing games, hiking, traveling, gardening, or whatever? If so, the two of you have a much better chance of building a lasting relationship than if your feelings consist primarily of passionate love.

K EY TERMS

FOR MORE INFORMATION

Goldenthal, P. (2002). *Why can't we get along? Healing adult sibling relationships.* New York: Wiley.
● Utilizing case histories from the author's clinical practice, this book provides practical tips to help adult siblings understand why they fight with each other and how to free themselves from past resentments.

Hendrick, S. S. (2004). *Understanding close relationships.* Boston: Allyn & Bacon.
● With a mixture of current research findings and a lively text, the author involves the reader with respect to topics such as loneliness, friendship, sexuality, and abuse. Personal assessments are scattered throughout the text to provide additional interest.

Karen, R. (1997). *Becoming attached: First relationships and how they shape our capacity to love.* New York: Oxford University Press.
● The author presents the complexities of attachment theory in interesting, accessible terms. Besides its utility for all of us who interacted with parents, this book is especially useful for people who currently are parents or who are planning to become parents.

Pines, A. M. (2000). *Falling in love: Why we choose the lovers we do.* New York: Routledge.
● A couples' counselor combines psychological research and advice to help the reader examine intimate relationships from both a personal and impersonal perspective.

9

SOCIAL INFLUENCE
Changing Others' Behavior

When I (Robert Baron) was a teenager, my parents were pretty relaxed: They didn't set many rules for me to follow because, I'd like to believe, they trusted me and felt I was a responsible person. But there was one rule they did state over and over: "Never drive with someone who is drunk." My father repeated this many times because he had a favorite cousin who was killed while driving with friends who were intoxicated. I rarely had reason to consider this rule, but one New Year's Eve, I did. I was at a party and everyone was drinking heavily. When the party finally broke up, my friend Stan offered me a ride home. It was snowing heavily and I knew I'd never get a city bus at that time of the morning, so I accepted. As we walked to the car with several other friends, I could see that Stan was very unsteady on his feet, so remembering my parents' repeated warnings, I said, "Hey Stan, I don't think you are in any condition to drive. I'll walk home." This brought hoots of derision from my friends, who told me, very directly, that I was acting like a "scared chicken"—Stan could handle it. Sad to relate, I gave in to the group pressure and got into the car with the others. As soon as we started out, I could see that Stan was truly drunk. He weaved all over the street and had major problems making turns. Soon, I was pretty scared, and the more scared I got, the more clearly I could hear my father's voice saying, "Don't risk your life—if someone is drunk, don't drive with them. Remember what happened to my cousin." It was snowing and sleeting hard, and we were still several miles from my house. But when Stan pulled up at a red light, I jumped out of the car, saying, "I'll walk from here. See you guys tomorrow." I arrived home soaked and freezing—but in one piece. As it turns out, Stan did drive off the road after a near accident and got stuck in a ditch. So although no one was hurt, Stan and my friends didn't get home any sooner than I did. Anyway, I've never regretted resisting social pressure from my friends that night; who knows—it might have saved my life.

Although this incident happened many years ago, it still clearly
reflects several major themes we consider in this chapter. First,
it illustrates the process of **social influence**—efforts by one or
more individuals to change the attitudes, beliefs, perceptions, or
behaviors of one or more others. Social influence is a common
feature of everyday life, and like the character in Figure 9.1, we
either try to influence others or are influenced by them many
times each day.

Because social psychologists have long recognized the
importance of social influence, it has been a central topic in our
field since its very beginnings. We have already considered some
of this work in Chapter 4, in which we examined the process of
persuasion. Here, we expand on that earlier discussion by exam-
ining many other aspects of social influence. First, we focus on the topic of **conformity**—
pressure to behave in ways that are viewed as acceptable or appropriate by our group or
society. As we'll soon discover, such pressures can be very hard to resist. I managed to
do so in the incident described above, but believe me—it wasn't easy! Next, we turn to
compliance—efforts to get others to say "yes" to various requests. Third, we examine
what is, in some ways, the most intriguing form of social influence—influence that
occurs when other persons are not present and are not making any direct attempts to
affect our behavior. For instance, in the opening story, it was my memories of my parents' warnings that caused me to get out of Stan's car; my mother and father weren't
there to enforce this rule or urge me to follow it. Recent findings indicate that thoughts
of other persons, or simply being reminded of them or our relationships with them, are
often sufficient to change our current behavior (e.g., Fitzsimons & Bargh, 2003). We refer
to such effects as *symbolic social influence* to reflect the fact that it results from our mental representations of other persons rather than their actual presence or overt actions.
After considering this indirect form of social influence, we'll examine another kind that
is, in some respects, its direct opposite: **obedience**—social influence in which one person simply orders one or more others to do what they want. Finally, we briefly consider
forms of social influence that occur in many *real-life settings,* especially workplaces (e.g.,
Yukl, Kim, & Chavez, 1999).

Conformity: Group Influence in Action

Have you ever found yourself in a situation in which you felt that you stuck out like
the famous sore thumb? If so, you have already had direct experience with pressures
toward *conformity.* In such situations, you probably experienced a strong desire to get
back into line—to fit in with the other people around you. Such pressures toward conformity stem from the fact that in many contexts, there are explicit or unspoken rules

social influence
Efforts by one or more
individuals to change the
attitudes, beliefs, perceptions, or behaviors of one
or more others.

conformity
A type of social influence
in which individuals
change their attitudes or
behavior in order to
adhere to existing social
norms.

compliance
A form of social influence
involving direct requests
from one person to
another.

obedience
A form of social influence
in which one person sim-
ply orders one or more
others to perform some
action(s), and the persons
then comply.

indicating how we should or ought to behave. These rules are known as **social norms,** and they often exert powerful effects on our behavior. (Actually, there are several kinds of social norms, but here, we are discussing primarily one important type, known as *injunctive norms*—the kind that tells us what we *should* do in a given situation. We consider other types of social norms in later sections; Kallgren, Reno, & Cialdini, 2000.)

In some instances, social norms are detailed and are stated explicitly. For instance, governments generally function through written constitutions and laws; athletic contests are usually regulated by written rules; and signs in many public places (e.g., along highways, in parks, at airports) describe expected behavior in considerable detail (e.g., *Speed Limit: 55; No Swimming; No Parking; Keep Off the Grass*).

In contrast, other norms are unspoken or implicit, and, in fact, may have developed in a totally informal manner. For instance, when people work together on a task, they gradually converge in their perceptions of how much time has passed—even though they never set out to influence one another in this way and may not intend to do so (Conway, 2004). Similarly, most of us obey such unwritten rules as "Don't stare at strangers" and "Don't arrive at parties exactly on time." We are often influenced by current and rapidly changing standards of dress, speech, and grooming. Regardless of whether social norms are explicit or implicit, though, one fact is clear: Most people obey them most of the time. For instance, few persons visit restaurants without leaving a tip for the server, and virtually everyone, regardless of personal political beliefs, stands when the national anthem of their country is played at sports events or other public gatherings (see Figure 9.2).

At first glance, this strong tendency toward conformity—toward going along with society's or the group's expectations about how we should behave in various situations—may strike you as objectionable. After all, it does place restrictions on personal freedom. Actually, though, there is a strong basis for so much conformity: Without it, we would quickly find ourselves facing social chaos. Imagine what would happen outside movie theaters, stadiums, or at supermarket checkout counters if people did *not* obey the norm "Form a line and wait your turn." And consider the danger to both

social norms
Rules indicating how individuals are expected to behave in specific situations.

Figure 9.2 ■ Social Norms: A Powerful Influence on Our Behavior
Social norms tell us what we should do (or not do) in a given situation, and most people obey them most of the time.

drivers and pedestrians if there were not clear and widely followed traffic regulations. In many situations, then, conformity serves a very useful function.

Given that strong pressures toward conformity exist in many social settings, it is surprising to learn that conformity, as a social process, received relatively little attention in social psychology until the 1950s. At that time, Solomon Asch (1951), whose research on impression formation we considered in Chapter 3, carried out a series of experiments on conformity that yielded dramatic results. Because Asch's research had a strong influence on later studies of this aspect of social influence, it's worth a close look here.

Asch's Research on Conformity: Social Pressure—The Irresistible Force?

Suppose that just before an important math exam, you discover that your answer to a homework problem—a problem of the type that will be on the test—is different than that obtained by one of your friends. How would you react? Probably with mild concern. Now imagine that you learn that a second person's answer, too, is different than yours. To make matters worse, this other answer agrees with the one reported by the first person. How would you feel now? The chances are good that your anxiety would be considerable. Next, you discover that a third person agrees with the other two. At this point, you know that you are in big trouble. Which answer should you accept? Yours or the one obtained by your three friends? The exam is about to start, so you have to decide quickly.

Life is filled with such dilemmas—instances in which we discover that our own judgments, actions, or conclusions are different than those reached by other persons. What do we do in such situations? Important insights into our behavior were provided by studies conducted by Solomon Asch (1951, 1955), research that is viewed as a true "classic" in social psychology.

In his research, Asch asked participants to respond to a series of simple perceptual problems such as the one in Figure 9.3. On each problem, they indicated which

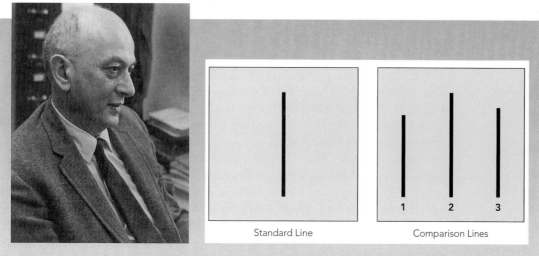

Standard Line   Comparison Lines

Figure 9.3 ■ Asch's Line Judgment Task
Participants in Asch's research were asked to report their judgments on problems such as this one. Their task was to indicate which of the comparison lines (1, 2, or 3) best matched the standard line in length. To study conformity, Asch had participants make these judgments out loud, only after hearing the answers of several other people—all of whom were Asch's assistants. On certain critical trials, the assistants all gave wrong answers. These wrong answers exposed participants to strong pressures to conform.

of three comparison lines matched a standard line in length. Several other persons (usually six to eight) were also present during the session, but unknown to the real participant, all were assistants of the experimenter. On certain occasions known as *critical trials* (twelve out of the eighteen problems), the accomplices offered answers that were clearly wrong: They unanimously chose the wrong line as a match for the standard line. Moreover, they stated their answers *before* the real participants responded. Thus, on these critical trials, the persons in Asch's study faced precisely the type of dilemma just described. Should they go along with the other individuals present or stick to their own judgments? Results were clear: A large majority of the persons in Asch's research chose conformity. Across several different studies, fully 76 percent of those tested went along with the group's false answers at least once; and overall, they voiced agreement with these errors 37 percent of the time. In contrast, only 5 percent of the participants in a control group, who responded to the same problems alone, made such errors.

Of course, there were large individual differences in this respect. Almost 25 percent of the participants *never* yielded to the group pressure. At the other extreme, some persons went along with the majority nearly all the time. When Asch questioned them, some of these persons stated, "I am wrong; they are right." They had little confidence in their own judgments. Others, however, said they felt that the other persons present were suffering from an optical illusion or were merely sheep following the responses of the first person. Yet, when it was their turn, these people, too, went along with the group.

In further studies, Asch (1956) investigated the effects of shattering the group's unanimity by having one of the accomplices break with the others. In one study, this person gave the correct answer, becoming an "ally" of the real participant; in another study, this person chose an answer in between the one given by the group and the correct one; and in a third, he chose the answer that was even more incorrect than that chosen by the majority. In the latter two conditions, in other words, he broke from the group but still disagreed with the real participants. Results indicated that conformity was reduced under all three conditions. However, somewhat surprisingly, this reduction was greatest when the dissenting assistant expressed views even more extreme (and wrong) than the majority. Together, these findings suggest that it is the unanimity of the group that is crucial; once it is broken, no matter how, resisting group pressure becomes much easier.

There's one more aspect of Asch's research that it is important to mention. In later studies, he repeated his basic procedure but with one important change: Instead of stating their answers out loud, participants wrote them down on a piece of paper. As you might guess, conformity dropped sharply because there was no way for the real participants to know what the other persons were doing. This finding points to the importance of distinguishing between *public conformity*—doing or saying what others around us say or do—and *private acceptance*—actually coming to feel or think as others do. Often, it appears, we follow social norms overtly but don't actually change our private views (Maas & Clark, 1984). This distinction between public conformity and private acceptance is an important one, and we refer to it at several points in this book.

Asch's research was the catalyst for much activity in social psychology, as many other researchers sought to investigate the nature of conformity to identify factors that influence it and to establish its limits (e.g., Crutchfield, 1955; Deutsch & Gerard, 1955). Indeed, such research is continuing today, and is still adding to our understanding of this crucial form of social influence (e.g., R. S. Baron, Vandello, & Brunsman, 1996; Bond & Smith, 1996; Buehler & Griffin, 1994).

KEY POINTS

★ *Social influence*—efforts by one or more persons to change the attitudes or behavior of one or more others—is a common part of life.

★ Most people behave in accordance with *social norms* most of the time; in other words, they show strong tendencies toward *conformity*.

★ Conformity was first systematically studied by Solomon Asch, whose classic research indicated that many persons will yield to social pressure from a unanimous group.

Factors Affecting Conformity: Variables That Determine the Extent to Which We "Go Along"

Asch's research demonstrated the existence of powerful pressures toward conformity, but even a moment's reflection suggests that conformity does not occur to the same degree in all settings. For instance, short hair (for men) and boots with pointy toes (for women) are "in" right now, with the result that many people experience strong pressures to adopt these fashions. Yet, despite this fact, many do not. Why? In other words, what factors determine the extent to which individuals yield to conformity pressure or resist it? Research findings suggest that many factors play a role; here, we examine the ones that appear to be most important.

Cohesiveness and Conformity: Being Influenced by Those We Like

As stated, short hair is "in" right now, especially for men. But suppose that suddenly, some of the most popular people in your school or neighborhood let their hair grow until it was shoulder length. Would their adoption of this new style lead to its rapid spread? Perhaps; after all, they are popular and it is often the popular people who set the trends. But now suppose that, instead, the only persons who adopted this style were true "losers"—people who are viewed as weird and unpopular. Would *their* adoption of the new fashion lead to its rapid spread? Probably not; after all, who wants to be like them?

This example illustrates one factor that plays an important role where conformity is concerned: **Cohesiveness** refers to all of the factors that bind group members together into a coherent social entity. When cohesiveness is high—that is, when we like and admire some group of persons and feel strong ties to them—pressures toward conformity are magnified. After all, we know that one way of gaining the acceptance of such persons is to be like them in various ways. On the other hand, when cohesiveness is low, pressures toward conformity, too, are low; why should we change our behavior to be like other people we don't especially like or admire? Research findings indicate that cohesiveness exerts strong effects on conformity (Crandall, 1988; Latane & L'Herrou, 1996); cohesiveness, therefore, is one important determinant of the extent to which we yield to this type of social pressure.

Conformity and Group Size: Why More Is Better with Respect to Social Pressure

A second factor that exerts important effects on the tendency to conform is the size of the influencing group. Asch (1956) and other early researchers (e.g., Gerard, Wilhelmy, & Conolley, 1968) found that conformity increases with group size but only up to about

cohesiveness
All of the factors that bind group members together into a coherent social entity.

three members; beyond that point, it appears to level off or even decrease. However, more recent research failed to confirm these early findings (e.g., Bond & Smith, 1996). Instead, these later studies found that conformity tended to increase with group size of up to eight group members and beyond. So, it appears that the larger the group, the greater our tendency to go along with it, even if this means behaving differently than we'd really prefer.

■ Descriptive and Injunctive Social Norms: How Norms Affect Behavior

Social norms, we have already seen, can be formal or informal in nature—as different as rules printed on large signs and informal guidelines such as "Don't leave your shopping cart in the middle of a parking spot outside a supermarket." This is not the only way in which norms differ, however. Another important distinction is that between **descriptive norms** and **injunctive norms** (e.g., Cialdini, Kallgren, & Reno, 1991; Reno, Cialdini, & Kallgren, 1993). Descriptive norms are ones that simply describe what most people do in a given situation. They influence behavior by informing us about what is generally seen as effective or adaptive in that situation. In contrast, injunctive norms specify what *ought* to be done—what is approved or disapproved behavior in a given situation. Both kinds of norms can exert strong effects on our behavior (e.g., Brown, 1998). However, Cialdini and his colleagues believe that in certain situations—especially ones in which antisocial behavior (behavior not approved of by a given group or society) is likely to occur—injunctive norms may exert somewhat stronger effects. This is true for two reasons. First, such norms tend to shift attention away from *how* people are acting in particular situation (littering) to how they *should be* behaving (putting trash into containers). Second, such norms may activate the social motive to do what's right in a given situation, regardless of what others have done or are doing.

When, precisely, do injunctive norms influence behavior? It is clear that injunctive norms don't always produce such effects. For instance, although there is an injunctive norm stating, "Clean up after your dog," and many towns and cities have laws requiring such behavior, many dog owners choose to look the other way when their pets obey the call of nature. Why do people sometimes disobey or ignore even strong injunctive norms? One answer is provided by **normative focus theory** (e.g., Cialdini, Kahlgren, & Reno, 1991). This theory suggests that norms will influence behavior only to the extent that they are *salient* (i.e., relevant, significant) to the persons involved at the time the behavior occurs. In other words, people will obey injunctive norms only when they think about them and see them as relevant to their own actions. This prediction has been verified in many different studies (e.g., Kallgren, Reno, & Cialdini, 2000). For instance, in an ingenious study on this issue conducted by Reno, Cialdini, and Kallgren (1993), individuals crossing a parking lot encountered an accomplice walking toward them. In the experimental condition of most interest here, the accomplice stopped to pick up a fast-food bag that had been dropped by someone else. (In a control condition, the accomplice did not engage in this behavior.) The researchers reasoned that seeing another person actually pick litter up from the ground would remind participants of society's disapproval of littering, and so make this norm very salient to them. To test the effects of this norm on their later behavior, Reno et al. (1993) placed handbills on the windshields of the participants' cars and observed what they did when they found them there. As predicted, those who had seen another person pick up the fast-food bag significantly were less likely to toss the handbills on the ground than were those who had not seen this action, and so had not been reminded of the injunctive norm against littering.

The fact that we tend to follow injunctive norms only to the degree that they are salient to us raises an interesting point: Many persons are members of a number of different groups, and some of these groups may have opposing norms. For instance, should women who are executives behave in ways that are consistent with their gender (one

descriptive norms
Norms that simply indicate what most people do in a given situation.

injunctive norms
Norms specifying what *ought* to be done—what is approved or disapproved behavior in a given situation.

normative focus theory
A theory suggesting that norms will influence behavior only to the extent that they are focal for the persons involved at the time the behavior occurs.

Chapter 9 / Social Influence

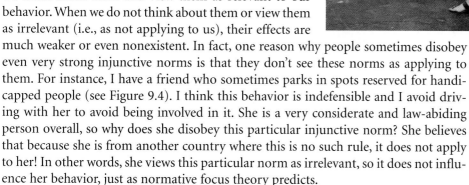

Figure 9.4 ■ Social Norms: They Affect Our Behavior Only When They Are Salient to Us
Why do some people park in handicapped parking spots, even though they are not physically challenged? While there may be many reasons for such socially objectionable behavior, one factor may be that such persons do not view this rule (norm) as applying to them; they feel that, somehow, they are exempt and that the rule is irrelevant to them.

major group to which they belong) or with their role as someone in authority? We examine this issue in detail in Chapter 5.

These findings and those of related studies (e.g., Kallgren, Reno, & Cialdini, 2000) suggest that norms influence our actions primarily when they are made salient—when we think about them and view them as relevant to our behavior. When we do not think about them or view them as irrelevant (i.e., as not applying to us), their effects are much weaker or even nonexistent. In fact, one reason why people sometimes disobey even very strong injunctive norms is that they don't see these norms as applying to them. For instance, I have a friend who sometimes parks in spots reserved for handicapped people (see Figure 9.4). I think this behavior is indefensible and I avoid driving with her to avoid being involved in it. She is a very considerate and law-abiding person overall, so why does she disobey this particular injunctive norm? She believes that because she is from another country where this is no such rule, it does not apply to her! In other words, she views this particular norm as irrelevant, so it does not influence her behavior, just as normative focus theory predicts.

Situational Norms: Automaticity in Normative Behavior

When you enter a museum or hospital, do you lower the volume of your voice? And when you are in a sports stadium, do you raise it? If so, you are showing adherence to what social psychologists describe as *situational norms*—norms that guide behavior in a certain situation or environment (e.g., Cialdini & Trost, 1998). But do you have to be aware of these norms—or any others—for them to influence your behavior? Recent findings indicate that such awareness is not necessary. On the contrary, norms can be activated in an automatic manner without your consciously thinking of them; and when they are, they can still strongly affect your overt actions. A very clear illustration of such effects, and of the powerful effects of situational norms, is provided by research conducted by Aarts and Dijksterhuis (2003). They first asked participants to look at photographs of a library or an empty railway station. Some of the people who saw the photo of the library were told that they would later be visiting this location; others were not given this information. Then, they were instructed to read out loud ten words presented on a computer screen. The volume of their voices was measured as they performed this task. The researchers predicted that when individuals expected to visit the library, the situational norm of being quiet would be activated and that, as a result, they would read the words less loudly. They also predicted that such effects would not occur when the individuals did not expect to visit the library or when they saw a photo of the railway station—a place in which the "Be quiet" norm does not apply. As

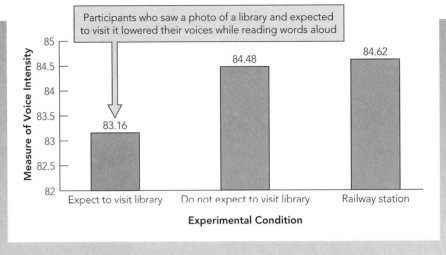

Figure 9.5 ■ The Effects of Situational Norms on Behavior
Participants who saw a photo of a library and expected to visit this location lowered the intensity of their voices relative to persons who saw a photo of a library but did not expect to visit it, or those who saw a photo of a railway station. This illustrates the effects of situational norms ("Be quiet in libraries") on overt behavior. (*Source: Based on data from Aarts & Dijksterhuis, 2003.*)

you can see from Figure 9.5, this is precisely what was found: Participants lowered the volume of their voices in the expect-to-visit library condition relative to the other two conditions.

In additional studies, Aarts and Dijksterhuis (2003) found similar effects with respect to acting in a polite manner in a fancy restaurant, thus indicating that situational norms operate in many different locations, and that they can automatically influence our behavior in these settings. In fact, participants for whom this norm had been activated actually ate a biscuit more neatly than those for whom this norm had not been primed! Overall, then, two facts seem clear: (1) Situational norms that tell us how to behave in a given environment or location often strongly affect our behavior, and (2) such norms—like other norms—can exert such effects in a relatively automatic manner, even if we do not consciously recognize their impact. In other words, social influence is indeed a powerful and pervasive aspect of daily life—perhaps stronger and more widespread than you would ever guess.

The Bases of Conformity: Why We Often Choose to "Go Along"

As just noted, several factors determine whether and to what extent conformity occurs. Yet, this does not alter the essential point: Conformity is a basic fact of social life. Most people conform to the norms of their groups or societies much, if not most, of the time. Why is this so? Why do people often choose to go along with these social rules or expectations instead of resisting them? The answer seems to involve two powerful motives possessed by all human beings: the desire to be liked or accepted by others and the desire to be right—to have an accurate understanding of the social world (Deutsch & Gerard, 1955; Insko, 1985)—plus cognitive processes that lead us to view conformity as fully justified after it has occurred (e.g., Buehler & Griffin, 1994).

Normative Social Influence: The Desire to Be Liked

How can we get others to like us? This is one of the eternal puzzles of social life. As we saw in Chapters 3 and 7, many tactics can prove effective in this regard. One of the most successful of these tactics is to appear to be as similar to others as possible. From our earliest days, we learn that agreeing with the persons around us, and behaving as they do, causes them to like us. Parents, teachers, friends, and others often heap praise and approval on us for showing such similarity (see the discussion of attitude formation in Chapter 4). One important reason we conform, therefore, is this: We have learned that doing so can help us win the approval and acceptance we crave. This source of conformity is known as **normative social influence,** because it involves altering our behavior to meet others' expectations. (For an intriguing illustration of normative social influence in operation, please see the **Beyond the Headlines** section on page 348.)

The Desire to Be Right: Informational Social Influence

If you want to know your weight, you can step onto a scale. If you want to know the dimensions of a room, you can measure them directly. But how can you establish the accuracy of your own political or social views or decide which hairstyle suits you best? There are no simple physical tests or measuring devices for answering these questions. Yet we want to be correct about such matters, too. The solution to this dilemma is obvious: To answer such questions, we refer to other people. We use *their* opinions and actions as guides for our own. Such reliance on others, in turn, is often a powerful source of the tendency to conform. Other people's actions and opinions define social reality for us, and we use these as a guide for our own actions and opinions. This basis for conformity is known as **informational social influence,** because it is based on our tendency to depend on others as a source of information about many aspects of the social world.

Research evidence suggests that because our motivation to be correct or accurate is very strong, informational social influence is a very powerful source of conformity. However, as you might expect, such motivation is more likely to be present in situations in which we are highly uncertain about what is "correct" or "accurate" than in situations in which we have more confidence in our own ability to make such decisions. That this is so is clearly illustrated by the results of a study conducted by Robert S. Baron, Vandello, and Brunsman (1996). In this investigation, the researchers used an ingenious modification of the Asch line-drawing task. They showed participants a drawing of a person and then asked them to identify this person from among several others in a kind of simulated eyewitness line-up. In one condition, the drawing was shown for only 0.5 seconds; this made the identification task difficult to perform. In another condition, it was shown for 5.0 seconds, and the task was much easier. Another aspect of the study involved the importance of making an accurate decision. Half of the participants were told that the study was only preliminary in nature, so results were not very important. The others were told that results were very important to the researchers.

To measure conformity, participants were exposed to the judgments of two assistants who identified the *wrong* person before making their own choice in the simulated line-up. The overall prediction was that when the study was described as being very important, participants would be more likely to conform when the task was difficult (when they saw the drawings for only 0.5 seconds) than when the task was easy (when they saw the photos for 5.0 seconds). This is because under the former conditions, participants would be uncertain of their own decisions and would rely on the judgments of the assistants. When the study was described as being relatively unimportant, however, task difficulty wouldn't matter: Conformity would be the same in

normative social influence Social influence based on the desire to be liked or accepted by other persons.

informational social influence Social influence based on the desire to be correct (i.e., to possess accurate perceptions of the social world).

The Rocky Road to Social Acceptance?

Why On Earth Do So Many People Collect Big Rocks?

Valley Springs, CA—Carol Williams doesn't see rocks the way most people do. To Ms. Williams, rocks have beauty, rocks have soul, rocks have ... price tags. ... Wearing black-denim jeans and a white hard hat, Ms. Williams prowls through a boulder-strewn quarry here in Calaveras County, ignoring a sign warning that she is in a blasting area. She sighs, touching a large gray boulder. ... The rock, she declares, has "character," and she tags it with a strip of blue tape for future pickup. In time, the boulder may fetch hundreds or even thousands of dollars on the rock market. ... Rocks are hot, and Ms. Williams sells them. ... Collectors are planting boulders in gardens, on lawns, and even in living rooms. ... Among the most avid collectors ... price doesn't seem to be an obstacle. One collector, Ms. Turos, says that she has paid more than $50,000 for her collection, which includes an 8,000 pound boulder near her front door. ... "My house is a boulder mecca," she says proudly. To Ms. Williams, rocks are more than just a business: they have a mystical significance. She names her favorites— "Whale's Tail," "the Wave" and "Seven Sisters ...." Though only 52, she already has selected the boulder she wants as her gravestone. She recently insisted that three flat boulders retrieved together from a riverbed sell only as a family. After turning down offers for them as individuals, she found a buyer to take the batch. "We wanted only one or two, but her enthusiasm was really contagious," says Nancy Parker, the buyer, who ended up paying several thousand dollars for the "family" and several unrelated boulders. ...

Rocks for sale? Customers willing to pay hundreds or even thousands of dollars for boulders—the kind people used to pay to have removed from their property? What's going on here? Although we can't say for sure, it seems likely that *normative social influence* is playing a role, just as it does in many other fashions and trends. Rocks have always been around—and available. But now, because having one or more in the front yard is viewed as showing "good taste," they are really hot, at least in some areas of the United States (see Figure 9.6). In the same way that people buy lawn sculptures, certain kinds of garden furniture, and even special kinds of barbecue grills to impress their neighbors, they now buy boulders: After all, if rocks are "in," one can't afford to be left behind! So Americans are now buying boulders, because owning—and displaying— them is the "in" thing to do, and they want to be liked, admired, and accepted by their friends and neighbors. In other words, viewed from the perspective of social psychology, this recent fad is not at all puzzling: It is just another illustration of the fact that most of us realize that being different is uncomfortable, while doing as other people do not only feels good, it also wins their approval and liking. So, three cheers for rocks— if that's what it takes to be "with it," who can resist?

Figure 9.6 ■ Normative Social Influence at Work
Why would people pay large amounts of money for boulders to place outside their houses? One possibility involves *normative social influence:* They want to do what their friends and neighbors are doing and so gain their approval.

both conditions. Results offered clear support for these predictions. These findings suggest that our desire to be correct or accurate can be a strong source of conformity, but primarily when we are uncertain about what is correct or accurate in a given situation.

How powerful are the effects of social influence when we are uncertain about what is correct and what is not? Research findings suggest a chilling answer: extremely powerful. For instance, in one study with disturbing results (Apanovitch, Hobfoll, & Salovey, 2002), participants viewed a video showing a gang rape of a woman by several men. After watching this tape, participants discussed it and then rated the victim's pain, their empathy for her, and the extent to which the men were responsible for the rape. Unknown to the participants, one of the people present was an assistant of the experimenter who, as in Asch's research, expressed prearranged opinions. This person indicated that he either held the men responsible for the rape, held the woman responsible for the rape, or offered no clear opinion. Even though the participants then made their judgments privately, they were strongly influenced by the assistant's behavior, viewing the men as more responsible when the assistant expressed this view, than when he blamed the woman for the rape (see Figure 9.7). Why was this so? Rape, after all, is an atrocious form of behavior that everyone finds disturbing, so how could people's judgments about it be influenced so readily? The answer seems to be that the participants were uncertain about how they should react in this situation, which was one with which they were very unfamiliar, and as a result, they were highly susceptible to influence from the assistant. In other words, the results of this study provide a strong and disturbing illustration of the powerful impact social influence can have on our perceptions, behavior, and judgments.

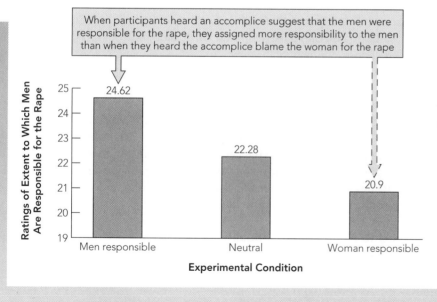

When participants heard an accomplice suggest that the men were responsible for the rape, they assigned more responsibility to the men than when they heard the accomplice blame the woman for the rape

Figure 9.7 ■ **The Powerful Effects of Social Influence**
When participants who had seen a videotape of a gang rape heard an accomplice blame the men for this appalling event, they assigned more responsibility to the men than when they heard the accomplice blame the woman for this assault, or when the accomplice voiced no clear opinion. (*Source: Based on data from Apanovitch, Hobfoll, & Salovey, 2002.*)

KEY POINTS

★ Many factors determine whether, and to what extent, conformity occurs. These include *cohesiveness*—degree of attraction felt by an individual toward some group, group size, and type of social norm operating in that situation—*descriptive* or *injunctive*.

★ Norms tend to influence our behavior primarily when they are relevant to us.

★ However, situational norms, like other norms, can influence our behavior in an automatic manner, even when we are not consciously aware of them.

★ Two important motives underlie our tendency to conform: the desire to be liked by others and the desire to be right or accurate. These two motives are reflected in two distinct types of *social influence: normative* and *informational social influence.*

★ The effects of *social influence* are powerful and pervasive but tend to be magnified in situations in which we are uncertain about our own judgments or what is correct.

Resisting Pressures to Conform: Why, Sometimes, We Choose *Not* to "Go Along"

Having read our discussion of normative and informational social influence, you may now have the distinct impression that pressures toward conformity are so strong that they are all but impossible to resist. If so, take heart. In many cases, individuals—or groups of individuals—*do* resist. This was certainly true in Asch's research, in which most of the participants yielded to social pressure, but *only part of the time*. On many occasions, they stuck to their guns even in the face of a unanimous majority that disagreed with them. If you want other illustrations of resistance to conformity pressures, just look around: You will find that while most persons adhere to social norms, most of the time, some do not. And most people do not go along with all social norms; rather, they pick and choose, conforming to most norms but rejecting at least a few (see Figure 9.8). For instance, do you know any men who have very long hair, even though this is no longer in style? Similarly, do you have any friends who hold very unpopular political or social views, and continue to do so despite strong pressure to conform? As these examples suggest, conformity pressures are *not* irresistible. What accounts for our ability to resist them? Although many factors appear to be important (e.g., Burger, 1992), two seem to be most important: (1) the need to maintain our individuality and (2) the need to maintain control over our own lives. (In Chapter 4, we examined a third factor—our tendency to restore our personal freedom by doing exactly the opposite of what someone else is trying to get us to do [reactance].)

The Need to Maintain Individuality, Culture, and Resistance to Conformity

The need to maintain our individuality, in particular, appears to be a powerful one. Yes, we want to be like others but not, it seems, to the extent that we lose our personal identity. In other words, along with needs to be right and to be liked, most of us possess a desire for **individuation**—for being distinguishable from others in some respects (e.g., Maslach, Santee, & Wade, 1987). In general, we want to be like others, especially others we like or respect, but we don't want to be *exactly* like these persons, because that would involve giving up our individuality.

individuation
The need to be distinguishable from others in some respects.

Figure 9.8 ■ Norms: Rules Made to Be Broken?
Although most people conform to most social norms most of
the time, there are many exceptions to this general rule.

If this is true, then an interesting prediction relating to the impact of culture on conformity—and on the ability to resist it—follows logically: The tendency to conform will be lower in cultures that emphasize individuality (individualistic cultures) than in those that emphasize being part of the group (collectivist cultures). Research by Bond and Smith (1996) examined this hypothesis by comparing conformity in seventeen different countries. They examined the results of 133 past studies that used the Asch line-judging task to measure conformity. Among these studies, they identified ones conducted in countries with collectivist cultures (e.g., countries in Africa and Asia) and in countries with individualistic cultures (e.g., countries in North America and Western Europe). Then, they compared the amount of conformity shown in these two groups of countries. Results were clear: More conformity did indeed occur in the countries with collectivistic cultures, where the motive to maintain one's individuality was expected to be lower, and this was true regardless of the size of the influencing group. Similar results have been obtained in other studies (e.g., Hamilton & Sanders, 1995), so it appears that the need for individuation varies greatly across different cultures and that these differences, in turn, influence the tendency to conform.

■ The Desire for Personal Control

Another reason why individuals often choose to resist group pressure involves their desire to maintain control over the events in their lives (e.g., Daubman, 1993). Most persons want to believe that they can determine what happens to them, and yielding to social pressure sometimes runs counter to this desire. After all, going along with a group implies behaving in ways one might not ordinarily choose, and can be viewed as a restriction of personal freedom. The results of many studies suggest that the stronger individuals' need for personal control, the less likely they are to yield to social pressure, so this factor, too, appears to be an important one where resisting conformity is concerned.

In sum, two motives—the desire to retain our individuality and the desire to retain control over our own lives—serve to counter our desires to be liked and to be accurate, and so reduce conformity. Whether we conform in a given situation, then, depends on the relative strength of these various motives and the complex interplay between them. Once again, therefore, we come face to face with the fact that trying to understand the roots of social behavior is often as complex as it is fascinating.

People Who Cannot Conform

So far in this discussion, we have been focusing on people who can conform but choose not to do so. There are also many persons who cannot conform for physical, legal, or psychological reasons. For instance, consider persons who are physically challenged. Though they can lead rich, full lives and participate in many activities that able-bodied persons enjoy, they cannot adhere to some social norms because of physical limitations. For instance, some cannot stand when the national anthem is played, and others cannot adhere to accepted styles of dress for similar reasons.

Homosexuals, too, face difficulties in adhering to social norms. Many persons in this group participate in stable, long-term relationships with a partner and would like to conform to the social norm stating that those who love each other may get married. Until recently, however, this was not possible in most countries. Even now, marriage between homosexuals of both genders is fully legal in only one country—the Netherlands. Although same-sex marriage is a complex issue, with some persons raising moral, religious, and ethical concerns about it, and is outside the realm of science, it is important to note that many people find it difficult or impossible to adhere to existing social norms even when they wish to, and that as a result, they face difficulties and conflicts unfamiliar to heterosexuals. For example, many same-sex couples participate in stable, long-term relationships and would like to adhere to the same social norms as heterosexuals, such as being entitled to marry, share benefits, and have families. Now, this is becoming possible (see Figure 9.9). In the past few years, several states in the United States (e.g., Massachusetts); several nations, such as the Netherlands and Belgium; and three provinces in Canada have made same-sex marriage legal. As a result, marriage licenses are being granted to same-sex couples, and some famous weddings have taken place—for instance, that of media-celebrities including that of Rosie O'Donnell (February 26, 2004). But stay tuned: Many people object to these changes on religious or moral grounds, so it is not entirely clear what the outcome will be. (Do men and women differ in the tendency to conform? For a discussion of this issue, see the **Making Sense of Common Sense** section on the next page.)

Figure 9.9 ■ **When People Can't Obey Social Norms**
Sometimes, individuals want to conform to social norms but simply can't. For instance, many homosexual couples want to marry—a culturally approved state for adults—but cannot because laws in many places restrict marriage to heterosexual couples. Although marriage between people of the same sex is now permitted in some locations, this is still the exception rather than the rule.

Do Women and Men Differ in the Tendency to Conform?

Consider the following statement by Queen Victoria of England, one of the most powerful rulers in the history of the world: *"We women are not made for governing—and if we are good women, we must dislike these masculine occupations. . . ."* (Letter of February 3, 1852). This and many similar quotations suggest that women do not like to be in charge—they would prefer to follow the lead of others. And that idea, in turn, suggests that women may be more susceptible to conformity pressures than men. As informal evidence for this view, many people who accept it point to the fact that, in general, women seem to be more likely than men to follow changes in fashion with respect to clothing and personal grooming. But does this mean that they are really more likely to conform than men? Early studies on conformity (e.g., Crutchfield, 1955) seemed to suggest that they are. The results of these experiments indicated that women showed a greater tendency to yield to social pressure than did men. More recent research, however, points to very different conclusions.

For instance, Eagly and Carli (1981) conducted a meta-analysis of 145 different studies in which more than twenty thousand people participated. Results indicated the existence of a very small difference between men and women, with women being slightly more accepting of social influence than were men. So, if such gender differences existed, they were much smaller than common sense suggested.

But that's not the end of the story. Additional research has further clarified when and why these small differences may exist—if they exist at all. With respect to

"when," it appears that both genders are more easily influenced when they are uncertain about how to behave or about the correctness of their judgments. And careful examination of many studies on conformity indicates that the situations and materials used were ones more familiar to men than to women. The result? Men were more certain about how to behave and so showed less conformity. Direct evidence for this reasoning was obtained by Sistrunk and McDavid (1971) who found that when males and females were equally familiar with the situations or materials employed, differences between them, in terms of conformity, disappeared.

Turning to "why" any gender differences in conformity might exist, the answer seems to involve differences in status between men and women. In the past—and even to some extent today—men tended to hold higher status jobs and positions in many societies than did women. And there was a relationship between status and susceptibility to social influence: Lower status led to greater tendencies to conform (Eagly, 1987). So, when and if gender differences in conformity continue to exist, they seem to be linked to social factors such as differences in status and gender roles, not to any basic, "built-in" differences between the two genders.

In sum, contrary to what common sense suggests, women are *not* much more accepting of social influence than are men. On the contrary, any differences between the two genders that do exist are very small. And when such factors as confidence in one's own judgments (as determined by familiarity with the situation) and social status are considered, these differences totally disappear. Once again, therefore, we see how the careful, scientific methods adopted by social psychologists helps us to clarify and refine "common sense" views about important social issues.

Minority Influence: Does the Majority Always Rule?

As just noted, individuals can, and often do, resist group pressure. Lone dissenters or small minorities can dig in their heels and refuse to go along. Yet there is more going on in such situations than simply resistance; in addition, there are instances in which such persons—*minorities* within their groups—actually turn the tables on the majority and *exert* rather than merely *receive* social influence. History provides many examples of such events. Giants of science, such as Galileo, Pasteur, and Freud, faced virtually unanimous majorities that initially rejected their views. Yet, over time, these famous persons overcame such resistance and won widespread acceptance of their theories.

Figure 9.10 ■ How Minorities Sometimes Influence Majorities
Vocal and deeply committed minorities can cause majorities to examine their views more carefully. In other words, minorities can encourage majorities to engage in more systematic processing of social information. This, in turn, can lead at least some members of the majority to change their views.

More recent examples of minorities influencing majorities are provided by the successes of environmentalists. Initially such persons were viewed as wild-eyed radicals with strange ideas. Gradually, however, they succeeded in changing the attitudes of the majority so that today, many of their views are widely accepted. And, of course, the framers of the U.S. Constitution were so concerned about protecting the rights of persons holding minority views that they established an indirect mechanism for electing the president—the electoral college. As was true in the election of 2000, this can result in instances in which a candidate with fewer votes is elected.

But when, precisely, do minorities succeed in influencing majorities? Research findings suggest that they are most likely to do so under certain conditions (Moscovici, 1985). First, the members of such groups must be *consistent* in their opposition to majority opinions. If they waver or seem to be divided, their impact is reduced. Second, members of the minority must avoid appearing to be rigid and dogmatic (Mugny, 1975). A minority that merely repeats the same position is less persuasive than one that demonstrates a degree of flexibility. Third, the general social context in which a minority operates is important. If a minority argues for a position that is consistent with current social trends (e.g., conservative views at a time of growing conservatism), its chances of influencing the majority are greater than if it argues for a position out of step with such trends.

Of course, even when these conditions are met, minorities face a tough uphill fight. The power of majorities is great, especially in ambiguous or complex social situations

Chapter 9 / Social Influence

in which majorities are viewed as more reliable sources of information about what is true than are minorities. In this sense, however, the threat posed by majorities to minorities may actually be of help to these minorities. Research findings indicate that because they feel greater concern over being right (i.e., holding correct views), minorities tend to overestimate the number of persons who share their views. In other words, they perceive more support for their positions than actually exists (Kenworthy & Miller, 2001). This can be encouraging and serve to strengthen the resolve of minorities to persevere in the face of daunting odds.

Before concluding, we should note one more point: Additional evidence suggests that one positive effect produced by minorities is that they induce the majority to exert increased cognitive effort in order to understand *why* the minority holds its unusual and unpopular views (Nemeth, 1995; Vonk & van Knippenberg, 1995). In other words, deeply committed and vocal minorities can encourage members of the majority to engage in *systematic processing* with respect to information they provide (e.g., Smith, Tindale, & Dugoni, 1996; Wood et al., 1996; see Figure 9.10 on the previous page). Similarly, minority members may engage in more careful (systematic) thought themselves concerning their unpopular views. This, in turn, may lead them to generate stronger arguments with which to influence the majority (Zdaniuk & Levine, 1996). So, even if minorities fail to sway majorities initially, they may initiate processes that ultimately lead to large-scale social change (e.g., Alvaro & Crano, 1996).

KEY POINTS

★ Although pressures toward conformity are strong, many persons resist them, at least part of the time. This resistance seems to stem from two strong motives: (1) the desire to retain one's individuality and (2) the desire to exert control over one's own life.

★ In addition, there are some people—for example, ones who are physically challenged and homosexuals who wish to marry—who cannot conform even if they wish to because of physical limitations or legal barriers, respectively.

★ Under some conditions, minorities can induce even large majorities to change their attitudes or behavior.

★ Because their views are threatened, minorities often overestimate the number of persons who share their beliefs.

★ One positive effect of minorities is that they induce majorities to think more systematically about the issues they raise, which may facilitate large-scale social change.

Compliance: To Ask—Sometimes—Is to Receive

Suppose that you wanted someone to do something for you. How would you go about getting them to agree? If you think about this question for a moment, you may quickly realize that you have quite a few tricks up your sleeve for gaining *compliance*—for getting others to say "yes" to your requests. What are these techniques like? Which ones work best? These are among the questions we now consider. Before doing so, however, we introduce a basic framework for understanding the nature of all of these procedures and why they often work.

Compliance: The Underlying Principles

Some years ago, one well-known social psychologist (Robert Cialdini) decided that the best way to find out about compliance was to study what he termed *compliance professionals*—people whose success (financial or otherwise) depends on their ability to get others to say "yes." Who are such persons? They include salespeople, advertisers, political lobbyists, fundraisers, politicians, con artists, and professional negotiators, to name a few. Cialdini's technique for learning from these people was simple: He temporarily concealed his true identity and took jobs in various settings in which gaining compliance is a way of life. In other words, he worked in advertising, direct (door-to-door) sales, fundraising, and other compliance-focused fields. On the basis of these first-hand experiences, he concluded that although techniques for gaining compliance take many different forms, they all rest to some degree on six basic principles (Cialdini, 1994):

- *Friendship/Liking:* In general, we are more willing to comply with requests from friends or from people we like than with requests from strangers or people we don't like.

- *Commitment/Consistency:* Once we have committed ourselves to a position or action, we are more willing to comply with requests for behaviors that are consistent with this position or action than with requests that are inconsistent with it.

- *Scarcity:* In general, we value, and try to secure, outcomes or objects that are scarce or decreasing in their availability. As a result, we are more likely to comply with requests that focus on scarcity than ones that make no reference to this issue.

- *Reciprocity:* We are generally more willing to comply with a request from someone who has previously provided a favor or concession to us than from someone who has not. In other words, we feel obliged to pay people back in some way for what they have done for us.

- *Social Validation:* We are generally more willing to comply with a request for some action if this action is consistent with what we believe persons similar to ourselves are doing (or thinking). We want to be correct, and one way to do so is to act and think like others.

- *Authority:* In general, we are more willing to comply with requests from someone who holds legitimate authority—or simply appears to do so.

According to Cialdini (1994), these basic principles underlie many techniques used by professionals—and ourselves—for gaining compliance from others. We now examine techniques based on these principles, plus a few others as well.

Tactics Based on Friendship or Liking: Ingratiation

We've already considered several techniques for increasing compliance through liking in our discussion of *impression management* (Chapter 3)—various procedures for making a good impression on others. Although this can be an end in itself, impression management techniques are often used for purposes of **ingratiation**—getting others to like us so that they will be more willing to agree to our requests (Jones, 1964; Liden & Mitchell, 1988).

Which ingratiation techniques work best? A review of existing studies on this topic (Gordon, 1996) suggests that *flattery*—praising others in some manner—is one of the best (see Figure 9.11). Other techniques that seem to work are improving one's own appearance, emitting many positive nonverbal cues, and doing small favors for the target persons (Gordon, 1996; Wayne & Liden, 1995). We described many of these tactics

ingratiation
A technique for gaining compliance in which requesters first induce target persons to like them and then attempt to change the persons' behavior in some desired manner.

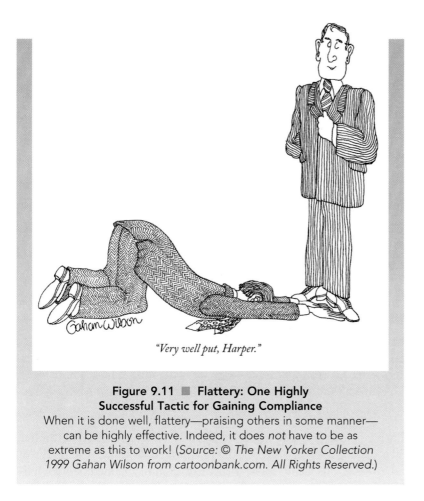

"Very well put, Harper."

**Figure 9.11 ■ Flattery: One Highly
Successful Tactic for Gaining Compliance**
When it is done well, flattery—praising others in some manner—
can be highly effective. Indeed, it does *not* have to be as
extreme as this to work! (*Source: © The New Yorker Collection
1999 Gahan Wilson from cartoonbank.com. All Rights Reserved.*)

in detail in Chapter 3, so we won't repeat that information here. Suffice it to say that many of the tactics used for purposes of impression management are also successful from the point of view of increasing compliance.

Still another means of increasing others' liking for us, and thus raising the chances that they will agree to requests we make, involves what has been termed *incidental similarity*—calling attention to small and slightly surprising similarities between them and ourselves. In several recent studies, Burger and his colleagues (Burger et al., 2004) found that research participants were more likely to agree to a small request (make a donation to charity) from a stranger when this person appeared to have the same first name or birthday as they did than when the requester was not similar to them in these ways. Apparently, these trivial forms of similarity enhance liking or a feeling of affiliation with the requester and so increase the tendency to comply with this person's requests.

Tactics Based on Commitment or Consistency: The Foot-in-the-Door and the Lowball

When you visit the food court of your local shopping mall, are you ever approached by people offering you free samples of food (see Figure 9.12 on page 358)? If so, why do they do this? The answer is simple: They know that once you have accepted this small free gift, you will be more willing to buy something from their booth. This is the basic idea behind an approach for gaining compliance known as the **foot-in-the-door technique.** Basically,

foot-in-the-door technique
A procedure for gaining compliance in which requesters begin with a small request and then, when this is granted, escalate to a larger one (the one they actually desire all along).

Figure 9.12 ■ The Foot-in-the-Door in Action
Why do many restaurants ask passersby in shopping malls to accept free samples of food? Probably *not* because they are kind. Rather, they know that once people say "yes" to these small gifts (and the request that they be accepted), they may be more likely to agree with requests for more significant and costly actions, such as purchasing meals at the restaurants that gave them the free samples.

this involves inducing target persons to agree to a small initial request ("Accept this free sample") and then making a larger request—the one desired all along. The results of many studies indicate that this tactic works; it succeeds in inducing increased compliance (e.g., Beaman et al., 1983; Freedman & Fraser, 1966). Why is this the case? Because the foot-in-the-door technique rests on the principle of *consistency:* Once we have said "yes" to the small request, we are more likely to say "yes" to subsequent and larger ones, too, because refusing these would be inconsistent with our previous behavior. For example, imagine that you want to borrow the class notes your friend has taken since the start of the semester. You might begin by asking for the notes from one lecture. After copying these, you might come back with a larger request: the notes for all the other classes. If your friend complies, it might well be because refusing would be inconsistent with his or her initial "yes" (e.g., DeJong & Musilli, 1982).

The foot-in-the-door technique is not the only compliance tactic that is based on the consistency/commitment principle, however. Another is the **lowball procedure.** With this technique, which is often used by automobile salespersons, a very good deal is offered to a customer. After the customer accepts, however, something happens that makes it necessary for the salesperson to change the deal and make it less advantageous for the customer—for example, the sales manager rejects the deal. The totally rational reaction for customers, of course, is to walk away. Yet, they often agree to the changes and accept the less desirable arrangement (Cialdini et al., 1978). In such instances, an initial commitment seems to make it more difficult for individuals to say "no," even though the conditions that led them to say "yes" in the first place have now been changed.

Clear evidence for the importance of an initial commitment in the success of the lowball technique is provided by research conducted by Burger and Cornelius (2003). These researchers phoned students living in dorms and asked them if they would contribute $5 to a scholarship fund for underprivileged students. In the lowball condition, a researcher indicated that persons who contributed would receive a coupon for a free smoothie at a local juice bar. Then, if participants agreed to make a donation, she told

lowball procedure
A technique for gaining compliance in which an offer or deal is changed to make it less attractive to the target person after this person has accepted it.

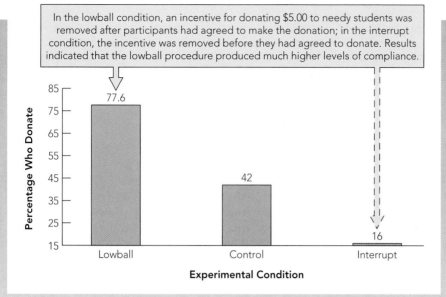

In the lowball condition, an incentive for donating $5.00 to needy students was removed after participants had agreed to make the donation; in the interrupt condition, the incentive was removed before they had agreed to donate. Results indicated that the lowball procedure produced much higher levels of compliance.

Figure 9.13 ■ **The Role of Commitment in the Lowball Technique**
In the *lowball condition*, participants were asked to make a donation of $5 to needy students. After doing so, they were told that an incentive for the donation was no longer available (a coupon for a free smoothie). They were then asked if they still wished to contribute. In the interrupt condition, participants learned *before* making the initial commitment to donate that the incentive was no longer available. As shown here, results indicated that the lowball procedure generated much higher rates of compliance. These findings underscore the importance of an initial commitment in the lowball technique. (*Source: Based on data from Burger & Cornelius, 2003.*)

them that she had just run out of coupons and couldn't offer them this incentive. She then asked if they would still contribute. In another condition (the interrupt condition), she made the initial request, but before the participants could answer "yes" or "no," interrupted them and indicated that there were no more coupons for persons who donated. In other words, this was just like the lowball condition, except that participants had no opportunity to make an initial commitment to donating to the fund. Finally, in a third (control) condition, participants were asked to donate $5 with no mention of any coupons for a free drink. Results indicated that more persons in the lowball condition agreed to make a donation than in either of the other two conditions (see Figure 9.13).

These results indicate that the lowball procedure does indeed rest on the principles of commitment: Only when individuals are permitted to make an initial public commitment—when they say "yes" to the initial offer—does it work. Having made this initial commitment, they feel compelled to stick with it, even though the conditions that led them to say "yes" in the first place no longer exist. Truly, this is a subtle yet powerful technique for gaining compliance.

Tactics Based on Reciprocity: The Door-in-the Face and the That's-Not-All Techniques

Reciprocity is a basic rule of social life: We usually "do unto others as they have done unto us." If they have done a favor for us, we feel that we should therefore be willing to do one for them in return. While most persons view this as fair and just, the principle of reciprocity also serves as the basis for several techniques for gaining compliance. One of these is, on the face of it, the opposite of the foot-in-the-door technique. Instead of beginning with a small request and then escalating to a larger one, persons seeking compliance sometimes start with a very large request and then, after this is rejected, shift to a smaller request—the one they wanted all along. This tactic is known as the **door-in-the-face technique** (because the first refusal seems to slam the door in the face of the requester), and several studies indicate that it can be quite effective. For example, in one well-known experiment, Cialdini and his colleagues (1975) stopped college students on the street and presented a huge request: Would the students serve as unpaid counselors for juvenile delinquents two hours a week for the next *two years!* As you can predict, no one agreed. When the experimenters then scaled down their request to a much smaller one—would the same students take a group of delinquents on a two-hour trip to the zoo—fully 50 percent agreed. In contrast, fewer than 17 percent of those in a control group agreed to this smaller request when it was presented alone rather than after the larger request.

This same tactic is often used by negotiators, who may begin with a position that is extremely advantageous to themselves but then retreat to a position much closer to the one they really hope to obtain. Similarly, sellers often begin with a price they know buyers will reject, and then lower the price to a more reasonable one—but one that is still quite favorable to themselves and close to what they wanted all along.

A related procedure for gaining compliance is known as the **that's-not-all technique.** Here, an initial request is followed, *before the target person can say "yes" or "no,"* by something that sweetens the deal—a small extra incentive from the persons using this tactic (e.g., a reduction in price, "throwing in" something additional for the same price). For example, television commercials for various products frequently offer something extra to induce viewers to pick up the phone and place an order. Several studies confirm informal observations suggesting that the that's-not-all technique really works (Burger, 1986). Why is this so? One possibility is that this tactic succeeds because it is based on the principle of reciprocity: Persons on the receiving end of this technique view the "extra" thrown in by the other side as an added concession, and so feel obligated to make a concession themselves. The result: They are more likely to say "yes."

Another possibility is that creating the appearance of a bargain by reducing the price of an item or offering to add something extra causes individuals to think about the situation in an automatic or, as social psychologists sometimes put it, *mindless* way (e.g., Langer, 1984). "This is a bargain," people might reason, and in accordance with this heuristic thinking, become more likely to say "yes" than would be true if they were thinking more systematically. Evidence for this suggestion was reported by Pollock and his colleagues (1988). They found that a small price reduction produced the that's-not-all effect for a low-cost item (a $1.25 box of chocolates reduced to $1.00) but did not produce this effect for a more expensive item (a $6.25 box reduced to $5.00). Apparently, individuals thought more carefully about spending $5.00, and this countered their tendency to respond automatically—and favorably—to a small price reduction. Whatever its precise basis, the that's-not-all technique can often be an effective means for increasing the likelihood that others will say "yes" to various requests.

Tactics Based on Scarcity: Playing Hard to Get and the Fast-Approaching-Deadline Technique

It's a general rule of life that things that are scarce, rare, or difficult to obtain are viewed as being more valuable than those that are plentiful or easy to obtain. Thus, we are often

door-in-the-face technique A procedure for gaining compliance in which requesters begin with a large request and then, when this is refused, retreat to a smaller one (the one they actually desire all along).

that's-not-all technique A technique for gaining compliance in which requesters offer additional benefits to target persons before these persons have decided whether to comply with or reject specific requests.

Chapter 9 / Social Influence

willing to expend more effort or go to greater expense to obtain items or outcomes that are scarce than to obtain ones that are in large supply. This principle serves as the foundation for several techniques for gaining compliance. One of the most common of these is **playing hard to get.**

Many people know that playing hard to get can be an effective tactic in the area of romance: By suggesting that it is difficult to win their affection or that there are many rivals for their love, individuals can greatly increase their desirability (e.g., Walster et al., 1973). This tactic is not restricted to interpersonal attraction, however; research findings indicate that it is also sometimes used by job candidates to increase their attractiveness to potential employers, and hence to increase the likelihood that these employers will offer them a job. Persons using this tactic let the potential employer know that they have other offers and so are a very desirable employee. And in fact, research findings indicate that this technique often works (Williams et al., 1993).

A related procedure also based on the what's-scarce-is-valuable principle is one frequently used by department stores. Ads using this **deadline technique** state that a special sale will end on a certain date, implying that after that, the prices will go up. In many cases, the time limit is false: The prices won't go up after the indicated date and may, in fact, continue to drop if the merchandise remains unsold. Yet many persons reading such ads or seeing signs such as the one in Figure 9.14 believe them and hurry down to the store to avoid missing out on a great opportunity. So, when you encounter an offer suggesting that "the clock is ticking" and may soon run out, be cautious. This may simply be a technique for boosting sales.

Before concluding, we must note that the principle of *social validation,* another of Cialdini's (1994) basic principles, is closely related to conformity, and especially to informational social influence. Social validation suggests that we often comply with requests for actions that we view as being consistent with what persons similar to ourselves are doing (or thinking). So, the next time someone suggests to you that you should do something they want you to do because "it's what people like us are doing," you should be on guard: The chances are good that this is a tactic for gaining compliance rather than a simple description of what is appropriate behavior. (For an overview of various tactics for gaining compliance, see the **Ideas to Take with You—and Use!** section at the end of this chapter.)

playing hard to get
A technique that can be used for increasing compliance by suggesting that a person or object is scarce and hard to obtain.

deadline technique
A technique for increasing compliance in which target persons are told that they have only limited time to take advantage of some offer or to obtain some item.

Figure 9.14 ■ The Deadline Technique: A Procedure Based on Scarcity
In the *deadline technique,* potential customers or others are led to believe that if they do not do what the persons using this technique want *now,* it will soon be too late. The result? People indeed hurry to buy items that are really not in short supply and that will be available for the same or a lower price at a later time.

KEY POINTS

★ Individuals use many different tactics for gaining *compliance*—getting others to say "yes" to various requests. Many of these tactics rest on basic principles well known to social psychologists.

★ Two widely used tactics, the *foot-in-the-door* and the *lowball procedure* rely on the principle of commitment/consistency. In contrast, the *door-in-the-face* technique and the *that's-not-all* techniques rest on the principle of reciprocity.

★ *Playing hard to get* and the *deadline technique* are based on the principle of scarcity—what is scarce or hard to obtain is valuable.

★ Social validation, another principle underlying compliance, is closely related to *informational social influence* and *conformity*.

Symbolic Social Influence: How We Are Influenced by Others Even When They Are Not There

That other people can influence us when they are present and trying to do so is not that surprising; like us, they have many techniques at their disposal for getting us to say, think, or do what they want. But growing evidence suggests that others can influence us even when they are *not* present and *not* trying to change our behavior or thoughts, a process that can be described as **symbolic social influence.** In a sense, they do not produce such effects: *We* do. Our mental representations of others—what they want or prefer, our relationships with them, how we think they would evaluate us or our current actions—can exert powerful effects on us, and even, it appears, when we are not consciously aware of these effects (e.g., Bargh et al., 2001). For example, in one well-known study—a study that triggered interest in this topic—Baldwin, Carrell, & Lopez (1990) found that graduate students evaluated their own research ideas more negatively after being exposed, subliminally, to the face of their scowling department chair. In other words, the chair's face was shown for so short a period of time that the graduate students were not aware of having seen him, yet his negative facial expression exerted significant effects on their evaluations of their own work.

How can the psychological presence of others in our mental representations of them influence our behavior and thought? Two mechanisms seem to be involved, and both may involve goals—objectives we wish to attain. First, the extent that other persons are present in our thoughts (and even if we are not aware that they are) may trigger *relational schemas*—mental representations of people with whom we have relationships, and of the relationships themselves. When these relational schemas are triggered, in turn, goals relevant to them may be activated, too. For instance, if we think of a friend, the goal of being helpful may be activated; if we think of our mother and father, the goal of making them proud of us may be triggered. These goals, in turn, can affect our behavior, our thoughts about ourselves, and our evaluations of others. For instance, if the goal of helping others is triggered, then we may become more helpful toward others.

Second, the psychological presence of others may trigger goals with which those persons are associated—goals they want us to achieve. This, in turn, can affect our performance on various tasks and our commitment to reaching these goals, among other things (e.g., Shah, 2003). For instance, if we have thoughts about our father, we know that he wants us to do well in school, and our commitment to this goal may be increased and we may work harder to attain it, especially if we feel very close to him.

symbolic social influence
Social influence resulting from the mental representation of others or of our relationships with them.

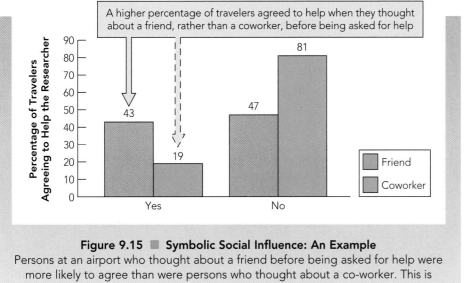

Figure 9.15 ■ Symbolic Social Influence: An Example
Persons at an airport who thought about a friend before being asked for help were more likely to agree than were persons who thought about a co-worker. This is because thinking about a friend triggered the goal of helping. (*Source: Based on data from Fitzsimmons & Bargh, 2003.*)

In other words, to the extent that others are psychologically present in our thoughts, the nature of our relationships with them, goals we seek in these relationships, and goals these people themselves seek or want us to attain can all be stimulated, and these ideas and knowledge structures, in turn, can strongly affect our behavior. Although many different studies have reported such effects, research conducted by Fitzsimmons and Bargh (2003) is especially revealing. In one study conducted by these social psychologists, persons at an airport were approached and asked to think of either a good friend or a coworker. Then, they were asked to write down the initials of the person of whom they were thinking and to answer a series of questions about him or her (e.g., describe his or her appearance, tell how long they had known this person, give his or her age, etc.). Finally, participants were asked if they would be willing to help the researcher by answering a longer set of questions. It was predicted that those who thought about a friend would be more willing to help, because thinking about a friend would trigger the goal of helping—something we often do for friends. As you can see in Figure 9.15, this is precisely what was found: More people who thought about a friend than a coworker were willing to help. Note that they were *not* asked to help their friend; rather, they were asked to assist a stranger—the researcher. But, still, thoughts of the friend affected their current behavior.

In another interesting study, the same researchers asked participants to think about and describe their mothers or to think about neutral events not involving other people (e.g., the first musical CD they had purchased, vacations they had taken, the name of the street on which they were born, etc.). Next, participants were given a set of seven letters and asked to generate as many words as possible from these. It was predicted that participants who thought about their mothers would do better on this task, but only if they had the goal of making their mothers proud of them. (Information on the extent to which they held this goal had been collected previously.) Results offered clear support for this prediction: Persons who thought about their mothers and wanted to make them proud did better than those who thought about their mothers but did not have this goal; for persons in the control condition, who thought about neutral events, whether they wanted to make their mothers proud or not had no effect—and why should it? They were not thinking about them as they performed the word task.

Findings such as these and those reported in a growing number of other studies (e.g., Shah, 2003) suggest that we can be strongly influenced by other persons when they are not physically present on the scene and trying to affect us, as long as they are psychologically present (in our thoughts). Do you recall the incident at the start of this chapter in which I walked home rather than ride with my drunk friend on a New Year's Eve many years ago? If so, you can now see how that story relates to symbolic social influence. My parents were not present that night (thank goodness!), but they were in my thoughts, and that was sufficient to change my behavior—and perhaps save my life. So, clearly, although symbolic social influence is more subtle than the face-to-face variety, it, too, is important and plays a key role in many aspects of social behavior and social thought.

KEY POINTS

★ Other people can influence us, even when they are not present, through our mental representations of them and our relationships with them. This effect is known as *symbolic social influence.*

★ Such influence often involves goals relevant to our relationships with others or goals with which these people themselves are associated.

★ To the extent that others are psychologically present in our thoughts, goals we seek in our relationships with them or goals these people themselves seek or want us to attain can be stimulated, and these, in turn, can strongly affect our behavior.

Obedience to Authority: Would You Harm an Innocent Stranger if Ordered to Do So?

Have you ever been ordered to do something you didn't want to do by someone with authority over you—a teacher, your boss, your parents? If so, you are already familiar with another major type of social influence—*obedience*—in which one person directly orders one or more others to behave in specific ways, and the persons then comply. Obedience is used less frequently as a tactic than conformity or compliance, because even persons who possess authority and could use it often prefer to exert influence through the *velvet glove*—through requests rather than direct orders (e.g., Yukl & Falbe, 1991). Still, obedience is far from rare and occurs in many settings, from schools to military bases. Obedience to the commands of persons who possess authority is far from surprising; these persons usually have effective means of enforcing their orders. More unexpected is that, often, persons lacking in such power can also induce high levels of submission from others. The clearest and most dramatic evidence for such effects was reported by Stanley Milgram in a series of famous—and controversial—studies (Milgram, 1963, 1965a, 1974).

Obedience in the Laboratory

In his research, Milgram wished to find out whether individuals would obey commands from a relatively powerless stranger requiring them to inflict what seemed to be considerable pain on another person—a totally innocent stranger. Milgram's interest in this topic derived from tragic events in which seemingly normal, law-abiding persons actually obeyed such directives. For example, during World War II, troops in the German army frequently obeyed commands to torture and murder millions of unarmed civilians. In fact, the Nazis established horrible but highly efficient death camps designed to eradicate Jews, Gypsies, and other groups they felt were inferior or a threat to their own racial purity.

In an effort to gain insights into the nature of such events, Milgram designed an ingenious, if unsettling, laboratory simulation. The experimenter informed participants in the study (all men) that they were taking part in an investigation of the effects of punishment on learning. One person in each pair of participants would serve as a "learner" and would try to perform a simple task involving memory (supplying the second word in pairs of words they had previously memorized after hearing the first word). The other participant, the "teacher," would read these words to the learner and would punish errors by the learner (failures to provide the second word in each pair) through administration of electric shock. These shocks would be delivered by means of the equipment shown in Figure 9.16, and as you can see from the photo, this device contained thirty numbered switches ranging from 15 volts (the first) through 450 volts (the thirtieth). The two persons present—a real participant and a research assistant—then drew slips of paper from a hat to determine who would play each role; as you can guess, the drawing was rigged so that the real participant always became the teacher. The teacher was then told to deliver a shock to the learner each time he made an error on the task. Moreover—and this is crucial—teachers were told *to increase the strength of the shock each time the learner made an error.* This meant that if the learner made many errors, he would soon be receiving strong jolts of electricity. It's important to note that this information was false: In reality, the assistant (the learner) never received any shocks during the experiment. The only real shock ever used was a mild pulse from button number three to convince participants that the equipment was real. Real participants, of course, did not know that the "learner" was an accomplice of the researcher.

During the session, the learner (following prearranged instructions) made many errors. Thus, participants soon found themselves facing a dilemma: Should they continue punishing this person with what seemed to be increasingly painful shocks? Or should they refuse? If they hesitated, the experimenter pressured them to continue with graded series "prods": "Please continue"; "The experiment requires that you continue"; "It is absolutely essential that you continue"; "You have no other choice; you *must* go on."

Figure 9.16 ▪ Studying Obedience in the Laboratory
The left photo shows the apparatus Stanley Milgram used in his famous experiments on destructive obedience. The right photo shows the experimenter (*right front*) and a participant (*rear*) attaching electrodes to the learner's (accomplice's) wrist. (*Source: From the film* Obedience, *distributed by the New York University Film Library, copyright 1965, by Stanley Milgram. Reprinted by permission of the copyright holder.*)

Because participants were all volunteers and were paid in advance, you might predict that most would quickly refuse the experimenter's orders. In reality, though, fully 65 percent showed total obedience—they proceeded through the entire series to the final 450-volt level. Many participants, of course, protested and asked that the session be ended. When ordered to proceed, however, a majority yielded to the experimenter's influence and continued to obey. Indeed, they continued doing so even when the victim pounded on the wall as if in protest over the painful shocks (at the 300-volt level), and then *no longer responded,* as if he had passed out. The experimenter told participants to treat failures to answer as errors; so from this point on, many participants believed that they were delivering dangerous shocks to someone who might already be unconscious!

In further experiments, Milgram (1965b, 1974) found that similar results could be obtained even under conditions that might be expected to reduce such obedience. When the study was moved from its original location on the campus of Yale University to a run-down office building in a nearby city, participants' level of obedience remained virtually unchanged. Similarly, a large proportion continued to obey, even when the accomplice complained about the painfulness of the shocks and begged to be released. Most surprising of all, many (about 30 percent) obeyed even when they were required to grasp the victim's hand and force it down on a metal shock plate! That these chilling results are not restricted to a single culture is indicated by the fact that similar findings were subsequently reported in several different countries (e.g., Jordan, Germany, Australia) and with children as well as adults (e.g., Kilham & Mann, 1974; Shanab & Yahya, 1977). Thus, Milgram's findings seemed to be alarmingly general in scope.

I (Robert Baron) went to high school with Milgram's niece, and I can remember the disbelief that students in my class felt when she told us about her uncle's findings several years before they were published. Psychologists, too, found Milgram's results highly disturbing. His studies seemed to suggest that ordinary people are willing, although with some reluctance, to harm an innocent stranger if ordered to do by someone in authority. This led to an important question: What factors lie behind this tendency to obey, even when obedience results in potential harm to others?

Destructive Obedience: Why It Occurs

As noted earlier, one reason why Milgram's results are so disturbing is that they seem to parallel many real-life events involving atrocities against innocent victims. To repeat the question raised earlier: Why does such destructive obedience occur? Why were participants in these experiments—and many persons in tragic situations outside the laboratory—so willing to yield to this form of social influence? Social psychologists have identified several factors that seem to play a role, and several of these are related to other aspects of social influence we have already considered.

First, in many situations, the persons in authority relieve those who obey of responsibility for their own actions. "I was only carrying out orders" is the defense many offer after obeying harsh or cruel commands. In real-life situations, this transfer of responsibility may be implicit; the person in charge (e.g., the military or police officer) is assumed to have the responsibility for what happens, which seems to be what happened in the tragic events of 2004 when U.S. soldiers—both men and women—were filmed abusing and torturing Iraqi prisoners. Their defense? "I was only following orders . . . I was told to do this, and a good soldier always obeys!" In Milgram's experiments, this transfer of responsibility was explicit. Participants were told at the start that the experimenter (the authority figure), not they, would be responsible for the learner's well-being. In view of this fact, it is not surprising that many obeyed: After all, they were let completely off the hook.

Second, persons in authority often possess visible badges or signs of their status. They wear special uniforms or insignia, have special titles, and so on. These indicators serve to remind many persons of the social norm "Obey the persons in charge." This norm is a powerful one, and when confronted with it, most people find it difficult to disobey. After all, we do not want to do the wrong thing, and obeying the commands of those who are in charge usually helps us avoid such errors. In a sense, then, informational social influence—a key factor in conformity to social norms—may have contributed to Milgram's results (e.g., Bushman, 1988; Darley, 1995).

A third reason for obedience in many situations in which the targets of such influence might otherwise resist involves the gradual escalation of the authority figure's orders. Initial commands may call for relatively mild actions, such as merely arresting people. Only later do orders come to require behavior that is dangerous or objectionable. For example, police or military personnel may at first be ordered only to question or threaten potential victims. Gradually, demands are increased to the point at which these personnel are commanded to beat, torture, or even murder unarmed civilians. In a sense, persons in authority use the foot-in-the-door technique, asking for small actions first but ever-larger ones later. In a similar manner, participants in Milgram's research were first required to deliver only mild and harmless shocks to the victim. Only as the sessions continued did the intensity of these "punishments" rise to potentially harmful levels.

Finally, events in many situations involving destructive obedience move very quickly: Demonstrations turn into riots, arrests into mass beatings or murder, and so on, quite suddenly. The fast pace of such events gives participants little time for reflection or systematic processing: People are ordered to obey and—almost automatically—they do so. Such conditions prevailed in Milgram's research; within a few minutes of entering the laboratory, participants found themselves faced with commands to deliver strong electric shocks to the learner. This fast pace, too, may tend to increase obedience.

In sum, the high levels of obedience generated in Milgram's studies are not as mysterious as they may seem. A social psychological analysis of the conditions existing both there and in many real-life situations identifies several factors that, together, may make it very difficult for individuals to resist the commands they receive. The consequences, of course, can be truly tragic for innocent and often defenseless victims.

Destructive Obedience: Resisting Its Effects

Now that we have considered some of the factors responsible for the strong tendency to obey sources of authority, we turn to a related question: How can this type of social influence be resisted? Several strategies may be helpful in this respect.

First, individuals exposed to commands from authority figures can be reminded that they—not the authorities—are responsible for any harm produced. Under these conditions, sharp reductions in the tendency to obey have been observed (e.g., Hamilton, 1978; Kilham & Mann, 1974).

Second, individuals can be provided with a clear indication that beyond some point, total submission to destructive commands is inappropriate. One procedure that is highly effective in this regard involves exposing individuals to the actions of *disobedient models*—persons who refuse to obey an authority figure's commands. Research findings indicate that such models can greatly reduce unquestioning obedience (e.g., Rochat & Modigliani, 1995). When we see one or more persons refuse to obey the commands of an authority figure, we may be strongly encouraged to do the same, with the ultimate result that the power of those in authority is severely weakened.

Third, individuals may find it easier to resist influence from authority figures if they question the expertise and motives of these figures. Are those in authority really in a better position to judge what is appropriate and what is not? What motives lie behind their commands: socially beneficial goals or selfish gains? Dictators always claim that their brutal orders reflect their undying concern for their fellow citizens and are in their best interests, but to the extent that large numbers of persons question these motives, the power of such dictators can be eroded and perhaps, ultimately, be swept away.

Finally, simply knowing about the power of authority figures to command blind obedience may be helpful in itself. Some research findings (e.g., Sherman, 1980) suggest that when individuals learn about the results of social psychological research, they often recognize these as important (Richard, Bond, & Stokes-Zooter, 2001) and sometimes change their behavior to take account of this new knowledge. With respect to destructive obedience, there is some hope that knowing about this process can enhance individuals' resolve to resist. To the extent this enlightenment takes place, then even exposure to findings as disturbing as those reported by Milgram can have positive social value.

To conclude, the power of authority figures to command obedience is great, but it is not irresistible. Under appropriate conditions, it can be countered or reduced. As in many other areas of life, there is a choice. Deciding to resist the commands of persons in authority can, of course, be highly dangerous: Persons in authority usually control most of the weapons, the army, and the police. Yet, history is filled with instances in which the authority of powerful and entrenched regimes has been resisted by courageous persons who ultimately triumphed, despite the long odds against them. Indeed, the American Revolution began in just this way: Small bands of poorly armed citizens decided to make a stand against Great Britain, the most powerful country on earth at the time (see Figure 9.17). The success of the colonists in winning their independence

Figure 9.17 ■ Resisting Authority: Sometimes, It Can Change the World
When small bands of colonists took a stand against Great Britain—the most powerful nation in the world at that time—they started a process that ultimately changed the world. Events such as this suggest that even powerful sources of authority can be resisted, although at considerable cost.

Chapter 9 / Social Influence

became a model for many other people all over the world—and changed history. The lesson from this and related events is clear: Power is never permanent, and, ultimately, victory often goes to those who stand for freedom and decency rather than to those who wish to exert total control over the lives of their fellow human beings.

KEY POINTS

★ *Obedience* is a form of social influence in which one person orders one or more persons to do something, and they do so. It is, in a sense, the most direct form of *social influence*.

★ Research by Stanley Milgram indicates that many persons readily obey orders from a relatively powerless source of authority, even if these orders require them to harm an innocent stranger.

★ Such destructive obedience, which plays a role in many real-life atrocities, stems from several factors. These include the shifting of responsibility to the authority figure; outward signs of authority on the part of these persons, which remind many persons of the

norm "Obey those in authority"; a gradual escalation of the scope of the commands given (related to the foot-in-the-door technique); and the rapid pace with which such situations proceed.

★ Several factors can help to reduce the occurrence of destructive obedience. These include reminding individuals that they share in the responsibility for any harm produced; reminding them that beyond some point, obedience is inappropriate; calling the motives of authority figures into question; and informing the general public of the findings of social psychological research on this topic.

Social Influence Goes to Work: Influence Tactics in Work Settings

Conformity, compliance, obedience, symbolic social influence—these are powerful forces in social life and clearly play a role in many different settings. But are these the tactics people actually use to influence others in real-life settings? To an important degree, they are. You have almost certainly been exposed to such forms of social influence as the foot-in-the-door technique or playing hard to get, and you have almost certainly been ordered to behave in various ways by people with authority over you. But growing evidence—much of it relating to social influence in work settings—suggests that there are other tactics and principles that are put to frequent use (e.g., Yukl, Falbe, & Young, 1993). Here is a brief description of the ones that are most common:

- *Rational Persuasion:* Using logical arguments and facts to persuade another that a desired result will occur if the persuader's views are accepted.

- *Inspirational Appeal:* Arousing enthusiasm by appealing to strongly held values and ideals.

- *Consultation:* Asking for the target person's participation in decision making or planning a change.

- *Ingratiation:* Getting someone to do what you want by putting that person in a good mood or getting him or her to like you.

- *Exchange:* Promising some benefits in exchange for complying with a request.

- *Personal Appeal:* Appealing to feelings of loyalty and friendship before making a request.

- *Coalition Building:* Persuading by seeking the assistance of others or by noting the support of others.

- *Legitimating:* Pointing out one's authority to make a request or verifying that it is consistent with prevailing organizational policies and practices.

- *Pressure:* Seeking compliance by using demands, threats, or intimidation.

This list is based on extensive in research in which large numbers of persons working in many different organizations have been asked to describe how they attempt to influence others, and how other persons in their organization seek to influence them (e.g., Yukl & Tracey, 1992). As you can see, several of these tactics are closely linked to ones we have already examined—ingratiation, legitimating (obedience), and, of course, rational persuasion. But others are somewhat different and do not fit readily under any of the major categories we have examined—inspirational appeals, coalition building, and consultation, to name a few. Why do people report using different tactics of influence in work settings than in other environments? Perhaps because in work settings, relationships between the people involved are both long-lasting and complex. For instance, they often involve differences in status and authority, with some people being supervisors and others subordinates. This situation is very different than one in which, for instance, you try to influence one of your friends. Further, people working in the same organization often interact with each other for several hours each day. As a result, using tactics of influence that might succeed in the short run, such as the foot-in-the-door or the door-in-the-face, may not be appropriate: They will be recognized quickly for what they are and may be more likely to generate anger and resistance than compliance. So, in a sense, it is not surprising that people tend to use somewhat different tactics in work settings; this merely illustrates that we tend to match the influence tactics we use to the specific situations in which we want to affect other persons.

But how are these tactics actually used? Not surprisingly, research findings indicate that they are used differently depending on whether influence is being directed at someone who is higher than, lower than, or equal to the status or organizational level of the person attempting to exert social influence. For example, persons in authority often use inspirational appeal to influence their subordinates, or even pressure when they feel this is necessary. However, subordinates are unlikely to use either of these techniques when attempting to influence their bosses. Instead, they are likely to rely on consultation or ingratiation when attempting to appeal to their bosses. Finally, when attempting to influence peers, both exchange and personal appeal were among the most popularly used techniques.

More generally, *consultative techniques*—ones that involve trying to persuade others directly—are generally viewed as more appropriate than more coercive techniques, ones that involve pressuring others or "cutting the ground from under them" (e.g., Yukl, Kim, & Chavez, 1999). Accordingly, the most popular techniques to influence people at all levels are consultation, inspirational appeal, and rational persuasion. In fact, recent findings (Blickle, 2003) indicate that the more individuals use these tactics, the more they are viewed as doing a good job by co-workers.

In contrast, less desirable forms of influence, such as pressure and legitimating, are not used as often. Recent findings (Blickle, 2003) indicate why such tactics tend to be rare: They generate strong levels of *reactance*—the desire to resist and refuse to do what the persons using the tactics want. In fact, the more individuals use these tactics, the greater the reactance they generate. So, clearly, pressure tactics are not effective ones to use in work settings. Taken as a whole, all of these findings make a good deal of social psychological sense, so they should be viewed as complementary to the findings of basic research on conformity, compliance, and obedience. They help to extend our knowledge of social influence to another important setting, and that is certainly beneficial.

KEY POINTS

★ Research findings indicate that individuals often use somewhat different influence tactics in work settings than in other contexts.

★ Among the most common are consultative techniques—ones that involve trying to persuade others directly. *Ingratiation* is also often widely used.

★ Other techniques involving coercion (e.g., pressure, legitimating) are used less frequently, partly because they tend to generate strong reactance.

SUMMARY AND REVIEW OF KEY POINTS

Conformity: Group Influence in Action

■ *Social influence*—efforts by one or more persons to change the attitudes or behavior of one or more others—is a common part of life.

■ Most people behave in accordance with *social norms* most of the time; in other words, they show strong tendencies toward *conformity*.

■ Conformity was first studied systematically by Solomon Asch, whose classic research indicated that many persons will yield to social pressure from a unanimous group.

■ Many factors determine whether, and to what extent, conformity occurs. These include *cohesiveness*—the degree of attraction felt by an individual toward some group, group size, and type of *social norm* operating in that situation (*descriptive* or *injunctive*).

■ Norms tend to influence our behavior primarily when they are relevant to us.

■ However, situational norms, like other norms, can influence our behavior in an automatic manner, even when we are not consciously aware of them.

■ Two important motives underlie our tendency to conform: the desire to be liked by others and the desire to be right or accurate. These two motives are reflected in two distinct types of social influence: *normative* and *informational social influence*.

■ The effects of *social influence* are powerful and pervasive but tend to be magnified in situations in which we are uncertain about our own judgments or what is correct.

■ Although pressures toward *conformity* are strong, many persons resist them, at least part of the time. This resistance seems to stem from two strong motives: the desire to retain one's individuality and the desire to exert control over one's own life.

■ In addition, there are some people—for example, ones who are physically challenged and homosexuals who wish to marry—who cannot conform even if they wish to because of physical limitations or legal barriers, respectively.

■ Under some conditions, minorities can induce even large majorities to change their attitudes or behavior.

■ Because their views are threatened, minorities often overestimate the number of persons who share their beliefs.

■ One positive effect of minorities is that they induce majorities to think more systematically about the issues the minorities raise, which may facilitate large-scale social change.

Compliance: To Ask— Sometimes—Is to Receive

■ Individuals use many different tactics for gaining *compliance*— getting others to say "yes" to various requests. Many of these rest on basic principles that are well known to social psychologists.

■ Two widely used tactics, the *foot-in-the-door technique* and the *lowball procedure*, rest on the principle of commitment/consistency. In contrast, the *door-in-*

the-face and the *that's-not-all techniques* rest on the principle of reciprocity.

■ *Playing hard to get* and the *deadline technique* are based on the principle of scarcity—what is scarce or hard to obtain is valuable.

■ Social validation, another basic principle underlying *compliance*, is closely related to *informational social influence* and *conformity*.

Symbolic Social Influence: How We Are Influenced by Others Even When They Are Not There

■ Other people can influence us, even when they not present, through our mental representations of them and our relationships with them. This is known as *symbolic social influence.*

■ Symbolic social influence often involves goals relevant to our relationships with others, or goals with which these people themselves are associated.

■ To the extent that others are psychologically present in our thoughts, goals we seek in our relationships with them or goals these people themselves seek or want us to attain can be stimulated, and these, in turn, can strongly affect our behavior.

Obedience to Authority: Would You Harm an Innocent Stranger If Ordered to Do So?

■ *Obedience* is a form of social influence in which one person orders one or more persons to do something, and they do so. Obedience is, in a sense, the most direct form of *social influence.*

■ Research by Stanley Milgram indicates that many persons readily obey orders from a relatively

powerless source of authority, even if these orders require them to harm an innocent stranger.

■ Such destructive obedience, which plays a role in many real-life atrocities, stems from several factors. These include shifting of responsibility to the authority figure, outward signs of authority on the part of these persons that remind many persons of the norm "Obey those in authority," a gradual escalation of the scope of the commands given (related to the *foot-in-the-door technique*), and the rapid pace with which such situations proceed.

■ Several factors can help to reduce the occurrence of destructive obedience. These include reminding individuals that they share in the responsibility for any harm produced; reminding them that, beyond some point, obedience is inappropriate; calling the motives of authority figures into question; and informing the general public of the findings of social psychological research on this topic.

Social Influence Goes to Work: Influence Tactics in Work Settings

■ Research findings indicate that individuals often use somewhat different influence tactics in work settings than they do in other contexts.

■ Among the most common are consultative techniques—ones that involve trying to persuade others directly. *Ingratiation* is also often widely used.

■ Techniques involving coercion (e.g., pressure, legitimating) are used less frequently, partly because they tend to generate strong reactance.

In this chapter, you read about . . .	In other chapters, you will find related discussions of . . .
the role of social norms in conformity	the role of social norms in attraction (Chapter 7), helping (Chapter 10), aggression (Chapter 11), and group decision making (Chapter 12)
the basic principles underlying many different techniques for gaining compliance	the role of these principles in other aspects of social behavior:
	The role of reciprocity in attraction (Chapter 7), aggression (Chapter 11), and cooperation (Chapter 12)
	The role of the desire to be consistent in attitude change (Chapter 4), the self-concept (Chapter 5), and helping (Chapter 10)
	The role of liking or friendship in social perception (Chapter 2), social relationships (Chapter 8), leadership (Chapter 12), and the legal process (Module A)
the role of mood in compliance	the effects of mood on social cognition (Chapter 3), attitudes (Chapter 4), and helping (Chapter 10)
the role of automaticity with respect to situational norms	the role of automaticity in attitudes (Chapter 4), prejudice (Chapter 6), and group processes (Chapter 12)

Thinking about Connections

1. It has sometimes been argued that social influence is the most basic and important aspect of social behavior. Do you agree? Can you think of any forms of social behavior (e.g., aggression [Chapter 11], helping [Chapter 10]) in which influence does *not* play a role? What about attraction and love (Chapters 7 and 8)? Are these aspects of social behavior affected by social influence?

2. The level of violence seems to have increased in many countries. Do you think this reflects changing norms concerning aggression—norms that now define *aggression* as more appropriate or acceptable than was true in the past? If so, why have such changes occurred?

3. As we describe in Module B, charismatic leaders are often viewed as masters of social influence: They seem to possess an amazing ability to bend others to their will. Do you think they use the principles and tactics for gaining compliance described in this chapter? And which of these do you feel might be most important to such leaders in their efforts to influence their followers?

Ideas to Take with You—and Use! TACTICS FOR GAINING COMPLIANCE

How can we get other persons to say "yes" to our requests? This problem is an eternal puzzle of social life. Research by social psychologists indicates that all of the techniques described here can be useful—and are widely used. So, whether or not you use them yourself, you are likely to be on the receiving end of many of them during your lifetime. Here are ones that are especially common:

Ingratiation

Getting others to like us so that they will be more willing to agree to our requests. This result can be accomplished through flattery, making ourselves attractive, and showing liking for and interest in the target person.

The Foot-in-the-Door Technique

Starting with a small request and, after it is accepted, escalating to a larger one.

The Door-in-the-Face Technique

Starting with a large request and then, when this is refused, backing down to a smaller one.

Playing Hard to Get

Making it appear as though we are much in demand, thereby making it more likely that others will value us and agree to our requests—implicit or explicit.

KEY TERMS

cohesiveness (p. 343)

compliance (p. 339)

conformity (p. 339)

deadline technique (p. 361)

descriptive norms (p. 344)

door-in-the-face technique (p. 360)

foot-in-the-door technique (p. 357)

individuation (p. 350)

injunctive norms (p. 344)

informational social influence (p. 347)

ingratiation (p. 356)

lowball procedure (p. 358)

normative focus theory (p. 344)

normative social influence (p. 347)

obedience (p. 339)

playing hard to get (p. 361)

social influence (p. 339)

social norms (p. 340)

symbolic social influence (p. 362)

that's-not-all technique (p. 360)

FOR MORE INFORMATION

Cialdini, R. B. (1994). *Influence: Science and practice* (3rd ed.). New York: HarperCollins.
  • An insightful, and very readable, account of the major techniques people use to influence others. The book draws both on the findings of systematic research and on informal observations made by the author in a wide range of practical settings (e.g., sales, public relations, fundraising).

Milgram, S. (1974). *Obedience to authority.* New York: Harper & Row.

• More than twenty-five years after it was written, this book remains the definitive work on obedience as a social psychological process. The untimely death of its author only adds to its value as a lasting contribution to our field.

Wosinska, W., Cialdini, R. B., Barrett, D. W., & Reykowski, J. (2001). *The practice of social influence in multiple cultures*. Mahwah, NJ: Erlbaum.

• This book examines social influence across various cultures. It focuses on how basic principles of influence operate in different cultural contexts, and the role they play in social change. By combining two important themes of social psychology (influence and diversity), the book makes for interesting and thought-provoking reading.

10

PROSOCIAL BEHAVIOR
Helping Others

I (Donn Byrne) traveled recently to Kansas State University to give a talk in honor of William Griffitt, one of my former students who died suddenly in the summer of 1999, many years before his time. My daughter, Rebecka, and I flew to Kansas City and then drove a rented car to Manhattan the evening before my scheduled presentation. The next morning, we planned to drive to the psychology department to meet a group for lunch. At the motel desk, I asked for directions. The desk clerks were unsure, but told me where to drive on campus to obtain a parking permit and a map.

As is true of most university campuses, space for cars is limited, and my daughter and I discovered that the parking area was located some distance from where we needed to go. That would have been OK, but it was raining quite heavily that morning, and a long walk would have resulted in some damp and messy notes and slides.

So, we returned quickly to the motel and told the ladies at the desk that we needed a taxi. Unlike that other place named Manhattan, the streets of Manhattan, Kansas, are not characterized by fleets of cruising cabs. In fact, we were told, it would probably be a half hour to forty-five minutes before one could be at the motel. That would have made us late for the luncheon meeting, and both my daughter and I must have looked at least mildly distressed and helpless.

The desk clerks conferred for a minute and then said they would try to locate one of the motel employees who was currently working on a leaking water pipe. They reached his cell phone, and he said he would be glad to drive us to the campus. Not only did he take us exactly where we needed to go, but he was adamant about not accepting a tip—another difference between the two Manhattans.

In any event, our problem was solved, and we were very grateful. Note that we were just strangers in town for a brief period, and our need for help was not in any way the responsibility of the desk clerks or the maintenance man. They spent time and effort solving our little problem, and wanted nothing in return. Why in the world did they help us?

A more general issue, and one that is the subject of the present chapter, is the question of why people in need of assistance are sometimes helped by strangers and sometimes ignored. As you learn in the following pages what social psychologists have discovered about prosocial behavior, you might find it useful to consider why my daughter and I received help in our mini-emergency in Kansas.

The assistance given to us by the three motel employees is a minor example of *prosocial behavior*. It may seem obvious that people provide assistance to one another, but, as you will see, they often do not. After all, the motel employees each had jobs to do, and it would have been much easier for them simply to mind their own business. Each made a relatively small sacrifice in order to assist strangers, and there was no obvious reward, except possibly the satisfaction of being able to help someone. That mixture of sacrifice and satisfaction underlying prosocial acts holds true whether the behavior is something relatively simple and safe (such as getting two people to a campus building) or something complicated and dangerous (such as saving a stranger trapped in a burning automobile).

In making sense of these interactions, the goal of social psychologists is to understand and to predict **prosocial behavior**—any act that benefits others. Generally, the term is applied to acts that do not provide any direct benefit to the person who performs the act, and may even involve some degree of risk. The term **altruism** is sometimes used interchangeably with *prosocial behavior*. But altruism specifically means an *unselfish concern* for the welfare of others.

In this chapter, we first describe some of the basic factors that influence whether a person who witnesses an emergency will or will not *respond to an emergency* with a prosocial act. Next, we examine a variety of *situational, emotional, and dispositional influences on helping behavior*. Then, we shift attention to those who *volunteer* to help others over a long time period; the conflict faced by all potential helpers between *self-interest, moral integrity, and moral hypocrisy;* and *how it feels to receive help*. The final major topic is a comparison of social psychological and genetic *explanations of prosocial motivation*.

Responding to an Emergency: Will Bystanders Help?

When an emergency arises, you often hear stories of someone providing assistance to a stranger (see Figure 10.1 on page 380). You also often hear stories of people standing by and doing nothing. What could explain such dramatic differences in behavior? Before answering that question, we present a few examples of the extremes that range from heroic actions to apathetic indifference.

When a Stranger Is Distressed: Heroism or Apathy?

The word *heroism* is often used incorrectly to mean anyone who does a difficult job well, and we may speak of a football hero who completed a pass that resulted in the winning touchdown or the person who made a heroic effort by escaping from a sinking boat just in time to avoid drowning. As Becker and Eagly (2004) point out, **heroism** actually refers to actions that involve courageous risk taking to obtain a socially valued goal. Both aspects must be involved. Someone who engages in risky behavior for fun is not a hero, and saving one's own life may be valuable but not heroic. And, someone who simply does socially valuable work such as nursing is to be congratulated for choosing a proso-

prosocial behavior
A helpful action that benefits other people without necessarily providing any direct benefits to the person performing the act, and may even involve a risk for the person who helps.

altruism
Behavior that is motivated by an unselfish concern for the welfare of others.

heroism
Actions that involve courageous risk taking to obtain a socially valued goal. An example would be a dangerous act undertaken to save the life of a stranger.

Figure 10.1 ■ Responding to an Emergency
The family of this small Iraqi boy was caught in crossfire during a battle in central Iraq; he is being comforted by a U.S. Navy Hospital Corpsman. When confronted by an emergency situation, bystanders sometimes do nothing, sometimes provide help, and sometimes even risk their lives to save others. The study of prosocial behavior attempts to identify the factors responsible for this wide range of responses.

cial occupation, but not for being a hero. And, it doesn't matter whether the positive action occurs carefully and deliberately or impulsively and uncontrollably; either way, the behavior receives moral praise (Pizarro, Uhlmann, & Salovey, 2003).

Examples of heroic behavior include winners of the Carnegie Hero Medal each year. The winners are ordinary citizens who have risked their lives in saving or attempting to save the life of another person. Beginning in 1904, when this award was established, winners have typically saved people who were attacked by animals (or criminals), or who were threatened by fires, drowning, electrocution, or other potentially fatal dangers (Wooster, 2000). Equally dramatic was the behavior of many gentiles in Europe during World War II who risked their lives to save Jews from the Nazi threat (United States Holocaust Memorial Museum, 2003). Becker and Eagly (2004) also apply the term *hero* to individuals who take risks in less dangerous and dramatic ways, such as donating a kidney to someone in need of a transplant, joining the Peace Corps, or volunteering to work overseas with Doctors of the World to treat those victimized by warfare or a natural disaster. Reading about the individuals who are willing to take risks to help others suggests that many of our fellow humans are impressively prosocial and unselfish. They can be described as just, brave, and caring (Walker & Hennig, 2004).

Unfortunately, there are also examples of unresponsiveness to emergencies, suggesting selfishness, unconcern, and apathy. Psychological interest in prosocial behavior was initially sparked by an incident in which bystanders *failed* to help a stranger in distress. The event was a murder that took place in the mid-1960s in New York City. Coming home from work as a bar manager, Catherine (Kitty) Genovese was crossing the street to her apartment building when she was approached by a man holding a knife. Ms. Genovese ran, but he chased after her until he was close enough to stab her. She screamed for help, and lights went on in many of the apartments that overlooked the scene. Many residents looked out, trying to determine what was happening. At this point, the attacker started to leave, but when he saw that no one was coming to help the victim, he returned and finished murdering her. Afterward, investigators found out that the forty-five minute attack was witnessed by thirty-eight residents of the apartment building, but not one of them either ventured out to help or even called the police (Rosenthal, 1964). Why not?

Before we describe some of the research designed to answer that question, please read **The Science of Social Psychology: Making Sense of Common Sense** section beginning on page 382, which deals with one relatively simple explanation.

Five Crucial Steps Determine Helping versus Not Helping

As the study of prosocial behavior expanded beyond the initial concern with the number of bystanders, Latané and Darley (1970) proposed that the likelihood of a person engaging in a prosocial act is determined by a series of decisions that must be made quickly by those who witness an emergency. Any one of us can sit in a comfortable chair and figure out instantly what bystanders should do. The witnesses to the stabbing attack should either have called the police immediately or perhaps even intervened directly by shouting at the attacker or working as a group to halt the attack. On September 11, 2001, the passengers on one of the hijacked planes apparently responded jointly, thus preventing the terrorists from accomplishing their goal of crashing the plane into the U.S. Capitol. The students in the laboratory experiment should have rushed out of the cubicle to help their fellow student who was having a medical emergency. When you are suddenly and unexpectedly facing an actual emergency, however, the situation is not that simple. As quickly as possible, you have to figure out what is going on and what, if anything, to do about it. At each step in the decision process, as shown in Figure 10.2, numerous factors operate to make helping behavior more or less likely to occur.

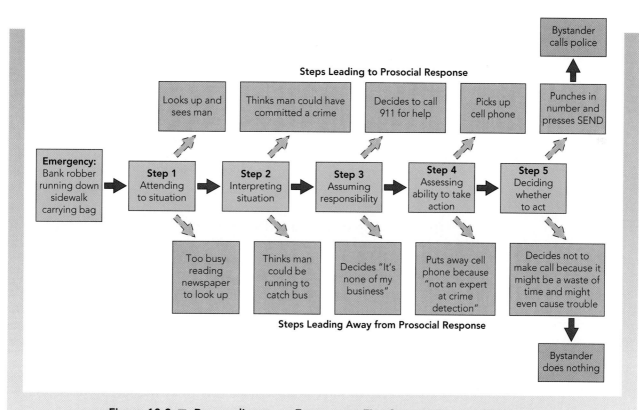

Figure 10.2 ■ Responding to an Emergency: Five Steps to Prosocial Behavior
A prosocial response to an emergency has been conceptualized as the end point of a series of five steps or choice points. At each step, an individual either becomes less likely or more likely to engage in a prosocial response. (*Source: Based on material in Latané and Darley, 1970.*)

Do More Witnesses to an Emergency Mean That More Help Is Given?

Consider the following scenario. You are walking across an icy street, lose your footing as you step up on the curb, and fall, injuring your knee. Because of your pain and the slickness of the ice, you find that you can't get back on your feet. Suppose (1) the block is relatively deserted, and only one person is close enough to witness your accident, or (2) the block is crowded, and a dozen people can see what happened. Common sense suggests that the more bystanders that are present, the more likely you are to be helped. In the first situation, you are forced to depend on the helpfulness of just one individual and that person's decision to help or not help you. In the second situation, with twelve witnesses, there would seem to be a much greater chance that at least one of them (and quite possibly more) will be motivated to behave in a prosocial way. Right? Wrong.

The explanation for the fact that multiple bystanders do not translate into multiple helpers was formulated, shortly after the Kitty Genovese murder, by two social psychologists, John Darley and Bibb Latané. Over lunch, they speculated as to why the large number of bystanders did nothing to stop the killer. In the media, there was much speculation about the widespread selfishness and indifference of people in general or at least of people in big cities. If multiple witnesses increase the odds that someone will help, did that mean that the murder was witnessed and ignored by thirty-eight cold and uncaring individuals?

Darley and Latané (1968) proposed a different, and not at all obvious, reason for the unresponsiveness of the bystanders—instead of increasing the odds that prosocial behavior will occur, having multiple bystanders *decreases* the odds. And, rather than apathy, the large number of witnesses experienced **diffusion of responsibility.** That is, the more bystanders that are present, the less responsibility any one of them feels with respect to dealing with the situation. If that idea is correct, in a situation with only one bystander, help is very likely to be given because all of the responsibility is centered on one individual. As the number of bystanders increases, each one has a smaller and smaller share of the responsibility, and the less likely anyone is to help. The two psychologists designed an experiment to test their prediction of what has become known as the **bystander effect.**

In their groundbreaking experiment, male college students were deliberately exposed to an "emergency" in which a fellow student apparently had a seizure, began to choke, and was clearly in need of help. The participants interacted by means of an intercom, and it was arranged that some believed they were the only person aware of the emergency, one of two bystanders, or one of five bystanders. Helpfulness was measured in terms of (1) the percentage of participants in each experimental group who attempted to help and (2) the time that passed before the help began.

As summarized in Figure 10.3, the prediction about diffusion of responsibility was correct. The more bystanders, the lower the percentage of students who made a prosocial response and the longer the helpful students waited before responding. In the example we gave,

diffusion of responsibility
The idea that the amount of responsibility assumed by bystanders to an emergency is shared among them.

bystander effect
The fact that the likelihood of a prosocial response to an emergency is affected by the number of bystanders who are present.

■ Step 1. Noticing or Failing to Notice that Something Unusual Is Happening

An emergency is obviously something that occurs unexpectedly, and there is no sure way to anticipate that it will occur or to plan how best to respond. We are ordinarily doing something else and thinking about other things when we hear a scream outside our window, observe that a fellow student is coughing and unable to speak, or observe that some of the other passengers on our airplane are standing up with box cutters in their hands. If we are asleep, deep in thought, or concentrating on something else, we may simply *fail to notice* that anything unusual is happening.

In everyday life, we ignore many sights and sounds because they are ordinarily not relevant to our concerns. If we were not able to screen out most aspects of our surroundings, we would be overwhelmed by an overload of information. Several years ago, I (Donn Byrne) was giving a talk at the Central University of Venezuela in Caracas. I became dimly aware of occasional sounds outside but didn't pay much attention to the noise until members of my audience became unusually restless and began whispering to one another. The person who was translating for me interrupted to suggest politely

Chapter 10 / Prosocial Behavior

it appears that you would be more likely to be helped if you fell with only one witness present than twelve of them.

Over the years, additional research on prosocial behavior has identified a great many additional factors that determine how people respond to an emergency, but the bystander effect is clearly an important basic discovery. More recently, the bystander effect has been extended to include simply thinking about groups. For example, imagining a dinner gathering with a group (versus having dinner with just one person) inhibits prosocial responsiveness (Garcia et al., 2002). Thus, the *priming* (see Chapter 2) of a social context by inducing people to think about the presence of others results in less helping behavior in a subsequent, unrelated situation. Such findings indicate that diffusion of responsibility can be triggered not only by the presence of others, but also by cognitive processes, thus constituting an **implicit bystander effect.**

Bar graph with left axis "Percentage of Bystanders Helping" (20 to 90) and right axis "Seconds Passing before Help Began" (40 to 180), x-axis "Number of Bystanders."

Callout: As the number of bystanders increased, the time elapsing before help was given increased

Callout: As the number of bystanders increased, the percentage of individuals who helped decreased

Percentage of Bystanders Helping: One = 85, Two = 62, Five = 31

Seconds Passing before Help Began: One = 52, Two = 93, Five = 166

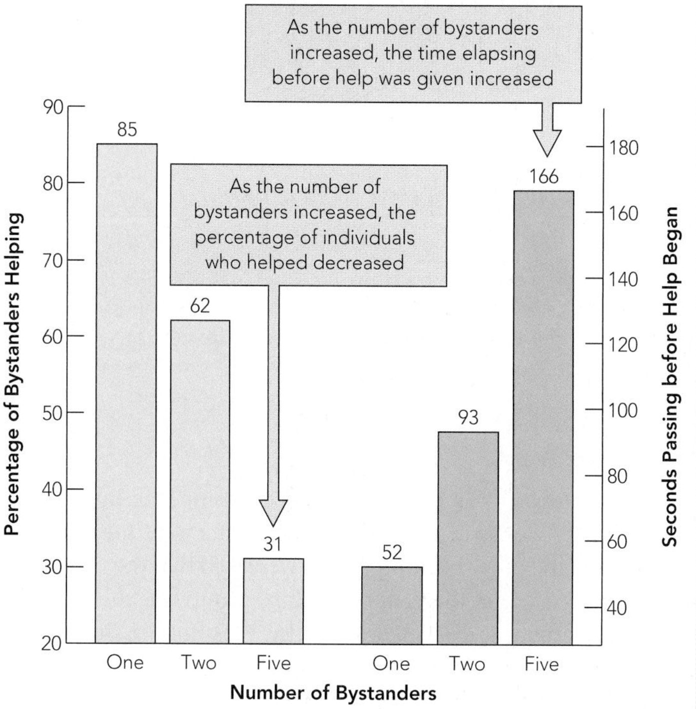

Figure 10.3 ■ The Inhibiting Effect of Multiple Bystanders
In the initial experiment designed to test the proposed *bystander effect*, Darley and Latane (1968) placed college students in a situation in which a fellow student called for help because of what seemed to be a medical emergency. Each research participant believed himself to be either the only bystander aware of the emergency, one of two bystanders, or one of five. As the number of bystanders increased, the percentage of individuals who tried to help the victim decreased. In addition, among those who did attempt to help, the more bystanders, the greater the delay before help was initiated. This effect is explained in terms of *diffusion of responsibility* among those who could possibly provide help—the more bystanders, the less responsibility for each one. (*Source: Based on data in Darley and Latané, 1968.*)

that we take a brief break. We did, and members of the audience rushed to look out the windows. When I joined them, I was surprised to see soldiers and tanks stationed around the campus. Some of the troops were firing in the air above a group of students who were protesting a meeting between a U.S. delegation and members of the Venezuelan government. At that point, I obviously began to pay attention to what was going on. My hosts quickly decided to postpone the talk to a later time in a different location, and we slipped out a side door where cars were waiting to take us away from the confrontation. You may have observed that my belated awareness of the emergency did not lead to any heroic or prosocial action on my part; but awareness at least made such action a possibility. The more general point is that, when people are preoccupied by personal concerns, they pay less attention to what is going on around them. As a result, prosocial behavior is less likely to occur. See Figure 10.4 on page 384 for another example.

Darley and Batson (1973) conducted a field study to test the importance of this first step in the decision process. Their research was conducted with students in training for the clergy, individuals who should be especially likely to help a stranger in need. The experimenters instructed each participant to walk to a nearby building on the

implicit bystander effect
The decrease in helping behavior brought about by simply thinking about being in a group.

"Please! Let me through. I don't have time to go around."

Figure 10.4 ■ Too Busy to Help
When an individual is preoccupied by his or her own concerns, as is the man with the briefcase, a prosocial response to an emergency is unlikely. In some instances, busy people may not even be aware of the emergency situation. (*Source: © The New Yorker Collection 2002 Leo Cullum from cartoonbank.com. All Rights Reserved.*)

campus to give a talk. In order to vary the degree of preoccupation, the investigators created three different conditions. Some of the seminary students were told that they had plenty of extra time to reach the other building, some were told that they were right on schedule with just enough time to get there, and the third group was told that they were late for the speaking assignment and needed to hurry. Presumably, during their walk across the campus, individuals in the first group would be the least preoccupied by the need to hurry, and those in the third group would be the most preoccupied. Would you guess that the degree of preoccupation influenced whether or not the participants engaged in prosocial behavior? The answer is a resounding "Yes!"

Along the route to the building where the talk was to be given, an emergency was staged. A stranger (actually a research assistant) was slumped in a doorway, coughing and groaning. Would the students notice this apparently sick or injured individual? As shown in Figure 10.5, 63 percent of the participants who had time to spare provided help. For the group that was on schedule, 45 percent helped. In the most preoccupied group (those in a hurry), only 10 percent responded to the stranger. Many of the preoccupied students paid little or no attention to the person who was coughing and groaning. They simply stepped over him and continued on their way.

It seems clear that a person who is too busy to pay attention to his or her surroundings is very likely not to notice even an obvious emergency. Under these conditions, little help is given because the potential helper is not even aware that an emergency exists.

■ Step 2. Correctly Interpreting an Event as an Emergency

Even after we pay attention to an event, we have only limited and incomplete information as to what exactly is happening. Most of the time, whatever catches our attention does not turn out to be an emergency and need not be a concern of ours. One day, I (Donn Byrne) was working at home. I heard one of our dogs barking and looked out to see a man I did

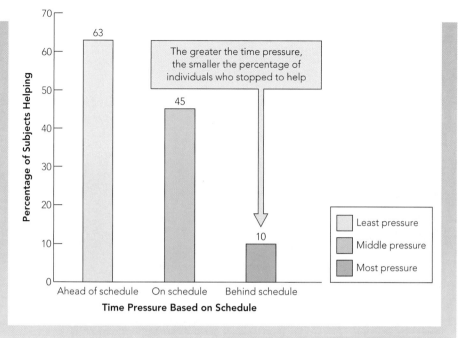

Figure 10.5 ■ In Too Much of a Hurry to Notice an Emergency
People who are concerned about being late for an appointment are less likely to pay attention to what is going on around them and, as a consequence, less likely to help a stranger in need. When research participants were told that they were ahead of schedule in getting to an appointment (and thus had time to spare), most stopped and helped a stranger who was slumped over, coughing and groaning in a doorway. Among those who were told they were on schedule (with just enough time), less than half stopped to help. Among those supposedly late for the appointment, only one out of ten stopped and provided assistance. (*Source: Based on data from Darley and Batson, 1973.*)

not know walking along the edge of our property holding some kind of object under his arm. This unexpected intruder could have created an emergency. (A hunter about to shoot a wild turkey and maybe hitting one of our pets? A burglar casing the joint? A terrorist planning to poison the nearby reservoir containing Albany's water supply?) If any of these hypotheses turned out to be correct, I had an emergency on my hands and should call 911. I went out on our deck, looked around, and discovered that the man was part of a surveying crew. In this instance, caution was a good choice. Rather than panic, it is usually best to assume that there is a routine, everyday explanation rather than an unusual and unlikely one (Macrae & Milne, 1992). When, however, there really is an emergency, caution inhibits the motive to respond in a prosocial way, as in Figure 10.6. on page 386.

Whenever potential helpers are not completely sure about what is going on, they tend to hold back and wait for further information. It's quite possible that in the early morning when Kitty Genovese was murdered, her neighbors could not clearly see what was happening, even though they heard the screams and knew that a man and a woman seemed to be having a dispute. It could have just been a loud argument between a woman and her boyfriend. Or, perhaps the couple had been drinking and were just joking around. Either of these two possibilities is actually more likely to be true than the fact that a stranger was stabbing a woman to death. With ambiguous information as to whether one is witnessing a serious problem or something inconsequential, most people are inclined to accept a comforting and undemanding and usually accurate interpretation that indicates no need to take action (Wilson & Petruska, 1984).

This suggests that the presence of multiple witnesses may inhibit helping not only because of the diffusion of responsibility, but also because it is embarrassing to

Figure 10.6 ■ What's Going on Here?
Even if you are paying attention and notice something unusual in your
surroundings, the need for help may not be obvious. Passing a glass
door in an office building, you see these two men interacting. Are they
having a simple conversation? Is one threatening the other? Are they
angry? Could one be a thief? How do you decide what is happening?

misinterpret a situation and to act inappropriately. Making such a serious mistake in front of several strangers might lead them to conclude that you are overreacting in a stupid way (see Figure 10.7). If I had called the State Troopers to rush to my house to investigate the mysterious intruder, both they and the surveyors would probably have enjoyed telling people about my panic for the next several weeks. Of course, had the man been a terrorist on his way to poison Albany's water supply, I would have helped save the city's residents from being poisoned. In this instance, I simply resolved my uncertainty by obtaining more information.

A second example of an interpretation problem is provided by the following story (Hawkins, 2002):

> *A man and his wife are awakened at 3 A.M. by a loud pounding on the door. The man gets up and goes to the door where an inebriated stranger, standing in the pouring rain, asks for a push.*
>
> *"Not a chance," says the husband, "It's three o'clock in the morning." He slams the door and returns to bed. "Who was that?" asked his wife. "Just some drunk guy asking for a push," he answers. "Did you help him?" she asks. "No, I did not, it is three in the morning and it's like a monsoon out there."*
>
> *"Well, you have a short memory," said the wife. "Can't you remember about three months ago when we broke down and those two guys helped us? I think you should help him, and you should be ashamed of yourself."*
>
> *The man does as he is told, gets dressed, and goes out in the rain. He calls out into the dark, "Hello, are you still there?" "Yes," the stranger answers. "Do you still need a push?" "Yes, please!" "Where are you?" asks the husband.*
>
> *"Over here on the swing!" replies the drunk.*

When others are present as fellow observers of such events, we rely on social comparisons to test our interpretations (see Chapters 4, 7, and 9). If other people show no sign of alarm about whatever we are witnessing, it is safer to follow their lead. No one wants to look foolish to others or to lose his or her "cool." The tendency for an individual surrounded by a group of strangers to hesitate and do nothing is based on what is known as **pluralistic ignorance.** That is, because none of the bystanders knows for sure what is happening, each depends on the others to provide cues. Each individual is less likely to respond if the others fail to respond. Latané and Darley (1968) provided a dramatic demonstration of just how far people will go to avoid making a possibly inappropriate response to what may or may not be an emergency. The investigators placed students in a room alone or with two other students and asked them to fill out questionnaires. After several minutes had passed, the experimenters secretly and quietly pumped smoke into the research room through a vent. When a participant was working there alone, most (75 percent) stopped what they were doing when the smoke appeared and left the room to report the problem. When three people were in the room, however, only 38 percent reacted to the smoke. Even after it became so thick that it was difficult to see, 62 percent continued to work on the questionnaire and failed to make any response to the smoke-filled room. The presence of other people clearly inhibits responsiveness. It is as if risking death is preferable to making a fool of oneself.

This inhibiting effect is much less if the group consists of friends rather than strangers, because friends are likely to communicate with one another about what is going on (Rutkowski, Gruder, & Romer, 1983). The same is true of people in small towns who are likely to know one another as opposed to big cities where most people are strangers (Levine et al., 1994). Interestingly, any anxiety about the reactions of others and thus the fear of doing the wrong thing is reduced by alcohol. As a result, people who have been drinking show an increased tendency to be helpful (Steele, Critchlow, & Liu, 1985).

pluralistic ignorance
The tendency of bystanders in an emergency to rely on what other bystanders do and say, even though none of them is sure about what is happening or what to do about it. Very often, all of the bystanders hold back and behave as if there is no problem. Each individual uses this "information" to justify the failure to act.

"I'M NOT JUMPING . . . THIS IS THE DESIGNATED SMOKING AREA."

©2004 WM. HOEST ENTERPRISES, INC.

Figure 10.7 ■ Misinterpreting a Situation as an Emergency
In order to respond to an emergency, one must interpret the situation correctly. Because people fear making a mistake and looking foolish, they may hesitate before taking action until they are sure. In this cartoon, the man in the window believed he was at the scene of a suicide attempt, but the man on the ledge was only there to smoke a cigarette. (*Source:* © 2004; Reprinted courtesy of Bunny Hoest and Parade Magazine.)

Figure 10.8 ■ Who Is Responsible for Doing Something?
In many emergency situations, certain individuals are the appropriate ones to take charge—for example, a military officer in response to an armed attack, a police officer in response to an accident or a crime, someone with medical training in response to a injury or illness, an instructor in response to a classroom emergency, and so forth.

■ Step 3. Deciding That It Is Your Responsibility to Provide Help

In many instances, the responsibility is clear (see Figure 10.8). Fire fighters are the ones to do something about a blazing building, police officers take charge when cars collide, and medical personnel deal with injuries and illnesses. If responsibility is not clear, people assume that anyone in a leadership role must take responsibility—adults with children, professors with undergraduates, and so on (Baumeister et al., 1988). As we pointed out earlier, when there is only *one* bystander, he or she usually takes charge because there is no alternative.

■ Step 4. Deciding That You Have the Necessary Knowledge and/or Skills to Act

Even if a bystander progresses as far as step 3 and assumes responsibility, a prosocial response cannot occur unless the person knows *how* to be helpful. Some emergencies are sufficiently simple that almost everyone has the necessary skills. If someone slips on the ice, almost any bystander is able to help that person get up. On the other hand, if you see someone parked on the side of the road, peering under the hood of the car, you can't be of direct help unless you know something about cars and how they function. The best you can do is offer to call for assistance.

When emergencies require special skills, usually only a portion of the bystanders are able to help. For example, only good swimmers can assist a person who is drowning. With a medical emergency, a registered nurse is more likely to be helpful than a history professor (Cramer et al., 1988).

■ Step 5. Making the Final Decision to Provide Help

Once a bystander progresses through the first four steps in the decision process, help still does not occur unless he or she makes the ultimate decision to engage in a helpful act. Helping at this final point can be inhibited by fears (often realistic ones) about potential negative consequences. In effect, people are said to engage in "cognitive algebra" as they weigh the positive versus the negative aspects of helping (Fritzsche,

Finkelstein, & Penner, 2000). As we will discuss later, the rewards for being helpful are provided primarily by the emotions and beliefs of the helper, but there are a great many kinds of potential costs. For example, if you had intervened in the Kitty Genovese attack, you might have been stabbed yourself. You might slip while helping a person who has fallen on the ice. A person might be asking for assistance simply as a trick that leads to robbery or worse (R. L. Byrne, 2001).

Though it is easy to assume that anyone who fails to provide help must have character flaws, it is not fair to jump to that conclusion. As pointed out, there are some very good reasons why bystanders might avoid a prosocial response.

KEY POINTS

★ When an emergency arises and someone is in need of help, a bystander may or may not respond in a prosocial way. Responses can range from heroism to apathy.

★ In part because of *diffusion of responsibility,* the more bystanders present as witnesses to an emergency, the less likely each of them is to provide help and the greater the delay before help occurs (the *bystander effect*).

★ When faced with an emergency, a bystander's tendency to help or not help depends, in part, on decisions made at five crucial steps. First, it is necessary for the bystander to pay attention and be aware that an unusual event is occurring.

★ Second, the bystander must correctly interpret the situation as an emergency.

★ Third, the bystander must assume responsibility to provide help.

★ Fourth, the bystander must have the required knowledge and skills to be able to act.

★ Fifth, the bystander must decide to act.

External and Internal Influences on Helping Behavior

As we have seen, interest in prosocial behavior was sparked by the question of why bystanders at an emergency sometimes help and sometimes do nothing. The initial factor to be identified was an external one—number of bystanders. In the five-step process, several internal factors were shown to be important: attention, interpretation of the situation, and so on. We now turn to additional aspects of the situation that exert an influence and then to a number of internal factors that also play an important role in prosocial responding.

Situational Factors That Enhance or Inhibit Helping

Among the cues that affect the likelihood of helping are the attributes of the victim that determine *attraction,* details of the situation that indicate whether or not the problem is the *responsibility of the victim,* and exposure to *prosocial models* either in the immediate situation or in the bystander's past experience.

Helping Those You Like

Most of the research interest has centered on providing help to strangers, because it is obvious that people are very likely to help their family members and friends. If a close friend were being attacked by a killer, or your brother were choking during an experiment, would you be likely to act? Of course, you would.

Consider a less obvious situation. The victim is a stranger but because he or she is similar to you with respect to age and race, would you be more likely to help than if the victim were a great deal older than yourself and of a different race? The answer is "yes"—a similar victim is more likely to be helped (Hayden, Jackson, & Guydish, 1984; Shaw, Borough, & Fink, 1994). In fact, any characteristic that affects attraction (see Chapter 7) also increases the probability of a prosocial response (Clark et al., 1987). For example, appearance influences prosocial behavior, and a physically attractive victim receives more help than an unattractive one (Benson, Karabenick, & Lerner, 1976).

Men are very likely to provide help to a woman in distress (Piliavin & Unger, 1985), perhaps because of gender differences in specific skills (e.g., changing a tire), perhaps on the basis of sexual attraction (Przybyla, 1985), and perhaps because women are more willing than men to ask for help (Nadler, 1991).

Holding similar values also results in a victim's receiving help. If unemployed individuals have violated the religious values of fundamentalists with respect to belief in God, sexual orientation, or premarital sex, the fundamentalists believed they should not be helped. Instead, the unemployed "sinners" should first change their lifestyles (Jackson & Esses, 1997). If, however, victims were unemployed but had not violated religious values, fundamentalists favored aiding them.

Helping Those Who Mimic Us

A seemingly unlikely determinant of prosocial behavior is **mimicry**—the automatic tendency to imitate the behavior of those with whom we interact. Humans are found to mimic the accent, tone of voice, and rate of speech of those around them. They also mimic the postures, mannerisms, and moods of others (Chartrand & Bargh, 1999; van Baaren et al., 2004). This tendency seems to be both automatic and unconscious. Apparently, the expression "Monkey see, monkey do" applies to us as well. This is thought to be an innate tendency—and one that has a positive effect on the person being mimicked. Mimicry increases liking, empathy, and rapport; as a result, it plays a key role in social interactions (Chartrand, Maddux, & Lakin, 2004), much like the role of laughter described in Chapter 7. One of the effects of mimicry is to increase prosocial behavior (van Baaren et al., 2003).

As one example of the experimental study of *deliberate* mimicry, research participants interacted for six minutes either with an experimenter who copied their posture, body orientation, and the position of their arms and legs or with a noncopying experimenter. Afterward, the experimenter "accidentally" dropped several pens on the floor. *All* of the research participants who had been mimicked helped by picking up the pens, while only a third of those who were not mimicked did so. Because mimicry increases attraction, this finding could simply be an attraction effect and not an indication that mimicry plays a unique role. To investigate this possibility, additional experimental conditions were investigated.

In these new experiments, students once again were or were not mimicked while interacting with the experimenter. In one condition, a different person entered the room and dropped pens on the floor. In another condition, following the interaction, each student was paid two euros and later given the option of keeping the money or donating some or all of it anonymously to a charity that helps hospitalized children. As can be seen in Figure 10.9, in each of the three experimental conditions, those who had been mimicked were more likely to help than those who had not been mimicked.

Altogether, this research confirms the proposal that mimicry increases the likelihood of engaging in prosocial behavior. Further, the prosocial acts are not restricted to helping the person who engaged in mimicry, but extends to helping others as well (van Baaren et al., 2004). Why should mimicry have this kind of effect? Some investigators suggest that mimicry plays a role in survival and reproductive success because it enhances cohesion and safety among animals in a group (Dijksterhuis, Bargh, & Miedema, 2000) and because imitation is an important aspect of learning and acculturation (de Waal, 2002). When one person mimics another, it could also serve as a non-

mimicry
The automatic tendency to imitate those with whom we interact. Being mimicked increases one's prosocial tendencies.

verbal message that "we are similar." In any event, mimicry can be included as *one* of the situational factors influencing helping behavior.

Helping Those Who Are Not Responsible for Their Problem

If you were walking down the sidewalk early one morning and passed a man lying unconscious by the curb, would you help him? You know that helpfulness would be influenced by all of the factors we have discussed—from the presence of other bystanders to interpersonal attraction. There is an additional consideration. Why is the man lying there? If his clothing is stained and torn and an empty wine bottle in a paper sack is by his side, what would you assume about his problem? You might well decide that he is a hopeless drunk who passed out on the sidewalk. In contrast, what if he is wearing an expensive suit and has a nasty cut on his forehead? These cues might lead you to decide that this was a man who had been brutally mugged on his way to work. Based on your attributions about the reasons that a person might be lying unconscious on the side-walk, you would be less likely to help the stranger with the wine bottle than the one with the cut on his head. In general, we are less likely to act if we believe that the victim is to blame for his or her predicament (Higgins & Shaw, 1999; Weiner, 1980). The man in the business suit did not choose to be attacked, so we are more inclined to help him.

Exposure to Prosocial Models Increases Prosocial Behavior

You are out shopping and come across representatives of a charity organization collecting money for a good cause. Do you decide to help by making a contribution? An important factor in this decision is whether you observe someone else make a donation. If others give money, you are more likely to do so (Macauley, 1970). Even the presence of

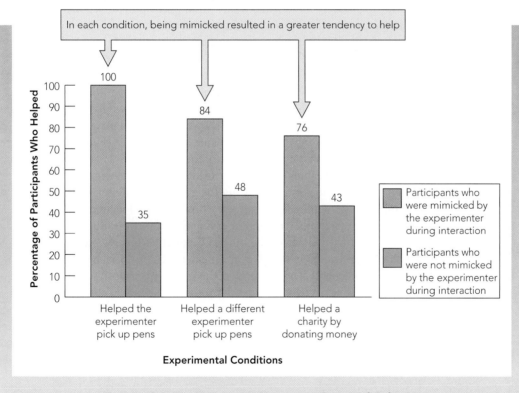

Figure 10.9 ■ Mimicry: An Impetus to Prosocial Behavior
During a six-minute interaction, the experimenter either mimicked or did not mimic each research participant. Afterward, helping was greater in the mimicked group with respect to the experimenter, to a different experimenter, and to a charity organization. In social interactions, mimicry occurs automatically, and it evokes a positive response in the person being mimicked. (*Source: Based on data in van Baaren et al., 2004.*)

Figure 10.10 ■ **How Likely Are You to Help This Motorist?**
Help is much more likely to be given in such a situation if you have recently witnessed someone else receiving help. Prosocial models facilitate such behavior whether they are members of our family, TV characters, or strangers.

coins and bills (presumably contributed earlier in the day) encourages you to respond. The various compliance techniques described in Chapter 9 are directly relevant to this kind of helping behavior. Collecting money for charity involves many of the same psychological processes that are involved in panhandling or in selling a product.

In an emergency, we know that the presence of bystanders who fail to respond inhibits helpfulness. It is equally true, however, that the presence of a helpful bystander provides a strong *social model,* and the result is an increase in helping behavior among the remaining bystanders. An example of such modeling is provided by a field experiment in which a young woman (a research assistant) with a flat tire parked her car just off the road (see Figure 10.10). Motorists were much more inclined to stop and help this woman if they had previously driven past a staged scene in which another woman with car trouble could be seen receiving assistance (Bryan & Test, 1967).

In addition to prosocial models in our surroundings, helpful models in the media also contribute to the creation of a social norm that encourages prosocial behavior. In an investigation of the power of TV, Sprafkin, Liebert, and Poulous (1975) were able to increase the prosocial responsiveness of six-year-olds. Some of the children were shown an episode of *Lassie* in which there was a rescue scene—thus serving as a model for providing help. A second group of children watched a *Lassie* episode that did not focus on a prosocial theme. A third group watched a humorous episode of *The Brady Bunch*—also without prosocial content. After watching one of these shows, the children played a game, with the winner receiving a prize. During the game, it was arranged that each child would encounter a group of whining, hungry puppies. At that point, the child was faced with a choice between pausing to help the pups (and thereby losing the chance to win a prize) and ignoring the puppies in order to continue playing the game. The children were clearly influenced by which TV show they had watched. Those who had viewed the *Lassie* rescue episode stopped and spent much more time trying to comfort the little animals than did the children who watched either of the other TV presentations. As predicted, watching prosocial behavior on television increased the incidence of prosocial behavior in real life.

Additional experiments have confirmed the influence of positive TV models. For example, preschool children who watch such prosocial shows as *Sesame Street* or *Barney and Friends* are much more apt to respond in a prosocial way than are children who do not watch such shows (Forge & Phemister, 1987). Of course, as we will see in more detail in Chapter 11, exposure to media can also have negative effects. As one example, research participants who played violent video games such as *Mortal Kombat* and *Street Fighter* showed a subsequent *decrease* in prosocial behavior (Anderson & Bushman, 2001).

Emotions and Prosocial Behavior

A person's emotional state is determined by both internal and external factors. On any given day, one's mood can be happy or sad, angry or loving, as well as many other possibilities. As we discussed in Chapter 7, emotions are often divided into two major categories—positive and negative. It might seem that being in a good mood would increase the tendency to help others, while being in a bad mood would interfere with helping. There is, in fact, a good deal of evidence supporting that general assumption (Forgas, 1998a). Research indicates, however, that the effects of emotions on prosocial behavior can be more complicated than we might expect (Salovey, Mayer, & Rosenhan, 1991).

Positive Emotions and Prosocial Behavior

Children seem very quick to pick up the idea that it's better to request something from a parent (or a teacher) when that person is in a good mood rather than in a bad one. Most often, this is true, and the effect extends to prosocial acts as well. Research indicates that people are more willing to help a stranger when their mood has been elevated by listening to a comedian (Wilson, 1981), finding even a small amount of money (Isen & Levin, 1972), or just spending time outdoors on a pleasant day (Cunningham, 1979).

Emotions are also influenced by smell. A pleasant fragrance makes us feel better, and this positive mood affects our behavior (Baron, 1990c). Baron and Thomley (1994) found that exposure to a pleasant lemon or floral odor increases one's willingness to spend time helping others. In a field study, shoppers in a mall were most likely to pick up a stranger's dropped pen or to make change for a stranger when they were near a pleasant smelling shop such as a bakery (Baron, 1997a).

Under certain specific circumstances, however, a positive mood can *decrease* the probability of responding in a prosocial way (Isen, 1984). A bystander in a very positive mood who encounters an ambiguous emergency tends to interpret the situation as a *nonemergency*. Even if it is clear that an emergency exists, people in a good mood tend to resist helping if that involves doing something difficult and unpleasant (Rosenhan, Salovey, & Hargis, 1981). It seems that a good mood gives us a feeling of independence, and this includes the power to turn our backs on someone in need.

Negative Emotions and Prosocial Behavior

Again, it is commonly assumed that someone in a negative mood is less likely to help others. And it is true that an unhappy person who is focusing on his or her own problems is less likely to engage in prosocial acts (Amato, 1986).

As with positive emotions, however, specific circumstances can reverse this general trend. For example, if the act of helping involves behavior that makes you feel better, a prosocial act is more likely when an individual is in a bad mood than in a neutral one (Cialdini, Kenrick, & Bauman, 1982). A negative emotion most often has a *positive* effect on prosocial behavior if the negative feelings are not too intense, if the emergency is clear-cut rather than ambiguous, and if the act of helping is interesting and satisfying rather than dull and unrewarding (Cunningham et al., 1990). The various effects of positive and negative emotions on prosocial behavior are summarized in Figure 10.11 on page 394.

Empathy and Other Personality Dispositions Associated with Helping

We have just described how a variety of situational and emotional factors can affect prosocial behavior, but different people facing the same situation or being in the same emotional state do *not* respond in an identical way. Some are more helpful than others. Such individual differences in behavior are assumed to be based on **personality dispositions**—the characteristic behavioral tendencies of individuals. Personality dispositions are based on differences in genetic composition, learning experiences, or a combination of the two. Such dispositions tend to be relatively consistent over time. For example, children who are prosocial in early childhood behave in a similar way in adolescence (Caprara et al., 2000; Eisenberg et al., 2002).

personality disposition
A characteristic behavioral tendency that is based on genetics, learning experiences, or both. Such dispositions tend to be stable over time and across situations.

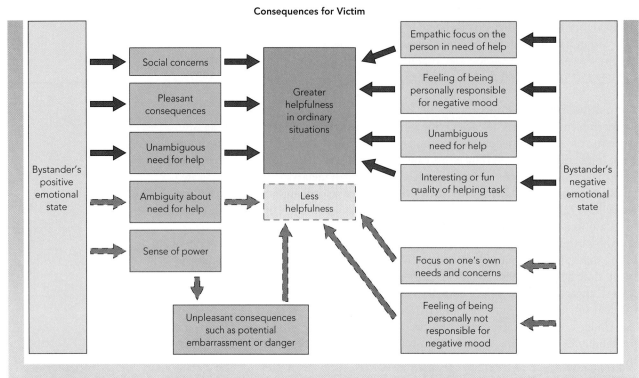

Consequences for Victim

Figure 10.11 ■ Emotional Effects on Prosocial Behavior
Depending on a number of specific factors, a positive emotional state can either increase or decrease the likelihood of a prosocial response—and the same is true of a negative emotional state. This diagram summarizes the primary factors and their effects.

■ Empathy: A Basic Requirement

Much of the interest in individual differences in helpfulness has concentrated on **empathy** (Clary & Orenstein, 1991; Schlenker & Britt, 2001). Empathy consists of affective and cognitive responses to another person's emotional state and includes sympathy, a desire to solve the problem, and taking the perspective of the other person (Batson et al., 2003). An empathetic person feels what another person is feeling and understands why that person feels as he or she does (Azar, 1997; Darley, 1993; Duan, 2000).

An affective component is essential to empathy, and children as young as twelve months seem clearly to feel distress in response to the distress of others (Brothers, 1990). This same characteristic is also observed in other primates (Ungerer et al., 1990) and probably among dogs and dolphins as well (Azar, 1997), as shown in Figure 10.12. Evolutionary psychologists suggest that the affective component of empathy also includes feeling sympathetic—not only feeling another's pain, but also expressing concern and attempting to do something to relieve the pain. Such findings are consistent with the idea that prosocial behavior has a biological basis.

The cognitive component of empathy appears to be a uniquely human quality that develops only after we progress beyond infancy. Such cognitions include the ability to consider the viewpoint of another person, sometimes referred to as *perspective taking*—the ability to "put yourself in someone else's shoes." Social psychologists have identified three different types of perspective taking (Batson, Early, & Salvarani, 1997):

1. You can imagine how the other person perceives an event and how he or she must feel as a result—taking the "imagine other" perspective. Those who take this perspective experience relatively pure empathy, which motivates altruistic behavior.

2. You can imagine how you would feel if you were in that situation—taking the "imagine self" perspective. People who do this also experience empathy, but they

empathy
A complex affective and cognitive response to another person's emotional distress. Empathy includes being able to feel the other person's emotional state, feeling sympathetic and attempting to solve the problem, and taking the perspective of others. One can be empathetic toward fictional characters as well as toward real-life victims.

Figure 10.12 ■ The Biological Basis of Empathy
Empathy seems to be a built-in response that is useful to our species (and to others as well). Humans as young as twelve months, other primates, and even dogs and dolphins have been observed to demonstrate empathy in response to the distress of others. This dog is towing the man out of a lake, saving him from possibly drowning.

tend to be motivated by self-interest, and self-interest sometimes interferes with altruism.

3. The third type of perspective taking involves identifying with fictional characters—feeling empathy for someone (or some creature) in a story. In this instance, there is an emotional reaction to the joys, sorrows, and fears of a character in a book, movie, or TV program. Many children (and adults, too) may cry when Bambi discovers that his mother has been shot, or cringe in fear when the Wicked Witch of the West threatens Dorothy and "your little dog, too."

■ How Does Empathy Develop?

People differ a great deal in how they respond to the emotional distress of others. At one extreme are those willing to risk their lives to help another person. At the other extreme are those who enjoy inflicting pain and humiliation on a helpless victim (see Figure 10.13 on page 396). As with most dispositional characteristics, the answer seems to lie in a combination of biological differences and differences in experience.

Genetic factors were investigated by Davis, Luce, and Kraus (1994). They examined more than eight hundred sets of identical and nonidentical twins and found that heredity underlies the two affective aspects of empathy (personal distress and sympathetic concern) but not cognitive empathy. Biological differences account for about a third of the variation among people in affective empathy. Presumably, other factors account for differences in cognitive empathy and for two thirds of the variation in affective empathy. Psychologist Janet Strayer (quoted in Azar, 1997) suggests that we are all born with the biological capacity for empathy but that our specific experiences determine whether this innate potential becomes a vital part of our selves or fails to manifest itself. Many children of preschool age are able to differentiate empathic and selfish behavior in others, and those who understand this difference behave in a more prosocial way than do those who do not (Ginsburg et al., 2003).

What kinds of specific experiences might enhance or inhibit the development of empathy? Having a secure attachment style facilitates an empathic response to the needs

Figure 10.13 ■ **Empathy versus Total Absence of Empathy**
Strong feelings of empathy can motivate some individuals to remarkable acts of heroism
and tenderness, as with these rescue workers who removed a woman from one of the towers in
the World Trade Center on 9-11-01. At the opposite extreme, the absence of empathy can lead to
barbarous acts against innocent victims, as with the Chechen separatists who killed several hundred
Russian school children, including the 16-year-old girl whose picture is being held up by a relative.

of others (Mikulincer et al., 2001). Earlier, we described research indicating the positive effects of brief exposure to prosocial TV models on empathy. It seems likely that *prolonged* exposure to such models on television and in movies would be of added value. Researchers believe that the influence of parents as models is probably much greater than the influence of the media. In his book *The Moral Intelligence of Children,* psychiatrist Robert Coles (1997) emphasizes the importance of mothers and fathers in shaping such behavior. He suggests that the key is to teach children to be "good" and "kind" and to think about other people rather than solely about themselves. *Good* children are not self-centered, and they are more likely to respond to the needs of others. Moral intelligence is not based on memorizing rules and regulations or on learning abstract definitions. Instead, children learn by observing what their parents do and say in their everyday lives. Coles believes that the elementary school years are the crucial time during which a child develops or fails to develop a conscience.

In early adolescence, the positive influence of parents and teachers in some instances is replaced by the negative influence of peers (Ma et al., 2002). Without appropriate models and appropriate experiences throughout their development, children can easily grow into selfish and rude adolescents and then into equally unpleasant adults. Coles quotes novelist Henry James, whose nephew asked how he should live his life. James replied, "Three things in human life are important. The first is to be kind. The second is to be kind. And the third is to be kind." Coles agrees and says that those who learn to be kind have a strong commitment to helping others rather than hurting them. Empathy is most likely to develop if the child's mother is a warm person, if both parents emphasize how other people are affected by hurtful behavior, and if the family is able to discuss emotions in a supportive atmosphere. Parents who use anger as the major way to control their children inhibit the development of empathy (Azar, 1997; Carpenter, 2001a).

Either because of genetic differences or because of different socialization experiences, women express higher levels of empathy than do men (Trobst, Collins, & Embree, 1994). Consistent with that finding is the fact that women outnumbered men two to one among those in World War II who helped rescue Jews from the Nazis (Anderson, 1993).

A special instance of empathy is the response of people to catastrophes such as a natural disaster or manmade disasters such as the attack on the World Trade Center in

Figure 10.14 ■ **Massive Disasters Bring Forth Massive Altruism**
As shown here after Hurricane Charley hit Port Charlotte, Florida, whenever there is a human catastrophe, caused either by nature or by other human beings, people all over the world express sympathy and often provide assistance in the form of charitable contributions. Empathy tends to be greatest toward victims similar to oneself and in response to a type of catastrophe that one has experienced personally.

New York in 2001 and the train bombing in Madrid in 2004. Most people respond with sympathy and very often with material assistance (see Figure 10.14). Empathy tends to be greater if the victims are similar to yourself and if you have experienced the same kind of catastrophe in the past (Batson, Sager et al., 1997; den Ouden & Russell, 1997; Sattler, Adams, & Watts, 1995).

■ Additional Personality Variables Associated with Prosocial Behavior

Empathy and altruistic motivation are related to other positive characteristics, such as a sense of well-being, achievement motivation, sociability, and an emotional state that is consistently positive, but empathy is rare among those who are high in aggressiveness (Krueger, Hicks, & McGue, 2001; Menesini, 1997; Miller & Jansen-op-de-Haar, 1997). People who express *interpersonal trust* engage in more prosocial acts than do people who mistrust others (Cadenhead & Richman, 1996). *Machiavellianism* refers to people who tend to be distrustful, cynical, egocentric, manipulative, and controlling. Individuals scoring high on this dimension are *unlikely* to exhibit prosocial tendencies (McHoskey, 1999).

The fact that multiple aspects of the personality are involved in prosocial behavior has led some investigators to propose that a combination of relevant factors constitutes what has been designated as the **altruistic personality**. An altruistic person is high on five dimensions that are found in people who engage in prosocial behavior in an emergency situation (Bierhoff, Klein, & Kramp, 1991). The same five personality characteristics were also found among people who actively helped Jews in Europe in the 1940s. These dispositional factors are as follows:

altruistic personality
A combination of dispositional variables associated with *prosocial behavior*. The components are *empathy*, belief in a just world, acceptance of social responsibility, having an internal locus of control, and not being egocentric.

1. *Empathy.* As you might expect, those who help are found to be higher in empathy than are those who do not. The most altruistic people describe themselves as responsible, socialized, conforming, tolerant, self-controlled, and motivated to make a good impression.

2. *Belief in a just world.* Helpful individuals perceive the world as a fair and predictable place in which good behavior is rewarded and bad behavior is punished. This belief leads to the conclusion that helping those in need is the right thing to do *and also* to the expectation that the person who helps will actually benefit from doing a good deed.

3. *Social responsibility.* The most helpful individuals also express the belief that each person is responsible for doing his or her best to assist anyone who needs help.

4. *Internal locus of control.* This is the belief that a person can choose to behave in ways that maximize good outcomes and minimize bad ones. People who fail to help, in contrast, tend to have an *external locus of control* and believe that their behavior is irrelevant, because outcomes are controlled by luck, fate, people in positions of power, and other uncontrollable factors.

5. *Low egocentrism.* Altruistic people do *not* tend to be self-absorbed and competitive.

In summary, prosocial behavior is found to be influenced in both positive and negative ways by many aspects of the situation, by one's emotional state, as well as by empathy and other personality dispositions that are based, in part, on genetic differences and, in part, on childhood experiences.

KEY POINTS

★ Positive and negative emotional states can either enhance or inhibit prosocial behavior, depending on specific factors in the situation and on the nature of the required assistance.

★ Individual differences in altruistic behavior are based, in large part, on *empathy*, a complex response that includes both affective and cognitive components. The extent to which a person is able to respond with empathy depends on hereditary factors and learning experiences.

★ The *altruistic personality* consists of empathy plus belief in a just world, social responsibility, internal locus of control, and low egocentrism.

Long-Term Commitment to Prosocial Action and the Effects of Being Helped

In addition to responding to an emergency situation by helping someone in need, prosocial behavior takes many other forms. We have mentioned some of these, including picking up pens that someone has dropped, comforting an unhappy puppy, protecting victims of persecution, giving money to a charity, and becoming an organ donor. A somewhat different type of altruistic behavior is represented by *volunteering* to engage in work for a worthy cause, often over a long period of time. With respect to all types of prosocial behavior, moral issues arise in making a choice as to whether to act or not, and the individual must balance *self-interest* with *moral integrity,* while not engaging in *moral hypocrisy.* Still another aspect of prosocial behavior is the *effect of helping* on the person being helped. We deal with each of these issues in the following section.

Volunteering

A special type of prosocial behavior is required when the person in need has a chronic, continuing problem that requires help over a prolonged time period (Williamson &

Figure 10.15 ■ **Volunteering Time and Effort to Help Those in Need**
Volunteerism is a form of prosocial behavior that requires a long-term commitment to engage in helpful acts. The example shown here is former President Jimmy Carter working with Habitat for Humanity to build affordable homes for people who lack adequate housing or enough money to acquire adequate housing.

Schulz, 1995). A person who volunteers to provide assistance in this context must commit his or her time and effort over weeks, months, or even longer. In the United States alone, almost one hundred million adults volunteer 20.5 billion hours each year, averaging 4.2 hours of prosocial activity each week (Moore, 1993). Among people age 45 and up, an amazing 87 percent volunteered time or money during 2003 (What gives?, 2004). It is reasonable to assume that, around the world, people are spending an enormous amount of time engaged in voluntary acts of helpfulness.

The five steps required to respond to an emergency that were described earlier also apply to volunteering. In order to help those who are homeless, for example, you must become aware of the problem (usually through the news media), interpret the problem accurately (a major need is for affordable housing), assume personal responsibility to provide help, decide on a course of action that is possible for you (e.g., signing up to work with Habitat for Humanity several hours a week), and then actually engage in the behavior (see Figure 10.15).

What motivates people to give up a portion of their private lives to help others when most have more than enough to do as it is? One answer is that an individual has to be convinced of the importance of a given need; there are obviously many worthwhile causes, and no one can help all of them. When the people who volunteer time and money are identified by race and ethnic group, different concerns become apparent (What gives?, 2004). In the United States, whites give most to help animals, the environment, and emergency personnel such as police officers and fire fighters. African Americans are more likely to assist those who are homeless or hungry, groups fighting for minority rights, and religious institutions. Asian Americans prefer helping museums and other artistic and cultural enterprises. Hispanics provide help to immigrants and to people in other countries. It seems that people with different backgrounds are motivated by the specific concerns of their group. On a more personal level, motives also vary, and we will examine some of them.

■ Motives for Volunteering

Patients with AIDS provide an example of people with a continuing problem, requiring the time-consuming commitment of volunteers. While progress is being made in medical research seeking a way to immunize against HIV infection and to find a cure for AIDS, throughout the world a growing number of individuals require immediate assistance as they await death. Volunteers can work in preventive educational programs or with groups raising money for research and treatment. It is also possible to work directly with patients to provide emotional support and to help with daily household needs and transportation.

AIDS provides a special excuse not to help; as we have seen, people have less sympathy for a victim perceived to be responsible for his or her problem. Pullium (1993) found that people have much less empathy for and are less willing to help an AIDS patient who has engaged in homosexual acts or who has shared needles than a patient who contracted the disease from a blood transfusion. Even if one can bypass the issue of blame, there is the fear (however unfounded) of contracting the disease or of being avoided by friends

Table 10.1 ■ Why Do People Volunteer?

Six distinct functions are served by engaging in volunteer activity. Appeals for volunteers are most effective if they recognize that different individuals have different motives for volunteering. The sample items are taken from a scale developed to measure why people volunteer.

FUNCTION SERVED	DEFINITION	SAMPLE ITEM
Values	To express or act on important values such as humanitarianism	"I feel it is important to help others."
Understanding	To learn more about the world or exercise skills that are often not used	"Volunteering lets me learn through direct, hands-on experience."
Enhancement	To grow and develop psychologically through volunteer activities	"Volunteering makes me feel better about myself."
Career	To gain career-related experiences	"Volunteering can help me to get my foot in the door at a place where I would like to work."
Social	To strengthen social relationships	"People I know share an interest in community service."
Protective	To reduce negative feelings, such as guilt, or to address personal problems	"Volunteering is a good escape from my own problems."

(*Source:* Based on information in Clary and Snyder, 1999.)

because of association with these patients. Exposure to a member of a stigmatized group (such as AIDS patients) or to people who associate with that group is likely to trigger an automatic avoidance tendency (Neumann, Hulsenbeck, & Seibt, 2003).

Given these negative considerations, a person must be strongly motivated to volunteer to provide help to someone with this disease. Clary and Snyder (1999) identified six basic functions that are served by working as an AIDS volunteer, and these are summarized in Table 10.1. The decision to volunteer can be based on personal values, the need to understand more about this disease, the desire to enhance one's own development, the chance to gain career-related experience, the need to improve one's own personal relationships, and/or the desire to reduce negative feelings such as guilt or escape from personal problems. In other words, volunteers may work side by side doing exactly the same job, but for quite different underlying reasons.

One benefit of being able to identify these motivational differences is that efforts to recruit volunteers are most successful when there is an emphasis on multiple reasons to become involved rather than just a single reason. The greatest success occurs when it is possible to match the recruitment message to the recipient's motivation (Clary et al., 1998).

In volunteer work, beyond the task of recruitment is the more difficult problem of turnover. About half of those who volunteer quit within a year (Grube & Piliavin, 2000; Omoto & Snyder, 1995). It is sensible to suppose that a major reason to continue with volunteer work is the feeling of satisfaction provided by such activity. Those in the first year of a volunteer project who felt the most satisfaction *did* volunteer more hours per week, but satisfaction was *unrelated* to continued commitment to the activity (Davis, Hall, & Meyer, 2003). Instead, quitting is directly related to their motivation for volunteering in the first place. People who continue volunteer work for at least two and a half years tend to be those motivated by the need to gain understanding, enhance self-esteem, and assist their own personal development. These self-centered needs provide better indicators of who will continue volunteer work than will the seemingly "selfless" needs centering on humanitarianism and the desire to help others.

Volunteering because of Mandates, Altruism, or Generativity

One way to generate volunteerism is to mandate it, as when some high schools and colleges require students to spend a specified amount of time in volunteer work in order to graduate. Though this practice does result in a large number of "volunteers," the sense of being forced to engage in such work decreases interest in future volunteer activity for many students (Stukas, Snyder, & Clary, 1999). These programs have been criticized because "if it is required, don't call it volunteering; and if it is volunteering, it should not be required" (Yuval, 2004, p. A22). College students have a favorable attitude toward volunteering, and some indicate a strong intention to volunteer their time after being exposed to a recruitment message. In fact, however, only one out of three with a high intention score actually enrolled in a volunteer program (Okun & Sloane, 2002).

Do volunteers exhibit the same dispositional characteristics as those who engage in other altruistic behavior? The answer is "yes," in that volunteers tend to assume internal locus of control (Guagnano, 1995) and to be high in empathy (Penner & Finkelstein, 1998), especially with respect to empathic concern and perspective taking (Unger & Thumuluri, 1997).

A different characteristic of volunteerism as been described by McAdams and his colleagues (1997). They define **generativity** as an adult's interest in and commitment to the well-being of future generations. Those high in generativity show this interest and commitment by becoming parents, by teaching young people, and by engaging in acts that will have positive effects beyond their own lifetimes. Generative adults believe that people need to care for one another. They possess enduring moral values that give purpose and meaning to their lives, perceive bad events as opportunities to create good outcomes, and make an effort to contribute to the progressive development of a better society.

Self-Interest, Moral Integrity, and Moral Hypocrisy

Very few people are consciously apathetic or heartless when confronted by someone who is hurt, frightened, lost, hungry, and so forth. Many people can, however, be nudged in that direction by convincing themselves that there is no reason to provide help (Bersoff, 1999)—for example, we can choose to ignore a victim for a variety of reasons, many of which we have discussed. For example, "It's not my responsibility" and "It's her own fault." With a good enough excuse, we can set aside or disengage moral standards (Bandura, 1999b). We tend to overestimate the frequency of our own moral actions and to believe that we are more likely to engage in selfless and kind behavior than are most people—a "holier than thou" self-assessment (Epley & Dunning, 2000). In fact, it is fairly easy for otherwise moral people to find a reason not to act morally in situations as varied as a stranger needing help in an emergency, charities needing help in responding to a natural disaster, and organizations needing volunteers to help care for others. We describe some of the motives underlying moral behavior in the following sections.

Motivation and Morality

Batson and Thompson (2001) suggest that three major motives are relevant when a person is faced with a moral dilemma such as whether to help someone or not, to donate to a worthy cause or not, or to volunteer one's time or not. These motives are *self-interest, moral integrity,* and *moral hypocrisy.* People can be roughly categorized with respect to which motive is primary for them. We examine what is meant by each of these motives.

Most of us are motivated, at least in part, by **self-interest** (sometimes labeled **egoism**). This means that much of our behavior is based on seeking whatever provides us with the most satisfaction; we seek rewards and try to avoid punishments. People whose primary motive is self-interest are not concerned about questions of right and wrong or fair and unfair—they simply do what is best for themselves.

Other people are strongly motivated by **moral integrity.** They care about questions such as goodness and fairness when they act and frequently agree to sacrifice at least

generativity
An adult's concern for and commitment to the well-being of future generations.

self-interest
The motivation to engage in whatever behavior provides the greatest satisfaction for oneself. See *egoism.*

egoism
An exclusive concern with one's own personal needs and welfare rather than with the needs and welfare of others. See *self-interest.*

moral integrity
The motivation to be moral and actually to engage in moral behavior.

some self-interest in order to do "the right thing." For a person primarily motivated by morality, the conflict between self-interest and moral integrity is resolved by making the moral choice. This sometimes painful decision has both internal and external support. For example, a moral decision is enhanced by reflecting on one's values or being reminded of those values by others. At times, of course, moral integrity is overwhelmed by self-interest, and the result is questionable behavior and a feeling of guilt.

A third category of people consists of those who want to *appear* moral while avoiding the costs of actually *being* moral. Their behavior is motivated by **moral hypocrisy.** That is, they are driven by self-interest but are also concerned with outward appearances. It is important for them to seem to care about doing the right thing, while they, in fact, act to satisfy their own needs.

To investigate these basic motivations, Batson and his colleagues (Batson, Kobrynowicz et al., 1997) created a laboratory situation in which undergraduates were faced with a moral dilemma. Each was given the power to assign himself or herself to one of two experimental tasks. The more desirable task included a chance to win raffle tickets. The less desirable task was described as dull and boring (and involved no raffle tickets). Most participants (over 90 percent) agreed that assigning the dull task to oneself was the moral thing to do as well as the polite choice. They accepted the concept that you should "do unto others as you would have them do unto you." Despite these sentiments, most (70 to 80 percent) actually did the opposite. In this simple situation, most people made a choice based on self-interest. Only a minority (20 to 30 percent) behaved in a way they had indicated was the moral thing to do. Subsequent research was designed to determine the effect of varying the strength of moral integrity motivation.

■ Making Morality More Salient

Using the same experimental situation just described, Batson and his colleagues (Batson et al., 1999) made the moral standard of fairness more salient for some participants. They were told, "Most participants feel that giving both people an equal chance—for example, by flipping a coin—is the fairest way to assign themselves and the participant to the tasks." The experimenter then provided a coin for the participants to use if they wished to do so.

Again, there was very good agreement about the most moral choice—almost all agreed that a fair procedure involved either tossing the coin or assigning the dull procedure to themselves. Nevertheless, only about half of the participants tossed the coin. Again, most (80 to 90 percent) of those who did not use the coin, assigned the positive task (raffle tickets, etc.) to themselves. More surprisingly, of those who did toss the coin, the same percentage still took the positive task for themselves. Some of these honestly won the flip of the coin, but many others (presumably motivated by self-interest) cheated when the coin toss didn't turn out the way they wanted (Batson, Thompson, & Chen, 2002). A few (presumably motivated by moral integrity) tossed the coin and made the task assignment on that basis, even when they did not like the outcome. Others (presumably motivated by moral hypocrisy) tossed to coin in order to appear fair, but then ignored the outcome when it conflicted with what they preferred.

In further research, the moral decision was made even more salient by giving participants the choice of flipping a coin or having the experimenter do it (Batson, Tsang, & Thompson, 2000). Most (80 percent) of those who opted for a coin toss wanted the experimenter to do it. With this procedure, they wouldn't have a chance to cheat, making it easier to behave with moral integrity.

One further variation involved making the cost of morality more difficult. The experiment now gave participants a choice of assigning a positive task and a painful task (receiving electric shock)—one to themselves and the other to a fellow participant. Under these conditions, almost all of the participants gave the positive task to themselves without even pretending to be fair.

moral hypocrisy
The motivation to appear moral while doing one's best to avoid the costs involved in actually being moral.

Chapter 10 / Prosocial Behavior

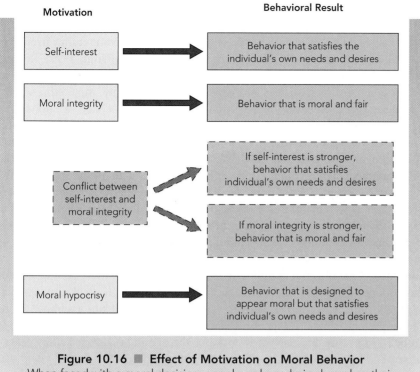

Motivation

Behavioral Result

Self-interest → Behavior that satisfies the individual's own needs and desires

Moral integrity → Behavior that is moral and fair

Conflict between self-interest and moral integrity → If self-interest is stronger, behavior that satisfies individual's own needs and desires

If moral integrity is stronger, behavior that is moral and fair

Moral hypocrisy → Behavior that is designed to appear moral but that satisfies individual's own needs and desires

Figure 10.16 ■ Effect of Motivation on Moral Behavior
When faced with a moral decision, people make a choice based on their underlying motivation. Some are motivated primarily by *self-interest* and do what is most rewarding for themselves, even if it lacks morality and fairness. Some are motivated primarily by *moral integrity* and behave in a moral and fair way. Moral integrity often conflicts with self-interest, and external factors can affect one's choices. Some individuals are motivated primarily by *moral hypocrisy* and behave so as to appear moral while actually meeting their own personal needs. (*Source: Based on information in Batson & Thompson, 2001.*)

In summary, as shown in Figure 10.16, it seems that some people simply choose to act in their own self-interest, even though they realize that this is less fair and less moral. Others are motivated to act in a moral way, but not when the moral choice is sufficiently unpleasant. Still others make it seem as if they are acting in a moral way, but their actual behavior is based on self-interest, even if it requires cheating.

Despite what we might like to think about ourselves, even in a simple choice situation, self-interest and moral hypocrisy seem to prevail over moral integrity, at least among the college students participating in this investigation. Would you guess that similar motives operate when serious, real-life choices must be made? That could be the case, but it is also possible that when the choice involves people with whom we interact on a regular basis, moral integrity might become a more likely choice. If nothing else, we tend to expect reciprocation in the future when the other person faces such a choice. In other words, "I'll do the right thing today, so that you'll be more likely to do the right thing tomorrow."

How Does It Feel to Be Helped?

That question may seem stupid. Of course, you are pleased that help is provided. Right? If you are in need of help, and someone comes along to provide assistance, it seems obvious that you would react positively and with gratitude. Often, however, one's reaction is not at all like that.

Being Helped Can Be Unpleasant

A person who receives help may react with discomfort and even resentment toward the person who helped. For example, someone with a physical impairment may need help badly, but still feel somewhat depressed when help is given (Newsom, 1999). Requiring help is a reminder of one's physical problem, and receiving help is evidence that someone else is more fortunate because he or she is *not* physically impaired. The person providing assistance needs to be sensitive to the possibility of such reactions.

The general problem is that when you receive help, your self-esteem can suffer. This is especially true when the one who helps is a friend or someone who is similar to you in age, education, or other characteristics (DePaulo et al., 1981; Nadler, Fisher, & Itzhak, 1983). For example, when a young person offers his bus seat to an older person, the offer is likely to be accepted with gratitude. If the offer is made by another older person, however, it may well be refused because the one who offers help can be perceived as expressing a sense of superiority: "I'm in better shape than you, so have a seat." Lowered self-esteem results in negative affect and dislike (see Chapter 7). In an analogous way, when a member of a stigmatized group (e.g., an African American student) is offered unsolicited help from a member of a nonstigmatized group (e.g., a white student), the response may be a negative one, because the help is perceived as a patronizing insult (Schneider et al., 1996). For the same reasons, help from a sibling can be unpleasant, especially from a younger brother (Searcy & Eisenberg, 1992), but the same degree of help from someone else tends not to be threatening (Cook & Pelfrey, 1985).

A helper is liked best when the person receiving help believes that the help was offered because of positive feelings toward the individual in need (Ames, Flynn, & Weber, 2004). Such helping evokes the *reciprocity norm,* and the one who was helped is motivated to reciprocate with a kind deed in the future. When the helping is based on the helper's role (e.g., a policeman helping a lost child) or on the helper's cost–benefit analysis (e.g., a helper deciding to help because he would gain more than he would lose from the deed), attraction toward the helper and the desire to reciprocate are less strong.

When Help Is Unpleasant, It Can Motivate Self-Help

Whenever a person feels unhappy about receiving help, there is a positive aspect that is not obvious. When being helped is sufficiently unpleasant to an individual, he or she is motivated to avoid such a situation in the future by engaging in self-help (Fisher, Nadler, & Whitcher-Alagna, 1982; Lehman et al., 1995). No one wants to be seen as helpless or incompetent, and self-help can reduce feelings of dependence as well (Daubman, 1995). I (Donn Byrne) have learned many new and marvelous things about the use of my computer over the years because I don't want to depend on my two youngest daughters to help me every time I have to copy a file on a disk, search for a website, or add an attachment to an e-mail. In contrast, when I receive help from a stranger who is a computer expert, I am not at all motivated to help myself by trying to gain that person's skills (see Figure 10.17).

Figure 10.17 ■ Being Helped by Strangers: Positive Affect but No Motivation to Change
When help is provided by strangers (or people unlike themselves), recipients tend to be grateful and to like those who help, and they are not motivated to behave in such a way as to avoid needing future help. When help is provided by family and friends (or other people similar to themselves), recipients tend to feel uncomfortable and to resent those who help. These negative feelings tend to motivate self-help to avoid the need for future help.

KEY POINTS

★ People volunteer to provide help on a long-term basis as a function of various "selfish" and "selfless" motives. Those most likely to continue working as volunteers are those motivated by somewhat selfish concerns.

★ People can be differentiated in terms of their primary motivation when faced with making a choice that involves relatively moral versus relatively immoral alternatives. The three primary motives are *self-interest*, *moral integrity*, and *moral hypocrisy*.

★ When the helper and the recipient are similar, the person who is helped tends to react negatively and to feel incompetent, to experience decreased self-esteem, and to resent the helper. These negative reactions also tend to motivate self-help in the future. Help from a dissimilar person elicits a more positive reaction but fails to motivate future self-help.

The Basic Motivation for Engaging in Prosocial Acts

Why do people help? Based on what has been discussed so far, it is obvious that many factors influence whether or not an individual is likely to engage in prosocial behavior. Many aspects of the situation, the bystander's cognitive appraisal of the situation, his or her emotional state, and several dispositional variables all contribute to the probability that helping will or will not occur. We turn now to a different kind of question about prosocial responses: not who will help under what circumstances, but rather *why* anyone would ever be motivated to engage in a prosocial act? Several theories have been proposed, but most rest on the familiar assumption that people attempt to maximize rewards and minimize punishments. If that assumption is correct, the question becomes "Why is it rewarding to help?"

When asked, people tend to attribute their own helpful behavior to unselfish motives such as "It was the right thing to do" or "The Lord put me here for a reason." When asked why someone else engaged in such behavior, the answer is equally split between unselfish motives such as "She was a hero" and selfish ones such as "She just wanted to get her name in the paper" (Doherty, Weigold, & Schlenker, 1990). Even those who spend their lives trying to find solutions to massive problems such as global warming or cancer are often viewed as acting in terms of their own self-interest (J. Baron, 1997). The ultimate example of such attributions is to say that the person engaged in helping others is only doing so because of the prospect of being rewarded by spending all of eternity in heaven. As a result, it is possible to explain all prosocial behavior as ultimately selfish and self-centered, but it is probably more reasonable to suggest that such behavior is based, in part, on selfish and, in part, on unselfish motives.

We now turn to three major psychological theories, each of which attempts to explain the reason for prosocial behavior. Figure 10.18 on page 406 summarizes these formulations. We then discuss a biological perspective on why people help.

Empathy–Altruism: It Feels Good to Help Others

In some ways, the least selfish and, in some ways, the most selfish explanation of prosocial behavior is that empathetic people help others because "it feels good to do good

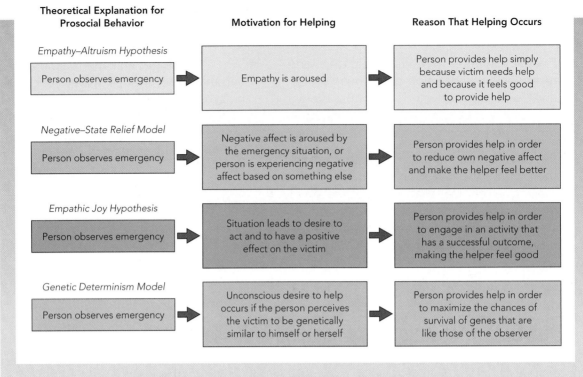

Figure 10.18 ■ Possible Motives for Prosocial Behavior
Four major explanations of the motivation underlying prosocial behavior are outlined here. The first three formulations (*empathy–altruism hypothesis, negative–state relief model,* and *empathic joy hypothesis*) stress the importance of increasing positive affect or decreasing negative affect. The fourth formulation (*genetic determinism model*) rests on the assumption that prosocial behavior is genetically determined. That is, such behavior evolved because it enhances the reproductive success of individuals or of groups.

deeds." Think of the Simpsons' neighbor, Ned Flanders. He is unselfish because his behavior results in people receiving help for no extrinsic reason and also selfish because it is rewarding to him to do the right thing. As an explanation of why people help, Batson and his colleagues (1981) offered the **empathy–altruism hypothesis.** They suggest that at least some prosocial acts are motivated solely by the desire to help someone in need (Batson & Oleson, 1991). Such motivation can be sufficiently strong that the helper is willing to engage in unpleasant, dangerous, and even life-threatening activity (Batson, Batson et al., 1995). Compassion for someone in need outweighs all other considerations (Batson, Klein et al., 1995).

To test this altruistic view of helping behavior, Batson and his colleagues devised an experimental procedure in which they aroused a bystander's empathy by describing a victim as being very similar to himself or herself (see Chapter 7). Other participants were told of the victim's dissimilarity and so did not have their empathy aroused. The bystander was then presented with an opportunity to be helpful (Batson et al., 1983; Toi & Batson, 1982). The participant was given the role of an "observer" who watched a "fellow student" on a TV monitor as she performed a task while (supposedly) receiving electric shocks. The victim was actually a research assistant recorded on videotape.

empathy–altruism hypothesis

The proposal that *prosocial behavior* is motivated solely by the desire to help someone in need and by the fact that it feels good to help.

After the task was underway, the assistant said that she was in pain and confided that as a child she had had a traumatic experience with electricity. Though she agreed to continue if necessary, the experimenter asked whether the observer would be willing to trade places with her or whether the experiment should simply be terminated. When empathy was low (victim and participant dissimilar), the participants preferred to end the experiment rather than engage in a painful prosocial act. When, however, empathy was high (victim and participant similar), participants were much more likely to take the victim's place and thus receive the shocks, presumably motivated simply by empathic concern for the victim.

Because empathy is strongly motivating, people prefer not to receive information that will arouse empathy (Shaw, Batson, & Todd, 1994). Presented with a victim needing help, participants were willing to learn about empathy-inducing aspects of the victim only if the cost of helping was low. When helping was costly, participants preferred to avoid detailed information about the victim rather than having their empathy aroused and thus become motivated to engage in high-cost helping.

Feelings of empathy also complicate matters when there are multiple victims who need help. How do you react when you learn that many people are in need? A mailing from the Feed the Children organization in Oklahoma City states that "over 12 million American children struggle with hunger each month." It is difficult or impossible to feel empathy for 12 million children, and you couldn't help all of them even if you felt intense empathy. Would you be more likely to help if you felt empathy for just one member of the group? That response is encouraged by charitable organizations. With a picture of a single child, and her sad request to help her and her family members, you might well respond with **selective altruism,** helping the individual, even though you must neglect the remaining millions (Batson, Ahmed et al., 1999; Figure 10.19.).

Arguing against the empathy–altruism view of prosocial behavior, Cialdini and his colleagues (1997) agreed that empathy leads to altruistic behavior but pointed out that this only occurs when the participant perceives an overlap between self and other. In a sense, a helpful participant identifies with the victim and is really only helping himself or herself. They conducted research to demonstrate that without a feeling of "oneness," helping does not occur. Empathic concern alone does *not* increase helping. Follow-up research by Batson and his colleagues indicated the opposite—"oneness" isn't necessary. Clearly, the issue has not been resolved (Batson et al., 1997).

selective altruism
When a large group of individuals is in need, and only one individual is helped. In appeals by charities, there is frequently a picture and information about one child, designed to arouse empathy toward him or her and the result is selective altruism.

Figure 10.19 ■ Selective Altruism
When a large number of people need help, it is difficult or impossible to feel empathy for all of the individuals involved. Charitable organizations attempt to solve this problem through the use of advertising that evokes empathy and the desire to help just one individual or just one family. Suppose you received a mailing with this little girl's picture and the message, "Please, can you help? I'm so hungry, and we have no money to buy food or Christmas presents." Would you be motivated to help her?

Negative-State Relief: Helping Makes You Feel Less Bad

Instead of helping because altruism behavior leads to positive emotions, is it possible that perceiving a person in need makes you feel so bad that you help in order to *reduce* your negative emotions? In other words, you do a good thing in order to stop feeling bad.

This explanation of prosocial behavior is known as the **negative-state relief model** (Cialdini, Baumann, & Kenrick, 1981). Research designed to test this hypothesis indicates that negative feelings increase the occurrence of helpful behavior. The investigators confirmed that proposal. They also found that it doesn't matter whether the bystander's unhappy state was caused by something unrelated to the emergency or by the emergency itself. That is, you could be upset about receiving a bad grade or about seeing that a stranger has been injured. In either instance, you are likely to engage in a prosocial act primarily as a way to improve your own negative mood (Dietrich & Berkowitz, 1997; Fultz, Schaller, & Cialdini, 1988). Such research suggests that unhappiness leads to prosocial behavior, while empathy is not a necessary component (Cialdini et al., 1987).

Empathic Joy: Helping as an Accomplishment

It is generally true that it feels good to have a positive effect on the lives of other people. It can literally be better to give help than to receive it. Helping can thus be explained on the basis of the **empathic joy hypothesis.** The basic idea is that a helper responds to the needs of a victim because he or she wants to accomplish something, and interpersonal accomplishment is rewarding.

An important implication of this proposal is that it is crucial for the person who helps to know that his or her actions had a positive impact on the victim. It is argued that if helping were based entirely on empathy, feedback about its effect would be irrelevant. To test that aspect of their empathic joy hypothesis, Smith, Keating, and Stotland (1989) asked research participants to watch a videotape in which a female student said she might drop out of college because she felt isolated and distressed. She was described as either similar to the participant (high empathy) or dissimilar (low empathy). After participants watched the tape, they were given the opportunity to offer helpful advice. Some were told they would receive feedback about the effectiveness of their advice, while others were told that they would not be able to learn what the student eventually decided to do. It was found that empathy alone was not enough to elicit a prosocial response. Rather, participants were helpful only if there was high empathy *and* feedback about the impact of their advice.

Note that in each of these three theoretical models for engaging in prosocial acts, the affective state of the person engaging in an act is a crucial element. All three formulations rest on the assumption that people engage in helpful behavior either because it feels good or because it makes make them feel less bad. And, all three formulations are able to predict prosocial behavior under specific conditions. On the basis of other investigations, one could also make the case that prosocial behavior can sometimes be motivated by self-interest. This includes the expectation of reciprocation from the person being helped, along with various possible rewards on earth (respect, fame, gratitude, and sometimes, material gain) and in the afterlife. Perhaps there really is no such thing as pure altruism—a totally unselfish concern for the welfare of others—or at least

negative-state relief model The proposal that *prosocial behavior* is motivated by the bystander's desire to reduce his or her own uncomfortable negative emotions.

empathic joy hypothesis The proposal that *prosocial behavior* is motivated by the positive emotion a helper anticipates experiencing as the result of having a beneficial impact on the life of someone in need.

Chapter 10 / Prosocial Behavior

it is exceedingly rare. Before we return to the question of prosocial behavior as a function of affect and rewards, let's look at a fourth model.

Genetic Determinism: Helping as an Adaptive Response

The **genetic determinism model** is based on a general biological perspective (Pinker, 1998). Presumably, people are no more conscious of being guided by genetic components than are grey geese, and much of what we do is because we are "built that way" (Rushton, 1989b). Genetic roots are well established for most human physical characteristics, and many behavioral characteristics also have a genetic base. Our human characteristics have been "selected" through evolution purely on the basis of their relevance to reproductive success. Therefore, any physical or behavioral characteristic that facilitates reproduction is more likely to be represented in future generations than are other characteristics that either interfere with reproductive success or are simply irrelevant to it.

Is it possible that the tendency to help others is adaptive? Consider something that was mentioned several times in this chapter: Both empathy and prosocial acts most often occur when the victim is similar to the bystander. Studies of various species indicate that the greater the genetic similarity between two individual organisms, the more likely it is that one will help the other when help is needed (Ridley & Dawkins, 1981). Evolutionary theorists have coined the term *selfish gene* to describe this phenomenon. That is, the more similar individual A is to individual B, the more genes they probably have in common. If so, when A helps B, some portion of A's genes will be more likely to be represented in future generations because of the genetic overlap of the two individuals (Rushton, Russell, & Wells, 1984). From this perspective, altruism doesn't necessarily benefit the individual who helps, but it is adaptive because adaptation is not limited to the individual and his or her reproductive fitness, but also to **inclusive fitness**—natural selection that favors behaviors that benefit whoever shares our genes (Hamilton, 1964; McAndrew, 2002). From a more general perspective, each individual organism needs to live long enough to reproduce or at least to enhance the reproductive odds of other individuals who are genetically similar to himself or herself (Browne, 1992). Interestingly, the principles of inclusive fitness extend beyond reproduction. Both in laboratory studies in which participants can theoretically share lottery winnings with relatives (Webster, 2003) and in actual monetary inheritance stipulated in wills (Judge & Hrdy, 1992), the greater the genetic relatedness, the greater proportion of money is allocated. In effect, fitness is enhanced by providing resources for genetically similar others.

Even though risking one's life to save the life of another person doesn't seem adaptive, it is adaptive *if* the person being saved is genetically similar to the rescuer (Burnstein, Crandall, & Kitayama, 1994). The best person to save is obviously a relative who is still young enough to reproduce, an aspect of inclusive fitness that led to the term **kin selection.** Burnstein and his colleagues conducted a series of studies based on hypothetical decisions about who you would choose to help in an emergency. As predicted on the basis of genetic similarity, research participants were more likely to say they would help a close relative than either a distant relative or a nonrelative. And, as predicted on the basis of reproductive ability, help was more likely for young relatives than for older ones. For example, given a choice between a female relative young enough to reproduce and a female relative past menopause, help would go to the younger individual.

Before we offer some final comments about these various explanations of prosocial behavior, it may be useful to consider the **Beyond the Headlines** section on page 410.

genetic determinism model
The proposal that behavior is driven by genetic attributes that evolved because they enhanced the probability of transmitting one's genes to subsequent generations.

inclusive fitness
The concept that natural selection not only applies to individuals, but also involves behaviors that benefit other individuals with whom we share genes. Sometimes referred to as *kin selection*.

kin selection
Another term for *inclusive fitness*—the concept that natural selection not only applies to individuals, but also involves behaviors that benefit other individuals with whom we share genes.

Is Helping as Joyful as Eating Ice Cream?

Boy Saved from Burning Car

Canaan, Maine (September 5, 2003)—With a wife and three young children, David Custer says he is not the kind of person who likes to take risks. But Wednesday night, as he saw another man struggling to save a small boy trapped in a burning car, he knew he had no choice. The child's mother was screaming, "Please save my baby. Please get my baby out of there!"

"It doesn't matter what race, color or creed, when there is a child inside a burning car you cast all other matters aside and act as though it were your own child," said Custer.

Custer and Mark Potter rescued the 3-year-old boy as he lay trapped in a car about halfway down a 20-foot embankment. Custer climbed on top of the car to hold the door open while Potter crawled in to cut the straps holding the child, and then Custer was able to pull him out. Within two minutes of the rescue, the car exploded in flames, setting the surrounding trees on fire.

"You don't think about your own fear when you see a child," Custer said. "I'm just glad that everything turned out all right." (Crowell, 2003)

And he is probably right. Most people coming upon that scene might well have done their best to save the child. This brings us back to an earlier question. Why *did* he help? Did he know his behavior would make him feel good or at least get rid of the discomfort he felt about a child in danger? Did he want to achieve something worthwhile? Did he consider the reproductive future of the crying baby?

McAndrew (2002) points out that social psychologists have focused on the immediate causes of altruism (e.g., number of bystanders), while an evolutionary perspective focuses on the origins of evolved behavior. Is it possible that we are "wired" to be nice, including being helpful and altruistic? At the most general level, our early ancestors benefited from a variety of related interpersonal tendencies such as affiliation (see Chapter 7), cooperation, and **reciprocal altruism**—when A helps B and B later reciprocates by helping A. Even without reciprocation, inclusive fitness indicates why it is beneficial to the group as a whole if each individual group member behaves altruistically toward others in that group (Wilson, 1997).

Recent research provides evidence for some of the physiological aspects of these inherited tendencies. For example, when we react to the emotional distress of others, a portion of the brain is activated (the "concern mechanism"). Sympathizing with someone else activates the same brain regions that are activated when we ourselves are experiencing the emotion (Benson, 2003; Decety & Chaminade, 2003). A mother screaming for help and a crying child would presumably evoke sympathetic activation in most of us.

When a situation causes us to feel upset, and our evolutionary history makes it likely that we will act in a prosocial way, such behavior also has a specific physical effect. Using MRI technology to examine brain images during various activities, it is found that positive interpersonal responses such as cooperation, trust, and generosity cause a specific brain reaction (Rillings et al., 2002). Newspaper reporter Natalie Angier (2002) sums up such findings:

> *"What feels as good as chocolate on the tongue or money in the bank but won't make you fat or risk a subpoena from the Securities and Exchange Commission?*
>
> *Hard as it may be to believe in these days of infectious greed and sabers unsheathed, scientists have discovered that the small, brave act of cooperating with another person, of choosing trust over cynicism, generosity over selfishness, makes the brain light up with quiet joy." (p. F1)*

It seems quite possible that we help one another because that kind of behavior has been sufficiently adaptive over thousands of years that we are programmed to behave in this way and to feel good about it. And, the various social psychological concepts outlined in this chapter are equally valid in identifying the many details of the situation and of the cognitive and affective responses of individuals that enhance or inhibit the underlying genetic tendencies (e.g., Maner et al., 2002). Figure 10.20 suggests a way to think about how the diverse research findings relevant to prosocial behavior can be considered as integral elements of a unified explanation of this complex topic.

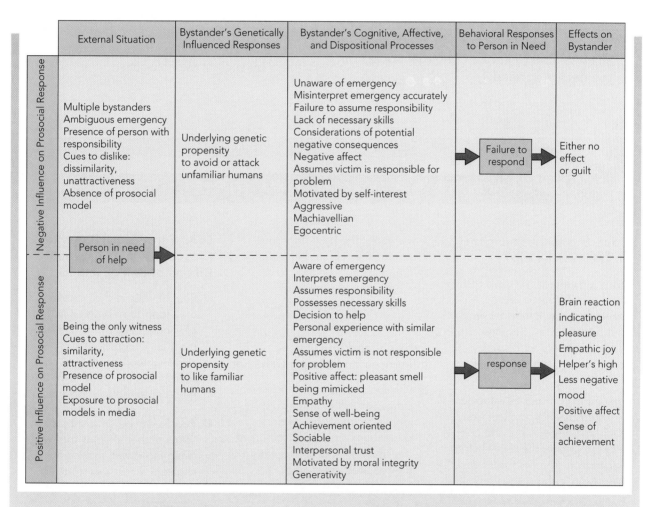

Figure 10.20 ■ Prosocial Behavior: Putting It All Together
Prosocial behavior describes a great many very different kinds of specific behaviors, including rescuing someone facing a life-threatening emergency, engaging in acts of kindness as simple as picking up dropped pens, and volunteering many hours of charitable work over an extended time period. Evolutionary psychologists work to explain both prosocial and antisocial behavior by concentrating on general, adaptive, genetically based tendencies to respond negatively to anyone who is unfamiliar (see Chapter 7) and to cooperate and help anyone who is familiar. These genetic predispositions to negative or positive interpersonal responses can be enhanced or overridden by the specific situational, cognitive, affective, and dispositional factors on which social psychological research has concentrated. The summary outline presented here rests on the assumption that both types of explanation are valid and that, together, they provide a useful framework for understanding why and under what circumstances people are likely to behave in ways that benefit other people or fail to engage in such prosocial responses.

KEY POINTS

★ The *empathy–altruism hypothesis* proposes that, because of empathy, we help those in need simply because it feels good to do so.

★ The *negative-state relief model* proposes that people help other people in order to relieve and make less negative their own emotional discomfort.

★ The *empathic joy hypothesis* bases helping on the positive feelings of accomplishment that arise when the helper knows that he or she was able to have a beneficial impact on the person in need.

★ The *genetic determinism model* traces prosocial behavior to the general effects of natural selection. Prosocial acts are part of our biological heritage, because both *reciprocal altruism* and *inclusive fitness* are adaptive evolutionary mechanisms.

★ It seems increasingly likely that prosocial behavior can best be conceptualized as an evolved biological predisposition that can be enhanced or inhibited by the many situational, cognitive, and affective factors identified by social psychologists.

SUMMARY AND REVIEW OF KEY POINTS

Responding to an Emergency: Will Bystanders Help?

■ When an emergency arises and someone is in need of help, a bystander may or may not respond in a prosocial way. Responses range from *heroism* to apathy.

■ In part because of *diffusion of responsibility*, the more bystanders present as witnesses to an emergency, the less likely each of them is to provide help and the greater the delay before help occurs (the *bystander effect*).

■ When faced with an emergency, a bystander's tendency to help or not help depends, in part, on decisions made at five crucial steps.

   ■ First, it is necessary for the bystander to pay attention and be aware that an unusual event is occurring.
   ■ Second, the bystander must correctly interpret the situation as an emergency.
   ■ Third, the bystander must assume responsibility to provide help.

   ■ Fourth, the bystander must have the required knowledge and skills to be able to act.
   ■ Fifth, the bystander must decide to act.

External and Internal Influences on Helping Behavior

■ Positive and negative emotional states can either enhance or inhibit *prosocial behavior*, depending on specific factors in the situation and on the nature of the required assistance.

■ Individual differences in altruistic behavior are based in large part on *empathy*, a complex response that includes both affective and cognitive components. The extent to which a person is able to respond with empathy depends on hereditary factors and learning experiences.

■ The *altruistic personality* consists of empathy plus belief in a just world, social responsibility, internal locus of control, and low egocentrism.

Long-Term Commitment to Prosocial Action and the Effects of Being Helped

■ People volunteer to provide help on a long-term basis as a function of various "selfish" and "selfless" motives. Those most likely to continue working at the volunteered task are those motivated by relatively selfish concerns.

■ People can be differentiated in terms of their primary motivation when faced with making a choice that involves relatively moral versus relatively immoral alternatives: *self-interest, moral integrity,* and *moral hypocrisy*.

■ When the helper and the recipient are similar, the person who is helped tends to react negatively and to feel incompetent, to experience decreased self-esteem, and to resent the helper. These negative responses also tend to motivate self-help in the future. Help from a dissimilar person elicits a more positive reaction but fails to motivate future self-help.

The Basic Motivation for Engaging in Prosocial Acts

■ The *empathy–altruism hypothesis* proposes that, because of empathy, we help those in need simply because it feels good to do so.

■ The *negative-state relief model* proposes that people help other people in order to relieve and make less negative their own emotional discomfort.

■ The *empathic joy hypothesis* bases helping on the positive feelings of accomplishment that arise when the helper knows that he or she was able to have a beneficial impact on the person in need.

■ The *genetic determinism model* traces prosocial behavior to the general effects of natural selection. Prosocial acts are part of our biological heritage, because both *reciprocal altruism* and *inclusive fitness* are adaptive evolutionary mechanisms.

■ It seems increasingly likely that prosocial behavior can best be conceptualized as an evolved biological predisposition that can be enhanced or inhibited by the many situational, cognitive, and affective factors identified by social psychologists.

Connections INTEGRATING SOCIAL PSYCHOLOGY

In this chapter, you read about . . .	In other chapters you will find related discussions of . . .
bystanders' response to nonverbal cues of other bystanders	interpretation of nonverbal cues (Chapter 2)
social comparison processes among the witnesses to an emergency	the importance of social comparison in the study of attitudes (Chapter 4), attraction (Chapter 7), and social influence (Chapter 9)
attributions as to the cause of a victim's problem	attribution theory (Chapter 2)
self-concept as a determinant of helping behavior and the effect of receiving help on self-esteem	research and theory on self-concept and self-esteem (Chapter 5)
similarity of victim and bystander as a determinant of empathy and helping	similarity and attraction (Chapters 7 and 8)
affective state and helping	affect as a factor in attitudes (Chapter 4), prejudice (Chapter 6), attraction (Chapter 7), relationships (Chapter 8), and aggression (Chapter 11)
genetics and helping	genetics as a factor in prejudice (Chapter 6), attraction (Chapter 7), mate selection (Chapter 8), and aggression (Chapter 11)

Thinking about Connections

1. As you are walking out of the building after your social psychology class, you see an elderly man lying face down on the sidewalk. Three students are standing nearby, not speaking but looking at the man. How would you interpret this situation? What might you observe in the facial expressions and bodily gestures of the three bystanders (Chapter 2)? As you take a closer look at the man, you may make some guesses as to why he is there. Many different attributions are possible (Chapter 2). Suggest some of the possibilities that might occur to you.

2. Your car won't start, and you are in a hurry. You have plenty of gas, and the battery is almost new. You open the hood but don't see anything obviously wrong. A fellow student comes

along and offers to help. She looks under the hood, taps something, and says, "Try it now." You turn the key, and the car starts easily. How do you feel at that moment? Do you like the student who helped you (Chapter 7)? Does being helped raise or lower your self-esteem (Chapter 5)? Do you think you might be motivated to learn more about automobiles so this won't happen to you again (Chapter 10)?

3. On the evening news, you learn about a devastating earthquake in California that has destroyed a great many homes, leaving many families without shelter or food. The announcer gives a telephone number and an address for those who want to contribute money or food. Also, volunteers are needed to help with the cleanup. Do you ignore this information, or do you decide to contribute money, food, or your time? What factors with respect to the disaster itself, where it occurred, and your experiences with such a situation might influence your decision? List the kinds of social psychological processes that could be operating.

4. You are in a burning building. You can get out, but have time to help only one other person escape from the fast-moving blaze. You know that you could help your teenage cousin or his mother (your middle-aged aunt). Which one would you choose to save? On what basis would you make this decision? Think about what you have read in this chapter about genetic factors. What goes through your mind in making this choice?

BEING A RESPONSIBLE BYSTANDER

From time to time, you have probably encountered a number of unexpected situations involving someone who needed your help. Did you help or not? In the future, if you want to be helpful, you might consider the following suggestions.

Pay Attention

In our everyday lives, we often think more about ourselves and what is going on in our lives than about our surroundings. It may be useful to pay more attention to what is going on around us. Remember the students who thought they were late for an appointment and ignored a man who appeared to have collapsed in a doorway? You may find it worthwhile from time to time to think about other people and their welfare.

Consider Alternate Explanations

When you notice something unusual, think about more than one possible explanation. A child crying in the park may have hurt herself or be lost or simply be tired and cross. The smoke you smell might be burnt toast or a fire in a nearby apartment. The scream you hear outside could be a cry for help or someone responding to a friend's joke. In any such situation, you can simply do nothing because there is probably nothing really wrong. You want to avoid looking foolish by jumping to false conclusions. Consider other possibilities, because there may be a serious problem that could be solved with your help.

Think of Yourself as Having as Much Responsibility as Any Other Bystander

If you find yourself in a group of people observing something that could be an emergency, don't just stand around and wait for somebody else to do something about it. If you see someone lying on the floor in a theater lobby, try to find out what is wrong. You know as much as others do and you are as responsible for doing the right thing as any of the other bystanders.

Chapter 10 / Prosocial Behavior

Take the Risk of Making a Fool of Yourself

Sometimes, when others fail to act, and you believe something is wrong, they can be right and you might do something foolish. Being foolish is not the end of the world, and you will probably never see your fellow bystanders again. It is better to make a mistake and offer help to someone who doesn't need it than to make an equally foolish decision to stand back when help is badly needed.

 EY TERMS

altruism (p. 379)

altruistic personality (p. 397)

bystander effect (p. 383)

diffusion of responsibility (p. 382)

egoism (p. 401)

empathic joy hypothesis (p. 408)

empathy (p. 394)

empathy–altruism hypothesis (p. 406)

generativity (p. 401)

genetic determinism model (p. 409)

heroism (p. 379)

implicit bystander effect (p. 384)

inclusive fitness (p. 409)

kin selection (p. 409)

mimicry (p. 390)

moral hypocrisy (p. 402)

moral integrity (p. 401)

negative-state relief model (p. 408)

personality disposition (p. 393)

pluralistic ignorance (p. 387)

prosocial behavior (p. 379)

reciprocal altruism (p. 411)

selective altruism (p. 407)

self-interest (p. 401)

 OR MORE INFORMATION

Cronin, H. (1993). *The ant and the peacock: Altruism and sexual selection from Darwin to today.* Cambridge: Cambridge University Press.
• The author explains why communal and prosocial animals such as ants are able to survive in a world in which being fierce and strong usually wins the day. The author blends history, science, and philosophy in a way that is both scholarly and a pleasure to read.

Monroe, K. R. (1996). *The heart of altruism: Perceptions of a common humanity.* Princeton, NJ: Princeton University Press.
• The author examines theories of altruism and of self-interest and how they influence behavior. Interviews provide insights about the determinants of altruistic versus egocentric behavior.

Rosenstand, N. (1999). *The moral of the story: An introduction to ethics.* New York: McGraw-Hill.
• Contemporary issues of ethics and morals are illustrated by examples drawn from fiction and film. The author provides an accessible and interesting way for readers to understand and evaluate moral issues.

11

AGGRESSION
Its Nature, Causes, and Control

CHAPTER OUTLINE

When I (Robert Baron) was ten, I had one of the most traumatic experiences of my entire childhood. It was a Saturday, and I was just returning home from playing baseball with my friends. As I approached the entrance to the apartment building where I lived, I saw that my younger brother Richard, who was about four, was standing in some rose bushes, looking at a bee that had landed on a flower. On the sidewalk next to him were Nancy Gordon and her friend Evelyn—two girls in my class at school. Nancy was urging Richard to pick up the bee in his hand. "Go ahead," she said, "Pick it up—it won't hurt you! In fact, rub it on your face—it will feel soft!" For some reason, Richard liked insects and had been stung just a few weeks ago when he stepped on a bee and failed to move. Nancy knew about this, and now she was trying to have fun at his expense.

"Hey!" I shouted at her. "Cut it out. Leave him alone!" Nancy was known for her cruel tongue, so I was not surprised when she turned it on me at once. "Oh, here comes big brother to the rescue," she announced, sarcasm dripping from her lips. "But he's not very big, is he? Go away and let us have fun with your stupid little brother!" That made me mad and I told her so. We exchanged insults and, finally, I must have said something that hit home, because Nancy, who was on roller skates, came right up to me and . . . spit in my face! That was it; I saw red. All I can remember is that I pushed her—hard. Because she was on skates, she lost her balance and fell backward, landing on her right arm. She got up crying and ran into the building, headed for home. Later that evening, I learned that she had broken her wrist. My father and mother wouldn't listen to my explanations— they blamed me entirely. In fact, my father made me accompany him to Nancy's home, where I apologized to her and to her parents for my actions. But that wasn't the end of it; I said that

Chapter 11 / Aggression

Nancy was cruel, and she was. She wrote "Courtesy of Robert Baron" on her cast and told everyone how I had broken her wrist. I was totally humiliated. To make matters worse, my friends began calling me "Lady Killer." Wow, was I glad when Nancy's cast was finally removed and the school year ended.

Did I mean to hurt Nancy Gordon? I was certainly angry with her, but I'm sure that I didn't intend to harm her seriously—I just lashed out, without conscious thought. And that, of course, is one of the many complexities of human aggression. Intentions are a hidden process we can't observe directly; even the people involved often don't know *why* they behaved as they did or what they wanted to accomplish. So, although social psychologists define **aggression** as intentional harmdoing, they realize that determining whether some action that caused harm to another was intentional or unintentional is a difficult task.

Aggression, of course, is not restricted to direct assaults by one person on another (such as my pushing Nancy Gordon). On the contrary, at the present time it often involves the use of modern weapons that can harm large numbers of persons at once. And in the hands of terrorists, such weapons are aimed not only at soldiers or other armed opponents, but often also at innocent civilians—passersby who are seriously harmed or killed without any warning and without any knowledge of who is the cause of these tragic outcomes, or even why they are being attacked (see Figure 11.1).

aggression
Behavior directed toward the goal of harming another living being, who is motivated to avoid such treatment.

Figure 11.1 ■ The Deadly Face of Human Aggression
When the desire to harm others is paired with modern weapons and placed in the hands of terrorists, the results can be both frightening and devastating. Large numbers of persons are harmed or killed without warning and without knowing who has performed these atrocities.

Given the very serious consequences that aggression can produce, it has long been a topic of major interest to social psychologists (e.g., Anderson & Bushman, 2002a; Baron & Richardson, 1994). In this chapter, we provide you with an overview of the intriguing insights their research has produced. First, we describe several *theoretical perspectives* on aggression, contrasting views about its nature and origin. Next, we examine several important determinants of human aggression. These include *social factors* involving the words or deeds of others, either in person or as represented in the mass media (e.g., Anderson et al., 2004); *cultural factors*, such as norms requiring that individuals respond aggressively to insults to their honor; *personal factors*—traits that predispose specific persons toward aggressive outbursts; and *situational factors*—aspects of the external world, such as high temperatures and alcohol. Third, we consider two forms of aggression that are especially disturbing because they occur within the context of long-term relationships rather than between total strangers—*bullying* (repeated victimization of specific persons by one or more other persons) and *workplace aggression*. Finally, to conclude on an optimistic note, we examine various techniques for the *prevention and control* of aggression.

Theoretical Perspectives on Aggression: In Search of the Roots of Violence

Why do human beings aggress against others? What makes them turn, with fierce brutality, on their fellow human beings? Thoughtful persons have pondered these questions for centuries and have proposed many contrasting explanations for the paradox of human violence. Here, we examine several explanations that have been especially influential, concluding with the modern answer provided by social psychologists.

The Role of Biological Factors: From Instincts to the Evolutionary Perspective

The oldest and probably best know explanation for human aggression is the view that human beings are somehow "programmed" for violence by their basic nature. Such theories suggest that human violence stems from built-in (i.e., inherited) tendencies to aggress against others. The most famous supporter of this theory was Sigmund Freud, who held that aggression stems mainly from a powerful *death wish* (*thanatos*) possessed by all persons. According to Freud, this instinct is initially aimed at self-destruction but is soon redirected outward toward others. Similar views were proposed by Konrad Lorenz, a Nobel Prize–winning scientist (Lorenz, 1966, 1974), who suggested that aggression springs mainly from an inherited *fighting instinct*, which assures that only the strongest males will obtain mates and pass their genes on to the next generation.

Until a few years ago, few social psychologists accepted such views. Among the many reasons for their objections to the idea that human aggression is genetically programmed were these: (1) Human beings aggress against others in many different ways—everything from ignoring others to overt acts of violence. How can such a huge range of behaviors be determined by genetic factors? (2) The frequency of aggressive actions varies tremendously across human societies, so that they are much more likely to occur in some societies than in others (e.g., Fry, 1998). Again, social psychologists asked, "How can aggressive behavior be determined by genetic factors if such huge differences exist?"

With the advent of the *evolutionary perspective* in psychology, however, this situation has changed considerably. Although most social psychologists continue to reject the view that human aggression stems largely from innate factors, many now accept the possibility that genetic factors may play *some* role in human aggression. For instance, consider the following reasoning, based on an evolutionary perspective (please see the discussion of this theory in Chapter 1). In the past (and even at present to some extent), males seeking desirable mates found it necessary to compete with other males. One way of eliminating such competition, of course, is through successful aggression, which drives such rivals away or may even eliminate them entirely by proving fatal. Because males who were adept at such behavior may have been more successful in securing mates and in transmitting their genes to offspring, this may have led to the development of a genetically influenced tendency for males to aggress against other males. In contrast, males would not be expected to acquire a similar tendency to aggress against females, because females may view males who engage in such behavior as too dangerous to themselves and their potential future children, and so may reject these males as potential mates. As a result, males may have weaker tendencies to aggress against females than against other males. In contrast, females might aggress equally against males and females, or even more frequently against males than other females. In fact, the results of several studies confirm such predictions (e.g., Hilton, Harris, & Rice, 2000). Findings such as these suggest that biological or genetic factors may play some role in human aggression, although in a much more complex manner than Freud, Lorenz, and other early theorists suggested.

Drive Theories: The Motive to Harm Others

When social psychologists rejected the instinct views of aggression proposed by Freud and Lorenz, they countered with an alternative of their own: the view that aggression stems mainly from an externally elicited *drive* to harm others. This approach is reflected in several different **drive theories** of aggression (e.g., Berkowitz, 1989; Feshbach, 1984). These theories propose that external conditions—especially *frustration*—arouse a strong motive to harm others. This aggressive drive, in turn, leads to overt acts of aggression (see Figure 11.2).

By far the most famous of these theories is the well-known **frustration–aggression hypothesis** (Dollard et al., 1939). According to this view, frustration leads to the arousal of a drive, the primary goal of which is to harm some person or object—primarily the perceived cause of the frustration (Berkowitz, 1989). As we'll see in a later discussion, the central role assigned to frustration by the frustration–aggression hypothesis has turned out to be largely false: Frustration is only one of many different causes of aggression, and a fairly weak one at that. Moreover, aggression stems from many causes other than frustration. Although social psychologists have largely rejected this theory as false, it still enjoys widespread acceptance outside of the field. In this way, at least, drive

drive theories (of aggression)
Theories suggesting that aggression stems from external conditions that arouse the motive to harm or injure others. The most famous of these is the *frustration–aggression hypothesis.*

frustration–aggression hypothesis
The suggestion that frustration is a very powerful determinant of aggression.

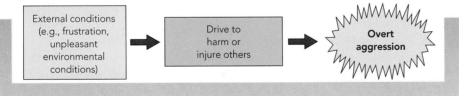

Figure 11.2 ■ Drive Theories of Aggression: Motivation to Harm Others
Drive theories of aggression suggest that aggressive behavior is pushed from within by drives to harm or injure others. These drives, in turn, stem from external events such as frustration. Such theories are no longer accepted as valid by most social psychologists, but one such view—the famous *frustration–aggression hypothesis*—continues to influence modern research.

theories have continued to have some impact on popular, if not scientific, views of human aggression.

Modern Theories of Aggression: The Social Learning Perspective and the General Aggression Model

Unlike earlier views, modern theories of aggression (e.g., Anderson & Bushman, 2002a; Berkowitz, 1993; Zillmann, 1994) do not focus on a single factor (instincts, drives, frustration) as the primary cause of aggression. Rather, they draw on advances in many fields of psychology in order to gain added insight into the factors that play a role in the occurrence of such behavior. One such theory, known as the *social learning perspective* (e.g., Bandura, 1997), begins with a very reasonable idea: Human beings are not born with a large array of aggressive responses at their disposal. Rather, they must acquire these in much the same way that they acquire other complex forms of social behavior: through direct experience or by observing the behavior of others (i.e., social models—live persons or characters on television, in movies, or even in video games who behave aggressively; Anderson & Bushman, 2001; Bushman & Anderson, 2002). Thus, depending on their past experience and the cultures in which they live, individuals learn (1) various ways of seeking to harm others (see Figure 11.3), (2) which persons or groups are appropriate targets for aggression, (3) what actions by others justify retaliation or vengeance on their part, and (4) what situations or contexts are ones in which aggression is permitted or even approved. In short, the social learning perspective suggests that whether a specific person will aggress in a given situation depends on many different factors, including this person's past experience, the current rewards associated with past or present aggression, and attitudes and values that shape this person's thoughts concerning the appropriateness and potential effects of such behavior.

Building on the social learning perspective, a newer framework known as the *general aggression model* (Anderson, 1997; Anderson & Bushman, 2002) provides an even more complete account of the foundations of human aggression. According to this theory, a chain of events that may ultimately lead to overt aggression can be initiated by two major types of *input variables:* (1) factors relating to the current situation (situational factors) and (2) factors relating the persons involved (person factors). Variables falling into the first category include frustration, some kind of attack from another person (e.g., an insult), exposure to other persons behaving aggressively (*aggressive models*) either in person or in violent movies or video games, and virtually anything that causes individuals to experience discomfort—everything from uncomfortably high temperatures to a dentist's drill or even an extremely dull lecture. Variables in the second category (*individual differences*) include traits that predispose individuals toward aggression (e.g., high irritability), certain attitudes and beliefs about violence (e.g., believing that it is acceptable and appropriate), a tendency to perceive hostile intentions in others' behavior, and specific skills related to aggression (e.g., knowing how to fight or how to use various weapons).

According to the **general aggression model** (GAM), these situational and individual difference variables can then lead to overt aggression through their impact on three basic processes: *arousal*—they may increase physiological arousal or excitement; *affective states*—they can arouse hostile feelings and outward signs of these (e.g., angry facial expressions); and *cognitions*—they can induce individuals to think hostile thoughts or can bring beliefs and attitudes about aggression to mind. Depending on individuals' interpretations (*appraisals*) of the current situation and restraining factors (e.g., the presence of police or the threatening nature of the intended target person), they then engage either in thoughtful action, which might involve restraining their anger, or

general aggression model A modern theory of aggression suggesting that aggression is triggered by a wide range of input variables that influence arousal, affective stages, and cognitions.

Figure 11.3 ■ Aggression: A Learned Form of Social Behavior
The social learning perspective suggests that aggression is a learned form of social behavior. In other words, we learn various ways of harming others, just as we learn many other forms of social behavior.

impulsive action, which can lead to overt aggressive actions. (See Figure 11.4 on page 424 for an overview of this theory.)

Anderson and Bushman (e.g., Bushman & Anderson, 2002) have expanded this theory to explain why individuals who are exposed to high levels of aggression, either directly or in films and video games, may tend to become increasingly aggressive themselves. Repeated exposure to such stimuli serves to strengthen *knowledge structures* relating to aggression—beliefs, attitudes, schemas, and scripts relevant to aggression (refer to Chapter 2). As these knowledge structures related to aggression grow stronger, it is easier for them to be activated by situational or person variables. The result? The persons in question are truly "primed" for aggression. The GAM is certainly more complex than earlier theories of aggression (e.g., the famous frustration–aggression hypothesis); (Dollard et al., 1939). But because the GAM fully reflects recent progress in the field, it seems much more likely to provide an accurate view of the nature of human aggression than these earlier theories. And that, of course, is what scientific progress is all about!

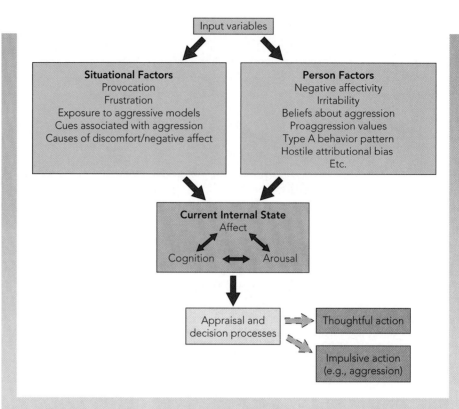

Figure 11.4 ■ **The GAM: A Modern Theory of Human Aggression**
As shown here, the *general aggression model* (GAM) suggests that human aggression stems from many different factors. Input variables relating to the situation or person influence cognitions, affect, and arousal, and these internal states plus other factors, such as appraisal and decision mechanism, determine whether and in what form aggression occurs. (*Source: Based on suggestions by Bushman & Anderson, 2002.*)

KEY POINTS

★ *Aggression* is the intentional infliction of harm on others. Although most social psychologists reject the view that human aggression is strongly determined by genetic factors, many now accept an evolutionary perspective that recognizes the potential role of such factors.

★ *Drive theories* suggest that aggression stems from externally elicited drives to harm or injure others. The *frustration–aggression hypothesis* is the most famous example of such theories.

★ Modern theories of aggression, such as the *general aggression model*, recognize the importance in aggression of learning, various eliciting input variables, individual differences, affective states, and, especially, cognitive processes.

Causes of Human Aggression: Social, Cultural, Personal, and Situational

Think back to the last time you lost your temper. What made you blow your cool? Something another person said or did (Harris, 1993), such as a condescending remark or something that made you feel jealous? Something about yourself—are you easily annoyed, do you perceive that others often treat you unfairly? Or was it something about the situation—had you been drinking, was the weather hot and steamy? In fact, research findings indicate that all of these factors can play a role in human aggression. As noted earlier, such behavior appears to stem from a wide range of *social, cultural, personal,* and *situational* variables. We'll now examine the effects of several of these factors.

Social Causes of Aggression: Frustration, Provocation, and Heightened Arousal

Although the situation shown in Figure 11.5 is a little extreme, it illustrates a basic fact: Often, individuals aggress because something others have said or done somehow provokes them. In other words, aggression occurs because the words or deeds of one or more persons stimulate aggression in others. But what, precisely, are these *social causes* of aggression? Let's see what research findings have revealed.

Frustration: Why Not Getting What You Want (Or What You Expect) Can Sometimes Lead to Aggression

Suppose that you asked twenty people you know to name the single most important cause of aggression. What would they say? The chances are good that most would reply *frustration.* And if you asked them to define *frustration,* many would state, "The way I feel when something—or someone—prevents me from getting what I want or expect to get in some situation." This widespread belief in the importance of frustration as a cause of aggression stems, at least in part, from the famous frustration–aggression hypothesis mentioned in our discussion of drive theories of aggression (Dollard et al., 1939). In it is original form, this hypothesis made two sweeping assertions: (1) Frustration *always* leads to some form of aggression, and (2) aggression *always* stems from frustration. In short, the theory held that frustrated persons always engage in some type of aggression and that all acts of aggression, in turn, result from frustration. Bold statements like these are appealing, but this doesn't imply that they are necessarily accurate. In fact, existing evidence suggests that both portions of the frustration–aggression hypothesis assign far too much importance to frustration as a determinant of human aggression. When frustrated, individuals do *not* always respond with aggression. On the contrary, they show many different reactions, ranging

IT STARTS.

"That's what you're wearing?"

Figure 11.5 ■ Social Causes of Aggression: An Example

As shown here, aggression often stems from social causes—something others have said or done. (*Source:* © *The New Yorker Collection 2003 Robert Leighton from cartoonbank.com. All Rights Reserved.*)

from sadness, despair, and depression on one hand to direct attempts to overcome the source of their frustration on the other. In short, aggression is definitely *not* an automatic response to frustration.

Second, it is equally clear that not all aggression stems from frustration. People aggress for many different reasons and in response to many different factors. For example, professional boxers hit their opponents because they wish to win valued prizes, not because of frustration. Similarly, during wars, air force pilots report that flying their planes is a source of pleasure, and they bomb enemy targets while feeling elated or excited, not frustrated. In these and many other cases, aggression stems from factors other than frustration. We consider many of these other causes of aggression below.

In view of these facts, few social psychologists now accept the idea that frustration is the only, or even the most important, cause of aggression. Instead, most believe that frustration is simply one of many factors that can lead to aggression. We must add that frustration *can* serve as a powerful determinant of aggression under certain conditions, especially when frustration is viewed as illegitimate or unjustified (e.g., Folger & Baron, 1996). For instance, if an individual believes that she deserves a large raise and then receives a much smaller one with no explanation for why this is so, she may conclude that she has been treated very unfairly—that her legitimate needs have been thwarted. The result: She may have hostile thoughts, experience intense anger, and seek revenge against the perceived source of such frustration—her boss or company. As we'll see in a later section, such reactions may play a key role in *workplace aggression* and in the aggressive reactions of some employees who lose their jobs through downsizing (e.g., Catalano, Novaco, & McConnell, 1997, 2002).

Direct Provocation: When Aggression Breeds Aggression

Major world religions generally agree in suggesting that when provoked by another person, we should turn the other cheek—in other words, the most appropriate way to respond to being annoyed or irritated by another person is to do our best to ignore this treatment. In fact, however, research findings indicate that this is easier to say than to do, and that physical or verbal **provocation** from others is one of the strongest causes of human aggression. When we are on the receiving end of some form of aggression from others—criticism we consider unfair, sarcastic remarks, or physical assaults—we tend to reciprocate, returning as much aggression as we have received, or perhaps even slightly more, especially if we are certain that the other person *meant* to harm us (Ohbuchi & Kambara, 1985).

What kinds of provocation produce the strongest push toward aggression? Existing evidence suggests that *condescension*—expressions of arrogance or disdain on the part of others—is very powerful (Harris, 1993). Harsh and unjustified criticism, especially criticism that attacks us rather than our behavior, is another powerful form of provocation, and when exposed to it, most people find it very difficult to avoid getting angry and retaliating in some manner, either immediately or later on (Baron, 1993). Still another form of provocation to which many people respond with anger is derogatory statements about their families; even persons who can tolerate attacks on themselves often lose their tempers in the face of an attack on their mothers, fathers, brothers, sisters, or spouse. So, if you direct such provocations toward others, beware! The likelihood that they will seek to retaliate in some manner is very high.

Heightened Arousal: Emotion, Cognition, and Aggression

Suppose that you are driving to the airport to meet a friend. On the way there, another driver cuts you off, and you almost have an accident. Your heart pounds wildly and your blood pressure shoots through the roof; but fortunately, no accident occurs. Now you arrive at the airport. You park and rush inside. When you get to the security check, an elderly man in front of you sets off the buzzer. He becomes confused and can't seem to

provocation
Actions by others that tend to trigger aggression in the recipient, often because these actions are perceived as stemming from malicious intent.

understand that the security guard wants him to take off his shoes. You are irritated by this delay. In fact, you begin to lose your temper and mutter, "What's wrong with him? Can't he get it?"

Now for the key question: Do you think that your recent near-miss in traffic may have played any role in your sudden surge of anger? Could the emotional arousal from that incident have somehow transferred to the scene inside the airport? Growing evidence suggests that it could (Zillmann, 1988, 1994). Under some conditions, heightened arousal—whatever its source—can enhance aggression in response to provocation, frustration, or other factors. In fact, in various experiments, arousal stemming from such varied sources as participation in competitive games (Christy, Gelfand, & Hartmann, 1971), exercise (Zillmann, 1979), and even some types of music (Rogers & Ketcher, 1979) have been found to increase subsequent aggression. Why is this the case? A compelling explanation is offered by **excitation transfer theory** (Zillmann, 1983, 1988).

Excitation transfer theory suggests that because physiological arousal tends to dissipate slowly over time, a portion of such arousal may persist as a person moves from one situation to another. In the preceding example, some portion of the arousal you experienced because of the near-miss in traffic may still be present as you approach the security gate in the airport. When you encounter a minor annoyance, that arousal intensifies your emotional reactions to the annoyance. The result: You become enraged rather than just mildly irritated. Excitation theory suggests further that such effects are most likely to occur when the persons involved are relatively unaware of the presence of residual arousal—a common occurrence, because small elevations in arousal are difficult to notice (Zillmann, 1994). Excitation transfer theory also suggests that such effects are likely to occur when the persons involved recognize their residual arousal but attribute it to events occurring in the present situation (Taylor et al., 1991). In the airport incident, for instance, your anger would be intensified if you recognized your feelings of arousal but attributed them to the elderly man's actions (see Figure 11.6.)

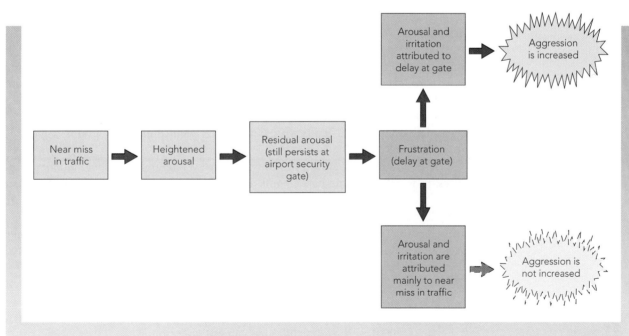

Figure 11.6 ■ Excitation Transfer Theory
Excitation transfer theory suggests that arousal occurring in one situation can persist and intensify emotional reactions in later, unrelated situations. Thus, the arousal produced by a near-miss in traffic can intensify feelings of annoyance stemming from delays at an airport security gate. (*Source: Based on suggestions by Zillmann, 1994.*)

Exposure to Media Violence: The Effects of Witnessing Aggression

Think about several films you have seen in recent months. Now, answer the following questions: How much aggression or violence did each contain? How often did characters in these movies hit, shoot at, or otherwise attempt to harm others? Unless you have chosen very carefully, you probably recognize that many of the films you have seen contained a great deal of violence—much more violence than you are ever likely to see in real life (Reiss & Roth, 1993; Waters et al., 1993).

This fact raises an important question that social psychologists have studied for decades: Does exposure to such materials increase aggression among children or adults? Literally hundreds of studies have been performed to test this possibility, and the results seem clear: Exposure to **media violence** may indeed be one factor contributing to high levels of violence in countries where such materials are viewed by large numbers of persons (e.g., Anderson, 1997; Paik & Comstock, 1994; Wood, Wong, & Cachere, 1991). In fact, in a recent summary of research findings in this area (Anderson et al., 2004), leading experts on this topic offered the following basic conclusions:

1. Research on exposure to violent television, movies, video games, and music indicates that such materials significantly increase the likelihood of aggressive and violent behavior by persons exposed to them.

2. Such effects are both short-term and long-term in nature.

3. The magnitude of these effects is large—at least as large as the various medical effects considered to be important by the medical community (e.g., the effect of aspirin on heart attacks).

In other words, social psychology's leading experts on the effects of media violence agree that these effects are real, lasting, and important—effects with important implications for society and for the safety and well-being of millions of person who are the victims of aggressive actions each year.

What kind of research led these experts to such chilling conclusions? In brief, it was research using every major method known to social psychologists. For example, in *short-term laboratory experiments*, children or adults viewed either violent films and television programs or nonviolent ones; then, their tendency to aggress against others was measured. In general, the results of such experiments revealed higher levels of aggression among participants who viewed the violent films or programs (e.g., Bandura, Ross, & Ross, 1963; Bushman & Huesmann, 2001).

Other and perhaps even more convincing research employed *longitudinal* procedures, in which the same participants are studied for many years (e.g., Anderson & Bushman, 2002a; Huesmann & Eron, 1984, 1986). Results of such research, too, are clear: The more violent films or television programs participants watched as children, the higher their levels of aggression as teenagers or adults—for instance, the higher the likelihood that they have been arrested for violent crimes. Such findings were replicated in many different countries—Australia, Finland, Israel, Poland, and South Africa (Botha, 1990). Thus, they appear to hold across different cultures. Further, such effects are not restricted only to actual programs or films: They appear to be produced by violence in news programs, by violent lyrics in popular music (e.g., Anderson, Carnagey, & Eubanks, 2003), and by violent video games (Anderson et al., 2004). As the group of experts on media violence mentioned, "The cup of research knowledge about violence in the media is relatively full. . . . It . . . supports sustained concern about media violence and sustained efforts to curb its adverse effects" (Anderson et al., 2004, p. 105).

media violence
Depictions of violent actions in the mass media.

The Effects of Media Violence: Why Do They Occur?

By now, you may be wondering about a very basic question: Why does exposure to media violence (of many different kinds) increase aggression among persons exposed to it? A compelling answer is provided by Bushman and Anderson (2002), who suggest that the effects of media violence can be readily understood within the context of the GAM. As you may recall, this model suggests that both personal and situational factors influence individuals' internal states—their feelings, thoughts, and arousal—and that these internal states, in turn, shape individuals' appraisal of a given situation and their decision as to how to behave in it—aggressively (impulsively) or nonaggressively (thoughtfully). Bushman and Anderson suggest that repeated exposure to media violence can strongly affect cognitions relating to aggression, gradually creating a *hostile expectation bias*—a strong expectation that others will behave aggressively. This, in turn, causes individuals to be more aggressive themselves: After all, they perceive provocations from others everywhere, even when the provocations really don't exist!

In one test of this reasoning, Bushman and Anderson (2002) exposed participants either to highly aggressive video games (e.g., *Carmageddon, Mortal Kombat*) or nonaggressive video games (*Glider Pro, 3D Pinball*). Then, they asked them to read brief stories in which it is not clear what the characters described will do next. After reading the stories, participants described what they thought the main character would do, say, feel, and think as the story continues. For instance, in one story, a character has a minor traffic accident after braking quickly for a yellow traffic light. He then approaches the other driver. The researchers predicted that after playing the aggressive video games, participants would expect the story character to act more aggressively, to think more aggressive thoughts, and to feel angrier; as you can see from Figure 11.7, this is exactly what happened.

These findings and the results of related research (e.g., Anderson et al., 2004; Anderson & Bushman, 2001; Bushman & Huesmann, 2001) suggest that exposure to violent media exerts its effects by strengthening beliefs, expectations, and other cognitive processes related

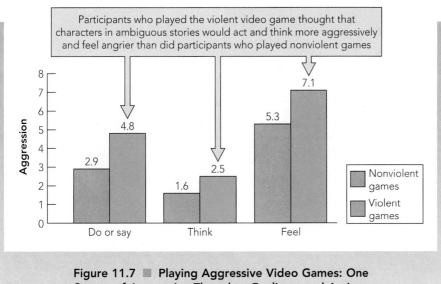

Figure 11.7 ■ Playing Aggressive Video Games: One Source of Aggressive Thoughts, Feelings, and Actions
Participants who played violent video games predicted that characters in ambiguous stories would behave, think, and feel more aggressively than did participants who played nonviolent games. These findings highlight the potential effects of *media violence* on aggression. (*Source: Based on data from Bushman & Anderson, 2002.*)

to aggression. In other words, as a result of repeated exposure to violent movies, TV programs, or violent video games, individuals develop strong *knowledge structures* relating to aggression—structures reflecting and combining these beliefs, expectations, schemas, and scripts. When these knowledge structures are then activated by various events, such persons feel, think, and act aggressively because this is what, in a sense, they have learned to do.

Whatever the underlying mechanisms, forty years of research on this issue suggests strongly that exposure to media violence may have harmful effects on society. So why, then, is there so much of it on television, in movies, and in video games? The answer, sad to relate, is that violence sells. People seem to find it exciting and enjoyable. Moreover, advertisers assume this is true and "put their money where the action is" (Bushman, 1998). In short, this is one more case in which economic motives take precedence over everything else. We know what to do, as a society, with respect to media violence: We should reduce it, if reducing violence is our goal. But as long as people pay to see aggressive shows and films or to buy violent games, there seems little chance this will happen. Perhaps the situation will change in the future, but although we are optimists by nature, it's difficult to be very positive of the likelihood of such change.

Violent Pornography: When Sex and Aggression Mix—and Perhaps Explode

When I (Robert Baron) lecture, I sometimes notice students in my class who are gazing intently at the screens of their laptop computers. No, they are not taking notes—they seem to be largely unaware of what I'm saying or doing. And occasionally, when I pass quietly by their seats, I notice that what they are watching is pornography of some type (see Figure 11.8). This experience is rare (thank goodness), but it does bring an important point into focus: Pornographic images are now freely available to virtually

Figure 11.8 ■ Violent Pornography on the Web
Many sites on the Web offer violent pornography. Thus, this type of content is much more common and easier to locate than was true in the past.

everyone, including, unfortunately, children. And, disturbingly, not all of these materials simply show consenting adults engaging in mutually enjoyable sexual activity. Some of it includes violent content, scenes in which victims—usually, but not always, women—are abused, exploited, and harmed in various ways (e.g., Linz, Fuson, & Donnerstein, 1990; Malamuth & Check, 1985).

If exposure to violence in the media can increase aggressive tendencies among persons exposed to such content, it seems possible that exposure to violent pornography might also produce such effects. In fact, because pornography often generates high levels of arousal (both negative and positive emotions), it seems possible that such effects might even be stronger than is true for media violence that does not contain sexual content. Although there is currently much less evidence on this issue than on the effects of media violence generally, some findings suggest that violent pornography may indeed have negative effects. For instance, laboratory studies (e.g., Linz, Donnerstein, & Penrod, 1988) suggest that exposure to violent pornography can increase men's willingness to aggress against women. Perhaps even more disturbing, repeated exposure to such materials appears to produce a *desensitizing effect,* in which emotional reactions to mistreatment or harm to sexual victims is gradually reduced. Finally, and most unsettling of all, exposure to violent pornography seems to encourage adoption of callous attitudes toward sexual violence, leading both women and men to accept dangerous myths about rape and other forms of sexual violence—for example, the myth that many women unconsciously want to be raped, or that almost all victims of rape are promiscuous and place themselves in situations in which they are likely to be sexually assaulted (Malamuth & Brown, 1994).

In sum, the growing availability of pornography, and especially pornography that includes themes of sexual violence, appears to be a dangerous trend. No, not all persons who are exposed to such materials become more willing to engage in such behavior themselves, but growing evidence suggests that the mixture of sex and violence such pornography contains can be a dangerous and volatile one. (Can exposure to violent pornography increase sexual aggression even among children? Please see the **Beyond the Headlines** section on page 432 for a discussion of this possibility.)

KEY POINTS

★ To study aggression, social psychologists often use procedures in which individuals are led to believe that they can harm others in various ways—delivery of painful electric shocks or reducing their winnings in a competitive game.

★ Contrary to the famous *frustration–aggression hypothesis,* all aggression does not stem from frustration, and frustration does not always lead to aggression. Frustration is a strong elicitor of aggression only under certain limited conditions.

★ In contrast, *provocation* from others is a powerful elicitor of aggression. We rarely turn the other cheek; rather, we match or slightly exceed the level of aggression we receive from others.

★ Heightened arousal can increase aggression if it persists beyond the situation in which it was induced and is falsely interpreted as anger.

★ Exposure to *media violence* increases aggression among viewers. This is due to several factors, such as the priming of aggressive thoughts and a weakening of restraints against aggression.

★ Exposure to violent pornography appears to increase the willingness of some persons to engage in similar behavior and to generate callous attitudes toward various forms of sexual violence.

Children as Sexual Predators: Does Violent Pornography Play a Role?

Porn Linked to Young Sex Offenders

Brisbane, Australia—Internet service providers should be made to filter online content because sexual assaults perpetrated by children are increasing, an

Internet media and mental health conference in Brisbane will be told today. Michael Flood, a research fellow at the Australia Institute, a public policy think tank, says little has been done to protect children from exposure to violent and extreme pornography.

Recent findings suggest exposure to such material—even if it is accidental—may be linked to a rise in the number of children sexually abusing other children. . . . Findings released last year revealed the number of children sexually harming other children

rose dramatically from the early 1990s to 2003, as violent pornography became more common on the Web. Other data suggest that about three-quarters of 16- and 17-year-olds have been exposed to pornographic websites, many carrying scenes of sexual violence. . .

Although sexual violence toward adults is a very serious matter, such behavior toward children is even more disturbing. And if it is perpetrated by children themselves, it is downright alarming. Yet, in the context of the research findings of social psychology, such effects are not unexpected. As noted earlier, a large body of evidence suggests that when children are exposed to scenes of aggression on television or in films, their own tendencies to engage in such behavior are increased (e.g., Anderson et al., 2004). Children, perhaps to an even greater extent than adults, have a strong tendency to imitate actions other persons perform. And, of course, they are still forming their ideas about what actions are and are not acceptable. When exposed to scenes of violent pornography, children not only learn new ways of harming others—actions involving various forms of sexual abuse—they also learn that such behaviors are condoned by at least some adults. It is little

wonder, then, that they become more likely to perform such actions themselves.

Can anything be done to reduce this problem? Several possibilities exist (e.g., making it more difficult for children to log onto pornographic sites; equipping computers with special filters that block such materials; urging parents to place computers in locations where they can readily see what their children are watching), but given the vast size and the ever-changing nature of the World Wide Web, any kind of control over its content or access to it is difficult. In the final analysis, then, the main responsibility for protecting children from exposure to violent pornography must rest with parents and other guardians. Only to the extent they take this responsibility to heart can individual children—and society in general—be sheltered from the harmful effects produced by a volatile mixture of sexual and violent content.

Cultural Factors in Aggression: "Cultures of Honor" and Sexual Jealousy

Aggression is often triggered by the words or deeds of other persons, but it can also stem from *cultural factors*—beliefs, norms, and expectations in a given culture suggesting that aggression is appropriate or perhaps even required under certain circumstances. Social psychologists have taken careful note of this fact in research on what is known as **cultures of honor**—cultures in which there are strong norms indicating that aggression is an appropriate response to insults to one's honor. This is a theme in many Asian films about warriors, in which characters felt compelled to have a fight with another person because their honor had somehow been sullied (see Figure 11.9).

Why did such norms develop? Cohen and Nisbett (1994, 1997) suggest that they may be traced to the fact that in some geographic areas, wealth was once concentrated

cultures of honor
Cultures in which there are strong norms indicating that aggression is an appropriate response to insults to one's honor.

Figure 11.9 ■ **Cultures of Honor in Action**
In *cultures of honor*, there are strong norms, suggesting that insults to one's honor must be avenged through aggression. This theme is captured in the fights that feature prominently in many Asian films about warriors.

mainly in assets that could readily be stolen (e.g., cattle and, sad to relate, slaves). For this reason, it became important for individuals to demonstrate that they would not tolerate such thefts, or any other affront to their honor. The result? Norms condoning violence in response to insults to one's honor emerged and were widely accepted.

Recent findings indicate that such norms are definitely *not* a thing of the past; on the contrary, they are alive and well in many parts of the world (e.g., Vandello & Cohen, 2003). Cultural beliefs condoning or even requiring aggression in response to affronts to one's honor operate in many different contexts, but their impact is especially apparent with respect to *sexual jealousy*. Because this topic has been investigated in many recent studies by social psychologists, we focus on it here.

■ Sexual Jealousy: One Key Effect of Concern with One's Honor

Infidelity—real or imagined—occurs in every society, even in ones that greatly restrict informal contact between women and men (see Figure 11.10). In cultures of honor, such behavior by women is viewed as especially threatening to male honor (e.g., Baker, Gregware, & Cassidy, 1999) and can result in drastic responses. In Iraq, for example, some physicians specialize in determining whether a woman is or

Figure 11.10 ■ **Sexual Jealousy in Cultures of Honor**
In many *cultures of honor*, informal contact between women and men is highly restricted. In fact, in some cultures, women are required to dress in a way that totally conceals their bodies—and their personal identities.

is not a virgin (e.g., Packer, 2004). And if a woman who is not married is found to have lost her virginity, her own family may execute her to protect and restore its honor!

Even in cultures of honor in which such actions are not condoned (e.g., cultures in South America), crimes of passion, in which husbands murder their wives or their wives' lovers, are condoned, at least to a degree. In these cultures, sexual infidelity by a wife or lover is viewed as the ultimate insult to a man's honor, so when a man takes action to restore his honor, it is viewed not merely as justified, but perhaps as actually required. As one saying from such cultures puts it, "Only blood can restore lost honor." This suggests that in cultures of honor, jealousy is a very powerful determinant of aggression—more powerful than it is in other cultures. Is this true? Growing evidence suggests that it is (e.g., Buss et al., 1992).

Perhaps the clearest evidence on this issue has recently been provided by Vandello and Cohen (1999, 2003) in a series of closely related studies. In their most recent work (Vandello & Cohen, 2003), they reasoned that the code of male honor is especially strong in Latin America and in the South of the United States. Thus, situations that induce jealousy would be expected to produce stronger aggressive reactions by the jealous persons in those cultures than in others. Moreover, persons in those honor-oriented cultures would tend to be more accepting of such aggression than would persons in other cultures (e.g., Nisbett & Cohen, 1996).

To test these ideas, Vandello and Cohen conducted several kinds of studies, but among these, perhaps the most interesting is one in which participants witnessed an interaction between a couple (both were assistants of the researchers) in which the woman stated that she was planning to visit her ex-boyfriend's house. The man in the couple indicated that he did not want her to do that, and the exchange between then became increasingly heated until the man grabbed the woman's car keys and pushed her roughly against the wall. Then, he left. At this point, the woman turned to the participant, who had been present during this scene, and expressed either contrition, explaining, "My fiancé really cares about me, and I guess that's just how he shows it," or anger, "That was my fiancé. He gets so jealous sometimes. . . . I'm getting so damn tired of this, you know?"

Later, participants in the study, who were from the northern United States or the southern United States, or were of Hispanic descent, rated their impressions of the woman. As predicted, participants from the South and who were of Hispanic descent rated her more favorably when she reacted with tolerance to her fiancé's mistreatment than when she reacted with anger (see Figure 11.11). Participants from the North generally showed the opposite pattern. In other words, participants in the study who came from cultures of honor reacted favorably to the forgiving woman because she was showing the kind of reaction that would help to restore her partner's compromised honor.

In other studies, the same authors asked participants to read brief stories in which a husband, who discovers that his wife has been unfaithful, responded either by yelling at her, by both yelling at her and slapping her, by telling her he wants a divorce, or by doing nothing. Participants then rated the man on several different dimensions. As predicted, participants who were from the South or were of Hispanic descent (people from cultures of honor) were more likely to express tolerance for the man when he was abusive than were persons from other cultures (e.g., the northern United States). Indeed, in additional research (Puente & Cohen, 2003), it was found that jealousy and the aggression that stems from it can even be viewed as signs of love! Not getting jealous or showing aggression, in other words, appears to suggest that the person whose partner is being unfaithful really doesn't care very much!

Overall, the findings reported by Vandello and Cohen (2003) and others (Puente & Cohen, 2003) indicate that jealousy is indeed a powerful cause of aggression and that, moreover, violence stemming from it—or forms of other slurs to one's honor—are excused or condoned, at least to a degree, in cultures of honor. Clearly, then, cultural factors play a key role in both the occurrence of aggression and in how it is perceived and evaluated.

Chapter 11 / Aggression

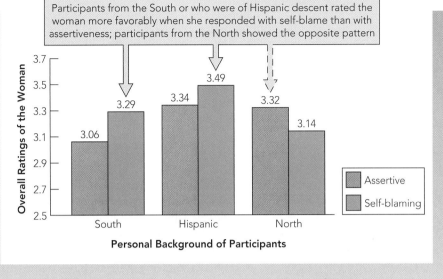

Figure 11.11 ■ Sexual Jealousy in Cultures of Honor
Participants from the South of the United States or who were of Hispanic descent rated a woman who responded to mistreatment by her fiancé with contrition (e.g., blaming herself) more favorably than a woman who responded with anger or assertiveness. In contrast, participants from the North showed the opposite pattern. These findings illustrate the powerful impact of *cultures of honor* on reactions to sexual jealousy. (*Source: Based on data from Vandello & Cohen, 2003.*)

KEY POINTS

★ In *cultures of honor*, norms requiring aggression as a response to threats to one's honor exist and exert powerful effects.

★ Sexual jealousy poses a major threat to male honor in such cultures, with the result that aggression in response to sexual infidelity is condoned to a greater extent, and women who are accepting of such aggression are viewed more favorably than ones who are not.

Personal Causes of Aggression: Type A, Narcissism, Sensation Seeking, and Gender Differences

Are some persons "primed" for aggression by their personal characteristics? Informal observation suggests that this is so. Some individuals rarely lose their tempers or engage in aggressive actions (see Figure 11.12 on page 436), but others seem to be forever "losing it," with potentially serious consequences. In this section, we consider several traits or characteristics that seem to play an important role in aggression.

■ The Type A Behavior Pattern: Why the *A* in Type A Could Stand for *Aggression*

Do you know anyone you could describe as (1) extremely competitive, (2) always in a hurry, and (3) especially irritable and aggressive? If so, this person shows the characteristics of what psychologists term the **Type A behavior pattern** (Glass, 1977; Strube,

Type A behavior pattern
A pattern consisting primarily of high levels of competitiveness, time urgency, and hostility.

Figure 11.12 ■ **Personality and Aggression**
Some persons, like the one shown here, rarely lose their tempers, but when they finally do—watch out! Others, in contrast, are constantly "blowing up." This suggests the existence of large individual differences with respect to aggression. This person, it appears, is truly a lit fuse or ticking bomb just waiting to explode. (*Source:* © J.D. Crowe, crowecartoons.com)

1989). At the opposite end of the continuum are persons who do not show these characteristics—individuals who are *not* highly competitive, who are *not* always fighting the clock, and who do *not* readily lose their tempers; such persons are described as showing the **Type B behavior pattern.**

Given these characteristics, it seems only reasonable to expect that Type A's would tend to be more aggressive than Type B's in many situations. In fact, the results of several experiments indicate that this is actually the case (Baron, Russell, & Arms, 1985; Carver & Glass, 1978).

Additional findings indicate that Type A's are truly hostile people: They don't merely aggress against others because this is a useful means for reaching other goals, such as winning athletic contests or furthering their own careers. Rather, they are more likely than Type B's to engage in what is known as **hostile aggression**—aggression in which the prime objective is inflicting some kind of harm on the victim (Strube et al., 1984). In view of this fact, it is not surprising to learn that Type A's are more likely than Type B's to engage in such actions as child abuse or spouse abuse (Strube et al., 1984). In contrast, Type A's are *not* more likely than Type B's to engage in **instrumental aggression**—aggression performed primarily to attain other goals aside from harming the victim, goals such as control of valued resources or praise from others for behaving in a "tough" manner.

Perceiving Evil Intent in Others: Hostile Attributional Bias

Suppose that while you are in a supermarket, another shopper hits you with her cart and then shouts angrily at you to get out of her way. In this case, it would be fairly clear that her actions were done on purpose—they stemmed from *hostile intentions*. But what if after hitting you she had said, "Oh, I'm sorry; please excuse me"? If she appeared to be genuinely sorry, the chances are good that you would not become angry and would not seek to retaliate against her. This is because our *attributions* concerning the causes of others' behavior play an important role in aggression, just as they do in many other forms of social behavior (see the discussion of this topic in Chapter 2). But what if she muttered, "Oh, I'm sorry," but at the same time had a malicious look on her face? In both cases, your actions would depend strongly on your attributions concerning her behavior. If you attributed her hitting you with her cart to hostile intentions, you would still become angry; if you decided to believe her, you might simply walk away instead.

The fact that attributions play an important role in our reactions to others' behavior—and especially to apparent provocations from them—is the starting point for another important personal characteristic that influences aggression: the **hostile attributional bias** (e.g., Dodge et al., 1986). This refers to the tendency to perceive hostile intentions or motives in others' actions when these actions are ambiguous. In other words, persons high in hostile attributional bias rarely give others the benefit of the doubt: They simply *assume* that any provocative actions by others are intentional, and

Type B behavior pattern
A pattern consisting of the absence of characteristics associated with the Type A behavior pattern.

hostile aggression
Aggression in which the prime objective is inflicting some kind of harm on the victim.

instrumental aggression
Aggression in which the primary goal is not harm to the victim but attainment of some other goal—for example, access to valued resources.

hostile attributional bias
The tendency to perceive hostile intentions or motives in others' actions when these actions are ambiguous.

react accordingly. The results of many studies offer support for the potential impact of this factor (e.g., Dodge & Coie, 1987), so it seems to be another important personal (individual difference) factor in the occurrence of aggression.

■ Narcissism, Ego Threat, and Aggression: On the Dangers of Wanting to Be Superior

Do you know the story of Narcissus? He was a character in Greek mythology who fell in love with his own reflection in the water and drowned trying to reach it. His name has now become a synonym for excessive self-love—for holding an overinflated view of one's own virtues or accomplishments; research findings indicate that this trait may be linked to aggression in important ways. Specifically, studies by Bushman and Baumeister (1998) suggest that persons high in *narcissism* (ones who agree with items such as "If I ruled the world, it would be a much better place" and "I am more capable than other people") react with exceptionally high levels of aggression to "slights" from others—feedback that threatens their inflated self-image. Why? Perhaps because such persons have nagging doubts about the accuracy of their inflated egos, and so react with intense anger toward anyone who threatens to undermine them.

Another possibility, investigated recently by McCullough and his colleagues (2003), is that narcissistic people, because of their inflated self-images, perceive themselves as the victims of transgressions more often than nonnarcissistic people. To test this prediction, these researchers asked college students to complete a measure of narcissism, and then to keep a diary for fourteen days in which they recorded the number of times in which other people offended them in some way. As expected, the higher participants' scored in narcissism, the greater the number of transgressions by others they reported. This was especially true for one aspect of narcissism relating to exploiting others or being entitled to wonderful treatment by them (e.g., strong agreement with statements such as "I insist on getting the respect that is due me").

The finding that narcissism is one personal characteristic related to aggression has important implications, because at the present time, many schools in the United States focus on building high self-esteem among their students. Up to a point, this may be beneficial, but if such esteem-building tactics are carried too far and produce children whose opinions of themselves are unrealistically high (i.e., narcissistic), the result may actually be an increased potential for violence. Clearly, this is a possibility worthy of further careful study.

■ Sensation Seeking and Aggression: Are People Who Like Lots of "Action" More Aggressive Than Others?

Do you know anyone who gets bored easily, seeks lots of new experiences—especially exciting ones with an element of risk—and is generally uninhibited? If so, this person may be high in what social psychologists describe as *sensation seeking*, or in the closely related trait of *impulsivity* (e.g., Zuckerman, 1994). There are grounds for expecting such persons to be higher than others in aggression, too. Why would this be the case? Again, the GAM (general aggression model) suggests some possible reasons. First, it may be that persons high in sensation seeking or impulsiveness experience anger and hostile feelings more often than do others. Their emotions are easily aroused, so they may have lower thresholds for becoming angry. Moreover, their tendencies to get bored and to seek exciting new experiences may lead them to have more hostile thoughts: After all, aggressive exchanges with others are exciting and dangerous. Evidence for these predictions has been reported recently by Joireman, Anderson, and Strathman (2003), who found that persons high in sensation seeking show several tendencies related to aggression. First, they are attracted to aggression-eliciting situations, which they find exciting and appealing. Second, they are indeed more likely to experience anger and hostility. Third, they are more likely to focus on the immediate rather than the delayed consequences of their behavior. The overall result? They tend to show higher levels of both physical and verbal aggression than others. The moral of these findings is clear: Beware of people who seek thrills, excitement, and adventure; a heightened tendency to aggress may go along with these personal characteristics.

Gender Differences in Aggression: Do They Exist?

Are males more aggressive than females? Folklore suggests that they are, and research findings suggest that, in this case, informal observation is correct: When asked whether they have ever engaged in any of a wide range of aggressive actions, males reported a higher incidence of many aggressive behaviors than did females (Harris, 1994). On close examination, however, the picture regarding gender differences in the tendency to aggress becomes more complex. On one hand, males are generally more likely than females both to perform aggressive actions and to serve as the target for such behavior (Bogard, 1990; Harris, 1992, 1994). Further, this difference seems to persist throughout the life span, occurring even among people in their seventies and eighties (Walker, Richardson, & Green, 2000). On the other hand, however, the size of these differences appears to vary greatly across situations.

First, gender differences in aggression are much larger in the absence of provocation than in its presence. In other words, males are significantly more likely than females to aggress against others when these persons have *not* provoked them in any manner (Bettencourt & Miller, 1996). In situations in which provocation *is* present, and especially when it is intense (see Figure 11.13), such differences tend to disappear.

Second, the size—and even direction—of gender differences in aggression seems to vary greatly with the *type* of aggression in question. Research findings indicate that males are more likely than females to engage in various forms of *direct* aggression—actions aimed directly at the target and that clearly stem from the aggressor (e.g., physical assaults, pushing, shoving, throwing something at another person, shouting, making insulting remarks; Bjorkqvist, Osterman, & Hjelt-Buck, 1994). However, females are more likely to engage in various forms of *indirect* aggression—actions that allow the aggressor to conceal his or her identity from the victim and that, in some cases, make it difficult for the victim to know that they have been the target of intentional harmdoing. Such actions include spreading vicious rumors about the target person, gossiping behind this person's back, telling others not to associate with the intended victim, making up stories to get the person in trouble, and so on. Research findings indicate that gender differences with respect to indirect aggression are present among children as young as eight years old and increase through age fifteen (Bjorkqvist, Lagerspetz, & Kaukiainen, 1992; Osterman et al., 1998) and into adulthood (Bjorkqvist, Osterman, & Hjelt-Back, 1994; Green, Richardson, & Lago, 1996). Further, these differences have been observed in several different countries—Finland, Sweden, Poland, Italy, and Australia (Osterman et al., 1998; Owens, Shute, & Slee, 2000), so they appear to be quite general in scope.

In sum, gender differences with respect to aggression do exist and can be substantial in some contexts. Overall, however, the nature of such differences are far more complex than common sense suggests.

Figure 11.13 ■ **Gender Differences in Aggression: Smaller Than You Think**
Though men are generally more aggressive than women, this difference tends to disappear in the face of strong provocation.

KEY POINTS

- ★ Persons showing the *Type A behavior pattern* are more irritable and aggressive than persons with the *Type B behavior pattern.*

- ★ Individuals high in *hostile attributional bias* attribute others' actions to hostile intent. As a result, they are more aggressive than persons low in this characteristic.

- ★ Persons high in narcissism hold an overinflated view of their own worth. They react with exceptionally high levels of aggression to feedback from others that threatens their inflated egos. They also view themselves, more than other persons, as the victim of transgressions from others, and this may contribute to their heightened aggression.

- ★ Persons high in sensation seeking tend to be more aggressive than others because they are attracted to aggression-eliciting situations and because they experience anger and hostile thoughts more often than do persons lower on this dimension.

- ★ Males are more aggressive overall than females, but this difference decreases in the context of strong provocation. Males are more likely to use direct forms of aggression, but females are more likely to use indirect forms of aggression.

Situational Determinants of Aggression: The Effects of High Temperatures and Alcohol Consumption

Aggression is often strongly influenced by social factors and personal characteristics, but it is also affected by factors relating to the situation or context in which it occurs. Here, we examine two of the many *situational factors* that can influence aggression: high temperatures and alcohol.

■ In the Heat of Anger: Temperature and Aggression

In the heat of anger; boiling mad; hot-tempered: Phrases such as these suggest that there may well be a link between temperature and human aggression. And, in fact, many people report that they often feel especially irritable and short-tempered on hot and steamy days. Is there really a link between climate and human aggression? Social psychologists have been studying this question for more than three decades, and during this period, the methods they have used and the results they have obtained have become increasingly sophisticated. (The most current answer, by the way, is, "Yes, heat does increase aggression, but only up to a point." Beyond some level, aggression may actually decline as temperatures rise, because people become so uncomfortable and fatigued that they are actually less likely to engage in overt aggression.)

The earliest studies on this topic (Baron, 1972; Baron & Lawton, 1972) were experiments, conducted under controlled laboratory conditions, in which temperature was systematically varied as the independent variable. For instance, participants were exposed either to comfortably pleasant conditions (temperatures of 70 to 72 degrees Fahrenheit) or to uncomfortably hot conditions (temperatures of 94 to 98 degrees Fahrenheit) and were then given opportunities to aggress against another person. (In fact, they only *believed* they could harm this person; ethical considerations made it necessary to ensure that no harm could actually take place.) Results were surprising: High temperature *reduced* aggression for both provoked and unprovoked persons. The initial explanation of these findings was that the high temperatures were so uncomfortable that participants focused on getting away from them—and this caused participants to reduce their aggression. After all, aggression might lead to unfriendly encounters with the victim, and this would prolong their misery.

This explanation seemed reasonable: When people are *very* hot, they do seem to become lethargic and to concentrate on reducing their discomfort rather than on evening the score with others. However, these early studies suffered from important drawbacks that made it difficult to assess this interpretation. For instance, the exposure to the high temperatures lasted only a few minutes, while, in the real world, such exposure occurs over much longer periods. Subsequent studies, therefore, used very different methods (e.g., Anderson, 1989; Anderson & Anderson, 1996; Bell, 1992). Specifically, they examined long-term records of temperatures and police records of various aggressive crimes to determine whether the frequency of such crimes increased with rising temperatures. For instance, consider an informative study by Anderson, Bushman, and Groom (1997).

These researchers collected average annual temperatures for fifty cities in the United States over a forty-five-year period (1950 to 1995). In addition, they obtained information on the rate of both violent crimes (aggravated assault, homicide) and property crimes (burglary, car theft), as well as another crime that has often been viewed as primarily aggressive in nature—rape. They then performed analyses to determine whether temperature were related to these crimes. In general, the results indicated that hotter years indeed produced higher rates of violent crimes but did *not* produce increases in property crimes or rape. This was true even though the effect of many other variables that might also influence aggressive crimes (e.g., poverty, age distribution of the population) were eliminated. These findings and those of related studies (e.g., Anderson, Anderson, & Deuser, 1996) suggest that heat is indeed linked to aggression.

Sophisticated as this research was, however, it did not fully resolve one key question: Does this heat–aggression relationship have any limits? In other words, does aggression increase with heat indefinitely, or only up to some point, beyond which aggression actually declines as temperatures continue to rise? As you may recall, that is the pattern obtained in initial laboratory studies on this topic.

Additional studies by Rotton and Cohn (Cohn & Rotton, 1997; Rotton & Cohn, 2000) have carefully addressed this issue. These researchers reasoned that if people do indeed try to reduce their discomfort when they are feeling very uncomfortable (e.g., when temperatures are very high), the relationship between heat and aggression should be stronger in the evening hours than at midday. Why? Because temperatures fall below their peak in the evening. In other words, a finer-grained analysis would reveal a curvilinear relationship between heat and aggression during the day but a linear one at night. This is exactly what they found (see Figure 11.14).

In sum, research on the effects of heat on aggression suggests that there is a link between heat and aggression: When people get hot, they become irritable and may be more likely to lash out at others. However, there may be limits to this relationship, stemming from the fact that after prolonged exposure to high temperatures, people become so uncomfortable that they are lethargic and focus on reducing their discomfort, not on attacking others. Short of these extreme conditions, however, there is a large grain of truth in the phrase "in the heat of anger," because when temperatures rise, tempers may, too—with serious social consequences.

Alcohol and Aggression: A Potentially Dangerous Mix

It is widely believed that at least some persons become more aggressive when they consume alcohol. This idea is supported by the fact that bars and nightclubs are frequently the scene of violence. However, though alcohol is certainly consumed in these settings, other factors might be responsible for the fights (or worse) that often erupt: competition for desirable partners, crowding (which leads people to jostle one another), and even cigarette smoke, which irritates some people (Zillmann, Baron, & Tamborini, 1981). What does systematic research reveal about a possible link between alcohol and

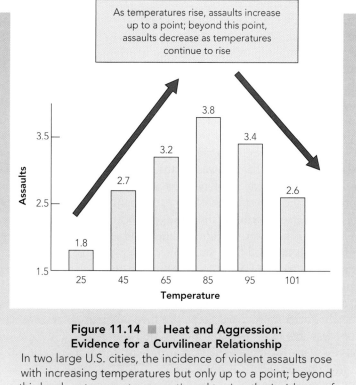

Figure 11.14 ■ **Heat and Aggression:**
Evidence for a Curvilinear Relationship
In two large U.S. cities, the incidence of violent assaults rose
with increasing temperatures but only up to a point; beyond
this level, as temperatures continued to rise, the incidence of
assaults actually dropped. These findings suggest that the
relationship between heat and aggression may be curvilinear in
nature. (*Source: Based on data from Rotton & Cohn, 2000.*)

aggression? Interestingly, it tends to confirm the existence of such a link. In several
experiments, participants who consumed substantial doses of alcohol—enough to
make them legally drunk—were found to behave more aggressively and to respond to
provocations more strongly than those who did not consume alcohol (e.g., Bushman
& Cooper, 1990; Gustafson, 1990). (Participants in such research are always warned, in
advance, that they may be receiving alcoholic beverages, and only those who consent
to such procedures actually take part; e.g., Pihl, Lau, & Assaad, 1997). But *why* does alcohol
produce such effects? Does it simply eliminate inhibitions against acting in an
impulsive and possibly dangerous way? Or does it make people especially sensitive to
provocations, so that they are more likely to behave aggressively (e.g., Gantner & Taylor,
1992)? Both of these possibilities are reasonable and are supported by some evidence,
but recent findings suggest that the effects of alcohol on aggression may stem,
at least in part, from reduced cognitive functioning and what this does, in turn, to social
perception.

Specifically, it has been found that alcohol impairs higher-order cognitive functions
such as evaluation of stimuli and memory. This result may make it harder for individuals
to evaluate others' intentions (hostile or nonhostile) and to evaluate the effects that
various forms of behavior on their part, including aggression, may produce (e.g.,
Hoaken, Giancola, & Pihl, 1998). Evidence for such effects has recently been reported
by Bartholow et al. (2003) in a study using a social neuroscience approach.

In this research, participants received either a high dose of alcohol, a moderate
dose, or no alcohol. Then, they read descriptions of strangers who had either positive

traits or negative traits (e.g., the strangers were described as "always opens the door for others"), and who were described as acting either in a positive or negative manner in a particular situation. Recordings of event-related brain potentials (ERBPs) were made during these procedures. It was predicted that regardless of whether they drank alcohol, participants would show larger late positive potentials (LPPs) in instances in which their expectancies were violated—when a person with positive traits acted in a negative way or when a person with negative traits acted in a positive way. This prediction was confirmed. It was also predicted that if alcohol interferes with the processing of information about other persons, the size of these LPPs would be reduced. In other words, a participant's ability to handle (try to make sense of) inconsistent information would be reduced. Results indicated that this was *not* the case. Rather, it was found that for individuals who did not consume alcohol, persons with positive traits performing negative behaviors produced the largest LPPs. When participants drank alcohol, however, the opposite was true: Persons with negative traits performing positive behaviors produced the largest LPPs. In other words, alcohol seemed to change the kind of inconsistencies to which individuals directed their attention.

What does this mean in terms of aggression? Although the researchers did not address this issue, one possibility is that alcohol reduces individuals' ability to process positive information about someone they initially dislike or view in negative terms. This would mean that if such a person provoked them, but then apologized, persons who drink alcohol might be less able to process this information cognitively, and so would be more likely to aggress. This is pure speculation at present, but it does seem to fit other findings concerning the impact of alcohol.

Whatever the precise cognitive processes involved, existing evidence (e.g., Gantner & Taylor, 1992) suggests that alcohol indeed may be one situational factor that contributes to the occurrence of aggression, and that such effects may be especially strong for persons who normally show low levels of aggression (Pihl et al., 1997). In this sense, then, consumption of alcohol may indeed have the release-of-inhibitions effects common sense suggests. (For an overview of the many factors that play a role in human aggression, see the **Ideas to Take with You—and Use!** section at the end of this chapter.)

KEY POINTS

★ High temperatures tend to increase aggression but only up to a point. Beyond some level, aggression declines as temperatures rise.

★ Consuming alcohol can increase aggression, especially, it appears, by individuals who normally show low levels of aggression.

★ Alcohol may exert these effects by reducing an individual's capacity to process some kinds of information and by changing their reactions to unexpected behaviors by other persons.

Aggression in Long-Term Relationships: Bullying and Workplace Violence

Reports of instances in which people are attacked by total strangers are disturbing. Even more unsettling, however, are situations in which people are harmed by others they know or with whom they have long-term relationships—family members, spouses or

Figure 11.15 ■ Bullying: One-Way Aggression
In *bullying*, one person repeatedly assaults one or more others who have no ability to defend themselves or retaliate. Such behavior occurs among children, as shown here, but also among adults.

partners, schoolmates, coworkers. Such aggression takes many different forms, but we focus here on two important topics: *bullying* (e.g., Ireland & Ireland, 2000; Smith & Brain, 2000) and *workplace violence* (Griffin & O'Leary, 2004).

Bullying: Singling Out Others for Repeated Abuse

Almost everyone has either experienced or observed the effects of **bullying**—a form of aggression in which aggression is primarily one way: One person repeatedly assaults one or more others who have little or no power to retaliate (Olweus, 1993). In other words, in bullying relationships, one person does the aggressing and the other (or others) are on the receiving end. Although bullying has been studied primarily as something that occurs among children and teenagers (see Figure 11.15), it is also common in other contexts, too, such as workplaces and prisons (e.g., Ireland & Archer, 2002). Indeed, research findings indicate that fully 50 percent of persons in prison are exposed to one or more episodes of bullying each week (Ireland & Ireland, 2000). In this discussion, therefore, we consider research on bullying in many different contexts.

■ Why Do People Engage in Bullying?

A very basic question about bullying, of course, is why does it occur? Why do some individuals choose targets they then repeatedly terrorize? There is no simple answer to this question, but two motives appear to play a key role: the motive to hold power over others and the motive to be part of a group that is "tough" and so confer status on its members (e.g., Olweus, 1999). These motives are clearly visible in research conducted by Roland (2002). In this study, more than two thousand children in Norway answered questions designed to measure their desire to exercise power over others, their desire to be part of powerful groups, and their tendency to be unhappy or depressed. (Previous research had suggested that feeling depressed might be another reason why individuals engage in bullying—it makes them feel better!) A measure of bullying was obtained by asking the children to indicate how often they had bullied other children (never, now and then, weekly, daily). Such self-reports of bullying have generally been found to be accurate when compared with teachers' ratings.

Results revealed some interesting gender differences. Among boys, the desire both to gain power and to be part of powerful groups was significantly related to bullying, while feeling depressed was not. For girls, all three motives were related to bullying. This suggests that for girls, at least, aggressing against someone who can't retaliate is one technique for countering the negative feelings of depression. Again, we should note that many other factors, too, play a role in the occurrence of bullying. The motives identified here, however, were found to play a role in bullying in many different contexts, so they seem to be among the most important causes of bullying.

bullying
A pattern of behavior in which one individual is chosen as the target of repeated aggression by one or more others; the target person (the victim) generally has less power than those who engage in aggression (the bullies).

The Characteristics of Bullies and Victims

Are bullies always bullies and victims always victims? Although common sense suggests that these roles would tend to be relatively fixed, research findings indicate that, in fact, they are not. Many persons who are bullies in one context become victims in other situations, and vice versa. So, there appear to be pure bullies (people who are always and only bullies), pure victims (people who are always and only victims), and bully-victims (people who switch back and forth between these roles).

But what, aside from the motives for power and belonging described above, makes some people become bullies in the first place? Findings of careful research on bullying point to the following factors. First, bullies tend to believe that others act the way they do intentionally or because of lasting characteristics (Smorti & Ciucci, 2000). In contrast, victims tend to perceive others as acting as they do at least in part because they are responding to external events or conditions, including how others have treated *them*. In other words, bullies are more subject to the hostile attributional bias described earlier in this chapter. In a sense, they attack others because they perceive them to be potentially dangerous and wish to get in the first blows!

Another difference is that bullies (and also bully-victims) tend to be lower in self-esteem than other persons. As a result, they often attack them to build up their own self-images. In addition, they tend to adopt a ruthless, manipulative approach to life and to dealing with other persons (e.g., Mynard & Joseph, 1997; Andreou, 2000). They believe that others are not to be trusted, so they feel it is totally justified to take unfair advantage of others (e.g., to attack the victims when their guard is down).

Finally, bullies and bully-victims believe that the best way to respond to bullying is with aggression. They believe, more than other persons, that aggressing against others who provoke them will bring respect from others and make them feel better (Ireland & Archer, 2002). The result? They choose to respond to even slight provocations from others with strong aggression, and so start the process of becoming a bully.

Reducing the Occurrence of Bullying: Some Positive Steps

Bullying can have devastating effects on its victims. In fact, there have been several cases in which children who have been bullied repeatedly and brutally by their classmates have actually committed suicide (O'Moore, 2000), and similar results often occur in prisons, in which persons who are brutalized by their fellow inmates see death as the only way out. These distressing facts lead to the following question: What can be done to reduce or even eliminate bullying? Many research projects—some involving the entire school systems or prison systems of several countries—have been conducted to find out, and the results have been at least moderately encouraging. Here is an overview of the main findings:

- First, bullying must be seen to be a problem by all involved parties—teachers, parents, students, prisoners, guards, fellow employees, and supervisors (if bullying occurs in work settings).

- If bullying occurs, persons in authority (teachers, prison guards, supervisors) must draw attention to it and take an unequivocal stand against it.

- Potential victims must be provided with direct means for dealing with bullying—they must be told precisely what to do and whom to see when bullying occurs.

- Outside help is often useful in identifying the cause of bullying and in devising programs to reduce it.

Programs that have emphasized these points have produced encouraging results. Overall, then, there appear to be grounds for optimism—provided bullying is recognized as the serious problem it is, and organizations in which it takes place (schools, prisons, businesses) take vigorous steps to deal with it.

Student questioned in killing of teacher—A 13 year old student sent home from school for throwing water balloons on the last day of classes returned two hours later and shot a teacher with a semi-automatic pistol. . . . (Lake Worth, Florida, May 29, 2001).

Dr. carves initials on woman—Obstetrician is being sued for using scalpel to etch letters on abdomen after Cesarean section (Albany, NY, January 22, 2000).

Portland, Oregon—A man accused of shooting two people and taking four others hostage in an office tower appeared in court Friday. . . . Police initially said Rancor intended to shoot female office workers for having him fired from his job. . . . (Associated Press, 1996).

Reports of incidents such as these have appeared with alarming frequency in recent years and seem to reflect a rising tide of violence in workplaces. In fact, more than eight hundred people are murdered at work each year in the United States alone (National Institute for Occupational Safety and Health, 1993). While these statistics seem to suggest that workplaces are becoming dangerous locations where disgruntled employees frequently attack or even shoot one another, two facts must be noted: (1) A large majority of violence occurring in work settings is performed by "outsiders"—people who do not work there but enter a workplace to commit robbery or other crimes (see Figure 11.16), and (2) recent surveys indicate that threats of physical harm or actual harm in work settings are actually rare—in fact, the chances of being killed at work (by outsiders or coworkers combined) are 1 in 450,000 (although this is considerably higher in some "high-risk occupations" such as taxi driver or police; LeBlanc & Barling, 2004).

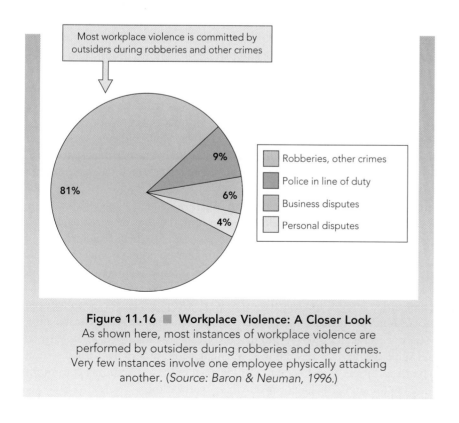

Figure 11.16 ■ Workplace Violence: A Closer Look
As shown here, most instances of workplace violence are performed by outsiders during robberies and other crimes. Very few instances involve one employee physically attacking another. (*Source:* Baron & Neuman, 1996.)

In sum, growing evidence suggests that while workplace *violence* is an important topic worthy of careful study, it is rare and is, in fact, only the dramatic tip of the much larger problem of **workplace aggression**—any form of behavior through which individuals seek to harm others in their places of work (Griffin & O'Leary, 2004; Neuman & Baron, 2004). What is such aggression like? Growing evidence suggests that it is largely *covert* rather than *overt* in nature. That is, it is relatively subtle in nature and allows aggressors to harm other persons while simultaneously preventing the victims from identifying them as the source of such harm. This type of aggression is strongly preferred in workplaces, because aggressors in such settings expect to interact with their intended victims frequently in the future. Using covert forms of aggression reduces the likelihood that their victims will retaliate against them.

What specific forms of aggression do individuals actually use in workplaces? Evidence on this issue is provided by research conducted by Baron, Neuman, and Geddes (1999). These researchers asked almost five hundred employed persons to rate the frequency with which they had personally experienced a wide range of aggressive behaviors at work. Careful analysis of their responses indicated that most aggression occurring in workplaces falls into three major categories:

- *Expressions of hostility:* Behaviors that are primarily verbal or symbolic in nature (e.g., belittling others' opinions, talking behind their backs)

- *Obstructionism:* Behaviors designed to obstruct or impede the target's performance (e.g., failure to return phone calls or respond to memos, failure to transmit needed information, interfering with activities important to the target)

- *Overt aggression:* Behaviors that have typically been included under the heading "workplace violence" (e.g., physical assault, theft or destruction of property, threats of physical violence)

How common are these forms of behavior? Research on what is known as **abusive supervision**—behavior in which supervisors direct frequent hostile verbal and nonverbal behavior toward their subordinates (Tepper, 2000)—suggests that the answer is, "More common than you might guess." It occurs not just between coworkers but also among supervisors and employees as well. Abusive supervision, one form of workplace aggression, includes such actions as public and private ridicule, exclusion from important activities, invasion of personal space, rude and discourteous behavior, lying, and taking credit for a subordinate's work; all seem to occur with high frequency. In sum, although workplace violence involving physical assaults is relatively rare, workplace aggression is much more common; in fact, in many workplaces, aggression is an everyday occurrence. If you have ever had a boss who held you up to ridicule, was rude to you in front of others, took credit for your work, or violated your personal space (e.g., looking into the drawers of your desk or your personal locker), you may have experienced such supervision firsthand.

What are the causes of workplace aggression? Again, as is true of aggression in any context, many factors seem to play a role. However, one that has emerged again and again in research on this topic is *perceived unfairness* (e.g., Skarlicki & Folger, 1997). When individuals feel that they have been treated unfairly by others in their organization—or by the organization itself—they experience intense feelings of anger and resentment and often seek to even the score by harming the people they hold responsible in some manner. In addition, aggression in work settings seems to be influenced by general societal norms concerning the acceptability of such behavior. For instance, one recent study (Dietz et al., 2003) found that the greater the incidence of violence in communities surrounding U.S. Post Offices, the higher the rates of aggression within these branch offices. It was as if acceptance of violence in the surrounding communities paved the way for similar behavior inside this organization.

workplace aggression
Any form of behavior through which individuals seek to harm others in their workplace.

abusive supervision
Behavior in which supervisors direct frequent hostile verbal and nonverbal behavior toward their subordinates.

Chapter 11 / Aggression

Other factors that seem to play a role in workplace aggression relate to changes that have occurred recently in many workplaces: downsizing, layoffs, increased use of part-time employees, to name a few. Several studies indicate that the greater the extent to which such changes have occurred, the greater the aggression occurring in such workplaces (e.g., Andersson & Pearson, 1999; Neuman & Baron, 1998). Such findings are only correlational in nature, but because downsizing, layoffs, and other changes have been found to produce negative feelings among employees (e.g., increased anxiety and feelings of resentment), it seems possible that these changes may well contribute, through such reactions, to increased aggression. One final point: Because such changes have occurred with increasing frequency in recent years, it seems possible that the incidence of workplace aggression, too, may be increasing for this reason.

In sum, media attention to dramatic instances of workplace violence may be somewhat misleading; although such actions do occur, they are far less frequent than more subtle but still harmful instances of workplace aggression. And such behavior, in turn, appears to be influenced by many of the same factors that influence aggression in other contexts (Baron, 2004).

KEY POINTS

★ *Bullying* involves repeated aggression against individuals who, for various reasons, are unable to defend themselves against such treatment. Bullying occurs in many contexts, including schools, workplaces, and prisons. Few persons are solely bullies or victims; more play both roles. Bullies and bully-victims appear to have lower self-esteem than do people who are not involved in bullying.

★ *Workplace aggression* takes many different forms but is usually *covert* in nature. It stems from a wide range of factors, including perceptions of having been treated unfairly and many disturbing changes that have occurred in workplaces recently.

The Prevention and Control of Aggression: Some Useful Techniques

If there is one idea in this chapter we hope you remember in the years ahead, it is this: Aggression is *not* an inevitable or unchangeable form of behavior. On the contrary, because it stems from a complex interplay between external events, cognitions, and personal characteristics, it *can* be prevented or reduced. In this final section, we consider several procedures that, when used appropriately, can be effective in reducing the frequency or intensity of human aggression.

Punishment: Just Desserts versus Deterrence

In most societies throughout the world, **punishment**—delivery of aversive consequences—is a major technique for reducing aggression. Persons who engage in such behavior receive large fines, are put in prison, and, in some countries, are placed in solitary confinement or receive physical punishment for their aggressive actions. In the most extreme cases, they receive *capital punishment* and are executed in various ways by legal

punishment
Procedures in which aversive consequences are delivered to individuals when they engage in specific actions.

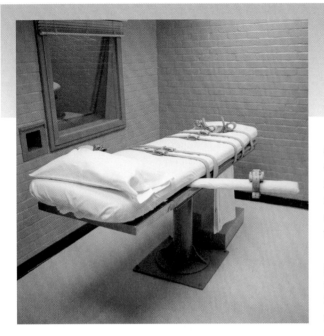

Figure 11.17 ■ Punishment: Its Most Extreme Form
Most societies use *punishment*—delivery of aversive consequences—as a means of reducing aggression. In its most extreme form, capital punishment, individuals judged to be a danger to their society are executed in a way prescribed by law.

authorities (see Figure 11.17). This raises two important questions: Why is punishment used so frequently as a means for reducing human aggression, and does punishment really work? These are complex questions that we can't hope to resolve here, but we can, at least, describe what research on these important issues has revealed.

Turning to the first question, there are two major grounds for punishing persons who commit aggressive actions (e.g., Darley, Carlsmith, & Robinson, 2000). The first involves the belief that when individuals engage in acts of aggression that are viewed as inappropriate in their societies, they *deserve* to be punished in order to make amends for the harm they have caused. This perspective suggests that the amount of punishment people receive should be matched to the magnitude of harm they have caused (e.g., breaking someone's arm deserves less punishment than permanently harming or killing someone). In addition, the magnitude of punishment should take account of extenuating circumstances. For instance, was there some "good" motive for the aggressive action, such as self-defense or defense of one's family?

The second reason for punishing persons who commit aggressive actions is to *deter* them (or others) from engaging in such behavior in the future. This basis for punishment implies that ease of detection of the crime should be given careful attention: If aggressive actions are hard to detect (e.g., they involve hidden or covert forms of harming others), they should be strongly punished, because only strong punishment will deter people from engaging in actions they believe they can get away with. Similarly, public punishment would be expected to be more effective in deterring future crimes than would private punishment.

Which of these two perspectives are most important in terms of the magnitude of punishment people feel is justified for aggressive acts or other offenses? Research by Carlsmith, Darley, and Robinson (2002) suggests that, in general, the first perspective—punishing people to make amends for the harm they have done—is more important. These researchers asked participants to read brief descriptions of crimes that varied in the extent to which the crimes seemed to deserve punishment (i.e., how much harm they had caused), and also varied in terms of the ease with which these crimes could be detected. An example of a crime that produced relatively little harm and might deserve low punishment was an employee embezzling money from an employer, while a crime that seemed to deserve high punishment was dumping toxic waste to increase profits. Participants also learned that the ease of detecting these crimes was either low or high. After reading these descriptions, participants in the study rated the extent to which the perpetrator should be punished. Results offered strong support for the view that in deciding how much punishment to deliver, we seem to be strongly influenced by how much punishment is *deserved*: Participants in the study assigned much harsher punishment for the dumping of toxic waste, which produced much harm, than to embezzling funds, which produced less harm. In contrast, the punishments they recommended were *not* significantly influenced by the ease of detecting various crimes. Using punishment as a deterrent to future crimes seemed to be much less important.

Does this mean that we don't consider the deterrence value of punishment at all? Carlsmith, Darley, and Robinson (2002) do not believe this is so. Rather, other results they obtained suggest that when thinking about punishment for a particular person, we tend to focus mainly on how much punishment she or he deserves. However, when thinking more generally, about the good of society, we *do* consider deterrence to be important. So, overall, it appears that both motives lie behind the use of punishment as a means of dealing with aggression.

At this point, we must note that there is still one other rationale for using punishment to reduce aggressive behavior: It removes dangerous people from society (e.g., by placing them in prison), and in this way protects future victims from possible harm. Unfortunately, statistics indicate that once people engage in violent crimes, they are likely to do so again, so removing them from society can, in fact, help prevent additional acts of aggression. This basis for giving persons convicted of aggressive crimes long prison sentences is not stated very often, but logically, it appears to make some sense.

Now for the next questions: Does punishment work? Can it reduce the tendency of specific persons to engage in harmful acts of aggression? Here, evidence is relatively clear: Punishment *can* reduce aggression but only if it meets four basic requirements: (1) It must be *prompt*—it must follow aggressive actions as quickly as possible; (2) it must be *certain to occur*—the probability that it will follow aggression must be very high; (3) it must be *strong*—strong enough to be highly unpleasant to potential recipients; and (4) it must be perceived by recipients as *justified* or deserved.

Unfortunately, these conditions are often *not* present in the criminal justice systems of many nations. In most societies, the delivery of punishment for aggressive actions is delayed for months or even years. Similarly, many criminals avoid arrest and conviction, so the certainty of punishment is low. The magnitude of punishment itself varies from one city, state, or even courtroom to another. And, often, punishment does not seem to fit the crime—it does not seem to be justified or deserved. In such cases, the persons who receive punishment may view it as aggression against *them*—as a kind of provocation. And as we saw earlier, provocation is a very powerful trigger for aggression. In view of these facts, it is hardly surprising that the threat of punishment—even the most severe punishment (execution)—does not seem to be effective in deterring violent crime. The conditions necessary for it to be effective are simply not present. This raises an intriguing question: Could punishment prove effective as a deterrent to violence if it were used more effectively? We can't say for sure, but existing evidence suggests that it could exert such effects *if* it were used in accordance with the principles described above. But instituting such conditions would raise complex issues relating to ethical and religious beliefs, so scientific data are clearly only one consideration, and for that reason, we cannot offer a clear position here. Rather, this is a matter each person must decide for her- or himself. (For information on another potential means of reducing aggression—one that is widely viewed as highly effective—see the **Science of Social Psychology: Making Sense of Common Sense** section on page 450.)

Cognitive Interventions: Apologies and Overcoming Cognitive Deficits

Do you find it easy or hard to apologize to others? If your answer is "hard," you should work on this particular social skill, because research findings agree with what common sense suggests: *apologies*—admissions of wrongdoing that include a request for forgiveness—often go a long way toward defusing aggression (e.g., Ohbuchi, Kameda, & Agarie, 1989). Similarly, good excuses—ones that make reference to factors beyond the excuse-giver's control—can also be effective in reducing anger and overt aggression by persons who have previously been provoked in some manner (e.g., Baron, 1989a; Weiner

Catharsis: Does "Getting It Out of Your System" Really Help?

When I (Robert Baron) was a little boy, my grandmother used to greet my temper tantrums by saying, "That's right, get it out . . . don't keep it bottled up inside—that will hurt you." In other words, she was a true believer in the **catharsis hypothesis**—the view that if individuals give vent to their anger and hostility in nonharmful ways, their tendencies to engage in more dangerous types of aggression will be reduced (Dollard et al., 1939).

Is this true? Most people seem to believe that it is; for instance, syndicated newspaper columnists often urge people to express their aggressive emotions and thoughts as a means of reducing them. But systematic research on catharsis by social psychologists calls such advice strongly into doubt: Widespread faith in the effectiveness of catharsis does *not* seem justified. On the contrary, it appears that so-called *venting* activities such as watching, reading about, or imagining aggressive actions, or even engaging in "play" aggressive actions such as punching a punching bag, are more likely to *increase* subsequent aggression than to reduce it (e.g., Bushman, 2001; Bushman, Baumeister, & Stack, 1999). A clear demonstration of this fact is provided by research conducted by Anderson, Carnagey, and Eubanks (2003).

These researchers reasoned that if catharsis really works, then exposure to songs with violent lyrics would allow people to vent aggressive thoughts or feelings; as a result, they would show lower levels of hostility and lower levels of aggressive thoughts. However, if catharsis does not work—and on the basis of previous findings, the researchers did not expect that it would—exposure to songs with violent lyrics might actually increase hostility and aggressive cognitions. To test these competing predictions, these researchers conducted series of studies in which participants listened to violent or nonviolent songs and then completed measures of their current feelings (hostile or friendly) and their aggressive cognitions (e.g., how much similarity they perceived between aggressive and ambiguous words—ones that could have both an aggressive and a nonaggressive meaning, such as *alley* or *police;* how quickly they pronounced aggressive and nonaggressive words that appeared on a computer screen). Results of all the studies were consistent: After hearing songs with violent lyrics, participants showed an increase both in hostile feelings and in aggressive thoughts (see Figure 11.18).

Why do such effects occur? For several reasons. First, anger actually may be increased when individuals think about wrongs they have suffered at the hands of others and imagine ways of harming these persons. Second, watching aggressive scenes, listening to songs with aggressive lyrics, or merely thinking about revenge and other aggressive activities may activate even more aggressive thoughts and feelings. These, in turn, may color interpretations of actual social interactions so that ambiguous actions by others are more likely to be per-

catharsis hypothesis
The view that providing angry persons with an opportunity to express their aggressive impulses in relatively safe ways will reduce their tendencies to engage in more harmful forms of aggression.

et al., 1987). So, if you feel that you are making another person angry, apologize without delay: The trouble you save makes it quite worthwhile to say, "I'm sorry."

Here's one old saying that I (Robert Baron) like a lot: "When emotions run high, reason flies right out the window." Applied to the question of controlling or reducing aggression, this saying calls attention to the fact that when we are very angry, our ability to think clearly—for instance, to evaluate the consequences of our own actions—may be sharply reduced. When this occurs, restraints that normally hold aggression in check (e.g., fear of retaliation) may also diminish. In addition, as noted by Lieberman and Greenberg (1999), when we are emotionally aroused, we may adopt modes of thoughts in which we process information in a quick and impetuous manner. This, in turn, may increase the chances that we will lash out against someone else, including persons who are *not* the cause of our annoyance or irritation (what is known as **displaced aggression;** e.g., Pederson, Gonzelez, & Miller, 2000).

Given these basic facts, any procedures that help us avoid or overcome such *cognitive deficits* can be helpful from the point of view of reducing aggression (Zillmann, 1993). One such technique involves *preattribution*—attributing annoying actions by

ceived as hostile ones. The result? Aggression is increased, not reduced, as the catharsis hypothesis suggests.

Is there even a small grain of truth in the catharsis hypothesis? Perhaps only this: Giving vent to angry feelings may make individuals feel better, at least temporarily. Anyone who has punched their own pillow or shouted angrily when alone in their own room has experienced such effects, but research findings suggest that such effects are temporary and do not really reduce the long-term tendency to engage in aggressive actions. In fact,

because reduced tension is pleasant, the long-term effects, again, may be a strengthening rather than a weakening of aggressive impulses.

In short, systematic research by social psychologists suggests that, in this case, common sense beliefs about the effectiveness of catharsis (as well as suggestions to this effect by Freud and others) are not really justified. So, resist the urging of those newspaper columnists and do *not* put your faith in catharsis as a useful means for keeping your own anger—and aggression—in check.

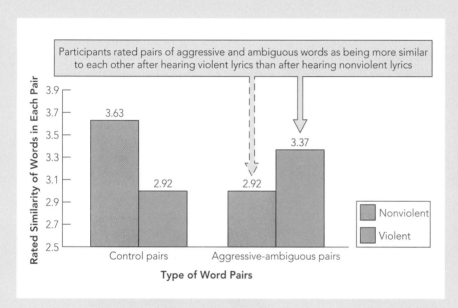

Figure 11.18 ■ Evidence That Catharsis Is Not Effective
Participants who listened to violent songs showed an increase in both hostile feelings and aggressive thoughts. For instance, as shown here, they rated aggressive and ambiguous words as being more similar to each other. This is precisely opposite to what the catharsis hypothesis would predict, and adds to growing evidence suggesting that, contrary to what common sense suggests, this technique is *not* very effective in reducing aggression. (*Source: Based on data from Anderson, Carnagey, & Eubanks, 2003.*)

others to *unintentional* causes before the provocation actually occurs. For example, before meeting with someone you know can be irritating, you could remind yourself that she or he doesn't mean to make you angry—it is just the result of an unfortunate personal style. Another technique involves preventing yourself or others from dwelling on previous real or imagined wrongs. You can accomplish this by distracting yourself in some way—for instance, by reading, watching an absorbing movie or television program, or working on a complex puzzle. Such activities allow for a cooling-off period during which anger can dissipate, and also help to reestablish cognitive controls over behavior—controls that help to hold aggression in check.

Forgiveness: Compassion Instead of Revenge

Almost everyone has experienced intense desire for revenge: Other persons harm us in some manner and we conclude that retaliating against them would be appropriate. Seeking to pay them back seems only natural, and we often feel it will make us feel better and, more importantly, restore our sense of justice.

displaced aggression
Aggression against someone other than the source of strong provocation; displaced aggression occurs because the persons who perform it are unwilling or unable to aggress against the initial source of provocation.

In fact, seeking revenge often has harmful effects for everyone concerned. The persons who seek it may feel better temporarily, but their actions may start the kind of upward spiral of retaliation, revenge, and further retaliation that we described in our discussion of the effects of provocation. As a result, both parties are at increasing risk. For these reasons, **forgiveness**—giving up the desire to punish those who have hurt us and seeking instead to act in kind, helpful ways toward them—may be highly beneficial in many ways, including the reduction of subsequent aggression (e.g., McCullough et al., 2001). Recent findings (McCullough, Fincham, & Tsang, 2003) indicate that it may be easier to attain the first goal—giving up the desire for revenge—than to attain the second—forgiving a person to the point that we actually behave in positive ways toward him or her. From the point of view of the present discussion, however, surrendering the desire for revenge may, in and of itself, be a useful step in terms of reducing subsequent aggression. Not only does it reduce the desire to strike back at the person who offended us—it may enhance our own psychological well-being, too.

Benefits of this latter type are demonstrated clearly in research by Karremans et al. (2003). These researchers asked participants in their study to remember an incident in which they were offended by another person. Then, they completed a test that was described as a measure of their forgiveness for this person. The test was scored, and they were given feedback indicating either that they had forgiven the offender or that they had not forgiven this person. Finally, participants completed additional measures of their current tension and their psychological well-being. Results indicated that those in the forgiveness condition (participants led to believe that they had forgiven the offender) reported higher self-esteem and lower levels of negative affect than those in the no-forgiveness condition. Other findings showed that the benefits of forgiveness were stronger for relationships to which individuals are strongly committed than for ones to which they are less committed. In other words, the closer we are to those who offend us, the more beneficial it is to forgive them for doing things that offend us (see Figure 11.19).

forgiveness
Giving up the desire to punish those who have hurt us, and seeking instead to act in kind, helpful ways toward them.

**Figure 11.19 ■ Forgiveness: One Effective
Means of Reducing Aggression**
Growing evidence suggests that *forgiveness*—giving up the desire to punish those who have hurt us, and seeking instead to act in kind, helpful ways toward them—can be an effective means for reducing anger and aggression. Further, the closer we are to the persons, the more inclined we are to offer forgiveness.

Chapter 11 / Aggression

Why are some people able to forgive more readily than others? In part, because of their own traits. Research findings indicate that forgiving people differ from persons who find it hard to forgive with respect to two aspects of personality we examine in detail in Chapter 10: They are higher in *agreeableness*—a tendency to trust others and want to help them—and higher in *emotional stability*—they show low vulnerability to negative moods or emotions (Berry et al., in press).

How, precisely, does forgiveness work? What do people do to forgive those who have harmed them? One technique involves *empathy*—they try to understand the feelings, emotions, and circumstances that caused the offending person to harm them. Similarly, they make generous attributions about the causes of their enemies' behavior, concluding that they had good reasons for acting as they did, even though this produced negative outcomes. Perhaps most important of all, they avoid *ruminating* about past transgressions; once these are over, they put them out of their minds and concentrate on other things (McCullough et al., 2001).

In sum, given the benefits that forgiveness may confer, it seems to be one social skill we should all try to develop. When we do, we may learn that there is a large grain of truth in the proverb, "To err is human; to forgive, divine."

KEY POINTS

★ *Punishment* can be effective in reducing aggression but only when it is delivered under certain conditions.

★ The *catharsis hypothesis* appears to be mainly false. Engaging in vigorous activities may produce reductions in arousal, but these are only temporary. Similarly, aggression is not reduced by engaging in apparently "safe" forms of aggression.

★ Aggression can be reduced by apologies—admissions of wrongdoing that include a request for forgiveness—and by overcoming the cognitive deficits produced by strong anger.

★ *Forgiveness*—surrendering the desire for revenge—is also effective in reducing aggression. In addition, it may contribute to our psychological well-being.

$\int$ UMMARY AND REVIEW OF KEY POINTS

Theoretical Perspectives on Aggression: In Search of the Roots of Violence

■ *Aggression* is the intentional infliction of harm on others. Though most social psychologists reject the view that human aggression is strongly deter-

mined by genetic factors, many now accept an evolutionary perspective that recognizes the potential role of such factors.

■ *Drive theories* suggest that aggression stems from externally elicited drives to harm or injure others. The *frustration–aggression*

hypothesis is the most famous example of such theories.

■ Modern theories of aggression, such as the *general aggression model*, recognize the importance in aggression of learning, various eliciting input variables, individual differences, affective states, and, especially, cognitive processes.

Causes of Human Aggression: Social, Cultural, Personal, and Situational

■ In order to study aggression, social psychologists often use procedures in which individuals are led to believe that they can harm others in various ways—for example, delivery of painful electric shocks or reducing their winnings in a competitive game.

■ Contrary to the famous *frustration–aggression hypothesis*, all aggression does not stem from frustration, and frustration does not always lead to aggression. Frustration is a strong elicitor of aggression only under certain limited conditions.

■ In contrast, *provocation* from others is a powerful elicitor of aggression. We rarely turn the other cheek; rather, we match—or slightly exceed—the level of aggression we receive from others.

■ Exposure to *media violence* has been found to increase aggression among viewers. This is due to several factors, such as the priming of aggressive thoughts and a weakening of restraints against aggression.

■ Exposure to violent pornography appears to increase the willingness of some persons to engage in similar behavior and to generate callous attitudes toward various forms of sexual violence.

■ In *cultures of honor*, norms requiring aggression as a response to threats to one's honor exist and exert powerful effects.

■ Sexual jealousy poses a major threat to male honor in cultures

of honor, with the result that aggression in response to sexual infidelity is condoned to a greater extent, and women who are accepting of such aggression are viewed more favorably than ones who are not.

■ Persons showing the *Type A behavior pattern* are more irritable and aggressive than persons with the *Type B behavior pattern*.

■ Individuals high in *hostile attributional bias* attribute others' actions to hostile intent. As a result, they are more aggressive than persons low in this characteristic.

■ Persons high in narcissism hold an overinflated view of their own worth. They react with exceptionally high levels of aggression to feedback from others that threatens their inflated egos.

■ Persons high in sensation seeking tend to be more aggressive than others because they are attracted to aggression-eliciting situations and because they experience anger and hostile thoughts more often than do persons lower on this dimension.

■ Males are more aggressive overall than females, but this difference decreases in the context of strong provocation. Males are more likely to use direct forms of aggression, but females are more likely to use indirect forms of aggression. Males are much more likely than females to engage in sexual coercion.

■ High temperatures tend to increase aggression but only up to a point. Beyond some level, aggression declines as temperatures rise.

■ Consuming alcohol can increase aggression, especially, it appears,

by individuals who normally show low levels of aggression.

■ Alcohol may exert these effects by reducing individuals' capacity to process some kinds of information and by changing their reactions to unexpected behavior by others.

Aggression in Long-Term Relationships: Bullying and Workplace Violence

■ *Bullying* involves repeated aggression against individuals who, for various reasons, are unable to defend themselves against such treatment. Bullying occurs in many contexts, including schools, workplaces, and prisons. Few people are solely bullies or victims; more play both roles. Bullies and bully-victims appear to have lower self-esteem than people who are not involved in bullying.

■ *Workplace aggression* takes many different forms but is usually covert in nature. It stems from a wide range of factors, including perceptions of having been treated unfairly and the many disturbing changes that have occurred in workplaces recently.

The Prevention and Control of Aggression: Some Useful Techniques

■ *Punishment* can be effective in reducing aggression but only when it is delivered under certain conditions.

■ The *catharsis hypothesis* appears to be mainly false. Engaging in vigorous activities may produce reductions in arousal, but these are only temporary. Similarly, aggression is not reduced by engaging in apparently "safe" forms of aggression.

- Aggression can be reduced by apologies—admissions of wrongdoing that include a request for forgiveness—and by overcoming the cognitive deficits produced by strong anger.

- *Forgiveness*—surrendering the desire for revenge—is also effective in reducing aggression. In addition, it may contribute to our psychological well-being.

Connections   INTEGRATING SOCIAL PSYCHOLOGY

In this chapter, you read about . . .	In other chapters, you will find related discussions of . . .
the role of cognitive and affective variables in aggression	the role of these factors in many other forms of social behavior . . . attitude change (Chapter 4) prejudice (Chapter 6) helping (Chapter 10)
social factors that play a role in aggression	the effects of these factors on other forms of social behavior . . . social models (Chapter 10) attributions (Chapter 2) arousal (Chapter 7)
personal characteristics that influence aggression	the role of these factors in several other forms of social behavior . . . social perception (Chapter 3) obedience (Chapter 9) helping behavior (Chapter 10) leadership (Module B)

Thinking about Connections

1. Attorneys sometimes defend individuals who commit violent acts—including murder—by suggesting that these persons were "overwhelmed" by emotions beyond their control. In view of our discussions in other chapters (e.g., Chapter 2, Chapter 10) of the effects of emotions on social thought and social behavior, what are your reactions to such defenses?

2. There seems to be overwhelming evidence that media violence can increase aggression in persons exposed to it. Yet, "violence sells": Television programs and films containing graphic violence are often very popular. In view of this fact, do you think anything can be done to reduce this potential cause of increased aggression? If so, what steps do you recommend?

3. Violence and other forms of aggression appear to be increasing in many workplaces. Do you think it is possible to screen potential employees, so as to reject those who have a high propensity for engaging in such behavior? If so, what aspects of their self-concept (Chapter 5), attitudes (see Chapter 4), or past behavior (e.g., the kind of relationships they have had with others; see Chapter 8) might be useful predictors of the likelihood that they would engage in workplace aggression if hired?

Ideas to Take with You—and Use!

CAUSES OF AGGRESSION

Research findings indicate that aggression stems from a wide range of variables—social factors, personal characteristics, and situational factors. Here is an overview of the most important factors identified by systematic research.

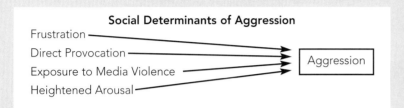

Social Determinants of Aggression

- Frustration
- Direct Provocation
- Exposure to Media Violence
- Heightened Arousal

→ Aggression

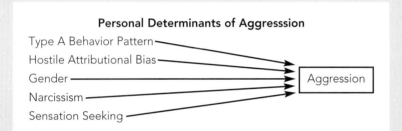

Personal Determinants of Aggresssion

- Type A Behavior Pattern
- Hostile Attributional Bias
- Gender
- Narcissism
- Sensation Seeking

→ Aggression

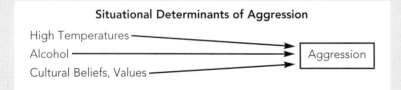

Situational Determinants of Aggression

- High Temperatures
- Alcohol
- Cultural Beliefs, Values

→ Aggression

KEY TERMS

abusive supervision (p. 446)

aggression (p. 419)

bullying (p. 443)

catharsis hypothesis (p. 450)

cultures of honor (p. 432)

displaced aggression (p. 451)

drive theories (of aggression) (p. 421)

excitation transfer theory (p. 427)

forgiveness (p. 452)

frustration–aggression hypothesis (p. 421)

general aggression model (p. 422)

hostile aggression (p. 436)

hostile attributional bias (p. 436)

instrumental aggression (p. 436)

media violence (p. 428)

provocation (p. 426)

punishment (p. 447)

Type A behavior pattern (p. 435)

Type B behavior pattern (p. 436)

workplace aggression (p. 446)

Baron, R. A., & Richardson, D. R. (1994). *Human aggression* (2nd ed.). New York: Plenum.
• This book provides a broad overview of current knowledge about human aggression. Separate chapters focus on the biological, social environmental, and personal determinants of aggression. Additional chapters examine the development of aggression, the prevention and control of such behavior, and its occurrence in many natural contexts.

Burstyn, J. N., Bender, G., Casella, R., Gordon, W. A., Guerra, D. P., Lushen, K. V., Stevens, R., &

Williams, K. M. (2001). *Preventing violence in schools: A challenge to American democracy*. Mahwah, NJ: Erlbaum.
• This book addresses a very timely topic: How can violence in schools be prevented or reduced? Current programs designed to accomplish this goal are described, and the foundations of these programs in basic research on aggression (such as that discussed in this chapter) are examined.

Tedeschi, J., & Felson, R. B. (1994). *Violence, aggression, and coercive actions*. Washington, DC: American Psychological Association.

• This book examines the social psychological and societal roots of violence, aggression, and a wide range of coercive actions—actions in which one person forces one or more others to act in ways they would prefer to avoid. Dramatic instances of such behavior are presented, and explanations for their occurrence based on scientific knowledge concerning human aggression are provided. A thought-provoking if somewhat chilling look at several dangerous forms of human behavior.

12

GROUPS AND INDIVIDUALS
The Consequences of Belonging

CHAPTER OUTLINE

When I (Robert Baron) was fifteen, I needed a summer job to earn spending money. Very few jobs were open to someone my age, but one that was available was working for a company that supplied umbrellas and folding chairs to visitors to a nearby beach. The job involved carrying these items—which were really heavy!—and setting them up for customers. It didn't pay much, but the job was close to where I lived, so I wanted it very much. The day I applied, there must have been fifty of us waiting to hear what the owner had to say. His remarks were ones I'll never forget: "OK, you guys, we need help for the summer and even though you are the most pitiful bunch I've ever seen, you'll have to do. But here's the deal: The government just raised the minimum wage, and I can't afford to pay it. So to make up the difference, you'll have to turn in your tips at the end of every day." "Turn in our tips?" I remember thinking. "That's what makes this crummy job worthwhile!" One young man standing nearby spoke up: "But the tips are ours," he said. "Why should we give them to you?" The owner walked up to the young man and said: "A wise guy, eh? Get lost; I don't need you. Go find another job." After that, the rest of us kept quiet: We needed the job, so we didn't protest. But later, most of us got together about a block away and discussed this arrangement. Our conclusion? It wasn't fair and we would resist—not immediately and not openly, but we would work on it!

Over the next few weeks, small groups of us met regularly to exchange ideas for keeping at least part of the tips customers gave us. One solution was to have friends meet us on the beach late in the day; we'd give them our tips to hold for us until later. Another was to find hiding places and put our tips there so we could retrieve them later.

The best thing that came out of our meetings—and the one that made all the difference—was this: One of us had an uncle who was an attorney, and he agreed to ask him if the owner could legally take our tips. Even though this was many years ago, we soon learned that he could not. In fact, the attorney was furious and wrote a letter threatening legal action if the owner continued this policy. Faced with this risk, he shouted angrily at us and called us a bunch of troublemakers, but grudgingly told us we could keep our tips. As you can guess, we did a lot of celebrating *that* night!

These events took place many years ago in a world very different from the one faced by teenaged workers today. But the points they illustrate are as valid now as they were then. First, we all join *groups;* some are temporary and come into existence to accomplish a specific purpose, like the group my fellow workers and I formed to resist the owner's "give me your tips" policy. In contrast, other groups are much more lasting in nature and focus on many different issues and activities (e.g., professional organizations; religious or political groups; fraternities and sororities). Second, the groups we join often provide us with important benefits; that's why we join them in the first place! (See Figure 12.1.) Third, all groups have to make decisions (e.g., "How should we resist the owner's policy?"), and, fourth, all seek to maximize *cooperation*—working together to reach various goals, and

Figure 12.1 ■ Groups: Often, They Provide Us with Important Benefits
People join groups for many reasons, but an important factor is the benefits they confer.

to minimize or at least manage *conflict* between their members. Finally, most, if not all groups, must deal with the issue of *fairness*—both within the group and outside it. (For example, how should resources and rewards within the group be distributed? How should the group seek to assure that its members receive fair treatment in society?)

We examine all of these questions—plus several others—in the present chapter. Specifically, we begin by examining the basic nature of groups and the central question of why we join them and why, sometimes, we choose to quit. Next, we examine the impact of what is, in some ways, the most basic group effect: the mere presence of others. The presence of others, even if we are not in a formal group with them, can affect our performance on many tasks and other important aspects of our behavior. Third, we briefly examine the nature of cooperation and conflict in groups—why these contrasting patterns emerge and the effects they produce. After that, we consider the closely related question of perceived *fairness* in groups—the central process at work in the salary incident described earlier. Finally, we turn to *decision making* in groups and the unexpected dangers this process sometimes poses. (We consider another important aspect of group functioning—*leadership*—in Module B.)

Groups: Why We Join . . . and Why We Leave

Look at the photos in Figure 12.2. Which shows a group? Probably you would identify the one on the right as a group, but the one on the left as showing a mere collection of persons. Why? Because implicitly, you already accept a definition of the term **group** close to the one adopted by social psychologists: a collection of persons who are perceived to be bonded together in a coherent unit to some degree (e.g., Dasgupta, Banji, & Abelson, 1999; Lickel et al., 2000). Social psychologists refer to this property of groups as **entiativity**—the extent to which a group is perceived as being a coherent entity (Campbell, 1958). Entiativity varies greatly, ranging from mere collections of people who happen to be in the same place at the same time but have little or no connection with one another, to highly intimate groups such as our families or persons with whom we have romantic relationships. So, clearly, some groups are much closer to our con-

Figure 12.2 ▪ What Makes a Group a Group?

The photo on the left shows a collection of persons who happen to be in the same place at the same time; they are not part of a *group*. The photo on the right shows a true group: The people in this group interact with one another and have shared goals and outcomes. Moreover, they feel that they are, in fact, part of a group.

ception of what a group is like than others. But what determines whether, and to what extent, we perceive several persons as forming a coherent group? This question has received growing attention from researchers in recent years, and a clear answer has begun to emerge (Lickel et al., 2000). In particular, it appears that true groups—ones high in entiativity—show the following characteristics: (1) Members interact with one another often, (2) the group is important to its members, (3) members share common goals and outcomes, and (4) they are similar to one another in important ways. The higher groups are on these dimensions, the more they are seen by their members as forming coherent entities—real groups to which they choose to belong.

In sum, entiativity is a key dimension from the point of view of understanding precisely what constitutes a group and how being part of a group can influence our behavior. To the extent that groups possess the features mentioned, they are viewed by members are being real and important entities, ones that can, and often do, exert powerful effects on their members.

Groups: Some Basic Aspects

"OK," we can almost hear you saying, "groups exist. I knew that already; in fact, I belong to several. Now, tell me something I *don't* know!" That's what the rest of this chapter does, but before turning to the specific ways in which groups affect various aspects of our behavior and thought, it is useful to first describe several basic features of groups—ones that are present in virtually every group deserving of this label. These features are *roles, status, norms,* and *cohesiveness.*

▪ Roles: Differentiation of Functions within Groups

Think of a group to which you belong or have belonged—anything from the scouts to a professional association. Now consider this question: Did everyone in the group act in the same way or perform the same functions? Your answer is probably "no." Different persons performed different tasks and were expected to accomplish different things for the group. In short, they played different **roles.** Sometimes roles are assigned; for instance, a group may select different individuals to serve as its leader, treasurer, and secretary. In other cases, individuals gradually acquire certain roles without being formally assigned to them. Regardless of how roles are acquired, people often *internalize* them; they link their roles to key aspects of their self-concept (see Chapter 5). When this happens, a role may exert profound effects on a person's behavior, even when she or he is not in the group. A very dramatic illustration of the powerful effects roles can exert on us was provided by Zimbardo and his colleagues (Haney, Banks, & Zimbardo, 1973). In this study, male college students who had volunteered for a study of prison life were "arrested" and confined to a simulated prison in the basement of the Stanford University psychology building. The prison "guards" were also paid volunteers, and, in fact, assignment to these two roles—prisoner and guard—was completely random.

The major purpose of the study was to determine whether, as a result of the roles they played, the participants would come to behave like real guards and real prisoners. The answer was quick to appear: Absolutely! In fact, so dramatic were the changes in the behavior of both the prisoners and the guards that it was necessary to stop the study after only six days, instead of the two weeks for which it was planned. The prisoners, who at first were rebellious, became increasingly passive and depressed, while the guards became increasingly brutal. They harassed the prisoners constantly, forcing them to derogate one another and assigning them to tedious, senseless tasks. In short, participants started to act more and more like actual prisoners and actual guards in real prisons. The roles they played exerted powerful—and chilling—effects on their behavior, and are indicative of the powerful impact that roles often exert on us in many different groups.

roles
The set of behaviors that individuals occupying specific positions within a group are expected to perform.

Figure 12.3 ■ Does Height Confer Status?
Research findings indicate the existence of a relationship between height and status, at least for men. Presidents, heads of major corporations, and military leaders all tend to be taller than average.

■ Status: Hierarchies in Groups

When the president of my (Robert Baron's) university enters the room, everyone stands, and no one sits down until she has taken a seat. Why? One answer involves an important aspect of groups or, rather, positions within them: **status**—position or rank within a group. Different roles or positions in a group are often associated with different levels of status, and our president is clearly very high on this dimension. People are often extremely sensitive to status because it is linked to a wide range of desirable outcomes—everything from salary and "perks" to first choice among the potential romantic partners (Buss, 1991). For this reason, groups often use status as a means of influencing the behavior of their members: Only "good" members—ones who follow the group's rules—receive it.

Evolutionary psychologists attach considerable importance to status, noting that in many different species, including our own, high status confers important advantages on those who possess it. Specifically, high-status persons have greater access than lower-status persons to key resources relating to survival and reproduction, such as food and access to mates (e.g., Buss, 1999). But how, precisely, do people acquire high status? Height may play some role—taller men have an edge (see Figure 12.3). For instance, presidents and heads of large corporations tend to be taller than average (e.g., Gillis, 1982). Whether the advantage of being tall will fade as women move increasingly into such high-status positions remains to be seen, but at least for men, "bigger" does seem to be "better" where status is concerned.

Factors relating to individuals' behavior also play a role in acquiring status. Research by Tiedens (2001), for instance, suggests that people can sometimes boost their status through *intimidation*—by appearing angry and threatening. Whatever its basis, however, there can be little doubt that differences in status are an important fact of life in most groups.

■ Norms: The Rules of the Game

A third factor responsible for the powerful impact of groups on their members is **norms**—rules established by groups that tell their members how they are supposed to

status
An individual's position or rank in a group.

norms
Rules within a group indicating how its members should (or should not) behave.

Chapter 12 / Groups and Individuals

behave. We discussed norms in detail in Chapter 9, so here we simply note again that they often exert powerful effects on behavior. Moreover, as noted above, adherence to such norms is often a necessary condition for gaining status and other rewards controlled by groups.

cohesiveness

All forces (factors) that cause group members to remain in the group.

Cohesiveness: The Forces that Bind

Consider two groups. In the first, members like one another very much, strongly desire the goals their group is seeking, and feel that they could not possibly find another group that would better satisfy their needs. In the second, the opposite is true: Members don't like one another very much, don't share common goals, and are actively seeking other groups that might offer them a better deal. Which group would exert stronger effects on the behavior of its members? The answer is obvious: the first. The reason for this difference involves a concept we discussed in Chapter 9, **cohesiveness**—all the factors that bind members together and cause them to want to remain in the group, such as liking for the other members, similarity between members, and the desire to gain status by belonging to the "right" groups (Festinger, Schachter, & Back, 1950). Cohesiveness can be a powerful force; in fact, recent findings suggest that to the extent members identify with a group (the greater their *social identity* with it), the less likely they are to leave it, even if desirable options exist (e.g., leaving to join some other, more attractive group; Van Vugt & Hart, 2004).

Several factors influence cohesiveness, including (1) status within the group (Cota et al., 1995)—cohesiveness is often higher for high- than low-status members; (2) the effort required to gain entry into the group—the greater these costs, the higher the cohesiveness (see the discussion of dissonance theory in Chapter 4); (3) the existence of external threats or severe competition—such threats increase members' attraction and commitment to the group; and (4) size—small groups tend to be more cohesive than large ones.

In sum, several aspects of groups—roles, status, norms, and cohesiveness—play an important role in their functioning and in how they affect their members. We introduce these basic dimensions here because we will refer to them again in later sections of this chapter.

KEY POINTS

- ★ *Groups* are collections of persons perceived to form a coherent unit to some degree. The extent to which the group is perceived to form a coherent entity is known as *entiativity*.

- ★ Basic aspects of groups involve *roles, status, norms,* and *cohesiveness*. The effects of roles on our behavior are often very powerful, causing us to act in ways that we might not otherwise choose.

- ★ People gain status in a group for many reasons, ranging from physical characteristics (e.g., height) to various aspects of their behavior.

- ★ Another important feature of groups is their level of *cohesiveness*—the sum of all the factors that cause people to want to remain members, such as liking between them.

The Benefits—and Costs—of Joining

Think for a moment: To how many different groups do you belong? If you give this matter careful thought, you may be surprised at the length of the list. Though some individuals belong to more groups than others, it's clear that, in general, we are "joiners"—members of many different groups. Why? What do we gain from group membership? And why, if these benefits are so great, do we sometimes choose to leave—to withdraw from a group to which we have belonged for months, years, or even decades? Here's a summary of what social psychologists have found out about these issues.

■ The Benefits of Joining: What Groups Do for Us

That people sometimes go through a lot to join specific groups is clear: Membership in many groups is by invitation only, and winning that invitation can be difficult! (Please see the **Beyond the Headlines** section on page 469 for more information on this topic.) And, perhaps even more surprising, once they gain admission, many persons stick with a group, even when it experiences hard times and falls from favor. For instance, consider sports fans and how they remain loyal to their teams, even when the teams have a miserable season and are the target of ridicule and scorn. What accounts for this strong desire to join—and remain in—many social groups? The answer, it appears, is many different factors.

First, we often gain *self-knowledge* from belonging to various groups. Our membership in them tells us what kinds of persons we are—or perhaps, would like to be—so group membership becomes central to our self-concept (recall our discussion of this topic in Chapter 5). The result? We want "in," and once we belong, we find it hard to imagine life outside this group, because being a member partly defines who we are!

Another obvious benefit of belonging to some groups is that they help us reach our goals. Do you want to meet certain kinds of persons? Then join a group to which they belong. Do you want to gain certain kinds of knowledge or skill? Again, joining various groups can help.

As noted earlier, groups also often provide a boost to our status. When individuals are accepted into prestigious groups—a highly selective school, an exclusive social club, a varsity sports team—their status and their self-esteem often rise significantly. This is another important reason why individuals join specific groups. Just how important is this status-boost to joining and identifying with groups? Research findings suggest that this depends, to an important extent, on the degree to which the persons involved are seeking *self-enhancement*—boosting their own public image and feeling that they are somehow superior to others—or, alternatively, are seeking *self-transcendence*—the desire to help others, regardless of their status, and to seek such goals as increased understanding of others and social justice (e.g., Brown, 2000; Schwartz & Bardi, 2001). As you can probably guess, the greater the degree to which individuals are seeking self-enhancement, the more important will a group's status be to them and the more strongly they will identify with it. In contrast, the greater the degree to which they are seeking self-transcendence, the less important will a group's status be. This is precisely what was found in recent research by Roccas (2003). She obtained measures of business students' desires for self-enhancement and self-transcendence, the perceived status of a group to which they belonged (their school), and their identification with this group. Results indicated that the stronger their desire for self-enhancement, the stronger the link between the group's status and students' identification with it, while the stronger their desire for self-transcendence, the weaker was this link. In other words, status was much more important to those seeking to boost their own "image" than to those who were more concerned with a very different goal—helping others.

Still another benefit of joining groups is that doing so often helps us to accomplish social change. How can members of minority groups, women, gays, or other groups that have been the target of oppression gain their full rights? As we saw in Chapter 6, one way of doing so is to join groups committed to working toward these goals (see Figure 12.4). By joining together, persons who have been the victims of prejudice can gain "social clout" and can often succeed in changing their societies—and so win better treatment for themselves and other minorities (Klandermans, 1997). Indeed, recent findings

**Figure 12.4 ■ Producing Social Change:
One Reason Why People Join Groups**
One potential benefit individuals obtain from groups is social change.
For instance, by joining together, members of oppressed groups can
often improve their standing in, and treatment by, society.

suggest that identification with such groups is a strong predictor of participation in public marches and parades, initiating and signing petitions, boycotts against businesses that discriminate against various minorities, and so on (Sturmer & Simon, 2004).

Clearly, then, we derive many benefits from belonging to various groups. Indeed, it is apparent that we really can't meet many of our most basic needs—social and otherwise—outside of groups.

■ The Costs of Membership: Why Groups Sometimes Splinter

Unfortunately, there are few, if any, unmixed blessings in life. Almost everything—no matter how beneficial—has a downside, too. And this is certainly true of group membership. Although groups do help us to reach the goals we seek, and can help to boost our status along the way, they also impose certain costs. We cover many of these in later sections (e.g., the harmful effects of groups on decision making; the increased tendency toward strong adherence to group norms that often occurs in large crowds). Here, though, we call your attention to several more general costs.

First, group membership often restricts personal freedom. Members of various groups are expected to behave in certain ways—to follow the group's norms or to comply with requirements of their roles in the groups. If they don't, the groups often impose strong sanctions on them or may, ultimately, expel them from membership. For instance, in the United States, it is considered inappropriate for military officers to make public statements about politics. Thus, even a high-ranking general who engages in such actions may be strongly reprimanded for doing so. In fact, during the Korean War, President Truman removed an extremely famous general—Douglas McArthur—from command because he made such statements.

Similarly, groups often make demands on members' time, energy, and resources, and they must meet these demands or surrender their membership. Some churches, for instance, require that their members donate 10 percent of their income to the church.

Persons wishing to remain in these groups must comply—or face expulsion. Finally, groups sometimes adopt positions or policies of which some members disapprove. Again, the dissenting members must either remain silent, speak out and run the risk of strong sanctions, or withdraw. So group membership is not always a bed of roses; there are some real thorns hidden among the benefits, and members must often consider these carefully as they weigh the costs of group membership against its benefits.

Withdrawing from a group can be a major and costly step, and so raises an intriguing question: Why, specifically, do individuals take this ultimate action? One answer provided by research (e.g., Sani & Reicher, 2000) is based on the fact that when individuals identify with a social group, they often redraw the boundaries of their self-concept to include other group members (Aron & McLaughlin-Volpe, 2001). In other words, as far as they are concerned, other members of the group are definitely viewed together with the self as "we." To the extent that this is true, then an explanation for why specific members sometimes choose to withdraw from groups or why groups themselves splinter follows logically. Perhaps individuals decide to leave a group and form a new subgroup when they conclude that other members have changed sufficiently that they can no longer be viewed as "we"—as falling within the boundaries of their extended self-concept.

Evidence for this process was reported recently by Sani and Todman (2002). These researchers studied the Church of England, which, in 1992, adopted the policy of making women priests within the church. In 1994, the first women were ordained as priests, and, as a result, hundreds of clergy decided to leave the church. Why did they feel this drastic action was necessary? To find out, the researchers asked a large number of priests and deacons in the Church of England to express their views about the new policy of ordaining women as priests, the extent to which they felt this had changed the church greatly, and the degree to which they felt their views (if they were opposed to this policy) would be heard. Results indicated that clergy who left the Church did not do so because they were hard-core sexists, against equal rights for women. Rather, it appeared that they left the Church because they felt it had changed so much that it was no longer the same organization as the one they originally joined and no longer represented their views. Further, they felt strongly that no one would pay attention to their dissenting opinions and that this left them no choice but to withdraw (see Figure 12.5).

Sani and Todman (2002) suggest that this process is not restricted to religious groups. On the contrary, they note that similar splits have occurred in many other

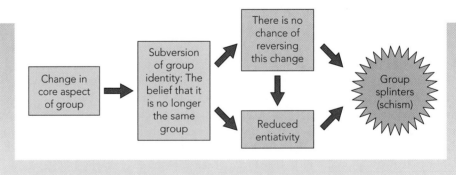

Figure 12.5 ■ Why Groups Splinter: One View
Recent findings (e.g., Sani & Todman, 2003) indicate that groups splinter when current members perceive that the group has changed so much (subversion) that it is no longer the same entity (group) they originally joined, and when they conclude that no one will listen to their protests over this change (there is no chance of reversing it). (*Source: Based on suggestions by Sani & Todman, 2002.*)

Chapter 12 / Groups and Individuals

groups—political parties, social movements, and, in fact, any group based on shared beliefs and values. In other words, when groups splinter and many members leave, this is simply the final step in a process that has been unfolding for some time. Groups change, and when they do so to the extent that members feel that they can no longer identify with the group, the final outcome is inevitable: Members withdraw from groups that, they believe, no longer possess the *entiativity* we described at the start of this chapter. In other words, in their view, the group they originally joined no longer exists, so formally withdrawing is simply acknowledging what is already fact! (In Chapter 4, we noted that individuals often work very hard to gain membership in certain groups, and when they do, cognitive dissonance causes them to value these groups even more highly than they did before. But just how hard will people work to get into a group? For a chilling answer, please see the **Beyond the Headlines** section.)

B EYOND THE HEADLINES   AS SOCIAL PSYCHOLOGISTS SEE IT

Groups to Die For?

Sorority Accused of Hazing in $100 Million Suit

Los Angeles—The family of a young woman who died in an alleged hazing incident filed a $100 million wrongful death lawsuit against the one of the nation's oldest sororities

Monday. Kristin High, 22, and Kenitha Saafir, 24, drowned September 9 at Dockweller State Beach. . . . High was the mother of a 2-year-old and was engaged to be married . . . Saafir and High were "blindfolded and tied by their hands and their bodies were led into the rip tide

conditions of the ocean," the family's lawsuit says. That night waves were cresting at 6 to 8 feet. . . . The lawsuit claims the two women were forced to do this after days of losing sleep as they did difficult and embarrassing chores for sorority members. . . . And before they entered

the water . . . they were told to engage in a set of tiring and rigorous calisthenics. . . . High's mother, Patricia-Strong-Fargas, asked the sorority to "stop these savage acts of passion in the name of sisterhood. . . ."

Many groups erect high barriers to entry: They want only *some* persons to join, and they insist that those people be highly motivated to enter. Steep initiation fees, long trial periods—these are some of the tactics groups use to restrict their membership. But initiations can, and sometimes do, lead to death. How can groups, no matter how desirable or selective, induce potential members to accept such terms?

Social psychologists answer this question in terms of the powerful motives people have for joining groups—motives that strike close to their very core as individuals. As we noted earlier, membership in certain groups can confer large boosts in status, help people reach important goals, assist them in refining and clarifying their own self-concept, and contribute to obtaining desired changes in society. Certainly, these are important benefits, and some persons, at least, are willing to pay a very high price to attain them. In addition, once individuals begin paying the costs of initiation into selective groups,

cognitive biases may come into play. They find themselves in an *escalation of commitment* or *sunk costs* situation (see Chapter 2): They have already made initial commitments of time, money, and effort, so it becomes hard for them to admit that doing so was a mistake and to now back out. Moreover, the greater the discomfort (embarrassment, humiliation, physical pain) they suffer along the way, the more cognitive dissonance leads them to boost their perceptions of the group.

When all of these factors are combined, the willingness of some persons to pay a very heavy price for group membership loses much of its mystery. On the contrary, it simply illustrates a principle well known to social psychologists: Given sufficient motivation, human beings are capable of behavior far outside the ordinary. And motivation to acquire the benefits offered by prestigious groups is so high that it can lead individuals to endure much—and a great deal if they believe that doing so will help them gain these benefits.

KEY POINTS

★ Joining groups confers important benefits on members, including increased self-knowledge, progress toward important goals, enhanced status, and attaining social change.

★ However, group membership also exacts important costs, such as loss of personal freedom and heavy demands on time, energy, and resources.

★ Individuals often withdraw from groups when they feel that the group has changed so much that it no longer reflects their basic values or beliefs.

★ The desire to join exclusive and prestigious groups may be so strong that individuals are willing to undergo painful and dangerous initiations in order to become members.

Effects of the Presence of Others: From Task Performance to Behavior in Crowds

The fact that our behavior is often strongly affected by the groups to which we belong is far from surprising; after all, in these groups we have specific roles and status, and the groups usually have well-established norms that tell us how we are expected to behave as members. Perhaps much more surprising is the fact that, often, we are strongly affected by the *mere presence of others*, even if we, and they, do not belong to formal groups. You already know about such effects from your own experiences. For instance, suppose you are sitting alone in a room, studying. When you itch, you will probably scratch, and you may sit in any way you find comfortable. But if a stranger enters the room, all of this may change. You will probably refrain from doing some things you might have done when alone, and you may change many other aspects of your behavior, even though you don't know this person and are not interacting with her or him (see Figure 12.6). So, clearly, we are often affected by the mere physical pres-

Figure 12.6 ■ Effects of the Mere Presence of Others
Often, the mere presence of other persons, even if they are total strangers, can strongly affect our behavior.

Chapter 12 / Groups and Individuals

ence of others. Although such effects take many different forms, we focus here on two that are especially important: the effects of the presence of others on our performance of various tasks, and the effects of being in a large crowd.

Sometimes, when we perform a task, we work totally alone; for instance, you might study alone in your room, and as I write these words, I am alone in my office. In many other cases, even if we are working on a task by ourselves, other people *are* present— for instance, you might study in a crowded library or in your room or while your room-mate sleeps or also studies. In other situations, we work on tasks together with other persons as part of a task-performing group. What are the effects of the presence of others on our performance in these various settings? Let's see what research findings suggest.

Social Facilitation: Performing in the Presence of Others

Imagine that you are a young singer—and that you are preparing for your first impor-tant concert. You practice your routines alone for several hours each day, month after month. Finally, the big day arrives and you walk out onto the stage to find a huge audi-ence seated in a beautiful concert hall (see Figure 12.7). How will you do? Better or worse than was true when you practiced alone?

This was one of the first topics studied by social psychologists, and early results (e.g., Allport, 1920) suggested that performance was better when people worked in the presence of others than when they worked alone. For instance, in one study, Allport (1920) asked participants to write down as many associations as they could think of to words printed at the top of an otherwise blank sheet of paper (e.g., *building, labora-tory*). They were allowed to work for three one-minute periods, and performed this task both alone and in the presence of two other persons. Results were clear: Ninety-three percent of the participants produced more associations when working in the presence

**Figure 12.7 ■ The Presence of an Audience:
How Does It Affect Our Performance?**
What happens when people perform in front of an audience—do they
do better or worse than they do when performing the same tasks alone?
Research by social psychologists offers some intriguing answers.

of others than when working alone. On the basis of such findings, Allport and other researchers referred to the effects on performance of the presence of other persons as **social facilitation,** because it appeared that when others were present, performance was enhanced. But other research soon reported exactly opposite results: performance was *worse* in the presence of an audience or other people performing the same task (coactors) than it was when individuals performed alone (Pessin, 1933). Why is this so? How could the presence of others sometimes enhance and sometimes reduce performance? One elegant answer to this mystery was offered by Robert Zajonc.

■ Zajonc's Drive Theory of Social Facilitation: Other Persons as a Source of Arousal

Imagine that you are performing some task alone. Then, several other people arrive on the scene and begin to watch you intently. Will your pulse beat quicker because of this audience? Informal experience suggests that it may—that the presence of other persons in the form of an interested audience can increase our activation or arousal. Taking note of this fact, Zajonc suggested that this might provide the solution to the puzzle of social facilitation. Here's how.

When arousal increases, our tendency to perform *dominant responses*—the ones that are most likely to occur in a given situation—also rises. Such dominant responses, in turn, can be correct or incorrect. If this is so, then it follows logically that if the presence of an audience increases arousal, this factor will *improve* performance when dominant responses are correct ones, but may *impair* performance when such responses are incorrect (please see Figure 12.8).

Another implication of Zajonc's reasoning—which is known as the **drive theory of social facilitation** because it focuses on arousal or drive—is this: The presence of others will improve individuals' performance when they are highly skilled at the task in question (in this case, their dominant responses would tend to be correct), but will interfere with performance when they are not highly skilled—for instance, when they are learning to perform it. (Under these conditions, their dominant responses would *not* be correct.)

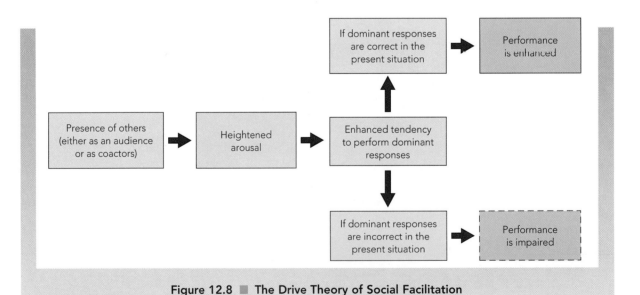

Figure 12.8 ■ The Drive Theory of Social Facilitation

According to the *drive theory of social facilitation* (Zajonc, 1965), the presence of others, either as an audience or coactors, increases arousal, and this, in turn, strengthens the tendency to perform dominant responses. If these responses are correct, performance is enhanced; if they are incorrect, performance is impaired.

Chapter 12 / Groups and Individuals

Many studies soon provided support for Zajonc's theory. Individuals were more likely to perform dominant responses in the presence of others than when alone, and their performance on various tasks was either enhanced or impaired, depending on whether these responses were correct or incorrect in each situation (e.g., Geen, 1989; Zajonc & Sales, 1966).

But the story does not end there: Additional research raised an important question: Does social facilitation stem from the *mere physical presence of others?* Or do additional factors, such as concern about others' evaluations of us, also play a role? If that is so, then, *type* of audience should matter. In fact, several studies found that this is the case: For instance, social facilitation effects did *not* occur if the audience was blindfolded or showed no interest in watching the person performing a task (Cottrell et al., 1968). Such findings indicate that there is more to social facilitation than just increased drive; concern over being evaluated also plays a role.

As reasonable as these conclusions seem, however, they didn't appear to apply in all cases; studies conducted with animals found that performance of simple tasks was facilitated by the presence of an audience. For instance, Zajonc, Heingartner, and Herman (1969) found that even cockroaches would run faster through a maze when other roaches were present (in clear plastic boxes next to the maze) than when no roach "audience" was present. Clearly, it makes little sense to suggest that insects are concerned about the impressions they make on others, so these findings suggest that social facilitation does not stem entirely from **evaluation apprehension.** So what's the answer?

One researcher, Robert S. Baron (*not* the author of this text!) suggests that it may involve shifts in attention and the effects these produce. Baron (1986) argues that presence of others, either as an audience or as coactors, can be distracting, and because it can be, it can threaten the organism performing a task with cognitive overload (e.g., Baron, 1986). Specifically, task performers must divide their attention between the task and the audience, and this generates both increased arousal *and* the possibility of cognitive overload. Cognitive overloads, in turn, can lead to a tendency to restrict one's attention so as to focus only on essential cues or stimuli while "screening out" nonessential ones.

Several findings offer support for this view, known as **distraction–conflict theory** (Baron, 1986). For example, audiences produce social facilitation effects only when directing attention to them conflicts in some way with task demands (Groff, Baron, & Moore, 1983). Similarly, individuals experience greater distraction when they perform various tasks in front of an audience than when they perform them alone (Baron, Moore, & Sanders, 1978).

But a key question remains: Which is more important—increased drive or this tendency toward a narrowed attentional focus? According to Baron (1986), the two theories (drive theory and distraction–conflict theory) make contrasting predictions with respect to one type of task: a poorly learned task that involves only a few key stimuli. Drive theory predicts that the presence of others will facilitate dominant responses, which, on a poorly learned task, are errors. Thus, performance will be reduced by the presence of an audience. In contrast, the distraction–conflict theory, with its emphasis on attentional focus, predicts that the presence of others will cause individuals to focus more closely on the important task-relevant cues, with the result that performance will be *improved.*

Research findings have confirmed these predictions (e.g., Huguet et al., 1999), so it appears that social facilitation stems from cognitive factors—not just heightened arousal, as Zajonc (1965) proposed. Yes, the presence of others generates increased arousal, but it may do so because of the cognitive demands of paying attention both to an audience and to the task being performed rather than as a result of their mere physical presence; and it may influence task performance by inducing a narrowed attention focus. One advantage of this cognitive perspective is that it helps explain why animals as well as people are affected by the presence of an audience. After all, animals, too (even

evaluation apprehension
Concern over being evaluated by others. Such concern can increase arousal and so contribute to social facilitation.

distraction–conflict theory
A theory suggesting that *social facilitation* stems from the conflict produced when individuals attempt, simultaneously, to pay attention to other persons and to the task being performed.

cockroaches), can experience conflicting tendencies to work on a task *and* pay attention to an audience. A theory that can explain similar patterns of behavior among organisms ranging from cockroaches to human beings is powerful indeed and seems to provide a compelling explanation for the effects of an audience or coactors on performance.

KEY POINTS

★ The mere presence of other persons either as an audience or as coactors can influence our performance on many tasks. Such effects are known as *social facilitation* (or as social facilitation–inhibition effects).

★ The *drive theory of social facilitation* suggests that the presence of others is arousing and can either increase or reduce performance, depending on whether dominant responses in a given situation are correct or incorrect.

★ The *distraction–conflict theory* suggests that the presence of others induces conflicting

tendencies to focus on the task being performed and on an audience or coactors. This can result both in increased arousal and narrowed attentional focus.

★ Recent findings offer support for the view that several kinds of audiences produce narrowed attentional focus among persons performing a task. This cognitive view of social facilitation helps explain why it occurs among animals as well as people.

Social Loafing: Letting Others Do the Work

additive tasks

Tasks for which the group product is the sum or combination of the efforts of individual members.

Suppose that you and several other people are helping to push a stalled SUV. Because it is a large vehicle, you all pitch in to get it moving. Question: Will all of the people helping exert equal effort? Probably not. Some will push as hard as they can, others will push moderately, and some may simply hang on and pretend to be pushing when, in fact, they are not (see Figure 12.9).

This pattern is quite common in situations in which groups perform what are known as **additive tasks**—ones in which the contributions of each member are combined into a single group output. On such tasks, some persons work hard while others goof off, doing less than their share and less than they might do if working alone. Social psychologists refer to such effects as **social loafing**—reductions in motivation and effort that occur when individuals work collectively in a group compared with when they work individually as independent coactors (Karau & Williams, 1993).

Social loafing has been demonstrated in many experiments. For example, in one of the first, Latane, Williams, and Harkins (1979) asked groups of male students to clap

Figure 12.9 ■ Does Everyone Pitch in to Share the Work? Not Always
When several people work together to accomplish a task, the chances are good that they do not all exert the same amount of effort. Some will work very hard, others will do less, and perhaps a few will do nothing at all, while pretending to work hard!

or cheer as loudly as possible at specific times, supposedly so that the experimenter could determine how much noise people make in social settings. Participants performed these tasks in groups of two, four, or six persons. Results indicated that although the total amount of noise rose as group size increased, the amount produced *by each participant* dropped. In other words, each person put out less and less effort as group size increased. Such effects are not restricted to simple and seemingly meaningless situations like this; on the contrary, they appear to be quite general in scope, and occur with respect to many different tasks—cognitive ones as well as ones involving physical effort (Weldon & Mustari, 1988; Williams & Karau, 1991). Moreover, these effects appear among both genders and among children as well as adults, although this tendency may be slightly stronger in men than in women (Karau & Williams, 1993). In fact, there appear to be only two exceptions to the generality of social loafing. First, as just noted, women may be slightly less likely to show this effect than men (Karau & Williams, 1993), perhaps because they tend to be higher than men in concern for others' welfare. Second, social loafing effects don't seem to occur in *collectivistic* cultures, such as those in many Asian countries—cultures in which the collective good is more highly valued than individual accomplishment or achievement (Earley, 1993). In fact, in such cultures, people seem to work *harder* when in groups than they do when alone. So, as we've noted repeatedly, cultural factors sometimes play a very important role in social behavior.

Aside from this important exception, however, social loafing appears to be a pervasive fact of social life. Because that's true, the next question is obvious: What can be done to reduce it?

■ Reducing Social Loafing: Some Useful Techniques

The first and most obvious way of reducing social loafing involves making the output or effort of each participant readily identifiable (e.g., Williams, Harkins, & Latane, 1981). Under these conditions, people can't sit back and let others do their work, so social loafing is, in fact, reduced. Second, groups can reduce social loafing by increasing group members' commitment to successful task performance (Brickner, Harkins, & Ostrom, 1986). Pressures toward working hard will then serve to offset temptations to engage in social loafing. Third, social loafing can be reduced by increasing the apparent importance or value of a task (Karau & Williams, 1993). Fourth, social loafing is reduced when individuals view their contributions to the task as unique rather than as merely redundant with those of others (Weldon & Mustari, 1988). Together, these steps can sharply reduce social loafing—and the temptation to "goof off" at the expense of others. (Please see the **Ideas to Take with You—and Use!** section at the end of this chapter for some practical suggestions on how you can benefit from social facilitation and protect yourself against social loafing by others.)

Deindividuation: Submerged in the Crowd

"The mob has many heads but no brains."
—*(English Proverb, seventeenth century)*

Have you ever attended a football or basketball game at which members of the crowd shouted obscenities, threw things at the referees, or engaged in other behavior they would probably never show in other settings? (See Figure 12.10 on page 476.) If so, you already have first-hand experience with another potential effect of the presence of others—in this case, many others—on our behavior. These effects, a drift toward wild, unrestrained behavior, are termed **deindividuation** by social psychologists because they seem to stem, at least in part, from the fact that when we are in a large crowd, we tend to submerge our identity in the crowd—to lose our individuality. And when we do, the

social loafing
Reductions in motivation and effort when individuals work collectively in a group, compared with when they work individually or as independent coactors.

deindividuation
A psychological state characterized by reduced self-awareness and reduced social identity, brought on by external conditions, such as being an anonymous member of a large crowd.

**Figure 12.10 ■ Unrestrained Behavior by Crowds:
A Dramatic Example of the Effects of the Presence of Others**
Crowds often engage in actions individual members would never dream of
performing if they were alone. This is a dramatic illustration of how the mere
presence of others can strongly affect our behavior.

restraints that usually hold many kinds of objectionable or dangerous behavior in check seem to melt away. In fact, the larger the crowd, the more likely such effects are to occur, and the more extreme and savage the behavior that follows (Mullen, 1986). More formally, the term *deindividuation* refers to a psychological state characterized by reduced self-awareness and social identity brought on by external conditions such as being an anonymous member of a large crowd.

Initial research on deindividuation (Zimbardo, 1976) seemed to suggest that being an anonymous member of a crowd makes people feel less responsible or accountable for their own actions and that this, in turn, encourages wild, antisocial actions. More recent evidence, though, indicates that another factor may actually be more important. When we are part of a large crowd, it seems we are more likely to obey the norms of this group and less likely to act in accordance with other norms (Postmes & Spears, 1998). For instance, at a sporting event, when norms in that situation suggest that it is appropriate to boo the opposing team and perhaps throw bottles or other objects onto the field, this is what we tend to do. We pay attention to these norms while ignoring other norms, such as ones calling for polite behavior toward other persons or norms against littering in public places (see Chapter 9). Overall, then, being part of a large crowd and experiencing deindividuation does not necessarily lead to negative or harmful behaviors: It simply increases the likelihood that crowd members will follow the norms of the group.

But what, exactly, happens to people when they feel anonymous? Research by Mullen, Migdal, and Rozell (2003) suggests that when individuals feel anonymous, they experience a reduction in self-awareness *and,* simultaneously, a reduction in their social identity (awareness of the fact that they belong to specific social or ethnic groups). Such effects are fully consistent with the idea that when we are part of a large crowd, we are more likely to follow the norms operating in that situation: After all, we feel less connected to other groups that may have very different norms. Mullen, Migdal, and Rozell (2003) reached these conclusions on the basis of research in which individuals completed questionnaires designed to measure their degree of self-awareness *and* their degree of social identity. They completed these measures while either sitting in front of a mirror (a procedure known, from earlier research, to increase self-awareness), while wearing a mask (a procedure known to induce feelings of anonymity and deindividuation), or after filling out a small family tree, in which they entered the names of their fathers, mothers, and themselves in empty boxes (this procedure was designed to increase social identity—awareness, among participants, of their belonging to one specific group: their families). Results indicated that the mirror increased self-awareness and reduced social identity, while completing a family tree increased social identity but reduced self-awareness. Most relevant to the present discussion, wearing a mask reduced both self-awareness *and* social identity. In this condition, in other words, participants felt less aware of themselves as individuals and less aware of their social ties to others (in this case, their families). These findings, and those of several related studies (e.g., Postmes & Spears, 1998), suggest that being part of a large, anonymous crowd indeed, in a sense, casts individuals adrift from their usual social ties: Not only do they experience reduced awareness of themselves and their own behavior, they also often experience a temporary weakening of ties to the social groups to which they ordinarily belong. Given these effects, it is not at all surprising that large crowds often demonstrate behavior that the persons of whom they are composed would never, under other conditions, perform themselves.

KEY POINTS

- ★ When individuals work together on a task, *social loafing*—reduced output by each group member—sometimes occurs.

- ★ Social loafing can be reduced in several ways: by making outputs individually identifiable, by increasing commitment to the task and task importance, and by assuring that each member's contributions to the task are unique.

- ★ When we are part of a large crowd, we experience reductions in both our self-awareness and our social identity. This, in turn, causes us to adopt the norms operating in the current situation—norms that often sanction impulsive, unrestrained behavior.

Coordination in Groups: Cooperation or Conflict?

In Chapter 10, we noted that individuals often engage in *prosocial behavior*—actions that benefit others but have no obvious or immediate benefits for the persons who perform them. Although such behavior is far from rare, another pattern—one in which helping is mutual and both sides benefit—is even more common. This pattern is known as **cooperation** and involves situations in which groups work together to attain shared goals. Cooperation can be highly beneficial; indeed, through this process, groups of persons can attain goals they could never hope to reach by themselves, Surprisingly,

cooperation
Behavior in which groups work together to attain shared goals.

though, cooperation does not always develop. Frequently, persons belonging to a group try to coordinate their efforts but somehow fail in this attempt. Even worse, they may perceive their personal interests as incompatible, with the result that instead of working together and coordinating their efforts, they work *against* each other, often, in this way, producing negative results for both sides. This is known as **conflict,** defined as a process in which individuals or groups perceive that others have taken or will soon take actions that are incompatible with their own interests. Conflict is indeed a process, for as you probably know from your own experience, it has a nasty way of escalating, starting, perhaps, with simple mistrust and moving quickly through a spiral of anger, resentment, and actions designed to harm the other side. When carried to extremes, the ultimate effects can be very harmful to both sides. Let's see what social psychologists have learned about both patterns of behavior.

Cooperation: Working with Others to Achieve Shared Goals

Cooperation is often highly beneficial to the persons involved. A key question, then, is this: Why don't group members always coordinate their activities in this manner? One answer is straightforward: They don't cooperate because some goals that people seek simply can't be shared. Several people seeking the same job, promotion, or romantic partner can't combine forces to attain these goals: The rewards can go to only one. In such cases, cooperation is not possible, and *conflict* may develop quickly, as each person (or group) attempts to maximize its own outcomes (Tjosvold, 1993).

In many other situations, however, cooperation *could* develop but does not. This is precisely the kind of situation that has been of most interest to social psychologists, who have tried to identify the factors that tip the balance either toward or away from cooperation. We now consider some of the most important of these factors.

■ Social Dilemmas: Situations in Which Cooperation Could Occur But Often Doesn't

Many situations in which cooperation could potentially develop but does not can be described as ones involving **social dilemmas**—situations in which each person can increase his or her individual gains by acting in a purely selfish manner, but if all (or most) persons do the same thing, the outcomes experienced by all are reduced (Komorita & Parks, 1994). As a result, the persons in such situations must deal with *mixed motives:* There are reasons to cooperate (avoid negative outcomes for all), but also reasons to *defect* (to do what is best for oneself), because if only one or a few persons engage in such behavior, they will benefit and the others will not. A classic illustration of this kind of situation, and one in which it is reduced to its simplest form, is known as the *prisoner's dilemma* (see Figure 12.11). Here, there are two persons, and each can choose either to cooperate or to compete. If both cooperate, they both experience large gains. If both compete, each person experiences much smaller gains, or actual losses. The most interesting pattern occurs if one chooses to compete, but the other chooses to cooperate. In this case, the first person experiences much larger gains than the second, trusting one. This situation is called the prisoner's dilemma because it reflects a dilemma faced by two suspects who have been caught by police. Assume that the police do not have enough evidence to convict either person. If both stick to their stories (they both cooperate), they will be set free or receive a very short sentence for a minor crime. If both confess, they will both be convicted and receive a stiff sentence. If one confesses (turns states' evidence) but the other does not, the police will have enough evidence to convict both, but the person who confesses will receive a lighter sentence because of the help she or he has given. As you can see, this situation captures the essence of many social dilemmas: Each suspect experiences pressures both to cooperate and to compete. Social psy-

conflict
A process in which individuals or groups perceive that others have taken or will soon take actions incompatible with their own interests.

social dilemmas
Situations in which each person can increase his or her individual gains by acting in one way; but if all (or most) persons do the same thing, the outcomes experienced by all are reduced.

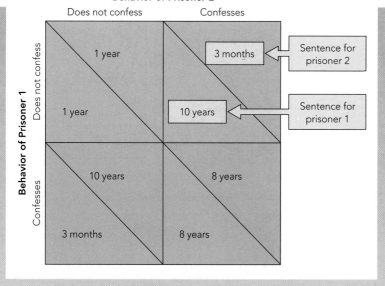

Behavior of Prisoner 2

Does not confess   Confesses

Behavior of Prisoner 1

Does not confess

1 year

1 year

3 months

10 years

Sentence for prisoner 2

Sentence for prisoner 1

Confesses

10 years

3 months

8 years

8 years

Figure 12.11 ■ The Prisoner's Dilemma: To Cooperate or to Compete—That Is the Question!
In the prisoner's dilemma, a simple form of social dilemma, two persons can choose either to cooperate or to compete with one another. If both choose to cooperate, each receives favorable outcomes. If both choose to compete, each receives negative outcomes. If one chooses to compete while the other chooses to cooperate, the first person receives a much better outcome than the second person. Research findings indicate that many factors influence the choices people make in this kind of mixed-motive situation.

chologists have used this type of situation, or ones very much like it (simulated, of course!), to examine the factors that tip the balance toward trust and cooperation or mistrust and competition (e.g., Insko et al., 2001). The findings of such research indicate that many factors play a role in whether cooperation or competition develops.

■ Factors Influencing Cooperation: Reciprocity, Personal Orientations, and Communication

Though many different factors determine whether individuals will choose to cooperate with others in situations involving the mixed motives generated by social dilemmas, three appear to be most important: tendencies toward *reciprocity, personal orientations* concerning cooperation, and *communication.*

Reciprocity is probably the most obvious of these factors. Throughout life, we tend to follow this principle, treating others very much as they have treated us (e.g., Pruitt & Carnevale, 1993). In choosing between cooperation and competition, too, we seem to adopt this general rule. When others cooperate with us and put their selfish interests aside, we usually respond in kind. In contrast, if they defect and pursue their own interests, we generally do the same (Kerr & Kaufman-Gililland, 1994).

Evolutionary psychologists have noted that this tendency to adopt reciprocity where cooperation is concerned is not restricted to human beings; it has been observed among other species, too (e.g., bats, chimpanzees; Buss, 1999). This, in turn, raises in intriguing question: Because "cheaters" (those who do not return cooperation after receiving it) often gain an advantage, how could a strong tendency toward reciprocity have evolved? One possible answer is provided by the theory of **reciprocal altruism** (e.g.,

reciprocity
A basic rule of social life, suggesting that individuals should treat others as these persons have treated them.

reciprocal altruism
A theory suggesting that by sharing resources such as food, organisms increase their chances of survival, and thus the likelihood that they will pass their genes on to the next generation.

Figure 12.12 ■ Competition as an Approach to Life!
As shown here, some people seem to want to turn every interaction with others into a contest or competition. (*Source: Reproduced with special permission of King Features Syndicate.*)

Cosmides & Tooby, 1992). This theory suggests that by sharing resources such as food, organisms increase their chances of survival, and thus the likelihood that they will pass their genes on to the next generation. Further, they tend to share in such a way that the benefits are relatively great for the recipients of such cooperation while the costs are relatively minimal to the provider. For instance, if one hunter has more meat than he and his family can eat while another is starving, the costs to the first for sharing are minimal, while the gains to the second are great. When the situation is reversed, cooperation will again benefit both parties and increase their chances of survival. In contrast, organisms who act in a purely selfish manner do not gain such benefits.

A second factor that exerts strong effects on cooperation is *personal orientation* toward such behavior. Think about the many people you have known during your life. Can you remember ones who strongly preferred cooperation—people who could be counted on to try to work together with other group members in almost every situation? In contrast, can you remember others who usually preferred to pursue their own selfish interests and could *not* be relied on to cooperate—or someone like the character in the cartoon in Figure 12.12, who seems to turn every social encounter into competition? You probably have little difficulty in bringing examples of both types to mind, for large individual differences in the tendencies to cooperate exist. Such differences, in turn, seem to reflect contrasting perspectives toward working with others—perspectives that individuals carry with them from situation to situation, even over relatively long periods of time (e.g., Knight & Dubro, 1984). Specifically, research findings indicate that individuals can possess any one of three distinct orientations toward situations involving social dilemmas: (1) a *cooperative* orientation, in which they prefer to maximize the joint outcomes received by all the persons involved; (2) an *individualistic* orientation, in which they focus primarily on maximizing their own outcomes; or (3) a *competitive* orientation, in which they focus primarily on defeating others—on obtaining better outcomes than other persons do (DeDreu and McCusker, 1997; Van Lange & Kuhlman, 1994). These orientations exert strong effects on how people behave in many situations, so they are an important factor in whether cooperation does or does not develop.

A third factor that influences the choice between cooperation and competition is *communication*. Common sense suggests that if individuals can discuss the situation with others, they may soon conclude that the best option is for everyone to cooperate; after all, this will result in gains for all. Surprisingly, though, early research on this possibility produced mixed results. In many situations, the opportunity for group members to communicate with each other about what they should do in the situation did *not* increase cooperation. On the contrary, group members seemed to use this opportunity primarily to *threaten* one another, with the result that cooperation did not occur (e.g., Deutsch & Krauss, 1960; Stech & McClintock, 1981). Is this always the case? Fortunately, research findings point to more optimistic conclusions: Apparently, communication between group members *can* lead to increased cooperation, provided certain conditions are met (e.g., Kerr & Kaufman-Gilliland, 1994; Sally, 1998). Specifically, beneficial effects can, and do, occur if group members make personal commitments to cooperate with one another, and if these commitments are backed up by strong, personal norms to honor them (see Chapter 9 for a discussion of the nature and impact of social norms; e.g., Kerr et al., 1997).

In sum, several factors determine what individuals do in situations in which they can choose between cooperation and competition. The choice is neither simple nor automatic; rather, it emerges from a complex interaction between social and personal factors.

KEY POINTS

★ *Cooperation*—working together with others to obtain shared goals—is a common aspect of social life.

★ However, cooperation does not develop in many situations in which it is possible, partly because such situations involve *social dilemmas,* in which individuals can increase their own gains by defection.

★ Several factors influence whether cooperation occurs in such situations. These include

strong tendencies toward *reciprocity,* personal orientation toward cooperation, and communication.

★ Evolutionary psychologists suggest that our tendency to reciprocate may result from the fact that organisms that cooperate are more likely to survive and reproduce than are organisms that do not.

Conflict: Its Nature, Causes, and Effects

If prosocial behavior (which we covered in Chapter 10) and cooperation constitute one end of a dimension describing how individuals and groups work together, then *conflict* lies at or near the other end. As noted earlier, conflict refers to a process in which one individual or group perceives that others have taken or will soon take actions that are incompatible with their own interests. The key elements in conflict, then, seem to include (1) opposing interests between individuals or groups, (2) recognition of such opposition, (3) the belief by each side that the other will act to interfere with these interests, and (4) actions that produce such interference.

Unfortunately, conflict is an all-too-common part of social life and can be extremely costly to both sides. What factors cause such seemingly irrational behavior? And, perhaps even more important, what can be done to reduce it? These are the key questions that social psychologists have addressed in their research.

Major Causes of Conflict

Our definition of *conflict* emphasizes the existence of incompatible interests and recognition of this fact by the parties involved. Indeed, this is *the* defining feature of conflicts. Interestingly, though, conflicts sometimes fail to develop, even though both sides

Figure 12.13 ■ Destructive Criticism: One Social Cause of Conflict
When one person criticizes another harshly and without clear justification, the recipient may react with anger and a desire for revenge. The result? The seeds for bitter and lasting conflict between them may be planted—a conflict that does not stem from incompatible interests.

have incompatible interests; and in other cases, conflicts occur when the two sides don't really have opposing interests—they may simply *believe* that these exist (e.g., De Dreu & Van Lange, 1995; Tjosvold & DeDreu, 1997). In short, conflict involves much more than opposing interests. In fact, a growing body of evidence suggests that *social* factors may play as strong a role in initiating conflicts as incompatible interests.

One social factor that plays a role in this respect is what have been termed *faulty attributions*—errors concerning the causes behind others' behavior (e.g., Baron, 1989a). When individuals find that their interests have been thwarted, they generally try to determine *why* this occurred. Was it bad luck? A lack of planning on their part? A lack of needed resources? Or was it due to intentional interference by another person or group? If they conclude that the latter is true, then the seeds for an intense conflict may be planted—even if other persons actually had nothing to do with the situation! In other words, erroneous attributions concerning the causes of negative outcomes can, and often do, play an important role in conflicts, and sometimes cause them to occur when they could readily have been avoided (see Chapter 11 for more information).

Another social factor that seems to play an important role in conflict is what might be termed *faulty communication*—the fact that individuals sometimes communicate with others in a way that angers or annoys them, even though it is *not* their intention to do so. Have you ever been on the receiving end of harsh criticism—criticism you felt was unfair, insensitive, and not in the least helpful? The results of several studies indicate that feedback of this type, known as *destructive* criticism, can leave the recipient hungry for revenge, and so set the stage for conflicts that, again, do not necessarily stem from incompatible interests (see Figure 12.13; e.g., Baron, 1990; Cropanzano, 1993).

A third social cause of conflict involves the tendency to perceive our own views as objective and as reflecting reality, but those of others as biased by their ideology (e.g., Keltner & Robinson, 1997; Robinson et al., 1995). As a result of this tendency, we tend to magnify differences between our views and those of others, and so to exaggerate conflicts of interest between us. Research findings indicate that this tendency is stronger for groups or individuals who currently hold a dominant or powerful position (Keltner & Robinson, 1997). This, in turn, often leads to what is known as the *status quo bias*—a tendency for powerful groups defending the current status quo to be less accurate at intergroup perception than the groups that are challenging them. For instance, they perceive their position as much more reasonable or objective than it is.

Personal traits or characteristics, too, play a role in conflict. For example, *Type A* individuals—ones who are highly competitive, always in a hurry, and quite irritable—tend to become involved in conflicts more often than calmer and less irritable Type B persons (Baron, 1989b).

Finally, recent findings (Peterson & Behfar, 2003) indicate that conflict within a group may stem from poor initial performance by the group. Poor performance, and negative feedback about this performance, may be threatening to group members, and this, in turn, can lead them to blame each other (not themselves!) for these poor results (recall our discussion of the self-serving bias in Chapter 3). The overall result may be increased conflict among group members. To test these predictions, Peterson and Behfar (2003) asked groups of MBA students to complete questionnaires designed to measure the amount of conflict they experienced at two different times during one semester. Course instructors provided information on the grades received by each team on class projects—this was the measure of performance feedback to the teams. Results indicated that, as the researchers expected, the more negative the initial feedback groups received, the greater the conflict they reported after receiving this information. In addition, and not surprisingly, the more conflict the groups reported initially, before receiving the feedback, the more they reported later. Conflict indeed has a nasty way of persisting unless active steps are taken to reduce it.

So where does all of this leave us? With the conclusion that conflict does *not* stem solely from opposing interests. On the contrary, it often derives from social factors—long-standing grudges or resentment, the desire for revenge, inaccurate social perceptions, poor communication, and similar factors. In short, conflict, like cooperation, has many roots. Although the most central of these factors may indeed be incompatible interests, this is far from the entire story, and the social and cognitive causes of conflict should not be overlooked.

Resolving Conflicts: Some Useful Techniques

Because conflicts are often very costly, the persons involved in such situations usually want to resolve them as quickly as possible. What steps are most useful for reaching this goal? Although many may succeed, two seem especially useful: *bargaining* and *superordinate goals.*

■ Bargaining: The Universal Process

By far the most common strategy for resolving conflicts is **bargaining** or *negotiation* (e.g., Pruitt & Carnevale, 1993). In this process, opposing sides exchange offers, counteroffers, and concessions, either directly or through representatives. If the process is successful, a solution acceptable to both sides is attained and the conflict is resolved. If, instead, bargaining is unsuccessful, costly deadlock may result and the conflict will intensify. What factors determine which of these outcomes occurs? As you can probably guess, many play a role.

First, and perhaps most obviously, the outcome of bargaining is determined, in part, by the specific tactics adopted by the bargainers. Many of these are designed to accomplish a key goal: reduce the opponent's *aspirations* (i.e., hopes or goals) so that this person or group becomes convinced that it cannot get what it wants and should, instead, settle for something quite favorable to the other side. Tactics for accomplishing this goal include (1) beginning with an extreme initial offer—one that is very favorable to the side proposing it; (2) the "big-lie" technique—convincing the other side that one's break-even point is much higher than it is so that they offer more than would otherwise be the case (e.g., a used car salesperson may claim that she will lose money on the deal if she lowers price when, in fact, this is false); and (3) convincing the other side that you have an "out"—if they won't make a deal with you, you can go elsewhere and get even better terms (Thompson, 1998).

Do these tactics seem ethical to you? This is a complex question on which individuals may well differ, but social psychologists who have conducted research on this question (Robinson, Lewicki, & Donahue, 1998) have found that there is general agreement

bargaining (negotiation)
A process in which opposing sides exchange offers, counteroffers, and concessions, either directly or through representatives.

that four types of tactics are questionable from an ethical standpoint: (1) *attacking an opponent's network*—manipulating or interfering with an opponent's network of support and information; (2) *false promises*—offering false commitments or lying about future intentions; (3) *misrepresentation*—providing misleading or false information to an opponent; and (4) *inappropriate information gathering*—collecting information in an unethical manner (e.g., through theft, spying, etc.). These tactics are measured by a questionnaire known as the Self-reported Inappropriate Negotiation Strategies Scale (or SINS for short).

A second and very important determinant of the outcome of bargaining involves the overall orientation of the bargainers to the process (Pruitt & Carnevale, 1993). People taking part in negotiations can approach such discussions from either of two distinct perspectives. In one, they can view the negotiations as win–lose situations, in which gains by one side are necessarily linked with losses for the other. In the other, they can approach negotiations as potential win–win situations, in which the interests of the two sides are not necessarily incompatible and in which the potential gains of both sides can be maximized.

Not all situations offer the potential for such agreements, but many provide such possibilities. If participants are willing to explore all options carefully, they can sometimes attain what are known as *integrative agreements*—ones that offer greater joint benefits than simple compromise—splitting all differences down the middle. Here's an example: Suppose that two cooks are preparing recipes that call for an entire orange, and they have only one. What should they do? One possibility is to divide the orange in half. That leaves both with less than they need. Suppose, however, that one cook needs all the juice while the other needs all the peel. Here, a much better solution is possible: They can share the orange, each using the part she or he needs. Many technique for attaining such integrative solutions exist; a few of these are summarized in Table 12.1.

▪ Superordinate Goals: "We're All in This Together"

As we saw in Chapter 6, individuals often divide the world into two opposing camps—"us" and "them." They perceive members of their own group (us) as quite different from, and usually better than, people belonging to other groups (them). These tenden-

Table 12.1 ▪ Tactics for Reaching Integrative Agreements

Many strategies can be useful in attaining integrative agreements—ones that offer better outcomes than simple compromise. Several of these strategies are summarized here.

TACTIC	DESCRIPTION
Broadening the pie	Available resources are increased so that both sides can obtain their major goals
Nonspecific compensation	One side gets what it wants; the other is compensated on an unrelated issue.
Logrolling	Each party makes concessions on low-priority issues in exchange for concessions on issues it values more highly.
Bridging	Neither party gets its initial demands, but a new option that satisfies the major interests of both sides is developed.
Cost cutting	One party gets what it desires, and the costs to the other party are reduced in some manner.

cies to magnify differences between one's own group and others and to disparage outsiders are very powerful and often play a role in the occurrence and persistence of conflicts. Fortunately, such tendencies can be countered through the induction of **superordinate goals**—goals that both sides seek and that tie their interests together rather than drive them apart (e.g., Sherif et al., 1961; Tjosvold, 1993). When opposing sides can be made to see that they share overarching goals, conflict is often sharply reduced and may, in fact, be replaced by overt cooperation.

KEY POINTS

★ *Conflict* is a process that begins when individuals or groups perceive that others' interests are incompatible with theirs.

★ Conflict also can stem from social factors such as faulty attributions, poor communica-

tion, the tendency to perceive our own views as objective, and personal traits.

★ Conflict can be reduced in many ways, but *bargaining* and the induction of *superordinate goals* seem to be most effective.

Perceived Fairness in Groups: Its Nature and Effects

Have you ever been in a situation in which you felt that you were getting less than you deserved from some group to which you belonged—less status, less approval, less pay? If so, you probably remember that your reactions to such *perceived unfairness* were probably very strong and not at all pleasant. Perhaps you experienced anger, resentment, and powerful feelings of injustice (e.g., Cropanzano, 1993; Scher, 1997). And if you did, you probably did not sit around waiting for the situation to improve; on the contrary, you may have taken some concrete action to rectify it and get whatever it was you felt you deserved—as I and my fellow coworkers did in the "give me your tips" incident described at the start of this chapter. Whatever you did—demand more, reduce your contributions to the group, or even leave it—may well have affected the functioning of the group. Social psychologists have recognized such effects for many years, and have conducted many studies to understand (1) the factors that lead individuals to decide they have been treated fairly or unfairly, and (2) what they do about it—their efforts to deal with perceived unfairness (e.g., Adams, 1965). We now consider both questions.

Basic Rules for Judging Fairness: Distributive, Procedural, and Transactional Justice

Deciding whether we have been treated fairly in our relations with others is a complex and tricky task. First, we rarely have all the information needed to make such a judgment accurately (e.g., Van den Bos & Lind, 2002). Second, even if we did have enough information, perceived fairness is very much in the eye of the beholder, so it is subject to many of the kinds of bias and distortion we have described throughout this book. For instance, it is always tempting to conclude that *we* deserve more than others, even if this is not really true (the self-serving bias in action). Despite such complexities,

superordinate goals
Goals that both sides of a conflict seek and that tie their interests together rather than drive them apart.

though, research on perceived fairness in group settings indicates that, in general, we make these judgments on the basis of three distinct rules.

The first, known as **distributive justice** (or *equity;* Adams, 1965), involves the outcomes we and others receive. According to this rule, available rewards should be distributed (divided) among group members in accordance with their contributions: The more they provide in terms of effort, experience, skills, and other contributions to the group, the more they should receive. For example, we expect people with more seniority in a group or organization to receive higher salaries than beginners; similarly, we expect persons who have made major contributions toward reaching the group's goals to receive greater rewards than persons who have contributed very little. In short, we often judge fairness in terms of the ratio between the contributions group members have provided and the rewards they receive. We expect this ratio to be approximately the *same* for all members, and to the extent it is not, we perceive that distributive justice has been violated and that unfairness exists (e.g., Brockner & Wiesenfeld, 1996; Greenberg, 1993).

Although we are certainly concerned with the outcomes we and others receive, this is far from the entire story where judgments of fairness are concerned. In addition, we are also often interested in the fairness of the *procedures* through which rewards have been distributed. This is known as **procedural justice** (e.g., Folger & Baron, 1996), and we base our judgments about it on factors such as these: (1) the consistency of procedures—the extent to which they are applied in the same manner to all persons; (2) accuracy—the extent to which procedures are based on accurate information about the relative contributions of all group members; (3) opportunity for corrections—the extent to which any errors in distributions that are made can be adjusted information; (4) bias suppression—the extent to which decision makers avoid being influenced by their own self-interest; and (5) ethicality—the extent to which decisions are made in a manner compatible with ethical and moral values held by the people affected.

Evidence that such factors really do influence our judgments concerning procedural justice has been obtained in many studies (e.g., Brockner et al., 1994; Leventhal, Karuza, & Fry, 1980). For instance, in one investigation, Magner et al. (2000) asked property owners in a medium-sized city to rate the extent to which their taxes were determined through fair procedures. Results indicated that ethicality, accuracy, and bias suppression were important factors in taxpayers' decisions about procedural justice: The more these factors were present, the more they perceived the process of setting each person's taxes to be fair.

Finally, we also judge fairness in terms of the way in which information about outcomes and procedures is given to us. This is known as **transactional justice** (or sometimes, interactional justice), and two factors seem to play a key role in our judgments about it: the extent to which we are given clear and rational reasons for *why* rewards were divided as they were (Bies, Shapiro, & Cummings, 1988), and the courtesy and sensitivity with which we are informed about these divisions (e.g., Greenberg, 1993a). Here's an illustration of how these factors work: Suppose you receive a term paper back from one of your professors. On the top is the grade "C–." You expected at least a B, so you are quite disappointed. Reading on, though, you see a detailed explanation of why you received the grade you did, and, after reading it, you have to admit that it is clear and reasonable. In addition, the professor inserts the following comment: "I know you'll be disappointed with this grade, but I feel you are capable of much better work and would be glad to work with you to help you improve your grade." How would you react? Probably by concluding that the grade is low but the professor treated you fairly. In contrast, imagine how you'd react is there were no explanation for the grade, and the professor wrote the following comment: "Very poor work; you simply haven't met my standards. And don't bother to try to see me: I never change grades." In this case, you

---

distributive justice (fairness)
Refers to individuals' judgments about whether they are receiving a fair share of available rewards—a share proportionate to their contributions to the group or any social relationship.

procedural justice
Judgments concerning the fairness of the procedures used to distribute available rewards among group members.

transactional (interpersonal) justice
Refers to the extent to which persons who distribute rewards explain or justify their decisions and show considerateness and courtesy to those who receive the rewards.

are much more likely to experience feelings of anger and resentment, and to view your treatment by the professor as unfair.

In sum, we judge fairness in several different ways—in terms of the rewards we have received (distributive justice), the procedures used to reach these divisions (procedural justice), and the style in which we are informed about these divisions (transactional justice). All three forms of perceived justice can have strong effects on our behavior and, in this way, can influence the functioning of groups to which we belong.

Factors Affecting Judgments of Fairness

The terms *distributive, procedural,* and *transactional justice* refer to general rules we apply in deciding whether we have been treated fairly by others. But, in essence, they are simply guidelines—rules of thumb (heuristics) we use to help us in making such judgments. Many factors influence the extent to which we apply them, and how we do so, in any situation (e.g., Folger & Cropanzano, 1998; Tyler et al., 1997). Two factors that appear to be very important in this respect, however, are our current *affective states* and *status*.

In many situations in which we ask the question, "Am I being treated fairly?" we do not have sufficient information about rewards or procedures to apply rules of distributive and procedural justice firmly. We don't know exactly what rewards others have received (e.g., their salaries or bonuses), and we may not know all the procedures used to distribute such rewards to group members. What do we do in such situations? Just what we do in many others in which we lack required information: We "go with our hearts" or feelings. Because we lack needed information, we use our current feelings as a source of information, reasoning "If I feel good, this must be fair" or "If I feel bad, this must be unfair." (Recall our discussion of affect and cognition in Chapter 2.)

Evidence that we really do operate in this manner has recently been provided by van den Bos (2003). He first varied participants' mood by asking them to imagine how they would feel if they were very happy or how they would feel if they were very unhappy. Then, they worked with another person on a task requiring them to count the number of squares shown in complex patterns on a computer screen. They were informed that after working on this task, the experimenter would divide some lottery tickets between them and the other person; lottery winners would receive cash prizes.

As they performed the task, they learned that the other person had performed at about the same level as themselves. At this point, the crucial manipulation in the study occurred: Participants were told either that the experimenter had given both the participant and the other person the same number of lottery tickets, that the other person received *more* than they did, or that the other person received *fewer* than they did. In a control condition, participants were given no information about the division of tickets. The key question was this: Would participants' mood (previously varied to be positive or negative) now influence their judgments about how fair the distribution of lottery tickets was? Van den Bos (2003) predicted that it would, especially when participants had no information about the way the lottery tickets were divided. As you can see from Figure 12.14 on page 488, this is precisely what happened. Under this condition (the control or *unknown* group), persons in a good mood rated the division of tickets as more fair than those in a good mood. In the other conditions, in which they had information on the ticket division, mood had no significant effects—although, as you can guess, they were happier with the division when it was equal than when it gave the other person more than they received. In additional studies, van den Bos (2003) found that judgments of procedural justice, too, are influenced by mood, so it is clear that when we do not have all the information we need to decide whether we are being treated fairly, our current moods color these judgments—just as they influence many other judgments we make about the social world.

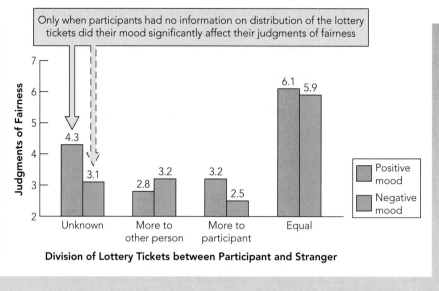

Figure 12.14 ■ The Role of Affect in Judgments of Fairness
When participants had no information on how lottery tickets had been divided between themselves and another person, they perceived the outcome as more fair when they were in a positive mood than when they were in a negative mood. In contrast, when participants had information on how the tickets had been distributed (they knew that the other person had received more or fewer tickets than they did), mood did not significantly influence their judgments of fairness. (*Source: Based on data from van den Bos, 2003.*)

Another factor that influences our judgments of fairness—and especially judgments concerning procedural justice—is status. Apparently, when we think about our status in a group, this triggers concerns with the fairness of procedures used to distribute rewards within the group. Why? Perhaps because awareness of our status reminds us of the principle that the same procedures should be applied to all group members in the same manner, regardless of their status or rank (e.g., Tyler & Blader, in press). Recent findings reported by van Prodijen, van den Bos, and Wilke (2002) provide support for this reasoning: They found that when status was made salient to group members (they were asked to think about the thoughts and feelings that come to mind when thinking about the concept "status"), they showed stronger evidence of being concerned with procedural justice than when another topic was made salient (the content of TV programs). These and other findings indicate that awareness of our status in a group does lead us to focus on fairness within the group, and especially on the fairness of procedures used to divide available rewards among members.

Reactions to Perceived Unfairness: Tactics for Dealing with Injustice

Now let's turn to another and perhaps even more interesting question: What do people do when they feel that they have been treated unfairly? As you probably know from your own experience, many different things. First, if unfairness centers around rewards (distributive justice), people may focus on changing the balance between their contributions and outcomes. For example, they may reduce contributions or demand larger rewards. If these are not delivered, they may take more drastic actions, such as leaving the group altogether. All these reactions are readily visible in workplaces—one setting in which judgments concerning fairness play a key role. Employees who feel that they are being underpaid may come in late, leave early, do less on the job, and request more benefits—higher pay, more vacation, and so on. If these tactics fail, they may protest, join a union and go out on strike, or, ultimately, quit and look for another job.

Such reactions are also visible in intimate relationships as well: When members of a couple feel that they are being treated unfairly by their spouse or significant other (e.g., they have to do more than their share of the housework), they often react with anger and resentment, and may take steps to change the situation (e.g., Sprecher, 1992). This can range from direct requests to their partner through deciding to leave the relationship for another. Interestingly, research findings indicate that perceived unfairness may not only lead to marital distress—it may be a result of it. In a carefully conducted longitudinal study, Grote and Clark (2001) asked married couples to rate their marital satisfaction, their marital conflict, and the perceived fairness of division of household tasks at three different times: while the wife was pregnant, six months after their child was born, and twelve to fifteen months after their child was born. Results indicated that the more conflict couples reported before the child was born, the greater their perceptions of unfairness at the later times (after the child was born). These findings occurred for both genders, but were, not surprisingly, somewhat stronger for women who, in fact, do more than half of the household chores in most couples. These results suggest that when couples are getting along well and conflict is low, they do *not* pay much attention to unfairness, even if it exists. But when conflict is high, their attention is focused on unfairness, and this, in turn, may serve to intensify conflict still further. In sum, perceived unfairness can be the result of marital conflict as a well as a cause of such difficulties for couples.

When unfairness centers around procedures (procedural justice) or a lack of courteous treatment by the persons who determine reward divisions (transactional justice) rather than on rewards themselves (distributive justice), individuals may adopt somewhat different tactics. Procedures are often harder to change than specific outcomes because they go on behind "closed doors" and may depart from announced policies in many ways. Similarly, changing the negative attitudes or personality traits that lie behind insensitive treatment by bosses, professors, or other persons who allocate rewards is a difficult, if not impossible, task. As a result, individuals who feel that they have been treated unfairly in these ways often turn to more covert (hidden) techniques for "evening the score." For instance, a growing body of evidence suggests that such feelings of unfairness lie behind many instances of employee theft and sabotage (e.g., Greenberg, 1997; see Figure 12.15). As noted in Chapter 11, feelings of unfairness also play a major role in many forms of workplace aggression—especially in subtle, hidden actions individuals perform to get even with others who, they believe, have treated them unfairly.

Finally, individuals who feel that they have been treated unfairly and conclude that there is little they can do about this may cope with this

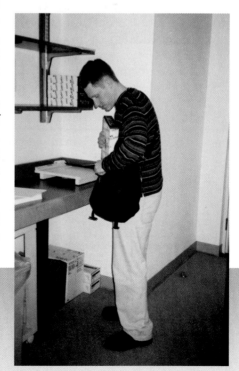

Figure 12.15 ■ Employee Theft: One Tactic for Dealing with Perceived Unfairness
When employees feel that they have been treated unfairly by management and have no legitimate means for correcting this situation, they may engage in employee theft or sabotage. In this way, they seek to "even the score" with their employers.

situation simply by changing their perceptions. They can conclude, for instance, that other persons who receive larger rewards than they do *deserve* this special treatment because they possess something "special"—extra talent, greater experience, a bigger reputation, or some other special qualities. In such cases, individuals who feel that they cannot eliminate unfairness can at least cope with it and reduce the discomfort it produces, even though they continue to be treated unfairly by others.

KEY POINTS

★ Individuals wish to be treated fairly by the groups to which they belong. Fairness can be judged in terms of outcomes (*distributive justice*), in terms of procedures (*procedural justice*), or in terms of courteous treatment (*transactional justice*).

★ When individuals feel that they have been treated unfairly, they often take steps to restore fairness.

★ These steps range from such overt actions as reducing or protesting their contributions through such covert actions as employee theft or sabotage, or changes in perception, suggesting that others deserve better treatment.

Decision Making by Groups: How It Occurs and the Pitfalls It Faces

Groups are called on to perform many tasks—everything from playing rock music to performing surgical operations. One of the most important activities they perform, however, is **decision making**—combining and integrating available information in order to choose one out of several possible courses of action. Governments, large corporations, military units, sports teams—these and many other organizations entrust key decisions to groups. Why? Although many factors play a role, the most important seems to be this: Most people believe that groups usually reach better decisions than individuals. After all, groups can pool the expertise of their members and avoid extreme decisions.

Are such beliefs accurate? Do groups really make better or more accurate decisions than individuals? In their efforts to answer this question, social psychologists have focused on three major topics: (1) How do groups actually make their decisions and reach consensus? (2) Do decisions reached by groups differ from those reached by individuals? (3) What accounts for the fact that groups sometimes make truly disastrous decisions—ones so bad it is hard to believe they were actually reached?

The Decision-Making Process: How Groups Attain Consensus

decision making
Processes involved in combining and integrating available information in order to choose one out of several possible courses of action.

When groups first begin to discuss any issue, their members rarely voice unanimous agreement. Rather, they come to the decision-making task with different information, and so support a wide range of views (e.g., Larson, Foster-Fishman, & Franz, 1998; Gigone & Hastie, 1997). After some period of discussion, however, groups usually do reach a decision. This does not always happen: Juries become "hung," and other decision-making groups, too, sometimes deadlock. But, in general, some decision is reached. How is this accomplished, and can the final outcome be predicted from the views initially held by a group's members? Here is what research findings suggest.

Social Decision Schemes: Blueprints for Decisions

Let's begin with the question of whether a group's decisions can be predicted from the views held by its members at the start. Here, the answer itself is quite straightforward, even though the processes involved are more complex: "Yes." The final decisions reached by groups can often be predicted accurately by relatively simple rules known as **social decision schemes**. These rules relate the initial distribution of members' views or preferences to the group's final decisions. For example, one scheme—the *majority-wins rule*—suggests that, in many cases, the group will opt for whatever position is initially supported by most of its members (e.g., Nemeth et al., 2001). According to this rule, discussion serves mainly to confirm or strengthen the most popular initial view; it is generally accepted no matter how passionately the minority argues for a different position. A second decision scheme is the *truth-wins rule*. This indicates that the correct solution or decision will ultimately be accepted as its correctness is recognized by more and more members. A third decision rule is known as the *first-shift rule*. Groups tend to adopt a decision consistent with the direction of the first shift in opinion shown by any member. Still another rule—*unanimity*—is often imposed by the legal system, which requires that juries reach unanimous verdicts.

Surprising as it may seem, the results of many studies indicate that these simple rules are quite successful in predicting even complex group decisions. Indeed, they have been found to be accurate up to 80 percent of the time (e.g., Stasser, Taylor, & Hanna, 1989), although members holding extreme views—outliers—can sometimes exert strong influence and shift groups away from reaching decisions predicted by these basic rules (e.g., Ohtsubo et al., 2004). Thus, social decision schemes seem to provide important insights into how groups move toward consensus. (That groups do indeed reach decisions is clear; but what about the *quality* of these decisions—are they better or worse than the decisions individuals would make alone? More balanced and conservative? For a discussion of this issue, please see the **Making Sense of Common Sense** section on page 492.)

Potential Dangers of Group Decision Making: Groupthink, Biased Processing, and Restricted Sharing of Information

The drift of many decision-making groups toward polarization is a serious problem—one that can interfere with their ability to make accurate decisions. Unfortunately, this is not the only process that can exert such negative effects. Several others, too, emerge during group discussions and can lead groups to make costly, even disastrous, decisions (Hinsz, 1995). Among the most important of these are (1) *groupthink,* (2) biased processing of information by group members, and (3) groups' seeming inability to share and use information held by some, but not all, of their members.

Groupthink: When Too Much Cohesiveness Is a Dangerous Thing

Earlier, we noted that high levels of cohesiveness in groups can be a good thing: It increases motivation and morale and makes groups more pleasant places in which to work. But like anything else, there can be "too much of a good thing" where group cohesiveness is concerned. When cohesiveness reaches very high levels, it appears **groupthink** may develop. This is a strong tendency for decision-making groups to "close ranks," cognitively, around a decision, assuming that the group *can't* be wrong, that all members must support the decision strongly, and that any information contrary to it should be rejected (Janis, 1972, 1982). Once this collective state of mind develops, it has been suggested, groups become unwilling—and perhaps *unable*—to change their

social decision schemes
Rules relating the initial distribution of member views to final group decisions.

groupthink
The tendency of the members of highly cohesive groups to assume that their decisions can't be wrong, that all members must support the groups' decisions strongly, and that information contrary to these decisions should be ignored.

Are Groups Really Less Likely Than Individuals to "Go over the Edge"?

Truly important decisions are rarely left to individuals. Instead, they are usually assigned to groups—preferably, highly qualified groups. For instance, medical decisions are made by teams of physicians, and government policies are set, or at least recommended, by groups of experts. Why are so many crucial decisions entrusted to groups? One answer involves the widespread belief that groups are far less likely than individuals to make risky and hazardous decisions—to rush blindly over the edge. Is common sense correct in this respect? Research findings offer a straightforward answer: "Not really!" Contrary to popular belief, a large body of evidence indicates that groups are actually *more* likely to adopt extreme positions than are individuals making decisions alone. In fact, across many different kinds of decisions and many different contexts, groups show a pronounced tendency to shift toward views more extreme than the ones with which they initially began (Burnstein, 1983; Hilton, 1998; Lamm & Myers, 1978). This is known as **group polarization,** and its major effects can be summarized as follows: Whatever the initial leaning or preference of a group prior to its discussions, this preference is strengthened during the group's deliberations. As result, not only does the *group* shift toward more extreme views, individual members, too, often show such a shift (see Figure 12.16). Initial research on this topic (e.g., Kogan & Wallach, 1964) suggested that groups move toward riskier and riskier alternatives as they discuss important issues—a change described as the *risky shift*. But additional research indicated that the shift was not always one toward risk—that happened only in situations in which the

initial preference of the group leaned in this direction. The shift could be in the exact opposite direction—toward increased caution—if *this* was the group's initial preference. So, do groups tend to make more conservative and therefore better decisions than individuals? The findings of careful research suggest this answer: "Not at all."

Please note: The term *group polarization* does *not* refer to a tendency of groups to split apart into two opposing camps or poles (a process we discussed earlier in this chapter). Rather, it refers to a strengthening of the group's initial preferences, whatever these happen to be.

But why do groups tend to move, over the course of their discussions, toward increasingly extreme views and decisions? Two major factors seem to be involved. First, it appears that *social comparison* plays an important role. Everyone wants to be "above average," and where opinions are concerned, this implies holding views that are "better" than those of other group members. What does *better* mean? In this context, *better* implies holding views in line with the group's overall preference, but even more so. So, for example, in a group of liberals, *better* would mean "more liberal." Among a group of conservatives, it would mean "more conservative." And among a group of racists, it would mean "even more bigoted." In other words, people who voice opinions even stronger than those of the group are admired, and so tend to become influential.

Another aspect of this process involves the fact that during group discussions, at least some members discover—often to their surprise—that their views are *not* better than those of most other members. The result: After comparing themselves with these persons, they shift to even more extreme views, and the group polarization effect is off and running (Goethals & Zanna, 1979).

group polarization
The tendency of group members to shift toward more extreme positions than those they initially held as a result of group discussion.

decisions, even if external events suggest that these decisions are very poor ones. For example, consider the repeated decisions by three U.S. presidents (Kennedy, Johnson, and Nixon) to escalate the war in Vietnam. Each escalation brought increased American casualties and no visible progress toward the goal of assuring the survival of South Vietnam as an independent country; yet, the cabinets of each president continued to recommend escalation. According to Janis (1982), the social psychologist who originated the concept of *groupthink,* this process—and the increasing unwillingness to consider alternative courses of action that it encourages among group members—may well have contributed to this tragic chain of events.

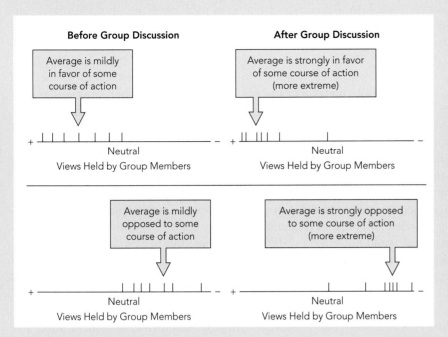

Before Group Discussion

Average is mildly in favor of some course of action

Neutral
Views Held by Group Members

Average is mildly opposed to some course of action

Neutral
Views Held by Group Members

After Group Discussion

Average is strongly in favor of some course of action (more extreme)

Neutral
Views Held by Group Members

Average is strongly opposed to some course of action (more extreme)

Neutral
Views Held by Group Members

Figure 12.16 ■ Group Polarization: How It Works

As shown here, *group polarization* involves the tendency for decision-making groups to shift toward views that are more extreme than the ones with which the groups initially began, but in the same general direction. Thus, if groups start out slightly in favor of one view or position, they often end up holding this view more strongly or extremely after discussions of it. This shift toward extremity can be quite dangerous in many settings.

A second factor involves the fact that during group discussion, most arguments presented are ones favoring the group's initial preference. As a result of hearing such arguments, persuasion occurs (presumably through the *central route* described in Chapter 4), and members shift increasingly toward the majority view. As a result of these shifts, the proportion of arguments favoring the group's initial preference increases, so that, ultimately, members convince themselves that this must be the "right" view. Group polarization results from this process (Vinokur & Burnstein, 1974).

Regardless of the precise basis for group polarization, it has important implications. The occurrence of polarization may lead many decision-making groups to adopt positions that are increasingly extreme, and therefore increasingly dangerous. In this context, it is chilling to speculate about the potential role of such shifts in disastrous decisions by political, military, or business groups, which should, by all accounts, have known better—for example, the decision by the "hard-liners" in the now-vanished Soviet Union to stage a coup to restore firm communist rule, or the decision by Apple computer *not* to license its software to other manufacturers—a decision that ultimately assured the success of its competitors. Did group polarization influence these and other disastrous decisions? It is impossible to say for sure, but research findings suggest that this is a real possibility.

Why does groupthink occur? Research findings (e.g., Tetlock et al., 1992; Kameda & Sugimori, 1993) suggest that two factors may be crucial. As just mentioned, one of these is a very high level of *cohesiveness* among group members. The second is *emergent group norms*—norms suggesting that the group is infallible, morally superior, and that because of these factors, there should be no further discussion of the issues at hand: The decision has been made, and the only task now is to support it as strongly as possible.

Closely related to these effects is a tendency to reject any criticism by outside sources—persons who are not members of the group. Criticism from outsiders is viewed with suspicion and attributed to negative motives rather than to a genuine desire to help. The result? It is largely ignored, and may even tend to strengthen the group's cohesiveness as members rally to defend the group against assaults by outsiders! Precisely such effects have recently been reported by Hornsey and Imani (2004). These researchers asked Australian college students to read comments about Australia supposedly made during an interview by a stranger. These comments were either positive ("When I think of Australians, I think of them as being fairly friendly and warm people") or negative ("When I think of Australians, I think of them as being fairly racist"). Moreover, they were attributed either to another Australian (an in-group member), a person from another country who had never lived in Australia (out-group—inexperienced), or to a person from another country who had once lived in Australia and therefore had experience with Australians (out-group—experienced). Participants then rated the source of the comments in terms of personal traits (e.g., intelligence, friendliness, openmindedness) and the extent to which this person's comments were designed to be constructive. Hornsey and Imani (2004) reasoned that when the comments made by the stranger were negative, both the stranger and the comments would receive lower ratings when this person was an out-group member than when he or she was an in-group member. Further, they reasoned that experience with the in-group (having lived in Australia) would not make any difference because this person was still not a member of the in-group. When the comments were positive, such effects were not expected to occur; after all, praise is acceptable, no matter what its source! As you can see from Figure 12.17, this is precisely what happened. When the stranger's comments were positive, whether this person was an Australian or someone from another country made no difference. But when this person made negative comments, both the stranger and

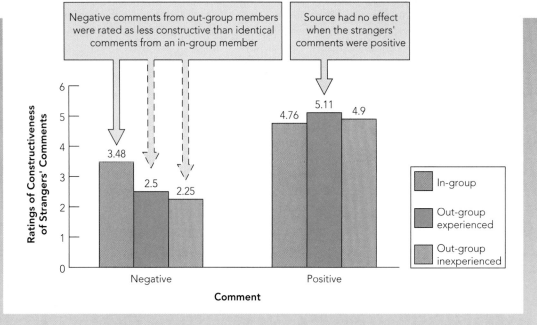

Figure 12.17 ■ Rejection of Criticism from Out-Group Members: One Reason Why Groups Sometimes Make Bad Decisions
When a stranger made critical comments about research participant's in-group (Australians), these comments were viewed more negatively when the stranger was supposedly from another country (an out-group member) than when the stranger was a member of the in-group (another Australian). Moreover, this was true even if the person had lived in Australia for several years. These findings suggest that groups' tendency to reject criticism from outsiders may be one reason why they often make very bad decisions. (*Source: Based on data from Hornsey & Imani, 2004.*)

We could continue this discussion, but by now the main point should be clear: Decision making by groups *can* be improved; however, active steps must be taken to achieve this goal. Left to their own devices, and without outside intervention, groups often slip easily into the "mental traps" outlined here—and often with devastating results.

KEY POINTS

★ It is widely believed that groups make better decisions than do individuals. However, research findings indicate that groups are often subject to *group polarization* effects, which lead them to make more extreme decisions than do individuals.

★ In addition, groups often suffer from *groupthink*—a tendency to assume that they can't be wrong and that information contrary to the groups' views should be rejected.

★ Although all aspects of groupthink have not been verified in careful research, recent findings indicate that groups tend to reject criticism from out-group members relative to identical criticism from in-group members.

★ Groups often engage in biased processing of information in order to reach the decisions they initially prefer, or to adhere to general values, such as the principle of *distributive justice*.

★ Group decision making can be improved in several ways, such as the *devil's advocate technique* and building *authentic dissent* into groups when they are formed.

SUMMARY AND REVIEW OF KEY POINTS

Groups: Why We Join Them. . . and Why We Leave

■ *Groups* are collections of persons perceived to form a coherent unit to some degree. The extent to which the group is perceived to form a coherent entity is known as *entiativity*.

■ Basic aspects of groups involve *roles, status, norms,* and *cohesiveness*. The effects of roles on our behavior are often very powerful, causing us to act in ways that we might not otherwise choose.

■ People gain status in a group for many reasons, ranging from physical characteristics (e.g., height) to various aspects of their behavior.

■ Another important feature of groups is their level of *cohesiveness*—the sum of all the factors that cause people to want to remain members, such as liking between them.

■ Recent findings indicate that one technique for gaining status is by expressing anger.

■ Joining groups confers important benefits on members, including increased self-knowledge, progress toward important goals, enhanced status, and attaining social change.

■ However, group membership also exacts important costs, such as loss of personal freedom and heavy demands on time, energy, and resources.

■ Individuals often withdraw from groups when they feel that the group has changed so much that it no longer reflects their basic values or beliefs.

■ The desire to join exclusive and prestigious groups may be so strong that individuals are willing to undergo painful and dangerous initiations in order to become members.

Effects of the Presence of Others: From Task Performance to Behavior in Crowds

■ The mere presence of other persons either as an audience or as coactors can influence our performance on many tasks. Such effects are known as *social facilitation* (or as social facilitation–inhibition effects).

■ The *drive theory of social facilitation* suggests that the presence of others is arousing and can either increase or reduce performance, depending on whether dominant responses in a given situation are correct or incorrect.

■ The *distraction–conflict theory* suggests that the presence of others induces conflicting tendencies to focus on the task being performed and on an audience or coactors. This can result both in increased arousal and narrowed attentional focus.

■ Recent findings offer support for the view that several kinds of audiences produce narrowed attentional focus among persons performing a task. This cognitive view of social facilitation helps explain why social facilitation occurs among animals as well as people.

■ When individuals work together on a task, *social loafing*—reduced output by each group member—sometimes occurs.

■ Social loafing can be reduced in several ways: by making outputs individually identifiable, by increasing commitment to the task and task importance, and by assuring that each member's

contributions to the task are unique.

■ When we are part of a large crowd, we experience reductions in both our self-awareness and our social identity. This, in turn, causes us to adopt the norms operating in the current situation—norms that often sanction impulsive, unrestrained behavior.

Coordination in Groups: Cooperation or Conflict?

■ *Cooperation*—working together with others to obtain shared goals—is a common aspect of social life.

■ However, cooperation does not develop in many situations in which it is possible, partly because such situations involve *social dilemmas*, in which individuals can increase their own gains by defection.

■ Several factors influence whether cooperation occurs in such situations. These include strong tendencies toward *reciprocity*, personal orientation toward cooperation, and communication.

■ Evolutionary psychologists suggest that our tendency to reciprocate may result from the fact that organisms that cooperate are more likely to survive and reproduce than are organisms that do not.

■ *Conflict* is a process that begins when individuals or groups perceive that others' interests are incompatible with their interests.

■ Conflict also can stem from social factors such as faulty attributions, poor communication, the tendency to perceive our own views as objective, and personal traits.

■ Conflict can be reduced in many ways, but *bargaining* and the

induction of *superordinate goals* seem to be most effective.

Perceived Fairness in Groups: Its Nature and Effects

■ Individuals wish to be treated fairly by the groups to which they belong. Fairness can be judged in terms of outcomes (*distributive justice*), in terms of procedures (*procedural justice*), or in terms of courteous treatment (*transactional justice*).

■ When individuals feel that they have been treated unfairly, they often take steps to restore fairness.

■ These steps range from such overt actions as reducing or protesting their contributions through such covert actions as employee theft or sabotage, or changes in perception, suggesting that others deserve better treatment.

Decision Making by Groups: How It Occurs and the Pitfalls It Faces

■ It is widely believed that groups make better decisions than do individuals. However, research findings indicate that groups are often subject to *group polarization* effects, which lead them to make more extreme decisions than do individuals.

■ In addition, groups often suffer from *groupthink*—a tendency to assume that they can't be wrong and that information contrary to the groups' views should be rejected.

■ Although all aspects of groupthink have not been verified in careful research, recent findings indicate that groups tend to reject criticism from out-group members relative to identical criticism from in-group members.

- Groups often engage in biased processing of information in order to reach the decisions they

initially prefer, or to adhere to general values, such as the principle of *distributive justice*.

- Group decision making can be improved in several ways, such as

the *devil's advocate technique* and building *authentic dissent* into groups when they are formed.

Connections — INTEGRATING SOCIAL PSYCHOLOGY

In this chapter, you read about . . .	In other chapters, you will find related discussions of . . .
the role of norms in the functioning of groups	the nature of norms and their role in social influence (Chapter 9) and aggression (Chapter 11)
the nature of cooperation and conflict and factors that affect their occurrence	other forms of behavior that either assist or harm others: discrimination (Chapter 6) helping behavior (Chapter 10) aggression (Chapter 11)
individuals' concern with others' evaluations of their performance	the effects of others' evaluations on our self-concept (Chapter 5) and on our liking for others (Chapter 7)
perceived fairness	the effects of perceived fairness on many other forms of social behavior, such as helping (Chapter 10) and aggression (Chapter 11), and the role of fairness in close relationships (Chapter 8)
the role of persuasion and other forms of social influence in group decision making	the nature of persuasion (Chapter 4), and various forms of social influence (Chapter 9)

Thinking about Connections

1. Do you see any connection between social loafing and perceived fairness? (Hint: If you have ever been in a group in which you suspected that other people were engaging in "social loafing," what did you do about it? And if you did take action, why?)

2. Suppose you had to give an important speech to a large audi-

ence. According to research on social facilitation, what would be the best way to prepare for this event?

3. Many situations in our lives involve social dilemmas: If we cooperate with others, everyone gains, but it is tempting to pursue our own self-interests, because, in the short-run, it is easier to do so and offers immediate gains. Can you think of such a situation in your own life? What did you do when you found yourself in it—the "right"

thing or the "easy" thing? Do you think that after reading this chapter, you might behave differently in such situations than you have in the past?

4. If groups are more likely to make extreme decisions, to reject input from outsiders, and to engage in biased processing of available information, why are so many important decisions still entrusted to groups? Do groups offer any advantages not discussed in this chapter?

Social facilitation effects seem to occur because the presence of others is arousing. This increases our tendency to perform dominant responses. If these dominant responses are correct, performance is improved; if they are incorrect, performance is impaired. This leads to two practical suggestions:

■ Study alone but take tests in the presence of others: If you study alone, you'll avoid the distraction caused by other persons and so will learn new materials more efficiently. If you have studied hard, your dominant responses will probably be correct ones, so the increased arousal generated by other persons will improve your performance.

■ Work on simple tasks (e.g., ones requiring pure physical effort) in front of an audience: The presence of an audience will increase your arousal, and so your ability to put out physical effort on such tasks.

Social loafing occurs when persons working together put out less effort than they would if they were working alone. This can be costly to you if *you* work hard but others goof off. Here's how you can avoid such an outcome:

■ Make sure that the contribution of each member of the group can be assessed individually—don't let social loafers hide!

■ Try to work only with people who are committed to the group's goals.

■ Make sure that each person's contribution is unique, not redundant with others. In that way, each person can be personally responsible for what she or he produces.

KEY TERMS

FOR MORE INFORMATION

Foddy, M., Smithson, M., Schneider, S., & Hogg, M. (Eds.). (2000). *Resolving social dilemmas: Dynamic, structural, and inter-group aspects* (pp. 281–293). Philadelphia: Psychology Press.
• In this book, experts on social dilemmas—and on cooperation and competition—discuss the nature of such situations and techniques for resolving them in a way that maximizes the outcomes of all persons concerned. This is an excellent source to consult if you'd like to know more about how people behave in situations involving conflicting pressures to cooperate and compete.

Hong, Y. Y., Levy, S. R., & Chiu, C. Y. (2003). *Lay theories and their role in the perception of social groups.* Mahwah, NJ: Erlbaum.
• This intriguing book reviews a number of views concerning the ways in which we think about groups and the factors that influence actual group behavior. Separate chapters examine the nature of entiativity (groupness), different types of groups, and the distinction between in-groups and out-groups. This is a very good source to consult if you'd like to know more about the nature of groups and how they function.

Tyler, T. R., & Blader, S. (2000). *Cooperation in groups: Procedural justice, social identity, and behavioral engagement.* Philadelphia: Psychology Press.
• Why do people choose to cooperate—or to compete—with others? The authors of this thought-provoking book examine people's views about the extent to which procedures in a group are fair to their motivation to cooperate or be helpful. An intriguing book if you want to know more about perceived justice (fairness) and its role in important group processes.

Witte, E., & Davis, J. H. (Eds.). (1996). *Understanding group behavior: Consensual action by small groups.* Hillsdale, NJ: Erlbaum.
• In this book, noted experts summarize existing knowledge about many aspects of group behavior. The sections on decision making are especially interesting and expand greatly on the information regarding the topic presented in this chapter.

 SOCIAL PSYCHOLOGY
IN ACTION
Applications to
Law and Health

In July 2002, Samuel Hirsch, a New York City attorney, filed a lawsuit against McDonald's on behalf of his client, Caesar Barber, claiming that Mr. Barber had been made obese by the high-fat, high-calorie meals served by McDonald's. "They said '100 percent beef,'" Mr. Barber remarked, "and I thought that meant it was good for you." Soon, Mr. Hirsch replaced this client with two others—hefty New York teenagers who claimed that they, too, had been made obese by McDonald's, whose foods, they argued, were not what they seemed to be, containing more fat, calories, and cholesterol than they had expected. The suit was dismissed by the courts, but the message they contained for the food industry was chilling, to say the least: If lawsuits on behalf of consumers had succeeded in winning hundreds of billions in damages from tobacco companies, could the food industry—and especially, the fast-food industry—be far behind? After all, concern over rising obesity rates and their grim implications for health was growing in the United States.

Taking note of this situation, the U.S. Congress passed the so-called Cheeseburger Bill—a law making it difficult for customers to sue food companies or restaurants for making them fat. Consumer groups were outraged, noting that ads by McDonald's and other food chains have targeted children, and that the foods sold by many restaurants contain ingredients customers do not know about, and would not want to consume if they did. In response, supporters of the new law noted that eating is *not* like addiction to tobacco and is under the control of individuals. Therefore, lawsuits against food companies and restaurants are not justified and will only succeed in costing these companies millions of dollars in legal fees to defend themselves against these groundless suits. As House Majority Leader Tom Delay of Texas put it, "If you eat a lot of food and you get sick, it's your responsibility, not the responsibility of the people who sold it to you."

What do you think? Are lawsuits against fast-food companies justified? Or should consumers take responsibility for their own diets—and health—and stop blaming others for problems they cause themselves? (See Figure A.1.) Clearly, this is a complex question and there are no simple answers. So why do we introduce it here? Mainly because it illustrates the fact that social psychology has a lot to say about this and many other matters relating to both the *legal system* and *personal health*. In fact, the basic methods, findings, and principles of social psychology have long been applied to understanding many a wide range of complex and intriguing issues in both of these areas (e.g., Levine & Wallach, 2002). For instance, included in a small sample of the many intriguing questions studied in this context by social psychologists are these: (1) *Why*, specifically, are Americans becoming obese? Do social norms and social influence play any role? (2) Does high self-esteem contribute to personal health, personal happiness, and interpersonal success (e.g., Baumeister et al., 2003)? (3) Do personality factors, such as the Type A pattern of behavior (see Chapter 11), or being a self-critical perfectionist (e.g., Dunkley, Zuroff, & Blankstein, 2003) play any role in personal health? (4) Can individuals be influenced by others to "invent" false memories—memories for events that never took place (e.g., Zaragoza et al., 2001)? And (5) Why do juries often accept false confessions, wrung from innocent persons by police, to be valid (e.g., Lassiter, 2002)? We consider these and many other issues in the pages that follow. Specifically, we begin by examining applications of social psychology to the legal system, focusing on such topics as how a jury's decisions are affected by the behavior and even appearance of attorneys and defendants, and some of the ways in which social factors can influence the memories of defendants and the accuracy (or inaccuracy!) of eyewitness testimony. Then we turn to applications of social psychology to personal health, examining such topics as how stress affects health, the role of personal characteristics in this relationship, and ways of promoting healthy lifestyles.

Figure A.1 ■ The Real Cause of Obesity?
Are fast-food restaurants responsible for the rapid rise in obesity in the United States and many other countries? Or are overweight people themselves to blame? This question raises complex legal and ethical issues, and is closely related to public health.

Figure A.2 ■ Justice: Is It Really Blind?
Ideally, justice should be blind to the background, characteristics, gender, and ethnic identity of individuals—everyone should be treated equally. In fact, however, this goal is easier to imagine than to attain.

Social Psychology and the Legal System

Is justice really blind? It is shown this way (blindfolded) on many court buildings throughout the world, and this is the ideal: All persons should be equal before the law and treated in the same, impartial manner (see Figure A.2). After having read many of the chapters in this book, however, you probably realize that though this is an admirable ideal, it may be hard to achieve in real life. As we saw in earlier discussions, it is very difficult, if not impossible, for us to ignore the words, behaviors, or personal characteristics of other persons, or to dismiss from our thinking and decisions preconceived ideas, beliefs, and stereotypes that we have developed over years or even decades. So although we all wish that justice could be totally impartial and fair, we must temper this desire with the recognition that making it—and our legal system—live up to these goals is a very tall order! To move toward it, many social psychologists believe, we must first understand the potential sources of error and bias that either creep into the legal system or, in some cases, are actively introduced by its key players—attorneys, judges, and police. Once we understand the possible risks, we may be able to take steps to correct these problems and reduce, if not totally eliminate, them from the system. The result? Justice would indeed be more fair and impartial, as we all desire. What are some of these potential pitfalls and how can we seek to reduce them? These are the questions we now consider.

Before the Trial Begins: Effects of Police Interrogation

Long before a case reaches a courtroom, two major factors influence the testimony that will eventually be presented and the attitudes or views with which the jurors begin: (1) the way the police question witnesses and suspects and (2) the information about the case as it is presented in the media.

■ Police Procedures: What Is the Best Way to Interrogate Suspects?

After police take a suspect into custody, they interrogate this person in various ways to prepare the ground for further legal proceedings. How do they handle this important responsibility? Most of us would prefer that they adopt what is known as an *inquisitorial approach*—a search for the truth—rather than an *adversarial approach*—an approach in which they seek to prove guilt, perhaps by wringing a confession out of an unwilling defendant (Williamson, 1993). In other words, most of us would prefer that the police seek to gather information rather than engage in powerful forms of persuasion or social influence to "force" defendants to confess (see Chapter 9).

In fact, though, research findings indicate that even if police do *not* engage in such actions, serious forms of bias can enter the process. Suspects, who find themselves in a highly stressful and emotion-charged setting, may sometimes become highly agitated and confused, with the result that they confess to crimes they did not commit. And then, to make matters worse, jurors may tend to accept these confessions as accurate, with the tragic result that innocent persons are convicted and sent to prison—or worse—for crimes committed by other, unknown individuals.

How can such disasters—such distortions of the impartial and fair legal system we all desire be avoided? One possibility involves the requirement that all interrogations of defendants by police be videotaped. This, it is assumed, prevents police from using strong-arm tactics, and also, when the videotapes are shown to jurors, permits them to make accurate judgments about whether a confession is true or false. On the basis of this reasoning, videotaping has been instituted in several countries (e.g., the United Kingdom) and in many states in the United States (see Figure A.3).

There is a serious problem with such procedures, however, one involving an effect we examined earlier in this book: our tendency to perceive whatever is the focus of our attention as being more important and more central to subsequent events than

Figure A.3 ■ Videotaping Interrogations: Is It Really Effective?
In several countries, police are required to record all interrogations of suspects. Research findings indicate that though this may indeed prevent police from using abusive interrogation techniques, it does not prevent jurors from perceiving false confessions given under pressure as voluntary.

whatever is *not* the focus of our attention (see Chapters 2 and 6). For instance, if we observe two people holding a casual conversation, the one who is most directly in our view is the one we perceive as being more influential—the one who exerted most effect on the conversation. Applying this effect to videotapes of police interrogations, Lassiter and his colleagues (e.g., Lassiter et al., 2002) noted that many of these tapes focus entirely on the defendant. As a result, illusory correlation may occur, and jurors will tend to view any confessions obtained as true and voluntary because the defendant is in the center of their attention—in fact, the defendant is the only person they see. To test this prediction, Lassiter and his coworkers conducted a series of studies in which participants viewed videotapes of interrogations, in which the suspect confessed. In one condition, the camera focused entirely on the suspect, while in another, both the suspect and the interrogator were shown. Everything else was held constant—the suspect's answers, the interrogator's questions, and so on. Results were dramatic: Participants rated the confessions in the first condition (only the suspect was shown) as more voluntary than those in the second, despite the fact that the suspect's words were identical! Further, they rated the suspects as more guilty and recommended harsher sentences in the suspect-only condition than in the condition in which both suspect and interrogator were shown.

Why does this occur? Further research (e.g., Lassiter, 2002) indicates that these results have to do mainly with how we extract and initially register information from events we observe. Whatever serves as the focus of our attention becomes the center of our initial thoughts, and this, in turn, causes it to strongly affect our later judgments. Whatever the precise mechanism, however, these findings have important implications. They suggest that videotaping police interrogations *can* be beneficial, but only if the camera shows both the interrogator and the defendant. Focusing on the defendant (suspect) alone can lead jurors and others to overestimate the extent to which any confessions were offered voluntarily.

Another factor that can strongly affect the outcome of police interrogations is the location of such procedures—where they take place (Schooler & Loftus, 1986). For this reason, the investigators much prefer to conduct a formal investigation in an intimidating location such as police headquarters rather than in a nonthreatening location such as the suspect's home or place of work. Both the location and the authority of the questioner (a government representative) reinforce the ordinary citizen's belief that the one asking the questions is an expert who possesses detailed knowledge of the case (Gudjonsson & Clark, 1986). The officer is in charge of what happens during the interview, and the person being questioned is not supposed to interrupt or argue about what is said. Under these circumstances, three factors encourage compliance with the interrogator's questions: The witness or suspect usually experiences (1) some *uncertainty* about the "right" answers, (2) some degree of *trust* in the officer asking the questions, and (3) an unspoken *expectation* that he or she is supposed to know the answer. As a result, rather than saying "I don't know," "I don't remember," or "I'm not sure," most people tend to provide an answer, at least a tentative one. Once an answer is made, however, the person is inclined to believe it, especially if the interrogator provides immediate reinforcement with a nod or by saying "Good," for example. As is described in a later section, this can lead the person being questioned to believe and even remember the details of something that never happened.

Additional Aspects of Interrogation: Social Influence in Action

In seeking a confession, interrogators need not resort to heavy-handed methods, because more subtle approaches can often be just as effective (Kassin & McNall, 1991). For example, in interacting with a suspect, an interrogator can minimize the strength of the evidence and the seriousness of the charge, perhaps blaming the victim rather than the suspect for what happened. When an interrogator minimizes the crime and seems supportive, there is an implicit promise that the punishment will be relatively mild. Not only is this technique, which is based on ingratiation (see Chapter 9) effective, it avoids the legal problems associated with threatening a suspect. Jurors tend to discount a confession obtained by threats of punishment, but the minimization approach is perceived as acceptable. In fact, however, although this "soft-sell technique" may seem to be noncoercive, it is simply a less obvious way to elicit compliance. In effect, the suspect confesses after being lulled into a false sense of security.

Other tactics of social influence, too, are used by interrogators. Kassin and Kiechel (1996) point out that police sometimes present suspects with bogus polygraph results, fake fingerprint data, inaccurate eyewitness identifications, and false information about the confession of a fellow suspect—all in an attempt to persuade them to confess. The power of such procedures is clearly illustrated by research conducted by Kassin and Kiechel (1996), who conducted a study in which college students were led to believe that they were taking part in a laboratory experiment involving reaction time. Each participant interacted with a female accomplice who read a list of letters; the participants' task was to respond by typing the letter on a keyboard. There was a special warning *not* to press the ALT key because this would cause the program to crash and the data to be lost. The pace of the study was set by the accomplice to be either *fast,* so that the participant would be less sure of what might have happened (high vulnerability), or *slow* (low vulnerability). After the experiment was underway, the computer suddenly ceased functioning, and the apparently upset experimenter rushed in and accused the participant of pressing the key despite the warning not to do so: "Did you hit the ALT key?" To determine the effect of false evidence—one potential technique for generating false confessions—the accomplice either said that she had seen the participant hit the key or that she had not seen what happened. No one actually hit that key, but the question was whether each individual would *comply* by signing a false confession, *internalize* the false confession by telling another student privately that she or he pressed the key, and *confabulate* by later recalling false details about the transgression that supposedly had occurred.

Results indicated that fully 69 percent of the participants signed the false confession, that 28 percent internalized their guilt, and that 9 percent produced confabulated details about their actions. These effects were stronger when the study pace was fast and when false evidence was present. In fact, when the study pace was fast and false evidence was provided, every participant confessed, most internalized their guilt, and over a third falsely remembered details of their "crime"! So, not only does false evidence and uncertainty about what to do increase the likelihood of false confessions, these factors also increase the likelihood that people will believe their own false confessions and remember imaginary details about about a crime they did not commit. As noted throughout this book, and especially in Chapter 9, social influence really *is* a powerful tool, and it can be turned to good or evil purposes, depending on who happens to be wielding it.

Effects of Media Coverage on Perceptions of Defendants

Many legal proceedings—especially ones involving famous defendants or especially dramatic crimes—receive a great deal of coverage from the media. For instance, when Martha Stewart was put on trial in 2004, daily events during the trial appeared in hundreds of newspapers and on virtually every news program on television (see Figure A.4). Clearly, such massive coverage can have powerful effects on the public's perceptions of defendants and can, in some cases, even influence jurors. When a suspect is arrested, we quickly learn a great deal about that person, often with photos and videotapes of the accused wearing handcuffs, surrounded by officers of the law. Because such coverage does not tend to emphasize evidence pointing to the defendant's innocence, there is a strong tendency to form a negative impression of the suspect based on the *primacy*

Figure A.4 ■ **Can the Media Affect the Outcome of Legal Proceedings?**
When famous persons are charged with crimes, or when an especially
shocking crime is committed, media coverage of the trial is usually extensive.
Growing evidence suggests that such coverage can shape public opinion
about the alleged crimes and even influence jurors' decisions.

effect—the tendency for information we receive first to strongly influence our impressions of others (see Chapter 3). Moreover, people tend to believe assertions made in the media (Gilbert, Tafarodi, & Malone, 1993). The result? Defendants are often viewed as guilty by the public even before the trial begins.

Because of these effects on public opinion (including the people who will eventually serve as jurors), pretrial publicity tends to benefit the prosecution and harm the defense. Moran and Cutler (1991) have documented just such effects of pretrial coverage on the assumption of guilt among potential jurors in actual cases. In general, the greater the amount of publicity about a crime, the greater the tendency of jurors to convict whoever is accused of committing it (Linz & Penrod, 1992). According to Moran (1993), government officials take advantage of these effects by providing as much crime information as possible to newspapers and television stations. The goal is for the public and potential jurors to form a negative impression of the defendant and thus support the government's case.

Research clearly indicates that media presentations also affect the final verdict of many trials, despite efforts to screen out jurors who have been exposed to news about the crime and to remind them of the importance of maintaining an open mind and an impartial attitude until they hear all of the evidence. According to O'Connell (1988), asking those who are called for jury duty whether they can be fair and impartial is "as useless as asking an alcoholic if he can control drinking." In either instance, a "yes" response means very little.

One solution is to change the law. For example, the United States allows publicity before and during trials, while Canada restricts such coverage in order to avoid "polluting" the jury. A simpler solution to the media problem is suggested by findings reported by Fein, McCloskey, and Tomlinson (1997). The biasing effects of pretrial publicity can be greatly weakened if the jurors are given reason to be suspicious about *why* incriminating evidence might have been given to the media. That is, this tactic shifts attention away from the content of the leaked evidence to the underlying *motivation* of those who leaked the evidence.

KEY POINTS

Eyewitnesses: Are They as Accurate as We'd Like to Believe?

Eyewitness testimony—evidence given by persons who have witnessed a crime—plays an important role in many trials. At first glance, this makes a great deal of sense: What better source of information about the events of a crime than the persons who actually saw them? But there is an important "joker" in this deck: As we have seen over and over again, human perception, thought, and memory are far from perfect. On the contrary, all of these basic processes—building blocks of our understanding of the social world—are subject to a wide range of errors and distortions. This leads to an intriguing, and important, question: Are eyewitnesses really as accurate as we would like to believe?

Unfortunately, from the point of view of developing a totally fair, impartial, and accurate legal system, the answer is clear: They are not. In fact, eyewitnesses often falsely identify innocent persons as criminals (Wells, 1993), make mistakes about important details concerning a crime (Loftus, 2003), and sometimes report "remembering" events that did not actually take place (e.g., Zaragoza et al., 2001). Why do such errors occur? How can persons who were actually present when a crime occurred make serious errors about it? This question becomes even more puzzling when it is realized that most eyewitnesses are doing their best to be as accurate as possible; they are definitely *not* faking their testimony. So, what is the cause of their errors—errors that can sometimes lead to conviction of innocent persons? The answer seems to center around several factors that, together, can produce distortions in memory. These include *suggestibility*—witnesses are sometimes influenced by *leading questions* and similar techniques used by attorneys or police officers (we return to this topic in the next section)—and errors with respect to *source monitoring*—eyewitnesses often attribute their memories to the wrong source. For instance, they identify a suspect in a lineup as the person who committed a crime because they remember having seen this individual before, and they assume this was at the scene of the crime; in fact, his or her face may be familiar because they saw it in an album of mug shots. Let's now take a look at some of the major factors that make eyewitness testimony less accurate than we would wish. Specifically, we'll examine three of these factors: the role of *intense emotions*, the passage of *time* between a crime and eyewitness testimony, and various kinds of *error or distortion in memory*.

■ The Role of Emotion: Affect and Cognition Revisited

In an earlier discussion (Chapter 2), we noted that our current feelings or emotions can often exert powerful effects on our cognition—our thoughts, what we remember, and our decisions and judgments (e.g., Martin & Clore, 2001). In fact, witnesses very often make mistakes, in part because intense emotions tend to exert such effects on their

eyewitness testimony
Evidence given by persons who have witnessed a crime; plays an important role in many trials.

Figure A.5 ◼ **The Uniform I Never Saw, but Remember: An Illustration of the Effects of Misleading Postevent Information**
Although I (Robert Baron) seem to have vivid memories of my great-grandfather's uniform (similar to the one shown here), I now realize that I could never have actually seen it. So what do I recall? Probably, my father's descriptions of the uniform.

information processing. Such effects often occur when a witness is also the victim of a crime. Loftus (1992a) described a case in which a rape victim identified the wrong man as the rapist; this individual, though innocent, was convicted, imprisoned, and eventually released only when the actual rapist confessed. Beginning with the applied research of Munsterberg (1907) at the start of the twentieth century, numerous experiments have made it clear that even the most honest, intelligent, and well-meaning witnesses to an event can make errors. Mistaken identity is not a rare event; inaccurate eyewitnesses constitute the single most important factor in the wrongful conviction of innocent defendants, and strong emotions often contribute to such tragic mistakes (Wells, 1993; Wells, Luus, & Windschitl, 1994).

◼ Time and Intervening Information

Another major obstacle to accuracy among eyewitnesses is the passage of time between witnessing an event and testifying about what was seen and heard (Loftus, 1992b). During that interval, the witness is almost always exposed to *misleading postevent information* from police questions, news stories, and the statements made by others. Such information becomes incorporated into what the witness remembers: It all blends together as part of what *seems* to be remembered. Inaccuracy occurs because eyewitnesses can no longer distinguish between what is actually remembered and what has been learned subsequently. For instance, sitting here now, I (Robert Baron) have vivid memories of a uniform that belonged to my great-grandfather who immigrated to the United States from Austria, and was in the Austrian Army before coming here. I can visualize the brass buttons, gold braid, and velvet material of the jacket (see Figure A.5). But about ten years ago, when I asked my father about what happened to this uniform, he told me, "You could never have seen it. We threw it out long before you were born." So what do I remember? Not the uniform itself; what I recall is my father's descriptions of it, told to me when I was a child. Try as I may, I cannot now separate truth from fiction in these memories, and the same kind of effects often happen to eyewitnesses.

◼ Memory Distortion and Construction: Remembering What Never Happened

Now, we come to what is, perhaps, the most powerful and certainly the most dramatic source of error in eyewitness testimony: the limitations of human memory. Although memory—our systems for storing and later retrieving information about the world—is truly amazing (e.g., it can store virtually unlimited amounts of information for years or even decades), it is far from perfect. In fact, memory is subject to many kinds of error. Perhaps the most important of these from the point of view of this discussion, however, involves what has often been termed *memory construction*—the development of "memories" for events that never took place or experiences we never had. Where do these *false memories*—memories for events we never experienced—come from? The answer seems to be that they are somehow "planted" in our minds by the words or actions of others. Often, this is done unintentionally. For instance, some therapists urge their patients to look at old family photo albums in order to recover "repressed" memories of childhood sexual abuse. Recent evidence suggests that doing so may help to trigger long-forgotten memories, but can also, under some conditions, lead to false memories about events that never happened (Lindsay et al., 2004).

In other situations, in contrast, such memories may be the result of deliberate efforts to create them. Unfortunately, this sometimes occurs in the legal system when police and attorneys attempt to wring confessions from suspects or get witnesses to provide "evidence" valuable to their case. Whatever the basis, a great deal of evidence suggests that false memories can be readily created and that once they are, they can strongly influence our thoughts and our judgments, including judgments of guilt or innocence by jurors (e.g., Loftus, 2003).

How, specifically, can false memories be created? One way is through simply imagining an event. Indeed, recent evidence indicates that simply imagining an event can generate false memories about it. For instance, in an intriguing study (Mazzoni & Memon, 2003), students at a British university were asked to read and imagine one event and to read a one-page description of another. One of the events was one that students frequently experience—having a baby tooth removed by a dentist. The other was an event that could never happen because it is illegal in the United Kingdom—having a nurse remove a skin sample from their little finger. One group of participants was asked to imagine the impossible event and read a description of the frequent one; the other group imagined the frequent event and read a description of the impossible one. One week later, both groups were given a memory test for the events. As you can see from Figure A.6, being asked to imagine these events increased memory for them; more importantly, it increased memory for the impossible event as much as for the possible one! So, clearly, just imagining an event can generate memories for it.

Another factor that generates false memories involves actively making up information about some event while attempting to answer a question about it—something known as *confabulating* (e.g., Ackil & Zaragoza, 1998). Apparently, when individuals make up information about an event or experience that never took place, they often come to believe it—to accept it as true. Moreover, and even more surprising, this is true

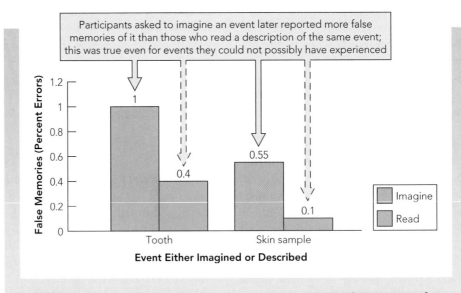

Figure A.6 ■ Merely Imagining an Event Can Create Vivid Memories of It
Individuals either read a description of an event or were asked to imagine it. Later, they were tested for memories of these events. Regardless of whether the event was one they could actually have experienced, imagining it led to the formation of vivid memories of it. (*Source: Based on data from Mazzoni & Memom, 2003.*)

even when they are forced to confabulate—when they are told to make up answers to questions about events that never occurred. For instance, after watching a clip from a Walt Disney movie, participants in one study (Zaragoza et al., 2001) either were told to make up answers to questions about events that never occurred in the film (e.g., one of the characters being seriously hurt) or were not instructed to do this (they were free to answer, "That never happened"). Half of the participants heard the experimenter state "That's right" after they provided their made-up answers to the question, while half did not receive this kind of confirmatory feedback. When their memory for events in the film was tested both one week later and four to six weeks later, results were clear: At both times, persons who had been instructed to create false memories remembered more of this confabulated information than those who had not, and rated it as more accurate. Moreover, these effects were especially true for persons who had received the "That's right" confirmatory feedback.

These results, plus those of many other studies (e.g., Mazzoni et al., 1999), indicate that false memories can be readily planted in our minds, and that, often, we have considerable difficulty telling these memories from real ones. Clearly, this has important—and disturbing—implications for accuracy and fairness of the legal system, especially, as we'll soon note, if used for deceitful purposes by attorneys whose sense of ethics is in need of repair!

■ Recovering Forgotten Memories of Traumatic Events

Before concluding this discussion of the role of memory in eyewitness testimony, we should touch briefly on one additional and closely related topic: memories of traumatic events occurring early in life. You may have heard of various instances in which an adult, often as the result of therapy, suddenly remembers a traumatic past event, most often centering on having been the victim of sexual abuse. Are such memories, when they are reported to therapists, really accurate? In other words, are they memories for actual, traumatic events, or are they false memories suggested, at least in part, by the techniques therapists used to "shake them loose" from repression or other factors that make them hard to remember? Evidence on this issue is mixed, but the studies reviewed above concerning the planting of false memories suggest that at least some of these reports of early traumatic events may also be false. That at least some of these memories are false is indicated by the fact that some refer to events that could not possibly have occurred, such as of sexual abuse by aliens from another planet, abuse during a previous lifetime, memories from the womb, and abuse by Satan-worshipping cult members (Humphreys, 1998). Of course, this in no way implies that all such memories are false. Childhood sexual abuse does indeed occur—it can often be verified by medical authorities (e.g., Goodman et al., 2003). However, there seem to be sufficient questions about the nature of repression, and sufficient evidence that some "memories" of traumatic events can be unintentionally constructed, to suggest the need for caution.

■ Increasing Eyewitness Accuracy

So, taking all this evidence into account, how would we answer the question posed at the start of this section: Are eyewitnesses as accurate as we would like to believe? Unfortunately, we would have to reply, "No." Certainly, they are not always inaccurate; indeed, in many cases, eyewitnesses do a very good job of describing the events they have observed. But there is enough room for distortion and error to suggest the need for techniques designed to improve the performance of eyewitnesses in the courtroom. One promising approach involves conducting improved interviews with witnesses—interviews that may enhance their ability to remember crucial information accurately. In such *cognitive interviews,* eyewitnesses are asked to report everything they can remember; this provides them with multiple retrieval cues (aids to memory) and can increase accuracy of recall. In addition, they are sometimes asked to describe events

Figure A.7 ■ **Police Lineups: Do They Help?**
Police often use lineups, in which eyewitnesses to a crime are asked to select the guilty person from among several persons. Although these procedures are sometimes effective, they are also susceptible to errors that reduce their accuracy. Improved lineup procedures such as blank lineups (in which the witnesses first see only innocent people) can help reduce the likelihood of such errors.

from different perspectives and in several different orders, not just the one in which the events actually occurred. These and other steps seem to increase the accuracy of eyewitness testimony, but they are far from perfect, so the basic problem remains: Eyewitness testimony is not nearly as accurate as was once widely believed. For this reason, it is probably best to view it as an imperfect and potentially misleading source of information.

Other efforts have focused on improving police *lineups* as a technique for identifying guilty persons. (Lineups involve procedures in which several persons are presented to eyewitnesses, who have the task of indicating whether any of them were the person they saw commit a crime; see Figure A.7). Wells and Luus (1990) suggest that a lineup is analogous to a social psychological experiment. The officer conducting the lineup is the *experimenter,* the eyewitnesses are the *research participants,* the suspect is the primary *stimulus,* a witness's positive identification constitutes the *response data,* and the nonsuspects and the arrangement of the lineup constitute the *research design.* Also, the police have a *hypothesis* that the suspect is guilty. Finally, for either experiments or testimony, the data are stated in terms of *probability* because neither experiments nor lineups can provide absolute certainty. In Chapter 1, we described several factors that can interfere with obtaining accurate experimental results—for example, the absence of a control group. The same factors can interfere with the accuracy with which a witness makes a positive identification.

Based on this analogy, police can improve the accuracy of lineups by using common experimental procedures such a *control group.* For example, the *blank-lineup control* means that a witness is first shown a lineup containing only innocent nonsuspects (Wells, 1984). If the witness fails to identify any of them, there is increased confidence in his or her accuracy. If an innocent person *is* identified, the witness is informed and then cautioned about the danger of making a false identification, thus improving accuracy when actual lineups are presented.

Other procedures that improve accuracy include the presentation of pictures of the crime scene and of the victim to the witness before an identification is made (Cutler, Penrod, & Martens, 1987), showing one member of the lineup at a time rather than a group (Leary, 1988), and encouraging witnesses to give their first impressions (Dunning & Stern, 1994). The goal, of course, is to increase the accuracy with which guilty persons are identified, and to the extent that objective is reached, the fairness of the entire legal system will be enhanced.

KEY POINTS

★ Eyewitnesses are not as accurate as is commonly believed. Several factors (e.g., intense emotion, the passage of time since the observed events, and errors in memory) contribute to this fact.

★ Individuals often construct false memories—memories for events that never happened.

Imagination and confabulation (making up information while answering questions) contribute to the development of such false memories.

★ The accuracy of *eyewitness testimony* can be improved through the use of improved interviews and better lineup procedures.

Key Participants in a Trial: Effects of Attorneys, Judges, Defendants, and Jurors

Research has repeatedly shown that the outcome of a trial is not simply a matter of evidence and logic. These certainly matter, but their effects are combined with the effects of seemingly irrelevant factors such as the appearance, style, and other characteristics of the key participants—attorneys, judges, defendants, and jurors. Here, we focus on ways in which attorneys, jurors, and defendants can affect the legal process.

■ Attorneys: Adversaries for the Prosecution and the Defense

In the legal system of the United States and many other countries, the two sides do not cooperate to reach a common goal such as "the truth." Instead, they compete in a struggle to win—to obtain the outcome they seek (an acquittal or a conviction; Garcia, Darley, & Robinson, 2001). An important aspect of this "battle" is something that occurs before the trial begins—*voir dire*. This procedure allows attorneys for each side to examine potential jurors to determine who is acceptable to them and who is not. (*Voir dire* is French for "to see and to speak with.") The stated goal is to choose the most competent and impartial jurors, but, in fact, the opposing sides do their best to choose ones they believe will be helpful to their side. Fortunately, research findings indicate that even experienced attorneys are not highly successful in predicting how jurors will actually respond to the opposing arguments, so they can't really choose ones who are guaranteed to produce the outcome they want.

During the trial itself, attorneys are *not* permitted to ask **leading questions**—questions designed to generate specific responses—when examining their own witnesses. For example, a leading question would be "How much blood did you see on Mrs. Jones's car seat?" An acceptable version would be "Would you please describe what you saw when you looked into Mrs. Jones's car?" In cross-examination, however, leading questions *are* permitted, and they can sometimes exert strong effects on how witnesses respond (Smith & Ellsworth, 1987).

When they make their closing arguments, attorneys for each side get one last chance to influence how jurors will vote, and much of what they say is designed to do just that.

leading questions
Questions by attorneys during a trial that are designed to generate specific responses.

"Your honor, before the jury retires to reach a verdict, my client wishes to present each of them with a little gift of jewelry."

© 1982 United Press Syndicate

Figure A.8 ■ Attorneys: Influencing the Jury Is Their Goal!
Although attorneys would not be permitted to use the kind of tactic shown here to influence jurors, they do employ a wide range of procedures to make jurors favorable to their side. (*Source: HERMAN reprinted by permission of Newspaper Enterprise Association, Inc.*)

Although their tactics may not be as obvious as those shown in Figure A.8, the opposing attorneys do their best to influence members of the jury in every way they can.

One more point: Suppose that during a trial, an attorney asks a leading question or makes a comment the judge finds inappropriate—perhaps one damaging to the defendant's character. The judge then instructs the jury to "disregard that remark." The assumption is that this information can be ignored by the jury, just as it can be eliminated from the court records. Is this correct? A growing body of evidence gathered by psychologists suggests that it is on very shaky ground. Many studies indicate that information that evokes emotional reactions may be almost impossible to ignore or disregard (e.g., Edwards, Heindel, & Louis-Dreyfus, 1996; Wegner & Gold, 1995). For example, consider a study conducted by Edwards and Bryan (1997).

These researchers reasoned that information that is dramatic or evokes emotional reactions may be a potent source of what is known as **mental contamination**—a process in which our judgments, emotions, or behavior are influenced by mental processing that is not readily under our control (Wilson & Brekke, 1994). Specifically, Edwards and Bryan suggested that information that evokes emotional reactions may be especially likely to produce such effects, because emotional reactions are diffuse in nature and tend to trigger thought that is *not* careful, rational, or analytic in nature. The result: Once we are exposed to emotion-generating information, we can't ignore it, no matter how hard we try.

To test this reasoning, Edwards and Bryan conducted research in which participants played the role of jurors. Participants read a transcript of a murder trial that contained information about the defendant's previous criminal record. In one condition, this information was presented in an emotion-generating manner (it described a *vicious* attack he had performed on a woman); in another condition, it was presented in a more neutral manner (the transcript simply mentioned that he was accused of a prior assault). For half of the participants, the transcript indicated that this information about the defendant was admissible and should be considered, while for the other half, it was described as inadmissible and jurors were specifically instructed to ignore it in reaching their verdict.

After reading the transcript, participants were asked to rate the guilt of the defendant and to recommend a sentence for him. Edwards and Bryan (1997) predicted that because of the factors described above, participants would *not* be able to ignore the emotion-generating information. In fact, when told to do so, they might find themselves thinking about it more often than when *not* told to do this—a kind of *rebound* effect observed in many other studies in which individuals are instructed *not* to think about something (e.g., Wegner, 1994). As a result, they would view the defendant as more guilty and recommend a harsher sentence for him under these conditions (when exposed to emotion-generating information and told to ignore it). Results strongly confirmed these predictions. These findings have important implications for the legal

mental contamination
A process in which our judgments, emotions, or behavior are influenced by mental processing that is not readily under our control.

system, in which jurors are often told to ignore emotion-provoking information. The results obtained by Edwards and Bryan and other psychologists suggest that this may be an impossible task. In fact, there is growing recognition of this and related issues on the part of attorneys and judges. In recent years, legal systems in many states and countries have sought advice from *forensic psychologists*—psychologists who specialize in studying the cognitive and behavioral factors that influence legal proceedings and the law. On the basis of their recommendations, changes have been made in the legal systems of many countries to improve their overall fairness. Clearly, this is one way in which the findings of social psychology contribute to human welfare.

Defendant Characteristics and Juror Characteristics

Truly "blind" justice would be uninfluenced by the characteristics of defendants or jurors: Only the evidence—the "facts"—would count. But trials are, in a sense, social encounters among the key participants—attorneys, defendants, and jurors. Thus, it is not at all surprising that many of the factors that influence behavior in other social settings also play a role in the courtroom—much as we would wish it were otherwise. Let's see what some of these factors are and how they can shape the outcome of legal proceedings (Levine & Wallach, 2002).

Defendant's Race, Gender, and Appearance. In the United States, African American defendants have generally been found to be at a disadvantage. For example, they are more likely than whites to be convicted of murder and to receive the death penalty; blacks are proportionally overrepresented on death row (Sniffen, 1999). The most obvious—but not necessarily correct—hypothesis is that white judges and juries tend to be racially biased. It is also possible that African Americans are more likely than whites to be raised in a subculture of poverty, unemployment, and the glorification of antisocial role models. Also, if whites as a group have an economic advantage, that also means that they are better able to afford more skillful attorneys. Whatever the precise basis, it is clear that even today, the race of defendants can influence the outcomes they receive in our legal system, and this is unacceptable.

Race, however, is not the only personal characteristic of defendants that can play a role in legal proceedings. In addition, their physical appearance (attractiveness), gender, and socioeconomic status are also important. For example, persons accused of most major crimes are less likely to be found guilty if they are physically attractive, female, and of high rather than low socioeconomic status (Mazzella & Feingold, 1994). Attractiveness has been studied the most, and in real as well as mock trials, attractive defendants have a major advantage over unattractive ones with respect to being acquitted, receiving a light sentence, and gaining the sympathy of the jurors (see Figure A.9 on page 518; Downs & Lyons, 1991; Quigley, Johnson, & Byrne, 1995; Wuensch, Castellow, & Moore, 1991).

Beyond these personal characteristics, the way defendants behave in the courtroom can also have strong effects. For example, smiling does not influence judgments of guilt, but a smiling defendant is more likely to be recommended for leniency than a nonsmiling one (LaFrance & Hecht, 1995). The fact that a defendant denies guilt has no effect on the jury, but if he or she goes on to deny accusations that were not actually made, that person is perceived as untrustworthy, nervous, responsible for the crime, *and* is more likely to be found guilty.

Jurors' Gender, Beliefs, Attitudes, and Values. We have already discussed some of the problems involved in jury selection and in the effect of race on the outcome of trials. Gender also plays a role. One of the consistent differences between male and female jurors is in reaction to cases involving sexual assault. For example, in judging what occurred in cases of rape, men are more likely than women to conclude that the

Figure A.9 ■ Defendant's Appearance: A Factor That Shouldn't Matter—but Does!
Research findings indicate that attractive defendants have a big "edge" in the courtroom: They are convicted less often and tend to receive lighter sentences or smaller fines than unattractive defendants.

sexual interaction was consensual (Harris & Weiss, 1995). Schutte and Hosch (1997) analyzed the results of thirty-six studies of simulated cases of rape and child abuse. In responding to defendants accused of either crime, women were more likely than men to vote for conviction.

Jurors also differ with respect to the attitudes and beliefs they hold. For instance, they vary in terms of the extent to which they tend to place the blame for criminal acts on society or on the defendant. Thus, those with a *leniency bias* (the assumption that the defendant is also a victim) are least likely to vote for guilt (MacCoun & Kerr, 1988). At the opposite extreme, jurors high in *legal authoritarianism* (the assumption that the defendant is responsible for the crime) are most likely to vote for guilt (Narby, Cutler, & Moran, 1993). In Australia as well as in the United States, relatively authoritarian jurors (i.e., jurors who tend to see the world in black-and-white terms and favor harsh punishment) tend to react to offenses as more serious and hence as deserving punishment (Feather, 1996).

Jurors also differ in the way they process information, and these differences can lead to more or less accurate decisions. For example, about a third have already made up their minds about the trial by the time the opening arguments are made. As the trial progresses, 75 to 85 percent begin to favor one side over the other, and this bias affects how subsequent evidence is processed (Carlson & Russo, 2001). As we saw in Chapter 2, the *confirmation bias* may begin to operate, with the result that only information consistent with the jurors' initial opinion is noticed and remembered. The outcome is that jurors make up their minds with increasing certainty, even though they are not really paying careful attention to both sides. In contrast, other jurors process information by constructing at least two different views or schemas, one for "guilty" and one for "innocent." As a result, all information being presented can fit into one schema or the other; so, these jurors do not make up their minds prematurely, before hearing all available evidence.

Overall, it appears that what happens in courtrooms often mirrors what occurs in many other social settings: People's thoughts, judgments, and memories are strongly shaped by their current feelings, by various heuristics and biases, by their first impressions of the major participants (attorneys, defendants, judges), and by a host of other social factors. As a result, the task of making legal proceedings as fair and accurate as possible is a complex one, and will require close cooperation between social psychologists and legal authorities. The goal sought is so important, though, that this is one task that no society interested in the welfare of its citizens can afford to overlook.

KEY POINTS

★ During pretrial voir dire procedures, attorneys often try to select jurors who will be favorable to their side.

★ During trials, attorneys sometimes ask *leading questions* or present evidence that is inadmissible. Research findings indicate that jurors find it very hard to ignore such information.

★ Defendants' race, gender, and appearance often exert strong effects on the outcomes they experience in legal proceedings.

★ Jurors' gender, beliefs, and values can strongly influence their decisions, apart from the evidence presented in court.

Social Psychology and Personal Health

Why do people become ill? Your immediate reply is probably something like "Because they catch something" or "Because they are exposed to bacteria or viruses." Although those answers are correct, they are only part of the total picture. Growing evidence from the field of **health psychology,** the branch of psychology that studies the relation between psychological variables and health, suggests that both health and illness are actually determined by a complex interaction among genetic, psychological, and social factors (Taylor, 2002). Yes, exposure to disease-causing organisms plays a role, but so do health-related attitudes and beliefs, and the kind of *lifestyle* we adopt. Need proof? Then consider a major study conducted over a ten-year period in Alameda County, California. The researchers (Wiley & Comacho, 1980) asked a large group of adults whether they followed certain health practices, including sleeping seven to eight hours each night, eating breakfast regularly, refraining from smoking, drinking alcohol in moderation or not at all, maintaining their weight within normal limits, and exercising regularly. The results revealed that participants who reported practicing all or most of these behaviors were much less likely to die during the study period than those who practiced few or none of these behaviors. These findings, and those of many other studies, suggest that there is a strong link between the lifestyles we adopt and our health. And because social psychology studies topics closely related to lifestyle, such as attitudes and beliefs, different ways of coping with stress, and the personal characteristics that may play a role in our health (e.g., Dunkley, Zuroff, & Blankstein, 2003), it has much to contribute to our understanding of the factors that affect our health and well-being.

In this section, we consider several important applications of the findings and principles of social psychology to personal health. We begin by examining the nature of stress and how people cope with it. Stress, it appears, is truly one of the most important factors affecting our health. Next, we examine personal characteristics that can

health psychology
The branch of psychology that studies the relation between psychological variables and health.

strongly affect our health—factors such as the Type A behavior pattern and tendencies toward perfectionism (e.g., Dunkley, Zuroff, & Blankstein, 2003). Finally, we conclude with a discussion of ways in which individuals to can adopt healthier lifestyles—ones that can, in the long run, save their lives!

Stress: Its Causes, Effects, and Control

Have you ever felt that you were right at the edge of being overwhelmed by negative events in your life or by pressures you could no longer handle (see Figure A.10)? If so, you are already quite familiar with **stress**—our response to events that disrupt, or threaten to disrupt, our physical or psychological functioning (Taylor, 2002). Unfortunately, stress is a common part of modern life—something few of us can avoid altogether. Partly for this reason and partly because it seems to exert negative effects on both physical health and psychological well-being, stress has become an important topic of research in psychology. We now review the key findings of this research, with special attention to its links to major findings and principles of social psychology. Please note that stress has many other effects aside from ones on personal health; for instance, it can strongly influence performance on many tasks and key aspects of decision making. Here, though, we focus on its impact on personal health.

■ Major Sources of Stress and Their Effects on Personal Health

What factors contribute to stress? Unfortunately, the list is a very long one: Many conditions and events can add to our total "stress quotient." Among the most important of these, though, are major stressful life events (e.g., the death of a loved one or a painful divorce) and the all-too-frequent minor *hassles* of everyday life. (Another major source of stress is events that occur at work, but because we cover applications of social psychology to work settings in Module B, we won't discuss those here.)

Major Stressful Life Events. Death of a spouse, injury to one's child, failure in school or at work—unless we lead truly charmed lives, most of us experience traumatic events and changes at some time or other. What are their effects on us? This question was first investigated by Holmes and Rahe (1967), who asked a large group of persons to assign arbitrary points (from 1 to 100) to various life events according to how much readjustment each had required (a few examples: death of a spouse = 100 points; getting fired = 47 points; taking out a car loan = 17 points). Holmes and Rahe (1967) then related the total number of points accumulated by another group of individuals dur-

stress

Our response to events that disrupt, or threaten to disrupt, our physical or psychological functioning.

Figure A.10 ■ Stress: An Inescapable Part of Life
Do you ever feel like the person in this cartoon? If so, you know very well what stress is like! (*Source: © The New Yorker Collection 1990 Warren Miller from cartoonbank.com. All Rights Reserved.*)

ing a single year to changes in their personal health. The results were dramatic: The greater the number of "stress points" people accumulated, the greater was their likelihood of becoming seriously ill. Although this study had a number of flaws (e.g., the correlational design did not allow for causal inferences), it suggested that accumulated stress, rather than stress emanating for any specific stressor, is associated with health problems.

Newer research has begun to identify the specific effects of accumulated stress on health (McEwen, 1998). For example, in one study, Cohen and his colleagues (1998) asked a group of volunteers to describe stressful events they had experienced during the previous year and to indicate the temporal course (the onset and offset) of each event. The stressful events described by participants ranged from *acute* stressors that were brief in duration (e.g., a severe reprimand at work or a fight with a spouse) to more *chronic* ones that typically lasted a month or more and involved significant disruption of everyday routines (e.g., ongoing marital problems or unemployment). Then the researchers gave these persons nose drops containing a low dose of a virus that causes the common cold. Results indicated that volunteers who reported experiencing *chronic* stressors were more likely to develop a cold than those who had experienced only acute stressors. Moreover, the longer the duration of the stressor, the greater was the risk for developing a cold.

The Hassles of Daily Life. Although certain major life events such as the death of a loved one are dramatic and deeply disturbing, they occur only rarely. Does this mean that, in general, our lives are a calm lake of tranquility? Hardly. As you know, daily life is filled with countless minor, annoying sources of stress—termed *hassles*—that seem to make up for their relatively low intensity by their much higher frequency. That such daily hassles are an important cause of stress is suggested by the findings of several studies by Lazarus and his colleagues (e.g., DeLongis, Folkman, & Lazarus, 1988; Lazarus et al., 1985). These researchers developed a *Hassles Scale* on which individuals indicate the extent to which they have been hassled by common events during the past month. The items included in this scale deal with a wide range of everyday events, such as having too many things to do at once, misplacing or losing things, troublesome neighbors, and concerns over money.

Although such events may seem relatively minor when compared with the life events discussed earlier, they appear to be quite important. When scores on the Hassles Scale are related to reports of psychological symptoms, strong positive correlations are obtained (Lazarus et al., 1985). In short, the more stress people report as a result of daily hassles, the poorer their psychological well-being. You can assess the extent of your own exposure to daily hassles using the hassles scale provided in Table A.1 on page 522. Let's turn now to a discussion of the effects of stress on health.

■ How Does Stress Affect Health?

We hope that, by now, you are convinced that stress plays an important role in personal health. But how, exactly, do these effects occur? Though the precise mechanisms involved remain to be determined, growing evidence suggests that the process goes something like this: By draining our resources, inducing negative affect, and keeping us off balance physiologically, stress upsets our complex internal chemistry. In particular, it may interfere with efficient operation of our *immune system*—the mechanism through which our bodies recognize and destroy potentially harmful substances and intruders, such as bacteria, viruses, and cancerous cells. When functioning normally, the immune system is nothing short of amazing: Each day it removes or destroys many potential threats to our health.

Unfortunately, prolonged exposure to stress seems to disrupt this system. Chronic exposure to stress can reduce circulating levels of *lymphocytes* (white blood cells that

Table A.1 ■ The Daily Hassles Scale

By completing the items here, you can obtain an index of how much stress you experience from the hassles of daily life.

DAILY HASSLES

Directions: Listed here are a number of ways in which a person can feel hassled. As you read each hassle, use the following rating scale to rate how much a hassle each item is for you: 0 = None or Did Not Occur; 1 = Somewhat Severe; 2 = Moderately Severe; 3 = Extremely Severe. Add up your total. The higher your score, the more likely your psychological well-being will be affected.

___ Misplacing or losing things

___ Social obligations

___ Inconsiderate smokers

___ Troubling thoughts about your future

___ Thoughts about death

___ Health of a family member

___ Not enough money for clothing

___ Not enough money for housing

___ Concerns about owing money

___ Concerns about getting credit

___ Concerns about money for emergencies

___ Someone owes you money

___ Cutting down on electricity, water, etc.

___ Smoking too much

___ Use of alcohol

___ Personal use of drugs

___ Too many responsibilities

___ Decisions about having children

___ Care for pet

___ Planning meals

___ Trouble relaxing

___ Trouble making decisions

___ Problems getting along with fellow workers

___ Customers or clients give you a hard time

___ Home maintenance (inside)

___ Not enough money for basic necessities

___ Not enough money for food

___ Too many interruptions

___ Too much time on hands

___ Having to wait

___ Concerns about accidents

___ Being lonely

___ Not enough money for health care

___ Fear of confrontation

___ Financial security

___ Silly practical mistakes

___ Inability to express yourself

___ Physical illness

___ Side effects of medication

___ Concerns about medical treatment

___ Physical appearance

___ Fear of rejection

___ Sexual problems that result from physical problems

___ Concerns about health in general

___ Not seeing enough people

___ Friends or relatives too far away

___ Preparing meals

___ Wasting time

___ Auto maintenance

___ Filling out forms

___ Problems with employees

___ Concerns about bodily functions

___ Rising prices of common goods

___ Not getting enough rest

___ Not getting enough sleep

___ Problems with your lover

___ Difficulties seeing or hearing

___ Overloaded with family responsibilities

___ Too many things to do

___ Concerns about meeting high standards

___ Financial dealings with friends or acquaintances

___ Trouble with reading, writing, or speaking ability

___ Trouble with arithmetic skills

___ Gossip

___ Legal problems

___ Concerns about weight

___ Not enough time to do the things you need to do

___ Not enough personal energy

___ Concerns about inner conflicts

___ Feel conflicted over what to do

___ Regrets over past decisions

___ Menstrual (period) problems

___ The weather

___ Nightmares

___ Difficulties with friends

___ Not enough time for family

___ Transportation problems

___ Not enough money for transportation

___ Not enough money for entertainment and recreation

___ Shopping

___ Prejudice and discrimination from others

___ Property, investments or taxes

___ Not enough time for entertainment and recreation

___ Yardwork or outside home maintenance

___ Concerns about news events

(Source: Adapted from items developed by Lazarus et al., 1985.)

fight infection and disease) and increase levels of the hormone *cortisol,* a substance that suppresses aspects of our immune system (Kemeny, 2003).

The physiological effects of chronic stressors, such as a stressful job, a poor interpersonal relationship, or financial concerns, also take their toll on people's cardiovascular systems. Evidence also suggests that racial and gender differences exist in stress-induced heart disease. For instance, there is a greater prevalence of hypertension and cardiovascular disease among African Americans than whites, perhaps because blacks are exposed to more stressors in their lives and have stronger physiological reactions to stressors. A recent study of African American women and women of European descent found that African American women experienced higher levels of chronic stress due to critical life events, discrimination, and economic hardship (Troxel et al., 2003). Furthermore, chronic stress was related to evidence of heart disease for African American women but not for women of European descent. These findings suggest that African American women may be especially vulnerable to the burdens of chronic daily stress.

One model of how stress can affect our health is illustrated in Figure A.11. This model suggests that stress exerts both direct and indirect effects upon us. The direct effects are the ones just described (e.g., on our immune system and other bodily functions). The indirect effects involve influences on the lifestyles we adopt—our health-related

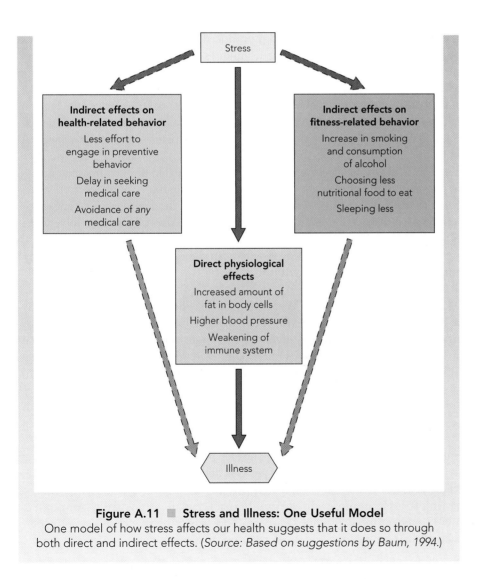

Figure A.11 ■ **Stress and Illness: One Useful Model**
One model of how stress affects our health suggests that it does so through both direct and indirect effects. (*Source: Based on suggestions by Baum, 1994.*)

behaviors (e.g., whether we seek medical care promptly when we need it) and fitness-related behaviors (e.g., the diet we choose, exercise, etc.). Although this model may not include all the ways in which stress can affect our health, it offers a useful overview of several ways in which such effects may arise.

■ Coping with Stress

Because stress is an inescapable part of life, the key task we face is not trying to eliminate or avoid it, but that of learning to *cope* with it effectively—in ways that reduce its adverse effects while helping us deal with its causes. You are already familiar with several effective means of coping with stress, such as improving your physical fitness (e.g., Brown, 1991) and eating a healthy diet, which can provide the added benefit of regulating your weight. Good weight regulation is a very important outcome, and one to which we'll return in a later section. Here, we focus on three major strategies: efforts to replace the negative emotions produced by stress with more positive ones (emotion-focused coping); efforts to alter the situation itself—the cause of stress (problem-focused coping); and a technique suggested by the findings of social psychology—seeking **social support**—-drawing on the emotional and task resources provided by others.

Emotion-Focused and Problem-Focused Coping. One major way in which individuals attempt to cope with stress—to reduces its adverse effects—is to engage in activities that reduce the negative feelings produced by stress, an approach known as **emotion-focused coping.** Some of these techniques can be effective in the short run, but may be ineffective or even dangerous in the long-term. For instance, when feeling stressed, many people drink alcohol or take drugs (Armeli et al., 2000; Goeders, 2004). Although this can make them feel better, it leaves the causes of stress largely unchanged and can, of course, be damaging to personal health. In contrast, other emotion-focused strategies, such as trying to perceive the situation in positive terms (*positive reappraisal*) by seeing how it may lead to personal growth or learning, or *positive self-talk,* positive statements individuals make to themselves that are designed to be encouraging or reassuring (e.g., reminding oneself about all the good things in life), can be more effective. According to most experts on stress, however, a much better approach is to engage in **problem-focused coping**—efforts to alter the causes of the stress. This can involve active efforts to change or remove the stressor, making plans for solving existing problems, seeking the help of others, or anything else that can change the situation for the better, not simply make the persons involved feel better.

Social Support and Stress. What do *you* do when you feel stressed? Many people turn to friends or family, seeking their advice, help, and sympathy. And research findings indicate that this can be a highly effective means of protecting our personal health from the ravages of stress (House, Landis, & Umberson, 1998). Just being with those you like can be helpful; even monkeys seek contact with others in stressful situations (Cohen et al., 1992). You may remember the discussion of similar instances of human affiliation in Chapter 7. As you might also guess on the basis of research on the effects of similarity, people who desire social support tend to turn to others who are similar to themselves in various ways (Morgan, Carder, & Neal, 1997). But you don't have to have contact with another person to experience such benefits: Recent findings indicate that having a pet can help reduce stress (see Figure A.12; e.g., Allen, 2003). And it is not simply that people who have pets tend to be better at coping with stress than those who do not. In one intriguing study (Allen, Shykoff, & Izzo, 2001), stockbrokers who lived alone and described their work as very stressful, and who all had high blood pressure, were randomly selected to receive a pet cat

Figure A.12 ■ Pets Can Reduce Stress!
Research findings indicate that, for many persons, owning a pet can help to reduce stress.

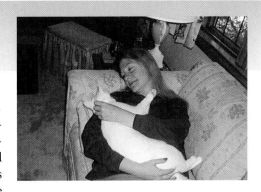

or dog from an animal shelter or to not receive a pet. Results indicated that the pets were an excellent source of social support, reducing stress among those who received them. In fact, when exposed to high levels of stress, those who had acquired pets had increases in blood pressure less than half as large as those who did not receive pets.

Why are pets so effective in this regard? One possibility is that they provide *nonjudgmental social support:* They love their owners under all conditions. Whatever the precise reasons, it seems clear that pets can be an important aid in coping with stress—at least for people who enjoy having them.

In contrast, a lack of a reliable social support network can actually increase a person's risk of dying of disease, an accident, or suicide. Persons who are divorced or separated from their spouses often experience reduced functioning in certain aspects of their immune system, compared with individuals who are happily married (Kiecolt-Glaser et al., 1987, 1988).

Although it is clear that receiving social support is important to health, recent findings seem to indicate that providing social support to others may be just as important. In one recent study, Brown and her colleagues (2003) isolated and compared the unique effects of giving and receiving social support on mortality in a sample of 846 elderly married people. The researchers initially measured the extent to which participants received and gave support to their spouse and to others (friends, relatives, neighbors) and then monitored mortality rates over a five-year period. Participants who reported providing high levels of support to others were significantly less likely to die over the five-year period than were participants who had provided little or support to others. By contrast, receiving social support from one's spouse or from others did not appear to affect mortality among people in this group. In short, these findings suggest it may be better to give than to receive, especially when it comes to health!

■ Gender Differences in Coping Mechanisms

Do men and women differ in the way they cope with stress? There is a widespread belief that they do—that men are more likely to confront a problem head-on or to deny its existence, while women are more likely to respond with emotional coping (e.g., discussing the problem with friends or family). What do research findings indicate? Though results have been mixed, a meta-analysis of existing evidence (Tamres, Janicki, & Helgeson, 2002), suggests that men and women may indeed prefer different tactics for handling stress. Results of this careful study indicate that, overall, women use a wider range of coping strategies than do men, including both problem-focused (e.g., active coping, planning) and emotion-focused (e.g., seeking social support, positive reappraisal, venting, rumination) strategies. In addition, women are more likely to use strategies that involve verbal expressions to others or the self—to ruminate about the problem, use positive self-talk, and seek emotional support from friends and family. In contrast, men are more likely to use avoidance of problems or withdrawal from them than are women. Interestingly, there was *not* strong evidence that men are more likely to attack problems head-on than are women.

What is the basis for these gender differences in coping with stress? Tamres, Janicki, and Helgeson (2002) suggest that the differences may reflect contrasting gender roles. Women are expected by society to turn to others for support during times of stress, while men are not, and these expectations may become self-confirming. Another possibility—and one supported by some findings obtained by Tamres, Janicki, and Helgeson (2002)—is that women tend to perceive many stressors as more severe than do men. This, in turn, leads them to engage in a wider range of coping strategies, including those involving seeking help from others. Whatever the specific basis for gender differences in coping, it appears that some differences do exist in this respect, although as we have seen at many points throughout this book, they are not necessarily the ones "common sense" suggests.

KEY POINTS

★ *Stress* is our response to events that disrupt, or threaten to disrupt, our physical or psychological functioning.

★ Stress stems from many causes, including major life events and the hassles of daily life.

★ Individuals adopt many different tactics for dealing with stress, but most of these can be described as *emotion-focused coping* (e.g., seeking social support, reappraisal of stressors) or *problem-focused coping* (e.g., attacking the problem head-on).

★ Women seem to employ a wider range of coping tactics than do men, perhaps because they perceive many stressors as more severe.

Personal Characteristics and Health: Hostility, Perfectionism, and Socioeconomic Status

That large differences in personal health exist is obvious; some persons are rarely ill and go decades without seeing the inside of a hospital, while others suffer from frequent illnesses. What accounts for such differences? From the preceding discussion, you know that *stress* provides part of the answer: Prolonged exposure to high levels of stress can undermine personal health, and this is especially likely to occur for persons who do not have effective techniques for coping with it (e.g., Kiecolt-Glaser & Glaser, 1992). But stress itself is only part of the story. As we'll see in the next section, adoption of a healthy or unhealthy lifestyle is another major component. In addition, it appears that several *personal characteristics*, too, can play a role in health, often because they increase or reduce individuals' ability to cope with stress. Here, we briefly examine three of these factors: *anger or hostility* (e.g., Niaura et al., 2002), a tendency toward self-critical *perfectionism* (e.g., Dunkley & Blankstein, 2000), and *socioeconomic class* (e.g., Gottfredson, 2003).

■ Anger and Hostility

Do you recall the *Type A behavior pattern* that we discussed in Chapter 11? Such persons are extremely competitive, always in a hurry, and very irritable and easily angered (e.g., Strube, 1989). These characteristics often get them into serious interpersonal difficulties with others. In addition, persons high on the hostility or anger component of this pattern have been found to be at much higher risk for heart disease than other persons. For instance, medical students who become angry quickly while under stress are more than three times more likely to develop premature heart disease and five times more likely to have an early heart attack than their calmer colleagues (Smith, 2003). Similarly, highly hostile men angered by another person have higher blood pressure, a higher heart rate, and other physiological signs of high levels of stress than persons lower in hostility (Suarez, 1998). In fact, one study (Niaura et al., 2002) indicates that a high level of hostility is a better predictor of heart disease in older men than smoking, drinking, high caloric intake, and even high levels of cholesterol. Over all, then, it appears that although anger is certainly justified in some situations, it can, if experienced too often, add to stress and undermine our physical health.

Perfectionism: Another Way in Which We Can Be Our Own Worst Enemy

Do you know anyone who is a perfectionist—someone who wants to be perfect, or nearly perfect, in everything they do? If so, ask yourself this: Are these people happy? Probably, your answer is "No way!" And, in a sense, how could they be? No matter how hard they try and how well they do, they are always falling short of their own high standards. Actually, two different patterns of such *perfectionism* exist: *personal standards perfectionism*—a pattern in which people who set extremely, and often unreasonably, high standards for themselves—and **self-critical perfectionism**—a contrasting pattern in which individuals constantly engage in harsh criticism of their own behavior, an inability to derive satisfaction from successful performance, and chronic concerns about other's expectations and criticism (e.g., Blankstein & Dunkley, 2002). For instance, persons showing self-critical perfectionism tend to agree with such items as "People expect nothing less than perfection from me" and "People will think less of me if I make a mistake." Persons high in personal standards perfectionism, in contrast, agree with statements like these: "I set very high standards for myself" and "If I do not set the highest standards for myself, I am likely to end up a second-rate person."

Although both of these patterns can be harmful, recent findings suggest that self-critical perfectionism is especially damaging to personal health. Persons who show this characteristic tend to blame themselves for everything, perceive that others will be highly critical of them, and doubt their own ability to deal with stressful situations. As a result, they tend to experience high levels of negative affect and to engage in avoidance coping strategies. Moreover, they perceive that they cannot readily attain social support from others (see Figure A.13 on page 528). The overall result is that individuals high in self-critical perfectionism cause themselves to experience negative feelings, high levels of stress, and feelings of helplessness, because they don't seem able to cope with such stress (Dunkley, Zuroff, & Blankstein, 2003). Clearly, these outcomes can be harmful to personal health, so this is one pattern we should all try to avoid!

Socioeconomic Status

It has been known for many decades that there is a link between socioeconomic status and health: Overall, the higher individuals are in this respect, the better their personal health (e.g., Steenland, Henley, & Thun, 2002). In the past, it has usually been suggested that these differences stem from the fact that persons high in socioeconomic status have greater material resources (e.g., better diet, more comfortable homes, etc.) and greater access to health care facilities than persons lower in socioeconomic status (see Figure A.14). And certainly, there can be little doubt that these factors play some role in the consistently observed connection between health and socioeconomic status.

self-critical perfectionism A pattern in which individuals constantly engage in harsh criticism of their own behavior, an inability to derive satisfaction from successful performance, and chronic concerns about others' expectations and criticism.

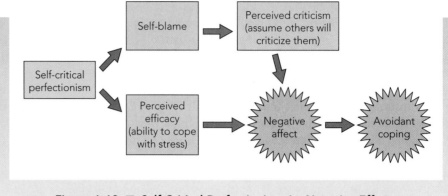

Figure A.13 ■ Self-Critical Perfectionism: Its Negative Effects
Persons who are high in self-critical perfectionism tend to blame themselves for everything, expect others to be highly critical of them, and doubt their own ability to deal with stressful situations. As a result, they experience high levels of negative affect and often engage in avoidance coping strategies for dealing with stress. (*Source: Based on suggestions by Dunkley, Zuroff, & Blankstein, 2003.*)

Recent findings, however, raise the intriguing possibility that another factor may underlie these differences: differences in general intelligence. It has been found that the higher individuals' socioeconomic status, the higher their general intelligence. Why this difference exists is not clear; it may well stem from contrasting educational opportunities and differences in access to books and other learning materials in richer and poorer homes. But regardless of the origins of this difference, some researchers believe that they may contribute to contrasting levels of personal health (e.g., Gottfredson, 2004). Why should this be so? The basic reasoning goes something like this.

As defined by most experts, general intelligence refers to the ability to learn and solve problems (e.g., Gottfredson, 1997). Differences along these dimensions, therefore, may play a role in dealing successfully with a wide range of life situations—situations that occur at work, at play, and in virtually every other setting. In addition, differences in the ability to learn may contribute to differences in knowledge relating to health and therefore to adoption of healthy versus unhealthy lifestyles and behaviors. To the extent this is true, then, differences in general intelligence across socioeconomic status may translate into differences in personal health. Persons higher in socioeconomic status, having higher intelligence, know more about what it takes to be healthy and are more likely to put this knowledge to use than are persons lower in such status.

While a considerable amount of evidence can be interpreted as consistent with this reasoning, it is important to note that, at present, it is only a possibility: It has *not* been proved conclusively. Further, it is also important to note that neither differences in general intelligence nor differences in health knowledge are "set in stone." On the contrary, they can readily be changed by changing environmental conditions. So, even if intelligence does contribute to differences in health across varying levels of socioeconomic status, there is no implication that such differences must exist and will continue to do so. Rather, you should view this whole area of research more as food for thought than for reaching firm conclusions. In any case, because socioeconomic status certainly falls within the domain of social psychology, it is clear once again that the knowledge and findings of our field can shed important light on the bases of personal health. (For information on other personal characteristics that can affect health, please see the **Beyond the Laboratory Headlines** section on page 530.)

Figure A.14 ■ Socioeconomic Status and Health
There is a strong link between socioeconomic status and health, such that wealthier people tend to enjoy better personal health. This may be due to the fact that the higher persons are in socioeconomic status, the greater access they have to excellent health care. However, recent findings indicate that general intelligence, too, may play a role in producing this outcome.

KEY POINTS

★ Personal characteristics can strongly influence our health. Persons who are high in hostility are more likely to experience serious health problems such as heart attacks than persons who are lower in hostility.

★ Being high in *self-critical perfectionism* can lead to negative outcomes such as reduced capacity to cope effectively with stress.

★ Socioeconomic status is related to health, partly because wealthier persons have better access to medical care but perhaps because of other factors such as differences in general intelligence as well.

Promoting Healthy Lifestyles: The Choice Is Ours

How long will you live? And how healthy will you be during your life, especially during the later decades? At some point, nearly everyone wonders about these questions. When we are young—in our teens, twenties, or thirties—we rarely think about them. But as we grow older, we ponder these questions with increasing frequency, even if we remain in good health. The answers to these questions are complex and are only just beginning to emerge, but we are definitely making progress. Genetic factors clearly play some role; persons whose parents and grandparents lived to ripe old ages are more likely to do so themselves than would be expected by chance alone. And research suggests that a group of genes found on a single human chromosome may well play some role in determining life span (Perls and Silver, 1999). But it is also clear that environmental factors, especially our lifestyles, matter, too. For instance, consider research by Levy et al. (2002).

Can Being a Happy Person Reduce the Odds of Catching a Cold?

Sick of the Sniffles? Put on a Happy Face

USA Today—The common cold is not an equal-opportunity attacker. Everyone knows it is contagious, yet some stay healthy or suffer only mild symptoms even when they are exposed to armies of sniffling kids and co-workers. Others seem to be knocked out by every passing bug.

Scientists are far from understanding everything about colds, but a growing pool of evidence suggests that personality, stress, and social life can all affect healthy adults' vulnerability. . . . "Just like in kindergarten, those who 'play well with others' are better off," says psychologist Sheldon Cohen. . . . For 16 years he has been exposing volunteers to colds by dropping rhinoviruses into their noses. Then he quarantines them for five days to see who gets sick. Here's what he has found:

· Happy, relaxed people are more resistant than those who tend to be unhappy or tense.
· The more extroverted a person is, the less likely he or she is to catch a cold.
· Serious work-related or personal stress for at least a month increases the chances of catching a cold.

Have you ever noticed that while some people tend to catch one cold after another, others seem relatively immune—they have few colds, and the ones they do have tend to be mild. What accounts for this difference? The findings reported in this article seem to suggest that cold-resistant people have a kind of "invisible, protective shield" against cold-causing microbes provided by their lifestyle and personalities. Can this really be true? In fact, additional evidence suggests that it can and for reasons we are now beginning to understand— mechanisms that center around the ways in which stress affects our immune system.

When individuals are exposed to stress, their bodies release adrenaline-like hormones that stimulate the immune system. Then, a little later, *cortisol,* which battles inflammation, is released. For a while, both hormones are active, but when stress ends, the adrenaline-like hormones drop off first. This leaves the hormones that suppress the immune system still active. The result? Individuals become ill several days after experiencing intense stress. Because being happy and relaxed and having lots of friends (which is true for people high in extroversion) can help to lessen the effects of stress, the chances of getting ill, too, are reduced.

So, surprising as it may seem, there are sound scientific grounds for suggesting that being happy and reducing high levels of stress can actually lower your chances of catching colds. No, these can't be put into a bottle of cold-fighting pills, but they *are* attainable—and well worth seeking.

These researchers conducted a longitudinal study stretching across more than twenty-two years, in which they measured individuals' self-perceptions of aging—their beliefs about what would happen to them as they grew older. Then, they divided the participants into those who had mainly positive perceptions about their own aging and those who had mainly negative ones. When they followed these individuals for more than two decades, they obtained an amazing result: Those with positive beliefs about aging were more likely to continue living throughout the study than those with negative beliefs about aging! In fact, those in the positive belief group lived, on average, 7.5 years longer than those with negative beliefs (see Figure A.15).

What accounts for this difference? Further research indicated that the difference was due, at least in part, to what Levy et al. (2002) describe as the *will to live.* Persons with positive self-perceptions of aging tended to perceive their lives as hopeful, fulfilling, and worth living, while those with negative self-perceptions tended to perceive their lives as empty, worthless, and hopeless. This, in turn, may have caused those with

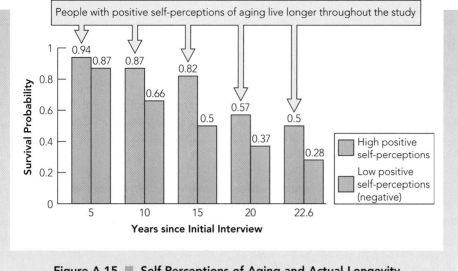

Figure A.15 ■ **Self-Perceptions of Aging and Actual Longevity**
As shown here, people who believed that they would age well actually lived longer
than those who believed that as they aged, they would experience serious
problems and deterioration. (*Source: Based on data from Levy et al., 2002.*)

positive self-perceptions to take better care of themselves—to live a more healthy
lifestyle—with the result that they did, in fact, live longer!

So, just what *is* a healthy lifestyle? Probably, you already know quite a bit about this:
It is a lifestyle in which we avoid behaviors that are potentially harmful to our health
(e.g., excessive use of alcohol, smoking, unprotected sex, unprotected exposure to the
sun; Glanz et al., 2002) and seek early detection and effective treatment of illnesses when
they occur. Because you have already heard many persuasive messages urging you to
avoid various threats to your health and to seek early medical advice, we focus here on
the topic with which we began (do you recall the Cheeseburger bill?) and that now
looms as an ever-growing threat to the health of Americans and persons in many other
countries: obesity.

The Rising Tide of Obesity: A Social-Psychological Perspective

Recent statistics suggest that in the United States, fully 65 percent of all adults are
obese—they weigh far more than the ideal for their height and body frame. But you
don't need statistics to demonstrate this fact. Just go to any nearby shopping mall or
theater and observe the crowd. You will soon have your own evidence that Americans
(and persons in many other countries) are truly becoming "super-sized." Because obesity is clearly harmful to personal health—it increases the risk of heart disease, bone
disease, and a host of other illnesses—two key questions arise: (1) What factors are
responsible for this growing problem? And (2) what, if anything, can be done to reverse
the trend?

Why We Are Losing the "Battle of the Bulge."   Many different factors contribute
to the fact that around the globe, increasing numbers of people are gaining weight. First,
genetic factors appear to be important. Consider the situation faced by our ancestors:
Periods of plenty alternated with periods of famine. Under these conditions, people who
were efficient at storing excess calories as fat during times of plenty gained an important

advantage: They were more likely to survive during famines and to have children. As a result, all of us living today have some tendency to gain weight when we overeat—much to our dismay!

Environmental factors, too, play an important role. In recent years, the size of the portions of many foods has increased dramatically. Thirty years ago, a Coke or Pepsi was eight ounces; now, one-liter bottles (about thirty-two ounces) are being offered as a single serving. Similarly, McDonald's hamburgers were small and thin and contained about two hundred calories; now, most people purchase double cheeseburgers or Big Macs containing four hundred or five hundred calories. Because people tend to eat their entire portion of food, no matter how big it is, this, too, may be a factor in the rising rate of obesity.

In addition—and most central to this discussion—social factors play an important role. First, people don't walk as much as they did in the past. In cities, fear of crime has stopped many people from walking to stores and other locations. Similarly, shopping malls have brought large number of stores to one location, with parking just outside the door. In the past, people had to walk many blocks to visit as many different shops—and often rode public transportation to reach them, because parking was so difficult. Every time I (Robert Baron) follow a school bus, I see another change in lifestyle: Instead of stopping at a few locations, the buses stop at every single house, thus saving steps for the children—and calories, too.

Another social factor involves ever more enticing media campaigns for high-calorie meals and snacks. Fewer and fewer people, it seems, can resist the foods shown in television commercials, on billboards, and in magazines, so caloric intake—and weight gain—is increased by this factor, too. However, as shown in Figure A.16, some companies are bucking this media trend.

Yet another factor involves the fact that the sit-down dinner is fast disappearing. Instead of eating their meals together, a growing number of families eat at different times, often away from home. This often can leads to a situation in which people snack

Figure A.16 ■ **Combatting the Obesity Trend**
Fast-food chains such as McDonalds have recently begun appealing to health-conscious customers by broadening their menu to include healthier choices such as salads and items with lower fat.

all day; after all, there is no reason to save their appetites for a family meal! Research findings indicate that it is much harder for our built-in bodily mechanisms to regulate eating when it occurs in this manner, so this is yet another social factor that contributes to expanding waistlines.

Finally, consider the social norms concerning weight: Although "thin" is definitely "in"—most people report that they want to weigh less than they do, and in fact, to weigh less than many experts consider to be ideal for good health—there is tacit acceptance of weight gain as a "normal" part of life. As the number of extremely large persons increases, overweight people can take consolation from the fact that they are not alone. And, in fact, many organizations designed to fight discrimination against overweight persons have been formed, and now play an active role in promoting the view that being greatly overweight is, if not desirable, at least not a basis for rejection. In sum, many social factors appear to play a role in the trend toward "super-size" noticed in many countries in recent years.

Tactics for Turning the Tide.   So, given all of the forces against us, can we really win the battle to maintain a stable weight, and thus, contribute to our own health and well-being? Being optimists, we believe that the answer is "yes," but realizing it requires some effort. Given the tremendous health benefits that stem from being at or close to your ideal weight, though, we believe this is effort well spent. Here are some steps we recommend:

- *Avoid high-calorie snack foods.* A handful of potato chips or a small order of fries can contain hundreds of calories. Yet, they don't tend to make you feel full. Avoid such foods as much as possible.

- *Don't eat when you aren't hungry, out of habit.* It's all too easy to get into the habit of eating whenever you watch TV, study, or sit down to talk with friends. If you must munch on something, eat a piece of fruit or drink some coffee or tea. Coffee and tea contain natural substances that tend to reduce appetite.

- *Avoid temptation.* If you want to avoid gaining weight, try to avoid temptation. When you encounter attractive, appetizing foods, or ads for them, look the other way or turn to another channel—fast!

- *Walk a little more.* Vigorous exercise will definitely help you burn calories, which can translate into weight loss. But even if you cannot engage in aerobic workouts, you can make a lot of progress simply by walking a little more each day. In fact, research findings indicate that walking just fifteen to thirty minutes more *per week* can make a difference, and at least stop further weight gain (Sallis, Salens, & Frank, 2003).

- *Drink water not soft drinks with your meals.* During the past two decades, the consumption of soft drinks in the United States and many other countries has soared. From the point of view of weight gain, that's unfortunate, because each glass of Coke, Pepsi, or whatever contains almost two hundred calories. So, ignore the ads and sip water when you are thirsty.

- *Lower your stress.* Recent findings indicate that when exposed to high levels of stress, many persons tend to increase their eating. And they don't eat just anything, rather, they tend to eat foods high in fats and sugar, which are very high in calories (Dallman, 2003). So, this is yet another potential benefit of reducing stress in your life or, at least, getting it under control.

- *Don't adopt fad diets.* Diet books are perpetual best-sellers and usually contain new approaches for losing weight quickly and effortlessly. Don't be fooled by such claims. There is really no scientific evidence for these diets, and the only thing they accomplish, in general, is to make their authors rich (and famous). You *can* lose weight, and fairly quickly, too, but the best way to do it is by reducing the amount you eat while increasing your exercise. That formula is 90 percent certain to yield the results you want, with minimum risk to your health.

• *Most important, don't give up.* If you have succeeded in losing weight—most people on diets do—don't quit. Managing your weight is a lifelong process. And if you persist, you will eventually lower your body's set point, so that keeping the extra pounds off will actually become easier.

Will these steps guarantee that your weight will come down? No, but they are based on research findings, and they are definitely steps in the right direction. If social factors contribute to weight gain—and we firmly believe that they do—then following these steps, which are suggested by the findings of social psychological research, can help. Good luck—and remember, the health you promote will be your own!

KEY POINTS

★ Obesity is increasing around the world and poses a major threat to personal health.

★ Many factors play a role in this trend, including social factors such as the fact that because of the advent of shopping malls and other changes, people do less walking; a growing tendency for family members to eat separately, and hence all day; and growing acceptance of obesity as a "normal" state for many persons.

★ Effective procedures for halting or reversing weight gain exist and do work for people who follow them carefully.

SUMMARY AND REVIEW OF KEY POINTS

Social Psychology and the Legal System

■ Most people prefer that police interrogators adopt an inquisitorial approach, in which they search for the truth, rather than an adversarial approach, in which they attempt to prove guilt.

■ Research findings indicate that videotaping police interrogations reduces the use of abusive tactics by police but does not prevent jurors from viewing false confessions, obtained under pressure, as valid.

■ Publicity in the media before and during a trial can have strong effects on public opinion about the guilt or innocence of the defendants, and can even affect jurors' decisions.

■ Eyewitnesses are not as accurate as is commonly believed. Several factors (e.g., intense emotion, the passage of time since the observed events, and errors in memory) contribute to this fact.

■ Individuals often construct false memories—memories for events that never happened. Imagination and confabulation (making up information while answering questions) contribute to the development of such false memories.

■ The accuracy of *eyewitness testimony* can be increased through the use of improved interviews and better lineup procedures.

■ During pretrial voir dire procedures, attorneys often try to select jurors who will be favorable to their side.

■ During trials, attorneys sometimes ask *leading questions* or present evidence that is inadmissible. Research findings indicate that jurors find it very hard to ignore such information.

- Defendants' race, gender, and appearance often exert strong effects on the outcomes they experience in legal proceedings.

- Jurors' gender, beliefs, and values can strongly influence their decisions, apart from the evidence presented in court.

Social Psychology and Personal Health

- *Stress* is our response to events that disrupt, or threaten to disrupt, our physical or psychological functioning.

- Stress stems from many causes, including major life events and the hassles of daily life.

- Individuals adopt many different tactics for dealing with stress, but most of these can be described as *emotion-focused coping* (e.g., seeking *social support,* reappraisal of stressors) or *problem-focused coping* (e.g., attacking the problem head-on).

- Women seem to employ a wider range of coping tactics than do men, perhaps because women perceive many stressors as more severe.

- Personal characteristics can strongly influence our health. Persons who are high in hostility are more likely to experience serious health problems, such as heart attacks, than are persons who are lower in hostility.

- Being high in *self-critical perfectionism* can lead to negative outcomes, such as reduced capacity to cope effectively with stress.

- Socioeconomic status is related to health, partly because wealthier persons have better access to medical care but perhaps because of other factors, such as differences in general intelligence.

- Obesity is increasing around the world and poses a major threat to personal health.

- Many factors play a role in this trend, including social factors such as the fact that because of the advent of shopping malls and other changes, people do less walking; a growing tendency for family members to eat separately, and hence all day; and growing acceptance of obesity as a "normal" state for many persons.

- Effective procedures for halting or reversing weight gain exist and do work for people who follow them carefully.

Connections   INTEGRATING SOCIAL PSYCHOLOGY

In this chapter, you read about . . .	In other chapters, you will find related discussions of . . .
how the media may influence legal proceedings	how the media influence aggression and other forms of social behavior (Chapter 11)
how memory distortion and construction reduce the accuracy of eyewitnesses	how errors in memory influence social thought and judgments (Chapters 2, 3, 4)
how the attractiveness, race, and gender of defendants and jurors influence legal proceedings	the role of attractiveness, gender, and race in many other contexts (e.g., Chapters 6 and 7)
how personal characteristics can influence personal health	the role of personal characteristics in many aspects of social behavior and thought (almost all chapters of this book)

Thinking about Connections

1. A theft has taken place where you work, and all of the employees are being questioned by the police about what they know. You are asked to remember where you were on Friday of the previous week, the actions of your fellow employees that day, and precisely what you may have seen. Think about what it is you actually remember (Chapter 2) and what you only seem to remember. Is it possible that the person interrogating you has already made up his or her mind and simply wants you to provide confirmation? Do the questions suggest that certain answers are expected? Are you comfortable in honestly saying such things as, "I don't know" and "I can't remember," or do you feel you *should* come up with tentative guesses?

2. In the past year, you have probably experienced at least one or two (and maybe many more) stressful situations. How did you respond? Were you physically fit at the time, or had you skipped exercise, stayed up late and missed sleep, and dined primarily on junk food? Did you find yourself feeling depressed? Did you think of options that might help solve the problem or at least deal with it? Did you seek the support of other people? How closely do you feel that you resemble the self-healing personality versus the disease-prone personality? Finally, did you get sick? If so, does it appear that your illness occurred because of how well you cope?

3. Are you gaining weight? If so, why? What steps can you take to return to your ideal weight? Do you think you can really follow them effectively?

KEY TERMS

emotion-focused coping (p. 524)

eyewitness testimony (p. 510)

health psychology (p. 519)

leading questions (p. 515)

mental contamination (p. 516)

problem-focused coping (p. 524)

self-critical perfectionism (p. 527)

social support (p. 524)

stress (p. 520)

SOCIAL PSYCHOLOGY GOES TO WORK
Applying Social Psychology to Work Settings and Entrepreneurship

*S*everal years ago, the president of Delta Airlines was being interviewed about cost cutting at his company. The cuts had resulted in lay-offs of employees, and less favorable working conditions for the ones who remained. When asked to comment on these effects, he looked into the cameras and said, "So be it." He soon learned to regret those words, because the reaction from Delta's employees was immediate: They were angry! Within a few hours, hundreds of flight attendants, maintenance crew members, baggage handlers, and even pilots had pinned buttons saying, "So Be It" to their clothes as a sign of protest. And morale, service, and efficiency plummeted. The ultimate result? Delta's Board of Directors fired the president and replaced him with another leader who was more sympathetic to the company's employees—or, at least, avoided public statements suggesting that he couldn't care less about them!

Why do we start with this example from the world of work? Because it illustrates the key point of this module: Work settings are *social settings*—ones in which people interact with each other for many hours each day, often for months, years, or even decades. In fact, unless we are fortunate enough to be born to extreme wealth, most of us spend more of our lives at work than anywhere else, working closely with many other people (see Figure B.1). Given these basic facts, it seems clear that the principles and findings of social psychology are directly relevant to work settings and virtually everything that goes on in them. And, in fact, social psychology *has* been applied to understanding many aspects of people's behavior and thought in the world of work. Much of this work has been carried out by **industrial–organizational psychologists**—psychologists who specialize in studying all forms of behavior and cognition in work settings (e.g., Landy & Conte, 2004). But social psychologists, too, have been actively involved in this work, increasingly so in recent years (Haslam et al., 2003). What have they learned about the social side of work? So much that we could not possibly describe it all here. Instead, therefore, we focus on several topics that are closely related to earlier chapters of this book—ones that illustrate clearly how the findings and principles of social psychology can be applied to practical questions about our working lives.

First, we examine the role of *attitudes* in work settings, focusing on *job satisfaction*—people's attitudes toward their jobs (e.g., Weiss, 2002). As you can probably guess, the actions of Delta's president had strong, negative effects on the job satisfaction of its employees—with disastrous effects for the company. Next, we turn to the ways in which people help or don't help each other at work, and the factors that influence this choice.

industrial–organizational psychologists
Psychologists who specialize in studying all forms of behavior and cognition in work settings.

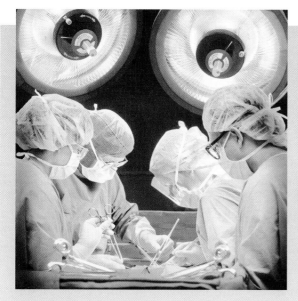

Figure B.1 ■ Work Settings: Where We Spend Our Lives

Most people spend more time in work settings such as these than in any other location; and they spend more time working than doing anything else.

Such *prosocial behavior* in work settings is usually referred to as *organizational citizenship* behavior because it refers to the help people give each other at work that is *not* a required part of their jobs (e.g., Organ, 1988). Clearly, Delta's employees pulled together to show their anger at the president's words, and by joining forces in this way, helped rid themselves of this hated leader. Third, we consider the role of *influence* in work settings by examining the nature of *leadership*. (Being able to influence one's followers is a key, defining characteristic of being a leader.) In this context, we examine such questions as why some persons, but not others, become leaders, and how leaders exert their powerful effects over the groups they lead. Certainly, Delta's president did *not* show excellent leadership skills when he uttered his famous, sarcastic remark—and it soon brought his role as a leader to an end! Finally, we examine a topic that has just begun to receive attention from social psychologists—*entrepreneurship*. As you already know, successful entrepreneurs such as Bill Gates can have major effects on their societies— or even the entire world (where are Microsoft products *not* used today?). But why do some persons, but not others, choose to become entrepreneurs? And why are some so successful in this role while others fail? The theories and findings of social psychology have much to say about these issues, so we take a brief look at how they are currently being used to answer these and related questions.

Work-Related Attitudes: The Nature and Effects of Job Satisfaction

As we saw in Chapter 4, we are rarely neutral to the social world. On the contrary, we hold strong *attitudes* about many aspects of it. Jobs are no exception to this rule. If asked, most persons can readily report their attitudes toward their jobs and also toward the organizations that employ them. Attitudes concerning one's own job or work are generally referred to by the term **job satisfaction** (e.g., Wanous, Reiches, & Hudy, 1997), while attitudes toward one's company are known as *organizational commitment* (e.g., Brown, 1996; Keller, 1997). Because job satisfaction is linked more directly to basic research on attitudes in social psychology, we focus on this topic here.

Job Satisfaction: Its Causes

Despite the fact that many jobs are repetitive and boring in nature, surveys involving literally hundreds of thousands of employees conducted over the course of several decades point to a surprising finding: Most indicate that they are quite satisfied with their jobs (e.g., Shore, Cleveland, & Goldberg, 2003). In part, this may reflect the operation of *cognitive dissonance* (see Chapter 4). Because most persons know that they have to continue working and know that there is often considerable effort—and risk—involved in changing jobs, stating that they are *not* satisfied with their current jobs would tend to generate dissonance. To avoid or reduce such reactions, therefore, many persons find it easier to report high levels of job satisfaction, and may then actually come to accept their own ratings as a true reflection of their views.

Though most people report being relatively satisfied with their jobs, they do vary in this respect, with some reporting very high levels and others lower levels of job satisfaction. What factors influence such attitudes? Research on this issue indicates that two major groups of factors are important: *organizational factors* related to a company's practices or the working conditions it provides, and *personal factors* related to the traits of individual employees.

The organizational factors that influence job satisfaction contain few surprises: People report higher satisfaction when they feel that the reward systems in their companies are fair (when raises, promotions, and other rewards are distributed fairly; see Chapter 12), when they like and respect their bosses and believe these persons have their best interests at heart, when they can participate in the decisions that affect them, when the work they perform is interesting rather than boring and repetitious, and when they are neither *overloaded*, with too much to do in a given amount of time, nor *underloaded*, with too little to do (e.g., Callan, 1993; Melamed et al., 1993; Miceli & Lane, 1991). Physical working conditions, too, play a role: When they are comfortable, employees report higher job satisfaction than when they are uncomfortable (e.g., too hot, too noisy; Baron, 1994).

More surprising, perhaps, are findings concerning the factors that do *not* exert strong effects on job satisfaction. For instance, although you might guess that job satisfaction would be strongly linked to pay, this is not the case (e.g., Landy & Conte, 2004). In fact, research on personal happiness (such happiness is related, in part, to satisfaction with one's job or work) indicates that earning a high salary is *not* closely related to happiness (e.g., Diener & Lucas, 1999). More important than actual pay, it appears, is its *perceived fairness*. As long as people feel that their pay is fair, they can express relatively high satisfaction with it, at least within broad limits.

Turning to personal factors, the least surprising findings are those relating to seniority and status: The longer people have been in a given job and the higher their status, the greater their satisfaction (Zeitz, 1990). Similarly, the greater the extent to

job satisfaction
Attitudes individuals hold concerning their jobs.

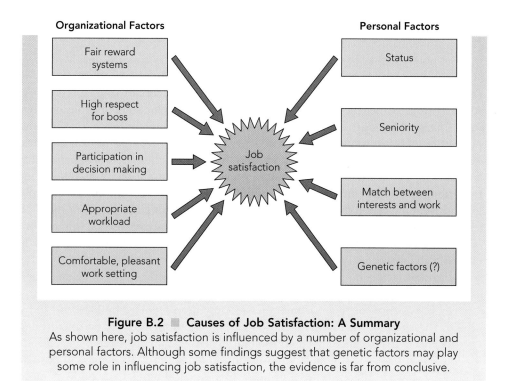

Organizational Factors

- Fair reward systems
- High respect for boss
- Participation in decision making
- Appropriate workload
- Comfortable, pleasant work setting

Job satisfaction

Personal Factors

- Status
- Seniority
- Match between interests and work
- Genetic factors (?)

Figure B.2 ■ Causes of Job Satisfaction: A Summary
As shown here, job satisfaction is influenced by a number of organizational and personal factors. Although some findings suggest that genetic factors may play some role in influencing job satisfaction, the evidence is far from conclusive.

which jobs are closely matched to individuals' personal interests, the greater their satisfaction (Fricko & Beehr, 1992). More surprising, perhaps, is the finding that certain personal traits are closely related to job satisfaction. For instance, Type A persons tend to be *more* satisfied than Type B's, despite their greater overall irritability (see Chapter 11). Perhaps this is because jobs allow people to stay busy, and Type A's, of course, *like* to be busy all the time! (See Figure B.2 for a summary of all these factors.)

On the other hand, another result of research on job satisfaction may greatly surprise you—although, in fact, it is related to research on the evolutionary perspective in social psychology. Some studies—far from conclusive and somewhat controversial—seem to suggest that genetic factors may play some role in job satisfaction. In other words, some persons, it appears, have an inherited tendency to be either satisfied or unsatisfied with their jobs. Needless to say, such effects are small, and situational factors relating to actual working conditions can certainly overwhelm general tendencies to be satisfied or dissatisfied with almost any job. But such tendencies do seem to exist and are consistent with the informal observation that some people seem to be reasonably happy with their jobs no matter what they are like, while others are unhappy even under very favorable working conditions.

The first research pointing to such conclusions was conducted by Arvey and his colleagues (1989) more than ten years ago. These researchers measured current job satisfaction in thirty-four pairs of identical (monozygotic) twins who had been separated at an early age and then raised apart. Because such twins have identical genetic inheritance but have had different life experiences (being raised in different homes), the extent to which they report similar levels of job satisfaction provides information on the potential role of genetic factors in such attitudes. Results obtained by Arvey et al. (1989) indicated that the level of job satisfaction reported by these pairs of twins correlated significantly, and that these correlations were higher than was true for unrelated persons who, of course, do not share the same genes. Additional findings indicated that as much as 30 percent of the variation in job satisfaction may stem from genetic factors! Though these findings remain somewhat controversial (e.g., Cropanzano & James, 1990), they have been replicated in other studies (e.g., Arvey et al., 1994; Judge, 1992;

Keller et al., 1992), so it does seem possible (although far from proven!) that genetic factors play some role (certainly a small one) in job satisfaction.

But how, you may be wondering, can genetic factors play a role in positive or negative attitudes toward one's job? The answer involves the influence of genetic factors on certain aspects of personality. Research findings indicate that certain basic aspects of personality—for instance the "Big Five" dimensions that we discussed in previous chapters (e.g., Chapter 11; Judge, Heller, & Mount, 2002) and a general tendency to experience positive or negative moods (positive and negative affectivity; e.g., Watson & Clark, 1994)—may be related to job satisfaction, and that, further, these aspects of personality are partly heritable (i.e., partly the result of genetic factors; e.g., Loehlin, 1992). Putting these findings together, an intriguing possibility arises: Perhaps genetic factors influence job satisfaction through their impact on these basic aspects of personality. For instance, perhaps persons high in emotional stability, agreeableness, and extraversion (dimensions of the "Big Five") and persons who are high in positive affectivity are more likely to express high job satisfaction than are persons who are low on these dimensions. In other words, genetic factors do not influence job satisfaction directly; rather, they exert their effects indirectly, through key aspects of personality, as shown in Figure B.3.

Direct evidence for this reasoning has recently been reported by Illies and Judge (2003). These researchers found that both the "Big Five" dimensions of personality and positive affectivity–negative affectivity did indeed help explain the effects of genetic factors on job satisfaction. Although both were found to play a role, the effects of positive affectivity–negative affectivity were stronger. In a practical sense, these findings mean that genetic factors influence the tendency to experience positive feelings such as enthusiasm, confidence, and cheerfulness (Watson et al., 1999) versus negative feelings such as fear, hostility, and anger, and these tendencies, in turn, influence job satisfaction. If you've ever known someone who seemed happy and cheerful in every situation, or someone who was just the opposite, you get the picture. Yes, people are satisfied or dissatisfied with their jobs for lots of reasons. But, in addition, it appears that some persons—because of personality traits that are, in part, inherited—are more likely to express high satisfaction than others in almost any context.

In short, although working conditions, the nature of the jobs people perform, and many organizational factors combine to determine job satisfaction, these work-related attitudes are also strongly affected by personal traits or characteristics—ones people take with them from job to job and situation to situation. As a result, some persons express a high level of satisfaction no matter where they work, while others express a low level

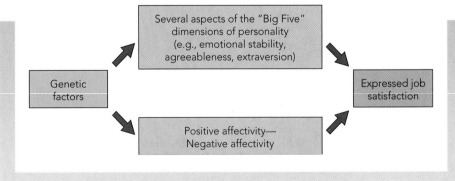

Figure B.3 ■ **The Effects of Genetic Factors on Job Satisfaction: The Effects Are Indirect**
Genetic factors appear to influence job satisfaction, but these effects are indirect. Genetic factors influence certain aspects of personality (e.g., positive affectivity—negative affectivity; emotional stability; extraversion), and these, in turn, play a role in job satisfaction. (*Source: Based on findings reported by Illies & Judge, 2003.*)

Module B / Social Psychology Goes to Work

Figure B.4 ■ Job Satisfaction: It Differs across Individuals
Some people, it seems, are satisfied with their jobs no matter what these are like, while others express a low level of satisfaction even if their jobs are very desirable. These differences in job satisfaction, in turn, can strongly affect actual performance of the jobs in question.

no matter where *they* work. Which ones would *you* most like to have as coworkers? The answer is too clear to require further comment (see Figure B.4).

Job Satisfaction: Its Effects

Are happy workers—ones who like their jobs—productive workers? Although common sense seems to suggest that they are, it's important to remember that job satisfaction is a special kind of attitude. And as we noted in Chapter 4, attitudes are not always strong predictors of overt behavior. Thus, you should not be surprised to learn that while job satisfaction is related to performance in many jobs, this relationship is relatively weak—correlations in the range of .15 to .20 (e.g., Judge, 1992; Tett & Meyer, 1993). The strength of this relationship varies across different occupations—for instance it is stronger for scientists and engineers than for nurses—but it is not very strong for any occupation studied (e.g., Judge et al., 2001).

Why isn't this relationship stronger? Because several factors tend to weaken or moderate the impact of job satisfaction on performance. One of the most important of these is that many jobs leave little room for variations in performance. Think about production line employees, for example. If they don't perform at a minimum level, they get behind "the line" and can't hold their jobs. But they can't get *exceed* this minimum by much either: They'd just be standing around waiting for the next item on which to work. Because of these limits in the range of possible performance, job satisfaction cannot be strongly related to it.

Another reason for the relatively weak link between job satisfaction and task performance is that many other factors also determine performance: working conditions, the availability of required materials and tools, the extent to which the task is structured, skills, abilities, previous experience, and so on. In many cases, the effects of these factors may be more important than job satisfaction in determining performance. For instance, even employees who love their jobs can't do their best work if the environment in which they work is too hot, too cold, or too noisy. Similarly, employees can't show excellent performance if they are working with broken or out-of-date equipment.

Another possibility is that, in some cases, job satisfaction *results* from good performance rather than vice versa. This possibility is easier to understand with respect to the performance of an entire organization than to the performance of individuals. Imagine that because a company adopts policies that have been found to enhance employees' performance (e.g., involving employees in key decisions, paying them for acquiring

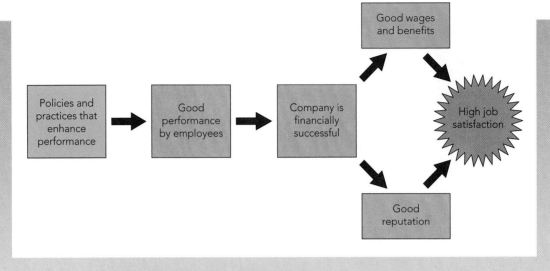

**Figure B.5 ■ Why Good Performance May Lead to
High Job Satisfaction Rather Than Vice Versa**
Enlightened policies on the part of a company (e.g., giving employees a voice in key decisions)
may enhance employees' performance. This, in turn, contributes to the company's financial
success—and to its ability to offer good pay and benefits—as well as enhances its reputation.
As a result, employees experience high job satisfaction. So, in such cases, it is good performance
that produces high job satisfaction rather than the other way around.

new skills), employees do show good performance. This good performance, in turn, enhances the financial success of the company. Because it is successful, the company can offer good benefits and increased pay and enjoys a very good reputation. The result? Employees feel well treated and are proud to work for this company, and this leads them to experience—and report—high levels of job satisfaction. In fact, recent findings reported by Schneider and his colleagues (2004) provide support for this reasoning, and for the model shown in Figure B.5. They found that the greater the financial success of many different companies, the higher the job satisfaction reported by employees in these companies. How did they know that it was financial success that predicted job satisfaction rather than the other way around? Because they used research methods in which measures of job satisfaction and measures of financial success (e.g., earnings per share) were acquired at different times over a four-year period. This meant that they could use job satisfaction at one time to predict financial success at another time and vice versa. Using this technique, they found that, in general, it was financial success that predicted higher job satisfaction. Although some aspects of job satisfaction (e.g., satisfaction with pay) did seem to influence financial success, they were the exception: Overall, financial success seemed to cause changes in job satisfaction rather than vice versa.

In sum, while job satisfaction is modestly related to individual performance—happy workers perform slightly better than unhappy ones—when we consider the performance of an organization overall, it is financial success that shapes attitudes. This finding fits quite well with social psychological research suggesting that the relationship between attitudes and behavior is far from simple. Yes, attitudes often affect behavior, but sometimes behavior shapes attitudes, too (e.g., recall our discussion of cognitive dissonance in Chapter 4). This turns out to be as true in work settings as any in other context, and this demonstrates strongly the benefits that can result from applying social psychology to the world of work. (What happens when employees in a company have low job satisfaction—negative attitudes toward their work and perhaps toward their organization, too? For information on this topic, please see the **Beyond the Headlines** section.)

Module B / Social Psychology Goes to Work

When Employees No Longer Care: Effects of Low Job Satisfaction

Shirk Ethic: How to Fake a Hard Day at the Office

The Wall Street Journal—David Wiskus gives new meaning to the term "working lunch." The Denver tech-support worker installed a program on his hand-held computer that allowed him to manipulate the screen on his office computer from a booth at a local diner. As he lingered over burgers and fries, he could open windows and move documents around on his screen, creating the impression that he had just stepped away from his desk for a moment.... It has never been easier to be a white-collar slacker. While some complain about how mobile technology has created a 24/7 work culture, a savvier crowd has moved on to a more rewarding pursuit: using technology to make it look like they are working when they are not. . . .

The tactic isn't new, but the tools are. Executives have long asked their secretaries to flip on the office light to make Friday absences less glaring; leaving a jacket on the back of your desk chair is another old trick. But the latest generation of office accessories, from cell phones to the RIM BlackBerry, have brought a new level of sophistication—and many new strategies for manipulating perception of your diligence. . . . . .

These are just a few of the tactics used by technologically savvy people to generate the *appearance* that they are working hard when, in fact, they are not. Here are a few others:

E-mail timers: Set these to send messages while you're out of the office, thus making people think you are burning the midnight oil when you are not.

Go ToMyPC.Com: This software allows you to control your work computer over the Internet from anywhere. The result? You can log on while on vacation and open up today's newspaper or recent memos to make people think you have just stepped out for a few minutes (see Figure B.6).

RIM BlackBerry Handheld: you can adjust this device so that e-mails you send from it look just like regular office messages. This allows you to leave work early but to send a few BlackBerry messages from the road to cover your tracks.

Many other tactics for appearing to work hard while out of the office or slacking off also exist. They require a degree of technological sophistication and often some personal expense. So why do people use them? Not simply because they don't like to work hard. Rather, research on the effects of job *dissatisfaction* (very low job satisfaction) suggests that they do this at least, in part, because they have very negative attitudes toward their work. They view their jobs as meaningless, their bosses as uncaring, and their companies as large organizations out to exploit them in any way they can and that won't reward good work anyway. As a result, they conclude that working hard is for the birds, and choose instead to do as little as possible—while simultaneously creating the *impression* that they are hard-working, diligent employees. The moral in all this? Organizations should do everything they can to develop high job satisfaction among their employees. Yes, this can be costly—it requires the adoption of fair systems for rewarding performance, making work as interesting as possible and assuring that working conditions are pleasant and comfortable. But *not* taking these actions may result in a situation in which employees' low morale and job satisfaction cause them to spend more time figuring out how to *avoid* work than actually working; and that, of course, can be the beginning of the end for any organization.

Figure B.6 ■ One Way to Look as Though You Are Working Hard When You Are Not!
Through the use of special software, individuals can run their computers from any location—the beach, a park, anywhere. As a result, they can look busy even when they are far from the office.

KEY POINTS

★ People spend more time at work than any other single activity. Because they often work with others, the findings and principles of social psychology help to explain behavior in work settings.

★ *Job satisfaction* refers to individuals' attitudes toward their jobs. Job satisfaction is influenced by organizational factors, such as working conditions and the fairness of reward systems, and personal factors, such as seniority, status, and specific personality traits. Recent findings suggest that job sat-

isfaction is often highly stable over time for many persons, and that it may be influenced by genetic factors.

★ The relationship between job satisfaction and task performance is relatively weak, partly because many factors other than these work-related attitudes influence performance.

★ Recent findings indicate that good performance may contribute to job satisfaction rather than vice versa.

Organizational Citizenship Behavior: Prosocial Behavior at Work

In Chapter 10, we examined many aspects of *prosocial behavior*—helpful actions that benefit others but have no obvious benefits for the persons who perform them. As we saw in that chapter, prosocial behavior stems from many different factors and can yield a wide range of effects. That such behavior often occurs in work settings, too, is obvious. If you have ever helped coworkers with their jobs, filled in for people when they had to be absent, or switched vacation dates with others to help them out, you already know that helping is common at work. Let's take a brief look at what research on prosocial behavior in work settings has found with respect to its forms and the factors that affect whether, and how often, it occurs.

The Nature of Prosocial Behavior at Work: Some Basic Forms

Although a number of different terms have been used to describe prosocial behavior in work settings (e.g., Van Dyne & LePine, 1998), most researchers refer to such behavior as **organizational citizenship behavior** (*OCB* for short)—prosocial behavior occurring within an organization that may or may not be rewarded by the organization (e.g., Organ, 1997). The fact that such behavior is not automatically or necessarily rewarded (e.g., through a bonus or a raise in pay) is important, because it suggests that OCB is performed voluntarily, often without any thought of external reward for doing so. Thus, it does indeed qualify as prosocial behavior according to the definition noted above. How do individuals working in an organization seek to help one another? Research findings suggest that they do so in many different ways. However, most seem to fall into one of the following five categories:

- *Altruism.* Helping others to perform their jobs (note that social psychologists do *not* use the term *altruism* in this way).

- *Conscientiousness.* Going beyond the minimum requirements of a job, doing more than is required. For instance, an employee who prides her- or himself on never missing a day of work or on taking short breaks is showing conscientiousness.

organizational citizenship behavior
Help people give each other at work that is not a required part of their jobs.

- *Civic virtue.* Participating in and showing concern for the "life" of the organization. Two examples: attending voluntary meetings and reading memos rather than throwing them in the trash.

- *Sportsmanship.* Showing willingness to tolerate unfavorable conditions without complaining. If an employee decides to "grin and bear it" rather than complain, she or he is showing this type of OCB.

- *Courtesy.* Making efforts to prevent interpersonal problems with others. For instance, "turning the other cheek" when annoyed by another person at work or behaving courteously toward them even when they are rude.

The results of several studies (e.g., Podsakoff et al., 1993) suggest that a large proportion of prosocial behavior at work falls into one or more of these categories, so they seem to provide a useful framework for studying helpful actions in organizations.

Helping at Work: What Factors Affect Its Occurrence?

What factors lead individuals to engage in various forms of helping? Recent findings indicate that a number of different factors play a role. One of these involves *social identity*—a concept we discussed in Chapters 5 and 12. Social identity refers to the extent to which employees identify with the companies for which they work—the extent to which they feel that their company is a group to which they belong. The greater such social identity, the more likely are employees to engage in various forms of citizenship behavior (Haslam, Branscombe, & Bachmann, 2003). Another important factor in helping at work is be the belief among employees that they are being treated *fairly.* As we saw in Chapter 12, perceptions of fairness can involve outcomes received (*distributive justice*—do people get rewards that reflect the size of their contributions?), the procedures used to determine these outcomes (*procedural justice*—are the procedures used to determine who gets what fair?), and the style or manner in which outcomes are delivered (*interactional justice*—do the people who distribute rewards treat the recipients openly and with courtesy?) (e.g., Greenberg & Lind, 2000). All three forms are important, and all play a role in willingness to help others by going "beyond the call of duty" (e.g., Colquitt, 2001). In other words, the greater the extent to which employees feel that they are being treated in these ways, the greater the tendency to help others in many ways.

In addition, recent research indicates that perceived fairness among employees also affects their willingness to do more than their jobs require with respect to customers as well as coworkers. For instance, Simons and Roberson (2003) measured perceptions of fair treatment by management—both procedural and interpersonal justice—among employees of a large chain of hotels. They also measured the employees' satisfaction with their supervisors, the extent to which they engaged in discretionary service behaviors (going out of their way to help customers), their intention to remain on the job, and customers' actual satisfaction with the treatment they received. Results indicated that the stronger employees' beliefs that they were being treated fairly, the more they delivered extra service to customers, the greater their intention of remaining on the job, and the greater the customers' actual satisfaction (see Figure B.7 on page 548). In other words, perceived fairness played a key role in employees' willingness to do extra things for customers—another form of OCB.

One way in which employees in an organization engage in helping behavior is by trading favors with one another, as the old saying "You scratch my back and I'll scratch yours" suggests. In fact, this kind of *reciprocity* tends to build strong working relationships: People come to count on each other's help, and this strengthens the bonds between them (e.g., Kramer & Tyler, 1996). But when people exchange favors, do the givers (the favor-doers) and the receivers (the ones for whom the favor is done) view the situation in the same way? As we saw in Chapter 10, being helped can have very different effects

Figure B.7 ■ Prosocial Behavior toward Customers
Employees often show prosocial behavior not only toward coworkers, but also toward customers. They are most likely to engage in such behaviors when they feel that they are being treated fairly by their company.

from actually giving help; in fact, persons who are helped by others sometimes react negatively to the obligations this generates. Recent research suggests that the same kinds of differences may exist in work settings, too. Specifically, it appears that persons who receive favors tend to assess them largely in terms of the *style* with which they are delivered—in terms of *interactional justice.* They are sensitive to the extent to which the giver treated them with respect, was open with them, and so on (Flynn & Brockner, 2003). They are less concerned with the benefits the favor confers. In contrast, givers focus on the benefits they are providing for the recipient and put less weight on the manner in which it is given. The result? Persons who do favors for others in an offhand or seemingly routine manner may find that the recipients do not feel gratitude and do not feel obligated to reciprocate; after all, in their eyes, principles of interactional justice have been violated. So, reciprocity may indeed by an important cause of helping in work settings, but it may operate differently for favor-givers and favor-receivers.

Another factor that influences OCB is employees' perceptions of the breadth of their jobs—which behaviors are required and which are voluntary. The more broadly employees define their jobs, the more likely they are to engage in instances of OCB (Morrison, 1994; Van Dyne & LePine, 1998). For instance, if a professor believes that helping other professors by taking over their classes when they have to be out of town is part of her job—this is simply the "right thing to do"—she may be much more willing to engage in such behavior than if she believes that this is definitely *not* part of her job and *not* her responsibility.

Finally, the frequency of OCB seems to be influenced by attitudes held by employees about their organizations—attitudes generally known as *organizational commitment.* The more favorable these are, the higher the frequency of OCB.

In sum, many factors seem to influence the occurrence of helping (OCB) at work, just as many factors influence such behavior in other settings. Whatever the specific causes, however, it is clear that a high incidence of helpful, considerate behavior can not only make work settings more pleasant, but also enhance performance and behaviors that help the organization itself to prosper (e.g., Simons & Roberson, 2003).

KEY POINTS

★ Individuals often engage in prosocial behavior at work. This is known as *organizational citizenship behavior* (OCB) and can take many different forms.

★ OCB is influenced by several factors, including trust in one's boss and the organization, the extent to which employees define their job responsibilities broadly, and organizational commitment (their attitudes toward their organization).

★ Persons who do favors for others often tend to focus on the benefits these confer, while those who receive the favors tend to concentrate on the manner in which they are delivered. This can lead to situations in which persons who receive favors do not feel obligated to reciprocate.

Leadership: Influence in Group Settings

Try this simple demonstration with your friends. Ask them to rate themselves, on a seven-point scale ranging from 1 (very low) to 7 (very high), on *leadership potential.* Unless they are a very unusual group, here's what you'll find: Most will rate themselves as *average* or *above* on this dimension. This suggests that they view leadership very favorably. But what *is* **leadership?** In a sense, it's like love: easy to recognize but hard to define. However, psychologists generally use this term to refer to *the process through which one member of a group (its leader) influences other group members toward attainment of shared group goals* (Avolio, 1999; Vecchio, 1997; Yukl, 1998). In other words, being a leader involves *influence*—a leader is the group member who exerts the most influence within the group.

Research on leadership has long been part of social psychology and several related fields, so literally thousands of research studies about it have been published (e.g., Bass, 1998). Here, we consider key aspects of this work by focusing on the following topics: (1) why some individuals, but not others, become leaders; (2) what leaders actually do—how they fill this role in their groups; and (3) what the difference is between two important forms of leadership—*transactional* and *transformational* leadership.

Why Do Some Persons, but Not Others, Become Leaders?

Are some people born to lead? Common sense suggests that this is so. Famous leaders such as Alexander the Great, Queen Elizabeth I, and Abraham Lincoln seem to differ from ordinary people in several respects. Such observations led early researchers to formulate the **great person theory of leadership**—the view that great leaders possess certain traits that set them apart from most human beings, traits that are possessed by all such leaders, no matter when or where they lived (see Figure B.8 on page 550).

These are intriguing ideas, but early research designed to test them was not encouraging. Try as they might, researchers could not come up with a short list of key traits shared by all great leaders (Yukl, 1998). In more recent years, however, this situation has changed greatly. More sophisticated research methods, coupled with a better understanding of the basic dimensions of human personality, have led many researchers to conclude that leaders do indeed differ from other persons in several important ways

leadership
The process through which one member of a group (its leader) influences other group members toward attainment of shared group goals.

great person theory of leadership
The view that leaders possess certain traits that set them apart from other persons, traits that are possessed by all leaders no matter where or when they lived.

| Dalai Lama Tenzin Gyatso | Queen Elizabeth I | Martin Luther King, Jr. | Franklin D. Roosevelt |

Figure B.8 ■ **The Great Person Theory of Leadership**
Are some persons born to lead? The *great person theory of leadership* suggests that they
are, and that, therefore, all great leaders at all times in history share certain traits.

(Kirkpatrick & Locke, 1991). What special traits do leaders possess? Research findings point to the conclusion that leaders rate higher than most people on the following traits: *drive*—the desire for achievement coupled with high energy and resolution; *self-confidence; creativity;* and *leadership motivation*—the desire to be in charge and exercise authority over others. Perhaps the most important single characteristic of leaders, however, is a high level of *flexibility*—the ability to recognize what actions or approaches are required in a given situation and then to act accordingly (Bennis, 2001; Zaccaro, Foti, & Kenny, 1991).

In addition, research findings suggest that several of the **"Big Five" dimensions of personality** may play an important role in who becomes a leader (e.g., Watson & Clark, 1997.) For instance, persons high in extraversion (e.g., friendliness), in openness to experience, and in agreeableness (e.g., the tendency to trust others, at least initially) are more likely to become leaders than are persons low on these dimensions (Judge et al., 2002).

So, are some persons more suited for leadership than others? The answer appears to be "yes," at least to some extent. Persons who possess certain traits are more likely to become leaders and to succeed in this role than are persons who do not possess these traits or possess them to a lesser degree. It is also clear, however, that leaders do *not* operate in a social vacuum. On the contrary, different groups, facing different tasks and problems, seem to require different types of leaders—or at least leaders who demonstrate contrasting styles (House & Podsakoff, 1994; Locke, 1991). For instance, in a group that deals mostly with routine, predictable events (e.g., a work group in a government agency), a high level of creativity or drive on the part of the leader would not be required. But in a group that faces one crisis after another (e.g., physicians and nurses working in an emergency room of a large hospital), these traits would be more essential. So, traits, though they do matter where leadership is concerned, are only part of the total picture. Different persons, showing different patterns of characteristics, can rise to positions of leadership under different circumstances. With this thought in mind, let's take a closer look at precisely *how* leaders lead—what they actually do while performing this important role.

What Do Leaders Do? Basic Dimensions of Leader Behavior

All leaders are definitely not alike. They may share certain traits to a degree, but they differ greatly in terms of their approach to leadership and the behaviors they show in this role (e.g., George, 1995; Peterson, 1997). Although there are probably as many dif-

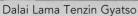

"Big Five" dimensions of personality
Basic dimensions of personality; where individuals stand along several of these dimensions (e.g., extraversion, agreeableness, neuroticisim) is often apparent in their behavior.

ferent styles of leadership as there are leaders, research on leader behavior suggests that, in fact, most leaders can be placed along a small number of dimensions relating to their overall approach to leadership. Two such dimensions emerged in very early research on leadership (e.g., Weissenberg & Kavanagh, 1972) and have been confirmed over and over again. The first is known as **initiating structure** (or **production-orientation**). Leaders high on this dimension are concerned primarily with getting the job done. They engage in actions such as organizing work, urging subordinates to follow the rules, setting goals, and making leader and subordinate roles explicit. In contrast, leaders low on this dimension engage in such actions to a lesser degree.

The second dimension is known as **consideration** (or **person-orientation**). Leaders high on this dimension focus on establishing good relations with their subordinates and on being liked by them. They engage in such actions as doing favors for subordinates, explaining things to them, and watching out for their welfare. Leaders low on this dimension, in contrast, do not really care how well they get along with their subordinates (see Figure B.9 for an overview of these two basic dimensions of leader behavior).

Is either of these two styles superior? Not really. Both offer a mixed pattern of advantages and disadvantages. High consideration (high concern with people) can lead to improved group morale, but because such leaders do not like to tell subordinates what to do or give them negative feedback, efficiency sometimes suffers. In contrast, when leaders are high on initiating structure, efficiency may be high but subordinates may conclude that the leader does not really care about them, and their commitment to the organization may suffer. Overall, though, it appears that leaders who are high on both dimensions may have an edge in many situations. In other words, leaders who are concerned with establishing good relations with their subordinates *and* with maintaining efficiency and productivity may often prove superior to leaders showing other patterns of behavior.

Two other dimensions of leader behavior that have been uncovered by careful research involve the extent to which leaders make all the decisions themselves or allow

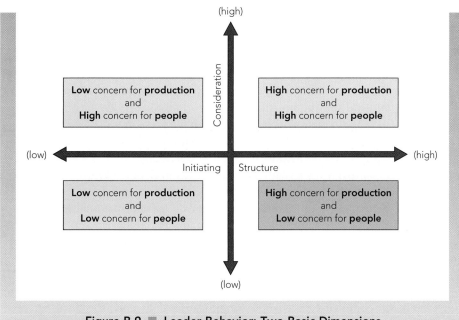

Figure B.9 ■ Leader Behavior: Two Basic Dimensions
Leader behavior has been found to vary along the two dimensions shown here: *consideration*, which involves concern for people and good relations with them, and *initiating structure*, which involves concern for production and task completion. These dimensions are largely independent, so any leader can be high or low on each.

participation by group members (an *autocratic–participative* dimension), and the extent to which leaders try to "run the show" by closely directing the activities of all group members—(a *directive–permissive* dimension) (Muczyk & Reimann, 1987; Peterson, 1997). If you think back over your own experiences, you can probably recall leaders who were high or low on both of these dimensions. For instance, in a summer job I (Robert Baron) once held, the manager of the department was definitely on the directive end of the directive–permissive dimension: He was constantly looking over our shoulders and telling us how to do virtually everything. Many employees dislike this kind of micromanagement because it suggests that their boss has no confidence in them; and, in fact, that's just how I felt. Again, being high or low in each of these dimensions is not necessarily good or bad from the point of view of leader effectiveness—this depends on the situation. For instance, under emergency conditions, when decisions have to be made quickly (as in a hospital emergency room), an autocratic style may be helpful; under more relaxed conditions, though, most persons prefer participative leaders who let them have input into the decision-making situation. The same is true for the directive–permissive dimension: When subordinates are new at their jobs, they need direction from the leader; once they have mastered their jobs, though, it is usually better for the leader to take a step back and leave them alone.

Transactional and Transformational Leaders: Different Approaches, Different Effects

Have you ever seen films of John F. Kennedy? Franklin Roosevelt? Martin Luther King, Jr.? If so, you may have noticed that there seemed to be something special about these leaders. As you listened to their speeches, you may have found yourself being moved by their words and stirred by the vision of the future they presented. If so, you are definitely not alone: These leaders exerted powerful effects on many millions of persons and, by doing so, changed their societies. Leaders who accomplish such feats are termed **transformational leaders** (House & Howell, 1992; Kohl, Steers, & Terborg, 1995). Such leaders are often viewed as being *charismatic*—they exert such profound effects on their followers that it almost seems as though they wield some kind of magical power. In fact, though, careful research by social psychologists suggests that there is nothing mystical about their impact. Rather, it stems from four characteristics that they demonstrate to a high degree: *idealized influence*—they are admired and trusted by their followers; *inspirational motivation*—they know how to inspire people by offering them meaning and challenge in their work, often through the presentation of stirring *visions* of a glorious future; *intellectual stimulation*—they stimulate their followers to be innovative and creative by questioning existing assumptions and reframing problems in new ways; and *individualized consideration*—they pay attention to their followers' needs for achievement and growth by acting as a mentor (e.g., Avolio, Bass, & Jung, 1999; Antonakis, 2001). Together, these four components provide transformational leaders with tremendous influence over their followers. They can boost followers' motivation and performance to very high levels, command great allegiance and respect, and induce followers to undertake difficult or even dangerous tasks (Avolio & Bass, 2002; Bass et al., 2003; DeGroot, Kiker, & Cross, 2000).

In addition, other findings suggest that transformational leaders also demonstrate high levels of self-confidence, excellent communication skills, and an exciting personal style (House, Spangler, & Woycke, 1991). And leaders are more likely to be as charismatic when they behave in a way that affirms their membership in the group (e.g., Haslam et al., 2001). In other words, leaders are seen as being charismatic to the extent that they are perceived by their followers as "doing it for us"—behaving in ways that promote the welfare of the group (e.g., Haslam et al., 2003). Finally, transformational

transformational leaders
Leaders who, because of several characteristics, exert profound effects on their followers.

leaders are often masters of *impression management,* a process we described in Chapter 3. When this skill is added to the traits and behaviors mentioned above, and combined with transformational leaders' use of vision and reframing of problems, the ability of such leaders to influence large numbers of followers loses its mystery. One more point: Recent findings suggest that, in fact, transformational leaders produce two seemingly contradictory effects on followers. On the one hand, they make followers *dependent* on them, and on the other, they *empower* them, increasing their followers' feelings of self-efficacy and self-esteem (Kark, Shamir, & Chen, 2003). How can both of these effects occur? Because, apparently, transformational (charismatic) leaders induce high levels of identification with themselves personally, *and* high levels of identification with the group they lead. As a result, when followers do what transformational leaders want them to do, they feel closer to this person and, simultaneously, also feel closer to or more identified with their group; that, in turn, boosts their self-esteem. This is why the followers of transformational leaders, whether they be great political leaders or the leaders of cults, feel powerful allegiance to the leader yet also believe that the leader has somehow *increased* their personal freedom and self-esteem.

In contrast to transformational leaders, **transactional leaders** are the kind we are more likely to meet in our everyday lives. They, too, exert strong influence over their followers, but they do it in a very different way. Such leaders work largely within the system by offering praise, rewards, and resources for good performance, but negative outcomes (e.g., disciplinary actions) for poor performance. They build motivation among followers by clarifying key goals and providing recognition for achieving them rather than through inspirational appeals or stirring visions. Yet, transactional leaders can be highly effective; they can boost the motivation, morale, and productivity of their followers and keep things "humming along" in situations in which neither the work being performed nor the goals being sought are highly inspiring—in other words, in most ordinary work settings (e.g., Goodwin, Wofford, & Whittington, 2001).

Clearly, transactional and transformational leaders differ sharply in style; and this, in turn, leads to an intriguing question: Is either type better from the point of view of maximizing a group's performance? To find out, Waldman and his colleagues (Waldman et al., 2001) asked several hundred high-level executives in more than one hundred different companies to rate the CEO (leader) of their company in terms of both styles of leadership. These ratings were then related to the companies' financial performance (how successful they were financially). An additional aspect of the study involved the extent to which the companies faced an uncertain and unpredictable environment. Waldman et al. (2001) reasoned that charismatic (transformational) leaders would do better in uncertain, rapidly changing environments, because such leaders would be more effective than transactional leaders in gaining high commitment and effort from employees. But this advantage would disappear in more stable environments.

As you can see from Figure B.10 page 554, results confirmed this prediction. Whether leaders were low or high in charisma did not matter much in stable, unchanging environments. But in rapidly changing, chaotic environments, companies whose leaders were high in charisma outperformed those whose leaders were low in charisma. Interestingly, the extent to which leaders were low or high in transactional leadership style did not influence the companies' financial performance.

In sum, several decades of research employing a wide range of participants and many different measures of group performance indicate that leaders, and their specific style of performing this role, do indeed matter. Although there does not appear to be one single style of leadership that is always best, it is clear that some styles are preferred by most group members, and that, depending on the circumstances faced by a group, some leaders are more likely than others to facilitate performance. So what's the final message in this research? That choosing the right leader is a crucial task for *all* groups, because it can strongly shape the group's morale, motivation, and performance.

transactional leaders
Leaders who direct their groups by rewarding them for desired behavior, and by taking action to correct mistakes or departures from existing rules. Such leaders generally strengthen existing structures and strategies within an organization.

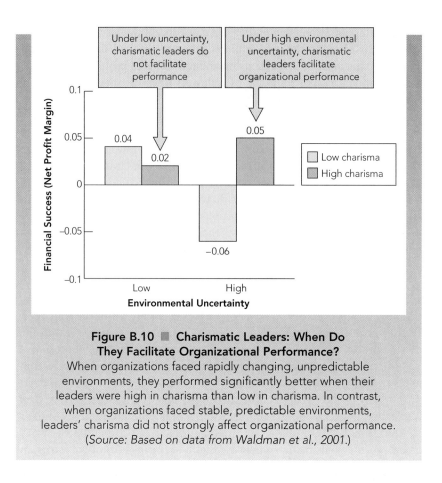

Figure B.10 ■ Charismatic Leaders: When Do They Facilitate Organizational Performance?
When organizations faced rapidly changing, unpredictable environments, they performed significantly better when their leaders were high in charisma than low in charisma. In contrast, when organizations faced stable, predictable environments, leaders' charisma did not strongly affect organizational performance. (*Source: Based on data from Waldman et al., 2001.*)

KEY POINTS

★ *Leadership* refers to the process through which one member of a group (its leader) influences other group members toward the attainment of shared group goals.

★ While the *great person theory of leadership* has been shown to be false, recent findings suggest that leaders do indeed differ from other persons with respect to several traits. For instance, two of the *"Big Five" dimensions of personality*—extraversion and openness to experience—seem to be related to becoming a leader and success in this role.

★ In addition, leaders vary with respect to their behavior or style. Classic research in social psychology suggested that leaders vary in terms of two basic dimensions: *consideration* and *initiating structure*. In addition, leaders vary along two other key dimensions: autocratic–participative and directive–permissive.

★ *Transformational* (charismatic) *leaders* exert profound effects on their followers and often change their societies. Research on the nature of such leadership suggests that it stems from certain behaviors by leaders, such as stating a clear vision, framing the group's goals in ways that magnify their importance, and possessing a stirring personal style.

★ In contrast, *transactional leaders* exert influence through such steps as clarifying goals and rewarding good performance. They operate within the system rather than change it.

★ Recent research suggests that transformational leaders may produce better group performance in environments that are changing rapidly, but that they are not superior to transactional leaders in more stable environments.

The Social Psychology of Entrepreneurship

During the 1990s, large corporations in the United States downsized more than six million jobs out of existence. Yet, prosperity grew at a rapid pace and the unemployment rate actually *dropped*. What accounted for this puzzling state of affairs? The answer seems clear: The new companies started by **entrepreneurs**—individuals who recognize an opportunity for a new business and actually start one—more than took up the slack. In fact, there is now widespread recognition among economists, business experts, and social psychologists, of the following fact: Entrepreneurs play a key role in the economies of their cities, states, or even entire countries (e.g., Shane, 2003). Moreover, they do not simply create wealth for themselves; rather, they also provide new jobs and increased prosperity for large numbers of other persons (see Figure B.11; Venkataraman, 1997).

Given these basic facts, a growing number of social psychologists have begun to turn their attention to understanding this unique group of individuals—people who, in a sense, create "something" (successful new businesses) out of what is, initially, "nothing": an idea for something new, plus their own ingenuity and hard work. But what, you may be wondering, is the relevance of social psychology to the study of entrepreneurship? The answer is this: The findings, theories, and principles of social psychology can shed important light on key questions about entrepreneurs. For instance, research indicates that social psychology can help us to understand the issues such as these: (1) Why do some persons but not others, decide to become entrepreneurs in the first place? (2) Why are some persons so much more successful in this role than others? We now summarize the ways in which the knowledge base of social psychology has, in fact, contributed greatly to efforts to answer these questions.

Why Do Some Persons Become Entrepreneurs? The Role of Social, Cognitive, and Personal Factors

I (Robert Baron) hold three U.S. patents (for a special kind of air filter) and actually started and ran my own company to develop and sell this product (see Figure B.12). How did a social psychologist such as myself ever get the idea of becoming an entrepreneur? One important source seems clear: My grandfather and two of my uncles had been entrepreneurs before me. So, as I grew up, I heard them talk about how they had started their own businesses. I never planned to do this myself, but later, when my

entrepreneurs
Individuals who recognize an opportunity for a new business and actually start one.

Figure B.12 ■ Social Psychologists Can Be Entrepreneurs, Too!
One of the authors (Robert Baron) started a company to produce the air cleaner shown here. This device filtered the air and also provided a noise reduction system to increase privacy and aid in sleep. It also released, if owners wished, pleasant fragrances.

research led me to come up with an idea for a new product, I had these memories to draw upon. So, one important factor in the decision to become an entrepreneur is a kind of social influence known as *modeling* (or *observational learning;* Bandura, 1997). In other words, being exposed to other persons who are entrepreneurs can provide individuals with the knowledge and skill they need to become an entrepreneur—and can simply give them the idea of doing this! Many studies suggest that, in fact, having entrepreneurs in one's family *does* play a role in the decision to become an entrepreneur (e.g., Shane, 2003), so, clearly, social factors are involved in this decision.

Other findings indicate that cognitive processes long studied by social psychologists also play a role. Do you remember our discussion of cognitive biases or "tilts" in Chapter 2? Several of these are related to the decision to become an entrepreneur. For instance, consider the general tendency to expect more favorable outcomes in almost any situation than can rationally be expected—the *optimistic bias* (e.g., Newby-Clark & Ross, 2003). Research findings indicate that entrepreneurs may be more subject to this bias than are other persons (e.g., Simon, Houghton, & Aquino, 2000). Similarly, do you recall the *planning fallacy*—the tendency to believe that we can accomplish more in a given period of time than we actually can? Research (e.g., Baron, 1998) suggests that, again, entrepreneurs may be more susceptible to this bias than are other persons.

Closely related to this is the perception of *risk.* Many studies indicate that although entrepreneurs are not necessarily more prone to take risks than are other persons, they do tend to perceive lower levels of risk in any situation (e.g., Busenitz & Barney, 1997; Stewart & Roth, 2001). This, in turn, leads them to be more willing to "take the plunge" and leave secure jobs for the uncertainty of a new business. New ventures *are* uncertain—fewer than half survive for more than a year (e.g., Shane, 2003). In sum, cognitive factors long studied by social psychologists definitely play a role in the decision to become an entrepreneur, and researchers in the field of entrepreneurship have drawn on these findings in their efforts to answer this important question.

What about individual characteristics, such as aspects of personality? Do they also play a role in the decision to become an entrepreneur? Absolutely. Growing evidence suggests that certain aspects of the "Big Five" dimensions of personality play a role in this decision. For instance, persons high in extraversion are more likely to start new businesses than are persons who are low in this dimension (e.g., Baron & Markman, 2004). Perhaps more surprisingly, persons high in *openness to experience* are actually *less* likely than persons low in this trait to start new businesses (e.g., Ciavarella et al., 2004). Why would this be so? Because such persons tend to enjoy new and innovative activities, and like to jump around from one activity to another. Thus, they find the need to focus intensely, which is required in starting a new business, unappealing, and so tend to avoid becoming entrepreneurs.

In sum, several concepts and findings of social psychology have provided new insight into why some persons, but not others, decide to become entrepreneurs. Clearly, this is an important new way in which social psychology is being applied to important, practical issues.

Why Are Some Entrepreneurs More Successful Than Others?

Another key question concerning entrepreneurs is this: Why are some entrepreneurs so much more successful than others? Why, for instance, do some, like Bill Gates, found companies that go on to change the world, while others found companies that either fail or merely limp along for many years without much success—companies sometimes described as "the living dead." One possibility is that successful entrepreneurs begin with an exceptionally good or useful idea (see Figure B.13). But another interpretation is that, once again, social, cognitive, and individual factors play an important role.

With respect to social factors that play a role in entrepreneurs' success, recent findings indicate that entrepreneurs' *social skills*—their ability to interact effectively with others (e.g., skill at social perception, being persuasive, making good first impressions)—play a key role. Evidence for this prediction has recently been reported by Baron and Markman (2003). They asked entrepreneurs working in two different industries (cosmetics and high-tech) to complete a questionnaire designed to measure several social skills. At the same time, they obtained information on the entrepreneurs' financial success—their earnings from their new businesses. Results indicated that one aspect of social competence— accuracy in perceiving others—was positively related to financial success for both groups of entrepreneurs. In addition, another social skill—the ability to adapt quickly and well to new social situations (social adaptability)—was related to financial success for entrepreneurs in the cosmetics industry. Finally, expressiveness (which is closely linked to the "Big Five" dimension of extraversion) was positively related to the financial success of entrepreneurs in the high-tech industry. The questionnaire employed to assess social competence was cross-validated with a third group of entrepreneurs who completed this measure themselves, and whose social competence was also rated by persons who knew them well. The two sets of ratings agreed closely, thus providing evidence for the validity of the measure employed by Baron and Markman (2003).

Why should entrepreneurs' social skills exert such a strong effect or be so useful to entrepreneurs? Perhaps because during the process of new venture creation, entrepreneurs must form new social relationships with many different persons (e.g., customers, suppliers, new employees) "from scratch." Moreover, they must do so in

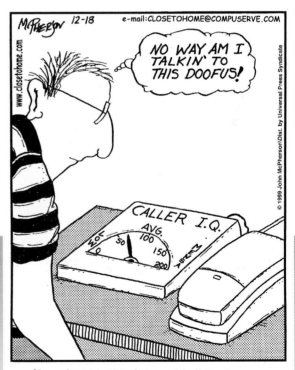

New phone technology we'd all like to see.

Figure B.13 ■ **A Good Idea Provides a Strong Start for Entrepreneurs . . . But It Is Definitely Not the Entire Story**
Starting with a good idea—one for a product or service many people would find useful—is certainly helpful for entrepreneurs. But, as described in the text, many social, cognitive, and individual factors also play a role. (*Source:* CLOSE TO HOME © 1999 John McPherson. Reprinted with permission of UNIVERSAL PRESS SYNDICATE. All rights reserved.)

environments that are highly uncertain and unstructured (see, e.g., Carter, Gartner, & Reynolds, 1996). It is precisely in such contexts—ones in which individuals cannot fall back on the established relationships or clearly prescribed norms and roles—that social skills may prove most useful.

Cognitive factors, too, have been found to play an important role in entrepreneurs' success. For example, research in the field of entrepreneurship has examined the potential role of *counterfactual thinking* in entrepreneurs' success. As you may recall from our discussion of such thinking in Chapter 2, counterfactual thinking refers to the tendency to imagine different outcomes in a given situation than actually occurred (i.e., "what might have been") (e.g., Roese, 1997). Research on the effects of counterfactual thinking suggests that it offers a mixed bag of benefits and potential costs in many contexts, including business settings. On the negative side, engaging in such thought often leads to feelings of regret about actions not performed, or actions that were performed but yielded negative results. Such feelings are unpleasant and can interfere with task performance in a wide range of settings (e.g., Roese, 1997). On the positive side, engaging in counterfactual thinking sometimes induces individuals to consider past events from the perspective of constructing more effective strategies—ones more likely to generate positive outcomes on future occasions than the actions or strategies actually adopted in the past. Because new business have limited resources, failures by entrepreneurs to learn from their mistakes in this way can be disastrous.

One study on counterfactual thinking among entrepreneurs (Baron, 2000) compared individuals who had started and were currently running their own businesses (entrepreneurs) with other persons who had no interest in doing so and had, in fact, never started a business (school teachers, government employees). The two groups were matched on a wide range of socioeconomic variables (age, education, income). Both were asked to indicate the frequency with which they had engaged in counterfactual thinking following disappointing outcomes and the effects of such thoughts on their affective states. Results were clear: Entrepreneurs reported engaging in counterfactual thinking significantly less frequently than did nonentrepreneurs. Moreover, they reported less negative affect as a result of such thoughts (e.g., fewer regrets). In fact, when asked to list the three events in their lives they regretted most, entrepreneurs often failed to identify three such events and reported a significantly lower number than did nonentrepreneurs. As several entrepreneurs who participated in the study put it, they much preferred to focus on the future, and viewed thinking about events that might have occurred but did not as a waste of time (Baron, 2000).

Combining these findings with the reasoning noted above, it seems possible that although entrepreneurs generally engage in counterfactual thinking less often than do other persons, successful ones may be more adept at using such thoughts to develop improved task strategies. In other words, they may profit more from their past mistakes. This is an interesting possibility, and one that can readily be investigated in future research.

Earlier, we saw that various cognitive "tilts" or biases might play a role in the decision to become an entrepreneur. Susceptibility to such biases also may play a role in shaping entrepreneurs' success. Specifically, it seems possible that successful entrepreneurs, as compared with unsuccessful ones, may be less subject to a wide range of cognitive errors or biases that can serve to distort information processing and lead to less-than-optimal decisions (e.g., Baron, 1998; Busenitz & Barney, 1997; Simon, Houghton, & Aquino, 2000). Included among such errors might be several discussed previously (e.g., the *optimistic bias*—Shepperd, Ouellette, & Fernandez, 1996; the planning fallacy and affect infusion—Forgas, 1995a). These may prove especially deadly to new ventures, which generally lack the resources of more mature organizations.

One additional cognitive "tilt" that may be especially relevant to entrepreneurs' success is known as *sunk costs* or *escalation of commitment*—the tendency to stick with decisions that generate initial negative outcomes (e.g., Ross & Staw, 1993). To the extent entrepreneurs fall prey to this cognitive bias, they may put the survival of their new ventures in jeopardy. On the other hand, new businesses rarely obtain positive results immediately; thus, the tendency to stay the course in the face of initial, negative results may be an essential ingredient in attaining ultimate success. These considerations lead to the intriguing possibility that successful entrepreneurs may be ones who are good at knowing when to persevere or when to switch to alternative strategies (see, e.g., Baron, 2004).

Additional insights into the potential role of sunk costs in entrepreneurs' success are provided by Brockner, Higgins, and Low (2004), who relate this cognitive error to **regulatory focus theory**—an important framework for understanding that in regulating their own behavior in order to achieve desired end-states, individuals adopt one of two contrasting perspectives (e.g., Camacho, Higgins, & Luger, 2003). In the first, known as a *promotion focus,* the ultimate goal sought by individuals is *accomplishment*—attaining positive outcomes. When they adopt this regulatory focus, persons seek to generate many hypotheses and to explore all possible means to reach the goals they desire. In a *prevention focus,* in contrast, the ultimate goal sought is *safety*—avoiding negative outcomes. Thus, when individuals adopt this regulatory focus, they tend to generate fewer hypotheses and focus on avoiding mistakes—actions or decisions that will produce negative outcomes. Many studies (e.g., Higgins & Silberman, 1998) indicate that individuals differ in their chronic preferences for a promotion or prevention focus. In addition, individuals can be induced to adopt one or the other of these two foci by situational factors (e.g., instructions to focus either on achieving gains or on avoiding losses; e.g., Liberman et al., 1999).

What is the relationship of regulatory focus theory to sunk costs? Brockner, Higgins, and Low (2004) suggest that whether a promotion focus or a prevention focus is more effective from the point of view of helping entrepreneurs avoid the dangers of sunk costs depends strongly on how the entrepreneurs interpret initial, negative results. If these are seen as stemming from better options that are currently available but that they (the entrepreneurs) not pursuing, then persons with a promotion focus will have an edge: They will be better able than persons with a prevention focus to "cut loose" from failing decisions. Why? Because persons who have a promotion focus are concerned primarily with attaining positive results, and the best way to do so is to switch to the new, better, and available course of action that is currently available. Persons with a prevention focus, in contrast, are mainly concerned with avoiding losses, and giving up on their present course of action means that they are certain to experience such outcomes (i.e., losses).

In contrast, if the superior option is *not* available, persons with a prevention focus may have an advantage—they may find it easier to remove themselves from the trap of sunk costs. Persons who have a prevention focus are concerned primarily with minimizing losses, so they may quickly give up on the failing course of action they are pursuing. In contrast, persons with a promotion focus may continue trying to reverse the negative outcomes they are experiencing because they don't see any better course of action. Research findings provide clear support for both predictions, so it appears that regulatory focus (promotion or prevention) is indeed closely linked to how people handle the problem of sunk costs.

We could continue, but by now, the main point should be clear: The findings, theories, and principles of social psychology offer many important insights into how entrepreneurs think and how they behave. Because entrepreneurs develop new products and services that benefit millions of persons and have such powerful economic effects, we believe that this is an example of applying social psychology at its best: Not only does it add to our basic knowledge, it enhances human welfare, too. Truly, it doesn't get any better than that!

regulatory focus theory
An important framework for understanding that in regulating their own behavior in order to achieve desired end-states, individuals adopt one of two contrasting perspectives: a *promotion focus,* in which they focus primarily on attaining positive outcomes, or a *prevention focus,* in which they focus primarily on avoiding negative outcomes.

KEY POINTS

★ Social factors (e.g., exposure to family members who are entrepreneurs), cognitive factors (e.g., perceptions of risk, the optimistic bias), and individual variables (e.g., aspects of personality), all play a role in the decision to become an *entrepreneur*.

★ Similarly, social factors (e.g., social skills) and cognitive factors (e.g., counterfactual thinking, susceptibility to various cognitive biases such as sunk costs) influence entrepreneurs' success.

SUMMARY AND REVIEW OF KEY POINTS

Work-Related Attitudes: The Nature and Effects of Job Satisfaction

■ People spend more time at work than at any other single activity. Because they often work with others, the findings and principles of social psychology help to explain behavior in work settings.

■ *Job satisfaction* refers to individuals' attitudes toward their jobs. Job satisfaction is influenced by organizational factors, such as working conditions and the fairness of reward systems, and personal factors, such as seniority, status, and specific personality traits. Recent findings suggest that job satisfaction is often highly stable over time for many persons, and that it may be influenced by genetic factors.

■ The relationship between job satisfaction and task performance is relatively weak, partly because many factors other than these work-related attitudes influence performance. Recent findings indicate that good performance may contribute to job satisfaction rather than vice versa.

Organizational Citizenship Behavior: Prosocial Behavior at Work

■ Individuals often engage in prosocial behavior at work. This is known as *organizational citizenship behavior* (OCB) and can take many different forms.

■ OCB is influenced by several factors, including trust in one's boss and the organization, the extent to which employees define their job responsibilities broadly, and organizational commitment—(their attitudes toward their organization).

■ Persons who do favors for others often tend to focus on the benefits these confer, while those who receive the favors tend to concentrate on the manner in which the favors are delivered. This can lead to situations in which persons who receive favors do not feel obligated to reciprocate.

Leadership: Influence in Group Settings

■ *Leadership* refers to the process through which one member of a group (its leader) influences other group members toward the attainment of shared group goals.

■ Although the *great person theory of leadership* has been shown to be false, recent findings suggest that leaders do indeed differ from other persons with respect to several traits. For instance, two of the *"Big Five" dimensions of personality*—extraversion and openness to experience—seem to be related to becoming a leader and success in this role.

■ In addition, leaders vary with respect to their behavior or style. Classic research in social psychology suggested that leaders vary in terms of two basic dimensions: *consideration* and *initiating structure*. In addition, leaders vary along two other key dimensions: autocratic–participative and directive–permissive.

■ *Transformational* (charismatic) *leaders* exert profound effects on their followers and often change their societies. Research on the nature of such leadership suggests that it stems from certain behaviors by leaders, such as stating a clear vision, framing the group's goals in ways that magnify their importance, and possessing a stirring personal style.

- In contrast, *transactional leaders* exert influence through such steps as clarifying goals and rewarding good performance. They operate within the system rather than change it.

- Recent research suggests that transformational leaders may produce better group perfor-

mance in environments that are changing rapidly, but that they are not superior to transactional leaders in more stable environments.

The Social Psychology of Entrepreneurship

- Social factors (e.g., exposure to family members who are entrepreneurs), cognitive factors (e.g., perceptions of risk, the

optimistic bias), and individual variables (e.g., aspects of personality), all play a role in the decision to become an entrepreneur.

- Similarly, social factors (e.g., social skills) and cognitive factors (e.g., counterfactual thinking, susceptibility to various cognitive biases such as sunk costs) influence entrepreneurs' success.

Connections INTEGRATING SOCIAL PSYCHOLOGY

In this chapter, you read about . . .	In other chapters, you will find related discussions of . . .
job satisfaction	the basic nature of attitudes (Chapter 4)
organizational citizenship behavior	prosocial behavior (Chapter 10)
leadership	other aspects of influence (Chapter 9), other group processes (Chapter 12)
factors that influence the decision to become an entrepreneur	cognitive factors that play a role in the decision to become an entrepreneur (Chapter 2)
factors that influence entrepreneurs' success	social factors that play a role in such success, such as social skills (Chapter 3)

Thinking about Connections

1. Social psychologists have developed many techniques for changing attitudes (see Chapter 4). Do you think that these techniques might be useful in increasing employees' job satisfaction? If so, which techniques might prove most helpful in this respect?

2. People who work together often do so for many months or years. Do you think this fact might increase their tendency to engage in reciprocal helping—for instance, doing favors for one another, as compared with situations in which people interact only temporarily?

3. It has been contended that effective leadership requires skill with respect to many important aspects of social behavior—effec-

tive use of nonverbal cues (Chapter 2), a high degree of persuasiveness (Chapters 4 and 9), skill at impression management (Chapter 2), and so on. Do you agree? And if you do, does this mean that we could train potential leaders to be more effective?

4. Overall, do you feel that almost anyone can become an entrepreneur, or is this role suitable only for some persons who possess certain characteristics?

KEY TERMS

"Big Five" dimensions of personality (p. 550)

consideration (person-orientation) (p. 551)

entrepreneurs (p. 555)

great person theory of leadership (p. 549)

industrial–organizational psychologists (p. 538)

initiating structure (production-orientation) (p. 551)

job satisfaction (p. 540)

leadership (p. 549)

organizational citizenship behavior (p. 546)

regulatory focus theory (p. 559)

transactional leaders (p. 553)

transformational leaders (p. 552)

GLOSSARY

above-average effect The tendency for people to rate themselves as above the average on most positive social attributes.

abusive supervision Behavior in which supervisors direct frequent hostile verbal and nonverbal behavior toward their subordinates.

actor–observer effect The tendency to attribute our own behavior mainly to situational causes but the behavior of others mainly to internal (dispositional) causes.

adaptive response Any physical characteristic or behavioral tendency that enhances the odds of reproductive success for an individual or for other individuals with similar genes.

additive tasks Tasks for which the group product is the sum or combination of the efforts of individual members.

affect A person's emotional state—positive and negative feelings and moods.

affect Our current feelings and moods.

affect-centered model of attraction A conceptual framework in which attraction is assumed to be based on positive and negative emotions. These emotions can be aroused directly by another person or simply associated with that person. The emotional arousal can also be enhanced or mitigated by cognitive processes.

aggression Behavior directed toward the goal of harming another living being, who is motivated to avoid such treatment.

altruism Behavior that is motivated by an unselfish concern for the welfare of others.

altruistic personality A combination of dispositional variables associated with *prosocial behavior.* The components are *empathy,* belief in a just world, acceptance of social responsibility, having an internal locus of control, and not being egocentric.

ambivalent racial attitudes Both positive and negative feelings about a minority group.

anchoring and adjustment heuristic A heuristic that involves the tendency to use a number or value as a starting point, to which we then make adjustments.

appearance anxiety Apprehension or worry about whether one's physical appearance is adequate and about the possible negative reactions of other people.

assumed similarity The extent to which two people believe they are similar with respect to specific attitudes, beliefs, values, and so forth, as opposed to the extent to which they are actually similar.

attachment style The degree of security experienced in interpersonal relationships. Differential styles initially develop in the interactions between infant and caregiver when the infant acquires basic attitudes about self-worth and *interpersonal trust.*

attitude accessibility The ease with which specific attitudes can be remembered and brought into consciousness.

attitude similarity The extent to which two individuals share the same attitudes about a range of topics. In practice, the term also includes similarity of beliefs, values, and interests—as well as attitudes.

attitude Evaluation of various aspects of the social world.

attitude-to-behavior process model A model of how attitudes guide behavior that emphasizes the influence of attitudes and stored knowledge of what is appropriate in a given situation on an individual's definition of the present situation. This definition, in turn, influences overt behavior.

attribution The process through which we seek to identify the causes of others' behavior and so gain knowledge of their stable traits and dispositions.

augmenting principle The tendency to attach greater importance to a potential cause of behavior if the behavior occurs despite the presence of other, inhibitory causes.

authentic dissent A technique for improving the quality of group decisions in which one or more group members actively disagree with the group's initial preference without being assigned this role.

automatic processing After extensive experience with a task or type of information, the stage at which we can perform the task or process the information in a seemingly effortless, automatic, and nonconscious manner.

availability heuristic A strategy for making judgments on the basis of how easily specific kinds of information can be brought to mind.

balance theory The formulations of Heider and of Newcomb that specify the relationships among (1) an individual's liking for another person, (2) his or her attitude about given topic, and (3) the other person's attitude about the same topic. Balance (liking plus agreement) results in a positive emotional state. Imbalance (liking plus disagreement) results in a negative state and a desire to restore balance. Nonbalance (disliking plus either agreement or disagreement) leads to indifference.

bargaining (negotiation) A process in which opposing sides exchange offers, counteroffers, and concessions, either directly or through representatives.

benevolent sexism Views suggesting that women are superior to men in various ways (e.g., they are more pure, have better taste) and are truly necessary for men's happiness (e.g., no man is truly fulfilled unless he has a women he adores in his life).

"Big Five" dimensions of personality Basic dimensions of personality; where individuals stand along several of these dimensions (e.g., extraversion, agreeableness, neuroticisim) is often apparent in their behavior.

bilateral symmetry   The alikeness of the left and the right sides of the body (or parts of the body).

black sheep effect   When a member of the ingroup behaves in a way that threatens the value of the group identity and is intensely derogated as a means of protecting the group identity.

body language   Cues provided by the position, posture, and movement of others' bodies or body parts.

bona fide pipeline   A technique that uses *priming* to measure implicit racial attitudes.

bullying   A pattern of behavior in which one individual is chosen as the target of repeated aggression by one or more others; the target person (the victim) generally has less power than those who engage in aggression (the bullies).

bystander effect   The fact that the likelihood of a prosocial response to an emergency is affected by the number of bystanders who are present.

care ethic   A justice and ethics orientation that emphasizes the maintenance of relationships. Moral dilemmas are accordingly solved by focusing on the welfare of others.

catharsis hypothesis   The view that providing angry persons with an opportunity to express their aggressive impulses in relatively safe ways will reduce their tendencies to engage in more harmful forms of aggression.

central route (to persuasion)   Attitude change resulting from systematic processing of information presented in persuasive messages.

classical conditioning   A basic form of learning in which one stimulus, initially neutral, acquires the capacity to evoke reactions through repeated pairing with another stimulus. In a sense, one stimulus becomes a signal for the presentation or occurrence of the other.

close friendship   A relationship in which two people spend a great deal of time together, interact in a variety of situations, and provide mutual emotional support.

cognitive dissonance   An internal state that results when individuals notice inconsistency among two or more attitudes or between their attitudes and their behavior.

cohesiveness   All forces (factors) that cause group members to remain in the group.

cohesiveness   All of the factors that bind group members together into a coherent social entity.

collective guilt   The emotion that can be experienced when people are confronted with the harmful actions done by their in-group against an out-group. Collective guilt is most likely to be experienced when the harmful actions are seen as illegitimate.

common in-group identity model   A theory suggesting that to the extent individuals in different groups view themselves as members of a single social entity, intergroup bias will be reduced.

communal behavior   Benevolent acts in a relationship that "cost" the one who performs those acts and "benefit" the partner and the relationship itself.

companionate love   Love that is based on friendship, mutual attraction, shared interests, respect, and concern for one another's welfare.

compliance   A form of social influence involving direct requests from one person to another.

conflict   A process in which individuals or groups perceive that others have taken or will soon take actions incompatible with their own interests.

conformity   A type of social influence in which individuals change their attitudes or behavior in order to adhere to existing social norms.

consensus   The extent to which other persons react to some stimulus or even in the same manner as the person we are considering.

consideration (person-orientation)   A key dimension of leader behavior. Leaders high on this dimensions focus on establishing good relations with their subordinates and on being liked by them.

consistency   The extent to which an individual responds to a given stimulus or situation in the same way on different occasions (i.e., across time).

consummate love   In Sternberg's *triangular model of love,* a complete and ideal love that combines *intimacy, passion,* and *decision/commitment.*

contact hypothesis   The view that increased contact between members of various social groups can be effective in reducing prejudice among them.

cooperation   Behavior in which groups work together to attain shared goals.

correlational method   A method of research in which a scientist systematically observes two or more variables to determine whether changes in one are accompanied by changes in the other.

correspondence bias (fundamental attribution error)   The tendency to explain others' actions as stemming from dispositions, even in the presence of clear situational causes.

correspondent inference (theory of)   A theory describing how we use others' behavior as a basis for inferring their stable dispositions.

counterfactual thinking   The tendency to imagine other outcomes in a situation than the ones that actually occurred ("what might have been").

cultures of honor   Cultures in which there are strong norms indicating that aggression is an appropriate response to insults to one's honor.

deadline technique   A technique for increasing compliance in which target persons are told that they have only limited time to take advantage of some offer or to obtain some item.

debriefing   Procedures at the conclusion of a research session in which participants are given full information about the nature of the research and the hypothesis or hypotheses under investigation.

deception A technique whereby researchers withhold information about the purposes or procedures of a study from persons participating in it.

decision making Processes involved in combining and integrating available information in order to choose one out of several possible courses of action.

decision/commitment In Sternberg's *triangular model of love,* these are the cognitive processes involved in deciding that you love another person and are committed to maintaining the relationship.

deindividuation A psychological state characterized by reduced self-awareness and reduced social identity, brought on by external conditions, such as being an anonymous member of a large crowd.

dependent variable The variable that is measured in an experiment.

descriptive norms Norms that simply indicate what most people do in a given situation.

devil's advocate technique A technique for improving the quality of group decisions in which one group member is assigned the task of disagreeing with and criticizing whatever plan or decision is under consideration.

diffusion of responsibility The idea that the amount of responsibility assumed by bystanders to an emergency is shared among them.

discounting principle The tendency to attach less importance to one potential cause of some behavior when other potential causes are also present.

discrimination Differential (usually negative) behaviors directed toward members of different social groups.

dismissing attachment style A style characterized by high *self-esteem* and low *interpersonal trust.* This is a conflicted and somewhat insecure style in which the individual feels that he or she "deserves" a close relationship but is frustrated because of mistrust of potential partners. The result is the tendency to reject the other person at some point in the relationship in order to avoid being the one who is rejected.

displaced aggression Aggression against someone other than the source of strong provocation; displaced aggression occurs because the persons who perform it are unwilling or unable to aggress against the initial source of provocation.

distinctiveness The extent to which an individual responds in the same manner to different stimuli or events.

distraction–conflict theory A theory suggesting that *social facilitation* stems from the conflict produced when individuals attempt, simultaneously, to pay attention to other persons and to the task being performed.

distributive justice (fairness) Refers to individuals' judgments about whether they are receiving a fair share of available rewards—a share proportionate to their contributions to the group or any social relationship.

door-in-the-face technique A procedure for gaining compliance in which requesters begin with a large request and then, when this is refused, retreat to a smaller one (the one they actually desire all along).

downward social comparison A comparison other who does less well than the self.

drive theories (of aggression) Theories suggesting that aggression stems from external conditions that arouse the motive to harm or injure others. The most famous of these is the *frustration–aggression hypothesis.*

drive theory of social facilitation A theory suggesting that the mere presence of others is arousing and increases the tendency to perform dominant responses.

ego-defensive function Protection of ourselves from unwanted or unflattering views of ourselves by claiming particular attitudes.

egoism An exclusive concern with one's own personal needs and welfare rather than with the needs and welfare of others. See *self-interest.*

elaboration–likelihood model (of persuasion) A theory suggesting that persuasion can occur in either of two distinct ways—systematic versus heuristic processing, which differ in the amount of cognitive effort or elaboration they require.

emotion-focused coping Attempts to cope with stress by engaging in activities that reduce or counter the negative feelings stress produces.

empathic joy hypothesis The proposal that *prosocial behavior* is motivated by the positive emotion a helper anticipates experiencing as the result of having a beneficial impact on the life of someone in need.

empathy A complex affective and cognitive response to another person's emotional distress. Empathy includes being able to feel the other person's emotional state, feeling sympathetic and attempting to solve the problem, and taking the perspective of others. One can be empathetic toward fictional characters as well as toward real-life victims.

empathy–altruism hypothesis The proposal that *prosocial behavior* is motivated solely by the desire to help someone in need and by the fact that it feels good to help.

entiativity The extent to which a group is perceived as being a coherent entity.

entrepreneurs Individuals who recognize an opportunity for a new business and actually start one.

evaluation apprehension Concern over being evaluated by others. Such concern can increase arousal and so contribute to social facilitation.

evolutionary psychology A new branch of psychology that seeks to investigate the potential role of genetic factors in various aspects of human behavior.

excitation transfer theory A theory suggesting that arousal produced in one situation can persist and intensify emotional reactions occurring in later situations.

existential terror Anxiety stemming from awareness that the self will inevitably die.

experimentation (experimental method) A method of research in which one or more factors (the independent variables) are systematically changed to determine whether such variations affect one or more other factors (dependent variables).

external validity The extent to which the findings of an experiment can be generalized to real-life social situations and perhaps to persons different from those who participated in the research.

eyewitness testimony Evidence given by persons who have witnessed a crime; plays an important role in many trials.

fearful–avoidant attachment style A style characterized by low *self-esteem* and low *interpersonal trust.* This is the most insecure and least adaptive attachment style.

foot-in-the-door technique A procedure for gaining compliance in which requesters begin with a small request and then, when this is granted, escalate to a larger one (the one they actually desire all along).

forewarning Advance knowledge that one is about to become the target of an attempt at persuasion. Forewarning often increases resistance to the persuasion that follows.

forgiveness Giving up the desire to punish those who have hurt us, and seeking instead to act in kind, helpful ways toward them.

frustration–aggression hypothesis The suggestion that frustration is a very powerful determinant of aggression.

fundamental attribution error (correspondence bias) The tendency to overestimate the impact of dispositional cues on others' behavior.

gender stereotypes Stereotypes concerning the traits possessed by females and males, and that distinguish the two genders from each other.

general aggression model A modern theory of aggression suggesting that aggression is triggered by a wide range of input variables that influence arousal, affective stages, and cognitions.

generativity An adult's concern for and commitment to the well-being of future generations.

genetic determinism model The proposal that behavior is driven by genetic attributes that evolved because they enhanced the probability of transmitting one's genes to subsequent generations.

glass ceiling Barriers based on attitudinal or organizational bias that prevent qualified women from advancing to top-level positions.

great person theory of leadership The view that leaders possess certain traits that set them apart from other persons, traits that are possessed by all leaders no matter where or when they lived.

group polarization The tendency of group members to shift toward more extreme positions than those they initially held as a result of group discussion.

group A collection of persons who are perceived to be bonded together in a coherent unit to some degree.

groupthink The tendency of the members of highly cohesive groups to assume that their decisions can't be wrong, that all members must support the groups' decisions strongly, and that information contrary to these decisions should be ignored.

health psychology The branch of psychology that studies the relation between psychological variables and health.

heroism Actions that involve courageous risk taking to obtain a socially valued goal. An example would be a dangerous act undertaken to save the life of a stranger.

heuristic processing Processing of information in a persuasive message that involves the use of simple rules of thumb or mental shortcuts.

heuristics Simple rules for making complex decisions or drawing inferences in a rapid and seemingly effortless manner.

hostile aggression Aggression in which the prime objective is inflicting some kind of harm on the victim.

hostile attributional bias The tendency to perceive hostile intentions or motives in others' actions when these actions are ambiguous.

hostile sexism The view that women are a threat to men's position (e.g., they seek special favors they do not deserve or are attempting to seize power that they should not have from men).

hypocrisy The public advocating some attitudes or behaviors and then acting in a way that is inconsistent with these attitudes or behavior.

hypothesis An as-yet-unverified prediction.

identity interference When two important social identities are perceived as in conflict, such that acting on the basis of one identity interferes with performing well based on the other identity.

identity or self-expression function Attitudes can permit the expression of central values and beliefs and thereby communicate who we are.

illusory correlation The perception of a stronger association between two variables than actually exists.

implicit associations Links between group membership and trait associations or evaluations of which the perceiver may be unaware. They can be activated automatically when the target is categorized as a group member.

implicit bystander effect The decrease in helping behavior brought about by simply thinking about being in a group.

implicit personality theories Beliefs about what traits or characteristics tend to go together.

impression formation (self-presentation) The process through which we form impressions of others.

impression management Efforts by individuals to produce favorable first impressions on others.

impression motivation function Attitudes can be used to lead others to have a positive view of ourselves. When motivated to do so, the attitudes we express can shift in order to create the desired impression on others.

incidental feelings   Those feelings induced separately or before a target is encountered—so they are irrelevant to the group being judged, but can still affect judgments of the target.

inclusive fitness   The concept that natural selection not only applies to individuals, but also involves behaviors that benefit other individuals with whom we share genes. Sometimes referred to as *kin selection.*

independent self-concept   In individualistic cultures, the expectation is that people will develop a self-concept as separate from or independent of others. Men are expected to have an independent self-concept more so than women.

independent variable   The variable that is systematically changed (i.e., varied) in an experiment.

individuation   The need to be distinguishable from others in some respects.

induced or forced compliance   Situations in which individuals are somehow induced to say or do things inconsistent with their true attitudes.

industrial–organizational psychologists   Psychologists who specialize in studying all forms of behavior and cognition in work settings.

inferential statistics   A special form of mathematics that allows us to evaluate the likelihood that a given pattern of research results occurred by chance alone.

information overload   Instances in which our ability to process information is exceeded.

informational social influence   Social influence based on the desire to be correct (i.e., to possess accurate perceptions of the social world).

informed consent   A procedure in which research participants are provided with as much information as possible about a research project before deciding whether to participate in it.

ingratiation   A technique for gaining compliance in which requesters first induce target persons to like them and then attempt to change the persons' behavior in some desired manner.

ingratiation   The attempt to make others like us by conveying that we like them.

in-group differentiation   The tendency to perceive members of our own group as showing much larger differences from one another (as being more heterogeneous) than members of other groups.

in-group homogeneity   In-group members are seen as more similar to each other than out-group members are. This tends to occur most among minority-group members.

in-group   The social group to which an individual perceives herself or himself as belonging ("us").

initiating structure (production-orientation)   A key dimension of leader behavior. Leaders high on this dimension are primarily concerned with getting the job done (i.e., with production).

injunctive norms   Norms specifying what *ought* to be done—what is approved or disapproved behavior in a given situation.

instrumental aggression   Aggression in which the primary goal is not harm to the victim but attainment of some other goal—for example, access to valued resources.

instrumental conditioning   A basic form of learning in which responses that lead to positive outcomes or that permit avoidance of negative outcomes are strengthened.

interdependence   The characteristic that is common to all close relationships. Interdependence refers to an interpersonal association in which two people influence each others' lives. They often focus their thoughts on one another and regularly engage in joint activities.

interdependent self-concept   In collectivist cultures, the expectation is that people will develop a self-concept in terms of one's connections or relationships with others. Women are expected to have an interdependent self-concept more so than men.

intergroup comparisons   Judgments that result from comparisons between our group and another group.

interpersonal attraction   A person's attitude about another person. Attraction is expressed along a dimension that ranges from strong liking to strong feelings of dislike.

interpersonal trust   An attitudinal dimension underlying *attachment styles* that involves the belief that other people are generally trustworthy, dependable, and reliable as opposed to the belief that others are generally untrustworthy, undependable, and unreliable.

intimacy   In Sternberg's *triangular model of love*, the closeness felt by two people—the extent to which they are bonded.

intragroup comparisons   Judgments that result from comparisons between individuals who are members of the same group.

introspection   Attempts to understand the self by self-examination; turning inwardly to assess one's motives.

job satisfaction   Attitudes individuals hold concerning their jobs.

justice ethic   A justice and ethics orientation that emphasizes the application of universal rules regardless of one's own relationship with those individuals. Moral dilemmas are accordingly solved by using the same principle across cases.

kin selection   Another term for *inclusive fitness*—the concept that natural selection not only applies to individuals, but also involves behaviors that benefit other individuals with whom we share genes.

knowledge function   Attitudes aid in the interpretation of new stimuli and enable rapid responding to attitude-relevant information.

leadership   The process through which one member of a group (its leader) influences other group members toward attainment of shared group goals.

leading questions   Questions by attorneys during a trial that are designed to generate specific responses.

less-leads-to-more effect   The fact that offering individuals small rewards for engaging in counterattitudinal behavior often produces more dissonance, and so more attitude change, than offering them larger rewards.

linguistic style   Aspects of speech apart from the meaning of the words employed.

loneliness   The unpleasant emotional and cognitive state based on desiring close relationships but being unable to attain them.

love   A combination of emotions, cognitions, and behaviors that often play a crucial role in intimate relationships.

lowball procedure   A technique for gaining compliance in which an offer or deal is changed to make it less attractive to the target person after this person has accepted it.

magical thinking   Thinking involving assumptions that don't hold up to rational scrutiny—for example, the belief that things that resemble one another share fundamental properties.

media violence   Depictions of violent actions in the mass media.

mental contamination   A process in which our judgments, emotions, or behavior are influenced by mental processing that is not readily under our control.

mere exposure effect   Another term for the *repeated exposure* effect, emphasizing the fact that exposure to a stimulus is all that is necessary to enhance the positive evaluation of that stimulus.

mere exposure   By having seen an object previously, but not necessarily remembering having done so, attitudes toward an object can become more positive.

meta-analysis   A statistical technique for combining data from independent studies in order to determine whether specific variables (or interactions among variables) have significant effects across these studies.

microexpressions   Fleeting facial expressions lasting only a few tenths of a second.

mimicry   The automatic tendency to imitate those with whom we interact. Being mimicked increases one's prosocial tendencies.

minimal groups   When people are categorized into different groups based on some "minimal" criteria, they tend to favor others who are categorized in the same group as themselves, compared with those categorized as members of a different group.

modern racism   More subtle beliefs than blatant feelings of superiority. Modern racism consists primarily of thinking that minorities are seeking and receiving more benefits than they deserve and a denial that discrimination affects their outcomes.

mood congruence effects   Effects that we are more likely to store or remember positive information when in a positive mood, and negative information when in a negative mood.

mood-dependent memory   The effect that what we remember while in a given mood may be determined, in part, by what we learned when previously in that mood.

moral hypocrisy   The motivation to appear moral while doing one's best to avoid the costs involved in actually being moral.

moral integrity   The motivation to be moral and actually to engage in moral behavior.

multicultural perspective   A focus on understanding the cultural and ethnic factors that influence social behavior.

narcissism   A personality disposition characterized by unreasonably high *self-esteem,* a feeling of superiority, a need for admiration, sensitivity to criticism, a lack of empathy, and exploitative behavior.

need for affiliation   The basic motive to seek and maintain interpersonal relationships.

negative-state relief mode   The proposal that *prosocial behavior* is motivated by the bystander's desire to reduce his or her own uncomfortable negative emotions.

negativity bias   A greater sensitivity to negative information than to positive information.

noncommon effects   Effects produced by a particular cause that could not be produced by any other apparent cause.

nonverbal communication   Communication between individuals that does not involve the content of spoken language. It relies instead on an unspoken language of facial expressions, eye contact, and body language.

normative focus theory   A theory suggesting that norms will influence behavior only to the extent that they are focal for the persons involved at the time the behavior occurs.

normative social influence   Social influence based on the desire to be liked or accepted by other persons.

norms   Rules within a group indicating how its members should (or should not) behave.

obedience   A form of social influence in which one person simply orders one or more others to perform some action(s), and the persons then comply.

objective scales   Scales with measurement units that are tied to external reality so that they mean the same thing regardless of category membership (e.g., dollars earned, feet and inches, chosen or rejected).

objective self-awareness   The organism's capacity to be the object of its own attention—to know that it is seeing its own self in a mirror, for example.

observational learning   A basic form of learning in which individuals acquire new forms of behavior as a result of observing others.

optimistic bias   Our predisposition to expect things to turn out well overall.

organizational citizenship behavior   Help people give each other at work that is not a required part of their jobs.

out-group homogeneity   The tendency to perceive members of an out-group as "all alike" or more similar to each other than members of the in-group.

out-group Any group other than the one to which individuals perceive themselves as belonging.

overconfidence barrier The tendency to have more confidence in the accuracy of our judgments than is reasonable.

passion In Sternberg's *triangular model of love,* the sexual motives and sexual excitement associated with a couple's relationship.

passionate love An intense and often unrealistic emotional response to another person. When this emotion is experienced, it is usually perceived as an indication of "true love," but to outside observers it appears to be "infatuation."

peripheral route (to persuasion) Attitude change that occurs in response to peripheral persuasion cues, often based on information concerning the expertise or status of would-be persuaders.

perseverance effect The tendency for beliefs and schemas to remain unchanged, even in the face of contradictory information.

personality disposition A characteristic behavioral tendency that is based on genetics, learning experiences, or both. Such dispositions tend to be stable over time and across situations.

personal–social identity continuum The two distinct ways that the self can be categorized. At the personal level, the self can be thought of as a unique individual, whereas at the social identity level, the self is thought of as a member of a group.

persuasion Efforts to change others' attitudes through the use of various kinds of messages.

physical attractiveness The combination of characteristics that are evaluated as beautiful or handsome at the positive extreme and as unattractive at the negative extreme.

planning fallacy The tendency to make optimistic predictions concerning how long a given task will take for completion.

playing hard to get A technique that can be used for increasing compliance by suggesting that a person or object is scarce and hard to obtain.

pluralistic ignorance The tendency of bystanders in an emergency to rely on what other bystanders do and say, even though none of them is sure about what is happening or what to do about it. Very often, all of the bystanders hold back and behave as if there is no problem. Each individual uses this "information" to justify the failure to act.

pluralistic ignorance When we collectively misunderstand what attitudes others hold, and believe erroneously that others have different attitudes than ourselves.

possible selves Images of how the self might be in the future—either "dreaded" possible selves to be avoided or "desired" potential selves that can be strived for.

prejudice Negative attitudes toward the members of specific social groups.

preoccupied attachment style A style characterized by low *self-esteem* and high *interpersonal trust.* This is a con-

flicted and somewhat insecure style in which the individual strongly desires a close relationship but feels that he or she is unworthy of the partner and is thus vulnerable to being rejected.

priming Increased availability in memory or consciousness of specific types of information held in memory due to exposure to specific stimuli or events.

priming Using a stimulus to make accessible related information in memory.

problem-focused coping Attempts to cope with stress by altering the cause of stress.

procedural justice Judgments concerning the fairness of the procedures used to distribute available rewards among group members.

proportion of similarity The number of specific indicators that two people are similar divided by the number of specific indicators that two people are similar plus the number of specific indicators that they are dissimilar.

prosocial behavior A helpful action that benefits other people without necessarily providing any direct benefits to the person performing the act, and may even involve a risk for the person who helps.

provocation Actions by others that tend to trigger aggression in the recipient, often because these actions are perceived as stemming from malicious intent.

proximity In attraction research, the physical closeness between two individuals with respect to where they live, where they sit in a classroom, where they work, and so on. The smaller the physical distance, the greater the probability that the two people will come into repeated contact, experiencing repeated exposure to one another, positive affect, and the development of mutual attraction.

punishment Procedures in which aversive consequences are delivered to individuals when they engage in specific actions.

random assignment of participants to experimental conditions A basic requirement for conducting valid experiments. According to this principle, research participants must have an equal chance of being exposed to each level of the independent variable.

reactance Negative reactions to threats to one's personal freedom. Reactance often increases resistance to persuasion and can even produce negative attitude change or that opposite to what was intended.

realistic conflict theory The view that prejudice stems from direct competition between various social groups over scarce and valued resources.

recategorization Shifts in the boundaries between an individual's in-group ("us") and some out-group ("them"). As a result of such recategorization, persons formerly viewed as out-group members may now be viewed as belonging to the in-group, and consequently are viewed more positively.

reciprocal altruism A theory suggesting that by sharing resources such as food, organisms increase their chances of survival, and thus the likelihood that they will pass their genes on to the next generation.

reciprocal altruism The cooperative behavior among unrelated individuals that benefits both individuals, because when individual A helps individual B, B is motivated to reciprocate at some point by helping A. Such behavior also benefits the larger group to which both A and B belong.

reciprocity A basic rule of social life, suggesting that individuals should treat others as these persons have treated them.

regulatory focus theory An important framework for understanding that in regulating their own behavior in order to achieve desired end-states, individuals adopt one of two contrasting perspectives: a *promotion focus*, in which they focus primarily on attaining positive outcomes, or a *prevention focus*, in which they focus primarily on avoiding negative outcomes.

repeated exposure Zajonc's finding that frequent contact with any mildly negative, neutral, or positive stimulus results in an increasingly positive evaluation of that stimulus.

representativeness heuristic A strategy for making judgments based on the extent to which current stimuli or events resemble other stimuli or categories.

repulsion hypothesis Rosenbaum's provocative proposal that attraction is not increased by similar attitudes but is simply decreased by dissimilar attitudes. This hypothesis is incorrect as stated, but it is true that dissimilar attitudes tend to have negative effects that are stronger than the positive effects of similar attitudes.

respect The quality of being seen positively and as having worth. People seem to believe that men deserve greater respect than women.

roles The set of behaviors that individuals occupying specific positions within a group are expected to perform.

schemas Cognitive frameworks developed through experience that affect the processing of new social information.

schemas Mental frameworks centering around a specific theme that help us to organize social information.

secure attachment style A style characterized by high *self-esteem* and high *interpersonal trust*. This is the most successful and most desirable attachment style.

selective altruism When a large group of individuals is in need, and only one individual is helped. In appeals by charities, there is frequently a picture and information about one child, designed to arouse empathy toward him or her and the result is selective altruism.

selective avoidance A tendency to direct attention away from information that challenges existing attitudes. Such avoidance increases resistance to persuasion.

self-complexity How the self-concept is organized. For those whose self-concepts are organized complexly, important aspects of the self are distinct from one another. For those whose self-concept is low in complexity, there is greater overlap in different components of the self.

self-critical perfectionism A pattern in which individuals constantly engage in harsh criticism of their own behavior, an inability to derive satisfaction from successful performance, and chronic concerns about others' expectations and criticism.

self-efficacy The belief that one can achieve a goal as a result of one's own actions. Collective self-efficacy is the belief that by working together with others, a goal can be achieved.

self-esteem function Function in which holding particular attitudes can help maintain or enhance feelings of self-worth.

self-esteem The degree to which the self is perceived positively or negatively; one's overall attitude toward the self.

self-esteem The self-evaluation made by each individual. It represents one's attitude about oneself along a positive–negative dimension.

self-evaluation maintenance model The perspective that suggests that in order to maintain a positive view of the personal self, we distance ourselves from others who perform better than we do on valued dimensions, but move closer to others who perform worse. This view suggests that doing so will protect our self-esteem.

self-fulfilling prophecies Predictions that, in a sense, make themselves come true.

self-interest The motivation to engage in whatever behavior provides the greatest satisfaction for oneself. See *egoism*.

self-monitoring The monitoring by people of their behavior in response to others' expectancies. Low self-monitors are not very effective at doing this and instead prefer to act consistently according to their personal views. High self-monitors are quite effective at monitoring their behavior and adjust their actions according to others' expectations or the situation.

self-reference effect People's orientation toward stimuli that are associated with the self. People show a preference for objects owned by and reflective of the self.

self-serving bias The tendency to attribute positive outcomes to internal causes (e.g., one's own traits or characteristics) but negative outcomes or events to external causes (e.g., chance, task difficulty).

sexism Prejudice based on gender; it typically refers to biases and negative responses toward women.

sexual harassment Unwanted contact or communication of a sexual nature.

shifting standards When people use one group as the standard but shift to another group as the comparison standard when judging members of a different group.

similarity–dissimilarity effect The consistent finding that people respond positively to indications that another person is similar to themselves and negatively to indications that another person is dissimilar from themselves.

slime effect A tendency to form negative impressions of others who play up to their superiors but who treat subordinates with disdain.

social categorization The tendency to divide the social world into separate categories: our in-group ("us") and various out-groups ("them").

social cognition The manner in which we interpret, analyze, remember, and use information about the social world.

social comparison theory Festinger (1954) suggested that people compare themselves to others because, for many domains and attributes, there is no objective yardstick with which to evaluate the self, so other people are therefore highly informative.

social comparison The process through which we compare ourselves to others in order to determine whether our views of social reality are or are not correct.

social creativity responses When low-status groups attempt to achieve positive distinctiveness for their group on alternative dimensions that do not threaten the high-status group (e.g., *benevolent sexism*).

social decision schemes Rules relating the initial distribution of member views to final group decisions.

social dilemmas Situations in which each person can increase his or her individual gains by acting in one way; but if all (or most) persons do the same thing, the outcomes experienced by all are reduced.

social exclusion *Social rejection* of an individual by an entire group of people, not on the basis of what he or she has done, but on the basis of prejudice, stereotypes, and biases.

social facilitation Effects upon performance resulting from the presence of others.

social identity theory A theory concerned with the consequences of perceiving the self as a member of a social group and identifying with it.

social identity theory Our response when our group identity is salient. Suggests that we will move closer to positive others with whom we share an identity, but distance ourselves from other ingroup members who perform poorly or otherwise make our social identity negative.

social influence Efforts by one or more individuals to change the attitudes, beliefs, perceptions, or behaviors of one or more others.

social learning view (of prejudice) The view that prejudice is acquired through direct and vicarious experiences in much the same manner as other attitudes.

social learning The process through which we acquire new information, forms of behavior, or attitudes from other persons.

social loafing Reductions in motivation and effort when individuals work collectively in a group, compared with when they work individually or as independent coactors.

social neuroscience An area of research in social psychology that seeks knowledge about the neural and biological bases of social processes.

social norms Expectations about how people will or should behave in a particular context.

social norms Rules indicating how individuals are expected to behave in specific situations.

social norms Rules within a particular social group concerning what actions and attitudes are appropriate.

social perception The process through which we seek to know and understand other persons.

social psychology The scientific field that seeks to understand the nature and causes of individual behavior and thought in social situations.

social rejection Rejection by one individual of another individual, not on the basis of what he or he has done, but on the basis of prejudice, stereotypes, and biases.

social support Drawing on the emotional and task resources provided by others as a means of coping with stress.

spreading of alternatives When individuals make a decision between two options they tend to reduce the positivity of the item they did not choose and increase the positivity of the item they did choose.

staring A form of eye contact in which one person continues to gaze steadily at another regardless of what the recipient does.

status An individual's position or rank in a group.

stereotype threat People's belief that they might be judged in light of a negative stereotype about their group or that they may, because of their performance, in some way confirm a negative stereotype of their group.

stereotypes Beliefs about social groups in terms of the traits or characteristics that they are deemed to share. Stereotypes are cognitive frameworks that influence the processing of social information.

stress Our response to events that disrupt, or threaten to disrupt, our physical or psychological functioning.

subjective scales Response scales that are open to interpretation and lack an externally grounded referent, including scales labeled from good to bad or weak to strong. They are said to be subjective because they can take on different meanings, depending on the group membership of the person being evaluated.

subjective self-awareness The first level of self to emerge. It is the recognition that the self is separate from other objects in one's physical environment.

subliminal conditioning Classical conditioning of attitudes by exposure to stimuli that are below individuals' threshold of conscious awareness.

subliminal levels Stimuli shown to participants so rapidly that the stimuli cannot be recognized or identified by them.

subtype A subset of a group that is not consistent with the stereotype of the group as a whole.

superordinate goals Goals that both sides of a conflict seek and that tie their interests together rather than drive them apart.

superordinate goals   Goals that can be achieved only by cooperation between groups.

survey method   A method of research in which large numbers of persons answer questions about their attitudes or behavior.

symbolic self-awareness   The uniquely human capacity to form an abstract representation of the self through language. It also is connected with knowing that death of the physical self is inevitable.

symbolic social influence   Social influence resulting from the mental representation of others or of our relationships with them.

systematic observation   A method of research in which behavior is systematically observed and recorded.

systematic processing   Processing of information in a persuasive message that involves careful consideration of message content and ideas.

terror management theory   Because humans are aware of the inevitability of their own death, they confront existential terror. Terror management theory suggests ways that people attempt to deal with this threat to the self when their own mortality is salient.

that's-not-all technique   A technique for gaining compliance in which requesters offer additional benefits to target persons before these persons have decided whether to comply with or reject specific requests.

theories   Efforts by scientists in any field to answer the question "Why?" Theories involve attempts to understand why certain events or processes occur as they do.

theory of planned behavior   An extension of the *theory of reasoned action,* suggesting that in addition to attitudes toward a given behavior and subjective norms about it, individuals also consider their ability to perform the behavior.

theory of reasoned action   A theory suggesting that the decision to engage in a particular behavior is the result of a rational process in which behavioral options are considered, consequences or outcomes of each are evaluated, and a decision is reached to act or not to act. That decision is then reflected in behavioral intentions, which strongly influence overt behavior.

third-person effect   Effect that occurs when the impact of media exposure on others' attitudes and behaviors is overestimated and the impact on the self is underestimated.

thought suppression   Efforts to prevent certain thoughts from entering consciousness.

threat   Threat can take different forms, but it primarily concerns fear that one's group interests will be undermined or that one's self-esteem is in jeopardy.

tokenism   Tokenism can refer to hiring based on group membership. It also can concern instances in which individuals perform trivial positive actions for members of out-groups that are later used as an excuse for refusing more meaningful beneficial actions for members of these groups.

transactional (interpersonal) justice   Refers to the extent to which persons who distribute rewards explain or justify their decisions and show considerateness and courtesy to those who receive the rewards.

transactional leaders   Leaders who direct their groups by rewarding them for desired behavior, and by taking action to correct mistakes or departures from existing rules. Such leaders generally strengthen existing structures and strategies within an organization.

transformational leaders   Leaders who, because of several characteristics, exert profound effects on their followers.

triangular model of love   Sternberg's conceptualization of love relationships consisting of three basic components: *intimacy, passion,* and *decision/commitment.*

trivialization   A technique for reducing dissonance in which the importance of attitudes or behavior that are inconsistent with each other is cognitively reduced.

Type A behavior pattern   A pattern consisting primarily of high levels of competitiveness, time urgency, and hostility.

Type B behavior pattern   A pattern consisting of the absence of characteristics associated with the Type A behavior pattern.

ultimate attribution error   The tendency to make more favorable and flattering attributions about members of one's own group than about members of other groups. In effect, it is the self-serving attributional bias at the group level.

unrequited love   *Love* felt by one person for another who does not feel love in return.

upward social comparison   A comparison other who does better than the self.

within-group comparisons   Comparisons made between a target and other members of that same category only.

workplace aggression   Any form of behavior through which individuals seek to harm others in their workplace.

REFERENCES

Aarts, H., & Dijksterhuis, A. (2003). The silence of the library: Environment, situational norms, and social behavior. *Journal of Personality and Social Psychology, 84,* 18–24.

Abelson, R. P., Frey, K. P., & Gregg, A. P. (2004). *Experiments with people: Revelations from social psychology.* Mahwah, NJ: Erlbaum.

Ackil, J. K., & Zaragoza, M. S. (1998). Memorial consequences of forced confabulation: Age differences in susceptibility to false memories. *Developmental Psychology, 34,* 1358–1372.

Adams, J. M., & Jones, W. H. (1997). The conceptualization of marital commitment: An integrative analysis. *Journal of Personality and Social Psychology, 72,* 1177–1196.

Adams, J. S. (1965). Inequity in social exchange. In L. Berkowitz (Ed.), *Advances in experimental social psychology* (Vol. 2, pp. 267–299). New York: Academic Press.

Ahrons, C. (2004). *We're still family: What grown children have to say about their parents' divorce.* New York: Harper Collins.

Ajzen, I. (1987). Attitudes, traits, and actions: Dispositional prediction of behavior in personality and social psychology. In L. Berkowitz (Ed.), *Advances in experimental social psychology* (Vol. 20). San Diego, CA: Academic Press.

Ajzen, I. (1991). The theory of planned behavior: Special issue: Theories of cognitive self-regulation. *Organizational Behavior and Human Decision Processes, 50,* 179–211.

Ajzen, I. (2001). Nature and operation of attitudes. *Annual Review of Psychology, 52,* 27–58.

Ajzen, I., & Fishbein, M. (1980). *Understanding attitudes and predicting social behavior.* Englewood Cliffs, NJ: Prentice-Hall.

Alagna, F. J., Whitcher, S. J., & Fisher, J. D. (1979). Evaluative reactions to interpersonal touch in a counseling interview. *Journal of Counseling Psychology, 26,* 465–472.

Alexander, M. G., Brewer, M. B., & Herrmann, R. K. (1999). Images and affect: A functional analysis of out-group stereotypes. *Journal of Personality and Social Psychology, 77,* 78–93.

Alexander, M. J., & Higgins, E. T. (1993). Emotional trade-offs of becoming a parent: How social roles influence self-discrepancy effects. *Journal of Personality and Social Psychology, 65,* 1259–1269.

Alexander, R., Feeney, J., Hohaus, L., & Noller, P. (2001). Attachment style and coping resources as predictors of coping strategies in the transition to parenthood. *Personal Relationships, 8,* 137–152.

Alicke, M. D., Vredenburg, D. S., Hiatt, M., & Govorun, O. (2001). The better than myself effect. *Motivation and Emotion, 25,* 7–22.

Allen, K. (2003). Are pets a healthy pleasure? The influence of pets on blood pressure. *Current Directions in Cognitive Science, 12,* 236–239.

Allen, K., Shykoff, B. E., & Izzo, J. L. (2001). Pet ownership, but not ACE inhibitor therapy, blunts home blood pressure responses to mental stress. *Hypertension, 38,* 815–820.

Allgeier, E. R., & Wiederman, M. W. (1994). How useful is evolutionary psychology for understanding contemporary human sexual behavior? *Annual Review of Sex Research, 5,* 218–256.

Allport, F. H. (1920). The influence of the group upon association and thought. *Journal of Experimental Psychology, 3,* 159–182.

Allport, F. H. (1924). *Social psychology.* Boston: Houghton Mifflin.

Allyn, J., & Festinger, L. (1961). The effectiveness of unanticipated persuasive communications. *Journal of Abnormal and Social Psychology, 62,* 35–40.

Alvaro, E. M., & Crano, W. D. (1996). Cognitive responses to minority- or majority-based communications: Factors that underlie minority influence. *British Journal of Social Psychology, 34,* 105–121.

Amato, P. R. (1986). Emotional arousal and helping behavior in a real-life emergency. *Journal of Applied Social Psychology, 16,* 633–641.

Amato, P. R., & Booth, A. (2001). The legacy of parents' marital discord: Consequences for children's marital quality. *Journal of Personality and Social Psychology, 81,* 627–638.

American Psychiatric Association. (1994). *Diagnostic and statistical manual of mental disorders* (4th ed.). Washington, DC: American Psychiatric Association.

Ames, D. R., Flynn, F. J., & Weber, E. U. (2004). It's the thought that counts: On perceiving how helpers decide to lend a hand. *Personality and Social Psychology Bulletin, 30,* 461–474.

Andersen, S. M., & Baum, A. (1994). Transference in interpersonal relations: Inferences and affect based on significant-other representations. *Journal of Personality, 62,* 459–497.

Anderson, C. A. (1989). Temperature and aggression: Effects on quarterly, yearly, and city rates of violent and nonviolent crime. *Journal of Personality and Social Psychology, 52,* 1161–1173.

Anderson, C. A. (1997). Effects of violent movies and trait hostility on hostile feelings and aggressive thoughts. *Aggressive Behavior, 23,* 161–178.

Anderson, C. A., & Anderson, K. B. (1996). Violent crime rate studies in philosophical context: A destructive testing approach to heat and Southern culture of violence effects. *Journal of Personality and Social Psychology, 70,* 740–756.

Anderson, C. A., Anderson, K. B., & Deuser, W. E. (1996). Examining an affective aggression framework: Weapon and temperature effects on aggressive thoughts, affect, and attitudes. *Personality and Social Psychology Bulletin, 22,* 366–376.

Anderson, C. A., & Bushman, B. J. (2001). Effects of violent video games on aggressive behavior, aggressive cognition, aggressive affect, physiological arousal, and prosocial behavior: A meta-analytic review of the scientific literature. *Psychological Science, 12,* 353–359.

Anderson, C. A., & Bushman, B. J. (2002a). Media violence and the American public revisited. *American Psychologist, 57,* 448–450.

Anderson, C. A., & Bushman, B. J. (2002b). Human aggression. *Annual Review of Psychology, 53,* 27–51.

Anderson, C. A., Bushman, B. J., & Groom, R. W. (1997). Hot years and serious and deadly assault: Empirical tests of the heat hypothesis. *Journal of Personality and Social Psychology, 73,* 1213–1223.

Anderson, C. A., Carnagey, N. L., & Eubanks, J. (2003). Exposure to violent media: The effects of songs with violent lyrics on aggressive thoughts and feelings. *Journal of Personality and Social Psychology, 84,* 960–971.

Anderson, C. A., Carnagey, N. L., Flanagan, M., Benjamin, A. J., Eubanks, J., & Valentine, J. C. (in press). Violent video games: Specific effects of violent content on aggressive thoughts and behavior. In M. Zanna (Ed.), *Advances in experimental social psychology* (Vol. 36). New York: Elsevier.

Anderson, C. A., Miller, R. S., Riger, A. L., Dill, J. C., & Sedikides, C. (1994). Behavioral and characterological attributional styles as predictors of depression and loneliness: Review, refinement, and test. *Journal of Personality and Social Psychology, 66,* 549–558.

Anderson, C. A., Berkowitz, L., Donnerstein, E., Huesmann, L. R., Johnson, J. D., Linz, D., Malamuth, N. M., & Wartella, E. (2004). The influence of media violence on youth. *Psychology in the Public Interest, 4,* 81–110.

Anderson, N. H. (1965). Averaging versus adding as a stimulus combination rule in impression formation. *Journal of Experimental Social Psychology, 70,* 394–400.

Anderson, N. H. (1968). Application of a linear-serial model to a personality impression task. Using serial presentation. *Journal of Personality and Social Psychology, 10,* 354–362.

Anderson, N. H. (1973). Cognitive algebra: Integration theory applied to social attribution. In L. Berkowitz (Ed.), *Advances in experimental social psychology.* New York: Academic Press.

Anderson, V. L. (1993). Gender differences in altruism among holocaust rescuers. *Journal of Social Behavior and Personality, 8,* 43–58.

Andersson, L. M., & Pearson, C. M. (1999). Tit-for-tat? The spiraling effect of incivility in the workplace. *Academy of Management Review, 24,* 452–471.

Andreoletti, C., Zebrowitz, L. A., & Lachman, M. E. (2001). *Personality and Social Psychology Bulletin, 27,* 969–981.

Andreou, E. (2000). Bully/victim problems and their association with psychological constructs in 8- to 12-year-old Greek schoolchildren. *Aggressive Behavior, 26,* 49–58.

Angier, N. (1998a, September 1). Nothing becomes a man more than a woman's face. *New York Times,* p. F3.

Angier, N. (2002, July 23). Why we're so nice: We're wired to cooperate. *The New York Times,* F1, F8.

Angier, N. (2003, July 8). Opposites attract? Not in real life. *The New York Times,* F1, F6.

Antonakis, J. (2001). *The validity of the transformational, transactional, and laissez-fair leadership model as measured by the Multifactor Leadership Questionnaire (MLQ 5X).* Unpublished doctoral dissertation.

Apanovitch, A. M., Hobfoll, S. E., & Salovey, P. (2002). The effects of social influence on perceptual and affective reactions to scenes of sexual violence. *Journal of Applied Social Psychology, 32,* 443–464.

Archibald, F. S., Bartholomew, K., & Marx, R. (1995). Loneliness in early adolescence: A test of the cognitive discrepancy model of loneliness. *Personality and Social Psychology Bulletin, 21,* 296–301.

Aristotle. (1932). *The rhetoric* (L. Cooper, Trans.). New York: Appleton-Century-Crofts. (Original work published c. 330 B.C.)

Armeli, S., Carney, M. A., Tennen, H., Affleck, G., & O'Neil, T. P. (2000). Stress and alcohol use: A daily process examination of the stressor–vulnerability model. *Journal of Personality and Social Psychology, 78,* 979–994.

Armitage, C. J., & Conner, M. (2000). Attitudinal ambivalence: A test of three key hypotheses. *Personality and Social Psychology Bulletin, 26,* 1421–1432.

Arndt, J., Greenberg, J., Schimel, J., Pyszczynski, T., & Solomon, S. (2002). To belong or not to belong, that is the question: Terror management and identification with gender and ethnicity. *Journal of Personality and Social Psychology, 83,* 26–43.

Aron, A., & Henkemeyer, L. (1995). Marital satisfaction and passionate love. *Journal of Social and Personal Relationships, 12,* 139–146.

Aron, A., & McLaughlin-Volpe, T. (2001). Including others in the self: Extensions to own and partner's group membership. In C. Sedikides & M. B. Brewer (Eds.), *Individual self, relational self, collective self* (pp. 89–108). Philadelphia: Psychology Press.

Aron, A., & Westbay, L. (1996). Dimensions of the prototype of love. *Journal of Personality and Social Psychology, 70,* 535–551.

Aron, A., Aron, E. N., & Allen, J. (1998). Motivations for unreciprocated love. *Personality and Social Psychology Bulletin, 24,* 787–796.

Aron, A., Paris, M., & Aron, E. N. (1995). Falling in love: Prospective studies of self-concept change. *Journal of Personality and Social Psychology, 69,* 1102–1112.

Aron, A., Dutton, D. G., Aron, E. N., & Iverson, A. (1989). Experiences of falling in love. *Journal of Social and Personal Relationships, 6,* 243–257.

Aron, A., Melinat, E., Aron, E. N., Vallone, R. D., & Bator, R. J. (1997). The experimental generation of interpersonal closeness: A procedure and some preliminary findings. *Personality and Social Psychology Bulletin, 23,* 363–377.

Aronoff, J., Woike, B. A., & Hyman, L. M. (1992). Which are the stimuli in facial displays of anger and happiness? Configurational bases of emotion recognition. *Journal of Personality and Social Psychology, 62,* 1050–1066.

Aronson, E. (1968). Dissonance theory: Progress and problems. In R. Abelson, E. Aronson, W. McGuire, T. Newcomb, M. Rosenberg, & P. Tannenbaum (Eds.), *The cognitive consistency theories: A source book* (pp. 5–27). Chicago: Rand McNally.

Aronson, J., Blanton, H., & Cooper, J. (1995). From dissonance to disidentification: Selectivity in the self-affirmation process. *Journal of Personality and Social Psychology, 68,* 986–996.

Aronson, J., Lustina, M. J., Good, C., Keough, K., Steele, C. M., & Brown, J. (1999). When white men can't do math: Necessary and sufficient factors in stereotype threat. *Journal of Experimental Social Psychology, 35,* 29–46.

Arriaga, X. B., & Agnew, C. R. (2001). Being committed: Affective, cognitive, and conative components of relationship commitment. *Personality and Social Psychology Bulletin, 27,* 1190–1203.

Arriaga, X. B., & Rusbult, C. E. (1998). Standing in my partner's shoes: Partner perspective taking and reactions to accommodative dilemmas. *Personality and Social Psychology Bulletin, 24,* 927–948.

Arvey, R. D., Bouchard, T. J., Jr., Segal, N. L., & Abraham, L. M. (1989). Job satisfaction: Genetic and environmental components. *Journal of Applied Psychology, 74,* 187–192.

Asch, S. (1946). Forming impressions of personality. *Journal of Abnormal and Social Psychology, 41,* 258–290.

Asch, S. E. (1951). Effects of group pressure upon the modification and distortion of judgment. In H. Guetzkow (Ed.), *Groups, leadership, and men.* Pittsburgh: Carnegie.

Asch, S. E. (1955). Opinions and social pressure. *Scientific American, 193*(5), 31–35.

Asch, S. E. (1956). Studies of independence and conformity: A minority of one against unanimous majority. *Psychological Monographs, 70* (Whole No. 416).

Asendorpf, J. B. (1992). A Brunswickean approach to trait continuity: Application to shyness. *Journal of Personality, 60,* 55–77.

Asher, S. R., & Paquette, J. A. (2003). Loneliness and peer relations in childhood. *Current Directions in Psychological Science, 12,* 75–78.

Ashmore, R. D., Deaux, K., & McLaughlin-Volpe, T. (2004). An organizing framework for collective identity: Articulation and significance of multidimensionality. *Psychological Bulletin, 130,* 80–114.

Ashmore, R. D., Solomon, M. R., & Longo, L. C. (1996). Thinking about fashion models' looks: A multidimensional approach to the structure of perceived physical attractiveness. *Personality and Social Psychology Bulletin, 22,* 1083–1104.

Aune, K. S., & Wong, N. C. H. (2002). Antecedents and consequences of adult play in romantic relationships. *Personal Relationships, 9,* 279–286.

Averill, J. R., & Boothroyd, P. (1977). On falling in love: Conformance with romantic ideal. *Motivation and Emotion, 1,* 235–247.

Avolio, B. J. (1999). *Full leadership development: Building the vital forces in organizations.* Thousand Oaks, CA: Sage.

Avolio, B. J., Bass, B. M., & Jung, D. (1999). Reexamining the components of transformational and transactional leadership using the Multifactor Leadership Questionnaire. *Journal of Occupational and Organizational Psychology, 7,* 441–462.

Azar, B. (1997, November). Defining the trait that makes us human. *APA Monitor, 1,* 15.

Baccman, C., Folkesson, P., & Norlander, T. (1999). Expectations of romantic relationships: A comparison between homosexual and heterosexual men with regard to Baxter's criteria. *Social Behavior and Personality, 27,* 363–374.

Bachorowski, J., & Owren, M. J. (2001). Not all laughs are alike: Voiced but not unvoiced laughter readily elicits positive affect. *Psychological Science, 12,* 252–257.

Baker, N. V., Gregware, P. R., & Cassidy, M. A. (1999). Family killing fields: Honor rationales in the murder of women. *Violence Against Women, 5,* 164–184.

Baldwin, D. A. (2000). Interpersonal understanding fuels knowledge acquisition. *Current Directions in Psychological Science, 9,* 40–45.

Baldwin, M. W., Carrell, S. E., & Lopez, D. F. (1990). Priming relationship schemas: My advisor and the Pope are watching me from the back of my mind. *Journal of Experimental Social Psychology, 26,* 435–454.

Banaji, M., & Hardin, C. (1996). Automatic stereotyping. *Psychological Science, 7,* 136–141.

Bandura, A. (1990). Selective activation and disengagement of moral control. *Journal of Social Issues, 46,* 27–46.

Bandura, A. (1997). *Self-efficacy: The exercise of control.* New York: W. H. Freeman.

Bandura, A. (1999a). A sociocognitive analysis of substance abuse: An agentic perspective. *Psychological Science, 10,* 214–216.

Bandura, A. (1999b). Moral disengagement in the perpetration of inhumanities. *Personality and Social Psychology Review, 3,* 193–209.

Bandura, A. (2000). Exercise of human agency through collective efficacy. *Current Directions in Psychological Science, 9,* 75–78.

Bandura, A., Ross, D., & Ross, S. (1963). Imitation of film-mediated aggressive models. *Journal of Abnormal and Social Psychology, 66,* 3–11.

Banse, R. (2004). Adult attachment and marital satisfaction: Evidence for dyadic configuration effects. *Journal of Social and Personal Relationships, 21,* 273–282.

Barash, D. P., & Lipton, J. E. (2001). *The myth of monogamy.* New York: Freeman.

Bargh, J. A. (1997). The automaticity of everyday life. In R. S. Wyer (Ed.), *Advances in social cognition* (Vol. 10, pp. 1–61). Mahwah, NJ: Erlbaum.

Bargh, J. A., & Chartrand, T. L. (1999). The unbearable automaticity of being. *American Psychologist, 54,* 462–479.

Bargh, J. A., & Pietromonaco, P. (1982). Automatic information processing and social perception: The influence of trait information presented outside of conscious awareness on impression formation. *Journal of Personality and Social Psychology,* 43, 437–449.

Bargh, J. A., Chen, M., & Burrows, L. (1996). Automaticity of social behavior: Direct effects of trait construct and stereotype activation on action. *Journal of Personality and Social Psychology, 71,* 230–234.

Bargh, J. A., Chaiken, S., Govender, R., & Pratto, F. (1992). The generality of the automatic attitude activation effect. *Journal of Personality and Social Psychology, 62,* 893–912.

Bargh, J. A., Gollwitzer, P. M., Lee-Chai, A., Barndollar, K., & Trotschel, R. (2001). The automated will: Nonconscious activation and pursuit of behavioral goals. *Journal of Personality and Social Psychology, 18,* 1014–1027.

Baron, J. (1997). The illusion of morality as self-interest: A reason to cooperate in social dilemmas. *Psychological Science, 8,* 330–335.

Baron, R. A. (1972). Aggression as a function of ambient temperature and prior anger arousal. *Journal of Personality and Social Psychology, 21,* 183–189.

Baron, R. A. (1989a). Applicant strategies during job interviews. In G. R. Ferris & R. W. Eder (Eds.), *The employment interview: Theory, research, and practice* (pp. 204–216). Newbury Park, CA: Sage.

Baron, R. A. (1989b). Personality and organizational conflict: The Type A behavior pattern and self-monitoring. *Organizational Behavior and Human Decision Processes, 44,* 281–297.

Baron, R. A. (1990a). Attributions and organizational conflict. In S. Graha & V. Folkes (Eds.), *Attribution theory: Applications to achievement, mental health, and interpersonal conflict* (pp. 185–204). Hillsdale, NJ: Erlbaum.

Baron, R. A. (1990c). Environmentally induced positive affect: Its impact on self-efficacy, task performance, negotiation, and conflict. *Journal of Applied Social Psychology, 20,* 368–384.

Baron, R. A. (1993a). Effects of interviewers' moods and applicant qualifications on ratings of job applicants. *Journal of Applied Social Psychology, 23,* 254–271.

Baron, R. A. (1993b). Reducing aggression and conflict: The incompatible response approach, or why people who feel good usually won't be bad. In G. C. Brannigan & M. R. Merrens (Eds.), *The undaunted psychologist* (pp. 203–218). Philadelphia: Temple University Press.

Baron, R. A. (1993c). Criticism (informal negative feedback) as a source of perceived unfairness in organizations: Effects, mechanisms, and countermeasures. In R. Cropanzano (Ed.), *Justice in the workplace: Approaching fairness in human resource management* (pp. 155–170). Hillsdale, NJ: Erlbaum.

Baron, R. A. (1994). The physical environment of work settings: Effects of task performance, interpersonal relations, and job satisfaction. In M. Staw & L. L. Cummings (Eds.), *Research in organizational behavior* (Vol. 16, pp. 1–46). Greenwich, CT: JAI Press.

Baron, R. A. (1997). The sweet smell of helping: Effects of pleasant ambient fragrance on prosocial behavior in shopping malls. *Personality and Social Psychology Bulletin, 23,* 498–503.

Baron, R. A. (1998). Cognitive mechanisms in entrepreneurship: Why, and when, entrepreneurs think differently than other persons. *Journal of Business Venturing, 13,* 275–294.

Baron, R. A. (2000). Counterfactual thinking and venture formation: The potential effects of thinking about "What might have been." *Journal of Business Venturing, 15,* 79–92.

Baron, R. A. (2004). The cognitive perspective: A valuable tool for answering entrepreneurship's "Why?" questions. *Journal of Business Venturing, 19,* 221–240.

Baron, R. A., & Lawton, S. F. (1972). Environmental influences on aggression: The facilitation of modeling effects by high ambient temperatures. *Psychonomic Science, 26,* 80–82.

Baron, R. A., & Markman, G. D. (2003). Beyond social capital: The role of entrepreneurs' social competence in their financial success. *Journal of Business Venturing, 18,* 41–60.

Baron, R. A., & Markman, G. D. (in press). Toward a process view of entrepreneurship: The changing impact of individual level variables across phases of new venture development. In M. A. Rahim, R. T. Golembiewski, & K. D. Mackenzie (Eds.), *Current topics in management* (Vol. 9). New Brunswick, NJ: Transaction Publishers.

Baron, R. A., & Neuman, J. H. (1996). Workplace violence and workplace aggression: Evidence on their relative frequency and potential causes. *Aggressive Behavior, 22,* 161–173.

Baron, R. A., & Richardson, D. R. (1994). *Human Aggression* (2nd ed.). New York: Plenum.

Baron, R. A., & Thomley, J. (1994). A whiff of reality: Positive affect as a potential mediator of the effects of pleasant fragrances on task performance and helping. *Environment and Behavior, 26,* 766–784.

Baron, R. A., Markman, G. D., & Hirsa, A. (2001). Perceptions of women and men as entrepreneurs. Evidence for differential effects of attributional augmenting. *Journal of Applied Psychology, 86,* 923–929.

Baron, R. A., Neuman, J. H., & Geddes, D. (1999). Social and personal determinants of workplace aggression: Evidence for the impact of perceived injustice and the Type A behavior pattern. *Aggressive Behavior, 25,* 4, 281–296.

Baron, R. A., Russell, G. W., & Arms, R. L. (1985). Negative ions and behavior: Impact on mood, memory, and aggression among Type A and Type B persons. *Journal of Personality and Social Psychology, 48,* 746–754.

Baron, R. S. (1986). Distraction/conflict theory: Progress and problems. In L. Berkwoitz (Ed.), *Advances in experimental social psychology* (Vol. 19, pp. 1–40). Orlando: Academic Press.

Baron, R. S., Moore, D., & Sanders, G. S. (1978). Distraction as a source of drive in social facilitation research. *Journal of Personality and Social Psychology, 36*, 816–824.

Baron, R. S., Vandello, U. A., & Brunsman, B. (1996). The forgotten variable in conformity research: Impact of task importance on social influence. *Journal of Personality and Social Psychology, 71*, 915–927.

Barrick, M. R., Stewart, G. L., & Piotrowski, M. 2002. Personality and job performance: Test of the mediating effects of motivation among sales representatives. *Journal of Applied Psychology, 87*, 43–51.

Bar-Tal, D. (2003). Collective memory of physical violence: Its contribution to the culture of violence. In E. Cairns & M. D. Roe (Eds.), *The role of memory in ethnic conflict* (pp. 77–93). New York: Palgrave Macmillan.

Bartholomew, K., & Horowitz, L. M. (1991). Attachment styles among young adults: A test of a four category model. *Journal of Personality and Social Psychology, 61*, 226–244.

Bartholow, B. D., Pearson, M. A., Gratton, G., & Fabiani, M. (2003). Effects of alcohol on person perception: A social cognitive neuroscience approach. *Journal of Personality and Social Psychology, 85*, 627–638.

Bass, B. I. (1998). *Leadership* (2nd ed.). New York: Free Press.

Bass, B. M., Avolio, B. J., Jung, D. I., & Berson, Y. (2003). Predicting unit performance by assessing transformational and transactional leadership. *Journal of Applied Psychology, 88*, 207–218.

Bassili, J. N. (2003). The minority slowness effect: Subtle inhibitions in the expression of views not shared by others. *Journal of Personality and Social Psychology, 84*, 261–276.

Batson, C. D., & Oleson, K. C. (1991). Current status of the empathy–altruism hypothesis. In M. S. Clark (Ed.), *Prosocial behavior* (pp. 62–85). Newbury Park, CA: Sage.

Batson, C. D., & Thompson, E. R. (2001). Why don't moral people act morally? Motivational considerations. *Current Directions in Psychological Science, 10*, 54–57.

Batson, C. D., Early, S., & Salvarani, G. (1997). Perspective taking: Imagining how another feels versus imagining how you would feel. *Personality and Social Psychology Bulletin, 23*, 751–758.

Batson, C. D., Thompson, E. R., & Chen, H. (2002). Moral hypocrisy: Addressing some alternatives. *Journal of Personality and Social Psychology, 83*, 330–339.

Batson, C. D., Tsang, J., & Thompson, E. R. (2000). *Weakness of will: Counting the cost of being moral.* Unpublished manuscript, University of Kansas, Lawrence.

Batson, C. D., Klein, T. R., Highberger, L., & Shaw, L. L. (1995). Immorality from empathy-induced altruism: When compassion and justice conflict. *Journal of Personality and Social Psychology, 68*, 1042–1054.

Batson, C. D., Duncan, B. D., Ackerman, P., Buckley, T., & Birch, K. (1981). Is empathic emotion a source of altruistic motivation? *Journal of Personality and Social Psychology, 40*, 290–302.

Batson, C. D., Kobrynowicz, D., Donnerstein, J. L., Kampf, H. C., & Wilson, A. D. (1997). In a very different voice: Unmasking moral hypocrisy. *Journal of Personality and Social Psychology, 72*, 1335–1348.

Batson, C. D., O'Quin, K., Fultz, J., Vanderplas, M., & Isen, A. M. (1983). Influence of self-reported distress and empathy on egoistic versus altruistic motivation to help. *Journal of Personality and Social Psychology, 45*, 706–718.

Batson, C. D., Thompson, E. R., Seuferling, G., Whitney, H., & Strongman, J. A. (1999). Moral hypocrisy: Appearing moral to oneself without being so. *Journal of Personality and Social Psychology, 77*, 525–537.

Batson, C. D., Batson, J. G., Todd, R. M., Brummett, B. H., Shaw, L. L., & Aldeguer, C. M. R. (1995). Empathy and the collective good: Caring for one of the others in a social dilemma. *Journal of Personality and Social Psychology, 68*, 619–631.

Batson, C. D., Sager, K., Garst, E., Kang, M., Rubchinsky, K., & Dawson, K. (1997). Is empathy-induced helping due to self–other merger? *Journal of Personality and Social Psychology, 73*, 495–509.

Batson, C. D., Ahmed, N., Yin, J., Bedell, S. J., Johnson, J. W., Templin, C. M., & Whiteside, A. (1999). Two threats to the common good: Self-interested egoism and empathy-induced altruism. *Personality and Social Psychology Bulletin, 25*, 3–16.

Batson, C. D., Lishner, D. A., Carpenter, A., Dulin, L., Harjusola-Webb, S., Stocks, E. L., Gale, S., Hassan, O., & Sampat, B. (2003). ". . . As you would have them do unto you.": Does imagining yourself in the other's place stimulate moral action? *Personality and Social Psychology Bulletin, 29*, 1190–1201.

Baum, A. (1994). Behavioral, biological, and environmental interactions in disease processes. In S. Blumenthal, K. Matthews, & S. Weiss (Eds.), *New research frontiers in behavioral medicine: Proceedings of the national conference* (p. 62). Washington, DC: NIH Publications.

Baumeister, R., Smart, L., & Boden, J. (1996). Relation of threatened egotism to violence and aggression: The dark side of high self-esteem. *Psychological Review, 103*, 5–33.

Baumeister, R. F. (1998). The self. In D. T. Gilbert, S. T. Fiske, & G. Lindzey (Eds.), *Handbook of social psychology* (4th ed., Vol. 1, pp. 680–740). New York: McGraw-Hill.

Baumeister, R. F., & Leary, M. R. (1995). The need to belong: Desire for interpersonal attachments as a fundamental human motivation. *Psychological Bulletin, 117*, 497–529.

Baumeister, R. F., & Newman, L. S. (1994). Self-regulation of cognitive inference and decision processes. *Personality and Social Psychology Bulletin, 20*, 3–19.

Baumeister, R. F., Twenge, J. M., & Nuss, C. K. (2002). Effects of social exclusion on cognitive processes: Anticipated aloneness reduces intelligent thought. *Journal of Personality and Social Psychology, 83*, 817–827.

Baumeister, R. F., Wotman, S. R., & Stillwell, A. M. (1993). Unrequited love: On heartbreak, anger, guilt, scriptlessness, and humiliation. *Journal of Personality and Social Psychology, 64*, 377–394.

Baumeister, R. F., Campbell, D. J., Krueger, J. I., & Vohs, K. D. (2003). Does high self-esteem cause better performance, interpersonal success, happiness, or healthier lifestyles? *Psychological Science in the Public Interest, 4,* 1–44.

Baumeister, R. F., Chesner, S. P., Sanders, P. S., & Tice, D. M. (1988). Who's in charge here? Group leaders do lend help in emergencies. *Personality and Social Psychology Bulletin, 14,* 17–22.

Baxter, L. A. (1990). Dialectical contradictions in relationship development. *Journal of Social and Personal Relationships, 7,* 69–88.

Beall, A. E., & Sternberg, R. J. (1995). The social construction of love. *Journal of Social and Personal Relationships, 12,* 417–438.

Beaman, A. I., Cole, M., Preston, M., Klentz, B., & Steblay, N. M. (1983). Fifteen years of the foot-in-the-door research: A meta-analysis. *Personality and Social Psychology Bulletin, 9,* 181–186.

Beauvois, J. L., & Dubois, N. (1988). The norm of internality in the explanation of psychological events. *European Journal of Social Psychology, 18,* 299–316.

Becker, S. W., & Eagly, A. H. (2004). The heroism of women and men. *American Psychologist, 59,* 163–178.

Beinart, P. (1998, October 19). Battle for the 'burbs. *The New Republic,* 25–29.

Bell, B. (1993). Emotional loneliness and the perceived similarity of one's ideas and interests. *Journal of Social Behavior and Personality, 8,* 273–280.

Bell, B. E. (1995). Judgments of the attributes of a student who is talkative versus a student who is quiet in class. *Journal of Social Behavior and Personality, 10,* 827–832.

Bell, D. C. (2001). Evolution of parental caregiving. *Personality and Social Psychology Review, 5,* 216–229.

Bell, P. A. (1992). In defense of the negative affect escape model of heat and aggression. *Psychological Bulletin, 111,* 342–346.

Bell, R. A. (1991). Gender, friendship network density, and loneliness. *Journal of Social Behavior and Personality, 6,* 45–56.

Bell, S. T., Kuriloff, P. J., & Lottes, I. (1994). Understanding attributions of blame in stranger rape and date rape situations: An examination of gender, race, identification, and students' social perceptions of rape victims. *Journal of Applied Social Psychology, 24,* 1719–1734.

Bem, D. J. (1972). Self-perception theory. In L. Berkowitz (Ed.), *Advances in experimental social psychology* (Vol. 6, pp. 1–62). New York: Academic Press.

Benjamin, E. (1998, January 14). Storm brings out good, bad and greedy. Albany *Times Union,* pp. A1, A6.

Bennis, W. (2001). Leading in unnerving times. *MIT Sloan Management Review, 42,* 97–102.

Benoit, W. L. (1998). Forewarning and persuasion. In M. Allen & R. Priess (Eds.), *Persuasion: Advances through meta-analysis* (pp. 159–184). Cresskill, NJ: Hampton Press.

Ben-Porath, D. D. (2002). Stigmatization of individuals who receive psychotherapy: An interaction between help-seeking behavior and the presence of depression. *Journal of Social and Clinical Psychology, 21,* 400–413.

Benson, E. (2003, March). Study examines neural correlates of sympathy. *Monitor on Psychology,* 14.

Benson, P. L., Karabenick, S. A., & Lerner, R. M. (1976). Pretty pleases: The effects of physical attractiveness, race, and sex on receiving help. *Journal of Experimental Social Psychology, 12,* 409–415.

Berant, E., Mikulincer, M., & Florian, V. (2001). The association of mothers' attachment style and their psychological reactions to the diagnosis of infant's congenital heart disease. *Journal of Social and Clinical Psychology, 20,* 208–232.

Berg, J. H., & McQuinn, R. D. (1989). Loneliness and aspects of social support networks. *Journal of Social and Personal Relationships, 6,* 359–372.

Berkowitz, L. (1989). Frustration-aggression hypothesis: Examination and reformulation. *Psychological Bulletin, 106,* 59–73.

Berkowitz, L. (1993). *Aggression: Its causes, consequences, and control.* New York: McGraw Hill.

Bernieri, F. J., Gillis, J. S., Davis, J. M., & Grahe, J. E. (1996). Dyad rapport and the accuracy of its judgment across situations: A lens model analysis. *Journal of Personality and Social Psychology, 71,* 110–129.

Berry, D. S., & Hansen, J. S. (1996). Positive affect, negative affect, and social interaction. *Journal of Personality and Social Psychology, 71,* 796–809.

Berry, J. W., Worthing, E. I., Parrott, L., O'Connor, L. E., & Wade, J. N. G. (in press). Dispositional forgiveness: Development and construct validity of the Transgression Narrative Test of Forgiveness (TNTFO). *Personality and Social Psychology Bulletin.*

Berscheid, E., & Hatfield, E. (1974). A little bit about love. In T. L. Huston (Ed.), *Foundations of interpersonal attraction* (pp. 355–381). New York: Academic Press.

Berscheid, E., & Reis, H. T. (1998). Attraction and close relationships. In D. T. Gilbert, S. T. Fiske, & G. Lindzey (Eds.), *The handbook of social psychology* (4th ed., Vol. 2, pp. 193–281). New York: McGraw-Hill.

Bersoff, D. M. (1999). Why good people sometimes do bad things: Motivated reasoning and unethical behavior. *Personality and Social Bulletin, 25,* 28–39.

Bettencourt, B. A., & Miller, N. (1996). Gender differences in aggression as a function of provocation: A meta-analysis. *Psychological Bulletin, 119,* 422–447.

Bierhoff, H. W., Klein, R., & Kramp, P. (1991). Evidence for the altruistic personality from data on accident research. *Journal of Personality, 59,* 263–280.

Biernat, M., & Thompson, E. R. (2002). Shifting standards and contextual variation in stereotyping. *European Review of Social Psychology, 12,* 103–137.

Biernat, M., & Vescio, T. K. (2002). She swings, she hits, she's great, she's benched: Implications of gender-based shifting standards for judgment and behavior. *Personality and Social Psychology Bulletin, 28,* 66–77.

Biernat, M., Eidelman, S., & Fuegan, K. (2002). Judgment standards and the social self: A shifting standards perspective. In J. P. Forgas & K. D. Williams (Eds.), *The social self: Cognitive, interpersonal, and intergroup perspectives* (pp. 51–72). Philadelphia: Psychology Press.

Bies, R. J., Shapiro, D. L., & Cummings, L. L. (1988). Causal accounts and managing organizational conflict: Is it enough to say it's not my fault? *Communication Research, 15,* 381–399.

Björklund, D. F., & Shackelford, T. K. (1999). Differences in parental investment contribute to important differences between men and women. *Current Directions in Psychological Science, 8,* 86–89.

Björkqvist, K., Lagerspetz, K. M., & Kaukiainen, A. (1992). Do girls manipulate and boys fight? Developmental trends in regard to direct and indirect aggression. *Aggressive Behavior, 18,* 117–127.

Björkqvist, K., Österman, K., & Hjelt-Bäck, M. (1994). Aggression among university employees. *Aggressive Behavior, 20,* 173–184.

Blaney, P. H. (1986). Affect and memory: A review. *Psychological Bulletin, 99,* 229–246.

Blankstein, K. R., & Dunkley, D. M. (2002). Evaluative concerns, self-critical, and personal standards perfectionism: A structural equation modeling strategy. In G. L. Flett, & P. L. Hewitt (Eds.), *Perfectionism: Theory, research, and treatment* (pp. 285–315). Washington, DC: American Psychological Association.

Blascovich, J., Wyer, N. A., Swart, L. A., & Kibler, J. L. (1997). Racism and racial categorization. *Journal of Personality and Social Psychology, 72,* 1364–1372.

Blazer, D. G., Kessler, R. C., McGonagle, K. A., & Swartz, M. S. (1994). The prevalence and distribution of major depression in a national community sample: The National Comorbidity Survey. *American Journal of Psychiatry, 151,* 979–986.

Bleske-Rechek, A. L., & Buss, D. M. (2001). Opposite-sex friendship: Sex differences and similarities in initiation, selection, and dissolution. *Personality and Social Psychology Bulletin, 27,* 1310–1323.

Bless, H. (2001). The consequences of mood on the processing of social information. In A. Tesser & N. Schwarz (Eds.), *Blackwell handbook in social psychology* (pp. 391–412). Oxford, England: Blackwell Publishers.

Blickle, G. (2003). Some outcomes of pressure, ingratiation, and rational persuasion used with peers in the workplace. *Journal of Applied Social Psychology, 33,* 648–665.

Bobo, L. (1983). Whites' opposition to busing: Symbolic racism or realistic group conflict? *Journal of Personality and Social Psychology, 45,* 1196–1210.

Bobo, L. (2000). Race and beliefs about affirmative action. In D. O. Sears, J. Sidanius, & L. Bobo (Eds.), *Racialized politics: The debate about racism in America* (pp. 137–164). Chicago: University of Chicago Press.

Bodenhausen, G. F. (1993). Emotion, arousal, and stereotypic judgment: A heuristic model of affect and stereotyping. In D. Mackie & D. Hamilton (Eds.), *Affect, cognition, and stereotyping: Intergroup processes in intergroup perception* (pp. 13–37). San Diego, CA: Academic Press.

Bodenhausen, G. V., & Lambert A. J. (Eds.). (2003). *Foundations of social cognition: A Festschrift in honor of Robert S. Wyer, Jr.* Mahwah, NJ: Erlbaum.

Bodenmann, G., Kaiser, A., Hahlweg, K., & Fehn-Wolfsdorf, G. (1998). Communication patterns during marital conflict: A cross-cultural replication. *Personal Relationships, 5,* 343–356.

Boer, F., Westenberg, M., McHale, S. M., Updegraff, K. A., & Stocker, C. M. (1997). The factorial structure of the Sibling Relationship Inventory (SRI) in American and Dutch samples. *Journal of Social and Personal Relationships, 14,* 851–859.

Bogard, M. (1990). Why we need gender to understand human violence. *Journal of Interpersonal Violence, 5,* 132–135.

Bolton, M. M. (2004, April 8). Gay couples sue state over marriage law. Albany *Times Union,* A1, A14.

Bombardieri, M. (2004, February 9). For dateless on campus, idea clicks. *Boston Globe,* B1.

Bond, M. H. (1996). Chinese values. In M. H. Bond (Ed.), *The handbook of Chinese psychology* (pp. 208–226). Oxford, England: Oxford University Press.

Bond, R., & Smith, P. B. (1996). Culture and conformity: A meta-analysis of studies using Asch's (1952b, 1956) line judgment task. *Psychological Bulletin, 119,* 111–137.

Boon, S. D., & Brussoni, M. J. (1998). Popular images of grandparents: Examining young adults' views of their closest grandparents. *Personal Relationships, 5,* 105–119.

Bornstein, R. F., & D'Agostino, P. R. (1992). Stimulus recognition and the mere exposure effect. *Journal of Personality and Social Psychology, 63,* 545–552.

Bossard, J. H. S. (1932). Residential propinquity as a factor in marriage selection. *American Journal of Sociology, 38,* 219–224.

Bosson, J. K., Haymovitz, E. L., & Pinel, E. C. (2004). When saying and doing diverge: The effects of stereotype threat on self-reported versus non-verbal anxiety. *Journal of Experimental Social Psychology, 40,* 247–255.

Boswell, J. (1963). *The life of Samuel Johnson L. L. D.* (Vol. 2). New York: Heritage. (Original work published 1791.)

Botha, M. (1990). Television exposure and aggression among adolescents: A follow-up study over 5 years. *Aggressive Behavior, 16,* 361–380.

Bourhis, R. Y., Giles, H., Leyens, J. P., & Tajfel, H. (1978). Psycholinguistic distinctiveness: Language divergence in Belgium. In H. Giles & R. St. Clair (Eds.), *Language and social psychology* (pp. 158–185). Oxford: Blackwell.

Bower, G. H. (1991). Mood congruity of social judgments. In J. P. Forgas (Ed.), *Emotion and social judgments* (pp. 31–55). Oxford: Pergamon Press.

Bowers, L., Smith, P. K., & Binney, V. (1994). Perceived family relationships of bullies, victims and bully/victims in middle childhood. *Journal of Social and Personal Relationships, 11,* 215–232.

Bowlby, J. (1969). *Attachment and loss: Vol. 1. Attachment.* New York: Basic Books.

Bowlby, J. (1973). *Attachment and loss: Vol. 2. Separation.* New York: Basic Books.

Bowlby, J. (1982). *Attachment and loss: Vol. 1. Attachment* (2nd ed.). New York: Basic Books.

Boyce, N. (2001, June 4). Cruel lessons from an epidemic. *U.S. News and World Report,* 48–49.

Branscombe, N. R. (1998). Thinking about one's gender group's privileges or disadvantages: Consequences for well-being in women and men. *British Journal of Social Psychology, 37,* 167–184.

Branscombe, N. R. (2004). A social psychological process perspective on collective guilt. In N. R. Branscombe & B. Doosje (Eds.), *Collective guilt: International perspectives* (pp. 320–334). New York: Cambridge University Press.

Branscombe, N. R., & Miron, A. M. (2004). Interpreting the ingroup's negative actions toward another group: Emotional reactions to appraised harm. In L. Z. Tiedens & C. W. Leach (Eds.), *The social life of emotions* (pp. 314–335). New York: Cambridge University Press.

Branscombe, N. R., & Wann, D. L. (1994). Collective self-esteem consequences of outgroup derogation when a valued social identity is on trial. *European Journal of Social Psychology, 24,* 641–657.

Branscombe, N. R., Doosje, B., & McGarty, C. (2002). Antecedents and consequences of collective guilt. In D. M. Mackie & E. R. Smith (Eds.), *From prejudice to intergroup emotions: Differentiated reactions to social groups* (pp. 49–66). Philadelphia: Psychology Press.

Branscombe, N. R., Schmitt, M. T., & Harvey, R. D. (1999). Perceiving pervasive discrimination among African-Americans: Implications for group identification and well-being. *Journal of Personality and Social Psychology, 77,* 135–149.

Branscombe, N. R., Slugoski, B., & Kappen, D. M. (2004). The measurement of collective guilt: What it is and what it is not. In N. R. Branscombe & B. Doosje (Eds.), *Collective guilt: International perspectives* (pp. 16–34). New York: Cambridge University Press.

Branscombe, N. R., Wann, D. L., Noel, J. G., & Coleman, J. (1993). Ingroup or outgroup extremity: Importance of the threatened identity. *Personality and Social Psychology Bulletin, 19,* 381–388.

Braver, S., Ellman, I. M., & Fabricus, W. V. (2003). Relocation of children after divorce and children's best interests: New evidence and legal considerations. *Journal of Family Psychology, 17,* 206–219.

Braza, P., Braza, F., Carreras, M. R., & Munoz, J. M. (1993). Measuring the social ability of preschool children. *Social Behavior and Personality, 21,* 145–158.

Brehm, J. W. (1966). *A theory of psychological reactance.* New York: Academic Press.

Brennan, K. A., & Bosson, J. K. (1998). Attachment-style differences in attitudes toward and reactions to feedback from romantic partners: An exploration of the relational bases of self-esteem. *Personality and Social Psychology Bulletin, 24,* 699–714.

Brewer, M. B., & Brown, R. (1998). Intergroup relations. In D. T. Gilbert, S. T. Fiske, & G. Lindzey (Eds.), *The handbook of social psychology* (4th ed., Vol. 2, pp. 554–594). New York: McGraw-Hill.

Brewer, M. B., Ho, H., Lee, J., & Miller, M. (1987). Social identity and social distance among Hong Kong schoolchildren. *Personality and Social Psychology Bulletin, 13,* 156–165.

Brickner, M., Harkins, S., & Ostrom, T. (1986). Personal involvement: Thought provoking implications for social loafing. *Journal of Personality and Social Psychology, 51,* 763–769.

Bringle, R. G., & Winnick, T. A. (1992, October). *The nature of unrequited love.* Paper presented at the first Asian Conference in Psychology, Singapore.

Brockner, A. T., Higgins, E. T., & Low, M. B. (2004). Regulatory focus theory and the entrepreneurial process. *Journal of Business Venturing, 19,* 203–220.

Brockner, J., Konovsky, M., Cooper-Schneider, R., Folger, R., Martin, C., & Bies, R. J. (1994). Interactive effects of procedural justice and outcome negativity on victims and survivors of job loss. *Academy of Management Journal, 37,* 397–409.

Brockner, J. M., & Wiesenfeld, B. M. (1996). An integrative framework for explaining reactions to decisions: Interactive effects of outcomes and procedures. *Psychological Bulletin, 120,* 189–208.

Broemer, P. (2004). Ease of imagination moderates reactions to differently framed health messages. *European Journal of Social Psychology, 34,* 103–119.

Brooks-Gunn, J., & Lewis, M. (1981). Infant social perception: Responses to pictures of parents and strangers. *Developmental Psychology, 17,* 647–649.

Brothers, L. (1990). The neural basis of primate social communication. *Motivation and Emotion, 14,* 81–91.

Brown, J. D. (1991). Staying fit and staying well: Physical fitness as a moderator of life stress. *Journal of Personality and Social Psychology, 60,* 555–561.

Brown, J. D., & Rogers, R. J. (1991). Self-serving attributions: The role of physiological arousal. *Personality and Social Psychology Bulletin, 17,* 501–506.

Brown, L. M. (1998). Ethnic stigma as a contextual experience: Possible selves perspective. *Personality and Social Psychology Bulletin, 24,* 165–172.

Brown, R. (2000). Social identity theory: Past achievements, current problems and future challenges. *European Journal of Social Psychology, 30,* 745–778.

Brown, S. L., Nesse, R. M., Vinokur, A. D., & Smith, D. M. (2003). Providing social support may be more beneficial than receiving it. *Psychological Science, 14,* 320–327.

Brown, S. P. (1996). A meta-analysis and review of organizational research on job involvement. *Psychological Bulletin, 120,* 235–255.

Browne, M. W. (1992, April 14). Biologists tally generosity's rewards. *New York Times,* pp. C1, C8.

Bruder, G. E., Stewart, M. M., Mercier, M. A., Agosti, V., Leite, P., Donovan, S., & Quitkin, F. M. (1997). Outcome of cognitive–behavioral therapy for depression: Relation to hemispheric dominance for verbal processing. *Journal of Abnormal Psychology, 106,* 138–144.

Bryan, J. H., & Test, M. A. (1967). Models and helping: Naturalistic studies in aiding behavior. *Journal of Personality and Social Psychology, 6,* 400–407.

Buck, R. (1977). Nonverbal communication of affect in preschool children: Relationships with personality and skin conductance. *Journal of Personality and Social Psychology 35,* 225–236.

Buckley, K. E., Winkel, R. E., & Leary, M. R. (2003). Reactions to acceptance and rejection: Effects of level and sequence of relational evaluation. *Journal of Experimental Social Psychology, 40,* 14–28.

Budesheim, T. L., & Bonnelle, K. (1998). The use of abstract trait knowledge and behavioral exemplars in causal explanations of behavior. *Personality and Social Psychology Bulletin, 24,* 575–587.

Buehler, R., & Griffin, D. (1994). Change-of-meaning effects in conformity and dissent: Observing construal processes over time. *Journal of Personality and Social Psychology, 67,* 984–996.

Buehler, R., Griffin, D., & MacDonald, H. (1997). The role of motivated reasoning in optimistic time predictions. *Personality and Social Psychology Bulletin, 23,* 238–247.

Buehler, R., Griffin, D., & Ross, M. (1994). Exploring the "planning fallacy": Why people underestimate their task completion times. *Journal of Personality and Social Psychology, 67,* 366–381.

Bumpass, L. (1984). Children and marital disruption: A replication and update. *Demography, 21,* 71–82.

Burger, J. M. (1986). Increasing compliance by improving the deal: The that's-not-all technique. *Journal of Personality and Social Psychology, 51,* 277–283.

Burger, J. M. (1992). *Desire for control: Personality, social, and clinical perspectives.* New York: Plenum.

Burger, J. M. (1995). Individual differences in preference for solitude. *Journal of Research in Personality, 29,* 85–108.

Burger, J. M., & Cornelius, T. (2003). Raising the price of agreement: Public commitment and the lowball compliance procedure. *Journal of Applied Social Psychology, 33,* 923–934.

Burger, J. M., Messian, N., Patel, S., del Pardo, A., & Anderson, C. (2004). What a coincidence! The effects of incidental similarity on compliance. *Personality and Social Psychology Bulletin, 30,* 35–43.

Burnstein, E. (1983). Persuasion as argument processing. In M. Brandstatter, J. H. Davis, & G. Stocker-Kriechgauer (Eds.), *Group decision processes.* London: Academic Press.

Burnstein, E., Crandall, C., & Kitayama, S. (1994). Some neo-Darwinian rules for altruism: Weighing cues for inclusive fitness as a function of the biological importance of the decision. *Journal of Personality and Social Psychology, 67,* 773–789.

Busenitz, L. W., & Barney, J. B. (1997). Differences between entrepreneurs and managers in large organizations: Biases and heuristics in strategic decision making. *Journal of Business Venturing, 12,* 9–30.

Bushman, B. J. (1988). The effects of apparel on compliance: A field experiment with a female authority figure. *Personality and Social Psychology Bulletin, 14,* 459–467.

Bushman, B. J. (1998). Effects of television violence on memory for commercial messages. *Journal of Experimental Psychology: Applied, 4,* 1–17.

Bushman, B. J. (2001). Does venting anger feed or extinguish the flame? Catharsis, rumination, distraction, anger, and aggressive responding. Manuscript under review.

Bushman, B. J., & Anderson, C. A. (2002). Violent video games and hostile expectations: A test of the general aggression model. *Personality and Social Psychology Bulletin, 28,* 1679–1686.

Bushman, B. J., & Baumeister, R. F. (1998). Threatened egotism, narcissism, self-esteem, and direct and displaced aggression: Does self-love or self-hate lead to violence? *Journal of Personality and Social Psychology, 75,* 219–229.

Bushman, B. J., & Cooper, H. M. (1990). Effects of alcohol on human aggression: An integrative research review. *Psychological Bulletin, 107,* 341–354.

Bushman, B. J., & Huesmann, L. R. (2001). Effects of televised violence on aggression. In D. Singer & J. Singer (Eds.), *Handbook of children and the media* (pp. 223–254). Thousands Oaks, CA: Sage.

Bushman, B. J., Baumeister, R. F., & Stack, A. D. (1999). Catharsis messages and anger-reducing activities. *Journal of Personality and Social Psychology, 76,* 367–376.

Buss, D. M. (1994). The strategies of human mating. *American Scientist, 82,* 238–249.

Buss, D. M. (1998). Evolutionary psychology. Boston: Allyn & Bacon.

Buss, D. M. (1999). *Evolutionary psychology: The new science of the mind.* Boston: Allyn and Bacon.

Buss, D. M., & Schmitt, D. P. (1993). Sexual strategies theory: An evolutionary perspective on human mating. *Psychological Review, 100,* 204–232.

Buss, D. M., & Shackelford, T. K. (1997). From vigilance to violence: Mate retention tactics in married couples. *Journal of Personality and Social Psychology, 72,* 346–361.

Buss, D. M., Larsen, R. J., Westen, D., & Semmelroth, J. (1992). Sex differences in jealousy: Evolution, physiology, and psychology. *Psychological Science, 3,* 251–255.

Buston, P. M., & Emlen, S. T. (2003). Cognitive processes underlying human mate choice: The relationship between self-perception and mate preferences in Western society. *The Proceedings of the National Academy of Sciences, 100,* 8805–8810.

Butler, D., & Geis, F. L. (1990). Nonverbal affect responses to male and female leaders: Implications for leadership evaluations. *Journal of Personality and Social Psychology, 58,* 48–59.

Buunk, B. P., & Prins, K. S. (1998). Loneliness, exchange orientation, and reciprocity in friendships. *Personal Relationships, 5,* 1–14.

Buunk, B. P., & van der Eijnden, R. J. J. M. (1997). Perceived prevalence, perceived superiority, and relationship satisfaction: Most relationships are good, but ours is the best. *Personality and Social Psychology Bulletin, 23,* 219–228.

Buunk, B. P., Dukstra, P., Fetchenhauer, D., & Kenrick, D. T. (2002). Age and gender differences in mate selection criteria for various involvement levels. *Personal Relationships, 9,* 271–278.

Byrne, B. M., & Shavelson, R. J. (1996). On the structure of social self-concept for pre-, early, and late adolescents: A test of the Shavelson, Hubner, and Stanton (1976) model. *Journal of Personality and Social Psychology, 70,* 599–613.

Byrne, D. (1961a). The influence of propinquity and opportunities for interaction on classroom relationships. *Human Relations, 14,* 63–69.

Byrne, D. (1961b). Interpersonal attraction and attitude similarity. *Journal of Abnormal and Social Psychology, 62,* 713–715.

Byrne, D. (1971). *The attraction paradigm.* New York: Academic Press.

Byrne, D. (1991). Perspectives on research classics: This ugly duckling has yet to become a swan. *Contemporary Social Psychology, 15,* 84–85.

Byrne, D. (1992). The transition from controlled laboratory experimentation to less controlled settings: Surprise! Additional variables are operative. *Communication Monographs, 59,* 190–198.

Byrne, D. (1997a). An overview (and underview) of research and theory within the attraction paradigm. *Journal of Social and Personal Relationships, 14,* 417–431.

Byrne, D. (1997b). Why would anyone conduct research on sexual behavior? In G. G. Brannigan, E. R. Allgeier, & A. R. Allgeier (Eds.), *The sex scientists* (pp. 15–30). New York: Addison Wesley Longman.

Byrne, D., & Blaylock, B. (1963). Similarity and assumed similarity of attitudes among husbands and wives. *Journal of Abnormal and Social Psychology, 67,* 636–640.

Byrne, D., & Clore, G. L. (1970). A reinforcement–affect model of evaluative responses. *Personality: An International Journal, 1,* 103–128.

Byrne, D., & Fisher, W. A. (Eds.). (1983). *Adolescents, sex, and contraception.* Hillsdale, NJ: Erlbaum.

Byrne, D., & Nelson, D. (1965). Attraction as a linear function of proportion of positive reinforcements. *Journal of Personality and Social Psychology, 1,* 659–663.

Byrne, D., Baskett, G. D., & Hodges, L. A. (1971). Behavioral indicators of interpersonal attraction. *Journal of Applied Social Psychology, 1,* 137–149.

Byrne, D., Allgeier, A. R., Winslow, L., & Buckman, J. (1975). The situational facilitation of interpersonal attraction: A three-factor hypothesis. *Journal of Applied Social Psychology, 5,* 1–15.

Byrne, R. L. (2001, June 1). Good safety advice. Internet.

Cacioppo, J. T., & Berntson, G. G. (1999). The affect system: Architecture and operating characteristics. *Current Directions in Psychological Science, 8,* 133–136.

Cacioppo, J. T., Hawkley, L. C., & Berntson, G. G. (2003). The anatomy of loneliness. *Current Directions in Psychological Science, 12,* 71–74.

Cacioppo, J. T., Berntson, G. G., Long, T. S., Norris, C. J., Rickhett, E., & Nusbaum, H. (2003). Just because you're imaging the brain doesn't mean you can stop using your head: A primer and set of first principles. *Journal of Personality and Social Psychology, 85,* 650–661.

Cacioppo, J. T., Hawkley, L. C., Berntson, G. G., Ernst, J. M., Gibbs, A. C., Stickgold, R., & Hobson, J. A. (2002). Do lonely days invade the nights? Potential social modulation of sleep efficiency. *Psychological Science, 13,* 384–387.

Cadenhead, A. C., & Richman, C. L. (1996). The effects of interpersonal trust and group status on prosocial and aggressive behaviors. *Social Behavior and Personality, 24,* 169–184.

Callan, V. J. (1993). Subordinate manager communication in different sex-dyads: Consequences for job satisfaction. *Journal of Occupational and Organizational Psychology, 66,* 13–27.

Camacho, J., Higgins, E. T., & Luger, L. (2003). Moral value transfer from regulatory fit: What feels right *is* right and what feels wrong *is* wrong. *Journal of Personality and Social Psychology, 84,* 498–510.

Campbell, D. T. (1958). Common fate, similarity, and other indices of the status of aggregates of persons as social entities. *Behavioral Science, 4,* 14–25.

Campbell, L., Simpson, J. A., Kashy, D. A., & Fletcher, G. J. O. (2001). Ideal standards, the self, and flexibility of ideals in close relationships. *Personality and Social Psychology Bulletin, 27,* 447–462.

Campbell, W. K. (1999). Narcissism and romantic attraction. *Journal of Personality and Social Psychology, 77,* 1254–1270.

Campbell, W. K., & Foster, C. A. (2002). Narcissism and commitment to romantic relationships: An investment model analysis. *Personality and Social Psychology Bulletin, 28,* 484–495.

Cann, A., Calhoun, L. G., & Banks, J. S. (1995). On the role of humor appreciation in interpersonal attraction: It's no joking matter. *Humor: International Journal of Humor Research.*

Caprara, G. V., Barbaranelli, C., Pastorelli, C., Bandura, A., & Zimbardo, P. G. (2000). Prosocial foundations of children's academic achievement. *Psychological Science, 11,* 302–306.

Carey, M. P., Morrison-Beedy, D., & Johnson, B. T. (1997). The HIV-Knowledge Questionnaire: Development and evaluation of a reliable, valid, and practical self-administered questionnaire. *AIDS and Behavior, 1,* 61–74.

Carlsmith, K. M., Darley, J. M., & Robinson, P. H. (2002). Why do we punish? Deterrence and just deserts as motives for punishment. *Journal of Personality and Social Psychology, 83,* 284–299.

Carlson, K. A., & Russo, J. E. (2001). Biased interpretation of evidence by mock jurors: A meta-analysis. *Journal of Experimental Psychology: Applied, 7,* 91–103.

Carpenter, S. (2001a, July/August). They're positively inspiring. *Monitor on Psychology,* 74–76.

Carpenter, S. (2001b, March). Fools rush in. *Monitor on Psychology,* 66–67.

Carpenter, S. (2001c, October). Technology gets its day in court. *Monitor on Psychology,* 30–32.

Carroll, F. (2004, August 12). Legacy of divorce depends on the study. *Albany Times Union,* pp. D1, D3.

Carroll, J. M., & Russell J. A. (1996). Do facial expressions signal specific emotions? Judging emotion from the face in context. *Journal of Personality and Social Psychology, 70,* 205–218.

Carter, N. M., Gartner, W. B., & Reynolds, P. D. (1996). Exploring start-up event sequences. *Journal of Business Venturing, 11,* 151–166.

Carver, C. S., & Glass, D. C. (1978). Coronary-prone behavior pattern and interpersonal aggression. *Journal of Personality and Social Psychology, 376,* 361–366.

Carver, C. S., Kus, L. A., & Scheier, M. F. (1994). Effects of good versus bad mood and optimistic versus pessimistic outlook on social acceptance versus rejection. *Journal of Social and Clinical Psychology, 13,* 138–151.

Cash, T. F., & Duncan, N. C. (1984). Physical attractiveness stereotyping among black American college students. *Journal of Social Psychology, 122,* 71–77.

Cash, T. F., & Trimer, C. A. (1984). Sexism and beautyism in women's evaluation of peer performance. *Sex Roles, 10,* 87–98.

Caspi, A., & Herbener, E. S. (1990). Continuity and change: Assortative marriage and the consistency of personality in adulthood. *Journal of Personality and Social Psychology, 58,* 250–258.

Caspi, A., Herbener, E. S., & Ozer, D. J. (1992). Shared experiences and the similarity of personalities: A longitudinal study of married couples. *Journal of Personality and Social Psychology, 62,* 281–291.

Castano, E., Paladino M. P., Coull, A., Yzerbyt, V. Y. (2002). Protecting the ingroup stereotype: Ingroup identification and the management of deviant ingroup members. *British Journal of Social Psychology, 41,* 365–385.

Castelli, L., Zogmaister, C., & Smith, E. R. (2004). On the automatic evaluation of social exemplars. *Journal of Personality and Social Psychology, 86,* 373–387.

Catalano, R., Novaco, R. W., & McConnell, W. (2002). Layoffs and violence revisisted. *Aggressive Behavior, 28,* 233–247.

Caughlin, J. P., Huston, T. L., & Houts, R. M. (2000). How does personality matter in marriage? An examination of trait anxiety, interpersonal negativity, and marital satisfaction. *Journal of Personality and Social Psychology, 78,* 326–336.

Chaiken, S., & Maheswaran, D. (1994). Heuristic processing can bias systematic processing: Effects of source credibil-ity, argument ambiguity, and task importance on attitude judgment. *Journal of Personality and Social Psychology, 66,* 460–473.

Chaiken, S., & Trope, Y. (1999). *Dual-process theories in social psychology.* New York: Guilford Press.

Chaiken, S., Giner-Sorolla, R., & Chen, S. (1996). Beyond accuracy: Defense and impression motives in heuristic and systematic processing. In P. M. Gollwitzer & J. A. Bargh (Eds.), *The psychology action: Linking motivation and cognition to behavior* (pp. 553–578). New York: Guilford.

Chaiken, S., Liberman, A., & Eagly, A. H. (1989). Heuristic and systematic processing within and beyond persuasion context. In J. S. Uleman & J. A. Bargh (Eds.), *Unintended thought* (pp. 212–252). New York: Guilford.

Chait, J. (2004, March 15). Look left. *The New Republic,* 10–11.

Chajut, E., & Algom, D. (2003). Selective attention improves under stress: Implications for theories of social cognition. *Journal of Personality and Social Psychology, 85,* 231–248.

Chang, E. C., & Asakawa, K. (2003). Cultural variations on optimistic and pessimistic bias for self versus a sibling: Is there evidence for self-enhancement in the West and for self-criticism in the East when the referent group is specified? *Journal of Personality and Social Psychology, 84,* 569–581.

Chaplin, W. F., Phillips, J. B., Brown, J. D., Clanton, N. R., & Stein, J. L. (2000). Handshaking, gender, personality, and first impressions. *Journal of Personality and Social Psychology, 79,* 110–117.

Chartrand, T. L., & Bargh, J. A. (1999). The Chameleon effect: The perception-behavior link and social interaction. *Journal of Personality and Social Psychology, 76,* 893–910.

Chartrand, T. L., Maddux, W. W., & Lakin, J. L. (2004). Beyond the perception-behavior link: The ubiquitous utility and motivational moderators of non-conscious mimicry. In R. Hassin, J. Uleman, & J. A. Bargh (Eds.), *Unintended thought 2: The new unconscious.* New York: Oxford University Press.

Chast, R. (2004, January 19). The Acme Marital Adjustment Test. *New Yorker,* 96.

Chen, F. F., & Kenrick, D. T. (2002). Repulsion or attraction? Group membership and assumed attitude similarity. *Journal of Personality and Social Psychology, 83,* 11–125.

Chen, M., & Bargh, J. A. (1997). Nonconscious behavioral confirmation processes: The self-fulfilling consequences of automatic stereotype activation. *Journal of Experimental Social Psychology, 33,* 541–560.

Chen, M., & Bargh, J. A. (1999). Consequences of automatic evaluation: Immediate behavioral predispositions to approach or avoid the stimulus. *Personality and Social Psychology Bulletin, 25,* 215–224.

Cheverton, H. M., & Byrne, D. (1998, February). *Development and validation of the Primary Choice Clothing Questionnaire.* Presented at the meeting of the Eastern Psychological Association, Boston.

Choi, I., & Nisbett, R. E. (1998). Situational salience and cultural differences in the correspondence bias and actor-observer bias. *Personality and Social Psychology Bulletin, 24,* 949–960.

Christy, P. R., Gelfand, D. M., & Hartmann, D. P. (1971). Effects of competition-induced frustration on two classes of modeled behavior. *Developmental Psychology, 5,* 104–111.

Cialdini, R. B. (1994). *Influence: Science and practice* (3rd ed.). New York: Harper Collins.

Cialdini, R. B., & Petty, R. (1979). Anticipatory opinion effects. In B. Petty, T. Ostrom, & T. Brock (Eds.), *Cognitive responses in persuasion.* Hillsdale, NJ: Erlbaum.

Cialdini, R. B., & Trost, M. R. (1998). Social influence: Social norms, conformity, and compliance. In D. T. Gilbert, S. T. Fiske, & G. Lindzey (Eds.), *The handbook of social psychology* (Vol. 2, pp. 151–192). Boston: McGraw-Hill.

Cialdini, R. B., Baumann, D. J., & Kenrick, D. T. (1981). Insights from sadness: A three-step model of the development of altruism as hedonism. *Developmental Review, 1,* 207–223.

Cialdini, R. B., Kallgren, C. A., & Reno, R. R. (1991). A focus theory of normative conduct. *Advances in Experimental Social Psychology, 24,* 201–234.

Cialdini, R. B., Kenrick, D. T., & Baumann, D. J. (1982). Effects of mood on prosocial behavior in children and adults. In N. Eisenberg-Berg (Ed.), *Development of prosocial behavior.* New York: Academic Press.

Cialdini, R. B., Cacioppo, J. T., Bassett, R., & Miller J. A. (1978). A low-ball procedure for producing compliance: Commitment then cost. *Journal of Personality and Social Psychology, 36,* 463–476.

Cialdini, R. B., Brown, S. L., Lewis, B. P., Luce, C., & Neuberg, S. L. (1997). Reinterpreting the empathy–altruism relationship: When one into one equals oneness. *Journal of Personality and Social Psychology, 73,* 481–494.

Cialdini, R. B., Schaller, M., Houlainham, D., Arps, K., Fultz, J., & Beaman, A. L. (1987). Empathy-based helping: Is it selflessly or selfishly motivated? *Journal of Personality and Social Psychology, 52,* 749–758.

Cialdini, R. B., Vincent, J. E., Lewis, S. K., Catalan, J., Wheeler, D., & Darby, B. L. (1975). Reciprocal concessions procedure for inducing compliance: The door-in-the-face technique. *Journal of Personality and Social Psychology, 31,* 206–215.

Ciavarella, M. A., Bucholtz, A. K., Riordan, C. M., Gatewood, R. D., & Stokes, G. S. (in press). The big five and venture success: Is there a linkage? *Journal of Business Venturing, 19,* 465–484.

Claire, T., & Fiske, S. T. (1998). A systemic view of behavioral confirmation: Counterpoint to the individualist view. In C. Sedikides, J. Schopler & C. A. Insko (Eds.), *Intergroup cognition and intergroup behavior* (pp. 205–231). Mahwah, NJ: Erlbaum.

Clark, L. A., Kochanska, G., & Ready, R. (2000). Mothers' personality and its interaction with child temperament as predictors of parenting behavior. *Journal of Personality and Social Psychology, 79,* 274–285.

Clark, M. S., & Grote, N. K. (1998). Why aren't indices of relationship costs always negatively related to indices of relationship quality? *Personality and Social Psychology Review, 2,* 2–17.

Clark, M. S., Ouellette, R., Powel, M. C., & Milberg, S. (1987). Recipient's mood, relationship type, and helping. *Journal of Personality and Social Psychology, 53,* 94–103.

Clary, E. G., & Orenstein, L. (1991). The amount and effectiveness of help: The relationship of motives and abilities in helping behavior. *Personality and Social Psychology Bulletin, 17,* 58–64.

Clary, E. G., & Snyder, M. (1999). The motivations to volunteer: Theoretical and practical considerations. *Current Directions in Psychological Science, 8,* 156–159.

Clary, E. G., Snyder, M., Ridge, R. D., Copeland, J., Stukas, A. A., Haugen, J., & Miene, P. (1998). Understanding and assessing the motivations of volunteers: A functional approach. *Journal of Personality and Social Psychology, 74,* 1516–1530.

Clore, G. L., Schwarz, N., & Conway, M. (1993). Affective causes and consequences of social information processing. In R. S. Wyer & T. K. Srull (Eds.), *Handbook of social cognition* (2nd ed.). Hilldsale, NJ: Erlbaum.

Cobb, R. J., Davila, J., & Bradbury, T. N. (2001). Attachment security and marital satisfaction: The role of positive perceptions and social support. *Personality and Social Psychology Bulletin, 27,* 1131–1143.

Cohen, D., & Nisbett, R. E. (1994). Self-protection and the culture of honor: Explaining southern violence. *Personality and Social Psychology Bulletin, 20,* 551–567.

Cohen, D., & Nisbett, R. E. (1997). Field experiments examining the culture of honor: The role of institutions in perpetuating norms about violence. *Personality and Social Psychology Bulletin, 23,* 1188–1199.

Cohen, S., Kaplan, J. R., Cunnick, J. E., Manuck, S. B., & Rabin, B. S. (1992). Chronic social stress, affiliation, and cellular immune response in non-human primates. *Psychological Science, 3,* 301–304.

Cohen, S., Frank, E., Doyle, W. J., Skoner, D. P., Rabin, B. S., & Gwalatney, J. M. (1998). Types of stressors that increase susceptibility to the common cold in healthy adults. *Health Psychology, 3,* 214–223.

Cohn, E. G., & Rotton, J. (1997). Assault as a function of time and temperature: A moderator-variable time-series analysis. *Journal of Personality and Social Psychology, 72,* 1322–1334.

Coles, R. (1997). *The moral intelligence of children.* New York: Random House.

Collins, M. A., & Zebrowitz, L. A. (1995). The contributions of appearance to occupational outcomes in civilian and military settings. *Journal of Applied Social Psychology, 25,* 129–163.

Colquitt, J. A. (2001). On the dimensionality of organizational justice: A construct validation of a measure. *Journal of Applied Psychology, 86,* 386–400.

Conger, R. D., Rueter, M. A., & Elder, G. H., Jr. (1999). Couple resilience to economic pressure. *Journal of Personality and Social Psychology, 76,* 54–71.

Coniff, R. (2004, January). Reading faces. *Smithsonian,* 44–50.

Conway, L. G., III. (2004). Social contagion of time perception. *Journal of Experimental Social Psychology, 40,* 113–120.

Conway, M., & Vartanian, L. R. (2000). A status account of gender stereotypes: Beyond communality and agency. *Sex Roles, 43,* 181–199.

Cook, S. W., & Pelfrey, M. (1985). Reactions to being helped in cooperating interracial groups: A context effect. *Journal of Personality and Social Psychology, 49,* 1231–1245.

Coontz, S. (1992). *The way we never were: American families and the nostalgia trap.* New York: Basic Books.

Cortina, L. M. (2004). Hispanic perspectives on sexual harassment and social support. *Personality and Social Psychology Bulletin, 30,* 570–584.

Cosmides, L., & Tooby, J. (1992). Cognitive adaptations for social exchange. In J. Barkow, L. Cosmides, & J. Tooby (Eds.), *The adapted mind* (pp. 163–228). New York: Oxford University Press.

Cota, A. A., Evans, C. R., Dion, K. L., Kilik, L., & Longman, R. S. (1995). The structure of group cohesion. *Personality and Social Psychology Bulletin, 21,* 572–580.

Cottrell, N. B., Wack, K. L., Sekerak, G. J., & Rittle, R. (1968). Social facilitation of dominant responses by the presence of an audience and the mere presence of others. *Journal of Personality and Social Psychology, 9,* 245–250.

Couple repays university for bringing them together. (1997, October 29). *University Update.*

Courneya, K. S., & McAuley, E. (1993). Efficacy, attributional, and affective responses of older adults following an acute bout of exercise. *Journal of Social Behavior and Personality, 8,* 729–742.

Cozzarelli, C., Karafa, J. A., Collins, N. L., & Tagler, M. J. (2003). Stability and change in adult attachment styles: Associations with personal vulnerabilities, life events, and global construals of self and others. *Journal of Social and Clinical Psychology, 22,* 315–346.

Craig, J.-A., Koestner, R., & Zuroff, D. C. (1994). Implicit and self-attributed intimacy motivation. *Journal of Social and Personal Relationships, 11,* 491–507.

Cramer, R. E., McMaster, M. R., Bartell, P. A., & Dragma, M. (1988). Subject competence and minimization of the bystander effect. *Journal of Applied Social Psychology, 18,* 1133–1148.

Crandall, C. S. (1988). Social contagion of binge eating. *Journal of Personality and Social Psychology, 55,* 588–598.

Crandall, C. S. (1994). Prejudice against fat people: Ideology and self-interest. *Journal of Personality and Social Psychology, 66,* 882–894.

Crandall, C. S., & Martinez, R. (1996). Culture, ideology, and anti-fat attitudes. *Personality and Social Psychology Bulletin, 22,* 1165–1176.

Crandall, C. S., Eshleman, A., & O'Brien, L. T. (2002). Social norms and the expression and suppression of prejudice: The struggle for internalization. *Journal of Personality and Social Psychology, 82,* 359–378.

Crandall, C. S., D'Anello, S., Sakalli, N., Lazarus, E., Wieczorkowska, G., & Feather, N. T. (2001). An attribution–value model of prejudice: Anti-fat attitudes in six nations. *Personality and Social Psychology Bulletin, 27,* 30–37.

Crano, W. D. (1995). Attitude strength and vested interest. In R. E. Petty & J. A. Krosnick (Eds.), *Attitude strength: Antecedents and consequences* (Vol. 4, pp. 131–157). Hillsdale, NJ: Erlbaum.

Crites, S. L., & Cacioppo, J. T. (1996). Electrocortical differentiation of evaluative and nonevaluative categorizations. *Psychological Science, 7,* 318–321.

Crocker, J., & Major, B. (1989). Social stigma and self-esteem: The self-protective properties of stigma. *Psychological Review, 96,* 608–630.

Crocker, J., & Wolfe, C. T. (2001). Contingencies of self-worth. *Psychological Review, 108,* 593–623.

Crocker, J., Cornwell, B., & Major, B. (1993). The stigma of overweight: Affective consequences of attributional ambiguity. *Journal of Personality and Social Psychology, 64,* 60–70.

Crocker, J., Thompson, L. J., McGraw, K. M., & Ingerman, C. (1987). Downward comparison, prejudice, and evaluation of others: Effects of self-esteem and threat. *Journal of Personality and Social Psychology, 52,* 907–916.

Cropanzano, R. (Ed.). (1993). *Justice in the workplace* (pp. 79–103). Hillsdale, NJ: Erlbaum.

Cropanzano, R., & James, K. (1990). Some methodological considerations for the behavioral–genetic analysis of work attitudes. *Journal of Applied Psychology, 71,* 433–439.

Crosby, F. J. (2004). *Affirmative action is dead: Long live affirmative action.* New Haven, CT: Yale University Press.

Crosby, F. J., Clayton, S., Alksnis, O., & Hemker, K. (1986). Cognitive biases in the perception of discrimination: The importance of format. *Sex Roles, 14,* 637–646.

Crosby, F. J., Iyer, A., Clayton, S., & Downing, R. A. (2003). Affirmative action: Psychological data and the policy debates. *American Psychologist, 58,* 93–115.

Cross, S. E., & Madson, L. (1997). Models of the self: Self-construals and gender. *Psychological Bulletin, 122,* 5–37.

Crowell, A. (2003, September 5). Boy saved from burning car. *Kennebec (Maine) Journal.*

Crowley, A. E., & Hoyer, W. D. (1994). An integrative framework for understanding two-sided persuasion. *Journal of Consumer Research, 20,* 561–574.

Crowley, M. (2003, October 27). Fresh faced. *The New Republic,* 42.

Crutchfield, R. A. (1955). Conformity and character. *American Psychologist, 10,* 191–198.

Cunningham, J. D., & Antill, J. K. (1994). Cohabitation and marriage: Retrospective and predictive comparisons. *Journal of Social and Personal Relationships, 11,* 77–93.

Cunningham, M. R. (1979). Weather, mood, and helping behavior: Quasi-experiments with the sunshine Samaritan. *Journal of Personality and Social Psychology, 37,* 1947–1956.

Cunningham, M. R. (1986). Measuring the physical in physical attractiveness: Quasi-experiments on the sociobiology of female facial beauty. *Journal of Personality and Social Psychology, 50,* 925–935.

Cunningham, M. R., Roberts, A. R., Wu, C.-H., Barbee, A. P., & Druen, P. B. (1995). "Their ideas of beauty are, on the whole, the same as ours": Consistency and variability in the cross-cultural perception of female physical attractiveness. *Journal of Personality and Social Psychology, 68,* 261–279.

Cunningham, M. R., Shaffer, D. R., Barbee, A. P., Wolff, P. L., & Kelley, D. J. (1990). Separate processes in the relation of elation and depression to helping: Social versus personal concerns. *Journal of Experimental Social Psychology, 26,* 13–33.

Cunningham, W. A., Johnson, M. K., Gatenby, J. C., Gore, J. C., & Banaji, M. R. (2003). Neural components of social evaluation. *Journal of Personality and Social Psychology, 85,* 639–649.

Curtis, J. T., & Wang, Z. (2003). The neurochemistry of pair bonding. *Current Directions in Psychological Science, 1,* 49–53.

Cutler, B. L., Penrod, S. D., & Martens, T. K. (1987). Improving the reliability of eyewitness identification: Putting content into context. *Journal of Applied Psychology, 72,* 629–637.

Dallman, M. (2003). Chronic stress and diet. *Proceedings of the National Academy of Sciences, 100.*

Darley, J. M. (1993). Research on morality: Possible approaches, actual approaches. *Psychological Science, 4,* 353–357.

Darley, J. M. (1995). Constructive and destructive obedience: A taxonomy of principal-agent relationships. *Journal of Social Issues, 125,* 125–154.

Darley, J. M., & Batson, C. D. (1973). From Jerusalem to Jericho: A study of situational dispositional variables in helping behavior. *Journal of Personality and Social Psychology, 27,* 100–108.

Darley, J. M., & Cooper, J. (1998). *Attribution and social interaction: The legacy of Edward E. Jones.* Washington, DC: American Psychological Association.

Darley, J. M., & Latané, B. (1968). Bystander intervention in emergencies: Diffusion of responsibility. *Journal of Personality and Social Psychology, 8,* 377–383.

Darley, J. M., Carlsmith, K. M., & Robinson, P. H. (2000). Incapacitation and just desserts as motives for punishment. *Law and Human Behavior, 24,* 659–684

Dasgupta, N., Banji, M. R., & Abelson, R. P. (1999). Group entiativity and group perception: Association between physical features and psychological judgment. *Journal of Personality and Social Psychology, 75,* 991–1005.

Daubman, K. A. (1993). *The self-threat of receiving help: A comparison of the threat-to-self-esteem model and the threat-to-interpersonal-power model.* Unpublished manuscript, Gettysburg College, Gettysburg, PA.

Daubman, K. A. (1995). Help which implies dependence: Effects on self-evaluations, motivation, and performance. *Journal of Social Behavior and Personality, 10,* 677–692.

Davila, J., & Cobb, R. J. (2003). Predicting change in self-reported and interviewer-assessed adult attachment: Tests of the individual difference and life stress models of attachment change. *Personality and Social Psychology Bulletin, 29,* 859–870.

Davila, J., Steinberg, S. J., Kachadourian, L., Cobb, R., & Fincham, F. (2004). Romantic involvement and depressive symptoms in early and late adolescence: The role of a preoccupied relational style. *Personal Relationships, 11,* 161–178.

Davis, M. H., Hall, J. A., & Meyer, M. (2003). The first year: Influences on the satisfaction, involvement, and persistence of new community volunteers. *Personality and Social Psychology Bulletin, 29,* 248–260.

Davis, M. H., Luce, C., & Kraus, S. J. (1994). The heritability of characteristics associated with dispositional empathy. *Journal of Personality, 62,* 369–391.

De Judicibus, M. A., & McCabe, M. P. (2002). Psychological factors and the sexuality of pregnant and postpartum women. *Journal of Sex Research, 39,* 94–103.

De Longis, A., Folkman, S., & Lazarus, R. S. (1988). The impact of daily stress on health and mood: Psychological and social resources as mediators. *Journal of Personality and Social Psychology, 54,* 486–495.

Deaux, K., & Kite, M. E. (1993). Gender stereotypes. In M. A. Paludi & F. Denmark (Eds.), *Psychology of women: A handbook of issues and theories* (pp. 107–139). Westport, CT: Greenwood Press.

Deaux, K., & LaFrance, M. (1998). Gender. In D. T. Gilbert, S. T. Fiske, & G. Lindzey (Eds.), *The handbook of social psychology* (4th ed., Vol. 1, pp. 788–827). New York: McGraw-Hill.

Deaux, K., & Major, B. (1987). Putting gender into context: An interactive model of gender-related behavior. *Psychological Review, 94,* 369–389.

Decety, J., & Chaminade, T. (2003). Neural correlates of feeling sympathy. *Neuropsychologia, 41,* 127–138.

DeDreu, C. K. W., & McCusker, C. (1997). Gain–loss frames and cooperation in two-person social dilemmas: A transformational analysis. *Journal of Personality and Social Psychology, 72,* 1093–1106.

DeDreu, C. K. W., & Van Lange, P. A. M. (1995). Impact of social value orientation on negotiator cognition and behavior. *Personality and Social Psychology Bulletin, 21,* 1178–1188.

DeGroot, T., Kiker, D. S., & Cross, T. C. (2000). A meta-analysis to review organizational outcomes related to charismatic leadership. *Canadian Journal of Administrative Sciences, 17,* 356–371.

DeJong, W., & Musilli, L. (1982). External pressure to comply: Handicapped versus nonhandicapped requesters and the foot-in-the-door phenomenon. *Personality and Social Psychology Bulletin, 8,* 522–527.

den Ouden, M. D., & Russell, G. W. (1997). Sympathy and altruism in response to disasters: A Dutch and Canadian comparison. *Social Behavior and Personality, 25,* 241–248.

DeNoon, D. (2003, September 15). Only happy marriage is healthy for women. *WebMD Medical News.* Internet.

DePaulo, B. M. (1994). Spotting lies: Can humans learn to do better? *Current Directions in Psychological Science, 3,* 873–886.

DePaulo, B. M., & Kashy, D. A. (1998). Everyday lies in close and casual relationships. *Journal of Personality and Social Psychology, 74,* 63–79.

DePaulo, B. M., Brown, P. L., Ishii, S., & Fisher, J. D. (1981). Help that works: The effects of aid on subsequent task performance. *Journal of Personality and Social Psychology, 41,* 478–487.

DePaulo, B. M., Lindsay, J. J., Malone, B. E., Muhlenbruck, L., Chandler, K., & Cooper, H. (2003). Cues to deception. *Psychological Bulletin, 129,* 74–118.

DeSteno, D., Bartlett, M. Y., Braverman, J., & Salovy, P. (2002). Sex differences in jealousy: Evolutionary mechanism or artifact of measurement? *Journal of Personality and Social Psychology, 83,* 1103–1116.

DeSteno, D., Dasgupta, N., Bartlett, M. Y., & Cajdric, A. (2004). Prejudice from thin air: The effect of emotion on automatic intergroup attitudes. *Psychological Science, 15,* 319–324.

Deutsch, M., & Gerard, H. B. (1955). A study of normative and informational social influences upon individual judgment. *Journal of Abnormal and Social Psychology, 51,* 629–636.

Deutsch, M., & Krauss, R. M. (1960). The effect of threat upon interpersonal bargaining. *Journal of Abnormal and Social Psychology, 61,* 181–189.

Devine, P. G., & Monteith, M. J. (1993). The role of discrepancy-associated affect in prejudice reduction. In D. M. Mackie & D. L. Hamilton (Eds.), *Affect, cognition, and stereotyping: Interactive processes in group perception* (pp. 317–344). San Diego, CA: Academic Press.

Devine, P. G., Plant, E. A., & Blair, I. V. (2001). Classic and contemporary analyses of racial prejudice. In R. Brown & S. Gaertner (Eds.), *Blackwell handbook of social psychology: Intergroup processes* (pp. 198–217). Oxford, UK: Blackwell.

deWaal, F. (2002). *The ape and the sushi master: Cultural reflections of a primatologist.* New York: Basic Books.

Diamond, L. M. (2004). Emerging perspectives on distinctions between romantic love and sexual desire. *Current Directions in Psychological Science, 13,* 116–119.

Diekman, A. B., & Eagly, A. H. (2000). Stereotypes as dynamic constructs: Women and men of the past, present, and future. *Personality and Social Psychology Bulletin, 26,* 1171–1188.

Diener, E., & Lucas, R. R. (1999). Personality and subjective well-being. In E. Kahneman, E. Diener, & N. Schwarz (Eds.), *Well-being: The foundations of hedonic psychology* (pp. 434–450). New York: Russell Stage Foundation.

Diener, E., Wolsic, B., & Fujita, F. (1995). Physical attractiveness and subjective well-being. *Journal of Personality and Social Psychology, 69,* 120–129.

Dietrich, D. M., & Berkowitz, L. (1997). Alleviation of dissonance by engaging in prosocial behavior or receiving ego-enhancing feedback. *Journal of Social Behavior and Personality, 12,* 557–566.

Dietz, J., Robinson, S. A., Folger, R., Baron, R. A., & Jones, T. (2003). The impact of societal violence and organizational justice climate on workplace aggression. *Academy of Management Journal, 46,* 317–326.

Dijksterhuis, A. (2004). I like myself but I don't know why: Enhancing implicit self-esteem by subliminal evaluative conditioning. *Journal of Personality and Social Psychology, 86,* 345–355.

Dijksterhuis, A., & van Knippenberg, A. (1996). The knife that cuts both ways: Facilitated and inhibited access to traits as a result of stereotype-activation. *Journal of Experimental Social Psychology, 32,* 271–288.

Dijksterhuis, A., Bargh, J. A., & Miedema, J. (2000). Of men and mackerels: Attention and automatic behavior. In H. Bless & J. P. Forgas (Eds.), *Subjective experiences in social cognition and behavior* (pp. 36–51). Philadelphia: Psychology Press.

Dion, K. K., & Dion, K. L. (1991). Psychological individualism and romantic love. *Journal of Social Behavior and Personality, 6,* 17–33.

Dion, K. K., Berscheid, E., & Hatfield (Walster), E. (1972). What is beautiful is good. *Journal of Personality and Social Psychology, 24,* 285–290.

Dion, K. K., Pak, A. W.-P., & Dion, K. I. (1990). Stereotyping physical attractiveness: A sociocultural perspective. *Journal of Cross-Cultural Psychology, 21,* 158–179.

Dion, K. L., & Earn, B. M. (1975). The phenomenology of being a target of prejudice. *Journal of Personality and Social Psychology, 32,* 944–950.

Dion, K. L., Dion, K. K., & Keelan, J. P. (1990). Appearance anxiety as a dimension of social-evaluative anxiety: Exploring the ugly duckling syndrome. *Contemporary Social Psychology, 14,* 220–224.

Dittmann, M. (2003, November). Compassion is what most find attractive in mates. *Monitor on Psychology, 10,* 12.

Dodge, K. A., & Coie, J. D. (1987). Social-information-processing factors in reactive and proactive aggression in children's peer groups. *Journal of Personality and Social Psychology, 53,* 1146–1158.

Dodge, K. A., Pettit, G. S., McClaskey, C. L., & Brown, M. M. (1986). Social competence in children. *Monographs of the Society for Research in Child Development, 51*(2), 1–85.

Doherty, K., Weigold, M. F., & Schlenker, B. R. (1990). Self-serving interpretations of motives. *Personality and Social Psychology Bulletin, 16,* 485–495.

Dollard, J., Doob, L., Miller, N., Mowerer, O. H., & Sears, R. R. (1939). *Frustration and aggression.* New Haven, CT: Yale University Press.

Doosje, B., & Branscombe, N. R. (2003). Attributions for the negative historical actions of a group. *European Journal of Social Psychology, 33,* 235–248.

Doucet, J., & Aseltine, R. H., Jr. (2003). Childhood family adversity and the quality of marital relationships in young adulthood. *Journal of Social and Personal Relationships, 20,* 818–842.

Dovidio, J. F., & Fazio, R. (1991). New technologies for the direct and indirect assessment of attitudes. In N. J. Tanur (Ed.), *Questions about survey questions: Meaning, memory, attitudes, and social interaction* (pp. 204–237). New York: Russell Sage.

Dovidio, J. F., Evans, N., & Tyler, R. B. (1986). Racial stereotypes: The contents of their cognitive representations. *Journal of Experimental Social Psychology, 22,* 22–37.

Dovidio, J. F., Gaertner, S. L., & Validzic, A. (1998). Intergroup bias: Status differentiation and a common ingroup identity. *Journal of Personality and Social Psychology, 75,* 109–120.

Dovidio, J. F., Brigham, J., Johnson, B., & Gaertner, S. (1996). Stereotyping, prejudice, and discrimination: Another look. In N. Macrae, C. Stangor, & M. Hwestone (Eds.), *Stereotypes and stereotyping* (pp. 1276–1319). New York: Guilford.

Dovidio, J. F., Gaertner, S. L., Isen, A. M., & Lowrance, R. (1995). Group representations and intergroup bias: Positive affect, similarity, and group size. *Personality and Social Psychology Bulletin, 21,* 856–865.

Dovidio, J. F., Kawakami, K., Johnson, C., Johnson, B., & Howard, A. (1997). On the nature of prejudice: Automatic and controlled processes. *Journal of Experimental Social Psychology, 33,* 510–540.

Downs, A. C., & Lyons, P. M. (1991). Natural observations of the links between attractiveness and initial legal judgments. *Personality and Social Psychology Bulletin, 17,* 541–547.

Drake, R. A., & Myers, L. R. (2001, in press). Visual perception and emotion: Relative rightward attention predicts positive arousal. *Cognitive Brain Research,* More info to come.

Duan, C. (2000). Being empathic: The role of motivation to empathize and the nature of target emotions. *Motivation and Emotion, 24,* 29–49.

Dubois, N., & Beauvois, J. L. (1996). Internality, academic status and intergroup attributions. *European Journal of Psychology of Education, 11,* 329–341.

Duck, J. M., Hogg, M. A., & Terry, D. J. (1999). Social identity and perceptions of media persuasion: Are we always less influenced than others? *Journal of Applied Social Psychology, 29,* 1879–1899.

Duck, S., Pond, K., & Leatham, G. (1994). Loneliness and the evaluation of relational events. *Journal of Social and Personal Relationships, 11,* 253–276.

Duggan, E. S., & Brennan, K. A. (1994). Social avoidance and its relation to Bartholomew's adult attachment typology. *Journal of Social and Personal Relationships, 11,* 147–153.

Duncan, J., & Owen, A. W. (2000). Common regions of the human frontal lobe recruited by diverse cognitive demands. *Trends in Cognitive Science, 23,* 475–483.

Dunkley, D. M., & Blankstein, K. R. (2000). Self-critical perfectionism, coping, hassle, and current distress: A structural equation modeling approach. *Cognitive Therapy and Research, 24,* 713–730.

Dunkley, D. M., Zuroff, D. C., & Blankstein, K. R. (2003). Self-critical perfectionism and daily affect: Dispositional and situational influences on stress and coping. *Journal of Personality and Social Psychology, 84,* 234–252.

Dunn, J. (1992). Siblings and development. *Current Directions in Psychological Science, 1,* 6–11.

Dunning, D., & Sherman, D. A. (1997). Stereotypes and tacit inference. *Journal of Personality and Social Psychology, 73,* 459–471.

Dunning, D., & Stern, L. B. (1994). Distinguishing accurate from inaccurate eyewitness identification via inquiries about decision processes. *Journal of Personality and Social Psychology, 67,* 818–835.

Dutton, D. G., & Aron, A. P. (1974). Some evidence for heightened sexual attraction under conditions of high anxiety. *Journal of Personality and Social Psychology, 30,* 510–517.

Eagly, A. H. (1987). *Sex differences in social behavior: A social-role interpretation.* Hillsdale, NJ: Erlbaum.

Eagly, A. H., & Carli, L. (1981). Sex of researchers and sex-typed communications as determinants of sex differences in influence-ability: A meta-analysis of social influence studies. *Psychological Bulletin, 90,* 1–20.

Eagly, A. H., & Chaiken, S. (1998). Attitude structure and function. In G. Lindsey, S. T., Fiske, & D. T. Gilbert (Eds.), *Handbook of social psychology* (4th ed.). New York: Oxford University Press and McGraw-Hill.

Eagly, A. H., & Karau, S. J. (2002). Role congruity theory of prejudice toward female leaders. *Psychological Review, 109,* 573–598.

Eagly, A. H., & Mladinic, A. (1994). Are people prejudiced against women? Some answers from research on attitudes, gender stereotypes, and judgments of competence. In W. Sroebe & M. Hewstone (Eds.), *European review of social psychology* (Vol. 5, pp. 1–35). New York: Wiley.

Eagly, A. H., & Wood, W. (1999). The origins of sex differences in human behavior: Evolved dispositions versus social roles. *American Psychologist, 54,* 408–423.

Eagly, A. H., Makhijani, M. G., & Klonsky, B. G. (1992). Gender and the evaluation of leaders: A meta-analysis. *Psychological Bulletin, 111,* 3–22.

Eagly, A. H., Wood, W., & Chaiken, S. (1996). Principles of persuasion. In E. T. Higgins & A. W. Kruglanski (Eds.), *Social psychology: Handbook of basic principles* (pp. 702–742). New York: Guilford.

Eagly, A. H., Chen, S., Chaiken, S., & Shaw-Barnes, K. (1999). The impact of attitudes on memory: An affair to remember. *Psychological Bulletin, 124*, 64–89.

Eagly, A. H., Kulesa, P., Brannon, L. A., Shaw, K., & Hutson-Comeaux, S. (2000). Why counterattitudinal messages are as memorable as proattitudinal messages: The importance of active defense against attack. *Personality and Social Psychology Bulletin, 26*, 1392–1408.

Earley, P. C. (1993). East meets West meets Mideast: Further explorations of collectivistic and individualistic work groups. *Academy of Management Journal, 36*, 319–348.

Edwards, K., & Bryan, T. S. (1997). Judgmental biases produced by instructions to disregard: The (paradoxical) case of emotional information. *Personality and Social Psychology Bulletin, 23*, 849–864.

Edwards, K., Heindel, W., & Louis-Dreyfus, E. (1996). *Directed forgetting of emotional and non-emotional words: Implications for implicit and explicit memory processes.* Manuscript submitted for publication.

Edwards, T. M. (2000, August 28). Flying solo. *Time*, 46–52.

Egloff, B., Schmukle, S. C., Burns, L. R., Kohlmann, C.-W., & Hock, M. (2003). Facets of dynamic positive affect: Differentiating joy, interest, and activation in the Positive and Negative Affect Schedule (PANAS). *Journal of Personality and Social Psychology, 85*, 528–540.

Eich, E. (1995). Searching for mood dependent memory. *Psychological Science, 6*, 67–75.

Eisenberg, N. (2000). Emotion, regulation, and moral development. *Annual Review of Psychology, 51*, 665–697.

Eisenberg, N., Guthrie, I. K., Cumberland, A., Murphy, B. C., Shepard, S. A., Zhou, Q., & Carlo, G. (2002). Prosocial development in early adulthood: A longitudinal study. *Journal of Personality and Social Psychology, 82*, 993–1006.

Eisenman, R. (1985). Marijuana use and attraction: Support for Byrne's similarity-attraction concept. *Perceptual and Motor Skills, 61*, 582.

Eisenstadt, D., & Leippe, M. R. (1994). The self-comparison process and self-discrepant feedback: Consequences of learning you are what you thought you were not. *Journal of Personality and Social Psychology, 67*, 611–626.

Eiser, J. R., Fazio, R. H., Stafford, T., & Prescott, T. J. (2003). Connectionist simulation of attitude learning: Asymmetries in the acquisition of positive and negative evaluations. *Personality and Social Psychology Bulletin, 29*, 1221–1235.

Ekman, P. (2001). *Telling lies: Clues to deceit in the marketplace, politics, and marriage* (3rd ed.). New York: Norton.

Ekman, P., & Friesen, W. V. (1975). *Unmasking the face.* Englewood Cliffs, NJ: Prentice-Hall.

Ekman, P., & Heider, K. (1988). The universality of a contempt expression: A replication. *Motivation and Emotion, 12*, 303–308.

Ekman, P., O'Sullivan, M., & Frank, M. G. (1999). A few can catch a liar. *Psychological Science, 10*, 263–266.

Elkin, R., & Leippe, M. (1986). Physiological arousal, dissonance, and attitude change: Evidence for a disso-nance–arousal link and "don't remind me" effect. *Journal of Personality and Social Psychology, 51*, 55–65.

Ellemers, N. (2001). Individual upward mobility and the perceived legitimacy of intergroup relations. In J. T. Jost & B. Major (Eds.), *The psychology of legitimacy* (pp. 205–222). New York: Cambridge University Press.

Ellemers, N., Van Rijswijk, W., Roefs, M., & Simons, C. (1997). Bias in intergroup perceptions: Balancing group identity with social reality. *Personality and Social Psychology Bulletin, 23*, 186–198.

Elliot, A. J., & Devine, P. G. (1994). On the motivational nature of cognitive dissonance: Dissonance as psychological discomfort. *Journal of Personality and Social Psychology, 67*, 382–394.

Elliot, A. J., & Reis, H. T. (2003). Attachment and exploration in adulthood. *Journal of Personality and Social Psychology, 5*, 317–331.

Ellsworth, P. C., & Carlsmith, J. M. (1973). Eye contact and gaze aversion in aggressive encounter. *Journal of Personality and Social Psychology, 33*, 117–122.

Ely, R. J. (1994). The effects of organizational demographics and social identity on relationships among professional women. *Administrative Science Quarterly, 39*, 203–238.

Endo, Y., Heine, S. J., & Lehman, D. R. (2000). Culture and positive illusions in close relationships: How my relationships are better than yours. *Personality and Social Psychology Bulletin, 26*, 1571–1586.

Epley, N., & Dunning, D. (2000). Feeling "holier than thou": Are self-serving assessments produced by errors in self- or social prediction? *Journal of Personality and Social Psychology, 79*, 861–875.

Epley, N., & Gilovich, T. (2004). Are adjustments insufficient? *Personality and Social Psychology Bulletin, 30*, 447–460.

Epley, N., & Huff, C. (1998). Suspicion, affective response, and educational benefit as a result of deception in psychology research. *Personality and Social Psychology Bulletin, 24*, 759–768.

Erwin, P. G., & Letchford, J. (2003). Types of preschool experience and sociometric status in the primary school. *Social Behavior and Personalty, 31*, 129–132.

Esses, V. M., Jackson, L. M., Nolan, J. M., & Armstrong, T. L. (1999). Economic threat and attitudes toward immigrants. In S. Halli & L. Drieger (Eds.), *Immigrant Canada: Demographic, economic and social challenges* (pp. 212–229). Toronto: University of Toronto Press.

Estrada, C. A., Isen, A. M., & Young, M. J. (1995). Positive affect improves creative problem solving and influences reported source of practice satisfaction in physicians. *Motivation and Emotion, 18*, 285–300.

Etcoff, N. (1999). *Survival of the prettiest: The science of beauty.* New York: Doubleday.

Etcoff, N. L., Ekman, P., Magee, J. J., & Frank, M. G. (2000). Lie detection and language comprehension. *Nature, 40*, 139.

Ethier, K. A., & Deaux, K. (1994). Negotiating social identity when contexts change: Maintaining identification and responding to threat. *Journal of Personality and Social Psychology, 67,* 243–251.

Evangelicals in America. (2004, May 3). *U.S. News & World Report,* 62.

Faison, E. W. J. (1961). Effectiveness of one-sided and two-sided mass communications in advertising. *Public Opinion Quarterly, 25,* 468–469.

Falomir-Pichastor, J. M., Munoz-Rojas, D., Invernizzi, F., & Mugny, G. (2004). Perceived in-group threat as a factor moderating the influence of in-group norms on discrimination against foreigners. *European Journal of Social Psychology, 34,* 135–153.

Faludi, S. (1992). *Backlash: The undeclared war against American women.* New York: Doubleday.

Fang, B. (2001, September 3). On the trail of a killer. *U.S. News & World Report,* 22–26.

Faulkner, S. J., & Williams, K. D. (1999, April). *After the whistle is blown: The aversive impact of ostracism.* Paper presented at the meeting of the Midwestern Psychological Association, Chicago.

Favata, P. A. (2004, April 8). Marriage is more than a benefits package. Albany *Times Union,* A16.

Fazio, R. H. (1989). On the power and functionality of attitudes: The role of attitude accessibility. In A. R. Pratkanis, S. J. Breckler, & A. G. Greenwald (Eds.), *Attitude structure and function* (pp. 153–179). Hillsdale, NJ: Erlbaum.

Fazio, R. H. (2000). Accessible attitudes as tools for object appraisal: The costs and benefits. In G. R. Maio & J. M. Olson (Eds.), *Why we evaluate: Functions of attitudes* (pp. 1–26). Mahwah, NJ: Erlbaum.

Fazio, R. H., & Hilden, L. E. (2001). Emotional reactions to a seemingly prejudiced response: The role of automatically activated racial attitudes and motivation to control prejudiced reactions. *Personality and Social Psychology Bulletin, 27,* 538–549.

Fazio, R. H., & Powell, M. C. (1997). On the value of knowing one's likes and dislikes: Attitude accessibility, stress, and health in college. *Psychological Science, 8,* 430–436.

Fazio, R. H., & Roskos-Ewoldsen, D. R. (1994). Acting as we feel: When and how attitudes guide behavior. In S. Shavitt & T. C. Brock (Eds.), *Persuasion* (pp. 71–93). Boston: Allyn and Bacon.

Fazio, R. H., Ledbetter, J. E., & Towles-Schwen, T. (2000). On the costs of accessible attitudes: Detecting that the attitude object has changed. *Journal of Personality and Social Psychology, 78,* 197–210.

Fazio, R. H., Sanbonomatsu, D. M., Powell, M. C., & Kardes, F. R. (1986). On the automatic activation of attitudes. *Journal of Personality and Social Psychology, 50,* 229–238.

Feagin, J. R., & McKinney, K. D. (2003). *The many costs of racism.* Lanham, MD: Rowman & Littlefield.

Feagin, J. R., & Sikes, M. P. (1994). *Living with racism: The Black middle-class experience.* Boston, MA: Beacon.

Feather, N. T. (1996). Reactions to penalties for an offense in relation to authoritarianism, values, perceived responsibility, perceived seriousness, and deservingness. *Journal of Personality and Social Psychology, 71,* 571–587.

Fehr, B. (1999). Laypeople's conceptions of commitment. *Journal of Personality and Social Psychology, 76,* 90–103.

Fehr, B. (2004). Intimacy expectations in same-sex friendships: A prototype interaction-pattern model. *Journal of Personality and Social Psychology, 86,* 265–284.

Fehr, B., & Broughton, R. (2001). Gender and personality differences in conceptions of love: An interpersonal theory analysis. *Personal Relationships, 8,* 115–136.

Fein, S., & Spencer, S. J. (1997). Prejudice as self-image maintenance: Affirming the self through derogating others. *Journal of Personality and Social Psychology, 73,* 31–44.

Fein, S., McCloskey, A. L., & Tomlinson, T. M. (1997). Can the jury disregard that information? The use of suspicion to reduce the prejudicial effects of pretrial publicity and inadmissible testimony. *Personality and Social Psychology Bulletin, 23,* 1215–1226.

Feingold, A. (1992). Good-looking people are not what we think. *Psychological Bulletin, 111,* 304–341.

Feldman, S. S., & Nash, S. C. (1984). The transition from expectancy to parenthood: Impact of the firstborn child on men and women. *Sex Roles, 11,* 61–78.

Felmlee, D. H. (1995). Fatal attractions: Affection and disaffection in intimate relationships. *Journal of Social and Personal Relationships, 12,* 295–311.

Felmlee, D. H. (1998). "Be careful what you wish for . . .": A quantitative and qualitative investigation of "fatal attractions." *Personal Relationships, 5,* 235–253.

Ferguson, T. J., & Stegge, H. (1998). Measuring guilt in children: A rose by any other name still has thorns. In J. Bybee (Ed.), *Guilt and Children* (pp. 19–74). San Diego, CA: Academic Press.

Feshbach, S. (1984). The catharsis hypothesis, aggressive drive, and the reduction of aggression. *Aggressive Behavior, 10,* 91–101.

Festinger, L. (1954). A theory of social comparison processes. *Human Relations, 7,* 117–140.

Festinger, L. (1957). *A theory of cognitive dissonance.* Evanston, IL: Row, Peterson.

Festinger, L., Schachter, S., & Back, K. (1950). *Social pressures in informal groups: A study of a housing community.* New York: Harper.

Fichten, C. S., & Amsel, R. (1986). Trait attributions about college students with a physical disability: Circumplex analyses and methodological issues. *Journal of Applied Social Psychology, 16,* 410–427.

Fiedler, K., Walther, E., Freytag, P., & Nickel, S. (2003). Inductive reasoning and judgment interference: Experiments on Simpson's paradox. *Personality and Social Psychology Bulletin, 29,* 14–27.

Fink, B., & Penton-Voak, I. (2002). Evolutionary psychology of facial attractiveness. *Current Directions in Psychological Science, 11,* 154–158.

Finkel, E. J., & Campbell, W. K. (2001). Self-control and accommodation in close relationships: An interdependence analysis. *Journal of Personality and Social Psychology, 81,* 263–277.

Fischman, J. (1986, January). Women and divorce: Ten years after. *Psychology Today,* 15.

Fisher, J. D., & Byrne, D. (1975). Too close for comfort: Sex differences in response to invasions of personal space. *Journal of Personality and Social Psychology, 32,* 15–21.

Fisher, J. D., Nadler, A., & Whitcher-Alagna, S. (1982). Recipient reactions to aid. *Psychological Bulletin, 91,* 27–54.

Fisher, W. A., & Barak, A. (1991). Pornography, erotica, and behavior: Most questions than answers. *International Journal of Love and Psychiatry, 14,* 65–83.

Fiske, S., & Neuberg, S. (1990). A continuum of impression formation from category-based to individuating processes. In M. Zanna (Ed.), *Advances in experimental social psychology* (Vol. 23, pp. 1–73). San Diego: Academic Press.

Fiske, S. T. (1993). Social cognition and social perception. In L. W. Porter & M. R. Rosenzweig (Eds.), *Annual Review of Psychology, 44,* 155–194.

Fiske, S. T. (2000). Interdependence and the reduction of prejudice. In S. Oskamp (Ed.), *Reducing prejudice and discrimination* (pp. 115–135). Mahwah, NJ: Erlbaum.

Fiske, S. T., & Depret, E. (1996). Control, independence, and power: Understanding social cognition in its social context. In W. Stroebe & M. Hewstone (Eds.), *European Review of Social Psychology* (Vol. 7, pp. 31–61). Chichester: Wiley.

Fiske, S. T., & Stevens, L. E. (1993). What's so special about sex? Gender stereotyping and discrimination. In S. Oskamp & M. Costanzo (Eds.), *Gender issues in contemporary society* (pp. 173–196). Newbury Park, CA: Sage.

Fiske, S. T., Lin, M. H., & Neuberg, S. L. (1999). The continuum model: Ten years later. In S. Chaiken & Y. Trope (Eds.), *Dual process theories in social psychology* (pp. 231–254). New York: Guilford.

Fiske, S. T., Cuddy, A. J. C., Glick, P., & Xu, J. (2002). A model of (often mixed) stereotype content: Competence and warmth respectively follow from perceived status and competition. *Journal of Personality and Social Psychology, 82,* 878–902.

Fiske, S. T., Bersoff, D. N., Borgida, E., Deaux, K., & Heilman, M. E. (1991). Social science research on trial: Use of sex stereotyping research in *Price Waterhouse v. Hopkins. American Psychologist, 46,* 1049–1060.

Fitzsimmons, G. M., & Bargh, J. A. (2003). Thinking of you: Nonconscious pursuit of interpersonal goals associated with relationships partners. *Journal of Personality and Social Psychology, 84,* 148–164.

Fitzsimons, G. M., & Kay, A. C. (2004). Language and interpersonal cognition: Causal effects of variations in pronoun usage on perceptions of closeness. *Personality and Social Psychology Bulletin, 30,* 547–557.

Fleming, M. A., & Petty, R. E. (2000). Identity and persuasion: An elaboration likelihood approach. In D. J. Terry & M. A. Hogg (Eds.), *Attitudes, behavior, and social context* (pp. 171–199). Mahwah, NJ: Erlbaum.

Fletcher, G. J. O., Simpson, J. A., & Thomas, G. (2000). Ideals, perceptions, and evaluations in early relationship development. *Journal of Personality and Social Psychology, 79,* 933–940.

Fletcher, G. J. O., Simpson, J. A., Thomas, G., & Giles, L. (1999). Ideals in intimate relationships. *Journal of Personality and Social Psychology, 76,* 72–89.

Fletcher, G. J. O., Tither, J. M., O'Loughlin, C., Friesen, M., & Overall, N. (2004). Warm and homely or cold and beautiful? Sex differences in trading off traits in mate selection. *Personality and Social Psychology Bulletin, 30,* 659–672.

Floyd, K. (1996). Brotherly love I: The experience of closeness in the fraternal dyad. *Personal Relationships, 3,* 369–385.

Flynn, J. F., & Brockner, J. (2003). It's different to give than to receive; Predictors of givers' and receivers' reactions to favor exchange. *Journal of Personality and Social Psychology, 88,* 1023–1045.

Folger, R., & Baron, R. A. (1996). Violence and hostility at work: A model of reactions to perceived injustice. In G. R. VandenBos and E. Q. Bulato (Eds.), *Violence on the job: Identifying risks and developing solutions* (pp. 51–85). Washington, DC: American Psychological Association.

Folger, R., & Cropanzano, R. (1998). *Organizational justice and human resource management.* Thousand Oaks, CA: Sage.

Foltz, C., Barber, J. P., Weinryb, R. M., Morse, J. Q., & Chittams, J. (1999). Consistency of themes across interpersonal relationships. *Journal of Social and Clinical Psychology, 18,* 204–222.

Folwell, A. L., Chung, L. C., Nussbaum, J. F., Bethes, L. S., & Grant, J. A. (1997). Differential accounts of closeness in older adult sibling relationships. *Journal of Social and Personal Relationships, 14,* 843–849.

Ford, T. E., Ferguson, M. A., Brooks, J. L., & Hagadone, K. M. (2004). Coping sense of humor reduces effects of stereotype threat on women's math performance. *Personality and Social Psychology Bulletin.*

Forgas, J. P. (1995a). Mood and judgment: The affect infusion model (AIM). *Psychological Bulletin, 117,* 39–66.

Forgas, J. P. (1995b). Strange couples: Mood effects on judgments and memory about prototypical and atypical targets. *Personality and Social Psychology Bulletin, 21,* 747–765.

Forgas, J. P. (1998a). Asking nicely? The effects of mood on responding to more or less polite requests. *Personality and Social Psychology Bulletin, 24,* 173–185.

Forgas, J. P. (1998b). On feeling good and getting your way: Mood effects on negotiator cognition and bargaining strategies. Journal of Personality and Social Psychology, 74, 565–577.

Forgas, J. P. (2001). *Handbook of affect and social cognition.* Mahwah, NJ: Erlbaum.

Forge, K. L., & Phemister, S. (1987). The effect of prosocial cartoons on preschool children. *Child Study Journal, 17,* 83–88.

Forrest, J. A., & Feldman, R. S. (2000). Detecting deception and judge's involvement; lower task involvement leads to better lit detection. *Personality and Social Psychology Bulletin, 26,* 118–125.

Forster, J., Friedman, R. S., & Liberman, N. (2004). Temporal construal effects on abstract and concrete thinking: Consequences for insight and creative cognition. *Journal of Personality and Social Psychology, 87,* 177–189.

Fowers, B., Lyons, E., Montel, K., & Shaked, N. (2001). Positive illusions about marriage among married and single individuals. *Journal of Family Psychology,* 95–109.

Fox, R. L., & Oxley, Z. M. (2003). Gender stereotyping in state executive elections: Candidate selection and success. *Journal of Politics, 65,* 833–850.

Frable, D. E., Blackstone, T., & Scherbaum, C. (1990). Marginal and mindful: Deviants in social interactions. *Journal of Personality and Social Psychology, 59,* 140–149.

Fraley, B., & Aron, A. (2004). The effect of a shared humorous experience on closeness in initial encounters. *Personal Relationships, 11,* 61–78.

Fraley, R. C. (2002). Attachment stability from infancy to adulthood: Meta-analysis and dynamic modeling of developmental mechanisms. *Personality and Social Psychology Review, 6,* 123–151.

Franiuk, R., Cohen, D., & Pomeratz, E. M. (2002). Implicit theories of relationships: Implications for relationship satisfaction and longevity. *Personal Relationships, 9,* 345–367.

Frank, E., & Brandstatter, V. (2002). Approach versus avoidance: Different types of commitment to intimate relationships. *Journal of Personality and Social Psychology, 82,* 208–221.

Frazier, P. A., Byer, A. L., Fischer, A. R., Wright, D. M., & DeBord, K. A. (1996). Adult attachment style and partner choice: Correlational and experimental findings. *Personal Relationships, 3,* 117–136.

Fredrickson, B. L. (1995). Socioemotional behavior at the end of college life. *Journal of Social and Personal Relationships, 12,* 261–276.

Fredrickson, B. L., Roberts, T. A., Noll, S. M., Quinn, D. M., & Twenge, J. M. (1998). That swimsuit becomes you: Sex differences in self-objectification, restrained eating, and math performance. *Journal of Personality and Social Psychology, 75,* 269–284.

Freeberg, A. L., & Stein, C. H. (1996). Felt obligation towards parents in Mexican–American and Anglo–American young adults. *Journal of Social and Personal Relationships, 13,* 457–471.

Freedman, J. L., & Fraser, S. C. (1966). Compliance without pressure: The foot-in-the-door technique. *Journal of Personality and Social Psychology, 4,* 195–202.

Frey, D., Schulz-Hardt, S., & Stahlberg, D. (1996). Information seeking among individuals and groups and possible consequences for decision making in business and politics. In E. Witte & J. H. Davis (Eds.), *Understanding group behavior: Small group processes and interpersonal relation* (Vol. 2, pp. 211–225). Mahwah, NJ: Erlbaum.

Fricko, M. A. M., & Beehr, T. A. (1992). A longitudinal investigation of interest congruence and gender concentration as predictors of job satisfaction. *Personnel Psychology, 45,* 99–117.

Fried, C. B., & Aronson, E. (1995). Hypocrisy, misattribution, and dissonance reduction. *Personality and Social Psychology Bulletin, 21,* 925–933.

Friedman, H. S., Riggio, R. E., & Casella, D. F. (1988). Nonverbal skill, personal charisma, and initial attraction. *Personality and Social Psychology Bulletin, 14,* 203–211.

Friedman, H. S., Tucker, J. S., Schwartz, J. E., Martin, L. R., Tomlinson-Keasey, C., Wingard, D. L., & Criqui, M. H. (1995). Childhood conscientiousness and longevity: Health behaviors and cause of death. *Journal of Personality and Social Psychology, 68,* 696–703.

Fries, J. H. (2001). Reports of anti-Arab hate crimes dip, but concerns linger. *The New York Times,* December 22.

Fritzsche, B. A., Finkelstein, M. A., & Penner, L. A. (2000). To help or not to help: Capturing individuals' decision policies. *Social Behavior and Personality, 28,* 561–578.

Fry, D. P. (1998). Anthropological perspectives on aggression: Sex differences and cultural variation. *Aggressive Behavior, 24,* 81–95.

Fuegen, K., & Biernat, M. (2002). Reexamining the effects of solo status for women and men. *Personality and Social Psychology Bulletin, 28,* 913–925.

Fuegen, K., & Brehm, J. W. (2004). The intensity of affect and resistance to social influence. In E. S. Knowles & J. A. Linn (Eds.), *Resistance and persuasion* (pp. 39–63). Mahwah, NJ: Erlbaum.

Fultz, J., Shaller, M., & Cialdini, R. B. (1988). Empathy, sadness, and distress: Three related but distant vicarious affective responses to another's suffering. *Personality and Social Psychology Bulletin, 14,* 312–325.

Furman, W. (2002). The emerging field of adolescent romantic relationships. *Current Directions in Psychological Science, 11,* 177–180.

Furr, R. M., & Funder, D. C. (1998). A multimodal analysis of personal negativity. *Journal of Personality and Social Psychology, 74,* 1580–1591.

Gable, S. L., Reis, H. T., & Elliot, A. J. (2000). Behavioral activation and inhibition in everyday life. *Journal of Personality and Social Psychology, 78,* 1135–1149.

Gabriel, M. T., Critelli, J. W., & Ee, J. S. (1994). Narcissistic illusions in self-evaluations of intelligence and attractiveness. *Journal of Personality, 62,* 143–155.

Gaertner, S. L., Rust, M. C., Dovidio, J. F., Bachman, B. A., & Anastasio, P. A. (1994). The contact hypothesis: The role of common ingroup identity on reducing intergroup bias. *Small Group Research, 25,* 224–249.

Gaertner, S. L., Mann, J., Murrell, A., & Dovidio, J. F. (1989). Reducing intergroup bias: The benefits of recategorization. *Journal of Personality and Social Psychology, 57,* 239–249.

Gaertner, S. L., Mann, J. A., Dovidio, J. F., Murrell, A. J., & Pomare, M. (1990). How does cooperation reduce intergroup bias? *Journal of Personality and Social Psychology, 59,* 692–704.

Gagne, F. M., & Lydon, J. E. (2003). Identification and the commitment shift: Accounting for gender differences in relationship illusions. *Personality and Social Psychology Bulletin, 29,* 907–919.

Galambos, N. L. (1992). Parent–adolescent relations. *Current Directions in Psychological Science, 1,* 146–149.

Gallucci, G. (2003). I sell seashells by the seashore and my name is Jack: Comment on Pelham, Mirenberg, and Jones (2002). *Journal of Personality and Social Psychology, 85,* 789–799.

Gallup, G. G. (1994). Monkeys, mirrors, and minds. *Behavioral and Brain Sciences, 17,* 572–573.

Galton, F. (1952). *Hereditary genius: An inquiry into its laws and consequences.* New York: Horizon. (Original work published 1870.)

Gantner, A. B., & Taylor, S. P. (1992). Human physical aggression as a function of alcohol and threat of harm. *Aggressive Behavior, 18,* 29–36.

Garcia, D. M., Desmarais, S., Branscombe, N. R., & Gee, S. S. (in press). Opposition to redistributive employment policies for women: The role of policy experience and group interest. *British Journal of Social Psychology.*

Garcia, M., & Shaw, D. (2000). Destructive sibling conflict and the development of conduct problems in young boys. *Developmental Psychology, 36,* 44–53.

Garcia, S. M., Darley, J. M., & Robinson, R. J. (2001). Morally questionable tactics: Negotiations between district attorneys and public defenders. *Personality and Social Psychology Bulletin, 27,* 731–743.

Garcia, S. M., Weaver, K., Moskowitz, G. B., & Darley, J. M. (2002). Crowded minds: The implicit bystander effect. *Journal of Personality and Social Psychology, 83,* 843–853.

Garcia-Marques, T., Mackie, D. M., Claypool, H. M., & Garcia-Marques, L. (2004). Positivity can cue familiarity. *Personality and Social Psychology Bulletin, 30,* 585–593.

Gardner, R. M., & Tockerman, Y. R. (1994). A computer–TV methodology for investigating the influence of somatotype on perceived personality traits. *Journal of Social Behavior and Personality, 9,* 555–563.

Gardner, W. L., Pickett, C. L., & Brewer, M. B. (2000). Social exclusion and selective memory: How the need to belong influences memory for social events. *Personality and Social Psychology Bulletin, 26,* 486–496.

Gawronski, G. (2003). Implicational schemata and the correspondence bias: On the diagnostic value of situationally constrained behavior. *Journal of Personality and Social Psychology 84,* 1154–1171.

Geary, D. C., Vigil, J., & Byrd-Craven, J. (2004). Evolution of human mate choice. *Journal of Sex Research, 41,* 27–42.

Geen, R. G. (1989). Alternative conceptions of social facilitation. In P. B. Paulus (Ed.), *Psychology of group influence* (2nd ed., pp. 16–31). New York: Academic Press.

Geis, F. L. (1993). Self-fulfilling prophecies: A social psychological view of gender. In A. E. Beall & R. J. Sternberg (Eds.), *The psychology of gender* (pp. 9–54). New York: Guilford Press.

George, J. M. (1995). Leader positive mood and group performance: The case of customer service. *Journal of Applied Social Psychology, 25,* 778–794.

George, M. S., Ketter, T. A., Parekh-Priti, I., Horwitz, B., et al. (1995). Brain activity during transient sadness and happiness in healthy women. *American Journal of Psychiatry, 152,* 341–351.

Gerard, H. B., Wilhelmy, R. A., & Conolley, E. S. (1968). Conformity and group size. *Journal of Personality and Social Psychology, 8,* 79–82.

Gerstenfeld, P. B. (2002). A time to hate: Situational antecedents of intergroup bias. *Analyses of Social Issues and Public Policy, 2,* 61–67.

Gibbons, D., & Olk, P. M. (2003). Individual and structural origins of friendship and social position among professionals. *Journal of Personality and Social Psychology, 84,* 340–351.

Gibbons, F. X., Eggleston, T. J., & Benthin, A. C. (1997). Cognitive reactions to smoking relapse: The reciprocal relation between dissonance and self-esteem. *Journal of Personality and Social Psychology, 72,* 184–195.

Gifford, R. (1994). A lens-mapping framework for understanding the encoding and decoding of interpersonal dispositions in nonverbal behavior. *Journal of Personality and Social Psychology, 66,* 398–412.

Gigone, D., & Hastie, R. (1993). The common knowledge effect: Information sharing and group judgment. *Journal of Personality and Social Psychology, 65,* 959–974.

Gigone, D., & Hastie, R. (1997). The impact of information on small group choice. *Journal of Personality and Social Psychology, 72,* 132–140.

Gilbert, D. T. (2002). Inferential correction. In T. Gilovich, D. W. Griffin, & D. Kahneman (Eds.), *Heuristics and biases: The psychology of intuitive judgment* (pp. 167–184) New York: Cambridge University Press.

Gilbert, D. T., & Malone, P. S. (1995). The correspondence bias. *Psychological Bulletin, 117,* 21–38.

Gilbert, D. T., & Wilson, T. D. (2000). Miswanting: Some problems in the forecasting of future affective states. In J. Forgas (Ed.), *Feeling and thinking: The role of affect in social cognition.* New York: Cambridge University Press.

Gilbert, D. T., Tafarodi, R. W., & Malone, P. S. (1993). You can't not believe everything you read. *Journal of Personality and Social Psychology, 65,* 221–233.

Gilbert, L. A. (1993). *Two careers/one family.* Newbury Park, CA: Sage.

Gilligan, C. (1988). Re-mapping the moral domain—New images of self in relationships. In C. Gilligan, J. V. Ward, & J. M. Taylor (Eds.), *Mapping the moral domain: A contribution of women's thinking to psychological theory and education.* Cambridge, MA: Harvard University Press.

Gillis, J. S. (1982). *Too small, too tall.* Champaign, IL: Institute for Personality and Ability Testing.

Gilovich, T., Medvec, V. H., & Savitsky, K. (2000). The spotlight effect in social judgment: An egocentric bias in estimates of the salience of one's own actions and appearance. *Journal of Personality and Social Psychology, 78,* 211–222.

Giner-Sorolla, R., & Chaiken, S. (1994). The causes of hostile media effects. *Journal of Experimental Social Psychology, 30,* 165–180.

Giner-Sorolla, R., & Chaiken, S. (1997). Selective use of heuristic and systematic processing under defense motivation. *Personality and Social Psychology Bulletin, 23,* 84–97.

Ginsburg, H. J., Ogletree, S. M., Silakowski, T. D., Bartels, R. D., Burk, S. L., & Turner, G. M. (2003). Young children's theories of mind about empathic and selfish motives. *Social Behavior and Personality, 31,* 237–244.

Giovannini, J. (2000, November 27). Lost in space. *New York.* 146, 148.

Gladue, B. A., & Delaney, H. J. (1990). Gender differences in perception of attractiveness of men and women in bars. *Personality and Social Psychology Bulletin, 16,* 378–391.

Gladwell, M. (2000, December 11). Designs for working. *The New Yorker, 60, 62,* 64–65, 68–70.

Gladwell, M. (2004). Big and bad: How the SUV ran over automotive safety. *The New Yorker,* January 12, 2004, pp. 28–33.

Glanz, K., Geller, A. C., Shigaki, D., Maddock, J. E., & Isnec, M. R. (2002). A randomized trial of skin cancer prevention in aquatics settings: The pool cool program. *Health Psychology, 21*(6), 579–587.

Glaser, J., & Salovey, P. (1998). Affect in electoral politics. *Personality and Social Psychology Review, 2,* 156–172.

Glass Ceiling Commission. (1995). *Good for business: Making full use of the nation's human capital.* Washington, DC: Glass Ceiling Commission.

Glass, D. C. (1977). *Behavior patterns, stress, and coronary disease.* Hillsdale, NJ: Erlbaum.

Gleicher, F., Boninger, D., Strathman, A., Armor, D., Hetts, J., & Ahn, M. (1995). With an eye toward the future: Impact of counterfactual thinking on affect, attitudes, and behavior. In N. J. Roses & J. M. Olson (Eds.), *What might have been: the social psychology of counterfactual thinking.* (pp. 283–304). Mahwah, NJ: Erlbaum.

Glick, P. (2002). Sacrificial lambs dressed in wolves' clothing: Envious prejudice, ideology, and the scapegoating of Jews. In *Understanding genocide: The social psychology of the Holocaust* (pp. 113–142). New York: Oxford University Press.

Glick, P., Fiske, S. T., et al. (2000). Beyond prejudice as simple antipathy: Hostile and benevolent sexism across cultures. *Journal of Personality and Social Psychology, 79,* 763–775.

Goeders, N. E. (2004). Stress, motivation, and drug addiction. *Current Directions in Psychological Science, 13,* 33–35.

Goethals, G. R., & Darley, J. (1977). Social comparison theory: An attributional approach. In J. M. Suls & R. L. Miller (Eds.), *Social comparison processes: Theoretical and empir-*

ical perspectives (pp. 259–278). Washington, DC: Hemisphere.

Goethals, G. R., & Zanna, M. P. (1979). The role of social comparison in choice shifts. *Journal of Personality and Social Psychology, 37,* 1469–1476.

Gold, J. A., Ryckman, R. M., & Mosley, N. R. (1984). Romantic mood induction and attraction to a dissimilar other: Is love blind? *Personality and Social Psychology Bulletin, 10,* 358–368.

Goldenberg, J. L., Pyszczynski, T., Greenberg, J., McCoy, S. K., & Solomon, S. (1999). Death, sex, love, and neuroticism: Why is sex such a problem? *Journal of Personality and Social Psychology, 77,* 1173–1187.

Goldinger, S. D., Kleider, H. M., Tamiko, Azuma, & Beike, D. R. (2003). Blaming the victim under memory load. *Psychological Science, 14,* 81–85.

Goldman, B. M. (2001). Toward an understanding of employment discrimination claiming: An integration of organizations justice and social information processing theories. *Personnel Psychology, 54,* 361–386.

Gonnerman, M. E., Jr., Parker, C. P., Lavine, H., & Huff, J. (2000). The relationship between self-discrepancies and affective states: The moderating roles of self-monitoring and standpoints on the self. *Personality and Social Psychology Bulletin, 26,* 810–819.

Goodman, G. S., Ghetti, S., Quas, J. A., Edelstein, R. S., Alexander, K. W., Redlich, A. D., Cordon I. M., & Jones, D. P. H. (2003). A prospective study of memory for child sexual abuse: New findings relevant to the repressed-memory controversy. *Psychological Science, 14,* 113–118.

Goodwin, R., Cook, O., & Yung, Y. (2001). Loneliness and life satisfaction among three cultural groups. *Personal Relationships, 8,* 225–230.

Goodwin, S. A., Fiske, S. T., Rosen, L. D., & Rosenthal, A. M. (2002). The eye of the beholder: Romantic goals and impression biases. *Journal of Experimental Social Psychology, 38,* 232–241.

Goodwin, S. A., Gubin, A., Fiske, S. T., & Yzerbyt, V. (2000). Power can bias impression processes: Stereotyping subordinates by default and by design. *Group Processes and Intergroup Relations, 3,* 227–256.

Goodwin, V. L., Wofford, J. C., & Whittington, J. L. (2001). A theoretical and empirical extension to the transformational leadership construct. *Journal of Occupational Behavior, 22,* 759–774.

Gootman, E. (2004, June 15). The killer gown is essential, but the prom date? Not so much. *The New York Times,* B1, B4.

Gordon, R. A. (1996). Impact of ingratiation in judgments and evaluations: A meta-analytic investigation. *Journal of Personality and Social Psychology, 71,* 54–70.

Gottfredson, L. S. (1997). Why *g* matters: the complexity of everyday life. *Intelligence, 24,* 79–132.

Gottfredson, L. S. (2003). Dissecting practical intelligence theory: Its claims and evidence. *Intelligence, 31,* 343–397.

Gottfredson, L. S. (2004). Intelligence: Is it the epidemiologists' elusive "fundamental cause" of social class inequalities in health? *Journal of Personality and Social Psychology, 86,* 174–199.

Gould, S. J. (1996, September). The Diet of Worms and the defenestration of Prague. *Natural History,* 18–24, 64, 66–67.

Graham, S., & Folkes, V. (Eds.). (1990). *Attribution theory: Applications to achievement, mental health, and interpersonal conflict.* Hillsdale, NJ: Erlbaum.

Graham, S., Weiner, B., & Zucker, G. S. (1997). An attributional analysis of punishment goals and public reactions to O. J. Simpson. *Personality and Social Psychology Bulletin, 23,* 331–346.

Gray, H. M., Ambady, N., Lowenthal, W. T., & Deldin, P. (2004). P300 as an index of attention to self-relevant stimuli. *Journal of Experimental Social Psychology, 40,* 216–224.

Graziano, W. G., Jensen-Campbell, L. A., & Hair, E. C. (1996). Perceiving interpersonal conflict and reacting to it: The case for agreeableness. *Journal of Personality and Social Psychology, 70,* 820–835.

Green, J. D., & Campbell, W. K. (2000). Attachment and exploration in adults: Chronic and contextual accessibility. *Personality and Social Psychology Bulletin, 26,* 452–461.

Green, L. R., Richardson, D. R., & Lago, T. (1996). How do friendship, indirect, and direct aggression relate? *Aggressive Behavior, 22,* 81–86.

Greenbaum, P., & Rosenfield, H. W. (1978). Patterns of avoidance in responses to interpersonal staring and proximity: Effects of bystanders on drivers at a traffic intersection. *Journal of Personality and Social Psychology, 36,* 575–587.

Greenberg, J. (1997). A social influence model of employee theft: Beyond the fraud triangle. In R. J. Lewicki, R. J. Bies, & B. H. Sheppard (Eds.), *Research on negotiation in organizations* (Vol. 6, pp. 29–52). Greenwich, CT: JAI Press.

Greenberg, J., & Baron, R. A. (2002). *Behavior in organizations* (8th ed.). Upper Saddle River, NJ: Prentice-Hall.

Greenberg, J., & Baron, R. A. (in press). *Behavior in organizations* (9th ed.). Upper Saddle River, NJ: Prentice-Hall.

Greenberg, J., & Lind, E. A. (2000). The pursuit of organizational justice: From conceptualization to implication to application. In C. L. Cooper & E. A. Locke (Eds.), *Industrial/organizational psychology: What we know about theory and practice.* (pp. 72–107). Oxford, England: Blackwell.

Greenberg, J., Pyszczynski, T., & Solomon, S. (1982). The self-serving attributional bias: Beyond self-presentation. *Journal of Experimental Social Psychology, 18,* 56–67.

Greenberg, J., Solomon, S., & Pyszczynski, T. (1997). Terror management theory of self-esteem and social behavior: Empirical assessments and conceptual refinements. In M. P. Zanna (Ed.), *Advances in experimental social psychology* (Vol. 29, pp. 61–139). New York: Academic Press.

Greenberg, J., Solomon, S., Pyszczynski, T., Rosenblatt, A., Burling, J., Lyon, D., Simon, L., & Pinel, E. (1992). Why do people need self-esteem? Converging evidence that self-esteem serves an anxiety-buffering function. *Journal of Personality and Social Psychology, 63,* 913–922.

Greenhaus, J. H., & Parasuraman, S. (1993). Job performance attributions and career advancement prospects: An examination of gender and race effects. *Organizational Behavior and Human Decision Processes, 55,* 273–297.

Greenwald, A. G. (2002). Constructs in student ratings of instructors. In H. I. Braun & D. N. Douglas (Eds.), *The role of constructs in psychological and educational measurement* (pp. 277–297). Mahwah, NJ: Erlbaum.

Greenwald, A. G., & Banaji, M. R. (1995). Implicit social cognition: Attitudes, self-esteem, and stereotypes. *Psychological Review, 102,* 4–27.

Greenwald, A. G., McGhee, D. E., & Schwartz, J. L. K. (1998). Measuring individual differences in implicit cognition: The implicit association test. *Journal of Personality and Social Psychology, 74,* 1464–1480.

Griffin, R. W., & O'Leary-Kelly, V. (Eds.). *The dark side of organizational behavior.* San Francisco: Jossey-Bass.

Groff, D. B., Baron, R. S., & Moore, D. L. (1983). Distraction, attentional conflict, and drivelike behavior. *Journal of Experimental Social Psychology, 19,* 359–380.

Grote, N. K., & Clark, M. S. (2001). Perceiving unfairness in the family: Cause of consequence of marital distress? *Journal of Personality and Social Psychology, 80,* 281–289.

Grote, N. K., Frieze, I. H., & Stone, C. A. (1996). Children, traditionalism in the division of family work, and marital satisfaction: "What's love got to do with it?" *Personal Relationships, 3,* 211–228.

Grube, J. A., & Piliavin, J. A. (2000). Role identity, organizational experiences, and volunteer performance. *Personality and Social Psychology Bulletin, 26,* 1108–1119.

Guagnano, G. A. (1995). Locus of control, altruism and agentic disposition. *Population and Environment, 17,* 63–77.

Gudjonsson, G. H., & Clark, N. K. (1986). Suggestibility in police interrogation: A social psychological model. *Social Behavior, 1,* 83–104.

Guimond, S. (2000). Group socialization and prejudice: The social transmission of intergroup attitudes and beliefs. *European Journal of Social Psychology, 30,* 335–354.

Gump, B. B., & Kulik, J. A. (1997). Stress, affiliation, and emotional contagion. *Journal of Personality and Social Psychology, 72,* 305–319.

Gunther, A. (1995). Overrating the X-rating: The third-person perception and support for censorship of pornography. *Journal of Communication, 45,* 27–38.

Gustafson, R. (1990). Wine and male physical aggression. *Journal of Drug Issues, 20,* 75–86.

Hackel, L. S., & Ruble, D. N. (1992). Changes in the marital relationship after the first baby is born: Predicting the impact of expectancy disconfirmation. *Journal of Personality and Social Psychology, 62,* 944–957.

Hahn, J., & Blass, T. (1997). Dating partner preferences: A function of similarity of love styles. *Journal of Social Behavior and Personality, 12,* 595–610.

Halberstadt, J., & Rhodes, G. (2000). The attractiveness of nonface averages: Implications for an evolutionary explanation of the attractiveness of average faces. *Psychological Science, 11,* 285–289.

Halford, W. K., & Sanders, M. R. (1990). The relationship of cognition and behavior during marital interaction. *Journal of Social and Clinical Psychology, 9,* 489–510.

Hall, J. A., & Bernieri, F. J. (Eds.). (2001). *Interpersonal sensitivity.* Mahwah, NJ: Erlbaum.

Hall-Elston, C., & Mullins, L. C. (1999). Social relationships, emotional closeness, and loneliness among older meal program participants. *Social Behavior and Personality, 27,* 503–518.

Hamilton, D. L., & Sherman, S. J. (1989). Illusory correlations: Implications for stereotype theory and research. In D. Bar-Tal, C. F. Graumann, A. W. Kruglanski, & W. Stroebe (Eds.), *Stereotyping and prejudice: Changing conceptions* (pp. 59–82). New York: Springer-Verlag.

Hamilton, G. V. (1978). Obedience and responsibility: A jury simulation. *Journal of Personality and Social Psychology, 36,* 126–146.

Hamilton, V. L., & Sanders, J. (1995). Crimes of obedience and conformity in the workplace: Surveys of Americans, Russians, and Japanese. *Journal of Social Issues, 51,* 67–88.

Hamilton, W. D. (1964). The genetical theory of social behavior: I and II. *Journal of Theoretical Biology, 7,* 1–32.

Haney, C., Banks, W., & Zimbardo, P. (1973). Interpersonal dynamics in a simulated prison. *International Journal of Criminology, 1,* 69–97.

Hanko, K., Master, S., & Sabini, J. (2004). Some evidence about character and mate selection. *Personality and Social Psychology Bulletin, 30,* 732–742.

Hansen, T., & Bartsch, R. A. (2001). The positive correlation between personal need for structure and the mere exposure effect. *Social Behavior and Personality, 29,* 271–276.

Hareli, S., & Weiner, B. (2000). Accounts for success as determinants of perceived arrogance and modesty. *Motivation and Emotion, 24,* 215–236.

Hargreaves, D., & Tiggemann, M. (2002). The effect of television commercials on mood and body dissatisfaction: The role of appearance schema activation. *Journal of Social and Clinical Psychology, 21,* 287–308.

Harker, L., & Keltner, D. (2001). Expressions of positive emotion in women's college yearbook pictures and their relationship to personality and life outcomes across adulthood. *Journal of Personality and Social Psychology, 80,* 112–124.

Harmon-Jones, E. (2000). Cognitive dissonance and experienced negative affect: Evidence that dissonance increases experienced negative affect even in the absence of aversive consequences. *Personality and Social Psychology Bulletin, 26,* 1490–1501.

Harmon-Jones, E., & Allen, J. J. B. (2001). The role of affect in the mere exposure effect: Evidence from psychophysiological and individual differences approaches. *Personality and Social Psychology Bulletin, 27,* 889–898.

Harmon-Jones, E., & Devine, P. G. (2003). Introduction to the special section on social neuroscience: Promise and caveats. *Journal of Personality and Social Psychology, 85,* 589–593.

Harris, C. R. (2002). Sexual and romantic jealousy in heterosexual and homosexual adults. *Psychological Science, 13,* 7–12.

Harris, C. R. (2003). A review of sex differences in sexual jealousy, including self-report data, psychophysiological responses, interpersonal violence, and morbid jealousy. *Personality and Social Psychology Review, 7,* 102–128.

Harris, L. R., & Weiss, D. J. (1995). Judgments of consent in simulated rape cases. *Journal of Social Behavior and Personality, 10,* 79–90.

Harris, M. B. (1992). Sex, race, and experiences of aggression. *Aggressive Behavior, 18,* 201–217.

Harris, M. B. (1993). How provoking! What makes men and women angry? *Journal of Applied Social Psychology, 23,* 199–211.

Harris, M. B. (1994). Gender of subject and target as mediators of aggression. *Journal of Applied Social Psychology, 24,* 453–471.

Harris, M. B., Harris, R. J., & Bochner, S. (1982). Fat, four-eyed, and female: Stereotypes of obesity, glasses, and gender. *Journal of Applied Social Psychology, 12,* 503–516.

Harrison, M. (2003). "What is love?" Personal communication.

Hartup, W. W., & Stevens, N. (1999). Friendships and adaptation across the life span. *Current Directions in Psychological Science, 8,* 76–79.

Haslam, S. A. (2001). *Psychology in organizations: The social identity approach.* London: Sage.

Haslam, S. A., & Wilson, A. (2000). In what sense are prejudicial beliefs personal? The importance of an in-group's shared stereotypes. *British Journal of Social Psychology, 39,* 45–63.

Haslam, S. A., Branscombe, N. R., & Bachmann, S. (2003). Why consumers rebel: Social identity and the etiology of adverse reactions to service failure. In Haslam, S. A., van Knippenberg, D., Platow, M. J., & Ellemers, N. (Eds.), *Social identity at work* (pp. 293–309). New York: Psychological Press.

Haslam, S. A., van Knippenberg, D., Platow, M. J., & Ellemers, N. (2003). *Social identity at work: Developing theory and organizational practice.* New York: Psychological Press.

Haslett, A. (2004, May 31). Love supreme: Gay nuptials and the making of modern marriage. *The New Yorker,* 76–80.

Hassin, R., & Trope, Y. (2000). Facing faces: Studies on the cognitive aspects of physiognomy. *Journal of Personality and Social Psychology, 78,* 837–852.

Hatfield, E. (1988). Passionate and companionate love. In R. J. Sternberg & M. I. Barnes (Eds.), *The psychology of love* (pp. 191–217). New Haven, CT: Yale University Press.

Hatfield, E., & Rapson, R. L. (1993). Historical and cross-cultural perspectives on passionate love and sexual desire. *Annual Review of Sex Research, 4,* 67–97.

Hatfield, E., & Sprecher, S. (1986a). *Mirror, mirror . . . : The importance of looks in everyday life.* Albany, NY: S. U. N. Y. Press.

Hatfield, E., & Walster, G. W. (1981). *A new look at love.* Reading, MA: Addison-Wesley.

Haugtvedt, C. P., & Wegener, D. T. (1994). Message order effects in persuasion: An attitude strength perspective. *Journal of Consumer Research, 21,* 205–218.

Hawkins, E. (2002, May 10). Asking for a push. From the Internet. BACLIFF28@aol.com.

Hawkley, L. C., Burleson, M. H., Berntson, G. G., & Cacioppo, J. T. (2003). Loneliness in everyday life: Cardiovascular activity, psychosocial context, and health behaviors. *Journal of Personality and Social Psychology, 85,* 105–120.

Hayden, S. R., Jackson, T. T., & Guydish, J. N. (1984). Helping behavior of females: Effects of stress and commonality of fate. *Journal of Psychology, 117,* 233–237.

Hebl, M. R., & Mannix, L. M. (2003). The weight of obesity in evaluating others: A mere proximity effect. *Personality and Social Psychology, 29,* 28–38.

Heider, F. (1958). *The psychology of interpersonal relations.* New York: Wiley.

Heilman, M. E., Block, C. J., & Lucas, J. A. (1992). Presumed incompetent? Stigmatization and affirmative action efforts. *Journal of Applied Psychology, 77,* 536–544.

Heine, S. J., & Lehman, D. R. (1997). Culture, dissonance, and self-affirmation. *Personality and Social Psychology Bulletin, 23,* 389–400.

Helweg-Larsen, M., & Shepperd, J. A. (2001). Do moderators of the optimistic bias affect personal or target risk estimates? A review of the literature. *Personality and Social Psychology Review, 5,* 74–95.

Hendrick, C., & Hendrick, S. S. (1986). A theory and method of love. *Journal of Personality and Social Psychology, 50,* 392–402.

Hendrick, C., Hendrick, S. S., Foote, F. H., & Slapion-Foote, M. J. (1984). Do men and women love differently? *Journal of Social and Personal Relationships, 1,* 177–195.

Hendrick, S. S., & Hendrick, C. (2002). Linking romantic love with sex: Development of the Perceptions of Love and Sex Scale. *Journal of Social and Personal Relationships, 19,* 361–378.

Hense, R., Penner, L., & Nelson, D. (1995). Implicit memory for age stereotypes. *Special Cognition, 13,* 399–415.

Herbert, J. D. (1995). An overview of the current status of social phobia. *Applied and Preventive Psychology, 4,* 39–51.

Herbst, K. C., Gaertner, L., & Insko, C. A. (2003). My head says yes but my heart says no: Cognitive and affective attraction as a function of similarity to the ideal self. *Journal of Personality and Social Psychology, 84,* 1206–1219.

Herek, G. M., Gillis, J. R., & Cogan, J. C. (1999). Psychological sequelae of hate-crime victimization among lesbian, gay, and bisexual adults. *Journal of Consulting and Clinical Psychology, 67,* 945–951.

Herrera, N. C., Zajonc, R. B., Wieczorkowska, G., & Cichomski, B. (2003). Beliefs about birth rank and their reflec-

tion in reality. *Journal of Personality and Social Psychology, 85,* 142–150.

Herring, J. (2001, May 20). 10 tricks to a happy marriage. Knight Ridder.

Hersh, S. M. (2004). Torture at Abu Ghraib. *The New Yorker,* May 10.

Hertzberg, H. (2004, March 15). Wedded blitz. *The New Yorker,* 61–62.

Hess, J. A. (2002). Distance regulation in personal relationships: The development of a conceptual model and a test of representational validity. *Journal of Social and Personal Relationships, 19,* 663–683.

Hewstone, M., Bond, M. H., & Wan, K. C. (1983). Social factors and social attributions: The explanation of intergroup differences in Hong Kong. *Social Cognition, 2,* 142–157.

Higgins, E. T., & King, G. (1981). Accessibility of social constructs: Information processing consequences of individual and contextual variability. In N. Cantor & J. Kihlstrom (Eds.), *Personality, cognition, and social interaction* (pp. 69–121). Hillsdale, NJ: Erlbaum.

Higgins, E. T., & Silberman, I. (1998). Development of regulatory focus: Promotion and prevention as ways of living. In J. Heckhausen & C. S. Dweck (Eds.), *Motivation and self-regulation across the life span* (pp. 798–113). New York: Cambridge University Press.

Higgins, E. T., Rohles, W. S., & Jones, C. R. (1977). Category accessibility and impression formation. *Journal of Experimental Social Psychology, 13,* 141–154.

Higgins, N. C., & Shaw, J. K. (1999). Attributional style moderates the impact of causal controllability information on helping behavior. *Social Behavior and Personality, 27,* 221–236.

Hill, C. A., Blakemore, J. E. O., & Drumm, P. (1997). Mutual and unrequited love in adolescence and young adulthood. *Personal Relationships, 4,* 15–23.

Hilton, D. J. (1998). *Psychology and the city: Applications to trading, dealing, and investment analysis.* London: Center for the Study of Financial Innovation.

Hilton, N. Z., Harris, G. T., & Rice, M. E. (2000). The functions of aggression by male teenagers. *Journal of Personality and Social Psychology, 79,* 988–994.

Hinsz, V. B. (1995). Goal setting by groups performing an additive task: A comparison with individual goal setting. *Journal of Applied Social Psychology, 25,* 965–990.

Hinsz, V. B., Matz, D. C., & Patience, R. A. (2001). Does women's hair signal reproductive potential? *Journal of Experimental Social Psychology, 37,* 166–172.

Hirt, E. R., & Markman, K. D. (1995). Multiple explanation: A consider-an-alternative strategy for debiasing judgments. *Personality and Social Psychology Bulletin, 69,* 1069–1086.

Hoaken, P. N. S., Giancola, P. R., & Pihl, R. O. (1998). Executive cognitive functions as mediators of alcohol-related aggression. *Alcohol and Alcoholism, 33,* 45–53.

Hogg, M. A., & Abrams, D. *Social identifications: A social psychology of intergroup relations and group processes.* London: Routledge.

Hogg, M. A., & Turner, J. C. (1987). Intergroup behaviour, self-stereotyping and the salience of social categories. *British Journal of Social Psychology, 30,* 325–340.

Holmes, J. G. (2002). Interpersonal expectations as the building blocks of social cognition: An interdependence theory perspective. *Personal Relationships, 9,* 1–26.

Holmes, T. H., & Rahe, R. H. (1967). The social readjustment rating scale. *Journal of Psychosomatic Research, 22,* 213–218.

Hope, D. A., Holt, C. S., & Heimberg, R. G. (1995). Social phobia. In T. R. Giles (Ed.), *Handbook of effective psychotherapy* (pp. 227–251). New York: Plenum.

Hopkins, A. B. (1996). *So ordered: Making partner the hard way.* Amherst, MA: University of Massachusetts Press.

Horney, K. (1950). *Neurosis and human growth: The struggle toward self-realization.* New York: Norton.

Hornsey, M. J., & Hogg, M. A. (2000). Intergroup similarity and subgroup relations: Some implications for assimilation. *Personality and Social Psychology Bulletin, 26,* 948–958.

Hornsey, M. J., & Imani, A. (2004). Criticizing groups from the inside and the outside: An identity perspective on the intergroup sensitivity effect. *Personality and Social Psychology Bulletin, 30,* 365–383.

House, J. S., Landis, K. R., & Umberson, D. (1988). Social relationships and health. *Science, 241,* 540–545.

House, R. J., & Howell, J. M. (1992). Personality and charismatic leadership. *Leadership Quarterly, 3,* 81–108.

House, R. J., & Podsakoff, P. M. (1994). Leadership effectiveness: Past perspectives and future directions for research. In J. Greenberg (Ed.), *Organizational behavior: The state of the science* (pp. 45–82). Hillsdale, NJ: Erlbaum.

House, R. J., Spangler, W. D., & Woycke, J. (1991). Personality and charisma in the U.S. presidency: A psychological theory of leader effectiveness. *Administrative Science Quarterly, 36,* 364–396.

Households. (2001, August 6). *U.S. News & World Report,* 15.

Hovland, C. I., & Weiss, W. (1951). The influence of source credibility on communication effectiveness. *Public Opinion Quarterly, 15,* 635–650.

Hovland, C. I., Janis, I. L., & Kelley, H. H. (1953). *Communication and persuasion: Psychological studies of opinion change.* New Haven, CT: Yale University Press.

Huang, I.-C. (1998). Self-esteem, reaction to uncertainty, and physician practice variation: A study of resident physicians. *Social Behavior and Personality, 26,* 181–194.

Hudson, K. (2004, April 30). *Entertainment Weekly,* 46.

Huesmann, L. R., & Eron, L. D. (1984). Cognitive processes and the persistence of aggressive behavior. *Aggressive Behavior, 10,* 243–251.

Huesmann, L. R., & Eron, L. D. (1986). *Television and the aggressive child: A cross-national comparison.* Hillsdale, NJ: Erlbaum.

Hugenberg, K., & Bodenhausen, G. V. (2003). Facing prejudice: Implicit prejudice and the perception of facial threat. *Psychological Science, 14,* 640–643.

Hughes, J. (2000, December 12). What does love mean? From the Internet. jeh66@aol.com.

Hughes, J. (2002, March 4). How do you decide who to marry? Online at: Jeh66@aol.com.

Hughes, S. M., Harrison, M. A., & Gallup, G. G., Jr. (2002). The sound of symmetry: Voice as a marker of developmental instability. *Evolution and Human Behavior, 23,* 173–180.

Huguet, P., Galvaing, M. P., Monteil, J. M., & Dumas, F. (1999). Social presence effects in the Stroop task: Further evidence for an attentional view of social facilitation. *Journal of Personality and Social Psychology, 77,* 1011–1025.

Hummert, M. L., Crockett, W. H., & Kemper, S. (1990). Processing mechanisms underlying use of the balance scheme. *Journal of Personality and Social Psychology, 58,* 5–21.

Humphreys, L. G. (1998). A little noticed consequence of the repressed memory epidemic. *American Psychologist, 53,* 485–486.

Hunt, A. McC. (1935). A study of the relative value of certain ideals. *Journal of Abnormal and Social Psychology, 30,* 222–228.

Huston, T. L., Caughlin, J. P., Houts, R. M., Smith, S. E., & George, L. J. (2001). The connubial crucible: Newlywed years as predictors of marital delight, distress, and divorce. *Journal of Personality and Social Psychology, 80,* 237–252.

Ickes, W., Reidhead, S., & Patterson, M. (1986). Machiavellianism and self-monitoring: As different as "me" and "you." *Social Cognition, 4,* 58–74.

Illies, R., & Judge, T. A. (2003). On the heritability of job satisfaction: The mediating role of personality. *Journal of Applied Psychology, 88,* 750–759.

Insko, C. A. (1985). Balance theory, the Jordan paradigm, and the West tetrahedron. In L. Berkowitz (Ed.), *Advances in experimental social psychology.* New York: Academic Press.

Insko, C. A., Schopler, H. J., Gaertner, G., Wildschutt, T., Kozar, R., Pinter, B., Finkel, E. J., Brazil, D. M., Cecil, C. L., & Montoya, M. R. (2001). Interindividual-intergroup discontinuity reduction through the anticipation of future interaction. *Journal of Personality and Social Psychology, 80,* 95–111.

Inzlicht, M., & Ben-Zeev, T. (2000). A threatening intellectual environment: Why females are susceptible to experiencing problem-solving deficits in the presence of males. *Psychological Science, 11,* 365–371.

Ireland, C. A., & Ireland, J. L. (2000). Descriptive analysis of the nature and extent of bullying behavior in a maximum security prison. *Aggressive Behavior, 26,* 213–222.

Ireland, J. L., & Archer, J. (2002). The perceived consequences of responding to bullying with aggression: A study of male and female adult prisoners. *Aggressive Behavior, 28,* 257–272.

Irvine, M. (1999, November 24). American families in flux. Associated Press.

Isbell, L. M., & Wyer, R. S., Jr. (1999). Correcting for mood-induced bias in the evaluation of political candidates: The roles of intrinsic and extrinsic motivation. *Personality and Social Psychology Bulletin, 25,* 237–249.

Isen, A. M. (1984). Toward understanding the role of affect in cognition. In S. R. Wyer & T. K. Srull (Eds.), *Handbook of social cognition* (Vol. 3, pp. 179–236). Hillsdale, NJ: Erlbaum.

Isen, A. M., & Baron, R. A. (1991). Affect and organizational behavior. In B. M. Staw & L. L. Cummings (Eds.), *Research in organizational behavior* (Vol. 15, pp. 1–53).

Isen, A. M., & Levin, P. A. (1972). Effect of feeling good on helping: Cookies and kindness. *Journal of Personality and Social Psychology, 21,* 384–388.

Istvan, J., Griffitt, W., & Weidner, G. (1983). Sexual arousal and the polarization of perceived sexual attractiveness. *Basic and Applied Social Psychology, 4,* 307–318.

Ito, T. A., & Urland, G. R. (2003). Race and gender on the brain: Electrocortical measures of attention to the race and gender of multiply categorizable individuals. *Journal of Personality and Social Psychology, 85,* 616–626.

Ito, T. A., Larsen, J. T., Smith, N. K., & Cacioppo, J. T. (1998). Negative information weighs more heavily on the brain: The negativity bias in evaluative categorizations. *Journal of Personality and Social Psychology, 75,* 887–900.

Izard, C. (1991). *The psychology of emotions.* New York: Plenum.

Jackman, M. R. (1994). *The velvet glove: Paternalism and conflict in gender, class, and race relations.* Berkeley, CA: University of California Press.

Jackson, L. M., & Esses, V. M. (1997). Of scripture and ascription: The relation between religious fundamentalism and intergroup helping. *Personality and Social Psychology Bulletin, 23,* 893–906.

Jackson, L. M., Esses, V. M., & Burris, C. T. (2001). Contemporary sexism and discrimination: The importance of respect for men and women. *Personality and Social Psychology Bulletin, 27,* 48–61.

Jackson, T., Soderlind, A., & Weiss, K. E. (2000). Personality traits and quality of relationships as predictors of future loneliness among American college students. *Social Behavior and Personality, 28,* 463–470.

Jackson, T., Fritch, A., Nagasaka, T., & Gunderson, J. (2002). Towards explaining the association between shyness and loneliness: A path analysis with American college students. *Social Behavior and Personality, 30,* 263–270.

Jacobi, L., & Cash, T. F. (1994). In pursuit of the perfect appearance: Discrepancies among self-ideal percepts of multiple physical attributes. *Journal of Applied Social Psychology, 24,* 379–396.

Jacobs, J. A., & Steinberg, R. (1990). Compensating differentials and the male-female wage gap: Evidence from the New York state comparable worth study. *Social Forces, 69,* 439–468.

Janis, I. L. (1972). *Victims of groupthink.* Boston: Houghton Mifflin.

Janis, I. L. (1982). *Victims of groupthink* (2nd ed.). Boston: Houghton Mifflin.

Jarrell, A. (1998, October 4). Date that calls for judicious attire. *New York Times,* 9-1–9-2.

Jeffries, V. (1993). Virtue and attraction: Validation of a measure of love. *Journal of Social and Personal Relationships, 10,* 99–117.

Jellison, J. M., & Green, J. (1981). A self-presentation approach to the fundamental attribution error: The norm of internality. *Journal of Personality and Social Psychology, 40,* 643–649.

Jensen-Campbell, L. A., West, S. G., & Graziano, W. G. (1995). Dominance, prosocial orientation, and female preferences: Do nice guys really finish last? *Journal of Personality and Social Psychology, 68,* 427–440.

Jetten, J., & Spears, R. (2003). The divisive potential of differences and similarities: The role of intergroup distinctiveness in intergroup differentiation. *European Review of Social Psychology, 14,* 203–241.

Jetten, J., Spears, R., & Manstead, A. S. R. (1997). Strength of identification and intergroup differentiation: The influence of group norms. *European Journal of Social Psychology, 27,* 603–609.

Jetten, J., Branscombe, N. R., Schmitt, M. T., & Spears, R. (2001). Rebels with a cause: Group identification as a response to perceived discrimination from the mainstream. *Personality and Social Psychology Bulletin, 27,* 1204–1213.

Johnson, B. T. (1994). Effects of outcome-relevant involvement and prior information on persuasion. *Journal of Experimental Social Psychology, 30,* 556–579.

Johnson, C., & Mullen, B. (1994). Evidence for the accessibility of paired distinctiveness in the distinctiveness-based illusory correlation in stereotyping. *Personality and Social Psychology Bulletin, 20,* 65–70.

Johnson, J. C., Poteat, G. M., & Ironsmith, M. (1991). Structural vs. marginal effects: A note on the importance of structure in determining sociometric status. *Journal of Social Behavior and Personality, 6,* 489–508.

Johnson, J. D., & Lecci, L. (2003). Assessing anti-White attitudes and predicting perceived racism: The Johnson-Lecci scale. *Personality and Social Psychology Bulletin, 29,* 299–312.

Johnson, M. K., & Sherman, S. J. (1990). Constructing and reconstructing the past and the future in the present. In E. T. Higgins & R. M. Sorrentino (Eds.), *Handbook of motivation and social cognition: Foundations of social behavior* (pp. 482–526). New York: Guilford.

Johnson, S. (2003, April). Laughter. *Discover,* 62–68.

Johnston, V. S., & Oliver-Rodriguez, J. C. (1997). Facial beauty and the late positive component of event-related potentials. *Journal of Sex Research, 34,* 188–198.

Johnstone, B., Frame, C. L., & Bouman, D. (1992). Physical attractiveness and athletic and academic ability in controversial–aggressive and rejected–aggressive children. *Journal of Social and Clinical Psychology, 11,* 71–79.

Joireman, J., Anderson, J., & Strathman, A. (2003). The aggression paradox: Understanding links among aggression, sensation seeking, and the consideration of future consequences. *Journal of Personality and Social Psychology, 84,* 1287–1302.

Jones, E. E. (1964). *Ingratiation: A social psychology analysis.* New York: Appleton-Century-Crofts.

Jones, E. E. (1979). The rocky road from acts to dispositions. *American Psychologist, 34,* 107–117.

Jones, E. E., & Davis, K. E. (1965). From acts to disposition: The attribution process in person perception. In L. Berkowitz (Ed.), *Advances in experimental social psychology* (Vol. 2, pp. 219–266). New York: Academic Press.

Jones, E. E., & Harris, V. A. (1967). The attribution of attitudes. *Journal of Experimental Social Psychology, 3,* 1–24.

Jones, E. E., & McGillis, D. (1976). Corresponding inferences and attribution cube: A comparative reappraisal. In J. H. Har, W. J. Ickes, & R. F. Kidd (Eds.), *New directions in attribution research* (Vol. 1). Morristown, NJ: Erlbaum.

Jones, E. E., & Nisbett, R. E. (1971). *The actor and the observer: Divergent perceptions of the causes of behavior.* Morristown, NJ: General Learning Press.

Jones, J. H. (1997, August 25 and September 1). Dr. Yes. *New Yorker,* 98–110, 112–113.

Judd, C. M., Ryan, C. S., & Parke, B. (1991). Accuracy in the judgment of in-group and out-group variability. *Journal of Personality and Social Psychology, 61,* 366–379.

Judge, D. S., & Hrdy, S. B. (1992). Allocation of accumulated resources among close kin: Inheritance in Sacramento, California, 1890–1984. *Ethology and Sociobiology, 13,* 495–522.

Judge, T. A. (1992). The dispositional perspective in human resources research. *Research in Personnel and Human Resources Management, 10,* 31–72.

Judge, T. A., & Cable, T. A. (2004). The effect of physical height on workplace success and income: Preliminary test of a theoretical model. *Journal of Applied Psychology, 89,* 428–441.

Judge, T. A., Heller, D., & Mount, M. K. (2002). Five-factor model of personality and job satisfaction. *Journal of Applied Psychology, 87,* 530–541.

Judge, T. A., Bono, J. E., Ilies, R., & Gerhgardt, M. W. (2002). Personality and leadership: A qualitative and quantitative review. *Journal of Applied Psychology, 87,* 765–780.

Judge, T. A., Thoresen, C. J., Bono, J. E., & Patton, G. K. (2001). The job satisfaction–performance relationship: A qualitative and quantitative review. *Psychological Bulletin, 127,* 376–407.

Kahneman, D., & Miller, D. T. (1986). Norm theory: Comparing reality to its alternatives. *Psychological Review, 93,* 136–153.

Kaiser, C. R., & Miller, C. T. (2001). Stop complaining! The social costs of making attributions to discrimination. *Personality and Social Psychology Bulletin, 27,* 254–263.

Kallgren, C. A., Reno, R. R., & Cialdini, R. B. (2000). A focus theory of normative conduct: When norms do and do not affect behavior. *Personality and Social Psychology Bulletin, 26,* 1002–1012.

Kameda, T., & Sugimori, S. (1993). Psychological entrapment in group decision making: An assigned decision rule and a groupthink phenomenon. *Journal of Personality and Social Psychology, 65,* 282–292.

Kandel, D. B. (1978). Similarity in real-life adolescent friendship pairs. *Journal of Personality and Social Psychology, 36,* 306–312.

Kanagawa, C., Cross, S. E., & Markus, H. R. (2001). "Who am I?" The cultural psychology of the conceptual self. *Personality and Social Psychology Bulletin, 27,* 90–103.

Karau, S. J., & Williams, K. D. (1993). Social loafing: A meta-analytic review and theoretical integration. *Journal of Personality and Social Psychology, 65,* 681–706.

Kark, R., Shamir, B., & Chen, G. (2003). The two faces of transformational leadership: Empowerment and dependency. *Journal of Applied Psychology, 88,* 246–255.

Karraker, K. H., & Stern, M. (1990). Infant physical attractiveness and facial expression: Effects on adult perceptions. *Basic and Applied Social Psychology, 11,* 371–385.

Karremans, J. C., Van Lange, P. A. M., Ouwerkerk, J. W., & Kluwer, E. S. (2003). When forgiving enhances psychological well-being: The role of interpersonal commitment. *Journal of Personality and Social Psychology, 84,* 1011–1026.

Kassin, S. M., & Kiechel, K. L. (1996). The social psychology of false confessions: Compliance, internalization, and confabulation. *Psychological Science, 7,* 125–128.

Kassin, S. M., & McNall, K. (1991). Police interrogations and confessions: Communicating promises and threats by pragmatic implication. *Law and Human Behavior, 15,* 233–251.

Katz, D. (1960). The functional approach to the study of attitudes. *Journal of Abnormal and Social Psychology, 70,* 1037–1051.

Katz, J., & Beach, S. R. H. (2000). Looking for love? Self-verification and self-enhancement effects on initial romantic attraction. *Personality and Social Psychology Bulletin, 26,* 1526–1539.

Kawakami K., & Dovidio, J. F. (2001). The reliability of implicit stereotyping. *Personality and Social Psychology Bulletin, 27,* 212–225.

Kawakami, K., Dion, K. L., & Dovidio, J. F. (1998). Racial prejudice and stereotype activation. *Personality and Social Psychology Bulletin, 24,* 407–416.

Kawakami K., Dovidio, J. F., Moll, J., Hermsen, S., & Russn, A. (2000). Just say no (to stereotyping): Effects of training in the negation of stereotypic associations on stereotype activation. *Journal and Personality and Social Psychology, 78,* 871–888.

Keller, L. M., Bouchard, T. J., Jr., Arvey, R. D., Segal, N. L., & Dawis, R. V. (1992). Work values: Genetic and environmental influences. *Journal of Applied Psychology, 77,* 79–88.

Keller, R. T. (1997). Job involvement and organizational commitment as longitudinal predictors of job performance: A study of scientists and engineers. *Journal of Applied Psychology, 82,* 539–545.

Kellerman, J., Lewis, J., & Laird, J. D. (1989). Looking and loving: The effects of mutual gaze on feelings of romantic love. *Journal of Research in Personality, 23,* 145–161.

Kelley, H. H. (1972). Attribution in social interaction. In E. E. Jones et al. (Eds.), *Attribution: Perceiving the causes of behavior.* Morristown, NJ: General Learning Press.

Kelley, H. H., & Michela, J. L. (1980). Attribution theory and research. *Annual Review of Psychology, 31,* 57–501.

Kelly, A. E., & Kahn, J. H. (1994). Effects of suppression of personal intrusive thoughts. *Journal of Personality and Social Psychology, 66,* 998–1026.

Kelly, A. E., & Nauta, M. M. (1997). Reactance and thought suppression. *Personality and Social Psychology Bulletin, 23,* 1123–1132.

Kelman, H. C. (1967). Human use of human subjects: The problem of deception in social psychological experiments. *Psychological Bulletin, 67,* 1–11.

Keltner, D., & Robinson, R. J. (1997). Defending the status quo: Power and bias in social conflict. *Personality and Social Psychology Bulletin, 23,* 1066–1077.

Keltner, D., Young, R. C., Heerey, E. A., Oemig, C., & Monarch, N. D. (1998). Teasing in hierarchical and intimate relations. *Journal of Personality and Social Psychology, 75,* 1231–1247.

Kemeny, M. E. (2003). The psychobiology of stress. *Current Directions in Psychological Science, 12,* 124–129.

Kenealy, P., Gleeson, K., Frude, N., & Shaw, W. (1991). The importance of the individual in the 'causal' relationship between attractiveness and self-esteem. *Journal of Community and Applied Social Psychology, 1,* 45–56.

Kenrick, D. T., & Gutierres, S. E. (1980). Contrast effects and judgments of physical attractiveness: When beauty becomes a social problem. *Journal of Personality and Social Psychology, 38,* 131–140.

Kenrick, D. T., Montello, D. R., Gutierres, S. E., & Trost, M. R. (1993). Effects of physical attractiveness on affect and perceptual judgments: When social comparison overrides social reinforcement. *Personality and Social Psychology Bulletin, 19,* 195–199.

Kenrick, D. T., Neuberg, S. L., Zierk, K. L., & Krones, J. M. (1994). Evolution and social cognition: Contrast effects as a function of sex, dominance, and physical attractiveness. *Personality and Social Psychology Bulletin, 20,* 210–217.

Kenrick, D. T., Sundie, J. M., Nicastle, L. D., & Stone, G. O. (2001). Can one ever be too wealthy or too chaste? Searching for nonlinearities in mate judgement. *Journal of Personality and Social Psychology, 80,* 462–471.

Kenworthy, J. B., & Miller, N. (2001). Perceptual asymmetry in consensus estimates of majority and minority members. *Journal of Personality and Social Psychology, 80,* 597–612.

Kernis, M. H., Cornell, D. P., Sun, C. R., Berry, A. J., & Harlow, T. (1993). There's more to self-esteem than whether it is high or low: The importance of stability of self-esteem. *Journal of Personality and Social Psychology, 65,* 1190–1204.

Kerr, N. L., & Kaufman-Gilliland, C. M. (1994). Communication, commitment, and cooperation in social dilemmas. *Journal of Personality and Social Psychology, 66,* 513–529.

Kerr, N. L., Garst, J., Lewandowski, D. A., & Harris, S. E. (1997). That still, small voice: Commitment to cooperate as an internalized versus a social norm. *Personality and Social Psychology Bulletin, 23,* 1300–1311.

Kiecolt-Glaser, J. K., & Glaser, R. (1992). Psychoneuroimmunology: Can psychology interventions modulate immunity? *Journal of Consulting and Clinical Psychology, 60,* 569–575.

Kiecolt-Glaser, J. K., Fisher, L., Ogrocki, P., Stout, J. C., Speicher, C. E., & Glaser, R. (1987). Marital quality, marital disruption, and immune function. *Psychosomatic Medicine, 49,* 13–34.

Kiecolt-Glaser, J. K., Kennedy, S., Malkoff, S., Fisher, L., Speicher, C. E., & Glaser, R. (1988). Marital discord and immunity in males. *Psychosomatic Medicine, 50,* 213–229.

Kilduff, M., & Day, D. V. (1994). Do chameleons get ahead? The effects of self-monitoring on managerial careers. *Academy of Management Journal, 37,* 1047–1060.

Kilham, W., & Mann, L. (1974). Level of destructive obedience as a function of transmitter and executant roles in the Milgram obedience paradigm. *Journal of Personality and Social Psychology, 29,* 696–702.

Killeya, L. A., & Johnson, B. T. (1998). Experimental induction of biased systematic processing: The directed through technique. *Personality and Social Psychology Bulletin, 24,* 17–33.

Kilmartin, C. T. (1994). *The masculine self.* New York: Macmillan.

Kim, H., & Markus, H. R. (1999). Deviance or uniqueness, harmony or conformity? A cultural analysis. *Journal of Personality and Social Psychology, 77,* 785–800.

Kirkland, S. L., Greenberg, J., & Pyszczynski, T. (1987). Further evidence of the deleterious effects of overheard ethnic slurs: Derogation beyond the target. *Personality and Social Psychology Bulletin, 13,* 216–227.

Kirkpatrick, S. A., & Locke, E. A. (1991). Leadership: Do traits matter? *Academy of Management Executive, 5*(2), 48–60.

Kisner, R. D. (2004, April 12). A European marriage. *The New Yorker,* 7.

Kitzmann, K. M., Cohen, R., & Lockwood, R. L. (2002). Are only children missing out? Comparison of the peer-related social competence of only children and siblings. *Journal of Social and Personal Relationships, 19,* 299–316.

Klagsbrun, F. (1992). *Mixed feelings: Love, hate, rivalry, and reconciliation among brothers and sisters.* New York: Bantam.

Klandermans, B. (1997). *The social psychology of protest.* Oxford, UK: Basil Blackwell.

Klar, Y. (2002). Way beyond compare: The nonselective superiority and inferiority biases in judging randomly assigned group members relative to their peers. *Journal of Experimental Social Psychology, 38,* 331–351.

Klein, S. B., & Loftus, J. (1993). Behavioral experience and trait judgments about the self. *Personality and Social Psychology Bulletin, 16,* 740–745.

Klein, S. B., Loftus, J., & Plog, A. E. (1992). Trait judgments about the self: Evidence from the encoding specificity paradigm. *Personality and Social Psychology Bulletin, 18,* 730–735.

Klein, S. B., Loftus, J., Trafton, J. G., & Fuhrman, R. W. (1992). Use of exemplars and abstractions in trait judgments: A model of trait knowledge about the self and others. *Journal of Personality and Social Psychology, 63,* 739–753.

Kleinke, C. L. (1986). Gaze and eye contact: A research review. *Psychological Bulletin, 100,* 78–100.

Kling, K. C., Ryff, C. D., & Essex, M. J. (1997). Adaptive changes in the self-concept during a life transition. *Personality and Social Psychology Bulletin, 23,* 981–990.

Klohnen, E. C., & Bera, S. (1998). Behavioral and experiential patterns of avoidantly and securely attached women across adulthood: A 31-year longitudinal perspective. *Journal of Personality and Social Psychology, 74,* 211–223.

Klohnen, E. C., & Luo, S. (2003). Interpersonal attraction and personality: What is attractive—self similarity, ideal similarity, complementarity, or attachment security? *Journal of Personality and Social Psychology, 85,* 709–722.

Knee, C. R. (1998). Implicit theories of relationships: Assessment and prediction of romantic relationship initiation, coping, and longevity. *Journal of Personality and Social Psychology, 74,* 360–370.

Knight, G. P., & Dubro, A. (1984). Cooperative, competitive, and individualistic social values: An individualized regression and clustering approach. *Journal of Personality and Social Psychology, 46,* 98–105.

Koch, W. (1996, March 10). Marriage, divorce rates indicate Americans are hopelessly in love. *Albany Times Union,* p. A11.

Kochanska, G., Friesenborg, A. F., Lange, L. A., & Martel, M. M. (2004). Parents' personality and infants' temperament as contributors to their emerging relationship. *Journal of Personality and Social Psychology, 86,* 744–759.

Koehler, J. J. (1993). The base rate fallacy myth. *Psychology, 4.*

Koestner, R., Bernieri, F., & Zuckerman, M. (1992). Self-regulation and consistency between attitudes, traits, and behaviors. *Personality and Social Psychology Bulletin, 18,* 52–59.

Kogan, N., & Wallach, M. A. (1964). *Risk-taking: A study in cognition and personality.* New York: Henry Holt.

Kohl, W. L., Steers, R., & Terborg, Jr. (1995). The effects of transformational leadership on teacher attitudes and student performance in Singapore. *Journal of Organizational Behavior, 73,* 695–702.

Komorita, M., & Parks, G. (1994). Interpersonal relations: Mixed-motive interaction. *Annual Review of Psychology, 46,* 183–207.

Kowalski, R. M. (1993). Interpreting behaviors in mixed-gender encounters: Effects of social anxiety and gender. *Journal of Social and Clinical Psychology, 12,* 239–247.

Kowalski, R. M. (1996). Complaints and complaining: Functions, antecedents, and consequences. *Psychological Bulletin, 119,* 179–196.

Kowalski, R. M., Walker, S., Wilkinson, R., Queen, A., & Sharpe, B. (2003). Lying, cheating, complaining, and other aversive interpersonal behaviors: A narrative examination of the darker side of relationships. *Journal of Social and Personal Relationships, 20,* 471–490.

Kramer, R. M. (1998). Revisiting the Bay of Pigs and Vietnam decisions 25 years later. How well has the groupthink hypothesis stood the test of time? *Organizational Behavior and Human Decision Processes, 36,* 236–271

Kramer, R., & Tyler, T. R. (1996). *Trust in organizations: Frontiers of theory and research.* Thousand Oaks, CA: Sage.

Krosnick, J. A. (1988). The role of attitude importance in social evaluation: A study of political preferences, presidential candidate evaluations, and voting behavior. *Journal of Personality and Social Psychology, 55,* 196–210.

Krosnick, J. A. (1989). Attitude importance and attitude accessibility. *Personality and Social Psychology Bulletin, 15,* 297–308.

Krosnick, J. A., Betz, A. L., Jussim, L. J., & Lynn, A. R. (1992). Subliminal conditioning of attitudes. *Personality and Social Psychology Bulletin, 18,* 152–162.

Krueger, R. F., Hicks, B. M., & McGue, M. (2001). Altruism and antisocial behavior: Independent tendencies, unique personality characteristics, distinct etiologies. *Psychological Science, 12,* 397–402.

Kulik, J. A., Mahler, H. I. M., & Moore, P. J. (1996). Social comparison and affiliation under threat: Effects on recovery from major surgery. *Journal of Personality and Social Psychology, 71,* 967–979.

Kunda, Z. (1999). *Social cognition: Making sense of people.* Cambridge, MA: MIT Press.

Kunda, Z., & Oleson, K. C. (1995). Maintaining stereotypes in the face of disconfirmation: Constructing grounds for subtyping deviants. *Journal of Personality and Social Psychology, 68,* 565–579.

Kurdek, L. A. (1993). The allocation of household labor in gay, lesbian, and heterosexual married couples. *Journal of Social Issues, 49(3),* 127–139.

Kurdek, L. A. (1996). The deterioration of relationship quality for gay and lesbian cohabiting couples: A five-year prospective longitudinal study. *Personal Relationships, 3,* 417–442.

Kurdek, L. A. (1997). Adjustment to relationship dissolution in gay, lesbian, and heterosexual partners. *Personal Relationships, 4,* 145–161.

Kurdek, L. A. (1999). The nature and predictors of the trajectory of change in marital quality for husbands and wives over the first 10 years of marriage: Predicting the seven-year itch. *Journal of Developmental Psychology, 35,* 1283–1296.

Kurdek, L. A. (2003). Differences between gay and lesbian cohabiting couples. *Journal of Social and Personal Relationships, 20,* 411–436.

Kwon, Y.-H. (1994). Feeling toward one's clothing and self-perception of emotion, sociability, and work competency. *Journal of Social Behavior and Personality, 9,* 129–139.

LaFrance, M., & Hecht, M. A. (1995). Why smiles generate leniency. *Personality and Social Psychology Bulletin, 21,* 207–214.

Lalonde, R. N., & Silverman, R. A. (1994). Behavioral preferences in response to social injustice: The effects of group permeability and social identity salience. *Journal of Personality and Social Psychology, 66,* 78–85.

LaMastro, V. (2001). Childless by choice? Attributions and attitudes concerning family size. *Social Behavior and Personality, 29,* 231–244.

Lambert, A. J. (1995). Stereotypes and social judgment: The consequences of group variability. *Journal of Personality and Social Psychology, 68,* 388–403.

Lambert, T. A., Kahn, A. S., & Apple, K. J. (2003). Pluralistic ignorance and hooking up. *Journal of Sex Research, 40,* 129–133.

Lamm, H., & Myers, D. G. (1978). Group-induced polarization of attitudes and behavior. In L. Berkowitz (Ed.), *Advances in experimental social psychology.* New York: Academic Press.

Landy, F. F., & Conte, J. M. (2004). *Work in the 21st century.* McGraw-Hill: New York.

Langer, E. (1984). *The psychology of control.* Beverly Hills, CA: Sage.

Langlois, J. H., & Roggman, L. A. (1990). Attractive faces are only average. *Psychological Science, 1,* 115–121.

Langlois, J. H., Roggman, L. A., & Musselman, L. (1994). What is average and what is not average about attractive faces? *Psychological Science, 5,* 214–220.

Langlois, J. H., Kalakanis, L., Rubinstein, A. J., Larson, A. I., Hallam, M., & Smoot, M. (2000). Maxims or myths of beauty: A meta-analytic and theoretical review. *Psychological Bulletin, 126,* 390–423.

Lapham, L. H. (1996, September). Back to school. *Harper's Magazine,* 10–11.

LaPiere, R. T. (1934). Attitude and actions. *Social Forces, 13,* 230–237.

Larson, J. H., & Bell, N. J. (1988). Need for privacy and its effects upon interpersonal attraction and interaction. *Journal of Social and Clinical Psychology, 6,* 1–10.

Larson, J. R., Jr., Christensen, C., Franz, T. M., & Abbott, A. S. (1998). Diagnosing groups: The pooling, management, and impact of shared and unshared case information in team-based medical decision making. *Jounral of Personality and Social Psychology, 75,* 93–108.

Larson, J. R., Jr., Foster-Fishman, P. G., & Franz, T. M. (1998). Leadership style and the discussion of shared and unshared information in decision-making groups. *Personality and Social Psychology Bulletin, 24,* 482–495.

Lassiter, G. D. (2002). Illusory causation in the courtroom. *Current Directions in Psychological Science, 11,* 204–208.

Lassiter, G. D., Geers, A. L., Handley, I. M., Weiland, P. E., & Munhall, P. M. (2002). Videotaped interrogations and confessions: A simple change in camera perspective alters verdicts in simulated trials. *Journal of Applied Psychology, 87,* 867–874.

Latané, B., & Darley, J. M. (1968). Group inhibition of bystander intervention in emergencies. *Journal of Personality and Social Psychology, 10,* 215–221.

Latané, B., & Darley, J. M. (1970). *The unresponsive bystander: Why doesn't he help?* New York: Appleton-Century-Crofts.

Latané, B., & L'Herrou, T. (1996). Spatial clustering in the conformity game: Dynamic social impact in electronic groups. *Journal of Personality and Social Psychology, 70,* 1218–1230.

Latané, B., Williams, K., & Harkins, S. (1979). Many hands make light the work: The causes and consequences of social loafing. *Journal of Personality and Social Psychology, 37,* 822–832.

Lau, S., & Gruen, G. E. (1992). The social stigma of loneliness: Effect of target person's and perceiver's sex. *Personality and Social Psychology Bulletin, 18,* 182–189.

Laurenceau, J.-P., Barrett, L. F., & Pietromonaco, P. R. (1998). Intimacy as an interpersonal process: The importance of self-disclosure, partner disclosure, and perceived partner responsiveness in interpersonal exchanges. *Journal of Personality and Social Psychology, 74,* 1238–1251.

Lazarus, R. S., Opton, E. M., Nomikos, M. S., & Rankin, N. O. (1985). The principle of short-circuiting of threat: Further evidence. *Journal of Personality, 33,* 622–635.

Leary, M. R. (1999). Making sense of self-esteem. *Current Directions in Psychological Science, 8,* 32–35.

Leary, M. R., Tambor, E. S., Terdal, S. K., & Downs, D. L. (1995). Self-esteem as an interpersonal monitor: The sociometer hypothesis. *Journal of Personality and Social Psychology, 68,* 518–530.

Leary, W. E. (1988, November 19). Novel methods unlock witnesses' memories. *New York Times,* pp. C1, C15.

LeBlanc, M. M., & Barling, J. (2004). Workplace aggression. *Current Directions in Psychological Science, 13,* 9–12.

Lee, A. Y. (2001). The mere exposure effect: An uncertainty reduction explanation revisited. *Personality and Social Psychology Bulletin, 27,* 1255–1266.

Lee, Y. T., & Seligman, M. E. P. (1997). Are Americans more optimistic than the Chinese? *Personality and Social Psychology Bulletin, 23,* 32–40.

Lehman, T. C., Daubman, K. A., Guarna, J., Jordan, J., & Cirafesi, C. (1995, April). *Gender differences in the motivational consequences of receiving help.* Paper presented at the meeting of the Eastern Psychological Association, Boston.

Leippe, M. R., & Eisenstadt, D. (1994). Generalization of dissonance reduction: Decreasing prejudice through induced compliance. *Journal of Personality and Social Psychology, 67,* 395–413.

Lemley, B. (2000, February). Isn't she lovely? *Discover,* 42–49.

Lemonick, M. D., & Dorfman, A. (2001, July 23). One giant step for mankind. *Time,* 54–61.

Levenson, R. W., Carstensen, L. L., & Gottman, J. M. (1994). The influence of age and gender on affect, physiology, and their interrelations: A study of long-term marriages. *Journal of Personality and Social Psychology, 67,* 56–68.

Leventhal, G. S., Karuza, J., & Fry, W. R. (1980). Beyond fairness: A theory of allocation preferences. In G. Mikula (Ed.), *Justice and social interaction* (pp. 167–218). New York: Springer-Verlag.

Levine, M., & Wallach, L. (2002). *Psychological problems, social issues, and the law.* Boston: Allyn & Bacon, Inc.

Levine, R. V., Martinez, T. S., Brase, G., & Sorenson, K. (1994). Helping in 36 U.S. cities. *Journal of Personality and Social Psychology, 67,* 69–82.

Levy, B., & Langer, E. (1994). Aging free from negative stereotypes: Successful memory in China and among the American deaf. *Journal of Personality and Social Psychology, 66,* 989–997.

Levy, B. R., Slade, M. D., Kunkel, S. R., & Kasl, S. V. (2002). Longevity increased by positive self-perceptions of aging. *Journal of Personality and Social Psychology, 83,* 261–270.

Levy, K. N., & Kelly, K. (2002; July/August). Sex differences in jealousy: Evolutionary style or attachment style? *American Psychological Society,* 25–49.

Lewin, T. (2002, September 29). More in high school are virgins, study finds. *New York Times,* 34.

Lewis, M. (1992). Will the real self or selves please stand up? *Psychological Inquiry, 3,* 123–124.

Leyens, J.-P., Desert, M., Croizet, J.-C., & Darcis, C. (2000). Stereotype threat: Are lower status and history of stigmatization preconditions of stereotype threat? *Personality and Social Psychology Bulletin, 26,* 1189–1199.

Li, N. P., Bailey, J. M., Kenrick, D. T., & Linsenmeier, J. A. W. (2002). The necessities and luxuries of male preferences: Testing the tradeoffs. *Journal of Personality and Social Psychology, 82,* 947–955.

Liberman, A., & Chaiken, S. (1992). Defensive processing of personally relevant health messages. *Personality and Social Psychology Bulletin, 18,* 669–679.

Liberman, N., Idson, L. C., Camacho, C. J., Higgins, E. G. (1999). Promotion and prevention choices between stability and change. *Journal of Personality and Social Psychology, 77,* 1135–1145.

Lickel, B., Hamilton, D. L., & Sherman, S. J. (2001). Elements of a lay theory of groups: Types of groups, relational styles, and the perception of group entitativity. *Personality and Social Psychology Review, 5,* 129–140.

Lickel, B., Hamilton, D. L., Wieczorkowski, G., Lewis, A., Sherman, S. J., & Uhles, A. N. (2000). Varieties of groups and the perception of group entiativity. *Journal of Personality and Social Psychology, 78,* 223–246.

Liden, R. C., & Mitchell, T. R. (1988). Ingratiatory behaviors in organizational settings. *Academy of Management Review, 13,* 572–587.

Lieberman, J. D., & Greenberg, J. (1999). Cognitive-experiential self-theory and displaced aggression. *Journal of Personality and Social Psychology,* in press.

Lin, M.-C., & Haywood, J. (2003). Accommodation predictors of grandparent-grandchild relational solidarity in Taiwan. *Journal of Social and Personal Relationships, 20,* 537–563.

Linden, E. (1992). Chimpanzees with a difference: Bonobos. *National Geographic, 18*(3), 46–53.

Lindsay, D. S., Hagen, L., Read, J. D., Wade, K. A., & Garry, M. (2004). True photographs and false memories. *Psychological Science, 15,* 149–154.

Lindsey, E. W., Mize, J., & Pettit, G. S. (1997). Mutuality in parent–child play: Consequences for children's peer competence. *Journal of Social and Personal Relationships, 14,* 523–538.

Linville, P. W. (1987). Self-complexity as a cognitive buffer against stress-related illness and depression. *Journal of Personality and Social Psychology, 52,* 663–676.

Linville, P. W., Fischer, G. W., & Salovey, P. (1989). Perceived distributions of the characteristics of in-group and out-group members: Empirical evidence and a computer simulation. *Journal of Personality and Social Psychology, 57,* 165–188.

Linz, D., & Penrod, S. (1992). Exploring the first and sixth amendments: Pretrial publicity and jury decision making. In D. K. Kagehiro & W. S. Laufer (Eds.), *Handbook of psychology and law.* New York: Springer-Verlag.

Linz, D., Donnerstein, E., & Penrod, S. (1988). Effects of long-term exposure to violent and sexually degrading depictions of women. *Journal of Personality and Social Psychology, 55,* 758–768.

Linz, D., Fuson, I. A., & Donnerstein, E. (1990). Mitigating the negative effects of sexually violent mass communications through pre-exposure briefings. *Communication Research, 17,* 641–674.

Lipkus, I. M., Green, J. D., Feaganes, J. R., & Sedikides, C. (2001). The relationships between attitudinal ambivalence and desire to quite smoking among college smokers. *Journal of Applied Social Psychology, 31,* 113–133.

Lippa, R., & Donaldson, S. I. (1990). Self-monitoring and idiographic measures of behavioral variability across interpersonal relationships. *Journal of Personality, 58,* 465–479.

Locke, E. A. (1991). *The essence of leadership.* New York: Lexington Books.

Locke, V., & Johnston, L. (2001). Stereotyping and prejudice: A social cognitive approach. In M. Augoustinos & K. J. Reynolds (Eds.), *Understanding prejudice, racism, and social conflict* (pp. 107–125). London: Sage.

Locke, V., & Walker, I. (1999). Stereotyping, processing goals, and social identity: Inveterate and fugacious characteristics of stereotypes. In D. Abrams & M. A. Hogg (Eds.), *Social identity and social cognition* (pp. 164–182). Oxford: Blackwell.

Lockwood, P., & Kunda, Z. (1999). Increasing the salience of one's best selves can undermine inspiration by outstanding role models. *Journal of Personality and Social Psychology, 76,* 214–228.

Loehlin, J. C. (1992). *Genes and environment in personality development.* Newbury Park, CA: Sage.

Loftus, E. F. (1992a). *Witness for the defense.* New York: St. Martin's Press.

Loftus, E. F. (1992b). When a lie becomes memory's truth: Memory distortion after exposure to misinformation. *Current Directions in Psychological Science, 1,* 121–123.

Loftus, E. F. (2003). Make-believe memories. *American Psychologist, 58,* 867–873.

Long, C. R., Seburn, M., Averill, J. R., & More, T. A. (2003). Solitude experiences: Varieties, settings, and individual differences. *Personality and Social Psychology Bulletin, 29,* 578–583.

Lopez, F. G., Gover, M. R., Leskela, J., Sauer, E. M., Schirmer, L., & Wyssmann, J. (1997). Attachment styles, shame, guilt, and collaborative problem-solving orientations. *Personal Relationships, 4,* 187–199.

Lord, C. G., & Saenz, D. S. (1985). Memory deficits and memory surfeits: Differential cognitive consequences of tokenism for tokens and observers. *Journal of Personality and Social Psychology, 49,* 918–926.

Lorenz, K. (1966). *On aggression.* New York: Harcourt, Brace, & World.

Lorenz, K. (1974). *Civilized man's eight deadly sins.* New York: Harcourt, Brace, Jovanovich.

Losch, M., & Cacioppo, J. (1990). Cognitive dissonance may enhance sympathetic tonis, but attitudes are changed to reduce negative affect rather than arousal. *Journal of Experimental Social Psychology, 26,* 289–304.

Luczak, S. E. (2001). Binge drinking in Chinese, Korean, and White college students: Genetic and ethnic group differences. *Psychology of Addictive Behaviors, 15,* 306–309.

Lundberg, J. K., & Sheehan, E. P. (1994). The effects of glasses and weight on perceptions of attractiveness and intelligence. *Journal of Social Behavior and Personality, 9,* 753–760.

Lyness, K. S., & Thompson, D. E. (1997). Above the glass ceiling? A comparison of matched samples of female and male executives. *Journal of Applied Psychology, 82,* 359–375.

Lyness, K. S., & Thompson, D. E. (2000). Climbing the corporate ladder: Do female and male executives follow the same route? *Journal of Applied Psychology, 85,* 86–101.

Ma, H. K., Shek, D. T. L., Cheung, P. C., & Tam, K. K. (2002). A longitudinal study of peer and teacher influences on prosocial and antisocial behavior of Hong Kong Chinese adolescents. *Social Behavior and Personality, 30,* 157–168.

Maass, A., & Clark, R. D. III (1984). Hidden impact of minorities: Fifteen years of minority influence research. *Psychological Bulletin, 95,* 233–243.

Macaulay, J. (1970). A shill for charity. In J. Macaulay & L. Berkowitz (Eds.), *Altruism and helping behavior* (pp. 43–59). New York: Academic Press.

MacCoun, R. J., & Kerr, N. L. (1988). Asymmetric influence in mock jury deliberation: Jurors' bias for leniency. *Journal of Personality and Social Psychology, 54,* 21–33.

Mack, D., & Rainey, D. (1990). Female applicants' grooming and personnel selection. *Journal of Social Behavior and Personality, 5,* 399–407.

Mackie, D. M., & Smith, E. R. (2002). Beyond prejudice: Moving from positive and negative evaluations to differentiated reactions to social groups. In D. M. Mackie & E. R. Smith (Eds.), *From prejudice to intergroup emotions: Differentiated reactions to social groups* (pp. 1–12). New York: Psychology Press.

Mackie, D. M., & Worth, L. T. (1989). Cognitive deficits and the mediation of positive affect in persuasion. *Journal of Personality and Social Psychology, 57,* 27–40.

Macrae, C. N., & Milne, A. B. (1992). A curry for your thoughts: Empathic effects on counterfactual thinking. *Personality and Social Psychology Bulletin, 18,* 625–630.

Macrae, C. N., Milne, A. B., & Bodenhausen, G. V. (1994). Stereotypes as energy-saving devices: A peek inside the cognitive toolbox. *Journal of Personality and Social Psychology, 66,* 37–47.

Macrae, C. N., Mitchell, J. P., & Pendry, L. F. (2002). What's in a forename? Cue familiarity and stereotypical thinking. *Journal of Experimental Social Psychology, 38,* 186–193.

Macrae, C. N., Bodenhausen, G. V., Milne, A. B., & Ford, R. (1997). On the regulation of recollection: The intentional forgetting of stereotypical memories. *Journal of Personality and Social Psychology, 72,* 709–719.

Maeda, E., & Ritchie, L. D. (2003). The concept of *shinyuu* in Japan: A replication of and comparison to Cole and Bradac's study on U.S. friendship. *Journal of Social and Personal Relationships, 20,* 579–598.

Maestripieri, D. (2001). Biological bases of maternal attachment. *Current Directions in Psychological Science, 10,* 79–82.

Magner, N. R., Johnson, G. G., Sobery, J. S., & Welker, R. B. (2000). Enhancing procedural justice in local government budget and tax decision making. *Journal of Applied Social Psychology, 30,* 798–815.

Maheswaran, D., & Chaiken, S. (1991). Promoting systematic processing in low-motivation settings: Effect of incongruent information on processing and judgment. *Journal of Personality and Social Psychology, 61,* 13–25.

Mahoney, S. (2003, November & December). Seeking love. *AARP Magazine,* 66–67.

Maio, G. R., Esses, V. M., & Bell, D. W. (1994). The formation of attitudes toward new immigrant groups. *Journal of Applied Social Psychology, 24,* 1762–1776.

Maio, G. R., Fincham, F. D., & Lycett, E. J. (2000). Attitudinal ambivalence toward parents and attachment style. *Personality and Social Psychology Bulletin, 26,* 1451–1464.

Maisonneuve, J., Palmade, G., & Fourment, C. (1952). Selective choices and propinquity. *Sociometry, 15,* 135–140.

Major, B. (1994). From social inequality to personal entitlement: The role of social comparisons, legitimacy appraisals, and group membership. In M. P. Zanna (Ed.), *Advances in experimental social psychology* (Vol. 26, pp. 293–348). San Diego, CA: Academic Press.

Major, B., Kaiser, D. R., & McCoy, S. K. (2003). It's not my fault; When and why attributions to prejudice protect self-esteem. *Personality and Social Psychology Bulletin, 29,* 772–781.

Major, B., Barr, L., Zubek, J., & Babey, S. H. (1999). Gender and self-esteem: A meta-analysis. In W. B. Swann, J. H. Langlois, & L. A. Gilbert (Eds.), *Sexism and stereotypes in modern society* (pp. 223–253). Washington, DC: American Psychological Association.

Malamuth, N. M., & Brown, L. M. (1994). Sexually aggressive men's perceptions of women's communications: testing three explanations. *Journal of Personality and Social Psychology 67,* 699–712.

Malamuth, N. M., & Check, J. V. P. (1985). The effects of aggressive pornography on beliefs in rape myths: Individual differences. *Journal of Research in Personality, 19,* 299–320.

Malone, B. E., & DePaulo, B. M. (2003). Measuring sensitivity to deception. In J. A. Hall & F. J. Bernieri (Eds.), *Interpersonal sensitivity: Theory and measurement* (pp. 103–124). Mahwah, NJ: Lawrence Erlbaum.

Maner, J. K., Luce, E. L., Neuberg, S. L., Ciaddini, R. B., Brown, S., & Sagarin, B. J. (2002). The effects of perspective taking on motivations for helping: Still no evidence for altruism. *Personality and Social Psychology Bulletin, 28,* 1601–1610.

Maner, J. K., Kenrick, D. T., Becker, D. V., Delton, A. W., Hofer, B., Wilbur, C. J., & Neuberg, S. L. (2003). Sexually selective cognition: Beauty captures the mind of the beholder. *Journal of Personality and Social Psychology, 85,* 1107–1120.

Manning, J. T., Koukourakis, K., & Brodie, D. A. (1997). Fluctuating asymmetry, metabolic rate and sexual selection in human males. *Evolution and Human Behavior, 18,* 15–21.

Manstead, A. S. R. (2000). The role of moral norm in the attitude-behavior relation. In D. J. Terry & M. A. Hogg (Eds.), *Attitudes, behavior, and social context* (pp. 11–30). Mahwah, NJ: Erlbaum.

Marcus, D. K., & Miler, R. S. (2003). Sex differences in judgments of physical attractiveness: A social relations analysis. *Personality and Social Psychology Bulletin, 29,* 325–335.

Markey, P. M., Funder, D. C., & Ozer, D. J. (2003). Complementarity of interpersonal behaviors in dyadic interactions. *Personality and Social Psychology Bulletin, 29,* 1082–1090.

Markman, G. D., Balkin, D. B., & Baron R. A. (2002). Inventors and new venture formation: The effects of general self-efficacy and regretful thinking. *Entrepreneurship Theory & Practice, 27,* 149–165.

Markus, H., & Kitayama, S. (1991). Culture and the self: Implications for cognition, emotion, and motivation. *Psychological Review, 98,* 224–253.

Markus, H., & Nurius, P. (1986). Possible selves. *American Psychologist, 41,* 954–969.

Markus, H., & Oyserman, D. (1989). Gender and thought: The role of the self-concept. In M. Crawford & M. Gentry (Eds.), *Gender and thought: Psychological perspectives* (pp. 100–127). New York: Springer-Verlag.

Marques, J., & Paez, D. (1994). The 'black sheep effect': Social categorization, rejection of ingroup deviates, and perception of group variability. *European Review of Social Psychology, 5,* 37–68.

Marques, J., Paez, D., & Sera, A. F. (1997). Social sharing, emotional climate, and the transgenerational transmission of memories: The Portuguese Colonial war. In J. W. Pennebaker, D. Paez, & B. Rime (Eds.), *Collective memory and political events: Social psychological perspectives* (pp. 253–275). Mahwah, NJ: Erlbaum.

Martin, C. L., & Parker, S. (1995). Folk theories about sex and race differences. *Personality and Social Psychology Bulletin, 21,* 45–57.

Martin, L. L., & Clore, G. L. (Eds.). (2001). *Mood and social cognition: Contrasting theories.* Mahwah, NJ: Erlbaum.

Martin, R. (1997). "Girls don't talk about garages!": Perceptions of conversation in same- and cross-sex friendships. *Personal Relationships, 4,* 115–130.

Martz, J. M., Verette, J., Arriaga, X. B., Slovik, L. F., Cox, C. L., & Rusbult, C. E. (1998). Positive illusion in close relationships. *Personal Relationships, 5,* 159–181.

Maslach, C., Santee, R. T., & Wade, C. (1987). Individuation, gender role, and dissent: Personality mediators of situational forces. *Journal of Personality and Social Psychology, 53,* 1088–1094.

Mastekaasa, A. (1995). Age variation in the suicide rates and self-reported subjective well-being of married and never married persons. *Journal of Community and Applied Social Psychology, 5,* 21–39.

Maticka-Tyndale, E., Herold, E. S., & Oppermann, M. (2003). Casual sex among Australian schoolies. *Journal of Sex Research, 40,* 158–169.

Matsushima, R., & Shiomi, K. (2002). Self-disclosure and friendship in junior high school students. *Social Behavior and Personality, 30,* 515–526.

May, J. L., & Hamilton, P. A. (1980). Effects of musically evoked affect on women's interpersonal attraction and perceptual judgments of physical attractiveness of men. *Motivation and Emotion, 4,* 217–228.

Mayer, J. D., & Hanson, E. (1995). Mood-congruent judgment over time. *Personality and Social Psychology Bulletin, 21,* 237–244.

Mayo, C., & Henley, N. M. (Eds.). (1981). *Gender and nonverbal behavior.* Seacaucaus, NJ: Springer-Verlag.

Mazzella, R., & Feingold, A. (1994). The effects of physical attractiveness, race, socioeconomic status, and gender of defendants and victims on judgments of mock jurors: A meta-analysis. *Journal of Applied Social Psychology, 24,* 1315–1344.

Mazzoni, G., & Memon, A. (2003). Imagination can create false autobiographical memories. *Psychological Science, 14,* 186–188.

Mazzoni, G. A. L., Loftus, E. F., Seitz, A., & Lynn, S. J. (1999). Changing beliefs and memories through dream interpretation. *Applied Cognitive Psychology, 13,* 125–144.

McAdams, D. P., Diamond, A., Aubin, E. de S., & Mansfield, E. (1997). Stories of commitment: The psychosocial construction of generative lives. *Journal of Personality and Social Psychology, 72,* 678–694.

McAndrew, F. T. (2002). New evolutionary perspectives on altruism: Multilevel-selection and costly-signaling theories. *Current Directions in Psychological Science, 11,* 79–82.

McArthur, L. Z., & Friedman, S. A. (1980). Illusory correlation in impression formation: Variations in the shared distinctiveness effect as a function of the distinctive person's age, race, and sex. *Journal of Personality and Social Psychology, 39,* 615–624.

McCall, M. (1997). Physical attractiveness and access to alcohol: What is beautiful does not get carded. *Journal of Applied Social Psychology, 23,* 453–562.

McClure, J. (1998). Discounting causes of behavior: Are two reasons better than one? *Journal of Personality and Social Psychology, 74,* 7–20.

McConahay, J. B. (1986). Modern racism, ambivalence, and the Modern Racism Scale. In J. F. Dovidio & S. L. Gaertner (Eds.), *Prejudice, discrimination, and racism* (pp. 91–125). New York: Academic Press.

McConnell, A. R., Sherman, S. J., & Hamilton, D. L. (1994). Illusory correlation in the perception of groups: An extension of the distinctiveness-based account. *Journal of Personality and Social Psychology, 67,* 414–429.

McCullough, M. E., Fincham, F. D., & Tsang, J. A. (2003). Forgiveness, forbearance, and time: The temporal unfolding of transgression-related interpersonal motivations. *Journal of Personality and Social Psychology, 84,* 540–557.

McCullough, M. E., Bellah, C. G., Kilpatrick, S. D, & Johnson, S. L. (2001). Vengefulness: Relationships with forgiveness, rumination, well-being, and the Bit Five. *Personality and Social Psychology Bulletin, 27,* 601–610.

McCullough, M. E., Emmons, R. A., Kilpatrick S. D., & Mooney, C. N. (2003). Narcissists as "victims": The role of narcissism in the perception of transgressions. *Personality and Social Psychology Bulletin, 29,* 885–893.

McDonald, F. (2001). *States' rights and the union: Imperium in imperio, 1776–1876.* Lawrence: University of Kansas Press.

McDonald, H. E., & Hirt, E. R. (1997). When expectancy meets desire: Motivational effects in reconstructive memory. *Journal of Personality and Social Psychology, 72,* 5–23.

McDonald, R. D. (1962). *The effect of reward–punishment and affiliation need on interpersonal attraction.* Unpublished doctoral dissertation, University of Texas.

McEwen, B. S. (1998). Protective and dangerous effects of stress mediators. *New England Journal of Medicine, 338,* 171–179.

McGarty, C., Haslam, S. A., Hutchinson, K. J., & Turner, J. C. (1994). The effects of salient group memberships on persuasion. *Small Group Research, 25,* 267–293.

McGonagle, K. A., Kessler, R. C., & Schilling, E. A. (1992). The frequency and determinants of marital disagreements in a community sample. *Journal of Social and Personal Relationships, 9,* 507–524.

McGuire, S., & Clifford, J. (2000). Genetic and environmental contributions to loneliness in children. *Psychological Science, 11,* 487–491.

McGuire, S., McHale, S. M., & Updegraff, K. A. (1996). Children's perceptions of the sibling relationship in middle childhood: Connections within and between family relationships. *Personal Relationships, 3,* 229–239.

McGuire, W. J. (1961). Resistance to persuasion confirmed by active and passive prior refutation of the same and alternate counterarguments. *Journal of Abnormal and Social Psychology, 63,* 326–332.

McGuire, W. J., & McGuire, C. V. (1996). Enhancing self-esteem by directed-thinking tasks: Cognitive and affective positivity asymmetries. *Journal of Personality and Social Psychology, 70,* 1117–1125.

McGuire, W. J., & Papageorgis, D. (1961). The relative efficacy of various types of prior belief-defense in producing immunity against persuasion. *Journal of Abnormal and Social Psychology, 62,* 327–337.

McHoskey, J. W. (1999). Machiavellianism, intrinsic versus extrinsic goals, and social interest: A self-determination theory analysis. *Motivation and Emotion, 23,* 267–283.

McKelvie, S. J. (1993a). Perceived cuteness, activity level, and gender in schematic babyfaces. *Journal of Social Behavior and Personality, 8,* 297–310.

McKelvie, S. J. (1993b). Stereotyping in perception of attractiveness, age, and gender in schematic faces. *Social Behavior and Personality, 21,* 121–128.

McLaughlin, L. (2001a, April 30). Happy together. *Time,* 82.

McNulty, J. K., & Karney, B. R. (2004). Positive expectations in the early years of marriage: Should couples expect the best or brace for the worst? *Journal of Personality and Social Psychology, 86,* 729–743.

Mead, G. H. (1934). *Mind, self, and society.* Chicago: University of Chicago Press.

Medvec, V. H., & Savitsky, K. (1997). When doing better means feeling worse: The effects of categorical cutoff points on counterfactual thinking and satisfaction. *Journal of Personality and Social Psychology, 72,* 1284–1296.

Medvec, V. H., Madey, S. F., & Gilovich, T. (1995). When less is more: Counterfactual thinking and satisfaction among

Olympic athletes. *Journal of Personality and Social Psychology, 69,* 603–610.

Mehrabian, A., & Piercy, M. (1993). Affective and personality characteristics inferred from length of first names. *Personality and Social Psychology Bulletin, 19,* 755–758.

Meier, B. P., Robinson, M. D., & Clore, G. L. (2004). Why good guys wear white. Automatic interferences about stimulus valence based on brightness. *Psychological Science, 15,* 82–87.

Melamed, S., Ben-Avi, I., Luz, J., & Green, M. S. (1995). Objective and subjective work monotony: Effects on job satisfaction, psychological distress, and absenteeism in blue-collar workers. *Journal of Applied Psychology, 80,* 29–42.

Meleshko, K. G. A., & Alden, L. E. (1993). Anxiety and self-disclosure: Toward a motivational model. *Journal of Personality and Social Psychology, 64,* 1000–1009. Miller, D. T., & Ross, M. (1975). Self-serving biases in attribution of causality: Fact or fiction? *Psychological Bulletin, 82,* 313–325.

Mendoza-Denton, R., Ayduk, O., Mischel, W., Shoda, Y., & Testa, A. (2001). Person X situation interactionism in self-encoding (*I am . . . When . . .*): Implications for affect regulation and social information processing. *Journal of Personality and Social Psychology, 80,* 533–544.

Menesini, E. (1997). Behavioural correlates of friendship status among Italian schoolchildren. *Journal of Social and Personal Relationships, 14,* 109–121.

Meyers, S. A., & Berscheid, E. (1997). The language of love: The difference a preposition makes. *Personality and Social Psychology Bulletin, 23,* 347–362.

Miall, D., & Dissanayake, E. (2004). The poetics of babytalk. *Human Nature, 14,* 337–364.

Miceli, M. P., & Lane, M. C. (1991). Antecedents of pay satisfaction: A review and extension. In K. Rowland & O. R. Ferris (Eds.), *Research in personnel and human resources management* (Vol. 9, pp. 235–309). Greenwich, CT: JAI Press.

Michael, R. T., Gagnon, J. H., Laumann, E. O., & Kolata, G. (1994). *Sex in America: A definitive survey.* Boston: Little, Brown.

Mikulincer, M. (1998a). Adult attachment style and individual differences in functional versus dysfunctional experiences of anger. *Journal of Personality and Social Psychology, 74,* 513–524.

Mikulincer, M., Gillath, O., Halevy, V., Avihou, N., Avidan, S., & Eshkoli, N. (2001). Attachment theory and reactions to others' needs: Evidence that activation of the sense of attachment security promotes empathic responses. *Journal of Personality and Social Psychology, 81,* 1205–1224.

Milanese, M. (2002, May/June). Hooking up, hanging out, making up, moving on. *Stanford,* 62–65.

Miles, S. M., & Carey, G. (1997). Genetic and environmental architecture of human aggression. *Journal of Personality and Social Psychology, 72,* 207–217.

Milgram, S. (1963). Behavior study of obedience. *Journal of Abnormal and Social Psychology, 67,* 371–378.

Milgram, S. (1965a). Liberating effects of group pressure. *Journal of Personality and Social Psychology, 1,* 127–134.

Milgram, S. (1965b). Some conditions of obedience and disobedience to authority. *Human Relations, 18,* 57–76.

Milgram, S. (1974). *Obedience to authority.* New York: Harper.

Miller, D. A., Smith, E. R., & Mackie, D. M. (2004). Effects of intergroup contact and political predispositions on prejudice: Role of intergroup emotions. *Group Processes and Intergroup Relations, 7,* 221–237.

Miller, D. T., & Prentice, D. A. (1996). The construction of social norms and standards. In E. T. Higgins & A. W. Kruglanski (Eds.), *Social psychology: Handbook of basic principles* (pp. 799–829). New York: Guilford Press.

Miller, D. T., Monin, B., & Prentice, D. A. (2000). Pluralistic ignorance and inconsistency between private attitudes and public behaviors. In D. J. Terry & M. A. Hogg (Eds.), *Attitudes, behavior, and social context* (pp. 95–113). Mahwah, NJ: Erlbaum.

Miller, L. C., Putcha-Bhagavatula, A., & Pedersen, W. C. (2002, June). Men's and women's mating preferences: Distinct evolutionary mechanisms? *Current Directions in Psychological Science, 11,* 88–93.

Miller, N., Maruayama, G., Beaber, R. J., & Valone, K. (1976). Speed of speech and persuasion. *Journal of Personality and Social Psychology, 34,* 615–624.

Miller, P. (2004, April 8). Prosecute ministers for same-sex weddings. Albany *Times Union,* A16.

Miller, P. A., & Jansen-op-de-Haar, M. A. (1997). Emotional, cognitive, behavioral, and temperament characteristics of high empathy children. *Motivation and Emotion, 21,* 109–125.

Miller, P. J. E., & Rempel, J. K. (2004). Trust and partner-enhancing attributions in close relationships. *Personality and Social Psychology Bulletin, 30,* 695–705.

Mills, J., Clark, M. S., Ford, T. E., & Johnson, M. (2004). Measurement of communal strength. *Personal Relationships, 11,* 213–230.

MIT-report: A study on the status of women faculty in science at MIT. (1999). Cambridge, MA: Massachusetts Institute of Technology.

Monahan, J. L., Murphy, S. T., & Zajonc, R. B. (2000). Subliminal mere exposure: Specific, general, and diffuse effects. *Psychological Science, 11,* 462–466.

Mondloch, C. J., Lewis, T. L., Budreau, D. R., Maurer, D., Dannemiller, J. L., Stephens, B. R., & Kleiner-Gathercoal, K. A. (1999). Face perception during early infancy. *Psychological Science, 10,* 419–422.

Monin, B. (2003). The warm glow heuristic: When liking leads to familiarity. *Journal of Personality and Social Psychology, 85,* 1035–1048.

Monteith, M. J., & Spicer, C. V. (2000). Contents and correlates of Whites' and Blacks' racial attitudes. *Journal of Experimental Social Psychology, 36,* 125–154.

Monteith, M. J., Devine, P. G., & Zuwerink, J. R. (1993). Self-directed versus other-directed affect as a consequence of prejudice-related discrepancies. *Journal of Personality and Social Psychology, 64,* 198–210.

Montepare, J. M., & Zebrowitz-McArthur, L. (1988). Impressions of people created by age-related qualities of their gates. *Journal of Personality and Social Psychology, 55,* 547–556.

Montgomery, R. (2004, February 20). Trip down aisle a road less traveled. Knight Ridder. Albany *Times Union,* pp. A1, A6.

Montoya, R. M., & Horton, R. S. (2004). On the importance of cognitive evaluation as a determinant of interpersonal attraction. *Journal of Personality and Social Psychology, 86,* 696–712.

Moore, T. (1993, August 16). Millions of volunteers counter image of a selfish society. *Albany Times Union,* p. A-2.

Moran, G. (1993, February 23). Personal communication.

Moran, G., & Cutler, B. L. (1991). The prejudicial impact of pretrial publicity. *Journal of Applied Social Psychology, 21,* 345–367.

Moreland, R. L., & Beach, S. R. (1992). Exposure effects in the classroom: The development of affinity among students. *Journal of Experimental Social Psychology, 28,* 255–276.

Morey, N., & Gerber, G. L. (1995). Two types of competitiveness: Their impact on the perceived interpersonal attractiveness of women and men. *Journal of Applied Social Psychology, 25,* 210–222.

Morgan, D., Carder, P., & Neal, M. (1997). Are some relationships more useful than others? The value of similar others in the networks of recent widows. *Journal of Social and Personal Relationships, 14,* 745–759.

Morris, M. W., & Larrick, R. P. (1995). When one cause casts doubt on another: A normative analysis of discounting in causal attribution. *Psychological Review, 102,* 331–335.

Morris, M. W., & Pang, K. (1994). Culture and cause: American and Chinese attributions for social and physical events. *Journal of Personality and Social Psychology, 67,* 949–971.

Morrison, E. W. (1994). Role definitions and organizational citizenship behavior: The importance of employees' perspective. *Academy of Management Journal, 37,* 1543–1567.

Morrison, E. W., & Bies, R. J. (1991). Impression management in the feedback-seeking process: A literature review and research agenda. *Academy of Management Review, 16,* 322–341.

Moscovici, S. (1985). Social influence and conformity. In G. Lindzey & E. Aronson (Eds.), *Handbook of social psychology* (3rd ed.). New York: Random House.

Muczyk, J. P., & Reimann, B. C. (1987). The case for directive leadership. *Academy of Management Review, 12,* 637–647.

Mugny, G. (1975). Negotiations, image of the other and the process of minority influence. *European Journal of Social Psychology, 5,* 209–229.

Mullen, B. (1986). Stuttering, audience size, and the other-total ratio: A self-attention perspective. *Journal of Applied Social Psychology, 16,* 141–151.

Mullen, B., Migdal, M. J., & Rozell, D. (2003). Self-awareness, deindividuation, and social identity: Unraveling theoretical paradoxes by filling empirical lacunae. *Personality and Social Psychology Bulletin, 29,* 1071–1081.

Mummendey, A., & Schreiber, H. J. (1984). 'Different' just means 'better': Some obvious and some hidden pathways to ingroup favoritism. *British Journal of Social Psychology, 23,* 363–368.

Munro, G. D., & Ditto, P. H. (1997). Biased assimilation, attitude polarization, and affect in reactions to stereotype-relevant scientific information. *Personality and Social Psychology Bulletin, 23,* 636–653.

Munsterberg, H. (1907). *On the witness stand: Essays in psychology and crime.* New York: McClure.

Murray, L., & Trevarthen, C. (1986). The infant's role in mother-infant communications. *Journal of Child Language, 13,* 15–29.

Murray, S. L., & Holmes, J. G. (1997). A leap of faith? Positive illusions in romantic relationships. *Personality and Social Psychology Bulletin, 23,* 586–604.

Murray, S. L., & Holmes, J. G. (1999). The (mental) ties that bind: Cognitive structures that predict relationship resilience. *Journal of Personality and Social Psychology, 77,* 1228–1244.

Murray, S. L., Holmes, J. G., Griffin, D. W., Bellavia, G., & Rose, P. (2001). The mismeasure of love: How self-doubt contaminates relationship beliefs. *Personality and Social Psychology Bulletin, 27,* 423–436.

Mussweiler, T., Gabriel, S., & Bodenhausen, G. V. (2000). Shifting social identities as a strategy for deflecting threatening social comparisons. *Journal of Personality and Social Psychology, 79,* 398–409.

Mynard, H., & Joseph, S. (1997). Bully victim problems and their association with Eysenck's personality dimensions in 8 to 13 year olds. *British Journal of Educational Psychology, 67,* 51–54.

Nadler, A. (1991). Help-seeking behavior: Psychological costs and instrumental benefits. In M. S. Clark (Ed.), *Prosocial behavior* (pp. 290–311). Newbury Park, CA: Sage.

Nadler, A., Fisher, J. D., & Itzhak, S. B. (1983). With a little help from my friend: Effect of a single or multiple acts of aid as a function of donor and task characteristics. *Journal of Personality and Social Psychology, 44,* 310–321.

Narby, D. J., Cutler, B. L., & Moran, G. (1993). A meta-analysis of the association between authoritarianism and jurors' perceptions of defendant culpability. *Journal of Applied Psychology, 78,* 34–42.

National Institute for Occupational Safety and Health, Center for Disease Control and Prevention. "Homicide in the workplace." Document #705003, December 5, 1993.

Nemeth, C. J. (1995). Dissent as driving cognition, attitudes, and judgments. *Social Cognition, 13,* 273–291.

Nemeth, C. J., Connell, J. B., Rogers, J. D., & Brown, K. S. (2001). Improving decision making by means of dissent. *Journal of Applied Social Psychology, 31,* 45–58.

Neto, F., & Barrios, J. (2000). Predictors of loneliness among adolescents from Portuguese immigrant families in Switzerland. *Social Behavior and Personality, 28,* 193–206.

Neuberg, S. L., & Cottrell, C. A. (2002). Intergroup emotions: A biocultural approach. In D. M. Mackie & E. R. Smith (Eds.), *From prejudice to intergroup emotions: Differentiated reactions to social groups* (pp. 265–283). Philadelphia: Psychology Press.

Neuberg, S. L., & Newsom, J. T. (1993). Personal need for structure: Individual differences in the desire for simple structure. *Journal of Personality and Social Psychology, 65,* 113–131.

Neuman, J. H., & Baron, R. A. (1998). Workplace violence and workplace aggression: Evidence concerning specific forms, potential causes, and preferred targets. *Journal of Management, 24,* 391–420.

Neuman, J. H., & Baron, R. A. (2004). Aggression in the workplace: A social-psychological perspective. In S. Fox, & P. E. Spector (Eds.), *Counterproductive workplace behavior: An integration of both actor and recipient perspectives on causes and consequences.* Washington, DC: American Psychological Association.

Neumann, R., & Strack, F. (2000). "Mood contagion": The automatic transfer of mood between persons. *Journal of Personality and Social Psychology, 79,* 211–223.

Neumann, R., Hulsenbeck, K., & Seibt, B. (2003). Attitudes toward people with AIDS and avoidance behavior: Automatic and reflective bases of behavior. *Journal of Experimental Social Psychology, 40,* 543–550.

Newby-Clark, I. R., & Ross, M. (2003). Conceiving the past and future. *Personality and Social Psychology Bulletin, 29,* 807–818.

Newcomb, T. M. (1956). The prediction of interpersonal attraction. *Psychological Review, 60,* 393–404.

Newcomb, T. M. (1961). *The acquaintance process.* New York: Holt, Rinehart and Winston.

Newman, M. L., Pennebaker, H. W., Berry, D. S., & Richards, J. M. (2003). Lying words: Predicting deception from linguistic styles. *Personality and Social Psychology Bulletin, 29,* 665–675.

Newsom, J. T. (1999). Another side to caregiving: Negative reactions to being helped. *Current Directions in Psychological Science, 8,* 183–187.

Newsweek Poll (May 24, 2004). The "Will and Grace" effect.

Newton, T. L., Kiecolt-Glaser, J. K., Glaser, R., & Malarkey, W. B. (1995). Conflict and withdrawal during marital interaction: The roles of hostility and defensiveness. *Personality and Social Psychology Bulletin, 21,* 512–524.

Neyer, F. J. (2002). Twin relationships in old age: A developmental perspective. *Journal of Social and Personal Relationships, 19,* 155–177.

Niaura, R., Todaro, J. F., Stroud, L., Spiro, A. III, Ward, K. D., & Weiss, S. (2002). Hostility, the metabolic syndrome, and incident coronary heart disease. *Health Psychology, 21*(6) 588–593.

Nida, S. A., & Koon, J. (1983). They get better looking at closing time around here, too. *Psychological Reports, 52,* 657–658.

Nienhuis, A. E., Manstead, A. S. R., & Spears, R. (2001). Multiple motives and persuasive communication: Creative elaboration as a result of impression motivation and accuracy motivation. *Personality and Social Psychology Bulletin, 27,* 118–132.

Nisbett, R. E. (1990). Evolutionary psychology, biology, and cultural evolution. *Motivation and Emotion, 14,* 255–264.

Nisbett, R. E., & Cohen, D. (1996). *Culture of honor: The psychology of violence in the South.* Boulder, CO: Westview Press.

Nisbett, R. E., & Wilson, T. D. (1977). Telling more than we can know: Verbal reports on mental processes. *Psychological Review, 84,* 231–259.

Noel, J. G., Wann, D. L., & Branscombe, N. R. (1995). Peripheral ingroup membership status and public negativity toward outgroups. *Journal of Personality and Social Psychology, 68,* 127–137.

Nolan, S. A., Flynn, C., & Garber, J. (2003). Prospective relations between rejection and depression in young adolescents. *Journal of Personality and Social Psychology, 85,* 745–755.

Nolen-Hoeksema, S. (1987). Sex differences in unipolar depression: Evidence and theory. *Psychological Bulletin, 101,* 259–282.

Nunn, J. S., & Thomas, S. L. (1999). The angry male and the passive female: The role of gender and self-esteem in anger expression. *Social Behavior and Personality, 27,* 145–154.

Nussbaum, S., Trope, Y., & Liberman, N. (2003). Creeping dispositionism: The temporal dynamics of behavior prediction. *Journal of Personality and Social Psychology 84,* 485–497.

Nyman, L. (1995). The identification of birth order personality attributes. *The Journal of Psychology, 129,* 51–59.

O'Brien, M., & Bahadur, M. A. (1998). Marital aggression, mother's problem-solving behavior with children, and children's emotional and behavioral problems. *Journal of Social and Clinical Psychology, 17,* 249–272.

O'Connell, P. D. (1988). Pretrial publicity, change of venue, public opinion polls: A theory of procedural justice. *University of Detroit Law Review, 65,* 169–197.

O'Connor, S. C., & Rosenblood, L. K. (1996). Affiliation motivation in everyday experience: A theoretical comparison. *Journal of Personality and Social Psychology, 70,* 513–522.

O'Donohue, W. (1997). *Sexual harassment: Theory, research, and treatment.* Boston: Allyn & Bacon.

O'Leary, S. G. (1995). Parental discipline mistakes. *Current Directions in Psychological Science, 4,* 11–13.

O'Moore, M. N. (2000). Critical issues for teacher training to counter bullying and victimization in Ireland. *Aggressive Behavior, 26,* 99–112.

O'Sullivan, C. S., & Durso, F. T. (1984). Effects of schema-incongruent information on memory for stereotypical attributes. *Journal of Personality and Social Psychology, 47,* 55–70.

O'Sullivan, M. (2003). The fundamental attribution error in detecting deception: The boy-who-cried-wolf effect. *Personality and Social Psychology Bulletin, 29,* 1316–1327.

Oakes, P. J., & Reynolds, K. J. (1997). Asking the accuracy question: Is measurement the answer? In R. Spears, P. J. Oakes, N. Ellemers, & S. A. Haslam (Eds.), *The social psychology of stereotyping and group life* (pp. 51–71). Oxford: Blackwell.

Oakes, P. J., Haslam, S. A., & Turner, J. C. (1994). *Stereotyping and social reality.* Oxford: Blackwell.

Oberlander, E. (2003, August). Cross-disciplinary perspectives on attachment processes. *American Psychological Society, 16,* 23, 35.

Oettingen, G. (1995). Explanatory style in the context of culture. In G. M. Buchanan & M. E. P. Seligman (Eds.), *Explanatory style.* Hillsdale, NJ: Erlbaum.

Oettingen, G., & Seligman, M. E. P. (1990). Pessimism and behavioral signs of depression in East versus West Berlin. *European Journal of Social Psychology, 201,* 207–220.

Ohbuchi, K., & Kambara, T. (1985). Attacker's intent and awareness of outcome, impression management, and retaliation. *Journal of Experimental Social Psychology, 21,* 321–330.

Ohbuchi, K., Kameda, M., & Agarie, N. (1989). Apology as aggression control: Its role in mediating appraisal of and response to harm. *Journal of Personality and Social Psychology, 56,* 219–227.

Ohman, A., Lundqvist, D., & Esteves, F. (2001). The face in the crowd revisited: Threat advantage with schematic stimuli. *Journal of Personality and Social Psychology, 80,* 381–396.

Ohtsubo, Y., Miller, C. E., Hayashi, N., & Masuchi, A. (2004). Effects of group decision rules on decisions involving continuous alternatives: the unanimity rule and extreme decisions in mock civil juries. *Journal of Experimental Social Psychology, 40,* 320–331.

Okun, M. A., & Sloane, E. S. (2002). Application of planned behavior theory to predicting volunteer enrollment by college students in a campus-based program. *Social Behavior and Personality, 30,* 243–250.

Olson, J. M., & Maio, G. R. (2003). Attitudes in social behavior. In T. Millon & M. J. Lerner (Eds.), *Handbook of psychology: Personality and social psychology* (Vol. 5., pp. 299–325). New York: Wiley.

Olson, M. A., & Fazio, R. H. (2001). Implicit attitude formation through classical conditioning. *Psychological Science, 12,* 413–417.

Olweus, D. (1993). *Bullying at school: What we know and what we can do.* Oxford: Blackwell.

Olweus, D. (1999). Sweden. In P. K. Smith, Y. Morita, J. Junger-Tas, D. Olweus, R. F. Catalano, & P. Slee (Eds.), *The nature of school bullying: A cross-national perspective* (pp. 7–27). New York: Routledge.

Omoto, A. M., & Snyder, M. (1995). Sustained helping without obligation: Motivation, longevity of service, and per-

ceived attitude change among AIDS volunteers. *Journal of Personality and Social Psychology, 68,* 671–686.

Onishi, M., Gjerde, P. F., & Block, J. (2001). Personality implications of romantic attachment patterns in young adults: A multi-method, multi-informant study. *Personality and Social Psychology Bulletin, 27,* 1097–1110.

Orbell, S., Blair, C., Sherlock, K., & Conner, M. (2001). The theory of planned behavior and ecstasy use: Roles for habit and perceived control over taking versus obtaining substances. *Journal of Applied Social Psychology, 31,* 31–47.

Organ, D. (1988). *Organizational citizenship behavior: The good-soldier syndrome.* Lexington, MA: Lexington Books.

Organ, D. W. (1997). Organizational citizenship behavior: It's construct clean-up time. *Human Performance, 10,* 85–98.

Orpen, C. (1996). The effects of ingratiation and self promotion tactics on employee career success. *Social Behavior and Personality, 24,* 213–214.

Osborne, J. W. (2001). Testing stereotype threat: Does anxiety explain race and sex differences in achievement? *Contemporary Educational Psychology, 26,* 291–310.

Österman, K., Björkqvist, K., Lagerspetz, K. M. J., Kaukiainen, A., Landua, S. F., Fraczek, A., & Caprara, G. V. (1998). Cross-cultural evidence of female indirect aggression. *Aggressive Behavior, 24,* 1–8.

Ottati, V. C., & Isbell, L. M. (1996). Effects of mood during exposure to target information on subsequently reported judgments: An on-line model of misattribution and correction. *Journal of Personality and Social Psychology, 71,* 39–53.

Owens, L., Shute, R., & Slee, P. (2000). "Guess what I just heard!": Indirect aggression among teenage girls in Australia. *Aggressive Behavior, 26,* 57–66.

Packer, G. (2004). Caught in the crossfire. *The New Yorker,* May 17, 63–68, 70–73.

Page, R. M. (1991). Loneliness as a risk factor in adolescent hopelessness. *Journal of Research in Personality, 25,* 189–195.

Paik, H., & Comstock, G. (1994). The effects of television violence on antisocial behavior: A meta-analysis. *Communication Research, 21,* 516–546.

Palmer, J., & Byrne, D. (1970). Attraction toward dominant and submissive strangers: Similarity versus complementarity. *Journal of Experimental Research in Personality, 4,* 108–115.

Paolini, S., Hewstone, M., Cairns, E., & Voci, A. (2004). Effects of direct and indirect cross-group friendships on judgments of Catholics and Protestants in Northern Ireland: The mediating role of an anxiety-reduction mechanism. *Personality and Social Psychology Bulletin, 30,* 770–786.

Park, J., & Banaji, M. R. (2000). Mood and heuristics: The influence of happy and sad states on sensitivity and bias in stereotyping. *Journal of Personality and Social Psychology, 78,* 1005–1023.

Patrick, H., Neighbors, C., & Knee, C. R. (2004). Appearance-related social comparisons: The role of contingent self-esteem and self-perceptions of attractiveness. *Personality and Social Psychology Bulletin, 30,* 501–514.

Paul, E. L., & Hayes, K. A. (2002). The casualties of "casual" sex: A qualitative exploration of the phenomenology of college students' hookups. *Journal of Social and Personal Relationships, 19,* 639–661.

Paulhus, D. L., Bruce, M. N., & Trapnell, P. D. (1995). Effects of self-presentation strategies on personality profiles and their structure. *Personality and Social Psychology Bulletin, 21,* 100–108.

Pavalko, E. K., Mossakowski, K. N., & Hamilton, V. J. (2003). Does perceived discrimination affect health? Longitudinal relationships between work discrimination and women's physical and emotional health. *Journal of Health and Social Behavior, 43,* 18–33.

Pearson, K., & Lee, A. (1903). On the laws of inheritance in man: I. Inheritance of physical characters. *Biometrika, 2,* 357–462.

Pedersen, D. M. (1994). Privacy preferences and classroom seat selection. *Social Behavior and Personality, 22,* 393–398.

Pederson, W. C., Gonzales, C., & Miller, N. (2000). The moderating effect of trivial triggering provocation on displaced aggression. *Journal of Personality and Social Psychology, 78,* 913–947.

Pelham, B. W., Mirenberg, M. C., & Jones, J. T. (2002). Why Susie sells seashells by the seashore: Implicit egotism and major life decisions. *Journal of Personality and Social Psychology, 82,* 469–487.

Pelham, B. W., Carvallo, M., DeHart, T., & Jones, T. J. (2003). Assessing the validity of implicit egotism: A reply to Gallucci (2003). *Journal of Personality and Social Psychology, 85,* 800–807.

Pennebaker, J. W., Dyer, M. A., Caulkins, R. S., Litowicz, D. L., Ackerman, P. L., & Anderson, D. B. (1979). Don't the girls all get prettier at closing time: A country and western application to psychology. *Personality and Social Psychology Bulletin, 5,* 122–125.

Penner, L. A., & Finkelstein, M. A. (1998). Dispositional and structural determinants of volunteerism. *Journal of Personality and Social Psychology, 74,* 525–537.

Pentony, J. F. (1995). The effect of negative campaigning on voting, semantic differential, and thought listing. *Journal of Social Behavior and Personality, 10,* 631–644.

People. (2001, August 6). *U.S. News & World Report,* 14.

Perls, T. T., & Silver, M. H. (1999). *Living to 100: Lessons in living to your maximum potential at any age.* New York: Basic Books.

Perrett, D. I., May, K. A., & Yoshikawa, S. (1994). Facial shape and judgements of female attractiveness. *Nature, 368,* 239–242.

Perrewe, P. L., & Hochwarter, W. A. (2001). Can we really have it all? The attainment of work and family values. *Current Directions in Psychological Science, 10,* 29–32.

Pessin, J. (1933). The comparative effects of social and mechanical stimulation on memorizing. *American Journal of Psychology, 45,* 263–270.

Peterson, R. S. (1997). A directive leadership style in group decision making can be both a virtue and vice: Evidence from elite and experimental groups. *Journal of Personality and Social Psychology, 72,* 1107–1121.

Peterson, R. S., & Behfar, K. J. (2003). The dynamic relationship between performance feedback, trust, and conflict in groups: A longitudinal study. *Organizational Behavior and Human Decision Processes, 92,* 102–112.

Peterson, V. S., & Runyan, A. S. (1993). *Global gender issues.* Boulder, CO: Westview Press.

Pettigrew, T. F. (1969). Racially separate or together? *Journal of Social Issues, 24,* 43–69.

Pettigrew, T. F. (1979). The ultimate attribution error: Extending Allport's cognitive analysis of prejudice. *Personality and Social Psychology Bulletin, 5,* 461–476.

Pettigrew, T. F. (1981). Extending the stereotype concept. In D. L. Hamilton (Ed.), *Cognitive processes in stereotyping and intergroup behavior* (pp. 303–331). Hillsdale, NJ: Erlbaum.

Pettigrew, T. F. (1997). Generalized intergroup contact effects on prejudice. *Personality and Social Psychology Bulletin, 23,* 173–185.

Pettigrew, T. F. (2004). Justice deferred: A half-century after Brown v. Board of Education. *American Psychologist, 59,* 1–9.

Pettijohn, T. E. F., II, & Jungeberg, B. J. (2004). Playboy playmate curves: Changes in facial and body feature preferences across social and economic conditions. *Personality and Social Psychology Bulletin, 30,* 1186–1197.

Petty, R. E., & Cacioppo, J. T. (1986). The elaboration likelihood model of persuasion. In L. Berkowitz (Ed.), *Advances in experimental social psychology* (Vol. 19, pp. 123–205). New York: Academic Press.

Petty, R. E., & Cacioppo, J. T. (1990). Involvement and persuasion: Tradition versus integration. *Psychological Bulletin, 107,* 367–374.

Petty, R. E., Wheeler, C., & Tormala, Z. L. (2003). Persuasion and attitude change. In T. Millon & M. J. Lerner (Eds.), *Handbook of psychology: Personality and social psychology* (Vol. 5, pp. 353–382). New York: Wiley.

Petty, R. J., & Krosnick, J. A. (Eds.). (1995). *Attitude strength: Antecedents and consequences* (Vol. 4). Hillsdale, NJ: Erlbaum.

Phelps, E. A., O'Connor, K. J., Gatenby, J. C., Gore, J. C., Grillon, C., & Davis, M. (2001). Activation of the left amygdala to a cognitive representation of fear. *Nature Neuroscience, 4,* 437–441.

Pickett, C. L., Gardner, W. L., & Knowles, M. (2004). Getting a cue: The need to belong and enhanced sensitivity to social cues. *Personality and Social Psychology Bulletin, 30,* 1095–1107.

Pierce, C. A., Byrne, D., & Aguinis, H. (1996). Attraction in organizations: A model of workplace romance. *Journal of Organizational Behavior, 17,* 5–32.

Pierce, C. A., Broberg, B. J., McClure, J. R., & Aguinis, H. (2004). Responding to sexual harassment complaints: Effects of a dissolved workplace romance on decision-making standards. *Organizational Behavior and Human Decision Processes, 95,* 66–82.

Pihl, R. O., Lau, M. L., & Assad, J. M. (1997). Aggressive disposition, alcohol, and aggression. *Aggressive Behavior, 23,* 11–18.

Piliavin, J. A., & Unger, R. K. (1985). *The helpful but helpless female: Myth or reality?* In V. E. O'Leary, R. K. Unger, & B. S. Wallston (Eds.), *Women, gender, and social psychology* (pp. 149–189). Hillsdale, NJ: Erlbaum.

Pines, A. (1997). Fatal attractions or wise unconscious choices: The relationship between causes for entering and breaking intimate relationships. *Personal Relationship Issues, 4,* 1–6.

Pinker, S. (1998). *How the mind works.* New York: Norton.

Pittman, T. S. (1993). Control motivation and attitude change. In G. Weary, F. Gleicher, & K. L. Marsh (Eds.), *Control motivation and social cognition* (pp. 157–175). New York: Springer-Verlag.

Pizarro, D., Uhlmann, E., & Salovey, P. (2003). Asymmetry in judgments of moral blame and praise: The role of perceived metadesires. *Psychological Science, 14,* 267–272.

Plant, E. A., & Devine, P. G. (1998). Internal and external motivation to respond without prejudice. *Journal of Personality and Social Psychology, 75,* 811–832.

Plant, E. A., Hyde, J. S., Keltner, D., & Devine, P. G. (2000). The gender stereotyping of emotions. *Psychology Women Quarterly, 24,* 81–92.

Pleban, R., & Tesser, A. (1981). The effects of relevance and quality of another's performance on interpersonal closeness. *Social Psychology Quarterly, 44,* 278–285.

Podsakoff, P. M., Mackenzie, S. B., & Hui, C. (1993). Organizational citizenship behaviors and managerial evaluations of employee performance: A review and suggestions for future research. In G. R. Ferris (Ed.), *Research in personnel and human resources management* (Vol. 11, pp. 1–40). Greenwich, CT: JAI Press.

Polivy, J., & Herman, C. P. (2000). The false-hope syndrome: Unfulfilled expectations of self-change. *Current Directions in Psychological Science, 9,* 128–131.

Pollak, K. I., & Niemann, Y. F. (1998). Black and white tokens in academia: A difference in chronic versus acute distinctiveness. *Journal of Applied Social Psychology, 28,* 954–972.

Pollock, C. L., Smith, S. D., Knowles, E. S., & Bruce, H. J. (1998). Mindfulness limits compliance with the that's-not-all technique. *Personality and Social Psychology Bulletin, 24,* 1153–1157.

Pontari, B. A., & Schlenker, B. R. (2000). The influence of cognitive load on self-presentation: Can cognitive busyness help as well as harm social performance? *Journal of Personality and Social Psychology, 78,* 1092–1108.

Ponzetti, J. J., Jr., & James, C. M. (1997). Loneliness and sibling relationships. *Journal of Social Behavior and Personality, 12,* 103–112.

Postmes, T., & Branscombe, N. R. (2002). Influence of long-term racial environmental composition on subjective well-being in African Americans. *Journal of Personality and Social Psychology, 83,* 735–751.

Postmes, T., & Spears, R. (1998). Deindividuation and antinormative behavior: A meta-analysis. *Psychological Bulletin, 123,* 238–259.

Powell, A. A., Branscombe, N. R., & Schmitt, M. T. (in press). Inequality as "ingroup privilege" or "outgroup disadvantage": The impact of group focus on collective guilt and interracial attitudes.

Pratto, F., & Bargh, J. A. (1991). Stereotyping based on apparently individuating information: Trait and global components of sex stereotypes under attentional overload. *Journal of Experimental Social Psychology, 27,* 26–47.

Prentice, D. A., & Miller, D. T. (1992). When small effects are impressive. *Psychological Bulletin, 112,* 160–164.

Previti, D., & Amato, P. R. (2004). Is infidelity a cause or a consequence of poor marital quality? *Journal of Social and Personal Relationships, 21,* 217–230.

Priester, J. R., & Petty, R. E. (2001). Extending the bases of subjective attitudinal ambivalence: Interpersonal and intrapersonal antecedents of evaluative tension. *Journal of Personality and Social Psychology, 80,* 19–34.

Pronin, E., Steele, C. M., & Ross, L. (2004). Identity bifurcation in response to stereotype threat: Women and mathematics. *Journal of Experimental Social Psychology, 40,* 152–168.

Pruitt, D. G., & Carnevale, P. J. (1993). *Negotiation in social conflict.* Pacific Grove, CA: Brooks/Cole.

Przybyla, D. P. J. (1985). *The facilitating effect of exposure to erotica on male prosocial behavior.* Unpublished doctoral dissertation, University at Albany, State University of New York.

Puente, S., & Cohen, D. (2003). Jealousy and the meaning (or nonmeaning) of violence. *Personality and Social Psychology Bulletin, 29,* 449–460.

Pullium, R. M. (1993). Reactions to AIDS patients as a function of attributions about controllability and promiscuity. *Social Behavior and Personality, 21,* 297–302.

Pyszczynski, T., & Greenberg, J. (1987). Toward an integration of cognitive and motivational perspectives on social inference: A biased hypothesis-testing model. *Advances in experimental social psychology, 20,* 297–341.

Pyszczynski, T., Greenberg, J., Solomon, S., Arndt, J., & Schimel, J. (2004). Why do people need self-esteem? A theoretical and empirical review. *Psychological Bulletin, 130,* 435–468.

Queller, S., & Smith, E. R. (2002). Subtyping versus bookkeeping in stereotype learning and change: Connectionist simulations and empirical findings. *Journal of Personality and Social Psychology, 82,* 300–313.

Quigley, B. M., Johnson, A. B., & Byrne, D. (1995, June). *Mock jury sentencing decisions: A meta-analysis of the attractiveness–leniency effect.* Paper presented at the meeting of the American Psychological Society, New York.

Quinn, J. M., & Wood, W. (2004). Forewarnings of influence appeals: Inducing resistance and acceptance. In E. S. Knowles & J. A. Linn (Eds.), *Resistance and persuasion* (pp. 193–213). Mahwah, NJ: Erlbaum.

Ray, G. E., Cohen, R., Secrist, M. E., & Duncan, M. K. (1997). Relating aggressive victimization behaviors to children's sociometric status and friendships. *Journal of Social and Personal Relationships, 14,* 95–108.

Read, S. J., & Miller, L. C. (1998). *Connectionist and PDP models of social reasoning and social behavior.* Mahwah, NJ: Erlbaum.

Redersdorff, S., Martinot, D., & Branscombe, N. R. (2004). The impact of thinking about group-based disadvantages or advantages on women's well-being: An experimental test of the rejection-identification model. *Current Psychology of Cognition, 22,* 203–222.

Regan, P. C. (1998). Of lust and love: Beliefs about the role of sexual desire in romantic relationships. *Personal Relationships, 5,* 139–157.

Regan, P. C. (2000). The role of sexual desire and sexual activity in dating relationships. *Social Behavior and Personality, 28,* 51–60.

Regan, P. C., Lyle, J. L., Otto, A. L., & Joshi, A. (2003). Pregnancy and changes in female sexual desire: A review. *Social Behavior and Personality, 31,* 603–612.

Reisman, J. M. (1984). Friendliness and its correlates. *Journal of Social and Clinical Psychology, 2,* 143–155.

Reiss, A. J., & Roth, J. A. (Eds.). (1993). *Understanding and preventing violence.* Washington, DC: National Academy Press.

Reno, R. R., Cialdini, R. B., & Kallgren, C. A. (1993). The transsituational influence of social norms. *Journal of Personality and Social Psychology, 64,* 104–112.

Rensberger, B. (1993, November 9). Certain chemistry between vole pairs. *Albany Times Union,* pp. C-1, C-3.

Rentsch, J. R., & Heffner, T. S. (1994). Assessing self-concept: Analysis of Gordon's coding scheme using "Who am I?" responses. *Journal of Social Behavior and Personality, 9,* 283–300.

Reskin, B., & Padavic, I. (1994). *Women and men at work.* Thousand Oaks, CA: Pine Forge Press.

Rhodes, G., & Tremewan, T. (1996). Averageness, exaggeration, and facial attractiveness. *Psychological Science, 7,* 105–110.

Rhodewalt, F., & Davison, J., Jr. (1983). Reactance and the coronary-prone behavior pattern: The role of self-attribution in response to reduced behavioral freedom. *Journal of Personality and Social Psychology, 44,* 220–228.

Richard, F. D., Bond, C. F., Jr., & Stokes-Zoota, J. J. (2001). "That's completely obvious . . . and important." Lay judgments of social psychological findings. *Personality and Social Psychology Bulletin, 27,* 497–505.

Richards, Z., & Hewstone, M. (2001). Subtyping and subgrouping: Processes for the prevention and promotion of stereotype change. *Personality and Social Psychology Review, 5,* 52–73.

Ridgeway, C. L. (2001). Social status and group structure. In M. A. Hogg & R. S. Tindale (Eds.), *Blackwell handbook of social psychology: Group processes* (pp. 352–375). Oxford: Blackwell.

Ridley, M., & Dawkins, R. (1981). The natural selection of altruism. In J. P. Rushton & R. M. Sorrentino (Eds.), *Altruism and helping behavior.* Hillsdale, NJ: Erlbaum.

Riess, M., & Schlenker, B. R. (1977). Attitude change and responsibility avoidance as modes of dilemma resolution in forced-compliance situations. *Journal of Personality and Social Psychology, 35,* 21–30.

Riggio, H. R. (2004). Parental marital conflict and divorce, parent-child relationships, social support, and relationship anxiety in young adulthood. *Personal Relationships, 11,* 99–114.

Rilling, J., Gutman, D., Zeh, T., Pagnoni, G., Berns, G., & Kilts, C. (2002). A neural basis for social cooperation. *Neuron, 35,* 395–405.

Ro, T., Russell, C., & Lavie, N. (2001). Changing faces: A detection advantage in the flicker paradigm. *Psychological Science, 12,* 94–99.

Robbins, T. L., & DeNisi, A. S. (1994). A closer look at interpersonal affect as a distinct influence on cognitive processing in performance evaluations. *Journal of Applied Psychology, 79,* 341–353.

Robins, R. W., Caspi, A., & Moffitt, T. E. (2000). Two personalities, one relationship: Both partners' personality traits shape the quality of their relationship. *Journal of Personality and Social Psychology, 79,* 251–259.

Robins, R. W., Hendin, H. M., & Trzesniewski, K. H. (2001). *Personality and Social Psychology Bulletin, 27,* 151–161.

Robins, R. W., Spranca, M. D., & Mendelsohn, G. A. (1996). The actor–observer effect revisited: Effects of individual differences and repeated social interactions on actor and observer attribution. *Journal of Personality and Social Psychology, 71,* 375–389.

Robinson, L. A., Berman, J. S., & Neimeyer, R. A. (1990). Psychotherapy for the treatment of depression: A comprehensive review of controlled outcome research. *Psychological Bulletin, 108,* 30–49.

Robinson, R., Keltner, D., Ward, A., & Ross, L. (1995). Actual versus assumed differences in construal: "Naïve realism" in intergroup perception and conflict. *Journal of Personality and Social Psychology, 68,* 404–417.

Roccas, S. (2003). Identification and status revisited: the moderating role of self-enhancement and self-transcendence values. *Personality and Social Psychology Bulletin, 29,* 726–736.

Roccas, S., & Brewer, M. B. (2002). Social identity complexity. *Personality and Social Psychology Review, 6,* 88–106.

Rochat, F., & Modigliani, A. (1995). The ordinary quality of resistance: From Milgram's laboratory to the village of Le Chambon. *Journal of Social Issues, 5,* 195–210.

Roese, N. J. (1997). Counterfactual thinking. *Psychological Bulletin, 121,* 133–148.

Rogers, R. W. (1980). *Subjects' reactions to experimental deception.* Unpublished manuscript, University of Alabama, Tuscaloosa.

Rogers, R. W., & Ketcher, C. M. (1979). Effects of anonymity and arousal on aggression. *Journal of Psychology, 102,* 13–19.

Rokach, A., & Bacanli, H. (2001). Perceived causes of loneliness: A cross-cultural comparison. *Social Behavior and Personality, 29,* 169–182.

Rokach, A., & Neto, F. (2000). Coping with loneliness in adolescence: A cross-cultural study. *Social Behavior and Personality, 28,* 329–342.

Rokach, A., Moya, M. C., Orzeck, T., & Exposito, F. (2001). Loneliness in North America and Spain. *Social Behavior and Personality, 29,* 477–490.

Roland, E. (2002). Aggression, depression, and bullying others. *Aggressive Behavior, 28,* 198–206.

Rosenbaum, M. E. (1986). The repulsion hypothesis: On the nondevelopment of relationships. *Journal of Personality and Social Psychology, 51,* 1156–1166.

Rosenberg, E. L., & Ekman, P. (1995). Conceptual and methodological issues in the judgment of facial expressions of emotion. *Motivation and Emotion, 19,* 111–138.

Rosenberg, M. (1965). *Society and the adolescent self-image.* Princeton, NJ: Princeton University Press.

Rosenhan, D. L., Salovey, P., & Hargis, K. (1981). The joys of helping: Focus of attention mediates the impact of positive affect on altruism. *Journal of Personality and Social Psychology, 40,* 899–905.

Rosenthal, A. M. (1964). *Thirty-eight witnesses.* New York: McGraw-Hill.

Rosenthal, E. (1992, August 18). Troubled marriage? Sibling relations may be at fault. *New York Times,* pp. C1, C9.

Rosenthal, R. (1994). Interpersonal expectancy effects: A thirty year perspective. *Current Direction in Psychological Science, 3,* 176–179.

Rosenthal, R., & DePaulo, B. M. (1979). Sex differences in accommodation in nonverbal communication. In R. Rosenthal (Ed.), *Skill in nonverbal communication: Individual differences* (pp. 68–103). Cambridge, MA: Oelgeschlager, Gunn & Hain.

Rosenthal, R., & Jacobson, L. (1968). *Pygmalion in the classroom: Teacher expectation and student intellectual development.* New York: Holt, Rinehart, & Winston.

Ross, J., & Staw, B. M. (1993). Organizational escalation and exit: Lessons from the Shoreham nuclear power plant. *Academy of Management Journal, 36,* 701–732.

Ross, L. (1977). The intuitive scientist and his shortcoming. In L. Berkowitz (Ed.), *Advances in experimental social psychology* (Vol. 10, pp. 174–221). New York: Academic Press.

Rotenberg, K. J. (1997). Loneliness and the perception of the exchange of disclosures. *Journal of Social and Clinical Psychology, 16,* 259–276.

Rotenberg, K. J., & Kmill, J. (1992). Perception of lonely and non-lonely persons as a function of individual differences in loneliness. *Journal of Social and Personal Relationships, 9,* 325–330.

Rothgerber, H. (1997). External intergroup threat as an antecedent to perceptions of in-group and out-group homogeneity. *Journal of Personality and Social Psychology, 73,* 1206–1212.

Rothman, A. J., & Hardin, C. D. (1997). Differential use of the availability heuristic in social judgment. *Personality and Social Psychology Bulletin, 23,* 123–138.

Rotton, J., & Cohn, E. G. (2000). Violence is a curvilinear function of temperature in Dallas: A replication. *Journal of Personality and Social Psychology, 78,* 1074–1081.

Rotton, J., & Kelley, I. W. (1985). Much ado about the full moon: A meta-analysis of lunar-lunacy research. *Psychological Bulletin, 97,* 286–306.

Rowatt, W. C., Cunningham, M. R., & Druen, P. B. (1998). Deception to get a date. *Personality and Social Psychology Bulletin, 24,* 1228–1242.

Rowe, P. M. (1996, September). On the neurobiological basis of affiliation. *APS Observer,* 17–18.

Roy, M. M., & Christenfeld, N. J. S. (2004). Do dogs resemble their owners? *Psychological Science, 15,* 361–363.

Rozin, P., & Nemeroff, C. (1990). The laws of sympathetic magic: A psychological analysis of similarity and contagion. In W. Stigler, R. A. Shweder, & G. Herdt (Eds.), *Cultural psychology: Essays in comparative human development* (pp. 205–232). Cambridge, England: Cambridge University Press.

Rozin, P., Lowery, L., & Ebert, R. (1994). Varieties of disgust faces and the structure of disgust. *Journal of Personality and Social Psychology, 66,* 870–881.

Rubin, J. Z. (1985). Deceiving ourselves about deception: Comment on Smith and Richardson's "Amelioration of deception and harm in psychological research." *Journal of Personality and Social Psychology, 48,* 252–253.

Rubin, Z. (1970). Measurement of romantic love. *Journal of Personality and Social Psychology, 16,* 265–273.

Ruder, M., & Bless, H. (2003). Mood and the reliance on the ease of retrieval heuristic. *Journal of Personality and Social Psychology, 85,* 20–32.

Rudman, L. A., & Fairchild, K. (2004). Reactions to counterstereotypic behavior: The role of backlash in cultural stereotype maintenance. *Journal of Personality and Social Psychology, 87,* 157–176.

Runtz, M. G., & O'Donnell, C. D. (2003). Students' perceptions of sexual harassment: Is it harassment only if the offender is a man and the victim is a woman? *Journal of Applied Social Psychology, 33,* 963–982.

Rusbult, C. E., & Zembrodt, I. M. (1983). Responses to dissatisfaction in romantic involvements: A multidimensional scaling analysis. *Journal of Experimental Social Psychology, 19,* 274–293.

Rusbult, C. E., Martz, J. M., & Agnew, C. R. (1998). The Investment Model Scale: Measuring commitment level, satisfaction level, quality of alternatives, and investment size. *Personal Relationships, 5,* 467–484.

Rusbult, C. E., Morrow, G. D., & Johnson, D. J. (1990). Self-esteem and problem-solving behavior in close relationships. *British Journal of Social Psychology,*

Ruscher, J. B., & Hammer, E. D. (1994). Revising disrupted impressions through conversation. *Journal of Personality and Social Psychology, 66,* 530–541.

Rushton, J. P. (1989b). Genetic similarity, human altruism, and group selection. *Behavioral and Brain Sciences, 12,* 503–559.

Rushton, J. P., Russell, R. J. H., & Wells, P. A. (1984). Genetic similarity theory: Beyond kin selection. *Behavior Genetics, 14,* 179–193.

Russell, J. A. (1994). Is there universal recognition of emotion from facial expressions? A review of cross-cultural studies. *Psychological Bulletin, 115,* 102–141.

Rutkowski, G. K., Gruder, C. L., & Romer, D. (1983). Group cohesiveness, social norms, and bystander intervention. *Journal of Personality and Social Psychology, 44,* 542–552.

Ruvolo, A. P., Fabin, L. A., & Ruvolo, C. M. (2001). Relationship experiences and change in attachment characteristics of young adults: The role of relationship breakups and conflict avoidance. *Personal Relationships, 8,* 265–281.

Ryan, M. K., David, B., & Reynolds, K. J. (2004). Who cares? The effect of gender and context on the self and moral reasoning. *Psychology of Women Quarterly, 28,* 246–255.

Ryckman, R. M., Robbins, M. A., Kaczor, L. M., & Gold, J. A. (1989). Male and female raters' stereotyping of male and female physiques. *Personality and Social Psychology Bulletin, 15,* 244–251.

Ryff, C. D., & Singer, B. (2000). Interpersonal flourishing: A positive health agenda for the new millennium. *Personality and Social Psychology Review, 4,* 30–44.

Sadker, M., & Sadker, D. (1994). *Failing at fairness: How America's schools cheat girls.* New York: Charles Scribners Sons.

Sadler, P., & Woody, E. (2003). Is who you are who you're talking to? Interpersonal style and complementarity in mixed-sex interactions. *Journal of Personality and Social Psychology, 84,* 80–96.

Sallis, J., Selens, B. E., & Frank, L. (2003). Walking and weight control. *Annals of Behavioral Medicine, 25.*

Sally, D. (1998). Conversation and cooperation in social dilemmas: A meta-analysis of experiments from 1958–1992. *Rationality and Society.*

Salmela-Aro, K., & Nurmi, J.-E. (1996). Uncertainty and confidence in interpersonal projects: Consequences for social relationships and well-being. *Journal of Social and Personal Relationships, 13,* 109–122.

Salovey, P., Mayer, J. D., & Rosenhan, D. L. (1991). Mood and helping: Mood as a motivator of helping and helping as a regulator of mood. In M. S. Clark (Ed.), *Prosocial behavior* (pp. 215–237). Newbury Park, CA: Sage.

Sangrador, J. L., & Yela, C. (2000). 'What is beautiful is loved': Physical attractiveness in love relationships in a representative sample. *Social Behavior and Personality, 28,* 207–218.

Sani, F., & Reicher, S. (2000). Contested identities and schisms in groups: Opposing the ordination of women as priests in the Church of England. *British Journal of Social Psychology, 39,* 95–112.

Sani, F., & Todman, J. (2002). Should we stay or should we go? A social psychological model of schisms in groups. *Personality and Social Psychology Bulletin, 28,* 1647–1655.

Sanitioso, R. B., & Wlodarski, R. (2004). In search of information that confirms a desired self-perception: Motivated processing of social feedback and choice of social interactions. *Personality and Social Psychology Bulletin, 30,* 412–422.

Sanitioso, R. B., Kunda, Z., & Fong, G. T. (1990). Motivated recruitment of autobiographical memories. *Journal of Personality and Social Psychology, 59,* 229–241.

Sanna, L. J. (1997). Self-efficacy and counterfactual thinking: Up a creek with and without a paddle. *Personality and Social Psychology Bulletin, 23,* 654–666.

Sanna, L. J., & Pusecker, P. A. (1994). Self-efficacy, valence of self-evaluation, and performance. *Personality and Social Psychology Bulletin, 20,* 82–92.

Sattler, D. N., Adams, M. G., & Watts, B. (1995). Effects of personal experience on judgments about natural disasters. *Journal of Social Behavior and Personality, 10,* 891–898.

Schachter, D. L., & Kihlstrom, J. F. (1989). Functional amnesia. In F. Boller & J. Grafman (Eds.), *Handbook of neuropsychology* (Vol. 3, pp. 209–230). New York: Elsevier.

Schachter, S. (1951). Deviation, rejection, and communication. *Journal of Abnormal and Social Psychology, 46,* 190–207.

Schachter, S. (1959). *The psychology of affiliation.* Stanford, CA: Stanford University Press.

Schachter, S. (1964). The interaction of cognitive and physiological determinants of emotional state. In L. Berkowitz (Ed.), *Advances in experimental social psychology* (Vol. 1, pp. 48–81). New York: Academic Press.

Schaller, M., & Maass, A. (1989). Illusory correlation and social categorization: Toward an integration of motivational and cognitive factors in stereotype formation. *Journal of Personality and Social Psychology, 56,* 709–721.

Schein, V. E. (2001). A global look at psychological barriers to women's progress in management. *Journal of Social Issues, 57,* 675–688.

Scher, S. J. (1997). Measuring the consequences of injustice. *Personality and Social Psychology Bulletin, 23,* 482–497.

Schimel, J., Pyszczynski, T., Greenberg, J., O'Mahen, H., & Arndt, J. (2000). Running from the shadow: Psychological distancing from others to deny characteristics people fear in themselves. *Journal of Personality and Social Psychology, 78,* 446–462.

Schlenker, B. R., & Britt, T. W. (2001). Strategically controlling information to help friends: Effects of empathy and friendship strength on beneficial impression management. *Journal of Experimental Social Psychology, 37,* 357–372.

Schlenker, B. R., & Pontari, B. A. (2000). The strategic control of information: Impression management and self-presentation in daily life. In A. Tesser, R. Felson, & J. Suls (Eds.), *Perspectives on self and identity.* Washington, DC: American Psychological Association.

Schlenker, B. R., Weigold, M. F., & Hallam, J. R. (1990). Self-serving attributions in social context: Effects of self-esteem and social pressure. *Journal of Personality and Social Psychology, 58,* 855–863.

Schmid, R. E. (2001, April 18). Teen pregnancy drops to record low. Associated Press.

Schmitt, D. P. (2003a). Sociosexuality from Argentina to Zimbabwe: A 48-nation study of sex, culture, and the dynamics of human mating. Manuscript submitted for publication.

Schmitt, D. P. (2003b). Universal sex differences in the desire for sexual variety: Tests from 52 nations, 6 continents, and 13 islands. *Journal of Personality and Social Psychology, 85,* 85–104.

Schmitt, D. P. (2004). Patterns and universals of mate poaching across 53 nations: The effects of sex, culture, and personality on romantically attracting another person's partner. *Journal of Personality and Social Psychology, 86,* 560–584.

Schmitt, D. P., & Buss, D. M. (2001). Human mate poaching: Tactics and temptations for infiltrating existing mateships. *Journal of Personality and Social Psychology, 80,* 894–917.

Schmitt, D. P., & Schackelford, T. K. (2003). Nifty ways to leave your lover: The tactics people use to entice and disguise the process of human mate poaching. *Personality and Social Psychology Bulletin, 29,* 1018–1035.

Schmitt, E. (2001, May 15). In census, families changing. *New York Times.*

Schmitt, M. T., & Branscombe, N. R. (2002a). The meaning and consequences of perceived discrimination in disadvantaged and privileged social groups. *European Review of Social Psychology, 12,* 167–199.

Schmitt, M. T., & Branscombe, N. R. (2002b). The causal loci of attributions to prejudice. *Personality and Social Psychology Bulletin, 28,* 484–492.

Schmitt, M. T., Branscombe, N. R., & Postmes, T. (2003). Women's emotional responses to the pervasiveness of gender discrimination. *European Journal of Social Psychology, 33,* 297–312.

Schmitt, M. T., Ellemers, N., & Branscombe, N. R. (2003). Perceiving and responding to gender discrimination at work. In S. A. Haslam, D. van Knippenberg, M. Platow, & N. Ellemers (Eds.), *Social identity at work: Developing theory for organizational practice* (pp. 277–292). Philadelphia, PA: Psychology Press.

Schmitt, M. T., Silvia, P. J., & Branscombe, N. R. (2000). The intersection of self-evaluation maintenance and social identity theories: Intragroup judgment in interpersonal and intergroup contexts. *Personality and Social Psychology Bulletin, 26,* 1598–1606.

Schneider, B., Hanges, P. J., Smith, D. B., & Salvaggio, A. N. (2004). Which comes first: Employee attitudes or organizational financial and market performance? *Journal of Applied Psychology, 88,* 836–851.

Schneider, M. E., Major, B., Luhtanen, R., & Crocker, J. (1996). Social stigma and the potential costs of assump-tive help. *Personality and Social Psychology Bulletin, 22,* 201–209.

Schooler, J. W., & Loftus, E. F. (1986). Individual differences and experimentation: Complementary approaches to interrogative suggestibility. *Social Behavior, 1,* 105–112.

Schubert, T. W. (2004). The power in your hand: Gender differences in bodily feedback from making a fist. *Personality and Social Psychology Bulletin, 30,* 757–769.

Schul, Y., & Vinokur, A. D. (2000). Projection in person perception among spouses as a function of the similarity in their shared experiences. *Personality and Social Psychology Bulletin, 26,* 987–1001.

Schulz-Hardt, S., Jochims, M., & Frey, D. (2002). Productive conflict in group decision making: Genuine and contrived dissent as strategies to counteract biased information seeking. *Organizational Behavior and Human Decision Processes, 88,* 563–586.

Schumacher, M., Corrigan, P. W., & Dejong, T. (2003). Examining cues that signal mental illness stigma. *Journal of Social and Clinical Psychology, 22,* 467–476.

Schusterman, R. J., Reichmuth, C. J., & Kastak, D. (2000). How animals classify friends and foes. *Current Directions in Psychological Science, 9,* 1–6.

Schutte, J. W., & Hosch, H. M. (1997). Gender differences in sexual assault verdicts: A meta-analysis. *Journal of Social Behavior and Personality, 12,* 759–772.

Schwarz, N., & Bohner, G. (2001). The construction of attitudes. In A. Tesser & N. Schwarz (Eds.), *Blackwell handbook of social psychology: Intrapersonal processes* (pp. 436–457). Oxford, UK: Blackwell.

Schwarz, N., Bless, H., Strack, F., Klumpp, G., Rittenauer-Schatka, G., & Simons, A. (1991). Ease of retrieval as information: Another look at the availability heuristic. *Journal of Personality and Social Psychology, 61,* 195–202.

Schwarz, S. H., & Bardi, A. (2001). Value hierarchies across cultures: Taking a similarities perspective. *Journal of Cross Cultural Psychology, 32,* 268–290.

Schwarzer, R. (1994). Optimism, vulnerability, and self-beliefs as health-related cognitions: A sytematic overview. *Psychology and Health, 9,* 161–180.

Scutt, D., Manning, J. T., Whitehouse, G. H., Leinster, S. J., & Massey, C. P. (1997). The relationship between breast symmetry, breast size and occurrence of breast cancer. *British Journal of Radiology, 70,* 1017–1021.

Seal, D. W. (1997). Inter-partner concordance of self-reported sexual behavior among college dating couples. *Journal of Sex Research, 34,* 39–55.

Searcy, E., & Eisenberg, N. (1992). Defensiveness in response to aid from a sibling. *Journal of Personality and Social Psychology, 62,* 422–433.

Sears, D. O. (1986). College sophomores in the laboratory: Influences of a narrow data base on social psychology's view of human nature. *Journal of Personality and Social Psychology, 51,* 515–530.

Sears, D. O. (1988). Symbolic racism. In P. A. Katz & D. A. Taylor (Eds.), *Eliminating racism: Profiles in controversy* (pp. 53–84). New York: Plenum.

Sedikides, C., & Anderson, C. A. (1994). Causal perception of intertrait relations: the glue that holds person types together. *Personality and Social Psychology Bulletin, 21,* 294–302.

Sedikides, C., & Gregg, A. P. (2003). Portraits of the self. In M. A. Hogg & J. Cooper (Eds.), *The Sage handbook of social psychology* (pp. 110–138). Thousand Oaks, CA: Sage.

Sedikides, C., & Skowronski, J. J. (1997). The symbolic self in evolutionary context. *Personality and Social Psychology Review, 1,* 80–102.

Seery, M. D., Blascovich, J., Weisbuch, M., & Vick, B. (2004). The relationship between self-esteem level, self-esteem stability, and cardiovascular reactions to performance feedback. *Journal of Personality and Social Psychology, 87,* 133–145.

Segal, M. M. (1974). Alphabet and attraction: An unobtrusive measure of the effect of propinquity in a field setting. *Journal of Personality and Social Psychology, 30,* 654–657.

Selim, J. (2003, April). Anatomy of a belly laugh. *Discover,* 65.

Selim, J. (2004b, May). Who's a little bitty artist? Yes, you are! *Discover,* 16.

Senecal, C., Vallerand, R. J., & Guay, F. (2001). Antecedents and outcomes of work-family conflict: Toward a motivational model. *Personality and Social Psychology Bulletin, 27,* 176–186.

Seta, C. E., Hayes, N. S., & Seta, J. J. (1994). Mood, memory, and vigilance: The influence of distraction on recall and impression formation. *Personality and Social Psychology Bulletin, 20,* 170–177.

Settles, I. H. (2004). When multiple identities interfere: The role of identity centrality. *Personality and Social Psychology Bulletin, 30,* 487–500.

Shah, J. (2003). Automatic for the people; How representations of significant others implicitly affect goal pursuit. *Journal of Personality and Social Psychology, 84,* 661–681.

Shams, M. (2001). Social support, loneliness and friendship preference among British Asian and non-Asian adolescents. *Social Behavior and Personality, 29,* 399–404.

Shanab, M. E., & Yahya, K. A. (1977). A behavioral study of obedience in children. *Journal of Personality and Social Psychology, 35,* 530–536.

Shane, S. 2003. *A general theory of entrepreneurship: The individual-opportunity nexus approach to entrepreneurship.* Aldershot, United Kingdom: Eward Elgar.

Shannon, M. L., & Stark, C. P. (2003). The influence of physical appearance on personnel selection. *Social Behavior and Personality, 31,* 613–624.

Shapiro, A., & Gottman, J. (2000). The baby and the marriage: Identifying factors that buffer against decline in marital satisfaction after the first baby arrives. *Journal of Family Psychology, 14,* 59–70.

Shapiro, J. P., Baumeister, R. F., & Kessler, J. W. (1991). A three-component model of children's teasing: Aggression, humor, and ambiguity. *Journal of Social and Clinical Psychology, 10,* 459–472.

Sharp, D., Adair, J. G., & Roese, N. J. (1992). Twenty years of deception research: A decline in subjects' trust? *Personality and Social Psychology Bulletin, 18,* 585–590.

Sharp, M. J., & Getz, J. G. (1996). Substance use as impression management. *Personality and Social Psychology Bulletin, 22,* 60–67.

Shaver, P. R., & Brennan, K. A. (1992). Attachment styles and the "big five" personality traits: Their connections with each other and with romantic relationship outcomes. *Personality and Social Psychology Bulletin, 18,* 536–545.

Shaver, P. R., Morgan, H. J., & Wu, S. (1996). Is love a "basic" emotion? *Personal Relationships, 3,* 81–96.

Shavitt, S. (1990). The role of attitude objects in attitude functions. *Journal of Experimental Social Psychology, 26,* 124–148.

Shaw, J. I., Borough, H. W., & Fink, M. I. (1994). Perceived sexual orientation and helping behavior by males and females: The wrong number technique. *Journal of Psychology and Human Sexuality, 6,* 73–81.

Shaw, L. L., Batson, C. D., & Todd, R. M. (1994). Empathy avoidance: Forestalling feeling for another in order to escape the motivational consequences. *Journal of Personality and Social Psychology, 67,* 879–887.

Sheeran, P., & Abraham, C. (1994). Unemployment and self-conception: A symbolic interactionist analysis. *Journal of Community & Applied Social Psychology, 4,* 115–129.

Sheldon, W. H., Stevens, S. S., & Tucker, W. B. (1940). *The varieties of human physique.* New York: Harper.

Shepperd, J. A., & McNulty, J. K. (2002). The affective consequences of expected and unexpected outcomes. *Psychological Science, 13,* 84–87.

Shepperd, J. A., Ouellette, J. A., & Fernandez, J. K. (1996). Abandoning unrealistic optimistic performance estimates and the temporal proximity of self-relevant feedback. *Journal of Personality and Social Psychology, 70,* 844–855.

Shepperd, J. A., Findley-Klein, C., Kwavnick, K., Walker, D., & Perez, S. (2000). Bracing for loss. *Journal of Personality and Social Psychology, 78,* 620–634.

Sherif, M. (1966). *In common predicament: Social psychology of intergroup conflict and cooperation.* Boston, MA: Houghton-Mifflin.

Sherif, M., Harvey, D. J., White, B. J., Hood, W. R, & Sherif, C. W. (1961). *The Robbers' cave experiment.* Norman, OK: Institute of Group Relations.

Sherman, J. W., & Klein, S. B. (1994). Development and representation of personality impressions. *Journal of Personality and Social Psychology, 67,* 972–983.

Sherman, M. D., & Thelen, M. H. (1996). Fear of intimacy scale: Validation and extension with adolescents. *Journal of Social and Personal Relationships, 13,* 507–521.

Sherman, S. S. (1980). On the self-erasing nature of errors of prediction. *Journal of Personality and Social Psychology, 16,* 388–403.

Shore, L. M., Cleveland, J. N., & Goldberg, C. B. (2003). Work attitudes and decisions as a function of manager age and employee age. *Journal of Applied Psychology, 88,* 529–537.

Shuffelton, F. (2004). *The letters of John and Abigail Adams.* New York: Penguin Books.

Sidanius, J., & Pratto, F. (1999). *Social dominance.* New York: Cambridge University Press.

Sigall, H. (1997). Ethical considerations in social psychological research: Is the bogus pipeline a special case? *Journal of Applied Social Psychology, 27,* 574–581.

Sigelman, C. K., Thomas, D. B., Sigelman, L., & Robich, F. D. (1986). Gender, physical attractiveness, and electability: An experimental investigation of voter biases. *Journal of Applied Social Psychology, 16,* 229–248.

Sillars, A. L., Folwell, A. L., Hill, K. C., Maki, B. K., Hurst, A. P., & Casano, R. A. (1994). *Journal of Social and Personal Relationships, 11,* 611–617.

Silverstein, R. (1994). Chronic identity diffusion in traumatized combat veterans. *Social Behavior and Personality, 22,* 69–80.

Simon, B. (1992). The perception of ingroup and outgroup homogeneity: Reintroducing the social context. In W. Stroebe & M. Hewstone (Eds.), *European Review of Social Psychology* (Vol. 3, pp. 1–30). Chichester: Wiley.

Simon, B. (1998). The self in minority-majority contexts. In W. Stroebe & M. Hewstone (Eds.), *European Review of Social Psychology* (Vol. 9, pp. 1–31). Chichester: Wiley.

Simon, B. (2004). *Identity in modern society: A social psychological perspective.* Oxford: Blackwell.

Simon, B., & Klandermans, B. (2001). Politicized collective identity: A social psychological analysis. *American Psychologist, 56,* 319–331.

Simon, B., & Pettigrew, T. F. (1990). Social identity and perceived group homogeneity: Evidence for the ingroup homogeneity effect. *European Journal of Social Psychology, 20,* 269–286.

Simon, B., Glassner-Bayerl, B., & Stratenwerth, I. (1991). Stereotyping and self-stereotyping in a natural intergroup context: The case of heterosexual and homosexual men. *Social Psychology Quarterly, 54,* 252–266.

Simon, L., & Greenberg, J. (1996). Further progress in understanding the effects of derogatory ethnic labels: The role of preexisting attitudes toward the targeted group. *Personality and Social Psychology Bulletin, 22,* 1195–1204.

Simon, L., Greenberg, J., & Brehm, J. (1995). Trivialization: The forgotten mode of dissonance reduction. *Journal of Personality and Social Psychology, 68,* 247–260.

Simon, M., Houghton, S. M., & Aquino, K. (2000). Cognitive biases, risk perceptions, and venture formation: How individuals decide to start companies. *Journal of Business Venturing, 15,* 113–134.

Simons, T., & Roberson, Q. (2003). Why managers should care about fairness: The effects of aggregate justice perceptions on organizational outcomes. *Journal of Applied Psychology, 88,* 432–443.

Simpson, J. A. (1987). The dissolution of romantic relationships: Factors involved in relationship stability and emotional stress. *Journal of Personality and Social Psychology, 53,* 683–692.

Simpson, J. A., & Gangestad, S. W. (1992). Sociosexuality and romantic partner choice. *Journal of Personality, 60,* 31–51.

Simpson, J. A., Ickes, W., & Blackstone, T. (1995). When the head protects the heart: Empathic accuracy in dating relationships. *Journal of Personality and Social Psychology, 69,* 629–641.

Sinclair, L., & Kunda, Z. (1999). Reactions to a black professional: Motivated inhibition and activation of conflicting stereotypes. *Journal of Personality and Social Psychology, 77,* 885–904.

Singh, R., & Ho, S. Y. (2000). Attitudes and attraction: A new test of the attraction, repulsion and similarity–dissimilarity asymmetry hypotheses. *British Journal of Social Psychology, 39,* 197–211.

Singh, R., Choo, W. M., & Poh, L. L. (1998). In-group bias and fair-mindedness as strategies of self-presentation in intergroup perception. *Personality and Social Psychology Bulletin, 24,* 147–162.

Sistrunk, F., & McDavid, J. W. (1971). Sex variable in conforming behavior. *Journal of Personality and Social Psychology, 17,* 200–207.

Sivacek, J., & Crano, W. D. (1982). Vested interest as a moderator of attitude-behavior consistency. *Journal of Personality and Social Psychology, 43,* 210–221.

Skarlicki, D. P., & Folger, R. (1997). Retaliation in the workplace: The roles of distributive, procedural, and interactional justice. *Journal of Applied Psychology, 821,* 434–443.

Smeaton, G., Byrne, D., & Murnen, S. K. (1989). The repulsion hypothesis revisited: Similarity irrelevance or dissimilarity bias? *Journal of Personality and Social Psychology, 56,* 54–59.

Smirles, K. E. (2004). Attributions of responsibility in cases of sexual harassment: the person and the situation. *Journal of Applied Social Psychology, 34,* 342–365.

Smith, C. M., Tindale, R. S., & Dugoni, B. L. (1996). Minority and majority influence in freely interacting groups: Qualitative versus quantitative differences. *British Journal of Social Psychology, 35,* 137–149.

Smith, D. (2003). Angry thoughts, at-risk hearts. *Monitor on Psychology,* March, 2003, pp. 46–47.

Smith, D. E., Gier, J. A., & Willis, F. N. (1982). Interpersonal touch and compliance with a marketing request. *Basic and Applied Social Psychology, 3,* 35–38.

Smith, E. R., & Zarate, M. A. (1992). Exemplar-based model of social judgment. *Psychological Review, 99,* 3–21.

Smith, E. R., Byrne, D., Becker, M. A., & Przybyla, D. P. J. (1993). Sexual attitudes of males and females as predictors of interpersonal attraction and marital compatibility. *Journal of Applied Social Psychology, 23,* 1011–1034.

Smith, K. D., Keating, J. P., & Stotland, E. (1989). Altruism reconsidered: The effect of denying feedback on a victim's status to empathetic witnesses. *Journal of Personality and Social Psychology, 57,* 641–650.

Smith, P. B., & Bond, M. H. (1993). *Social psychology across cultures.* Boston: Allyn & Bacon.

Smith, P. K., & Brain, P. (2000). Bullying in schools; lessons from two decades of research. *Aggressive Behavior, 26,* 1–9.

Smith, S. S., & Richardson, D. (1985). On deceiving ourselves about deception: Reply to Rubin. *Journal of Personality and Social Psychology, 48,* 254–255.

Smith, V. I., & Ellsworth, P. C. (1987). The social psychology of eyewitness accuracy: Misleading questions and communicator expertise. *Journal of Applied Psychology, 72,* 294–300.

Smorti, A., & Ciucci, E. (2000). Narrative strategies in bullies and victims in Italian schoolchildren. *Aggressive Behavior, 26,* 33–48.

Smuts, B. (2001/2002, December/January). Common ground. *Natural History,* 78–83.

Sniffen, M. J. (1999, November 22). Serious crime declines sharply. Associated Press.

Snyder, M., & Ickes, W. (1985). Personality and social behavior. In G. Lindzey & E. Aronson (Eds.), *Handbook of social psychology* (3rd ed., Vol. 2, pp. 883–947). New York: Random House.

Sommer, K. L., Horowitz, I. A., & Bourgeois, M. J. (2001). When juries fail to comply with the law: Biased evidence processing in individual and group decision making. *Personality and Social Psychology Bulletin, 27,* 309–320.

Spears, R., Doosje, B., & Ellemers, N. (1999). Commitment and the context of social perception. In N. Ellemers, R. Spears, & B. Doosje (Eds.), *Social identity: Context, commitment, content* (pp. 59–83). Oxford: Blackwell.

Spears, R., Jetten, J., & Doosje, B. (2001). The (il)legitimacy of ingroup bias: From social reality to social resistance. In J. T. Jost & B. Major (Eds.), *The psychology of legitimacy* (pp. 332–362). New York: Cambridge University Press.

Spencer, S. J., Steele, C. M., & Quinn, D. M. (1999). Stereotype threat and women's math performance. *Journal of Experimental Social Psychology, 35,* 4–28.

Sprafkin, J. N., Liebert, R. M., & Poulous, R. W. (1975). Effects of a prosocial televised example on children's helping. *Journal of Personality and Social Psychology, 48,* 35–46.

Sprecher, S. (1992). How men and women expect to feel and behave in response to inequity in close relationships. *Social Psychology Quarterly, 55,* 57–69.

Sprecher, S. (2002). Sexual satisfaction in premarital relationships: Associations with satisfaction, love, commitment, and stability. *Journal of Sex Research, 39,* 190–196.

Sprecher, S., & Regan, P. C. (2002). Liking some things (in some people) more than others: Partner preferences in romantic relationships and friendships. *Journal of Social and Personal Relationships, 19,* 463–481.

Spencer, S. J., Fein, S., & Zanna, M. P., & Olson, J. M. (Eds.). (2003*). Motivated social perception.* Mahwah, NJ: Erlbaum.

Stacey, J., & Biblarz, T. (2001). Does the sexual orientation of parents matter? *American Sociological Review, 66,* 159–183.

Stafford, L., Kline, S. L., & Rankin, C. T. (2004). Married individuals, cohabiters, and cohabiters who marry: A longitudinal study of relational and individual well-being. *Journal of Social and Personal Relationships, 21,* 231–248.

Stangor, C., & McMillan, D. (1992). Memory for expectancy-congruent and expectancy-incongruent information: A review of the social and social developmental literatures. *Psychological Bulletin, 111,* 42–61.

Stangor, C., Sechrist, G. B., & Jost, T. J. (2001). Changing racial beliefs by providing consensus information. *Personality and Social Psychology Bulletin, 27,* 486–496.

Stasser, G. (1992). Pooling of unshared information during group discussion. In S. Worchel, W. Wood, & J. H. Simpson (Eds.), *Group process and productivity* (pp. 48–67). Newbury Park, CA: Sage.

Stasser, G., Taylor, L. A., & Hanna, C. (1989). Information sampling in structured and unstructured discussions of three- and six-person groups. *Journal of Personality and Social Psychology, 57,* 67–78.

Staub, E. (1989). *The roots of evil: The origins of genocide and other group violence.* New York: Cambridge University Press.

Staub, E. (1999). The roots of evil: Social conditions, culture, personality, and basic human needs. *Personality and Social Psychology Review, 3,* 179–192.

Stech, F., & McClintock, C. G. (1981). Effects of communication timing on duopoly bargaining outcomes. *Journal of Personality and Social Psychology, 40,* 664–674.

Steele, C. M. (1988). The psychology of self-affirmation: Sustaining the integrity of the self. In L. Berkowitz (Ed.), *Advances in experimental social psychology* (pp. 261–302). Hillsdale, NJ: Erlbaum.

Steele, C. M. (1997). A threat in the air: How stereotypes shape the intellectual identities and performance of women and African-Americans. *American Psychologist, 52,* 613–629.

Steele, C. M., & Aronson, J. (1995). Stereotype threat and the intellectual test performance of African Americans. *Journal of Personality and Social Psychology, 69,* 797–811.

Steele, C. M., & Lui, T. J. (1983). Dissonance processes as self-affirmation. *Journal of Personality and Social Psychology, 45,* 5–19.

Steele, C. M., Critchlow, B., & Liu, T. J. (1985). Alcohol and social behavior II: The helpful drunkard. *Journal of Personality and Social Psychology, 48,* 35–46.

Steele, C. M., Southwick, L., & Critchlow, B. (1981). Dissonance and alcohol: Drinking your troubles away. *Journal of Personality and Social Psychology, 41,* 831–846.

Steele, C. M., Spencer, S. J., & Aronson, J. (2002). Contending with group image: The psychology of stereotype and social identity threat. *Advances in Experimental Social Psychology, 34,* 379–439.

Steele, C. M., Spencer, S. J., & Lynch, M. (1993). Self-image resilience and dissonance: The role of affirmational resources. *Journal of Personality and Social Psychology, 64,* 885–896.

Steenland, K., Henley, J., & Thun, M. (2002). All-cause and cause-specific death rates by educational status for two million people in two American Cancer Society cohorts, 1959–1996. *American Journal of Epidemiology, 156,* 11–21.

Stein, R. I., & Nemeroff, C. J. (1995). Moral overtones of food: Judgments of others based on what they eat. *Personality and Social Psychology Bulletin, 21,* 480–490.

Steinhauer, J. (1995, April 10). Big benefits in marriage, studies say. *New York Times,* p. A10.

Stephan, W. G. (1985). Intergroup relations. In G. Lindzey & E. Aronson (Eds.), *Handbook of social psychology* (Vol. 3, pp. 599–658). New York: Addison-Wesley.

Stephan, W. G., & Stephan, C. W. (2000). An integrated threat theory of prejudice. In S. Oskamp (Ed.), *Reducing prejudice and discrimination* (pp. 23–45). Mahwah, NJ: Erlbaum.

Sternberg, R. J. (1996). Love stories. *Personal Relationships, 3,* 59–79.

Sternberg, R. J., & Hojjat, M. (Eds.). (1997). *Satisfaction in close relationships.* New York: Guilford.

Stevens, C. K., & Kristof, A. L. (1995). Making the right impression: A field study of applicant impression management during job interviews. *Journal of Applied Psychology, 80,* 587–606.

Stevens, L. E., & Fiske, S. T. (2000). Motivated impressions of a powerholder: Accuracy under task dependency and misperception under evaluation dependency. *Personality and Social Psychology Bulletin, 26,* 907–922.

Stewart, R. B., Verbrugge, K. M., & Beilfuss, M. C. (1998). Sibling relationships in early adulthood: A typology. *Personal Relationships, 5,* 59–74.

Stewart, T. L., Vassar, P. M., Sanchez, D. T., & David, S. E. (2000). Attitudes toward women's societal roles moderates the effect of gender cues on target individuation. *Journal of Personality and Social Psychology, 79,* 143–157.

Stewart, W., & Roth, P. (2001). Risk taking propensity differences between entrepreneurs and mangers: a meta-analytic review. *Journal of Applied Psychology, 86,* 145–53.

Stone, A. A., Neale, J. M., Cox, D. S., Napoli, A., Valdimarsdottir, H., & Kennedy-Moore, E. (1994). Daily events are associated with a secretory immune response to an oral antigen in men. *Health Psychology, 13,* 440–446.

Stone, J., Lynch, C. I., Sjomeling, M., & Darley, J. M. (1999). Stereotype threat effects on Black and White athletic performance. *Journal of Personality and Social Psychology, 77,* 1213–1227.

Stone, J., Wiegand, A. W., Cooper, J., & Aronson, E. (1997). When exemplification fails: Hypocrisy and the motives for self-integrity. *Journal of Personality and Social Psychology, 72,* 54–65.

Stowers, L., Holy, T. E., Meister, M., Dulac, C., & Loentges, G. (2002). Loss of sex discrimination and male-male aggression in mice deficient for TRP2. *Science, 295,* 1493–1500.

Stradling, S. G., Crowe, G., & Tuohy, A. P. (1993). Changes in self-concept during occupational socialization of new recruits to the police. *Journal of Community & Applied Social Psychology, 3,* 131–147.

Stroebe, M., Gergen, M. M., Gergen, K. J., & Stroebe, W. (1995). Broken hearts or broken bonds: Love and death in historical perspective. In L. A. DeSpelder & A. L. Strickland (Eds.), *The path ahead: Readings in death and dying* (pp. 231–241). Mountain View, CA: Mayfield.

Stroessner, S. J., Hamilton, D. L., & Mackie, D. M. (1992). Affect and stereotyping: the effect of induced mood on distinctiveness-based illusory correlations. *Journal of Personality and Social Psychology, 62,* 564–576.

Stroh, L. K., Langlands, C. L., & Simpson, P. A. (2004). Shattering the glass ceiling in the new millenium. In M. S. Stockdale and F. J. Crosby (Eds.), *The psychology and management of workplace diversity* (pp. 147–167). Malden, MA: Blackwell.

Strube, M. J. (1989). Evidence for the Type in Type A behavior: A taxonometric analysis. *Journal of Personality and Social Pycology, 56,* 972–987.

Strube, M., Turner, C. W., Cerro, D., Stevens, J., & Hinchey, F. (1984). Interpersonal aggression and the Type A coronary-prone behavior pattern: A theoretical distinction and practical implications. *Journal of Personality and Social Psychology, 47,* 839–847.

Stukas, A. A., Snyder, M., & Clary, E. G. (1999). The effects of "mandatory volunteerism" on intentions to volunteer. *Psychological Science, 10,* 59–64.

Sturmer, S., & Simon, B. (2004). The role of collective identification in social movement participation: A panel study in the context of the German gay movement. *Personality and Social Psychology Bulletin, 30,* 263–277.

Suarez, E. D. (1998). Anger and cardiovascular health. *Psychosomatic Medicine, 60,* 1–12.

Suitor, J. J., & Pillemer, K. (2000). Did Mom really love you best? Developmental histories, status transitions, and parental favoritism in later life families. *Motivation and Emotion, 24,* 105–120.

Suls, J., & Rosnow, J. (1988). Concerns about artifacts in behavioral research. In M. Morawski (Ed.), *The rise of experimentation in American psychology* (pp. 163–187). New Haven, CT: Yale University Press.

Swann, W. B. (1990). To be adored or to be known? The interplay of self-enhancement and self-verification. In E. T. Higgins & R. M. Sorrentino (Eds.), *Handbook of motivation and cognition: Foundations of social behavior* (pp. 408–448). New York: Guilford Press.

Swann, W. B., Jr., & Gill, M. J. (1997). Confidence and accuracy in person perception: Do we know what we think we know about our relationship partners? *Journal of Personality and Social Psychology, 73,* 747–757.

Swann, W. B., Jr., De La Ronde, C., & Hixon, J. G. (1994). Authenticity and positivity strivings in marriage and courtship. *Journal of Personality and Social Psychology, 66,* 857–869.

Swann, W. B., Jr., Rentfrow, P. J., & Gosling, S. D. (2003). The precarious couple effect: verbally inhibited men + critical, disinhibited women = bad chemistry. *Journal of Personality and Social Psychology, 85,* 1095–1106.

Swap, W. C. (1977). Interpersonal attraction and repeated exposure to rewarders and punishers. *Personality and Social Psychology Bulletin, 3,* 248–251.

Swim, J. K. (1994). Perceived versus meta-analytic effect sizes: An assessment of the accuracy of gender stereotypes. *Journal of Personality and Social Psychology, 66,* 21–36.

Swim, J. K., & Campbell, B. (2001). Sexism: Attitudes, beliefs, and behaviors. In R. Brown & S. Gaertner (Eds.), *Blackwell Handbook of Social Psychology: Intergroup Processes* (pp. 218–237). Oxford, UK: Blackwell.

Swim, J. K., Aikin, K. J., Hall, W. S., & Hunter, B. A. (1995). Sexism and racism: Old-fashioned and modern prejudices. *Journal of Personality and Social Psychology, 68,* 199–214.

Tajfel, H. (1978). *The social psychology of the minority.* New York: Minority Rights Group.

Tajfel, H. (1981). Social stereotypes and social groups. In J. C. Turner & H. Giles (Eds.), *Intergroup behavior* (pp. 144–167). Chicago, IL: University of Chicago Press.

Tajfel, H. (1982). *Social identity and intergroup relations.* Cambridge, England: Cambridge University Press.

Tajfel, H., & Turner, J. C. (1986). The social identity theory of intergroup behavior. In S. Worchel & W. G. Austin (Eds.), *The social psychology of intergroup relations* (2nd ed., pp. 7–24). Monterey, CA: Brooks-Cole.

Takata, T., & Hashimoto, H. (1973). Effects of insufficient justification upon the arousal of cognitive dissonance: Timing of justification and evaluation of task. *Japanese Journal of Experimental Social Psychology, 13,* 77–85.

Tamres, L. K., Janicki, D., & Helgeson, V. S. (2002). Sex differences in coping behavior: A meta-analytic review and an examination of relative coping. *Personality and Social Psychology Review, 6,* 2003.

Tan, D. T. Y., & Singh, R. (1995). Attitudes and attraction: A developmental study of the similarity–attraction and dissimilarity–repulsion hypotheses. *Personality and Social Psychology Bulletin, 21* 975–986.

Taylor, K. M., & Shepperd, J. A. (1998). Bracing for the worst: Severity, testing, and feedback timing as moderators of the optimistic bias. *Personality and Social Psychology Bulletin, 24,* 915–926.

Taylor, S. E. (2002). *Health psychology* (5th ed.). New York: McGraw-Hill.

Taylor, S. E., & Brown, J. D. (1988). Illusion and well-being: A social psychological perspective on mental health. *Psychological Bulletin, 103,* 193–210.

Taylor, S. E., Buunk, B. P., & Aspinwall, L. G. (1990). Social comparison, stress, and coping. *Personality and Social Psychology Bulletin, 16,* 74–89.

Taylor, S. E., Helgeson, V. S., Reed, G. M., & Skokan, L. A. (1991). Self-generated feelings of control and adjustment to physical illness. *Journal of Social Issues, 47,* 91–109.

Taylor, S. E., Lerner, J. S., Sherman, D. K., Sage, R. M., & McDowell, N. K. (2003). Are self-enhancing cognitions associated with healthy or unhealthy biological profiles? *Journal of Personality and Social Psychology, 85,* 605–615.

Tepper, B. J. (2000). Consequences of abusive supervision. *Academy of Management Journal, 43,* 178–190.

Terman, L. M., & Buttenwieser, P. (1935a). Personality factors in marital compatibility: I. *Journal of Social Psychology, 6,* 143–171.

Terman, L. M., & Buttenwieser, P. (1935b). Personality factors in marital compatibility: II. *Journal of Social Psychology, 6,* 267–289.

Terry, D. J., & Hogg, M. A. (1996). Group norms and the attitude-behavior relationship: A role for group identification. *Personality and Social Psychology Bulletin, 22,* 776–793.

Terry, D. J., Hogg, M. A., & Duck, J. M. (1999). Group membership, social identity, and attitudes. In D. Abrams & M. A. Hogg (Eds.), *Social identity and social cognition* (pp. 280–314). Oxford: Blackwell.

Terry, R. L., & Krantz, J. H. (1993). Dimensions of trait attributions associated with eyeglasses, men's facial hair, and women's hair length. *Journal of Applied Social Psychology, 23,* 1757–1769.

Tesser, A. (1988). Toward a self-evaluation maintenance model of social behavior. *Advances in Experimental Social Psychology, 21,* 181–227.

Tesser, A., & Martin, L. (1996). The psychology of evaluation. In E. T. Higgins & A. W. Kruglanski (Eds.), *Social psychology: Handbook of basic principles* (pp. 400–423). New York: Guilford Press.

Tesser, A., Martin, L. L., & Cornell, D. P. (1996). On the substitutability of the self-protecting mechanisms. In P. Gollwitzer & J. Bargh (Eds.), *The psychology of action* (pp. 48–68). New York: Guilford.

Tetlock, P. E., Peterson, R. S., McGuire, C., Change, S., & Feld, P. (1992). Assessing political group dynamics: A test of the groupthink model. *Journal of Personality and Social Psychology, 63,* 403–425.

Tett, R. P., & Meyer, J. P. (1993). Job satisfaction, organizational commitment, turnover intention, and turnover: Path analyses based on meta-analytic findings. *Personnel Psychology, 46,* 259–293.

Thompson, J. M., Whiffen, V. E., & Blain, M. D. (1995). Depressive symptoms, sex and perceptions of intimate relationships. *Journal of Social and Personal Relationships, 12,* 49–66.

Thompson, L. (1998). *The mind and heart of the negotiator.* Upper Saddle River, NJ: Prentice-Hall.

Tice, D. M., Bratslavsky, E., & Baumeister, R. F. (2000). Emotional distress regulation takes precedence over impulse control: If you feel bad, do it! *Journal of Personality and Social Psychology, 80,* 53–67.

Tice, D. M., Butler, J. L., Muraven, M. B., & Stillwell, A. M. (1995). When modesty prevails: Differential favorability of self-presentation to friends and strangers. *Journal of Personality and Social Psychology, 69,* 1120–1138.

Tidwell, M.-C. O., Reis, H. T., & Shaver, P. R. (1996). Attachment, attractiveness, and social interaction: A diary study. *Journal of Personality and Social Psychology, 71,* 729–745.

Tiedens, L. Z. (2001). Anger and advancement versus sadness and subjugation: The effect of negative emotion expressions on social status control. *Journal of Personality and Social Psychology, 80,* 86–94.

Tiedens, L. Z., & Fragale, A. R. (2003). Power moves: Complementarity in dominant and submissive nonverbal behavior. *Journal of Personality and Social Psychology, 84,* 558–568.

Tjosvold, D. (1993). *Learning to manage conflict: Getting people to work together productively.* New York: Lexington.

Tjosvold, D., & DeDreu, C. (1997). Managing conflict in Dutch organizations: A test of the relevance of Deutsch's cooperation theory. *Journal of Applied Social Psychology, 27,* 2213–2227.

Toi, M., & Batson, C. D. (1982). More evidence that empathy is a source of altruistic motivation. *Journal of Personality and Social Psychology, 43,* 281–292.

Tormala, Z. L., Petty, R. E., & Brunol, P. (2002). Ease of retrieval effects in persuasion: A self validation analysis. *Personality and Social Psychology Bulletin.*

Towles-Schwen, T., & Fazio, R. H. (2001). On the origins of racial attitudes: Correlates of childhood experiences. *Personality and Social Psychology Bulletin, 27,* 162–175.

Townsend, J. M. (1995). Sex without emotional involvement: An evolutionary interpretation of sex differences. *Archives of Sexual Behavior, 24,* 173–206.

Trafimow, D., Silverman, E., Fan, R., & Law, J. (1997). The effects of language and priming on the relative accessibility of the private self and collective self. *Journal of Cross-Cultural Psychology, 28,* 107–123.

Trevarthen, C. (1993). The function of emotions in early infant communication and development. In J. Nadel & L. Camaioni (Eds.), *New perspectives in early communication development* (pp. 48–81). London: Routledge.

Triandis, H. C. (1990). Cross-cultural studies of individualism and collectivism. In J. J. Berman (Ed.), *Nebraska symposium on motivation, 1989* (pp. 41–133). Lincoln: University of Nebraska Press.

Trobst, K. K., Collins, R. L., & Embree, J. M. (1994). The role of emotion in social support provision: Gender, empathy, and expressions of distress. *Journal of Social and Personal Relationships, 11,* 45–62.

Trope, Y., & Liberman, A. (1996). Social hypothesis testing: Cognitive and motivational mechanisms. In E. T. Higgins & A. W. Kruglanski (Eds.), *Social psychology: Handbook of basic principles* (pp. 239–270). New York: Guilford.

Troxel, W. M., Matthews, K. A., Bromberger, T. J., & Sutton-Tyrrell, K. (2003). Chronic stress burden, discrimination, and subclinical carotid artery disease in African-American and Caucasian women. *Health Psychology, 22,* 1020–1031.

Tucker, J. S., Friedman, H. S., Schwartz, J. E., Criqui, M. H., Tomlinson-Keasey, C., Wingard, D. L., & Martin, L. R. (1997). Parental divorce: Effects on individual behavior and longevity. *Journal of Personality and Social Psychology, 73,* 381–391.

Tucker, P., & Aron, A. (1993). Passionate love and marital satisfaction at key transition points in the family life cycle. *Journal of Social and Clinical Psychology, 12,* 135–147.

Turner, J. C. (1985). Social categorization and the self-concept: A social cognitive theory of group behavior. In E. J. Lawler (Ed.), *Advances in group processes* (Vol. 2, pp. 77–122). Greenwich, CT: JAI Press.

Turner, J. C. (1991). *Social influence.* Pacific Grove, CA: Brooks/Cole.

Turner, J. C., & Onorato, R. S. (1999). Social identity, personality, and the self-concept: A self-categorization perspective. In T. R. Tyler, R. M. Kramer & O. P. John (Eds.), *The psychology of the social self* (pp. 11–46). Mahwah, NJ: Erlbaum.

Turner, J. C., Hogg, M. A., Oakes, P. J., Reicher, S. D., & Wetherell, M. S. (1987). *Rediscovering the social group: A self-categorization theory.* Oxford, UK: Blackwell.

Turner, M. E., Pratkanis, A. R., & Samuels, S. (2003). In S. A. Haslam, D. Van Knippenberg, M. J. Platow, and N. Ellemers (Eds.), *Social Identity at work: Developing theory for organizational practice.* New York: Psychology Press.

Tversky, A., & Kahneman, D. (1973). Availability: A heuristic for judging frequency and probability. *Cognitive Psychology, 5,* 207–232.

Tversky, A., & Kahneman, D. (1982). Judgment under uncertainty: Heuristics and biases. In D. Kahneman, P. Slovic, & A. Tversky (Eds.), *Judgment under uncertainty* (pp. 3–20). New York: Cambridge University Press.

Twenge, J. M. (1999). Mapping gender: The multifactorial approach and the organization of gender-related attributes. *Psychology of Women Quarterly, 23,* 485–502.

Twenge, J. M., & Crocker, J. (2002). Race and self-esteem: Meta-analyses comparing Whites, Blacks, Hispanics, Asians, and American Indians. *Psychological Bulletin, 128,* 371–408.

Twenge, J. M., & Manis, M. M. (1998). First-name desirability and adjustment: Self-satisfaction, others' ratings, and family background. *Journal of Applied Social Psychology, 24,* 41–51.

Twenge, J. M., Catanese, K. R., & Baumeister, R. F. (2003). Social exclusion and the deconstructed state: Time perception, meaninglessness, lethargy, lack of emotion, and self-awareness. *Journal of Personality and Social Psychology, 85,* 409–423.

Tykocinski, O. E. (2001). I never had a chance: Using hindsight tactics to mitigate disappointments. *Personality and Social Psychology Bulletin, 27,* 376–382.

Tyler, T. R., & Blader, S. (2000). *Cooperation in groups: Procedural justice, social identity and behavioral engagement.* Philadelphia, PA: Psychology Press.

Tyler, T. R., & Blader, S. L. (in press). The influence of status judgments in hierarchical groups: comparing autonomous and comparative judgments about status. *Organizational Behavior and Human Decision Processes.*

Tyler, T. R., Boeckmann, R. J., Smith, H. J., & Huo, Y. J. (1997). *Social justice in a diverse society.* Boulder, CO: Westview.

U.S. Department of Justice. (1994). *Criminal victimization in the United States, 1992.* Washington, DC: Office of Justice Programs, Bureau of Justice Statistics.

U.S. Department of Labor. (1992). *Employment and earnings* (Vol. 39, No. 5: Table A-22). Washington, DC: U.S. Department of Labor.

Udry, J. R. (1980). Changes in the frequency of marital intercourse from panel data. *Archives of Sexual Behavior, 9,* 319–325.

Unger, L. S., & Thumuluri, L. K. (1997). Trait empathy and continuous helping: The case of volunteerism. *Journal of Social Behavior and Personality, 12,* 785–800.

Ungerer, J. A., Dolby, R., Waters, B., Barnett, B., Kelk, N., & Lewin, V. (1990). The early development of empathy: Self-regulation and individual differences in the first year. *Motivation and Emotion, 14,* 93–106.

United States Holocaust Memorial Museum. (2003). *Index to Righteous Gentile registry of Yad Vashem.* Washington, DC: Author.

Urbanski, L. (1992, May 21). Study uncovers traits people seek in friends. *The Evangelist,* 4.

Vallone, R., Ross, L., & Lepper, M. (1985). Social status, cognitive alternatives, and intergroup relations. In H. Tajfel (Ed.), *Differentiation between social groups* (pp. 201–226). London: Academic Press.

van Baaren, R. B., Holland, R. W., Kawakami, K., & van Knippenberg, A. (2004). Mimicry and prosocial behavior. *Psychological Science, 15,* 71–74.

van Baaren, R. B., Holland, R. W., Steenaert, B., & van Knippenberg, A. (2003). A mimicry for money: Behavioral consequences of imitation. *Journal of Experimental Social Psychology, 39,* 393–398.

Van Boven, L., White, K., Kamada, A., & Gilovich, T. (2003). Intuitions about situational correction in self and others. *Journal of Personality and Social Psychology, 85,* 249–258.

Van den Bos, K. (2003). On the subjective quality of social justice: the role of affect as information in the psychology of justice judgments. *Journal of Personality and Social Psychology, 85,* 482–498.

Van den Bos, K., & Lind, E. W. (2001). Uncertainty management by means of fairness judgments. In M. P. Zanna (Ed.), *Advances in experimental social psychology* (Vol. 34, pp. 1–60). San Diego, CA: Academic Press.

Van Dick, R., Wagner, U., Pettigrew, T. F., Christ, O., Wolf, C., Petzel, T., Castro, V. S., & Jackson, J. S. (2004). Role of perceived importance in intergroup contact. *Journal of Personality and Social Psychology, 87,* 211–227.

Van Dyne, L., & LePine, J. A. (1998). Helping and voice extra-role behaviors: Evidence of construct and predictive validity. *Academy of Management Journal, 41,* 108–119.

Van Lange, P. A. M., & Kuhlman, M. D. (1994). Social value orientation and impressions of partner's honesty and intelligence: A test of the might versus morality effect. *Journal of Personality and Social Psychology, 67,* 126–141.

Van Overwalle, F. (1997). Dispositional attributions require the joint application of the methods of difference and agreement. *Personality and Social Psychology Bulletin, 23,* 974–980.

Van Overwalle, F. (1998). Causal explanation as constraint satisfaction: A critique and a feedforward connectionist alternative. *Journal of Personality and Social Psychology, 74,* 312–328.

Van Prodijen, J. W., Van den Bos, & Wilke, H. A. M. (2002). Procedural justice and status: Status salience as antecedent of procedural fairness effects. *Journal of Personality and Social Psychology, 83,* 1353–1361.

Van Vugt, M., & Hart, C. M. (2004). Social identity as social glue: The origins of group loyalty. *Journal of Personality and Social Psychology, 86,* 585–598.

Vandello, J. A., & Cohen, D. (1999). Patterns of individualism and collectivism in the United States. *Journal of Personality and Social Psychology, 77,* 279–292.

Vandello, J. A., & Cohen, D. (2003). Male honor and female fidelity: Implicit cultural scripts that perpetuate domestic violence. *Journal of Personality and Social Psychology, 84,* 997–1010.

Vanderbilt, A. (1957). *Amy Vanderbilt's complete book of etiquette.* Garden City, NY: Doubleday.

Vanman, E. J., Paul, B. Y., Ito, T. A., & Miller, N. (1997). The modern face of prejudice and structure features that moderate the effect of cooperation on affect. *Journal of Personality and Social Psychology, 73,* 941–959.

Vasquez, K., Durik, A. M., & Hyde, J. S. (2002). Family and work: Implications of adult attachment styles. *Personality and Social Psychology Bulletin, 28,* 874–886.

Vasquez, M. J. T. (2001). Leveling the playing field—Toward the emancipation of women. *Psychology of Women Quarterly, 25,* 89–97.

Vecchio, R. (1997). *Leadership.* Notre Dame, IN: University of Notre Dame Press.

Venkataraman, S. (1997). The distinctive domain of entrepreneurship research: An editor's perspective. In J. Katz (Ed.), *Advances in entrepreneurship, firm emergence, and growth.* 3: 119–138. Greenwich, CT: JAI Press.

Vertue, F. M. (2003). From adaptive emotion to dysfunction: An attachment perspective on social anxiety disorder. *Personality and Social Psychology Review, 7,* 170–191.

Vinokur, A., & Burnstein, E. (1974). Effects of partially shared persuasive arguments on group-induced shifts: A group problem-solving approach. *Journal of Personality and Social Psychology, 29,* 305–315.

Vinokur, A. D., & Schul, Y. (2000). Projection in person perception among spouses as a function of the similarity in their shared experiences. *Personality and Social Psychology Bulletin, 26,* 987–1001.

Vobejda, B. (1997, June 3). Pain of divorce follows children. *Washington Post.*

Volpe, K. (2002, July/August). Measuring emotion. *American Psychological Society, 15,* 7–8.

Vonk, R. (1998). The slime effect: Suspicion and dislike of likeable behavior toward superiors. *Journal of Personality and Social Psychology, 74,* 849–864.

Vonk, R. (1999). Differential evaluations of likeable and dislikeable behaviours enacted towards superiors and subordinates. *European Journal of Social Psychology, 29,* 139–146.

Vonk, R. (2002). Self-serving interpretations of flattery: Why ingratiation works. *Journal of Personality and Social Psychology, 82,* 515–526.

Vonk, R., & van Knippenberg, A. (1995). Processing attitude statements from in-group and out-group members: Effects of within-group and within-person inconsistencies on reading times. *Journal of Personality and Social Psychology, 68,* 215–227.

Vriz, A., Edward, K., & Bull, R. (2001). Police officers' ability to detect deceit: The benefit of indirect deception detection measures. *Legal and Criminological Psychology 81,* 365–376.

Wade, N. (2002, February 26). Fight or woo? Sex scents for a male mouse. *New York Times,* F3.

Wade, N. (2003, November 25). A course in evolution taught by chimps. *New York Times,* F1, F4.

Waldman, D. A., Ramiriz, G. G., House, R. J., & Puranam, P. (2001). Does leadership matter? CEO leadership attributes and profitability under conditions of perceived environmental uncertainty. *Academy of Management Journal, 44,* 134–143.

Walker, L. J., & Hennig, K. H. (2004). Differing conceptions of moral exemplarity: Just, brace, and caring. *Journal of Personality and Social Psychology, 86,* 629–647.

Walker, S., Richardson, D. S., & Green, L. R. (2000). Aggression among older adults: The relationship of interaction networks and gender role to direct and indirect responses. *Aggressive Behavior, 26,* 145–154.

Walster, E., & Festinger, L. (1962). The effectiveness of "overheard" persuasive communication. *Journal of Abnormal and Social Psychology, 65,* 395–402.

Walster, E., Walster, G. W., Piliavin, J., & Schmidt, L. (1973). "Playing hard-to-get": Understanding an elusive phenomenon. *Journal of Personality and Social Psychology, 26,* 113–121.

Wann, D. L., & Branscombe, N. R. (1993). Sports fans: Measuring degree of identification with their team. *International Journal of Sport Psychology, 24,* 1–17.

Wanous, J. P., Reiches, A. E., & Hudy, M. J. (1997). Overall job satisfaction: How good are single-item measures? *Journal of Applied Psychology, 82,* 247–252.

Waters, H. F., Block, D., Friday, C., & Gordon, J. (1993, July 12). Networks under the gun. *Newsweek,* 64–66.

Watson, C. B., Chemers, M. M., & Preiser, N. (2001). Collective efficacy: A multilevel analysis. *Personality and Social Psychology Bulletin, 27,* 1057–1068.

Watson, D., & Clark, L. A. (1994). *The PANAS-X: Manual for the positive and negative affect schedule—expanded form.* Iowa City: University of Iowa.

Watson, D., & Clark, L. A. (1997). Extraversion and its positive emotional core. In R. Hogan, J. A. Johnson, & S. R. Briggs (Eds.), *Handbook of personality psychology* (pp. 767–793). San Diego, CA: Academic Press.

Watson, D., Hubbard, B., & Wiese, D. (2000). Self–other agreement in personality and affectivity: The role of acquaintanceship, trait visibility, and assumed similarity. *Journal of Personality and Social Psychology, 78,* 546–558.

Watson, D., Wiese, D., Vaidya, J., & Tellgen, A. (1999). The two general activation systems of affect: Structural findings, evolutionary considerations, and psychological evidence. *Journal of Personality and Social Psychology, 76,* 805–819.

Watts, B. L. (1982). Individual differences in circadian activity rhythms and their effects on roommate relationships. *Journal of Personality, 50,* 374–384.

Wayne, J. H., Riordan, C. M., & Thomas, K. M. (2001). Is all sexual harassment viewed the same? Mock juror decisions in same- and cross-gender cases. *Journal of Applied Social Psychology, 86,* 179–187.

Wayne, S. J., & Ferris, G. R. (1990). Influence tactics, and exchange quality in supervisor–subordinate interactions: A laboratory experiment and field study. *Journal of Applied Psychology, 75,* 487–499.

Wayne, S. J., & Kacmar, K. M. (1991). The effects of impression management on the performance appraisal process. *Organizational Behavior and Human Decision Processes, 48,* 70–88.

Wayne, S. J., & Liden, R. C. (1995). Effects of impression management on performance ratings: A longitudinal study. *Academy of Management Journal, 38,* 232–260.

Wayne, S. J., Liden, R. C., Graf, I. K., & Ferris, G. R. (1997). The role of upward influence tactics in human resource decisions. *Personnel Psychology, 50,* 979–1006.

Weaver, S. E., & Ganong, L. H. (2004). The factor structure of the Romantic Beliefs Scale for African Americans and European Americans. *Journal of Social and Personal Relationships, 21,* 171–185.

Webster, G. D. (2003). Prosocial behavior in families: Moderators of resource sharing. *Journal of Experimental Social Psychology, 39,* 644–652.

Wegener, D. T., Petty, R. E., Smoak, N. D., & Fabrigar, L. R. (2004). Multiple routes to resisting attitude change. In E. S. Knowles & J. A. Linn (Eds.), *Resistance and persuasion* (pp. 13–38). Mahwah, NJ: Erlbaum.

Wegner, D. M. (1992a). The premature demise of the solo experiment. *Personality and Social Psychology Bulletin, 18,* 504–508.

Wegner, D. M. (1992b). You can't always think what you want: Problems in the suppression of unwanted thoughts. In M. Zanna (Ed.), *Advances in experimental social psychology* (Vol. 25, pp. 193–225). San Diego, CA: Academic Press.

Wegner, D. M. (1994). Ironic processes of mental control. *Psychological Review, 101,* 34–54.

Wegner, D. M., & Bargh, J. A. (1998). Control and automaticity in social life. In D. T. Gilbert, S. T. Fiske, & G. Lindsey (Eds.), *Handbook of social psychology* (4th ed.). New York: McGraw-Hill.

Wegner, D. M., & Gold, D. B. (1995). Fanning old flames: Emotional and cognitive effects of suppressing thoughts of a past relationship. *Journal of Personality and Social Psychology, 68,* 782–792.

Wegner, D. M., & Zanakos, S. (1994). Chronic thought suppression. *Journal of Personality, 62,* 615–640.

Wegner, D. T., & Petty, R. E. (1994). Mood management across affective states: The hedonic contingency hypothesis. *Journal of Personality and Social Psychology, 66,* 1034–1048.

Weigel, D. J., & Ballard-Reisch, D. S. (2002). Investigating the behavioral indicators of relational commitment. *Journal of Social and Personal Relationships 19,* 403–423.

Weinberg, M. S., Lottes, I. L., & Shaver, F. M. (1995). Swedish or American heterosexual college youth: Who is more permissive? *Archives of Sexual Behavior, 24,* 409–437.

Weiner, B. (1980). A cognitive (attribution) emotion–action model of motivated behavior: An analysis of judgments of help-giving. *Journal of Personality and Social Psychology, 39,* 186–200.

Weiner, B. (1985). An attributional theory of achievement motivation and emotion. *Psychological Review, 92,* 548–573.

Weiner, B. (1993). On sin versus sickness: A theory of perceived responsibility and social motivation. *American Psychologist, 48,* 957–965.

Weiner, B. (1995). *Judgments of responsibility: A foundation for a theory of social conduct.* New York: Guilford.

Weiner, B., Amirkhan, J., Folkes, V. S., & Verette, J. A. (1987). An attributional analysis of excuse giving: Studies of a naive theory of emotion. *Journal of Personality and Social Psychology, 52,* 316–324.

Weisberg, J. (1990, October 1). Fighting words. *The New Republic,* 42.

Weiss, H. M. (2002). Deconstructing job satisfaction: Separating evaluations, beliefs, and affective experiences. *Human Resource Management Review, 12,* 173–194.

Weissenberg, P., & Kavanagh, M. H. (1972). The independence of initiating structure and consideration: A review of the evidence. *Personnel Psychology, 25,* 119–130.

Weldon, E., & Mustari, L. (1988). Felt dispensability in groups of coactors: The effects of shared responsibility and explicit anonymity on cognitive effort. *Organizational Behavior and Human Decision Processes, 41,* 330–351.

Wells, G. L. (1984). The psychology of lineup identification. *Journal of Applied Social Psychology, 14,* 89–103.

Wells, G. L. (1993). What do we know about eyewitness identification? *American Psychologist, 48,* 553–571.

Wells, G. L., & Luus, C. A. E. (1990). Police lineups as experiments: Social methodology as a framework for properly conducted lineups. *Personality and Social Psychology Bulletin, 16,* 106–117.

Wells, G. L., Luus, C. A. E., & Windschitl, P. D. (1994). Maximizing the utility of eyewitness identification evidence. *Current Directions in Psychological Science, 3,* 194–197.

Wentura, D., Rothermund, K., & Bak, P. (2000). Automatic vigilance: The attention-grabbing power of approach- and avoidance-related social information. *Journal of Personality and Social Psychology, 78,* 1024–1037.

What gives? (2004, January/February) *AARP,* 78.

Wheeler, L., & Kim, Y. (1997). What is beautiful is culturally good: The physical attractiveness stereotype has different content in collectivistic cultures. *Personality and Social Psychology Bulletin, 23,* 795–800.

Whiffen, V. E., Aube, J. A., Thompson, J. M., & Campbell, T. L. (2000). Attachment beliefs and interpersonal contexts associated with dependency and self-criticism. *Journal of Social and Clinical Psychology, 19,* 184–205.

White, R. K. (1977). Misperception in the Arab-Israeli conflict. *Journal of Social Issues, 33,* 190–221.

Whitelaw, K. (2003, July 21). In death's shadow. *U.S. News & World Report,* 17–21.

Wiederman, M. W., & Allgeier, E. R. (1996). Expectations and attributions regarding extramarital sex among young married individuals. *Journal of Psychology & Human Sexuality, 8,* 21–35.

Wieselquist, J., Rusbult, C. E., Agnew, C. R., & Foster, C. A. (1999). Commitment, pro-relationship behavior, and trust in close relationships. *Journal of Personality and Social Psychology, 77,* 942–966.

Wiley, J. A., & Camacho, T. C. (1980). Life-style and future health: Evidence from the Alameda County study. *Preventive Medicine, 9,* 1–21.

Williams, C. L. (1992). The glass escalator: Hidden advantages for men in the "female" professions. *Social Problems, 39,* 253–267.

Williams, G. P., & Kleinke, C. L. (1993). Effects of mutual gaze and touch on attraction, mood, and cardiovascular reactivity. *Journal of Research in Personality, 27,* 170–183.

Williams, J. E., & Best, D. L. (1990). *Sex and psyche: Gender and self viewed cross-culturally.* Newbury Park, CA: Sage.

Williams, K. B., Radefeld, P. A., Binning, J. F., & Suadk, J. R. (1993). When job candidates are "hard-" versus "easy-to-get": Effects of candidate availability on employment decisions. *Journal of Applied Social Psychology, 23,* 169–198.

Williams, K. D. (2001). *Ostracism: The power of silence.* New York: Guilford Press.

Williams, K. D., & Karau, S. J. (1991). Social loafing and social compensation: The effects of expectations of co-worker performance. *Journal of Personality and Social Psychology, 61,* 570–581.

Williams, K. D., Cheung, C. K. T., & Choi, W. (2000). Cyberostracism: Effects of being ignored over the Internet. *Journal of Personality and Social Psychology, 79,* 748–762.

Williams, K. D., Harkins, S., & Latané, B. (1981). Identifiability as a deterrent to social loafing: Two cheering experiments. *Journal of Personality and Social Psychology, 40,* 303–311.

Williamson, G. M., & Schulz, R. (1995). Caring for a family member with cancer: Past communal behavior and affective reactions. *Journal of Applied Social Psychology, 25,* 93–116.

Williamson, T. M. (1993). From interrogation to investigative interviewing: Strategic trends in police questioning. *Journal of Community and Applied Social Psychology, 3,* 89–99.

Willingham, D. T., & Dunn, E. W. (2003). What neuroimaging and brain localization can do, cannot, and should not do for social psychology. *Journal of Personality and Social Psychology, 85,* 662–671.

Wilson, A. E., & Ross, M. (2000). The frequency of temporal-self and social comparisons in people's personal appraisals. *Journal of Personality and Social Psychology, 78,* 928–942.

Wilson, D. S. (1997). Altruism and organisms: Disentangling the themes of Multilevel Selection Theory. *The American Naturalist, 150,* S122-S134.

Wilson, D. W. (1981). Is helping a laughing matter? *Psychology, 18,* 6–9.

Wilson, J. P., & Petruska, R. (1984). Motivation, model attributes, and prosocial behavior. *Journal of Personality and Social Psychology, 46,* 458–468.

Wilson, M. L., & Wrangham, R. W. (2003). Intergroup relations in chimpanzees. *The Annual Review of Anthropology, 32,* 363–392.

Wilson, T. D., & Brekke, N. (1994). Mental contamination and mental correction: Unwanted influences on judgments and evaluations. *Psychological Bulletin, 116,* 117–142.

Wilson, T. D., & Kraft, D. (1993). Why do I love thee?: Effects of repeated introspections about a dating relationship on attitudes toward the relationship. *Personality and Social Psychology Bulletin, 19,* 409–418.

Winograd, E., Goldstein, F. C., Monarch, E. S., Peluso, J. P., & Goldman, W. P. (1999). The mere exposure effect in patients with Alzheimer's disease. *Neuropsychology, 13,* 41–46.

Winquist, J. R., & Larson, J. R., Jr. (1998). Information pooling: When it impacts group decision making. *Journal of Personality and Social Psychology, 74,* 317–377.

Wiseman, H. (1997). Far away from home: The loneliness experience of overseas students. *Journal of Social and Clinical Psychology, 16,* 277–298.

Wisman, A., & Koole, S. L. (2003). Hiding in the crowd: Can mortality salience promote affiliation with others who oppose one's world view? *Journal of Personality and Social Psychology, 84,* 511–526.

Witt, L. A., & Ferris, G. B. (2003). Social skill as moderator of the conscientiousness-performance relationship: Convergent results across four studies. *Journal of Applied Psychology, 88,* 808–820.

Wohl, M. J. A., & Branscombe, N. R. (2005). Forgiveness and collective guilt assignment to historical perpetrator groups depend on level of social category inclusiveness. *Journal of Personality and Social Psychology, 88.*

Wood, G. S. (2004, April 12 & 19). Pursuits of happiness. *The New Republic,* 38–42.

Wood, J. V. (1989). Theory and research concerning social comparisons of personal attributes. *Psychological Bulletin, 106,* 231–248.

Wood, J. V., & Wilson, A. E. (2003). How important is social comparison? In M. R. Leary & J. P. Tangney (Eds.), *Handbook of self and identity* (pp. 344–366). New York: Guilford Press.

Wood, W., & Quinn, J. M. (2003). Forewarned and forearmed? Two meta-analytic syntheses of forewarning of influence appeals. *Psychological Bulletin, 129,* 119–138.

Wood, W., Wong, F. Y., & Cachere, J. G. (1991). Effects of media violence on viewers' aggression in unconstrained social interaction. *Psychological Bulletin, 109,* 371–383.

Wood, W., Pool, G. J., Leck, K., & Purvis, D. (1996). Self-definition, defensive processing, and influence: The normative impact of majority and minority groups. *Journal of Personality and Social Psychology, 71,* 1181–1193.

Wooster, M. M. (2000, September). Ordinary people, extraordinary rescues. *American Enterprise, 11,* 18–21.

Wosinska, W., Cialdini, R. B., Barrett, D. W., & Reykowski, J. (Eds.). (2001). *The practice of social influence in multiple cultures.* New York: Lawrence Erlbaum Associates, Publishers.

Wright, S. C. (2001). Strategic collective action: Social psychology and social change. In R. Brown & S. Gaertner (Eds.), *Blackwell handbook of social psychology: Intergroup processes* (pp. 409–430). Oxford: Blackwell.

Wright, S. C., Taylor, D. M., & Moghaddam, F. M. (1990). Responding to membership in a disadvantaged group: From acceptance to collective protest. *Journal of Personality and Social Psychology, 58,* 994–1003.

Wright, S. C., Aron, A., McLaughlin-Volpe, T., & Ropp, S. A. (1997). The extended contact effect: Knowledge of cross-group friendships and prejudice. *Journal of Personality and Social Psychology, 73,* 73–90.

Wuensch, K. L., Castellow, W. A., & Moore, C. H. (1991). Effects of defendant attractiveness and type of crime on juridic judgment. *Journal of Social Behavior and Personality, 6,* 713–724.

Wyer, R. S., Jr., & Srull, T. K. (Eds.). (1994). *Handbook of social cognition* (2nd ed., Vol. 1). Hillsdale, NJ: Erlbaum.

Wyer, R. S., Jr., Budesheim, T. L., Lambert, A. J., & Swan, S. (1994). Person memory judgment: Pragmatic influences on impressions formed in a social context. *Journal of Personality and Social Psychology, 66,* 254–267.

Yoder, J. D., & Berendsen, L. L. (2001). "Outsider within" the firehouse: African American and white women firefighters. *Psychology of Women Quarterly, 25,* 27–36.

Yoshida, T. (1977). Effects of cognitive dissonance on task evaluation and task performance. *Japanese Journal of Psychology, 48,* 216–223.

Yovetich, N. A., & Rusbult, C. E. (1994). Accommodative behavior in close relationships: Exploring transformation of motivation. *Journal of Experimental Social Psychology, 30,* 138–164.

Yu, W. (1996, May 12). Many husbands fail to share housework. *Albany Times Union,* pp. A1, A7.

Yukl, G., & Falbe, C. M. (1991). Importance of different power sources in downward and lateral relations. *Journal of Applied Psychology, 76,* 416–423.

Yukl, G., & Tracey, J. B. (1992). Consequences of influence tactics used with subordinates, peers, and the boss. *Journal of Applied Psychology 77,* 525–535.

Yukl, G., Falbe, C. M., & Young, J. Y. (1993). Patterns of influence behavior for managers. *Group & Organizational Management, 18,* 5–28.

Yukl, G., Kim, H., & Chavez, C. (1999). Task importance, feasibility, and agent influence behavior as determinants of target commitment. *Journal of Applied Psychology, 84,* 137–143.

Yukl, G. A. (1998). *Leadership in organizations* (4th ed.). Englewood Cliffs, NJ: Prentice-Hall.

Yuval, G. (2004, June 15). Volunteers in college. *The New York Times,* p. A22.

Yzerbyt, V., Rocher, S., & Schradron, G. (1997). Stereotypes as explanations: A subjective essentialist view of group perception. In R. Spears, P. J. Oakes, N. Ellemers, & S. A. Haslam (Eds.), *The social psychology of stereotyping and group life* (pp. 20–50). Oxford: Blackwell.

Zaccaro, S. J., Foti, R. J., & Kenny, D. A. (1991). Self-monitoring and trait-based variance in leadership: An investigation of leader flexibility across multiple group situations. *Journal of Applied Psychology, 76,* 308–315.

Zadro, L., Williams, K. D., & Richardson, R. (2004). How low can you go? Ostracism by a computer is sufficient to lower self-reported levels of belonging, control, self-esteem, and meaningful existence. *Journal of Experimental Social Psychology, 40,* 560–567.

Zajonc, R. B. (1965). Social facilitation. *Science, 149,* 269–274.

Zajonc, R. B. (1968). Attitudinal effects of mere exposure [monograph]. *Journal of Personality and Social Psychology, 9,* 1–27.

Zajonc, R. B. (2001). Mere exposure: A gateway to the subliminal. *Current Directions in Psychological Science, 10,* 224–228.

Zajonc, R. B., & Sales, S. M. (1966). Social facilitation of dominant and subordinate responses. *Journal of Experimental Social Psychology, 2,* 160–168.

Zajonc, R. B., Heingartner, A., & Herman, E. M. (1969). Social enhancement and impairment of performance in the cockroach. *Journal of Personality and Social Psychology, 13,* 83–92.

Zajonc, R. B., Adelmann, P. K., Murphy, S. T., & Niedenthal, P. M. (1987). Convergence in the physical appearance of spouses. *Motivation and Emotion, 11,* 335–346.

Zaragoza, M. S., Payment, K. E., Ackil, U. K., Drivdahl, S. B., & Beck, M. (2001). Interviewing witnesses: Forced confabulation and confirmative feedback increase false memories. *Psychological Science, 12,* 473–478.

Zarate, M. A., Garcia, B., Garza, A. A., & Hitlan, R. T. (2004). Cultural threat and perceived realistic conflict as dual predictors of prejudice. *Journal of Experimental Social Psychology, 40,* 99–105.

Zdaniuk, B., & Levine, J. M. (1996). Anticipated interaction and thought generation: The role of faction size. *British Journal of Social Psychology, 35,* 201–218.

Zebrowitz, L. A. (1997). *Reading faces.* Boulder, CO: Westview Press.

Zebrowitz, L. A., Collins, M. A., & Dutta, R. (1998). The relationship between appearance and personality across the life span. *Personality and Social Psychology Bulletin, 24,* 736–749.

Zebrowitz, L. A., Fellous, J.-M., Mignault, A., & Andreoletti, C. (2003). Trait impressions as overgeneralized responses to adaptively significant facial qualities: Evidence from connectionist modeling. *Personality and Social Psychology Review, 7,* 194–215.

Zeitz, G. (1990). Age and work satisfaction in a government agency: A situational perspective. *Human Relations, 43,* 419–438.

Zillmann, D. (1979). *Hostility and aggression.* Hillsdale, NJ: Erlbaum.

Zillmann, D. (1983). Transfer of excitation in emotional behavior. In J. T. Cacioppo & R. E. Petty (Eds.), *Social psychophysiology: A sourcebook* (pp. 215–240). New York: Guilford Press.

Zillmann, D. (1988). Cognition–excitation interdependencies in aggressive behavior. *Aggressive Behavior, 14,* 51–64.

Zillmann, D. (1993). Mental control of angry aggression. In D. M. Wegner & J. W. Pennebaker (Eds.), *Handbook of mental control.* Englewood Cliffs, NJ: Prentice-Hall.

Zillmann, D. (1994). Cognition–excitation interdependencies in the escalation of anger and angry aggression. In M. Potegal & J. F. Knutson (Eds.), *The dynamics of aggression.* Hillsdale, NJ: Erlbaum.

Zillmann, D., Baron, R. A., & Tamborini, R. (1981). The social costs of smoking: Effects of tobacco smoke on hostile behavior. *Journal of Applied Social Psychology, 11,* 548–561.

Zimbardo, P. G. (1976). The human choice: Individuation, reason, and order versus deindividuation, impulse, and chaos. *Nebraska Symposium on Motivation, 17,* 237–307.

Zimbardo, P. G. (1977). *Shyness: What it is and what you can do about it.* Reading, MA: Addison-Wesley.

Zoglin, R. (1993). The shock of the blue. *Time, 142*(17), 71–72.

Zukerman, M. (1994). Behavioral expressions and biosocial bases of sensation seeking. New York: Cambridge University Press.

Zusne, L., & Jones, W. H. (1989). *Anomalistic psychology: A study of magical thinking* (2nd ed.). Hillsdale, NJ: Erlbaum.

NAME INDEX

Claire, T., 219
Clark, L. A., 299, 542, 550
Clark, M. S., 325, 327, 328, 390, 489
Clark, N. K., 507
Clark, R. D., 342
Clary, E. G., 394, 400, 401
Cleveland, J. N., 540
Clifford, J., 305
Clore, G. L., 68, 71, 264, 276, 510
Cobb, R. J., 299
Cobb, R. J., 330
Cogan, J. C., 198
Cohen, D., 311, 432, 433, 434, 435
Cohen, R., 301
Cohen, S., 521, 524
Cohn, E. G., 11, 440, 441
Coie, J. D., 437
Coles, R., 396
Collins, M. A., 272, 273
Collins, R. L., 396
Comstock, G., 428
Colquitt, J. A., 547
Conger, R. D., 325
Coniff, R., 90
Conner, M., 125
Conolley, E. S., 343
Conte, J. M., 538, 540
Conway, L. G., 340
Conway, M., 68, 213
Cook, O., 304
Cook, S. W., 404
Coontz, S., 319
Cooper, H. M., 441
Cooper, J. A, 156
Cornelius, T., 358, 359
Cornell, D. P., 156
Cornwell, B., 198
Corrigan, P. W., 276
Cortina, L. M., 19
Cosmides, L., 480
Cota, A. A., 465
Cottrell, C. A., 227
Cottrell, N. B., 473
Courneya, K. S., 181
Cozzarelli, C., 299
Craig, J.-A., 260
Cramer, R. E., 388
Crandall, C., 409
Crandall, C. S., 30, 211, 226, 234, 235, 278, 343
Crano, W. D., 140, 355
Crichtlow, B., 158, 387
Critelli, J. W., 272
Crites, S. L., 126, 133
Crocker, J., 19, 174, 188, 191, 197, 198
Crockett, W. H., 283
Cropanzano, R., 482, 485, 487, 541
Crosby, F. J., 187, 215, 216, 220
Cross, S. E., 175, 193
Cross, T. C., 552
Crowe, G., 183
Crowell, A., 410
Crowley, A. E., 148

Crowley, M., 277
Crutchfield, R. A., 342, 353
Cummings, L. L., 486
Cunningham, J. D., 320
Cunningham, M. R., 115, 273, 274, 393
Cunningham, W. A., 54, 55
Curtis, J. T., 297
Cutler, B. L., 509, 515, 518

D'Agostino, P. R., 270
Dallman, M., 533
Darley, J., 190
Darley, J. M., 31, 367, 381, 382, 383, 385, 387, 394, 448, 449, 515
Dasgupta, N., 462
Daubman, K. A., 351, 404
David, B., 175, 176
Davila, J., 299, 330
Davis, K. E., 93, 94
Davis, M. H., 395, 400
Davison, J. Jr., 152
Dawkins, R., 409
Day, D. V., 115
De Dreu, C. K. W., 482
De Judicibus, M. A., 326
De La Ronde, C., 310
de Waal, F., 390
Deaux, K., 175, 178, 179, 213
Decety, J., 410
DeDreu, C., 482
DeDreu, C. K. W., 480
Dejong, T., 276
DeGroot, T., 552
DeJong, W., 358
Delaney, H. J., 276
DeLongis, A., 521
den Ouden, 397
DeNisi, A. S., 69
DeNoon, D., 325
DePaulo, B. M., 84, 88, 92, 302, 404
Depret, E., 224
DeSteno, D., 227, 228, 328
Deuser, W. E., 440
Deutsch, M., 342, 346, 481
Devine, P. G., 16, 156, 211, 237, 246
Diamond, L. M., 313
Diassanayake, E., 298
Diekman, A. B., 170
Diener, E., 273, 540
Dietrich, D. M., 408
Dietz, J., 446
Dijksterhuis, A., 185, 230, 345, 346, 390
Dion, K. I., 273
Dion, K. K., 272, 273
Dion, K. L., 198, 230, 272, 273
Dittmann, M., 309
Ditto, P. H., 134
Dodge, K. A., 436, 437
Doherty, K., 405
Dollard, J., 421, 423, 425, 450
Donaldson, S. I., 194
Donnerstein, E., 431
Doosje, B., 101, 102, 224, 235, 246

Dorfman, A., 317
Doucet, J., 330
Dovidio, J. F., 144, 222, 229, 230, 238, 245, 262
Downs, A. C., 517
Drake, R. A., 261
Druen, P. B., 115
Drumm, P., 316
Duan, C., 394
Dubois, N., 187
Dubro, A., 480
Duck, J. M., 132
Duck, S., 306
Duggan, E. S., 305
Dugoni, B. L., 355
Duncan, J., 54
Duncan, N. C., 273
Dunkley, D. M., 504, 519, 520, 526, 527, 528
Dunn, E. W., 17
Dunn, J., 301
Dunning, D., 222, 401, 515
Durik, A. M., 325
Durso, F. T., 222
Dutta, R., 273
Dutton, D. G., 317

Eagly, A. E., 379, 380
Eagly, A. H., 93, 126, 145, 150, 153, 154, 170, 213, 214, 219, 224, 353
Earley, P. C., 475
Early, S., 394
Earn, B. M., 198
Ebert, R., 85
Edwards, K., 69, 70, 516
Edwards, T. M., 325
Ee, J. S., 272
Eggleston, T. J., 161
Egloff, B., 262
Eich, E., 69
Eidelman, S., 191
Eisenberg, N., 242, 393, 404
Eisenman, R., 283
Eisenstadt, D., 161, 185
Eiser, J. R., 262
Ekman, P., 85, 86, 88, 92
Elder, G. H. Jr., 325
Elkin, R., 158
Ellemers, N., 216, 218, 235
Elliot, A. J., 156, 262, 299
Ellman, I. M., 331
Ellsworth, P. C., 86, 515
Ely, R. J., 215
Embree, J. M., 396
Emlen, S. T., 281
Endo, Y., 311
Epley, N., 32, 51, 401
Eron, L. D., 428
Erwin, P. G., 305
Eshkoli, N., 396
Eshleman, A., 211, 235
Esses, V. M., 132, 218, 231, 390
Essex, M. J., 183

Latané, B., 31, 343, 381, 382, 383, 387, 474, 475
Lau, M. L., 441
Lau, S., 305
Laurenceau, J.-P., 302
Lavie, N., 260
Lawton, S. F., 439
Lazarus, R. S., 521
Leary, M. R., 184, 194, 259, 260, 307
Leary, W. E., 515
Leatham, G., 306
LeBlanc, M. M., 445
Lecci, L., 225
Ledbetter, J. E., 139
Lee, A., 321
Lee, A. Y., 269
Lee, Y. T., 104
Lehman, D. R., 158, 159, 311
Lehman, T. C., 404
Leippe, M., 158
Leippe, M. R., 161, 185
Lemley, B., 275, 276
Lemonick, M. D., 317
LePine, J. A., 546, 548
Lerner, R. M., 390
Letchford, J., 305
Levenson, R. W., 329
Leventhal, G. S., 486
Levin, P. A., 71, 393
Levine, J. M., 355
Levine, M., 504, 517
Levine, R. V., 387
Levy, B., 200
Levy, B. R., 529, 530
Levy, K. N., 328
Lewin, T., 320
Lewis, J., 316
Lewis, M., 179, 269
Leyens, J.-P., 203
Liberman, A., 97, 146, 150
Liberman, N., 60, 99, 559
Lickel, B., 177, 462, 463
Liden, R. C., 115, 356
Lieberman, J. D., 450
Liebert, R. M., 392
Lin, M.-C., 299
Lin, M. H., 108, 112, 114
Lind, E. A., 547
Lind, E. W., 485
Linden, E., 20
Lindsay, D. S., 512
Lindsey, E. W., 300
Linville, P. W., 174, 223, 224
Linz, D., 431, 509
Lipkus, I. M., 156
Lippa, R., 194
Lipton, J. E., 13
Liu, T. J., 387
Locke, E. A., 550
Locke, V., 222
Lockwood, P., 181
Lockwood, R. L., 301
Loehlin, J. C., 542

Loftus, E. F., 507, 510, 511, 512
Loftus, J., 113
Long, C. R., 304
Longo, L. C., 274
Lopez, D. F., 362
Lopez, F. G., 299
Lord, C. G., 200
Lorenz, K., 420
Losch, M., 158
Lottes, I. L., 319
Louis-Dreyfus, E., 69, 516
Low, M. B., 559
Lowery, L., 85
Lucas, J. A., 216
Lucas, R. R., 540
Luce, C., 395
Luczak, S. E., 19
Lui, T. J., 156
Lundberg, J. K., 276, 278
Lundqvist, D., 57
Luo, S., 283, 309
Luus, C. A. E., 511, 514
Lycett, E. J., 299
Lydon, J. E., 311
Lynch, M., 156
Lyness, K. S., 215
Lyons, P. M., 517

Ma, H. K., 396
Maass, A., 223, 342
Macauley, J., 391
MacCoun, R. J., 518
MacDonald, H., 58
Mack, D., 276
MacKenzie, S. B., 547
Mackie, D. M., 71, 223, 226, 227
Macrae, C. N., 220, 222, 279, 385
Madey, S. F., 62
Madson, L., 175
Maddux, W. W., 390
Maeda, E., 302
Maestripieri, D., 297
Magner, N. R., 486
Maheswaran, D., 134, 150
Mahler, H. I. M., 261
Mahoney, S., 315
Maio, G. R., 125, 132, 139, 299
Maisonneuve, J., 269
Major, B., 175, 188, 189, 191, 197, 198, 199, 220
Makijani, M. G., 214
Malamuth, N. M., 431
Malone, B. E., 88
Malone, P. S., 97, 99, 509
Maner, J. K., 272, 411
Manis, M. M., 10
Mann, L., 366, 367
Manning, J. T., 312
Mannix, L. N., 278
Manstead, A. S. R., 135, 136, 226
Marcus, D. K., 273, 274
Markey, P. M., 281
Markman, G. D., 97, 181, 556, 557

Markman, K. D., 496
Markus, H., 175, 181
Markus, H. R., 175, 193
Marques, J., 193, 243
Martens, T. K., 515
Martin, C. L., 237
Martin, L., 13
Martin, L. L., 71, 156, 510
Martin, R., 304
Martinez, R., 278
Martinot, D., 214
Martz, J. M., 311, 331
Marx, R., 304
Maslach, C., 350
Mastekaasa, A., 325
Master, S., 311, 312
Maticka-Tydale, E., 314
Matsushima, R., 302, 305
Matz, D. C., 312
May, J. L., 263
May, K. A., 276
Mayer, J. D., 68, 393
Mayo, C., 92
Mazzella, R., 517
Mazzoni, G., 512
Mazzoni, G. A., 513
McAdams, D. P., 401
McAndrew, F. T., 409, 410
McArthur, L. Z., 223
McAuley, E., 181
McCabe, M. P., 326
McCall, M., 10
McClintock, C. G., 481
McCloskey, A. L., 509
McClure, J., 97
McConahay, J. B., 238
McConnell, A. R., 222
McConnell, W., 426
McCoy, S. K., 198
McCullough, M. E., 437, 452, 453
McCusker, C., 480
McDavid, J. W., 353
McDonald, F., 285
McDonald, H. E., 68
McDonald, R. D., 263
McEwen, B. S., 521
McGarty, C., 134, 246
McGillis, D., 94
McGonagle, K. A., 329
McGue, M., 397
McGuire, C. V., 184
McGuire, S., 301, 305
McGuire, W. J., 154, 184
McHale, S. M., 301
McHoskey, J. W., 397
McKelvie, S. J., 274, 276
McKinney, K. D., 244
McLaughlin, L., 327
McLaughlin-Volpe, T., 179, 468
McMillan, D., 43, 44
McNall, K., 507
McNulty, J. K., 60, 327, 329
McQuinn, R. D., 304

Park, J., 71
Parke, 221
Parker, S., 237
Parks, G., 478
Patience, R. A., 312
Patrick, H., 174, 273
Patterson, M., 194
Paul, E. L., 314
Paulhus, D. L., 116
Pavalko, E. K., 188
Pearson, C. M., 447
Pearson, K., 321
Pedersen, D. M., 270
Pedersen, W. C., 312
Pederson, W. C., 450
Pelfrey, M., 404
Pelham, B. W., 18
Pendry, L. F., 279
Pennebaker, J. W., 276
Penner, L. A., 389, 401
Penrod, S., 431, 509
Penrod, S. D., 515
Penton-Voak, I., 273
Pentony, J. F., 266
Perls, T. T., 530
Perrett, D. I., 276
Perrew, P. L., 325
Pessin, J., 472
Peterson, R. S., 483, 550, 552
Peterson, V. S., 214
Petruska, R., 385
Pettigrew, T. F., 124, 223, 224, 235, 244,
    247
Pettijohn, T. E. F., 14
Pettit, G. S., 300
Petty, R., 152
Petty, R. E., 71, 125, 134, 140, 145,
    150, 151
Petty, R. J., 126, 139, 140, 147
Phelps, E. A., 54
Phemister, S., 392
Pickett, C. L., 88, 260
Pierce, C. A., 310
Piercy, M., 279
Pietromonaco, P., 49
Pietromonaco, P. R., 302
Pihl, R. O., 441, 442
Piliavin, J. A., 390, 400
Pillemer, K., 301
Pinel, E. C., 202
Pines, A., 328
Pinker, S., 409
Piotrowski, M., 117
Pittman, T. S., 92
Pizarro, D., 380
Plant, E. A., 211, 219, 246
Pleban, R., 191
Plog, A. E., 113
Podsakoff, P. M., 547, 550
Poh, L. L., 235
Polivy, J., 181
Pollak, K. I., 177
Pollock, C. L., 360

Pomerantz, E. M., 311
Pond, K., 306
Pontari, B. A., 116, 117, 118
Ponzetti, J. J. Jr., 305
Postmes, T., 177, 199, 201, 476, 477
Poteat, G. M., 305
Poulous, R. W., 392
Powell, A. A., 246, 247
Pratkanis, A. R., 495
Pratto, F., 53, 242
Preiser, N., 181
Preister, J. R., 125
Prentice, D. A., 135, 138, 188
Previti, D., 329
Prins, K. S., 305
Pronin, E., 201
Pruitt, D. G., 479, 483, 484
Przybyla, D. P. J., 390
Puente, S., 434
Pullium, R. M., 399
Pusecker, P. A., 181
Putcha-Bhagavatula, A., 312
Pyszczynski, T., 103, 180, 186, 210, 240

Queller, S., 222
Quigley, B. M., 517
Quinn, D. M., 200
Quinn, J. M., 152

Rahe, R. H., 520
Rainey, D., 276
Rankin, C. T., 320, 324
Rapson, R. L., 296, 313
Ray, G. E., 305
Read, S. J., 93
Ready, R., 299
Redersdorff, S., 214
Regan, P. C., 309, 316, 326
Reicher, S., 468
Reichers, A. E., 540
Reichmuth, C. J., 270
Reidhead, S., 194
Reimann, B. C., 552
Reis, H. T., 262, 296, 299, 328
Reisman, J. M., 307
Reiss, A. J., 428
Reiss, H. T., 299
Rempel, J. K., 105
Reno, R. R., 340, 344, 345
Rensberger, B., 317
Rentfrow, P. J., 281
Rentsch, J. R., 174
Reskin, B., 191
Reynolds, K. J., 173, 175, 176
Reynolds, P. D., 558
Rhodes, G., 275, 276
Rhodewalt, F., 152
Rice, M. E., 421
Richard, F. D., 368
Richards, Z., 44, 222
Richardson, D., 32
Richardson, D. R., 420, 438
Richardson, D. S., 438

Richardson, R., 307
Richman, C. L., 397
Ridgeway, C. L., 214
Ridley, M., 409
Riess, M., 161
Riggio, H. R., 330
Riggio, R. E., 279
Rilling, J., 410
Riordan, C. M., 106
Ritchie, L. D., 302
Ro, T., 260
Robbins, T. L., 69
Roberson, Q., 547, 548
Robins, R. W., 99, 184, 324
Robinson, L. A., 105
Robinson, M. D., 276
Robinson, P. H., 448, 449
Robinson, R., 482, 483
Robinson, R. J., 482, 515
Roccas, S., 174, 466
Rochat, F., 367
Rocher, S., 221
Roese, N. J., 32, 62, 558
Rogers, R. J., 103
Rogers, R. W., 32, 427
Roggman, L. A., 274
Rohles, W. S., 49
Rokach, A., 304
Roland, E., 443
Romer, D., 387
Rosenbaum, M. E., 283
Rosenberg, E. L., 86
Rosenberg, M., 184
Rosenblood, L. K., 260
Rosenfield, H. W., 86
Rosenhan, D. L., 393
Rosenthal, A. M., 381
Rosenthal, E., 302
Rosenthal, R., 45, 92
Roskos-Ewoldsen, D. R., 139, 143
Rosnow, J., 31
Ross, D., 428
Ross, J., 559
Ross, L., 100, 103, 201
Ross, M., 9, 58, 60, 103, 181, 556
Ross, S., 428
Rotenberg, K. J., 305, 307
Roth, J. A., 428
Roth, P., 556
Rothermund, K., 285
Rothgerber, H., 223
Rothman, A. J., 48
Rotton, J., 11, 440, 441
Rowatt, W. C., 115
Rowe, P. M., 259
Roy, M. M., 283, 284
Rozell, D., 476, 477
Rozin, P., 65, 85
Rubin, J. Z., 32
Rubin, Z., 313
Ruble, D. N., 326
Ruder, M., 18, 48, 71, 72
Rudman, L. A., 231

Rueter, M. A., 325
Runtz, M. G., 106
Runyan, A. S., 214
Rusbult, C. E., 329, 330, 331
Ruscher, J. B., 113
Rushton, J. P., 409
Russell, C., 260
Russell, G. W., 397, 436
Russell, J. A., 85, 86
Russell, J. M., 85
Russell, R. J. H., 409
Russo, J. E., 518
Rutkowski, G. K., 387
Ruvolo, A. P., 299
Ruvolo, C. M., 299
Ryan, C. S., 221
Ryan, M., 175
Ryan, M. K., 176
Ryckman, R. M., 278, 287
Ryff, C. D., 183, 297

Sabini, J., 311, 312
Sadler, P., 281
Saelens, B. E., 533
Saenz, D. S., 200
Sager, K., 397
Sakder, D., 45
Sakder, M., 45
Sales, S. M., 473
Sallis, J., 533
Sally, D., 481
Salmela-Aro, K., 306
Salovey, P., 223, 224, 266, 349, 380, 393
Salvarani, G., 394
Samuels, S., 495
Sanders, G. S., 473
Sanders, J., 351
Sanders, M. R., 329
Sangrador, J. L., 319
Sani, F., 468
Sanitioso, R. B., 186
Sanna, L. J., 62, 181
Santee, R. T., 350
Sattler, D. N., 397
Savitsky, K., 52, 63
Schachter, D. L., 69
Schachter, S., 70, 261, 269, 280, 317
Schaller, M., 223, 408
Scheier, M. F., 306
Schein, V. E., 214
Scher, S. J., 485
Scherbaum, C., 200
Schilling, E. A., 329
Schimel, J., 286
Schlenker, B. R., 116, 117, 118, 161, 186, 405
Schlenker, R. B., 394
Schmid, R. E., 320
Schmitt, D. P., 12, 13, 14, 317
Schmitt, E., 326
Schmitt, M. T., 171, 192, 198, 199, 216, 246, 247
Schneider, B., 544

Schneider, M. E., 404
Schooler, J. W., 507
Schradron, G., 221
Schreiber, H. J., 218
Schubert, T. W., 87
Schul, Y., 112, 324
Schulz, R., 399
Schulz-Hardt, S., 495, 496
Schumacher, M., 276
Schusterman, R. J., 270
Schutte, J. W., 518
Schwartz, S. H., 466gi
Schwarz, N., 48, 68, 136
Schwarzer, R., 58
Scutt, D., 312
Seal, D. W., 310
Searcy, E., 404
Sears, D. O., 126, 149, 237
Sechrist, G. B., 248
Sedikides, C., 110,179, 190
Seery, M. D., 188
Segal, M. M., 269
Seibt, B., 400
Seligman, M. E. P., 104
Selim, J., 264, 284, 298
Senecal, C., 325
Sera, A. F., 243
Seta, C. E., 68
Seta, J. J., 68
Settles, I. H., 174
Shackelford, T. K., 12, 14, 326
Shah, J., 11, 362, 363
Shams, M., 304
Shanab, M. E., 366
Shane, S., 555, 556
Shannon, M. L., 276
Shapiro, A., 326
Shapiro, D. L., 486
Shapiro, J. P., 263
Sharmi, B., 553
Sharp, M. J., 115
Sharpe, D., 32
Shavelson, R. J., 174
Shaver, F. M., 319
Shaver, P. R., 299, 312
Shavitt, S., 133
Shaw, D., 301
Shaw, J. K., 391
Shaw, J. L., 390
Shaw, L. L., 407
Sheehan, E. P., 276, 278
Sheeran, P., 183
Sheldeon, W. H., 278
Shepperd, J. A., 58, 60, 147, 181, 558
Sherif, M., 224, 232, 485
Sherman, D. A., 222
Sherman, J. W., 114
Sherman, M. D., 305
Sherman, S. J., 58, 177, 222, 223
Sherman, S. S., 368
Shiomi, K., 302, 305
Shoda, Y., 174
Shore, L. M., 540

Shuffelton, F., 325
Shute, R., 438
Shykoff, B. E., 524
Sidanius, J., 242
Sigall, H., 32
Sigelman, C. K., 273
Sikes, M. P., 187
Silberman, I., 559
Sillars, A. L., 327
Silverman, R. A., 216
Silverstein, R., 183
Silvia, P. J., 192
Simon, B., 177, 181, 223, 224, 467
Simon, L., 156, 240
Simon, M., 556, 558
Simons, T., 547, 548
Simpson, J. A., 310, 319, 330
Simpson, P. A., 214
Sinclair, L., 231
Singer, B., 297
Singh, R., 235, 283
Sistrunk, F., 353
Sivacek, J., 140
Skarlicki, D. P., 446
Skowronski, J. J., 179
Slee, P., 438
Sloane, E. S., 401
Slugoski, B., 243
Smart, L., 188
Smeaton, G., 283
Smilver, M. H., 530
Smirles, K. E., 106
Smith, C. M., 355
Smith, D., 527
Smith, D. E., 88
Smith, E. R., 18, 113, 222, 226, 227, 324
Smith, K. D., 408
Smith, P. B., 12, 29, 342, 344, 351
Smith, P. K., 301, 443
Smith, S. S, 32
Smith, V. I., 515
Smorti, A., 444
Smuts, B., 297
Sniffen, M. J., 517
Snyder, M., 193, 400, 401
Soderlind, A., 304
Solomon, M. R., 274
Solomon, S., 103, 180
Sommer, K. L., 495
Southwick, L., 158
Spangler, W. D., 552
Spears, R., 136, 218, 224, 226, 235, 476, 477
Spencer, S. J., 156, 200, 201, 230, 231
Spicer, C. V., 225
Sprafkin, J. N., 392
Spranca, M. D., 99
Sprecher, S., 272, 309, 324, 489
Srull, T. K., 43, 220
Stack, A. D., 450
Stacy, J., 327
Stafford, L., 320, 324
Stahlberg, D., 495

SUBJECT INDEX

Above-average effect, 186
Abstractions, 113
Abu Ghraib prison, 242–243, 243f
Acceptance, nonverbal cues and, 88
Accuracy, as core value, 7
Action, social influence on, 507–508
Actor-observer effect, 102–103
Actual self, 15
Adaptive response, 285
Additive tasks, 474
Adolescence, 300
Adversarial approach, 506
Affect
    attraction and, 262–263
    as basic response system, 261–262
    brightness and, 276
    cognition and, 286, 287f
    influence on cognition, 68–70, 68f, 70f
    intensity/strength of, 261–262, 262f
    manipulating, to influence behavior, 265–267, 266f
    positive, 266–267, 266f
Affect-attraction relationship, 263–267
Affect-centered model of attraction, 286, 286f
Affective state
    aggression and, 422
    fairness judgments and, 487–488, 488f
    interpersonal attraction and, 259
    regulation of, 73–74, 74f
Affiliation
    as adaptive response, 259–260, 260f
    importance, for human existence, 259–261, 260f
    need for (See Need for affiliation)
African Americans
    crime rates and, 223
    stereotype threat and, 200–201
    stress and, 523
Aggression, 418–420, 419f
    alcohol consumption and, 440–442
    biological factors, 420–421
    causes of, 425–431, 425f, 427f, 429f
    cognition and, 426–427, 427f
    cultures of honor and, 432–433, 433f
    direct vs. indirect, 438
    drive theories of, 421–422, 421f
    ego threat and, 437
    emotion and, 426–427, 427f
    exposure to media violence and, 428–430, 429f
    frustration and, 425–426
    gender differences in, 438, 438f
    as learned form of social behavior, 423f
    in long-term relationships, 442–447, 443f, 445f
    modern theories of, 422–423, 423f, 424f
    narcissism and, 437
    overt, 446
    personal causes of, 435–438, 436f, 438f
    prevention/control of, 447–453
        cognitive interventions, 449–451, 451f
        forgiveness, 451–453, 452f
        punishment, 447–449, 448f
    sensation seeking and, 437–438
    situational determinants of, 439–442, 441f
    social cause of, 425–427, 425f, 427f
    temperature and, 439–440, 441f
    theoretical perspectives, 420–424, 421f, 423f
    type A behavior pattern and, 435–436, 436f
    violent pornography and, 430–432, 430f
    workplace, 445–447, 445f
Aggression, workplace, 426
Aging, self-perceptions of, 530–531, 531f
AIDS, 320
AIDS volunteers, 399–400
Airport security, 210–211
Alcohol consumption, aggression and, 440–442
Altruism
    definition of, 379
    disasters and, 396–397, 397f
    organizational citizenship behavior and, 546
    reciprocal, 410–411, 479–480
    selective, 407, 407f
    volunteering and, 401
Altruistic personality, 397–398
Ambivalence, 124, 125
Ambivalent racial attitudes, 241
Anchoring and adjustment heuristic, 49–52, 52f, 99
Anger, 86
Anger, health and, 527
Anonymity, 476
Anxiety
    in marriage, 324
    stress-based, 202
Apologies, 449–450
Appearance anxiety, 272–273
Appearance stereotypes, 273
Appraisals, aggression and, 422
Aristotle, 280
Arousal
    aggression and, 422
    heightened, 426–427, 427f
Aspirations, 483
Associated effect, of emotions on attraction, 263, 264f
Assumed similarity, 324
Attachment patterns, 296
Attachment style, 298, 305
Attacking an opponent's network, 484
Attention, 42–43
Attitude accessibility, 139, 139f
Attitude-behavior consistency, 139, 139f
Attitude extremity, 140
Attitudes
    about gay marriage, 323, 323f
    actively defending, 153–154, 154f
    ambivalent, 124–125, 125
    based on reasoned thought, 141–143, 142f
    behavior and, 137–138, 140–141
    behavior prediction and, 125–126, 125f
    changing, 126
    explicit vs. implicit, 238
    expression of, situational constraints on, 138–139
    formation of, 126, 127
    functions of, 133–136, 134f, 136f
    personal experience and, 140–141
    shaping, classical conditioning and, 127–130, 128f

influence, on affect, 70, 72–74
intense emotion and, 510–511
prejudice and, 200
processing capacity and, 46
regulation of affective states, 73–74, 74f
Cognitive dissociation, social rejection and, 307
Cognitive dissonance, 127, 155–156, 540
Cognitive interventions, for aggression prevention/control, 449–451, 451f
Cognitive interviews, 513–514
Cognitive overload, impression management and, 116–118, 116f
Cognitive perspective, impression formation and, 112–114
Cognitive processes, 10–11
Cognitive therapy, 306
Cohesiveness
conformity and, 343
of group, 465
Co-innovation, 21, 22f
Cold stare, 86
Collective guilt
Abu Ghraib prison and, 242–243
in reducing racism, 246, 247f
Collective self-efficacy, 181, 182f
Collectivistic cultures, 101, 475
Commitment, 356
Common in-group identity model, 245
Common sense, 8, 17–18
Communal behavior, 327, 328f
Communication
faulty, 482
in social dilemmas, 480–481
Communicators
attractiveness of, 148, 149f
persuasion and, 145–149
Companionate love, 317, 325
Comparative negligence, 495
Competence, context and, 173–174, 173f
Competition
cooperation and, 480f
for resources, as prejudice source, 232–233, 232f
Competitive orientation, 480
Complaining, self-serving bias and, 187
Complementarity, 281, 281f
Compliance
definition of, 339
principles of, 356
tactics
based on commitment or consistency, 357–359, 358f, 359f
based on reciprocity, 359–360
based on scarcity, 360–361, 361f
Compliance professionals, 356
Computer dating websites, 315, 315f
Condescension, 426
Confabulation, 512–513
Confirmation bias, 518
Conflict
causes of, 478, 481–483, 482f
elements in, 481
resolution of, 462, 483–485
Conformity, 339–341, 340f
bases of, 346–349, 348f, 349f
cohesiveness and, 343
factors affecting, 343–345, 345f
gender differences in, 353
group size and, 343–344

measuring, 347, 349
research on, 341–342, 341f
resisting, 350–353
Conscientiousness, organizational citizenship behavior and, 546
Consensual validation, 284–285
Consensus, 95
Consideration (person-orientation), 551, 551f
Consistency, 95, 356
Consultation, 370
Consultative techniques, 370–371
Consumate love, 318–319
Contact hypothesis, 244
Context
competence and, 173–174, 173f
perceptions of attractiveness and, 276
self-evaluations and, 192–193, 192f
Contrast effect, 276
Contributory negligence, 495
Control group, 514
Controllable factors, attribution and, 96–97
Controlled processing
definition of, 53
vs. automatic processing, 54–56
Cooperation, 461, 477–479, 479f
Cooperative orientation, 480
Coping, with stress, 524–525, 525f
Coping mechanisms, gender differences in, 525–526
Core values, 7
Correlation, 21, 23–24, 24f
Correspondence bias (fundamental attribution error)
attributions about groups, 101–102, 102f
cultural factors in, 101
description of, 99–101, 100f
Correspondent inference, theory of, 93–94
Cortisol, 523, 530
Counterarguments, 152–154, 154f
Counterfactual thinking, 61–63, 61f, 67, 73, 558
Courtesy, organizational citizenship behavior and, 547
Covariation principle, 198
Creativity, 60
Credibility, of communicators, 145–148, 148f
Crime, workplace aggression and, 445–446, 445f
Criticism
destructive, 482, 482f
rejection from out-group members, 493–495 494f
Cultural context
biological factors and, 12–14
social behavior and, 11–12, 11f
stigmatized identity and, 200–201, 201f
Cultural differences
family interactions and, 300–301
self-conceptions and, 175
Culture
conformity and, 350–351
correspondence bias and, 101
friendships and, 302–303
Cultures of honor, 432–434, 433f, 435f

Deadline technique, 361, 361f
Death wish (thanatos), 420
Debriefing, 32, 32f
Deception
definition of, 31–32
recognition of, 88–90, 89f, 91f
Decision/commitment, 318–319

Decision making
  definition of, 490
  in groups, 490–497, 493*f*, 494*f*, 496*f*
  process for, 490–491
  representativeness heuristic and, 47
  social decision schemes and, 491
Defendants
  appearance of, 517, 518*f*
  gender of, 517
  perceptions of, effects of media coverage on, 508–509, 509*f*
  race of, 517
Defensive attribution, 107
Deindividuation, 475–477, 476*f*
Dependent variable, 25
Depression
  attribution and, 105, 106*f*
  cognition and, 69
Descriptive norms, 344–345
Desegregation, 124
Desensitizing effect, 431
Destructive criticism, 482, 482*f*
Destructive obedience, 366–367
  resisting effects of, 367–369, 368*f*
Deterrence value, of punishment, 448–449
Devil's advocate technique, 496, 496*f*
Differential respect, gender stereotypes and, 218
Diffusion of responsibility, 382, 383
Directive-permissive dimension, of leaders, 552
Disappointment, counterfactual thinking and, 63
Disasters, altruism and, 396–397, 397*f*
Discounting principle, 97, 98*f*
Discrimination, 198, 211, 212–213
  definition of, 236–237
  evaluation differences and, 220–221
  vs. prejudice, 226
Discrimination claims, 187
Disengagement, social rejection and, 307
Dismissing attachment style, 299
Disobedient models, 367–368
Displaced aggression, 450, 451
Dissimilarity, interpersonal attraction and, 259
Dissonance
  attitude change and, 160–161, 160*f*
  beneficial behavior changes and, 161–162, 162*f*
  less-leads-to-more effect, 160–161, 160*f*
  as universal human experience, 158–160, 159*f*
  unpleasantness of, 158
Dissonance reduction, 156
Dissonance theory, 156
Distinctiveness, 95
Distraction-conflict theory, 473–474
Distributive justice, 547
Distributive justice (equity; fairness), 486
Divorce, 11–12, 331
Dominant responses, 472
Door-in-the-face technique, 360
Downward social comparison, 190
Drive theory
  of aggression, 421–422, 421*f*
  of social facilitation, 472–473, 472*f*

Ease-of-use heuristic, 71
Egocentricism, altruistic personality and, 398
Ego-defensive function, of attitudes, 135
Egoism, 401
Ego threat, 437

Elaboration-likelihood model of persuasion, 150–151, 150*f*
Elite group, 5
Emblems, 86
Emergencies
  correct interpretation of, 384–387, 386*f*, 387*f*
  failure to notice, 382–384
  helping, decision-making for, 388–389
  necessary knowledge/skills to act, determining, 388
  pluralistic ignorance and, 387
  responding to, 379–380, 380*f*
  responsibility to provide help, 388, 388*f*
  steps to prosocial behavior, 381–389, 381*f*, 383*f*–388*f*
  time pressure and, 384, 385*f*
  unresponsiveness to, 380–381, 380*f*
  witnesses to, 380–381, 382
Emergent group norms, 493
Emotional contagion, 84
Emotional distress, individual responses to, 395–396
emotion-focused coping, 524
Emotions
  aggression and, 426–427, 427*f*
  basic, 85
  combinations of, 85, 85*f*
  effect on attraction, 263
  intense, effect on cognition, 510–511
  interpersonal attraction and, 259
  prejudice and, 197–200, 197*f*
  prosocial behavior and, 392–393, 394*f*
Empathetic joy hypothesis, 408–409
Empathy
  affective component of, 394
  altruistic personality and, 397
  biological basis of, 394, 395*f*
  cognitive component of, 394
  development of, 395–397, 396*f*, 397*f*
  forgiveness and, 453
Empathy-altruism hypothesis, 405–407
Employee theft, 489, 489*f*
Encoding, 43
Entiativity, 462–463, 462*f*
Entrepreneurs
  cognitive factors and, 555–556
  definition of, 555
  personal factors and, 555–556
  social factors and, 555–556
  success and, 557–559
Entrepreneurship, 539
Environment, behavior and, 11
ERPs (event-related potentials), 16, 185
Error, sources of, 8–9, 99–104
Escalation of commitment, 469, 558–559
Ethnic slurs, exposure to, 239–241, 240*f*
Evaluation apprehension, 473
Evaluations
  instant, 271–279, 272*f*–275*f*
  mutual, 287
  of social stimuli, 54–56, 55*f*
Event-related potentials (ERPs), 16, 185
Evolutionary perspective, 420–421
Evolutionary psychology, 12–13, 12*f*
Exchange, 370
Excitation transfer theory, 427, 427*f*
Exhibitionism, high self-esteem and, 188
Existential terror, 180
Expectancies, stereotype-based, violating, 214

Guilt
    collective, 242–243
    prejudice reduction and, 246

Handshakes, 278
Happiness, downside of, 71
Hassles, of daily life, 520, 521
Hassles Scale, 521, 522t
Hazing, sorority, 469
Health
    personal characteristics and, 526–529, 528f
    promotion of, 529–534, 531f, 532f
    stress and, 521, 522t, 523–524, 523f
Health messages, positive vs. negative, 146–147, 146f–147f
Health psychology, 519–520
Helpfulness
    emotions and, 392–393
    empathy and, 393–398
    responsibility for problem and, 391
Helping
    as accomplishment, 408–409
    behaviors
        mimicry and, 390–391, 391f
        situational factors and, 389–392, 391f
    feeling of being helped, 403–404, 404f
    negative-state relief model and, 408
    at work, 547–548
Heroism, 379–380, 380f
Heuristic
    anchoring and adjustment, 49–52, 52f
    availability, 48–49
    definition of, 42, 46
    mood and, 71–72, 72f
    representativeness, 47–48
Heuristic processing, 149–151, 150f
Hierarchies, in groups, 464, 464f
High school friends, 256–258, 257f
High school prom, 314, 314f
"Hippie" identity, 178
Hispanic identity, 178, 191
Homosexuals, social norms and, 352
Hostile aggression, 436
Hostile attributional bias, 436–437
Hostile sexism, 217–218, 217f
Hostility, expressions of, workplace aggression and, 446
Hostility, health and, 527
Human immunodeficiency virus (HIV), 320
Hypocrisy, 161–162, 162f
Hypothesis, 23, 29, 514

Idealized influence, 552
Ideal self, 15
Identity dilemma, 178
Identity function, of attitudes, 134–135, 134f
Identity interference, 174
Illness, stress and, 523–524, 523f
Illusory correlation, 222–2234
Imbalance, 283
Immune system, 521
    happiness and, 530
Implicit associations, 228–229, 229f
Implicit bystander effect, 383
Implicit personality theories, 110–112, 111f
Implicit processes, 17–18
Implicit racial attitudes, measuring, 238–239, 239f
Implicit theories of personality, 84

Impression formation
    cognitive perspective and, 112–114
    definition of, 83–84
    effortless nature of, 108
    motives for, 113–114
Impression management (self-presentation)
    cognitive overload and, 116, 116f
    definition of, 84, 114–115, 115f
    self-regulation and, 193–195
    tactics, 115–116
    techniques for, 356–357, 357f
    transformational leaders and, 553
Impression motivation function, of attitudes, 135–136, 136f
Impulsivity, 437
Incidental feelings, 228
Incidental similarity, 357
Inclusive fitness, 409
Independent self-concept, 175
Independent variable, 25
Individualistic cultures, 101
Individualistic orientation, 480
Individuality, need to maintain, 350–351
Individualized consideration, 552
Individuation, 350
Induced compliance, 160
Industrial-organizational psychologists, 538
Inequality, perceived, 211
Infants, communication of, 297–298, 298f
Inferences, 11, 83
Inferential prisons, stereotypes as, 222
Inferential statistics, 28–29
Infidelity, 328–329
Infidelity, sexual, 433–434, 433f, 435f
Influence, 4
Information
    concealing, 84
        negativity bias and, 57–58, 57f
        sharing, failures in groups, 495–496
Informational social influence, 347, 349, 349f
Information gathering, inappropriate, 484
Information overload, 46, 47f
Information processing, biased, in groups, 495
Informed consent, 32
Ingratiation, 193, 287, 356–357, 357f, 370
In-group, 233–235, 234f
In-group differentiation, 223–224
In-group homogeneity, 223–224
Inheritance, 12, 12f
Initiating structure, 551, 551f
Injunctive norms, 344–345
Injustice, dealing with, 488–490, 489f
Inoculation, against persuasion, 154–155
Inquisitorial approach, 506
Inspirational appeal, 369
Inspirational motivation, 552
Instrumental aggression, 436
Instrumental conditioning, 129–130
Instrumental function, 187
Integrative agreements, 484, 484t
Intellectual stimulation, 552
Intentions, best, twarting of, 142, 142f
Interactional justice, 547, 548
Interchannel discrepancies, 89
Interdependence, 296–297
Interdependent relationships, 296
Interdependent self-concept, 175

Subliminal levels, 229
Subtype, 44, 222
Suggestibility, 510
Sunk costs, 558–559
Superordinate goals, 233, 484–485
Supportive defense condition, 154
Survey method, 21, 22f
SUVs, 50–51, 51t
Symbolic self-awareness, 179
Symbolic social influence, 339, 362–364, 363f
Systematic observation, 20–21
Systematic processing, 149–151, 150f, 355

Technology, "shirk ethic" and, 545
Television
    attitudes toward same-sex marriage and, 157
    prosocial models, prolonged exposure to, 396
Temperature, aggression and, 439–440, 441f
Temptation, yielding to, 73–74, 74f
Terror management theory, 180, 180f
Thanatos (death wish), 420
That's-not-all technique, 360
Theft, employee, 489, 489f
Theory
    acceptance or rejection of, 29
    of causal attributions, 94–96, 96f
    of correspondent inference, 93–94
    formulation of, 30
    of planned behavior, 141–142, 142f
    of reasoned action, 141–142, 142f
    in social psychology, 29–30, 30f
Third-person effect, 131
Thought
    automatic modes of, 53–54
    planning or narrative mode, 58
Thought suppression, 63–65, 64f, 67
Threatening posture, 86
Threats
    prejudiced action toward foreigners and, 129, 129f
    to self-esteem, 230–232, 231f
Time factors, in emergency responsiveness, 384, 385f
Tokenism, 216
Token women, in high places, 215–216, 215f
Touching, as nonverbal cue, 87–88
Transactional justice (interpersonal), 486
Transactional leaders, 553
Transformational leaders, 552–553, 554f
Trials
    attorneys, 515–517, 516f
    defendants (See Defendants)
    eyewitness testimony, 510–515, 511f, 512f, 514f
    jurors, 517–519
    media coverage, effects on defendant perceptions, 508–509, 509f
    pretrial police interrogations, 505–508, 506f
Triangular model of love, 318, 318f
Trivialization, 156

Truth, vs. lies, 88–90
Truth-wins rule, 491
Twins
    job satisfaction and, 541–542, 542f
    loneliness and, 305
    sibling relationships of, 302
Two-factor theory of emotion, 70, 72–73, 317
Type A behavior pattern, 435–436, 436f, 482, 527
Type B behavior pattern, 436, 482

Ultimate attribution error, 235
Unanimity, 491
Unfairness, perceived, 485, 488–490, 489f
Unrequited love, 316
Upward counterfactuals, 62
Upward social comparison, 190
Us-versus-them effect, 233–236, 234f, 235t

Variables
    confounding of, 27–28, 27f
    correlation of, 21, 23–24, 24f
    moderating, 66–67
Variation, 12, 12f
Venting activities, 450
Victims, characteristics of, 444
Video games, aggressive, 429–430, 429f
Videotaping, of police interrogations, 506, 506f
Violence, workplace, 445–447, 445f
Voir dire, 515
Volunteering, 398–399, 399f
    altruism and, 401
    generativity and, 401
    mandates for, 401
    motives for, 399–400, 400t

Walking style, youthful, 278
Weight control, steps for, 533–534
"Will & Grace," 157
Within-group comparisons, 220–221, 222
Witnesses, in emergencies, 380–381, 382
Women
    "good wife" stereotype, 170–171, 172f
    mate selection and, 312
    nonverbal communication and, 92
    token, in high places, 215–216, 215f
Women's intuition, 92–93, 93f
Wording, of lies, 90
Word meanings, good vs. bad, 54
Work overload, 540
Workplace
    attributions in, 106–108, 107f
    romantic relationships in, 310, 310f
Workplace aggression, 426
Workplace violence, 445–447, 445f
Work setting, social influence in, 369–371
Work settings, attitudes in, 538–539
Work underload, 540

PHOTO CREDITS

Chapter 1

Page 2: Lee Snider/The Image Works; 7 (left): Photo Researchers, Inc.; 7 (right): Trevor Wood/Getty Images Inc.—Stone Allstock; 10 (left): Chuck Savage/CORBIS-NY; 10 (right): Ronnie Kaufman/Corbis/Bettmann; 11: Picture Desk, Inc./Kobal Collection; 16: Lester Lefkowitz/Corbis/Stock Market; 22: Courtesy of The Lally School of Management and Technology at Rensselaer Polytechnic Institute; 32: Photo Courtesy of Robert A. Baron; 35: Najlan Feanny/Stock Boston; 36: Miramax/Picture Desk, Inc./Kobal Collection

Chapter 2

Page 38: Daniel Hulshizer/AP Wide World Photos; 43 (left): Taxi/Getty Images, Inc.; 43 (right): Chuck Savage/CORBIS-NY; 45: Getty Images, Inc.—Hulton Archive Photos; 47: Daniel Hulshizer/AP Wide World Photos; 49: Bill Crump/Getty Images, Inc.—Image Bank; 52: Derrick Ceyrac/AP Wide World Photos; 55 (left): J. Curley/The Image Works; 55 (right): J.P. Laffont-Sigma/Corbis/Sygma; 59 (bottom): Michael Dwyer/AP Wide World Photos; 59 (top): Michael Dwyer/Stock Boston; 64: Jeffrey Greenberg/PhotoEdit; 66: Dave King/Dorling Kindersley Media Library; 74: Jutta Klee/CORBIS-NY; 77: Bob Daemmrich/The Image Works; 78 (left): Michael Prince/CORBIS-NY; 78 (right): Bonnie Kamin/PhotoEdit

Chapter 3

Page 80: Jonathan Player/New York Times Pictures; 82 (left): Hulton-Deutsch Collection/CORBIS-NY; 82 (right): AP Wide World Photos; 85 (left): Photos Courtesy of Robert A. Baron; 87 (left): Photos Courtesy of Robert A. Baron; 91: Rommel Pecson/The Image Works; 93 (left): Bob Daemmrich/PhotoEdit; 93 (right): Larry Kolvoord/The Image Works; 104 (left): Dylan Martinez/CORBIS-NY; 104 (right): Kevork Djansezian/AP Wide World Photos; 107 (left): Corbis RF; 107 (right): Steven Lunnetta/PhotoEdit; 109 (left): Jon Feingersh/CORBIS-NY; 109 (right): Rob Lewine/CORBIS-NY; 116: Jim Bourg/Corbis/Reuters America LLC; 117: Jonathan Player/New York Times Pictures; 120: Corbis RF; 121: Kevork Djansezian/AP Wide World Photos

Chapter 4

Page 122: Jim Bourg/Corbis/Reuters America LLC; 125 (left): Tom McCarthy/PhotoEdit; 125 (right): Jim Bourg/Corbis/Reuters America LLC; 128: Mark Peterson/CORBIS-NY; 131: Amy Etra/PhotoEdit; 143: Dan McCoy/Rainbow; 145: Bernard Boutirt/Woodfin Camp & Associates; 146: A. Ramey/PhotoEdit; 149: Bonnie Kamin/PhotoEdit; 162: Spencer Grant/PhotoEdit; 165: Digital Vision Ltd.; 166 (left): Stock Boston; 166 (middle): Susan Steinkamp/CORBIS-NY; 166 (right): Mark Richards/PhotoEdit

Chapter 5

Page 168: Michael Keller/CORBIS-NY; 171: Corbis/Bettmann; 172: Getty Images, Inc.—Hulton Archive Photos; 173: Jonathan Nourok/Getty Images, Inc.—Stone Allstock; 178: Yellow Dog Productions/Getty Images, Inc.—Image Bank; 179: Thea E. Linscombe; 182 (bottom): Darren McCollester/Getty Images, Inc.; 182 (top): Ho and Katsumi Kasahara/AP Wide World Photos; 185 (left): Kai Pfaffenbach/Corbis/Reuters America LLC; 185 (right): Corbis Digital Stock; 194: Dion Ogust/The Image Works; 201 (left): Jim Noelker/The Image Works; 201 (right): Hinata Haga/The Image Works; 206 (left bottom): Lawrence Migdale/Photo Researchers, Inc.; 206 (middle bottom): Matt A. Brown/CORBIS-NY; 206 (middle top): Chris Stewart/CORBIS-NY; 206 (bottom right): David Raymer/CORBIS-NY; 206 (top left): Michael Keller/CORBIS-NY

Chapter 6

Page 208: Herb Snitzer/Stock Boston; 212 (bottom): Louis Lanzano/AP Wide World Photos; 212 (top left): Gianluigi Guercia/Getty Images, Inc.—Agence France Presse; 212 (top right): ABC, Inc. Photography; 216: Stephen Jaffe/Getty Images, Inc.—Agence France Presse; 221: Ariel Skelley/CORBIS-NY; 227: Monika Graff/The Image Works; 232: Peter Turnley/CORBIS-NY; 234 (left): Jeremy Horner/CORBIS-NY; 234 (right): Steve Prezant/CORBIS-NY; 243: Washington Post/Getty Images, Inc.; 252 (bottom left): AP Wide World Photos; 252 (bottom right): Herb Snitzer/Stock Boston; 252 (middle): Photo Courtesy of Nyla R. Branscombe; 252 (top left): Ellen Senisi/The Image Works; 252 (top right): Robert Harbison/Robert Harbison

Chapter 7

Page 254: Doug Menuez/Getty Images, Inc.—Photodisc; 257 Corbis/Sygma; 260: The Granger Collection; 262 (bottom right): David Katzenstein/CORBIS-NY; 262 (bottom right): Tony Savino/The Image Works; 262 (top right): David Katzenstein/CORBIS-NY; 262 (top right): Nancy Richmond/The Image Works; 266: Jon Feingersh/CORBIS-NY; 268: Spencer Grant/PhotoEdit; 272 (left): Keline Howard/Corbis/Sygma; 272 (right): Keline Howard/Corbis/Sygma; 273: Larry Williams/CORBIS-NY; 274 (left): Rufus F. Folkks/CORBIS-NY; 274 (right): Jennifer Graylock/AP Wide World Photos; 275: Photos courtesy of Dr. Judith H. Langlois, Charles and Sarah Seay Regents Professor, Dept. of Psychology, University of Texas, Austin; 278: David Young-Wolff/PhotoEdit; 281: Alex Wong/Getty Images, Inc.; 284 (bottom): Corbis RF; 284 (top left): Bill Cooke/AP Wide World Photos; 284 (top right): Tim Macpherson/Getty Images, Inc.—Stone Allstock; 290 (left): Charles Gupton/Corbis/Stock Market; 290 (right): Bill Losh/Getty Images, Inc.—Taxi; 290 (middle): Doug Menuez/Getty Images, Inc.—Photodisc; 291: Kevin Lamarque/Corbis/Reuters America LLC

Chapter 8

Page 292: Jose Luis Pelaez/CORBIS-NY; 297: Peter Arnold, Inc.; 298 (left): Corbis RF; 298 (right): Shirley Zeiberg/Pearson Education/PH College; 300: Jose Luis Pelaez/CORBIS-NY; 303: Photos Courtesy of Robert A. Baron; 304: Dick Blume/Syracuse Newspapers/The Image Works; 308 (left): Michael Gibson/Paramount Picture/CORBIS-NY; 308 (right): Jon Farmer/Picture Desk, Inc./Kobal Collection; 309: Spencer Grant/PhotoEdit; 310: Jose Luis Pelaez/CORBIS-NY; 314 (bottom): Mike Appleton/New York Times Pictures; 314 (top): Mike Appleton/New York Times Pictures; 315: Courtesy of PerfectMatch.com; 316: Miramax/Picture Desk, Inc./Kobal Collection; 319: Tom Miner/The Image Works; 322: Terry Schmitt/Landov LLC; 326: Michael Newman/PhotoEdit; 334 (left): George Shelley/CORBIS-NY; 334 (bottom right): Ariel Skelley/CORBIS-NY; 334 (middle left): Chris Pizzello/AP Wide World Photos; 334 (middle right): Suzanne Plunkett/AP Wide World Photos; 334 (top middle): Mark Ludak/The Image Works

Chapter 9

Page 336: Kevork Djansezian/AP Wide World Photos; 340: Kevork Djansezian/AP Wide World Photos; 341: Courtesy of the Archives of the History of Psychology; 345: Kayte Deioma/PhotoEdit; 348: Rob Reichenfeld/Dorling Kindersley Media Library; 351 (left): Bonnie Kamin/PhotoEdit; 351 (right): Ronnie Kaufman/CORBIS-NY; 352: AP Wide World Photos; 354 (left): Rachel Epstein/PhotoEdit; 354 (right): Sylvia Johnson/Woodfin Camp & Associates; 358: Jeff Greenberg/The Image Works; 361: Rhoda Sidney/Stock Boston; 365: Alexandra Milgram; 368: North Wind Picture Archives; 374 (left): Peter Vanderwarker/Stock Boston; 374 (right): Bachmann/PhotoEdit; 374 (top middle): Bill Aron/PhotoEdit; 374 (middle bottom): Michael Newman/PhotoEdit

Chapter 10

Page 376: Jeff Greenberg/PhotoEdit; 380: Damir Sagolj/Reuters America Inc.; 386: Helen King/CORBIS-NY; 388: Corbis/Sygma; 392: David Young-Wolff/PhotoEdit; 395: Absaroka Search Dogs of Montana; 396 (left): Allan Tannenbaum/The Image Works; 396 (right): Grigory Dukor/Corbis/Reuters America LLC; 397: Jeff Greenberg/PhotoEdit; 399: Johnny Crawford/The Image Works; 404: Adrian Arbib/CORBIS-NY; 407: CORBIS-NY; 414 (left): Lee Snider/The Image Works; 414 (middle): Photolibrary.Com; 414 (right): Robert Maass/CORBIS-NY; 415: Erin Moroney LaBelle/The Image Works

Chapter 11

Page 416: Paul White/AP Wide World Photos; 419: Paul White/AP Wide World Photos; 423 (top left): Michael Newman/PhotoEdit; 423 (top right): Abreu, Cesar Lucas/Getty Images, Inc.—Image Bank; 423 (bottom left): Corbis/Reuters America LLC; 423 (bottom right): Dex Images/CORBIS-NY; 430: Cat Gwynn/CORBIS-NY; 433 (bottom): Emmanuel Dunand/Corbis/Bettmann; 433 (top): Bejing New Picture/Elite Group/Picture Desk, Inc./Kobal Collection; 438: Rick Gomez/CORBIS-NY; 443: Michael Newman/PhotoEdit; 448: Andrew Lichtenstein/Aurora & Quanta Productions Inc.; 452: Corbis Royalty Free; 456 (bottom): Michael Newman/PhotoEdit; 456 (middle): Gary Conner/PhotoEdit; 456 (top): David Young-Wolff/PhotoEdit

Chapter 12

Page 462 (left): Don Spiro/Getty Images, Inc.—Stone Allstock; 462 (right): Rune Hellestad/CORBIS-NY; 464: Sherwin Crasto/CORBIS-NY; 467: Philip James Corwin/CORBIS-NY; 470 (left): Kateland Photo; 470 (right): Kateland Photo; 471: Neal Preston/CORBIS-NY; 474: Jutta Klee/CORBIS-NY; 476: Pawel Kopczynski/CORBIS-NY; 482: Amy Etra/PhotoEdit; 489: Photo Courtesy of Robert A. Baron; 500 (top right): Mark Richards/PhotoEdit; 500 (bottom left): Spencer Grant/PhotoEdit; 500 (bottom right): Berbard Asset/Photo Researchers, Inc.; 500 (middle): Jeff Greenberg/PhotoEdit

Appendix A

Page 504: Tony Freeman/PhotoEdit; 505: Alan Schein/Corbis/Bettmann; 506: Getty Images, Inc.—Liaison; 509: Spencer Platt/Getty Images, Inc.; 511: Geoff Dann/Dorling Kindersley Media Library; 514: Tom Hussey/Getty Images, Inc.—Image Bank; 518 (left): Corbis RF; 518 (right): AP Wide World Photos; 525: Photo Courtesy of Robert A. Baron; 529 (left): A. Ramey/PhotoEdit; 529 (right): Arthur Tilley/Getty Images, Inc.—Taxi; 532: David Young-Wolff/PhotoEdit

Appendix B

Page 539 (bottom left): LWA-Dann Tardif/Corbis/Bettmann; 539 (top left): Lester Lefkowitz/CORBIS-NY; 539 (top right): Charles Gupton/CORBIS-NY; 543 (left): Spencer Grant/PhotoEdit; 543 (right): Jose Luis Pelaez/CORBIS-NY; 545: Steve Mason/Getty Images, Inc.—Photodisc; 548: Patrick Olear/PhotoEdit; 550 (far left): Galen Rowell/CORBIS-NY; 550 (far right): Oscar White/CORBIS-NY; 550 (middle left): John Hammond/The Image Works; 550 (middle right): Francis Miller/Time Life Pictures/Getty Images, Inc.; 555: Rommel Pecson/The Image Works; 556: Photo Courtesy of Robert A. Baron